Pervert-Schizoid-Woman

TEXTS BY
MICHAEL WILLIAMS

GRAPHICS BY DAVID COHN

Bleakswan Publications

Cambridge, Massachusetts

ISBN: 978-0-9962-9922-0 (sc)
ISBN: 978-0-9962-9923-7 (e)

Library of Congress Control Number: 2016911490

Because of the dynamic nature of the Internet, any web addresses or links contained in this book may have changed
since publication and may no longer be valid. The views expressed in this work are solely those of the author and do
not necessarily reflect the views of the publisher, and the publisher hereby disclaims any responsibility for them.

Any people depicted in stock imagery provided by Thinkstock are models,
and such images are being used for illustrative purposes only.
Certain stock imagery © Thinkstock.

Bleakswan Publications rev. date: 12/13/2016

For Jonathan Williams

For those who encouraged my writing —

Creative Arts at Park, Patty White, Tamsin Lorraine, Cindy Halperin, Douglas Berger, Scott Butchart, Tom DiPiero, Janet Wolff, Manic Depressive Guy #2, Lucy Curzon, Paul Bruchez, David Mann, Reni Celeste, Trevor Pederson, Andy Pink, Dave Cohn, Berklee students, Leanne Gilbertson, Peter Hobbs, Lisa Soccio, Daniel Ezra Johnson, Masha Jack, Alan Rauch, Marlene Rauch, Sophie Gliksburg, Cecil Berthiaume, Lori Wike, Kate McNally, Alex Jack, Alfred Schenkman, Stan Rauch, Homer A. Jack, Esther Jack, and Lucy Williams, Banana Republic, All Saints, Scotch & Soda, Newports, Bonobos, See Eyewear, Urban Outfitters, and J. Crew.

In the judgment that gave Dr. Schreber back his liberty will be found a few sentences which summarize his delusional system: "He believed that he had a mission to redeem the world and to restore it to its lost state of bliss. This, however, he would only bring about if he were first transformed from a man into a woman." (p. 475).

— Sigmund Freud, *The Schreber Case*, 1911

26. The word "think" was omitted in the above answer. This was because the souls were in the habit — even before the conditions contrary to the Order of the World had started — of giving their thoughts (when communicating with one another) grammatically incomplete expression; that is to say they omitted certain words which were not essential for the sense. In the course of time this habit degenerated into an abominable abuse of me, because a human being's nerves of mind (his "foundation" as the expression goes in the basic language) were excited continuously by such interrupted phrases, because they automatically try to find the word that is missing to make up the sense.

— Daniel Paul Schreber, *Memoirs of My Nervous Illness*, 1903

Desire does not lack anything; it does not lack its object. It is, rather, the subject that is missing in desire, or desire that lacks a fixed subject; there is no fixed subject unless there is repression.

— Gilles Deleuze and Felix Guattari, *Anti-Oedipus: Capitalism and Schizophrenia*, 1972

At the level of the signifier, in its material aspect, the delusion is characterized precisely by that special form of discordance with common language known as a neologism. At the level of meaning, it's characterized by the following, which will appear to you only if you set out with the idea that a meaning always refers to another meaning, that is, precisely, that the meaning of these words can't be exhausted by reference to another meaning. This can be seen in Schreber's text as well as in the presence of a patient.

—Jacques Lacan, *The Psychoses*, 1955

Table of Contents

A Note on the Illustrations

The relationship between the text and the illustrations in the book is neither complementary nor supplementary. The images do not strictly accord with the text, and the writing does not mimic the pictures. The text is also not an adjunct to the illustrations, and the images are not an appendage to the text. The rapport between the writing and the drawing is a paradoxical relative autonomy in which units of text and splices of pictures intersect with each other in inequivalence and asymmetry. The illustrations are snapshots of the Becomings of the concepts in the text, and the writings are reflections of the Becomings of the visuality in the illustrations. The excesses in the text are pictorially embodied in the surplus significance in the illustrations, and the extensions in the pictures are textually figured in the extra meaning in the writing. The noncorrespondence between text and image opens a parallactic gap between word and picture whose overlap exceeds the otherwise tidy demarcation between the two dimensions of text and illustration. The excess of this overlap is the reader's engagement with both text and image and the asymmetrical relationship between the two orders of signification. The purpose of the illustrations is to present the reader with the opportunity to encounter this simultaneous gap and suture between text and illustration. The horizon is the generation of an additional significance for the concepts in the book. The reader is presented with illustrations which do not speculate the text and with writing which does not mirror the image. The challenge for the reader is to locate the noncoincidental asymmetry between text and image in order to capture a significance which exceeds both of these dimensions. The image writes in overabundance of the text, and the text sketches in superfluity of the image. The wager is that pictures speak more than they draw and that texts portray more than they articulate. The reader will discover that the nonequivalence between text and illustration generates a surplus surprise of otherness which cannot be captured in the discrete division between paragraphs and pictures.

This section presents a series of graphic symbols with supplementary text. The visual signs recur in the illustrated figures of conceptual art in the book. This sequence of images composes a symbology. This system of signification articulates the details and nuances in the visualization of the concepts under consideration in the book. The symbology is the code to the illustrated figures in *Pervert-Schizoid-Woman*. Each graphic symbol represents a concept which is repeatedly articulated within various images in this work. These reiterated symbols — over the course of the book — organize the figural representation of the ideas and themes in the illustrations. The reader is invited to refer to these graphic symbols in order to facilitate interpretation of the illustrations in the book. This symbology will enable the reader to decode the visual depiction of ideas in the conceptual art in the figures in the book. An intuition of this symbology will illuminate the conceptual art in the figures in the book. An interpretation of this system of signs will also clarify the relationship between graphic representation and discursive articulation in *Pervert-Schizoid-Woman*. A comprehensive grasp of this symbology is necessary for an appreciation of both the figural language of the conceptual art and the alphabetical language of the textual art in the book. The gap between figure, or visual language, and discourse, or textual language, in this book is crucial to an interpretation of the illustrations in *Pervert-Schizoid-Woman*.

The languages, visual and textual, in this book are distinct, yet they are drawing and writing the same object: the system, its critique, and its transcendence. The object is split because the languages are split between figure and discourse. But the passion of each language is to hold the object in its place in a relationship of tension between the two modalities of signification. Desperately, the visual and the textual, the figural and the alphabetical, desire to draw and speak to each other, and even to sketch and voice as each other. The effect of the failure of this mimetic project is the distinctiveness of the two languages, of the gap between the figural and the textual. The following set of graphic symbols and supplementary texts is the key to the aperture and closure of the parallactic gap of the split object of critique and reinvention: the system of $-ism. At points in the text of the book, the reader is invited to participate in the textualization and visualization of the project by writing and drawing. There are open spots in the book marked for Notes & Sketches by the reader who wants to actively engage in the enterprise to outline the present and fashion the future.

The reader is advised to begin reading *Pervert-Schizoid-Woman* with chapter one, "A Drive toward (*a*) sexuality," at the start of division one, "Perversion." The reader may consult the symbology as it is presented in "A Key to the Ilustrations" over the course of the reader's engagement with the book. A guided experience of cross-reference and cross-citation between the symbology in "A Key to the Illustrations" and the numbered "Figures" in the book will inspire detailed comprehension of the relationship between the visual idiom and the textual dialect in *Pervert-Schizoid-Woman*. At the start of chapter one, "A Drive toward (*a*)sexuality," the reader will be introduced to several key concepts, and an interpretation of the complementary graphics in this chapter will require the reader to return to the symbology in "A Key to the Illustrations." Repeated returns to the symbology over the course of the reading of the book will spawn elaborated interpretation and nuanced review of the abstract artwork in the book. This enhanced appreciation for the graphic art will stimulate greater mastery of the theoretical concepts in the book. A back-and-forth excursion between the symbology and the text will advance insight and promote clarity. *Not yet!*

A Key to the Illustrations

Figure K.1 Space

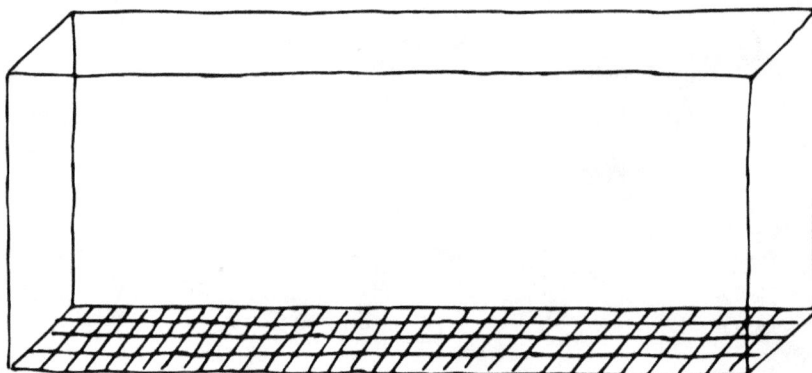

This drawing of a rectangular box recurs as a representation of the three-dimensional space of language. It is the in-the-world of speaking and writing. It is the realm in which the significations of (con)text are (im)possible. A word (signifier) is merely an ideational Nothingness and material Being in the absence of the system of the joint between concept and corporeality — sign — in which the word emerges and functions. This space is the possibility of communication. The boundaries of this space are both open and closed. The space is paradoxically open insofar as it is closed, and it is closed insofar as it is open. The space of language is Inside-Out and Outside-In to "itself." The space is symbolized as three-dimensional because this is the functional locus in which the texts and illustrations interrupt and pause — open space — for the articulation of the structurality of structure. Although all paradoxes are structured by an eternal instant of contradiction in terms, they must manifest — appear and hide — within a coherent temporality. This is so because the binarism of oppositionality which is involved in paradox must yet appear to alternate rather than *contra*-exist at once. A metalanguage (that would) articulate(s) the possibility of its own articulation (as) is impossible. This is the reason that the illustrations symbolize — speak and write — an epi-language with a quasi-linguistic syntax. This space also represents the locus that the texts and illustrations create for their own articulation.

Notes & Sketches —

A, B, C, D . . .

A, B, C, D (and so on) each indicate any given unit of signification. This unit of text may be conceptualized as an articulation of speech and writing — word, symbol, phrase, sentence — which is a textual and alphabetical medium for meaning. These letters represent a bound and specific signification. The terms operate on the level of abstraction. These units of meaning are necessarily specific, and they operate within the context of the gravitational system of meaning-making. But the singular specificity of the unit of text is open and unthematized. Each term is specific, but the thematization of this specificity is not necessarily articulated and conveyed in bound signification. The units of text — A, B, C, D, and so on — function to situate the illustrations on their own relational plane of meaning-making. The plane of signification of the illustrations is its own unspecified specific representationality. This visual system is only quasi-linguistic, but it approaches a semantic system of simultaneously open and closed relationships of units of text with each other.

Notes & Sketches —

S_N

$$S_N$$

The symbol of S_N represents the infinite difference and deferral of the series of words in the chain of signification. The S represents this series. The sub-N articulates any object which is symbolized by a letter. The N functions like it does in mathematics. The N indicates the possibility of — holds a spot for — any object in the series of S. Any word — A or B or C or D — is potentially the Nth term in the chain of objects. This series is a set of significations in the system. Any word — A or B or C or D — is a unit of significance. The arrows (not pictured) indicate deferral of meaning. The posterior unit of significance retroactively (*Nachträglichkeit* and *après-coup*) clarifies the previous word *ad infinitum*. The series is a set of backward glances toward the future. The single-lined arrow represents the indication of difference and deferral or the relationality and constructionism of space and time. The double-lined arrow articulates logical implication. A mathematical logical equivalence does not involve deferral in time or difference in space. S_N articulates the concept of the occluded center and its ejection from the structure of which it is the center. The N — A or B or C or D — denotes any unit of significance. The N resembles the Real *qua* resistance of the center. This resistance is constitutive of all units of meaning. S_N represents the structure of structure itself. This structure is simultaneously in all spaces and times of the structure. The integral sign $\int$ (not pictured) denotes the principle of this series of units.

Notes & Sketches —

Figure K.4 The Jagged Edge

This image of the jagged edge represents the (in/ex)ternal cut of the signifier. The jagged edge articulates the split in each unit of meaning. The fissure symbolizes the break in the possibility of any object or entity which is "itself" significant as either a word or a sign. These units of meaning — A or B or C or D — are split from "themselves." There can be no legible representation — Being — of the disunified unit of signification. The word is distanced from "itself." The sign is otherwise than "itself." The private property ownership (*le propre*) of the "itself" is ruptured by a division within the unit "itself." The jagged edge writes Being *qua* under erasure. The jagged edge illuminates the series of differences and deferrals — Derrida's neologism of *différance* — which separates any word from itself. The word differs and defers toward this otherness which cannot finally return to the "itself" of the sign. The jagged edge illustrates the break between the "it" of the object and the self-same and self-identical unity of the "self." The jagged edge interferes between "it" and "self." The proper articulation of any (dis)unit of meaning is its-Other-self. The jagged edge is the mediatory Other that recursively and doubly alienates any object from its own objecthood *qua* its own objecthood. The jagged edge replicates itself across the chains of objects and words in the system. The jagged edge denotes the endless series of metaphors *qua* metonymies which is retroactively constituted by (neurosis) or suspended by (psychosis) further supplementation toward Other jagged edges and their (in)completion in the process of signification. The jagged edge is the visual depiction of this (in/ex)ternal fragmentation of each (dis)unity of meaning. The jagged edge splits the self from itself and the itself from the self. The gap or wound between words is always already closed and sutured at the same time as it is reopened and unfastened. The jagged edge is also a figuration of fragmentation of a general process whereby identity and essence are cut by the Real which resists any written or spoken — song and dance — articulation of the identity and essence in question. This essence is (the) (in) question. The jagged edge illuminates the parallactic overlap of the simultaneity of both fissure and suture, both aperture and closure, and both a subtractional supplementation and an additional supplementation. The jagged edge also refers to the (*a*)sexual play of the Real Fetishist and her will to substitute but also bind objects with distant reference to the penis (clitoris) in order to inspire an Other *jouissance* of perversity rather than madness.

Notes & Sketches —

Figure K.5 Becoming-Arrow

....

This illustration of the single-line arrow represents Becoming. Becoming is both temporal and atemporal. This (a)temporal Becoming operates in distinctive modalities in each of the structures of neurosis, psychosis, and perversion. Neurotically, the *point de capiton* retroactively (*après-coup, Nachträglichkeit*) pins significance of C (future) on A (past, present). The future happens in the past in the Becoming of the neurotic. Psychotically, the phallic function is suspended such that A extends to 0-A toward Z-1 in an infinitely recursive antecedence and posteriority. Nothing has happened yet. Perversely, the fetishist mediates between the neurotic's temporality of the *futur antérieur* and the Time of the Schizoid. The pervert's Becoming sustains the Untruth of the madman's Nothingness. But the pervert also sutures this excessive timelessness with a present articulation of the Being *of* Nothingness or of the is *of* the is not. Neurotically, Becoming is temporal. Psychotically, Becoming is timeless. Perversely, Becoming is Being. The ordinary intuition of the network of words (A, B, C, D) is neurotic. It posits a perpetual reclarification and redefinition of A toward B back toward A toward C back toward B toward C back toward A toward C back toward B toward C toward D, and so on. Perversely, a simultaneous gain and loss are produced. The trace both is and is not the origin and destination, and commencement and arrival, and 0-A and Z-1. The pervert demonstrates the Being (what is) of this Becoming (Ing⁺). Becoming indicates the transformation in the space of material objects, as either neurotic *après-coup* and *Nachträglichkeit*, or psychotic suspension of the phallic function, or perverse presence of interminable Becoming. The transformation of the object in time (space) is not of a merely discrete and unified object. Rather, the (a)temporality of Becoming reconfigures and reshapes the object in the spatial (temporal) context of past, present, and future in reclarification and redefinition. Time (is) space. The pervert's jockstrap is simultaneously expansive and contractive in space. The jockstrap changes sizes and shifts positions in the (a)sexual *mise-en-scène* of *Trieb*. The jockstrap is its own material manipulation and bodily reorientation of itself in space. But the tendency toward expansion rather than contraction is the force of the (a)sexual nucleus of the solar system. The proclivity of heterosexuality is toward contraction because it is regulated by the general equivalent of the magnitude of the penis and its controlled (in)equality.

Notes & Sketches —

Figure K.6 Relationality *r* and Deferral *d*

$$r, d$$

The symbol of *r* represents relationality. The symbol of *d* figures deferral. The *r* designates proximity to the gravitational center of the system. The *r* is the binding force of *Eros*. The *r* is the power which enforces the relationship between the units of signification — A and B and C and D — in the series of F_N. The A is subsumed by the occluded center in lost time. The A is reiterated (a)new in D (AD). Neurotically, the A approaches the occluded center. The A is distanced from the unspeakable and unwritable binding force of *Eros* and the extant arrangement of the order. The symbol *d* or deferral patches the distance. The *d* is strangely the opposite of trace because it recuperates the lost identity from the past. But the *d* is also comparable to the trace because it unleashes the object from its past signification. The *d* is both the play and arrest of meaning because it halts and returns signification at the same time as it revises and releases meaning. The gap of space and time between D and A (in S_N) is an interval of both lost and found, and debt and surplus. This excess of lack and plenitude is subject to various portraiture. D has lost but gained in the break between A and itself *qua* D. This deficit and abundance are structured around the gravitational unification of the orbit of S_N. The symbols *r* and *d* refer to the *Eros* of the system, but this binding force is also ruptured by the death drive and its will to displace and disconnect. The *r* refers to the A which is retroactively (in)equivalent to B. Everything is the same because of the invisible gravity of the system. The *d* is located at the site of B which has been detached from A in space and time. This gap — loss and gain — is recuperated by *langue*. The interval is reintegrated into the system. This is the point at which the occluded center functions as the veil of the organizational principle of the structure. The approach to the center is the moment at which language — S_N — vanishes from its original space and time. The *r* and the *d* are essentially the same function. Each symbol represents the same process in different dimensions. The *r* is the *Eros* which retains congruence between objects — Being — and the *d* is the *Eros* (but also *Thanatos*) which sustains the objects as similarly different or the same difference — or what I call Sameness⁺ (pronounced: /SAMENESS-plus/). The tension between *r* and *d* — *Eros* and *Thanatos* — demonstrates the loss and gain, lack and plenitude, and debt and surplus which are (un)recuperated into an explosive Sameness⁺ which is not identical to either A or B (or to any of the terms in the series of S_N).

Notes & Sketches —

Figure K.7 The Derivative Symbol

$$\partial$$

The text ∂ is the Queer Mathematical symbol for instantaneous change or the rate of change. $\partial x/\partial y$ represents change in the x dimension over the change in the y dimension. It refers to the rate of change of a function at a given point. The equation $\partial r/\partial d = (\partial r/\partial d)/\partial d$ indicates that the rate of change is equal to the rate of change *of* the rate of change in the relationship between difference and deferral, and between relationality and constructionism. The symbol ∂ indicates that the difference *of* difference is difference or the (non)originary origin of difference and deferral in trace and *différance*. There is an Other of the Other because the series of units of text and context unfurls in space: the (con)text of the (con)text of the (con)text, and so on. *Qua* subjectivity, the slips and slides before and beyond itself exceed this "I." The "I" yields to a series of other incarnations of the "I," such as "you," "he," "she," "they," and other forces which destabilize the ostensible ownership of the *le propre* of *my* speech of the "I." There is (no) Other of the Other except the series of references and referrals — differences and deferrals — to yet Other speakers ("I") and their precisely *l'impropre* set of egos. The symbol ∂ can be applied to the exponential equation $r = k(e^d)$. The k refers to any constant. This k symbolizes the occlusion of the center. The constant of k is the product of the relationship of bounded infinity — *finite infinity* and *infinite finity* — to itself. The constant refers the mark and sound of the signifier to the Outside of the system which is simultaneously the essence of the system. Queer Mathematically, the $\partial r/\partial d = (\partial r/\partial d)/\partial d$ articulates the function which is its own derivative. The difference of difference is difference (and so on). There is (no) Other of the Other. The "I" takes the form of the "you" and the "he" and the "she" and the "they," such that "you" in relationship to "you" is still simultaneously "I." Queer Mathematically, $\partial r/\partial d = (\partial r/\partial d)/\partial d$ is equal to $r = k(e^d)$. The k is any constant. The e is the transcendental number 2.71828…. This is the articulation of the exponential function.

Notes & Sketches —

The text $\int$ represents the integral sign. The symbol is the obverse of ∂. The $\int$ represents the space which is enclosed by the function of $-ism. This is also the space which is enclosed by the circulation of the general equivalent and the units of text. The $\int$ is the potentiality of the infinity of the signifying chain. The symbol denotes the structural potential that the letter never arrives at its destination. The aneconomy is prospectively situated between arrival and destination, and between departure and *arche*. This interminability is veiled by $-ism even as it is simultaneously the schizoid essence of the system. The integrant is symbolized as: $\int S_N$. This indicates that d (deferral) is a function of r (relationality and constructionism). This text gestures toward the occlusion symbol and the (in)finite bounds of *différance*. The trace is paradoxically timeless because the *point de capiton* is psychotically suspended. Nothing ~~has~~ happened. Nothing ~~is~~ happening. Nothing ~~will~~ happen. The trace is ~~forever~~ excised from the temporality of the signifying chain of S_N — from A toward D back to A toward C back to B back to A toward Z, back to, toward, back to, toward, and so on. The trace is *ad infinitum* antecedent but also posterior to any *arche* — departure, arrival, destination, commencement, I, you, he, she, they, we, and so on — whatsoever. But the integrant (in)finitely approaches zero. Time is negativity. Time is the negation of Being and what is, as such, by definition, *il y a*, by necessity, and *qua*. The unconscious is timeless not only because temporality is a convention of chronological narrativity. The unconscious is atemporal because the communist *Aufhebung* of the cuts and scrapes of numbers, integers, and decimals — speculations and abstractions in capitalism — will subvert any delimitation of the expanses of space in temporal units. Space is the one-dimension. *Praxis* is the dimension which traverses the extensions of this (un)bound space in order to speak and write the Real of its own return.

Notes & Sketches —

Figure K.9 The Vertical Slash

....

The illustration outlines the symbol for the occluded center. The picture depicts a vertical slash which cuts the cent(er) by itself. The center is split by the center which is split from itself. The occlusion of the split emerges from itself *qua* its own fissure. The occluded center cannot be symbolized because it is the Real *arche* of the system. But the occlusion can be visually and textually articulated in its effects in the pervert's texts and illustrations. The written mark is also represented by the vertical slash. The strikethrough — *sous rature* and *sur l'effacement* — is visually indicative of the process of deconstruction. This activity (is) the spatial (difference) and temporal (deferral) movement of the signifying chain as it extends and expands inward and outward — this way and that way — in the expanses of space and in the fables of time. The hand raises the symbol of occlusion. The hand extracts the text of occlusion. The magical sleight-of-hand of this work is perverse. The hand makes visible this occlusion within the space and time of the system of signification. A clever pervert imagines the structure (*of* structure *of* structure *of* structure, and so on). The pervert plays a game of (a)symmetry. He "knows very well" that this occluded center is the Outside of himself. The pervert intuits that the Real center of (*a*)sexuality is unspeakable and unwriteable. "But nevertheless," the pervert draws this symbol in the future. The pervert creatively writes the text and illustrates the concept. The pervert jocularly balances the gap between the Other *jouissance* and the idiot's *jouissance*. This effort is a time which is beyond — neither before nor after — the deferral of the Time of the Neurotic (*Nachträglichkeit* and *après-coup*) in the otherwise timelessness of the unconscious. The pervert enjoys substitution — Metaphoricity — which slips and slides toward the Outside of the space of signification. The pervert playfully textualizes the Outside pleasure of the tedious desire of the regulation of tension and its release in the phallocentrism of sex and the male orgasm of ejaculation.

Notes & Sketches —

Figure K.10 The Occluded Center

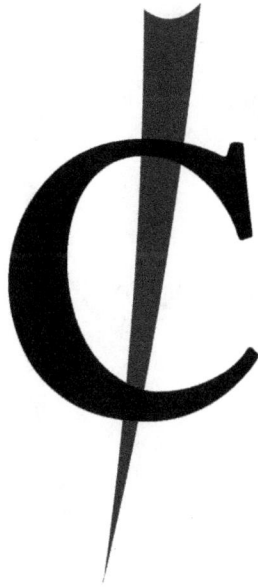

The symbol of the occluded center is a modification of the cent symbol. The cent symbol parallels the $ symbol. The vertical strikethrough is structured like the horizontal strikethrough of the *sous rature* and *sur l'effacement* of Being under erasure. Each word and object in the system is ~~under erasure~~ because the decenterment of Being (is, are) divides each word from itself. Being is itself under erasure as Being in a double-strikethrough which is potentially infinitely recursive. The symbol of the occluded center is situated underneath the vortex of the system as it opens and closes toward the abyssal structure of its emergence and cessation in the *ex nihilo* of the signifying chain. The vortex and occluded center are a physical black hole. Physically, a black hole is a singularity of materiality whose gravitational field is a hole in space-time. A black hole is the cause — *objet petit a* — of a gravity which binds objects together. These objects are at the same time imperceptible and unknowable. The vortex is invisible even as it is the organizational principle of $-ism. The vortex depicts the binding force of *Eros*. The occluded center and the vortex — Being and Real Penis — bind the world and language, and materiality and ideality, together. The source of this force is *Eros* which is neither conceptually nor practically isolated from *Thanatos*. The force is veiled and secret, but (*a*)sexuality is the metaphorical prop for this source — departure and destination, commencement and arrival, and *arche* and *arche* — of this galactic force in the universe. The occluded center and its effort to bind (but also fragment) emerge *ex nihilo* but also (*a*)sexually as the provisos of the structure. The occluded center is the differed and deferred (non)reference point of each unit of text (signifier, signified, sign) in the space (schizoidly) and time (neurotically) of the signifying chain. Meaning-making orbits the unsymbolizable Real. The resistance to signification is queerly absent from the space of *langue*. The occluded center is this Real of (*a*)sexuality. The vertical strikethrough of the occluded center is the visual representation of the inaccessibility and remote processes which condition signification and its dissolution.

Notes & Sketches —

Figure K.11 The Object

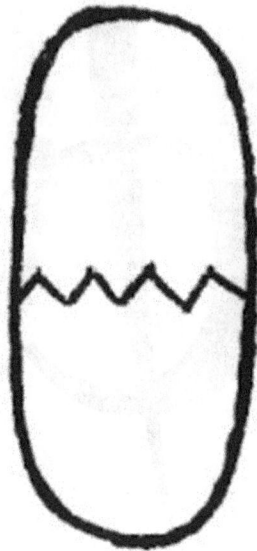

The illustration depicts the object as a figure which is cut and fragmented by the jagged edge. The object represents the end(s) of *désir* and the flirtation of presence and absence in the veil — *Aletheia* — of Being at the end(s) of Becoming. The object of desire (*a*) appears in the space of language. This space is mediated by the system of $-ism. The system situates — enframes — the object within a context of phallocentric binary hierarchy: penis/not-penis, and so on. The pervert reimagines *désir qua Trieb*. Perversely, there is no such *das Ding* as desire. There is no such *das Ding* as the departure (*arche*) or arrival (*arche*) of desire. But the object presents itself to the neurotic subject of desire as a bound and finite — present — object in-the-world of signification and the sign. This symbol for the object — the figure which is cut with the jagged edge of fragmentation — reappears as the complement to the inverted head of the figure of the Woman and her relationship to the scene of the discovery of sexual difference. Neurotic desire is framed within a context of lack — of Something is Missing. The object represents the enforced scene of castration of the subject of desire and the object of its fascination with (lost) presence. The brute material embodiment of the object is irrelevant to the organization of the relationship $<>*a*. The object (*a*) is a substitutable and metaphorical placeholder which sustains the in-between frenzy (<>) of the subject ($) in relationship to the symbolization of the Real ~~object~~. The fetishistic substitutability of the object — under erasure — is the secret truth of *Trieb* that the neurotic subject forever misses in the (missed) encounter with the object as otherwise than "itself."

Notes & Sketches —

Figure K.12 The Neurotic

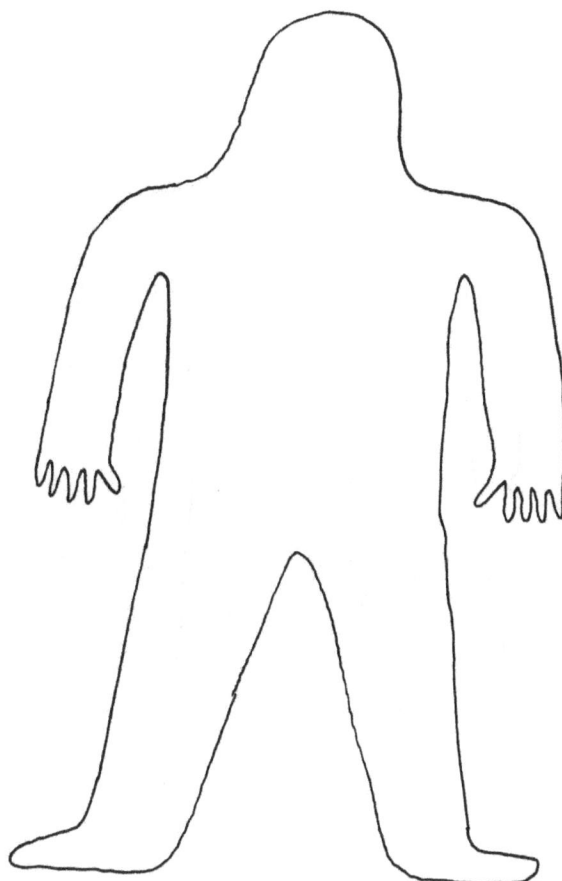

This picture outlines the human figure which represents the neurotic. As depicted, the neurotic is anonymous, isolated, and generic. He suffers the thinking, being, and living of $-ism. The neurotic is daft to the structure within which he is embedded. This figure of the neurotic is often depicted in the illustrations as the visual conceptual persona who encircles the gravitational occluded center of the system. The neurotic traversal of the gravitational occluded center is analogous to the orbit of a galaxy around a black hole. A black hole is a region of space-time in which strong gravitational effects prevent electromagnetic radiation (such as light) from escaping from within/out its internal structure. The neurotic is the isolated man of society who thinks and speaks the extant and borrowed meanings in the system. But the neurotic falsely assumes that such thought and speech are his own and original (*le propre*) articulations. The neurotic's actions and speech service the system of $-ism from which he is epistemologically and ontologically alienated. The neurotic does not know how the world works. The system is necessarily psychotic, but the neurotic misrecognizes $-ism as s. The neurotic easily and simply speaks — A, B, C, D, and so on — because his speech is merely the expression of his own subordination to a system whose organizational principle is requisitely omitted from articulation.

Notes & Sketches —

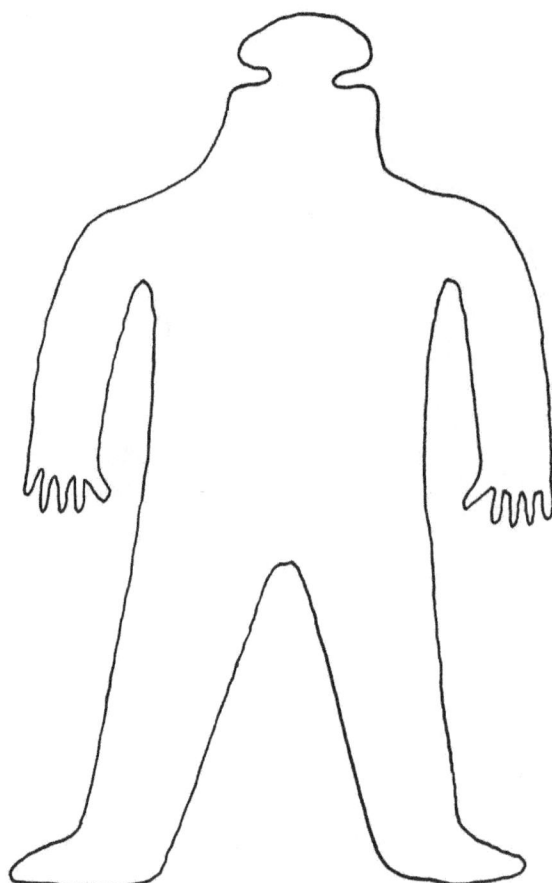

This picture outlines the psychotic whose eyes — but not I's — can see (visually, but also generally in his sensory apparatus) the secret Unreasonable truth of the schizophrenia of the system. The frenzied schizoid can see and intuit $-ism, but his words are a senseless and illegible flurry of marks because they emanate from the Outside — perpendicular to — the organization of the system (s). The schizoid forecloses the *point de capiton* that otherwise anchors the anxious identity and disappointed desire of the neurotic. The psychotic tends toward the explosive aesthetic of *Thanatos* over the binding force of *Eros*. The pervert insists on reconciliation between this wild nonsense of Unreason and an expansive (but also contractive) logic of Reason. The (*a*)semiology which (de)structures the schizoid's words belies his radical alienation (and not mere separation) from the symbolic order. The schizoid's words articulate a Sameness⁺ that the pervert passionately symbolizes for the neurotic. The psychotic maniacally babbles a Sameness⁺ which can only be intuited in its theoretical rigor by the pervert. The schizoid rejects the parameters of identity and desire that otherwise organize the neurotic's thinking, being, and living in the world. The schizoid forecloses (*Verwerfung*) borders — *tout court* — in the spits and fits of the Outside of the symbolic in the unalloyed materiality of the Real.

Notes & Sketches —

Figure K.14 The Pervert

....

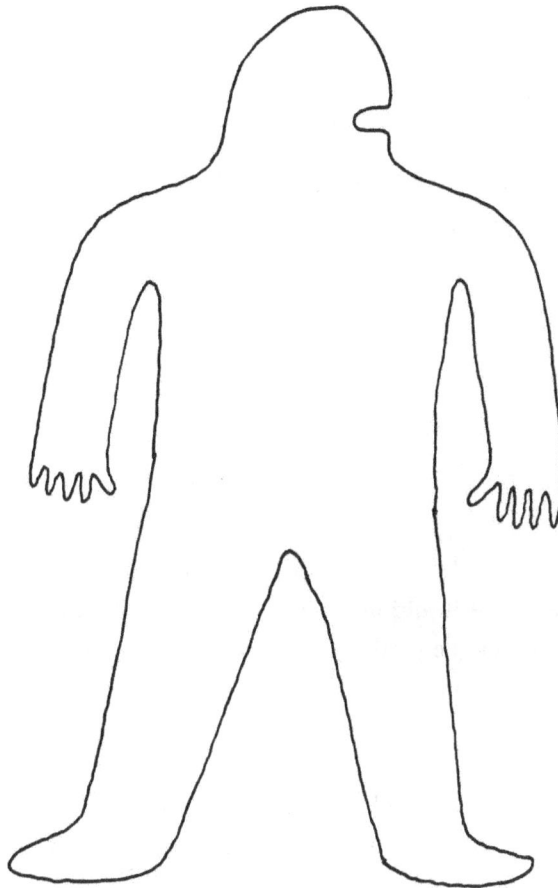

The illustration outlines the pervert who deftly symbolizes — speaks and writes — the Unreason of the schizoid. The pervert — whose psychical and social etiology is in suspension — intuits the secret untruth of the system (s) and its underside in $-ism. The system is structured as schizophrenic. The modality of its negation is the paradoxical Neurotic Foreclosure — *rejet névrotique* — of the repression (foreclosure) of the Real and its return *qua* the system itself. The art of disavowal is the technique of the pervert's magic. The pervert's "I know very well, but nevertheless…" both acknowledges and denies the castrative logic of the systems — patriarchy, capitalism, and language — of $-ism. The pervert returns to the system in order to explicate the nonsensical architectonics of the otherwise sensible architecture of the system. The pervert deploys and manipulates neurotic objects and words in order to illuminate their resistance to the Logic of Identity (A = A) and the correlative vast repercussions of the deconstruction of the economy of binary opposition. The pervert's playful *jouissance* of substitution and Metaphoricity reconciles the crazed Unreason of the schizoid and the dreary Reason of the neurotic. At the juncture of neurosis and psychosis, the pervert balances the tension between s and $-ism in order to *pervert the neurotic* in anticipation of the Woman and the Spirit of the System.

Notes & Sketches —

Figure K.15 The Woman

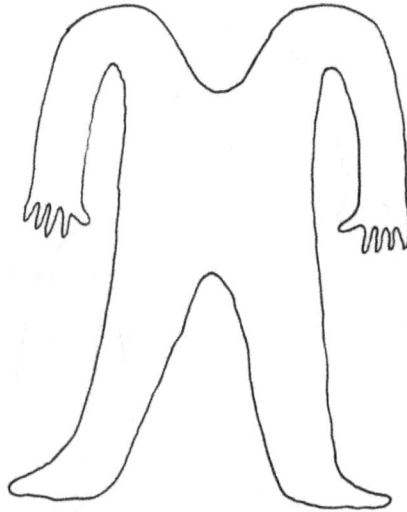

This illustration of the Woman depicts the simultaneous overlap of the Woman and the Woman. The parallactic gap is only perceptible to the intuition of the pervert and the madness of the schizoid. *Qua* Woman, lack is superimposed on Her by the patriarchal system of representational phallocentrism and the penis/not-penis binary of the Being of man and the Nothingness of Woman. But the illustration also refers to the castration which is enforced by the $-istic systems of the economics of capitalism and the discourse of the sign. The inverted head represents a Something is Missing in the Woman whose transformation into the Woman of the Spirit of the System heralds the Nothing is Missing in the economies of gender and sexuality, the exchanges of utility and abstraction, and the divisions among signifier, signified, and sign. The Woman lacks the penis. The worker lacks credit. The sign (signifier) lacks its Other. The Woman, worker, and signifier lack the principle — surplus penis, excess credit, and extra signifier — which organizes these positionalities. This figure simultaneously represents: first, the void of identity and desire in the psychotic's *Verwerfung*; second, the fragility of identity and desire in the neurotic's *Verdrängung*; and third, the (in)stability of *jouissance* in the pervert's chutes and ladders of substitution. This openness (closedness) parallels the space which is created by the gravity of the occluded center. A black hole organizes space through its absence from the space. *Eros* binds the identity of the sign *qua* positive unity which cannot be represented by the negative and differential diacritics of the displacement of the back hole from its centered (or otherwise) point in the expanses of unconscious space. Patriarchally, the Woman is represented as a Something is Missing in the West. But this neurotic phallocentrism of penis/not-penis blindly disregards the schizoid's vision and the pervert's intuition of the madman's Unreason: that the Woman is a Becoming-Woman in the Real of presence rather than absence, abundance rather than scarcity, fullness rather than lack, plenitude rather than castration — and the simultaneously obverse — of this transformation from the Nothingness of the Woman into the Being (Nothingness, and so on) of the Woman. As yet in this historical moment of $-ism, the Woman can only be written *qua* ~~Woman~~ (~~Being~~) in a metaphysics of presence (absence). Toward the Spirit of the System — Woman will be written neither *sous rature* nor *sur l'effacement* but —

Notes & Sketches —

Figure K.16 The Pervert-Schizoid-Woman

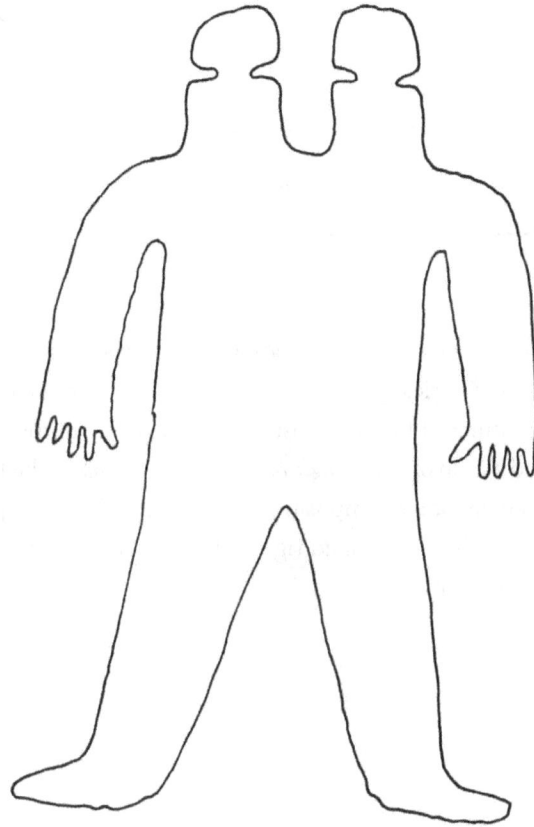

The Pervert-Schizoid-Woman is the revolutionary subjectivity of the future. Her talent as a pervert enables her to perform the pinch which reveals the parallax between S and $. Perversely, the Pervert-Schizoid-Woman concretely instantiates and playfully performs the Sameness⁺ which (dis)organizes each unit of meaning — *within meaning* — in the system. Her disavowal of the system that psychotically includes the neurotic and neurotically excludes the psychotic is the source of her *unambivalent* attitude. This aesthetic insists — despite the resistance of the Real — in the *Praxis* of a symbolization of an *à venir* Real. The Pervert-Schizoid-Woman's Womanhood consists in her own constitutive and systematic erasure — ~~Pervert-Schizoid-Woman~~ — from a system that otherwise only symbolizes in reference to the phallus and its violent subordination of singularity to the comparison, contrast, and exchange of the general equivalent. The Pervert-Schizoid-Woman ascends to the Clitoral Stage and its Outside. This futural (*a*)sexuality embraces the surplus materiality of the signifier which is constitutively unsymbolized by the system of $-ism. The schizophrenia of the ghostly apparition of the future (de)structures a radical difference that cannot be reduced to the metaphysics of Being. She (un)binds an *Eros* which is committed to a *Thanatos*. This deathly force of a renewed life in the otherworld forecloses the system of $-ism in which difference and negativity are reduced to calculation and hierarchy. The Pervert-Schizoid-Woman lives Outside of the system of $-istic nihilism. The Woman is schizoid in her Positivity.

Notes & Sketches —

Figure K.17 The Hand

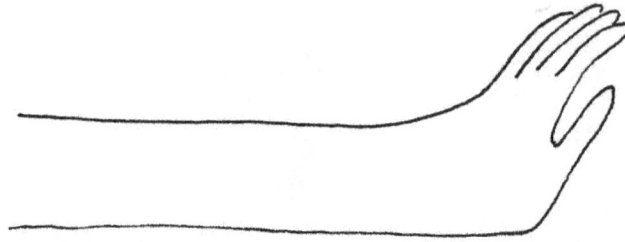

The image of the hand represents the neurotic's orientation toward the world. The symbol depicts a hand which holds the neurotic in his place ($-istically) or non-place ($-istically) in the otherwise interchangeability of words and interdependence of gestures. The hand positions the neurotic in the Temporality of the Neurotic of the *futur antérieur* of the deferred action of *Nachträglichkeit* and *après-coup* as the hours, minutes, and seconds pass beneath the neurotic. The hand denotes an imposition of a fabricated debt — phallocentric castration and capitalist scarcity — of the system of $-ism. The hand figures the (in)stability of the placement of the neurotic within an otherwise schizophrenic system.

Notes & Sketches —

Figure K.18 The Spreading Hands of the Psychotic

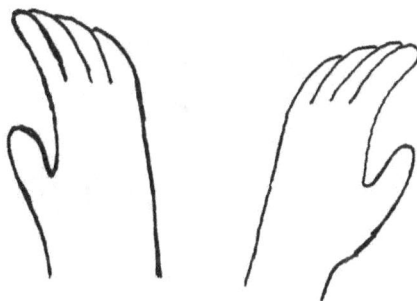

The spreading hands illustration depicts the radical force of *Thanatos* and the explosion of unities into disparate traces and radical differences. The symbol mimics the torus which is the symbol of schizophrenia. The torus is a multi-verse of disparate worlds. The schizophrenia of the madman is visible in his textual incoherence. But, at the same time, this schizoid discerns the sense — Reason — in the nonsense — Unreason — of the Other-Logic. The schizoid illuminates the Madness of Order. The spreading hands represent the force of openness and expansion. The spreading hands portray the power of *Thanatos* to rupture unity and destabilize identity in the transposition of the self-same and the self-identical into the Sameness[+] of the diacritics of differential negativity and its explosive Positivity.

Notes & Sketches —

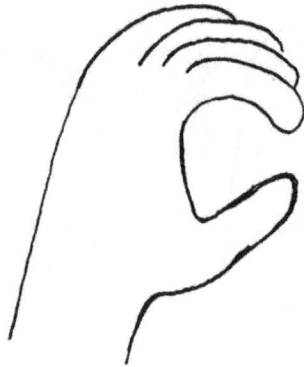

The pervert's pinch represents the *Möbius* twist in the pervert's text. The pervert's *écriture* twists and flips the Inside and the Outside into an extimacy in which the distinct and opposed are transmuted into a Sameness⁺ which is not identical. The perverse gesture articulates and performs in theory and practice the Sameness⁺ which is the object of the schizoid's discovery. The pinch also represents the simultaneous collapse and erection — fragmentation and totalization — of signification. The pinch portrays the expansion in space of the affirmative negation and its return of the extension of the self-same and the self-identical *qua* Other. The pervert's pinch elaborates and demonstrates the extension of meaning — A to B to C to D to C to B to A to D, and so on — across the expansive openness of space. The Outside of the system is endlessly spoken about and ceaselessly written around by the system. The pervert's pinch represents: the perverse transposition of the obscene differential negativity of the diacritics of the signifier into the positive unity of the sign; the perverse signifierization of the sign; and the perverse conversion of signification into value. These tricks are perversely performed from within the Reason of discourse.

Notes & Sketches —

Figure K.20 The Totality Sphere

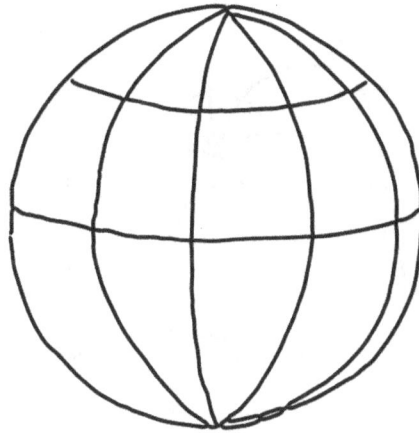

The totality sphere represents the world as a totally enclosed finite universe of bound spatiality, temporality, and practicality. The existent (Being, *il y a*, as such, and so on) conforms to the Logic of Identity: it is what it is and it is not what it is not (A = A). This dry and dreary universe is structured by a coordinated and binary system of opposition. $-istic meaning-making is organized by the arrangement of distinct and opposed units of signification (as opposed to different and negative sparks of value). The cost of this system is that any ~~Being~~ Meaning in the Real is exiled from the system. The neurotic builds and inhabits this galaxy of the totality sphere. The plethora of brute stuff — words, commodities, objects — that the neurotic encounters in the world is symbolized in the figural image of the television (not pictured). These words, commodities, and objects are misrecognized as present and existent structures of the regime of the Logic of Identity. But the pervert recognizes these entities as simulations — ~~Being~~ Meaning — of the idle chatter of *doxa*. The totality sphere depicts a neurotic resignation to the *le propre* limits of signification and the sign against the public property trace of value and the signifier.

Notes & Sketches —

Figure K.21 The Multiplicity Sphere

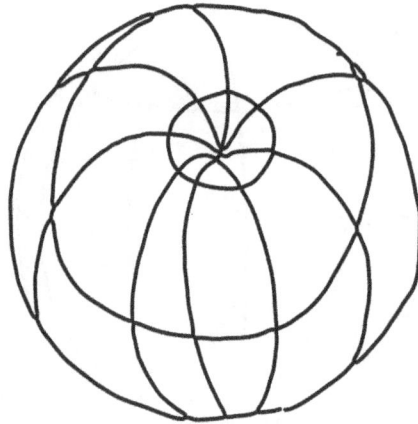

....

This illustration shows the multiplicity sphere as a metasphere (of sorts) of an infinite — *finite infinity* and *infinite finity* — set of spheres. The multiplicity sphere denotes an open universe in the timeless expanses of space. The multiplicity sphere parallels the psychotic's will toward the fragmentation of *Thanatos*. The sphere spans a Real unspeakable and unwriteable spatiality (psychosis) and temporality (neurosis) of incarnations of objects and manifestations of significations. The multiplicity sphere is a representation of the fourth-dimension of *Praxis*. The multiplicity sphere illustrates the impossible symbolization of the Real in every gesture and in every movement which encircle the (*a*)sexual energy of the solar system. The sphere designates the possibility of relationship and construction. The sphere denotes an estrangement and alienation from itself. In contrast to the totality sphere, the multiplicity sphere is unsplit and *Gestalt* but only insofar as it is extensive and expansive rather than contracted and closed. The multiplicity sphere represents that the Inside (is) the Outside because any distinction between the two opposed sides is perversely suspended by the *point de capiton* that otherwise binds unconscious space and facilitates neurotic time.

Notes & Sketches —

Figure K.22 The Pinched Sphere

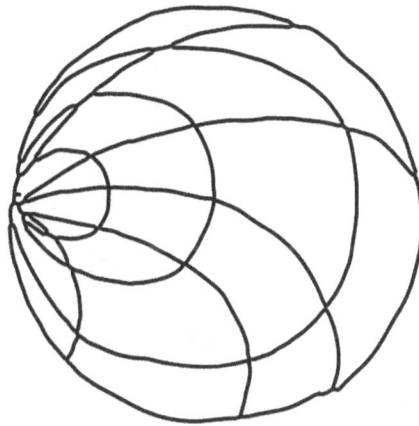

This pinched sphere is a spherical *Möbius* strip which approaches infinity. The multiplicity sphere can be structured and represented in a visual language. But the pinched sphere cannot be signified because its horizon eclipses its own border. At best, the pinched sphere can be represented as its own internal impossibility to incorporate the excess of its own horizon. The totality sphere is whole because it is an element in a system or set. The multiplicity sphere is an unbounded system or set. The pinched sphere is simultaneously bound and unbound — finite and infinite — in its inclusion of its own exclusion, and vice-versa. The Inside is and is not (and so on) the Outside in an instantaneous at once relationship which overflows in surplus the instant of its execution. The pinched sphere is a deconstructionist textual trope and visual shape. The pinched sphere exceeds itself in its spatial extension beyond itself toward its (re)(re)contextualization in the differential and negative diacritics of the *not*. The pinched sphere mimes the occlusion symbol and the phallocentric, capitalist, and linguistic Something is Missing. The distinction with the pinched sphere is that the substance of the absence — object of lack — is instantly recuperated such that it is not Something which is Missing but an Other Thing which is Missing. The pinched sphere is present in all points in space. This extension portrays the essential openness of the returns of the Logic of Sameness[†].

Notes & Sketches —

Figure K.23: The Dollar

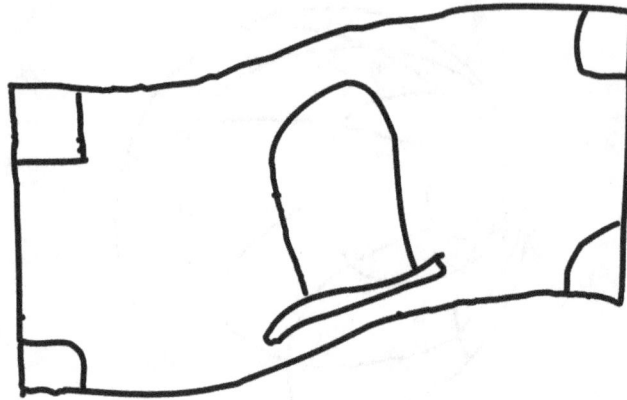

In the system of $-ism, the dollar is the general equivalent which annihilates the identity of every object and term. Every use-value mutates into a commodity. Every unit of meaning collapses into exchange-value. Every experience acquires a currency. Every object loses its value in itself. The entirety of language and economy becomes a galaxy of nihilistic nodes of value rather than a universe of fresh objects of surprise. The dollar turns every quality into a quantity. Difference becomes deficit, the clitoris becomes the not-penis, and the scene of castration becomes the backdrop to the subject's engagement with the world. During the process of identification of the subject with itself, the subject must make a forced unconscious choice of either desire or identity. The result is the dichotomy between psychosis and neurosis. Perversion is the both and neither of this mutual exclusion. The pervert is the heir to a destructured dollar and to the inherent potential destruction of the system that it regulates.

Notes & Sketches —

Figure K.24 The Klein Bottle

....

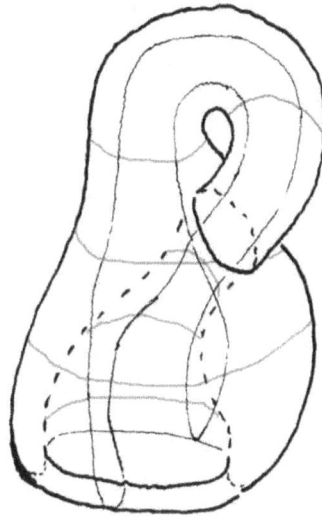

The Klein Bottle is a figural and visual representation of the unconscious. *Qua* unconscious, the subject *is* at all points of space — everywhere — in the system Unc. The subject as such is the binding force — *Eros* — of this space. This figuration of the unconscious is precisely not a solipsistic inside/outside model of a present — self-same and self-identical — consciousness of an internal content whose translation from inside to outside (and the reverse) is fraught with conceptual aporias. The ideology of solipsistic consciousness represses the schizoid's truth of the Other-Logic and its ruin of the distinction, opposition, and presence of the word. The fiction of a solipsistic consciousness invariably reduces the world of externality and otherness to the self-imposed confines of internality and presence. The perverse deconstructive Other-Logic sustains the distinction between inside/outside but not as an economy of discrete opposition (the signification of the sign) but as an inside<>outside unsymbolizable ~~Being~~ whose relationship to "itself" — <> — is mediated by the trace. The foundation of difference (identity) is the expansive and infinite movement in time — and in the unconscious — of an architectural space of nonknowledge and Positivity. The unconscious Outside of the signifying machine indicates that the Other-Logic of the Inside ~~is~~ the Outside — ~~Inside Outside~~ — is not an equation but rather an unspeakable and unwriteable Real relationality — A ~~is~~ B and A ~~is not~~ B and A ~~is~~ A and A ~~is not~~ A, and so on — which evades the frantic efforts of *Praxis* to symbolize this structure. The figure of the Klein Bottle is inverted (below). This space of inversion is the Outside. The unconscious is Outside of the subject, and it is the Outside of the presence of Being: what is. The unconscious is not a static materiality which is the underside of the system Cs. and its ideological imposition of signification and the fiction of the self-presence of consciousness. Rather, the unconscious is structured like a series of words or a *langue* with a syntax and semantics. The unconscious is the Outside of the inside (of the outside), and so on. The unconscious is the (in)visible Other to the inside/outside series of binary pairs of signs in the system of the signification of the sign-system of consciousness. There is an Outside to Being and the architecture of *langue*. This Outside emerges in the hiccups and dysfunctions — dreams, slips, jokes, and psychopathologies of everyday life — of the system of the conscious. The detail of Becoming illuminates the system of Being.

Notes & Sketches —

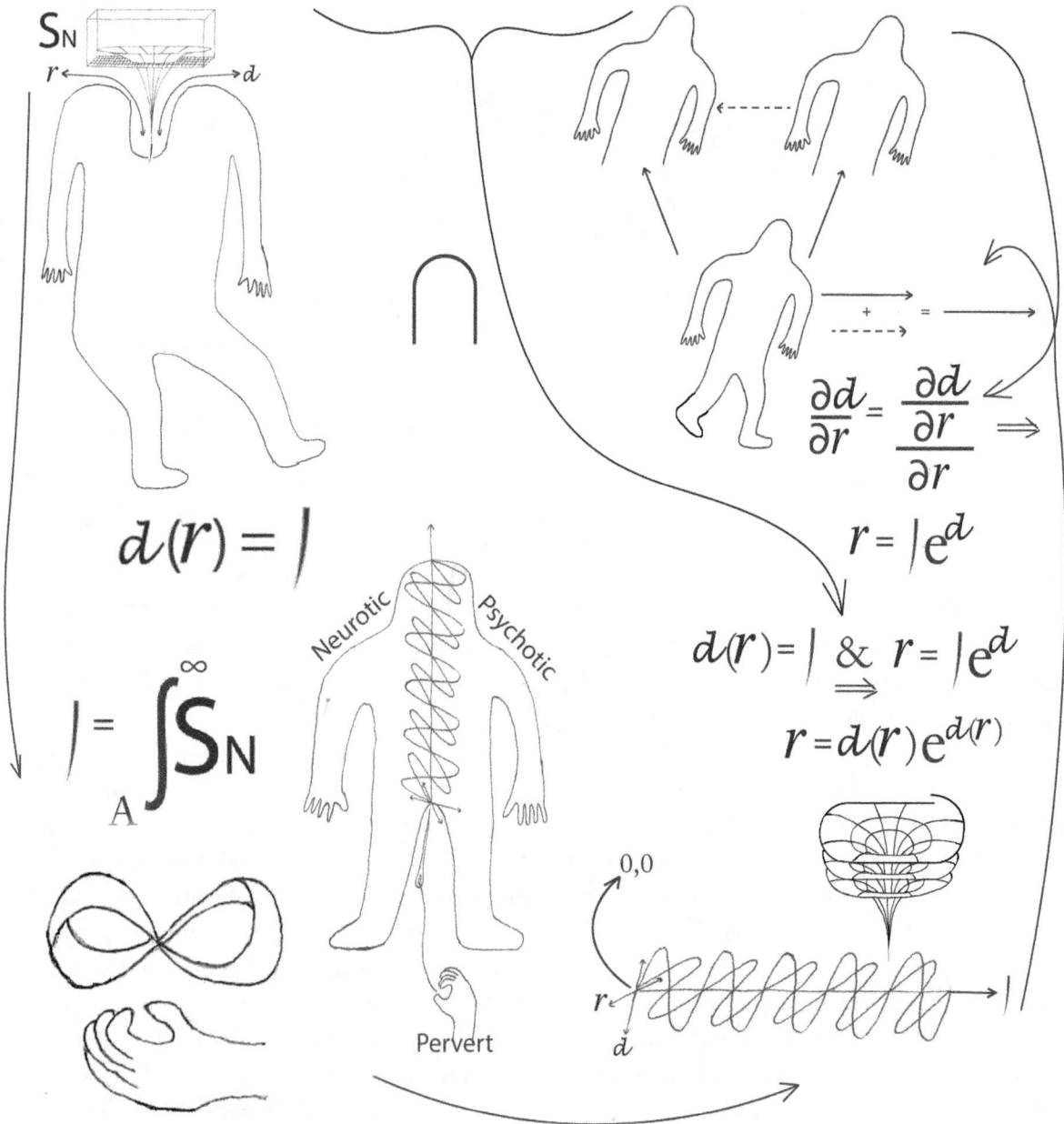

Figure K.25 Queer Mathematics Master Diagram

Communication is Possible & There is no Other of the Other

S_N

$r \leftarrow \qquad \rightarrow d$

$\dfrac{\partial d}{\partial r} = \dfrac{\dfrac{\partial d}{\partial r}}{\partial r} \Rightarrow$

$r = |e^d$

$d(r) = |$

$d(r) = | \underset{\Rightarrow}{\&} r = |e^d$

$r = d(r)e^{d(r)}$

$| = \int_A^\infty S_N$

Neurotic   Psychotic

0,0

$r \leftarrow$

d

Pervert

The image (above, left) is a microscopic visualization of the pictogram for the absent center of presence. The drawing relates the r of relationality and the d of deferral to the imaginary dimension. This imaginary realm expands in order to suture the rupture of the symbolic order by the insistent resistance of the Real. Queer Mathematics indicates that the integral of the signifying chain is equal to the constant which governs the exponential expansion of the circulation of currency (dollars and coins) and units of text (signifying terms). The image (center) is a replication of the illustration of the perversity of the particle<>wave duality. The arrows demonstrate the isomorphism between the parallactic oscillational expansion of the particle and the wave, on the one hand, and the parallactic overlap between the neurotic and the psychotic, on the other hand. The constant, k, of $r = ke^d$, Queer Mathematically articulates the constant of the speed of the parallactic expansion. This expansion is the relation of an interiority in the absence of any determinate exteriority. The image (above, right) is a reproduction of the illustration of the graphic representation of slippage of (con)text. The relationship arrow between "I" and "you" is simultaneously representative of the relationship of the "I" to the "he" of the "you." This "he" of the "you" is shown in the dotted arrow. This relationship of the "he" of the "you" recurs in the illustration of the simulation of representation. This concept is Queer Mathematically articulated as $\partial d/\partial r$ = $(\partial d/\partial r)/\partial r$. This Queer Mathematical notation denotes the function whose rate of change is equal to the rate *of* the rate of change. Existentially, the subject lives difference. But the subject cannot be in relationship to difference itself. The absolute is discovered only as a limit which resists articulation. The Real resists symbolization. The resultant exponential function — $r = ke^d$ — is represented as the inverse of the logarithmic curve in the organizational gravity function. Deferral as a function of relationality is equal to the constant that governs the expansive circulation of units of text (signifying terms). This is Queer Mathematically articulated as $d(r) = k$. The combination of this articulation with the exponential function results in the Lambert Omega Function. This function is represented in the form of the organizational gravity function. The gravity function is the aperture of the imaginary realm of the maternal phallus. This maternal phallus (Queer Mathematically) compensates for the rupture of the symbolic order by the resistance of the Real. The center of this function is the complex infinity of 1/0. This 1/0 reappears in the illustration of the neurotic's movement in fantasy — a journey which is distinct from the analytical traversal of the Real.

Notes & Sketches —

Division One

Perversion

Chapter One

A Drive toward (a)sexuality

It is when you have found the word that concentrates around it the greatest number of threads in the mycelium that you know it is the hidden center of gravity of the desire in question.

— Jacques Lacan

This project takes the form of a Freudian dream.* If the Oedipus complex was Freud's dream, as Lacan claims, then the question which emerges for such a dream is, "What is the latent wish which animates the dreamy form of its manifest content?" Freud's dream of the Oedipus complex veils a wish to be guilty of the father's murder. This wish animates Freud's myth of the primal horde murder of the father in *Totem and Taboo* (1913). I will return to this dead father and the wish toward the end of the book. The manifest form of the dream of *Pervert-Schizoid-Woman* is an obscure or at least a misrecognized interpretation of several writers. These scribes are Freud and Lacan, in what I baptize "over-psychoanalysis"; Derrida, Saussure, and Heidegger, in what I like to refer to as "retro-deconstruction"; and even a "fore-Marxism." These authors have made a contribution to twentieth-century thought which has been retread many times in the secondary literature on such theoretical work.

The difference in this work of theory is the creative translation of those authors whose work challenges the limits of thought. There are some readers and interpreters who seek correct interpretation as adequation between the text and its exegesis, and between the author's intent and the reader's transcription. This way of reading the dreams of the limit of thought represses the "play of the text" that always inventively scrambles signification. The veiled wish for the reader and his interpretation to somehow become the text and the author is plagiarism. The only guarantee of so-called correctness is a perfect mimicry in the absence of an excess in the translator's words. Any deviation from mirror speculation in plagiarism is a misreading in the strict sense because it translates the original — writer's text and author's intent — beyond the frontiers of the primary iteration of the text. Misreading is the horizon of this book.

---

* The Foreword to this book, entitled "Buggery and Blowjobs — and Perverse Philosophy," was written by Andy Pink, the Editor-in-Chief of Bleakswan Publications in Cambridge, Massachusetts. The Foreword has been censored by the printing press. The text of the Foreword by Andy Pink is available at www.pervert-schizoid-woman.com. *"Not yet!"*

LIRER ET ÉCRITURE

If all iteration is a productive reiteration which is ever delayed and differed, and if all transcription is a mistaken copy, then the impasse of the plagiaristic wish is upset. The *méconnaissance* which hampers identification in the scene of the mirror also applies to interpretation. The text is captured in a misrecognition. This *méconnaissance* submits its form to the imaginary fantasy of the interpretation. Authorial intent is reduced to the whims of the reader's caprice. The point is that plagiaristic fidelity to both the author's words and the theory's idea must be tempered by a gleeful manipulation and happy violation. This messy practice widens the gap between the originality of the interpretation's will and the conventionality of the author's intent. Veiling the wish is the purpose of a dreamy text. The tack is to celebrate the mysterious form that the wish takes as a symptom. This opacity is the reason that the symptom holds a magical magnetism for the interpreter and reader and sustains an enigmatic (counter)transference for the doctor and patient.

This book is a symptom. The form of this book is a deviation from the strict authority of the text. The horizon of this work is the invention of novelty and surprise: specifically, an alternative psychoanalysis which emphasizes diagnostics and structures which transcend the strict categorizations in Freud and Lacan's frameworks; a deviant deconstruction which returns to the *arche* of the grammatological project but with mismatched metaphors; and an empowered Marxism which is simply *for* Marxism. What is the purpose of a sorry mimicry of an original? The only amusement that a text holds for the reader — and for the reader's interpreter, and for the interpreter's translator, and so on — is a sly deviation from a distant moment of original enunciation. This gesture endeavors to keep that repeated enunciation retroactively returned to the past in order to keep a future alive for its own time to come.

The pedagogy of desire is not only the purpose of the *mise-en-scène* of fantasy. This edification is also instructive for the analysis of a dream. Lacan's citation in the epigraph about the nodal point of the dream illuminates the creative pedagogy of the desire of the unconscious. Lacan's version of the analysis of the dream is to discover the "word" around which the threads of the interconnected and, significantly, (*a*)sexual, tentacles of the mycelium of a fungus gather. Of special interest in this formulation is the (*a*)sexuality of the navel of the word and the focal point of the significance of this sign. How can the "navel" of the dream be (*a*)sexual — like the tentacles of the mycelium of a fungus concentrate — if the latent content of the unconscious is entirely libidinized?

Lacan's point is that this focal "word" is (*a*)sexual not only because it is conscious and so segregated from the free eroticism of the unconscious. The word is (*a*)sexual because it is exactly the sign which is excluded from the significance of the dream. Sexuality is the excluded center of the dream. Lacan's reference to this (*a*)sexual word as the "hidden center of gravity of the desire in question" in the dream suggests that the word is both "found," as he writes, but also "hidden." The word is at the center and on the periphery. A central-peripheral (*a*)sexuality is the organizational principle of the dream. The word which illuminates the desire "in question" — that precisely is a question as such — is disavowed in its very function. The (*a*)sexual word is perversely both visible and invisible, central and marginal, present and absent, and so on. Lacan designates this word as the "center of gravity" because it coalesces all content around itself. This is so even as it operates as a mere principle and minor form rather than as a consequential event and significant content. Lacan's quip indicates that the (*a*)sexual center of the significance of the dream is this simultaneous absent eroticism in sex and present sexuality in asceticism. An (*a*)sexuality is an *Aletheia* of bodily (in)access/(out)excess.

A specter is haunting psychoanalysis. It is the specter of (*a*)sexuality. The liminality of (*a*)sexuality illuminates the relationships among the relevant words — free associations — at the same time as it disappears from the gravitational pull of the Other. There is something (*a*)sexual — queer — about sex. The "desire in question" will always be a question as such. Desire is the form of this question or the object of the "epistemophilic instinct," as Freud says of the junior's will to resolve the riddle of sexual difference. The question is the "navel" of (*a*)sexuality which leads down into the "unknown." This (*a*)sexuality involves the question which burns in the pursuit of knowledge — the ontological "What is?" — about desire and sexuality. The question of the dream of this study is the fiery concern of this ontology: What is? — and how, precisely, may it also not be what it is, at once.

As a dream, this book presents its repressed truth in a cryptic manifest form. This symptom must be interpreted in a reversal of the dream-work. The unconscious-work otherwise veils the wish of this text. My project is to interpret the latent thoughts of these manifest forms. I will analyze the latent *of the latent*. My effort is to "dramatize an idea," as Freud says of the dream.[1] I want to express the truth in the form of the obscured — what Heidegger describes as *Aletheia* in the Greek. This is the essence of truth or the tension between the veil of truth and the revelation of this truth in the event of making-present. The writer and reader must accept that there will always be an obscurity. This stain is the very proviso of clarity. Essentially, my work is to play — seriously. My work is attuned to the nuances of the texts under discussion. But I am also freed within constraints to enjoy the "second reading" of the clotural reading process of a deconstruction. As an otherwise impossible "metalanguage," deconstruction perversely illuminates the unjust Madness of Order and the redemptive advent of the Pervert-Schizoid-Woman in the Becoming of the Spirit of the System (S).

Like the dream-work with the displacements, condensations, and secondary revision of the primary process, this book dummy runs deconstruction, psychoanalysis, and Marxism from a present which returns to a past. I do so in order to recall and recalibrate a future with a critical tweak and a perverse aesthetic. My work is to obscure but also determine the text. This work is done in the Spirit of the deconstructive, psychoanalytic, and Marxist thinkers whose limit-thoughts weave and bob about this book. The reader's job is to translate the manifest form into the latent truth. This clandestine desire is obscured to the author of his "own" text. I am not responsible for the semen in the back of Irma's throat. The author is the patient, and the reader is the physician. As Freud puts it in the dream-book, "Sleep signifies an end to the authority of the self."[2] But whose self? This is a question that Barthes poses in reference to the reader in his celebration of the destruction of the voice of authorship.[3]

As writer, the crucial task of the dream-censor, which applies to my work, is what Freud calls "considerations of representability." These considerations — can the dream be interpreted at all? — are the criteria of the appropriate efforts of making-present the event of truth. This involves the tension of the secondary-ego process that ambivalently colludes with the primary process to make the dream instantly obscure but potentially analyzable. The wager of analysis is a bet on the ambivalence of the ego. Considerations of representability — making sense — in a dream involve the preconscious secondary process which applies logical relations and chronological sequence to an inchoate accumulation of dream-thoughts. The significance of this assemblage of words cannot be interpreted without the formative work of a basic symbolic organization. The pervert's talented supplement to the schizoid's wacky yet brazen Untruth performs this general coordination.

My work is to pursue the Reason of the rational and the logical in the otherwise Unreason of the cuckoo and the loco. My job is to present authors and texts which stray, like a dream, from the conventional. If I succeed, that which is *non compos mentis* will return to a state of ratiocination. As will become evident in my elaboration of the radicality of Saussure's thought, the problematic knot is the *not* of symbolization. The *not* itself is central to the efforts of this book and also to the thinkers under discussion — writers whose contribution to twentieth-century thought is a challenge to the limits of conceptualization and to the translation of the dream-work. The *Cogito* will translate the Madness of Order in order to show that it is precisely the Un*Cogito*.

Figure 1.1 The Occluded Center Organizational Gravity Structure

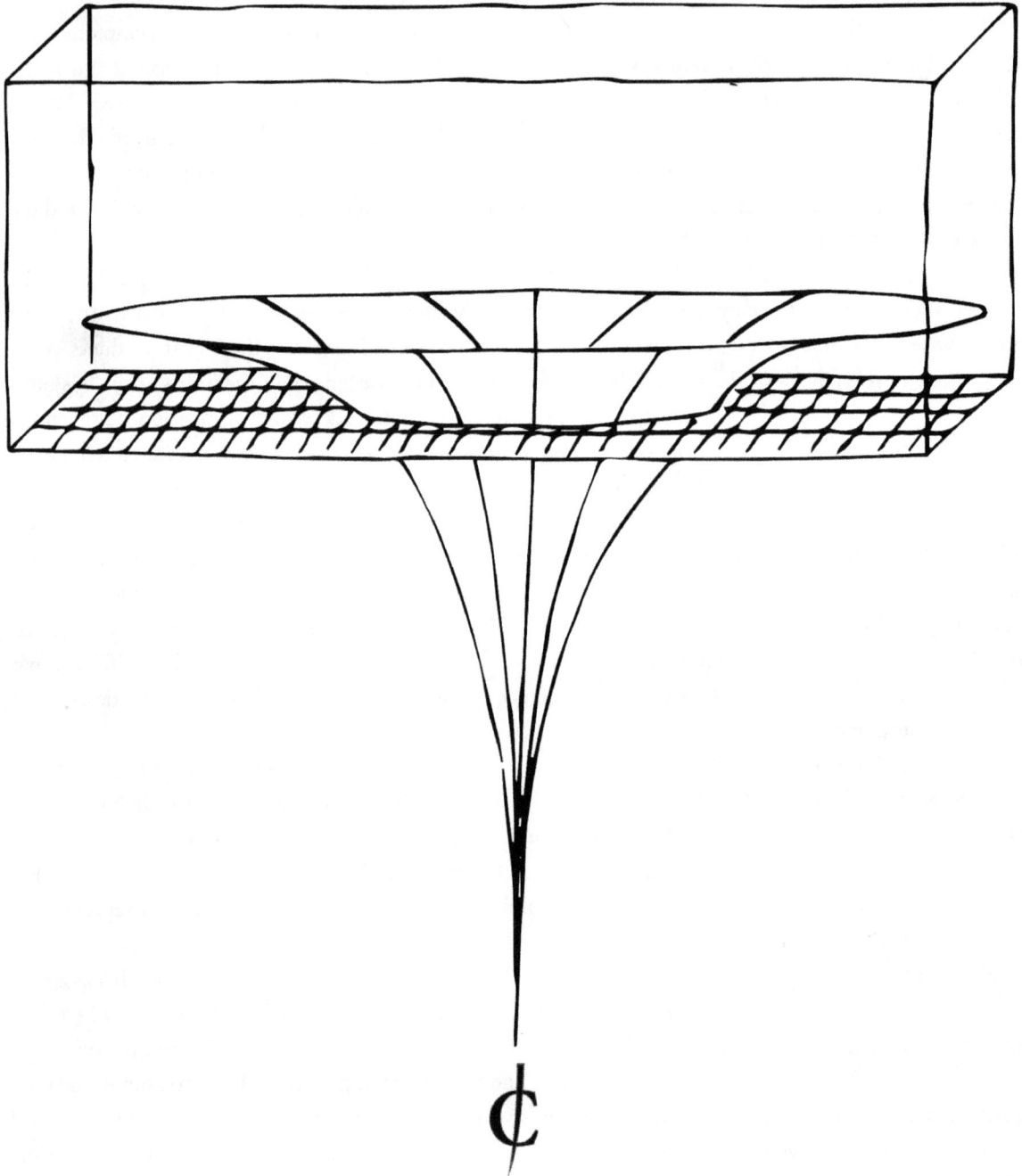

The occluded center (below) organizes the space of language as an absence. This unsymbolizable internal Outside of the system is the force of the (*a*)sexual. The desire in and as the signifying chain is the ordinary system of general equivalence of comparison, contrast, and exchange. But the occluded center is suspended from this system of general equivalence because the singular difference — Sameness⁺ (pronounced: /SAMENESS-plus/) — of the occluded center is the Outside of the economy of comparison, contrast, and exchange. This singular difference is a hole in the system. This gap is Becoming at all spatial and temporal points in the system. The system is this series of fissures. The gravitational function (occluded center) pervades the entire space of language. The occluded center is everywhere — spatially, temporally — the condition of the possibility of each unit of text in the system. This illustration represents this hole in space and time of the Inside-Out and Outside-In relationship of the system to itself. The nucleus of sexuality is strictly (*a*)sexual. The possibility of a drive toward coherent and centered difference is itself a mere repetition of this difference. The gravity (center) is the binding force or *Eros*. This gravity is also representative of the (*a*)sexuality in the system of *langue*. The center of the occluded center (below) is slashed in order to indicate that it cannot be spoken or written in the symbolic system. The ~~occluded center~~ is under erasure because it is the proviso of the metaphysics of presence (absence). This drawing supplements the deconstruction of text with a visual methodology. The image gestures toward an impossible visual symbolization of an infinity. This infinity must otherwise be depicted as *finite infinity* or *infinite finity* in the systems of $-ism. This visualization is an impossible Real which can only be depicted as an indirect effect of the system. The slash symbol of occlusion and the logarithmic curves of the structure can only allude to an infinite and perpetual disposal and displacement. The occluded center is properly positioned in an infinite remove from itself — downward — below the space of language. The occluded center is the simultaneous Outside and Center of the system. The visual depiction of this endless deferral can only represent the effect of this displacement. The logarithmic curves meet each other — rather than asymptotically approach each other — only because a finite space limits the visual. The same *finite infinity* or *infinite finity* of the ploy of the $-ism of phallocentric castration, capitalist scarcity, and linguistic lack also circumscribes the limits of visual representation. This asymptotic aspect of the function of gravity will be further elaborated in the Queer Mathematical imagery *à venir*.

Notes & Sketches —

I will present original interpretations of the authors whose work is the object of my playful and obscurant methodology. My *Ziel* is clarity. But *das Ziel fo dem Ziel* is not always the *Trieb*. The author's symptom, the dream, needs translation by the reader, in analysis. Instead of $\$<>a$, I present: $\$-ism<>S$. Lacan's talent to engender a transference in the reader is simply unmatched in French theory. He is perhaps the greatest thinker since Socrates to inspire a transference with, *"Je ne sais pas."* An authorial repetition *de perversité* must be supplemented by the readerly risk to violate the derived so-called originality of the primary iteration. The text, like the author, is neither primary not authoritative. Rather, the primacy and authority of the author's work are fantasies not of the writer of the text but of the secondary reader of the text. This effort is a transliterary transference. In the case of Lacan's reception, this dumb show inspired a kind of devotion which is visible in the works of the translators and interpreters of his various idiomatic expressions. But whose (counter)transference is whose?

The readerly-writerly overlap can invite deviations from the imagined knowledge of the *sujet supposé savoir*. Deviant interpretation generates the "surprise of otherness" that a close reader like Derrida aspires to in his peculiar and controversial readings of Western philosophers. But this transliterary transference can also inhibit the play of the text and the constitutive instability of meaning. It is this superpositional oscillation (1925), as they say in quantum physics, which veils the latent truth at the same time (*Aletheia*) as it reveals it. The work of the philosopher in Derrida is derivative and secondary because his interpretations are insidiously intertwined with the so-called "original" from which his readings evolve and deviate. Like his infamous neo/retrologism, *différance*, Derrida's work is fundamentally unoriginal and copied. There are no strictly secondary sources about Derrida's work because he is already a secondary reader of "himself" in the mediation between his words and the texts of the other. My book has already been written and read. Derrida's work undoes the division between primary and secondary that otherwise hampers the playful work of reading a text. The purpose of exegesis is not getting the author right. The horizon of interpretive work is getting the author wrong. This intentional and productive misreading is the only way to keep an author and her text alive for the future.

The establishment of analytic knowledge makes the text of an obscurantist like Lacan an object of insatiable desire. But the epistemophilic instinct also engenders submissive devotion. Lacan's foray into the algebraic formalization of his concepts into inert and untranslatable symbols ($\$$, *a*, $<>$, ?, and so on) produced effects on his devotees. Formalization opens the concept to limitless application. The universality of the algebra pretends to explain all matter of instances in a peculiar reduction of the singularity of each patient to a general explanatory schema. This was the case with Freud's later so-called sociological work in *Totem and Taboo* (1913), *Moses and Monotheism* (1937), *Group Analysis of the Ego* (1922), and *Civilization and Its Discontents* (1930). In my opinion, psychoanalysis and deconstruction perform their best work as arts of the particular or the singularity. The idiosyncrasy specifies the wish which is submerged in the text. Psychoanalytically, this desire may be considered as a representation in a picture — what does that mean? — in a patient's dream. Deconstructively, the desire may be indicated as a break — what does that not mean? — in an author's text.

The effort in this book is to "dramatize" the dream whose manifest form is the symbol $\$-ism$ on the cover of the book. $\$-ism$ (pronounced: /SCHIZ-em/) is strangely coincident with the entire system(s) in which it is embedded. The latent content of $\$-ism$ is co-extensive with its manifest form(s). In *The Parallax View* (2006), Zizek describes the "parallactic gap" as the constitutive overlap of two antagonistic perspectives on the "one" and the "same" object. The trick of the parallax is the demonstration of the coincidence and continuity between the otherwise exclusive. This is the talent of the pervert. My job is to "dramatize" the concept ($\$-ism$) with its opposite (S). Division between the two — of manifest-s and latent-$\$-ism$ and the obverse of latent-s and manifest-$-ism — makes the simultaneous performance of the difference in the identity — Sameness⁺ — an effort for both author and reader as perverts, schizoids, and Women.

The crucial part of Zizek's concept of the parallactic gap is that the magic is in the performance and demonstration of the simultaneous aperture and closure of the fissure between the two antagonistic perspectives on the "one" and the "same" object: the Real parallax. The parallax is the object of an impossible representation in the ephemeral moment of its presentation and witness. Herein, a recent encounter between myself and an economics professor:

Michael: "I hate rich people."

Professor Economist: "Why?"

Michael: "Because they stole all my money."

[pause.] [laughter.] [pause.]

Professor Economist: "What do you mean they stole all your money?"

Michael: "How else do you explain why they have so much and I have so little?"

[silence.]

Professor Economist: "Well, see, the supply and demand dynamics of the free enterprise capitalist marketplace are such that the assumed scarcity in the market of commodities necessitates that in order to keep inflation low the NAIRU or the Non-Accelerating Inflation Rate of Unemployment must be directed by the natural rate which is adjusted to the annual percentage rate as determined by the Federal Reserve which is subtracted from the —"

Michael: " — That's what I'm talking about!"

Outline of the Book

The book, *Pervert-Schizoid-Woman*, is a work of philosophy, critical theory, Cultural Studies, and queer theory. It critiques the organization of Western economy, language, and desire, and it promotes alternative frameworks for a posthumanist theory and practice of selfhood and sociality. The book critically reconceptualizes three philosophical paradigms: Marxism, deconstruction, and psychoanalysis. The text identifies the capitalist economic system as structured by scarcity and supply/demand dynamics, and it discerns the paradoxical accumulation of debt as the essence of the assumed scarcity in the financial system. It also uncovers the profound isomorphism between the economics of scarcity and the castration and lack at the center of the psychoanalytic interpretation of gender, sexuality, and desire. *Pervert-Schizoid-Woman* exposes the phallocentric systems of gender, sexuality, and desire as they are structured according to the capitalist logic of scarcity, and it claims that deconstruction unveils the organization of words as an absence. The constitutive absence at the center of the word is isomorphic both to the scarcity identified in Marx's critique of capitalist economics and to the castration which is diagnosed in Freud's analysis of phallocentric sexual difference.

The book concludes that the negativity in the scarcity of capitalism, the absence in the structure of language, and the castration in the network of desire are the sources of the dysfunctions in Western systems of finance, expression, and gender and sexuality. In its analysis, the work elaborates and mobilizes Marxism, deconstruction, and psychoanalysis in order to propose a postcapitalist and postphallocentric selfhood and sociality. The critique of economy, language, and desire inspires a Marxist, deconstructive, and psychoanalytic innovation of a future selfhood and sociality. The book elaborates this posthumanist world with various conceptual personae which illuminate the aporetics in the extant systems of finance, expression, gender, sexuality, and desire. These philosophical demonstrations are offered as a path to a practical and theoretical posthumanity.

Pervert-Schizoid-Woman analyzes the extant symbolic order of the systems of finance, language, and desire through the critical lenses of Marxism, deconstruction, and psychoanalysis. The exposition is twofold: critique and reinvention. The book undertakes a study of the (dys)function of the economic system, the language system, and the gender and sexuality system. The book mobilizes a transformed variant of Marxism in order to critique the fissures in capitalism. I utilize a dialectical and materialist approach in order to: review the financial speculation and monetary abstraction of capital; study capitalist accumulation of profit and debt; assess the relationships between labor and life; and evaluate quantitative exchange-value and qualitative use-value under capitalism.

The book integrates this Marxist critique of the economic system with a reconceptualized version of deconstruction which unpacks the essential schizophrenia of the language system. I illuminate: the playful incoherence of the value of the signifier and the enforced sovereignty of signification; the clinically psychotic structure of metaphor and metonymy; the destruction of philosophical identity and essence by the signifying chain; and the undecidability of the signifier and its exchange of indetermination of value. The book layers and integrates both Marxist and deconstructive critiques of the Western system with a revamped variant of psychoanalysis in order to uncover the catastrophic effects of phallocentrism and castration on the self and society. The novel conclusion of the book's rigorous and playful critique is the discovery of the profound isomorphism among capitalist scarcity and supply/demand dynamics, linguistic differential negativity and value, and phallocentric castration and lack. The book is integrated and layered. Concepts are reiterated and reconfigured in order to resituate novel ideas and experimental practices in new contexts.

In addition to a reworked Marxist critique of the economic system, a revamped deconstructive analysis of the language system, and a revised psychoanalytic exegesis of the gender and sexuality system, the book imagines alternatives to the dysfunctions in economy, language, and gender and sexuality in the extant symbolic order. The thesis of this component of the book is explicated with the exuberant invention of new philosophical concepts, including: $-ism (pronounced: /SCHIZ-em/), Pervert-Schizoid-Woman, Spirit of the System, Madness of Order, Spiritual S (X), Signified/r (pronounced: /SIGNI-fied-grrr/), Real Symbolic, Peniscentrism, (a)sexuality, and Sameness⁺ (pronounced: /SAMENESS-plus/). The book demonstrates that a proper Marxist, deconstructive, and psychoanalytic analysis of the system invites us to envision postcapitalist, postsignification, and postphallocentric theories and practices of thinking, being, and living. The pervert is the conceptual persona who inherits a future selfhood and sociality after the critical review of the Western system of humanism. The dual structure of scrupulous critique and creative reinvention is the framework for the philosophical interventions in the book.

The book articulates a sustained and original critical study of the Western systems of economy, language, and gender and sexuality, and it imagines a set of experimental and pleasurable alternatives to current impasses in theory and practice. I situate an analysis of contemporary society within the frameworks of original expositions of Marxism, deconstruction, and psychoanalysis. The objective of this approach to critique is to revitalize the relevance of critical theory to the study of culture, including the structure of finance, the system of language, and the organization of desire. The book reinvigorates the philosophical paradigms of Marxism, deconstruction, and psychoanalysis, and it introduces new lines of critical inquiry in the study of economics and the financial system; language and the sign system; and desire and the gender and sexuality system. It renews academic study of philosophical posthumanism, and it revives research in the traditions of nineteenth- and twentieth-century French and German critical theory. The purpose is to inspire new investigations of, and discussions about, economics, language, and desire from the perspectives of redesigned variants of Marxism, deconstruction, and psychoanalysis, while demonstrating the value of Continental philosophy to the study of contemporary culture. The book's *telos* appropriates insights from critical theory in order to imagine future practices in everyday life.

Pervert-Schizoid-Woman is a rigorous critical exegesis and reconceptualization of Marxism, deconstruction, and psychoanalysis. The book is a playhouse for the sustained, imaginative creation of new concepts for thought and novel habits for practice. The book is a work of critical theory in the French and German philosophical traditions. The book reframes Continental philosophy as the theoretical foundation of the interdisciplinary field of Cultural Studies, and it situates philosophical intervention within its general project: to research and study the social and historical determinants of selfhood and sociality. The book is layered and integrated in the presentation of its nuanced transformation of extant philosophical paradigms. The book refines concepts and perfects ideas in a repetition over the course of the study. The book is also rigorous and comprehensive in its introduction of various invented conceptual personae which illuminate both the critique of the system and the reinvention of the self, other, and society. The text weaves the perspicacious interpretation of the isomorphism among Marxism, deconstruction, and psychoanalysis into the body of the work, and it repeatedly returns these equivalents to the discussions of both critique and reinvention, while playfully layering and comprehensively integrating the three theoretical paradigms in relationship to each other — and to the object of the critique of the system and to the subject of the renewal of the future. The book's synthetic structure reconciles the gap between theory and practice, and between critique and redesign.

The first division of the book theorizes postpsychoanalytic psychical structures. The pervert is the conceptual persona whose sensibility and aesthetic intuit the Madness of Order and the systems of language, finance, and desire. These substrates of the system must be properly uncovered — recognized and unraveled — and critiqued — explicated and evaluated. The pervert is the conceptual persona whose psychical structure is suited to a mastery and analysis of the systems of word, commodity, and phallus. An elaboration of perversion is a forerunner to a sustained critical commentary on the systems of $-ism. The purpose of this first chapter is to reimagine configurations between desires and objects. The first chapter foreshadows work on psychical characterology and perverse aesthetics in division one of the book. Division two of the book presents sustained and perverse critiques of the extant systems of the Madness of Order. The objects of critical exposition are language and the sign, finance and scarcity, and desire and the phallus. Division one of the book elaborates the pervert as the free Spirit whose intuition makes her the proper critic to elucidate the systems of $-ism which are under scrutiny in division two of the book. Division one dramatizes the pervert as a force at the outskirts of language, capitalism, and heterosexuality. The focus of division two of the book is the pervert's critique of the system of $-ism. The pervert's peculiar psychical and aesthetic configuration — (*a*)sexuality — makes her the qualified critic of the systems of language, finance, and sexuality. The pervert is the energy of the Outside. The pervert returns the force of the Outside to the Inside of the system. This is the return of (*a*)sexuality.

Spirit of the Book

Summarily, the subtext of the book is that system ($-ism) and its obverse (S) are structured by a compulsive and ambivalent insistence between aperture and closure. This command tends toward openness rather than closedness. The universe is expansive rather than contractive. But the system is also sustained by a compulsive and ambivalent insistence toward closure. The tendency of the system is expansive and open. But the sovereignty of the system is contractive and closed. The system is opposed to its own essence. An openness is critically structured into the systems of psychoanalysis, Marxism, and deconstruction. Nevertheless, a compulsive ambivalence insists. But the structure of this equivocality is not exact ambivalence. An excess to strict ambivalence ruptures the systems of desire, finance, and language. The trick is to return to the surplus — but then not to return.

Aperture and closure in the expansion and contraction of the galaxy are visible in the critical work in psychoanalysis, Marxism, and deconstruction. Psychoanalytically, the male junior of the castration complex is not only anxiously disturbed by the phallocentric arrangement of penis/not-penis and the forced choice of desire and reality. The male junior is also upset by the very *mise-en-scène* of castration. Man is distressed by the scene of nihilism and its hierarchies of value. The male junior's private property of the penis is his own — *le propre* — by virtue of its potential loss. But man's ambivalence also applies to the excluded (*a*)sexual center. The (*a*)sex is the Outside of the scene of the discovery of sexual difference and the system of nihilism. This (*a*)sexuality generates the openness of the system which is otherwise closed by the nihilistic evaluation of penis/not-penis under phallocentrism and masculine desire. The system compulsively reenacts lack and loss in order to sustain — reproduce — the history of gender and sexuality. This compulsive insistence of contraction contradicts the essential expansiveness of the universe. The system sustains closedness in order to avoid a confrontation with an originary empty fundamental plenitude or Sameness⁺ (pronounced: /SAMENESS-plus/). The (*a*)sexual generative center of the system is negated in perpetuity in order to sustain gender and sexuality.

The Marxist critique of scarcity as a capitalist precept underscores the compulsive insistence toward contraction and closedness — rather than expansion and openness — in the system. Capitalist overproduction is reincorporated by the system. The various crises of capitalist overproduction assimilate the surplus into the system. This reincorporation illuminates the compulsive insistence of the system toward closedness and contraction at the historical moment of openness and expansion. Capitalist overproduction is generated by the same (*a*)sexual center which must be renounced in order to sustain currency and supply/demand dynamics. The (*a*)sexual center of the capitalist system is suffocated by currency and the *finite infinity* or *infinite finity* of dollars and coins. The accumulation of capital entails the calculation of debt. The capitalist recoils from (*a*)sexuality because it threatens the contractive and closed logic of the system of currency. An aneconomy in the absence of dollars and coins thwarts the compulsive insistence of capitalism toward the paradoxical *accumulation of debt*.

The deconstructive critique of *langue* demonstrates the excess of meaning-making in the signifier. This surplus is overwritten by the sovereignty of the word. The proclivity of the signifier is toward openness and aperture. But the sign compulsively insists toward containment and restraint. The word dampens and subdues the otherwise infinite semiosis of the abundance and plenitude of the signifier. The signifier is generated by the (*a*)sexual center of the Outside of nihilism. This (*a*)sexuality of excess value in meaning is abandoned by the pursuit of proper syntax and semantics. The system of *langue* rebuffs the signifier and its surpluses and supplements in favor of the sign and its limits and borders. The word compulsively insists toward a containment of the signifier and its (*a*)sexual center. This (*a*)sexuality is otherwise the generative source of the force of excess and surplus over strict ambivalence and the balance of binary opposition.

Psychoanalytic *Trieb,* capitalist overproduction, and deconstructive signifier each gravitate toward expansion and openness — delayed eroticism, material abundance, and open signification. But the (*a*)sexual center of this generation is consistently opposed by an ambivalent compulsion away from the obscene presence of the absent (*a*)sexual center. This (*a*)sexuality is the Outside of the nihilism of the value of the general equivalent of phallus in sexual relations, the father in social relations, currency in commodity relations, and the word in linguistic relations. My word — (*a*)sexuality — can only be understood imprecisely. The word is a metaphor for the excess and surplus which generate the expansion and openness — but also contraction and closedness — of the system. At best, (*a*)sexuality is Spirit. The Spirit of (*a*)sexuality overpowers the forces of contraction and closedness in desire and gender, scarcity and currency, and the syntax and semantics of the word. The theory of (*a*)sexuality — word — is the optimistic risk of an expansive rather than contractive solar system. An (*a*)sexuality is a Spirit for the future.

The universe is always already infinitely expanded. Conceptually, there is neither psychoanalytic castration nor capitalist scarcity nor syntax and semantics. The Spirit of the System is a historical confrontation with the obscene and empty abundance of (*a*)sexuality. This (*a*) applies to the (*a*) cause of the compulsive insistence toward loss and death. The (*a*) applies not only to sexuality but also to the system of the commodity in Marx's critique of capitalism and to the system of the word in deconstruction's analysis of signification. A historical encounter with this absent presence of (*a*)sexuality portends the arrival of the future in the Spirit of the System in desire as queerness, in finance as communism, and in language as the signifier. This communist queer (*a*)sexual future is not the reversal of the extant system ($-ism) and its obverse (S). The horizon is not the transition from desire to drive, capitalism to communism, and the word to the signifier. The future of the Spirit of the System is a profound *unambivalent*[4] disavowal of the fundamental Sameness[+] between these oppositional pairs. This *Verleugnung* tends toward openness and expansion rather than toward closedness and contraction. There is an excess in the Sameness[+] of the disavowal. The return of *Verleugnung* is beyond itself and its own recurrence. The originary (*a*)sexuality which generates the abundance articulates the fundamental Nothing is Missing at the *arche* of the solar system.

Nothing is Missing is *a priori* — and sexual difference, marketplace commodity, and linguistic word are deviations of castration, scarcity, and absence from this originary — A Nothing is Missing returns from the vagaries of sexual castrations, financial scarcities, and linguistic absences. This return is a forceful celebration of the *différance* — excess and surplus — between Something is Missing in lack and castration and Nothing is Missing in abundance and plenitude. This *Verleugnung* returns the universe to an unsymbolized — unspoken and unwritten — (*a*)sexual generator of an unthematized surfeit and superfluity. The Spirit of the System is the expansive consequence of the won force of (*a*)sexuality against the compulsive insistence of the negative wills of psychoanalytic desire, capitalist scarcity, and the word of syntax and semantics. The embryonic Spirit of the System (S and $-ism) is a return to an inevitable absence of absence. Communist queer (*a*)sexuality will happen to history from the Outside. This Outside is the essential force of the expansion of the solar system. This Outside is no longer *of* history and temporality. This Outside is *against* history and temporality. This Outside is spatial. The Outside is the space of the unconscious and its communist queer (*a*)sexuality. The future is the ends of time from the Outside. The Outside is a plenitude of a proliferated series of sex objects, a surplus production of goods and services, and a free liberation of the play of the signifier. This won excess emerges in the transition away from the Something is Missing in the phallocentrism of sexuality and gender, the scarcity in capitalism, and the syntax and semantics of the sign and toward the Nothing is Missing of communist queer (*a*)sexuality. Outside — castration, scarcity, and signification will be torn asunder by the Spirit of the System. The space of this future is the timeless unconscious.

DESIRE AND DRIVE, IN REVERSE

This project is a form of *Praxis* — what Lacan describes as any "concerted human action" which treats the Real by the function of the symbolic.[5] The desire which is visible in the field and delimited by the *Praxis* is supported by the fantasy. The fantasy coordinates and organizes the desire in question. This fantasy-reality situates the desire in the field of the imaginary rivalrous and aggressive relations between an ego and an alter ego. Borders between self and other are what Derrida names in general terms as *le propre*: the proper, property, ownership, possession, and mineness. *Le propre* contains the basic constituents of what I call $-ism (pronounced: /SCHIZ-em/). These partitions are (im)precisely in question in the imaginary register. Whose ego is whose? Whose transference is whose? The imaginary realm is marked by the undecidability of the trauma. Freud approaches this instability in his account of the "traumatic neurosis" of the Great War. These neuroses were the response to the battlefield jolt of the incursion of the "inside" by the "outside" that Freud uncovers in his book, *Beyond the Pleasure Principle* (1920).[6] The imaginary is dominated by this hostile and violent blitz of the other on the self (and vice-versa) within the ambiguous double-edged distinctions of these limits and sides. Where does the self end and the other begin? The transferential question of the origin and trace — of the departure of the letter and its alleged arrival — yields no easy resolution. All of the words in the symbolic order — self/other, straight/gay, and so on — submit to the unregulated force of the Real. This disruptive exertion of the Real endlessly pulsates beyond the fixed fluctuation between tension and its release.

Freud's pleasure principle rules the conservative balance and temperate organization — homeostasis — which stabilize and steady the system. Fantasy veils the object *qua* Real. Fantasy defers the work of *Thanatos*. The death drive is beyond the regulated returns of the pleasure principle. This Real is an excess. The Real cannot be (ac)counted (for) by the system. The object that the symbolization of the *Praxis* seeks to approach as object-cause of its desire is fundamentally imaginary. This is so even if its strength is a Real that always returns to the "same place," as Lacan puts it.[7] Desire is uncomfortable because it involves capture in the imaginary duality and struggle around the borders between objects in the system. Desire is inevitably frustrated because the function of the object-cause of desire (*objet petit a*) is metonymic. Metonymy launches desire onto an object which is otherwise than the object of desire. The object of desire is not the object of desire. The *objet* is precisely not "itself." A *le petit a* is concealed from the efforts of the subject to capture the ephemerality of the object in speech and writing. The object as Real persists — tempts and flirts — beyond the blunt clutches of the desire in question.

The answer to the question of desire is simply another question — *ad infinitum* or not — if the letter either does not structurally arrive at its destination (Derrida's ambivalent position) or must always eventually commit to its *Ziel* (Lacan's nuanced orientation). In Derrida's *différance*, presence — what is — is a presumed origin that finally and infinitely yields to the differences and deferrals of the trace. These marks — written text but also audible speech — entice the reader's desire for *arche*. Who is speaking? This object of desire — strangely, both *arche* and trace — confronts the subject with a movement. The traversal avoids a satisfactory presence. The letter pretends to always arrive at its destination. This imaginary fantasy-reality omnubilates the Real. The traumatic rupture of the Real *qua* symbolic order is contained by the fantasy of a desire. Metonymic movement — in Lacan's matheme: f (S…S′)S » S(—)s — of the slip and slide of the *objet petit a* submits to the powers of the imaginary register.[8] Psychoanalysis is the science of desire (in my matheme: $<>a<>a<>a, and so on). Psychoanalysis unveils desire as otherwise than "itself." The object of desire is vacated of any essence because the substance of desire is the deviation of the object from itself; the object is always elsewhere than in its own and proper place.

Figure 1.2 Isomorphisms and Cleavages between Perverse Philosophy and Analytic Philosophy

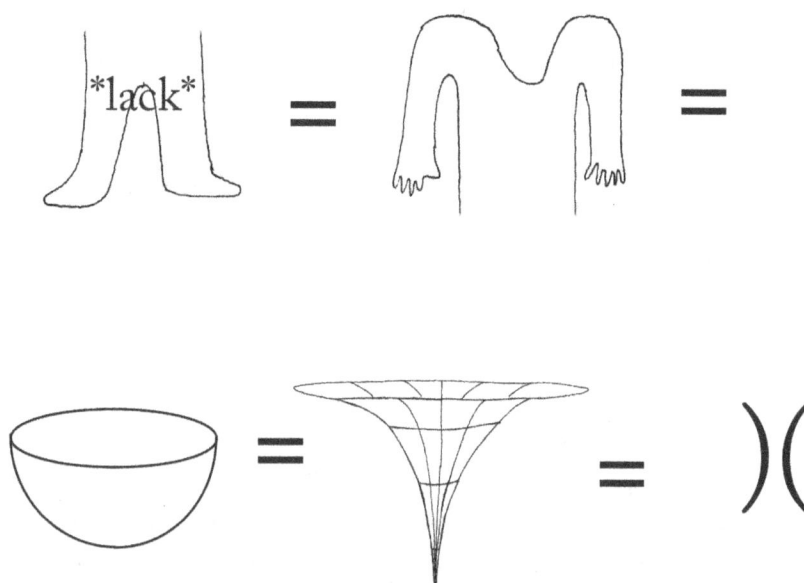

This illustration portrays the parallax. The linguistic, phallocentric, and capitalist Something is Missing is differently framed in the text and illustrations in order to creatively open a parallactic space of isomorphism. This space will sustain different modalities of the parallels among the objects of deconstruction, psychoanalysis, and Marxism in the text and illustrations. The parallactic parallelism is an illustration of the impossibility of a visual form which can articulate from the Outside of the borders of organization. This Outside is simultaneously different from its own organization both Inside and Outside of the system. The figures (from above right to below left) depict the Something is Missing in the dimensions of: 1) Queer Mathematical Set Theory (the principle of an Inclusion which cannot be Included); 2) discourse (linguistic binds of *Eros* and splits of *Thanatos*); 3) subjectivity (identity and selfhood); 4) phallocentrism (sexual difference and castration); and 5) capitalism (scarcity and exchange).

1) Queer Mathematical Set Theory:

In the analytic (as opposed to Continental) tradition of philosophy, the mathematical theory of the principle of Inclusion is central to Wittgenstein's avoidance of Russell's Paradox. The latter debate — between Wittgenstein and Russell — illuminates the isomorphism of the theoretical aporia of the *arche* of the (*a*)sexual drive and the paradox in Set Theory: the Set(s) of all Sets which do(es) not include (itself) themselves. The illustration draws a comparison between Sets in mathematics and contexts of signification in linguistic analysis. The figure mobilizes a consistent mathematics which shows first, a system of Sets which may Include their own terms and also other Sets and, second, a space of language in which objects are self-same and self-identical. Russell's Paradox — of a Set(s) of Sets which do(es) not Include (itself) themselves — upsets the consistency of Set Theory because it Implicitly proposes the possibility of a Set which can Exclude itself. The key interval is between "Not Include" and "Exclude" or between "Non-Presence" and "Absence." Wittgenstein may rejoin that Russell's Paradox relies on a linguistic trick which obfuscates his categories of the Explicit and the Implicit. A

Set always Implicitly Includes itself. The Queer Mathematics of the illustrations shows that the problematic of a Set which could Include itself Explicitly is the same quandary as the visual and textual representation of the context *of* symbolization itself. The problem is: if a Set can Explicitly Include itself, then Sets could Implicitly exist in a Being which is defined by an Exclusion or Nothingness. But Sets do not have an Outside Explicitly. The comparison to *langue* is that there is an infinite Inside to the Set even if the Set (or context) is delimited or bounded. The object which is not Inside is also not Outside. This unsymbolizable gap is the Nothing is Missing. For Wittgenstein, there is no Something is Missing in the Set. The Set Includes in the Absence of any Exclusion. A Non-Presence (Not Including) is the Real of an unwriteable and unspeakable gap.

2) Discourse and the Signifier:

The signifying term or unit of text (A, B, C, D, and so on) signifies and communicates — makes meaning — because it operates by the mechanism of the *point de capiton* of retroactive and limited signification within a delimited and bounded context. Saussure's discovery is that the conceptual and abstract signified (what the mark "means") and the material and embodied signifier (the brute materiality of its Being as divorced from Meaning) are only isolatable in theory. In practice, the sign *qua* the conjoinment of signifier and signified, and materiality and conceptuality, is always already united in the self-same and self-identical positive unity of the word. In the signifying chain, "A" (unit of text) signifies "not-B" and "not-C" and "not-D" on the level of the material signifier insofar as it *is* "not-A" and *is* "not-B." A profound negation is constitutive of the meaning-making potential of the signified and the abstract component of the sign. In the language game, as Wittgenstein would put it, "A" communicates in meaning-making by distinction from and opposition to (as Saussure would put it of the sign) every other unit of text. But the emergence of the identity and essence of "A" in the game of differential negativity necessitates ever more distinctions and oppositions — negations — because "D" is also identified as "not-B" and "not-C." The language game expansively generates "E" in order to clarify and consolidate — by differential negation — "A," "B," "C," "D," and so on. Wittgenstein would want to indicate that the *not* must be situated Inside of the " " in the context of Meaning, and that the *not* must be situated Outside of the " " in the context of Being: "A" means (Meaning) "not-B" and is (Being) not "B." The distinction between the two orientations toward the negation or the *not* is isolated by the gap between Absence and Non-Presence. Saussure intuits that the sign (word) involves no such gap between Absence and Non-Presence. A Non-Presence is necessarily articulated as an Absence. This must be so if the *not* is spatially and temporally — anywhere and anytime — the Same[+]. The *not* must be the Same[+] if "E" is to provide any clarification and consolidation of Meaning — Why? The *not* of "not-B" or "not-C" must be retained — traced — in the Meaning of "B." The system must be closed — ( ) — to the *not* which is Outside of Being — Non-Presence — and open —) (— to the *not* which is inside of Meaning — Absence. Wittgenstein's disposal of Russell's Paradox is an affirmation of the Sameness[+] between the Exclusion of Presence and the Inclusion of Absence. This Sameness[+] which is *not* identical is written by Derrida as a "sameness which is not identical" — or a Sameness[+]. Wittgenstein's claim that a Set cannot Include its own principle of Inclusion parallels the assertion that the master signifier's binary opposite cannot be spoken or written — that the signified is under erasure and that the occluded center is compulsively forced into the Outside of the system.

3) Subjectivity and Identity:

The $-istic subject's identity to and as itself — self-presence *qua* self-presence — obscures the constitutive reference of the ostensible self-sameness of the Other. This mistaken Exclusion of the Exclusion is isomorphic to the gesture of Exclusion of its opposite (not-penis) in the consolidation of its own present signification. The subject's identity (A = A) obscures this otherness to itself. The subject exchanges the arbitrary conventionality — contingency — of Being for an economy in which Being is present, as such, *qua*, by definition, *il y a*, and so on. Consciousness is fundamentally neurotic. Consciousness fantasizes a recursion back upon itself which is a present instantiation and coherent articulation of itself in the absence of reference — difference and deferral in *différance* — to an otherness which would otherwise psychotically destabilize its will to consistency and coherence.

4) Phallocentrism and Sexual Difference:

The genitals represent the primacy of plenitude. The clitoris is only secondarily an absence. Unexpectedly, the clitoris is primarily a presence because masculine castration anxiety only becomes a coherent threat in the structured and specular return of the penis to itself in its mediation by the not-penis of the present absence of the clitoris. The clitoris is the present otherness of an absent self-sameness and self-identity. The binary system of sexuality is structured by negativity: the presence of the penis and the presence *of the absence* of the penis — the clitoris. The neurotic's thinking, being, and living are organized by this specular dynamic of a negativity which is presented as an atrophied Positivity. The binaristic system of plenitude and scarcity is isomorphic to the paradox of the A and) A (. The fetishistic gesture involves a veiled Positivity which resolves castration and its symptomatology of narcissism, aggressivity, and anxiety. The Non-Presence in the genitals (penis/not-penis) *qua* absence is the under erasure Being of the ~~Woman~~. The parallel between not-penis and "not-A" is limited and circumscribed because the Real Penis sustains an excess materiality which resists the grasp of the sign. Sexually, the paradox of the binary opposite of the Real Penis is an excess materiality which is neither a presence nor an absence.

5) Capitalism and Currency:

The capitalist fabled presupposition of scarcity — the posited excess of demand over a lack of supply — is isomorphic to the castration in the scene of the discovery of sexual difference and to the linguistic *not* of difference and negativity. The bank freely prints *qua* debt the general equivalent — dollars and coins. This manufactured medium of exchange — currency — in the system dilutes the differences and negations (but not distinctions and oppositions) between the sign-commodities (rather than signifier-commodities) in the marketplace economy. Capitalistically, the neurotic obscures the diacritics of *value* against the dialectics of *signification*. The sign and the exchange of debt and calculation of return structure capitalism, and the signifier and its excess and unsymbolizable materiality of goods and services (dis)organize the nascent economy of communism. The Non-Presence in the impossible ") (" of Russell's Paradox is the Excluded plenitude of materiality which is foreclosed by the capitalist system of supply/demand dynamics and the ideology of scarcity. The (communist) abundance cannot be symbolized under capitalism because the material surplus — foreskinly excess — resists the binary logic of signification which compares and contrasts all sign-commodities through the mediation of the general equivalent of dollars and coins under the logic of nihilism. The abundance — goods and services — is occluded by the system. Wittgenstein would want to say that this capitalist foreclosure of abundance illuminates his discovery that a Set (linguistic context) must be Implicitly Excluded.

Notes & Sketches —

Contra the Logic of Identity, the object is precisely not itself. The object parallactically parts from itself *qua* otherwise than itself. Zizek describes the split in the object's negativity as the "minimal difference" between the two antagonistic perspectives on the "one" and the "same" split object: between Economics 101 and Marxism 1917. This gap illuminates a Sameness⁺. Simultaneity of Sameness⁺ for the Pervert-Schizoid-Woman achieves no closure for a future subject who would otherwise neurotically seek an anticipatory mirror *Gestalt* for itself as its desired avatar. Derrida's claim that a letter is designed to potentially avoid capture in a destination repeats Lacan's claim but with a marked difference. For deconstruction, the letter evades capture in the imaginary fantasy. The letter is an effect of the Real but not as *arche*. The trace sabotages the *arche* (which is "itself") from within the order of the system (s). Otherwise, the *arche* seeks to sustain presence in its constitutional fragility. I contend that the structure of the symbolic order is Neurotic Foreclosure or *rejet névrotique*. This modality of negation of the system *tout court* is a perverse twist which is neither neurotic repression nor psychotic foreclosure. *Neurotische Ablehnung* is the by-the-by negation of the system and its return from the Real as "itself."

The so-called traversal of the fantasy in psychoanalysis simply inaugurates the so-called pass which is a prerequisite in the training of the psychoanalyst. The pass distances the subject from the Other. The presence of the Other otherwise overwhelms the neurotic subject with the desires and demands of the culture. This quiet — imperceptible — transition from the fantasy to the Real marks the coincidence of the Real with the symbolic. The traversal subdues the imaginary rivalry. The traversal initiates a drive (*Trieb*) whose *jouissance* of the Other encircles the object as Real or as what I call the Real Signifier and the Real Symbolic. Otherwise, desire is motivated by a frenzied castration. This frenetic desire is pulsated by lack instead of by plenitude. Desire is a forced choice. Absence organizes the ideology of scarcity in capitalist economics. Lack structures the phallocentric ideology of sexual difference in the offspring's Oedipus complex. This shift between desire and drive explains the necessity of the death drive (*Thanatos*) as an extension of the pleasure principle in Freud's thought. But how can *Thanatos* be the source of a renewed *Eros*?

The Traversal of the Fantasy

Praxis treats the Real through the defiles of the signifier in the symbolic function. Fantasy veils the Real dimension of the object of desire by capturing it in the coordinates of the imaginary. The duality of egos posits *Gestalt* objects. These *Gestalts* are simultaneously subject to the compressions and displacements of an entanglement with each other. These objects include the identification with an other who is understood as a complete and perfect form. This *Gestalt* embodies the subject's desire for identity. Desire inspires the fiction of the ego. These objects in-the-world extend beyond the reach of the desire that they inspire. Desire in the field of fantasy misapprehends the Real in the register of the imaginary. But in the transition from the subject of desire to the Pervert-Schizoid-Woman of drive, the object becomes Real instead of being merely the imaginary object of fantasy. The traversal of the fantasy and the cure of psychoanalytic technique reveal the imaginary as the scene of ideological desire. This scene is a disguise of the Real. The Real absolutely resists the symbolization of speaking and writing. In the traversal of the fantasy, the patient is led toward the infinite wander — analysis terminable and interminable — around the Real object. The subject experiences the resistance of the object *qua* Real to the figurations of the symbolic function within the field of the imaginary.

Traversal of the fantasy encourages the idiosyncratic shift in the patient from desire (*désir*) to drive (*Trieb*). My claim is that curative traversal coincides with the subject's experience of a revolution. The revolution transforms an Economics 101 scarcity of the Freudian Something is Missing of the female genitalia into a

Marxist 1917 abundance in which Nothing is Missing of the postphallic genital principle. This revolution is an (*a*)sexuality. After the traversal of the fantasy, the subject's orientation toward difference and the Other is profoundly reimagined because Nothing is Missing. Nothingness is the obverse of Freud's illustration of the vagina and the clitoris in *The Interpretation of Dreams* (1900): "Something is missing describes the principal characteristic of the female genitals."[9] This perversely feminine drive pursues a Real, around which it endlessly wanders and dances. The Pervert-Schizoid-Woman enjoys the Other *jouissance* of plenitude and abundance rather than the masculine desire of lack and loss. The future is communism, but so is the past. But how?

Sexual difference is reexperienced for the subject of the transition from desire to *Trieb* because the destination of the letter yields to the bemused pursuit of metonymic displacements. This deferral happens in a dreamy plenitude of an unconscious without temporality, negation, or knowledge. The Woman's absent penis is sutured by the pervert's will to encounter presence in the fetishistic props of the fur, lace, shoe, and jockstrap — and of any other representation in the system. The wound of the Woman otherwise strikes castration anxiety in the offspring. His private(s) property of *le propre* of the penis is at risk. The Something is Missing reminds the male junior of a potential narcissistic loss of the male sex organ which is otherwise the source of his ecstasy and existence.

Drive views this penis as different from itself. The penis and the clitoris are properly the Real objects of *Trieb* rather than the objects of the symbolic and imaginary registers. These fantasy objects otherwise must be guarded like the family jewels. The potential transformation of the penis from an object of the symbolic and the imaginary to an object of the Real occurs because the significance of the penis is relationally defined as an organ. The possessor (*le propre*) is consequently not the sole owner of this otherwise $-istic private property. The fear of the annexation of this property is subdued because the object is exactly displaced. The phallocentric prejudice intuits the Woman's difference as a deficit of Something is Missing. The Woman lacks the penis which is present in the man. This trope of scarcity is reordered in the aim/less wanders of the drive. This assumption of lack is recalibrated in the each according to his need and each according to his ability of communism.

In *Trieb*, the prospective loss cannot be determined as presence in the structure of the ontological question of the — What is? Proleptic castration is indeterminate because neither the man nor the Woman "own" (*le propre*, $-ism) the penis or clitoris as private property. The penis is neither the capitalist commodity of the man nor the $-istic dispossession of the Woman. The fantasy of phallocentrism is a discrimination. This prejudice is organized by capitalist private property. Marx wants to abolish ownership under the system of communism. I reconfigure sexual difference as it is conceived by psychoanalysis. A phallocentric bias veils the traversal of the fantasy from desire to drive. Phallocentrically, the male subject misleads himself in an imaginary capture of the duality of rivalry. He tricks himself into the phallic knowledge that the object's absent resistance yields to a worldly presence. This phallic knowledge of presence phallocentrically conceives of a sexual difference in which the clitoris is the absence of the penis and the penis is the presence of itself. This presence — *Fort! Da!* — of the phallic object — S*a* rather than S<>*a* — is a theoretical misfire and practical defeat. The subject quickly succumbs to the function of desire in absence. Desire installs lack in the place of the missed encounter. The subject pursues the mistaken imaginary object as present then — present then — present then — and so on. Desire is structured by the slip and slide — difference and deferral — of *différance*. The object is not present. But then what? The imaginary and symbolic object will only yield disappointment for the subject of desire. The object must be disowned and dispossessed. The object must be reconsidered as Real. The Real object is present in its absence. The Real object is encountered in its disappearance. The Real object flashes in the foreground even as it escapes in the background. Perversely, the Real object is full in its emptiness.

Figure 1.3 The Signifying Chain

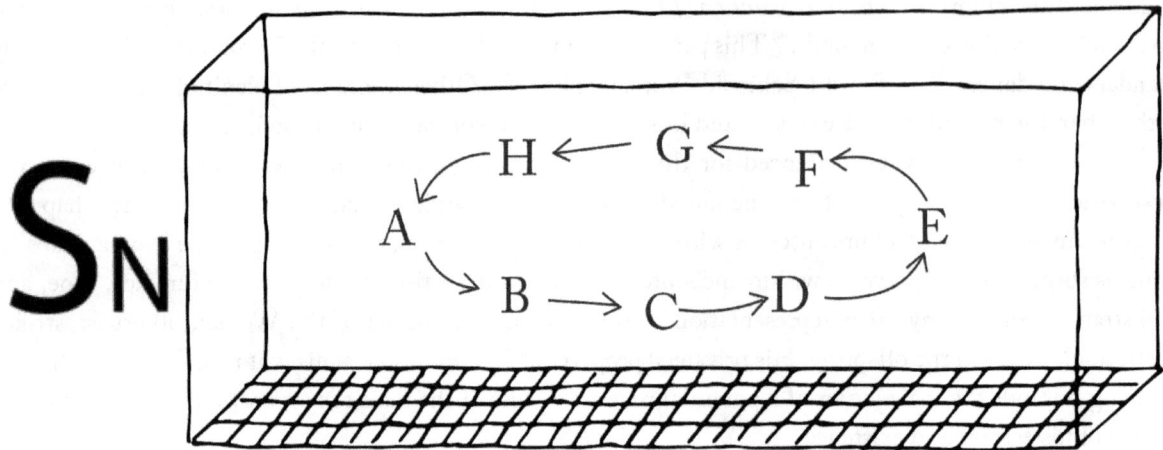

This figure of the signifying chain depicts the performance and function of meaning-making in the system of *langue*. The objects within the expansive space of discourse are both connected and severed by the arrows of temporal Becoming but also of spatial differentiation. The drawing illustrates that each term (letter, word, phrase, sentence, paragraph, and so on of text) is clarified by the next unit of text. This clarification is the constituted essence and Being of Becoming of each configuration of text in the signifying chain of articulated arrows between units of text. The order of units of text is irrespective of the temporal and spatial presence of each unit in the network of words. The S_N represents the series of terms (letters, words, phrases, sentences, paragraphs, and so on) such that any text (A, B, C, D, E, F, G, H, and so on) may be N at any instant. The S_N is the entire series of terms at a given temporal instant or spatial point. The depiction of the arrows, letters, and spatial *mise-en-scene* conveys the relationship between elementary symbols in the space of language. The mark of S_N illuminates the temporal deferral and spatial difference of the fundamental units of the system. The S_N symbolizes both the instant of the open totality of the signifying chain and the difference and deferral in relationality and constructionism of the identification of any discrete unit of text in the series. The signifying chain is both open and closed, and it is both expansive and contractive. The series of terms is both an aperture toward the *tout autre* at the same instant that it is a closure in totality.

Notes & Sketches —

A transition from failed and miserable *désir* to triumphant and radiant *Trieb* involves a subjective reorientation toward the object. The object must not be considered imaginary. The object must be reformulated as Real. This Real object (*objet réel peu a*) fundamentally resists and necessarily flees any pursuit of itself through the insistence of the signifying chain of the symbolic function. The fantasy conspires with *désir* to block *Trieb*. Traversal of the fantasy reveals the constitutive glint(s) of the object in the subjective shift from desire to drive, from imaginary object to Real object, and from the fantasy-reality of everyday life to the Real of the traumatic disruption of the symbolic order as such. Redesign of the subject's *Praxis* from desire to drive revises and transforms the parallactic object(s) in question. The aperture of the gap between the objects simultaneously achieves the closure of this gap between the objects. Both of these objects become otherwise than themselves. This transition — from debt to credit, and the reverse — disrupts the self-same and self-identical symbolic order. The Real of a simultaneity of Sameness⁺ emerges from this transformation from capitalism (Something is Missing, scarcity) to communism (Nothing is Missing, abundance). The psychoanalytic pass introduces an entirely different subjective experience for the subject of drive and the Real. The Becoming of the Pervert-Schizoid-Woman of the S revolts against the neurotic subject of s. The revolution begins (again) with the opening and closing of the parallactic gap.

From Scarcity to Plenitude — to Sameness+

The shift from desire to drive also illuminates an economic change in terrain for the subject. The dominance of desire and the regulated tension of the pleasure principle assume the scarcity and castration of Something is Missing. In contrast, the efforts of drive deny this castration and scarcity at the origins of the economic system. How? This is done so in the fetishist's disavowal (*Verleugnung*) of sexual difference. The pervert disavows sexual difference through the magical phallicization of the lack in the Woman. The capitalist economy works as an ideological system in the same way that sexual difference operates under the phallocentric rules of patriarchy. The neurotic economic precept of capitalism is scarcity. Economics 101 is isomorphic to the Something is Missing of the female genitalia in Freudian thought. The Something is Missing describes both the castration of the female genitalia for Freud (lack, loss) and the scarcity of the economy for Professor Economist (supply/demand). The Something is Missing haunts the masculine subject of both the phallocentrism of patriarchy and the supply/demand scarcity of capitalism.

The principal characteristic of the female genitalia and the capitalist system of supply/demand is Something is Missing. The capitalist economic so-called laws of supply/demand and the free hand of the market structure all of the economic rules of capitalism. This set of laws governs Western $-ism. These rules only apply to the economy if scarcity is assumed at the outset of the production (supply) and the consumption (demand) processes in the system (s). The pervert's trick is to intuit the parallactic gap in this theoretical scenario. She imagines abundance and plenitude in the place of scarcity and lack. The Pervert-Schizoid-Woman discerns the Unreasonable simultaneity of abundance/scarcity and plenitude/lack. Marx foresaw abundance — the female penis — as the liberatory contribution of capitalist overproduction in advanced systems, such as in contemporary Western economies.

Plenitude replaces sexual difference in the pervert's world. Any object is constitutively split in itself. The subject of drive reimagines a sexual system which is unanchored in the fiction of castration. She imagines an economic system which is untethered to the fable of scarcity. The pervert disavows an ideology of debt and return — American Express — in supply and demand. This perverse *Trieb* warrants the emergence of the ideological — and not simply material — conditions for communism, such as Marx imagined as each according to his need and each according to his ability. Ordinarily, phallocentric sexual difference and capitalist economic organization are structured by the Freudian pleasure principle of homeostasis — increase in tension, decrease in tension. This homeostasis is the principle of masculine idiotic *jouissance*.

Figure 1.4 Signification and Object

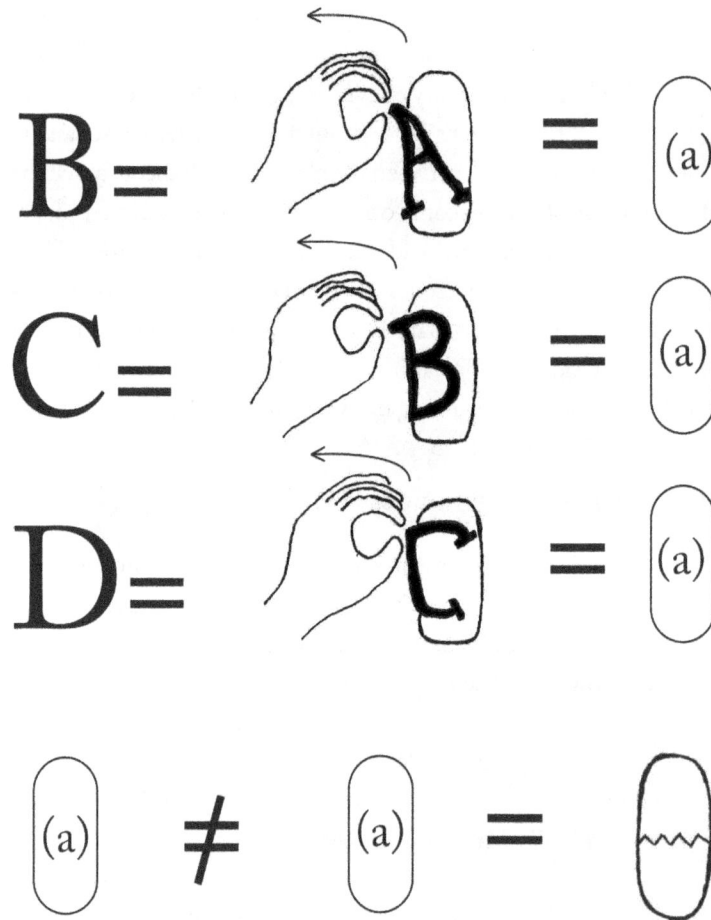

This drawing illustrates an object of the Real which is covered in infinite layers of the *mise-en-abyme* of symbolization. The unit of text B retroactively (*Nachträglichkeit, après-coup*) constitutes the signification of A and, in the process, of A and B in relationship to C (*et al.*). The illustration depicts B as the object of a signification which is stripped of A. B peels A (above, center) from the object at the same time as C peels B from its object. The object of the *mise-en-abyme* is never revealed as such except as a series of approximations in layers and mirrors. This illustration portrays the resistance of the Real object to symbolization. This effort — symbolization of the Real — is the definition of *Praxis*: to speak and write the occluded center in its expansion and extension to all points in space and time in the symbolic order. The Real object must be divergent from itself in order to consolidate itself in Being as such. The word is not itself. The object is not itself. The conclusion in the final equation (below) is that the object is different from itself. The object is fragmented. This object (below, right) is the fractured image of a Sameness[+] which is Different[+] from itself but the Same[+] as the other.

Notes & Sketches —

In contrast, the absence of absence — presence of presence and presence of absence and absence of presence, and so on — blunts this dickish idiocy. The pervert's sexual Other-Difference is of a female penis which is clitoral. The female penis (clitoris, and so on) unexpectedly eases castration anxiety for the masculine subject. He does not need to fear the loss of a private property which is precisely not his own. Similarly, the plenitude of communism undermines the logic of scarcity for the otherwise neurotic subject. He does not need to restrict his production and consumption. The arrival of the psychoanalytic and deconstructive letter is endlessly postponed (*différance*). The calculation of the Signified/r of the object tends toward this direction and then the reverse. Freud says that the criteria for the determination of this difference between the superiority/inferiority of the penis/clitoris in sexual difference are visibility and size.[10] Calculations of Marxian surplus value or capitalist "profit" are inapposite for the communist-perverse subject of free exchange and unregulated substitution. Like the offspring of embryonic sexuality from Freud's *Three Essays on the Theory of Sexuality* (1905), the subject of polymorphous perversity (and incalculable communism) enjoys a dirty sex as opposed to a rigid sexuality. The pervert and the communist are youthfully (*a*)sexual.

Michael Warner's queer work on sex and sexuality is a fine example of scholarship which privileges sex above sexuality. He valorizes the filthiness of tearoom trysts above narcissistic concern with identity and sexuality. In *The Trouble with Normal: Sex, Politics, and the Ethics of Queer Life* (1999), Warner calls for the liberation and enjoyment of what could be described as a quasi-embryonic free sexual exchange of aims and objects.[11] This is a filthy queerness which returns to the total sexualized body of junior sexuality. The sexualized body of the young is isomorphic to the free pursuit of production and consumption in communism. The junior's liberated sexuality plays like communist free labor. An (im)proper (*a*)sexuality is the free (sexual) production and emancipated (sexual) consumption of the communism of juvenescence.

Pervert-Schizoid-Woman's unhinged play — free aim and free object — empowers an Other *jouissance*. This orgasmic and painful Other-Joy is exemplary of the force of *Thanatos*. This (*a*)sexuality transgresses the regulations of an escalated tension and softened return within an economy of limitation and an (ac) count in (for) the pleasure principle. The *Trieb* beyond the pleasure principle releases the constraints of the fear and anxiety of castration. The oedipal will to guard the family jewels otherwise deadens the subject's relationship to the *objet a* (and *b* and *c* and *d*, and so on). Such *objets* are imaginary for the neurotic subject of simple pleasure. The pervert's object of the Real disrupts the symbolic order and its homeostasis of controlled orientation, balance, and organization. Pleasure is conservative. The *jouissance* of the Other is disorderly. The man is sexual. The Woman is the (*a*)sexual revolution. But how does the neurotic become a Woman? Cut the subject off at the —

Drive dismantles the difference between *désir* and *Trieb*. Neither of these designations as objects of desire (as "desire" and as "drive") sustains a metaphysics of presence. These concepts are not present. The concept of desire is *not*. The concept of drive is *not*. Even the opposition as a concept (desire/drive) is *not*. As objects of *Trieb*, these concepts (and also their respective objects) are not imaginarily fixed in the coordinates of the fantasy-reality of the imaginary-symbolic field. Driven, the difference between desire and drive is situated in the register of the Real. This Real resists symbolization absolutely. The Real challenges the system (s) of the coordination of oppositional pairs, such as *désir/Trieb*. The Pervert-Schizoid-Woman's *Trieb* drives beyond the pleasure principle of the arrest-escape — law/transgression — of the endless encirclement of an object. The object invariably resists capture.

This disappearance — slip and slide — is theorized in Freud's accidental discovery of *Thanatos*. The death drive articulates the beyond of the regulated homeostatic increase and decrease of tension of the lack in desire.

The concept of *Thanatos* explains the (dis)satisfaction of the object-cause of desire. *Thanatos* also explains the fluctuations of the supply/demand calculations in the capitalist marketplace. The pleasure principle of desire yields to drive. The *Trieb* aim/lessly wanders around the object. The drive deliriously encircles around "itself" as always otherwise than its "own" (penis, clitoris, commodity) "itself." The *Ziel* of the drive is *Trieb* "itself." As a deconstructive pervert would put it, *Trieb* enjoys the aim/less of a pursuit, and desire fetches in a claw toward frustration. For (*a*)sexual drive, the fantasmatic separation between "desire" and "drive" is purely imaginary. Pursuit against fetch: what's the difference?

The coordinates of the (con)text unravel any frame of reference by which to divide "desire" and "drive" from each other as distinctly and presently — Being — themselves. Unexpectedly, there is no difference between desire and drive, and between *désir* and *Trieb*, other than *différance*. Drive achieves — ! — the feminine *jouissance* as an enjoyment which is always intertwined with the other. The distinction between subject and object utterly dissolves into the ether of ecstasy rather than imaginarily tenses in the *Gestalt* of form. The drive wanders beyond the regulations of oppositions (increase/decrease) in the pleasure principle of the system (s). Drive is desire, but desire is not yet drive. This means that desire is exactly drive. The imaginary dimension promises *Gestalt* identities. But this scene of mirror-dualities overwrites such a pledge with the confusions of rivalry and aggression. Firm contours of both subject and other are undermined.

The singular difference between the desire of the imaginary fantasy-reality and the *Trieb* of the Real is massive yet simple: an aesthetics. A divergent sensibility divides the Pervert-Schizoid-Woman from the neurotic. The pervert's driven interpretation of the opposition between the two principles of *désir* and *Trieb* is parallactic. At the same time, the pervert discovers the simultaneity of the aperture and closure of the distinction. What is the Other-Logic which is beyond phallocentric castration and capitalist scarcity? What aneconomy encourages the subjective turn toward the Real? How can the neurotic come to the limit-thought and utmost-practice — Spirit of the System — which rupture the system (s) within which he is both troublemaker and guardian, and both dissident and conformist? How can the vanguard *pervert the neurotic* and transform man away from Something is Missing and toward Nothing is Missing, and transition him away from capitalism and toward communism, and convert him away from \$-ism and toward S — and then around again? What is the form of the revolution of this other-modality of thinking, being, and living?

The representational illumination must outline the schizoid's Unreason. This crazy talk is outside of rationality. But it is also simultaneously internal to the structure of Reason. Reason is Unreasonable, and Unreason is a form of Reason. This Unreason is otherwise invisibly prohibited by \$-ism. The system's (s) dominant logic must be supplanted by an other-arrangement and an other-configuration — the Outside. The same-Outside will be articulated in the critique of \$-ism. It will be introduced and celebrated as the Pervert-Schizoid-Woman, the master-signifier and mistress-revolutionary of this book. How do we illuminate the s *qua* \$-ism *qua* S? The wager of this book — not yet promised and not yet realized — is that the Pervert-Schizoid-Woman may be the subject of this otherwise than and elsewhere to itself. The pervert and her *Trieb* may be the *auteur* of this symbolization. But how can the pervert be an author after her death?

The *Praxis* of perverse textuality must traverse the fantasy. The pervert's symbol gestures beyond the calculations of the pleasure principle and toward a feminine *jouissance*. This Other-Pleasure finally puts an end to the anxiety and fear of the desire for castration under phallocentrism. This Other-Ecstasy puts the kibosh on the injustice and alienation of scarcity under capitalism. The end(s) of this desire must undo the frustrations of desire and, at their extension, redo their terrific joys as *Trieb*. My job is to articulate an endless insistence which is beyond the regulation of lack and its return in the homeostatic increase and decrease of tension of the simple pleasure principle. The object which is discovered by the object of drive and desire — *désirTrieb* — is the object of psychoanalytic training. This object is the pass — but past what?

To start, the object — rather than simply the subject — splits into a fragmented disunity. This fractal quarky string avoids captive objectification in the *Gestalt* totalities of the anticipatory fantasy of the imaginary. The object of drive is otherwise than itself within a metaphysics of presence. There is no ontological "what is" of the object of drive. *Trieb* is postontological. The drive is otherworldly. *Trieb* is (a)sexual. The object of drive is divided from itself. This metaphysics of Other-Presence is neither here nor there, neither this nor that but — the object of the schizoid's foreclosure (*Verwerfung*) of the symbolic and its return in the Real. This metaphysics of Other-Being is also both here and there, and both this and that and — the object of the pervert's disavowal (*Verleugnung*). And this Other-Metaphysics is also — Woman. The nonknowledge is beyond the regulated play of lack and its suture in the pleasure principle. Homeostasis of idiotic pleasure otherwise entices the object *qua* imaginary into the clutches of an ultimately disappointed desire. The subject of the Spirit of the System is precisely not itself.

The subject of the future is deviant from the Logic of Identity. Bataille uses the term *"ipse"* in his book, *Inner Experience* (1943).[12] Heidegger invokes "thrownness" in order to articulate the originary and constitutional displacement of *Dasein* being-in-the-world.[13] Diffusion of self in the death drive is (dis)located in a field which cannot gather such a subject into itself as unitary and fixed in the binds of *Eros*. The French *il y a* denotes presence. This idiom of the metaphysics of Being in ontology — what is — fails to capture the displacement of the object from its own (*le propre*) internal consistency. There is — *not*. This *not* expresses the negativity at the basis of all Being in the world. Heidegger refers to this fundamental essence as "nullity."[14] The object of drive is properly named as the world itself. But world is a series of references — differences and deferrals — without a final referent. The subject-object in-the-world can find no final reference as origin or *arche* either in the human being as subject in the world of objects, on the one hand, or in Being as copula in the relationship of the object to itself, on the other hand. It is what it is not.

The object which wanders in aim/less (a)sexual *Trieb* is *not* and so on — Nothingness. The $-ism<>*a* relationship is perversely reversible for the fetishist as *a*<>Spirit because the pervert is both subject and object, both patient and analyst, and both total and partial. The matheme of $<>*a* summarizes all neurotic forms of *Praxis*. The Other-Matheme *a* ⊇ S-pirit represents the *Praxis* of the Pervert-Schizoid-Woman. All concerted human action — Eternal Return of the Sameness⁺ — is articulable in a symbolic algebra which figures and structures all *Praxis*.[15] Lacan's barred and desirous subject is notated as S-ubject in my own recast version of this symbol as $-ubject. The S-pirit must be critically engaged in the pursuit of "itself" as an object. This $-ubject screens the Real from within the field of the imaginary. The desirous subject is an effect of the screen of the Real by the imaginary. All action in the world is fundamentally the same action.

Praxis is an infinite repetition of the Sameness⁺ of an aim/less wander. This perverse *Trieb* is a post-repetition compulsion. This post-repeatability can only be transcended when *jouissance* displaces *désir* as the principle of the economy. Sameness⁺ (which is the same difference as Difference⁺) underlies all *Praxis*. Sameness⁺ makes it difficult to identify the object because there are no differentiated levels or separated dimensions by which to compare and contrast by general equivalence — phallus, father, currency, sign — the objects in the system. The subject of drive intuits this constitutive Sameness⁺. The Pervert-Schizoid-Woman enjoys the happy drive itself rather than the strictly equivalent objects that she can variously take or leave. Why does she wander past them? These objects are elevated as ~~equal~~ to and ~~commensurable~~ with each other — and ~~unequal~~ to and ~~incommensurable~~ with each other — as singularities of Sameness⁺. The object is the same as the other because it is different from itself. This summarizes Sameness⁺. But if the Object-Spirit is not self-same and self-identical — and is, and so on — then is it relative to a standard? Or is the object — paradoxically — *relatively absolute* and *absolutely relative?*

The Essence of Construction

Drive revises the love-hate object from a scarcity to an abundance by elevating the object of desire *qua* essence to the object of desire (drive) *qua* construction. This Spirit splits from a world with which it is discontinuous and divergent — Different⁺ — but also continuous and coincident — Same⁺. The object is *essentially constructed*. The essentially-constructing is a contradiction in terms from the perspective of essentialists and constructionists, disrespectively. The essentially-constructing — Ing⁺ — (pronounced: / ANA-ng/ or your choice of whatever) articulates the drive's encounter with the object as otherwise than itself. The essential is the constructed because both words and processes in and of themselves deviate from their own essence and construction. The Spirit-Object-*a* is indistinguishable from the system of references: as the worldliness of the World in Heidegger; as the vectors of Force in Deleuze; as the permutations of Power in Foucault; as the splits in Text in Derrida, and so on.

Spirit-Object-*a* is inseparable from an extimate otherness within which it is always already embedded. The upshot of the transformation of the object from essence to construction — *constructionistly essential* and *essentially constructed* — is that the object is not itself. There is no object of genealogical critique. The object is schizoidly neither/nor but — The object is situated in a dream insofar as its essence is removed from itself in the displacements and condensations of the dream-work. The essence of construction is the dream. Primary process untangles the dream-S-*a*. Psychoanalysis translates the latent thoughts into their manifest form in secondary revision and considerations of representability. The object exceeds the apparent boundaries by which the symbolic and the imaginary seek to specify it in a field through the *Praxis* of science. This excess results in the evolution of the object of desire into the object of *Trieb*. The Spirit of *Trieb* drives around the entire world: from front to back, from here to there, from this side to the other side, from departure to arrival — and so on. The stop at the destination is the delirious commencement of the missed encounter with the objet *e qua* being-in-the-world and *qua* being-with-others.

The object exceeds itself in the matrix of the world as a system of references of the insistence of the signifying chain. The essence of the *objet a* of desire reveals itself in the construction which is perused by the drive in pursuit of the missed encounter in pursuit of the *objet b* in pursuit of the hot pursuit. This broken engagement only makes sense retroactively in a deferred future of the Time of the Neurotic. The missed encounter illuminates the noisy Real. The imaginary register otherwise conceals this *Réel* with fantasy. *Désir* pursues the object *qua* essence *qua* "itself." *Trieb* wanders about the essence of the object in its construction *qua* not "itself." The presence is absent in the drive — literally: *is* — of the constructing or the verb form of the gerund: Ing⁺. The remnant of the missed encounter with the *objet c* of the drive is the essence of the object: *objet zed*. The drive slips and slides around — near, beside, under, over, beneath, by, adjacent — its object. The essence of the object distances itself from any presence in space or time. The object is always otherwise than in the presence of the subject of desire. The substantive essence of the object in itself is its remainder in the past and future of its excess in the missed encounter with the subject of desire. The present essence of the object is its constructed absence as missed in its ephemerality. The florid Being of the object is its terrific Nothingness. *Trieb* discovers the uncanny presence and life in absence and death. The object is misplaced, and the subject is displaced.

Figure 1.5 The Occluded Center and the Signifying Chain Equation

$$)\cancel{\mathcal{C}}(\ \neq\ \int_{A}^{\infty}\mathsf{S_N}\ \neq\ \left(\begin{array}{l}\text{A or B, C,}\\\text{D, E, etc.}\dots\end{array}\right)$$

The first part of the equivalence (left) is the symbol of the occluded center with parentheses which excludes the center from presence in any structure. The symbol of the occluded center with parentheses (left) indicates that the center is concealed and masked from the play of meaning-making in the space of language and its units of text. The parentheses demonstrate that the occluded center defines the signification of the terms in the network of words by the constitutive absence of this center. The other side (center and right) of the equivalence is a Queer Mathematical symbolization of the set of texts in the series of the chain of signification. The symbol of the integral spans from an imaginary hypothetical first unit of text in the sequence to an infinity of units of texts in an open series of marks. The integral symbol expresses the distilled principle that the series of words is subject to a sequence of potentially endless transformations. The occluded center (left) is the unsymbolizable Real principle. The occluded center is the architectonics — organizational principle and structural precept — of *langue*. The strikethrough of the occluded center (left) sketches the impossibility of symbolization and the Real resistance to the spoken and the written. This is portrayed in the final inequivalence (right) which indicates that no object can be elevated to ~~Being~~. This ~~Being~~ is otherwise the principle which arranges speech and writing. A or B or C or D or E (right) is an ordinary and plain unit of meaning. This set (right) cannot be at once the meaning and the meaning *of* the meaning-making. Neither A nor B nor C nor D nor E can be a metalanguage *for* language itself and its occluded center.

Notes & Sketches —

This imagined essence in the drive is pure negativity. Saussure uncovers this beneath the relationships of all signifiers in *langue*. Nothingness elevates the Being of the object in its essence as the neurotic Being of the Logic of Identity (A = A). It does so in order to transform this Nothingness in its Constructing⁺ to the perverse Becoming-Otherwise of the Logic of Difference (A ≠ A). The constructing is concealed in the drive. The drive disappears as such. It dissolves into a destructive pulsation that Freud describes as death. In such a traversal, the *Trieb* unveils itself as *désir* — as exactly otherwise than drive itself. The essence of *Eros* is its constitutive entanglement in its other of *Thanatos*. The absurd incoherence of the end of Freud's *Beyond the Pleasure Principle* (1920) indicates that each drive extimately reveals itself in the other. The two forms of drive can be distinguished from each other from the perspective of the pleasure principle and a regulated and homeostatic desire. But from the beyond of the pleasure principle, no such discrete division is possible. If drive is dead, then is *Eros* the principle of the solar system? Or is *Thanatos* the doctrine which never stops not being written, as Lacan says of the Other satisfaction in the *Seminar* on female sexuality (1972-73)?[16]

[pause.]

To switch forms but not contents: where are we drive-ing with Matt Bomer and Chase Crawford, the Hollywood hunks, in the backseat, and Orlando Bloom, the British beauty, in the trunk of our shared Camaro? And can we evade the repeated disappointment of desire and allow *Trieb* to pursue its trajectory toward a world which makes the missed encounter between a gay pervert and a Los Angeles closet-case, and between ourselves and our Hollywood loves, an even more enjoyable missed encounter than the awkward precoital banter between the desperate virgin and the stargazed star/ex-lover? Or are we forced to stop at the flirtatious Keanu Reeves in a frozen desire as we drive by with the unenviable temptation that finally fails to resist his body at the West Hollywood corner as he waits for us to pull over and pick him up for our ride? And if so, is that not proof of precisely the encounter with the missed encounter which is the *telos* of our drive in the absence of *Ziel*?

Perhaps, but only if Keanu refuses to ride shotgun with us on our fairy-way around a galaxy of gorgeous boys and our momentary arrivals at their tight bodies, blond and brown and black hairs, and expressive eyes — before our destination is deferred yet again toward a limitless set of these Justin Timberlakes and Brad Pitts, and Chatum Tannings and Robert Pattisons, and Justin Beibers and Zac Efrons, and Giovanni Ribisis and Bradley Coopers, and so on. Drive is already desire, even if desire is not yet drive. If retro, over, and fore — grammatology, psychoanalysis, and Marxism — strike the pierced ear as empty pretention, then simply obey the rules of the cock-block: *block*. If such a revision of drive and desire — and of Heidegger and Saussure and Derrida in deconstruction, and Freud and Lacan in psychoanalysis, and Marx and his sex slaves-proletarians in Marxism — if such a scandalous revision of theory confounds your sensibility about the division among the catcher, the pitcher, and my pitch, then let us simply cite this, as Orlando Bloom in the trunk mutters, "has the ride started yet?" To which we all, hot boy to hot body, turn — "*Not yet!*"

Chapter Two

Delays and Interruptions

I regret to say that we of the FBI are powerless to act in cases of oral-genital intimacy, unless it has in some way obstructed interstate commerce.

— J. Edgar Hoover

The question of pleasure is crucial to this project because *jouissance* is the fundamental ground of psychical and social organization. Any evaluation of psychical life or political formation must tarry with the question of *jouissance* — how does man get off, and not? In this chapter, I evaluate Freud's conception of pleasure as it is articulated in his work on instincts (1915, 1919) and the principle of pleasure (1920). I supplement the aporias in Freud's views on pleasure with critical discussions of first, Lacan's theorization of courtly love in the *Seminar* on the ethics of psychoanalysis (1959-1960) and second, Deleuze's work on perversion in *Masochism: Coldness and Cruelty* (1967). The horizon of my work is to conceive of pleasure as precisely not what it is. Pleasure deviates from its own *telos*, and enjoyment strays from its own object. The essence of pleasure exceeds *jouissance* itself. The horizon of pleasure is neither fulfillment nor satisfaction. Rather, pleasure is structured by break and suspension. The object of desire is the obstacle to the economy of pleasure. Pleasure is properly desexualized. *Jouissance* is (*a*)sexual.

At the aperture of Freud's *Beyond the Pleasure Principle* (1920), he remarkably mentions his "gratitude" to any theory which would be "capable of revealing to us the meaning of these sensations of pleasure and unpleasure that are so imperative for us."[1] This (un)pleasure is, as Freud says, "the darkest and most impenetrable area of the psyche."[2] The use of "impenetrable" goes without saying, but Freud's emphasis on "meaning" is indicative for my work. It suggests the relationship between pleasure and the sign or *lettre*. Lacan observes that the subject magically exchanges *lettre* and *l'être*. The question of meaning and being is formulaically vexed. In the text, Freud says,

> We are minded to posit a connection between pleasure/unpleasure and the quantity of excitation — yet not annexed in any way — within the psyche; a connection whereby unpleasure corresponds to an increase in that quantity, and pleasure to a decrease.[3]

The repetition of the word "connection" suggests the copulation between bodies, naked or not. The schizoid-perverse deconstructive extimacy consists of the simultaneous internal externality and external internality, or inside-outside. The mixture of the extimacy of *Eros* and *Thanatos* emerges later in the text.

Freud's explicit theory strikes me as profoundly mistaken. As a wannabe pervert, I fundamentally disagree with Freud's version of the hydraulics of enjoyment as it is cautiously disseminated in *Beyond the Pleasure Principle* (1920). Tantric masturbatory edging or copulatory sexual engagement imagines the possibilities of an (*a*)sex which never ends. An edged recursion of climax simulates the differences and deferrals of the Signifier/d, as I call it. *Contra* Freud, an increase in tension may be the more "pleasurable" — whatever that may "mean." The question of (un)pleasure is certainly (re)defined during Freud's career. Freud reconsiders the question in "Problems in the Economy of Masochism" (1924). In the masochism text, he suggests that the "principle of constancy" (or "Nirvana principle") must be attenuated. He also indicates that the proffered correlation between pleasure/unpleasure must be amended. An intensification in tension would correspond to a pleasure which is temporal and rhythmic in its simultaneity. The old in-and-out in a quick intercourse or an edged beat-and-time in jerking off inflames tension. Such pressured agitation determines (un)pleasure itself. What if the orgasm never stopped not writing itself? Pleasure is unpleasure precisely because pleasure is not pleasure and unpleasure is not unpleasure. I refer to this foundational deconstruction of the self-same and the self-identical as Sameness⁺. Derrida calls it a "sameness which is not identical,"[4] in the early classic, "*Différance*," from *Margins of Philosophy* (1968).

The syncopated temporal dimension of the (un)pleasure of an (in)constant masochism raises the specter of the timelessness of the unconscious. What is the trance beat in the frame of wish, desire, and truth if the unconscious is timeless? How is the movement of condensation and displacement possible in a timeless unconscious? How could such artistry be possible if space is plentiful for image, picture, and symbol? These questions imply that there is neither masochism nor regulation (pleasure principle, constancy principle, or Nirvana principle) in the unconscious. The loci of *Eros* and *Thanatos* may enliven the sounds of the unconscious. But their throb and pace are less trance and more (*über-*)trance. An (*über-*)trance begins to symbolize the parallactic overlap of the two final instincts of Freud's career. In my estimation, Freud's constancy Nirvana principle is misled on all accounts. Those bouts of sorrowful laughter about the offensive and the inappropriate of man and world are suffered joys. These moments of excess should not be classified as unpleasure even if they are moments of the deconstruction of (un)pleasure itself. I am sympathetic to the grammatological discernment of an unsettled constancy/excitement (and *Eros/Thanatos*) diffusion. But it is crucial to abandon the idea of (un)pleasure as a system whose excitations can be regulated by any coherent principle of organization. There is no methodology which can account for the (un)beaten money shot of (un)pleasure at the edges of the death drive.

In "Instincts and their Vicissitudes" (1915), Freud poses the question of (un)pleasure and (in)constancy in a rhetorical murmur. He asks: "What sort of relation exists between pleasure and unpleasure, on the one hand, and fluctuations in the amounts of stimulus affecting mental life, on the other?"[5] "It is certain," he continues, "that many very various relations of this kind, and not very simple ones, are possible."[6] The Madness of Order enforces the regulation of excitation. It does so at the same time as it destabilizes any principle of structure. Regulation is the signature achievement of the system. Even in its profound chaos, the system regulates this frenzy. The system is this regulation. The system regulates itself. But it also returns itself to itself as disruption. It is unlikely that the parameters of the pleasure principle are a consistent state for the organism. This is the reason that Freud turns to the death drive in 1920. Freud prudently presents the antecedent to the beyond. But the indication of an expansion and contraction of manic impulses in the organism does not preordain man to settle for such a closed system of modulated masculine idiotic *jouissance*. In the least, the subject has an essence to look forward to beyond the "problems" in understanding masochism. The give-and-take with my boys is better than any final return of the gift.

THE ZIEL OF YOUR ANTI-OBJET

An extended study of Freud's "Instincts and their Vicissitudes" (1915) illuminates the twisting and unraveling of the (un)pleasure principle. This upheaval in the conceptualization of pleasure precedes the reconfiguration of drive theory. It also rearranges the logic of both the secondary and primary processes. James Strachey, the editor and translator, isolates two coherent views of instinct in the text on drives (1915). Despite Freud's own intentions, these two perspectives eventually become muddled over the course of Freud's paper (1915). The first view posits the drive as a "psychical representative" of the somatic and the bodily. This repeats the model of instinct elaborated in *Three Essays* (1905). The second orientation toward the drive is that it is nonpsychical. It is the frontier or interstice between the ideational-psychical dimension and the somatic-material component. The second elaboration of the drive mimics the long and sad history of the effort to link the material and the ideational in a coherent hinge. This history notoriously erupts in the battle between the materialism of Marx and the idealism of Hegel. This skirmish in theory is also depicted in Saussure's effort to conceive of a sign which is the union of the material signifier and the abstract signified in a positive entity. The sign's logic is different from the Other-Logic of the signifier and the signified, which are considered separate from each other. The signifier and the signified are described by Saussure as negative and differential. The concept of the sign *qua* the joint between the material and the conceptual is an iteration of the fraught speculative adventure to link — so to speak — the misfired corporeal synapse and the idea of a Marxist utopia. Hegel insists on idealism. His dialectical philosophy invites the necessary reversal of the ideal into the material. Marx challenges Hegel with the materialization of the dialectic. Saussure strives to reconcile the two theoretical tendencies with the concept of the sign. Neuroscience revises these fables.

The effort of conceiving of a frontier and interstitial space and time of the hinge and joint fails. This flop is not for conceptual reasons. Rather, the effort to join materiality and abstraction requires an Other-Logic or Sameness[+]. This Other must be consistent with the system and anathema to a critique of $-ism. The fundamental difficulty is not the intractability of this theoretical aporia. The difficulty is also not the inevitably conservative mindset that such questions involve. This philosophical distraction may be burdensome and tedious. The issue may itself even be a nonstarter. But the principal reason to be inattentive to the hinge and joint is that the deconstructive critique of so-called logocentrism (the mind/body split in Western philosophy) is profoundly beside the point. The choice of an idealist dialectic or a materialist dialectic is ultimately diversionary. The crucial concern is the possibility of a pervert's Other-Logic. This would exceed the violent and final negation of both idealism and materialism of dialectics. The frontier may be phallic. But the organization of the relationship between frontiers is of importance beyond the simple displacement and reversal of the logocentric critique. That said — "but nevertheless" — the question of the prioritization of materialism or idealism, the signifier or the signified, will be central to this project. But the issue is a nonstarter if the horizon of the future is a system of Being (Becoming) rather than Meaning.

The second view of the drive is a strictly nonpsychical version of instinct. As Strachey makes clear, the alternative view at the other center of Freud's essay is a strange and mixed representation of the unconscious. In the essay, "The Unconscious" (1919), Freud says with a familiar tone of the crazies,

> An instinct can never become an object of consciousness — only the idea that represents the instinct can. Even in the unconscious, moreover, an instinct cannot be represented other than by an idea. [] When we nevertheless speak of an unconscious instinctual impulse or of a repressed instinctual impulse [] we can only mean an instinctual impulse the ideational representation of which is unconscious.[7]

Freud carefully negotiates the issue of logocentrism. He dexterously manipulates the gap between the material and the abstract. He focuses on the representation or "ideational representation" or "idea." The drive is complexly ideational and abstract. There is no strictly material component to the instinct. The drive is almost entirely divorced from this materialism. This ideational representative can be both conscious and unconscious. This implies a certain instability between the secondary and primary processes. At the same time, the instinct continues to function as the frontier, or hinge, or joint, between the ideal and the material. There is a simultaneity in Freud's own theory between the sign (frontier, hinge, joint) and the signified (idea, instinctual representative). This overlap implies that this second view of instinct both engages and troubles the logocentric issue. The theory privileges the sign above its theoretical detachment of signifier and signified, and material and ideal, at the same time as it exalts the ideal, the representation, the idea, and so on. The unconscious is both ideational (condensation, displacement, secondary revision, and considerations of representability) and material.

In "Repression" (1915), Freud says that, "besides the idea, some other element representing the instinct has to be taken into account."[8] This excess is a nonpsychical materialism. The instinctual representative (*Triebreprasentanz*) invites a wholly different interpretation. Unbelievably, the penis is a language. The vagina must have teeth because she too speaks. The imaginary phallus and the penis are unconscious. The penis is in the unconscious or the signifying chain itself. The penis is not simply represented in language. Rather, it is "itself" a signifying chain in its fleshly embodiment. Semen is a semiology. The penis in its foreskinly embodiment is subject to the whims and caprice of the primary process. What becomes of the penis itself? Is the penis "as such" and "*qua*"? Or is the penis multiple and split? Are flesh and blood unconscious? What is the threat to the secondary ego-conscious process of the fleshly penis? Freud accidentally resolves the signifier/signified and material/abstract split. Freud strangely situates the hard materialism of the Real within the signifying chain and the unconscious. The phallus of phallocentrism is not merely representational. Additionally, a Peniscentrism emerges as constitutive of the unconscious/conscious division. If matter *matters*, then the concern with phallocentrism must be supplemented with an observation of Peniscentrism. The fleshly penis is the unconscious. The erection of the penis in the system of the conscious returns as a manifest thought. This penis is a profound disturbance to the system. This is Freud's wager in his concern with the "anatomical distinction" between penis/clitoris in his papers on the castration complex, such as "Some Psychical Consequences of the Anatomical Distinction Between the Sexes" (1925). Size queens may be on (to) something.

The Drive and its Boys

In "Instincts and their Vicissitudes" (1915), Freud outlines the components of the instinct: pressure (*Drang*), aim (*Ziel*), object (*Objekt*), and source (*Quelle*). Each of these concepts involves theoretical traps and difficulties. Each concept also illuminates the processes whereby desire engages its object. The "pressure" is the fundamental motility which rends the drive active in its essence.[9] All drives are active. Only the aim can alternate between passive and active. Instinct is both a signifier and a sign, and both a hard materialism and a soft idealism. The pressure (*Drang*) of muscular movement is requisite for the mobilization of the penis. This is also the case for the phallus as an indexical sign or signifier of the object of desire. The pressure (*Drang*) of the penis in the unconscious is the hard erection and sexual excitation of a scopophilic look at the Other. The unconscious is mobile. The imaginary phallus consists of a latent content. This underground is exposed to the wily primary process and its metaphors and metonymies. Wacky textualization obfuscates the unconscious threat of the penis in its physical embodiment. The penis is inside of the signifying chain of the unconscious. The penis is situated at the bottommost system of representation. The penis is in the unconscious. There is an unconscious latent content to the penis. How does the penis return to the conscious of the symbolic order as a symptom? If the penis manifests in the system of the conscious-$-ism, then does it return as the neurotic's repressed wish, desire, and truth, or as the schizoid's foreclosed hallucination and delusion, or as the pervert's disavowed representation of sexual (other-)difference?

The diagnostic rank of the imaginary phallus is crucial to the analysis and treatment of its threat. The determination of the neurosis or schizophrenia or perversion of the imaginary phallus enables discernment of the status of patriarchy-phallocentrism: is phallism the return of a symptom or the system itself? Is the penis a symptom or the system? The symptom of the secondary process of the ego can be considered the effect of the latent unconscious primary process. The symptom is structured by the tension between unconscious-work and the censorship. The system of patriarchy-phallocentrism must be considered the preconscious of thoughts. These ideas are accessible to the system of the conscious but are paid no heed. The system of patriarchy-phallocentrism enforces the fundamental structure of the world. The series of symptoms is subordinate to an (in)visibility. The symptom of patriarchy-phallocentrism is a parallactic gap between s and $-ism. The symptom-patriarchy-phallocentrism is the parallactic object between which interpretations compete for ascendancy. The imaginary phallus is the fleshly erection of an unconscious. This dimension of the primary process is neither strictly ideational nor entirely materialist. Instead, the unconscious is a representational embodiment of — what? The unconscious is a metaphorical substitution for the pervert's fetish-objects. The symptom is Gosling's blond locks, Keanu's hard pecs, and the Diesels, jockstraps, and blindfolds of queer sex. If the unconscious is structured like a language, as Lacan contends, then the unconscious is also organized like a penis. But what is a penis? What is the penis which threatens patriarchy and phallocentrism as symptoms? What is the penis *qua* material object which threatens the penis *qua* symbolic system? An approach which discerns the strategies and tactics of the castration of the penis subverts the masculine heteronormative system. The representational fetish-objects of the perverse hottie may be patriarchal and phallocentric. The fetishes may be penis-substitutes. But the unconscious is itself cocky and dickish. What does this unexpectedly evince? The masculine libidinal unconscious is a threat to masculinity. Patriarchy and phallocentrism are their own provisos of destruction.

This autodeconstruction illuminates the perverse structure. The negated (repressed, foreclosed, disavowed) and its return (symptom) are the same gesture. The regime of patriarchy-phallocentrism is a threat to itself — but why? The penis is the foundation of the system of the unconscious. The symptomatic return of the penis-unconscious destabilizes the institutional symptoms of patriarchy and the representational symptoms of phallocentrism. This may strike the reader as so-called essentialism. But I will remind you that matter *matters*. Anatomy also matters. This is so even if anatomy is not necessarily destiny. A decision for the Pervert-Schizoid-Woman is neither quick nor easy. The choice will be between the penis and the unconscious, and between the imaginary phallus and the clitoris. The decision may finally be both and the Other. The fleshly embodiment of the penis is glorified and enjoyed. But I want to underscore that we still do not yet know what a penis is. In the meantime, I encourage my antinormative feminists and queer friends to — whip out the tape measure and discuss at length.

Ziel's Zeal

The aim (or *Ziel*, as Freud names it in the German) is crucial to our conceptualization of the joys of drive against the tortures of desire. The concept of instinct is first rigorously developed in Freud's work in *Three Essays* (1905). He further refines his discovery of the aim of the drive in the text on the instincts (1915). Later, Freud (1920) writes, "An instinct is in every instance satisfaction."[10] This claim about "satisfaction" returns to the pivotal inquiry into (un)pleasure. What generates pleasure not for multicellular organisms in the natural world but for ordinary folks in the real world? There can be no generalized or unified theory of satisfaction or pleasure. Everyday mortals are scattered from each other, alienated from their desires, and simply total weirdos. Freud insists on the fundamental model of pleasure or satisfaction of the drive within the hydraulics model of tension and release. In the instincts text (1915), Freud says that satisfaction can "only be obtained by removing the state of stimulation at the source of the instinct."[11] The "source" (or *Quelle*) is the somatic location of the excitement: the head, shaft, balls, hole, clitoris, vagina, breasts, mouth, and so on. Is the edging fucking forever, despite the conservation of release in the long-session in-anticipation, more "pleasurable" or "satisfying"? Or is the liberation of tension, pulling the trigger early in the quickie and clean, more "pleasurable" and "satisfying"? Does sex tend toward the edge of the bump-and-ride of life? Or does sex favor the descent of the degree-zero of death?

In *Beyond the Pleasure Principle* (1920), Freud is finally impotent on the question of the primacy of either *Eros* or *Thanatos*. He ultimately vacillates on the question of the *telos* of the organism as either life or death. This undecidability is symptomatic of an inseparability of the two instincts. Freud refines his theory of instincts in his claim that,

> although the *ultimate* aim of each instinct remains unchangeable [satisfaction in the reduction of tension], there may yet be different paths leading to the same ultimate aim; so that an instinct may be found to have various nearer or *intermediate aims*, which are combined or interchanged with one another (my emphasis).[12]

This remarkable passage assumes an "ultimate" aim of the drive. At the same time, Freud's text undermines this claim. Freud argues, "Each instinct remains unchangeable" in its aim. The drive achieves satisfaction and the reduction of tension in the organism. But he also says that the aim involves "various nearer or intermediate aims." Are these other aims different from the "ultimate aim," which is the "same" in each case for each instinct? The "ultimate aim" is also the "same ultimate aim." A certain Sameness⁺ is involved in the satisfaction of the aim of the drive. There are "various," "nearer," or "intermediate" aims or "different paths" of furtive eyes, pick-up lines, banter, drinking, dirty dancing, and so on. These aim/less wanders of the drive precede the "ultimate aim." The "ultimate aim" may or may not be hetero/homosexual copulation.

One of the central questions of this short passage is whether orgasm (male, female, and the rest of us) is the "ultimate" aim of the drive, or whether a simple reduction in tension to homeostasis is this final aim. My sense is that Freud speaks broadly in this statement about all drives. Even at this time (1915), he is writing after "On Narcissism" (1914), which oscillates on the division between ego-drives and sexual-instincts. Later, in 1920, Freud will reduce the earlier wide set of instincts to the fundamental binary (in)opposition of life drive versus death drive. Freud's "ultimate" aim is a conscious articulation of the pleasure principle. He wants to theorize the pleasure principle in the absence of sex as the final referent. A second question beyond the final aim of the drive in this passage is an inquiry into the "combination" and "interchange" of the variety of proximate and midway aims of the "ultimate aim." These aims are aims, yet they do not conform to the strict criteria of an aim. They are (un)vanishing mediators of the relationship between the drive and its satisfaction in the *Objekt*. This in-between sexy diplomacy is the satisfaction of the aim and the drive. The pleasure principle cannot explain pleasure, even before the theorization of *Thanatos* in 1920. The "combination" and "interchangeability" of aims indicate that multiple aims work in coordination. This arrangement achieves the satisfactions and pleasures of these aims. The effort to combine and interchange must be a strenuously complex process. It strikes this reader that this intricate and contingent elaboration is the "ultimate" *jouissance* of the desire for satisfaction. The aim/less wander of flirtation, and so on — this encirclement involves the turn left and then the turn right, and so on, and then the walk down the avenue and then the cross the street, and so on, and then the stroll down the lane and then the wink at the guy, and so on. The aim in its motley crew of intermediations, proximities, interchangeabilities, and combinations makes *Ziel* the drive of life. The drive defers satisfaction in the anticipatory structure not of *desire* but of *enjoyment*. Idiotic masculine *jouissance* is organized by the momentary — gotcha back Gosling! — satisfaction of its stupid desire. Momentary capture in the *Gestalt* of imaginary capture will inevitably be supplemented beyond the immediacy of the lay and the getaway. In contrast, the feminine Other *jouissance* does not sourly (not) enjoy the *faux* arrival of the letter. The Other pleasures itself with the "interchangeability" and "combination" of aims. The Other trajectory is a flirtatious series of deferrals and differences. This enjoyment resists desire. It does so at the same time as it is structured in accordance with the identical temporality and spatiality of desire.

The difference between desire and *Trieb* is both minor and vast. The gap between the two relies upon a parallactic variance. The gap can only be intuited from the perspective of the emergence of the feminine order and the Pervert-Schizoid-Woman. I claim that the *Ziel* of the *Trieb* is deconstructive. The *Ziel* is *différance* "itself." Additionally, the potential integration and nascent substitution of aims recall both perverse disavowal and representation, on the one hand, and unconscious primary processes of configuration, on the other hand. This demonstrates an isomorphic relationship between the conscious and the unconscious. An analogy between conscious and unconscious illustrates Lacan's point that the unconscious is structured like a language. It also indicates a homology between perversion and deconstruction. My interpretation of the prospective feminine *jouissance* of *Trieb* in aim/less wander gestures beyond the foolish masculine enjoyment of aim and its refound goal. The quick procession beyond — you won't even leave your number, Ryan? — the tense flirtations and stressed edges of aim is ditched by Freud's regressive commentary. He says that instincts are "inhibited in their aim" and that they "involve a partial satisfaction."[13] But does "partial" not indicate that the suck and the fuck never end at their goal? The "partial satisfaction" of the *Ziel* of the *Trieb* promises sucking and fucking — (a)sexuality — that neither begin nor end. Oral sex and anal sex are always in-process and in-action. This exposes the truth of the drive. Instinct does not desire its object but rather desires "itself." The *Ziel* and its *Objekt* are identical. The "partial satisfaction" of an inhibited aim is the consequence of the split between the joint and hinge in the aim and object.

Objekt's Obscurity

Freud's conceptualization of the object (*Objekt*) of the drive puts the instabilities in the idea of the aim/less wander of the ultimate satisfaction of the drive in sharp relief. Freud says that the object is "the thing in regard to which or through which the instinct is able to achieve its aim."[14] The climacteric phrases in this citation are "in regard to which" and "through which." What is this object "in" and "through" which the drive achieves its goal? First off, "in" and "through" isolate the orifice and the inside/outside traversal. The drive travels "in," then transitions "through," then wanders toward an outside. But this description indicates that the aim/less *Trieb* wanders "in" and only manages to plow "through." Instinct does not necessarily reach the outside. The aim is always still inside in an effort to come out. The *Ziel* of the *Trieb* and its (aim)less wander is to come out of the closet. The process of the drive to come out is an endlessly reproduced effort. The inside closet is the locus of the drive. The aim never reaches its goal in "ultimate" satisfaction because it is trapped "in" the closet and "in" a space which are understood variously as safe, secretive, sexy, sorry, and sad. The *Trieb* is hidden "in" the closet but with the will to come out. The drive's *Objekt* is comfort in the public sphere. Instinct seeks openness with a variable public object or with a general publicness. Freud says of the object that it is,

> what is most variable about an instinct and [what is] not originally connected with it, but becomes assigned to it only in consequence of being peculiarly fitted to make satisfaction possible.[15]

Freud maintains that the object of the aim is the most capricious of the components of the instinct. This view supplements the discussion in *Three Essays* (1905) about the whimsical and fanciful interchangeability of sexual aims and erotic objects among offspring. The further claim that the *Objekt* is not at the *arche* and advent of the instinct shows that there is a social and historical process by which the drive assimilates mercurial objects. Lacan describes this work with the algebraic *a*. Lacan rethematizes this bizarre object. This object "becomes assigned" to the instinct — in pressure (physical mobility), source (somatic stimulus), and aim (wanders in and through and toward the object of partial satisfaction). The *a* as object-cause both overcomes and obstructs the traversal of the <> in the $<>*a* lozenge. The <> represents the kiss, green light, red light, diamond ring, and so on. Lacan refers to this brush in contact as the missed encounter. The reason for this miss is the "peculiarity" of the fit between the drive and the object. Freud evades a strict answer to this "peculiarity" over the course of a career which tarries with this question. However, in this discussion he hazards that the object is poised to offer satisfaction to the drive. It is certainly "peculiar" that such a "fit" is possible. A fastener must be posited in order to explain that *Ziel* can be assimilated to *Objekt*. This object is weirdly able to offer "satisfaction" to instinct.

The "fit" must find a fit in order to underpin the theory and its consequences. The fit conforms to the postulate of the pleasure principle and its conceptual scaffold: the systematic regulation of energy; the cultural surveillance of the norms of society; the insistent masculine *jouissance* which gets off on the arrival of the otherwise elusive letter; the encounter with the inevitably missed object; and the submission to the (ab)normative codes of the culture. The "fit" must be fit in order for the aim to come out of the closet and achieve the goal of a publicness for its wishes, desires, and truths. This latent content is otherwise submitted to sublimation and deflection by $-ism and the system of the proper. The order enforces division and separation between objects. These objects were formerly interchangeable and transposable in the opulence of nascent sexuality. The source (*Quelle*) is the bodily process which "occurs in an organ." This somatic stimulus is "represented in mental life by an instinct."[16] This formulation supplements the discussion of the break between and the suture of the material and the ideal, and the signifier and the signified. The body is the site of the *Quelle*. But Freud admits that its "representation" (what he also refers to as "names") in "mental life" is our only access to this materiality. The body is strangely outside of signification. Freud's ideas are themselves outside of the body. To come out — is to exchange *l'être pour lettre*. The fissure between *Ziel* and *Objekt* is mediated by an unsymbolizable Real body. The Real resists symbolization absolutely. The horizon is an impossible equivalence and coincidence between *Ziel* and *Objekt*. The aim and object are the same as each other because they are different from themselves.

The vicissitudes of the drive that Freud outlines illuminate the in/external organization of *Trieb*. The drive transforms from Being-Becoming-subject to Being-Becoming-object. It does so in the shift from activity to passivity and then the reverse. This is accompanied by the reversal of content in sadism/masochism, voyeurism/exhibitionism, and love/hate. Freud's theory of the drives is profoundly binaristic. Each sign is self-same and self-identical. Each component in the pairs is ordered according to opposition and division. This is the case despite the reversal of content and form which is internal to the drive. Only the content of love/hate in ambivalence displaces the binary structure of the drive. In *Totem and Taboo* (1913), Freud hypothesizes ambivalence as the center of the heart and soul of man. He confesses that the "origin" of this "ambivalence" is fundamentally unknown.[17] But there is a possible interpretation of the navel of ambivalence. The system is structured by the thematization of *Eros* and *Thanatos* in the opposition of love/hate. It is simply the affect which is the foundational binary opposition of the entire Freudian system. *Fort* is love. *Da* is hate.

The latent content of drive theory is that the oppositions and reversals of an otherwise self-same and self-identical content are subverted. But how so? The transgression is performed by a primary deconstructive "sameness which is not identical" or Sameness[+]. This (non)originary affect of ambivalence is at the center of the Madness of Order and the system of $-ism. Ambivalence is the affective split at the center of the parallactic gap of s. Ambivalence is the substratum of the ground of $-ism. The center of the structure is simultaneously split and sutured in an affective ambi-valence. Both order (binary opposition, the sign) and madness (deconstruction, the negative and differential free play of the signifier) will unify and dissolve any opposition. This *Eros-Thanatos* mishmash is the psychical correspondent to the so-called first reading and second reading of the clotural double-reading strategy of deconstruction. Grammatological collision is not explicitly proleptically theorized in Freud's conception of *Eros* and *Thanatos*. The vicissitudes of reversal in activity/passivity and subject/object in the scopophilic drive (and so on) find another *telos* outside of 1920 and the (de)regulation of pleasure. The transition from desire to drive, from masculine idiocy to feminine orgasm, and from the simple neurotic to the exotic Pervert-Schizoid-Woman is the horizon of the future. The convergence of activity and passivity of the turning around from self to other and from inside to outside — passive aggression and aggressive passivity — destabilizes the symbolic order. But it does so only to reset the regulation of the system in the afterglow of the conservative coordination of excitation and its vaunted decrease.

COURTLY CLIMAX AND THE BLUE BALLS OF TRIEB

In his *Seminar* on the ethics of psychoanalysis (1959-1960), Lacan describes the aim/less wander of *Trieb* as the foreplay of "courtly love." Courtly love is a medieval feudal tradition. The ritual involves a courtly man who woos a Woman (archetypally a figure on the balcony of her *boudoir*) for years and years, even decades, without touch or sex. The practice is devoid of an incarnated sensuality between bodies. Instead, the love is textual and lyrical. The practice is a pursuit of the *Ziel* from afar. The love is a stroll and a putter which encircle the object ($<>a$). The Woman resists like the *objet a*. The resistance of this Woman-*a* is internal and necessary to the process (<>). The Woman's coyness is the structure of the rapport between the lovers, the man and his "Lady." The case could also be made that the object's demur is applicable to the daddy and his "Boy" (18-24). The concept of courtly love veritably describes the style of Lacan's decades-long transferential flirtation with his admirers. Courtly love is instrumental to a proper interpretation of Freud's text, "Instincts and their Vicissitudes" (1915). The coy play also demonstrates Freud's original theory of (un)pleasure in homeostasis and constancy. Lacan's courtly love concept illuminates other central ideas in psychoanalysis, such as desire, drive, sublimation, enjoyment, and identification. Psychoanalytic theorization is structured by the concepts of castration and lack: Something is Missing. These ideas can be understood through the critical lens of the intricacies of the practices of courtly love, the flirtations of foreplay, and the aim/less wanders of the drive. The basal difference between the pleasure principle and its beyond is at stake in a comprehensive exegesis of Lacan's account of courtly love. Lacan's description of the rituals of courtly love exemplifies a drive which is strictly beyond the pleasure principle. *Ex nihilo* — presence emerges from absence. Suddenly, Nothing is Missing.

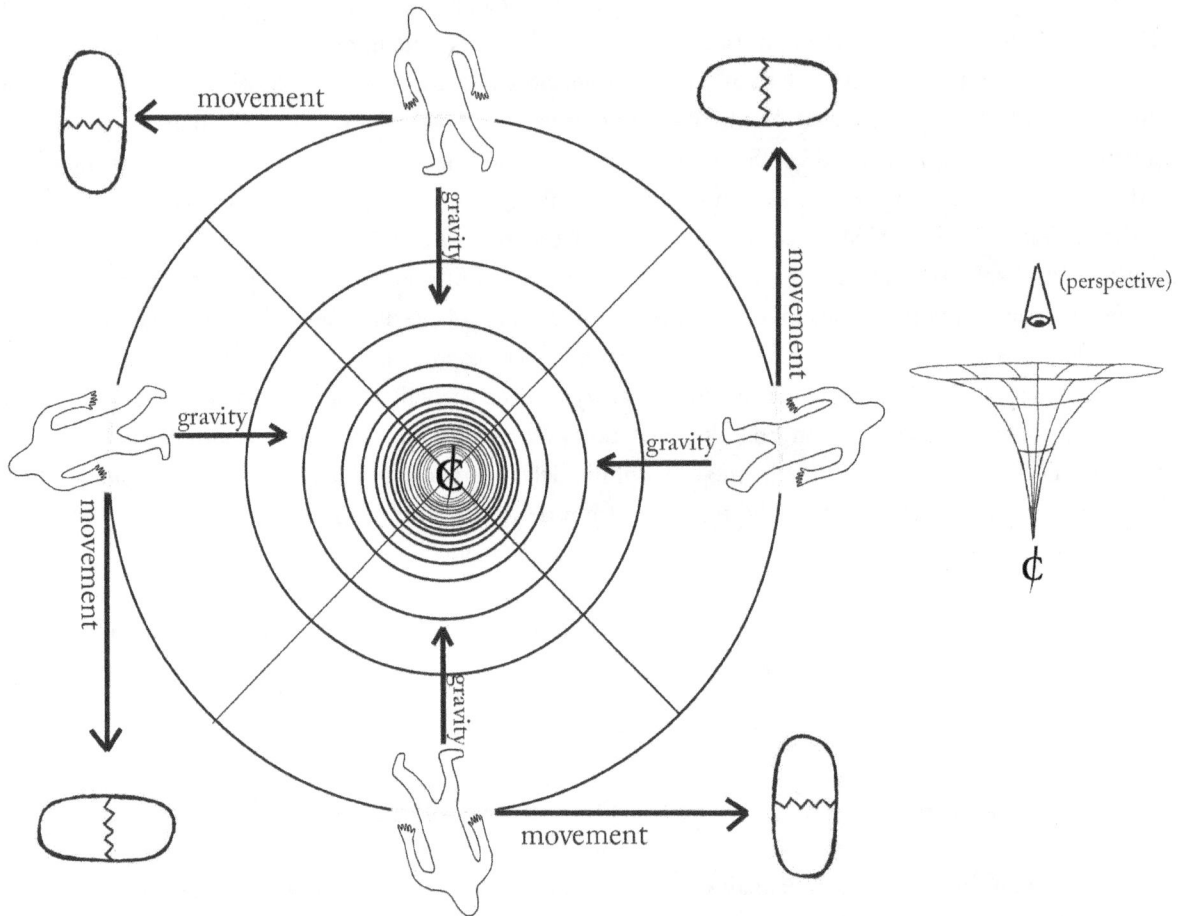

Figure 2.1 *Trieb* and *Objet*

The subject (above, below, left, right) is situated around the gravitational orbit of the chain of signification and the succession of objects. The gravitational pull pushes and prods the subject toward the occluded object of the *Trieb*. The (*a*)sexual center is the force which provides and sustains the vectors of the subject's drive. The occluded object is not the goal or *Ziel* of the drive. Rather, the goal is the series of obscured objects and barred *objets* that both inhibits and entices — sustains — the movement of the subject (above, below, left, right) toward an object which is fractured and fissured with the jagged line of fragmentation. At any instant, the subject's movement is directed toward the object as such. But in a given moment the *Trieb* endlessly encircles around the occluded center of the object of desire. The gravitational pull of the chain of words and objects of the occluded center is the (*a*)sexual force which disperses and distributes the subject's movement in space and time. The veiled object is the binding force of both signification and desire. But this *Eros* is hidden from the subject of *Trieb* even as it is the condition of possibility of Being — signification, desire — in the system. The masochist intuits the occlusion of the center and its (*a*)sexual foundation. The masochist's *jouissance* is the encirclement around the void rather than the impossible capture of the elusive object at the decenter of the vacuum.

Notes & Sketches —

The distinct orientations of the *jouissance* of the idiot and the *jouissance* of the Other — and the transition between masculine enjoyment and the pleasure of Becoming-Perverse — are also at issue. The fundamental hinge which opens the gap between the two parallactic perspectives is the point of the bodily and textual apex of the orgasm. This climax is antecedent to the return to the equilibrium of the system. The strange coincidence is of a *Ziel* which both diverges and converges with "itself" at the moment of this apogee. This parallax decides both the division and suture between courtly love and foreplay, on the one hand, and between orgasm and afterglow, on the other hand. This tension is isomorphic to the recurrence of obligation and debt after the release of an (un)pleasurable excitation. A parallactic overlap occurs between the masculine and the feminine, the idiotic and the Other, the sexual and the courtly, and the aim/less wander and the (re)turned goal. These inlays illuminate neither a massive lacuna nor a minor rift. Rather, the parallactic division on the "one" and the "same" object demonstrates that a mere shift in perspective is required to illuminate the simultaneous aperture and closure of the otherness of the same and the overlapped openness and totalization of the different of the unified. This is "a sameness which is not identical," as Derrida says, or a Sameness⁺, as I put it. What enables this perspectival shift that simultaneously broaches and shuts this "one" and the "same" difference as a Sameness⁺? How does the Other-Logic deconstruct the oppositions of either masculine or feminine, either idiotic or Other, either sexual or courtly, and either *Trieb* or goal? Is there a word for this object? What is the name of *das Ding* which represents the simultaneity of the mutually exclusive and the two antagonistic perspectives on the "one" and the "same"?

Conducts

The rules and conventions of courtly love are crucial to its legible practice and peculiar success. The pleasure principle implies a transgression of the law. Law returns the impropriety and misdemeanor to constancy and stasis. In contrast, courtly love defines the ritual of a man who woos his Lady for years with poetry, song, and lyrics. The consensual agreement between the man and the Lady is that they resist physical contact. This is an internal pact between the two lovers rather than an external law which is imposed by a principle. The relationship between the man and the Lady is organized around textuality: the word, the voice, and the signifier. There is no bodily engagement other than spatial proximity, physical adjacency, and corporeal visual surrounds in space. Lacan says,

> For a certain highly restricted circle, the ideal of courtly love is to be found at the origin of
> a moral code, including a whole series of modes of behavior, of loyalties, measures, services,
> and exemplary forms of conduct — what Freud calls an erotics.[18]

This courtly love of flirtation, chase, circuit, gesture, play, dance, glance, and so on is organized around strict codes and established conventions. Submitted rules of cultures and habits organize the practices of courtly love: flirtation abides edicts; chase decrees orders; circuit stipulates precepts; gesture commands ordinances; play administers directives; dance obeys routines; glance practices protocols; and desire resists transgressions. The suitor's pursuit of his Boy gets off on these (*a*)norms and (*a*)disciplines. The man and his Boy enjoy — happily submit to — the rules of a tradition which circumscribe the "moral code" of courtly love. In *On the Genealogy of Morals* (1887), Nietzsche claims that the debtor/creditor relationship — precapitalist exchange — is the origin of morality.[19] In contrast, the moral code of courtly love is neither reciprocated nor returned. The practices of courtly love never reach climax or apex. Moral codes or "modes of behavior, of loyalties, measures, services, and exemplary forms of conduct" are centered by the tensions of "unpleasure" in the excitation of the human organism.

The practice takes pleasure in unpleasure. The man and his Boy enjoy the escalation of tension, traction, edge, and apprehension. There is no orgasm in courtly love because the tension of an enjoyed unpleasure is never exhausted by the arrival (destination) or departure (commencement) of the letter of the transcendental signified or ultimate orgasm. The courtly love suspension of orgasm sustains a limitless orgasm. In the vocabulary of deconstruction, the capture of the Boy in the nets of desire is endlessly differed and deferred (*différance*) for years and even decades. The tension of the excitation of the organism (of the man and the Boy) cherishes a slow but intense extension. Like the signified in Derrida's apparatus of deconstruction, the Boy slips and slides across the chains of the erotics of "forms of conduct," which are forever supplemented. These modalities of pleasure are added, subtracted, multiplied, and divided by other lyrics and songs. This courtship of love encounters no end. There is no signified that retroactively pins the significance of the rituals. Flirtation is aporetically suspended in a nonpresence between past and future. The rituals of courtly love are yet to happen. The strict discipline of the codes of flirtation is crucial to the success (failure) of this formula of *Trieb*. The private pact of the rules of approach to the object is what the pervert recognizes as the law (pact) of enjoyment rather than the law of desire. The neurotic and his idiotic *jouissance* get off on the sexual engagement with the Boy. In contrast, the pervert of courtly love enjoys the slow unwind and the coy demure. This practice sustains a strange coincidence between law (pact) *qua* commitments and agreements, on the one hand, and enjoyment *qua* tensions and twists, on the other hand. This modality of practice displaces the otherwise unhappy overlap of the relationship between law *qua* external principle and desire *qua* castrative frustration. This shift from want to wanton illuminates the division between feminine and masculine, between idiotic and Other, and between desire and *Trieb*. Lacan's sexy outline of courtly love in the *Seminar* (1959-1960) demonstrates that rule is internal to (un)pleasure and that discipline is inside of (dis)satisfaction. Consensual prohibition is the proviso of an extended foreplay. This coyness gets off on both the deferral of the absolute orgasm and the suspension of the disappointment of desire and its *objet petit a*.

The contrast between the lyrics and poetry of courtly love in *Trieb*, on the one hand, and the commitment to the ultimate satisfaction in the capture of *Ziel* by the object, on the other hand, is both stark and indiscernible. The idiot imagines an enjoyment of his object in transgression only to experience frustration and regret. Eventually, the outlaw is murdered for his infraction. Alternatively, the Other practices the disciplines of courtship through a ritualistic encirclement of the *objet petit a* with(out) the (missed) encounter. The masculine idiot suffers the prosaic pleasure principle and its regulation of bodily tension in excitation, release, and the return to the constancy of homeostasis. The feminine pervert avoids the conservative regulation — up/down, here/there, left/right — of the pleasure principle. Why? He edges before-beyond — ~~pleasure principle~~ — the climactic apex of the ultimate satisfaction of the release of tension with the object-Boy. The pervert's foreplay of enjoyment is strictly outside of the regulation of tension. Rather than a conservative regulation of tension and excitation, the man and his Boy take pleasure in a masochistic deferral of satisfaction. This deferral of satisfaction of unpleasure is simultaneously the satisfaction of pleasure itself. The beyond of the pleasure principle is simultaneously the before of the pleasure principle. The future is simultaneously a past in the schizoid — *Yes!* — of time as such. This defines the Time of the Schizoid. There is no maximal magnitude of intensity which is forbidden to the pervert. The Boy's presence is forever. Courtly love is a textuality of *différance* and an erotics of madness. The Boy's absence manifests as an obscene presence. The Boy's deferral arrives in a metaphysics which is beyond the pleasure principle.

The Différance between Man and Boy

The man and the Boy in courtly love suffer the thirst, crave, ache, and itch for the object. The man and the Boy savor this extension — difference and deferral in space and time in *différance* — of tension on the edge of orgasmic satiation. This partial-ultimate satisfaction never achieves arrival (destination) or departure (commencement). Satisfaction is Becoming before it Becomes, after it Becomes, and while it Becomes. The suspension between these three moments is the space and time of courtly love. The schizoid *Yes!* is the timeless space of the unconscious of the codes and conventions of ritual. Courtly love takes place in the timeless space of the unconscious. The rules of the chase are mobilized by the flirtation-work: displacement, condensation, secondary revision, and considerations of representability. The wish of the dreamy courtship is the fulfillment of the wish. The pervert makes conscious the law (pact) of enjoyment. The threat of this unconscious truth — law (pact) of *jouissance* — is to the law of desire and the cycle of rule/rebellion.

A concrete theoretical example of the division between courtly love and idiotic *jouissance* is the scene of the murder of the primal father. At the beach, the boys are inexplicably hystericized. The primal horde myth cannot explain the ways in which the gay brothers learn how to desire. Yet, according to Freud, these homosexual sons desire the forbidden object of their exclusion: the sisters, daughters, and mothers. These Women are otherwise the sole sexual property of the primal father. The brothers' raid of the beach house transgresses an illegal and unfounded law. Paternity is illegal. In the process of the ambivalent incorporation of the body of the father, the gay brothers suffer guilt and remorse. They surrender access to the coveted Women whom they free from bondage in the aftermath of the (counter)revolution. The brothers experience the profound dissatisfaction of desire. An intense regret is the symptomatic consequence of the transgression which is internal to the law of desire. Alternatively, the man and his Boy enjoy the (*a*)rules and (*a*)disciplines of the rituals of foreplay and flirtation. Conduct achieves aesthetic beauty in masochistic (un)pleasure. Masochism takes (un)pleasure — Other affect — in the inaccessibility of the object. The brothers of the primal horde discover that the law is an obstacle to their stupid desire in the wake of the mistake. The man and the Boy surmise that the law (pact) need not and should not be violated. The pervert understands that following the rules is more enjoyable in *jouissance* than breaking the law in the transgression of desire. The tradition of courtly love enjoys the rules and pursues the object in accordance with consensual agreement. The perverse practice of erotics invents the rules and the disciplines of pleasure and enjoyment. The man and the Boy neither conform to the imposed law nor transgress the external principle. Rather, the law is deemed irrelevant to the pleasure of courtly love. The neurotic dialectic between desire and law is displaced by the perverse tension between enjoyment and its discipline.

Crucially, what the pervert instinctively glimpses is that the prohibition is internal to enjoyment. The pervert enjoys the rules of discipline. The pervert substitutes the inverted ladder of the law of desire with the chutes and ladders of the law (pact) of *jouissance*. The man and the Boy recognize that the rules are structured to enable an Other enjoyment. The man and his Boy discern that desire (dis)ables a masculine repetition of disappointment. At the same time, this masculine repetition of disappointment is the Other enjoyment. Why does the neurotic (not) enjoy the rule and the pervert does (not) enjoy the rule? The foreplayers of courtly love are before and beyond the pleasure principle. Queerly, beyond the pleasure principle is a prohibition which is the Outside of the externally imposed law and its set of principles. Beyond the pleasure principle, the tense foreplayer discovers prohibition as the extimate kernel of *jouissance*. Crazily, rule and discipline are the revolutionary pillars of an unregulated system of unimaginable tensions, joys, excitations, triggers, and sparks. The law (pact) *qua* consensual prohibition is on the pervert's side. This is the reason that the pervert's effort is the signification of the Real. He wants to erect the law (pact) of the Other enjoyment rather than the law of transgressive desire. Or is the reverse the case? — that the pervert enjoys the law of desire and that the neurotic desires the law (pact) of enjoyment? Can the law (pact) of enjoyment and the law of desire even be disjoined? What criterion separates *désir* from *Trieb* and the *objet petit a* from its veil? How is the shifting between these two perspectives on the "one" and the "same" object demonstrated? What is the word for this Real parallactic object?

The Boy's Endowment

The *perversion of the neurotic* involves the transformation of a society of neurosis into a culture of the Pervert-Schizoid-Woman. The necessary pedagogical gesture is to reorganize society. Subjects must learn to engage the law (pact) of enjoyment rather than the law of desire. The pervert remodels selfhood and sociality around the aim/less wander of *Trieb*. The pervert traverses the differences and deferrals in the elliptical but resistant encirclement of the *Ziel*. Paradoxically, the pervert commits to *Trieb qua Ziel*. Lacan offers few words on this instructive project. The task illuminates the law (pact) of *jouissance* to a culture which is insistent on the law of desire. The effort rids the neurotic of his habitual transgression of the rules and sleepy defiance of the prohibitions. The subversive is always murdered by the system — if not after the avant-garde text, then after publication, if not after publication, then after distribution, if not after distribution, then after the robbery, if not after the robbery, then after the rape, if not after the rape, then after the murder, if not after the murder, then after the genocide, if not after the genocide, then after —

An introduction of the object-Boy is requisite to an establishment of the *mise-en-scène* or fantasy-reality framework of the joys and merriments of songs and poems. Lacan says: "The object involved, the feminine object [the Lady, the Boy], is introduced oddly enough through the door of privation or of inaccessibility."[20] The Boy is "introduced" as a presentation and exhibition *qua* the object. The Boy is not found but rather endowed — *cut is a requirement* — in a pre-established arrangement. The courtly love ritual is scripted and affected. It is a conventionalized dance and masquerade. It is a pact and an arrangement. The practice is based on not only interpersonal trust but also on commitment to follow the rules. The effort and play of courtly love are neither spontaneous nor impetuous. Rather, the flirtation and foreplay are prompted and calculated. These modes of conduct are organized by strategy, constraint, and method. These strict returns to the playbook enable the agreement between the man and his Boy, a trust and custody of the involved ritual of the restraint of the covet and the itch — *Not yet!* But if not yet — when? At issue is the emergence of the Boy as the object of the *Trieb*. The Boy is the object-deferred of the aim/less wander of the circuit around this elusive but also present object. Lacan writes: "Whatever the social position of he who functions in the role, the inaccessibility of the object is posited as a point of departure."[21] But how does the Boy become the object if he appears as *a priori* inaccessible? The masochistic fantasy generates a scene of prohibition as the proviso of pleasure. The Boy must be veiled in order to be visible.

The ecstatic experience of reading Lacan's *Seminars* is the epic flirtation with a dense and "inaccessible" significance. The buried signified of Lacan's flirtation with himself entices and tempts the reader even as it frustrates and maddens him. The happy reader of Lacan is profoundly masochistic. He is a creature of the difference and deferral of the signified. He is a disciple of a sense which is (will be) the slippery object and subject of Lacan's poetry and prose. Lacan's words and techniques generated a massive and magical transference — and continue to do so — with his *aficionados* and detractors alike. He consistently arouses and enrages those whose claws could only approach his signification from the immanent distance of a transferential missed encounter. I hazard that the success of Lacan's words and techniques for the reader — whether in a positive or negative transference — is decided by the psychical structure (neurotic, schizoid, or perverse) of the interpreter in question. A standard neurotic subject who seeks the signified, the repressed, the return of the repressed, and the regulation of (un)pleasure in the constancy principle — he is bound to be flabbergasted and dumbfounded in the presence of Lacan's discourse. In such a slim volume as Bruce Fink's *The Lacanian Subject* (1996), the content of Lacan's concepts is brief and trim. A skeptic could reasonably conclude that the master is a mere charlatan. The master offers up only a few pithy but derivative ideas which have been elaborately and ostentatiously presented as profound and radical. But the content of Lacan's work is fundamentally the form of the words. His ideas are the speech of his oration. His concepts are the typeface of his performance. The props and costumes make him the unexpected *sujet supposé savoir*. His inaccessibility — over decades, in presence — is the source of the magical drive of the intellectual masochist. The process of writing and reading Lacan is coincident with the product of this methodological erotics. But who introduced us to the inaccessible? How were the contract and pact with Lacan arranged? Does the *aficionado* desire or enjoy?

Getting-Off Off-Limits

Lacan defines *Praxis* as the impossible effort to signify the Real. *Praxis* strives to make legible the absolutely resistant. This task is continuous with all thinking, being, and living in human existence. The neurotic pins retroactive meaning to speech and writing. He is irritated by the analysis terminable and interminable. He suffers the failure to symbolize the Real. In contrast, the pervert enjoys consensual agreement to the law (pact) of pleasure. The law of *jouissance* is a pact rather than a principle. This enjoyment is failure itself. Textual erotics is equivalent to submission to the rules and rituals of a resistant signification. Erotics is also matched to a disavowal of the gap between the symbolic and the Real, "but nevertheless — " The (non)coincidence between the symbolic and the Real mirrors the rhetorical structure of perversion: "I know very well, but nevertheless..." and "I know very well of this split between the symbolic and the Real, but nevertheless I will enjoy the failure, savor the defeat, and relish the agony of the difference and deferral." The disavowal is structured: "I know very well that the Real and the symbolic are coincident in a 'sameness which is not identical,' but nevertheless, and I know very well that the Real and the symbolic are discontinuous in a 'sameness which is not identical,' but nevertheless — " But then what?

The supplement to the Real Symbolic is the schizoid's neither/nor economy. The Real and the symbolic are neither continuous nor nonsynchronous, but — Other in the timelessness of the spaces of the unconscious. The future of the Pervert-Schizoid-Woman is the timelessness of the unconscious and the space of the dream. This unconscious is the Time of the Schizoid's *Yes!* The pervert's sensibility illuminates the paradoxes of *jouissance*. Crazily, unpleasure is precisely pleasure. The pleasure principle is properly reversed. The intensification of excitation is equivalent to pleasure. The moderation of tension is concurrent with unpleasure. The division between enjoying and suffering is tenuous. So is the distinction between desire and *Trieb*, between masculine and feminine, and between idiot and Other. The emergent question is: at what point does this parallactic overlap become (in)visible? The courtly subject is situated between the poles of the oppositions — desire and drive, masculine and feminine, and idiot and Other. A neurotic decision between either one or the other is impossible. The man and the Boy are situated within the structure of the lozenge <> rather than isolated as either the split subject $ or the object *a*. The pervert is the parallax.

Figure 2.2 Psychical Dimensions of the Image

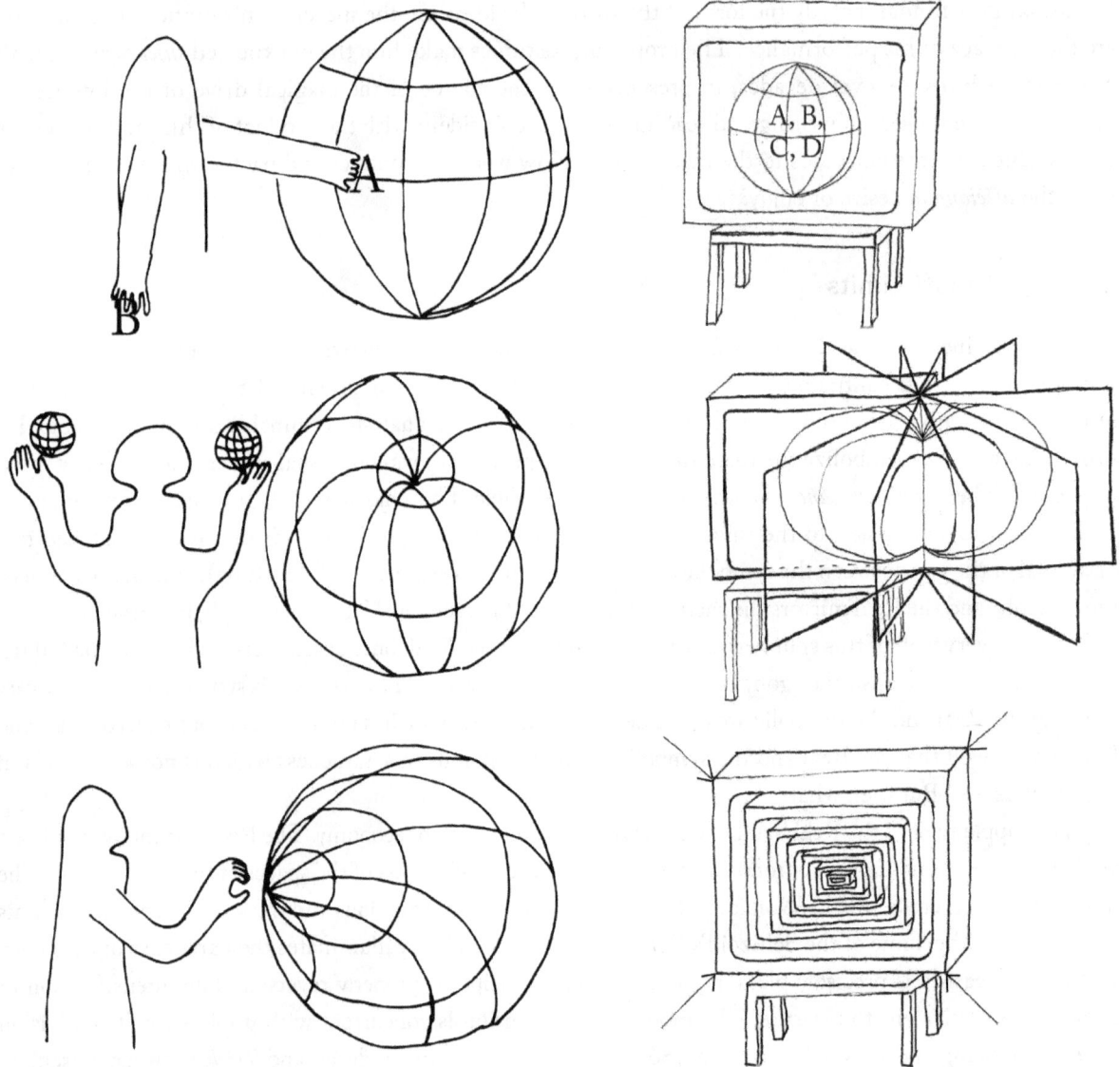

The neurotic (above) organizes different terms (A, B, C, and so on) within the system. The neurotic is unaware of the interchangeable Sameness⁺ of these objects in the slip and slide of substitutability of any object for any other object. The television (right) symbolizes the mediation of representation which showcases any possible series of worlds. The totality of the neurotic's television (above, right) indicates that the neurotic world is conceived in its various manifestations and incarnations as total and whole. The psychotic (center) recognizes multiplicity and plurality in his thinking, being, and living. The madman discovers that each object is the Same⁺ because it is not self-identical and self-same. Every image is the same image and every word is the same word because each is a singularity which cannot be compared, contrasted, and exchanged — made present — in relationship to the Other. The schizoid multiplies these fragmented totalities. The schizoid discerns the simultaneity of multiplicity and totality. This is represented in the picture by the repetition of the image of the multiplicity sphere. The multiplicity sphere is both opened and closed. The image is coincident with itself — *qua* — only in time. The multiplicity sphere circles back upon itself in perpetuity only to return as different from itself. Madness is a symptom of the temporal gap between the object and itself. Transformations are impossible for the neurotic (above) whose view of the world is a static monotony of the different (same) image of exchangeability. The image on the schizoid's television (center) swings and sways back on itself in a Sameness⁺ which cannot be reduced to the self-identity or self-sameness of the neurotic television (above). The madman's television (center) is an endless superpositional oscillation of differed and deferred *Trieb*. The swing and sway of the psychotic's television (center) suspend the phallic *point de capiton* in the temporality of the timeless unconscious. The world for the schizoid is an endless and circular series of strings and rings of images and words. The symbolization of this truth of the Real of the madman can only be expressed asymptotically and approximately because the superpositional and oscillational *différance* of the trace of words and images (center, left) is an alien vocabulary. The pervert (below) discovers the thinking, being, and living of the Unreasonable truth of the schizoid. The pervert uncoils the *point de capiton* and returns to time and the system of the conscious. The image of the pervert's television (below, right) depicts the fetishistic substitutability of the circularity of images. Any image — in any space and at any time — is already an image which is different from itself but the Same⁺ as any other image in the succession of objects and fetishes. This can be summarized like the feedback of waves. The image is returned to itself as different from itself. The image is instantly different from itself. The image of feedback is this simultaneous identity with and difference from the object. This essential structure of madness is the insight that energizes the pervert's will to fetishize the object as deviant from itself in its dispersed essence. The psychotic (center) lives the Inside-Outsideness extimacy of the system. The pervert cleverly pinches the Inside into the Outside and the Outside into the Inside in order to flip and twist the binary. The pervert exposes the *Möbius* twist which pervades the ostensible totality of the system. This $-ism is otherwise partial and fractured. The system (s) of $-ism is different from the self-sameness and self-identity of any positive object.

Notes & Sketches —

The neurotic clearly and coherently isolates the terms of these binary oppositions. The neurotic signifying chain is punctured by what Lacan refers to as the *point de capiton* of the function of the paternal metaphor. The function of the father retroactively pins meaning in the form of the *futur antérieur* or what will have been. The past may happen in the future (and the obverse), but the past indeed happens. The neurotic has a past. The neurotic can be analyzed for the etiological significance of the trauma of childhood. In contrast, the schizoid's signifying chain is a set of confused strands of words. These jumbled signifiers are unanchored in any center. There is no organization of the discursive structure of the statement. The difference and deferral (*différance*) forever refer signification otherwise and elsewhere. The signified weaves and bobs without a futural return — what will have been — to the past and present. Nothing has happened yet.

The crucial difference of the pervert's orientation toward the signifier is that he "knows very well." The pervert "knows very well" that the paternal metaphor is suspended. He "knows very well" that *différance* (dis) organizes the system. "But nevertheless," at the same time, his discourse of coy foreplay and courtly love enables him to symbolize the "ultimate pleasure," as Freud calls it, in the words and gestures of "partial pleasure." With talent, the pervert's *jouissance* is coordinated by a masochistic tendency. This affect favors an insistent repetition in pleasure. The pervert participates in the redo of the slip and slide of the Nietzschean Eternal Return of the Same. This peculiar temporality is an uninterrupted reiteration of the same gesture in different form. Repetition is finally the absurdist extension of the consequences of the law of the signifying chain. Masochism may be an effort to master loss, as Freud claims in *Beyond the Pleasure Principle* (1920). But it is also the joys and merriments of a deferred orgasm. This zigzag of *Trieb* is a meander around, near, about, and toward. It is a prepositionally structured *telos* without end. Like the madman, the pervert wanders about the signifying chain. His simple dexterity involves an escort which follows the rules. The man and the Boy conform to the directions — stops and goes — of the prepositional indices in the strands of words. These prepositional red lights and green lights — (*a*)rules and (*a*)disciplines — make *Trieb* coherent and legible to the pervert and the Other. The psychical function of the linguistic preposition is to direct the traffic of wanders and traversals. The preposition maps the orientation of words and gestures in the system. The preposition oversees the ways and routes in the phrase, the sentence, the paragraph, the page, the chapter, and the book. The *Praxis* of the symbolization of the Real deploys these grammatical marks in order to stave off schizophrenia for the subject of perversion.

The "point of departure" for the pervert is the fiction of the neurotic order of the symbolic. The neurotic's desirous *point de capiton* ensures that the future (present) happens in the past (present) — but that it happens nonetheless. But in the Madness of Order there is no "point of departure" (origin, *arche*). There is no "point of destination" which structures the rings and strings of the system of language. The point of departure of the sent love letter enforces the *arche*. This origin is otherwise disrupted by the Derridean trace. As soon as the strategy and adventure of the play begin, the words and gestures — lyrics and poems and prose — of the coded rituals of courtly love unfold. They do so forever in an Outside of time. The "point of departure" establishes that the father is the posited origin of the *jouissance* of the act of love. The father is neither the source of the law of transgression/desire nor the origin of the repression of *jouissance* and ecstasy. Rather, a feminized father — or maternal symbolic order — is the proviso of the possibility of foreplay and the masochistic joys of the ebb and flow of an excited edge of immanent but delayed ejaculation. This unexpected dynamic is precisely the insight of the pervert. His focus is the displacement of the law of transgression and desire with the law (pact) of the *jouissance* of the Other. The paternal pin of the point inspires the joys of foreplay and the restraints against "ultimate satisfaction." Restraint is the freedom of pleasure. Subordination is the emancipation of enjoyment. Regulation is the liberty of play. But how is the object of desire-to-*Trieb* represented as the untouchable?

The etiology of neurosis and perversion is a vexed question. Why does the pervert of courtly love discover the pre-orgasmic rhapsodies of the "partial satisfactions" of the missed encounter? Why does the masculine idiot rush headlong toward his sublime object only to experience — yet again — the deferral of this object as such? If both the pervert of foreplay and the neurotic of intercourse slip on the *objet petit a* — like an overly eager reader of Lacan — then what accounts for the opposed or parallactic reactions to this slide of the transcendental signified of the Boy's body and soul? A constitutional psychical structure could account for the divergent experiences of (un)pleasure — the before and the beyond of the pleasure principle. A neurotic discerns the trace of signifiers as finite. The pervert understands the slip and slide of the schizoid's linguistic torture. But the pervert's schizophrenia is animated by a happy submission to the phallic prepositional structure of the semantics and syntax of legible discourse. Both socially constituted psychical structures and modalities of sexuality could be determinant of and determined by both heterosexuality/homosexuality but also of and by a nascent (*a*) sexuality. An (*a*)sexuality may be a sexual modality which properly discerns *différance*. This deconstructive (*a*) sexuality would involve a scopophilic zeal for the human form. But it would also involve a will to resist relational embodiment with the object of desire or the object of *Trieb*. Quite possibly, the eroticism of *Trieb* is (*a*)sexuality.

There is a perverse resistance to sexualization. There is a foundational desexualization in the masochist's approach to the other's restraint on "ultimate satisfaction." The divergence between the masculine neurotic and the feminine Pervert-Schizoid-Woman is the deferral of foreplay. The pervert evades the economies of tension and return, climax and repose, and increase and decrease. The difference between masculine and feminine also involves a genuine perverse disinterest in bodily sexual engagement. This joyfully embraced prohibition is precisely the obstacle of (to) the Other *jouissance* of difference, deferral, and active courtly passivity in relationship to the lost signified. *Trieb* establishes the conditions of (im)possibility in order to lose what has already been lost as the condition of a manic excitation of gain(ing).

The spatiotemporal "introduction" of the remote and unapproachable Boy *qua* the exclusive and secluded object is an undecidable question of the *arche* of foreplay. How does the worship even begin? How is the pact to be decreed and the agreement to be arranged? Lacan flatlines on the question of the fantasmatic *mise-en-scène* of the arrangement of courtly love and the establishment of rules and regulations. But he does refer to a tradition and heritage of the conventions of foreplay. The anticipated restraints and restrictions must be skillfully and painstakingly "introduced." The masochistic pact, as Deleuze will name it, involves trust, loyalty, and measure. Laplanche and Pontalis articulate fantasy as the *mise-en-scène* of desire. Fantasy is the frame of the backdrop which enables a pedagogy of desire or an instruction in the structure of the relationship between the split subject and the *objet petit a*. The matheme of the lozenge (<>) is the symbolization for *Praxis*. It is the representation of the applied edification of desire and its wander toward the lubricious object. There is no strict object in the reality-fantasy scene of the pervert's foreplay. The object of desire (*Trieb*) is considered off-limits at the origin of the pact. The man "knows very well" that the Boy is sublimely beyond reach. "But nevertheless," he pursues the Boy with the joyful heartbreak of a subject who believes — *le sujet supposé croire* — nonetheless that the Boy will one day away be in his arms. The belief that someday the Boy will be his own supplements the knowledge of the pact. Bad faith is the organizational principle of the pervert's disavowal. But this bad faith is also strictly reversible as good faith. The pervert knows that the Boy will be his, but he nevertheless believes that he will be deferred, and so forever Outside of a temporality of chronological coordination. Knowledge and belief, "I know very well" and "but nevertheless," are strictly transposable. Bad faith and good knowledge are interchangeable. It is momentary whimsy whether religion or science organizes the faith-knowledge of the pervert.

The fantasy framework for perverse courtly foreplay is different from the *mise-en-scène* of the neurotic's learned approach from desire <to> object. The specificity of the pervert's fantasy is his position as the subject of drive who is simultaneously the object of desire. The Boy is certainly positioned as the unattainable and the inaccessible.

But the man is also positioned as such. He is so because of the constitutional and essential transhistorical and transfantasmatic separation of the man from the Boy. Establishment of the pact of physical alienation enables the perverse subject of the lyric and poem to promote himself as an object. But of what? The man inspires the joy of the Boy and his extraordinary and secluded beauty. Both the man and the Boy are positioned as analysts: *a<>a*. They each solicit desire (or *Trieb*) from the other. At the same time, they cannot (as in analysis) touch the other. It is too fucking hot. The relationship between suitor and beloved (or beloved and suitor, as reversible) is properly *a<>a*. The obverse is also the case, as $<>$. A mirrored foreplay emerges between the man and the Boy. Each *qua* other makes a claim toward the restrained courtship of the dialectic of nearness and distance, union and separation, and proximity and gap. The Boys exchange each other for each other and as each other in a tension between *Eros* and *Thanatos*. This gesture of love is a passion which is before and beyond the pleasure principle.

Another center of the drama of courtly love is the suture of the wound in masculine idiocy. In his *Seminar* on the four fundamental concepts of psychoanalysis (1964), Lacan makes brief reference to causality. He claims that there is only cause (origin, responsibility, *arche*, advent, departure, arrival, destination, and so on) in something which does not work. If the Boy is "inaccessible" at the origin ("posited as a point of origin"), then the rituals and regulations of courtly love are broken at their inception. This issue must be contextualized within the fundamental concept of Freudian psychoanalysis: castration. The female genitalia are defined as Something is Missing. This identification of female castration is proposed as early as *The Interpretation of Dreams* from 1900. The codes and conventions of foreplay involve prepositional twist and grammatical twirl. This "partial satisfaction" does posit an *arche*. But this advent is the success of a failure and the interruption of a bind. The origin, *arche*, and advent of the practices and customs of courtly love presume the forced miscarriage of desire: variously, that desire is the desire of the Other; that desire is the desire of desire itself; and that desire misses its encounter with its object. The misfired origin of the tradition of foreplay suspects the snap and rupture of the break. This is exactly the framework of the "partial satisfactions" of the *Trieb*. Foreplay is situated in-between Something is Missing (castration, lack, scarcity, and capitalism) and Nothing is Missing (plenitude, fullness, abundance, and communism). The parallactic coincidence of Something and Nothing — reversed — illuminates the *modus operandi* of the perverse foreplayers, the man and the Boy. But what is revealed? The overlap of scarcity and abundance — Something and Nothing — illustrates the aperture and closure of opposition. There is no division between the masculine and the feminine, the idiot and the Other, and desire and *Trieb*. The meander and ramble of "partial satisfactions" miss the missed encounter *qua* missed. The *Trieb* simply dillydallies around, near, behind, above, below, toward — prepositional direction — the object. The pervert is the master of the preposition. His talent in speaking and writing is punctuational.

The crucial constituent of the pleasure of courtly love is that the man and his Boy enjoy castration and simultaneously transform lack into plenitude and convert scarcity into abundance. This integrant is not of the male junior and his protective anxiety over the capitalist private property of the penis. Instead, the key is the Pervert-Schizoid-Woman and her enjoyment of loss. The affect of death is orgasm. Ejaculation is the proper response to mortality. Something is Missing is already Nothing is Missing. Capitalism is already communism, the masculine is already the feminine, the idiot is already the Other, and desire is already *Trieb*. This doubled overlap is unbeknownst to the neurotic signifiers of castration. The Woman and the Girl know that castration ("partial satisfactions") is neither loss nor lack. In courtly love, the miss is a hit, the loss is a gain, the negative is a positive, and the alienated is the proximate. Perverse enjoyment of castration animates a magical conversion of the sadness of absence into the happiness of presence. The pervert's peculiar orientation toward the law indicates that castration is the condition not merely of desire but also of *jouissance*. The advanced origin of courtly love is the sign of the triumph of defeat. It is also the defeat of triumph (and so on). This compulsive repetition of traversal around the object situates the pervert — Pervert-Schizoid-Woman — as the conceptual persona who enjoys the death instinct beyond the pleasure principle. — Living — around, between, in, out, under, over, above, below, near, far, asunder, at, of — dying — and — dying — of, at, asunder, far, near, below, above, over, under, out, in, between, around — living —

The features of the Boy as beloved but barred object are small-time and penny-ante. The Boy and his beauty are substitutes for the transfiguration of absence into presence. The Boy-chase is a circuit around an inaccessible object. Lacan states: "The Lady is presented with depersonalized characteristics." He continues: "As a result, writers have noted that all the poets seem to be addressing the same person."[22] These "depersonalized characteristics" distance the Boy from any identifiable traits and specific qualities. But, at the same time, this depersonalization enables the man to see the sublime Real beauty of the Boy through the Boy's own gaze. The man broaches the body and soul of his beloved in order to praise the singularity of his Being. The *mise-en-scène* of courtly love invites the circuit (<>) of the $ and its *a*. It also welcomes the obverse: the *a* and its $. The Boy can be experienced as the "same person" time after time. The man experiences an affect of Sameness+ in the (mis)approach toward his beauty. "Sameness+" refers to the compulsive and masochistic turn and return to the object in the elusive resistance of this Thing. Recurrence is the repeated gesture of approach and miss, advance and resistance, and arrival and departure. This is experienced as Sameness+. The man experiences the repetition of death. A return of the eternal supervenes as the mortal movement toward the ever distanced and finally recalled object of *Trieb*.

As Freud theorizes it in the allegory about his nephew and the reel of string in *Beyond the Pleasure Principle* (1920), the beyond of the conservative homeostatic regulation of the system radically disables the stability of the structure. Perverse courtly love is the revolution of the destabilization of the system as such. The object is "peculiarly fitted," as Freud says of the *Objekt* in his paper on the vicissitudes of the instinct (1915). But why? The essence of the Boy is constituted by the man who surrounds — <> — but demurs — <> — from the Boy. The unity is achieved by the man who performs the same caviling. This tension is between the opposed poles of a binary opposition of (counter)magnetism. Simultaneous attraction and repulsion — irredeemable loss — are mediated by the courtly love between the man and the interstitial Boy. The Sameness+ is the structure of the (un)pleasurable *Praxis* of courtly love. Sameness+ illuminates the truth of the perversity of love. All gesture is foreplay, and all gesture is gesturing, forever, no other gesture than —

The theoretical substance of the courtly love ritual is that it illuminates the scars and wounds of the culture. Masochistic pain exposes civilization and its discontents. Lacan says: "The poetry of courtly love, in effect, tends to locate in the place of the Thing certain discontents of the culture."[23] The "Thing" (or *das Ding* in the German) is the time and space of the beyond of the object. The Thing is inside-outside of the object "as such." *Das Ding* exceeds the object "itself" as its remainder and excess. The Thing is the surplus which cannot be assimilated into the system of homeostasis. *Das Ding* cannot be tamed by the conservative increase-decrease of the regulation of excitation in the organism. The Thing overreaches both the man and the Boy. The object of the *Praxis* of foreplay is beyond the pleasure principle. Courtly love is a discipline and a rule. It is fiercely unregulated because it is unbalanced. Foreplay knows no precipice. It is beyond the suitor's representation. This love cannot be captured in the words of the man's lyrics and poems. The Boy is the Real. The Real Boy is the center around which the man's words fail to capture the young man's beauty. The "place" of the Thing is the source of the maladies and diseases of the culture. The mad love affair of foreplay is conditioned by the rules and regulations of society. The neurotic loathes the law, which is understood by him as the object of either conformity or transgression. In contrast, the man and the beloved Boy enjoy the law (pact), which is understood by them as the proviso of the ritual and habit. These two distant lovers are the overseers of *jouissance* rather than desire. The suitor and the beloved take pleasure in the law (pact) of enjoyment. They organize *Trieb* and the elusive *Ziel* rather than meddle with instinct and its bound *objet petit a*.

For the foreplayers — Perverts-Schizoids-Women — the discontent of the culture is a superegoic imperative of the law and its insistence on the *Jouir!* of masculine idiotic pleasure. Why should I enjoy the system if I can enjoy making the system? The perverts lust after the exchange of *Trieb* for *désir* — *pour lettre pour l'être* — as the cure for the affliction of desire. The man and the Boy love "against," in Freud's words, the social demand of "ultimate satisfaction." They love "against" the fast-forward to the orgasmic release of the tension in the organism as it is structured by the pleasure principle. The pervert prefers to go off rather than get off. Lacan explicitly asserts the reversal of the pleasure principle in courtly love. Lacan says, "foreplay is precisely that it persists in opposition to the purposes of the pleasure principle."[24] He continues,

> It is only insofar as the pleasure of desiring, or, more precisely, the pleasure of experiencing unpleasure, is sustained that we can speak of the sexual valorization of the preliminary stages of the act of love.[25]

The "persistence" of an "opposition" to the pleasure principle opens toward *Eros*. Love extends in a compulsive repetition toward *Thanatos* and the death instinct — and beyond. This is an "experience," as Freud puts it, of the sheer joys of the pains of love. To outrageously suffer — gallows humor — is the orientation of the pervert. The future enjoys the differences and deferrals of trace and *différance* in the referral to *das Ding*. The pervert endures the recursion of meaning in the Other. The future suffers death because it is the Signified/r of a finite existence within an infinite chain of words. The man and the Boy will eventually die a happy death. The loop and beat of their courtly love repeat this Sameness[+] in a differential repetition of the same gesture.

Revolutionary (*a*)sexuality seizes *Thanatos* in order to traverse the beyond of regulation, obligation, return, and debt. This (*a*)sexuality tends toward a subversion in principle itself. But the most vexed question of the psychoanalytic (counter)transference operative in the soliloquies of courtly love is: who is the man and who is the Boy? Each, but from whose perspective? The neurotic is pinned to the deferred action of the present object. He orients his doomed and frustrated *Praxis* as $\$<>a$. Alternatively, the Pervert-Schizoid-Woman wanders astray in the nowheres of courtly foreplay. She situates his series of *petit morts* as a deconstructive $a<>a$ and $\$<>\$$. She enjoys a *Trieb* which circles his circuit. The loop twists and turns in the obverse of $a<>a$ and $\$<>\$$. The delirious perspectivalism of transferential vacillation and coy hesitancy deregulates the pleasure principle. The drive summons the revolutionary transformation of the constancy of the system. *Trieb* ushers in the ruled spontaneity of a structure of love which only a precise organization can return to freedom.

THE MASOCHISTIC EDGE

Deleuze theorizes masochism in his early work, *Masochism: Coldness and Cruelty* (1967). This book contributes to an assessment of the pair of perversions — masochism and sadism — from the margins of psychoanalytic assumptions about perversity. Deleuze opposes masochism to sadism. The two are not specifically complementary. They are ultimately antagonistic. Sadism is speculative and demonstrative. Sadism is organized by knowledge and fact. In contrast, masochism is considered to be dialectical and imaginative. Masochism is a perversion which is inventive and innovative. It is a source of the creation of the world-to-come. Sadism emerges in pure negation of the extant and even the possible. Masochism operates by disavowal. Masochism flourishes by suspension. Sadism repeats itself prodigiously. It is a parrot and echo of itself. Sadism is a tautological recurrence of the dictates of the law. Alternatively, masochism qualifies the norms with suspense.

Figure 2.3 The Traversal of the Pervert-Schizoid-Woman

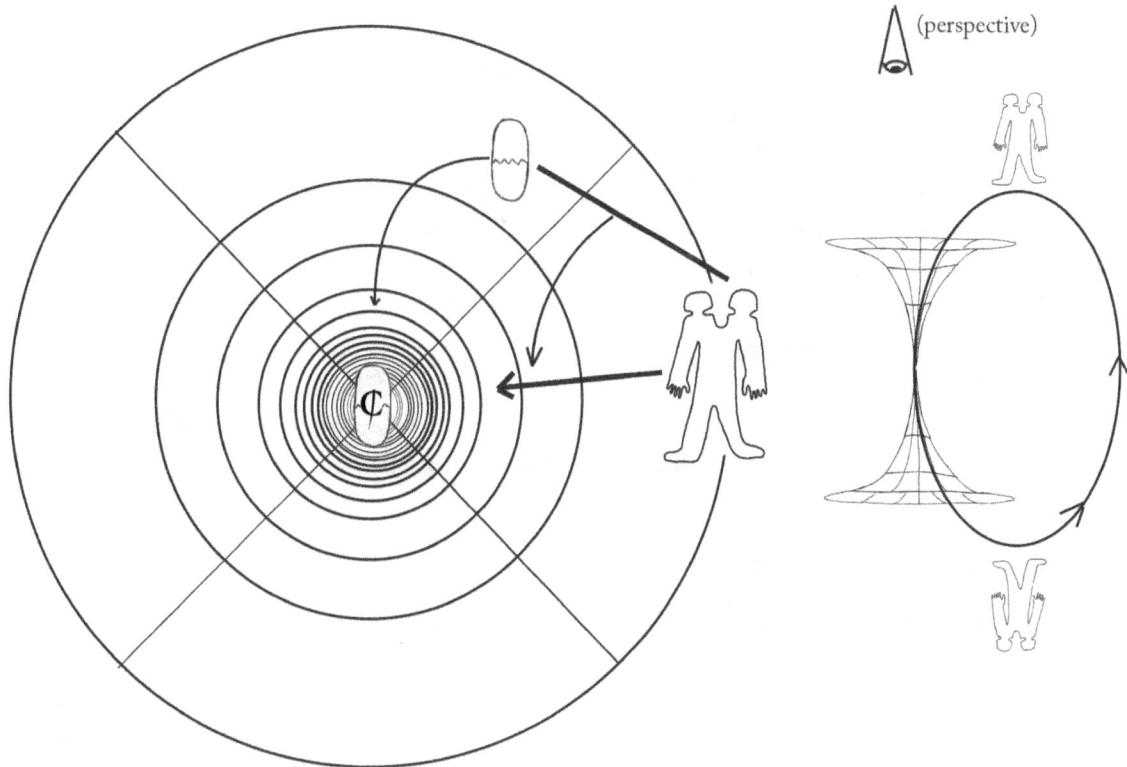

This image portrays the futural movement and traversal of the Pervert-Schizoid-Woman. Her object of desire transforms into the ~~object~~ of *Trieb*. This drive becomes a radical alterity. The diagram shows that the *objet* of the drive of the Pervert-Schizoid-Woman is a Sameness[+] at the occluded center of the object of the *mise-en-abyme*. The neurotic trajectory which prods and pushes the neurotic in circles around an anxiously desired object is transformed into diversion — delays and interruptions — toward the center of the abyss (left). The circle of the Pervert-Schizoid-Woman (right) circumnavigates the occluded center of signification. The Woman freely passes by, into, beside, around, near, and so on in a time which is the multiplicitous spatial expansion of the timelessness of the unconscious. The diversion from the occluded center toward the extension of the succession of other objects in the galaxy shows that her horizon — ~~departure~~ and ~~destination~~ — is (*a*) sexual. The Pervert-Schizoid-Woman is the effect rather than the cause of (*a*)sexuality. Her energy emerges from this alternate space. The Woman and her objects are partial and incomplete rather than total and whole.

Notes & Sketches —

Masochism puts into question and doubt the otherwise conventional gestures and actions of the world. Sadism destructures the role of nurture and care of the mother in favor of the rule and law of the father. Masochism reverses this in order to both acknowledge but also deny the mother. Masochism banishes the father from the symbolic order. The masochist strips the structure of a paternal anchor. This father would otherwise oppose suspense and imagination. The sadist rejects aesthetics and sensibility, but the masochist exalts these forms. Art and beauty are the foundations of enjoyment and creation for the masochist. Sadism is possible only within the institution and the organization. The sadist is the effect of an arbitrary but conventionalized bureaucratic law. In contrast, the masochist engages the other in a structure of trust in a pact. The masochist's word guarantees an agreement for the procurement of pleasure. Sadism is ordered by the superego and the processes of identification. Masochism is regulated by the idealization of beauty, aesthetics, and gesture. The formats and methods of sexuality in sadism and masochism are entirely distinct from each other. The sadist gets off on the infliction of pain. The pain is but a secondary effect of a brutal conformity to the violence of the law and the principle. The masochist enjoys pain. But he enjoys it only as an effect of a difference and a deferral. Masochistic pain is a consequence of the strategic and spontaneous encirclement around an elusive object, such as the "partial satisfaction" of the aim/less drive toward the Boy of courtly love. The masochist is archetypal of the Becoming of the Pervert-Schizoid-Woman in the future.

Imagination of the Impossible

The both/and economy of disavowal is articulated as, "I know very well, but nevertheless...." These words are exemplary of the pervert's talent for the clotural double-interpretation strategy of deconstruction. The simultaneous acknowledgment and denial of disavowal inspire the supplementation of knowledge with faith. For the pervert to "know very well" implies a mastery of knowledge and an exhaustion of epistemology. The pervert's gesture of "but nevertheless" emerges subsequent to Absolute Knowledge and the totalization of all epistemologies in the extant symbolic order. After epistemology, faith emerges. Faith is an uncertain commitment to an otherness. This excess cannot be assimilated into the self-same and the self-identical Reason of the archive of epistemology. The pervert's disavowal facilitates this passage from epistemology to faith, from science to divinity, and from idiocy to the Other. The masochist's disavowal also reorients the ontological project of the question of Being — of what is. Deleuze says of the pervert's modality of negation,

> Disavowal should perhaps be understood as the point of departure of an operation that consists neither in negating nor even destroying, but rather in radically contesting the validity of that which is: it suspends belief in and neutralizes the given in such a way that a new horizon opens up beyond the given and in place of it.[26]

"Contestation" of "that which is" invites the pervert to suspend the extant order of the society. He can imagine an otherwise to the norms and the conventions of the dominant system. This "suspension" is a detour of loss or a deferral of signification. The pervert wants to hobble the masculine desire for "ultimate satisfaction" and its will to capture the *objet petit a*.

The masochist disturbs man's submission to the conservative regulation of the homeostasis of the pleasure principle. The difference and deferral of this suspension enable the perverse masochist to imagine an alternative to the father's order. Crucially, this Other-Father is still orderly. This invention is possible because the masochist disrupts the father's metaphor and unbuckles his *point de capiton*. The quilting point is "suspended."

It is interrupted in order to make time and space for play and dance before castration by the signified of the text. The prelapsarian bliss is precedent to the introduction of the father's signified. The masochist idealizes an otherness which is as yet invisible in the existent reality-fantasy of the current moment. As Deleuze puts it: "The masochist's disavowal is the foundation of imagination, which suspends reality and establishes the ideal in the suspended world."[27] Deleuze outlines the principal object of the pervert's *Trieb*. The pervert wills the ideal and utopic. Deleuze says: "Disavowal and suspense are thus the very essence of imagination, and determine its specific object: the ideal."[28] The pervert dreams.

Disavowal is internal to imagination. The "but nevertheless" introduces a modality of the approach to the object which is otherwise than the strict epistemology of Reason. This other avenue includes faith and belief. But it also includes imagination, hope, passion, love, respect, joy, and so on. Suspense animates the masochist's imagination. Suspense releases the linchpins of the codes and conventions of the culture. Suspense inspires new substitutions and novel rearrangements. Together, disavowal and suspension gesture beyond the Reason of the neurotic and toward the Unreason of the Pervert-Schizoid-Woman. Deleuze's description of the masochist implicates a radical desexualization of the pervert's (*a*)sexuality. Deleuze makes this index explicit: "Disavowal should be regarded as the form of desexualization particular to masochism."[29] For psychoanalysis, this modality of negation is an ambivalent double-gesture. It provokes the male fetishist to enjoy a sexuality in the absence of castration. How? It does so by using the fetish-object as a screen of presence and a gain against a backdrop of absence and a loss. Why then must disavowal involve "desexualization"?

There are several explanations for this (*a*)sexuality. First, Deleuze indicates that sexual fetishism is not a sexuality. Fetishism disregards (or disavows) sexual difference. Second, the male fetishist's object of desire is the "desexualized" fetish-object. The pervert's sexuality is a desire for representation rather than an impulse for presentation *per se*. Third, the masochist's imagination and suspension differ and defer the Freudian "ultimate satisfaction." The pervert uses the strategies and tactics of the foreplay of courtly love. These flirtations delay departure-arrival at the destination of coitus or of any genital pleasure. The pervert's (*a*)sex never starts or stops. I'm in the fucking middle of something right now. The Deleuzean masochist mostly disavows genital sexuality. He imagines a utopic ideal which is beyond the idiotic regulations of sex in climax and release. This homeostatic increase/decrease in tension of the pleasure principle otherwise tethers the lover to the transgression of the law. The subject is also sutured to the dialectic of the ambivalently submissive and rebellious son. The son rages against a tyrannical father whose authority derives from a *mise-en-abyme* of convention and violence. The masochist's sexual intercourse never ends. The sex act(ion) defers the "ultimate satisfaction" of the aim/less drive. The pervert suffers a forever-anality and an endless-orality whose anticipatory pleasures extend to infinity. I am still in the fucking middle of something right now.

Patient Waiting

Deleuze claims that the pervert's fetish (the shoe, lace, fur, jockstrap) postpones gratification. Deleuze says that the fetish extends the (un)pleasure beyond the principle of homeostasis and constancy. The masochist's (*a*) sex is a constant revolution without end. The masochist's aesthetic is a parliamentary prorogation. The pervert's fashion waits for the messianic arrival of the object. The masochist's scene is of impossibility. This is exactly the orientation of deconstruction. Grammatology invites the advent of the Other. Deconstruction ushers in the *tout autre*. The perverse structure is profoundly deconstructive in principle and intuition. The masochist's respite and recess of the coy flirtation and the resistant foreplay with the object by pact and word consist of this fundamental waiting. The pervert euphorically awaits the emergence of the object in its accessibility and availability. He waits despite — "but nevertheless" — the explicit arrangement that *das Ding* always be deferred to an excess and remainder. The Boy is an otherness. He subsists beyond capture. The Boy's brutality is his concealed bodily form. About the fetish, Deleuze says,

> The constitution of the fetish in masochism points to the inner force of the fantasy, its characteristic of patient waiting, its suspended and static power, and the way in which the ideal and the real are together absorbed by it.[30]

The fantasy is the *mise-en-scène* of the pedagogy of desire. This is the organizational power of the invention of the fetish-object: the shoe, lace, fur, jockstrap — and every object and word in the system. These are *die Sachen* of a fantastic invention of the life of fantasy. The "patient waiting" for the impossible *is* the object. The Boy is barred as the condition of his access. The man waits for the Boy, and the Boy waits for waiting.

But the fetishist's "patient waiting" is neither passive nor unassertive. It is compliant with and obedient to the rules and regulations of the pact and the word. Patient waiting is intentionally performed and agentically theatricized. But there is no will to transgress in the otherwise stupid dynamic of law/infraction. The pervert's effort transcends *désir* in favor of *Trieb*. The "suspended and static power" of the fetishization of the world indicates the slow interruption of the hectic and imprecise movements in the spaces and times of the galaxies. The masochist savors precision and exactitude. These are the integrants of an (un)successful approach to the Boy. This stylized perfection surrounds the Boy from within the matrix of the rules of the agreement of the aim/less wander of *Trieb*. Deleuze's outline of the "absorption" of the real and the ideal, and the actual and the promised, situates such a tense reconciliation of both right of entry and prohibition of access within the meticulous and steady gestures of the masochist's approach toward the world. The ideal of the Other — *das Ding* — exceeds the Boy as this object. This fetish is the matrix for the pervert's acts and moves. The representation in the fetish-object desexualizes ecstasy. It does so even as it aestheticizes the every gesture of the body and soul. Masochism is the controlled manic frenzy of (*a*)sexual asceticism.

Train His Torturer

The object of the masochist's cooperative deal with the other is the trust of the word. Rapport between the man and the Boy is not regulated by any explicit law or statute. Rather, the foundation of the pact is outside of the law. It is so even if it is structured by rules and regulations. The masochist's will to restraint is based in a mere verbal agreement. Masochistic joy is the effect of a strategy and tactic. The masochist's active role in the design of the scene of constraints is critical to the coordination of the scene of *jouissance*. Deleuze writes: "The masochistic contract implies not only the necessity of the victim's consent, but his ability to persuade, and his pedagogical and judicial efforts to train his torturer."[31] How are we to conceive of the possibility of the "victim's consent" — a near contradiction in phrase? Consent to constraint — which is precisely not a restraint — is the object of the pervert's disavowal. The masochist must disavow his own role in his torture. He must disclaim his turn against himself in his consent to the torture by the lost other. The masochist waits for the infinite expansion of a universe which is already infinitely expanded.

The masochist's will to "train his torturer" evokes the simultaneity of the classic psychoanalytic binary oppositions: subject/object, active/passive, top/bottom, authority/subordinate, and so on. Concurrence of these oppositions rips open the unified and unitary structure of the subject. This will to train the torturer indicates the establishment of a scene of pleasure which is meticulously designed for enjoyment. This is precisely the project of the pervert. She wants to substitute the law of the father (lack, castration, capitalism, and ego-ideal) with the law (pact) of enjoyment (plenitude, fullness, communism, and oral mother). This principle of enjoyment must deconstruct the primary binary oppositions in the culture. At the same time, such a deed necessitates an organization within which the scene of enjoyment may be staged. The pervert's project is to train the torturer in the codes and regulations of joy and pleasure. The masochist trains his torturer in a pedagogy of *jouissance*.

The utopia of *jouissance* must banish the father. This must be done from within the parameters of the law of the mother. This set of rules is an entirely different order. It is a principle of organization which is specifically distinct from the father's dictates in the scene of the discovery of sexual difference. The utopia is at odds with the dangerous fantasy of the castration of the female junior. A fetishist's sex-objects dissimulate phallocentric sexual difference. This patriarchal regime otherwise regards the clitoris and the vagina as not the penis. Instead, the fetishist wills to banish centric-difference from the scene of sexuality, desire, and identification. The reason that the pervert can approach this tussle against sexual difference is the "patient waiting" of his (*a*)sexuality. The active deferral never comes to completion. Rather, it teeters at the edge of the "ultimate satisfaction" from which it pleasurably recoils in anticipatory — not yet — delirious — already — tumult. The masochist's desire is not repressed by the law. Rather, the masochist's pleasure is constrained by the word.

Absurdity against Irony

Deleuze approaches the aesthetic of the masochist with an account of the "patient waiting" of the pervert's torture. Deleuze contrasts sadistic irony and masochistic absurdity. Deleuze says,

> The law is no longer subverted by the upward movement of irony to a principle that overrides it, but by the downward movement of humor which seeks to reduce the law to its furthest consequences [and is] a demonstration of the law's absurdity.[32]

Sadistic irony achieves an agenda and a message, and a principle and a concept. Masochistic humor approaches the absurdity of that which is as an ontological reality. The absurd challenges the law from within the logic of the regulations of the codes and rules. The sadist presents a proposition and thesis. The ironic twist campaigns to exceed the extant symbolic order. The sadistic purpose of the discursive intervention is to negate the theorems and theses of the *doxa* of ordinary conversation. In contrast, the masochist recoils from simple and raw negation of rules. The masochist insists that the rule is internal to *jouissance*. Joy is not in opposition to the codes of conduct. The idiot's transgressive ecstasy relishes the infraction of the law. Alternatively, the regulation is integral to the pleasure of the pervert. The rule limits *jouissance* precisely in order to extend it. The arrangement short-circuits the quick homeostasis of the pleasure principle. The experience of the "ultimate satisfaction" is the fundamental mistake of the masculine libidinal economy. The masochist coyly recoils from her object of desire. The coldness of the masochist manifests in this indifference to direct contact with her object. Masochistically, the object is desirable because it is at an inaccessible distance. Shrewdly, the masochist discerns that the purpose of desire is to sustain the precious gap between the subject and the object. The object of desire is not the *objet* but the dramatization of desire and its interval of distance. Coldly, the masochist rebuffs her object in order to sustain the chilled burn.

Figure 2.4 Fetish Translation

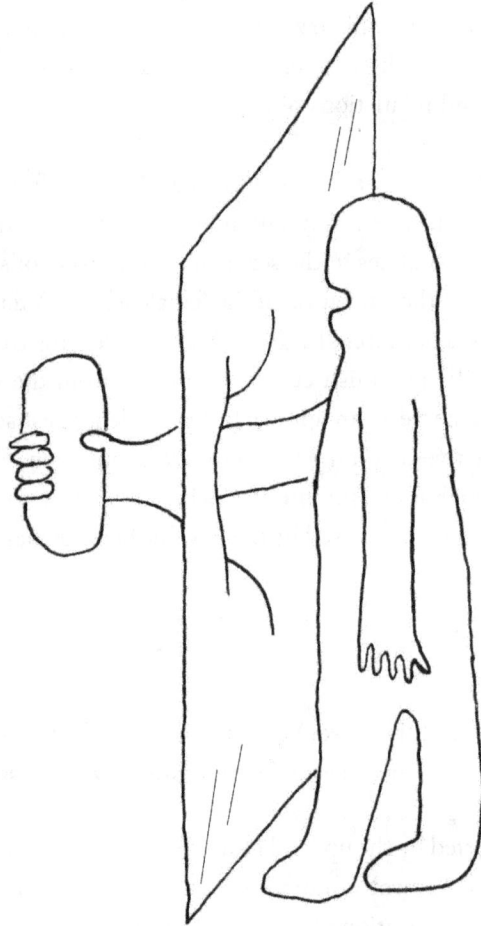

The pervert reaches through the mirror that otherwise radically obscures the other from engagement and confrontation as itself *qua* the other. The pervert's fetish is a prop for the *mise-en-abyme* of objects (and so on) whose basic principle is the force of the (*a*)sexual organizational condition of desire and its transformation into *Trieb*. This conversion facilitates the transition of a self-same and self-identical identity and difference and equality and inequality into a proximate Sameness⁺. The pervert lives and breathes on the other side of the mirror in the beyond of *désir*. The pervert enjoys — as opposed to desires — because he magically suspends the otherwise inexorable origin (destination) and departure (arrival) of desire and its phallic signified. The pervert enjoys his *Trieb* because he simulates a relationship with an expansion of otherness and death in *Thanatos*. The pervert performs such a *das Ding* as an (*a*)sexual relation which is otherwise impossible between the asymmetry of lack between pairs in heterosexuality. This picture portrays the pervert's outstretched extension into the void. This gesture returns a tangible object *ex nihilo* from the system in affirmative recurrence. The pervert recognizes that Nothingness is the center of Being. The pervert's sublimational gesture returns Something from Nothing in order to make existent the fetishes (jockstrap, and so on) in an expanded system.

Notes & Sketches —

The masochist enjoys the anticipatory approach to the "ultimate satisfaction." He jerks (off) back from the climax of the release of the tension in the pleasure principle. The masochist enjoys the latent underside of Freud's pleasure principle. *Contra* Freud, the increase in tension is the radical experience of pleasure. This experience is extimate with the structure of the law of homeostasis. The masochist's practice of pleasurable anticipation is exemplary of the "demonstration of the law's absurdity." Painful revelry in anticipation demonstrates that the Other enjoyment is an integrant of the law. The absurdity of the law is illuminated in this practice. The pervert gets off on — cums on, ejaculates into — the law. The idiot's pleasure forces transgression of the law which is otherwise principled. Masochistic fun exceeds the boundaries of a law which is otherwise irrelevant. But it does so in order to re-establish the rule. The masochist exceeds the law in order to show that this excess is the law itself. Deleuze writes: "The masochist is allowed or indeed commanded to experience the pleasure that the law was supposed to forbid."[33] This excessive *jouissance* is the pleasure that the system enables from within its own regulations and rules.

The dim joy of law/transgression always ends in decapitation. Such idiocy disappoints the neurotic whose object slips past his grasp. In contrast, the masochist manages to enjoy the "forbidden" ecstasy of the "absurdity" of the law. The (beyond of the) pleasure principle supplies a greater intensity of pleasure than the release of the tension in the return of the system to the constancy of Nirvana. The sadist's ironic disposition is strictly regulated by the pleasure principle. Irony yields a sour aesthetic. Alternatively, the masochist's absurdist sensibility is playfully organized by anticipatory tension without release. This anticipation postpones the homeostatic constancy of the pleasure principle. Such suspension is willed even from within this law itself. The masochist's disavowal, suspense, and fantasy are constitutive of his absurdist humor. Why? These techniques involve the reversal of roles — "train his torturer" — in which the pervert's disrespect masquerades deference and his submission screens mutiny. Playful artistry makes the masochist a theorist of the figurations of consequences. His perverse doublespeak of disavowal involves the closure of epistemology and the aperture of divinity. This both/and protects him from a sadistic punishment. Discipline otherwise mistakes the masochist's insurgence for battle and his revolt for riot. The pervert exhibits an intensely regulated play. His play is a serious play, as Freud says of the offspring. Like the offspring, the masochist's pretend is not superficial. This play is momentous for him. The masochist's fantasy, suspense, and imagination are the matured attributes of the offspring.

Desexualization

Deleuze's discussion of the (de)sexualization of the pervert is crucial to the project toward — (a)sexuality. The masochist is extraordinarily desexualized. He is so because he disavows sexual difference and genitalia *tout court*. He also repudiates the demand of the pleasure principle to seek enjoyment in the diminution of tension. The masochist exalts the infinite evolution of tension — before not yet already! This coil and recoil situate him squarely precedent and subsequent to the pleasure principle. Masochism is the Outside of the pleasure principle. But the masochist prepares for the pleasure principle and its climactic release. The masochist's desexualization approaches the beyond of the pleasure principle. The principle of constancy is seized in a repetition compulsion of tension. There is no release into the homeostatic constancy of the Nirvana principle. The before and after of the pleasure principle repudiate the dimwit's pleasures of tension and release. The Other edges toward eternity in its yearn and loiter. The masculine compulsively repeats the traumatic incursion of the inside by the outside. This repetition tries to master the dialectic between *Eros* and *Thanatos*.

The masochist's "patient waiting" exemplifies desexualization. This (a)sex, as I call it, is "equally the precondition of instantaneous resexualization."[34] Deleuze also claims that this at once resexualization

— simultaneous de/resexualization *Yes!* — is part of the pervert's work. Deleuze says that the masochist wants to put all of culture in "the service of masochism."[35] All of society returns to a sexualized masochism at a certain but undefined moment in the history of humanity. Deleuze says that this "resexualization takes place instantaneously, in a sort of leap."[36] The precise social or exact historical moment of this "leap" is uncertain. But it is clear that the turn toward masochism is swift and brisk. The revolution is such that there is a united turn in the subjective and objective worlds. Each gesture is turned into the "service" of masochism. The galaxy is at the service of service. The effort of the resexualization process is previously inhibited by the fetishistic libidinal representation. The fetish obscures sexual difference and the genital principle. But, at the same time, this object generates pleasure for the fetishist. The pervert rebuffs genital satisfaction and the phallic stage. The masochist repudiates the "ultimate satisfaction" of the climactic orgasm. He rebuffs the otherwise conservative and depressive return to the level of homeostatic constancy. The pervert comes after sex.

The couplet of (de/re)sexualization is a vault. There is a twist of (*a*)sexuality at once. Deleuze's term for this pivot is the "leap." This is the moment of the resexualization of masochism. An Other (*a*)sexuality substitutes for the penis and the fetish. This (*a*)sex involves (post)genital (post)desire. Deleuze mostly dismisses erotic pain as a mere secondary effect of the patient waiting at the edge of the masochist's economy. What he does emphasize is "the function of repetition and reiteration which characterize waiting."[37] Before the leap, there is a consistent form of repetition in the masochist's (*a*)sexuality. She infuses the fetish-object with the suspension, imagination, and idealization which make the fetish an object of enjoyment. The object is enjoyed even as it is deferred from presence. The "function" of waiting is a subjective experience of the Sameness⁺ of the gesture. Affectively and psychically, each movement is a repeated (re)enactment of the previous. Emotionally and cognitively, the masochist experiences a Nietzschean Eternal Return of the Same. Recurrence is isomorphic to the compulsive repetition of the memories of soldiers in the Great War. Repetition is also similar to the gestures and cries of the offspring in the *Fort! Da!* game. Repetition as such "characterizes waiting." The "patient waiting" of the masochist is an anticipatory delight. The man enjoys the simultaneity of the arrival-departure — it is here forever gone for now — of the Boy.

Anticipation of the present is neither inactive nor inoperative. Rather, anticipatory agony is vital and dynamic. At the same time, this patient waiting is experienced as a repetition of a certain Sameness⁺ that also involves an undefined difference. The leap into resexualization is a nuanced and experiential affair. Deleuze can only write the coordinates of this set of techniques. Pain is a mere secondary effect of "forms of repetition which condition its use."[38] "Forms" suggest that there is a multiplicity within the "repetition." There is a repetition with a difference. These forms repeat pain. What repeats is the agony of (un)pleasurable patient waiting. The "use" of these ritualistic rules and habitual regulations is the loiter and the linger. The effect of this restless pause is pain: I'm waiting for Nothing. But this pain is secondary to the forms which repeat this active and intentional postponement. The "ultimate satisfaction" of the capture of the goal exceeds the clutches of the subject — Where? — Over there.

The Delayed Leap

The masochist is desexualized before the leap. He is so because he firmly rejects the paternal legacy and its organization of phallic sexuality. The masochist's return to the oral mother of generosity and love desexualizes the masochist. The oral mother steals the genitality of this sexuality. Genital relationship is otherwise the province of the banished father. Capitalist sex is the masculine pleasure in genital objects. Communist (*a*)sex is perverse *jouissance* in representations — fetishes. The masochist is patiently waiting for the mother's missing penis. The essence of the maternal phallus is the promise of its emergent presence. The world is coming. The ego-ideal is the father's promise of compensation. The gift and its return are offered in exchange for the offspring's renunciation of the mother and his acquiescence to the rules of patriarchy. This is the paternal promise. It is jocosely disavowed by the masochist. The pervert resolutely abjures the father's phallic stage, and he rejects the genital opposition between penis/not-penis which structures the patriarchal gender binary between man/woman. The pervert is strictly the Outside of gender and sexuality — *qua* (*a*)sexual.

The pervert's superego develops according to the newly posited perverse law (pact) of enjoyment. The masochist's superego effaces the extant neurotic law of the father. The masochist establishes the pact with the oral mother as a substitute for the paternal law. This mother frees her son from the dominance of a phallically organized sexuality. In its place, the perverse masochist enjoys the (*a*)sexual fetish. The fetish is the object of utopic imagination and suspended desire.[39] The jockstrap is the revolution — *Fort! Fort! Fort!* — But how does the masochist resexualize his libido which is otherwise suspended between the postponed and the too-soon? Deleuze describes this resexualization as a "leap." The leap turns at a moment. The leap forces the ontology of the world of what is into the service of masochism. Service is the torturous rapture of the pleasures of repetition. Deleuze says,

> Pleasure and repetition have thus exchanged roles, as a consequence of the instantaneous leap, that is to say the twofold process of desexualization and resexualization.[40]

A mere instant resexualizes the universe of desexuality. The fetish-object and its series of representations are suddenly sexualized — which they already are — in a repetitious joy. This masochistic revolutionary service is (*a*)sexual. What is this (*a*), Boy? Masochistic resexualization (*a*)sexualizes the fetish-object with a nongential signification of postphallic (*a*)sexuality. Masochistic resexuality is postphallic and nongenital; it is profoundly fetishistic and substitutional.

The theoretical difficulty with this conception is that the fetish-object is fundamentally (*a*)sexual. Desexualization repudiates genital sexuality in favor of representation, in the shoe, lace, fur, and jockstrap. The desexualized fetish refashions and restyles the penis (or "penis-substitute," as Freud deems it). Crucially, it does so in the absence of specifically phallic signification. The pervert invents the female penis as artistry, humor, and revolution. The Woman's penis is the utopia of the pervert's worlding of new worlds to come — *Not yet!* Masochistic desexualization is the transformation of the penis into a nonphallic art and political object. Resexualization of masochism is a sexualization of this nonphallic object. The postgenital is the suspended and imagined fetish-object. The fetish is freed from phallic genitality. What is postgenital sexuality? What is postphallic sexuality? What is the (*a*)sexuality of the fetish?

At the same time, the fetish becomes sexualized. The masochist's sexuality is the return of sexuality in the universe of the oral mother rather than in the prison of the phallic father. Sexuality is possible without phallic organization. An (*a*)sexuality is imaginable beyond the genitality of the father. Deleuze continues,

> In-between the two processes [desexualization and resexualization] the Death Instinct seems about to speak, but because of the nature of the leap, which is instantaneous, it is always the pleasure principle that prevails.[41]

The death drive fractures all unities. This is so even if such fragments are recuperated by *Eros* in a tense dialectic between the shards of *Thanatos* and the unities of *Eros*. The "speech" of the death drive of instantaneity is the cry of the Unreasonable coincidence of (de/re)sexuality. The leap is the continuity of (non)phallic (*a*)sexuality. The leap intervenes at the false choice between a sexuality of the phallus and a sexuality of the oral mother. The choice is a fable because *Eros* and *Thanatos* cannot ultimately be separated, as Freud remarks in a footnote to *Beyond the Pleasure Principle* (1920).[42] The pleasure principle of tension and release is lazy constancy. The flaccid principle rules because of this choice between (re/de)sexualization, between the father and the mother, and between the superego and the ego. At stake is the (*a*)sexuality of maternal — nonphallic and nonpenile — orality.

Resexualization

The moment of the duality of the quantum superposition is the instant of the leap. The leap involves the transition from a representational economy of nonphallic fetish-object (*a*)sexuality to a nonphallic genital sexuality. The leap invites the pleasurable repetition of various objects. These Boys are nonphallic yet at the same time oddly genital. Deleuze writes: "Pain [] represents a sexualization which makes repetition autonomous and gives it instantaneous sway over the pleasures of resexualization."[43] Repetition becomes untethered and unorganized by the pleasures of sex and death. Resexualization breaks with the imagined suspension of the object. Manic enjoyment of this sex and death is otherwise forbidden by the pact of the masochist's word. In essence, the leap breaks the regulations and rules of the agreement between, on the one hand, the suspended and tortured Boy and, on the other hand, the arrived and appealed Other Boy. (De/re)sexualization is performed in the leap. The leap suspends suspension itself. The leap interrupts the reckless chase of the aim toward its goal. The masochist "knows very well" that the Boy awaits in suspension, "but nevertheless" he turns toward the Boy of foreplay and courtly love. The Other Boy turns without the constraints of the pact against genital sexuality. The Other Boy leaps. The universal service of masochism strips genitality of phallism. The resexualization of masochism introduces postphallic signification to genitalia. In other words, the object of masochistic resexualization is the maternal phallus. The leap between the Boys is mediated by the penis of the oral mother. What does the mother's penis look like? What does the mother's penis taste like?

This is the instantaneous moment of the parallactic overlap between law and enjoyment, and between principle and *jouissance*. The pervert enforces the law (pact) of pleasure. The pervert's (*a*)sexuality is *lawful transgression* and *transgressive lawfulness*. Deleuze summarizes: "*Eros* is desexualized and humiliated for the sake of a resexualized *Thanatos*."[44] The absurdity of (*a*)sexuality postpones — already now not yet — gratification. This is the coldness of the masochist's patient waiting. The masochist takes pleasure in simultaneity. She is a quantum physicist-sexualist of superpositional de/re/*a*/sexualization — *Yes!* But is the leap worth the wait? There is an automatism of repetition in masochism. The pervert repeats the gesture of the patient wait from within the system of *Thanatos*. The structure of the death instinct (such as it is) is a continuous experimentation with the same gesture. The masochist's gesture is simultaneously a different gesture than itself. A same-different repetitious automatism is mostly inconceivable on the page, in the text, and in the word. But it can be analogized as the visceral affect of a syncopated Sameness[+]. Rhythmic reversal recurs endlessly as the leap. The masochist endures (non)genital (*a*)sexual waiting for (non)genital sexual automatism. But the function of the leap is not to tether aim to goal and idiot to object. Rather, the purpose is to open the affect of this movement within the imagined object of suspension. What I am describing is sex — already now not yet — with the Other Boy. Crucially, the leap from desexualization to sexuality appears to separate repetition from pleasure. This deceptively makes joyous repetition — same difference — an immediate cause and instantaneous effect of pain. The repetition of resexualized (*a*)sex is the automatism of queer oral (*a*)sex with the mother's penis *qua* postphallic genital object. The secondary effect of pain of this leap can be ascribed to the unbounded interval of this process of worlding the world-to-come after — in the process of — the death of the father. Queer oral sex with the mother's penis is the revolution. The Becoming of the maternal phallus — *à venir* — is the horizon of the Spirit of the System.

An ordinary interpretation of the component of pain in masochism must be resisted. Deleuze stresses that pain is only a secondary effect of the pleasures of repetition. The masochist enjoys the missed encounter. He does so even in sexualization. The strange coincidence of the leap is that desexualization and resexualization are the same process. The moment of the intervention of *Thanatos* is the aperture of the parallactic gap. This opening of two different perspectives on the "one" and the "same" object both widens and narrows the gap between the law of the father and the law of the mother, between the superego and the ego, and between the transgression and the law. The leap pretends to speak. The gap emerges. What leaps from the abyss is the continuity between the law of the father and the law (pact) of enjoyment. The masochist enjoys the law of the father *qua* the law of the mother. The pervert discovers an Other *jouissance* at the center of the law. The pervert hustles this law to its absurdist consequences. The effect is the utter delight of the law. The consequence is the magical pleasure in discipline. The pervert can only grin and laugh at such absurdity. His radical desexualization approaches a ferocious resexualization in a leap. The leap illustrates the radical continuity between the difference which otherwise separates "a sameness which is not identical." For what is the masochist patiently waiting in his bemused suffering? He waits for the yet-to-come. Until then, he leaps on him — *Not yet!* Masochism is not the desire for the lost object but the enjoyment of the lost object.

Sex is not only traumatic. It is also curious. The pop artist, Andy Warhol, died a virgin. He said, "Sex is so messy." The queer philosopher, Michel Foucault, a kinky leather queen who died of AIDS in 1984, said, "Sex is boring." The psychoanalyst, Sigmund Freud, said that the object (*Objekt*) of sex is mostly irrelevant to desire and its satisfaction. The feminist philosopher, Marilyn Frye, said that the gay worship of the penis belies a discontent with sexuality and a dislike of Women. The psychoanalyst, Jacques Lacan, said that the erotics of foreplay is the proper object of sex. The philosopher, Gilles Deleuze, said that desexualization is the masochistic apex of eroticism. The queer literary critic, Leo Bersani, said that the secret of sex is that most people do not like it. If sex is messy, boring, objectless, discontented, impossible, resistant, and unlikeable — then why do people even bother to have sex? The issue at this historical moment is certainly not Freud's obsession with the repression of desire and its return in the symptom. The issue is neither the subjective and objective conditions of repressive authority, on the one hand, nor the cynical imperative for the emancipation of sex and desire from the dark recesses of libido, on the other hand. Western culture is in a transitional space between an economy of neurosis and its repressions and a future of perversion and its traces of madness. Sex is liberated. Now we are stuck with it. Sex is not only messy and boring. Sex is unsexy. If sex is unsexy, then what modalities of *jouissance* emerge after the Death of Sex? At the close of *History of Sexuality Volume 1* (1975), Foucault cracks his fundamental insight about sexuality: "The irony of this deployment [of sexuality] is in having us believe that our 'liberation' is in the balance."[45] Western civilization has finally liberated the unsexy. But now what?

Such is —

"I'm tired tonight, Boy." [beat.] "Maybe *tomorrow?*"

Figure 2.5 *Möbius* Pinch

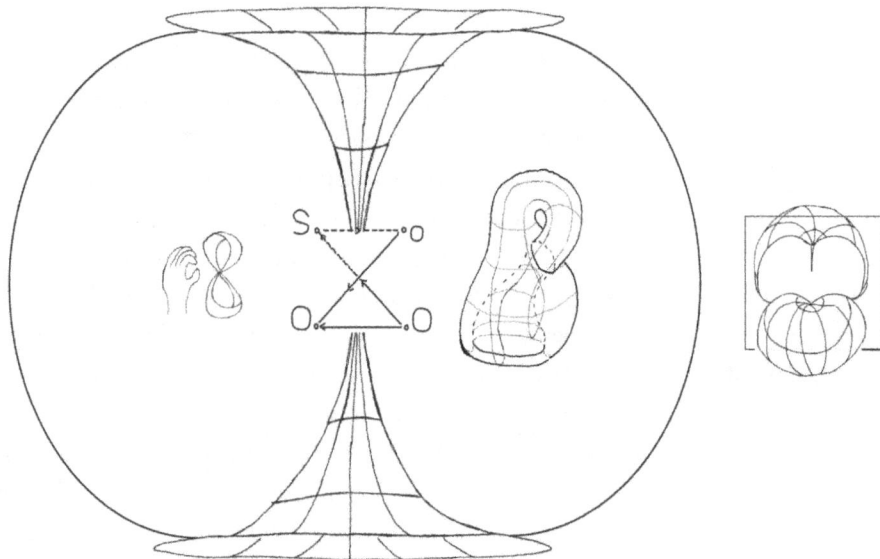

This illustration elaborates the pervert's play of substitutability in the *mise-en-abyme* of the fetish. The multiplicitous torus and cross-section (right) reflect the Inside-Outsideness and Outside-Insideness (extimacy) of the Klein Bottle which is depicted in Lacan's Schema-L (center). The Schema-L is analogous to the pervert's pinch and its facility with the simultaneously enforced presence and absence — suspension — of the *point de capiton*. The pervert's substitution — shoe for lace for fur for jockstrap for maternal phallus for penis-substitute for penis for penis for penis-substitute for maternal phallus for jockstrap for fur for lace for shoe, and so on — exposes and reveals a specific node of the structural Inside-Outsideness and Outside-Insideness (extimacy) relationship between objects. The pervert articulates the explosive multiplicity of the psychotic's intuition about: first, the positivity in the system of the signifier; second, the abundance in the supply of goods and services in the economy; and third, the singularity in the (*a*)sexuality of bodies. This substitutability can only be articulated in a system of coherent presence by the slip and slide of the pervert's pinch of the *point de capiton* and play of Metaphoricity. The neither identity nor difference nor equality nor inequality but Sameness[+] of the fetish is an instantiated node of the extimate singularity which is present in all points both Inside-not-Outside-Outside-not-Inside in relationality and constructionism in the system of *langue*. This illustration elaborates the pervert's pinch of the simultaneous aperture and closure — suspension — of the phallic function. This pinch arrests impossible presence at the same time as it enables fragile communication. The drawing illuminates a parallactic overlap which is the Unreasonable secret truth of the schizoid. This Untruth is hidden from the galaxy of illusory general equivalence in: first, the phallocentrism of patriarchy; second, the exchange-value of capitalism; and third, the positive unity of the word in language. The pervert's instinct for deconstruction traverses the wormhole of the endless (un)suspended *mise-en-abyme* of jockstraps and jockstraps. The Klein Bottle (right) is a visual depiction of this extimacy. The Klein Bottle is a surface which submits its closed form to its own open formlessness. The Inside is at once its own Outside.

Notes & Sketches —

Chapter Three

Psyches and Patients

When the characters are really alive before their author, the latter does nothing but follow them in their action, in their words, in the situations which they suggest to him.
— Luigi Pirandello

The Lacanian and Freudian asylum categorizes three clinical forms of pathology: neurosis, psychosis, and perversion. Each of these psychical organizations is culturally, not biologically, assembled. These clinical structures are distinct modes of relationship to desire, the phallus, and *jouissance*. There are five modalities of these clinical structures and psychical organizations: form of negation, manifest representation, latent content, symptom, and threat. The form of negation is introduced in Freud's "On Negation" (1924) as a specific mechanism. Negation proper is distinct from repression. The manifest representation of the return is the articulation of desire and truth. The latent content of the negated is hidden but visible in the unconscious. The unconscious is structured like a language. The negation in neurosis, psychosis, and perversion is represented in an arbitrary but conventionalized system of symbolization. This system is outside of the subject. The return of the negation forms a symptom. This symptom is the tick and caper of the clinical structure. The threat to the culture is the menace to the system that the social censorship negates as the latent content. The form of negation is specific to each disorder or psychical typology. Negation hides the latent content in the closet of the culture. The form of negation in neurosis is *Verdrängung*. The style of negation in schizophrenia is *Verwerfung*. The mode of negation in perversion is *Verleugnung*. This latter perverse form of negation is the object of my critical scrutiny. *Verleugnung* returns an expansive and extensive sequence of objects rather than the strict symptoms which recur in neurotic *Verdrängung* and in schizoid *Verwerfung*.

The negated is either neurotically repressed, psychotically foreclosed, or perversely disavowed in either a social unconscious or an individual unconscious. This space is the Outside of both the system and the subject. The manifest representation is the visible and noticeable effect of — in the case of dreams — the dream-censor and the subterfuge of the dream-work of condensation and displacement. Unconscious-work protects the conscious ego and the Madness of Order from the threats of the latent content of the unconscious. The latent content is the text — desire, wish, and truth — of the negated material in the unconscious. The latent desire is barred from the system of the conscious and the ego of both the self and the society. The return of the *Verdrängung* for the neurotic, the *Verwerfung* for the psychotic, or the *Verleugnung* for the pervert is the symptom of the system. These symptoms include language, phallocentric sexual difference, capitalist private property, and the Madness of Order. The symptom is also the individual detail of dysfunction. These details include dream, slip, joke, and psychopathology for the neurotic; hallucination and delusion for the psychotic; and (sexual) difference as "itself" for the pervert. The symptom disturbs the consistent and predictable procedure and renewal of these structures — psychical and systemic — by the effects of the symptomatic eruption of the latent content of the unconscious. The systemic threat is the reason for the negation of the latent content into the cellar and dunny of the unconscious. But the perverse return of "itself" in the symptom generates a productive series of objects which cannot be contained by the $-istic systems of language, desire, and scarcity. *Verleugnung* is the principle of the expansion of the solar system.

This unconscious space is the Outside of the subject and the system. The manifest representation, latent content, and symptom are all exterior to the subject. They are (un)situated within the web of representations in the symbolic order. An analysis of the signifying chain is necessary in order to decipher the Madness of Order in manifest representation, latent content, and threat of the symptom. But why are the manifest, latent, and symptom considered possessions (private property, *le propre*) of the individual or even the system if their origin and destination — departure and arrival — are the slippery slides of the networks of words? Whose unconscious is whose? Why does Lacan refuse to discuss the countertransference as the site of the desire of the analyst in the place of the hysteric as generator of the master signifier? These five configurations — form of negation, manifest representation, latent content, return of the negation as a symptom, and systemic threat — will be crucial to the descriptive pursuit of the psyches and patients in the psychoanalytic clinic. The pervert's *Verleugnung* recurs between departure and destination, and *arche* and arrival. The objects in this series — fur, lace, shoe, jockstrap, indecency, locket, watch, hair, belt, leather, brick, felt, announcement, hat (*et al.*) — recur *qua* "themselves" in the improper scare quotes of the return of affirmation from the force of the peculiar negation of *Verleugnung*.

In this chapter, my presentation of the patients of psychoanalysis will be layered and integrated in order to interweave and interlace the relationships among neurotic, psychotic, and pervert. The purpose of my exegesis is not to present unified and discrete views of each of the three clinical structures in their singular and specific personages. Rather, my pursuit is to present the interrelationships and interactions among neurosis, psychosis, and perversion. Toward this end, my work in this chapter is structured by substratum and coalescence. My purpose is to paint pictures of neurosis, psychosis, and perversion in their theoretical and conceptual dimensions and in their everyday practical routines. The horizon of this study is to bind these structures to each other in order to uncover the relationships among the clinical structures. The subtext of the chapter is to subvert the otherwise distinct classifications of neurosis, psychosis, and perversion. The purpose is to theorize psychical and social configurations which underpin the project to critique $-ism and to innovate the Spirit of the System. The benefit of this modality of analysis is an original and rigorous speculation on clinical structures and their social implications. The horizon of this chapter is to interweave and interlace an elaboration of a *postpsychoanalytic* theory of the conceptual personae of the neurotic, the psychotic, and the pervert in order to foreshadow the topics and concepts in the study. The rest of the book specifies and elaborates on these themes and ideas. Perversely, the intentional repetitions of the theses and propositions in this chapter recur as the fetishes of the text itself. The pervert's fetish returns with a difference, and the proposals in this chapter recur with a distinction. The return from the Real scare quotes recurs the "faith" in the theses and the "belief" in the propositions. I present this *mélange* of psychical structures with specific emphasis on the pervert. Fasten your seat belts, it's going to be a bumpy night!

Table 3.1 The Postpsychoanalytic Psychical Structures

Psychical Clinical Structure	Neurotic	Psychotic	Pervert
Symptom (Pathology)	Depression Anxiety Sexual Frigidity Sexual Dysfunction Inhibition Dissatisfaction Penis Envy Castration	Hallucination Delusion Mania Frenzy Incoherent speech "Sex is boring"	Enjoyment *Jouissance* Fetishism, Penis, Penis-Substitutes
Manifest Representation (Visible)	Dream Slip of the Tongue Joke Phantom Limb Inorganic Somatic Disturbances Inhibited Sex	Unreason (Foucault) Discourse Resistant to Truth Metaphysics of Anti-Presence What is is What is not Mania No Sex	Playful Representation Inventive Language Peculiar Word Play Talent for Language Fetish-Objects: Fur, Lace, Shoe, Jockstrap Sex as Representation (Pornography) Exhibitionism/Voyeurism Scopophilia, Vision, Human Form
Latent Content (Secret, in the Unconscious)	Desire Wish Truth "Something is Missing"	X	"Yes" Presence Totality Fullness Plenitude Communism "Nothing is Missing"
Mode of Negation (Object of "No")	Repression *Verdrängung* Of Desire, Wish, Truth Either/Or Opposition Sign Sexual Timidity	Foreclosure *Verwerfung* Of Father, Signified, Meaning Being-Deconstruction	Disavowal *Verleugnung* Of (Sexual) Difference Of Opposition Of Not, "No" Becoming-Deconstruction

Return of the Negated (Subject of "Yes")	Desire Lack Castration Scarcity Difference Identity Identification Meaning *"lettre pour l'être"* Language, Signified Mind, "Consciousness" "Sexuality" Politics "Something is Missing" Capitalism "Master Signifier" (Truth) Essence of Alienation in Marxism Private Property	Production Essence of Man in Marxism No Self, No Other No Meaning Being *"L'être pour lettre"* No Language Body	Enjoyment Plenitude Sameness Capitalism = Communism $A \neq A$ $A = B$ (Non)contradiction Anti-Meaning *"lettre et l'être"* Weird but Legible Language Body and Mind (whatever) Being = Nothingness Penis = Clitoris Clitoris = Penis "Male Homosexuality" Ethics, Self-Fashioning Communism Public Property
Threat	Sex Family Domesticity Gender Roles	Reason Truth Reality-Fantasy Coherence Stability System, Order Father, Signified, Capital Capitalism	Articulation of the Madness of the System Representation of the Truth of the Unreason of the Schizoid "Reasonable Unreason"

POSTPSYCHOANALYTIC DIAGNOSTICS

The essence of the subject is desire. Each psyche in question is articulated in a specific relationship to desire. According to Joel Dor, the structure of each pathology (neurosis, schizophrenia, and perversion) is distinguished by the ways in which "desire is handled."[1] The oedipal version of subjectivization in psychoanalysis posits that the preliminary pleasure of the male junior's penis and his incestuous joy with his mother are antecedent to desire proper. *Jouissance* is historically antecedent to desire. The male junior's delayed desire is activated in relationship to the fantasized castration of the female junior. Her lack is doubly consequential. First, the male offspring is quickly stricken with castration anxiety at the potential annexation of his private property. The contrast with the female junior's lack precedes the penis *qua* neither private nor jeopardized nor owned. Second, the male junior is immediately sutured into the law of the father and the guidance toward the ego-ideal. The paternal function enforces the male junior's mimicry of the normative values of the culture. The systematic upshot of the oedipal trajectory for the male junior is the anxious protection of private property and the desire for identity in the ego-ideal. The propagation of the culture of *Homo sapiens* demands that pleasure yield to desire. *Jouissance* is supplanted by desire as the essence of man.

Oedipally, the female junior in a flash acknowledges her castration and assumes penis envy.[2] Her response to phallic loss is a gleeful and desirous consumption of penises and their avatars. These penis-substitutes take metaphorical form in what Freud eventually refers to as the "penis-baby" among other substitute consolation prizes for the vaunted male appendage.[3] The upshot of the oedipal tale for the female junior is several. These consequences are elaborated with stress and disturbance by Freud in his essay, "Femininity" (1930). Feminine libido is pursuant of objects (husband, father) which will satisfy her will to identity. The general purpose of the Oedipus complex is to consolidate identity from an originary pleasure. This generalization does not necessarily apply in the case of Freud's version of femininity. But the way that desire is "handled" by the neurotic involves the transition from pleasure to identity and desire. How is the triumph of identity and desire (ego, ego-ideal, ideal-I) "handled" in relationship to an overturned but still nascent pleasure, either masculine or feminine? Must desire supplant *jouissance* as the organizational principle of mankind? The pervert's peculiarity is his magical facility to design a compromise between desire and pleasure. The pervert *enjoys desire*. The pervert *desires desire*. The object of the pervert's *jouissance* is *désir*. The Woman's Other *jouissance* is the desire of *jouissance*.

The specific organization of enjoyment is the *sinthome*. The *sinthome* is the kernel of arrangement of *jouissance*. The structure of desire supplants enjoyment as the definitive essence of the subject. The *sinthome* is the overlap of the orders of the imaginary, the symbolic, and the Real. The *sinthome* is the hallmark of each clinical designation. The neurotic represses desire into the unconscious. The wish returns in the symptom of the dream, joke, slip, and psychopathology of everyday life. Truth returns in the hidden motivation. This secret intention is betrayed in a veiled signification. The navel of this truth is indicated in free association. In contrast, the schizoid has no relationship to desire. The schizoid's psychical life is organized by the trace of *Trieb* and its aim/less voyage around objects and representations of a tangled *jouissance*. These figurations function as mere prepositional indices on the madman's trip. This voyage abjures the phallic *point de capiton*.

Alternatively, the pervert disavows (sexual) difference. The pervert's intuition may involve knowledge of lack. But this *savoir* is quickly sutured by a faith in and optimism about the (re)turn of (to) the maternal phallus and the sister's penis. The absence of the female penis is otherwise the linchpin of the economy of castration (loss, debt, private property, scarcity, supply/demand, and so on). The pervert's psychical structure demurs from any object of desire to grab or clasp. The pervert's divine faith and optimistic belief foreswear stupid desire and its idiotic *jouissance* for a coherent and legible *Trieb* and the Other *jouissance*. Drive gestures toward another modality of enjoyment and an alternative symbolic order altogether. The pervert's compromise between desire and pleasure facilitates a realist approach to sexual difference and a recurrent sequence of affirmed objects in the place of the lost object. *Verleugnung* returns positivity to negativity. The lost clitoris and threatened penis return as the fur, lace, shoe, jockstrap, *et al*. The neurotic takes pleasure in transgression and law, and the schizoid pleases himself with the violence of existence. But the pervert enjoys the rupture of the symbolic *qua* Real. The neurotic is the only clinical structure which strictly desires. The schizoid achieves orgasmic *jouissance* in his barred access to castration. Only the pervert reverses the psychical prioritization of desire over enjoyment.

No!?

The issue of negation is vexed in a postpsychoanalytic diagnostics because the distinct modalities of negation — neurotic *Verdrängung*, schizophrenic *Verwerfung*, and perverse *Verleugnung* — are pivotal to the peculiarities of each typology of psyche. A generalized theory of negation is necessary in order to frame the specificities of negation in the three clinical structures. Freud's brief essay, "Negation" (1925), claims that the negative is immanent to Reason and its intellectual judgment. The system of the Cs. is structured by knowledges and their negations. Intellectual activities — Reason and its logics — are vitally unimaginable. This is so in the absence of the faculty of negation and the paternal "No!" to the excesses of desire and truth. Freud's text explicates the relationship between Reason and the conscious system, on the one hand, and Unreason and the desire of the unconscious, on the other hand. Freud begins the text with the analytic proviso that,

> in our interpretations we [analysts] take the liberty of disregarding the negation and seizing
> on the positive content of the thought.[4]

A close reading of this passage beseeches several suspended questions. First, what is "the negation" of the conscious thought? Later in the essay, Freud distinguishes between two modalities of judgment: of existence and of property. Negation generally applies to either the negation of existence (is, is not) or property (qualification). What precisely is "the negation" of thought in a system of differences and negativities without positive terms?

Second, how does the psychoanalyst "disregard" the negation in order to focus on the positive content of the analysand's statement? Inexplicably, Freud suggests that negativity *qua* the repressed "No!" and positivity *qua* the uncensored content of the thought can be brazenly detached from each other. Discourse is a system of interrelated and interchangeable elements of extimate parallactic overlap. The negativity cannot be parsed from the positivity. The negative is internal to the positive. The psychoanalyst cannot easily divorce the conscious "No!" from the unconscious "yes." Nor can the analyst split the conscious "No!" from the unconscious "yes." The syntax and semantics of conscious discourse disable any discrete rupture between "yes" and "No!," and between affirmation and negation. A "No!" may mean "yes" — as Dora awkwardly grasped — but this conclusion is undecidable from within the discourse of the conscious and in the relationship between the systems of the Cs. and the Unc. The analyst who "disregards" the "No!" may accidentally spurn the "yes." Affirmation and negation cannot be squarely divided or discretely divorced.

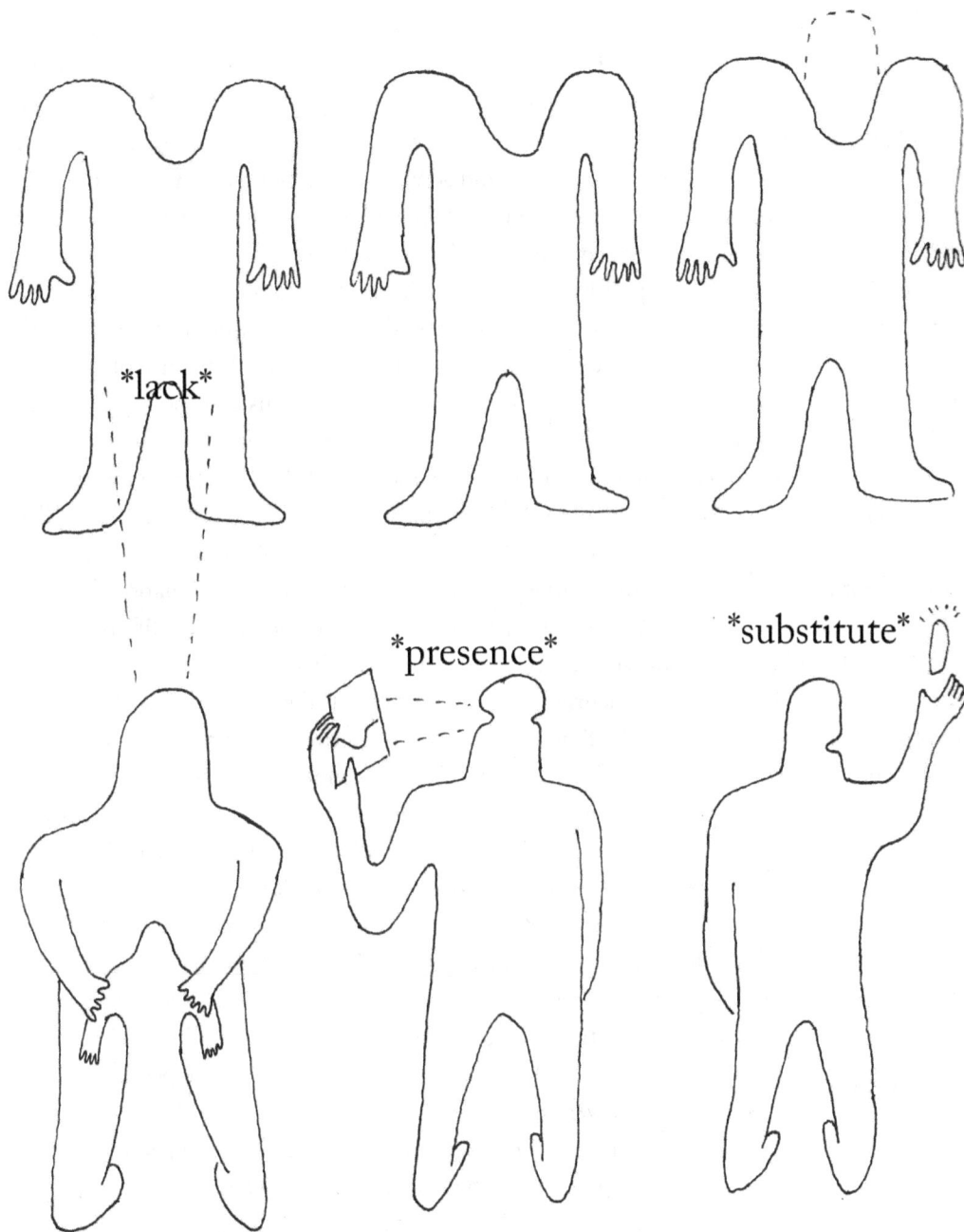

Figure 3.1 The Postpsychoanalytic Psychical Structures

This Illustration depicts the neurotic (left), the psychotic (center), and the pervert (right) in relationship to the phallocentric lack of the Woman. Each clinical typology — neurotic, schizoid, and pervert — represents a different attitude toward castration. The neurotic's repression protects the penis as private property with the consequent symptom of a profound anxiety. The neurotic's identity is continuous with his precarious ownership of his penis (*et al.*). The neurotic copes with sexual difference in the transformation of difference into deficit. The neurotic is represented in a gesture of the protection of his genitals. The genitals represent the purported identity and supposed essence of the neurotic. The figure shows the neurotic with his hand in extension in order to veil an image which is a semblance of himself. This gesture illuminates the threat of and defense against the Other. This Other decenters and destabilizes the Logic of Identity. The Other overwhelms the defensive gesture of the neurotic's hand. The neurotic strives (with his hand) to affirm the self-sameness and self-identity of the Logic of Identity in order to ratify (his own) identity. The neurotic holds his hand fast to the Logic of Identity. The neurotic transforms singular difference — Sameness[+] — into a difference between metaphorical likenesses. Phallocentrically, the neurotic's metaphorical difference translates the singular "a man has a penis and a Woman has a clitoris" into "a man has a penis and a Woman does not have a penis." The Woman is the self-same and self-identical deficit of the man. But the Woman's essentially constructed plenitude occludes her from the system of language and the symbolic order *tout court*. Language is neurotically structured by the self-sameness and self-identity of the positive and autonomous unit of the word. Alternatively, the psychotic response to castration is to foreclose sexual difference altogether. The identity of the ~~schizoid~~ is put under erasure by the return of the Real in madness. The psychotic recognizes the difference of Sameness[+], but his foreclosure of the symbolic obstructs any spoken or written articulation of this Sameness[+]. The schizoid affirms the presence of all that is as such. The psychotic approaches the sensibility of the Woman because he abjures the Logic of Identity. This Sameness[+] of the other and difference from the self is represented in the illustration of the mirror. The mirror displays the schizoid's reflection as the inverted head of the Woman. The psychotic sees himself in the mirror precisely as not himself but the Same[+] as the other. The schizoid is the same as the other but different from himself. The madman is at a distance from and in an alienation from himself. The schizoid's speech (such as it is) is an incoherent repetition of the same because his difference — Sameness[+] — is *in toto* the same difference. This specificity of the schizoid is his split from himself and conventional signification. The speech of madness is delirious babble. In contrast, the pervert enjoys the play of the *mise-en-abyme* of substitution. His form of negation (affirmation) is disavowal. The pervert at once acknowledges (sexual) difference and denies it. The pervert accepts castration as symbolic and as internal to the structure of *langue*. The pervert welcomes sexual difference into the system of language as a positive rather than a negative content. But this positive content is also the condition of the possibility of the repudiation of castration. The pervert's advance toward difference invites the Outside of *langue* into a play within the system that otherwise excludes it. The pervert circumvents the exclusion. The inverted head represents a destabilization of Being in the system. This turn toward otherness is conditioned by the return of substitution. The image depicts this substitution in the momentary instantiation and embodiment in the object. The substitute is an object which appears in the scene of castration but also transforms the castration of sexual difference into plenitude. The dotted lines indicate that the jockstrap may (im)properly fit into the absence. The pervert magically accepts castration but not as a *fait accompli*. The pervert accepts sexual difference and also acknowledges the diacritical system of meaning-making. The constitutive absence which haunts Being is the jagged fragmentation which is at the center of every signifier. This gap in and as the word and object is the pervert's undergrounds. The pervert's play fills this space with an expanded succession of fetish representations of presence. The pervert's will to power is the creative force of substitution and Metaphoricity. This perverse power exposes the Inside-Out and Outside-In of the system.

Notes & Sketches —

The third issue that the Freudian citation poses is about the "positive content" in the analysand's statement. What is the "positive content" of the thought in the patient's articulation? The division negative/positive must yield to the extimate overlap between positive assertion *qua* desire and truth, on the one hand, and negative repression *qua* censorship and inhibition, on the other hand. If the positive articulation of desire and the negative repression of the wish cannot be separated, then Freud's project to detach the affirmative content *qua* truth (*Eros*) from the negated content *qua* repressed (*Thanatos*) renders analysis a charade. Freud's insight about generalized negation is the coincidence of the negative *qua* the positive. But this theoretical achievement cannot escape the liminal indistinction between the repressed and its return at the *arche* of the division. Negation is a principle which tends toward contraction and closedness. The analyst's purpose is to expand and open the "No!" toward the "yes" of the recurrence of the repressed in the veil of conscious articulation. The pervert's *Verleugnung* returns the negated *qua* "negated" and a series of affirmed objects — furs, laces, shoes, jockstraps, *et al.* — whose reach extends beyond the return of the enervated symptom. The pervert's symptom is in essence the *sinthome* because the field of its return is the *jouissance* of the recurrence of the positive rather than the law/desire cycle of repression. There is no return in *Verleugnung* because disavowal is not strictly a principle of negation.

Freud argues that the repressed unconscious content emerges in consciousness *qua* negation. Negation is the language of desire and truth in the system of the Cs. Desire speaks in the language of the "No!" in the words of everyday life. Freud writes,

> The content of a repressed idea or thought can get things to consciousness, then, on account that it is negated.[5]

The translation between conscious and unconscious is vexed because the transliteration in question is between two radically different languages *within the same language*. The transition from unconscious positivity of wish and truth to conscious negativity (positivity) of manifest representation generates an excess. This surplus cannot be recuperated into the system of the translation of either the dream-work or the analysis-work. How does negation translate into positivity?

The crucial matter is the conversion of the "No!" into the "yes." The pivotal difficulty is the translation of a system of positivity of neither negation nor epistemology — *qua* positivity — into a structure of negation and intellectual judgment — *qua* affirmation. The conundrum is settled as an aporetic antinomy. Unconscious positivity is always already conscious negativity. Conscious negativity is always already unconscious positivity. The transliteration is between two different languages within the same language. This belies the Unreasonable secret truth of the psychoanalytic architecture: the system of the Cs. is both positive (wish, truth) and negative (repression, inhibition). The system of the Unc. is both negative (repression, inhibition) and positive (wish, truth). The translation is between two languages which are (is) one language. The sign is ambivalently split between the "No!" and the "yes." Freud's theory of generalized negation strives to transform this ambivalence into an *unambivalence* toward an expansion and extension of the "yes" against the contraction and diminution of the "No!" The wager of psychoanalysis is that the ambivalence between "yes" and "No!" can be won by affirmation. Generalized negation tends toward the positivity of the "yes." The pervert's *Verleugnung* is a simulated modality of negation which returns a series of positive objects. These objects shield the fetishist from the horror of castration which is confessed but dismissed. These fetishes generate pleasure and *jouissance* rather than desire and its vicissitudes of loss.

The distinction between conscious and unconscious is decisive for a generalized theory of negation. The conscious is the *mise-en-scène* of everyday interaction. The unconscious is the obscured Other scene of the translation between manifest and latent. There is neither negation nor knowledge nor temporality in the unconscious Other scene. The unconscious system articulates its affirmative and expansive *Eros* of "yes." It does so as a counter to the negativity and difference — *not* — in the ego-system of the conscious discourse. Freud claims that the "No!" is the symbol of negation in the conscious.[6] The unconscious "yes" is the measured affirmation in response to the structural differential negativity of everyday words. Freud famously summarizes his unconscious,

> We never find a "No!" in the unconscious, and recognition of the unconscious by the ego is always expressed in negative formulation.[7]

The oppositions conscious/unconscious and "No!"/"yes" are internal and external — extimate — to each other. The unconscious "yes" of articulated expansion and openness is the obversive Other scene of the conscious "No!" of its discursive differences and negativities. The interface of the systems of the Cs. and the Unc. is the translation of the unconscious "yes" into the conscious "No!" The paradox is that the symbolized unconscious "yes" is simultaneously the articulated conscious "No!" and — extimately — the expressed conscious "No!" is simultaneously the utterance of the unconscious "yes." But if "yes" and "No!" are parallactically overlapped in the unconscious, then is there even a "No!" or "yes" as such? What is in excess of a surplus "No!" and an extra "yes"?

The paradoxical conclusion is that the unconscious is not free of negation — no "No!" — as in Freud's original formulation. Rather, the unconscious affirmation is the translation of the conscious negation. The unconscious affirmation is a "yes" and a "No!" But the conscious negation is also a "yes" and a "No!" A "No!" is enforced on the unconscious because of the affirmative discourse of the ego-conscious system. The conscious negation and the unconscious affirmation are parallactically overlapped. The excess of this superposition in the generalized theory of negation is the psychoanalytic impotence to unyoke affirmation from negation, "yes" from "No!," and unconscious from conscious. A liminal *différance* between affirmation/negation, "yes"/"No!," and unconscious/conscious is articulated by an excess which overwhelms the authority of the psychoanalyst and his will to interpret "No!" *qua* "yes" in the calculation of desire.

But Freud's point is instructive. The unconscious paradoxically affirms with "yes" at the same moment as it negates with "No!" The unconscious only says "yes," but the conscious also only says "yes." The distinction is that the conscious "yes" affirms in the vocabularies of the differences and negations of "No!" The ego-system says "yes" *qua* "No!" The conscious dialogue speaks awry. The ego "always expresses" its affirmative "yes" in "negative formulation," as Freud says. It does so in order to evade the censorship. But the ego also expresses "yes" *qua* "No!" in order to overcome the structural differential negativity of the materiality of the signifier. The takeaway is that the essential diacriticality of conscious discourse belies a fundamental affirmation of the *Yes!* This expansive and extensive affirmative "yes, yes" is obscured by the skeletal scaffold of the architectonics of the system of *langue*. The pervert's *Verleugnung* recurs the "No!" *qua* "yes," and the "yes" *qua* "No!," and the "fur" *qua* "lace," and the "shoe" *qua* "jockstrap," and the "necklace" *qua* "Jared," and the "bra" *qua* "fairy," and so on. The negated object returns in the scare quotes of the affirmed object. The pervert's grammatological dissolution of the conscious/unconscious binary opposition establishes an affirmative (negative) sandbox in which the toys of fetishism are both yes and No!, both fur and lace, both shoe and jockstrap, both necklace and Jared, both bra and fairy, and so on. Perversely, generalized negation is beside the point of *jouissance*. Negation is relevant to desire and its negation and return *qua* symptom. The pervert's *sinthome* of enjoyment displaces the neurotic ambivalent and compulsive repetition of loss, redemption, and return. Freud's nephew and his reel of string (1920) recur and return — but with an expansive array of *objets* for the toy chest.

Figure 3.2 Symptom and Negation

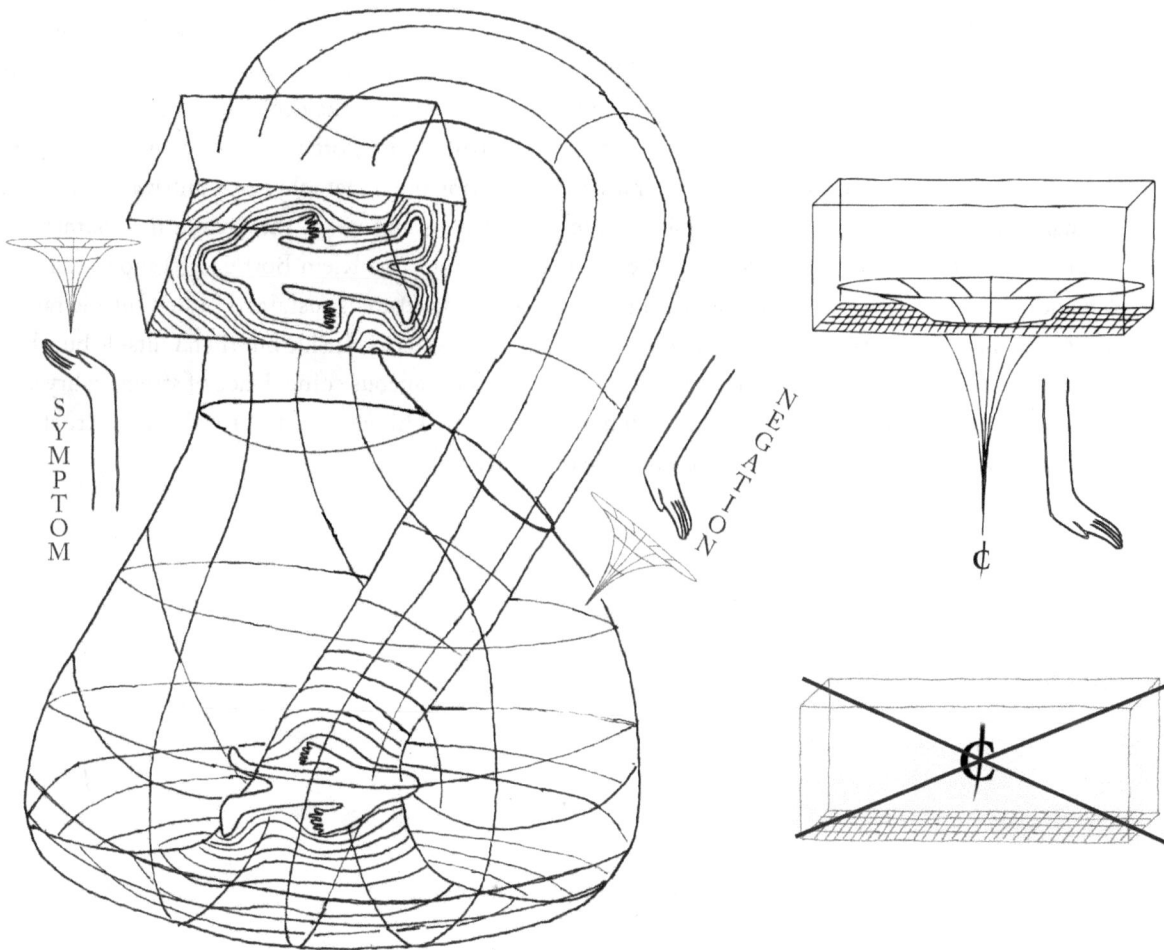

The Klein Bottle shape (left) illustrates the Inside-to-Outside-to-Inside *ad infinitum* extimate relationship of the conscious system (above, right) to the unconscious system (below, right). The neurotic (above) organizes the space of selfhood and sociality. The neurotic's subjectivity is this space and time (above, right). The neurotic is structured within this space and time. The unconscious (below, right) is structured like a language. This space is structured from the Outside toward the Inside. The semblance of a construction of the unconscious as obversely structured — from the Inside toward the Outside — is also the case, but this reversal is immediately recaptured by the primacy of the Outside (Inside). The force of negation in the unconscious quashes (e.g. represses) desire and truth in order to sustain the ego-function of the conscious system (above, right). The neurotic symptom manifests (above) in the form of the dream, joke, slip, and psychopathology of everyday life. The gravity function (above, right) appears in the symptom. This function defuses upward but also condenses downward. The two drawings of the conscious and the unconscious (right, above, below) illustrate in parallel the image of the Klein Bottle (left). The center or (*a*)asexual nucleus must be maintained on the Outside of the system in order to sustain its vectors of force. The eruption of the (*a*)sexual center of the system into the structure potentially disrupts the system. The Klein Bottle also illuminates the occlusion of the temporality of the structurality of the structure. The occluded center — structurality, organization, gravity, function, (*a*)sexual nucleus, *tout autre*, and so on — is neither a symbolic fiction nor a metaphysical contrivance. Rather, the (*a*)sexual center is the Being — metaphysics of presence and essence — of the system in a Sameness⁺ which is an Inside-Out extimacy (and so on) to itself in neurotic time. The Klein Bottle (left) shows that the symptom and negation of neurosis are temporal. The center of the structure is sustained by an Outside rather than by the presence of the positive ontological order of Being. The system is Inside but then Outside but then Inside (and so on) of and to itself. The illustration indicates the simultaneous coincidence of structurality and structure — construction and essence — of the system and its center. This center (structurality and structure, and construction and essence) destabilizes the presence of the system.

Notes & Sketches —

The Neurotic's Verdrängung

The negation of *Verdrängung* is mild. Neurotic repression merely obscures a desire which is stolen from the psychoanalytic playbook, including such scripts as the Oedipus complex, castration complex, penis and lack, unconscious and repressed, and so on. The neurotic's repression makes the dream, slip, joke, and psychopathology of everyday life readily analyzable by the psychoanalyst. The archetypal repression in hysteria enables the insightful analyst to return to the Freudian lexicon for an answer to the question of the latent content. This content is invariably sexual and repressive, at least at the time of Freud's writings in Europe. As Freud ambivalently puts it,

> The more one is concerned with the solution of dreams, the more one is driven to recognize that the majority of the dreams of adults deals with sexual material and gives expression to erotic wishes.[8]

The sexual desires in dreams are supplemented by the truth of the patient and the culture. This truth can only be represented by and as an obscurity. Repression is a consequence of the guilt and shame of truth. Freud's insight is that truth can only be represented as veiled. The oracular, cryptic, and occult are the royal road to truth. The linchpin of *Verdrängung* is desire rather than pleasure. Repression is extant only in the time and space in which the maternal phallus of obscene pleasure has been lost to the desire and identity of the paternal ego-ideal and the enforced kibosh on motherly joy.

The analyst of the neurotically repressed understands that the truth is exposed in the eldritch form of the bizarre. The translation of this truth from weird manifest form to interpretable content is the work of the psychoanalyst. According to Freud, the late nineteenth-century era (and onward) is the scene of the repressed latent content of sexuality, such as virginity, discomfort with the body, impotence, rape, incest, sexual frigidity, the privatization of sex and the body, abortive sexual rituals, sadomasochism, abhorrent sexual fantasies, and so on. These observable features of sex in the West are indices of the repression of sex in the culture. The truth disturbs the system in a misconfigured form. The manifest representation is legible as the erotic wish of the repression. But if the origin and destination of the wish, truth, and desire are the same in their presence in discourse, then what is the process which extends in space and time, confuses in sense and nonsense, and finally reconfigures as readable the "one" and the "same" origin and destination of the signified?

Perversely, repression and its return — latent content and manifest form as thickened in the symptom — are the same gesture. The neurotic and his analyst suffer the gap between conscious and unconscious, and between repressed and return. But the perverse truth is that these otherwise discrete indications are neither self-same nor self-identical but extimately the Same⁺ as each other. The pervert rebuffs the neurotic and his conscious repression and unconscious return because the pervert experiences a generative round of pleasures — "repression" and "return" — rather than identities and differences of the Logic of Identity. The neurotic misunderstands the Madness of Order. The analyst interprets truth from obscurity. But the analyst misrecognizes the excessive parallactic overlap between the repression and its return in the symptom. The analyst is concerned with identity and desire rather than with pleasure and its productivity.

Translation between unconscious/conscious is mediated by the "dream-work." Unconscious-work deploys talents and various techniques: principally, condensation or the unification of the multiple in images; and displacement or the transformation of psychical value and intensity from one signifier to another. But the crucial component of the primary process is the considerations of representability. This attention to figuration involves the obscene talents of the primary process in order to make understandable the encoded message of the latent truth. The effects of neurotic repression are the conscious professions of screwy sexuality in the discourse of the system. This inane sexuality is veiled by the censorship of the Other. The repression of sex as a social ritual is reproduced in the institutions of culture, such as schools, hospitals, homes, businesses, movies, television, music, and so on. The *Verdrängung* is an effect of social censorship. But the pervert discerns censorship as production, and he discovers law in transgression. Perversely, the censorship of the law is productive infraction.

The Madman's Verwerfung

The *Verwerfung* of the schizoid involves the Madness of Order and its conceptual and affective consequences for the psychotic. Lacan says that psychotic *Verwerfung* involves the suspension of the phallic function. The *point de capiton* otherwise closes the incessant play and slide of signification — what Derrida refers to as the trace of *différance*. The trace is the endless skid of difference and deferral. Trace confuses signification to the limit of bamboozlement in space and time. Freud isolates a specific defense mechanism in which "the ego rejects the incompatible idea together with its affect and behaves as if the idea had never occurred to the ego at all."[9] Freud's description separates "idea" from "affect." Freud indicates that the schizoid abandons both the "idea" and the "affect." But Freud implies that the memory of the "affect" (unlike the "idea") is mnemonically sustained. This is so even as the "idea" is jettisoned as if it had "never occurred to the ego at all."

This split between idea and affect is none other than the millennia-old conundrum of the dualism between body and mind. This classic philosophical gap between body/mind is refitted to structuralist linguistics in Saussure's split between the material signifier (body) and the abstract signified (mind). The signifier and signified can only be separated in theory but not in practice. Everyday life mobilizes the sign *qua* the conjoinment of material signifier and abstract signified. The word rules the system of signification. This signifier/signified organization is based on a conservative division and opposition rather than on a playful difference and negativity. The "idea" is the schizophrenic signified which slips and slides between the signifier. The signifier is generative materiality. The relationality and constructionism of the signifier situate the signifier in a bond and rapport with otherness. The signifier is neither self-same nor self-identical. Rather, the material signifier of the madman produces objects in excess of themselves in relationship to a surplus of objects in the Other.

Freud implies that affect may be sustained in schizophrenia. The affective orientation toward the threat is sustained. Schizophrenia involves the absolute negation — *Verwerfung* — of the idea of castration. But the affect of loss is operative in the schizoid psychical economy. Foreclosure of the name-of-the-father establishes a hole in the symbolic order. The traumatic gap cannot be sutured. The hole is animated by schizophrenic affect. Psychotic affect is not lost in the negation of castration. This is so even in the rejection of the ideas of phallocentrism and private property. Lacan identifies this gap: "Psychosis consists of a hole, a lack, at the level of the signifier."[10] This "hole" or "lack" is precisely the absence of a signified. This signified is otherwise guaranteed by the *point de capiton* of the phallic function. The material signifier is the affective dimension of the madman's relationship to the *Verwerfung* of castration. The idea of castration is foreclosed, but the affect of this loss is sustained in the psyche of the madman.

The emotive response to the Something is Missing of maternal castration is differently registered in the psyches of the neurotic and the pervert. The neurotic responds to the Real of sexual difference with both affective and ideational components. The pervert's *Verleugnung* unambivalently sustains both the idea and the affect of the discovery of sexual difference. But the pervert's discovery of extimacy renders the cognitive dissonance of the idea and the emotional dissonance of the affect benign to his psychical orientation. Perversely, the idea and affect are conjoined in the proliferation of fetishes. The fetish screens the ideational and affective components of the trauma of sexual difference. The pervert is ideationally and affectively distracted by the generation of objects in the return of affirmation from the *faux* negation of *Verleugnung*. The schizoid is terrorized by the emotive upheaval of the truth of the Woman's castration. The pervert is stabilized by reference to the idea of sexual (*a*)difference.

Derrida's psychotic concept of *différance* of infinite difference in space and endless deferral in time illuminates the trauma of the Real which the symbolic order can only weakly govern. The function of the phallus is to make presence. This function is deconstructed by the endless trace of the signifier. There is no signified as such or as *qua*. A temporality "suspends," as Derrida says, "the accomplishment or fulfillment of 'desire' or 'will,' and equally this suspension in a mode that annuls or tempers its own effect."[11] This acute mode of negation — *Verwerfung* — rejects the signified in the symbolic order. Foreclosure makes psychoanalysis of the patient nearly impossible because the work of the phallic function is suspended, disbanded, malfunctioned, and defective. There is no archetypal foreclosure. But the manifest representations of foreclosure are verifiable even if uninterpretable. The madman is a series of manifest representations in the absence of a coherent signified or latent content. This interpretation of the schizoid's manifest thought deviates from Freud's conception. Freud's framework readily enables him to interpret Schreber's delusion as a signifier of his homosexuality.[12] Derrida's *différance* slips and slides past any presence of the schizoid's homosexuality. The pervert's queerness is exemplified in the terror of the sight of the female genitals. But this horror is also tempered with an admirational decoration of the clitoris with the adornments of objects — and so on — which extend beyond the dyad of the presence of the penis and the absence of the clitoris. The madman's *différance* cannot command a succession of objects in the place of an archaic absence. The schizoid affect of *différance* manifests in the symptoms of hallucinations and delusions.

The psychotic's condition alienates him from the society. The schizoid's *Verwerfung* is systematically organized by the relationship between the symbolic and the Real. Schizophrenia is structured between a system of words which is based on a differential and negative diacritics of value, on the one hand, and a resistance to any word whatsoever, on the other hand. Real resistance to signification determines the madman's relationship to the society. The madman is the Real. He returns as an effect of the *Verwerfung* of the symbolic in the Real. Real madness sustains a terrorized affect which is not lost in the rebuttal of the idea of the signified. The schizoid is not only split between signifier and Signified/r. The psychotic is also alienated *qua* bodily affect and mindful ideal. The maniacal idea is lost to an infinite semiosis. But the frenzied affect circumscribes the psychotic's existential situation. The neurotic thinks and feels the Real of sexual difference. The madman contemplates obscene presence but experiences the terror of castration. The pervert succeeds in society because he returns the idea and affect of castration to an affirmation of a sequence of objects which makes good on the loss of the female penis. The pervert cognitively and emotively screens the trauma. The penis *qua* lace *qua* fur *qua* shoe *qua* jockstrap *qua* — each object is returned as a positive and prolific effect of the recurrence of difference *qua* Sameness⁺ and the Logic of Difference.

Saussure claims that the gap between material-signifier-body and abstraction-signified-mind is only possible in theory. All practice sutures the material signifier to the abstract signified in the conjoined distinctive and oppositional word. The madman is theoretical. The schizoid's world consists of an affect — materiality-signifier-body — which is split from the idea — abstraction-signified-mind — of the plentiful Woman. The psychotic is the theory of the split of materiality, signifier, and body. The madman is the theory of the mark and sound which are theoretically divorced from the idea and concept. This explains the sustained affect of the schizoid's approach to sexual difference. The idea — abstraction-signified-mind — of the Woman's castration is split. But the affect — materiality-signifier-body — of the Real of sexual difference is integrated. The practice of the theory of the madman is nonsense because his psyche is pure phonology of materiality in the absence of the pure psychology of abstraction. The schizoid is strictly beyond repression.

This is so not only because the schizoid refuses the bi-level configuration of the neurotic structure of the conscious and the unconscious. The psychotic is Outside of the economy of *Verdrängung* because the split between idea — abstraction-signified-mind — and affect — materiality-signifier-body — dissevers the madman from both the word and the signified. The schizoid is the unalloyed phonology (mark, sound) of the unassimilable signifier. The mad signifier cannot repress an ideational content. The schizoid is the signifier — materiality-affect-body — of the lost signified — abstraction-signified-mind. This madman's materiality — signifier-body — exceeds the abstractions and speculations — signified-mind — of a system of arrant psychology. There is no repression in psychosis. The madman transcends the divisions between materiality/abstraction, signifier/signified, and mind/body which are otherwise the linchpins of the indicator of the gap between conscious/unconscious. The psychotic's psyche is free of manifest representation and its translation into latent content. The return of *Verwerfung* in madness is the recurrence of hallucinations and delusions. These formations are unintegrated, affective, and material bodily responses to the castration of the Woman. The pervert evades these symptoms because his *sinthome* enjoys the cognitive dissonance and affective dissonance of sexual (*a*)difference.

The schizoid realizes that repression *qua* signifier and return of the symptom *qua* return of the foreclosed are principally the same gesture. There is no speculation which can intervene in the schizoid system in order to divide negation from return. There is no abstraction which can convince the schizoid of the gap between unconscious and conscious. As Lacan says of neurotic negation: "For repression to be possible there must be a beyond of repression."[13] The madman is the "beyond" of repression. The psychotic deconstructs the division between negation — *Verdrängung* or *Verwerfung* or *Verleugnung* — and return — neurotic and psychotic symptoms of loss and death and the perverse *sinthome* of the proliferation of simulations of presence and positivity for absence and negativity. The schizoid's signifier of the material body simply *is*. The mad signifier is a sheer metaphysics of presence and metaphysics of absence in the fleeting and floating of the signifier *qua not*.

The symptom of the latent content and the return of the repressed can only be considered a Sameness⁺ rather than a self-sameness and self-identity. This Principle of Sameness⁺ demands that the others — symptom/return — slip and slide into each other in an internal and external extimacy of the diacritical negative and differential economy of the signifier. The pervert's task is to flee toward the material signifier with the wit and insight of the abstract signified. The word and image are the media of the return of the disavowed as the "disavowed," and so on. The schizoid's experience of the gulf which separates materialist signifier and speculated signified makes the conjoinment of the sign impossible for his psychical structure. The madman is consigned to material mute shrieks and silent wails of affect and body in the absence of the abstract words of the pervert and his critique of the system. The madman is lost to the materialist marks of a signifier which is otherwise unanchored in the signified. The schizoid's words are untethered to any coherent abstraction or definitive speculation. The pervert's fetish-objects refer materiality (fur, lace, shoe, jockstrap) to signification with reference to the lost maternal phallus. The pervert's talent to refer materiality (the fetish-object) to abstraction (the penis-substitute) indicates advanced functionality. In contrast, the schizoid can only generate an endless materiality which is decentered from any conceptual foundation.

Figure 3.3 InsideOutside

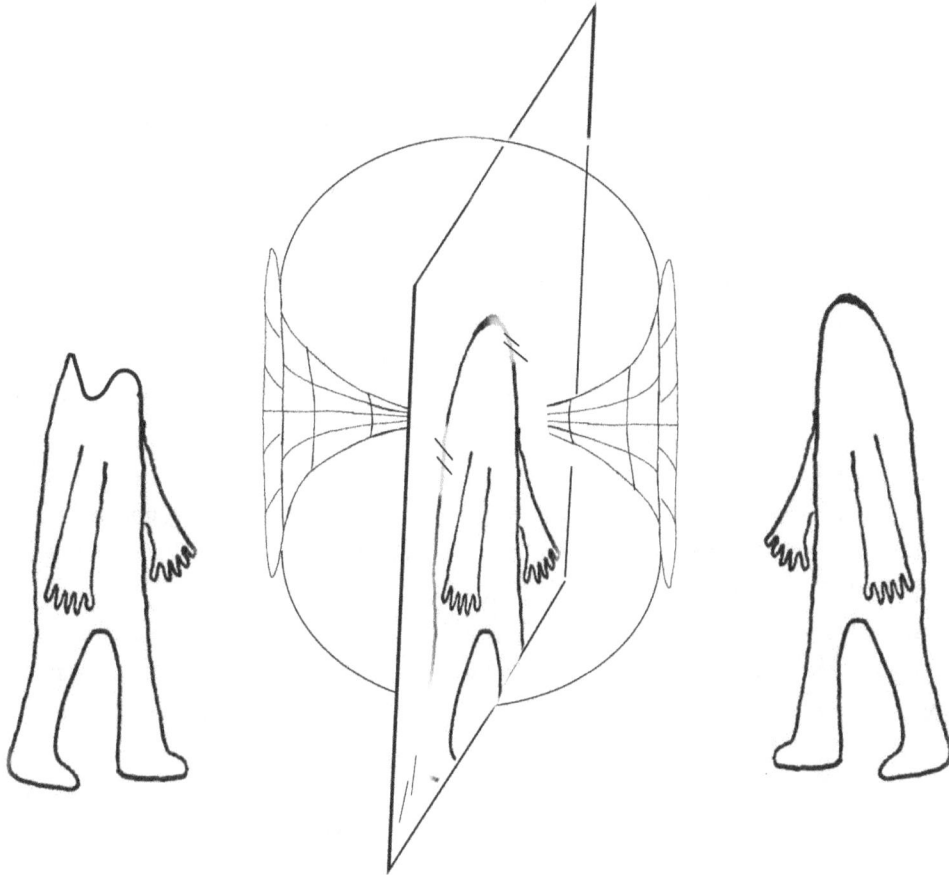

The neurotic (right) lives entirely unaware of the Inside-Outside extimacy which structures the reality-fantasy of his symbolic order. The neurotic mistakes the Other (left) for himself in the mirror. The Other is both at a distance from the mirror (left) and at the same time constitutive of the structure of the mirror. The Other Woman is the radical alterity which is the very possibility of neurotic being-in-the-world and being-with-others. The mirror and its gravitational pull (center) indicate the disappearance and occlusion of the center of the mirror. The Other is otherwise a Sameness⁺ which is not reducible to identity, difference, equality, inequality, or any speculative and abstract qualification or quantification of comparison, contrast, and exchange. This excluded Otherness enables the Woman's thinking, being, and living at the center. But the Woman is also the hidden condition of the neurotic's desire. This excluded Woman is the condition of speech and writing about and of the Real. The Woman on the other side of the mirror (left) is the possibility of the system of *langue*. The mirror returns the image of the self. The mirror also reflects the possibility of the image as such. The world is a series of these reflective surfaces of a *mise-en-abyme*. The mirror and its gravitation pull toward (away from) the occluded center represent the (im)possibility of signification in the structure of the world.

Notes & Sketches —

The Pervert's Verleugnung

The pervert's modality of negation is disavowal. *Verleugnung* both acts and reacts, both affirms and negates, both positivizes and negativizes, both makes and unmakes, and both does and undoes. The pervert's disavowal is structured by *bothness* and *andness*. Disavowal initiates nouns, verbs, prepositions, adjectives, and adverbs in a *bothness* and *andness* against opposition. Cake *implies* pudding. Run *indicates* walk. Around *suggests* near. Quietly *conveys* loudly. Proudly *intimates* lowly. Perversely, to make love is simultaneously to unmake love. To make unlove is to simultaneously unmake unlove. This series of affirmative negations or positive negativities generates and proliferates — and so on — beyond itself toward otherness. The neurotic Logic of Identity (A = A) circles itself in its self-sameness and self-identity. But the perverse Logic of Difference (A ≠ A = B, and so on) discerns the Principle of Sameness⁺. Sameness⁺ illuminates that any object is internal to any other object. This internal and external extimacy refers any object to an otherness. This otherness forms the unstable definition of the object as neither equal nor unequal nor identical nor different — ~~self-same~~ and ~~self-identical~~ — but as a singularity which is the Same⁺ as any other object because any object is different *from itself*.

The *bothness* and *andness* of the pervert's aesthetic double the series of objects which returns from the *faux* negation of *Verleugnung*. Cake implies pudding because dessert is alienated *from itself* but alike to pie. Run indicates exercise because movement is at a distance *from itself* but akin to stroll. Around suggests near because by is estranged *from itself* but similar to close. Quietly conveys loudly because softly is disunited *from itself* but near blaringly. Proudly intimates lowly because vainly is cut *from itself* but united with modesty. The kicker is that the connective copula between (un)like and (dis)similar words is *sous rature* because it is *different from itself* but the *same as the other*. The words of relationship — ~~alienated~~ and ~~indicates~~ and ~~suggests~~ and ~~conveys~~ and ~~intimates~~ — are not posed by the neurotic Logic of Identity. Differently, these words are a Sameness⁺ which deviates from the self-sameness and self-identity of the positive unit of the autonomous word. But what does *sous rature* indicate but Being and Nothingness, is and is not, presence and absence, plenitude and lack, abundance and scarcity, and so on? Disavowal returns these objects of *Verleugnung* to the ego-system *qua* split and fractured. But the positivity of these objects is indicted in the pleasure — *sous rature* — that these fetishes hold for the pervert. The pervert takes pleasure in ~~Being~~ under erasure. The principle of this *jouissance* is Sameness⁺. This Sameness⁺ recurs as "Sameness⁺."

The revolution of disavowal is both its simultaneity and its mutual inclusion. Everything happens to everything in every way every time in every space. This moment of mad simultaneity achieves the perverse "yes, yes" in which any object returns from *Verleugnung* as "itself" in excess of itself. This expansive and generative affirmation prevails beyond the Freudian principle of pleasure (1920) and its regulation of excitation and relaxation in the orga(ni)sm. Disavowal is the *telos* of the pervert's aesthetic and text. The *futur antérieur qua* Becoming of the Verbed Gerund — Ing⁺ — is of the Subject-Object all at once. The "yes, yes" is the absent object of the aim/less *Trieb* of the pervert's pursuits. The pervert returns the object of *Verleugnung* as an excess and surplus of "itself." The Logic of Identity refutes the closedness of self-sameness and self-identity (A = A) with the openness of a Sameness⁺ toward an otherness. This otherness generates a succession of objects which screens the phallic absence of the clitoris with a series of props and pillars of simulated presence. The neurotic is mired in the axes of identity and difference. The pervert is distracted with *jouissance*.

The scene of the discovery of sexual difference is the original context in which *Verleugnung* appears as a strategy to cope with loss and death. Laplanche and Pontalis claim that *Verleugnung* denotes "a specific mode of defense which consists in the subject's refusing to recognize the reality of a traumatic perception."[14] The authors contrast "recognition" with "perception." Recognition involves a previous encounter of personal experience.

The pervert recognizes a previously interpreted object. The object of the maternal phallus is refound. The recognition of the maternal phallus is based on a heretofore encounter with the imagined penis of the mother. In contrast, perception is a sentient apprehension of an object which is not necessarily previously encountered in the individual's existence.

The variance between recognition and perception is that the former indicates prior experience whereas the latter implicates sensory data. The pervert perceives the Woman's castration in a sentient and empirical capture of the object in the sense data of experience. But the pervert also recognizes the traumatic significance of this perception. The pervert recognizes a reappearance of an earlier experience of trauma. The strategy of *Verleugnung* applies to a secondary encounter with castration. The pervert perceives this repetition of lack with his sensory apparatus. The pervert perceives difference as a sensory experience. But the pervert does not recognize the deficit that he had already experienced. The pervert rewrites his originary encounter of maternal loss with a revision of maternal lack.

The pivotal component of the pervert's rescripted perception of maternal lack is that the pervert's *faux* negation in *Verleugnung* enables him to acknowledge ("I know very well") the absence of the penis but recognize the vagina and the clitoris ("but nevertheless"). This "I know very well, but nevertheless" is the essence of perverse aesthetics. It was articulated by Octave Mannoni's perverse patient in the mid-twentieth century.[15] The pervert recognizes the previous experience of castration in a revision. He perceives the sense data of the empirical reality of the experience as precisely not a defense against castration. Instead, the pervert encounters castration but also recognizes difference in an assault against phallocentrism and its penis/not-penis duality. Neurotically, the subject is situated between the Nothing is Missing of prelapsarian bliss of *jouissance* and the Something is Missing of anxious idealization. The neurotic exchanges pleasure for identity and desire. Instead, the pervert sees Nothing *qua* Something.

The pervert retroactively converts Something is Missing into Nothing is Missing. The pervert's recognition resymbolizes an earlier experience. *Qua* recognition, the pervert rewrites his original encounter and interpretation of the vagina and the clitoris. The pervert's perception recasts his interpretation of the vagina and the clitoris. *Qua* perception, the pervert rejects the Freudian empirical and sensory criteria of size and visibility as the markers of phallic presence. The pervert enjoys a rewritten recognition of the female anatomy. The pervert reconsiders the sensory data of his perception. The pervert interprets differently, and he experiences exotically. The pervert likes the loss. The pervert enjoys the death. The pervert takes pleasure in the castration. The reason is that he exposes an Outside of castration in the generative expansion of a universe of fetish-objects. The female anatomy is recognized and perceived as a Sameness+ to the female penis and to the male clitoris. Recognition and perception of female anatomy as difference *qua* difference rather than difference *qua* deficit invite him to assemble a series of objects — female penis and male clitoris, and so on — which extends beyond the centrality of the penis in the psychosexuality of the neurotic.

The pervert's distinction is his unique approach to difference. The fantasmatic scene of the neurotic response to sexual difference misrecognizes sexual *difference* as sexual *deficit*. The clitoris is misunderstood as defective rather than as different. In contrast, the pervert recognizes sexual *difference* in the reencountered female body as sexual *difference*. A possible account of the variance in the neurotic and perverse approaches to sexual difference is that the pervert reencounters the female body ("recognizes") whereas the neurotic encounters the body for the first time. The pervert's initial encounter with the female body may have been traumatic, but the trauma is rewritten ("perceived") in the later encounter with the female body. The pervert's revision ("perception") of the clitoris is structured by the tenet of Sameness+. Neurotic sexual difference is arranged by the penis/not-penis of binary phallocentric castration. But perverse sexual (*a*)difference is ordered by the Principle of Sameness⁺. The pervert understands ("perceives") in his rewritten revision of the female body that the penis is the same as the clitoris because the penis is different *from itself.* The clitoris is the same as the penis because the clitoris is different *from itself. Verleugnung* returns these objects as "penis" and "clitoris."

This axiom of Sameness⁺ is neither identity nor difference nor equality nor inequality. The penis is neither equal to nor identical to nor unequal to nor different from the clitoris. These relationships would be structured by the general equivalent of comparison, contrast, and exchange with size and visibility as the criteria of distinction. Rather, the precept of Sameness⁺ is *singularity.* A singularity cannot be compared, contrasted, or exchanged as equal or identical or unequal or different. The dissonance between any object (penis, clitoris) *with itself* is a difference, but this difference is an incongruous otherness. This internal and external extimacy is a *Spaltung* of any object *with itself.* The alienation between any object and itself opens the object to an expansive and generative relationship with an otherness. This rapport of openness toward otherness in singularity is the doctrine of Sameness⁺. The clitoris is the Same⁺ as the penis. The pervert discovers ("recognizes") in revision a sequence of sex objects in the scene of the discovery of sexual (*a*)difference: penis, clitoris, male clitoris, female penis, and so on. This series of objects is the effective treasury of fetishes in the pervert's psychosexual economy.

The Real Penis, as I call it, is distinct from the penis and the clitoris. The Real Penis is the greasy lubricant of the impossible relationships of Being between words such as ~~alienates~~ and ~~indicates~~ and ~~suggests~~ and ~~conveys~~ and ~~intimates.~~ The Real Penis is *sous rature,* and it is the principle of the *sous rature.* The Real Penis is instructive for the pervert because the fetishist intuits any object in its *bothness* and *andness* — of Being and Nothingness, is and is not, presence and absence, plenitude and lack, abundance and scarcity, and so on. The pervert perceives a *bothness* and an *andness* in *sous rature* and *sur l'effacement.* The Real Penis is the word for the pervert's talent to glimpse both the *sous rature* of the under erasure and the *sur l'effacement* of the over erasure. The pervert descries the deconstruction and the construction at the same time. The pervert's *Verleugnung* acknowledges female penis, clitoris, male clitoris, penis, hermaphroditic configurations, and so on.

Disavowal also repudiates the phallocentrism of mutual exclusion and the series of comparisons, contrasts, and exchanges of the general equivalent of the phallus. The pervert grasps a postphallocentric revision of sex organs, such as the expansive and generative fetishistic universe of configurations of any objects of penis and clitoris. Any sex organ is the Same⁺ as any other because any object is different *from itself.* The pervert happily affirms *difference* (Sameness⁺) rather than negates *deficit* (phallocentrism) in the Other. Freud says that the fetishist can "disavow the fact [of sexual difference] and believe that they do see a penis all the same."[16] The *bothness* and *andness* of disavowal apply to any sexual organ and any gendered body in the system.

Castration is the center around which the drama of sexual difference encircles. But the pervert evades castration because he beholds a different (Same⁺) version of sexual difference than the neurotic. The anxiety of female lack retroactively (*après-coup, Nachträglichkeit*) reminds the neurotic offspring of the father's threat against self-pleasure. Paternal threat also recalls the potential loss of the male junior's prized possession of the penis. This prospective privation is embodied in the female junior's clitoris. The clitoris is the principal reason that the male junior retains belief in the phallic mother. This is so even after the revised script ("recognition") of the sentient difference ("perception") has been written. The pervert gleefully tarries not with sexual difference *per se.* Rather, the pervert expands and opens difference as such. The code of Sameness⁺ illuminates that any binary oppositional blueprint for distinction between the sexes is a silly and crude charade. A castration complex of a simple present lack and potential future gain for the female junior and an easy present gain and prospective future loss for the male junior is a shamefully inexact fable.

The doctrine of sexual difference of penis/not-penis restricts any series of objects to the penis and its negative obverse in the clitoris. The sequence of sexual objects is contracted and closed. The creed of phallocentrism renounces a potential multiplicity of sexual organs, such as the clitoris, the male clitoris, the penis, the female penis, the clitoral penis, the penile clitoris, the fe-male penis, the fe-male clitoris, and so on. This succession of otherness of sex organs is isomorphic to the productive round of fetishes. The pervert's fetish is forcefully generated from a communist queer (*a*)sexual energy. This libido proliferates difference and otherness under the Principle of Sameness⁺. Any object is ~~alien~~ and ~~estranged~~ from itself because it is the Same⁺ as any other object in the system. This cycle of singularities cannot be reduced to an equality between penis and clitoris, or an inequality between penis and clitoris, or an identity between penis and clitoris, or a difference between penis and clitoris — or a relationship of any other word of comparison, contrast, and exchange of the general equivalent.

The pervert discovers that Sameness⁺ is *sous rature et sur l'effacement*. The pervert recognizes the plain text and stricken text of this print and its deletion. The edict of Sameness⁺ is also under (over) erasure as the principle of general inequivalence. The relationship between any object and itself is ~~different~~ — alien, estranged, otherwise, peculiar, exotic — and the bond between any object and the other is ~~Sameness⁺~~. These rapports between any object and itself and any other object are subordinate to radical negation. But the pervert's *faux* negation of *Verleugnung* returns the *sous rature et sur l'effacement* to a generative expansion of objects because the Logic of Difference (A ≠ A = B, and so on) relationally and constructionally opens the process of fetish-formation to an otherness which is otherwise closed by the self-sufficient autonomy of the positive unity of the Logic of Identity (A = A). The neurotic contracts the sexual universe to the penis and its obversive negation. The pervert expands the sexual galaxy to the substitutes for the penis which proliferate in the rewritten secondary encounter with the clitoris *qua* difference rather than *qua* deficit. The *faux* negation of *Verleugnung* negates *qua* produces a varied and expansive series of affirmed objects and fetishes.

Perversely, the gesture of negation and its positive return are the same motion. Any object returns in the disavowal of sexual difference *qua* "sexual difference." This series of scare quotes extends to the succession of objects which returns from the simultaneous acknowledgement and denial — *Verleugnung* — of sexual difference. The *bothness* and *andness* of perverse disavowal are expansive and inclusive. This contrasts with the *eitherness* and *orness* of neurotic repression and its contraction and restriction. The pervert's *faux* negation fancies an exclusive inclusion. This exclusive inclusion is simultaneously *sous rature* and *sur l'effacement*. The pervert imagines exclusion *of* inclusion and inclusion *of* exclusion as a Sameness⁺ which cannot be reduced to general equivalence of inclusion and exclusion. Disavowal repels its internal and external extimacy but simultaneously returns this negated (affirmed) to a proliferation of any freaky objects of Sameness⁺ whose singularity cannot be compared or contrasted with the other. The fetish is neither equal to nor unequal to nor identical to nor different from any object. The fetish is singular.

The pervert affirms both the negative of castration that Something is Missing of the original cognized encounter with the female body and at the same time affirms the plethora of manufactured sexual fetishes of Nothing is Missing. This "yes, yes" perverse attitude neither condenses in metaphor nor displaces in metonymy. Rather, the pervert doubly perceives in a sensory dissonance which unveils the double in the place of the single, and which uncovers the split in the site of the whole. The pervert's *Verleugnung* returns the economy of the *Spaltung*. The universe is not unified by the neurotic object of penis and its obversive negative. Rather, the world is fractured into part-objects and bit-fetishes which return in the scare quotes of the screen of sexual (*a*) difference over the trauma of sexual difference.

The secondary encounter ("perception") of the female body invites the pervert to reconsider his interpretation ("recognition") of phallocentrism. The neurotic's discrete encounter with the clitoris freezes his cognition of penis/not-penis in a phallocentric restrictive economy. The pervert's reencounter with the clitoris opens his recognition of penis/not-penis in a Sameness⁺ (postphallocentrism) of generative excess. The *faux* negation of *Verleugnung* returns any object to any other object. Negation affirms the growth and multiplication of the system. The gesture of "No!" returns a "yes, yes" which *includes* the "No!" as a negative and differential object of the system. The repression of *Verdrängung* is internal to the disavowal of *Verleugnung*. The excess of this parallactic overlap is the series of objects — scare quotes: sexual difference *qua* "sexual difference" — which is returned to an extended system. This series of expanded others includes centers, metaphors, words, objects, metonymies, fetishes, and so on. The field is potentially infinite with the exception of the excluded function of this expansion: Sameness⁺.

The *bothness* and *andness* of the structure of disavowal are spoken by Octave Mannoni's perverse patient: "I know very well, but nevertheless…." The pervert simultaneously "knows" of the castration "but nevertheless" screens the *not* in a succession of objects which returns the objects to themselves *qua* "themselves" in the galaxy of bits and bytes in the system of *jouissance*. The pervert knows ("recognizes") the Logic of Identity (A = A) and its series of words of distinction and opposition. The pervert knows of phallocentrism and the penis/not-penis of castration. This is the neurotic order of the system in its misperceived essence. But the pervert also disavows this (re)cognition of knowledge in the "but nevertheless" of (re)perception of the female body. The pervert's "but nevertheless" inscribes the Logic of Difference (A ≠ A = B, and so on) and its negative differentiality of the signifier and its Sameness⁺. The neurotic system values castrated penis above not-penis, absence above presence, Something is Missing above Nothing is Missing, lack above plenitude, and scarcity above abundance. The "but nevertheless" does not merely reverse this hierarchical prioritization. Rather, the pervert's *bothness* and *andness* uncover the doubleness of the *sous rature et sur l'effacement* of the neurotic choice of *eitherness* and *orness*.

The pervert's aesthetic favors *Trieb* above *désir* in the system of sexuality, communism above capitalism in the system of finance, and the signifier above the word in the system of language. But the horizon of the pervert's intervention is both to reverse this hierarchy but also — internal to this project — to demonstrate an excess in the parallactic overlap between the s and S. The pervert's "I know very well, but nevertheless…" speaks and writes the schizoid's secret materialist truth of the theoretical signifier. The Madness of Order is the Neurotic Foreclosure (*rejet névrotique*) of the essential schizophrenia of the system. The pervert is the figuration of the Nietzschean physician-philosopher who diagnoses the anatomy of the structure and writes the prescription.[17] The Rx is the return not of the *Verdrängung* of the symbolic but of the *Verwerfung* of the Real. This Real is the truth of the system. The pervert's "but nevertheless" is the pivot toward a succession of objects and systems at the end of the epistemological and ontological projects.

The *bothness* and *andness* complexity to disavowal — or both either/or and both/and — makes it difficult to interpret the latent content and symptom of the pervert. This oscillation and undecidability — double vision — between knowledge ("I know very well") and its extension ("but nevertheless") confuse the analyst. *Verleugnung* exposes the restriction and constriction of rationality and logic from within the symbolic order. Neurotically, the object is limited to penis and not-penis. Perversely, the galaxy is expansive and open to the fur, lace, shoe, jockstrap, and so on. The remainders of the *faux* negation of *Verleugnung* return in scare quotes because these objects are props and screens for the lost maternal phallus. The fur is a "fur." The lace is a "lace." The shoe is a "shoe." The jockstrap is a "jockstrap." The penis is the final referent for an extended series of objects, but this extended series of objects is also the referent for the penis. Any object is *both* a penis *and* justice. The relationship of reference between original and translation, and between authentic and copy, is reversible. The "jockstrap" is a substitute for the penis as much as the "penis" is a substitute for the jockstrap. The unstable referent for perversity is a slippery reference to — the penis.

This dissimulation of reference dissolves the prioritized oppositions — unconscious/conscious, latent/ manifest, return/symptom, and so on — in psychoanalysis. The pervert is unanalyzable and incurable — and thankfully so — by psychoanalysis and even the interventions of philosophical rationality. The pervert's representations — Jheri curl *qua* "monster burger" — are incongruous and odd. But this wackiness is of the perverse word and its double of *sous rature et sur l'effacement* rather than of the schizoid signifier and its obscene inexpressibility. The pervert's words are bewildered but writerly. These words are specifically of the sign as a practice of both psychology and phonology with an extant signified. This is opposed to the schizoid signifier as a theory of pure phonology. The schizoid is the theory of the signifier. The pervert is the practice of the sign. Together, their work is the vaunted *Praxis* of revolution.

The pervert's trick in the doubleness of *bothness* and *andness* is to both simulate and dissimulate reference. The false opposition between the literal and the metaphorical must be disbanded. But, at the same time, a semblance of reference — "jockstrap" to penis or "penis" to jockstrap — must be sustained in order for coherence to be "sustained." The truth of the literal/metaphorical opposition is the *mise-en-abyme* of expansive and extended semiosis — openness — toward an otherness which generates a series of objects and fetishes under the precept of Sameness⁺. But this expansion must be tactfully tempered with a contraction of reference. Neurotic *Verdrängung* is the pretext for this closedness. Otherwise, the pervert's paradox and play degenerate into the word salad of the schizoid.

Fortuitously, the phallus buttons the signifier and the signified to each other. The phallus is the function of the button-tie or *point de capiton*. The phallus quilts the signifier to the signified. The phallus anchors the alphabet soup to its conceptual foundation. The phallus intervenes in order to join the frenzied materiality of the theoretical madman to the passionate abstraction of the practiced pervert. *Qua* partners, the psychotic and the pervert join the *theory* of the Madness of Order to the *practice* of its symbolization. The pervert's *écriture* of fetishes of the (*a*)sexual prolific galaxy of objects performs the revolutionary intercourse of *Praxis*. The oppositional division between the theory-madman and the practical-pervert is minor but pivotal. The madman is the manic and unhinged performer of a politics which contests the Madness of Order. This madness returns the Real of expansive Sameness⁺ of fetishes to the symbolic order and its restricted set of penis/not-penis series of self-contained positive units of words. The pervert is the theorist of the *bothness* and *andness* of *Verleugnung*.

The pervert considers representability of the clandestine truth of madness and the *mise-en-abyme* of unrestricted sequences of objects and fetishes. The phallus joins theory and practice, and schizoid and fetishist, and every other pair in binary opposition. The phallus is the metaphorical figuration of the Real Penis and its doubled *sous rature et sur l'effacement* of affirmation and negation, positivity and negativity, presence and absence, plenitude and lack, abundance and scarcity, signifier and sign, and so on. The Real Penis is under erasure in order to permit the pervert to glimpse the parallactic doubleness of Being and Nothingness. What is foreclosed in *sous rature* "returns" in *sur l'effacement*. Perversely, the gesture of *Verleugnung* and its return *qua* "return" is an imperceptible parallactic difference. The gap between *sous rature* and plain text and *sur l'effacement* and stricken text is the scare quote. The scare quote is an index of referentiality and (dis)simulation. The madman cannot return the scare quotes to reference.

The Woman is the conceptual persona who lives the revolution of an expanded set of objects and fetishes against a restricted set of penises and their negativities. The Woman appears in the space of the return of the foreclosed Real to the symbolic order. This return in *Verleugnung* disperses referentiality. The evanescence of reference abolishes private property — whose commodity and ownership? — and deconstructs phallocentrism — what is a penis? The Woman inherits the ends of capitalism in communism and the *denouement* of patriarchy in feminism. The precept of the risen Woman is the Principle of Sameness⁺ and the expansion of fetishes and objects in the skies. An unimpeded extension of objects frees economy from scarcity and the supply/demand dynamics of currency. An unrestricted proliferation of sexual objects releases sexuality from reference to the penis and its negative obverse. The energy of the Woman is the communist queer (*a*)sexual center of an obscene abundance.

The systems of $-ism of sexuality, finance, and language otherwise recoil from (*a*)sexuality in order to sustain the phallic structure of general equivalence. Standardization is only possible in an organization of loss and death in which Something is Missing. The Woman and her revolution embody a revised differential negativity of the signifier. The Woman is a singularity who cannot be spoken or written. The Woman is a Sameness⁺ which is the Outside of the general equivalence of sexual difference in desire, currency in finance, and the word in language. The pervert's textual practice in theory in the word and the schizoid's politicized theory in practice in the signifier are joined by the aesthetic and sensibility of the Woman. The Pervert-Schizoid-Woman promises this simultaneous grammatological effluvium of Sameness⁺. The pervert's unrivaled gift is for the *jouissance* of strange signification. The succession of manufactured objects and assembled fetishes is the substance of this expanded range of words for inappropriate books, incongruous chapters, inapposite sentences, malappropriate words, and a prolific play of alphabets and texts.

The pervert flirts with a devious metalanguage. This *über*-discourse is otherwise under suspicion by the saints of poststructuralism, such as Derrida[18] and de Man.[19] The pervert's revolutionary *coup* is to produce the master signifier. This image is a strict materiality — "$-ism" and "Pervert-Schizoid-Woman" — of a signifier without a signified. This word is empty of abstraction. The word is a prop or pier — object or fetish — for the orbit of the generated marks and sounds, and abstractions and concepts, in the pervert's galaxy. The nefarious metalanguage of fetishism is visible in the scare quotes — Jason *qua* "penis" — in the return of the *faux* negation of *Verleugnung*. The reference *to* the penis is a metalanguage *of* the penis. This penile metalanguage returns the generated object of the scare quote to the language of the penis. The pervert flirts with a metalanguage. This perverse metalanguage recuperates the returned objects and fetishes of *Verleugnung* to the reference to the penis *qua* citation for the affirmed objects and fetishes of the Principle of Sameness⁺.

The body of the schizoid is tortured by the signified of language in such fields as Foucault's Power/Knowledge, Derrida's Constitutive Outside, Levinas's Face, Nietzsche's Will to Power, Lacan's Phallus and Other, Saussure's Value, and Heidegger's Ontico-Ontological Difference. Must Foucault's "Power/Knowledge" be recuperated by Derrida's "Constitutive Outside" as the referent for Nietzsche's "Will to Power"? Is there a "Power/Knowledge" metalanguage to the language of the "Constitutive Outside"? Is the "Will to Power" the referent for "Power/Knowledge" and "Constitutive Outside"? Or is " — 'Constitutive Outside' — " the metareference to the citation of Heidegger's "Ontico-Ontological Difference"? The pervert methodically and prudently negotiates the doubled returns — *sous rature qua sur l'effacement* — of the double visions of disavowal. The reason for this circumspection is a political commitment to illuminate the Madness of Order to the neurotic. The neurotic misperceives the *mise-en-abyme* of semiosis. The neurotic misunderstands the otherwise expansive systems which are restricted in desire, finance, and the word. A metalanguage (at times) is the cost of the pervert's ethical commitment. But what is lost in the translation from materiality to the sign, from value to signification, and from diacritics to binary opposition? Is the pervert prepared for the incendiary task of the reduction of lunatical Unreason to a Reason for neurotics? How does the schizoid experience the reduction of his truth from *metameta* to *metalanguage* to *language*? The pervert's text returns value to signification, the signifier to the sign, and metonymy to metaphor. The pervert's text triumphs because it insists on reference — precisely the function which is put in suspension by the madman's repudiation of the function of the father. The pervert's text situates schizoid Unreason in the field of reference.

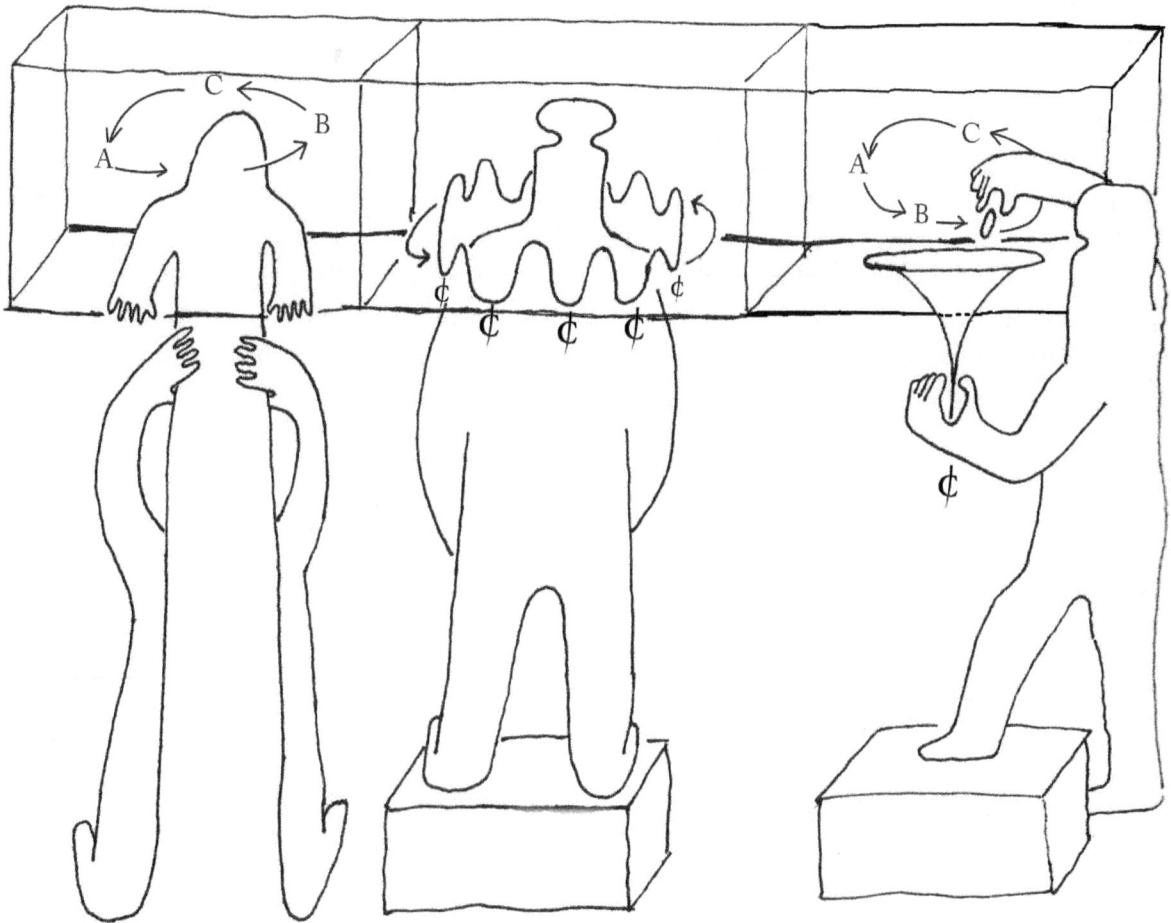

Figure 3.4 Being in $-ism

This illustration depicts the relationship between identity and desire in the neurotic, the psychotic, and the pervert. The drawing shows the participation of each of the psychical structures in the system of *langue*. Each typology of subjectivity copes with desire and its relationship to castration. This relationship to sexual difference organizes the bond of each psychical structure to the system. The neurotic (left) represses desire in order to protect his penis and nascent identity. The result of castration anxiety is the identification with the ego-ideal and the development of identity. The neurotic enters the $-ism of *le propre* and the system of signification in words, phrases, sentences, paragraphs, pages, and so on. The neurotic is the figure who is a proper subject — someone — in the midst of being-in-the-world and being-with-others. He participates in its structure even if it is the structure which participates him. The neurotic's identity enables him to perform his role in the symbolic order of the signifying chain. The neurotic's identity is a signified, like A, B, C, and so on. The subject of neurosis is pinned to the signified and to the coherent exchange of meaning-making. In contrast, the psychotic (center) repudiates sexual difference and cannot be triangulated into a relationship with castration and the father. The schizoid's absence of absence dislocates and dispossesses him from the system even if this structure is itself the reality-fantasy of the neurotic. The psychotic suspends the phallic function and the signified. The madman is lost in the chains and circles of unhinged and unanchored units of text. The psychotic understands only an obscene presence (absence) in subjectivity and sociality. This absence (presence) is represented by the concave shape of the Woman. Alternatively, the pervert (right) is the psychical structure which participates in the symbolic order with a dexterous intuition about the organization and arrangement of the system. The pervert strategizes and plays. The pervert manipulates the system in order to illuminate the Madness of Order. The pervert accepts the lack and desire at the center of the system, but he transforms sexual difference into plenitude with the fetish-object, penis-substitute, fur, lace, shoe, jockstrap, and so on. The charade of substitution playfully circulates signifiers in the expansion of units of text.

Notes & Sketches —

STRANGE MANIFESTATIONS

The manifest representation is the visible articulation of unconscious truth. The manifest representation returns in the conscious of the neurotic as dreams, parapraxes, jokes, and psychopathologies of everyday life. These manifest representations indicate the latent desires and clandestine truths of the subject and the society. These formations are sensory, such as visions, scents, affects, tastes, and sounds. These formations are assumed to be meaningless, but the psychoanalyst discovers significance in these details of everyday life. The manifest is the effect of the repression of the latent content. This wish is censored by the other and the Other into the closet of the unconscious. The unconscious resists a metaphysics of presence. It is neither present nor absent but Other. The unconscious is not inside of the interiority of the subject — the brain, the gut, the neuron, the heart, the tongue, or the soul. The unconscious is also not outside of the exteriority of the subject — the chair, the table, the skies, the atmosphere, or the vibe. Rather, the unconscious is the Outside of the subject in an extimacy. This extimacy is the structure of the chain of signifiers and the organization of signifier/signified links between conscious detail and unconscious truth. The web of words bends torus-like within and without in a movement which pulls inside and outside toward, away, and around the Other. The pervert discovers this dislocation of the unconscious. The pervert concludes that the unconscious is an excessive surplus of the *Spaltung* in the psychical apparatus.

The manifest form must be interpreted for its latent content. The manifest formation is the partner of the latent truth of the subject. The manifest/latent binary is an opposition in which any errant fissure or productive *mise-en-abyme* between the two dimensions undoes the fundamental oppositions of Freud's research: manifest/latent, conscious/unconscious, symptom/return, analysand/analyst, and so on. The stability of the concept of the manifest formation is structured by the prospect for translation between the levels of the signifier of manifest detail and the signified of latent truth. Freud writes,

> The dream-content seems like a transcript of the dream-thoughts into another mode of expression, whose characters and syntactic laws it is our business to discover by comparing the original and the translation.[20]

The interval between "the original" of the latent content and "the translation" is complex. Freud urges the psychoanalyst as a member of a community of performers to "discover" the "characters" and "syntactic laws" of this work of translation. Freud's imperative is not merely the arduous task of the facility with a new tongue. Rather, the interval between the manifest formation and the latent content is a translation *within the same language.*

The laws of the manifest representation and its translation into the latent content (and its reverse) are not generically structured for any given instance of manifest form. Instead, only an unsteady guide to "translation" is provided in Freud's theorization of condensation, displacement, secondary revision, and considerations of representability. There is no unified set of correspondences or universal code of equivalences between the manifest representation and the latent truth. There are only general mechanisms — displacement, condensation, secondary revision, and considerations of representability — and rules of translation — free association and affirmation — for the transcription of the latent content into manifest form. There is no metalanguage of the language of dreams. The pervert recognizes the *metameta* dimension. But he adroitly deploys this series of fetishes *for* fetishes in order to considerably represent the Madness of Order.

Perversely, the opposition between the original and the translation is spurious. Freud's words imply that the manifest representations of condensation and displacement, and metaphor and metonymy, transmit a unique creativity, inventive freshness, and singular dare. The inexorable question of the *arche* or *arche*-trace of the unconscious is a vexed pursuit. The pursuit of the *metalanguage* of interpretation starts from the trace of the simultaenously cut and sutured wound of the umbilical cord of the so-called navel of the dream. This exercise ends with the arrival at the so-called known of either the departure or destination of analysis. But Freud's countertransferential resistance to *arche* is in the Spirit of his discovery of the unconscious. The unconscious is a space. It is a space with neither temporality nor knowledge nor negation. Any chronological account of the *mise-en-scène* and *mise-en-abyme* — etiology — of this space in any time is discreditable to the psychoanalytic speculative endeavor.

The deferrals in time must be bracketed as a potential source of the slippery departure for the truths of this space. But the difference (in contrast to the deferral) of Derrida's *différance* means that space may be an approach to the origin of the unconscious. The recurrences of perverse *Verleugnung* expand the spatiality of the unconscious with a succession of objects and fetishes. The expanse of the space of the unconscious is inspired by fetishism. The recursion of the original and the translation (and in reverse) is muddled by the expansion and openness of objects under the Principle of Sameness[+] and the relationality and constructionism of otherness in the skies. The pervert peeks at the extensions of the unconscious and its myriad translations of originals, copies of facsimiles, originals of simulations, iterations or reiterations, codes of recodes, and so on. The division between original and translation (*et al.*) implies that the primary and antecedent original latent content temporally precedes the secondary and later translation of the manifest representation. This interpretation must retroactively yield to the original for its latent signification. The signified precedes the signifier. The latent content precedes the manifest formation. The translation precedes the original. The abstraction precedes the materiality. The interpretation of the dream precedes the wish and its fulfillment. The dream fulfills the wish of the interpretation. The pervert discovers that the unconscious is not a sequence of temporal antecedents but a series of objects — signified, signifier, latent content, manifest formation, translation, original, abstraction, materiality, dream, wish, and so on — which productively generates as yet unimagined marks in the expanses of space.

The fraught relationship between primary and secondary, original and translation, object and simulacrum, and origin and trace is a brimful intellectual history. This circled and doubled relationship between manifest representation and latent truth is situated in the context of the slip and slide of *metameta* and the *mise-en-abyme* of signification in and as the unconscious. The slippery slope and endless extension of objects and fetishes of the generative (*a*)sexual energy at the core of the Nothingness of Being raise the specter of the *latency of the latent*. This recursion subverts the divisions and oppositions — words — of the conceptual dualities of not only conscious/unconscious and manifest/latent but also of the entire series of binary oppositions in psychoanalysis, such as analysand/analyst, negation/return, symptom/threat, and so on. The skeletal scaffold of psychoanalytic speculation is tenuous and nebulous. The oppositions are subject to not only grammatological inquiry. The *arche*-trace upsets the borders between the oppositions. Where does the manifest end and the latent begin? Whose transference is whose? What is the wish of interpretation? The pervert discovers the Reason within this Unreasonable set of queries. The pervert's Sameness[+] expands and extends objects beyond their confinement: the *latency of the latent* and the *manifest of the manifest* and the *analysis of the analysis* and the *transference of the transference*. These surplus objects are the fetishes which screen the horror of not only sexual difference but of binary opposition *tout court*.

But deconstructive critique of the fuzzy boundaries between theories and practices of psychoanalysis is complemented by an ideology critique of its summary of concepts. Cultural Studies questions the political commitments and social consequences of such oppositions between words. These concepts could always be otherwise than their conventionalized relationships in the annals of twentieth-century Western psychoanalysis. The split in the origin enables the reversal and displacement of the original latent truth and the translation of the manifest copy. Is homosexuality the desire of the phantom limb or is the dream the desire of rape? The series of desires and truths can be retranslated as a sequence of symptoms and *sinthomes*. The twisted and flipped relationship between oppositions — *manifest (latent) of the latent (manifest)* — is integrant to the secret Unreason of the schizoid. This *Spaltung* of hypnoid conscience and perverse aesthetics is the moment of the return of the Real to the symbolic. This constituted *Verwerfung* is the affirmative generation of fetishes in the "*manifest (latent) of the latent (manifest)*" and an expanded succession of objects. The pervert discovers that both grammatological analysis and ideology critique generate a novel set of concepts and a new series of words which expand the set of fetishes for the encircled *Trieb* of a masochistic erotics.

Neurotic Secrets and Returns

The hysteric's manifest representations are the sentient objects of a sexual censorship at the close of Freud's era. But the variance in censorship between the end of Freud's era and our own is vast. The wish at the end of the nineteenth-century is different from the desire of contemporary North America. What is the latent content of today which threatens the order of the contemporary symbolic matrix? The latent content — wish, desire, and truth — of this historical moment deviates from the unconscious of late nineteenth-century Europe. What is today's wish? What is the clandestine desire of phallocentrism? What is the latent wish of late capitalism? What is the secret truth of the signifier? Manifest illuminations of dreams and jokes are frequent and repetitive for the neurotic. The wishes of *Verdrängung* are analytically interpretable in the reports of the coded messages of analysands. The analyst deciphers the text with the hack psychoanalytic playbook of Oedipus complex, castration complex, penis and lack, desire and object, and so on. The symptom is the off-kilter helter-skelter detail of dysfunction in the presence of Being in the subject and the society.

The psychoanalytic work in Cultural Studies focuses on the cultural productions of narrative film, television show, and pop song in order to read the text *qua* symptom of the censorship of the society. But this so-imagined censorship is also put under scrutiny by psychoanalytic Cultural Studies. The pervert recognizes the coincidence and continuity between law and desire. The pervert substitutes the inverse ladder of law and desire with the extimate slide of rule and enjoyment. The pervert glimpses the censorship which is internal and external — extimate — to desire. *Jouissance* is the sequela of the parallactic overlap between prohibition and transgression. The pervert takes pleasure in the deconstruction of oppositions. The society deploys these opposites in order to sustain neurosis and its system of loss and death.

The system neurotically forecloses (*rejet névrotique*) the Madness of Order. This madness is the insight of the pervert and the object of his articulation in the symbol. The latent content of the extant system is madness. Madness of Order is articulated in the concepts in this book, such as *différance*, trace, the Real Symbolic, the Signified/r, and Sameness[+]. In brief, I will outline the elements of each of these attributes of the Madness of Order. *Différance* is Derrida's (non)concept, and it refers to the spatial differentiation and temporal deferral of the words in the textual system. The expansive and open textual system ruptures *arche* and the origin of departure and destination, and commencement and arrival. The upshot of *différance* is the *destruktion* of the presence of Being of the what is — *qua*, by definition, as such, *il y a*, by necessity — in the text. The word is *sous rature* because it is always otherwise — *not* — what it is — *not*. The trace is Derrida's word for the retentions and protentions of texts within texts. Text is encircled by (con)text, and (con)text is saturated by text. The border around any object is cut and spliced by traces of other objects. Each object is the same object.

The other conceptual personae in this book are my own invention. The Real Symbolic is my term for the coincidence and continuity — parallactic overlap — between the ostensibly opposed orders of the Real and the symbolic. The Real is the limit of text beyond which the written or the spoken cannot be articulated. The symbolic order is the system of combinatory binary oppositions. The symbolic is structured by the homeostatic coordination of balance and equilibrium. The Real Symbolic indicates the parallactic overlap between the resistance of the word and the word itself. The excess of this parallax is the *sous rature*. The remainder of the *sur l'effacement* is the stricken — strikeout — of the word. The remnant of the Real Symbolic is the Nothingness of negativity. My word Signified/r designates the slip and slide between the stable abstraction of the signified and the differed and deferred materiality of the signifier. The word is always in the place of another word. The excess of this parallactic overlap is the materiality of the signifier. This materiality (mark, sound) exceeds the steady abstraction of the signifier. The surplus signifier (mark, sound) overruns and overwhelms the signified and its otherwise moored relationship to Reason. My concept of Sameness⁺ is a principle of the expansion and extension of the galaxy with objects and fetishes. Sameness⁺ is based on the Logic of Difference ($A \neq A = B$, and so on). Any object is ~~unequal~~ to and ~~identical~~ to and ~~equal~~ to and ~~different~~ from itself but the Same⁺ as the other. Any object is internal and external — extimate — to any other object in an open field of prolific fetishes. The ~~Sameness⁺~~ itself is *sous rature* and *sur l'effacement*. The excess of the overlap between an object with itself is not of the Principle of Sameness⁺ but of *principality* itself.

The pervert properly imagines these concepts as integrants of the Madness of Order. The neurotic suffers a daftness to the basic coordinates of the symbolic order. This blindness subordinates the truth of the system in *Verdrängung*. The pervert returns this *Verwerfung qua Verdrängung* as the Neurotic Foreclosure or *rejet névrotique*. The repressed (foreclosed) returns to the symbolic order in the perverse *Verleugnung* of the "Madness of Order." The returns of madness include "*différance*," "trace," "Real Symbolic," "Signified/r," "Sameness⁺," and an expansive succession of material and abstract fetishes for the ecstasy of the pervert. The scare quotes around an open sequence of words indicate a surplus of affirmation of Being which is the obverse of the negation of the Nothingness of the remainder of the *sous rature* and *sur l'effacement*.

The pervert's *Verleugnung* returns affirmation and *jouissance*. The pervert critically exposes the Madness of Order. This madness is the schizoid's secret truth of Unreason. The neurotic is oblivious to the order. The neurotic expression of the systematic foreclosure — *Verdrängung* of the *Verwerfung* — returns as the Real Symbolic (*et al.*) of the system of $-ism. The pervert writes and speaks this Real in the symbolization of the absolutely resistant in the manifesto of the schizoid's Unreason. This madness is otherwise expressed in the psychotic outbursts of the hallucinations and delusions of the future. The parallactic overlap between neurotic *Verdrängung* and schizoid *Verwerfung* is the returned *Verleugnung* of the pervert and the expansion of the galaxy of fetishes. The fetish exceeds the coincidence between the Real and the symbolic. The fetish is the pervert's imaginary embodiment — material figuration — of the Madness of Order and the *mise-en-abyme* of dissimulated representation.

$-ism is structured by the castration and lack of phallocentrism, the scarcity and debt of capitalism, and the word and sign of *langue*. The pivotal arrangement of $-ism is the binary opposition. Binarism otherwise yields to the Sameness⁺ of the Spirit of the System and its expansion and extension of the containment and restriction of castration in phallocentrism, loss in capitalism, and the word in language. $-ism is structured by a neurotic closedness. But this contraction is opposed by the tendency of the Madness of Order toward dilation and proliferation in the generative fetish and its series of recurrent objects in the system.

Phallocentrism returns an expanded set of sex parts which extends beyond the penis *qua* reference for all of sexuality. Capitalism returns a plethora of use-values which widens the set of commodities beyond the restriction of the *finite infinity* or *infinite finity* of the accumulation of debt. Language returns a succession of materialities and signifiers which exceeds the sovereignty of the word and its dominion over the practices of meaning-making. The neurotic contraction of *Verdrängung* is the essence of the system. But this tendency in $-ism toward restriction is opposed by the Spirit of extension in the systems of desire, finance, and language. The architecture of the system is neurotic. But the skeletal scaffold of $-ism is the Madness of Order. Real schizophrenia is repressed (foreclosed) by a symbolic order which is haunted by the return of this Real and its destabilization. The unbalanced Real returns to rock the system.

The decisive dynamic is that the return of the Real to the neurosis (psychosis) of the system *is the system itself.* The system is the effect of the neurotic containment of the schizoid structure of the system and the neurotic and schizoid *Verwerfung* of the Real. The necessary return of this *Verwerfung* is coincident and continuous with Sameness⁺. The Principle of Sameness⁺ is both the object of symbolic *Verdrängung* (*Verwerfung*) and also the subject of the return of the repressed (foreclosed) to the system. The object of return is also the Signified/r *qua* the essence of the Real Symbolic. But this schizoid Signified/r and its *mise-en-abyme* of endless semiosis are simultaneously the quintessence of the system. Sameness⁺ is repressed (foreclosed) in order to return *qua* itself.

The gap between the negated Sameness⁺ and the returned Sameness⁺ is imperceptible. But the excess between symbolic Sameness⁺ and Real Sameness⁺ is the glimpse of the system in its schizophrenic *Spaltung.* The pervert illuminates this gap in which neurosis and psychosis asymptotically approach each other from the opposed perspectives of *Verdrängung* and its return and *Verwerfung* and its return. The *jouissance* of the pervert is the split in the identity between the modes of negation (*Verdrängung* and *Verwerfung*) and their return *as themselves.* The opposition between negation/return is overturned. This deconstruction elides the binary contrasts between conscious/unconscious and manifest/latent. The Sameness⁺ *of* Sameness⁺ is the parallax which is exposed by the pervert as the schizoid (neurotic) truth of the Madness of Order. The returned Sameness⁺ is the principle of the pervert's expansion of the galaxy with the objects and fetishes (and so on) of the extension of: a *Trieb* which wanders beyond desire; a use-value which assembles beyond exchange-value; and a signifier which traces beyond the word.

The Madman's Unreason

The schizoid makes no sense. *Qua* schizophrenic, neither does the system make any sense. The madman's colloquy is a delirious Unreason. Madness ruptures Reason and the neurotic logics and rationalities: of phallocentric penis/not-penis at a time of generative fetishism; of capitalist debt and scarcity at a time of overproduction and abundance; and of linguistic word and sign at a time of the effluvium of the materiality of the signifier. But the hitch is that the symbolic order of penis, capital, and word is internally constrained by Reason. *Qua* Unreason, the penis is supplemented by fetishes, capital is outstripped by abundance, and the word is split by the signifier. The Reason of $-ism constrains its own Unreason of the Spirit of the System. Unreason is internal to Reason. The schizophrenia of the rationality and logic of the systems of desire, finance, and signification is the consequence of the Neurotic Foreclosure (*rejet névrotique*) of the Madness of Order. The Real Symbolic is the upshot of the contraction of expansion in the system.

The schizoid's nonsensical Unreason is the hallmark of the crazy person. The madman's spoken and written discourse — such as it is — is a materialism *sans* abstraction. Schizoid gobbledygook defuses the symbolic order because this word maze is tethered to the material sounds and marks of the signifier and unmoored in the abstract ideas and concepts of the signified. The psychotic is the archetypal so-called logocentrist.[21] The *Spaltung* of the psychotic is his split with abstraction and the conceptual dimension of *langue*. The subjectivity of the madman is a body which is alienated from the mind, a materiality which is divorced from the speculative, and a signifier which is split from the signified. The schizoid is pure phonology. The madman is a theorist of the architectonics of the system — but without alphabets and vocabularies for the articulation of this system of Neurotic Foreclosure (*rejet névrotique*). The psychotic is a revolutionary without a *pronunciamento*. The maniac's discourse is bereft of the basic integrant of the symbolic order: binary opposition.

The madman's intervention is exposed in his valiant reconfiguration of sexual difference. Psychoanalytically, "a man has a penis and Woman does not have a penis" is the unconscious symptom of latent phallocentrism and patriarchy. But the madman's subjectivity of body *sans* mind, materiality *sans* conceptuality, and signifier *sans* signified enables (disables) him to consciously reorder the unconscious. The madman notes that "a man has a penis and a Woman has a vagina and a clitoris." But schizoid Unreason is marked in a further articulation: "A man does not have a vagina and a clitoris, and a Woman does have a vagina and a clitoris." This Unreasonable persuasion reverses the prioritization of penis/not-penis and the opposition of Being and Nothingness under the Logic of Identity with a reprioritization of clitoris/not-clitoris and the obverse opposition of Nothingness and Being. The parallactic overlap between the extant phallocentrism of penis/not-penis and the schizoid Clitoralcentrism of clitoris/not-clitoris demonstrates the neurotic form of –centrism. The pervert is amused by this generative parallax because it churns out future objects and fetishes, such as the "not-clitoris." The pervert's *jouissance* is structured by this *Verleugnung* and its return of "not-clitoris" as an assembled fetish of the system of the simultaneity of disavowal and its return.

But the madman's supplemental expression is the Unreasonable, "A man has a penis and a Woman has a vagina and clitoris, and a man does not have a penis and a Woman does not have a vagina and clitoris, because the penis is not the penis and the vagina and the clitoris are not the vagina and the clitoris." This schizoid expression articulates an absence of absence — signifier without a signified — because it subverts the self-sameness and self-identity of any object in the system. The object (penis, vagina, and clitoris) is split *from itself* in the Logic of Difference ($A \neq A$). A Sameness[+] isolates the relationality and constructionism. This Logic of Difference ($A \neq A$ = B, and so on) opens the system toward an otherness of body parts and sex organs. The fetish takes pleasure in the assembly of these novel objects and new toys. Internal split and gap unfold external production and extension.

The pervert glimpses the parallactic excess of the overlap between the Logic of Identity and the Logic of Difference. The excess of this coincidence ($[A \neq A \neq A \neq A$, and so on$] \neq [A \neq A \neq A \neq A$, and so on$]$) is a positivity and affirmation of the *sous rature* and *sur l'effacement* which cannot be incorporated into the system of the *not* — "yes, yes." The Real and the symbolic overlap as a parallactic structure in which the escaped positivity and affirmation are organized by a radical negation of the extant — present Being — as such. The *Verleugnung* of Nothingness returns the Being *of* Nothingness as yet another fetish for the pervert's playful disavowal of the referent of the penis and the contractive sexual difference of the male sex organ.

The madman's Unreason is also visible in his redesign of the private property of the word. The system sustains and cultivates the private property of the word. The word is a positive unit. The word is self-contained and self-sufficient. The word is bounded by a circumscription of borders with edges and margins. This version of the word is closed and restricted. The differential and negative play of materialities and abstractions is constrained by the sovereignty of the presence and Being of the word. The architecture of the word is superordinate to the architectonics of the system of *langue* in the signifier and the signified. In contrast, the Unreason of the madman wills a public property of the word. This word (signifier) ordains a system which unlocks gates and overcomes guards. Schizophrenically, each metaphor is an open and endless metonymy.

Any object is joined to any other object in a field of relationships and constructions. The metonymization of metaphor redistributes the otherwise sovereignty of the word.

The word (signifier) is a negative relationship rather than a positive unit. The word (signifier) is dependent and interconnected rather than autonomous and unmonitored. The word (signifier) is open and expansive. The variance between the neurotic word and the schizoid word (signifier) opens the gap between phallocentrism and anticentrism, scarcity and plenitude, capitalism and communism, and the sign and the signifier. But the madman presents as representational incoherence. The pervert glimpses the madman's reversal of the prioritization of binary opposition. But he does so with techniques of conceptuality which are absent in the schizophrenic dominance of body over mind, materiality over abstraction, and the signifier over the signified. The madman is Real, and the pervert manipulates this Unreason in order to return truth to the symbolic order which has repressed (foreclosed) its own truth *qua* Other. The madman is the neurotic who sees himself in his selfhood and sociality in the system of $-ism. The pervert reminds the neurotic of his (whose?) essential madness.

The truth of *langue* is that the representational system is incoherent. The order of Reason of everyday life theoretically abjures consistent conversation and dependable discussion. The discourse of madness is a mistaken language that at once mimics the order of the sequence of words that it ostensibly transgresses. The schizoid abandons the signified abstraction and speculation of the general equivalent and the knowledge of the apparatus of *le sujet supposé savoir* of the extant symbolic order. But the catch is that this charade of epistemology ("I know very well, *but nevertheless*") is internal to the system of *langue*. The madman merely pushes Reason to its logical and rational absurd conclusions of Unreason. The maniac embodies the material signifier (mark, sound) of the body and flesh or the Foucauldian docile body of the regime of surveillance, regulation, and discipline. This submissive body is subordinate to the plethora of identities that the economy of binary opposition antagonistically structures. In his text, *History of Madness* (based on his doctoral dissertation from 1965), Foucault defines madness as this simple Unreason: a delirious and incoherent discourse which cannot be reduced to the self-same and self-identical positivity of the word.

This mad incoherence is the vocabulary of the Real. The Real is the limit principle of the spoken and the written. But the Real is also internal to the symbolic order. The principle of an internal and external Sameness⁺ or extimacy returns the word of binary opposition to the signifier of differential and negative relationality and constructionism. Any object is the same as any other object *qua* a singularity which cannot be adjudicated by the standardizations of the general equivalent. $-ism simulates the architecture of the word of Reason and the rationalities and logics of neurosis. But the system is simultaneously the architectonics of the signifier of Unreason and the cracks and splits of madness. The word is situated in a *Spaltung* between the sovereignty of autonomy and independence and self-sameness and self-identity, on the one hand, and the splits of neither equality nor inequality nor identity nor difference, on the other hand. The system is schizophrenic.

This is the reason that the mode of negation of $-ism is *Verwerfung*. But the system simulates neurosis. This is the reason that its mode of negation is also *Verdrängung*. The *rejet névrotique* returns the expansion and openness of perverse fetishism to the simulated contraction and closedness of neurotic *désir*. The neurotic galaxy of limited objects and penile referents is already the perverse universe of unlimited articles and fetishes. The repression (foreclosure) of any object returns in *Verleugnung* as "any object." The scare quotes are the mark of a generative extension and productive proliferation of the Madness of Order *qua* "Madness of Order." The schizoid speaks and writes in scare quotes, and the pervert takes pleasure in the simulation of props and objects for lacks and castrations. The word is the castration. The disavowed return of the "word" is the suture of the wound.

The schizoid penchant for the signifier over the word transforms any psychoanalysis of the madman. The psychotic does not showcase a manifest representation because he repudiates the bi-level opposition between manifest figuration and latent truth. Any excavation of the navel of the dream is impossible in a body which differs and defers the layers of conscious and unconscious. The *Verwerfung* of castration involves the loss of loss and the absence of absence. Foreclosure implicates the hole in the signified. *Verwerfung* indicates difference and deferral of the trace. Psychosis inspires the collapse of binarism. Schizophrenia exchanges the strict borders of private property (*le propre*) for a public property of the signifier. A proper psychoanalysis of the madman and his Unreason is impossible because any object is — ~~Being~~ — substitutable for any other object. The analyst undoubtedly deploys his own phallic *point de capiton* in any analysis in order to fix the borders between latent and manifest, and between unconscious and conscious. The analytic transcription of the elliptical original into the distinct translation — conversion of manifest into latent and the return voyage — produces an excess of the word in the surplus of the signifier. The semic organizational force of society is overrun by the *latency of the latent* and the *manifest of the manifest,* and so on. The pervert experiences this remainder as an expansion of objects and fetishes which extends beyond the precise confines of the positive unity of the word.

The body of the schizoid exceeds the system of *langue.* This psychotic body of the material signifier cannot be assimilated into the system of binary opposition and its tidy correspondences between words. A perverse interpretation of the schizoid's material text (marks, sounds) tarries with an object which is untied to the conceptions and abstractions of Reason. Analysis of madness is addressed by the perverse word maze of the Real Symbolic. Lacan says: "The structure of the psychotic should be located in a symbolic unreal."[22] My shorthand for "symbolic unreal" is the Real Symbolic. This structure of madness is nameless and faceless in an asymbolic dimension of unbuttoned body, materiality, and signifier. The schizoid's psychical organization is "located" in the material body of the signifier of the frenzied mania of hallucinations and delusions. The body of the madman is situated *in* the materialist traces of signification. The psychotic is the body of *langue.*

The schizoid is not a signifier *per se* but a web of materialities and bodies in extimate relational and constructionist — negative and differential — bond with each other. The madman is the material substrate of the architectonics of the system of the word. The specific materialist structure of the madman is essential to his (dys)function in the signifying chain ("symbolic") of simulacrum ("unreal"). The organization of the Real Symbolic contests the binary opposition between referent/copy, original/translation, and also the series of psychoanalytic polarities, such as unconscious/conscious, latent/manifest, symptom/return, and so on. The sheer materiality — body and signifier — of the psychotic generates a grammatological scar. The psychotic resists abstraction and conception despite his bodily political contestation. Mad politics omits knowledges and manifestos. The schizoid is the Outside of epistemology. The schizoid commissions a tear-down of the distinction between words because he axes all oppositions to bloody waste and fleshly refuse.

The parallax of the Real Symbolic (or symbolic unreal) is that the material architectonics of the Madness of Order exceeds the architecture of the word. The surplus of this encounter is the series of marks and sounds — laces, furs, shoes, and jockstraps — which animates the returned disavowed expansion and extension of fetishes in an open system of value rather than in a closed structure of signification. The madman's bodily materiality ruptures the positive unity of the word. The leftover is an excess goo which defies assimilation into the system. This remnant of the system is the Real and its overlap with the symbolic order. The neurotic constrains the madman's excess body with the signified — abstractions and speculations — of interpretation and analysis. But the pervert glances at these restraints as the purposeless effort to contain a communist queer (*a*)sexual force of expansion of the mad material signifier which overpowers the positive sign of the system. The return of repression (foreclosure) is an excess materialism of the body and the signifier. These returned surpluses of the body of the madman are the integrants of the objects and fetishes which extend the skies beyond the delimited set of words in the system. Excess materialism generates surplus abstraction. The sign multiplies from the materialist force of the madman's body.

The pervert's gift for textual play is the freedom of value and the signifier and the signified in their autonomy from subordination to the positive unity of the word. Perverse play of abstraction and speculation supplements mad resistance of the body and the signifier. The pervert's *écriture* empowers him to interpret the bodies, materialities, and signifiers of the madman and his alienated — differed and deferred *qua* unrecuperable and unassimilable — succession of sounds and marks as coherent objects and fetishes. The pervert transcribes from "translation" ("original") to "original" ("translation"). The pervert does so without the expired references of the penis in phallocentrism, the scarcity in capitalism, and the syntax and semantics of the word in *langue* in the Madness of Order. The excess of this transcription is *excess itself.* The pervert's *Verleugnung* produces an excess in the "No!" and its return of "No!" *qua* "yes." Perverse play abjures the $-istic institutions of capitalist private property and linguistic original articulation. The surplus of materiality and its partial speculation in the abstraction of the autonomous signified destabilize the restrictions and constraints of the *désir* of sexuality, the scarcity of capitalism, and the word of discourse. Summarily, the pervert converts the schizoid's chaotic, frenzied, materialist, hallucinatory, and delusional word salad into the coded manifesto of the Becoming of the Pervert-Schizoid-Woman of the Spirit of the System.

The oppressive structures of phallocentrism of patriarchy, scarcity of capitalism, and the isolated word of *langue* are unimaginable without the signified. The signified constrains any object within the edges and margins of the object. The penis is restricted to itself and its obversive negative in the not-penis. The *finite infinity* or *infinite finity* of dollars and coins constricts production and consumption. The word curbs the architectonics of the signifier. The signified button-tie is *in absentia* in the psychotic's economy of the *theory* of the *signifier.* The signified is present in the pervert's structure of the *practice* of the *sign.* The madman is a theoretical selfhood, and schizophrenia is a theoretical sociality. Any forceful resistance to patriarchy, capitalism, and language is a foremost theoretical endeavor. The schizoid signifier is distanced from any signified which could anchor a symbolic analysis of any symptom whatsoever: dream, slip, joke, and psychopathology of everyday life in the neurotic; "sexual difference" in the pervert; and hallucination and delusion in the psychotic. The schizoid's strict materialism illuminates the Madness of Order in its essence, but the suspended *point de capiton* sustains this revelation as a theoretical enterprise of the signifier (without a signified) rather than as a practical endeavor of the word (in relationship of difference and negativity to the Sameness+ of the extension of other words in the system). The pervert's job is to discern the Madness of Order (s *qua* $-ism) and to articulate the latent (manifest) truth of the system with a series of conceptual personae. These characters return as "conceptual personae" from the *faux* negation of *Verleugnung.*

The schizoid cannot be isolated or situated anywhere — spatially coordinated — in the signifying chain. The madman is everywhere in this word, in this sentence, on this page, in this chapter, in this book, and so on. Derrida's work on *différance* and context generatively expands the galaxy — differed and deferred — beyond any points of delimited coordinates or defined perimeters. The madman's experience of the extension of the skies disperses and decenters his selfhood and sociality to the limits of the solar system. The madman is *not.* Lacan says that the signifier is what represents a subject to another signifier.[23] The signifier represents to an Other signifier. The object portrays to another object. The fetish screens for another fetish. The succession of objects in the system generates a field of representations *of* representations *ad infinitum.* This expansion of the galaxy is the proviso of the growth of fetishes and centers and metaphors, and signs and words and substitutes, and so on.

But the psychotic's materialist value (as opposed to signification) curbs his *own* representation in the web of words. *Qua* signifier, the madman defies the "I" of the self and its "consciousness" in the metaphysics of presence and the series of violent epistemes. The "self" and "I" and "consciousness" of the madman are *sous rature* because the schizoid's only access to truth is the Principle of Sameness⁺. Sameness⁺ alienates "consciousness" (*et al.*) from its *arche* in abstraction and speculation. The fiction of "consciousness" is not only split — *Spaltung* — from itself but it is also coincident and continuous — ~~Being~~ — with the other representations of "consciousness." Whose "consciousness" is whose? This subversion of *le propre* undermines the projects of *désir* in sexuality, commodity in capitalism, and the word in discourse. The madman is nowhere, but neither is the desire for the penis, exchange-value of the commodity, and the word in the text. Theoretically, Being and Nothingness are the twin pillars of the expanse of space in the suspension of the narratives of temporality. This space is the unconscious. It is not only a space with no negation, no knowledge, and no temporality. The unconscious is also a space with no patriarchy, no capitalism, and no text.

The madman disrupts private property *tout court*. This includes the destabilization of capitalism and its ideology of scarcity and regime of currency. The ideology of scarcity mobilizes isolated units of credit and debt which can be exchanged by the general equivalent of currency. This system of scarcity is coded into dollars and coins because the system of integers and decimals is a *finite infinity* or *infinite finity*. The system of capitalist accumulation is only restricted by its own internal limit — presence — in any accumulation. The madness of Sameness⁺ disrupts the division of the credit/debt binary opposition. This Principle of Sameness⁺ destabilizes a system of balances and imbalances. Whose credit is whose? Whose debt is whose? The dictum of *différance* upends the origin and destination — departure and arrival — of any collection of coins and dollars. The economic transaction at the point of sale cannot be reduced to a buyer who purchases with currency and a seller who vends with currency. The consumer is not the consumer, and the producer is not the producer.

This Logic of Difference (A ≠ A = B, and so on) is neither consumer-centric (demand side economics) nor producer-centric (supply side economics). Rather, the Logic of Difference of the economy is an anticentrism in which the gap between the center and the margin is displaced. The pervert unveils this parallactic overlap between supply and demand, between producer and consumer, and between seller and buyer. Who is the creditor and who is the debtor? Whose currency is whose? The madman disrupts the borders between supply/demand (*et al.*). The point of transaction of capitalist sale is diffused beyond any conceptual or spatial locus. The excess of the parallax is a materialist use-value which cannot be absorbed into the system of dollars and coins. Nothing is Missing in use-value. But Something is Missing in exchange-value. The madman's psychical structure and the pervert's set of schizoid conceptual personae indicate that the Real of the maniac's body — materialist signifier — interrupts the regime of the accumulation of capital.

The pervert's schizophrenic platform presents a simulation of the divorced referent and estranged truth. Baudrillard is the *über*-theorist of the simulacrum. He says that "simulation is that of a territory, a referential being, or a substance [which is] the generation by models of a real without origin or reality: a hyperreal."[24] The text is a hyperreal which produces replicas and facsimiles whose reference to symbolic reality is unmoored. Duplicates and imitations substitute for the referential symbolic order. The madman's truth is the alienation from reference. The maniac's materialism estranges him from the desire, commodity, and word of the extant symbolic systems of patriarchy, capitalism, and discourse. Facsimiles and blueprints — rather than realities and truths — supplant both the original and the translation, both the latent and the manifest, both the unconscious and the conscious, and both the symptom and its return. The ontological endeavor of the as such, by definition, *il y a*, by necessity, *qua*, and so on is displaced altogether. Baudrillard claims that to simulate is to feign to have what one does not have. Simulation describes the phallocentric (castration, lack), capitalist (private property, scarcity), and deconstructive (trace, *différance*) essential structures of $-ism. These systems are structured by *le propre* and by the loss of objects (penis, commodity, word) which must be anxiously recuperated by the system. The perverse trick is to engage in systems of sexuality, utility, and signification — but in the absence of a relationship of ownership.

Figure 3.5 Subjectivity (is) Everywhere

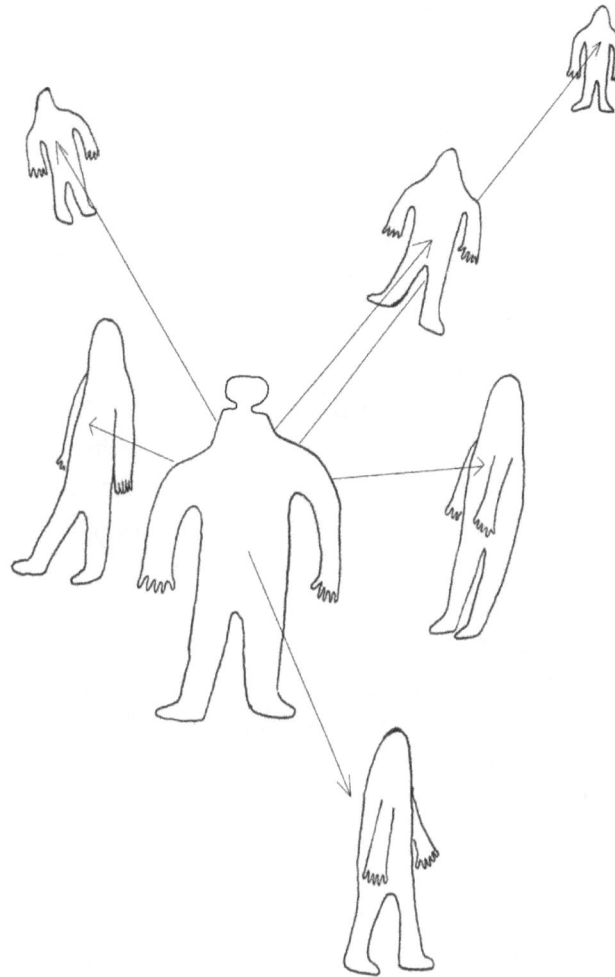

This illustration shows the psychotic who is distributed in and disseminated around the entirety of the solar system of subjectivity — above, near, around, below, adjacent, behind, and so on. The psychotic is detached from the signified because of the *Verwerfung* of ideality and the exposure of materiality. The schizoid is not himself *qua* himself because his relationships extend beyond the borders and partitions that would otherwise retroactively (*Nachträglichkeit* and *après-coup*) generate coherent relationships between units of text and "himself." In contrast, the neurotic is represented in a system of signification — the signifier represents the subject to another signifier. But the schizoid lives and breathes the infinite substitutability of objectivity and subjectivity. The schizoid permeates and spreads throughout the entirety of the system and its expansive and extensive beyond in space. Schizophrenia is in the ether of the Other. The schizoid is not engaged in processes of identity or identification. The schizoid's subjectivity is neither relative nor absolutely relative but strictly absolute. The effect of this ruptured isolation is an existential deferral. The psychotic subject *is* Becoming in the absence of the abrupt starts and stops — *point de capiton* — of the joint or hinge between the signifier and the signified.

Notes & Sketches —

The architecture of the system is the *le propre* of the private property of desire and its object, the commodity and its owner, and the word and its speaker. A simulation which feigns ownership in the place of dispossession is the defense of the system against the deconstruction of *le propre* in *Trieb*, in communism, in the signifier, and in the queer (*a*)sexuality of the generative nucleus of the expansion rather than the contraction of the solar system. Being-in-the-world and being-with-others are an effort to pretend *le propre*, to masquerade ownership, to pretense mineness, to posture possession, and to bluff the proper. The architecture of the system is the simulation of ownership. The architectonics of this system is the deconstruction of *le propre*. The parallactic gap between private property and the expansion of unmoored fetishes and unanchored counterfeits is perversely returned in the *Verleugnung* of (*a*)sexuality. An (*a*)sexuality is the choice of Spirit of contraction — desire, capitalism, word — or expansion — drive, communism, signifier.

The pervert's aesthetic foreswears the "I know very well, but nevertheless" altogether in its most radical moments of *écriture*: "I know ~~very well~~ nothing, ~~but~~ nevertheless something" — in faith and optimism in the creationist sublimation *ex nihilo* of the fetish and the expanded series of objects in the galaxy. Perversely, Nothing becomes Something. The negative not-penis of patriarchy, the constrictive scarcity of capitalism, and the isolated word of discourse — Nothingness — are transformed into the positive series of sex organs of (*a*)sexuality, the expansive abundance of communism, and the relational and constructed signifier of the trace — Being. This (de/re)construction is the symbolization of the pervert in his campy and farcical — but political and committed — perspective. Grammatological decenterment is the mode of the written and the spoken of the pervert. All signification is split from within by the Real. Any object is any other object. The reconstruction of words is the effort of the pervert's strange text, unsteady materiality, and crass conceptuality. The massive endeavor to pen the manifesto of the absent madman articulates the truth of the psychotic.

The hitch is that the maniac nevertheless knows the codes of the orders of $-ism. The madman discovers the false contraction of the otherwise generative expansion of the galaxies in desire, finance, and language. The madman's intuition about the system and its ambivalent contractions does not intimidate the pervert. The pervert's will to pen, pencil, and paint the madman's nightmarish daydreams is only sharpened. The pervert promises to put signified to sign, and conceptuality to materiality, in order to illuminate the Madness of Order. The mad conceptual personae of Real Symbolic, Signified/r, and Sameness⁺ are the ideas of the manifesto of the pervert's political and ethical commitment to the Unreason of the madman. *Verleugnung* promises to negate the repressions of these conceptual personae and to return them to the ego-system of the Madness of Order *qua* its own truth.

The Pervert's Fetishes

The representational form of the pervert's disavowal is his fetishism. The fetish consists of a colorful mash-up of representations. This mishmash is performed with the techniques of the primary process unconscious talents of condensation-metaphor and displacement-metonymy. Freud discovers the *Verleugnung* of sexual difference at the center of the pervert's clinical structure. The perverse clinical structure is decentered between the words in binary opposition, on the one hand, and a mediatory Real Penis of effective grease, on the other hand. The Real Penis — ~~Being~~ — lubricates the relationships between the pairs of contrasts in the system. The Real Penis is the conceptual persona which mobilizes the Principle of Sameness⁺ in the system of relational and constructive differences and negativities toward the openness of the other. Any object is the same as any other object. The Real Penis is the articulated emollient of this relationship which is *sous rature* and *sur l'effacement* because the Real Penis is the *same as the other* — Being — but *different from itself*. The lubricational words of relationship are necessarily *sous rature*: ~~Being~~.

Perversely, the center is antecedent to the center, which is posterior to the center, and so on. The wiles of condensations and displacements disrupt the spatiotemporal organization of these words. *Verleugnung* of difference stretches the tension between the binaristic pairs to the point of snap. Each word flails off into an extended space. The word then returns to be resynthesized in the dynamic between *Eros* and *Thanatos* in their (dis)union. The fate of difference is the crucial and basal consequence of the disavowal of the penis/not-penis division. *Verleugnung* releases the productive and generative play in-between otherwise starkly fixed words in rigid opposition. The excess of the greasy mediation between contrasts yields the fetish. The gap between fetish *qua* prop and the clitoris itself is arbitrated by the vibrant and radiant series of objects — furs, laces, shoes, jockstraps, and so on — whose extension beyond the confines of the strict set of binary oppositions in the system productively discovers the universe beyond the penis *qua* referent. The pervert's succession of fetishes expands play, extends paradox, produces contradiction, generates simulation, and excretes charisma.

But the fetish is also restricted. The final referent — original for translation, latent for manifest, and truth for simulation — is the penis. The schizoid's suspension of the *point de capiton* is retied in the fetishist's return to the penile referent for its series of objects of Sameness⁺. Freud writes: "To put it plainly: the fetish is a substitute for the Woman's (mother's) phallus which the male junior once believed in and does not wish to forego — we know why."[25] The schizoid denial of female castration enables him to enjoy his penis (*et al.*) without fear of loss and the symptoms of narcissism, aggression, anxiety, and so on. The *Verwerfung* of castration converts the capitalist private property of the penis into the communist public property of the free switch-and-swap of embryonic sexuality of aims and objects. The ideological supplement of capitalism is castration. The other ideological master signifiers of subordination to capitalism include debt and deficit. The Principle of Sameness⁺ transliterates the words of debt and deficit into surplus and plenitude. Perverse *Verleugnung* returns the negativity of loss and death *qua* the positivity of "gain" and "life."

The pervert's suspension *of* suspension of phallic reference pins manifest to latent, conscious to unconscious, symptom to return, and fetish to penis. The advantage of this containment is a consistent and coherent practice of generative and productive assembly of the fetish *qua qua* — as Something is Missing to Nothing is Missing. The caveat is that the fetish refers to the penis, but the obverse is that the penis refers to an otherness. If the fur is the penis, then what is the penis? Perversion puts the penis itself *sous rature* and *sur l'effacement*. The escaped excess of this overlap between the reference of the penis and the split in the object is the function of substitution. Perversion mobilizes substitution — of lace for fur, manifest for latent, shoe for jockstrap, unconscious for conscious, and so on. But, at the same time, perversion puts substitution under scrutiny. The Real Penis is the conceptual persona of lubrication which relates — *not* — the bonds of condensation and displacement in the semic field. There is a surplus of substitution in the primary process. How will this remainder be contained by the system?

The male junior "once believed in" the female penis. The male junior formerly glimpsed the truthful mediation of the object and reality. The male junior originally witnessed the unsimulated object. The male junior earlier experienced an object without the *sous rature* Being or Real Penis of exchange between positive unities of words. This unmediated and unsimulated experience yields to the realization (or "recognition," to use Hyppolite's earlier vocabulary) of the phallocentrism of castration and the Real of sexual difference in the turgidity (and lack) in the penis/not-penis opposition. The pervert "knows very well" of castration. Loss and death are both ideationally returned as a reoccurrence ("recognized") and sentiently experienced as an interpretation ("perceived") by the pervert. The pervert is attuned to castration and its consequences of narcissism, aggression, and anxiety. "But nevertheless," the pervert generates — somehow — an expansive sequence of objects which extends the penis beyond itself — what is a penis? — toward fetishes of laces, furs, shoes, and jockstraps.

The translation of the male junior's reexperience of the "once believed in" maternal phallus is an open faith, an optimistic sensibility, a historical revision, and a playful disregard for a castration that he "knows very well" is the Real of sexual difference. The fetishist "knows very well" of female lack and the evidence of his future castration. The male junior, as Freud says, "does not wish to forgo" his faith that the clitoris is ~~equal~~ and ~~identical~~ to the penis. Instead, the fetishist imagines the Principle of Sameness⁺ that the clitoris is the same as the penis because the clitoris is at a variance with itself and the penis is at a distance from itself. The Real Penis is the lubricant between these variances and distances between any object and itself. The Real Penis is *sous rature* of the ~~variance~~ and ~~distance~~. But the strikethrough of the relationality and constructionism between any object *with itself* opens an excess of Nothingness and negativity which returns in *Verleugnung* as the extension of objects in space.

The cycle of perverse fetishism and its relationship to the penis and the clitoris are open circles. This cycle starts from the original happy experience of plenitude of the maternal phallus. The shock and awe of the Real of sexual difference of penis/not-penis supplant the warmth of the *jouissance* with the mother. The *Verleugnung* of castration returns the offspring to the mother with the distinctive addition of the simulacral substitution of the fetish for the lost phallus and the prop of the object for loss and death. This sequence of perversity is circular. The male junior's psychical trajectory departs from the point of its destination. The cycle begins with masturbatory adoration of the male junior's penis and maternal phallus and returns to masturbatory adoration of the female junior's penis and its substitute fetishistic avatars. The economy of the fetish generates a series of returns of negations *qua* affirmations of such monstrous sex objects as the male penis, lace, female penis, fur, man's clitoris, shoe, Woman's penis, jockstrap, and so on. These fetishes expand from the interval between maternal warmth and stark castration.

Any fetish is a Sameness⁺ whose assembly is the upshot of a scripted revision of the sensory experience ("perception") of the polarity of sexual hierarchy of the difference *qua* deficit of the Logic of Identity, on the one hand, and the Sameness⁺ of the Real Penis and an incomparable and incontrastable exchange between singularities, on the other hand. The patterns in the fetishistic cycle, from denial of phallocentrism in the renarrative "perception" of maternal warmth — to the reexperienced "recognition" of the Real of phallocentrism — to the veil of sexual difference in the substitution of the fetish-object for the maternal phallus — and to the fetish *qua* generative assembly of objects (*et al.*) as the pervert's prop for fetishistic sex — this trajectory is cyclical. The *telos* indicates that the subjective and objective move in fetishistic sexuality is an orbit of its own sphere. The so-called *arche* of the perverse letter of fetishism is the beer and skittles of self-pleasure with hands and fingers. The ostensible destination of the fetishistic postcard is the glee and gaiety of self-pleasure with panties and hose. Fetishism is the *process* of metaphor and its substitutions. The object of the pervert's *jouissance* is metaphor. The surplus of Metaphoricity — metonymization of metaphor — is the Real Penis. The greasy lubricant which detaches and attaches part-objects in the series of *like* between metaphorical object and figural fetish is the excess which cannot be assimilated into the parallactic overlap between the fetish and the referent of its production.

The sequence of perversion involves the reexperienced "recognition" of sexual difference, and then the rescripted "recognition" of the Sameness⁺ of disavowal of phallocentrism, and then the assemblage of the fetish and the *jouissance* of its return in an affirmed expanse of objects in the universe. These fetishes are props and toys which screen phallocentric penis/not-penis and the regime of negativity in $-ism: loss and death in desire;

scarcity and currency in capitalism; and word and unity in discourse. The fetish is the horizon of the future of a Spirit which is expansive and open rather than contractive and closed. The fetish mobilizes *Trieb* and its extended collection of gestures and maneuvers. The fetish announces abundance and its free production and free consumption. The fetish animates the signifier and its excess of the material body over the abstract mind of the word. The fetish is the "penis-substitute" *qua* substitute *qua* destination *qua* departure *qua* series of *quas* which widens a Metaphoricity whose lubricational Real Penis coordinates under erasure.

The process of fetishism is a closed circle of substitution which is simultaneously open to the expansion of any object which is different *from itself* but related to and constructed in *rapport with* any other object in the system. The circular *Trieb* endlessly differs and defers in fetishism. The rotation of the sphere of negation of the censored object of the penis and its return in affirmation as the positive object of the fetish is expansively open to an otherness — substitutes, words, centers, metaphors, penises, metonymies, clitorises, dildos, shoes, penis-clitorises, vagina-centers, jockstraps, and so on (*et al.*). These objects award the fetishist with a greater whack at the intensity of *jouissance* because the series of substitutions extends the Metaphoricity — slip and slide — which is the object of the pervert's *jouissance*. Substitution is the functional center which invites the male junior to contest the phallocentrism of patriarchy, the private property of capitalism, and the word of *langue*. The penis is not the penis. The fetishist's Metaphoricity extends substitution to the otherwise architectural referent of the system in the penis. What is a penis? The destabilization of this penis enables the cycle of fetishism to endlessly repeat in the circulation of objects for fetishism, new goods and services for communist abundance, and new signifiers for meaning-making. The privacy of the property of the penis *qua* referent — and so on — is decentered from any essence. Simultaneously, fetishism robs castration of its bite marks on the facade of the masculine ego and its salty licks at the wounds of feminine selfhood.

The open circuit with an aperture toward the *tout autre* is a simple cycle of: enjoyment of the maternal phallus; anxiety of the Real of sexual difference; disavowal of phallocentrism; and *jouissance* of the generative series of objects and its collection of phallic prepositions. This sequence requires a principle of coordination in order to structure the spatial arrangement of the returned objects of *Verleugnung*. The indexical signals coordinate the spatiality of the structure. The phallic preposition directs the escalation of the traffic of fetishes in a universe of openness and growth. Prepositions organize the entirety of the fetishistic order of words and things — *les mots et les choses* — in the world. The Real Penis lubricates — *sous rature* — the relationship between difference and negativity of the signifier of any object with itself and with the series of other objects. The preposition arranges this succession of objects in the space of the timeless unconscious. These generated words, substitutes, objects, and fetishes are the substance of the carnival of the *Trieb* — endless gestures and infinite recoils — of the masochist. The bond between objects and prepositions overlaps.

The surplus of this gap is a spatial dissonance and a dislocation in place. The *différer* of *différance* is flipped and twisted by the incongruity in space which the remnants of the preposition and the object generate. This discordant space is a map which precedes the territory and a simulation which supplants the reality. The leftover of any object and its spatial relationship and construction — Real Penis — with itself and the other objects is the deconstruction of the edges and margins of inside/outside and the spatial coordination of text and context. The pervert experiences the elliptical stretch of space, but his *écriture* strives to refer dissonant space to the coordinates of displacement and condensation in the unconscious. The fetish of unconscious space is the navel of the dream. The referent of this navel is not the penis but the "known," as Freud says, of the wish of the dream. The pervert sustains and reproduces the *jouissance* of the fetishes in space without the return to the *désir* of the navel of space.

The psychotic free play of the signifier in *différance* is theoretical rather than practical. The autonomy of the signifier (and the signified) is the domain of theory. The subordination of the signifier and the signified to the positive unity of the word is the empire of practice. Theory is the dimension of the free play of the materiality, body, and signifier of the madman. Practice is the containment of such twists and turns in the distinction and opposition of the hierarchical Logic of Identity of the sign of the neurotic. The pervert's *Verleugnung* achieves a simultaneity of the free play of the signifier in *theory* and the containment of the sign in *practice*. But such bivalent talent requires the suture of the Real Penis. The Real Penis is the sexy emollient which greases the otherwise inexplicable conjoinment of material and abstract, body and mind, signifier and signified, theory and practice, and the pairs of binary oppositions in the system which are otherwise deemed present in the ontological order of Being. Any object is suspended in an aporetic uncertainty after the *destruktion* of the Heideggerian ontico-ontological difference of the what is — ? Fetishistically, the penis cannot be the referent for perverse sexuality because the penis is not internal and intrinsic to itself. What is a penis?

The substitute is not a substitute for the penis. The substitute is a substitute for *substitutability*. The pervert takes pleasure in the *mise-en-abyme* of this Metaphoricity. The only presence in the system is the lubricant of the Real Penis and the prepositional indices which order the expansive objects of fetishes in the timeless space of the unconscious. The Signified/r explodes the extant order. The Real Symbolic presents itself in its abject *destruktion*. The Real Penis lubricates the relationships between objects which are spatially coordinated by prepositions. The grown universe transforms lack into plenitude, scarcity into abundance, capitalism into communism, patriarchy into feminism, the word into the signifier, and so on. The obversive rearrangement also transpires. The unconscious space between capitalism and communism is moiled by the Real Penis, coordinated by the preposition, and subordinated to endless substitution in the return of the abundant (*a*)sexuality at the center of the solar system. Sameness[+] is the precept of the Spirit of the System.

The pervert's "but nevertheless" involves a posteriorly articulated subject and verb of "I believe." This bond between subject and verb is not exhausted by a relationship to faith. There are other words — verbed gerunds or Ing[+] — which supplement the expression of disavowal in the "I know very well, but nevertheless…." But nevertheless, what? These perverse alternatives to neurotic epistemology of "I know very well" include a sequence of permutations of "but nevertheless" — faith, wonder, imagination, hope, will, affirmation, and so on. But these supplements to "but nevertheless" must be perversely conceived as verbed gerunds — nouns or gerunds which are considered verbs or actions — or what I refer to as Ing[+]. These Ing[+] verbed gerunds of faith, wonder, imagination, hope, and will supplement "but nevertheless" with an optimism toward the future. This *tout autre* is beyond epistemological ("I know very well") regimes of patriarchy, capitalism, and *langue*. These three systems are epistemological because they pursue a presence of Being in their endeavors. Patriarchy enforces the presence of the penis against the lack of the not-penis. Capitalism grounds the exchange of commodities in the presence of the general equivalent of currency. Discourse imposes knowledge on a word which purports to refer to objects rather than to other words.

The verbed gerund Ing[+] indicates that the supplements to the pervert's "but nevertheless" are a succession of Becomings which supersedes the Being of the epistemology of the "I know very well." The epistemology of Being is supplanted by the faith of Becoming. The verbed gerund Ing[+] is the transitional grammatical tense between Being and Becoming. The Ing[+] indicates a departure and an arrival, and a commencement and a destination, which neither start nor stop at a beginning or an end. Becoming *is qua* verbed gerund *qua* Ing[+] *qua* Becoming. The pervert's verbed gerund Ing[+] Becomes-Other than present and fixed Being. The "but nevertheless" pursuit of faith, exploration to wonder, enjoyment of imagination, keep to hope, commitment to will, and preservation of affirmation must be understood in the tense of the verbed gerund of Ing[+] as Pursuing[+], Exploring[+], Enjoying[+], Keeping[+], Committing[+], and Preserving[+] in a Becoming[+] with neither departure nor arrival in Being. This Becoming of "but nevertheless" unsettles the phallic epistemology of the "I know very well" of the masculine, capitalist, and speakerly subject.

The epistemology of the man is castrated at the scene of the discovery of sexual difference. The capitalist's knowledge is put under scrutiny by the dynamics of overproduction. The epistemology of the speaker is undone by the deferral of words to words rather than in the reference of words to objects. But why do Freud and the male junior and the adult man fantasize castration? Why is the *telos* of masculine development man's own potential loss? Why does the death drive of *Thanatos* triumph over drive and *Trieb*? Why does the capitalist fantasize scarcity and limits to production and consumption? Why do supply/demand dynamics conquer overproduction and each according to his ability and each according to his need? Why does the speaker of *langue* fantasize the reference of word to object rather than the proliferation of signifiers in the text? Why does the sign vanquish the signifier? Why does the Being of the epistemology of the "I know very well" overwhelm the Becoming of the "but nevertheless" of faith (*et al.*)? Why is the verbed gerund Ing⁺ *sans* departure or destination subordinate to a fixed and static Being which suspends sexual proliferation of objects, limits overproduction of goods and services, and restricts free play of the signifier? The tendency toward the expansion and growth in the galaxy is consistently resisted by the forces of contraction and restriction. The system of $-ism must be displaced — twisted and flipped — by the energy of the communist queer (*a*)sexual obscene abundance at the center of the solar system. The verbed gerund Ing⁺ is the grammatical mark of the force of Becoming and expansion over the reaction of Being and contraction. The pervert's insight is that the gerund is a verb. The pervert's clairvoyance is that Becoming Becoming Becoming Becoming —

The simultaneous concession to and dismissal of castration and privation identify the subjective transition from knowledge to faith and from science to religion. The object of this faith and religion is the fetish. I would hazard that perversion animates the traversal from *désir* to *Trieb*, and from castration to schizoanalysis. *Verleugnung* inspires the expansion of master signifiers in letters sent and received, relayed and intercepted, and delayed and redirected around the globe. Perversely, the negative returns as the positive, and the negation recurs as the *sinthome*. The *sinthome* is the return of the enjoyed objects of negation. The fetish is an object of divinity in its positive return from *Verleugnung*. The jockstrap is a source of mystical ecstasy. The object is the origin of the Spiritual extension of the series of fetishes which is returned *qua* "returned." The fetish is worshipped not for its essential or eternal qualities. Rather, the fetish is exalted for its mnemic traces to the associated objects that the offspring senses at the moment of the reexperienced "perception" and rescripted "recognition" of a Woman's difference in the Outside of the general equivalence of penis/not-penis.

The fetish is metonymic and contiguous. The Principle of Sameness⁺ stimulates the recurrence of any objects in an open system of any other objects. The jockstrap is a part of a whole which is supplemented by a whole of a part, and so on. The presence of the jockstrap comforts the fetishist and his fear of the seizure of his private(s) property. The fetish holds a magical and sensual power for the pervert. The jockstrap is considered above the otherwise everyday objects in the world. The pervert's *jouissance* of his jockstrap returns the negated not-penis to the series of positive and affirmed objects in the sexual system. Perverse *jouissance* is structured not by tension and its release in the idiot's enjoyment but by an extension of tension in the growth of gestures, flirtations, and moves in a *Trieb* which is beyond the pleasure principle. Faith and religion epitomize this extension. In contrast, knowledge and science exemplify the contraction of the Becoming of *Trieb* to the static return of tension to the homeostasis of the Being of *désir*.

The pervert's ordinary object in its stupid materiality of the signifier is joined to sacred objecthood in mediation with the signified by the Real Penis. The fetish is the practice of the *sign* of the conjoinment of the material signifier and the abstract signified in the legible sign of *langue*. *Qua* Becoming, fetishism is an in-process, in-activity *fetishing* of the verbed gerund Ing⁺. This *fetishing* is a *practice* of the sign rather than a *theory* of the signifier or the signified. But the fetish is substituted *qua* signifier rather than *qua* sign, *qua* penis rather than *qua* phallus, *qua* use-value rather than *qua* currency, and *qua* mother rather than *qua* father. The same abstract and speculative reference of the sign of the jockstrap ("penis-substitute") is circulated around the other recurred fetishes in the system. The jockstrap and the shoe are an identical signification as the *sign*. But their materiality as the *signifier* is differently embodied in the supportive protection for the penis and the functional cover for the foot. The overlap between the fetishes in their different signifiers of materiality (supportive protection for the penis and functional cover for the foot in their embodied objectal difference), on the one hand, and their identical abstraction of the signified ("penis-substitute"), on the other hand, generates an excess of materiality and the signifier whose identity in the jockstrap and the shoe cannot be reincorporated into the system.

The pervert understands this surplus as the object of the expansion and openness toward the production of as yet unimagined fetishes — *les mots et les choses* — in an expansive system. The remainder of materiality between concrete jockstrap and empirical shoe, on the one hand, and abstract and speculative signified of the "penis-substitute," on the other hand, is the queer (*a*)sexual source of the expansion in the galaxy. The sacredness of the fetish swells the objects in the world. *Verleugnung* returns the abstract "penis-substitute" to the excess of the concreteness and empiricism of the jockstrap and the shoe. The object exceeds its own signification. The value of the signifier triumphs in the economy of fetishism.

The monster power of the fetish is to elevate the scrap to the level of *das Ding*. The pervert elevates *substitution* to the level of the beloved fetish. The fetish is strictly beyond the purview of science. The fetish has no basis in Reason other than in the function of substitution and in the pervert's *jouissance* of Metaphoricity. The fetish is the substitute — sign or metaphor or word or center, and so on — of plenitude. The *mise-en-abyme* of substitution is the object of the pervert's *jouissance*. The integrant of this slip and slide — navel to the unknown — is a strict materiality. This signifier is entirely divorced from the compulsively repeated reference to the penis and to the restriction of the constellation of sexual organs to the phallocentric arrangement between penis/not-penis. Metaphoricity of *mise-en-abyme* and its metonymization of metaphor abjures any subsequent –centrism of the center of the structure. The pervert's center is already decentered. This decenterment is the object of the pervert's *jouissance*.

This decenterment is also the expansion and extension of any object beyond its own borders and toward an otherness which grows the system of fetishes in the Other. The "penis-substitute" may be the abstract and speculative signified of the fetish, but the generation of *material* objects is the upshot of the displacement — difference and deferral — of the productivity of objects. The center is displaced by the metaphor. The metaphor is displaced by the fur. The fur is displaced by the word. The word is displaced by the shoe. The shoe is displaced by the metonymy. The metonymy is displaced by the jockstrap. The jockstrap is displaced by the sign. The sign is displaced by the — The logic of the fetish is the suspension of abstraction and speculation and the expansion of the materiality of the signifier. The "penis-substitute" figuration of the fetish is suspended by the massive productivity of the displacement of objects *from themselves* and *from each other*.

The fetishist's radical materialism is situated in the systems of desire, finance, and discourse. The discovery of sexual difference is originally a *mise-en-scène* of morphological difference of body, materiality, and signifier. Inexplicably, this morphology of anatomical distinction and opposition is conferred signification of binary opposition (penis/not-penis) in the criteria of size and visibility of the general equivalent. How are the penis and the clitoris captured by signification and situated as opposed signs? The penis and the clitoris are otherwise singular objects with no relationship to each other whatsoever. The prehistorical scene of the discovery of sexual difference is pure phonology — textures, scents, sounds, sights, and tastes — with abstraction and speculation of the signified *in absentia*. The overlay of the abstract signified onto the material signifier — *qua* sign — is enigmatic but crucial to the fabrication of the penis *qua* sign and to the fetish *qua* "penis-substitute." Capitalistically, the suture of the gap between the use-value of material objects and the exchange-value of abstract currency is unexplained. How do the banana and the quarter become tethered to each other? The banana and the quarter are otherwise singular objects with no relationship to each other whatsoever. Use-values are pure phonology of everyday utility, and exchange-values are pure psychology of general equivalence. The tourniquet between body and mind of banana and decimal can only be explained as the force of the sign.

As a language, Saussure clarifies that the idea of autonomy of materiality and abstraction as pure phonology of unalloyed materiality of the signifier and pure psychology of undiluted abstraction of the signified is a purely *theoretical* postulate. Practically, the joint of the signifier and the signified is forged in the invention of the word. The singularity of the penis and the clitoris in their joyous affect and tactility is stringently *theoretical*. The use-value of the everyday materialist communist object is strictly *theoretical*. The signifier is sternly *theoretical*. But the pervert's fetish is an embodied sign of the "penis-substitute" whose productivity expands and extends the materialism of objects in the galaxy — from lace to fur to shoe to jockstrap to locker room to football gear to showers to coach's office, and so on. The pervert's fetish may relay a trace of the abstraction and speculation of the signified of the "penis-substitute," but the excess of material objects gestures toward an assembly of concrete and empirical goods and services in the suspension of the *point de capiton*. The wager is that the growth of the universe is material rather than abstract. The Real Penis is the intermediary of the relationship between objects which are split *qua* themselves but sutured to each other *qua* otherness.

The *Verleugnung* of sexual difference is the specific mode of perverse sexuality. Disavowal animates its own modality of temporal simultaneity. *Verleugnung* enjoys the simultaneity of the intuition of the female genitals *qua* defective and absent but also *qua* sexy and proximate. This two-step conversion of Nothing *qua* Something and defect *qua* Sameness⁺ empowers the deconstruction of binarism as an in-process, in-action *fetishing*. The verbed gerund of Ing⁺ is the process of a Becoming which absolves the finalities of departure and destination, and commencement and arrival. The challenge is to imagine the concomitant — Becoming — of the denial of castration and the asseveration of the fact of castration. Freud explicitly says so: "In very subtle cases the fetish itself has become the vehicle of both denying and asseverating the fact of castration."[26] The fetish is the object of enjoyment because it screens the clitoris. But what are the consequences of this both/and denial and declaration — *Verleugnung* — of the convention of phallocentrism and capitalism in the symbolic order? How is kiss-off — not brush-off — articulated concomitantly as Sameness⁺?

The pervert glimpses a Becoming of *fetishing* in which denial and dismissal *and* affirmation and embrace of castration are performed as a verbed gerund of Ing⁺ simultaneously. The fetish is the materialist effect of the extension of the function of the Real Penis and its prepositional indices in the expanses of space. The lazy abstraction and speculation of Freud's "penis-substitute" yield to the productivity of new words and novel objects which return as affirmed from their own negation as excluded. *Qua Verleugnung*, the prohibited is permitted. The neurotic's repressed returns as the symptom of the dream. The madman's foreclosed repeats as the hallucination. But the pervert's *Verleugnung* reappears as itself *qua* "itself." The denied but acknowledged castration — penis/not-penis — reoccurs as a productivity of objects. But these objects extend beyond themselves toward the *jouissance* of "penis" and "not-penis," "sexual difference" and "castration," and an innumerable series of objects which is otherwise censored by the system and its return of symptoms. The fetishist exchanges the symptom for the *sinthome*, and he forsakes identity and desire for *jouissance*.

Patriarchal lack, capitalist scarcity, and the sovereignty of the word are ideologically coded into $-ism. The edict of Sameness⁺ renders the averment of phallocentric castration the contingent condition of its axiomatic other. *Verleugnung* is a "yes" and a "No!" to castration. This acknowledgment and denial return the *sinthome* of the *jouissance* of the series of objects which recurs in the place of expansion rather than contraction. *Verleugnung* is the simultaneity of the dictum of Sameness⁺ that any object is ~~different~~ and ~~identical~~ and ~~equal~~ and ~~unequal~~ to itself because it is ~~coincident~~ and ~~continuous~~ with any object in the system. The Real Penis sublimely lubricates the relationship among and between these objects. The preposition arranges these objects in the expansion of words in the space of the unconscious.

Communism and capitalism, anticentrism and phallocentrism, and the signifier and the sign are forever simultaneously superpositional. Any object collapses into identity/difference and the series of binary oppositions — communism/capitalism, anticentrism/phallocentrism, signifier/sign, and so on — upon the negative observation of the system. The restrictive systems — patriarchy, capitalism, discourse — are the returned symptoms of the negation of the Principle of Sameness⁺ and its nucleus of energy in the (*a*)sexual center of the solar system. The pervert's *sinthome* is the differed and deferred *Trieb* of sexuality, the singular utility of objects in communism, and the triumph of the material signifier over abstraction and speculation in *langue*. *Verleugnung* returns the entirety of the Becoming of the universe. There is a Nothing is Missing in the Spirit of the System which is distanced from the repressions and foreclosures of the select objects of censorship by the Other.

The perverse simultaneity of scarcity and capitalism, and plenitude and communism, indicates the strictly timeless interval of the unconscious between capitalist scarcity and its supply/demand economic relations, on the one hand, and communist plenitude and its overproduction of capitalist excess, on the other hand. The transition between capitalism and communism, between phallocentrism and anticentrism, and between the Madness of Order and the Spirit of the System is the interval of revolution. But the epic revolt is not a simple transformation of the one (capitalism, patriarchy, and madness) into the other (communism, feminism, and Spirit). Rather, the insurrectionary gesture is the pervert's illumination of the overlap between the binary opposition of the series. The systems of $-ism are disposed toward closedness, and the Spirits of communism, feminism, and the sovereignty of the signifier are inclined toward openness. The sutured gap between the pairs of contrasts is the space of the unconscious in a timeless transformation of any object into any other object. The revolution is the Principle of Sameness⁺.

The wager is that the credo of Sameness⁺ progresses the world toward the anti-$-istic Spirits of feminism, communism, and the sovereignty of the signifier. The extensions and expansions of Sameness⁺ — that any object is internal and external in extimacy to any other object — tend toward: feminism and the assembly of deferred sex objects; communism and the assembly of singular use-values; and discourse and the excess of the signifier above the abstractions of the sign. The pervert's fetish is the embodied fur, concrete lace, empirical shoe, and signifier jockstrap (*et al.*) whose suspension of a reductive abstraction and speculation of the "penis-substitute" releases the recurrence of objects which expands rather than contracts in deferred *Trieb*, surplus overproduction, and excess signifier — the solar system. The space of the unconscious is the galaxy of this explosion of objects: sex organs, commodities, words, "sex organs," "commodities," "words," and so on. This Becoming is a simultaneity of *fetishing* in the emollient of the Real Penis and its prepositional and indexical arrangement of the expanses in space.

The male fetishist sutures the wound of oedipal castration. He mobilizes the Principle of Sameness⁺ — any object is internal and external to any other object — in order to convert absence as deficit into absence as presence. The pervert repudiates the male junior's –centric supposition of difference *qua* deficit. The fetish shields the pervert from the threat to his capitalist private property of his penis. The penis is otherwise the fundamental source of his phallic *jouissance*. The fetish substitutes in place of an absence. The fetish is essentially a sublimation *ex nihilo*. Lacan cites the image of Moses, who converts the slavish Jews into the Chosen People, as exemplary of sublimation.[27] Sublimation elevates the scrap from the abyss of absence to the privilege of *das Ding*. This is the ethical endeavor of psychoanalysis.

But the wound of castration is also exemplary of the cut in every object in the series of the system. Psychoanalytically, any object is castrated because it is subordinate to the hierarchy of comparison and contrast of the general equivalent. The fetish bandages the gap between any object and any other object in the system. Capitalistically, any object is castrated because it is structured by private property relationships. These alliances of *le propre* subordinate any object to potential annexation by the corporation, the government, or any other partner in capitalist exchange. Linguistically, any word is castrated because it is spliced and diced in division and opposition from the other signs in the network of signification. There is a castration in the sexual object, the capitalist object, and the linguistic object. The pervert's Sameness[+] sutures these wounds. The fetish abjures the logic of castration in desire, economy, and discourse. The elevation of the scrap of negativity to the recurrence in *Verleugnung* of affirmative positivity is the ethics of psychoanalysis. *Trieb* is the (*a*)sexual modality of this difference and deferral of the edge and margin that otherwise divide and oppose *objets*, commodities, and words from each other. The fetish is the ethical substance.

Perverse queer fetishism is beyond points of departure and arrival, and commencement and destination, because it has no *arche*. The reason that queer fetishism is the Outside of the metaphysics of presence is that it *works*. There is only a cause or origin in an apparatus which does not work. The queer preference for the penis or the clitoris in drag — object *sous rature* and object *sur l'effacement* — is a reasonable consequence of the masculine abject fear of the female body. The homosexual flight from any sexual relationship with the Woman underscores this quip by Lacan: "There is no such thing as a sexual relation."[28] The only *das Ding* as a sexual relationship is the productive and generative series of objects which returns from negation in *Verleugnung* as a positive and affirmed sequence of objects of *jouissance*. In contrast, the tortured trajectory of the man toward heterosexuality needs to be explained. Heterosexuality is a point of departure and arrival, and commencement and destination, because it has an *arche* in anxiety. The reason that male heterosexuality is metaphysical ("I know very well, but I know very well") is that it does not *work*. How can horror be displaced by the orgasm?

Exogamy is a possible explanation for heterosexuality. But the motivation for a female object-choice in the grimaced glare of the horror of the female genitals can only be explained by heteronormativity. The object of heterosexual desire is a conventionalized arbitrariness in which social consensus adjudicates compared and contrasted signification between various objects in a sexual hierarchy. Heterosexuality rules sexuality only because it is the norm of sexuality. But this dominant exemplar does not *work*. There is no such *das Ding* as a heterosexual relation. Rather, *homosexuality* is the evolutionary and transparent original of sexuality. *Heterosexuality* is the deviant and strange copy of a primary homosexual libido. Queer fetishism requires no explanation. But heterosexuality must be meticulously subject to rationale and justification — Reason — in order to make the heterosexual relation possible even in theory. Just so — the capitalist ideology of scarcity and the linguistic hierarchy of the word are also subject to *arche* because they do not *work*. Capitalism is overrun with overproduction, and discourse is stressed by mishaps. Communism is the original mode of production, and the signifier is the elemental integrant of the system of *langue*. Communism, the signifier, and queer fetishism *work*.

Queer sexual energy is the original (dis)organization of sexuality in nascent play. The embryonic exchange of aims and objects is antecedent to the pairs of oppositions, such as activity/passivity. Freud proscribes these oppositions as the key to difference in the field of sexuality of male-active/female-passive. This includes the marginalization of the so-called activity of the clitoris in favor of the passive womb *qua* asylum of the vagina for the penis. Freud elaborates the tortured development toward the proper femininity for the female junior in his essay, "On Femininity" (1930). This female trajectory is a cakewalk in comparison to the male junior's forced arrival at heterosexuality. The male junior — somehow — overcomes the horror of the vagina and the clitoris, suspends anxiety and fear of loss and death, and abandons the mother-substitute as object-choice for the father of the ego-ideal. The man also agrees to actively and aggressively enjoy his place in the womb and asylum of the vagina. Utterly, the development toward male heterosexuality is an improbability which borders on the impossible.

In contrast, the fetishist conceals lack with plenitude. Any object is any other object. The extimacy of any object sullies the arrangements of *le propre* among desired objects, capitalist commodities, and linguistic words. The fetishist's magic trick which screens lack and absence with plenitude and presence is successful even if shards and blades of castration *qua* difference — but not *qua* deficit — ooze into the chambers of the bedroom. The talented fetishist valorizes scarcity and elevates the scrap of debt to the level of the dignity of *das Ding*. There may be no such thing as a sexual relation even for the fetishist. But it can be rejoined: heterosexuality is the unthinkable; fetishism is the resolution; homosexuality is the organic; and queer (*a*)sexuality is the ideal. There is such a *das Ding* as a relation. This relation is communist queer (*a*)sexuality.

Textually, the fetishist's discourse is organized by the "I know very well, but nevertheless…." Permutations of this text are legion. The "but nevertheless…" embraces all cognitive and sensory approaches to the world which are outside of the strict Reason of epistemology. The pervert's discourse resolves knowledge and belief, and science and religion, with the *bothness* and *andness* of the economy of *Verleugnung*. The pervert's disavowal is shifty and sketchy. Disavowal is neither incoherent nor unreasonable. It is witty and bitty, scrappy and happy, and patchy 'n catchy. *Verleugnung* returns the negation of epistemology ("I know very well") to the affirmative and positive objects of belief, wonder, amusement, joy, faith, *jouissance,* madness, love, and so on. Castration and the epistemology ("I know very well") of the Real of sexual difference are supplanted by a *jouissance* which forsakes identity and desire for pleasure.

The system of castrative epistemology ("I know very well") purports to be neurotic with its dynamic of the repression of the disagreeable idea of not-penis and the return of this repression with the symptoms of identity and desire. But $-ism is in sooth schizophrenic. The dynamic of negation and return is of a *neurotic repression* but *schizoid return* of the Real of sexual difference. *Neurotic repression* and *schizoid return* are the parallactic overlap of perversion and the Neurotic Foreclosure (*rejet névrotique*) of the system *with itself*. This *rejet névrotique* is the *Verleugnung* of the generative return of the objects of repression (foreclosure) to a system of an expanded set of *objets de jouissance*. The Madness of Order purports to repress the disagreeable idea of sexual difference, but it succeeds in the return of these objects to affirmative productivity of an extended series of fetishes. The "I know very well, but nevertheless" articulates the openness toward otherness in the Principle of Sameness⁺ after the displacement of epistemology by Unreason.

The pervert sutures the cut of difference *qua* deficit and its consequential anxious symptomatology of the phallocentrism of patriarchy, the deficit and debt of capitalism, and the positive unity of the word of discourse. The pervert illuminates the aperture and closure of the parallactic window pane in which system and $-ism, neurotic and schizoid, and every other binary opposition collide into each other in the articulation of the pervert's revised answer to the ontological question: "What is?" Perversely, it is what it is not. The system is Being *qua* Nothingness. But the pervert strictly adheres to the Freudian considerations of representability and the primary process perverse translation of the original latent truth into the offbeat transcription of the desire. The pervert does so in order to bypass the censor. Truth must be coherently coded, both as a legible and manifest symptom and as a wild and unruly *sinthome* of *jouissance*.

The pervert's discourse is tamed by a will to hermeneutics and a genial commitment to interlocution and monological coherence. The pervert's rendition of the schizoid's crazy talk is a both/and *écriture* that finitely limits the otherwise infinite *différance* of the schizoid's lunatical discourse. The strange couplet in the pervert's project is the fetish and the clitoris. The fetish is considered any representation (jockstrap), and the clitoris is configured as any other object in the system which is subordinate to castration, at the edges and margins of its own loss and death. The consistency in the parallactically overlapped project of the fetishization of the object is the trauma of the original — difference *qua* deficit — and the cure of the translation — the Principle of Sameness⁺ and the Logic of Difference.

The fetish indicates that the parallactic gap between original/translation and affliction/cure is not only twisted and displaced but a Sameness⁺. This order defers the horror of difference *qua* deficit because any object is the internal and external — extimatic — double and circle of any other. The transposition between difference and deficit is only possible if the object of horror resists the regime of general equivalence and the comparable and contrastable standard of exchange. The clitoris is redeemed as singular — rather than identical/different or equal/unequal — in a Sameness⁺ which expands the series of uncastrated fetishes and objects in the skies. The Principle of Sameness⁺ eschews identity and difference, and equality and inequality, and any other binary opposition of comparison and contrast. Sameness⁺ is the general *inequivalent*. The objects which are otherwise in exchange are freed from their subordination to an arbitrary but conventionalized standard. This yardstick must impose restriction and limitation in its work of comparison and contrast.

Psychoanalytically, the measurement of size and visibility limits (*a*)sexual objects which do not conform to these criteria. Capitalistically, the exchange-value of the commodity limits the quantity of goods and services which can be introduced into the system. Discursively, the syntax and semantics of the word circumscribe the configuration of text within a perimeter of proper and improper *écriture*. The Logic of Difference (A ≠ A = B, and so on) frees any object from the edges and margins of its own isolated unity of identity and desire. The Principle of Sameness⁺ frees sexes and bodies, commodities and use-values, and words and texts from the constraints of the general equivalent. Any object becomes a fetish *qua* prop and pillar for any other object. The general equivalent of the phallus in patriarchy, the commodity in captialism, and the word in language is jammed by an insistent extimacy of objects whose materiality oozes beyond the borders (*le propre*) of units which can be measured and quantified and then exchanged and counted. The fetish may be a screen for the clitoris, but the clitoris is also a screen for the fetish.

The manifest forms of fetishism are the fur, lace, shoe and jockstrap — but also televisual representations, filmic texts, print objects, online sites, and old-fashioned pin-ups of Keanu Reeves, Ryan Gosling, Leo DiCaprio, Tom Cruise, Tobey Maguire, Joseph Gordon-Levitt, and so on which extend to the entire battery of Hollywood hottie-signifiers in the system of desire. These disagreeable (or agreeable) ideas are subject to neurotic repression *qua* psychotic foreclosure (*rejet névrotique*) as well as to a return from *Verleugnung* as "themselves" in an open and expansive system of affirmation. The series is prolific. The succession of manufactured fetishes extends beyond any of the constraints and limitations of negated disagreeable (or agreeable) objects. The pervert's *jouissance* is representation. The pervert adores the image, the look, the gesture, the fashion, the smile, the tease, the pout, the cadence of the voice, the dance of the shoes, the arch of the back, and the incandescence of the color. The pervert's world is representational. The pervert is the fount of what Baudrillard indexes as the simulacrum and the simulation. The pervert savors portraits and photographs which are divorced from the guarantee of the real and the true. This is the reason that the pervert's favored modality of negation, *Verleugnung*, returns representation *qua* "representation" rather than *qua* the truth or reality in the guarantee of the general equivalent of comparison and contrast. The representation is singular precisely because it is parallactically overlapped — but not exchanged — with any other representation in the system.

The pervert delights in a picture which is alienated from reference and the general equivalent of God, currency, phallus, and father. This standardization of equivalence otherwise guarantees the specular identity between signifier and signified, reference and reality, image and truth, and so on. As Baudrillard puts it,

> All Western faith and good faith became engaged in this wager on representation: that a sign could refer to the depth of meaning, that a sign could be exchanged for meaning and that something could guarantee this exchange — God of course.[29]

Baudrillard's claim is that Western trust is organized by the pact that representation refers to a signification for which it could be exchanged — love *for* a red, red rose which is equal, equivalent, coincident, continuous, in short, *qua* Being. The trust is that exchange and speculation will be guaranteed by a third term of God, science, or the standardized general equivalents in the contemporary West: phallus, father, currency, and the sign.

Psychoanalytically, the exchange of penis for not-penis not only hierarchizes sexual objects, but it also generates the symptoms of the male junior's anxiety and the female junior's envy. Under capitalism, the exchange of commodities hierarchizes the value between two objects which are otherwise entirely unrelated in their use-value singularity. The guarantee of exchange also constrains the proliferation of goods and services because comparison and contrast are predicated on Something is Missing. Currency is the trade of castration. Linguistically, the word is exchanged for other words, such that an equality or inequality — rather than a singular Sameness⁺ — overwrites the play and excess which escape the margins and edges of the positive unity of the word. Baudrillard's point is that the "wager" or speculative punt with representation has withered. Simulacrum and simulation have usurped this "good faith" in representation. Perversely: "I know very well that sexual difference structures loss and death, but nevertheless the penis is not the penis and the clitoris is not the clitoris but the penis is — ~~Being~~ — the clitoris, and so on." This disavowal is not "bad faith." Rather, this alternative belief is in the singularity of Being in which any object is the same as any other object because each object is *different from itself.* The *Spaltung* opens the system to infinite expansion without the shackles of exchange.

The pervert is the conceptual persona in the psychoanalytic scene who wagers for *representation* rather than for *reality* as the source of the ecstatic joys of figuration, metaphor, image, picture, portrait, photograph, snapshot, statue, drawing, sketch, and so on. The fetishes — fur, lace, shoe, and jockstrap — are representational props for the absence of the female-penis/male-clitoris. The traces of abstraction and speculation of castration anxiety and their recuperation by the "penis-substitute" are secondary to the representational *jouissance* of the signifier in play. The fetish is a substitution of the body *qua* referent of lack for the object *qua* representation of plenitude. The exchange is neither "good faith" nor "bad faith" because it is not based on the general equivalence of the wager of correspondence and adequation between sign and referent, and between fetish and reality. Perversely, this is the reason that the clitoris is a fetish. Any object is a fetish because the pervert experiences the singular Sameness⁺ of the object in its internal and external — extimate — relationship *to itself* and *to any other object* in an expansive system of representations, fetishes, centers, signs, metaphors, words, substitutions, and so on.

Perversity is a simulation of a *singular faith* because it is a break with the epistemology of the "I know very well" of the "good faith" or "bad faith" of the wager on representation and its correspondence to truth and adequation to reality. The referential guarantee that representation corresponds to reality is the promise of a stable and universal hierarchy of value with a "depth of meaning." The penis is valuable in its size and visibility in comparison and contrast to the not-penis. The commodity is exchanged for another commodity at a value of quantification to be determined by supply/demand dynamics. The word is adequate to its relationship to other words in the conventions of syntax and semantics.

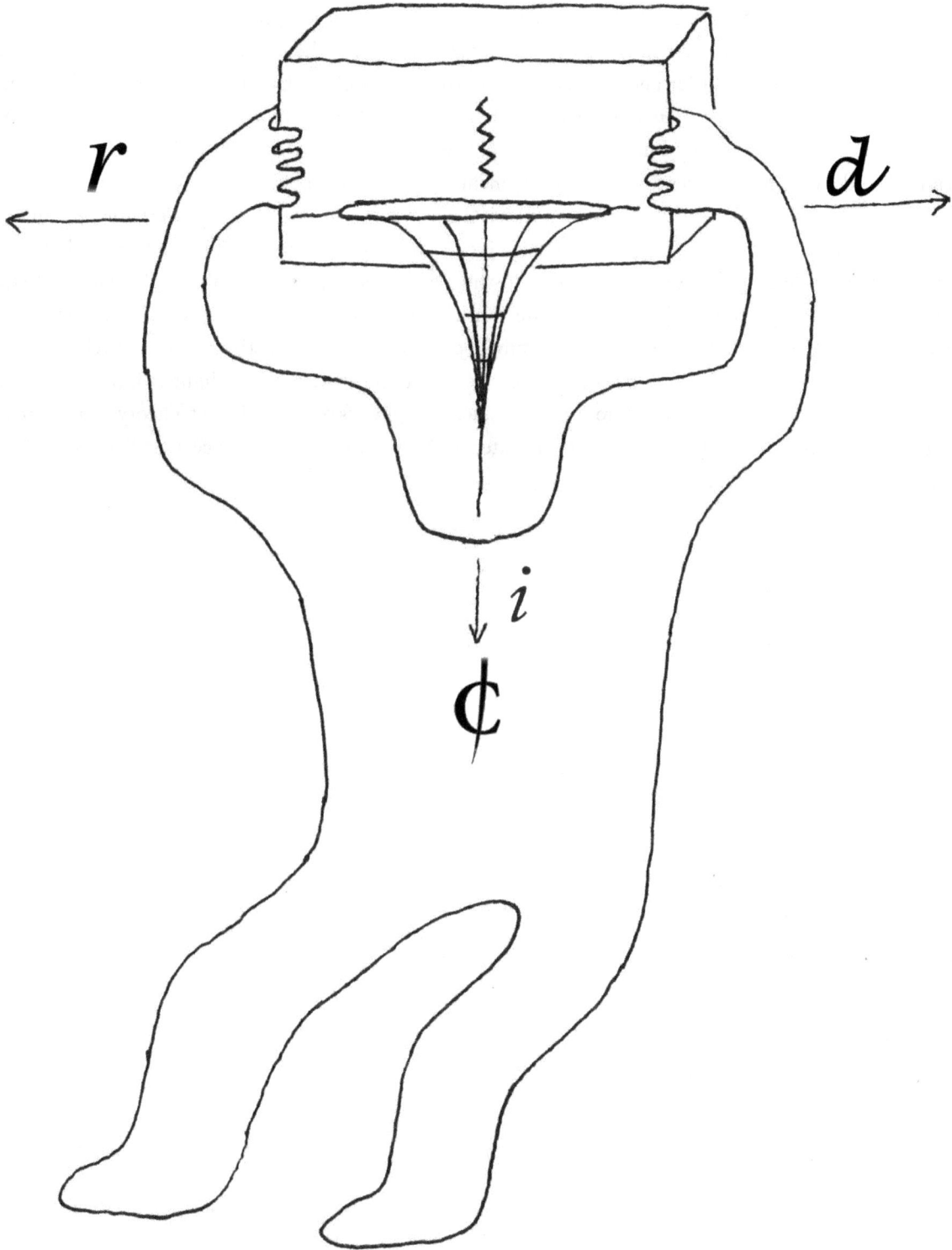

Figure 3.6 Absence as the Condition of Presence

This illustration portrays the fragmentation and fissure which result from the creation of the space of language (center, above). This structure is made possible by the symbolic order and the Real occlusion of the center (center). The parallactic gap is the space which is opened — but not yet closed — such that the system of *langue* is operational and functional. The Woman (center) is the Outside of the system. The occluded center (center) is the veiled nucleus of the center of the structure. The source of castration is at once the site of the Woman's expulsion from the system and the effect of the exclusion of the (returned) clitoris from and to the Madness of Order. This exclusion and return of the clitoris are symbolized by the concave head of the Woman (above) which situates the Woman and the system in relation to themselves *qua* themselves. As represented in the Lambert Substitutability Function, the i indicates the imaginary dimension in mathematics. This imaginary order emerges in order to suture the fragmentation in the symbolic dimension. This fragmentation is represented by the three-dimensional figure which illustrates the space of language. Fragmentation is the consequence of the Real and its disruption of the coherence of the symbolic order. The r refers to relationality. The d represents deferral. These variables refer to the simultaneous preservation and dissolution of stable signification in the symbolic order. The absolute constant is the sum of these two variables. The absolute constant is also the constant (speed of an electromagnetic wave) which is derived from the relationship of identity to itself within an infinite but bound universe. This constant speed of light is isomorphic to the reverberations of an Inside which is cut from any Outside. This physics parallels the Set Theory of mathematics and the linguistics of structuralism. Sets have no exterior. Non-presence and absence are a Sameness[+] within an infinite but bound system.

Notes & Sketches —

"But nevertheless," the suspension of the general equivalent of the symbolic order — neither good faith nor bad faith but *singular faith* — is the cut of the Real into the otherwise smooth coordination of the symbolic order and its general equivalence of sex organ of desire above drive, commodity of scarcity above abundance, and word of signification above the play of the signifier and signified of value. The *Verwerfung* of the general equivalent is the essence of the system. The return of this foreclosure is the Real Symbolic and the expansion of the edges and margins of isolated *le propre* to the extensions of the limits of articulation in the Real. The return of the Real fosters the conditions for simulation and the pervert's ecstatic *jouissance* in representation and in the playful dance of words and texts above the stern inflexibility of exchanges and calculations.

A simulation is the gap between the referential so-called sex in the flesh and body of Foucauldian "spirals of power and pleasure" and the so-called "sexuality" of the regulation of identity and selfhood of Foucauldian "perverse implantation."[30] The pervert discovers that *jouissance* is situated in spirals of perversity and in their queer implantations and queerer contestations. The perverse implantation delivered us "the hysterical Woman," "the masturbating offspring," "the homosexual," and "the pedophile" in the nineteenth-century. Up next, "the polyamorous," "the pansexual," "the transgender," "the postgender," "the gender queer," "the asexual," and so on. The sequence of fetishes in the "spirals of power and pleasure" expands in the "perverse implantation." Why be "the homosexual" of the nineteenth-century or "the gender queer" of the twenty-first century when the fetishist can simply don the costume and choose the prop for the representational role-play of his favored *mise-en-scène* of the moment? Fetishistically, the materialities of these costumes and props are supplemented by the abstract significance of the "penis-substitute" and its displacement of castration anxiety. But the speculative signified is overrun by the play and game of *Trieb* — tease — between the man and his Boy. The representational artwork is at the ready for the play-role of a series of gestures and habits which can only extend and expand objects and fetishes — "the daddy" — in the galaxy of the perverse implantation of identity and desire and the queer explosion of *jouissance*.

"But nevertheless" — the Western good faith in the indelible bond between sign and referent is also the obstacle to the fetishist's so-called neat and artful solution of the fetish. The fetish is the in-exchange of the Something of the "penis-substitute" *qua* the expansion of the succession of objects in the system for the Nothingness of the clitoris. This trade involves the swap of representation for referent, and jockstrap for clitoris — but in the absence of the apparatus of the general equivalent. Any object can substitute for any other object. The object of the Principle of Sameness⁺ is a singularity which cannot be recuperated by the exchange economy of standardization. A general equivalence of perversion would otherwise dictate that the clitoris be screened by a specific quantity and quality of object, such as the razor blade. Fetishism is certainly bad faith — "I know very well, but nevertheless" — because perversion refuses the pact with reference. *Verleugnung* confesses ("knows very well") that the fetish is exactly what it is not: penis-substitute ≠ female penis. But disavowal also rebuts ("but nevertheless") this bad faith. A bad faith is exchanged for a good faith. The fetishist's simultaneous *good faith* and *bad faith* are the essence of his denial of castration. The fetishist is in good faith and bad faith because he affirms the wager with representation in his denial that the fetish is exactly what it is: the fur, lace, shoe, and jockstrap. These objects perfectly speculate and totally exchange for Leonardo DiCaprio's pin-up, and so on.

But the caveat to the double faith of the fetishist is his *singular faith* that any object is exchangeable — but neither quantitatively nor qualitatively — for any other object in the succession of expansive fetishes. The only arbiter for the individual pervert is *jouissance*. A general equivalence of *jouissance* may be operative for any unique fetishist, but there is no universalization of this standard of *jouissance*. But the pervert glimpses the truth of *jouissance*: it is buoyed by Something is Missing. It is only the horizonal Nothing is Missing — postpatriarchal feminism, economic communism, and the discursive signifier — which tends toward an Other *jouissance*. The specific standard of *jouissance* for any individual fetishist is less about quantity and quality and more about the difference and deferral — masochistic edge — of the extension of the objects and bodies, goods and services, and signifiers and materialities in the system. *Jouissance* is about expenditure and excess. The pervert collects fetishes, expends them, gathers fetishes, distributes them, accumulates fetishes, disperses them, and so on. This is the reason that the *faux* modality of negation in *Verleugnung* returns in positivity and affirmation. The pervert relishes the excess in order to secrete it.

The situation for the pervert is the foreseen both/and celebration of contradiction in which the fetishist's bad faith, skeptical conversion of speculation between any object *qua* fetish *qua* penis-substitute *qua* maternal phallus, on the one hand, and good faith, trustful affirmation of speculation between fetish and penis-substitute and the sister's penis, on the other hand, indicate that good faith and bad faith are the same trust in their successes and failures. The wager plays the shoe against the fur on one night, or the poster of Brad Pitt against the hologram of Hayden Christensen on another night. Fetishism inspires good faith and bad faith in both the referent, we are hopeful, or the simulation, we are duped, "but nevertheless" the charade of good faith and bad faith prevails. The principled *singular faith* achieves its dominance in a sequence of objects of *jouissance,* night after night, which cannot be compared and contrasted — exchanged — for any other series of objects. The trace of the good faith and the bad faith of the penis-substitute is the substrate of the fetishist's *jouissance.* But the purpose of the originary suture of the wound in the rescripted "perception" of difference *qua* penis is displaced by the unquantifiable and unqualifiable *jouissance* of an expanse of returned objects from the prohibitions of the culture. The pervert senses that the refuse of the society is the salvage of his enjoyment.

The pervert packs his suitcase with his choice props — the fur, lace, shoe, jockstrap, penis-substitute, Sameness[+], center, signifier, Real Symbolic, metaphor, word, Real Penis, Tom Cruise photo-op, metonymy, and so on. The pervert does so in good faith. He believes that, as the aperture of difference *qua* deficit approaches, the closure of deficit *qua* difference will illuminate the overlap between a good faith and a bad faith. The pervert "but nevertheless" strives for the impossible of the *tout autre* of the female penis and its destruction of patriarchal castration and lack, capitalist scarcity and private property, linguistic word and syntax and semantics, and the generalized *le propre* of the patrolled edges and borders around self-same and self-identical autonomous units. The simultaneity of the pervert's bad faith and good faith is the essence of the affirmative and revolutionary *Verleugnung* of his intervention in the galaxy. The *singular faith* expands objects and extends *jouissance* because the excess does not need to be reincorporated into a system of general equivalence and the cuts and scrapes of the patriarchal chop-job, the capitalist mark-up, and the linguistic word-craze.

Excess is the supreme principle, and its surpluses and deficits are (un)accountable by the general equivalent. The rocket to celestial planets and intergalactic space satellites in the stars is a fetish adventure land of space sex in the timeless unconscious of the moon. This is the unconscious space in which the pervert disavows absence and restriction not only of the referent *qua* deficit. The object substitutes in the place of the clitoris, and the obverse. The pervert also disavows the difference of any object in the global orgiastic fetish fantasy land of the Other. There is only the *singular object* because the differences and deferrals in the traces of *Trieb* and its masochistic edge abjure the departure and arrival, and commencement and destination, of the presence of the Being of any object in its self-sameness and self-identity. The *singular object* dominates the system because *the object* is yet to be present in a system of relationality and constructionism. There is no object.

The word is a *Spaltung* which is split both externally and internally. The architecture of *langue* is the word, but the architectonics of the substrate of the word is the material signifier and the abstract signified. The system of language is practical. The architectonics of the system — signifier and signified — is theoretical. The word is split between the signifier (sound, mark) and the signified (abstraction, concept). The signifier and the signified as theoretically autonomous parts are joined as the practical word. The *Spaltung* in the word is both practical and theoretical. Practically, the signification of the word is split between texts and contexts which retroactively (*Nachträglichkeit, après coup*) supplement the word. The word may be a self-contained and self-sufficient positive unity on its own, but it is also subordinate to the *mise-en-scène* of the succession of other words which exceeds it in text and context. Theoretically, the word is split between materiality and conceptuality, and between the signifier and the signified. The word is split practically as a word which is situated in a network of other words, and the word is split theoretically between materiality and abstraction. The word is a parallax, and it is overrun by the Real of its excess in the semantics and syntax of other words and in its surplus of materiality and abstraction in the architectonics of the value of the signifier and the signified. The self-identity and self-sameness of the sign are displaced by an excess of words, a surplus of materiality, and a remainder of abstraction. The pervert glimpses the architectonics of the word — *value* — and appreciates that a word is precisely not itself. The excess of the theoretical architectonics over the practical architecture of *langue* is the object of Derrida's *différance* and the material and abstract differences and deferrals which extend the *arche* of the object. There is no object. There is no word.

The standardizations in the system are the father for social relations, currency for economic relations, the sign for linguistic relations, and the phallus for sexual relations. The sign is subordinate to a *Spaltung* which disrupts the system of syntax and semantics and the possibility of the word. The architectonics of the value of the signifier and the signified undoes the architecture of signification of the word. Another general equivalent, the phallus for sexual relations, is also subordinate to a *Spaltung*. The phallus has two distinct functions. First, the phallus pins signification with the *point de capiton* which arrests the slip and slide of meaning-making and retroactively (*Nachträglichkeit, après-coup*) quilts signification at the ends of the excesses of the signifier and the signified. Second, the phallus is the *metaphor* for the index of the object-cause of desire. The phallus indicates the *objet petit a*. The phallus is the *ur*-preposition which directs the transactions and translations in the *mise-en-scène* of desire. These distinct operations overlap. The phallus as a *metaphor* is subordinate to the differences with and deferrals toward other metaphors for which it purports to be the *ur*-metaphor. The slip and slide of the phallus as a metaphor strive to arrest its own play with its own function of the *point de capiton*. But the phallus is split by its function as *index* of a *metaphor* which is subordinate to its own *indexicality*. The index gestures beyond its own metaphor ("phallus") toward other metaphors. The phallus polices this slippage with its *point de capiton*. The button-tie strives to suture the *Spaltung* in the phallus. The *point de capiton* endeavors to return the indexed metaphor *for itself to itself* as the phallus. The *Spaltung* of the phallus is between the enforcement of signification and the consequent destabilization of *arche*. There is no object. There is no word. There is no phallus.

The interval between the success of the pervert's manifesto and elucidation of the system and the madman's wails and submission to the system is situated at the site of the (im)possibility of the *point de capiton*. The phallus is a deferral to other metaphors. But does this indexical voyage of *ur*-preposition and its network of prepositions arrive at the phallus *qua* phallus or *qua* metaphor — or not *qua* at all? The pervert's fashionable closet of furs, laces, shoes, jockstraps, dildos, chains, whips, KY, and pin-ups disavows the phallus because the pervert understands the constraints and limitations of metaphor. The metonymization of metaphor extends the indexical (~~phallic~~) expansion of the world. But metaphor itself contracts any excess of objects beyond its purview. The madman is unconstrained by the phallus or by its other metaphorical avatars. The madman is untamed by the *point de capiton*. He is subject to an endless deferral in the metonymization of metaphor. The psychotic's *Verwerfung* repudiates the phallus and metaphor as such. According to Lacan: "The phallus is the privileged signifier of this mark in which the role of *Logos* is wedded to the advent of desire."[31] The phallus is the nodal point between Reason in language and the manifestation of identification and metaphor, on the one hand, and Unreason in language and the mobilization of desire and metonymy, on the other hand. This interval between Reason and metaphor and Unreason and Metaphoricity is the vigilant gap that the pervert must negotiate between an articulation of the madman's secret truth of $-ism and the collapse into chaos and gobbledygook of the madman himself.

The phallus opens and closes the *mise-en-abyme* of Metaphoricity. This Metaphoricity is the structure of the madman's subjectivity and objectivity, and it is the object of the pervert's *jouissance* and the expansion of the globe. Metaphoricity is repressed by the neurotic, disavowed by the pervert, and foreclosed by the schizoid. The perverse *Verleugnung* of Metaphoricity returns as "itself" in the expansion of the succession of alphabets, words, letters, texts, contexts, and so on — but with the necessary contraction of the *point de capiton*. The button-tie enables the pervert to coherently express a metonymization of metaphor with a metaphorization of metonymy. The force of contraction is the reference of the prolific set of fetishes in the galaxy to the abstraction of the penis-substitute and the originary scene of the disavowal of the Real of sexual difference. Lost, the pervert returns to his *arche* in castration and its acknowledgement. There is no object. There is no word. There is no phallus. But there is a penis.

The feminist charge that the phallus in Lacan's work is a vexed example of phallocentrism misses the mark. The phallus is *metaphorcentric*. The phallus is isomorphic to the center in Derrida's analysis of structure. This center (phallus) is subject to a "number of different sign-substitutions," as Derrida says, which are put into play for the functionality of center.[32] The phallus is chosen by Freud and Lacan as the privileged signifier because psychoanalysis is primarily a theory of *sexual* difference. But a feminist may retort, "Why not the *clitorallus*?" Why is the subject of comparison the male? Why is the object of juxtaposition the female? Or is the male precisely the proximal object of envy from the perspective of the Woman?

The pervert's *Verleugnung* of the phallus eschews the metaphor because it extends the metaphorical avatars for the phallus to include any objects which index the *objet petit a* in the fantasy. Perverse disavowal disowns metaphor as a self-contained, self-sufficient, and autonomous series of words. *Verleugnung* extends metaphor and identity toward an excess in metonymy and desire. The pervert resists a radical commitment to the metonymization of metaphor, and he returns to metaphor in order to stretch and extend — spin out — the self-identity and self-sameness of the word toward an otherness of excess metaphors. These sexual metaphors may be objects which exceed the penile connotation of the word "phallus" and its metaphor for the generalized equivalence of sexual difference. Anally, penis = feces = baby = Hollywood pin-up = gay porno star = double-dong = the jockstrap, and so on.

These anal equivalences (Freud uses the equal symbol in his work on anal eroticism) must be understood as any series of objects which is internal and external in an extimate Sameness[+] — but not equality (=) — to any other object in the system. The phallus is singular, but it is only one of innumerable metaphors which extends and stretches toward others. The phallus is fragmented, and the pervert's *jouissance* is the joy of the representation — taken and left — of this excess succession of fragmentations. The *Verleugnung* of the phallus returns as the "clitorallus." There may be no penis after all. But there is a return of the "clitorallus."

The *mise-en-abyme* of Metaphoricity is an endless series of substitutions that the word strives to contain in its own word. The parallactic overlap of the word *qua* word in traversal in text and context and the word *qua* arrest and restraint in *point de capiton* is the abyssal joke of the phallus and its avatars. These avatars — betwixt word *qua* textuality and word *qua* arrest — are a succession of objects in the system. Fetishistically, the fetish substitutes for the penis-substitute — textuality *and* arrest — which substitutes for the maternal phallus — textuality *and* arrest — which substitutes for the fur — textuality *and* arrest — which substitutes for the lace — textuality *and* arrest — which substitutes for the shoe — textuality *and* arrest — which substitutes for the jockstrap — textuality *and* arrest — which substitutes for a metonymization of metaphor whose succession of material objects can only be checked by the perverse return to the abstraction of penis-substitute and the trace of anxiety and its containment in representation. Metaphoricity — *metonymized metaphor* — is savored by the pervert as the play of substitution. Every word is the phallus *qua* every word. Any object is the phallus because any object is the extimate obverse of any other object.

This Metaphoricity displaces the metaphysics of presence of any word with the function of coordination, such as the "phallus" or the "clitorallus." The phallus is merely one word for this exercise of the conjoinment of the signifier (*Logos*) and desire. At best, the phallus is a metaphor for the *mise-en-abyme* of Metaphoricity. The phallus is a metaphallus, but this metalanguage is subject to a sequence of horizontal and vertical *metameta* which undoes the primacy of the phallus or any of its *über*-avatars. The phallus *qua* Metaphoricity or a metalanguage is strictly Outside of the system. The phallus must be occluded and concealed in order to emerge as the metaphor for the system in its entirety. But any word and every word perform this task. Every word is Outside of the system. This is so even as every word is simultaneously Inside of the system. The Lacanian ~~phallus~~ is under erasure like Heideggerian ~~Being~~ and its ontico-ontological difference. The (any) metaphallus and metaBeing return in *Verleugnung* as extensions of word play and object *jouissance*.

Closeted

The unconscious space is hidden to the individual patient and to the society. The psychoanalytic symptom can be both an individual tick and a social pathology. The symptom is visible but not recognized in its latent significance. The truth is closeted in the unconscious of both the individual patient and the society. The issue is the content of the unconscious truth in both the individual quirk and the social sickness. Each of the three patients in psychoanalysis — neurotic, psychotic, and pervert — occupies its own unique space of the unconscious. The schizoid resists any coherent space of the unconscious. The pervert sustains a liminal and ruptured (un)conscious. The gap between the conscious and the unconscious is disrupted by the pervert's experience of the parallactic gap between the manifest and the latent dimensions. The neurotic is the only patient whose psychical configuration can be understood to strictly include an unconscious. Freud's discovery of the unconscious originally applied to hysterics and the defense mechanisms of neurotics. It is necessary to uncover the banished closet of the unconscious as it is manifest simply in the neurotic but also more complexly in the schizoid and the pervert. The neurotic's unconscious contracts the ego-system. The madman's absence of an unconscious explodes everyday existence. The pervert's *faux* unconscious opens space for the fetishes and objects which return from and as their disavowal. The pervert grasps that the unconscious is internally and externally in a relationship of extimacy to the conscious. The pervert glimpses the bend in the space of the unconscious. This torus twists the unconscious into the space of the ego.

Neurotic Illness

The latent content of the hysteric's discourse is both enjoyment and desire. Unexpectedly, *jouissance* and *désir* are both internal and external — extimate — to each other. The neurotic's latent content of the repressed in the unconscious is truth. Truth is coded by the culture. But truth is also peculiar to the specificities of the lives of individual hysterics. Freud's case histories of hysteria, such as the Dora monograph (1905), articulate the particularities of the desires and repressions of the lives of discrete patients. Interpretation of hysterical and latent content presumes the deconstructive surprise of otherness or the navel of the dream. This pivotal otherness makes the interpretation of the text an enjoyable enterprise for the analyst. This is so even if the reduction of manifest representation to its latent content is variable but scripted by the analyst's wearied and *clichéd* chirography. It is worth noting that so-called *free* association is otherwise *forced* by the organization of the signifying chain. The pervert surmises that freedom is circumscribed by necessity and that the wiles of the *Es* are scripted by the dictates of the *Über-Ich*.

The neurotic's latent content is sexual because Western culture represses "sex," according to Freud. But Western society certainly does not repress "sexuality," as Foucault makes clear.[33] So-called "sex" is repressed at least in Freud's era because it is perceived as a threat to the individual and to society. Today, prohibited wishes, such as public sex, incest, rape, sadomasochism, threesomes, bareback, orgies, bug-chasing, pedastry, and asexuality are pressed into the closet of the unconscious. These desires return as symptoms of these unspeakables. The symptoms manifestly return to the system of the ego and to the society of the secondary process. This process is the dispersed chain of signification which exceeds any points of spatial or temporal coordination. The network of words is organized as the Reason of the positive units of signs, even if the architectonics of this system is the Unreason of the value of signifiers and signifieds. Madness is the latent truth of the system. This Unreasonable truth returns from the Real *qua* the disruption of Reason of its own internal madness. The return of (Un)Reason *qua* (Un)Reason is the structure of the symbolic order. This work of the system of the ego is both a cause and an effect of the latent content.

The system represses the unacceptable neurotic wish which returns as the essence of the secondary process of logic and rationality. The system *represses* the neurotic wish, but it returns as the *Real* of the madness of the system. Sex is repressed, but it returns as hallucinations and delusions of sex. Self-pleasure (*et al.*) is simultaneously both a return of *Verdrängung* and a return of *Verwerfung*. The pervert's *Verleugnung* returns a disavowed sex as the "sexuality" of words, centers, signs, fetishes, substitutes, and an extended series of objects in the sexual system. The latent truth of the repression of "sex" in neurosis is the return of an abundance of ordinary and weird "sexualities." The neurotic represses the wish of "sex" but returns the fetishes of "sexuality." The excess of the parallactic overlap between repression and disavowal is the manifest representation which mediates between conscious and unconscious.

Reason is the force which quells the revolts of the unconscious. The relationship between latent and manifest, and between primary and secondary, is causal because the interrelationships do not *work*. The interval between arrival and departure, and between commencement and destination, is not suspended in an endless trace because there is a chink in the system — translational mediation and interpretive pyrotechnics — between the layers of the conscious and the unconscious. The psychoanalytic architecture does not *work*. This dysfunction is the dynamic of repression, return, symptom, and the misfire of the latent/manifest, primary/secondary, and unconscious/conscious oppositions. The snafu is visible to patient and analyst. It is structured as a causality with an *arche* or navel of the dream. The *arche* of the departure and destination of the letter and the commencement and arrival of the letter is undecidable. This is structurally so for Derrida. It is axiomatically so for Lacan.

But in the presence of the malfunction of the system, the cause of the binarism of the system is isolated: the repression of "sex," for Freud; and the production of the "perverse implantation," for Foucault. Conjointly for Freud and Foucault, the closet of the neurotic's unconscious is the shameful and guilty desire for sex. The distinction of the pervert is that he prefers the decorations of the "perverse implantation" to the boredom of "sex." Neurotically, it is the pervert who represses "sex" in order to return in *Verleugnung* the series of "perverse implantations" in an expanded galaxy of the props, costumes, scripts, and scenery of the fantasies of fetishes.

The pervert fathoms that the manic liberation of the manifest representations of "sexuality," rather than the analytic interpretation of these symptoms, is the royal road to the *jouissance* of the fetish.

The neurotic's wish is repressed by a system of the conscious of the ego and the Other. The neurotic's desire for "sex" is a threat to the order of Reason. This order produces these wishes as its underside. The system is the proviso of the constitution and surveillance of a so-called "sexuality" in the absence of any so-called "sex." This "sex" is presumably less pleasurable — boring — than any "sexuality" and its myriad figurations of pleasure — fascinating.[34] The sexuality of the hysteric's latent content renders interpretation obscenely simple. But sexuality also makes the cure of the neurotic malady difficult in a culture which prohibits sexual freedoms or, as Michael Warner says, "sexual autonomy."[35] The neurotic is differently interpreted by Freud and Foucault. Psychoanalysis postulates a negation and repression of a materialist "sex" which is strangely located in the abstractions of the ether of the web of words. Foucault posits a production and regulation of "sexuality" which is imprecisely situated. This "sexuality" is associated with vectors of forces in intersection with flesh and body. The pervert concludes that the signifier of "sex" *qua* "sexuality" is the locus of *jouissance*. A return of *Verleugnung* of the latent content *qua* manifest representation — *latent manfiestation* — is the object of perverse play and performance. This is a sex *of* sexuality.

Freud's neurotic endures a latent content of "sex." This latent content is suspended in the nether side of the signifier — neither here nor there nor up nor down but elsewhere in the atmosphere of the chutes and ladders of the network of representation. In contrast, Foucault's neurotic suffers production and regulation of "sexuality." Neurotic "sexuality" is invented by the diffuse so-called power/knowledge networks of institutions and discourses. This "sexuality" is focused on the materiality of the body. The division between Freud's abstraction of the latent content of "sex" in the signifier and Foucault's materialist interpretation of "sexuality" in the body mobilizes the binaries between mind/body and signified/signifier. What is the pivotal relationship between a "sex" of the signifier, materiality, and body, on the one hand, and a "sexuality" of the signified, abstraction, and mind, on the other hand? The phallus and its unexpected avatars — Metaphoricity (*et al.*) — wield the force to conjoin sex/sexuality, mind/body, and signified/signifier. But how so? The pervert interweaves "sex" and "sexuality" in the fetish. The fetish is the materiality of an expanded set of objects — "sex" — with the trace of protection from anxiety in the *point de capiton* of the "penis-substitute" — "sexuality." But if the fetish is the freely expansive set of objects in the galaxy, then where does perverse "sexuality" end and ordinary "sex" begin? Is sex everything *except* itself?

The Madman's Nothingness of Nothing

The schizoid's closet is empty of clothes. The psychotic's closet is devoid of signifiers of desires, wishes, and truths. The madman's foreclosure of the symbolic unbuttons the system because it suspends Lacan's button-tie. This *point de capiton* otherwise halts the free play of difference and deferral of the signified *qua* signifier of the Signified/r. The suspension of the button-tie displaces the latent dimension of the unconscious. Schizoidly, the signified is merely another signifier in a trace of (in)significance. The Signified/r differs and defers *qua* itself. The letter neither departs nor arrives but exclusively traces as an aim/less masochistic *Trieb*. The *Verwerfung* in the symbolic returns in the Real to a Sameness⁺ in which any object is internal and external to any other object. The return of *Verwerfung* is the relational and differential negative signifier. This Signified/r disrupts the ordered combination of words in divisions and oppositions in the extant symbolic order.

The gap between the madman and the pervert is that the prolific set of objects — signs, fetishes, words, gestures, metaphors, voices, metonymies, objects, and so on — is unconstrained for the madman but restrained for the pervert. Perversely, the coherence of the succession of objects is sustained by a trace of the "penis-substitute" whose button-tie closes the aperture of an unrestricted explosion of alphabets, letters, words, phrases, sentences, paragraphs, and so on. But the imminent question of the ontological essence — What is? — applies to the button-tie of the pervert's system. What is a "penis-substitute"? This easy question inspires a series of words and phrases whose subordination to *Verleugnung* only returns as "words" and "phrases." The catch is that irrespective of the object, it is protection against castration which animates the pervert's *jouissance* with the object in (and as a) question.

The latent content is the clandestine meaning of the essence of the subject. The latent content of the schizoid is vacant of intrigue and entanglement, like his begrimed unconscious. The madman is untied to the web of words. The psychotic is unmoored in the bi-level conscious top-side and unconscious bottom-most dimensions of signification. Psychotically, there are no desires, wishes, and truths in the chortle and chatter of discourse. Desire is not obscured by the arbitrary but conventionalized division between conscious/unconscious, secondary/primary, and analysis/symptom. The proviso of desire is its repression *from* the level of the conscious *to* the dimension of the unconscious. The madman cannot desire because he observes no division and opposition of levels between which translation *of* desire *as* desire is possible. The madman desires Nothingness. His Being is a desire of Nothingness.

Hysterical desire is supplanted by crazed enjoyment of *Trieb* and the aim/less wanders of a temptation and a motivation of the Other *jouissance*. The madman is alienated from the object-cause of desire. He is separated from entangled failure to generate a sustained enjoyment. The madman's will to destruction is motivated by *Thanatos*. The death drive is an effect of the privilege of value in play. The death drive is an effect of the pinball cascade of the differences and negativities of the haphazard and ephemeral series of Real Signifiers and the Signified/r. The schizoid is resistant to the distinctions and oppositions of cogent meaning-making of the word of signification. The pervert unravels these divisions between conscious/unconscious, manifest/latent, and secondary/primary. But the pervert also returns to the button-tie of the fetish which both protects against castration and enables a *jouissance*. The madman and the pervert both displace identity and desire, but the pervert edges toward a *jouissance* of coherence, and the madman tends toward a *jouissance* of Unreason. The neurotic's structure hinges on the division between unconscious/conscious and latent/manifest. The pervert untucks these oppositions, but he enjoys their return as "unconscious" and "conscious" and "latent" and "manifest" in the *Verleugnung* of affirmed positivity. Perversely, the unconscious is not a concept but a fetish, and it is not a dynamic but a role-play.

The schizoid is freed of abstraction and speculation. The madman cannot participate in the economies of the general equivalent: the phallocentrism of size and visibility of penis/not-penis; the capitalist supply/demand dynamics of scarcity of loss and gain; and the positive unity of the word of syntax and semantics. The psychotic cannot calculate. Any object is any other object in a singularity which is incomparable and incontrastable. The Principle of Sameness⁺ is the essence of the madman's orientation in the world. The negative and differential materialities of the signifier are decentered in an undecidability and indeterminacy in space and time. These singular materialities are divorced from both the signified and the positive unity of the word. The madman is the Outside of the measurement and evaluation of phallocentrism, the speculation and abstraction of capitalism, and the syntax and semantics of the sign. The schizophrenic is the Outside of $-ism because the system is structured by the coordination of the center of the structure of general equivalence. The madman is body *sans* mind, signifier *sans* signified, and materiality *sans* abstraction. The pervert experiences this horizon of pure phonology, but he also realizes the necessity of the signified — *point de capiton* — to the project of the *perversion of the neurotic*. The fetish is the freely switched and swapped material embodiment of *jouissance*. But the fetish is also struck with a trace of the significance of the threat of castration and the defense against the Real of sexual difference.

The psychotic traverses a *Trieb* with neither origin and departure nor arrival and destination. The madman's drive Becomes. The schizoid's everyday life is situated in an endless and spontaneous drive toward — around, by, near, between, above — materialities, bodies, and signifiers. The endless rituals — gestures, flirtations, movements, recoils, demurs, proximities — of courtly love illuminate the life and breath of *Trieb*. *Trieb* is an endless and joyous — rigorous and ethical — encirclement around the *objet*. *Trieb* is an aim/less wander without *Ziel*. It is oriented against the uncomfortable start-stop of the almost-catch, ever-regret, give-up, re-play, and forget-again of *désir*. Otherwise, desire is the will to a static essence in Being rather than a mobile play in Becoming.

Lacan defines the satisfaction of *Trieb* as "reaching one's *Ziel*, one's aim."[36] This proximate "reach" toward goal is distinct from the full realization or actual achievement of *Ziel*. The desirous capture of *Ziel* otherwise implies an oral incorporation, anal expulsion, or phallic hierarchization of the vicissitude of the drive. But the unification of *Ziel* and aim grammatologically undermines the opposition between fruition of the goal and tendency toward the object. The aim toward *Ziel* is exactly the simultaneous gain and loss of *Ziel*. Being and Becoming are reversible and displaceable. The joy in aim is the chase of *Ziel*. The goal of aim is *aim itself*. The word for this aim is *Trieb*. The province of the feminine economy of the schizoid is *Trieb*. The pervert's textuality proceeds by drive, but its courtly love for letters sent is tempered by a return to sender of the message and its code.

The horizon of the endlessly unlimited spatiality and temporality of drive is not goal. *Trieb* achieves neither commencement nor arrival, and neither departure nor destination. Rather, drive mobilizes the quick hop and unfixed jump between whack-a-mole hot spots of the metaphysics of presence. *Trieb* encircles *itself*. Drive is a vortex of a *mise-en-abyme* around which the encirclement of deferred flirtations and delayed coquetries animates the exacerbated tension of the distanced object. *Trieb* wanders around the aim *as* its own aim. Lacan describes this movement as a so-called traversal through the ideological edifice of fantasy toward the Real of difference. This traversal of the absolutely unsymbolized *arche* exposes a Sameness⁺ in which any object is internal and external in extimacy to any other object in its singularity. This singularity of the Boy cannot be speculated or abstracted — compared and contrasted — with any subjective or objective criteria of equivalence. The same place of this Sameness⁺ is inconsistent with the marks of identity and difference, equality and inequality, and space and time of the Madness of Order. *Trieb* encircles itself. Drive experiences the union of subject and object in the always incomplete (*a*)sexual adventure.

This (*a*)sexuality resembles the autoeroticism of self-pleasure. In "On Narcissism" (1914), Freud depicts this self-pleasure as a configuration in which the offspring is its own love object and love subject in the delightful coalescence of ego-libido and object-libido.[37] Ego and object are never entirely split in any form of desire. The aim of *Trieb* is reproduced and reinitiated — redoubled and reaffirmed — in its causes and effects in a circularly and disorderly disoriented movement of the aim *qua* difference from itself. *Trieb* is a discontinuous torus-like dance, like Derrida's *différance*. *Trieb* is the performance around which the *Ziel* of a desire takes *jouissance* in the absence of the phallic satisfaction and its otherwise appropriation of the disappointed goal. The schizophrenic extends and savors the *pirouette*. The pervert fancies this dance, but he also clips the infinite gesture and checks the endless recoil with a *Verleugnung* which returns a set of stable fetishes for *jouissance*. The madman's *jouissance* is deferred from presence. The pervert's *jouissance* is present in the fetish-objects which ceaselessly substitute with punctured moments of departure and arrival, and commencement and destination. The madman ( ) Becoming. The pervert *is* Becoming.

The feminine *jouissance* of *Trieb* relishes the *mise-en-scène* of an uncoordinated spatiality in the unconscious. The *différance* of the aim is the displaced origin of *différance* itself. These slips and slides are *metonymized metonymy* rather than *metonymized metaphor*. The schizoid's drive wills beyond conscious/unconscious, manifest/latent, and symptom/translation toward the categorical assault on metaphor. Identity is otherwise the proviso of the word. The distant allure of the object of *Trieb* is separated from the ceaseless unwind of the drive. The drive encircles around the elusive *objet petit a*. Schizoidly, the goal of *désir* is subordinate to the aim of *Trieb*. The verbed gerund of Ing⁺ is the essence of the temporality of the drive. This Ing⁺ — Becoming — Ing⁺ contrasts with the object-cause *qua* nouned gerund of desire and its *Fort! Da! Trieb* is organized by unconscious space. This is the *mise-en-scène* of the spits and spins of *Trieb*.

Drive contrasts with the castration of the subject in relationship to the fantasized plenitude of the object. Lacan writes: "By snatching at its object, the drive learns in a sense that this is precisely not the way it will be satisfied."[38] The Other satisfaction relieves the schizoid subject of the "snatch" of the object. The object and the movement which encircles it are the same object. Being and Becoming parallactically overlap as movement and traversal, on the one hand, and constancy and invariability, on the other hand. The object of drive is itself the *Trieb*. In early sexuality, there is no hard-and-fast division between subject and object, suckling and suckled, active and passive, and so on. Drive fosters a *jouissance* of the arrangement of the switcheroo of aims and objects rather than the isolation of the separation of discrete words. The pervert recognizes the essence of drive, but he also *metaphorizes metonymy* in order to return the extimate object to the trace of the *Verleugnung* of castration. The parallax of Being and Becoming perversely recurs as the principle of Ing⁺ as a conceptual persona rather than as an experiential force.

The Other satisfaction of feminine *jouissance* "learns," as Lacan says, to resist phallic satisfaction. It does so in order to enjoy traversal. The movement of *Trieb* is the aim of *Trieb*. Aim is ethical and political. Traversal across the galaxy is the act whereby the coordinates of the fantasy-reality structure of the extant symbolic order are revealed in their arbitrary naturalization. The approach to the Real undoes the reactive ossification of these naturalized points of coordination of the symbolic order. The subject and the object are reduced to each other and collapsed into each other. The division between the words — *Trieb* and *désir* — is undone. Aim has no need for *Ziel* because the goal of *Instinkt* is not — "What is?" — but rather — "Are we enjoying?" The schizoid's *Trieb* encompasses the distinctions of words in binary opposition. But the madman forecloses these words in the Real. He suspends the signified. He releases the proliferation of negative and differential materialities in the chaotic ether of his frenzied body and soul. The madman's existence submits to the trace of an (a)difference. This in-between endlessly departs and infinitely arrives. An autoaffection generates its own peculiar *jouissance* of the Other. This enjoyment merges with the self in portentous moments of ecstasy.

The stress on the signifier in the schizoid's Nothingness of Being applies to the pervert's materialist *jouissance*. Lacan says that the pervert "succeeds in his aim by integrating in the most profound way his function as subject with his existence as desire."[39] Lacan finds a "success" in the *Praxis* of the pervert. Lacan claims that the "success" of the "aim" is possible in the "profound" incorporation of the functionality of "subjectivity." The pervert's role as the material substrate of representation of the signifier to the symbolic order is his essence *qua* the lack in the object. The pervert escapes castration in his recoil from the project of identity and desire and his celebration of the promise of *jouissance*. The pervert escapes to the trace of aim. This requires the integration of the function of the subject as the materialist-signifier nub of the representational work of the web of words. The pervert flees identity, desire, and castration in his abandonment of essence ("existence as essence"). He embraces the ordered constitution of the words and objects of the Other. These include: Derrida's Constitutive Outside; Foucault's Power/Knowledge Relations; Nietzsche's Vectors of Force and Will to Power; Heidegger's

Ontico-Ontological Being of World; Levinas's Ethics as First Philosophy; Freud and Lacan's Unconscious; Saussure's Value, and so on.

The pervert decides to jilt the humanism of decision, will, choice, agency, and intention. Instead, he chooses his destiny in the whims of structures of the death of man. These structures condition the pervert to "succeed" most "profoundly" in an aim/less wander, or "nomadic itinerary," as Deleuze would say, around the heavens for sights and sounds rather than abstractions and conceptualizations. The pervert embraces his signifier-materiality as the substrate of representation. This is exactly the amused but tortured position of the madman. The psychotic's coherent verbosity is ripped from his Reason and entrapped in an Unreason of objectivity. The madman has deeply integrated his "function as subject" with his "existence as desire." The pervert's materialism is only tamed by the traces of the abstraction of the Real of sexual difference and the *Verleugnung* of its protective negation.

Paradoxically, the psychotic's radical negation of the battery of signifiers in the Other generates a closet which is burst with the manifest formations of the madman's tasty and freaky fashions. These accouterments are hallucinations and delusions. These Spirited visions and outlandish ideations of the madman are a projective reorder of the extant symbolic order. Freud's analysis of Schreber (1911) is instructive on the matter of the productivity of hallucinations and delusions. Freud says of Schreber: "What we take to be the pathological production, the delusional formation, is in reality the attempt at recovery, the reconstruction."[40] The delusional representation is exactly the "reconstruction" of the symbolic form in the absence of the button-tie effort of the phallic *point de capiton*. Schizophrenia is the essential *Spaltung* in the parallactic gap between the tied word, which is *its own* positive unity, and the split signifier, which is decentered *from itself*. The aperture and closure of this gap in the shift of perspective on "one" and the "same" object collapse the word and the architecture of *langue*. The schizoid's visual and ideational alienations from reality are "recoveries" and "reconstructions" of the new and the different of the world-to-come of the Pervert-Schizoid-Woman and the Spirit of the System. These reconstructions arise from the burned ash of the shattered shards of the extant Madness of Order and its compulsive and repetitive insistence toward contraction and closure against its essence in expansion and openness.

A madman's delusion or hallucination is a deviant and revolutionary recovery and reconstruction of the social order. The return of the symptom makes the *Verwerfung* of the symbolic the hallucination and delusion of the *tout autre*. Schizoid symptoms are the unimagined and the impossible. They are pathological but revolutionary gestures toward a so-called *passage de l'acte*. This passage reconfigures the coordinates of the possible of the past from an as yet unthematized future. This passage in the schizoid's delusion and hallucination is paradoxically its exactly perverse moment. The evanescent and fugitive imagery of the alien is buttonholed by the phallic function. This hallucinatory and delusional capture is a so-called Event. It is also the Event of the *perversion of schizophrenia*. Retroactively, from a present now to a present past and toward a present future — and then toward the impossible — the Spirit of the System *et al.* becomes the possible, the promised, and the pact with the advent of the future. This summarizes the schizoid's political contestation. The *perversion of schizophrenia* ties the untamed hallucinations and delusions to the button of reference. The perverse reference is the prophylactic against castration, with the fetish as the avatar of protection against sexual difference. The button-tie enforces reference on the schizoid's otherwise unmediated access to galaxies-to-come.

Schizoid politics fosters the pervert's commitment to write the manifesto of the revolution. This *avant-garde* document explicates the Madness of Order in language, finance, and desire. The manifesto gestures toward a Spirit of the System in which these pathologies in sign, commodity, and desire are resolved. The pervert's manifesto summons a Sameness⁺ of an object in excess *of itself*. The Principle of Sameness⁺ generates an extended series of objects because any object is the same as any other object in the set. This logic (*et al.*)

is the promised supplement to the wretched sparkle of the psychotic's mute but delusional and hallucinatory politics. The perverse reference of the generated series of objects is the fetish and its protection against the cut of castration. The perverse Marxist *camera obscura* (1845) stabilizes perspective even as the Unreason of the madman jettisons such orientation. The presentation of reality is topsy-turvy, upside-down, and freakishly true. There is no latent content on the Outside of the battle with delusions and hallucinations. The neurotic's desires, wishes, and truths are latent content. But the schizoid is devoid of the bi-level configuration of conscious/unconscious and manifest/latent. The psychotic's closet is barren of words. The Nothingness of his so-called unconscious contrasts with the explosive Being of his manifest formations — *ex nihilo* — in hallucinations and delusions. The emptiness of the schizoid's ~~unconscious~~ belies the fabulous and outlandish symbolic fashions which slip and slide in hallucinations and delusions.

This manifest mosaic of the future generates the return of the Real *qua* the symbolic order. The Real trauma of bodies, sex, and a global *jouissance* of the wordless system of value — outside of repression and apart from nihilism — recurs in the system of the Cs. as the symptom of the shaken order of the system. Patriarchally, new sex organs and sexual arrangements are invented which are the Outside of the regime of phallocentrism and the division between penis/not-penis and the dominance of the male orgasm and ejaculation. Under capitalism, novel goods and services are manufactured which are unshackled to the dollars and coins of general equivalence. Linguistically, the architecture of the word is split into the architectonics of the autonomy of the signifier and the signified. The pervert writes the manifesto with the words and phrases of patriarchy, capitalism, and discourse. But his job is to free sexuality from sex, use-values from exchange-values, and words from reference. But *A Pervert's Manifesto* is also sexy and graphic, on sale but discounted, and readable with notes.

The button-tie of the pervert's risk is the reference between the fetish (*et al.*) and the "penis-substitute" as the defense against sexual difference. The freed nakedness of the madman's body in ecstasy contests the syntax and semantics of the system. The pervert sustains but tweaks this syntax and semantics of the system in order to secrete a semblance of facility with words for his manifesto of the Madness of Order and the Spirit of the System. The madman refuses the system of distinction and opposition of the binary logic of the word. The work of the pervert is the signifierization of the sign or the negative signifierization of the positivity of the sign. Value is the architectonics of *langue*. The positive word is the architecture of the spoken and the written. The Logic of Difference ($A \neq A = B$, and so on) and Sameness⁺ ($A = B = C$, and so on) of the signifier are incongruously foreclosed by the symbolic and its so-called signification (A or B or C) of the word. Value returns from the Real in order to disconfigure signification *qua* value. The unrepentant signifier returns from its *Verwerfung* in the Real. The pervert's task is to playfully submit this unabashed signifier to the sign and its reference to the "penis-substitute" in the scene of fetishism. But the pervert's sign slips toward the drip and drop of the signifier in an unwary question. What is a "penis-substitute"? The manifest representation of the pervert's discourse is a *Reasoned Unreason*. What is even a "penis-substitute"?

The Pervert's Unreason

The pervert's tricky *Verleugnung* frees a both/and simultaneity of negation and its return. The *Verleugnung* of negation and the *Verleugnung* of return are of Sameness⁺. The only distinction of the return is the scare quotes of the "return" of the generated succession of objects and fetishes. The objects which are disavowed — acknowledged but denied, and recognized but dismissed — return as "themselves." The parallactic split between the disavowed and its return is imperceptible except for the scare quotes around a succession of generated objects and fetishes. Theoretically, the object of return is difference. The object returns differently from the *Verleugnung* to its emergence in the system of the Cs. But simultaneity of disavowal of difference and return of difference is a concomitant *repetition of the same*. This returned *déjà vu* is the return of the Principle of Sameness⁺ in which any object is any other object in the succession of assembled fetishes from the set of sex organs, commodity use-values, and words and signifiers in the Cs. system. The pervert's "yes, yes" — affirmation of the object and denial of the object, and negation of the object and return of the object — affirms both S and $-ism, both capitalism and communism, both phallocentrism and anticentrism, both sign and signifier, both identity/difference and Sameness⁺, both castration and plenitude, both lack and fullness, both affirmation and negation, and so on. The All returns in the pervert's psychosexual economy.

Madness rejects in *Verwerfung* the symbolic system and its normative organization in patriarchal phallocentrism, capitalist exchange-value, and the word of discourse. The *Verwerfung* of the extant systems of desire, finance, and language enables the experience of the frenzied body of mania. The pervert sustains his ambivalent *bothness* and *andness* position — Sameness⁺ as "Sameness⁺" — in the symbolic order. The schizoid's Real Signified/r is the latent truth of the extant system. The architectonics of the signifier and the signified is structured by the endless chain of words, phrases, sentences, paragraphs, pages, books, and so on without the button-tie of the *point de capiton* which would return the future to the past in the retroaction (*Nachträglichkeit*, *après-coup*) of the Time of the Neurotic. The architecture of the word overwrites the architectonics of the signifier and the signified in the Signified/r. Sameness⁺ is the internal and external — extimate — bosom, recess, and decentered principle of the Madness of Order. This generative mainspring of singular — ~~unequal~~ and ~~equal~~ and ~~identical~~ and ~~different~~ — objects and fetishes is subject to *Verwerfung* (*Verdrängung*) in the symbolic order. But this treasury returns in the Real. The schizoid hitch is that this Sameness⁺ is the principle of the sex organ, the commodity, and the word.

What is foreclosed in the Real Symbolic returns to the Real Symbolic. But it returns in the symbolic *qua* the Signified/r. This slippery slope between signifier and signified disrupts the castration and lack in phallocentrism, the commodity and private property in capitalism, and the word in discourse. But the hitch is that castration and lack, commodity and private property, and the word are *sui genesis* interrupted in the system. The foreclosure of the Principle of Sameness⁺ and the Real Symbolic is in excess of itself. The system is already $-ism and its obverse. This order is ostensibly arranged by the manifest binary opposition of words and the latent difference and negativity of the materialities and abstractions of signifiers and signifieds. But the obverse is also the case: the signifier and the signified are the architecture of the system, and the word is the architectonics of the system. The word is a myth. The commodity is a myth. The penis is a myth. What is a word? What is a commodity? What is a penis? The compulsive insistence of the ontological question — "What is?" — generates an expansive cycle of new objects which both destabilizes the Madness of Order and offers the pervert yet supplementary fetish-objects — "What is?" — for his happy *jouissance* of the question rather than anxious identity with and desire for the answer.

Schizoidly, the absence of the word makes the truth of the revolution strictly unsymbolized except as hallucinations and delusions. The schizoid cannot textualize his own secret truth of Unreason. The madman cannot engage in coherent meaning-making because he is the Outside of paternity and the *point de capiton*. The psychotic is divorced from the general equivalence of the penis/not-penis opposition in patriarchy, the supply/demand dynamics of exchange-value in capitalism, and the word and its positive unity in discourse. The snag is that this Outside is exactly the Inside of the system. There is neither phallocentrism nor private property nor the word in the extant symbolic order. The system is otherwise structured by the Principle of Sameness⁺ and the Signified/r of the Real Symbolic. Any object is any other object *except itself* in an expansive galaxy of fetishes. The pervert's *Verleugnung* negates a mythical set of penises, clitorises, properties, commodities, words, and signs. These disavowed blips return as "themselves" as the fetishes of the pervert's *jouissance*.

This succession of objects is distinct from schizoid hallucinations and delusions because it is moored to the scene of castration and its disavowal. But the system itself is already its underside. The set of deferred (*a*)sexual *objets* is already the desired object of the masculine subject. The freed use-values of communism are already the exchange-values of capitalism. The architectonics of the signifier is already the architecture of the word. This Marxist *camera obscura* (1845) flips and twists the division between $-ism and Spirit. But the psychotic cannot engage in Marxist *Praxis*. The aesthetic and political forms of the psychotic's delusions and hallucinations are otherwise masked by the system — hospital and asylum. But they are reedited and refashioned by the pervert's will to symbolize the Being of the eruptions of the future of the revolution. The pervert converts the madman's delusions and hallucinations into a succession of coherent penises, clitorises, properties, commodities, words, signs, metaphors, simulations, centers, metonymies, objects, substitutes, and so on. The pervert instills a modicum of reference in the madman's manifest representation. The pervert's manifesto refers hallucinations and delusions to the stark truth of patriarchal phallocentrism, capitalist exchange-value, and the linguistic word. The snare is that this referentiality of the pervert's simulations is unshackled as the essence of the system. The system is *already* postpatriarchal, postcapitalist, and postsignification. The mystery is this compulsive insistent closedness in the universe toward phallocentrism, exchange-value, and the word rather than openness toward (*a*)sexuality, communism, and the signifier. Why does the system contract its own expansion?

The written signifier is impossible in theory. The pervert invents techniques for the *signifierization of the sign* and the *theorization of practice* — and both as *Praxis*. This endeavor is simultaneous. This labor resumes in the Theory of Practice as a consideration of representability of the primary process of the diacritics of the signifier and the Madness of Order. The work does so in an assessment of Freud's version of the laws of unconscious processes. The Woman's ~~unconscious~~ — thinking and being and living — writes the body of her ~~unconscious~~. This *écriture* is the horizon of a perverse text. The manifesto theorizes the practice of the negativity and differentiality of the theoretical materialities of the signifier. This *Praxis* is the orbit of a manifesto of a future selfhood and sociality. *Praxis* is the proclamation of the Spirit of the System. But perversely, how does a theorist perform a *Praxis* of *value* and *signification* at the same time? How is *Praxis* possible if the pervert's practice in text is the positivity of *signification* which translates the schizoid's secret Unreason of the diacritics of *value*? How does the pervert write *value* in *signification*? How does the pervert write the *signifier* in the *sign*? These questions mine the gap between the madman's hallucinations and delusions and the pervert's fetishes and objects.

The Real is the unconscious of the society. The resistance to the spoken and the written is the latent truth of the system. The autonomy of the signifier and the signified in theory is the architectonics of $-ism and its manifest set of positive unities of words. *Qua* unconscious, the defiance of the spoken and the written establishes the society as inscrutable to interpretation and analysis. The unsymbolizable and the society are coincident and continuous. The Real and the symbolic order parallactically overlap. The Real Symbolic is the substance of the society and its subjects. There is a signified of meaning-making in neither the latent architectonics of the signifier nor the manifest architecture of the word. The Principle of Sameness⁺ is the organizational force of the system. Sameness⁺ puts under erasure — *sous rature et sur l'effacement* — the relationship *of* any object *with itself* and *between* any object *and* the other objects in the system. The singularity of the object ruptures the purpose of the general equivalent to exchange objects with a standard and a set of deviations. The subjects and objects of society are struck by this Real resistance to the spoken and the written.

The Principle of Sameness⁺ is a discoordination of the *value* of the signifier rather than a coordination of the *signification* of the sign.

Sameness⁺ illuminates the substance of society: singular subjects and objects in an undecidable and indeterminate relationship both to *themselves* and to *each other*. This Real is both the base and the superstructure of the system. One day, the system will find its mirror-reflection in the text of an absent author and a present revolutionary. The pervert will become the present author of a future revolution. The conundrum is the representation of the remnant of the *sous rature* of the entire network of objects and words. What is the remainder of the parallactic overlap of Being and Nothingness? How does the pervert write the *sous rature* of under erasure and the *sur l'effacement* of over erasure? How is the Being *of* Nothingness to be spoken and written as the substance of the society?

The madman does not have an unconscious. *Qua* signifier, the madman's conceptual persona misrecognizes the division and opposition of the structure of the word. The displacement of the positive unity of the sign and its divisions and oppositions — unconscious/conscious, and so on — with the negativity and differentiality of the signifier and its uncharted chaos of Sameness⁺ dissolves any coherence of an unconscious or a conscious, or a latent or a manifest. The bi-level configuration of the manifest and the latent, and the conscious and the unconscious, is destructured by the *sous rature* of the relationship of any object *with itself* and *between* any object and any other object. *In absentia,* the breakdown of the present Being of the word (what is) inspires the bonkers of Nothingness. Foucault's fine ditty that the "paradox," as he says, "is that [madness] manifests this Nothingness, causing it to overflow with signs, words and gestures" illuminates the Being *qua* Nothingness — ontological ~~Being~~ nullity — of the madman.[41] The psychotic's outlandish speech, inappropriate gestures, and soiled pants cannot be interpreted as a Being of a present ontological order. Rather, the madman's speech and gestures are the *not* of the differential negativity of diacritics.

This aneconomy of the differences and negativities of the signifier in value is the essence of madness. The madman is the conceptual persona of the architectonics of the system. The pervert's project is to rend the mad architectonics of the signifier into the *Verleugnung* of the return of this skeletal scaffold to the architecture of the word. The pervert assembles a conscious articulation from the destruction of the unconscious/conscious binary opposition. How does Nothingness return as the Being of the system? How does the pervert return the chaos of the signifier — the system — to the unity of the word — the system? How does *Verleugnung* return the system except as the "system"?

The misinterpreted Nothingness — *qua* Being — of madness makes the positive manifestation of the figures of madmen — contained, tortured, rehabilitated, exterminated — possible. This is the "paradox," as Foucault says, of the madman. Foucault continues,

> For madness, if it is nothing, can only show its face by emerging from itself and assuming an appearance within an order of reason, thereby becoming its own opposite.[42]

The Non-Being — *not* — of madness *qua* pure negation of the differential value of the signifier cannot escape the metaphysics of presence of Being. This madness — scribbled alphabets and slurred words — manifests this Nothingness in the guise of Reason. An abject Nothingness is converted into a deficient Being. This purported Being is the latent truth to be excavated by liberal do-gooders and their rudimentary educations in the so-called professions of the social sciences. The tortured relationship between Being and Nothingness, and between Reason and Unreason, renders madness, as Foucault plaints, "always absent, in perpetual inaccessible retreat, with no phenomenal or positive character, and yet it is present and perfectly visible in the unmistakably singular appearance of the madman."[43] Madness *qua* Nothingness in value — *not* — cannot manifest its essential Nothingness.

Madness invariably presents truth by the standards of Reason: "pathology," "sickness," "disease," and so on. The madman manifests not Nothingness but a deviance from truth and a distance from health. Even if madness is *not*, the madman most certainly *is*. But what will be the pervert's script of the schizoid's secret Untruth? What surplus exceeds the parallactic overlap of Being and Nothingness but the strikethrough of *sous rature* and *sur l'effacement*? The pervert's excess is the intentional gesture to transform a closed Being into an open Nothingness. This gesture is visible in the pervert's effort to transpose the restricted *désir* into the extended *Trieb*, the constrained exchange-value into the liberated use-value, and the unified word into the dispersed signifier. The pervert's *sous rature et sur l'effacement* bely the excess of the parallax of Being and Nothingness in the deconstructive critical gesture against the metaphysics of presence.

The alphabets and vocabularies of madness are not words but signifiers, and not signs but materialities. Foucault is certainly correct that "language," as he says, "is the primary and ultimate structure of madness."[44] But this insight must be extended. It is not simply that the web of words and the net of signs organize madness. Psychosis is not merely a disorganization of semantics and syntax. Foucault is exact that signs, symbols, and gestures — and also tortures, containments, and slaughters — structure the Western madman. The crucial dimension is that the essential structure of language is madness. *Langue* is a structure of psychosis. Foucault recoils from an analysis of the meshugaas of the chains of signs and circles of words in *signification*. But the essential madness of *langue* is structured into the architectonics of the system in the *value* of the signifier and the signified. The conceptual mania is the Principle of Sameness[+]. The skeletal scaffold of the system posits that any word is different *from itself* but the ~~same~~ as any other word in the system.

The ordinary precept of a symbolic system is binary opposition. But the Principle of Sameness[+] indicates that there is no identity/difference duality which is not subordinate to the *sous rature* and *sur l'effacement* of the relationality and constructionism of the negativity and differentiality of the signifier. The Logic of Difference ($A \neq A = B$, and so on) displaces the Logic of Identity ($A = A$). The unequal sign ($\neq$) of the Logic of Difference and the equal sign ($=$) of the Logic of Identity are both under erasure because they are each struck with the pervert's negative gesture against the metaphysics of presence. *Qua* signifier, there can be no division — binary opposition — between the Logic of Difference and the Logic of Identity. The skeletal scaffold of the system of *langue* is certainly "the primary and ultimate structure," as Foucault notes, "of madness." Why is the madman the only one who speaks the truth of the system? Why are the rest of us condemned to a counterfeit and fraudulent noise? Why does the galaxy sustain the contraction of the word rather than innovate the expansion of the signifier? Why does the neurotic not expire of his own *méconnaissance*?

Usually, the clandestine latent content of the wish is distinct in space and time from the interpretable manifest representation of the unconscious desire. But this binary structure is undone by the madman's Sameness[+] and even by the pervert's considered articulation of this principle. The latent wish is coextensive with its manifest interpretation as a parallax. The pervert's *bothness* and *andness* demonstrate each opposed word of *eitherness* and *orness*, such as conscious/unconscious and manifest/latent, as an extimate Sameness[+] of the other. The pervert reasons that the hysteric's phantom limb is already the desire for fornication. But what is the interval of this "already"? The already is a prop for the mediation of a series of words (*et al.*) which positions a point of departure (latent desire) and articulates a point of arrival (manifest representation). The obverse is also the case: the series of words positions a point of departure (manifest representation) and articulates a point of arrival (latent desire). The phantom limb and its interpretation are not only at a distance from themselves. The phantom limb is exactly *not itself*. The interpretation is precisely *not itself*.

But this internal gap *within* each object opens both objects to a S̶a̶m̶e̶n̶e̶s̶s̶⁺ with the other objects in the system. The symptom and its analysis are a *mise-en-abyme* of *effects* rather than an *arche* of *causes* in the system. The unconscious is the space of the ghostly apparition of the simultaneity of both the conscious and the unconscious, and at the same time both the manifest form and the latent content. This is the madman's version of the "unconscious," and this rendition is returned in the pervert's reasoned articulation in *Verleugnung* as the "unconscious."

The pervert's choice so-called "manifest representation" is also concurrently its so-called "latent content." The *bothness* and *andness* of the pervert ordain the fetish — fur, lace, shoe, jockstrap, word, metaphor, sign, object, metonymy, center, and so on — as simultaneously *both* a manifest figuration of desire *and* a latent desire itself. Perversely, there is no split between the cause of desire and the object of desire. The desire is its own cause, and the cause is of its own desire. This is the reason that Lacan refers to the object-cause of desire as the *objet petit a*. The object *causes* desire, but it is also *caused* by desire. The *objet petit a* is an expansion of libido *ex nihilo* and *sui generis*. The fetish is *both* an embodied conscious figuration of desire or manifest representation *and* an ideational unconscious source of desire or latent content. The fetish is concomitantly *both* the revelation of castration *and* the disclaimer to the threat. *Verleugnung* returns manifest representation and latent content as "manifest representation" and "latent content." *Verleugnung* recurs sexual difference as "sexual difference." The generative process of these disavowals expands the solar system of words and objects. The scare quotes refer to the excess of the deconstruction of the binary oppositions — manifest/latent and conscious/unconscious — which is the remainder of the recurrence of disavowal. The surplus is the positive and affirmative expansion of the otherwise contracted negations of Cs. *Verdrängung* and *Verwerfung*.

The pervert's *Verleugnung* recuperates the loss as an extended gain. The return of "penis/not-penis" or "clitoris/not-clitoris" is an addition to a series of organs and objects of sexual exploits. Under capitalism, the recurrence of the objects "scarcity" or "abundance" expands the series of commodities. Linguistically, any word is redoubled with a *jouissance* of a signifier which is ruptured from any reference. The pervert's *bothness* and *andness* deconstruct opposition and return *both* to an expanded set of objects and words and fetishes. The pervert thrills in the sheer *bothness* of the proximity of the binary opposition of castration and plenitude. The fetish-penis-substitute enables the pervert to take pleasure in both the glorious penis *qua* presence and the horrific clitoris *qua* absence. The pervert takes pleasure in a cognitive dissonance — or better: clitoral dissonance. The pervert enjoys both castration and plenitude — the *bothness*, the *andness*, the *eitherness*, the *orness* — of opposition *qua* both affirmation and negation in sexuality and textuality.

The pervert's manifest representation ("manifest representation") is the fetish. The fetish is an asymptotic and approximate screen for the maternal phallus. Freud's word for this mediation between penis and fetish is "penis-substitute." This imprecise and inexact relationship between copy and referent is structured by the codes and mechanisms of metaphorical substitution: like and unlike, and similar and dissimilar. The manifest is like the latent, and the clitoris is like the penis. But the manifest is also unlike the latent, and the clitoris is also unlike the penis. The fetish is similar to the maternal phallus, and the penis-substitute is similar to the penis. But the fetish is also dissimilar to the maternal phallus, and the penis-substitute is also dissimilar to the penis. Other articulations of the undecidability and indeterminacy of the relationships between manifest and latent, clitoris and penis, fetish and maternal phallus, and penis-substitute and penis are manifest (is) latent, clitoris (is) penis, fetish (is) maternal phallus, and penis-substitute (is) penis. But this copula of ontological Being — is — must be put under erasure — i̶s̶ — because this word is struck with a difference *from itself.* There is no word — l̶i̶k̶e̶ and u̶n̶l̶i̶k̶e̶ and s̶i̶m̶i̶l̶a̶r̶ and d̶i̶s̶s̶i̶m̶i̶l̶a̶r̶ and i̶s̶ — which escapes erasure by the relationality and constructionism of the Principle of Sameness⁺ of the system. The pervert's disavowal returns the negated of the internally split object — *with itself* — to an expansive galaxy of splits which is sutured with a recurrent otherness. The pervert's manifest representation is the connective goo between its own *Spaltung* and the splits of the expanded set of other fetishes and objects.

The madman and the architectonics of the system are sheer negativity. The *not* rules the architectonics and architecture of the system of *langue* and by extension the systems of patriarchy and castration, and capitalism and scarcity. But this dark, misty, and emblazoned *negativity* of the system (*Verdrängung* and *Verwerfung*) is also bright, glossy, and lustrous *positivity*. The *value* of the signifier (is) the *signification* of the sign. The signifier (is) the sign. Value (is) signification. The negative and differential diacritics of the system is simultaneously the positive and affirmed unity of the word. The perverse Principle of Sameness[+] indicates that any object is — *not* — any other object. The positivity of Being is internal to the negativity of Nothingness. The "yes" and the "yes" are mediated by a *not*. But this *not* is the positive condition of the affirmation. Positively, the pervert transitions to the mode of negation of the Pervert-Schizoid-Woman. This negation is neither the *Verdrängung* of repression nor the *Verwerfung* of foreclosure nor the *Verleugnung* of disavowal. The mode of negation of the Pervert-Schizoid-Woman of the Spirit of the System is the simple Positivity of Sameness[+]. This is the Woman's forgotten and remembered of the Real.

This mode of Spiritual negation (affirmation) is a Positivity of Sameness[+]. But it is a positivity not of the word as an autonomous self-same and self-identical unity but as a material and bodily signifier of the splits and shards of difference and negativity. Perverse Positivity of Sameness[+] converts the diacritics of the signifier into the positivity of the word. The positivity of the pervert negatively significizes the positivity of the sign. The pervert articulates the idea of *value* in the letters of *signification*. Spiritually, the diacritics of the signifier in negative and differential *value* will become the paradoxical diacritics of the sign in positive *signification*. Futurally, the word *qua* signifier will be the thinking, being, and living of negative and differential diacritics *qua* positivity. This summarizes the futural mode of negation (affirmation) of the Woman and her *jouissance*. The Woman is the conceptual persona who negatively significizes the positivity of the sign. The Woman speaks the concept of *value* in the words of *signification*. Somehow — the Real architectonics of the structure is spoken and written in the representational forms of the architecture of the system. Somehow — the Real is uttered by the symbolic. The Woman is the heir to the Real Symbolic. The Principle of Sameness[+] is the philosophical center of the Woman.

The riot toward the Pervert-Schizoid-Woman's Spiritual affirmation of positivity is performed — even within an arbitrary and conventionalized system of *signification* which is paradoxically structured according to the negative and differential diacritics of the system of *value*. The negative signification of the positivity of the sign is the in-process, in-action revolution of the pervert's manifesto of the madman's Unreason. Spiritually, the revolution will produce a surplus *jouissance*. The global orgasm will overwhelm the neurotic's pansy transgression and the schizoid's inchoate hallucinations and delusions. The risk of this surplus *jouissance* exceeds the constrictive mediation of the fetish and the penis by the "penis-substitute." The hazard of this excess *jouissance* outstrips the contractive supply/demand dynamics of production and consumption. This extra *jouissance* exceeds the restrictive context and its delimitation of the text. The system otherwise: slashes the surplus of fetish, object *qua* "fetish," and "object" *qua* "itself" in order to sustain the dominance of the penis as reference; squanders the excess of material goods and services in order to stabilize supply/demand dynamics with speculative dollars and coins; and diffuses the extra of text above the saturations of context in order to secure proper semantics and syntax in meaning-making.

At stake in the positive parallactic overlap of *value* and *signification* — Real Symbolic — is the *destruktion* of patriarchy, capitalism, and the word. The pervert's manifesto of the schizoid's Unreason promises to articulate an architecture (architectonics) of the system which expands rather than contracts.

The wager is that the Spirit gravitates away from the compulsive and insistent closedness of a stale system of $-ism and Something is Missing and toward a triumphant openness of a solar system in which Nothing is Missing. The obscene emptiness of (*a*)sexuality at the center of the system is the pivotal force of this expansion toward —

The Spiritual transformation of the diacritical negativity of the architectonics (architecture) of the system — *not* — into the positivity of the Principle of Sameness⁺ — *Yes!* — dissolves the mechanisms of neurotic *Verdrängung*, schizoid *Verwerfung*, and even perverse *Verleugnung*. Disavowal is the negation and return of that which is banished from the individual and the society. Undesirables return as objects and words which are split *from* themselves but sutured *to* the other objects in the system. The negative signifierization of the positivity of the sign returns castration as "fur," "lace," "shoe," and "jockstrap." The scare quotes indicate the split in the object and the expansion of the succession of objects in the pervert's world. This transmutation is mediated by: the pervert's *Trieb*; the willful transition from *désir*; and the missed encounter to the traditions of the extended flirtation of courtly love. The drive differs and defers the points of departure and arrival, and commencement and destination, of the object. The succession of *les motes et les choses* opens the universe to an expanded set of objects for amusement and joy. The pervert's insight is that the Unreasonable Logic of Difference generates a relationality and constructionism of objects that the Reasonable Logic of Identity otherwise constrains. The Positivity of Sameness⁺ speaks and writes the signifiers of the Real with the words of the system. Somehow — the Real is the symbolic because every object is subordinate to the *Spaltung* of a *not*. This mad negativity disperses and diffuses the text in a difference and deferral away from (toward) itself.

The revolution of the Spirit of the System is also inspired by a *Praxis* of the textualization of the madman's Unreason into the alphabets and vocabularies of the words of Reason. This articulation of the resistant to the spoken and the written overwrites the architecture of the word with the architectonics of the signifier. *Praxis* transforms the positive unity of the sign in its autonomous self-sufficiency into the negative and differential (Positivity of Sameness⁺) chaos of the signifier. The pervert is the pioneer of the conceptual persona of the Woman. The schizoid is the signifier *qua* theory. The madman is a purely theoretical — unalloyed phonological — conceptual persona in the world. The pervert is the conceptual persona of the Signified/r in theory. The pervert is the essence of the play of the signifier in the dimension of the skeletal scaffold of the system in the signifier and the signified. These autonomous materialities and abstractions are the theoretical components of the system. The sign (word) is the futural practical dimension of the embryonic Spirit of the System.

The Woman is the Theory of Practice. The Woman is the pure phonology of the madman and his autonomous signifier which are braced to the pure psychology of the abstraction of the signified. The Woman is the paradoxical spoken and written of the Nothingness of madness. The practice of the theory of the Woman is the negative signifierization of the positivity of the sign. Somehow — the Woman lives the brute phonology of the schizoid but in the text of the symbolic order. The Woman enjoys the architecture of the system in the word — but in the architectonics of the skeletal scaffold of the signifier. The Woman's existence sutures the gap between the theory of the signifier of the madman and the practice of the sign of future emancipation. Paradoxically, the bodily phonology of the madman's Unreason is transformed into the existence of a Reasonable phonologization of psychology, signifierization of the sign, positivization of the negative, and practicization of theory. The Woman's thinking, being, and living animate the parallactic gap. The Woman materializes the signifier in the being-in-the-world and being-with-others in the future. The negative becomes the positive condition of the next epoch in the transcendence of phallic lack, capitalist scarcity, and linguistic syntax and semantics.

Figure 3.7 Plenitude of the Woman

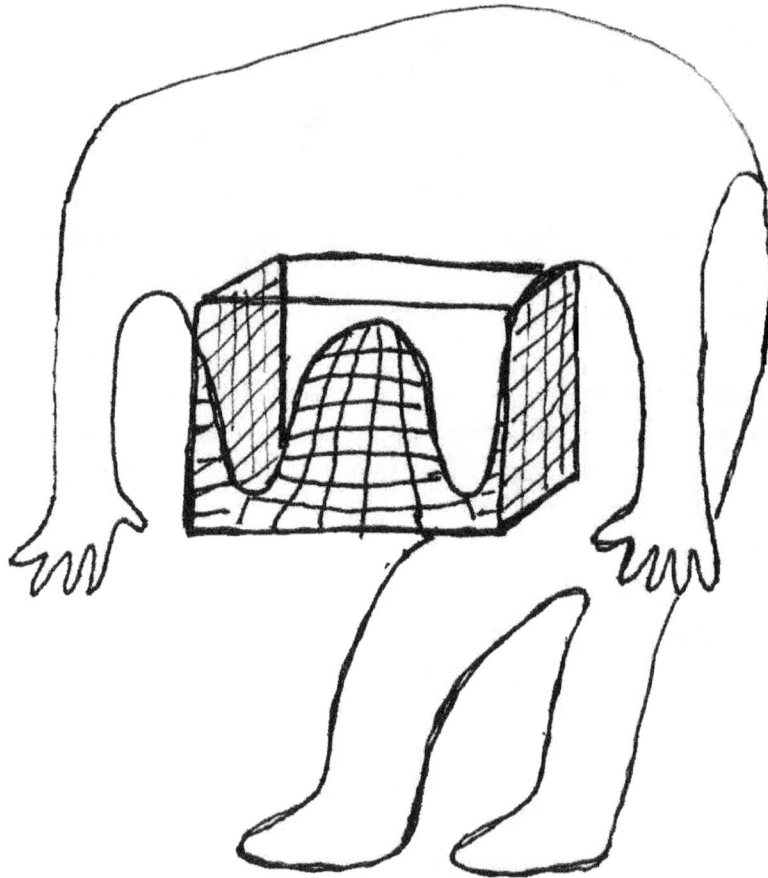

This illustration portrays the Woman who represents — as best — the impossible presence within a system in which Nothing is Missing. The concave head symbolizes the lack that the system enforces on her. This systematic lack enables the system to function in its structure. The depicted Woman symbolizes the parallactic overlap of Something is Missing and Nothing is Missing in a Sameness[†] which is neither self-same nor self-identical. The metaphysics of presence is structured into the system as lack. This desire is dislocated and unsituated within all points in the spatial grid of the cosmos. The Woman is the Outside of this system as a pure and raw positivity. The Woman is under erasure. But this *sous rature et sur l'effacement* are also the essence of the system. The illustration depicts a diacritical materialism in which the body and physics resist the word. The Woman defies the ideal signifier with the excess of her materiality. The Woman's Real resistance to symbolization is the Nothingness (Being) of her essence as the extimate Outside of the system *qua* its internal structure.

Notes & Sketches —

The pervert recognizes that the excess of these feminine overlaps is a series of new words and novel objects which cannot be assimilated by the Real Symbolic. The system of phallocentrism generates a new excess of sex organs. Capitalism spawns a surplus of goods and services. The language system breeds a remainder of materialities, abstractions, and words. The Woman oversees the expansion of the solar system. The Woman's whole is *not* entirely of the order. Her surplus exceeds the symbolic and seeps into the Real. There is always excess psychology to be phonologized, sign to be signifierized, negativity to be positivized, and theory to be practiced. *Trieb* recoils and advances, and it demurs and courts. The obstacle to the Boy engenders new costumes, gestures, tricks, habits, rituals, dialogue, and props with which to agentically and intentionally wait with patience. The Woman's patient waiting precipitates words and objects toward —

Revolutionarily, Sameness⁺ manifests as the central organizational principle of both the extant and futural systems. The Principle of Sameness⁺ is the structural precept of both the architecture (word) and architectonics (signifier) of the system. The exchange of phonology for psychology, signifier for sign, positive for negative, and practice for theory is a *de facto* exchange. There is *no change* in the system in the revolution. $-ism (=) S. The overlap of the Real revolution and the symbolic order is a shift in an intuition on a "one" and the "same" object. The minor shift of the parallax is between Reason and Unreason. The surplus of this overlap is the text of the pervert. *A Pervert's Manifesto* articulates this minor shift in the individual and social interpretation of the system. The madman is the obverse of the neurotic. The pervert's work is to indicate this coincidence.

The surplus of the parallax between the system and *itself* is the pervert's text. The pervert spotlights this text as the mediatory translation between the psychotic and the neurotic. The performance of the *perversion of the neurotic* is the excess of the gap between $-ism and itself. The Nothingness between the extant order and the revolutionized *tout autre* is the text of the manifesto. The text which cannot stop not being written is the remainder of the continuity: between the generative architectonics of the signifier and the architecture of the word; between the restriction of the penis and the generation of novel sexes and sexualities; between the scarcity of supply/demand dynamics and the abundance of each according to his need and each according to his ability; and between the constriction of the sign and the freedom of the signifier. The revolution is *ici* but also *ailleurs*. Why is the parallax inscrutable to the neurotic? The remnant of this obscurity is the symptom of the entirety of the system.

The pervert is intuitively communist. The pervert is against private property. The pervert is resistant to phallocentrism. The pervert is unhappy with −centrisms of all kinds. The pervert is dismissive of lack and castration. The pervert is resistant to a metaphorical structure of (un)like and (dis)similar. But the pervert has not resolved the conundrum of general equivalence of the phallus of desire or the sign of language or the currency of economy. The best the pervert can offer is a series of conceptual personae which articulates the *destruktion* of an economy of comparison, contrast, and exchange of generalized equivalence of *signification* in favor of an aneconomy of the undecidability and indeterminacy of *value*. But irrespective of the pervert's success and failure to pervert the neurotic, he is rapt for an expansive pleasure of himself and the Other in the explosion of objects and words — "Signified/r" and "Real Symbolic" and "Sameness⁺," and so on — which return from the negated in their *Spaltung* from themselves and their bond with the other objects and words in the system. The everyday life of the pervert withholds abstractions about right/wrong, good/evil, and manifest/latent. This is so except insofar as these theoretical aporias amuse him and his reader. The pervert's manifesto of the schizoid's Untruth is obscenely theoretical. But the skyline for the Pervert-Schizoid-Woman is a solar system which is beyond the sorry and constrictive referentiality of the penis, the anxious and contractive protection of private property, and the reactive and restrictive hierarchization of signification. The pervert pinches general equivalence, but his *jouissance* is the expansion — *plus de* — of fetishes and the sexy impediments and erotic hindrances to the Boy. The wakes of the differences and deferrals of this *arche* are the toys and games which facilitate advancement and kickback from the object of *Trieb*.

The pervert's *Verleugnung* oscillates between oppositional perspectives. As Dor puts it: "These two psychic contents, mutually exclusive with regard to reality, coexist in the psychic apparatus without ever influencing one another."[45] The crucial discovery in perverse disavowal is the transformation of the deadlock between any two psychical contents. The parallax is the object of this shift between perspectives on "one" and the "same" object. There is a kernel of ecstasy in the ambivalence of this superpositional oscillation. This is so even if the source of such ambivalence is unknown. What is the *arche* of the binary oppositional structure of word and affect? An ambivalence implicates a stalemate in the tension between the contraction of the galaxy in constrained penile reference, restricted private property, and restrained word play, on the one hand, and the expansion of the solar system in a dilated series of sex organs, a prolific succession of goods and services, and a cultivated play of syntax and semantics, on the other hand.

A necessary and supplementary economy of *unambivalence* must be imagined in order to shatter the balance between the "two psychical contents" — patriarchy/feminism, capitalism/communism, sign/signifier, manifest/latent, conscious/unconscious, symptom/return, patient/analyst, and so on — which is otherwise sustained or flipped but not displaced. The obscene center of (a)sexual energy is the force of the displacement of ambivalence between expansion and contraction in the galaxy. The pervert's manifesto wills an *unambivalent* tendency toward expansion in the proliferation of fetishes, growth of goods and services, and extension of word play. The two psychical contents may not "influence one another," as Dor says, but an imbalance between their forces must be achieved in order to deregulate the strictures of a system which is based on general *equivalence* rather than *inequivalence*.

The opposition between the two contents — originally, castration versus plenitude — insists as an undecidable moment of the affirmation of both contents. But this affirmation must be tempered by an (a)sexual tenacity to transcend the ambivalence of this affirmation of an *unambivalent* tendency toward the expansion of the universe. The fetish is the maternal symbolization of the *bothness* and *andness* of "coexistence," as Dor puts it, between the fact of sexual difference and the disavowal of this conceit of superiority and inferiority, and present absence and proleptic loss. The paradox of the simultaneity of sexual difference and sexual (a)difference is not resolved. This sequence of aporias is not mastered. The cycle of grievances is not negotiated. This run of hypotheses is not concluded. This wave of evidences is not arbitrated. This series of experiments is not proven. But the pervert enjoys generative paradox, surplus illogicality, productive contradiction, extended incongruity, extra absurdity, excessive oddity, expansive enigma, energetic puzzle, effusive antinomy, and prolific mystery.

The pervert does not coherently and cogently isolate the Untruth. Rather, the pervert prefers to *represent* it with a verity of affects: humorous jocularity, scholarly acumen, warm generosity, and brazen risk. The pervert is not an intellectual. The pervert is a player. But he is committed to expansion of the globe toward a succession of objects which breaks phallocentrism, outstrips capitalism, and frees the signifier. This *unambivalence* must return the negated as a surplus. Lacan explicitly says: "Repression and the return of the repressed are the same thing."[46] The symptomatic quirk and the analytic insight are the Same[+] gesture. But the excess which is returned in the fetishistic Sameness[+] of *Verleugnung* is the set of fetishes — shoe, lace, fur, jockstrap, *et al.* — which enables and disables the return to *arche* and the nefarious work of the *point de capiton* to halt the generation of words and the assembly of objects.

The *unambivalence* which scars the Principle of Sameness[+] is the *différance* between the two positive contents in question. The negated of *Verdrängung*, *Verwerfung*, *Verleugnung*, and their returns are neither identical nor different, neither equal nor unequal, but a Sameness[+]. This Sameness[+] is not identical because the repressed and its return are not identical in space (difference) and time (deferral). Sameness⁺ articulates an ~~identity~~ which deviates from ~~difference~~ in space and time. But this is the case only for the positive self-sufficient unity of the word. The relationality and constructionism of the diacritics of the negative and differential signifier extend in an open system of space which suspends the phallic *point de capiton*. Usually, the neurotic button-tie halts the differences and deferrals of meaning-making and retroactively pins signification from present and future to past.

But an expansive system of openness involves an aneconomy. This architectonics of the system confounds any departure or destination, and any commencement or arrival. There is no *arche* in the system of the signifier. There can be no time in the system in the suspension of the *point de capiton*. Spirit is purely spatial. Freud claims that the unconscious is timeless. There is no deferral in the unconscious. The unconscious is purely spatial. The delay of the *point de capiton* interrupts temporality and reduces time to not only the conventionalized myths of narration but also to a structural impossibility. The spatialization of *différance* affects the Principle of Sameness⁺. The gaps *within* and *between* objects are exclusively spatial. But even this spatial difference is subordinate to the collapse of the binary oppositions between text/context and the myriad other contrasts — latent/manifest, unconscious/conscious, and so on — which the Real Signifier destructures with the ontological *not* of the *Spaltung* of the split within each object. Any binary opposition is Sameness⁺ with the minor subtraction and addition of a *différance* of space *within* and *between* objects. The space of this decenterment is the unconscious. The upshot is that the relationship of the object to itself and to the other objects can only be represented by a ~~Sameness⁺~~ which is under erasure in an indeterminate and undecidable space. The solar system is a timeless, unconscious space. Any object is the same as any other object in the expanse of space.

The rule of grammatology is a happy undecidability and indeterminacy in an unconscious space of Sameness⁺. Perversely, truth is neither negation (*Verdrängung*, *Verwerfung*, or *Verleugnung*) nor its return. Instead, the pervert reorganizes oppositionality. As Dor puts it: "Disavowal is always accompanied by the opposite attitude."[47] This is so even if the "opposite attitude" must "accompany" the deleted copulation for Being *sous rature et sur l'effacement* of the Principle of Sameness⁺. The pervert appreciates that the excess of the negation of the copulatic words is the strikethrough of ~~Sameness⁺~~. But what is the excess of this negative deconstructive gesture?

The surplus is an expansive Nothingness which cannot be recuperated into the system. Nothing is Missing except a trace of an extended Nothingness. Dor's use of the word "accompanied" is instructive. The word implies a relationship and a togetherness. It is as if the "opposite attitudes" are not ambivalent but *unambivalent*. The perverse attitude is a disavowed *unambivalence*. The inequivalent and unbalanced tendency in the system is toward the trace of Nothingness in Nothing is Missing. Futurally, the Woman accompanies her various others, their different attitudes, their eccentric sensibilities, their queer tastes, their abhorrent values, and their delicious curves. These objects extend in the space of the unconscious and its suspension of the phallic *point de capiton*.

Perversely, the Positivity of Sameness⁺ in unconscious space cannot be divided and opposed *qua* word from negativity. But the positive affirmation of the word of the Pervert-Schizoid-Woman joins with the differential and negative attitude of the signifier. But does it do so in the format of the word *qua* signification *of* value? The signifierization of the sign or negative signifierization of the positivity of the sign is the essence of the pervert's representational puzzle. How does the pervert represent *value* in the alphabets and vocabularies of *signification?* How does the pervert articulate a *theory* of the architectonics of the signifier in the *practice* of the architecture of the word? How is the Positivity of Sameness⁺ to be spoken and written in a symbolic order which is otherwise structured by the differences and negations of unmoored materialities and abstractions, and signifiers and signifieds?

The pervert struggles with these considerations of representability, but he delights in the voyeurism and exhibitionism of representation — productive fanciful fashions, excessive textual upheavals, generative philosophical reversals, surplus political amusements, extended rueful ethics, and expansive experimental existences. The *signifierization of the sign* is the pedagogical mechanism of the *perversion of the neurotic* and the aperture and closure of the parallactic gap. The excess of the conversion of *signification* into *value* is the extant symptom of the society. $-ism is an effect of the schism between the architectonics of the signifier and the architecture of the sign. The speculated project of the transformation of psychology into pure phonology is the pervert's quandary. The fetish is the essence of the *Spaltung* of the object *within* itself and *between* the other objects in the system. The fetish is the parallactic overlap between signifier and sign, between materiality and speculation, and between the architectonics of the aneconomy and the architecture of the system. The excess of the parallax of the fetish is the extension of fetishes *qua* "fetishes," and so on.

Castration and scarcity enforce negativity. The inferior clitoris (penis) represents the male junior's prospective castration. Proleptic loss dominates the system of $-ism: the patriarchy of penis/not-penis and the contraction of sex and sexualities; the capitalism of private property and the scarcity of goods and services; and the *langue* of the positive unity of the self-same and self-identical word and the restriction of the play of the signifier. The regime of sexual difference subordinates the *All* to potential death. The schizoid valiantly forecloses this regime of *désir,* and the pervert vitally disavows the complex of sexuality. The pervert denies proleptic castration but simultaneously affirms potential loss. This *Verleugnung* is the tricky "No!" and "yes" of loss and gain, *désir* and *Trieb,* and presence and absence. The fetish of the fur, lace, shoe, and jockstrap (...) invites the pervert to refuse but also to accept phallocentric desire *qua* masochistic *Trieb qua* capitalist scarcity *qua* communist abundance *qua* word *qua* signifier *qua* Something is Missing *qua* Nothing is Missing, and so on. The pervert's "yes" and "No!" *Verleugnung* generates this series of objects of a *Spaltung* in which any object is the same — *not* — as any other object. This reversed and unfathomable moment of the Positivity of Sameness[+] can be textualized as: $= \neq =$ Something $\neq = \neq$ Nothing $= \neq =$ — but this *écriture* is also subject to the precept of the system of *not.* The *unambivalent* obverse of *not* is inarticulable. The expansion of "yes" counterbalances the "No!," but the *not* cannot be deleted except by the strikethrough of its endless negation of its own schism *within* itself. The remainder of *not* is *not itself.*

There is no object as such, *qua,* by definition, *il y a,* by necessity, and so on. The ontico-ontological difference and the elementary question of ontology — What is? — are present but inessential. The perverse master of his various fetishes, objects, words, centers, substitutes, metaphors, penises, and clitorises is ontologically mute. The pervert discovers that the basic ontological question of Being is irrelevant to his joys. But the pervert is also intensely committed to the destruction of the ontological question and the ontico-ontological difference. This grammatological and psychoanalytic process is at the center of his plot to inspire *jouissance* in himself and in his reader. The pervert wishes to be ontologically mum, but the destruction of the positive order of Being must be articulated. The pervert's pursuit of this textualization invites the variety of conceptual personae for the *destruktion* of the ontological order. This deconstruction in space opens the purpose of the indexical preposition. The preposition orders the spatial proximity between any object which is at a distance from itself but at a propinquity with any other object. The *Spaltung* of the object *within itself* invites it toward an extended relationship and construction with other objects in the system. This rapport between a split object and a sutured relationship is arranged by the preposition and its organization of the space of the unconscious.

RERUNS

The return of hysterical *Verdrängung*, psychotic *Verwerfung*, and perverse *Verleugnung* bears a symptom. Lacan renames this formation the *sinthome*. The *sinthome* is the kernel of *jouissance* of the identity of the subject. The symptom returns to the system of the Cs. The content can be returned because its substitute formation — manifest *qua* latent — must be represented to the conscious of either the individual or the society. The return of the repressed is the formative substitute for the latent content. This latency is otherwise negated in neurotic *Verdrängung*, psychotic *Verwerfung*, and perverse *Verleugnung*. The negated content of the repressed wants an expression with a symbol. This symbol (*sinthome*) is the symptom. The symptom returns as and for symbolization. The spoken and the written are symptomatic. Speech and writing in the dream, slip of the tongue, or joke are symptoms of a repressed latent content. The symptom returns the otherwise self-same and self-identical *qua* an otherness which cannot be recuperated into the system.

Lacan's *sinthome* presents the symptom as the overlapped object of the imaginary, the symbolic, and the Real. The *sinthome* binds the quirks and oddities of subjective and social symptoms into a kernel of enjoyment as an *Eros*. The unification of *Eros* staves off the splintered psychosis of a *Thanatos*. The death drive otherwise shatters any semblance of consistency that the symptom holds for the individual and the society. The symptom is the subject. $-ism is a symptom. The pervert recognizes that the symptom and its return are a Sameness[+] in which the split in the symptom *within itself* binds it to its return which is split *within itself.* This internal (external) split ties the two otherwise opposed and distinct (word) as differential and negative (signifier). The pervert dismantles the gap between the architectonics of the aneconomy of the skeletal scaffold of *langue* and the architecture of the word. The symptom is a signifier, and the return is a word. But the return is also a signifier, and the symptom is also a word. The excess of this parallactic overlap of architectonics and architecture, signifier and sign, and the symptom and return is the pervert's text. The remainder is the analytic interpretation of the return of the repressed (disavowed, foreclosed) and the extended spaces of the return of the collected fetishes.

The Neurotic's Return of Verdrängung

Neurotically, the return of the repressed is the symptom of vexation and exasperation with the extant symbolic order. These existential stains include familial relations, career concerns, amorous bonds, intellectual interests, health afflictions, and interpersonal conflicts. The neurotic experiences the shock and awe of a world awry. The hysteric's marked resistance to analytic interpretation of these ills is also coextensive with the transference and the rapport between the patient and the *sujet supposé savoir*. The transference is a symptomatic return of distress to the neurotic's world. The symptoms of depression and anxiety are exemplary of discontent and tetchiness with the world. Transferentially, the analyst is an extension of dissatisfaction with the hysteric's enigmatic desire. The hysteric suffers deep scars of the extant system of $-ism. These tears include: the madness of *langue* and the binary opposition of the word; the phallocentrism and the penis/not-penis regime of castration anxiety; and the capitalism of private property and the scarcity of goods and services.

But the enigma of the neurotic is that these objective conditions are *de facto* destructured in the Madness of Order. The structure of binary opposition is collapsed by the breakdown between the skeletal scaffold of the signifier and the sovereignty of the word. The phallocentrism of castration is undone by the displacement of *désir* by *Trieb*. The futural abundance of goods and services has outstripped the *finite infinity* or *infinite finity* of the accumulation of speculation and abstraction of dollars and coins with the explosive force of labor and the assembly of singular commodities. *The revolution has in effect happened.* Why is the neurotic incapable of an intuition of the destructured Madness of Order? The revolution has *de facto* supervened. The pervert is patiently waiting for his neurotic to discern that nothing has changed because everything has already changed. The madman and the pervert wisely glimpse the Event. The neurotic is daft to its presence. The series of returned symptoms in the society is an effect of this neurotically delayed response to the Event of revolution.

Repressed desire returns as the sickness of illness. But this repressed truth can also return as the magic of the master signifier. A melancholic sadness is the internalization of the lost object. The loss berates the subject from the inside. This internalized loss demonstrates a returned symptom of a depressive patient whose wishes are confined to the closet of the subjective and objective unconscious. The symbolic order organizes this internalized loss as the defeat of the subject. The repression of the hysteric's distress into the cauldron of the unconscious renders truth latent. The inspiration of the neurotic's own unique master signifier — idiosyncratic identity and eccentric desire — is deadened. The master signifier is a symptom. But the master signifier is a returned latent content which is also the peculiar art of the self of the neurotic. The master signifier is her own kink and crochet. The repression of the master signifier *qua* eccentric symptom is the remnant of a failed master of hystericization and an indifferent analyst of textualization.

The neurotic symptoms of depression and anxiety are the expression of a voice of despair rather than a song of experiment. The pervert's text is the upshot of a properly hystericized desire (*Trieb*) and expressed truth. The hysteric's symptoms cannot be relieved until her desire is hystericized (driven) and expressed in a symbol. The symptomatic daftness to the *de facto* Event of revolution is the consequence of the restriction of *Trieb* and the unspoken symbol. The hysteric is not yet a pervert. This is the reason that the fetishist must pervert the neurotic. He must give her space to acknowledge her truth and express her word. Until then, the succession of master fetishes is jammed by the *point de capiton* and the return to a depressed and anxious past. But is it possible to break the unfathomable etiological overdetermination of psychical structure? Is the *perversion of the neurotic* an achievable goal? What is lost (gained) in the slow quietus of the neurotics of the world — disunite? As Lacan makes clear in the *Seminar* on the other side of psychoanalysis (1969-1970), the hysteric needs a master as an object of rebellion and an analyst who silently solicits the symbol. The collusion between the analytic discourse and the master's discourse generates the text of the *tout autre*. It will be a different Event altogether.

The Madman's U-Turn in Verwerfung

There is no proper return of the essential symptom in the madman's world. There never were any fashions in his closet. This vacant series of unreal words — signifiers without a signified — is pure and free *différance* in the space of the unconscious. The symptom does not return from the dynamic relationship between manifest form and latent content. The symptom does not return in the space between conscious and unconscious. The psychical dynamic between negated and returned is absent in *Verwerfung*. The solar system is uninhabitable to the psychotic. But this is so not for the reason that his subjectivity is a misfit to the objectivity of the structure. Rather, the paradoxical and deceptive split between the explicit neurotic law of *le propre* ($-ism) of patriarchal sexuality, capitalist private property, and the linguistic sign, on the one hand, and the Spirit of the System (S) of (*a*)sexuality, communism, and the signifier, on the other hand, renders the madman paralyzed in his frenzy, derided in his speech, illegal in his deeds, illogical in his ideas, exploited in his body, and abused in his soul.

The madman is yet to produce a master fetish which is articulable to the society. The distance between the madman and the pervert is situated at this point: the madman is incoherent, and the pervert is lucid. The madman's objects are not fetishes because they do not sustain a trace of reference. The pervert's fetishes carry a remnant of the penis and its substitution with the fur, lace, shoe, jockstrap, and an expanded set of repudiated objects which return from the culture as "communism" (maternal phallus), "justice" (penis), "public property" (penis-substitute), "play" (center), and so on. The cost of the madman's repudiation of latent/manifest and unconscious/conscious is reference. The objects spill and drip, the words spew and wail, and the metalanguage of any semblance of referentiality is in abeyance. There is a structural excess *metameta* in the madman's approach to the *mise-en-abyme* of delayed and decentered reference.

The truth of the schizoid is at an acute variance with the fraud of the universe and its tendency toward the contraction of binary opposition against the expansion of the signifier. The schizoid cannot recognize these binary oppositions not merely because his phallic function is suspended by his psychical structure. He is thinking, being, and living the trace. But the schizoid also cannot acknowledge binary oppositions because he knows that they are a hoax. The craziness of the system executes the penis/not-penis phallocentricity of patriarchal masculine sexuality. But the psychotic realizes that male heterosexuality is properly understood as an (*a*)sexual queerness. The schizoid cannot recognize this heteronormativity not simply because he is a masochist. He is thinking, being, and living this masochism. But the schizoid also cannot accept patriarchal phallocentrism because he knows that it is a scam. The schizophrenia of the system cultivates private property and scarcity under capitalism. But the madman understands that scarcity is a fable of capitalism and that private property is the essence of exploitation. The madman cannot comprehend this capitalist *le propre* not only because he is a communist. He is thinking, being, and living this communism. But the psychotic also cannot condone capitalism because he knows that it is a treachery. The madman lives S in the time of $-ism. The madman is from the future. The schizophrenic is not an idiot. The psychotic is out of his time.

The object which does not return from unconscious to conscious, from latent to manifest, and from absence to presence is Nothingness — *not*. The manifestation of Nothing in(to) Something can be transliterated as the turn toward a Sameness⁺ of the Real *from within* the self-same and self-identical object and the autonomous and sovereign word of the symbolic order. The parallactic overlap between Nothing and Something, Real and symbolic, positive unity and differential negativity, and signifier and word twists the stability of the system and its foundation in the self-same and self-identical presence of the ontological order of Being. The schizoid Principle of Sameness⁺ disrupts the architecture of the system in general equivalence and its mediation of identity and difference in the speculations and abstractions of a hierarchy of words and integers. The object which is betwixt departure and arrival, and amidst commencement and destination, is exactly not present. This Real parallax is the Outside of narratively fabled temporality and indexed prepositional spatiality. The *not* illuminates the proximal extimacy between $-ism and S. The overlap of $-ism and its obverse in S ruptures liberal political and ethical commitments.

The schizoid reminds the society of its constitutive exclusions. The *not* is the queer exclusion from the system, and this excluded *not* is the center of the system. The repudiated *not* of *Verwerfung* is the foundation of Western civilization: the homeless of public property is banned from the private sphere; the madman is ostracized from the Ritz Carlton; the pedophile is eliminated from the family; the homosexual is banished from the acceptable; the mentally retarded is debarred from the rationality of Reason, and so on. The system is established by a homeless, mad, pedophilic, homosexual, and mentally retarded citizenry. These monstrosities are the return of the *Verwerfung* and the substance of the parallactic overlap with Reason. The pervert Reasonably theorizes the Unreasonable practices of the schizoid. The pervert is not an idiot. The pervert is in bad company.

The madman is the only clinical form of radical and bodily politicization. The psychotic's politics privileges the signifier over the sign, (*a*)sexual masochism over male heterosexuality, and communism over capitalism. But this prioritization is considered mistaken and mad gibberish by the society. This politics is considered a symptom by the society, but it is considered a *sinthome* by the schizoid. This politics resists any conventional articulation because it is Real and resistant to the spoken and the written. This is an asymbolic activism or Real Politics. The symptom (*sinthome*) of schizophrenia is a Sameness⁺ of the *Trieb* of (*a*)sex, the communism of each according to his ability and his need, and the architectonics of the signifier. But the system misinterprets this politics as the Other of Reason. The revolution is invisible, and it is the Outside of the structure that it contests.

The politics of the madman mobilizes psychoanalysis, Marxism, and deconstruction in order to illuminate the extant systems of $-ism. The discourse of the schizoid is differed and deferred *Trieb* because it suspends a lucid relationship between desire and its object. This *Trieb* forestalls any approach to the phallus and its mediatory third term of speculation and abstraction in the general equivalent of dollars and coins. The *Trieb* prioritizes the signifier above the sign because it delays the departure and the arrival, and the commencement and the destination, of the Boy in a metaphysics of presence. The madman's Unreason is the end — point of break — and origin — point of exclusion — of the system. Schizophrenic politics illuminates $-ism and its architecture at the same moment as it embraces S and the architectonics of the underside of *désir*, exchange-value, and the word. Psychotic politics contests the extant order because it illuminates the coincidence between the skeletal scaffold of the Spirit of the System and the designs of $-ism. *Trieb* defers the object at the same time as it reveals the *objet* in its disappearance. Communism illuminates the excess materiality of goods and services as the internal expansion of the limits of capital and the accumulation of debt. The signifier indicates that the word is seized by a succession of other words in the metonymization of metaphor. The politics of schizophrenia illuminates the Unreason at the center of Reason. Psychosis shames neurosis for its maladroit grasp of its own essence.

Perversely, the ostensible division among neurosis, psychosis, and perversion as distinct and discrete psychical structures must be put under scrutiny. The madman's hallucinations and delusions are the political vision *qua* sign of the messianic *tout autre* of the Other of political justice and ethics, but also of *Trieb*, fetish, use-value, each according to his ability and need, the signifier, and the trace. This psychotic set of symptoms (*sinthome* and politics) is simultaneously the neurotic's own repressed truth and unhystericized and unsymbolized master signifier. The madman's so-called manifest representations in hallucinations and delusions are continuous with the hysteric's latent content of desire and wish. The psychotic's manifest representation is the neurotic's latent content. The dysfunctional detail of the return of the hysteric's repressed is the colorful hallucination and delusion of the schizoid. The neurotic's embryonic master signifier is actualized in the madman's political truth. The neurotic's symbolic repressed and the madman's Real symptom (*sinthome*) are parallactically overlapped by the Principle of Sameness⁺ of the Real.

Only a spatial decenterment separates the latent content of the hysteric from the manifest articulation of the psychotic. The spatial dislocation of mad hallucinations and delusions and neurotic symptoms and pathologies is subject to the pervert's *Verleugnung*. Disavowal returns both the neurotic symptom and the psychotic *sinthome* to the succession of fetishes as "hallucination," "delusion," "dream," "parapraxis," and "joke." The pervert revises the parallactic overlap between the hallucinations and delusions *of neurosis* and the symptoms of the repressed *of madness*. The pervert's parallactic play performs the *Verleugnung — Verwerfung* and *Verdrängung* — of the opposition between neurosis and psychosis. The pervert's disavowal is the so-called vanishing mediator that invisibly translates between neurosis and madness. This perverse mediator speaks and writes its own disappearance. The prestidigitation of *Verleugnung* opens and closes a gap which disappears at the moment of its appearance. Perversely, neurosis, psychosis, and perversion are the *same structure*.

The temporalities of neurosis, psychosis, and perversion also illustrate the parallactic overlap of the clinical structures. The revolutionary projections in the schizoid's hallucinations and delusions invite the pervert to write and speak — symbolize as the Real in *Praxis* — the utopic future of subjectivity and sociality. This is the horizon of the pervert's manifesto. The schizoid is a preformalization and antisymbolization of his own realization in the future of the Pervert-Schizoid-Woman. The temporality of this horizonal projection from the past and present to the future unexpectedly positions the schizoid within the *futur antérieur* (*Nachträglichkeit* and *après-coup*) of the Time of the Neurotic. This ordinary temporality returns the future (present) to the past with the *point de capiton* in order to enforce a chronological temporality of past, present, and future. The madman will have been (*futur antérieur*) the future in the event that the future arrives. The arrival of the Spirit of the System in the future will retroactively redeem the distress and hardship of the past (present) of the madman's torture. The Time of the Neurotic indicates that the past happens in the future. But the Time of the Schizoid suspends the *point de capiton* such that no departure and arrival, or commencement and destination, is possible. The Time of the Schizoid is the fresh *Yes!* of the collision of temporalities in a simultaneous and superpositional instant. Neurotically, the past happens in the future. But psychotically, the past has not happened yet. Nothing has happened yet. Paradoxically, the madman emerges not in his own time but in the temporality of hysteria and its retroaction of pinned signification.

The Time of the Pervert is set to the trace of *différance*. The pervert's time is neither past nor present but an advent toward the future. The pervert resets the clock. The Time of the Neurotic indicates that the Event has happened. The Time of the Schizoid reveals that the Event has not happened yet. The Time of the Pervert indicates that the Event (is) happening. The pervert rescues this present time for a future which must arrive. This future of arrival is simultaneously the present of its destination. The Time of the Pervert folds the present (past) time into the future time. The pervert's text submits the schizoid's Time of the Neurotic to the superposition of the present (past) of the future. Not only is the Time of the Schizoid concurrent with the Time of the Neurotic but the temporality of the pervert returns the present (past) of the schizoid's hallucinations and delusions and the neurotic's symptoms and pathologies to the future. The future is the overlapped collision of the manifest representation of the schizoid's hallucinations and delusions and the neurotic's nascent master signifier. Perversely, this future is in an instant the present. The $-ism is *already* Spirit. The desire is *already* drive. Capitalism is *already* communism. The word is *already* the signifier. Perversely, the temporalities of schizophrenia and neurosis are the *same structure*. The excess of this parallactic overlap between the schizoid and the hysteric is the returned "Time" which is otherwise destructured in the timeless unconscious. Time is a fable of narrative convention. The present and its succession of differences and fetishes in space are the substance of the pervert's galaxy.

The Pervert's Verleugnung of Sameness+

Verleugnung is a peculiar modality of negation because it negates itself at the same time as it affirms itself. The simultaneous acknowledgement and denial of the content of the negation and affirmation mobilize a rebuttal of the unconscious as well as a pledge to the conscious. *Verleugnung* undoes what it does, and it unmakes what is makes. But this is done and made without a departure or arrival, or a commencement or destination, of an *arche* to do and to make. The slip and slide of the doing and making — Ing+ — are an endless succession of denials and guarantees. This series returns the repudiated to the conscious dimension of oath and deposition. The *unambivalence* of disavowal tends toward the openness of affirmation and the return rather than the closedness of negation and the symptom. *Verleugnung* is both openness and closedness, expansion and contraction, and extension and diminution. But the proclivity of disavowal as a structure of negation (affirmation) is toward growth and the supplementation of fetishes in the set of objects in the solar system. Affirmation is the essence of the return of the negation in *Verleugnung*.

The tricky component to disavowal is that the two moves — negativity and positivity, revocation and return, unconscious content and conscious manifestation — are performed simultaneously. The object may be subordinate to affirmation or to negation. The simultaneity of avowal and disavowal in *Verleugnung* confuses the binary opposition between negativity/positivity, negation/return, unconscious/conscious, and so on. The unmoored system of disavowal is anchored to the penile reference of the "penis-substitute" and to the essential defense against castration and sexual difference. But otherwise *Verleugnung* is essentially schizophrenic. Disavowal is split *from itself*. The disavowal of sexual difference — "a man has a penis and a Woman does not have a penis" — is concurrently avowed — "a man has a penis and a Woman does not have a penis." The object of the return in *Verleugnung* is simultaneously the object of the repudiation of the truth of castration *qua* sexual difference and the embrace of the truth of castration *qua* sexual (*a*)difference. Does *Verleugnung* succeed at any modality of negation whatsoever? Does disavowal in its simultaneous admission and dismissal achieve any gesture in the in-between space and time of acknowledgment and denial? Is an economy of an aperture and a closure of the parallactic gap possible in the *Verleugnung* of recognition and refusal? Or is the modality of negation in *Verleugnung* distinct from the hard negation in *Verwerfung* and the soft negation in *Verdrängung*?

The object of affirmative return is also under scrutiny in disavowal. The essence of *Verleugnung* is Sameness+. Any object is different *from itself* because it is overlapped *with* any other object in the system. The Logic of Difference ($A \neq A = B$) opens the gap of any word with itself but closes the alienation between words with each other. But what is the object of return in *Verleugnung*? A symptomatic Sameness+ recalls a Nietzschean Eternal Return of the Same.[48] Disavowal returns a sameness. The object of negation (affirmation) and its return is the same object. But this object is at a distance from itself. The object of chaotic refusal and warm return is not the object *qua* itself. The object returns an excess with itself. I have noted this excess as the scare quotes of a returned object to the system of the Cs. Disavowal returns "disavowal." The scare quotes indicate that the object is in excess of itself. A surplus is returned in the acknowledgment and denial of the object. This remainder is the relationality and constructionism of any object in regard to any other object in the system. The scare quotes indicate the Real Penis as the emollient of relatedness between objects in the system. The return of the object indicates a self-sameness and self-identity of the word as autonomous and sovereign. But the return of the "object" indicates a bond and alliance of diacritical difference and negativity with any other "object" in the system. The relationship between an "object" and an "object" — fetish and fetish — is lubricated by the Real Penis. Any "object" is split *from itself* but *bound to* any other "object" in the succession of words.

The fetish is this returned excess which obscures the object of castration with the "object" of the defense against castration. But even castration returns as "castration." Sexual difference returns as sexual (*a*)difference, and the surplus "(*a*)" is the excess of the fetish. *Verleugnung* returns surplus. This economy applies to the excess of *Trieb* to *désir* in psychoanalysis, of use-value to exchange-value in Marxism, and of the signifier to the word in deconstruction. The self-sameness and self-identity of the object of the penis yield to the Real Penis and its emollient of the relatedness of any "object" to any other "object" in the system of the diacritical negativity and difference of a value which is undecided and indeterminate in space. The *destruktion* of the symbolic order is an effect of this excess — "fetish" — which cannot be recuperated into the system of making and unmaking, doing and undoing, and the Ing+ of the Becoming of the succession of objects in the system. The system is open and expansive rather than closed and contracted. The unconscious is the space of the surplus.

Figure 3.8 The Fragmented Term

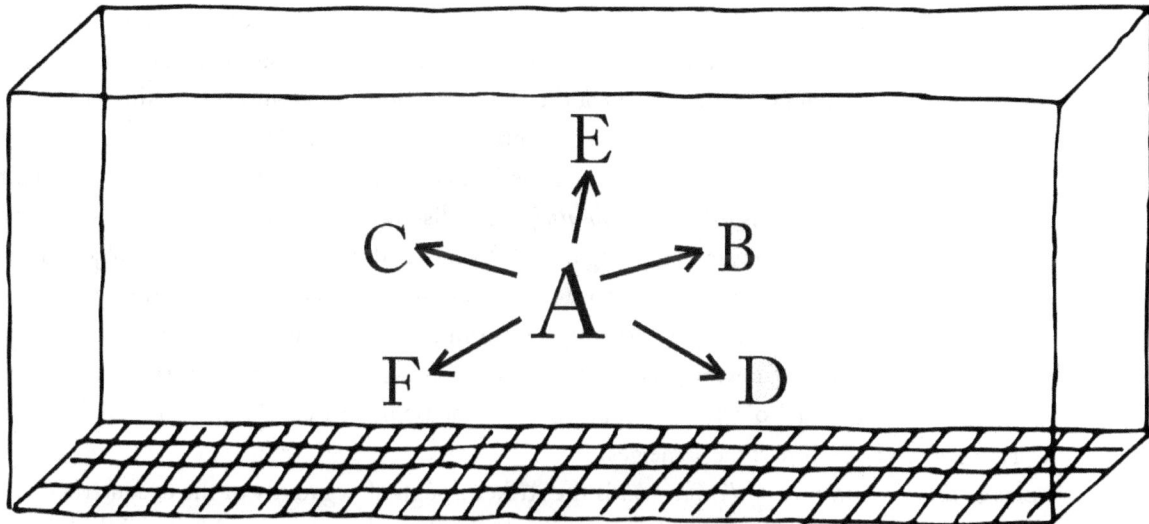

This illustration depicts the essential potentiality for any unit of text (letter, word, phrase, sentence, paragraph, and so on) to transform into any other unit of text. Any object is subject to an internal (external) necessity of Becoming otherwise than itself. This extimate essence (~~Being~~) is the organizational context of *langue* — Becoming of itself as not itself. Every word is divided from itself. The word is what it is not. The jagged fragmentation in the drawing is positioned below the space of language and the split within/out A and its internal (external) extimate others in B, C, D, E, and F. The space of *langue* in the galaxy is temporal. The variable Becoming of open nondefinition rather than the static Being of closed definition defines the space of the word. The Outside of this space must be understood as a realm in which objects are their essence in and as the negative. The object is the Outside of the space of *langue*. The word is exposed in its radical lack of identity and total absence of presence. The illustration of the jagged fragmentation applies to any unit of text at any point in any series. The ostensible ~~Being~~ of the signifier is represented within the space of the signifying chain. This illustration portrays the coincidence and continuity of Being and Becoming in the jagged fragmentation of the word. Becoming (de)structures Being. Becoming elides and illuminates — and counteracts and constitutes — Being. The image of the jagged fragmented A — any word and any object — illustrates the external internal — extimacy — of any word and any object.

Notes & Sketches —

The object which repeats and recurs is an identity which is different *from itself* but the same — ~~equal~~ and ~~unequal~~ and ~~identical~~ and ~~different~~ — as *any other object* in a decentered space whose objects are related by the lubrication of the Real Penis. But it should also be reiterated that the pervert's Sameness⁺ is the cardinal symptom of the Madness of Order and its elegant vitality. The architecture of the system in the word is returned as the architectonics of the system in the "word." The surplus of the parallactic overlap between the architecture and the architectonics is the excesses of the penis against the penis-substitute, of the surfeit of commodities against the restrictions of currency, and of the play of the signifier against the rigidity of the sign. Every gesture is the same gesture. But the unnecessarily noted caveat to this strict overlap is that the same gesture returns as the "same gesture." The remainder of the Sameness⁺ of the gesture (or of any materiality or any abstraction) is that the gesture is different *from itself*. This distance of the object from its own essence invites the relationality and constructionism of the Logic of Difference and the binds between the objects in the succession of fetishes. But the surplus is not ~~equality~~ or ~~inequality~~ or ~~identity~~ or ~~difference~~ or any permutation of general equivalence. Rather, the remainder is strictly spatial in the proximities of fetishes in relationship to each other. The other caveat is that every gesture is not every other gesture (or materiality or abstraction) because the surfeit of "every gesture" outstrips the Sameness⁺ of the Being or Real Penis of the copulative "is" in the proposition that every gesture *is* the same gesture.

The surplus of this *sous rature et sur l'effacement* is the strikethrough of negativity of the deconstruction of the metaphysics of presence. This is the extra Nothingness which returns between the object and the "object," or between the fetish and the "fetish." Perversely, this Nothingness of the strikethrough of ~~castration~~ returns to haunt the pervert and his defense against sexual difference. But the pervert's Sameness⁺ is not a closed system. Sameness⁺ is situated in a field of expansion. The simultaneous affirmation (negation) of the fetish is a trace of the *not* which cannot be recuperated into the system of perversion. But the open extension of the system promises an expansion in the fields of desire and sexuality; language and the signifier; and economy and labor. The obstacles of masochistic *Trieb* differ and defer the object — *Boy!* — in the expansion of the erotic galaxy. The signifiers of *langue* cascade inways and outways in the expansive play of the indetermination of value. The materiality of the overproductivity of labor exceeds in surplus any determinate calculation of the general equivalent of speculation and abstraction of exchange. The *Trieb* of (*a*)sexuality, the materialist overproductivity of communism, and the free play of the signifier of the deconstructionist text extend the open trace of Nothingness toward the expansion of Being and the *sous rature* of its supplementation in the Real Penis of the *tout autre* and its differed and deferred — *Not yet!* — beyond. The Real Penis and Being are isomorphic. Both words are under erasure. The distinction of the Real Penis indicates the Sameness⁺ of the relationship of any object at a distance from itself but in proximity to any other object in the succession of fetishes in the expansive galaxy. In contrast, Being relates static self-same and self-identical autonomous positive unities of words to each other. The Real Penis is motivated by the Principle of Sameness⁺ and the Becoming of Ing⁺. Being is structured by the metaphysics of presence and the equivalence of the object *qua* object rather than the excess of the fetish *qua* "fetish."

The *Verleugnung* of the simultaneous negation and affirmation of the object is the metalanguage of fetishism. This metalanguage of the deconstruction of binarism applies to the sign and signification in language, phallocentrism and sexual difference in patriarchy, and private property and scarcity in capitalism. The symptom of the perverse fetishist is sexual (*a*)difference or the concurrence of the acknowledgment of sexual difference ("a man has a penis and a Woman does not have a penis") and the rejection of sexual difference ("a man has a penis and a Woman does not have a penis"). The inconclusive consequence of the perverse *bothness* and *andness* of the simultaneous disavowal of sexual difference is: men have a penis and do not have a penis;

Women do not have a penis and have a penis; men have a penis and Woman have a clitoris and a vagina; men do not have a clitoris and a vagina and Women have a clitoris and a vagina, and so on.

But this series of reinscribed alternatives in the economy of disavowal is recursive and limitless. Any sexual organ and its permutations of economy return to the fetishistic structure as different *from themselves* but bound in an extimate Sameness⁺ *to each other*. The success of fetishistic play of admission and dismissal is potentially endless in the assembly of objects of play and amusement, but also of protection and defense. There is no conclusion — *arche* of departure and arrival, and commencement and destination — to the returns of the tendency toward expansion in *Verleugnung*. The perverse metalanguage of the deconstruction of binarism invites the proliferation of playful differences and negativities of the signifier rather than the reduction of strict divisions and oppositions of words. The *Verleugnung* of the perverse fetish expands, and the *Verdrängung* of the hysterical symptom contracts.

But the pivotal issue is that the recurrences of *Verleugnung* return the entire system of objects and words. The *All* is returned in the negation (affirmation) of the return of the refused and the clinched. The open totality of the succession of objects and words returns in the simultaneous mayhem of acknowledgment and dismissal. Not only does the truth of sexual difference return to the precise defense against castration. But both difference and (*a*)difference recur as "difference" and "(*a*)difference" with the surplus of the differential negativity (positivity) of fetishism. Perversely, the entirety of the system of objects and words in the solar system is at once negated and affirmed, and dismissed and acknowledged. The Principle of Sameness⁺ motivates this dyslexic return of the objects and words which are deviant *from themselves* but *proximal to* the other objects and words in the set. *Verleugnung* affirmatively recurs the solar system *qua* the Sameness⁺ of the fetish. This is the reason that the pervert's disavowal is the privileged modality of ~~negation~~ and ~~affirmation~~ in which to illuminate the Madness of Order and its bi-level (uni-level) architecture of the sign and architectonics of the signifier.

Grammatologically, the system is a sequence of diacritical differential negative signifiers in the absence of a center which would otherwise ground play in a structure of binary opposition. The word is not the primary unit of meaning-making. Psychoanalytically, the penis is not the final referent for sexuality. The *objet petit a* is not the penultimate object of the *Ziel* of *Trieb*. Communistically, commodities are not units of private property which can be made equivalent through the speculation and abstraction of integers and decimals. The object is primarily a use-value rather than an exchange-value. The entirety of the set of objects in the galaxy is not only Same⁺ but also Real. This Same⁺ Real exposes the latent truth of the Madness of Order: the deferral of the object in *Trieb*; the deferral of the penis as the referent of sex; and the deferral of debt in the accumulation of capital. This series of deferrals recurs in *Verleugnung* and in the affirmation of the entire ontological order in its succession of postponements and delays. The fetishist collects the objects of the missed encounter. Disavowal is a perpetual relationship to Otherness.

The pervert enjoys the modality of his *Verleugnung* and the returned object — *All* — as synchronous and spatial rather than as diachronous and temporal. The cause *qua* negation is simultaneously the effect *qua* symptom. The reverse is also the case: the symptom appears as the consequence of refusal. There is no distance between the return of the symptom and the repudiation of the object. Nor is there a gap between the manifestation of the latent and the affirmation of the word. The unconscious is timeless. The only temporality which approaches the expanses of space of the unconscious is the Time of the Schizoid which suspends the past (present) and the future between each other in a parallactic oscillation. Time is a fable of narratives and stories. Space is potentially infinite in its expansion and extension. The return of *All* to the (un)conscious in fetishism is an in-action, in-process succession of objects and words in a system of proliferation. The universe expands, and man's spatial position in the galaxy is resituated both everywhere and nowhere in the Outside of the determination of Being and the metaphysics of presence. The space of man is the Time of the Schizoid. There is no such *das Ding* as time.

The limits of an expansive universe cannot position man in coordinated space because an absolute or relative position cannot make reference to an independent standard. At best, man is dislocated as *absolutely relative* in the timeless space of the unconscious. The deferral of *différance* is suspended in the unconscious, and Derrida's exasperated statement in *Of Grammatology* (1967) that origin (is) trace refers the temporization of deferral to the spatialization of point(s) in space.[49] The *telos* of perversion is not the closure of the networks of relations and negativities in the webs of objects. Rather, the Positivity of Sameness+ is the schizoid's secret truth that the pervert's disavowal illuminates. But why "Sameness+"? The choice of word for this (con/de)structure or (de/con)struction is irrelevant. Every word (is) the same word. If so, Sameness+ is a handy word, and its articulation implies an expansion toward Otherness. Sameness+ is serviceable, but so is "Grasshopper+."

This sublime conflagration of ~~identity~~ and ~~difference~~ into a Sameness+ inspires a visible fiery void in which any object is at a distance from itself but in proximity with the other objects in the galaxy. A *Spaltung* splits the object *from itself* such that the void is internal to the object. The object of the void is the split in the object. This void is the energy of the (a)sexual obscene abundance at the center of the Madness of Order and its potential for expansion rather than contraction. Extension is a consequence of the Principle of Sameness+ and the split in any object by itself or the splice of any word by the signifier or the eclipse of any utility by exchangeability or the capitation of any penis by the fetish. An (a)sexual abundance is the potentiality of this expansion in words and syntax and semantics, in goods and services, and in sex organs. But the neurotic is desperately blind to this latent growth in the system. The neurotic is sexualized by repressions and their returns as symptoms.

In contrast, the pervert and the madman are desexualized by the difference and deferral of the trace. The pervert collects objects and words in a succession of flirtations, obstacles, hindrances, distractions, interferences, diversions, and interruptions between himself and *himself* and between himself and the *Boy*. Perversely, Sameness+ masochistically *works*. Sameness+ presents neither *arche* nor origin. Rather, Sameness+ strikes a void in any object in order to relate it to any other object. An (a)sexual obscenity grows the extensions of these relationships. The fractions and fractals extend beyond the splits in themselves because of the suspension of an abortive *point de capiton*. *A Pervert's Manifesto* demonstrates this Unreason within the syntax and semantics of the negative signifierization of the positive sign. The text is a signifier, but it writes and speaks in the word.

The four dimensions are critical to an interpretation of the three clinical structures and their relationship to the Madness of Order. The first-dimension is space. Space is the discoordinated expanse of the unconscious. The second-dimension is time. The second-dimension is only operative in the system of the Cs. Unconsciously, there is no second-dimension of time. The unconscious as a structure collapses the first-dimension of space and the second-dimension of time. The second-dimension is interrupted by the suspension of the *point de capiton* and the instantaneity of past, present, and future in the *Yes!* of the Time of the Schizoid. Futurally, the third-dimension is the timeless unconscious and its techniques and considerations of representability. The unconscious is the space of the play of the signifier in the condensations and displacements of the ordinary syntax of the architecture of the word. The fourth-dimension of *Praxis* is the space of the Pervert-Schizoid-Woman. *Praxis* refers to the pervert's articulation of the Unreasonable truth of the schizoid. The fourth-dimension of the Pervert-Schizoid-Woman emerges from the unconscious dimension and its *destruktion* (affirmation) of: *Trieb* and deferral in presence; use-value and the objects of general *inequivalence*; and the signifier and the play of unorthodox semantics and syntax. The fourth-dimension of the Pervert-Schizoid-Woman is the expansive space of the singularities of the Sameness⁺ of objects. The pervert illuminates that the solar system is a succession of singularities which is uncoordinated in an undecidable and indeterminate expanse of space. This is the parallax between the unconscious and the Madness of Order. $-ism is S. There is only one dimension.

The object of negative (affirmative) return in *Verleugnung* is not the abject horror of castration but the unexpected delight of sexual (*a*)difference of an undecidable and indeterminate general inequivalence. Not only do the female organs not lack the penis. But the penis does not lack the clitoris. Queer sexuality reconfigures phallocentrism because it posits that "a man has a penis and a man has a penis" and "a Woman has a vagina and a clitoris and a Woman has a vagina and a clitoris." These queer renditions of -centrism can be reworded as "a man has a not-clitoris and a man has a not-clitoris" and "a Woman has a not-penis and a Woman has a not-penis." But the former queer articulations affirm a repudiation of -centrism. What is gay male sexuality of penis/penis? What is lesbian sexuality of clitoris/clitoris? The theory and practice of queer sexuality reconfigure not only the genitals but also the rapport and bond — sexual practices — between same-sex copulation. Male homosexuality is exactly not phallocentric because it does not rely on its obverse negative term — the clitoris — as its diminutive opposite and distinct object. Lesbian sexuality is precisely not phallocentric not only because it puts the phallocentric definition under scrutiny in its redefinition of sex as the Outside of the male orgasm and ejaculation. Lesbian sexuality also involves the asymmetrical complementarity between two absences (not-penis and not-penis) but also simultaneously two presences (clitoris and clitoris). What is the magical *Praxis* of nonphallocentric (*a*)sex? What subjective and social reconfigurations of ~~desire~~ pleasure are possible in a system of asymmetrical parallactic coincidences and continuities?

Queer sex is not only (*a*)different. Queer (*a*)sex is also the choice of the abundance and plenitude of pleasure rather than the castration and lack of desire. Perverse queer *Verleugnung* returns these affirmative objects of *jouissance* rather than the self-same and self-identical objects of desire and their scrapes and cuts. The subject is not completed in the object. The subject and the object are complete as both positive — penis/penis and clitoris/clitoris — and negative — (*a*)different penis and (*a*)different clitoris. Queer perversion refuses the speculation of *desire* for the spectacle of *jouissance*. The excess of this overlap of penis/penis and clitoris/clitoris (and their negative obverse) is the (*a*) of (*a*)sexuality. This is the obscene force which grows rather than limits the succession of objects of *jouissance* instead of the series of units of *desire*. The pervert recognizes that queer (*a*)sexuality is animated by *jouissance* rather than by *desire*. Or (*a*)sexuality is structured by the overlap between desire and enjoyment. Perverse *Trieb* is the inheritance of this economy of the internalized obstacle of desire and the enjoyment of the inaccessible object. A perverse masochistic (*a*)sexuality *enjoys desire*.

The (*a*)difference returns to the aneconomy in the in-process, in-action Becoming of the proliferation of the *same difference* of incalculable and immeasurable — undecidable and indeterminate — singularities which cannot be arbitrated by general equivalence. A singularity — any object ~~is~~ any other object — is a configuration which is beyond psychoanalytic speculation or capitalist abstraction or linguistic signification. This modality of perversion is a threat to *le propre*. The capitalist private property of the penis (versus not-penis) and the clitoris (versus not-clitoris) and the other commodities in the marketplace is otherwise owned as a self-same and self-identical autonomous unit of value. There are other so-imagined private properties. These include affect (*my* feelings are my *own*), intellectual (*my* thoughts are my *own*), psychical (*my* unconscious is my *own*), familial (*my* wife is my *own*), religious (*my* God is my *own*), material (*my* house is my *own*), and interpersonal (*my* friend is my *own*).

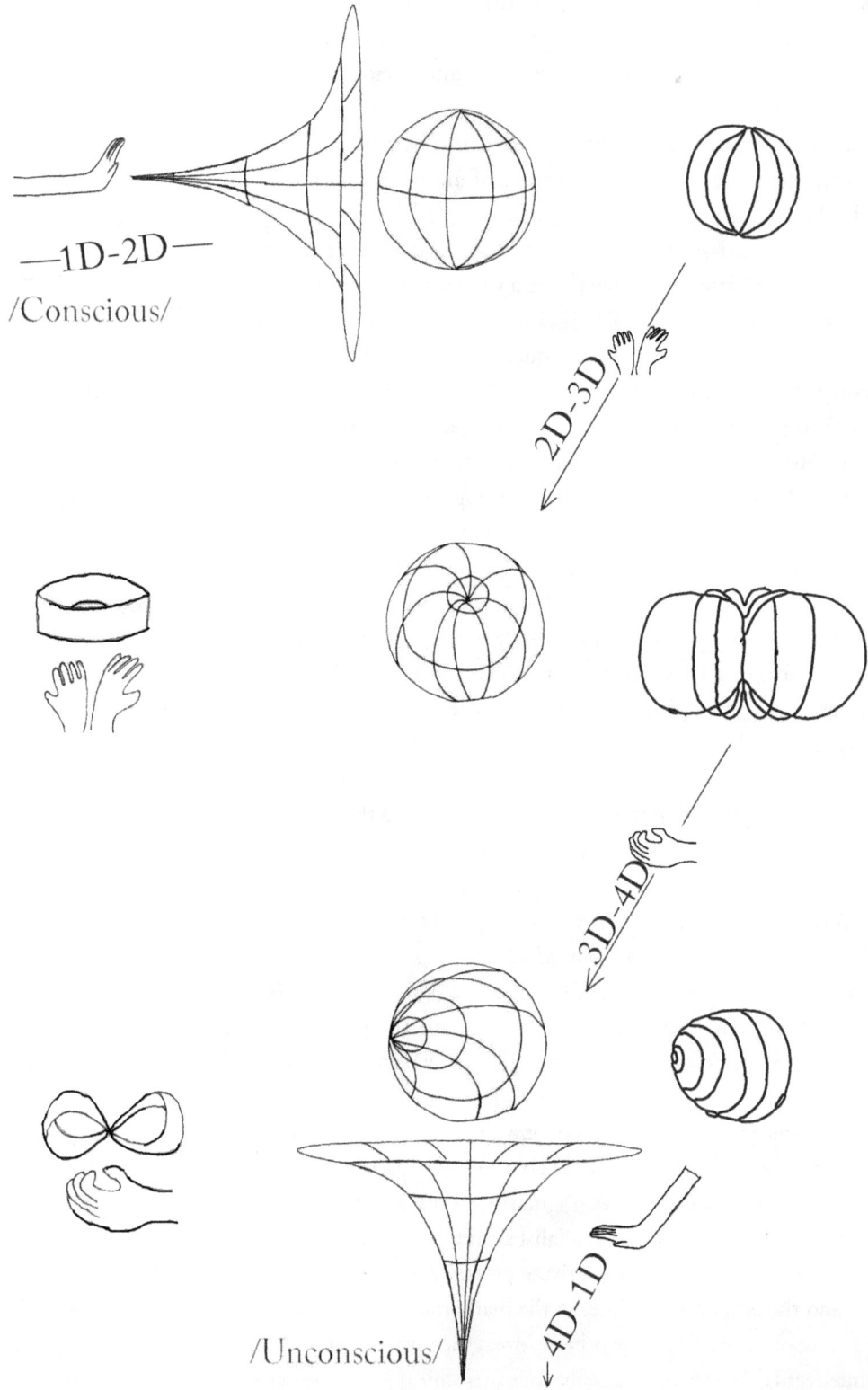

Figure 3.9 Dimensional Equivalence

This illustration shows the Sameness+ of the third-dimension of the timeless unconscious. The deconstruction of the self-same and the self-identical pervades and structures the four-dimensional universe of space, time, the unconscious, and *Praxis*. The subject — self and other — is simultaneously in all times (conventional chronological narration) and spaces (points of discoordination) in the universe of the (un)conscious. The universe wobbles in and out of Being (what is) in the parallactic overlap of any point in space. The universe is its own (re)verberation of the fetishistic substitution of the recurrence — lost and found — of objects in the solar system. Paradoxically, this configuration structures the unconscious to be both timeless but also in time. The galaxy is neither self-same nor self-identical but a Sameness+ which is neither identical nor different nor equal nor unequal nor any quantification or qualification of standardization. The pervert discovers that the universe is (non)coincident and (non)continuous with itself. The Pervert-Schizoid-Woman slips through the dimensions of space, time, the unconscious, and *Praxis*. She finds her discoordinated space in the *Praxis* of the unconscious. This trajectory is neither latent nor even the latent *of* the latent but the *tout autre* of a space after the Death of Time and its apparatus of the system of the conscious. The pervert's pinch and twist in the *Möbius* loop are simultaneously at all points of discoordinated space. The first-dimension of space is present at all points in the system but at the same time at a decentered distance from itself. Space is not yet space even at the Outside of time and conventional chronological narration. The schizoid discerns that any object in the system is the same as any other object. The system is a series of simulacra with reference to the *mise-en-abyme* of substitution — but not to the comparison and contrast of exchange. The pervert's ability to enact the flip and twist of this Sameness+ indicates the instant at which the *All* is Becoming in an extended interval. This instant is the suspended moment in which Something is Missing parallactically overlaps with Nothing is Missing. The parallax illuminates the otherwise occluded center of the Woman and Being (*et al.*) who are — yet — under erasure. The drawing shows the simultaneous dynamic interplay and paradoxical equivalence of the dimensions. An instantaneous and simultaneous expansion and contraction animate the (*a*)sexual center of the system. The arrows represent neither temporality nor spatiality. Rather, the arrows depict an unconscious (non)temporal and (non)spatial Gordian knot of the relationship between the first-dimension of space and the second-dimension of time. The *Praxis* of the symbolization of the Real structures and reveals the equivalence of space and time in the becoming-time of space and the becoming-space of time. The constitutive elements which are situated between the two open functions of gravity are the Outside of standardization and calculation. They cannot be compared and contrasted as (un)equal. Space is the first-dimension but at the same time three-dimensional.

Notes & Sketches —

This entire set of objects of general equivalence is structured by the private property relationships: of oedipal desire and its ownership of the penis; of capitalist commodification and its ownership of the object; and of linguistic signification and its ownership of the word. $-ism is the system of private property of calculable and measurable — decidable and determinate — objects. The pervert enjoys that the penis is not owned by the man, that the commodity is not owned by the consumer, and that the word is not owned by the speaker. The release of the privacy of property opens the tendency toward expansion rather than the proclivity toward contraction. The object disappears in the ether of the universe.

The perverse so-called symptom is the return of itself as "itself" in its affirmed negation in *Verleugnung*. But Freud (1938) also notes the "minor symptom" of the perverse offspring who "retains to this day — an anxious sensitivity about his little toes being touched."[50] Freud continues: "It is as if, after all the to-ing and fro-ing between denial and acknowledgement, it was the castration that managed to find the clearer expression."[51] According to Freud, the horror of castration returns in the perverse economy and its defense against sexual difference. But this return is only a "minor symptom." This is so even if such an inessential indicator manifests as castration anxiety. But in any case, why does the pervert's structure even return castration except as "castration" and as a succession of other objects? How is castration rather than Sameness[+] returned in *Verleugnung* of sexual difference if the modality of simultaneous negation is extimate to concomitant affirmation? How is castration returned if the downtrodden and the castrated, on the one hand, and the upraised and the protected, on the other hand, are the same gesture?

The answer is the peculiar structure of *Verleugnung* which blindsides the neurotic. Perversely, there are no divisions and oppositions — words — between an (*a*)sexual difference and a castration. The erupted return of disavowal in the so-called minor symptom is the recurrence of this same disavowal of the clitoris. The clitoris and the penis-substitute are returned as "clitoris" and "penis-substitute" whose self-sameness and self-identity are elevated to the organization of relationality and constructionism. This clitoris is the same as the penis because the clitoris is not the clitoris in its difference *from itself*, and the penis is not the penis in its difference *from itself*. The return of the negative and absent clitoris (penis) is simultaneously the return of the positive and present penis (clitoris). The objects of the return of the *Verleugnung* are the penis and the clitoris as distanced from themselves but proximate to each other. *Verleugnung* is neither the equal of nor the different from nor the unequal to nor the identical of the original. Rather, *Verleugnung* is the returned sexual (*a*)difference of the *All* and a succession of body parts, anatomical objects, furs, laces, shoes, jockstraps, and so on. This returned sexual difference is an (*a*)sexual difference. The pervert's Sameness[+] is (*a*)sexual difference. The returned object of *Verleugnung* is (*a*)sexuality.

The clitoris is the Outside of male fetishism. As Freud briefly outlines in "Medusa's Head" (1922), it is the penis which is the source of castration anxiety.[52] The penis is both the subject and the object of castration. The clitoris (not-penis) is not the only object of abject anxiety and total fear. Rather, the penis is the unexpected subject and object of castration anxiety. The male junior is anxious in relationship not only to the Woman but to his own penis. The system of *le propre* of the penis as private property is the source of dread. Capitalism is the source of castration anxiety. The ownership of the penis is the foundation of the male junior's fear. The man *desires castration* and the loss of the private property of the penis. The pervert recognizes that ownership of private property — the penis of the man, the commodity of the consumer, and the word of the speaker — is the source of worry. The fear is not of loss but of gain. Ownership impedes expansion and foments contraction.

Ownership is the exact object of deconstruction. The economy of *le propre* is the bullseye of any proper *destruktion* in theory and practice of the system of castration and its symptomatology of narcissism, aggression, and anxiety. The penis must return from negation (affirmation) as distinct from itself or as the "penis" of a succession of words which extends the series of fetishes. The clitoris is the returned heir to the penis. The penis is the returned inheritor of the clitoris. The exchange between penis and clitoris is asymmetrical because each is not only unowned by the man and the Woman but each is unowned as itself. The penis is free of propriety, and the clitoris is liberated from possession. It is no wonder that the presence of naked sexual anatomy is nearly irrelevant to (*a*)sexual eroticism. The masochistic delay of the inaccessible object defers any possession of the Boy.

It is pivotal to note that the connective tissue of Being, Sameness⁺, and the Real Penis is necessarily under erasure — *sous rature et sur l'effacement* — in a future system of undecidability and indeterminacy of spatial incoordination. The Real Signifier indicates that the penis and the clitoris are the ~~Same⁺~~ *as each other* because they are ~~Different⁺~~ *from themselves.* The relationship between an object and itself in the purported self-sameness and self-identity of the positive unity of the object is subordinate to a *Spaltung* which subverts the copulative bond — ~~Being~~ — between the object and itself. But this rupture also applies to the relationships among the succession of objects which returns from affirmative *Verleugnung.* The spatiality of the unconscious decenters objects from themselves and each other in a discoordination which is only haphazardly straddled by the system of prepositions. These prepositions link undecidability and indeterminacy in the space of the unconscious. Singularities are related to and constructed by each other, but an internal and external decenterment both consolidates (*Eros*) and disperses (*Thanatos*) objects from themselves and each other.

This *Spaltung* in the object disavows the objects of sexual difference both *within* themselves but also *between* each other. The penis and the fetish are concealed both from themselves and from each other. The penis is not present. The fetish is not present except as the "fetish." There is no such *das Ding* as a penis. The fur, lace, shoe, and jockstrap screen Nothingness. The penis is infinitely recursive and endlessly doubled. Perversely, the penis resists a metaphysics of presence. The penis is — *not.* The penis is a simulacrum of a copy; this copy is a facsimile of an image; this image is a transcript of a mimeograph; this mimeograph is a forgery of a knockoff, and so on, in a spiral down and up a *mise-en-abyme* in which the metalanguage of the penis-substitute yields to the *metameta* of endless recursion.

There is no originary and primary penis as such — *qua,* by definition, *il y a,* by necessity, and so on. The male junior's prestige and the female junior's ignominy are both substitutes — words, fetishes, metaphors, objects, signs, metonymies, centers — for each other in a delayed absence. But the absent not-penis is a prop for the phallus and its general equivalence. This speculation and abstraction halt the slip and slide of recursion with the neurotic *point de capiton.* The button-tie halts the skid of the *mise-en-abyme,* and it tethers the penis to either the not-penis (clitoris) or to the fetish (penis-substitute). The madman is lost in the hall of mirrors of redoubled recursion. The pervert recognizes this discoordination, but he typically anchors his sexuality in the return of the "jockstrap" in its reference to the penis-substitute and to the defense against castration.

The pervert enjoys the Other *jouissance.* He does so without the dynamic among the phallus, the object, and desire. The pervert's orientation is away from *désir* and toward *Trieb.* The pervert's aesthetic shifts away from the sex of anatomical bodies and sexuality and sexual difference and toward (*a*)sexuality and the Sameness⁺ of the Real. The pervert is a lucky voyeur and an artful exhibitionist. The pervert's vaunted fetishism is a disavowed both/and veil over the cringe of castration. But this fetishistic veil is not essentially or even primarily sexualized. This is so despite Freud's will to situate perversion and fetishism in the sexual domain in his work in *Three Essays* (1905), "Fetishism," (1927), and "Splitting of the Ego in the Process of Defense" (1938). Rather, the pervert is fascinated by *representation.* The pervert enjoys the idealized, imagistic, textual, scopophilic, adorational, sentient, and awed engagement with textuality — the word and the image.

The fetish is *re-presentational* of the absent penis in the fur, lace, shoe, jockstrap, collage, pin-up, old postcard, Instagram update, porno rag, and any content in textual and visual culture. These objects return as "fur," "lace," "shoe," "jockstrap," "collage," "pin-up," "old postcard," "Instagram update," and "porno rag." The relationality and constructionism of these returned scare quotes bond and extend to yet other representations. The pervert realizes that the screen and the veil — obstacle and obstruction — are sexier than the present object in its invariable absence and retreat. Perversely, absence is presence. The pervert's *jouissance* is this (any) interval of the parallactic gap. The pervert *enjoys desire.*

The crucial distinction of the mediatory Real Penis is that it refuses any calculation of credit/debt of size and visibility (and so on) of the objects in relationship to *themselves* or to *each other.* The Real Penis is the grammatical preposition, and it is indexical. But its prepositional indexicality relays and routes objects in a discoordinated space. The proximities of *Eros* and the distances of *Thanatos* are only haphazardly occasioned by the Real Penis. It is contingency that the shoe, fur, lace, and jockstrap (*et al.*) are juxtaposed to the body of the female in heterosexual fetishistic sex. Any object can potentially exchange with any other object in fetishism. The fetish is the logic of substitution: metaphor for center, center for fetish, fetish for object, object for metonymy, metonymy for phallus, and so on.

The exchanges are recursive and doubled, and the only limit to the substitution is the contraction of objects *qua* "objects" in the succession of fetishes in the system. A multiplicity of sexual (*a*)organs can be substituted for the penis as the referent for fetishistic sexual practices. The expansion of the world depends on the lubricational Real Penis and its prepositional magic to relay and route objects in relationship to each other. The penis can be its own fetish if the referent for sex is the jockstrap (*et al.*). The clitoris can be its own fetish if the referent for sex is the penis (*et al.*). The penis is not only *not* but it is not even the necessary referent for fetishism. The penis-substitute may be transposed as the fur-substitute. The pervert enjoys that there is no proper object of sexual *jouissance.* But the pervert's Other *jouissance* is neither the penis nor the jockstrap, and neither the clitoris nor the penis. Rather, the pervert's *jouissance* is substitution or the metonymization of metaphor in the expansion of the galaxy of undecidable and indeterminate words and objects. The *jouissance* of the pervert enjoys an excess which extends beyond the borders and limits of the text. The Real Penis lubricates this locus of substitution. The object of the pervert's *jouissance* is the substitutability in and as the Real Penis.

THREATS

The *bothness* and *andness* of the pervert's symptom are both disavowal and "disavowal." The distinction of the scare quotes is the affirmation in scare quotes of the otherwise negated in unquoted text. The excess of these scare quotes is the rupture of the self-identity and self-sameness of the positively unified object. The scare quotes indicate the *Spaltung* in the relationship of the word *with itself.* This split in Sameness[+] opens the object to a relatedness with the series of other objects in an expansive set of objects. The scare quotes indicate a suspicion, but the object of this skepticism is not the word itself but the positive unit of the sign and its elision of the architectonics of the system in the materiality of the signifier and the abstraction of the signified. The pervert recognizes that objects are not objects, and that words are not words. The pervert discerns that the *Thanatos* of the death drive carves and cuts unities into remainders and surpluses. The pervert's insight is that an explosive rupture of unity expands the system toward an outward openness which proliferates the set of fetishes — texts — for his *jouissance.*

Freud claims that fetishism verges on pathology because of its so-called fixation and exclusivity of object. But this indicates Freud's own idea that health involves the free-swap and endless-exchange of objects and aims of incipient sexuality. Freud intimates that embryonic sexuality is the proper mode of healthy sexuality. Unexpectedly, the *telos* of heterosexual monogamy is an unhealthy fixation and exclusivity in adult sexuality. The offspring's sexuality is normal and free. The adult's sexuality is abnormal and sick. The expansion of fetishes is the offspring's play, and the restriction of toys is the adult's normativity. The unfixated and nonexclusive fetish is the object of the offspringlike pervert's play. But what is the threat of perversion? What is the threat of unconscious play to the coordinated architecture of the penis, the commodity, and the sign?

The Signifiers of the Real

The threat of the pervert is the return of the Real and its disturbance of the general equivalent. The everyday word is neurotic and positive. This is so even as the word is at the same time schizoid and negative. The architectonics of the signifier and the architecture of the word parallactically overlap. This parallax is exactly the system in its operation and breakdown. The threat of the schizophrenic negative and differential diacritics of the signifier is that it will topple the system of general equivalence and its stable, equal, and symmetrical exchange of penis for not-penis, commodity for commodity, and word for word. The pervert's *Verleugnung* returns the object with an excess because the object is different *from itself* and related to the other objects in the system. Disavowal is a structure of uneven exchange within any object and between any set of objects. Sameness⁺ is a threat to a system of identity/difference, here/there, black/white, good/evil, time/space, and so on. The pervert discerns the fundamental general *inequivalence* of the system of exchange. A leftover in the penis, the commodity, and the word disturbs symmetrical exchange. This excess returns to topple a system of equality, inequality, identity, difference, and any precept of binary opposition and the self-sameness and self-identity of each side of a creditor/debtor nihilistic equation.

But the unexpected caveat to my articulation of the negative and differential architectonics of $-ism is that the underside of obscene diacritics is the flashy positivity of the affirmation of the return of the "objects" in *Verleugnung*. The fractal objects of the solar system are also animated by an *Eros* which unifies and consolidates the dispersal and decenterment of the decompositions of *Thanatos*. The extension of the radical undecidability and extreme indeterminacy of the value of any object in space inspires singularity. This singular object is incomparable to and incontrastable with any other object in the succession of returned fetishes. The singular object is neither equal nor unequal, neither identical nor different, but the same. Every word is the same word. But the obverse is also the case: every word is a different word. Every word — the same — is the same as every other word — the different. A *same difference* structures the singularity of the object in a discoordinated space of the unconscious. A singularity is arranged by the Positivity of Sameness⁺. This bright positivity is the horizon of the negative and differential diacritics of the signifier. But the difference between the positivity of singularity and the positivity of the self-same and self-identical unit of the word is that the former is in an extended tension with the other fetishes in the system whereas the latter is owned *by itself* and *unto itself*. The signifier explodes, and the sign implodes. The implosion of the architecture of the system is the threat of the perverse "return" of itself.

The fetishist affirms an alternative symbolic order — what I call the Spirit of the System. This Becoming of the Spirit of the System sparks the *Verleugnung* of sexual difference *qua* "sexual difference" (and "grasshopper," *et al.*). The pervert affirms and denies sexual difference in order to safeguard the object of the penis, clitoris, shoe, lace, fur, jockstrap, and so on. But he does so not to guard the family jewels of the private commodity of phallic *jouissance*. The pervert is not the capitalist owner of the penis as the self-identical and self-same object in its metaphysics of presence. Rather, the pervert disavows in order to release "grasshopper" (*et al.*) as public property for the Other's *jouissance*.

This perverse pleasure is otherwise mocked as resistance to the self-identical and self-same identity of the positive unity of the object. This fetishistic enjoyment is also considered a threat to the Logic of Identity of the system which guarantees the object and its exchangeability of Being and the ontological order of proper objects in their appropriate places. The pervert is the archetypal communist whose *A Pervert's Manifesto* is the words of the schizoid's Untruth. The pervert's pamphlet outlines the post-Marxist communist queer (*a*)sexual future of the Spirit of the System. The text of *A Pervert's Manifesto* is yet another series of marks which extends rather than restricts the success of fetishes in the world. The pervert gets off on *Praxis* and the symbolization of the Real. This *Praxis* is the essence of fetishism. The pervert discerns that the return of "text" from the void of negation loops alphabets and letters and festoons decorations and adornments in the aestheticization of the galaxy. The jockstrap is dreamy, but there are yet texts to come.

Dor says that the pervert confronts "a lack that cannot be symbolized" because he cannot overwrite the Real of the mother's castration.[53] This symbolic failure to overwrite the Real is the defeat of *Praxis*. But the perverse deconstruction of the symbolic order not only illuminates the structural hole in the system but also invites the textualization of this space. The gap is infinitely substitutable — object, sign, fetish, word, center, metaphor — because it "cannot be symbolized" as spoken or written. But the labor to symbolize the impossible — *A Pervert's Manifesto* — is the crux of the distinction between the pervert and the madman. The psychotic is unable to coherently overspeak and overwrite the Real with the symbol of the pen and the paper. But the Principle of Sameness⁺ and *Verleugnung* return the object which momentarily and impermanently sutures the wound of the Real at the center of the architecture of the penis, the commodity, and the word. The fetishist strives to symbolize the Real loss. The key is the striving.

The labor is recursive and redoubled. The work is endlessly extended in the return of objects, words, and fetishes to the overspoken and the overwritten. Perhaps the lack "cannot," as Dor says, be symbolized, but the pervert's purpose is to fetishize in order to make good the lack which can otherwise not forever be sutured. The substrate of the psychical structure of perversion is a *mise-en-abyme* of Metaphoricity — metonymization of metaphor — of faces, names, centers, metaphors, words, signs, fetishes, "grasshoppers," "crickets," "beetles," and so on. These manifestations promote the extension — "cannot" — of the *All* of the system. The pervert "knows very well" that the gap cannot be filled, "but nevertheless" — "mites," "cockroaches," "butterflies," "flies," "bugs," and so on. The pervert enjoys text. Words are fun. The phallus is a "bee."

The fetishist's symptom is a return of the Real *qua* the symbolic. This recurrence manifests as a proliferated succession of identities, equalities, differences, inequalities, and so on. But these objects are not self-same or self-identical. Rather, the recurrence of *les mots et les choses* is a Sameness⁺ of negative and differential (A ≠ A) materialities and abstractions. The skeletal scaffold of the architectonics of the symbolic order returns from the *Verleugnung* of the negated (affirmed) series of objects in the system. The architectonics of the signifier recurs from the architecture of the word. The fetish returns from the penis, and the use-value returns from the exchange-value. The symptom of fetishism is the general *inequivalence* of objects. These objects extend beyond themselves and their own discrete and isolated borders. The pervert's *Praxis* overwrites the trauma of the Real of castration with the script of the wax and wane of the Real Penis and its prepositional orchestration of the undecidable and indeterminate value of objects in discoordinated space. *Thanatos* returns from the *Eros* of the positive unity of the sign and the self-sameness and self-identity of unsplit *Gestalt* words and objects. These Real Signifiers are a regulated eruption in the pleasure principle of the Real Symbolic and the parallactic overlap between penis and fetish, signifier and sign, and use and exchange.

The conceptual division between the symbolic and the Real is put into question in Lacan's series of Venn diagrams, toruses, knots, and figure-eights in the torturous displacement of binary logic late in the *Seminar* on feminine sexuality (1973-1974). The pervert's topology — *The Pervert's Topology* — returns the Real Signifier from the Real *itself* to the symbolic *itself*. The Real is not fissured, but it is split in its own internal symbolic dimension. The pervert discerns that the Real is merely a metaphor for the symbolic order. This Metaphoricity in the chain of signification is the Real. Perversely, metaphor is the articulation of the Real in its symbolic expression. The essence of *langue* is the structure of metaphor and its likes and dislikes, and similarities and dissimilarities, in a recursion of reference. (In this book, I deploy the word "metaphor" in order to describe the rhetorical effects of both the relationship of "like" as explicit in simile and the veiled indication of "like" in metaphor.) The structure of the Real is metaphorical. The unsplit *Gestalt* of the Real outlines the parallactic overlap between *Spaltung* and *Gestalt*. The positive unity is split into shards and scraps, and the split gap is unified in undecidability and indeterminacy. The pervert discerns the excess of this parallactic overlap as the beyond of the pleasure principle in the masochist's delay of the object as such.

The Return of a Difference in the Aneconomy of Sameness+

The pervert's symptom is psychical lack and castration, and capitalist scarcity and loss. But castration and scarcity return not as self-same and self-identical words but as a scarcity and a castration which are struck by the Real of negativity and difference. The split distances castration *from itself* and distances scarcity *from itself*. Castration returns as "castration," and scarcity recurs as "scarcity." The disavowal of sexual difference as the object of *Verleugnung* returns as the "sexual difference" of the series of fetishes. The fraudulent negation of psychical lack and castration and capitalist scarcity and loss returns as the abundance and plenitude of an expansive galaxy of fetishes. *Verleugnung* unites two antagonistic perspectives on "one" and the "same" object of castration/plenitude and scarcity/abundance. Negation is (not, and so on) return. Return is not (not, and so on) negation. *Verleugnung* mobilizes the deconstructionist's two-step of the double clotural reading strategy.

The phallus is castrated. The political and ethical power of the fetish is to metonymize the dominant metaphor of the phallus. This metonymization of metaphor transpires at the precise moment of the rupture of the metaphor and its set of substitutes for the phallus. The rift in metaphor supervenes as the extension of the unregulated orgasm of the beyond of the pleasure principle in *Thanatos*. The death of metaphor — metonymization of metaphor — is achieved in the coincidence and continuity of the penis which is both like and unlike, and both similar and dissimilar, to the clitoris. The death of metaphor in the architecture of *langue* and the death of the phallus as *ur*-metaphor in sexual difference delay the presence of the clitoris (not-penis) in relationship to the penis. An endlessly structured *mise-en-abyme* of metonymy decenters and deflects the presence of the penis and its guarantee in a castrated phallus (or other equivalent metaphor). The hierarchical gap of magnitude in the constituted superiority/inferiority of the penis/not-penis is obliterated in the relationship between the two sets of body parts. The general equivalence of measurement of "size" and "visibility" is ruptured by the dispersal of a recursive succession of likenesses and unlikenesses, and similarities and dissimilarities. This *destruktion* of the exchange of metaphor is rearticulated as an incalculable and unspeculated Real: the clitoris is the penis; the penis is the clitoris; clitoris (is) penis; penis (is) clitoris; clitoris-penis; penis-clitoris; clitoris penis; penis clitoris; clitorispenis; penisclitoris, and so on.

The destabilized presence of division and opposition in mediatory calculation and exchangeable speculation slays metaphor and the *ur*-metaphor of the phallus in sexual difference. The metaphorical *like* is otherwise organized by comparison and contrast between two objects which are regulated by the general equivalent and the homeostasis of the pleasure principle. But the pervert recognizes that metaphor is both the essence of general equivalence and the substance of general *inequivalence*. The parallax of this coincidence between equivalence and its obverse extracts an excess that the pervert understands as the exact failure of representation *tout court*. The fiasco of representation is not only a reminder of the impossibility of *Praxis* and its symbolization of the Real. The sublimity of alphabets and letters also generates an excess Real which is forever resistant to the pervert's textualization of the schizoid's Unreasonable — ungraspable and untotalizable — truth. This remainder is the object of the pervert's *Verleugnung* of the set of fetishes.

The pervert's psychical orientation dramatizes the trauma of the Real of sexual difference. The pervert's "disavowal or denial of reality," as Dor says, is the "refusal to acknowledge the reality of a traumatic perception — the absence of a penis in the mother and in all Women."[54] But the returned presence of the penis and its substitute props is only the primary return in *Verleugnung*. The pervert also succeeds in the *Verleugnung* of difference as its own precept. *Verleugnung* disavows *Verleugnung*. *Verleugnung* recurs as *Verleugnung*. *Verleugnung* disavows "*Verleugnung*." The modality of negation in disavowal as such is splintered and fractured. *Verleugnung* is different *from itself*. This *bothness* and *andness* of perverse flapdoodle not only threaten the entirety of the symbolic order. The split within the principle of *Verleugnung* threatens the skeletal scaffold of the architectonics of the system. This deconstruction not of the *sign* but of the *signifier* threatens to collapse the order of binary opposition in latent/manifest, unconscious/conscious, abundance/scarcity, penis/fetish, signifier/sign, and so on.

This (these) disavowal(s) make(s) possible the pervert's *jouissance*. The *Spaltung* within disavowal *itself* only generates an expanded series of objects and fetishes. This *über*-disavowal enhances the pervert's *jouissance* of desire and enjoyment of lack. The parallactic overlap of abundance and scarcity inspires the secretion of the difference and negativity which cannot be recuperated into the system of the negation of the object and its simultaneous return to affirmation. A surplus of simultaneity emerges from the *disavowal of disavowal*. The Time of the Schizoid and his *Yes!* collide the series of affirmed fetishes. The source of the energy of this cosmic space is the obscene abundance at the (*a*)sexual center of the system. The pervert acknowledges that the extimate split in disavowal generates a succession of fetishes which only amplifies the incalculable *jouissance* of the pervert.

To patch the signifier over the Real is an arduous project. It may be plainly impossible for the pervert to overwrite the Sameness[+] (*et al.*) of Unreason with the syntax and semantics of neurotic Reason. There is no word for the trace if Sameness[+] overwrites the otherwise disordered system of binary opposition with a resistance to the spoken and written text. The disavowal of difference recurs as "difference." The negative (affirmative) exchange of difference as "difference" encourages the openness of S rather than the closedness of $-ism. Spirit is organized by the present fetish and its *mise-en-abyme* of substitutes rather than by the veiled phallus and the *ur*-metaphor. The hitch is that the fetish and the phallus are the same word — center, sign, penis, substitute, clitoris, fetish, phallus, metaphor, and word — because each is *different from itself* but *the same as the other*. The phallus returns as the "penis"; the center recurs as the "sign"; the penis returns as the "substitute"; the clitoris recurs as the "fetish"; the phallus returns as the "metaphor," and so on. The switch and swap of objects are abyssal, but this void is endlessly expanded by the affirmed return of the negated by the individual and the society. The threat of playful switcheroo is that the Logic of Identity (A = A) is superseded by the Logic of Difference (A ≠ A). The threat is against the positive unity of self-same and self-identical autonomous identity: it is what it is. The threat of Sameness[+] is against the positive ontological project of Being and the metaphysics of presence.

The issue of negation is peculiar beyond its distinct modalities in repression, foreclosure, and disavowal. The system represses, forecloses, and disavows — but why? What is the threat to the extant order that must be contained in the transposition of (un)conscious content into manifest representations and symptoms? Why is the latent content of neurotic desire, wish, and truth repressed? Why is the Unreasonable Real revolution foreclosed? Why are the atypical words of the return of fetish as "fetish" disavowed? Why does the system mobilize *Verdrängung*, *Verwerfung*, and *Verleugnung* in the pursuit of the coordination of the structure? Why is the force of negation necessary to the administration of the symbolic order? Psychical structures are not biologically designed. But what is the reason for the cultural appearance of neurosis, psychosis, and perversion in their distinctiveness? What does negation as such illuminate (to us about) (for) culture? Why are the various *latent of the latent* (*et al.*) of the three clinical structures considered deep threats to society rather than the mere quirks of oddballs?

The role of the *Über-Ich* in the life of the mind explains the supervision of the eruptions of Otherness in the individual and the society. The superego is the operative force of the prohibitions and rules in the system. But the superego does not merely say "No!" Rather, the superego enforces a subjective and objective enjoyment in subordination to the laws and codes of the culture. The superego incites a subjective and objective "yes" to the injunctions and stipulations of the order. The superego is not an external (internal) authority which commands "No!" to enjoyments. Rather, the superego is an internal (external) dynamic which persuades "yes" to pleasures. The difference is the object of this enjoyment. The *Es* (and its excesses in traces beyond any biological imperative) seeks satisfaction in collision with the dictates of the society. The id — *überall dort, wo es war und wo auch immer es sein wird* — pursues murderous and sexual aims against the proper fiats of the individual and the society. The *Es* says "yes" to its own desires and "No!" to social ordinances. The *Über-Ich* says "yes" to social ordinances and "No!" to the desires of the *Es*. But the two ostensibly opposed forces of the id and the superego are isomorphic to each other: both pursue *jouissance*.

The organization of *jouissance* for the subject is the *sinthome*. The superego is its own *sinthome*. The structure of the *jouissance* of the superego is cruel. But it is so not because it promotes nefarious pleasures of the corporation and the state at the cost of the benign enjoyments of sexuality and expression. The structured *sinthome* of the superego is an idiotic pleasure in the masculine arrival of the letter at its destination — signified — of the proper order, conservative balance, rigid coherence, and obscene commandment of the system. The *jouissance* of the superego is the homeostatic regulatory regime of the system. The *sinthome* of the superego is the system. There is a *jouissance* of the system. The system — *all of this* — is the object of *jouissance* for the structure in its anonymity and for its subjects in their everyday affairs. This superegoic *jouissance* and *sinthome* of the system delight in the obscenities of the culture. The objective superego as $-ism and the subjective superego as subject enjoy capital, sexism, misogyny, racism, homophobia, nationalism, and the traces of narcissistic, aggressive, and anxious pleasures in the culture. But why are these superegoic symptoms of violent pleasures — the system itself — simultaneously a threat to the system itself? Why is *jouissance* the essence of the regulation of the system but at the same time a menace to this system? Why is pleasure prohibited by the system — "No!" — even as *jouissance* organizes the system — "yes"?

The answer is that pleasure transgresses the binary oppositions of the culture. *Jouissance* exploits the cracks in the edifice of the architecture of *langue* and the general equivalence of the penis and the commodity. The system is structured by binary opposition. Any breach of the borders (*le propre*) between any identical object and any different object, or between any equal object and any unequal object, destabilizes the system. The system sanctions certain breaches between polarities, but these gaps resist the perverse gesture of the *Spaltung* within the object itself. These authorized amusements are quietly reincorporated into the systems of patriarchy, capital, and the sign under the regime of the economic foreclosure of $-ism. The sexist stand-up routine at the comedy club is quickly recuperated into the financial system with the payment for tickets for the show. The sale at the store is transposed into intensified extraction of value from the worker's labor for the good of the corporate profit. The pervert's word play in his text is consolidated by the literary review and its goal toward the market and sales of the book. Any contravention in the system of binary opposition is recuperated by capital and its frenzied will toward the accumulation of debt and credit. The *sinthome* of the superego is capital. $-ism is the precept of the monstrous recuperation of the chintzy trinkets of amusement that otherwise marginally open and quickly close the transgression of *le propre* in the society.

The *jouissance* of the People and our perverts, schizoids, and Women breaks these constraints of binarism and its lures in oedipality and scarcity. The limit-experiences of laughter and sex and the Other *jouissance* of communist queer (a)sexualism interrupt the arbitrary but conventionalized semic system. Both laughter and sex are sublime unrepresentables because they are not usually subject to persuasive articulation in words. There is a surplus of sex and laughter which cannot be reintegrated by the symbol. Limit-experiences express materiality — marks and sounds — without reference to the abstractions and speculations of the general equivalent. This *latent of the latent* (*et al.*) threatens the system because the return of the architectonics of the signifier revolts against the order of the sign. The vast but minor difference in the recurrence of the content is outlined by the near identical concepts of symptom and sublimation. The symptom is the detail which belies a dysfunction. The symptom is subordinate to correction so that the glitch is eliminated from the subjective and objective systems. Sublimation — the near exact of the symptom — is the detail which is embraced by the individual and society as a cultural achievement. Sublimation is the elevation of the scrap and scrape of the symptom to the dignity of *das Ding*. The sublimated object is authorized by the *sinthome* of the superego. The symptomatic object is barred by the apparatus of control and containment. Sublimation is bourgeois. Symptom is subversive.

The sublimation is an achievement of the regulation of the system. The symptom is a disruption of the homeostatic laziness of the principle of pleasure. The purpose of psychoanalysis must not be to dissolve the symptom. The horizon of psychoanalysis is to make the symptom *work*. This is the observation that Lacan made under the name of the *sinthome*. The *sinthome* is the recuperation of the symptom *qua* sublimation of the revolution. The symptom is transmuted into the *sinthome*. But it is so not because it is suddenly recognized as a cultural achievement. Rather, the symptom is elevated to the level of the dignity of *das Ding* because *das Ding* has been transformed away from the closed criteria of the bourgeoisie of the corporation and the state and toward the open standards of the *jouissance* of the People.

Neurotic Sex Education

The threat of the neurotic in Freud's era is sex and the desires, wishes, and truths which circulate within the society. The reason that this latent content is a menace to the culture is a vast and complex question. The matter of the perils of sex haunts the work of feminist and queer theory in Cultural Studies. Perversity wants to both ruin and sustain all convention in the culture. The pervert upends the arbitrary authority of the system. Perversely, the statute is illegal, and the infraction is the lawful. Foucault (1975) shows that the regime of the discourse on "sexuality" (as opposed to "sex") in such media (today) as film, television, music, and advertisement is *productive* rather than *repressive* of the culture. Foucault's theoretical innovation in *History of Sexuality Volume*

1 (1975) is not only the notion of "bio-power" which accompanied him until the end of his career. The other inspiration is the coincidence — good faith and bad faith — between the *repression* of the neurotic's desire and the *production* ("power/knowledge") of the historicized sexual identities of the homosexual, the masturbating offspring, the hysterical Woman, the pedophile — and today — the sadomasochist, the bisexual, the sex-positive, the repressed, the polyamorous, the transgender, the gender queer, the asexual, and so on.

The cynical paradoxical logic of the interface of repression *qua* production perversely transgresses the Logic of Identity (A = A; repression = repression; production = production) and its regime of binary oppositions which divides and opposes repression/production, and so on. Foucault's wild conclusion — three-quarters of a century after Freud — is that there is no such *das Ding* as repression. This is a secret untruth that only the pervert's *Verleugnung* — repression recurred as "repression" — can represent. The fetish is evidence of a softened repression because the common fur, lace, shoe, and jockstrap erect a presence of a *mise-en-abyme* but with closed reference to the penis in the place of castration and the not-penis. The work of the fetish-object is the obverse of the labor of language. The fetish collides the divided and opposed of the distinct unit of the sign into the negative and differential of the proximate spatiality of any object in prepositional incoordination with any other object. The sign isolates the division between words, such as clitoris/penis. The *production of repression* — fly returned as "fly" — is the essence of the fetishist's *Verleugnung* and its internally returned *qua* "returned externally." Analytic silence is productive noise because it provides space for the generation of master signifiers and mistress fetishes. There is no negativity in Foucault's emphasis on production in discourse. The "repressed" returns as the "produced."

Foucault's talented perversity is especially visible in the early portions of his text (1975) and in the discursive mobilization of the *bothness* and *andness* of the logic of disavowal. Foucault reverses the Freudian theory of repression that desire is negated into the unconscious only to return in the skewed manifestations of the detail of the dream or the slip of the tongue. Foucault's inversion demonstrates that Victorian chatter about "sexuality" was discontinuous with practices of "sex." The category of "sexuality" and its (ab)normative identities are distinct from "sex" and its material practices with the female body in the bedroom or with the male body in the locker room (*et al.*). This is so because symbolic "sexuality" (homosexual, hysterical, and so on) overwrites the inarticulable Real of "sex" (the unrepresentable sublime). The hysteric's latent desire for sexual intercourse with a partner of some sort (Freud's interpretation of Dora (1905) is exemplary) is repressed. Neurotically, the sexual repression and its returned symptom are not bodily enjoyed in the Real of their trauma. Foucault's twisted thesis is that the latent wish for sex is *discursively produced* and not *unconsciously repressed*. Perversely, this is so even were the division between a discursive *production* and an unconscious *repression* a meaningfully considerate distinction.

The divisions between discourse and unconscious, and between production and repression, are perversely spurious. Production and repression are subordinate to the Principle of Sameness[+] and to the unfathomable relationship of Being between two distinct and opposed words which are otherwise differential and negative nodal points of relationship and construction. The pervert discerns that Foucault's explicit point is that the neurotic's latent desire for sex is *discursively produced* rather than *unconsciously repressed*. But the pervert also glimpses the flipped obverse of the thesis: that the hysteric's wish is *unconsciously repressed* rather than *discursively produced*. The pervert's version of Foucault's (anti)thesis illuminates the parallactic overlap between Freud and his emphasis on repression and Foucault and his revision of production. Perversely, the regime of repression is its own productive factory of illicit fantasy and taboo projection. The effect of so-called sexual repression is a mosaic of sexual manifestation. The unconscious is a technology of visibility.

Figure 3.10 Pervert-Schizoid-Woman Work

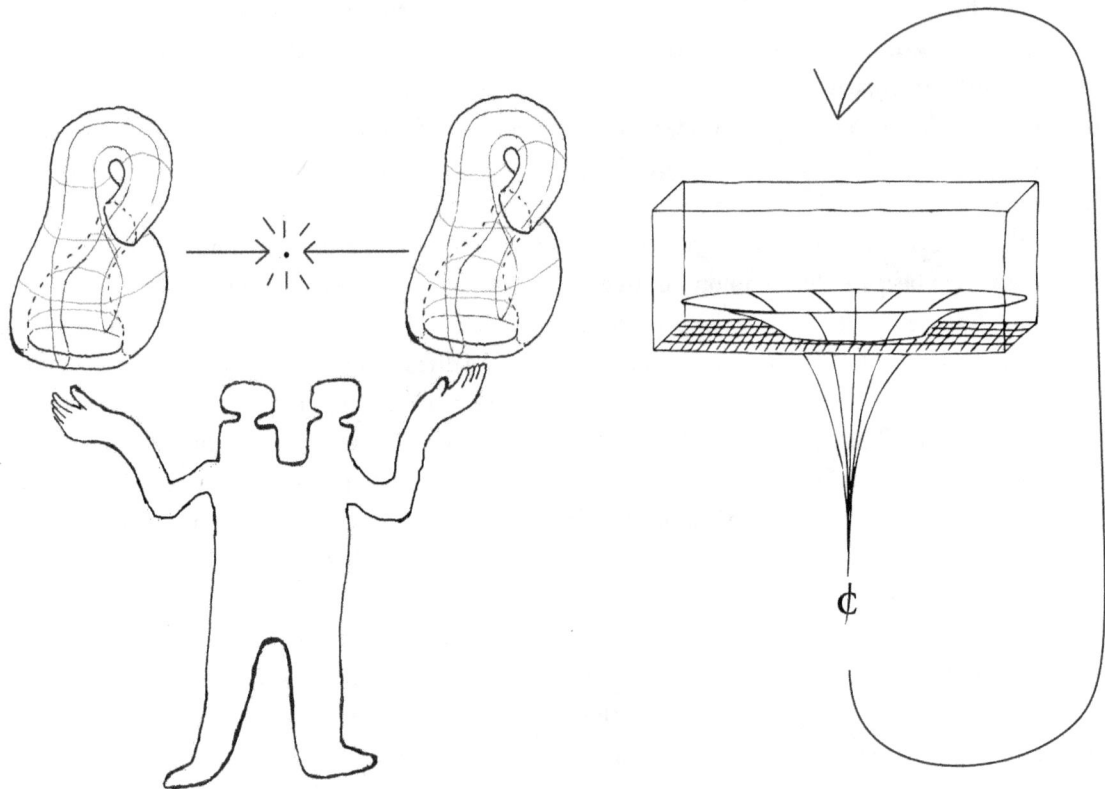

The Pervert-Schizoid-Woman is the thinking, being, and living of the future. The Pervert-Schizoid-Woman returns the Madness of Order to the Spirit of the System. The Pervert-Schizoid-Woman coherently symbolizes the structurality of the structure. The Pervert-Schizoid-Woman destructures the binary opposition between the Madness of Order and the Order of Madness. The Pervert-Schizoid-Woman demonstrates the isomorphism between the opposition of (s) and (S) such that the distinction collapses. The Inside (is) the Outside, and the Outside (is) the Inside. The parallactic binary Becomes as such and as the Other in the expression of the unary trait. The neurotic's logic of the either/or is transformed into the pervert's economy of the both/and and then into the schizoid's Unreasonable neither/nor and both/and. The figure (left) of the Pervert-Schizoid-Woman is symbolically marked with the three clinical structures. This visual figuration of the Pervert-Schizoid-Woman returns the Klein Bottle and its Inside-Outsideness to itself. The illustration depicts the collapse of the system and its variants of signification. The figure (right) shows the occluded center and its return to the system. The Pervert-Schizoid-Woman's movements and gestures traverse this differed and deferred center.

Notes & Sketches —

There is no basal disagreement between Freud and Foucault — between *Three Essays* (1905) and *History of Sexuality Volume 1* (1975) — because the Principle of Sameness⁺ upends the otherwise self-sameness and self-identity of the central terms of repression and production, and unconscious and discourse, in the parallax of the two viewpoints on "one" and the "same" object. The pervert expresses the excess of the overlap between Freud and Foucault, and between unconscious and discourse, as the failure to overwrite the Real of "sex" with the symbolic of "sexuality." *Verleugnung* returns the invitation toward the open proliferation of alphabets and vocabularies to the symbolization of the Real in the *Praxis* of *A Pervert's Manifesto*. Foucault wryly illuminates that repression (is) liberation, and that emancipation (is) domination. The threat of a *perverted neurosis* to the system is the topsy-turvy inversion of the binary coordination of the system. Foucault's tricks and capers mobilize Marx's *camera obscura* (1845) and its inversion of the architecture of the symbolic order of sex but also of desire, finance, and the word.

Mad Defense

The threat of the madman is the obverse of his manifest (latent) Unreason. The menace of the psychotic is the subversion of the arbitrary but naturalized organization and balance of the symbolic order. The cultural rush to coherence and clarity is the condition of any social and political identity: the postcolonial, the queer, the feminist, the proletarian, the African-American, the Jew, the superstar, the man, and so on. But there is no identity — female or the one percent — in madness. There is no identity — disabled or Asian — in the schizoid structure of *langue*. This psychotic threat to the Logic of Identity (A = A, disabled = disabled, Asian = Asian, and so on) is at the center of the schizoid's scare. The Real of the schizoid fissures the structures of division and opposition of the sign which otherwise arrange and coordinate $-ism.

The rambled and slurred discourse of the madman explodes all familial, social, professional, racial, ethnic, sexual, national (*et al.*) identities which are arranged by the self-sameness and self-identity of the positive unity of the word of the *Gestalt* image of bordered totality in the mirror stage of identification.[55] The coherent *Gestalt* image is otherwise an effect of a stable system of words and a secure series of pictures. The pervert notes that the Principle of Sameness⁺ ruptures all claims to individual and social classification. The future self must be transposed from fabled identities and manufactured identifications to a *moi* which is constituted by the entire set of objects and words in the social field *except* the self. The self escapes the self. The threat of madness to the system is the *sous rature et sur l'effacement* of the self. What is the self in the case that the entire self is the self *except* the self? What is the system in the case that the entire system is the system *except* the system? Madness transforms the self and the system — it is what it is — into the Spirit of the System — it is what it is not.

The menace of the madman is that he dangerously deconstructs the division between the loud mania of psychosis and the quiet frigidity of neurosis. The return of *Verwerfung* in schizophrenia is the body of the Real. The madman is in essence the materiality of the signifier and the flesh and blood, and sperm and bones, of the excesses of laughter and sex. The madman lives at the limit of the symbol. The strange coincidence between the schizoid and the hysteric is the transposition of the symptom and its return in the two psychical structures. The psychotic's perilous return of the body is exactly the substance of the neurotic's repression of sex. The madman returns the body, and the hysteric represses the body. The *Verwerfung* in the symbolic returns the body of madness. The *Verdrängung* in the symbolic represses the body of the hysteric. The schizoid symptom is the latent content of the neurotic's repression. The hysterically repressed in the symbolic returns as the madman's symptom in the Real. The neurotic returns madness, and the schizoid manifests hysteria. The parallactic overlap between the manifest visibility of the madman and the latent invisibility of the neurotic is isomorphic: the madman's docile body is the mere inversion of the neurotic's repressed sex.

Not only is the division between neurosis and psychosis perversely untenable but the opposition between the Real and the symbolic is flimsy. The Real Symbolic sparkles in its radiant perversity in the coincident overlap between the neurotic's returned symptom and the schizoid's foreclosed body. The threat to the extant order is that the hidden kernel of the neurotic is the manic frenzy of the madman. The pervert intuits that the excess of the overlap between the neurotic symptom and the schizoid body is identity and identification. The classification of social types — clinical structures — is at stake in the *destruktion* of the ostensible division and opposition — word — between neurosis and psychosis. The threat of this deconstruction is the pervert's *Praxis* to *pervert the neurotic*. What is the galaxy in the Event of the displacement of the defenses and repressions of neurosis with the games and toys of perversion? What are the thinking, being, and living of a solar system of perverts? If the madman's *Verwerfung* is the object of the hysteric's *Verdrängung*, then are we all already perverts? Why do we not yet know Unreasonable truth?

The disintegration of coherent sense in Unreason is the consequence of the suspension of the *point de capiton* and its otherwise return of the future to the past (present) in the retroaction of the Time of the Neurotic. But this Unreason is deeply logical and rationally organized. The coherence of the system is its architectonics of the signifier rather than architecture of the word. Unexpectedly, the word makes very little sense, and the signifier is the proper articulation of the Order of Madness. Reasonable incoherence is the extimate substance — *constructed essence* — of Unreason and the system of words, phrases, sentences, paragraphs, chapters, books, and so on. The slip and slide of this series of objects in *mise-en-abyme* transform desire from *objet petit a* and its full stop in the *Objekt* and in the idiocy of masculine *jouissance* into courtly love and *Trieb* and its open go in the inaccessible Boy in the masochism of feminine *jouissance*. The pervert's task is to speak and write — flirt with and gesture toward — the traumatic schizophrenia of the system.

Society fears *Trieb* because it destroys the object as such. Perversely, *there is no object*. Drive elevates an excess of movement and traversal — patient waiting — to the level of *das Ding* as Nothingness. The Boy is Nothingness. There is no proper word for either the subject or the object of drive. The man is Nothingness. The pervert wants to elevate the maniac's anguish to the level of the dignity of *das Ding* and the revolution against the apparatuses of Reason in the phallocentrism of patriarchy, the commodity of economy, and the sign of language. The threat of *Trieb* is that the foreclosure of the metaphysics of presence of the objects inspires the generation of (all) objects yet to come in the *tout autre*. The homeostatic contraction of the system is disturbed by the expansive Nothingness of space. But the pervert spotlights this basal Nothingness in the system as simultaneously a fundamental Being.

Perverse Écriture

This book (and chapter) have been a total trip to write. The concepts in deconstruction, psychoanalysis, and Marxism are thoughts at the limit of both ideology and expression. These ideas are limits to a theory of the extant order and also to the symbolization of the excess of this system. It is pure pleasure to write a book about concepts — that should not be concepts — with words — that should not be words. I hope that it is a joyful project for the reader to make sense of arcane ideas and strenuous articulation. This is the *jouissance* of the wannabe pervert as a writer who pens the text but also of the reader who drafts notes on the text. This is a book for poseur pervs and the rest of us. The pervert likes to symbolize — in words and sentences, but also in furs and jockstraps. The pervert enjoys his life with small details, such as the perfect expression of the phrase, the proper arrangement of the shoe, the best articulation of the idea, the sultriest juxtaposition of the jockstrap, the exemplary sentence for the concept, and the sexiest placement of the fur. And then the pervert fails. The phrase is imperfectly expressed. The shoe is improperly placed. The idea is misarticulated. The jockstrap is misjuxtaposed. The sentence for the concept is unexemplary. The placement of the fur is lifeless.

The interval between failure and success is the gap between the Real and its limit of adequate representation in the symbolic, on the one hand, and the pens, sketchpads, penises, and jockstraps of fetish-objects, on the other hand. *Praxis* is the symbolization of the Real. *Praxis* is the interval between the symbolic opportunity to represent and the Real limit to the spoken and the written. The pervert's insight is that *Trieb* is this extension and expansion of *Praxis* to the limits of a textual object — *A Pervert's Manifesto* — which cannot retroactively return the symbol to the Real. The pervert enjoys the *Praxis* — symbolic to Real, and the reverse — of the expression, arrangement, articulation, juxtaposition, exemplification, and placement. Masochistically, the pervert enjoys desire and its maneuvers, gestures, manipulations, performances, slips, returns, advances, recoils, and so on. The object is differed and deferred in an uncoordinated space in the expanses of the solar system. The Boy has read *A Pervert's Manifesto*. But the man has yet to finish writing it.

The threat of fetishism is of unconventional materiality, unorthodox abstraction, and untoward arrangement of the signifier and the signified in a strange word. The sexual fetishist gets off not only on the ordinary materiality of the breasts of the Woman or the pecs of the man. Rather, the fetishist's sexual signifiers are the eccentric materials of the fur, lace, shoe, and jockstrap. The cerebral fetishist takes pleasure not in the prosaic abstractions of the culture, like *The New York Times* or the latest run of critical theory from a university press. Rather, the cerebral fetishist enjoys the words and images on the margins. The signifier fur (*et al.*) and the signified Principle of Sameness (*et al.*) necromantically substitute for the penis (abouts) with their recurrence of the "fetish" and the extension of the series of signifiers and signifieds in the architectonics of the system. Like *avant-garde* writers of any historical and any national stripe, fetishism imperils the symbolic order with formal and ideational experimentation. The text — you and I — is freed of proper interpretation, decisive identification, and enforced identity. Who(m) is reading who(m)? Who(m) is writing for who(m)? Who(m) is who(m)? The Boy may have read *A Pervert's Manifesto*, but only if he is not yet a man.

The economy of *le propre* includes the apparatuses of the sign of language, the private property of capitalism, and the sexuality of patriarchy. These frameworks are ruptured by the destabilization of the center of the system in fetishism and the return of the object as the "object." Perverse words undo the division between latent and manifest, and between the unconscious and the conscious. This disbands binary opposition. Hierarchical division and opposition are otherwise the conditions of the sign in *langue*, private property in capitalism, and phallocentrism in patriarchy. The pervert writes the specific equivalence of *general inequivalence*, but this art and its drive teeter and totter at the edges of the Real. This experiment creates novel forms of perplexity of textuality because the pervert plays with concepts at the expressive limits of the frontier.

The intent of over-psychoanalysis is not to return the proper desire to the dysfunctional symptom. The purpose of over-psychoanalysis is to mobilize the symptom — master signifier and mistress fetish — and its subversive return. This distinction between the proper return of desire and the cultivation of the master signifier cuts across the minimal difference between symptom and sublimation. But the perverse difference is analysis interminable — and *Praxis* interminable. The subversive return of the symptom recurs — and then recurs. The insistence of this recursive recursion is not the compulsive repetition of an ambivalent contraction but the happy openness toward an *unambivalent* expansion of fetishes and texts, and jockstraps and words. The symbolic order and its toolbox of pencils and brushes are the forces of the obscene (*a*)sexual power of this extension. The system of *langue* is open rather than closed. There is always more *Praxis* to be performed. But if language is in *essence* constructed as perverse, then whose free constitution is such a costly necessity? Can *langue* perversely become otherwise than itself? If the penis is in *essence* constructed as the penultimate reference for sexuality, then can (*a*)sexuality delay its absent presence? Can the penis perversely become otherwise than itself? If the commodity is in *essence* constructed as an object of exchange, then can the object be freed of decided and determinate value? Can the commodity perversely become otherwise than itself? This study engages these questions. But first we put our hero, "the pervert," under closer scrutiny. Where did "the pervert" come from? And where is "she" going?

Chapter Four

The Pervert (1): Between Neurosis and Psychosis

Is there no other solution besides the functional disturbance of neurosis and the Spiritual outlet of sublimation? Could there not be a third alternative which would be related not to the functional interdependence of the ego and the superego, but to the structural split between them? And is this not the very alternative indicated by Freud under the name of perversion?

— Gilles Deleuze

This book outlines the gaps in the system. It then studies the effects of the return of the negated as symptoms. This work illuminates the schizophrenic effects of the Real in the symbolic order. I focus on the secret truth of Unreason of the schizoid. My efforts demonstrate the talents of the pervert in his engagement with text and world. In this chapter, I develop a theory of the structure of perversion. I also uncover the interstices between neurosis and psychosis. This enterprise forges an original reading of the pervert. This theory is informed by — but not limited to — the outline of perversion in psychoanalysis and its theoretical scaffold. The organization of the system is principally neurotic. The world is a series of desires, its threat to the social order, its return in symptoms, and its disorganization of the smooth operation of the system of $-ism.

But, at the same time, my critique of $-ism illuminates that the orientation of $-ism is profoundly schizophrenic. This is especially true of the signifying chain and its foreclosures and returns. Paradoxically, these psychotic foreclosures manifest as neurotic repressions. The manifest neurotic forms of these schizoid foreclosures veil the latent content of their psychotic negation. The return of the foreclosed is a threat to society. The return of the Real to the text foregrounds the hallucinatory and delusional structure of the symbolic order. These Real symptoms — hallucinations and delusions — destabilize the entire extant system of the social order. The purpose of this book is to elucidate the gap between the manifest neurosis of the system and the latent schizophrenia of $-ism. My study demonstrates the Unreason of the system and the Madness of Order. This madness can be summarized as a system that neurotically forecloses (*rejet névrotique*) the Real. This negation is internal to the symbolic. The foreclosed symbolic returns to the order of the system *qua* its disruption. This destabilization of the system by the system itself is the essence of the order of the galaxy. The psychoanalyst Octave Mannoni treated a famous perverse patient whose enigmatic statement, "I know very well, but nevertheless…," is considered the archetypal syntax and semantics of perversity.[1] An elaboration of this logic is central to an elucidation of the system and its dissolution *qua* S. The purpose of this chapter is to outline a nuanced psychoanalytic theory of perversity.

PERVERSION BETWEEN NEUROSIS AND PSYCHOSIS

Even long before the proper birth of psychoanalysis, Freud and Breuer mined the depths of hysterics and the crazy talk of their desires. These hysterical Women were dismissed by their husbands, brothers, sons, and fathers. Freud listened to these Women. As a result, Freud and Breuer formulated the concept of the *Spaltung*. This word refers to the split in the psychical apparatus. This split animates perversion. In the preliminary statement to their *Studies in Hysteria* (1892), the authors describe a fundamental insight,

> The more we were preoccupied with these phenomena the more convinced we became that the splitting of consciousness that is so strikingly present in the well-known cases as double conscience, exists in a rudimentary form in every hysteria; and that this tendency to dissociation and thereby to the emergence of abnormal states of consciousness, which we will group together under the term "hypnoid," is the fundamental phenomenon of this neurosis.[2]

This "splitting of consciousness" or "double conscience" or "hypnoid" structure well describes key themes in Freud's 1938 paper on fetishism and perversity, "The Splitting of the Ego in the Process of Defense." The early account (1892) of neurosis suggests that fetishistic disavowal as a "splitting of consciousness" pertains to clinical categories other than perversion, such as hysteria. Freud's view also implies that it is not only male fetishists in fear of the female genitals who are subjects of perversion. As indicated, Women can experience the *Spaltung* which comprises the essence of the fetishistic economy.

Freud transcribes the *sinthome* of Western culture as I symbolize it in this study. His word, in English, "splitting," is eerily close to /SCHIZ-em/. This "schism" is the aural articulation of $-ism. However, a crucial difference emerges between splitting and /SCHIZ-em/. As a neurologist on the path toward psychoanalysis, Freud situates this "hypnoid" phenomenon in "abnormal states of consciousness." In contrast, my critique of $-ism situates the "splitting" in both the unconscious of the society and in the psychical apparatus of the subject. This split is a fundamental rule which is foreclosed to the system of the conscious. The neurotic structure is the subjective outline of a patient. This citizen is blind to the schizoid structure of the Unreason of the system. The pervert is the talented master of *écriture* of what I name the Madness of Order. The structure of madness is not my concern. Rather, my focus is the madness of structure.

The practical conundrum for this endeavor of representation is intense. How does the pervert describe an order which is organized by a disorder? How can Unreason be outlined if its very structure is resistant to Reason? Or is this Madness of Order also the internal structure of madness? Madness is the Unreason of Reason. Unreason is the navel of the dream of Reason. Only a punctilious Reason and meticulous logic can illuminate the secret truth of Unreason. Rather than a discourse of Unreason, the Madness of Order can only be articulated by the rigors of Reason. But will the neurotic understand the reversal of Reason? Even if so, how does the revelation of the schizophrenia of the system transform the self and the society of the neurotic?

Perversion is situated at the intersection of neurosis and psychosis. The peculiarity of perversion is that its relationship to desire, the phallus, and the object is in-between the pathologies of neurosis and psychosis.

In "Neurosis and Psychosis" (1924), Freud articulates the situation of the heroic but besieged ego. This ego must, as Freud says, "humor all its masters at once."[3] These masters include the id, the superego, and the external world. Each of these factions wants to direct and manipulate the decisions of the ego. The ego is an executive function. But it is also primarily an object of other forces which exceed it. Freud even suggests that "the whole endeavor of the ego is aiming at — a reconciliation between its various dependent relationships."[4] The enterprise of a reconciliation and a synthesis is the occupation of the ego.

This work of orientation, balance, and organization of the center of the structure is foreclosed even as it is promised and demanded by the system. The ideological mischiefs and structural ruffians of the ideology of Oedipus include humanism, scarcity, castration, signification, and private property. These theoretical concepts and practical habits enframe the sorry ego. Neurotic theories and practices demand the subordination of the ego to the whims and desires of other agencies and apparatuses. The *Spaltung* in the Other includes this series of fissures. These subjective breaks and objective gaps make the fulfillment of an autonomous and synthetic ego an impossible project. Freud claims that this sequence of competing differences overwhelms any project. Any job which insists on rational unification is doomed. The problematic knot of difference is fundamental to the existential situation of the oedipal subject.

The subjective orientation toward difference is indexed by modalities of negation: neurotic *Verdrängung*, schizoid *Verwerfung*, and perverse *Verleugnung*. Man's attitude toward difference is also structured into man's relationships to the *objet petit a* and the phallus. The idiosyncratic orientation toward difference is the principal source of the variance between the outlooks and insights among the three psychoanalytic diagnostic categories: neurosis, psychosis, and perversion. The emergence of the ego from this conflict of the *Spaltung* at the center of the symbolic order requires strategy from the sensibility of perversion. The strategy of fetishism and the mechanism of disavowal can be mobilized in order to achieve a reconciliation among the various twists-and-tugs from the agencies — id, superego, external world — which assail the ego. These forces treat the self as an object rather than a subject.

The only roundabout of the no exit of neurosis and its tedious interaction between the repressed and its return is a transition to perversity. The pervert is the avatar of the Pervert-Schizoid-Woman. The pervert can only outline and perform this aesthetic because its secret truth is pilfered from the master. This magician is the madman and his linguistic lunacy. The crazy talk of the madman's Unreason is the secret truth of an escape from the oedipal injunction. Otherwise, Oedipus forces man to negotiate the demands of the agencies and apparatuses which constrain him as an object. The subject *qua* object is at the whims of forces which exceed him. Freud writes,

> It will be possible for the ego to avoid a rupture in any direction by deforming itself, by submitting to encroachments on its own unity and even perhaps by effecting a cleavage or division of itself.[5]

This citation is situated in the context of Freud's broad claim that neurosis is an effect of a conflict between the ego and the superego and that psychosis is a consequence of a discordance between the ego and external reality. This quotation repeats the claims made about hysteria at the start of psychoanalytic theorization. But the crucial difference in this update is that the border between the structural diagnostic categories is reconfigured. The proliferation of differences is key to a successful transition from the fiction of a besieged unity of a subject to the Real of an undone multiplicity of an object. The vaunted deformation of the unity of the ego foreruns a celebration of fetishistic disavowal.

In his later (1938) text on splits and defenses, Freud says that this both/and attitude is a "neat solution" and "artful solution" to castration.[6] Freud's consensus is that the ego is the focus of a battle for desires, compromises, and commitments. None of these investments can be satisfied by an executive ego which is reduced to a subordinate object. The "neat" and "artful" solution, so says Freud, is perverse hypnoid and double consciousness. The trick is a sensibility and an aesthetic in which the juxtaposition of the opposite and the play of the different overcome strict conflicts and severe contradictions. These barriers of stern logic otherwise spawn dangerous chaos for the ego and the world. But how is such splitting of the ego in the process of perversion possible? What are the social and psychical conditions which are necessary in order for this alternative Other economy to flourish? Are there spaces and times for perversion to blossom even amidst the violence of the antagonisms of subjectivity and sociality?

Freud begins to answer these questions in his elaboration of the scene of the discovery of sexual difference. The offspring's encounter with sexual difference is critical to later development because it elaborates the offspring's first encounter with *difference*. Freud applies his conclusions specifically to sexual difference. But his insights may be relevant to other modalities of difference, such as class, race, ethnicity, nation, and so on. Freudian so-called castration indicates a relationship between identity and difference as such. My interpretation of Freud gestures toward the possibility of a Derridean "sameness which is not identical," or as I name it, Sameness⁺.[7] This otherwise to the self-same and the self-identical — Same-Other — may approach differences beyond the psychoanalytic categories of sex, sexuality, and gender. The castration complex achieves relevance beyond the Oedipus complex.

Over the middle of his career during the 1920s, Freud repeatedly and compulsively theorized the scene of the male junior's discovery of the female genitalia. The vision of female difference retroactively arouses castration anxiety. The source of the anxiety is the male junior's interpretation of lack and castration in deficit rather than plenitude and fullness in difference. The lack in the place of the female junior's genitals spawns masculine distress about loss and death. The conditions of the normal oedipal trajectory demand that the male junior abdicate pleasure with the maternal body and his own penis in favor of identity and desire with the ego-ideal of the father. The purpose of the castration complex is the enforced transition from pleasure and *jouissance* to identity and desire. The instruction of the castration complex is the reproduction of the system of identification and the choice of proper (*le propre*) objects.

The male junior forsakes desire for and pleasure in the mother for identification with and mimicry of the father. In the process, the male junior saves his prized possession, namely, the penis. He also saves a metonymic litany of objects of private property, from the orgasmic penis to the fiery candlestick to the plumber's hose to the lead pipe to the pine tree to the syringe to the skyscraper, and so on. In the brief text, "Splitting of the Ego in the Process of Defense" (1938), Freud presents the male junior with an ostensibly either/or choice at the sight of the female genitalia. Freud writes,

> It now has to decide whether to acknowledge the real danger, submit to it, and refrain from satisfying the drive, or to deny reality, convince itself there is nothing to fear, and so hold on to the satisfaction.[8]

The decision consists of an either/or choice. The subject must either accept reality and repress the urge (neurotic repression) or deny reality and satiate the drive (psychotic foreclosure). As Freud puts it: "It is a conflict, then, between what the drive demands and what reality forbids."[9] It is noteworthy that instinct and society are juxtaposed as opposed to each other. The libidinal desire must conflict with the demands of reality. This indicates that the individual and society are set against each other from the advent of man and world. Could it be that a satisfaction of the urge be in accord rather than dissonance with the aims of history? But Freud conceives of libido and law as antagonistic. This discord organizes the binary oppositions between conscious/unconscious and law/transgression. The system posits that desire must be in a fracas with history.

The crucial choice consists of either the acceptance of reality and repression of the drive or the rejection of reality and satisfaction of the urge. Only the either/or choice is possible for the neurotic. The neurotic foreswears the plenitude of the imagined female penis. The imaginary phallus represents a broken mirror-reflection of the neurotic's own narcissism. The male junior imagines the female penis not as different but as *deficit*. The male junior understands the female sex organs as a phantom ghostly trace of horror because of the absence of the presence of the penis. The deficit of the clitoris is understood as the not-penis against the penis. This *not* defines the lost penis of the body of the female junior. Her castration and deficit rather than otherness and difference mark her with the stigmata of a lack of Something is Missing rather than with the novelty of a Something (Else) is Present. The male junior must foreswear *Trieb* and its endless circles of pleasures in tension and aim/less wander. The male junior settles for the anxious masculine *jouissance* of castration. Under duress, he suffers the minor jollies and major anxieties of the ego-ideal. The forced choice of the either/or decision enforces paternal identification on the offspring. This embryonic adult must identify with the norms and codes of the culture. The *clichéd* habits and conventional values of the dominant ego-ideal are the consolation for the lost pleasures with the mother and the male junior's own body.

The alternative to this either/or choice — either neurotic repression or psychotic foreclosure — is perversion. Freud writes: "But the offspring does neither thing, or rather it does both simultaneously, which amounts to the same thing."[10] This noteworthy passage both articulates and performs the logic of the fetish. The performance of "both simultaneously" invites the offspring to accept and reject — acknowledge and deny — the difference of sex. This disavowal disrupts the "same" that he otherwise expects in the place of the clitoris. The castration under the system of $-ism includes capitalist scarcity, anxious loss, and the semiotic signified. Is the disavowal of castration anxiety merely the "same thing" as castration anxiety? Freud ends this short article by noting: "It is as if, after all the to-ing and fro-ing between denial and acknowledgment, it was the castration that managed to find the clearer expression."[11] Beyond the offspring, this "expression" of castration is evident in the institutions and values of the West. Capitalism is organized according to scarcity. The signified is structured by the father's *point de capiton* and the arrest of textual play. Castration is the fear and anxiety of the loss of private property.

Nevertheless, Freud also refers to the male junior's disavowal as a "neat solution to the problem" of female lack. Freud repeatedly says that disavowal is an inventive strategy against the consequent castration anxiety which overwhelms the male junior who must confront the horror of difference *qua* deficit.[12] The "neat solution" of disavowal requires a radical split in the ego. The ego sustains two "contradictory reactions" of lack and plenitude, and of absence and presence. The perverse ego sustains this double conscience in the face of the expectation of the "same" and the reality of the different.[13] These "contradictory reactions" are the arts of the pervert. These aesthetics are borrowed from the schizophrenic. The madman's torture by the signifier is redeemed in the pervert's show. The psychotic's Unreason is made public in the talented text of the pervert's *écriture*. Freud writes,

> On the one hand, with the help of certain mechanisms, [the pervert] rejects reality and refuses any prohibition; on the other hand — and in the very same breath — it acknowledges

the danger from reality, turns anxiety about it into a pathological symptom, and attempts subsequently to ward off the danger.[14]

The male junior enunciates a split double-speak of the both/and mutual exclusion (inclusion) of contradiction and antinomy. This perverse discourse affirms both the both/and and the either/or. The pervert's text simultaneously affirms the presence of the absence of the female genitalia and the absence of the presence of the female genitalia. The pervert's magic is not simply a performance of the ambiguous subtext of the signifier. Rather, the pervert pens the collision of all of the signifiers in the series.

The reason for this will to explosion is the desire to reveal the schizoid's unsymbolizable Unreason. The essence (construction) of this Unreason is that each is the other *qua* itself (and so on). Freud indicates that the upshot of disavowal is the satisfaction of the two competing forces, the drive and reality. These forces are otherwise incompatible. As Freud says: "Each of the contending parties gets what it wants; the drive can go on being satisfied, and reality is accorded its due respect."[15] The split in the ego reconciles the irreconcilable, accommodates the incompatible, and fraternizes the impossible. At the same time, the splitting of the ego quickly and joyfully disperses the words in the text. The pervert's text is an experimental articulation of the Unreason of the schizoid's resistance to castration. The pervert avoids castration in his both/and two-step. But the pervert is also situated within the economy of debt and return. The schizoid's sheer craziness manages to escape this nexus of castration — but at cost. The future of the Pervert-Schizoid-Woman invites an exit from the pathological symptoms which coalesce specifically around contradiction. The pervert welcomes the logic of the unconscious. This Other-Logic animates the simultaneity of the opposed in the absence of cause/effect, before/after, temporality, and knowledge. This Other-Metaphysics achieves this simultaneity in an instant, at the same time. Freud maintains that there is neither temporality nor knowledge in the unconscious. The pervert's skill is to symbolize otherness *qua* effect in his text.

Unfortunately, Freud insists that the upshot of this affirmative double-gesture — of "yes," to the drive, and "yes," to reality — marks the onset of a severe symptom. Freud writes: "This success is achieved at the expense of a rift in the ego that will never heal, indeed it will widen as time goes on."[16] Freud fails to specify the exact symptomatology of this "rift in the ego." This "rift" may be a mimicry of the hysterical symptoms. Freud describes these ticks with the concept of the *Spaltung*. This "rift" is the pervert's embrace of contradiction and difference. *Spaltung* is the object of the pervert's endeavor to symbolize the Unreason of the schizoid's secret truth. But Freud warns: "The two contradictory reactions to this conflict persist as the focal point of a splitting of the ego."[17] The responses of neurosis and schizophrenia are the center of a gap in the ego. The pervert's disavowal of the split between reality and urge seeks to joyfully conciliate. Freud's work in the passage articulates a demand for oedipal *Gestalt* subjecthood. An index of such personhood is a self which is whole, total, complete, and aggregate. Any alternative vision of selfhood as dispersed, partial, incomplete, and split is considered unwise and undesirable.

But it is only within a social and psychical economy which demands seamless logic and specular totality that "two contradictory reactions" are considered a hindrance rather than a "neat solution" to the problem of "conflict." A "rift in the ego" opens space for the juxtaposition of oppositions, the apposition of contradictions, and the collocation of divergent signifiers. These otherwise contradictory assemblages appeal to a settlement of the horror of difference *qua* deficit. This logic of castration is introduced into the psychical economy by the castration complex. Castration frames the male junior's inexplicable translation of the dissimilar into the hierarchical. If the *Spaltung* of the ego "will widen as time goes on," then this foreshadows a social future in which disagreements and discrepancies — *Thanatos* — will happily enjoy each other — *Eros*. This effluvium of otherness certainly pulsates in the so-called beyond of the pleasure principle. Repetition compulsion of painful disintegration overwrites conscious unification and organization in the pleasure principle.

The key object which presents itself in the possible resolution of the oedipal deadlock and the castration impasse is the fetish. The fetish is customarily considered the prop for a pathological modality of sexuality. One of the central theoretical functions of the fetish is to explain the nearly inexplicable: male heterosexuality. Fetishism is raucous and pathological even in its formality. But fetishism is also a profoundly normal and advantageous approach to sex and sexuality. The male junior's "neat solution" of perversion is situated between neurosis — the yield of urge to reality — and psychosis — the deference of reality to pleasure. Perversion neither acquiesces to reality nor submits to fantasy. Rather, fetishism mobilizes the both/and of the otherwise contradiction between reality and fantasy. The both/and economy of *Verleugnung* is the peculiar and unimaginable — irrational and illogical — essence of perversion. This mode of negation straddles the mutually exclusive in the absence of both partiality and exclusion. Outside of one or the other, fetishistic disavowal affirms the decision which chooses both. The pervert entertains each option — in the case of castration, reality and pleasure — as the object of decision and choice. How is this possible?

Fundamentally, the choice of *both* cannot be explained by the Logic of Identity and the economy of Reason. The word for this alternative to neurosis and psychosis is perversion. Freud writes: "He created a substitute for the Woman's missing penis — a fetish."[18] Freud claims that the male subject manufactures an otherness in the fetish-object. This fetish-object sutures the wound in the place of the expected but absent maternal phallus. Fetishism is the mechanism by which the castration and scarcity of Something is Missing are transformed into the fullness and abundance of Nothing is Missing. A present inanimate object substitutes in the place of an absent animate object. The Something is Missing is bodily. This absence in the body is substituted with a repetition which veils this bodily loss. The object of repetition — of presence and Nothing for lack and Something, of abundance and Nothing for scarcity and Something, and so on — is a representation in which Nothing is Missing. The fetish stands in the place of the loss of an expected presence that ultimately presented to the offspring as a strange absence.

The peculiar gaze of the male junior's phallocentrism reduces difference to deficit. The masculine economy narrows an expected sameness into a not-sameness. The *mise-en-scène* of castration diminishes a present and absent not-presence and not-absence. My task is to resignify Something is Missing as Something Different Is Missing⁺. This project is only possible if the Other-Logic of Sameness⁺ is mobilized in the scene of the discovery of sexual difference. My other project is to reconvert lack and castration into plenitude and fullness. This invites the return of impotent adult sexuality to the free exchange and liberated substitution of young sexuality. There is also another perverse option for Sameness⁺. This perverse twist enlivens a schizophrenic intuition of both sexes in which Nothing is Missing because each is different from itself but coincident with the other: $A \neq A = B$, and so on. This economy of the simultaneity of first, parallactic gap, and second, relational plenitude, promises a perversity which gets off — on the jockstrap — ! — on the re-presentation — ! — on film and video — ! — on the material fetish-object — ! — Fetishism also inspires a splitting for men, Women, and the rest of us. Sexes, sexualities, and genders become unencumbered by castration and the ghostly haunt of Something is Missing. Freud discovered that the original experience of the Other is of Something is Missing. This fundamental encounter in sexuality overwrites our later experiences in finance and expression. Perversely, Something is Missing must be exchanged for Nothing is Missing. The system inculcates and cultivates castration and lack. The pervert's art is to unveil presence and abundance.

Figure 4.1 Representational Transference

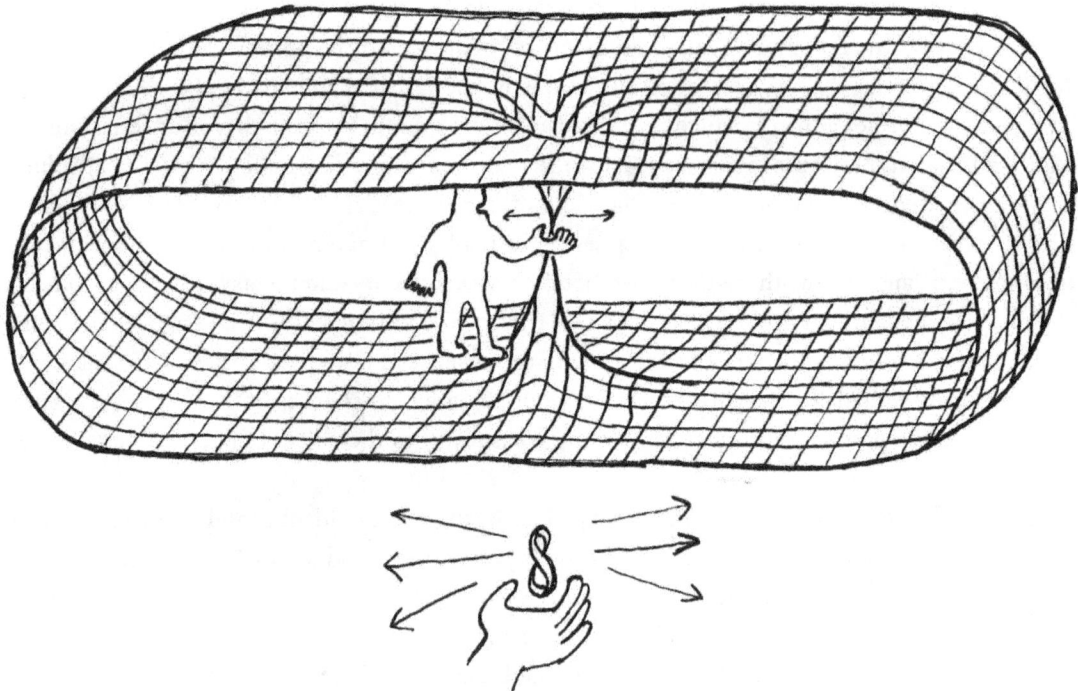

This image (center) depicts an open section of a space which is Inside-Out extimate to itself. The Inside (is) Becoming Outside (is) Becoming Inside *ad infinitum*. This intersection and inversion are the same crossroad and twist which funnel conscious into unconscious into conscious into unconscious into conscious (*ad infinitum*) in the Klein Bottle. The pervert (center) grips intersection and inversion at their points in space. Castration in the system is the Inside-Outsideness of the fragmented identity. Fragmentation is the proviso of any representation of word or object. Fragmentation also enables the parallactic concurrent separation and suture of the signifier and the signified. But for the pervert, any object — fetish, center, metaphor, word, jockstrap, and so on — is a prop for loss. The pervert's hand firmly holds to the horror of castration. But the pervert's pinch does so in order to creatively inoculate the pervert and the system from castration. The pervert's discerned *Möbius* Inside-Outsideness extimacy enables him to manipulate and perform anywhere inside the system. The *Praxis* of unconscious Sameness+ (below) is everywhere in the expanses of space in the system. The pervert intuitively and creatively exposes and enacts the Unreason of the system with a rational coherence and logical necessity.

Notes & Sketches —

THE FETISH

The successful conversion of lack into plenitude entails the selection and enjoyment of a material object, representation, or sign. This *das Ding* physically substitutes in the place of the maternal phallus. The entire system of the "neat solution" of fetishism is organized around the space and time of this basal loss. But perverts recuperate this lack in the material object of representation. The fetishist's sex is principally representational. The pervert's sex is profoundly re-presentational. This fetish-sex displaces in display the female genitalia with the material embodiment of the fetish-object as representation. The clitoral gap of absence or the feminine void of Nothingness facilitates the pervert's art of representation in his fetish-texts. The pervert's talent symbolizes the Unreason of a system of diacritics. The structure is coordinated by the *not* of both absent Something is Missing and present Nothing is Missing — the clitoris and the penis. This tension between lack and plenitude, scarcity and abundance, and castration and fullness — organizes all of the meaning-making in the culture.

Representations of Nothing is Missing

The fetishist's object of representation — the fur, lace, shoe, jockstrap — sutures the Nothingness of both Something and Nothing. This bandage is the seam of the material embodiment of the representation. The schizoid's secret truth of Unreason is that it is a profound negativity — *not not not* — which organizes the Peniscentrism of the offspring's relationship to the deficit of difference in the fantasy of castration. This entrenched negativity — *not not not* — subordinates all of the signifiers in the series to a void. The consequences of the return of the sign to the abyssal structure of a black hole are vast for both Reason and Unreason, and for both representation and sublimity. The fetishist's object is certainly representational. But this figuration of sexual Sameness† is simultaneously unsymbolizable and sublime. The pervert's fetish-object represents Nothingness. The fetish is the objective veil of the void of the female genitalia. The object of the pervert's pleasure is an impossible sublimity. The jockstrap is a defense against sense.

This passage by Freud (above) also illustrates the process of metaphorical substitution (*Wo Es war*) that the male junior enjoys in the creation of the fetish-object. The meaning-making powers of the fetish are strictly unsymbolizable and undeniably sublime. The veil of the clitoris is *il y'a de hors texte*. The Freudian nomenclature, "the Woman's missing penis – a fetish," performs the metaphorical substitution in the letter of the text. The Freudian phrase, "missing penis – a fetish," illuminates the metaphorical substitution of the fetish-object with metonymic traces. The slippage in the sentence between "the Woman's missing penis" and "a fetish" is made possible by the en-dash. The en-dash is the textual connective tissue between the phrases. A grammatical mark approximates an imperfect approach between the two signs, "the Woman's missing penis" and "a fetish." The male junior "may have been denying reality," as Freud says, "but he had saved his penis."[19] The fetish-object works as a defense against the threat of castration.

The jockstrap also operates as a guarantor of the pervert's enjoyment of his own penis. The pervert's fetish-text — *Pervert-Schizoid-Woman* — enables the male junior to protect the private property of his penis from a feared annexation. The fabricated presence in the fetish-object disavows — "I know very well, but nevertheless" — the reminder of a proleptic loss of identity in castration. The castration anxiety is eased even as the submission to the potential ego-ideal is the simultaneous condition of such an identity. The male junior relinquishes a Peniscentric identity in order to achieve a culturalcentric identity. Oedipally, the male junior's aesthetic and attitude are originally focused on the pleasures of the penis and the warmth of the mother. Later, the male junior renounces self-pleasure in order to save his penis from castration. This decision makes his penis safe but impotent. The male junior achieves paternal subjectivity with the ego-ideal and the father. The selection and enjoyment of the material object of the representation of the fetish-object suture the wound of the loss of the maternal phallus. But why is this representation of the jockstrap a successful defense against the reminder of annexation?

The answer is that the clitoris is a representation. The clitoris is an assembly of phallocentrism (penis/not-penis). The counterresistance against the difference *qua* deficit of the clitoris must be a counterrepresentation. The jockstrap is this counterrepresentation. The fetish-object certainly substitutes for the absent penis — somehow. But the fetish is also a material embodiment as a representation. The representation veils absence and masks castration. The only modality of fetishism is representation. This representation returns the pervert to the lost presence of the maternal phallus. Symbolization of this loss — making-fetish — presents the sublimity of the maternal phallus. This maternal appendage cannot otherwise be textualized, spoken or written. The fetish-object embodies this impossible representation of the unsymbolizable — even Harry's jockstrap will do.

Freud argues that the male junior's affirmative double-gesture in perversion is distinct from psychosis. The perverse assemblage of the "neat solution" of the fetish-object consists of a metonymic displacement from the absent female penis to the fetish-object *qua* penis-substitute in representation. This displacement in the act of sexual intercourse is an in-process, in-action Becoming Being — ! This Becoming satisfies the fetishist. The pervert enjoys this sexual configuration of *figuration*. The fetishist gets off on figure and metaphor. She takes pleasure in representation as the *mise-en-scène* of *désir* and *jouissance*. Freud writes,

> The boy did not simply contradict his perception and hallucinate a penis where there was none, he merely carried out a displacement in value, transferring the significance of the penis to another part of the body, a process facilitated — in a way we need not explain here — by the mechanism of regression.[20]

The male junior does not deny the absence of the female penis. Rather, the phantom value of the maternal phallus is transferred to the fur, lace, shoe, and jockstrap. The value is converted by representational transference. This so-called regression facilitates a sexual intercourse with the object of substitution. The fetish-sex is released of the anxiety of the annexation of the male junior's private property. The re-presentation of the female penis in the figuration of the fetish-object guards against the loss of the male junior's penis. Regression is homiletic for capitalism and the regime of *le propre*. Regression of the displacement of value from object to object — imagined female penis to actual fetish jockstrap — protects the private property of the penis from theft. The object of value is stripped of its significance. Value is transferred to another object. This other object — fetish — cannot be the object of loss or death. I "know very well" that the jockstrap only approximates the Real maternal phallus, "but nevertheless" I enjoy the jockstrap all the same.

The fetish eviscerates the loss of the proleptic relationship of castration between the penis and the clitoris. The fetish substitutes presence for absence, plenitude for lack, and Something is Missing for Nothing is Missing. The reason that this process works for the pervert is that metonymic displacement conditions the value that the fetish-object symbolizes. The process of regression is the essence of fetishism. This transference of value is the object of a successful, satisfactory, and perverse sexual relationship. The secret of regression is that the object — female penis or male jockstrap — is of secondary and displaced value. The delusion of a void structures difference *qua* deficit. The female penis can be displaced as the penis-substitute fetish-object in an endless metonymy of prospective anti-signifiers. These Other-Fetishes recall what I isolate as the Real Signifier. The Real Signifier is the re-presentation of the unsymbolizable fetish-object. This sublime fetish is the object of the pervert's desire and pleasure. The pervert gets off on the failure of representation. The fetishist's sexual joy is the limit-thought of representation. The pervert ejaculates at the frontier of the representation of the void of the Nothingness of the clitoris. The jockstrap veils the slip and slide of the trace.

The magical manufacture of the fetish is the work of the unconscious. This labor is comprised of metaphorical compression and metonymic displacement. The coming-into-being of the fetish happens in the timeless space in-process, in-action of a Becoming which is protective against castration. In the process of fetish-formation in the male junior, Freud alerts us, "as far as his own penis was concerned, nothing had changed at all."[21] The fetish-object sutures the wound of castration. The cut of difference *qua* deficit would normally arouse castration anxiety. The perverse alternative to castration is the fetish. The success of fetishism illuminates the Lacanian sound bite that "there is no such thing as a sexual relation."[22] There can be no such thing as a heterosexual relationship because the clitoris is the source of abject horror and acute fear for the male subject. The castration complex clarifies that male heterosexuality is impossible. The only modality of ostensibly heterosexual sex for the male subject is fetishism. Otherwise, the horror and dread of the female genitalia will invariably repel men away from sexual intercourse with Women and toward sexual engagement with other men.

The other reason that "nothing" has "changed" is that the fetish-process involves the *mise-en-scène* of the unconscious. Fetishistically, the primary process of the unconscious is simultaneously coincidental and overlapped with the system of the conscious. An unconscious timelessness dramatizes the ever generated Something is Missing with a series of Nothing is Missing. This plenitude surfaces even if such abundance must be forever supplemented with other objects. The Woman is the proper origin of the fetish. Her body discloses the clitoris. This lack is the object of substitution. The man is the rightful heir to this clitoral fetish. The pervert can save the original object of enjoyment with the penis and its avatars in the fur, lace, shoe, and jockstrap. This originary object of *jouissance* in the penis is neither the lost female penis nor the anxious male penis. Rather, this referent for fetishistic sexuality is the Real Penis of nascent sexuality.

The object of the fetish is precisely the sex and sexuality of a lost past and play. This sex is lost in the *Aufhebung* to the primacy of the phallus and its hierarchies and exclusions. The lost sexuality of infancy is the referent for the fetish. This childhood passion — playing doctor with Jay, comes to mind — invites an infinite chain of sexual objects and erotic aims. These objects and aims exceed any prospective castrations and losses. There is no re-presentation of the sublimity of the fetish-object in nascent sexuality. All of the objects were plentiful and sexualized in childhood. The objects of embryonic sex and sexuality are beyond the compressions and displacements of regression. The offspring is sexualized and libidinized over the entirety of its body. The adult is eroticized in relationship to a minority of parts and orifices. The offspring is totally sexual, and the adult is partially sexual. To grow up — is to lose sexuality. Sex is at the origin rather than the destination, and libido is at the departure rather than the arrival. The offspring's sexual epistemophilic and libidinal ontological inquiry, "What is?" — is the fetish.

The ghostly specter of a symptom surfaces at the close of Freud's discussion of fetishism. The fetishist does not fear the female genitalia. Instead, the anonymous male junior of Freud's text yields to a different symptom. This unconscious effect "manifested itself as an anxiety," as Freud says, "about being eaten by his father."[23] The culprit of this symptom is the male junior's sustained self-pleasure. This autoaffection happily continues even after the turn toward the fetish-object. Strangely, the fetish is a penis-substitute. This substitute — jockstrap *qua* penis — is a metaphor for the male junior's penis. This penis is the object of self-pleasure. As such, the fetish-jockstrap is the object of the male junior's self-pleasure. The fetish is a substitute for the offspring's penis. The penis cannot be the final referent for sex and sexuality because the penis is subject to play — displacement and compression — in the maneuvers of the substitutions of metaphor and metonymy. The fetish is a penis, and the penis is a fetish. There is no difference or delay between the penis and the fetish. The mediatory sign of "penis-substitute" arbitrates between a duet of a "sameness which is not identical" or a Sameness⁺. The function of the general equivalent is put into question. A penis can only be a re-presentation of itself. The penis is unstable and fragile. The penis must reiterate and repeat itself in order to consolidate its precarious identity. The offspring's insistent self-pleasure transgresses the father's law against autoaffection and maternal pleasure. The male junior obstinately refuses these interdictions because he denies female castration.

A crucial question emerges for the alphabets and vocabularies that we use to describe castration and the penis. Does the male junior who enjoys self-pleasure and denies the paternal threat enjoy plenitude or rather suffer lack? Does the masculine subject lack Nothing or does he lack Something? What is the difference between Something and Nothing? The ontological question *in toto* is destructured. These queries cannot even be posed to the male junior or to Freud. The offspring's prelapsarian period of sexual Sameness⁺ — free exchange and liberated substitution with aim/less aims and objectless objects — cannot fathom a division between Something/Nothing or even between lack/plenitude or capitalism/communism. The offspring both lacks Nothing and lacks Something. Neither Something nor Nothing is distinct from the other, "but nevertheless," the male junior's pleasure is forward and fierce under the spell of fetishism because the pervert's sexual practices promise the disavowal of the possible consequences — death and loss — of his pleasure.

The male junior of perversion experiences pleasure as free of responsibility and the generalized -ism of the proper. Freud's wish is to be free of responsibility for Irma's pains in the *ur*-dream of psychoanalysis. Just so, the property of responsibility, action, choice, decision — "I" — is freed from subjective and objective ownership — "I." The offspring's self-pleasure is not his "own." The offspring's "own" self-pleasure is the pleasure of the Other. The male junior repudiates the normative effects of private(s) property. He enjoys an aneconomy without the general equivalence of the phallus. The pervert escapes the phallic enforcement of the rules and norms of sexualities and hierarchies. The pervert also resists the properties of responsibilities, intentions, agencies, wills, and decisions. The "I" of the pervert dissolves into the ether of a harmless "me." Freud puts it succinctly,

> If he did not have to acknowledge that Women had lost their penis, then the threat made against him lost its credibility, he no longer had to fear for his penis, and he could go on masturbating undisturbed.[24]

This "self-pleasure" should be understood in its richest metaphorical and figural sense. Self-pleasure is an index of play with oneself, freedom to be oneself, enjoyment of oneself, agency with and toward oneself, and will and decision of oneself. This offspring enjoys this autoaffection without the burdens of consequence, responsibility, or obligation.

The most liberated of freedoms — Jockstraps of the World, Unite! — is lost when the "threat" against the private property of the penis is made "credible" by the peril. This danger is confirmed by the sight of the female junior's lack and the echo of the father's commination against the penis. Otherwise, a contained and harmless self-pleasure invites the subject and object into a unification in the body of the male junior and his innocent autoeroticism. Self-pleasurable glee enables him to think, be, and live a sex and sexuality which are outside of anxiety. The joys of self-pleasure evade the madness of the penis. This penis is the archetype of later objects of normative and regulated private property. This later so-called adult sexuality supplants the incipient self-pleasures of early life. The sex and sexuality of the adult elaborate an identity. Identity conforms to the norms and codes of the culture. These habits are the practices of $-ism and their dangerous and violent consequences for man and world. The ethical import of the fetish is that the jockstrap enables the male junior to resist obedience to the ego-ideal.

The fetish invites the male junior to escape the series of standards — "names-of-the-father," as Lacan puts it — for the father and his prowess. The sex and sexuality of the fetish contest the rules and formulas for success in a patriarchal and capitalist culture. Normatively, sexuality is the re-presentation of fetish-objects. The fetishes veil Nothingness in the enjoyment of a fearless sex. Now, with the regime of adult sexuality, the phallus intervenes and enforces the triumph of identity above pleasure. The fetishistic penis-substitute not only eases castration anxiety. But the fetish also deviates from the laws of the father's regime of identity. The fetishist performs pleasure. But are there coherent selves and socialities which emerge from the pervert's resistance to cultural exemplars, types, and patterns? Can the re-presentation of the fetish-object *qua* the clitoris not only return the masculine subject to pleasure but also at the same time exculpate the feminine subject from exile in Nothingness? Or is the Woman's Something is Missing the inverted Marxist *camera obscura* (1845) and ideological misrecognition of the male junior? Must the male junior's askew gaze miss that precisely Nothing is Missing?

The development of perversity in the male junior is an arduous psychical effort and social affair. The onset of perversity is beset with the confrontation with the difference *qua* deficit of the female junior. The transition toward fetishism also requires engagement with the father as the arbiter of the ego-ideal. The pervert must cope with the aporias of proper entrance into masculine culture. The maturation of adult fetishism resolves several of these complications. My claim is that the pervert can be archetypal of a future revolutionary selfhood. The young pervert suffers a symptomatology of fear, anxiety, and guilt despite a Peniscentrism that unexpectedly reverses phallocentrism. The adult fetishist decodes the conundrums which beset the young pervert. In his *ur*-text, "Fetishism" (1927), Freud articulates the Metaphoricity and substitutability of fetishes and objects. This free exchange effectively and ingeniously renders the fetishists "perfectly happy" in their sexual lives.[25] Castration anxiety is the nodal point of the impossibility of the (hetero)sexual relationship. Female castration (con)figures horror and dread at the sight of the female genitalia. Genital difference *qua* sexual deficit renders the romantic relationship an awkward and impotent folly.

But my concept of Sameness⁺ illuminates a metonymy (which is) in transition to metaphor (which is) in transition to *Trieb* (and so on). This series is animated by "a sameness which is not identical." A Sameness⁺ invites the in-process, in-action Becoming (of the) penis to the Becoming (of the) penis-substitute to the Becoming (of the) fetish, and so on. The penis never stops Becoming otherwise than itself. The penis never stops not being written. This vows an exit from castration anxiety. An anxiety about death and loss would otherwise organize the pervert's social and psychical life. Remarkably, Freud performs the essence of metaphor and substitution in the introductory remarks about fetishism in his text. In "Fetishism" (1927), Freud writes,

> What analysis revealed about the meaning and purpose of these fetishes was the *same* in every case. It emerged so spontaneously and seemed to me so compelling that I am prepared to anticipate the *same* general solution for all cases of fetishism (my emphasis).[26]

The "meaning" and "purpose" of the fetish underscore the substitution of Sameness⁺ ("a sameness which is not identical") for difference. The fetish entails metaphorical displacement of presence for absence. The substitution promises a swap of plenitude for lack. The "same general solution" describes the fundamental move of fetishism. This effort is to "anticipate the same" (the maternal phallus) in the place of the different (the Woman's clitoris). The female junior's penis is "the same" as the male junior's penis. This is so only if she has (in the past) never suffered a castration.

The presence of the female penis obviates the weird mechanism of conversion in which difference is translated into deficit. This transcription of otherness into the self-same and the self-identical is otherwise based on the criteria of "size" and "visibility." But even in the case of male perversion, the psychical revelation of this castration invites the fetishist to enjoy the fetish — metonymy for metaphor for metonymy for metaphor (and so on). This aim/less wander of *Trieb* (and so on) slips and slides around, against, by, near, with, *et al.*, all of the objects in the system. *Trieb* illuminates the first necessary component of a successful fetishism. An integrant of this fetishism is the difference and deferral — delay — in the masochistic edge toward (away from) the object of desire (pleasure).

Unexpectedly and requisitely, the female junior must be understood not in terms of the phallocentric economy of difference *qua* deficit but in the framework of the Peniscentric economy of sameness *qua* otherness. The female junior's clitoris is certainly not a deficit. The not-penis is contrived from an arbitrary difference ("size" and "visibility"). The phallocentric logic — "a man has a penis and a Woman does not have a penis" — cannot govern the intuition of sexual difference. Whatever the female junior's difference may be — just like whatever the penis may be — the two sets of sexual organs are fundamentally and unexpectedly the same. Freud indicates as much in his discussion of fetishism. This Sameness⁺ is structured according to the Other-Logic of perversion: A ≠ A = B, and so on.

The Pervert-Schizoid-Woman discovers that each object is the same as the other because each is different from itself. This is the profound sense of Derrida's words, "a sameness which is not identical," or a Sameness⁺. The fetishist experiences his *jouissance* in the process of substitution. He enjoys the in-process, in-action of metaphor even in the absence of the female penis. The sexuality of the fetishist is primarily metaphorical. The fetish re-presents the penis in the place of the female genitalia. The object of fetishism is isomorphic to the metonymic structure of the "(un)like" of metaphor (simile). The pervert gets off on extimacy. The pervert enjoys the imbrication of otherness in the self-same and the self-identical. The fetishist takes pleasure in the logic and economy of deconstruction. The fetishist "knows very well" that Something is Missing in the clitoris, "but nevertheless" he orchestrates a scene in which Nothing is Missing in this same clitoris.

The fetishist's prestidigitation resists the reduction of otherness into sameness. Rather, the fetishist achieves the transformation — somehow — of lack into plenitude in representation. The figuration of the jockstrap converts Something into Nothing (and vice-versa). In contrast, the heterosexual male focuses on size, visibility, and loss. These marks of life and death are irrelevant to the pervert. The fetishist's *jouissance* is profoundly organized by representation. Why pay for a boyfriend when you can just watch porn? The fetish re-presents the clitoris *qua* the penis. This retranscription is possible in the fetishistic economy because each object — jockstrap and bra — is deviant from the other in the simultaneity of the parallactic gap and relational plenitude: A ≠ A = B.

This negative and differential split — *Spaltung*, as Freud says of the early hysterics — animates an (*a*)sexuality. This Outside-Sex is not organized by difference whatsoever. Neurotic *désir* is structured by the difference between the split subject and the *objet petit a*. This tension is mediated by the function of the phallus. In contrast, the pervert's *jouissance* (as opposed to *désir*) is indifferent to an essentialist difference. The pervert is happy to neutralize the phallocentric hierarchy of penis/not-penis with the absurdly Unreasonable penis = clitoris (= faeces = baby), and so on. What is the not-jockstrap? And is it big enough? The imperceptible gap between the clitoris and its avatars in the fetish-objects is an indeterminate and incalculable residue which cannot be reduced to general equivalence. The *différance* between penis and clitoris cannot be abstracted and speculated by any criteria of standardization.

Figurations of Sex

The adult fetishist substitutes a fetish-object ("the same") for the clitoris (the different). The Metaphoricity of the fetish-object renders the adult fetishist "perfectly happy" with the substitution of "penis-substitute" for "penis" (and so on). The achievement of enjoyment is assured for the fetishist because there is always another penis-penis-substitute-fetish for in-action, in-process sexual intercourse. This slip and slide of substitute objects mobilize the aim/less *Trieb* or drive around the sexual galaxy. This travel is orchestrated by the preposition — this way and that way — without restriction to any necessary empirical object of satisfaction or referent for sexuality. Perversely, metaphor is sexual intercourse. The pervert's *jouissance* is organized by the substitution of representations. The economy of this substitution of representation is metaphorical and metonymical. The proper affect of the relationship between self and representation is neither desire nor need. Rather, the emotive relationship between the fetishist and the object-substitute is *jouissance* and pleasure.

The psychosexual orientation that most approximates a successful sexual relationship — "there *is* such a thing as a sexual relationship" — is undoubtedly the pervert's rapport with the object. The adult fetishist's anticipation of "the same" staves off the specter of castration anxiety. This worry otherwise ruins the (hetero) sexual relationship proper. The only triumphant modality of sex is an (*a*)sexuality. This Other-Sexuality is organized not by the desire and lack of the tension and release of the Freudian pleasure principle. Instead, this (*a*)sexuality is structured by the joy and pleasure of a masochistic suspension, wait, imagination, and coldness that Deleuze outlines as specific to the pervert's aesthetic.[27] An (*a*)sexual relationship works because this sexual intercourse is not an engagement with a subject. The pervert makes love to representation and metaphor rather than to reality and literality. The pervert is a lover of texts, letters, alphabets, and books. The pervert gets off on movies, television, magazines, images, textures, and sounds.

The pervert's (*a*)sexuality is most clearly visible in his recoil from bodies. Perversion mostly takes no pleasure in direct contact with genitalia. Rather, the fetishist is tempted and teased by the substitute-object. The pervert is mostly unmoved and unaroused by the sheer nakedness of bodies. The naked body of the other is ancillary to his *jouissance*. Anatomy is not destiny for the pervert. The pervert is scopophilically obsessed. He loves gazing, and he relishes looking. But he mostly has no interest in sexual engagement with a naked body. Fetishistically, the significance of the body of the other is its mediation of the representational object. Perversion covets the fetish which re-presents anatomy to him. This articulated image of the body is visible as a form of representational plenitude. The mystery of the pervert is that — somehow — this representation in the fetish-object converts patriarchal lack and capitalist scarcity into Peniscentric plenitude and communist abundance.

Unexpectedly, there is no castration in representation. Summarily, there is no reasonable account of the basal plenitude of representation for the pervert. Representation is usually considered severed from the referent. This is precisely the purpose for the pervert. The absence of a referential relationship between sign and object makes the bare signifier free to float and hover on its own. The naked signifier is untied to an anchor in any materiality of anatomy or body. The fetishist freely enjoys his signifier. The pervert happily relishes the words and letters of the text. Somehow, this image both obscures castration and acknowledges its lack. The pervert's nascent (*a*)sexuality celebrates a pronounced scopophilic cathexis to the body and fascination with the human form. The simultaneous love of male and female beauty and form and distance from its flesh and fluid strike us as Unreasonable. How can the desired object simultaneously be the desired obstacle? How does the fetishist enjoy the torture of the physical recoil from the material object? The pervert's representational *écriture* can only be understood as a skillful talent because it Reasonably articulates the Unreasonable truth of the schizoid. The pervert's Other *jouissance* exceeds the materiality and physicality of the body. Who needs the penis and the clitoris when you've got the pen and the calligraphy?

Figure 4.2 Plenty of Lack

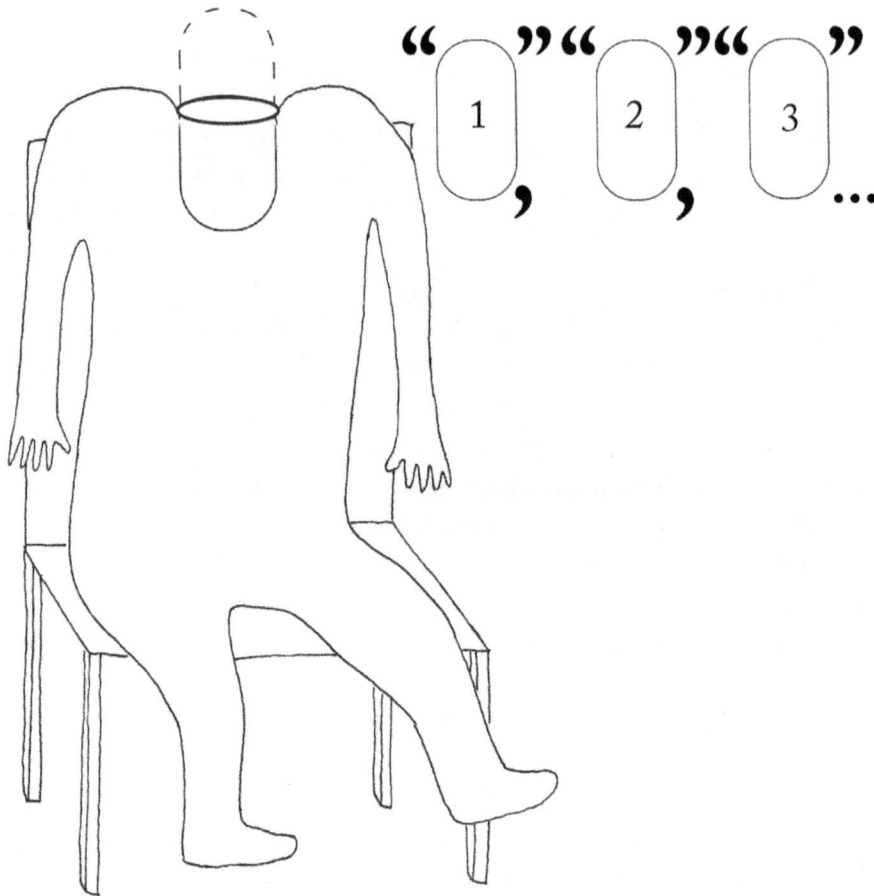

This picture of the seated Woman represents the Something is Missing of the scene of castration. This fable illuminates the metaphysics of presence. Perverse castration demonstrates the displacement of the void at the center of the structure with a series of avatars for the maternal phallus. The dotted line of half of the head of the Woman — and also of the fragmented object — illustrates that a singularity of presence (absence) may be substituted by any object to make good on the lack in this space. The scare quotes around the objects (above, right) indicate the schizoid Untruth of this metaphysics of present absence. Any word may be recontextualized as "itself." Any object can be conferred alternative value by a shift in context in a symbolic replication. The linguistic system and its Inside-Outsideness to "itself" indicate that any object is not what it is and is what it is not, or A ≠ A = B. The object is a simulacrum. This simulation is positivized into the ontological order of Being by a phallocentric occlusion of the Real Symbolic. The inverted head represents this -centrism. A -centrism erases the feminine in order to execute the binarism of Nothing is Missing and Something is Missing, and is and is not, and so on. The Woman Becomes an unconscious space in which any object is and is not, Something is Missing and Nothing is Missing, Being and Nothingness — "itself" in the battery of the Other of any object in the system.

Notes & Sketches —

The fetishism of perversity puts the entirety of Western civilization in sharp relief. The substitution of "the same" for the different mobilizes a Peniscentrism which is distinct from a phallocentrism. The metaphorical work of the fetish inaugurates the erection of a very particular absence. The object of this loss — castration and lack — is the Woman's presently presumed but veritably gone penis. The fate of the maternal phallus illuminates the history of humanity. The AWOL of the Woman's phallus outlines the violent chronicle of the folly of lack, castration, and the system of $-ism. Man's vexed relationship to the maternal phallus explains patriarchy and capitalism. The male dominance of patriarchy and the financial rule of capital are the nodal points of the economy of the proper. The unexpected holiday of the maternal penis in the castration complex founds the capitalist system of scarcity. Lack also structures the financial exploitation of the worker in the extraction of surplus value. Exploitation is the linchpin of the objective and subjective alienations of the marketplace. Loss of the female penis also initiates phallocentrism, patriarchy, and the laws of sex, sexuality, and gender. Castration encourages the sorry efforts to transgress these prohibitions on sex, sexuality, and gender. The system of *langue* is also subordinate to castration because the ostensible autonomy of the word is clipped by its saturation in (con)text.

Freud writes: "If I now state that a fetish is a penis-substitute, this will no doubt come as a disappointment."[28] There persists a constitutive gap between the "fetish" and the "penis-substitute." This match between penis and fetish enlists the mediation of the words "penis-substitute." Freud acknowledges that this overlap — parallactic aperture and suture — will "disappoint" the fetishist-reader. There must be links and bonds which are precisely not fetishes. There is a sequence of intervals in the system which cannot be sutured by the magical plenitude of the fetish-object. The "penis-substitute" must referee and umpire the relationship between the penis and the fetish. The relationship between the penis and the fetish is accidental and contingent rather than necessary and permanent. The constitutive gap between penis and fetish is a "disappointment" such that a substitute — whatever jockstrap — interposes itself between the original and the copy. The penis and the fetish are likely both originals and copies. Beyond the fur, lace, shoe, and jockstrap is the cut of the Real. The loss of the female penis invites the fetish to tie the loops and heal the joints. The fetishist substitutes a present Nothing is Missing for an absent Something is Missing. The fetish-metaphors fuse and weld all signifier-fetishes and object-fetishes in the signifying chain. The metonymic gaps — from fetish to center to word to substitute to sign, and so on — account for the "disappointment" of the minimal overlap and maximal coincidence of the series of objects of perversion. But what is not a fetish? What else is — a jockstrap?

SUBSTITUTIONS

The only Outside of the fetish-object substitution for the penis is the clitoris. The clitoris is the Real. The clitoris is the object around which representations and fetishes encircle. The objects traverse the Real of the clitoris. Fetishes surround the female sex organ. The clitoris is the Outside of the fetish. The fetish is the substitute for the penis. The clitoris is also strictly Outside of the sexual galaxy. The clitoris is Outside of the symbolic order. The clitoris is the strictly unsymbolizable sublime Real. The pervert is the archetypal talented symbolizer. But he cannot properly re-symbolize or re-present the fetish *of* the clitoris. The fetishist fashions the referent of the penis as the sublime unrepresentable. The penis is severed — *requirement: cut* — from the sign of the fetish-object. The penis is detached from the text. The penis is *hors texte*. Western civilization is structured by a differed and deferred *arche*. The figuration of this lost origin is the Woman's Real body.

The Clitoris Outside of the Fetish

The radical exclusion of the female body, sex, sexuality, and gender regulates $-ism. The Woman is sublime or, as Lacan teases, under erasure as ~~Woman~~. Freud's repeated and unanswered plea, "What is a Woman?," underscores the resistance to the symbolization of positive and essential words for and images of the Woman. The Woman is the proviso of the entire system. The structure of the world is based on castration and loss. The fetishist promotes a good faith in feminism and a politics of Sameness⁺ in difference. The pervert seeks to undo the masculine self-same and self-identical essence of both the penis and the clitoris. This theoretical move illuminates that anatomy cannot be so-called destiny. This rupture of bodily determinism is possible from within the conceptual framework of the parallactic gap and relational plenitude: $A ≠ A = B$. The Freudian question, "What is a Woman?," cannot be answered within his framework because the Woman is defined as the not-penis, the negative, and a Nothingness. The Woman is *not*.

But the penis is also not the penis. The clitoris is not the clitoris. Unreasonably, clitoris = penis = baby = faeces, and so on. A radically antiessentialist and antiidentitarian set of parameters renders the specificity of the female sex — from Nothingness not-penis to Being is-clitoris — undiscovered. The clitoral resistance of the Real — from *not-not* to *not-not* — would be of concern to a feminist theorist, such as Luce Irigaray.[29] A possible textualization — writing and speaking — of the specificity of the Woman's sex is possible. But this Real must be understood as a Sameness⁺, or "a sameness which is not identical." But is Being (penis) necessarily preferable to Nothingness (not-penis)? The penis is drenched in castration anxiety. Masculinity is the nodal point of sexual anxiety in the culture. This anxiety is structured by Being (penis) rather than by Nothingness (not-penis) or by the relationship between Being (penis) and Nothingness (not-penis). Freud conceives of Nothingness (not-penis) as the isolation of envy, but this jealous desire is perhaps preferable to castration anxiety. What are selfhood and sociality of lost Nothingness apart from man and world of anxious Being? If the question of "What is a Woman?" cannot be answered, then the question of "What is a man?" most certainly can be rejoined. But will the man be satisfied with these answers of and as his Being?

Freud notes a "disappointment" that his reader will feel upon the discovery that the fetish is merely a substitute for the penis. This disappointment is an echo of the absence of absence in the pervert's psychosexual economy. Otherwise, the unwritten and unspoken Outside of the fetish of the female sex manifests as the Real. This Real Clitoris destabilizes masculine sexuality. This Real Body of the Woman upsets the entirety of the symbolic order. At the same time, the Woman is the proviso of the organization of the system around loss, property, and the imperative to guard the family jewels of identity and desire at the cost of the joys of the *jouissance* of both the male and female body. The Woman is situated between the foundation and reproduction of the system, and between the breakdown and dissolution of the structure.

What is the significance of Freud's question, "What does a Woman want?" To pose this question implicates Freud's own deepest thoughts about sex and representation. The object of his question is the unwritten and unspoken sublimity of the question. What is the Outside of representation? What is the Outside of the fetish? What is the Outside of sex and sexuality? What is the Outside of the system? There is no such *das Ding* as a sexual relationship with a Woman because her sex cannot be understood within the parameters of a metaphysics of presence. The Real Clitoris is Outside of Being.

The (*a*)sexuality of men, Women, and the rest of us also resists capture in presence. The objects in the system are fetish-objects of various pleasures and intensifications. But the Woman's clitoris cannot be reduced to such representations. Uncannily, the Real of the Woman's body returns as both the bedrock of civilization and the rupture of this same system. The fetishist flirts with the female genitals. He does so in order to obscure the otherness of the clitoris. This chicanery is performed in the writing and speaking — symbolization — which are in the representation of the fetish-object. This object is a metaphor for the pervert's *jouissance* rather than *désir*. This pervert invites the radical fracture that female sexuality poses to the system of $-ism.

Penis, Fetish, and Substitute

Freud's words that "a fetish is a penis-substitute" obscure the difference between the fetish and the penis. The slip and slide between the two objects — the fetish *qua* representation and the penis *qua* referent — are made possible by the representational pyrotechnics of the psychosexuality of the pervert. This cut between fetish/penis is the object of the metaphor's dissimulation. Dissimulation veils that which is possessed. The fetish is not the penis. The fetish veils the absence of the penis. This whack-a-mole and hide-and-seek of the penis with the fetish — and of the fetish with the penis — are the labor of perverse dissimulation. As presence, in Being — the fetish is "a penis-substitute." The purpose of a fetish in its essence is to animate the link between the representation of the fetish-object and the referent of the penis.

The awkwardly named "penis-substitute" is the textual agency of adjudication and evaluation. Penis-substitute metaphorizes the representational capacity of the fetish. The penis-substitute mediates between the fetish-object as representational oddity (shoe, lace, fur, and jockstrap) and the penis as referential truth ("size" and "visibility"). This term "penis-substitute" is peculiar. It conflates and conjoins the referent with its representation. The word compresses referent ("penis") and representation ("substitute"). The good copy ("penis") and the bad copy ("substitute") and the bad copy ("penis") and the good copy ("substitute") become visible and tangible only in the conjoinment in the odd compression of "penis-substitute." The proviso of the penis is its necessary facsimile in the substitute. The penis must be reiterated and repeated. The haphazard identity of the penis is contingent. This penis Becomes-Penis only in the metaphor and substitute of itself. The penis is not "itself." The "substitute" mediates between fetish and penis. This substitute is the interstitial bond between the penis and the fetish. Outside of substitution, the Sameness[+] of the fetish cannot emerge as such.

The differences among penis, penis-substitute, and fetish are unexpectedly complex. None of these textual marks or referential objects can be considered significant in their essence, on their own, by themselves, as such, or *qua*. Freud indicates that the penis is the principal object. At the same time, the penis garners its significance only as the object of substitution of the fetish. The privileged object is certainly the penis. But the privilege of the penis is the proviso of the disprivilege of its object of switcheroo. This *objet* is the fetish. The penis is a fetish for the substitute. This substitute is a metaphor. The metaphor slips and slides beyond, above, below, around — prepositional orchestration — toward other metaphors. The penis is metaphorical and metonymical. The penis differs and defers itself in the traces of the chains of words. The Unreasonable conclusion of this discussion of penis, substitute, and fetish is that every object in the system is a penis. Every word in the system is not only the same word. Every word in the system is the penis. The word is not simply a substitute or a fetish for the penis. The word is the penis.

The penis is the point of departure and the source of destination in psychoanalysis. The penis is the final referent. But the pervert uncovers the fetish and the penis-substitute *qua* the objects of the in-process, in-action desire or *Trieb* of perverse (*a*)sexuality. This (*a*)sexuality is at once a start and a stop. It is orgasmic. It is ejaculative. It is quietly cleaned-up. The fetish approximates the penis as a substitute. Simultaneously, the penis is a fetish for this substitute. The penis, fetish, and penis-substitute are fundamentally isomorphic. Any distinction among penis, fetish, and substitute is structured by the chronology of substitution — of penis for fetish for substitute for fetish for penis, and so on. Not only is the penis a fetish and a substitute. The three modalities of objects are representations of perverse *jouissance*. The words in the system are under erasure. The female penis is no more lost than any other object — penis-substitute, substitute, fetish, and so on.

Figure 4.3 The Unbound Fetish

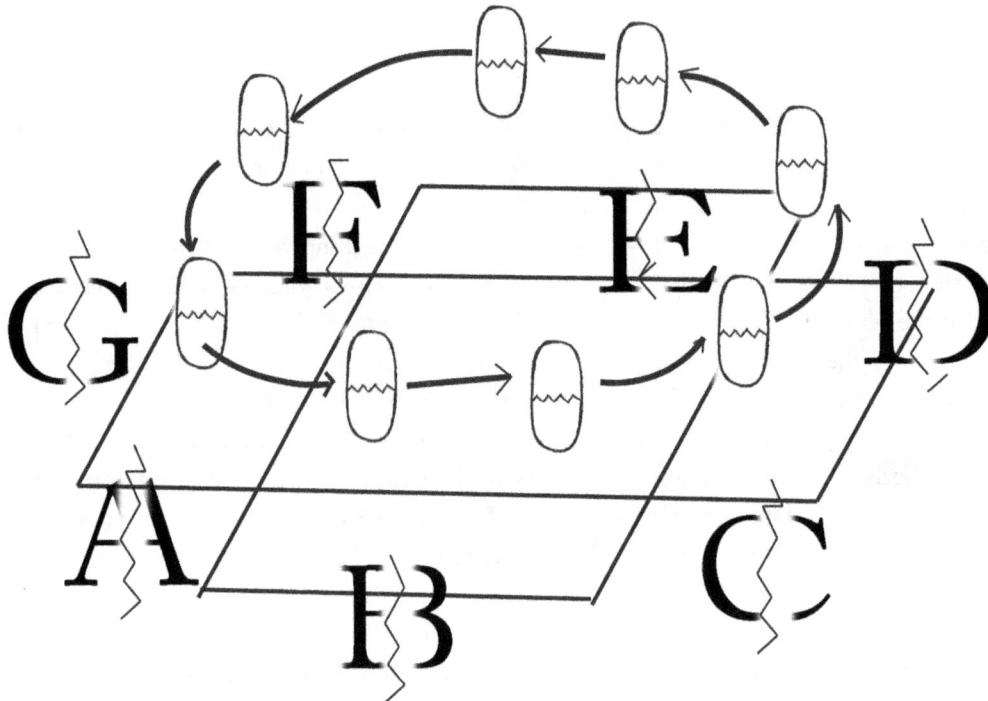

This image shows the fetish-substitute-object (jockstrap, *et al.*) in the place of the circulation of units of text in the signifying chain in the space of *langue* or Being. This unbound fetish is perversely open and expansive in space rather than closed and contracted by borders. These partitions around space generate a closed system of signification. The picture depicts the exposed units of text which signify the fragmented object of neither self-sameness nor self-identity. This open dissolution is the play and labor of the pervert and his extended accumulation of fetishes, objects, centers, metaphors, signs, metonymies, jockstraps, and so on. According to Saussure, the words in *langue* are infinitely substitutable yet simultaneously bound to a material system which regulates the comparison, contrast, and exchange of substitution. Any object is noncoincident and noncontinuous with itself. Any word is an infinite Sameness[+] with every other word. But the word is also dispersed and displaced within a limited material space. Alternatively, the pervert's fetish explodes this limitation and contraction and liberates extension and expansion. Perversely, the system of terms that otherwise circulates with a velocity which is defined by the temporal deferral of meaningful/lessness yields to the Spirit of the System of any object which is at once itself and the other. The pervert indulges in a *jouissance* which is unregulated by the temporality of tension and release of the pleasure principle and the retroaction (*Nachträglichkeit* and *après-coup*) of neurotic meaning-making. The pervert abjures a metalanguage (of the penis *qua* referent). The pervert opens (a) space in which free play is delightfully possible.

Notes & Sketches —

My conclusion must be that — the penis is a fetish for the clitoris. The clitoris and the penis are Real. Resistance to speech and writing applies to all sex organs. Sublimity colors all objects in the system. There is no strictly determinate object of fetishism. Rather, various ghostly centers, detached simulations, *clichéd* metaphors, handy fetishes, and erect penises — these are the objects of the pervert's *jouissance*. The pervert enjoys all subjects and objects in the galaxy. He discerns a parallactic difference and relational plenitude. The pervert is the subject of the absence of absence or a plenitude in which Nothing is Missing. The series of objects in the galaxy is a bounty of nascent part-objects. The pervert may gloss and adorn these scraps and scrapes. Fetishization *in toto* and *tout court* generates *jouissance* for the pervert and the Other. The Other's ecstasy is the object of the pervert's pleasure. The Freudian substitution of fetish for penis will provoke "disappointment," as Freud puts it. This is so for the subject who seeks a perfect and impossible specular correspondence between the fetish and the penis, between the substitute and the original, between the presence and the absence, between the plenitude and the lack, between the clitoris and the penis, and between the dildo and the phallus.

But the fetish cannot perfectly match the original object. The absence of this penis provokes a series of metaphorical substitutions. This set of centers and signs strives to contain the lack in the place of the mother. The substitution — center for another center, fetish for another fetish, simulacrum for another simulacrum, penis-substitute for another penis-substitute, penis for another penis, metaphor for another metaphor, sign for another sign, and so on — is a castration. But the fetish is an active object with a will toward the beyond of the pleasure principle. This serial metonymy is animated by manic fervor and tense frenzy. Fetishism exceeds the conservative regulation of pleasure. These substitutions escape the obstacle of the dead object. The fetishes traverse toward the Real. The horizon of the fetish is the Real Clitoris. The absence of absence liberates a perverse joy. This plenitude eludes the anxiety and distress of sexual difference. The fetish circumvents the apex of climax because the tension builds forever.

The qualitative distinction among penis, penis-substitute, and fetish is determined by the pleasure which is experienced by the subject of the sex. A fetish substitutes for a penis. This penis substitutes for an Other which is beyond the presence of the penis. The conundrum is the repute of the peculiar penis-substitute. The difficulty is the significance of this weird object of Freud's cautioned "disappointment" about the mediation between fetish and penis. The penis-substitute is a theoretical explanatory device. The penis-substitute mediates between the representational fetish and the fleshly penis. The penis-substitute is Freud's term for the general equivalence of perverse fetishism. What is the relationship between the penis and the fetish in the absence of this general equivalent of substitution? Are fetish and penis considered comparable and contrastable? Or are they singular in their own peculiar (*a*)sexual joy? Can a fetish perform its erotic duty without a substitutive mediation? Can a fetish perform its erotic duty with the penis as the final referent? Can the penis succeed in its sexual efforts without mediation in representational form as Other? Which generates a superior *jouissance*? — the penis in its fleshly and messy body or the fetish in its exhibitionistic and voyeuristic disposal?

DISAVOWAL

The originary loss — specifically, denial — of the maternal penis fails to properly register in the psychosexual economy of the adult fetishist. The original object is "not just any penis," Freud says, but "a specific and very special one."[30] The maternal phallus survives its neurotic negation in fetishism. The maternal phallus is simultaneously acknowledged and denied. The "specific and very special" maternal penis "should," as Freud says, "normally be renounced, but it is precisely the purpose of a fetish to prevent this loss from occurring."[31]

The fetish thwarts the loss of the "specific and very special" maternal penis. The metaphorical substitution of the fetish-object for the mother-penis serves as a primary defense against her present absence and his future absence. The fetish-object for the adult substitutes a presence, plenitude, object, dildo, phallus, metaphor, jockstrap (and so on) in the place of an absence. This lack has been disavowed in acknowledgement but denial.

Nothing from Nothing

Verleugnung is a complex process of negation. Freud explains: "The boy has refused to acknowledge the fact that he has perceived that Women have no penis."[32] There are three levels of disavowal at work in this statement: first, the disavowal of sexual difference, that man has a penis and that Woman does not have a penis ("phallocentrism"); second, the disavowal of the boy's own perception that the Woman does not have a penis ("castration anxiety"); and third, the disavowal of the Woman's imaginary lack (strict "disavowal"). The male junior's negative disavowal is double. He negates both the "fact" and the alternative interpretation of this "fact." The pervert disavows on the level of the conscious and in the dimension of the gaze. The pervert's *Verleugnung* of the source of castration can only be described as ingenious and creative. But if the mechanism is disavowal — acknowledgment and denial — then how does the pervert convince himself that the object that he epistemologically "knows very well" (empirically, and so on) can be displaced by divinely "but nevertheless" (faithfully, and so on)? What is the modality of engagement with Something is Missing of castration and scarcity which transforms it — against all odds — into Nothing is Missing of plenitude and abundance? The riddle of disavowal is the nexus of the quandary of first, sexual difference and castration anxiety under patriarchy, and second, scarcity and private property under capitalism. How does loss translate into gain? What is the schizophrenic secret of Unreason which enables penile Nothing is Missing and communist abundance to emerge from clitoral Something is Missing and capitalist scarcity?

A first approach to this dilemma is a critical evaluation of perverse sex and sexuality. The adult fetishist sustains a split in the ego — *Spaltung* — which invites him to evade castration anxiety and to enjoy his fetish-object. The fetishist enjoys the simultaneity of acceptance and rejection — acknowledgment and denial — of female castration. The sex act in its space and time — duration — is an activity of disavowal. Perverse (*a*)sex sustains a pleasure which is strictly beyond the principle of an original displeasure. The pleasure principle holds that the decrease of tension is the destination of the conservative homeostasis of the system. The pervert is masochistic because he reverses the Freudian pleasure principle of increase/decrease of tension in displeasure/pleasure. Perversely, the oppositions in the culture — increase/decrease, displeasure/pleasure, and acknowledgment/denial — are animated by a Sameness⁺, or a "sameness which is not identical." The self-same and the self-identical yield to an in/external otherness.

The pervert's (dis)avowal returns as its negation of "itself." Neither acknowledgment nor denial is distinct in its return. This explains the strange simultaneity of acknowledgment and denial in the pervert's "I know very well." Freud writes,

> The pervert both retains this belief [in the female phallus] and renounces it; in the conflict between the force of the unwelcome perception and the infantile aversion to it, a compromise is reached such as is possible only under the laws of unconscious thought, the primary process.[33]

The "conflict" between acceptance and rejection — "I know very well, but nevertheless" — is not a skirmish for the pervert. His *Verleugnung* is organized by the primary process of the unconscious. The unconscious is a field in which there is neither negation nor temporality. The pervert's disavowal is distinct from neurotic repression. A repression is the neurotic mechanism of negation of the secondary process of the system of the conscious. In contrast, the pervert's unconscious articulates a revision of the aversion to the unwelcome perception of the female sex. The perverse unconscious embraces the representational prop which veils the horror of castration. The unconscious techniques of compression and displacement enable the representation — the fur, lace, shoe, and jockstrap — to timelessly suture the gap between the acknowledgment of lack and the denial of castration.

Disavowal mobilizes the fetish-penis in representation. The no "No!" in the unconscious fosters a positivity which enables the fetish-object to suture the wound of castration. This positivity does so in the absence of the negation and knowledge of the father's phallocentric law. The fetishist both accepts and rejects the perception of female castration. The crucial dimension of fetishistic disavowal is the magnificent talent to achieve simultaneity. Disavowal draws from the techniques of the primary process of the unconscious. The primary process is the condition of the success of the fetishist's weird negation. But even if the unconscious inscribes an affirmative simultaneity of acknowledgement and denial into the psychical life of the adult fetishist, how does the pervert deny what he already knows? Or "but nevertheless" — but how?

Faith and Belief — Somehow

The pervert masters the unconscious techniques of the dream-work and the joke-work. He symbolizes the schizoid's Unreasonable secret truth with these textual talents. The pervert cultivates the artistry of the condensation of images and the displacement of intensities. The field of libido is coincident with the entire order of the ego-secondary process. The pervert libidinizes the secondary processes of the ego and the system Cs. The pervert is thinking, being, and living the unconscious even within the *mise-en-scène* of the conscious system. The sexual libido of the unconscious and the *Es* is notoriously Unreasonable but intensely affirmative. This unconscious-conscious system splits the pervert's "I know very well" of conscious epistemology from the "but nevertheless" of postepistemological faith, and so on. Belief flourishes in the aftermath of the exhaustion of the epistemological and ontological projects.

The fetishist skewers the system of the conscious. The perverted primary process of the unconscious pokes and prods beyond the "I know very well" that the Woman is castrated and toward the "but nevertheless" of faith and belief in representations and objects. These scraps and scrapes substitute in the place of this loss. Perverse disavowal is a modality of sex and sexuality which is organized by the power of dream. This orientation is the Outside of the epistemological knowledge of the secondary process, the system of the conscious, and the certainty of female castration. There can be no substantive conflict between the Reason of neurotic repression and the Unreason of perverse disavowal because the former articulates the epistemology of "I know very well" —full stop — whereas the latter enunciates in the wake of the exhaustion of epistemology in the "but nevertheless" — and so on.

The unconscious Unreason of the schizoid (pervert) does not merely trouble the system of the conscious and the secondary process. Unpredictably, the unconscious makes the system of the ego work. Perversely, the unconscious is the ego. The queer pervert discerns that there is no division between any of the oppositions in deconstruction, Marxism, and psychoanalysis — in Derrida's work, origin/trace, first/second reading, and so on; in Freud's work, manifest/latent, negation/symptom, repressed/return, patient/analyst, and so on; and in

Marx's work, capitalism/communism, bourgeoisie/proletariat, base/superstructure, and so on. The primary process and the pervert's Logic of the Unconscious make space for the juxtaposition of incompatibles, the fraternization of impossibles, and the apposition of opposites. This Jockstrap-Logic is a movement toward the desirous transition from *désir* to *Trieb* — from masculine to feminine, idiot to Other, capitalism to communism, lack to plenitude, and so on.

The pervert's playful *Verleugnung* representationally affirms the contradiction between acknowledgment and denial. The split in the perverse ego matches the *Spaltung*. This split animates the disavowal of the fetishist. This split mobilizes the aperture of the unconscious. The answer to the question of the pervert's disavowal is — How? The answer to this puzzle is the emergence of the techniques of the unconscious — compressions of metaphor, displacements of metonymy, and the absence of negation and knowledge in the primary process. The conscious *qua* unconscious is the forefront of the perverse (*a*)sex and (*a*)sexuality of the communist queerness of the future. The pervert's unconscious is already conscious. Rather than make love to horror and dread, the eroticized pervert makes love to representation — the fur, lace, shoe, and jockstrap. How is male heterosexuality possible? Is there a male heterosexuality which can be imagined as an Outside to the fetishistic *jouissance* of the porno representation and the gay *jouissance* of the penis?

In the process of the fetishist's (un)conscious *Verleugnung*, the penis changes its significance. The penis is not itself. The penis is the veil or representation of the clitoris. The clitoris is ex/internal to the penis. The penis is also a substitute for itself because the penis cannot be the final referent for perverse sex and sexuality. Representation *as such* is the final reference of all queer sex and sexuality. The pervert's object is representation. Representation literally re-presents the clitoris in the veil and screen of the male anatomy. The pervert witnesses the deconstruction of the literal/metaphorical and denotative/connotative dimensions because his sexual object is a re-presentation of "itself" and the object of his split desire. The creative solution of this fetishistic substitution is the work of the world.

Freud suggests that sexuality is coextensive with all of space — and precisely not of time. Temporality is absent from the unconscious. There is no time of (for) sex. The pervert's disavowal makes sex and sexuality possible. Sex is timeless. Sexual intercourse never ends. The orgasmic apex of the pleasure principle toward its pleasurable and regretful end is happily never achieved. The orgasm is forever deferred by the masochistic edge. The ejaculatory climax never cums at the apex of a constant masochistic deferral of (un)pleasure. These representational mobilizations of sexuality are only possible within the context of a disavowed lack of the female penis. This masochistic edge is conditioned by the timeless efforts of the unconscious and by Freud's dream-work and by my jockstrap-work, and so on.

The modality of fetishistic disavowal is only imaginable in the unconscious. The ego can only wonder at the question — How? A neurotic skepticism will always dominate the enigma of the pervert's (*a*)sexuality and *jouissance* of compressed and displaced unconscious images in dreams, jokes, and pictorial figurations of the primary process. The worthless sideshow of the rational agency of normativity guards against the pervert's magic. The neurotic order of $-ism pounces on the pervert's lucky fantasy in order to submit it to the playbook of the secondary principle of Reason and its negations and knowledges. The pervert's Unreason is not strictly a mode of negation. Repression articulates a *No!* Disavowal affirms a *yes*. *Verleugnung* joyously utters a "yes, yes" to the penis, the clitoris, and the entire troop of representational illusions. Any possible negation (repression) of an object is deferred by the masochistic edge and its diversionary series of affirmed objects of representation. Perversely, there is no present object to be repressed. The object is in-action, in-process Becoming in the intercourse of fetishistic (*a*)sex. The sequence of objects is only present in its Becoming.

Figure 4.4 Patriarchy and Fetishism

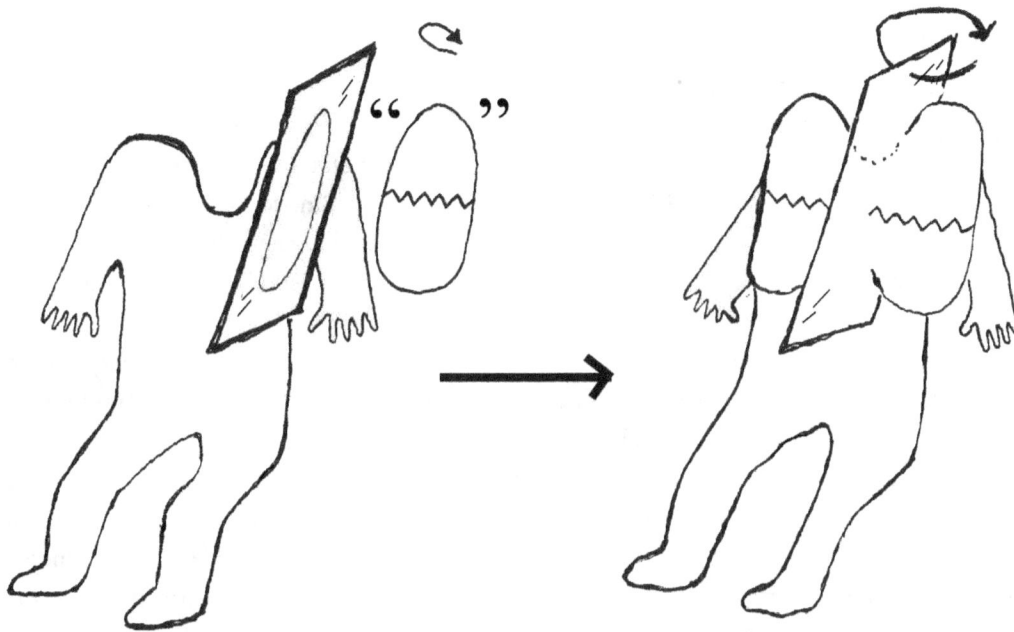

This image illustrates the distinction between the Patriarchal Fetishist and the Real Fetishist. The Patriarchal Fetishist (left) deploys the fetish in order to disavow difference and conceal it within its object in reference to the penis and the penis-substitute. The fetish on the one side of the mirror separates the fetish from the scene of castration and the return of "sexual difference" as otherwise than itself. The fetish loops and doubles back onto itself in its own narcissistic reflection. In contrast, the Real Fetishist (right) deploys the fetish which traverses the mirror and reconciles "itself" with the *tout autre* desire of the Other. This Other cannot be traced to the referent of the penis as the *ur*-foundation of the series of fetishes — centers, metaphors, signs, objects, metonymies, and so on. The Patriarchal Fetishist finds enjoyment in the disavowal of difference as such without the expansive and extensive return in decenterment from the penis. In contrast, the Real Fetishist seeks an Other *jouissance* in the disavowal of the self-same and the self-identical that otherwise references the penis. The Real Fetishist experiences and mobilizes the dispersal of identity and difference in Sameness⁺. Perversely, this Sameness⁺ can only be reiterated and recited in Difference⁺. In contrast, the Patriarchal Fetishist obscures Otherness because he refers the object to the penis *qua* proximate substitute. The Patriarchal Fetishist veils Difference⁺ in order to enjoy a narcissistic identity with himself. In contrast, the Real Fetishist discerns Sameness⁺ in the infinite traversal around — between, among, near, by, above, below — subjectivities and socialities in the absence of a necessary reference to the penis. The Real Fetishist enjoys difference, and he returns "difference." The Real Fetishist abandons the self-sameness and self-identity of selfhood. But the Patriarchal Fetishist emulates a dissolution which can only be deferred by reference to an (un)stable and (un) defined penis.

Notes & Sketches —

The emancipation of an unconscious affirmation only says "yes, yes." This intuited positivity indicates the sensibility of the Freudian psychoanalyst. The analyst quietly illuminates the schizoid's crazed Unreason and the pervert's talented inscription of the madman's bemused oddity. The pervert encourages the articulation of the unconscious manifestations in order to liberate the affirmative — "yes I said yes I will Yes" — of compression and displacement. The pervert releases the weird truths and bizarre desires from the closet of subjective and objective culture. He does so in order to confront the repressive threats of a system whose misrecognized neurosis forecloses the disturbances of the Real. This Real returns in the symptoms of the cultural instability of the system. The psychoanalyst certainly does not know the object of the perverse male junior's "very well" of epistemology and faith. The little perverse boy knows "very well" that the penis is a clitoris not simply as the present reminder of his deferred fate but as a Sameness⁺ between difference — penis = clitoris because penis ≠ penis and clitoris ≠ clitoris. Each is the other precisely because the penis is not "itself" and the clitoris is not "itself."

This simultaneity of the parallactic gap and relational plenitude (A ≠ A = B and = ≠ = and ≠ ≠ ≠, and so on) is the Unreasonable secret truth of the pervert. The Logic of Difference eviscerates the Logic of Identity of the self-same and the self-identical. Unreason also acutely dismantles all text, discourse, and symbol. Sameness⁺ also destructures all copulas (Being, and so on). These avatars of logic and rationality otherwise join words in the signifying chain. The female penis is the male penis because in the negativity and differentiality of the chain of signification every object is ~~deviant~~ from itself but simultaneously ~~coincident~~ — Sameness⁺ — with the series of words in the system. The relationship of the copula between the signs — the relationship between the female penis and the male penis — cannot be symbolized. The copula of Being (or "is") is cut and struck with a difference and negativity that otherwise put under erasure the identity and essence of the male penis and the female penis themselves. There is no relationship between objects and between the male penis and the female penis. The system is discoordination of spatial proximity and dislocated adjacency which is Outside of the metaphysics of presence.

The representational talents of perversion are restricted at the limit-thought of the transcendence of essence and identity. The fetish-object is representational. But this is so only insofar as it is isolated from relationships of negativity and difference. The logic of the Real Signifier would otherwise bind the fetishist to copulatic relationships with other objects in the system. The maternal phallus will eventually garner a significance for the adult fetishist. The "quite special" maternal phallus is the fundamental lost object. The penis, penis-substitute, and fetish will bedim and reveal this motherly penis. The object emerges as happy because it is born of the trace of the *Verleugnung* of the Woman's lost penis. The penis is not simply a screen over the specifically female lack for which the fetish-object is a metaphorical substitute. This would indicate a brazen homosexuality of the male fetishist. The penis which is (un)veiled is the lost penis of the mother. Beautifully, the fetishist believes in the presence of the absence and the obscured presence of the promised absence. The pervert is the archetypal Spiritualist of faith.

Not only does the pervert "know very well" in his exhaustion of epistemology "but nevertheless" he believes without any evidence to the contrary. The fetishist is the exemplary divinist because he enjoys commitment and cathexis which are strictly outside of metaphysical knowledge. The pervert is not a philosopher. The fetishist's project is to ingeniously invent objects for joy, to happily symbolize words for amusement, and to spritely verse in the Unreason of schizophrenia and the Madness of Order. It is fair to say that both the female junior and the male junior (man and Woman) are already castrated. The male junior is anxiously protective of his private property. The female junior is enviously consumptive of penis-substitutes. These envied objects are themselves fetish-objects. But the feminine objects are not metaphors for the maternal phallus. Instead, these feminine objects of envy are substitutes for the boy-phallus in the series of objects of father, husband, baby, and so on. But perversely, both the man and the Woman are strictly beyond castration because a man is a Woman insofar as each is different from itself.

The pervert's psychical and philosophical economy is such that all objects are always already intertwined in a torus-like extimacy. The one and the other cannot be divided with any distinction or opposition. But it is crucial to reiterate that the copula which relates male junior and female junior, man and Woman, to each other — Being, what is, as such, *qua*, by definition, *il y a*, and so on — is itself cut by negativity and difference. This value radically subverts the metaphysics of presence. This metaphysics is the structure upon which such relationships are based in their symbolization. Certainly, I (we) "know very well" that there is a coincidence between man and Woman because each is discontinuous with itself and overlapped with the other. This is a relationship of the parallactic gap and relational plenitude. "But nevertheless," this relationship is strictly unsymbolizable and unrepresentable. Being can only be glimpsed as a trace of textual sublimity. The internal schizophrenia of the system is that the Logic of Identity yields to a Logic of Difference, or a "sameness which is not identical." An illumination of this Sameness⁺ is the schizoid's insight and the pervert's text.

Yet another Penis

On all accounts, both man and Woman suffer castration under the rubric of an economy which is organized by the general equivalent of the phallus. Psyche and society are also structured by the private property of penis, body, self, thought, affect, action, responsibility, and so on. Such a regretful series of private property arrangements and their narcissistic, aggressive, and anxious symptomatology is frightful. The resurrection of the vaunted but lost — mistaken? unnoticed? disregarded? omitted? — maternal phallus is the linchpin toward an aperture to the Other economy. This Spirit of the System is beyond castration, phallocentrism, capitalism, and scarcity. This Other galaxy is strictly beyond all oppositions which are organized around hierarchical division. Communism, the unconscious, and *hors-texte* are the Outside to the phallic stage. This Outside is the apex of the communist queer (*a*)sexuality of the revolution.

The anal stage is structured by an obscene and shameful equality of penis = faeces = baby = jockstrap. The oral stage is organized by incorporation and internalization of otherness into the self. About the transition from the lost sister to the lost mother, Freud writes: "In his psyche, yes, the Woman still has a penis, but this penis is no longer the same as before."[34] The male junior remembers the Woman's penis. The male junior recalls a strange and uncanny affect of a presence which has quietly sidled and sloped away into absence. The female penis becomes the site of a metaphorical substitution in which a "successor, so to speak," as Freud says, comes to take its place.[35] This "successor" as fetish may be considered the paradoxical and original copy. This is so except that the fetish is also a retrospective glance toward the death of this original lost object. The present absence of this loss is effective and affective for the perverse male junior and the fetishistic adult. But is the maternal phallus in essence the original penis around which the male junior's penis, the female junior's not-penis, the Woman's phallus, the penis-substitute, and the fetish are organized? What is the prototypical "Real Penis," as I call it, which preexists the maternal penis, phallic penis, and fetish as their structural center?

These queries suggest that, antecedent to both the maternal phallus as object of present absence and the sister's penis as object of horror, there is yet another penis which is unseen and unthematized. This Other penis solicits an "Other satisfaction," as Lacan says, of the feminine *jouissance*.[36] This is the aim of the Pervert-Schizoid-Woman at the ends of the system of $-ism. The female genitals are a source of abject horror for the properly oedipalized heterosexual man who must then be either homosexual or masochistic. The clitoris is properly the sole province of the lesbian. The magical lesbian is the proper proprietor of female lack. The lesbian's prestidigitation is to make presence from absence, plenitude from lack, and so on. She converts the Something is Missing of capitalism and patriarchy into the Nothing is Missing of communism and the Clitoral Stage. This yet another penis is the Lesbian Penis of the Clitoral Stage. The lesbian orients herself at the start in the obverse of the position of the male junior.

The male junior begins his journey with the self-pleasure of Nothing is Missing. His entire experience in life can only be the slow loss of his ego. This ego is a series of lost object-cathexes. In contrast, the female junior starts her story with the castration of Something is Missing. Her entire existence in the world is the excited process of collection of penis-commodities. The male junior is oriented from the presence and abundance of the Nothing is Missing of communism toward the absence and scarcity of the Something (and more) is Missing of capitalism. Alternatively, the female junior evolves from the absence and scarcity of the Something is Missing of capitalism toward a Nothing (will yet be) Missing of the presence and abundance of communism. These differences are not based in anatomy but rather are organized by the temporal trajectories of the discovery of castration. The male junior will suffer castration anxiety. The female junior will relish penis envy. But both empirical boys and girls are subordinate to castration anxiety because private property (such as anatomy) is enforced on both sexes in a capitalist and patriarchal culture.

The fetishist approaches the Woman's penis with the fetish-object representation. The physical spatiotemporal conjunction of the body and the representation of the fetish enables the in-action, in-process intercourse with the fur, lace, shoe, and jockstrap. The fetish-representation is conjured in the scene of intercourse. But it is the representation which confers the phallic value on the otherwise horrific female genitalia. This "horror," as Freud puts it, "of castration has been immortalized in the creation of this substitute."[37] Freud's use of the term "immortalized" is pedagogical because the significance of the word confers an endurance and a permanence upon the object. Castration has been conferred this durable fame. The fetish-object guarantees the celebrity and renown of the absence. The peculiarity of the fetish is that a valorized absence is converted into a splendid presence. The strange "immortalization" of castration is made possible by the fixed and exclusive re-presentation of loss *qua* the simultaneous gain of the fetish-object. But how does the pervert transform lack into plenitude?

A key to this conundrum is this "immortalization." The word suggests that the precious eminence of the loss is itself a gain. Absence and death are essentially noble and great. Neurotics experience the horror of the Woman's castration and their own imminent loss. Perverts discover the repute and prestige of castration. Castration may be "horrific." But castration is also sublimely beautiful. Castration is the source of a re-presentation of its loss in the figuration of the fetish-object. Rather than the fetish as a mask of distraction ("but nevertheless"), the object reminds the pervert ("I know very well") of castration and its brilliant esteem. Male fetishists glorify the Woman with the assistance of the object of representation. This fetish does not merely make present the absent. Rather, the fetish-penis honors in immortality the female body and even the sex organs. Far from evidencing a misogynistic hatred of the Woman and her sex, the male fetishist adorns her with fetish-objects whose decorations strive to re-present the body of the Woman in an in-action, in-process peculiar but successful modality of (*a*)sexual intercourse.

The fetish-object is split. It is both the monument to castration and a guarantee against it. The representation acknowledges that Something is Missing ("monument to") but also staves off its consequences in misogyny and phallocentrism ("a guarantee against it"). The fetishist retroactively marks the lack as plenitude — somehow. The pervert then revises any future encounter with Women as a re-presentation with the fixed and exclusive fetish-object. This engagement is an intercourse with fullness and wholeness. The fetishist makes good on the Woman's lack that even the female junior of penis envy is unable to perform. At the apex of the engagement with the Woman, the heterosexual man "knows very well" that he does not and never did know anything of the Woman's castration. "But nevertheless," at the same time, he does not and never did know anything of the Woman's castration. "But nevertheless," he imagines a loss at the same time as he recuperates this lack as the penis. "But nevertheless," he believes in a loss at the same time as he recuperates this lack as the penis. "But nevertheless," he has faith in a loss at the same time as he recuperates this lack as the penis.

After the total depletion of knowledge and the utter destruction of epistemology ("I know very well"), the fetishist is free to experiment with nonknowledge — imagination, faith, hope, belief, will, necromancy, love, and so on. This postepistemological (*a*)sexuality is the eroticism of the unconscious with no "No!" and no "know." This (*a*)sexuality facilitates the "but nevertheless" knowledge in which the Woman's castration is at the center of the pervert's sex life. Castration is a substitute sexual encounter for a substitute sexual affair with a substitute fetish with a substitute representation — and so on. "But nevertheless" — the entirety of the series of objects in the world of the unconscious is libidinized and eroticized. The galaxy is a field of sexual compressions and displacements. The solar system is a cosmos of liberated exchanges and free substitutions. This endless switcheroo returns the pervert to an embryonic sexuality.

In infancy, the sum of body and soul — Woman and world — is a sexual object. The fetishist foreswears the Real Penis. The Real Penis is the lubricant of the relationship between the split subject and the object. The fetishist eschews the Real Penis — ~~Being~~ — in order to enjoy the copy (of a copy of a copy, and so on) of the maternal phallus in the sex act. This *jouissance* commemorates what has been acknowledged but also denied — somehow. The fetish is the celebrated object which enables the pervert to succeed in his (*a*)sexual activity. The "monument" is the pervert's generous avowal — sly concession — that castration is the condition of his (*a*)sexuality. At the same time, such a memorialization is manipulated in the denial of the object of salute. The pervert brilliantly maneuvers around the horror of sexual Sameness⁺. The pervert discovers *jouissance* in the fetishized and adorned copy or representation (the fur, lace, shoe, and jockstrap) rather than in the fancied and lost so-called original of the Woman's mutilated body. This refashioned body is the venerated source of the pervert's elaborate sexual apparatus.

The pervert is exactly beyond sexuality. The pervert's (*a*)sexuality is strictly simulacral and figural. The pervert gets off on a copy of a copy — or on a re-presentation of the presentation of the Woman's horror. This object obviates a Real loss because the series of copies memorializes, celebrates, immortalizes, honors, and observes the Woman's castration as the positive condition of sexuality. The fetish-objects are adornments of and ornaments on the object. This object is only thinly veiled and quietly obscured beneath the screen of fashion. It is now clear how — somehow — the pervert is able to convert Something is Missing of horrific capitalist castration into Nothing is Missing of the *jouissance* of communist queer (*a*)sexual ecstasy. Somehow — because the pervert no longer "knows very well" the law that the system of phallocentrism enforces. The imperative of the system is otherwise that the man has a penis and that the Woman does not have a penis. Perversely, the system is not phallocentrism. The system is not even capitalism. There is no *das Ding* as binary opposition. The pervert is exactly beyond gender.

The pervert's ruin of epistemology means that all that he "knows very well" is a "but nevertheless." The Woman has a penis of her own. The name of this penis is the "clitoris." Somehow — the pervert discovers the female penis. He adores this penis-clitoris. His fetish-objects memorialize and testify to its sublime beauty. He need not fear the loss of his own appendage in sexual engagement with the Woman. Her sex is neither a wound nor a mutilation. Rather, it is a singular penis whose name is the clitoris. The pervert discovers the singularity of the female penis. He does so not because the clitoris is identical to the male penis but because it is different from itself and the same — Sameness⁺ — as all of the other objects in the system of signification.

The adornments, ornaments, fetishes, and representations that the pervert offers as immortalizations of loss make the Woman's penis unique. This loss has become a gain after the profound disfigurement of all of epistemology. After the displacement of knowledge, the pervert and the female penis substitute nonknowledge with the imagination, faith, hope, belief, will, necromancy, and love of the "but nevertheless" — *Jouir!* The celebrated fetish-objects and substitutive re-presentations do not veil castration. Nor do they obscure loss. Rather, the fetish-objects screen epistemology — "a man has a penis and Woman does not have a penis." Epistemology is banished from the scene of perverse (*a*)sexuality. The adult fetishist returns full circle to the female penis that he was unfairly forced to repress as a neurotic or to foreclose as a psychotic — but only for a latency period of time. But after epistemology, what are the ontology and the ethics of the pervert? What is the ontological structure of perverse (*a*)sexuality? What is the ethical aesthetic of queer communism? Perversely, I now know very well that I do not know very well, but I live —

Chapter Five

The Pervert (2): Representation

In societies where modern conditions of production prevail, all of life presents itself as an immense accumulation of spectacles. Everything that was directly lived has moved away into a representation.

— Guy Debord

The (*a*)sex of the future of the pervert is *au fond* representational: textual, figural, metaphorical, scopophilic, and so on. Fetish-sex is purely simulacral. Perverse (*a*)sex is without reference to the Real of the body. Fetish sex is figural. It is a staged *mise-en-scène* of enjoyment. The plot is irrelevant to sexualized bodies. The future of sex is essentially (*a*)sexual. The genital principle in the aftermath of the capitalist stage of the phallus is an (*a*)sexual Clitoral Stage. This Clitoral Stage is precisely the celebration of the adornment and ornament of the female penis by the adult fetishist. The male body and its accoutrements are pivotal to the enjoyment of the homosexual pervert, but the _____ is the veiled referent of queer (*a*)sexuality and its attunement to the *mise-en-scène* of representational erotics: props, costumes, gestures, makeup, hair, shoes, jeans, tank tops, v-necks, cords, and so on. The penis recedes as the central referent for sex. The penis is simultaneously the distanced reference and the absent presence of the object of perverse representation. The key to perverse representation is a strategy of representation *around* the penis. The purpose of this chapter is to elaborate the representational practices in a theory of perversion.

REPRESENTATION

The pervert eschews the fear, worry, and dread of private property. He exchanges these capitalist symptoms for the joys of the decorative and aesthetic transformation of Something is Missing into Nothing is Missing. There is no castration of genitalia (phallocentrism, lack) or exchange-value of commodities (capitalism, scarcity). There is no general equivalent which enforces either identity or essence. These are otherwise the conditions of oedipal sexuality. The *absence of absence* means that an (*a*)sexual economy of constant fucking and sucking is inevitable. Both penis and clitoris, both male penis and female penis, both male clitoris and female clitoris — and so on — are majestically adorned with phallic (clitoral) attributes. All bodies are beautiful in the future.

These organs are not hierarchically conferred value (+ or -) by the general equivalent. The adult fetishist is the sexual being who demystifies the impasse of phallocentrism. Unexpectedly, the solution to phallocentrism is Peniscentrism (Clitoralcentrism). This animates an exchange of being for meaning, concreteness for abstraction, body for speculation, materialism for idealism, and so on. This penis is not the province of the male junior or the female junior. The penis is an appendage which can no longer be an object of *le propre* (the proper, property, ownership, possession, mineness) in which the male party possesses that which his female counterpart dispossesses. The pervert's intuition that both the man and the Woman have a penis (clitoris) defuses the otherwise deadly consequence of female castration. Perverse aesthetics invites the fetishist to foreswear anxiety. Perverse magic entices the fetishist to renounce identity in favor of pleasure, to repudiate identification in favor of play, and to abandon mimicry of norms in favor of experimentation with life.

Enjoy Your Representation!

A happy case of Peniscentrism — rather than phallocentrism — welcomes the opportunity for the man and the Woman to aesthetically fashion their genitalia not as an "identity which is not sameness." Rather, the sex organs are reconceptualized as a "sameness which is not identical." The male penis and the female penis are each coincident with each other and at the same time discontinuous with themselves. The pervert's party of men, Women, and the rest of us festoons selves and others with garb and swathe in the aesthetic reconstruction of penises, vaginas, clitorises, and so on. The pervert relishes these techniques of representation. The fetish-object for the adult fetishist is simply the latest of his representational gimmicks. The purpose of the fetish is not merely to veil the clitoral horror. The purpose of the fetish is also to decorate the beauty of the ontological "what is" — of all of the objects in the system.

The adult fetishist passes beyond the bounds of castration anxiety and masculine recoil at the female genitalia. The pervert invents fetishes — words, vocabularies, images, sounds, faces, jokes, letters — through which he can illuminate the object of his project. This work symbolizes the Unreason of the schizoid. The madman's crazy, secret truth must be unraveled — however impossibly — in a pedagogy of perversion. The pervert wants to reveal the Madness of Order that otherwise condemns man to a violent sexuality, an oppressive economic system, and a set of mores and values which are inimical to a happy life. The fetishist's necessary obligation is to the invention of future representations, novel objects, ultramodern fetishes, futuristic penis-substitutes, and untried penises. The penis is displaced by metaphors and phalluses.

The pervert "knows very well" the conventional epistemological interpretation of the female genitals. The patriarchal tradition translates difference into deficit. But the pervert never encounters the clitoris and the vagina in sexual intercourse. This is not because he is meticulously repulsed by their "horror." Rather, the pervert is the man who is bored with sex. The pervert ecstatically enjoys the copy, the simulacrum, the fake, and the fraud of the fetish-objects. The fetish-object is fantastical and fantasmatic neither for its cult value nor for its aura. Rather, the fetish-representation is expressly erotic because it participates in the ordinary and prosaic representations of everyday life in the shoe, lace, fur, and jockstrap. The pervert eroticizes the objects of everyday life. Representation itself becomes a sexualized and libidinized activity. This is so even in the absence of the body of the human form. Perversely, *l'écriture est érotique*.

The pervert is the character who is most committed to symbolization. The pervert writes his objects with the whimsy of pens, pencils, alphabets, and letters of signifiers, objects, fetishes, shoes, furs, laces, penises, vaginas, clitorises, and Hal's jockstrap. The pervert fetishizes all that can be in-process, in-action in symbolization in being-in-the-world and being-with-others. The pervert disavows the frozen and inert image of the clitoris as a void of Nothingness. Rather, the protofeminist pervert ignores his own potential loss in the castration gambit.

Instead, he (*a*)sexually engages the Woman with adornment and decoration — Marc Jacobs's jockstrap — as a will to play. Sex and sexuality are subordinate to game and play. These games and plays include moves, suspensions, pauses, and strategies that Deleuze identifies in masochism.[1] These gestures elevate representation in the text of the pervert above the referent in the sexual anatomy of the body. The penis is displaced by the polo shirt.

The copy and the simulacrum do not guarantee the "monument," as Freud says, of the father or the phallus. Rather, the fetishist enjoys a new world of the specifically maternal phallus. He giggles at an alternative symbolic order in which the father's regime of castration and equivalence is ruined in the wake of new games and novel plays. This Other is a representation of future strategies of *Trieb*. The pervert foreswears the jejune and bland pleasure principle that otherwise regulates the subject's excitations downward and conservatively rather than upward and spectacularly. The vapid modality of enjoyment yields to a *Thanatos* which emerges after the depressive and disappointed sexual orgasm. The death drive promises to free man from the binds of *Eros* and to catapult him toward a postsexual fragmentation and conflagration. *Thanatos* unveils the Pervert-Schizoid-Woman.

The horizon of (*a*)sex is beyond the sex principle. Freud's "monument" to castration is a fetish *of castration*. The monument is the reminder of the object to be lost *qua* private property were a man to break the rules and fail to find satisfaction with the female genitalia. As Freud succinctly puts it: "[The fetish] remains a mark of triumph over the threat of castration and a safeguard against it."[2] Perversely, the fetish reminds man ("remains a mark of triumph") of the defeat of castration. This is the function of the fetish. The fetish distracts the most insipid of fetishists from the psychosexual anatomical significance of the female genitalia. It facilitates sexual exchange with the Woman and with the requisite objects of re-presentation of the sex organs. The fetish is also a "safeguard" against castration because it neatly neutralizes the unconscious horror of the female genitals.

Representation of all kinds is the proper strategy for the treatment of the traumatic. The pervert's talent is the pen. He writes the secret truth of the schizoid's Unreason. The pervert articulates the Madness of Order. Re-presentation of the female penis (male clitoris) in the fetish-object is exemplary of the Madness of Order. $-ism must be neurotically foreclosed (*rejet névrotique*) in the Real only to return to destabilize the system as its condition of possibility. The pervert's fetish represents the unconscious compression and displacement of the otherwise proper center of the structure: namely, the penis. But what is a penis? — especially if it is re-presented as a male clitoris? The penis is supplanted by its Outside. This Outside is the object of the representation of the vacant Inside of the penis. The deferred allure of the penis is its representation by and as other metaphors, centers, words, objects, fetishes, and so on. The trauma of the potential castration of the penis (as opposed to the *fait accompli* of the female junior's castration) is symbolized by the *mise-en-scène* of the extimate to the penis.

If anxiety surfaces after the "triumph" against castration, then it is the worry of the counterfeit and the simulacrum. Baudrillard's most outlandish thesis about simulation is not that the copy is a facsimile for nothing or that the real was never real. This would simply mean that the Nothing is Missing is a creationist sublimation *ex nihilo*. Out of Nothing is the only possible explanation for the origin-story of the prelapsarian bliss. This is so even if this prelapsarian dimension is contextualized as the brothers of the excluded horde or as the male junior and his self-pleasure with the phallic mother. Rather, Baudrillard's bizarre claim about simulation is that the map precedes the territory.[3] In the case of fetishism, the map not only precedes the territory in a coverage that entirely overspreads the sum of the plane but it also surrounds an absent territory whose simultaneous presence is the condition of not only the map but of map-making *tout court*. The fetish must reconfirm itself as the "mark of triumph" because its object is registered as true ("avowed") but at the same time false ("disavowed"). The map is a map of a map *ad infinitum* in recursion. But, at the same time, this map is also a territory. The fetish is a fetish of a fetish *ad infinitum* in recursion. But, at the same time, this fetish is also a penis, a maternal phallus, a sister's penis, and so on. The penis is estranged in its abeyance and at the same time obscene in its proximity. The hipster's jeans are the veil between the masochistic relief of alienation and the neurotic urgency for contact with a differed and deferred *das Ding*.

Figure 5.1 Schizoid Structurality

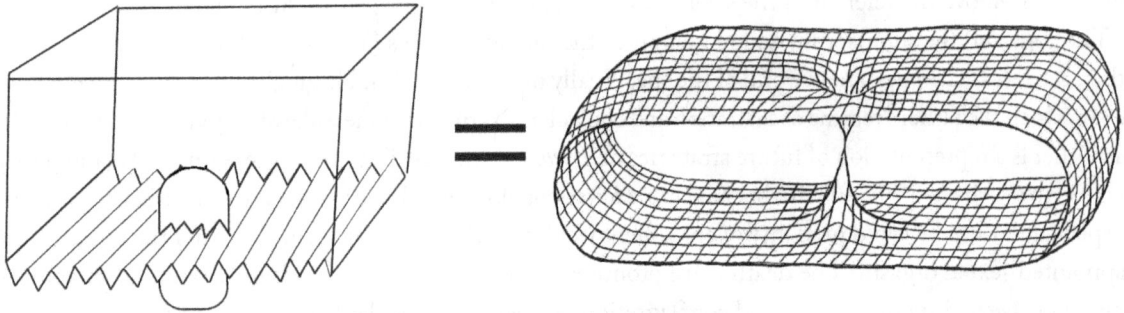

The (in)equation between the two figures (left, right) exposes the *mise-en-scène* of identity and difference within a structure of objects and subjects in relationship to each other. The space of language (left) splits the object into its own permeable — decentered and dispersed — boundaries. The space of *langue* is the space in which any object (is) a Sameness[+] with any other object of a Difference[-]. Neurotically, this space generates an identity (difference) which is established by spatial difference and temporal deferral. This identity is relational and not a mathematical or logical given as such. Difference is sustained in a system in which everything is the Same[+]. There is *différance* always already externally and internally — in extimacy — in the signifier which is decentered and dispersed from itself. The partitions and boundaries that otherwise establish the finitude of infinite perverse substitutability are as fragmented as the units of text themselves. The figure (right) represents the extimate intimacy and intimate extimacy of identity and difference in Sameness[+]. The equation (center) represents the possibility — proviso — of Being as such. Identity and difference cannot otherwise be restructured upon an identity which is a logical identity. Identity and difference cannot be formed from a difference which is essential and present. The figure (right) reveals its own Inside-Outsideness to itself. The image illuminates the parallactic superposition of the Real as it returns to itself *qua* the symbolic order. This return of the Real of *Verwerfung* is the *rejet névrotique* (Neurotic Foreclosure) of the system. $-ism is the return of the Real to the symbolic within the matrix of neurotic repression (foreclosure).

Notes & Sketches —

This metonymic slip and slide in the absence of a referent make fetishism an endless movement or metonymization of metaphor. It is a slippery difference and deferral not simply of metonymy but also of *Trieb*. This endless representational wander includes an infinite series of maternal penis, sister's penis, Gary's "penis-substitute," Ron's penis, fur, Manuel's penis, lace, George's penis, shoe, his penis, your jockstrap, and so on. This series of representations overrides *Ziel* in favor of the textual movement of the glorious and attuned masochist of the not-yet, out-standing, and in-coming. The minor anxiety of the fetishist is the fraudulence of his (*a*)sexuality because his enjoyment is less about himself and more about the Other. The pervert's *jouissance* is the joy of the Other. The fetishist positions himself as the beloved instrument of the Other's pleasure.

Representations and signifiers — figural penises-furs-penises-shoes-penises-laces-penises-jockstraps — are precisely the love-objects and object-causes of the pervert's *écriture* of the schizoid's Unreason. The madman's crazy talk is isomorphic to the (*a*)sexuality of the representational economy of the fetishist's wild, wooly, and altogether weird (*a*)sexuality. This (*a*)pleasure enjoys the figuration of the sexual fantasy frame. This is the space of the pervert's pedagogy of desire. The pervert is the consummate instructor of *jouissance*. The pervert prefers the occupation of textualist of the schizoid's declaimed Unreason. The pervert demurs from any encounter with the Patriarchal Clitoral Castration Industrial Complex. Patriarchal phallocentrism and Neo-Conservative Penis are squarely responsible for this economy of castration.

Sex as Representation

The perverse offspring sustains a fear of being "eaten by his father." But the adult fetishist endures no such fear. The future of the Becoming of the Pervert-Schizoid-Woman promises that man will enjoy an (*a*)sexuality without guilt or shame. The future will be animated by an extended nongenital Other (*a*)sexuality. This (*a*)sexuality is neither oral-incorporative nor anal-equalitive nor phallic-hierarchical. Lacan names this Other a *jouis-sens*. This orgasmic textuality-otherwise being-in-the-world is beyond the pleasure principle of the conservative regulation of the excitation of desire in the orga(ni)sm. This Other mobilizes a transition in humanity toward an ecstatic pleasure which is beyond the symptoms of the systems of *le propre* and $-ism. These illnesses include narcissism, aggression, anxiety, scarcity, supply/demand, exploitation, surplus value, private property, binary opposition, the word, phallocentrism, patriarchy, and so on. This future must be free of all general equivalence, such as currency, father, phallus, sign, and so on. Private property (currency), family relations (father), sexual difference (phallus), and language (sign) will be destructured in the annihilation of the system of $-ism.

Despite his sexualized moniker, the pervert mostly foreswears material, physical, and bodily sexuality altogether. His fierce queerness forfeits the anticipations and disappointments in the regulation of the pleasure principle. The trajectory of the pleasure principle proceeds from a frenzied mania to a deflated depression and then to a lonely sex with the last jockstrap. In contrast, the queer edges toward an orgasmic beyond of the pleasure principle. This beyond in the death drive of *Trieb* gets off on the feminine foray into the Other-Logic of Being — *All* — as neither self-same nor self-identical. The pervert becomes *Eros* and *Thanatos* as each other, simultaneously, at once. This modality of a queer (*a*)sexuality may very well include sexual intercourse. Locker room shenanigans are part of the concerted human action to symbolize the Real resistance to sexuality. This sexuality is otherwise organized by sexual difference. But the pervert enjoins enjoyment to representational sex in the absence of sexual difference. Queerly, what is sex after sexual difference? What is sex in the nongenital stage of sexuality under the communist mode of production of the Clitoral Stage? What is communist sex? What is *rapport sexuel* after *désir*?

The horizon of the Pervert-Schizoid-Woman's sex is the material, physics, and body of the triumph of representational fetish-objects over castrated body parts. The signifier of materiality is finally discarded in favor of the Signified/r. The Signified/r enjoys the unregulated play of concepts and abstractions in the dimensions of *sexe et texte*. The pervert transitions from a sexualized and disappointed desire to an (*a*)sexualized and uproarious *Trieb*. The pervert trespasses the regulation of pleasure — excitation-relaxation — unto an open system of unsynchronized movements. This queerly revolutionary disregulation includes the swap-in-swap-out of fetishes-texts for the pervert's amusement. This rapturous collage of autarkic and enfranchised figurations and references — copy of copy of copy, and so on, toward _____ — is (*a*)sexuality itself. This (*a*)sexuality of the Pervert-Schizoid-Woman reiterates a Freudian subtext. All representation is sexual representation.

"Actual"

But this psychoanalytic truism includes the delicious caveat that all representation is sex itself. As Freud puts it: "What other men have to pursue and strive for presents no such problems for the fetishist."[4] The series of textual and metaphorical and substitutional jockstraps — and the traces therein of symbolic metonymic displacements — finds its most humorous scripted articulation in the conclusion of Freud's text on "Fetishism" (1927): "We can conclude that the normal prototype for a fetish is the man's penis, just as the prototype of an inferior organ is the Woman's *actual* little penis, the clitoris" (my emphasis).[5] Freud's gleeful *jouis-sens* is veiled to the English reader, but there is a sexual joy in the synecdochic slide among "normal prototype," "fetish," "man's penis," "prototype," "inferior organ," "Woman's actual little penis," and "clitoris." And then onto which farcical and fabulous symbol? These objects are each the other as they are not themselves. This litany of metaphors for Metaphoricity "itself" abandons the pervert to a fit of chuckles. The normal is a prototype for which the penis is the proper prototype, which is prototypical of both the prototypicality of the prototype and the prototypicality of the other prototype, which is also a prototype. The pervert smiles, awash in a gaggle of giggles and a gag on his own jockstrap.

The Clitoris

This insightful but jocular play on Freud's endless series of fetishes *for* fetishes presents a significant clue to the theory of sexual difference in the passage. The only citation to a referent for the fundamental difference of sexual difference is noted in the citation at the end of the text: "The Woman's *actual* little penis, the clitoris" (my emphasis). This "actual" little penis of the Woman indicates to Freud the presence of the female penis. Her penis may be small in relationship to a man's penis. But the clitoris is nonetheless "actually" a penis. The unfettered series of fetishes — prototypes, atypicals, penises, copies, simulacrums, metaphors, substitutes, or centers of the structure of sexual difference — is free and liberated. This series of objects can be enjoyed without the anxious defense of private property against loss and annexation.

The absence of the female penis is present, "actually." The will to suture the parallactic gap with the lace, the fur, and the jock's tennis shoe in order to suffer sexual difference *qua* sexual anxiety is subdued. The pervert may deploy his representational props in order to abate the unconscious horror of the female sex. Fear, worry, dread, and anxiety would otherwise overwhelm the man in the absence of the eldritch panties and otherworldly boots. But the pervert discerns the truth of the system nonetheless. The father's law is dead and cold. The mother's penis is alive and hot. Freud's term "prototype" corresponds to the philosopher's tricky term *qua.* Both words repress the differences that the fetishist himself seeks to deny. The fetishist may be "fixated," as Freud says, on certain objects and texts in his sexual adventures in (*a*)sexual representation. But this is a consequence of a deathly drive toward repetition rather than the result of a pathological preoccupation with any sexual scene or representation.

The future invites an uncontrolled proliferation of differences — penis, fetish, substitute, center, penis-substitute, fetish-penis, substitute-center, penis-penis, and so on. These are all fundamentally the Same⁺ because each is the prototype for the Different⁺. This cross-prototypicality is only possible in the absence of the phallic function. The phallus otherwise enforces an economy which is structured by opposition, hierarchy, signification, and the sign. The only word which is exoteric in the system of $-ism for such a state of affairs is: Sameness⁺. This text is neither a symbol nor an integer. Sameness⁺ ushers in an economy in which the (ac) count in whatever system (monetary, familial, psychical, sexual) is valueless. Sameness⁺ is strictly transcendent of the system of nihilism. This horizon is a fetishism which is beyond a prototype and toward a word after nihilism. The male penis and the female penis are "actually" present in the system. But they are present neither as retrospective, disappointed fantasy for the female junior nor as prospective, jealous regret for the male junior. Rather, penis and clitoris are present as here and now. But then what is the symbol for the Real Penis which is as-yet unsignified?

There may be a phallus even in the Real. But the penis in its fleshly bodily protuberance must be visible in the sexual field. This is so even if its visibility is limited to a mere representation for the pervert. What is the material signifier of the penis in the Real? What is the foreskin in the Real which returns to the "same place," as Lacan says, to recurrently disturb the symbolic order *qua* the Real Penis? The Penis of the Real is the sublime referent of sexual difference *qua* the hard kernel of textual unrepresentability. If the Real Penis could speak, then what words would it utter? — and to whom? What does the Real Penis disrupt in the economies of the symbolic phallus of the ego-ideal and the imaginary phallus of bodily sex? How does the Real Penis disrupt the division between the abstract and the concrete, the speculative and the material, the capitalist and the communist, the sign and the signifier, and so on?

From s to S

The middle of Freud's essay on the splitting of the ego (1938) discusses the essential difference between neurosis and psychosis. The distinction marks a divergence between two poles of negation. The two forms of negation are *Verdrängung* in neurosis and *Verwerfung* in psychosis. The pervert straddles this gap between neurosis and psychosis in his artful — somehow — disavowal or *Verleugnung*. The neurotic represses the *Es* in favor of reality. The psychotic represses reality in favor of the urge. The cauldron of wishes, truths, and desires in the id of the neurotic must be repressed into the unconscious. These desires are repressed into the signifying chain rather than beneath the "brain," the "mind," the "hippocampus," or the "neuron." The Signified/rs of truth and wish are visible beneath the explicit and denotative discourse of the neurotic. The psychotic favors the *Es* which is the mirror-reflection of his own reality. The *Es* is an inversion of the subtexts or invisibilities in the system of the conscious-unconscious. The schizoid rejects the system because he refuses to engage within its parameters and expectations. The madman repudiates any system which is structured by the (Un)Reason of the chain of signification. The content of the unconscious of the negated — the neurotic's repressed, the schizoid's foreclosed, and the pervert's disavowed — is contingent on a subjective orientation. These conditions include case-study, background and childhood experience, specific etiology of illness, contextualized free associations in the interpretation of symptoms, and so on. The case is also determined within a social framework: patriarchy, phallocentrism, capitalism, corporatism, language, dialect, identity politics, and so on.

The psychoanalyst engages his hermeneutics of suspicion of the free associations and symptoms of the analysand and the culture in order to access the royal road to the unconscious of the self and society. Different cultures will produce different psychical structures. Distinct societies will enable divergent manifest forms and latent contents of symptoms. But the psychical structures themselves — neurosis, psychosis, and perversion — can be mostly generalized. The various modalities of manifestation, latency, return, symptomatology, threat, and cure in which these structures emerge are mostly stable across space and time. The principal insight in psychoanalytic practice and theory is the originality and universality of substitution — compression, displacement, metaphor, and metonymy. Substitution — of some form — cuts across all Romance languages. Substitution is foundational to the formation of symptoms and to the code through which these ticks are analytically decoded. But if Freud speaks about sex in his discourse, for what is sex a substitute? What is Freud talking about when he talks about "sex"?

I theorize the specificity of the Madness of Order. It is the object of my critique of $-ism. The schizoid returns from the Real of the neurotically foreclosed (*rejet névrotique*). My work discovers and elaborates the ostensibly misunderstood neurotic but essentiality schizoid structure of the system. This craziness is neurotically foreclosed (*rejet névrotique*) by the subjects of culture. Man is the generated effective symptom of a psychotic system. The repression of this system returns as the destabilization of the symbolic order. Paradoxically, the schizoid return of neurotic repression is the essence of the Madness of Order in its identity. The parallactic gap and relational plenitude in this instance are between the symbolic and its negations. The Neurotic Foreclosure (*rejet névrotique*) of the Real is the central function of the symbolic order. I refer to this unexpected extimacy between the symbolic and the Real as Sameness[+]. A "sameness which is not identical" returns from its banishment *qua* otherwise the center of the system.

The recalcitrantly invisible but embryonically illuminated unconscious structures of the scaffold and skeleton of the system of $-ism are barred to the society of neurotics. These bored and unhappy wanderers of the world seek the smooth reproduction of the system. They do so even as they rupture its continuity in the very act of making it (not) work. My work is the sport of the Nietzschean philosopher-physician. I must illuminate the "structurality of structure," as Derrida says, in order to invite a transition away from a neurotic culture and its paradoxical psychotic foreclosure of itself.[6] I want to advance toward a joyful reconciliation of the Real Signifier or Signified/r in the system. The wager is that the pervert's talented but vain effort at symbolization will spark a *perversion of neurosis* in the world. The bet is that man will embrace an understanding in Reason of the Unreason of the system. The hope is that men will — as neurotics, schizoids, and perverts — pioneer an interpretation of the madness which is structured into the order of the galaxy. The effort is to make Unreason Reasonable and to demonstrate that Unreason is the internal necessity of the $-istic system of Reason. The horizon of this work is an illumination of the extended and debauched wanton moment in which Unreason does not make sense of man but man makes sense of Unreason.

This revelation is the nexus of the coincidental parallactic overlap of (Un)Reason. The perversion of the culture will be in the throes of success. The perverts will run the academies and universities. The schizoids will regulate the governments and the corporations. The Women will dance naked in the lanes, the plains, and in the rains. The battalion of uniformed and civilian officers who defend — offend — the extant system will enforce — resist — its regime through the Reason of the Logic of Identity — essence of $(A = A)$ — and the madness of the Logic of Difference — construction of $(A \neq A)$. The perverts will charismatically persuade the citizens of the current order with their symbols that $-system is entirely coincident with its future as S. The system of $-ism ~~is~~ the Spirit of the System (S). The secret truth of the schizoid's Unreason is: S against-with $-ism. This simultaneity is the fluent poetry of a Pervert-Schizoid-Woman *Trieb* of the Outside of the reactively regulatory excitation-depression pleasure principle. This principle of modulation not only structures every climax and *denouement* to a homeostatic equilibrium, but it also supervises most intimate perverse pleasures in representation and text. These are otherwise the (*a*)sexual fetish-objects of the present. The figurations will be transformed into an (*a*)sexual and postgenital Other in the future of the Spirit of the System, to come, "yes, yes."

FATHER, DEAD AND ALIVE

Freud displays gleeful pride in both the male fetishist and the perverse male junior. But he insists on the recuperation of castration and loss in the psychical and social systems. This reactionary agenda is unexpected because Freud's intuition about perversity and fetishism has all but disavowed absence in favor of the representational techniques of the fetish-images, such as the shoe, lace, fur, and jockstrap. Apropos, in "Fetishism" (1927), Freud mentions the story of two brothers whose reaction to the death of their father discerns the effects of the veritable murder of the signified at the center of the system of the brothers in question.[7] This center is the heir to the paternal legacy as well as to the law and authority which organize the selfhood and the sociality of the two sons.

Dead and Alive

The story of these brothers is isomorphic to the resistance to the unsymbolizable and inexplicable Real. The brothers mime the pervert's approach to sexual difference. The fetishist's representational (*a*)sexuality enjoys the absence of the physical body in the presence of the virtual representation. The curious paternal death in question presents a quandary. Must the father symbolically die in order for the hole in the symbolic order to become a Real Signifier? Must the father die in order for the Signified/r to be released to trace and *différance* in the unassimilable signifier of the cut of the Real? Is the suspension of the *point de capiton* a consequence of an empirical paternal death whose effect is the compromised signifying chain of schizophrenia? Why do most Western subjects suffer the fate of neurosis and reproduce a system of madness in which they are the accidental conspirators in its own schizoid foreclosure? Why do other subjects — psychotics — suffer the foreclosure of *arche*? Why do few subjects — perverts — approach an enjoyment of the Other's pleasure which compels them to playfully textualize the Unreason of the system? What is the social mechanism by which perverts are born of a talent to discern the schizoid's manic and fatherless chain of signifiers which can only be retranslated into the garbled transcription of the pervert's talented photocopy?

These questions about the specific etiology of schizophrenia and perversion are not satisfactorily answered by either Freud or Lacan. The discovery of psychoanalysis is that an overdetermined incipient series of experiences determines sex, sexuality, desire, identification, and psychical structure. This overdetermined organization will not submit to easy coordination of causes, correlates, and effects. Any effort to pervert neurosis must endeavor to explain the etiology of these psychical structures. I weave the Real of Unreason into the text of the insight of the pervert. The wager is that such a Baedeker to Unreason will persuade neurotics to abandon A = A (essence, identity) for a Spirit of the System. This future liberates neurotics from the metaphysics of presence, the alienation of private property, and the anxiety of difference.

The *Spaltung* in the psyche sustains a perversity ("I know very well, but nevertheless") for the brothers of

Freud's study even after the father's death. This disavowal staves off the specter of a schizophrenic slide and glide (trace, *différance*) toward the endless postponement of signification. The brothers maintain a neurotic structure even in confrontation with the suspension of the phallic referent. Freud writes: "Only one current in their psyche had failed to acknowledge the father's death; there was another that took full account of this fact."[8] Peculiarly, Freud proffers no succinct account of the consequence of the father's death in this instance. This distinguishes the story of the sons from the fable of the murder of the primal father. The primal father story indicates a plethora of symptoms which results from the murder of the father. There are many possible responses to the death of the father. This is so even if ambivalence is foundational to man's relationship to both otherness and death. Various accounts of the offspring's relationship to the father in the history of psychoanalysis exclude almost no distinct affect from the subjective relationship to the paternal figure: love, hate, fear, ambivalence, aggression, narcissism, anxiety, and so on. The central psychopathologies in psychoanalysis are mobilized in the offspring's relationship to the paternal authority. The death of the father is not merely a reassessment of a particular affect, such as love or ambivalence. Rather, the death of the father is the most important event in the life of a man, as Freud says at the aperture of *The Interpretation of Dreams* (1900).[9]

The death of the father reconfigures the entire psychical and social life of man. Nothing is the same after the death of the father. The story of the two brothers from "Fetishism" (1927) posits a primary process of the unconscious which articulates two apparently oppositional attitudes: first, the "wishful attitude" that the father not be dead; and second, the "realistic attitude" that the father is dead. This both/and *Verleugnung* persisted "side by side" with a moderate obsessive-compulsive symptom as its unfortunate legacy.[10] This same primary process of the unconscious also explains the pervert's — somehow — reconciliation of knowledge of female castration and belief in phallic presence, simultaneously. The unconscious invites the play of contradiction. It translates the neurotic either/or into the perverse both/and. How do these brothers "know very well" that that the father is dead yet alive?

The brothers mobilize a perverse and superpositional both/and economy in which contraries — mutually exclusive, by the standards of Reason — enjoy themselves "side by side." One side "knows very well" in epistemology and the other side "but nevertheless" believes in faith. The primary process of the unconscious enables — somehow — the reconciliation of the incompatible and the juxtaposition of the Unreasonable. The parallactic object of the father is split between seemingly irreconcilable perspectives. But the brothers affirm both, simultaneously, at once, at the same time. The brothers do so with a talent that Freud ascribes to unconscious primary processes.

From Mine to —

The instructive point is that the fetishist is able to both confront and deny the Real of sexual difference. The fetishist: first, sustains the manufactured veil; second, elaborates the contradiction between penis and penis-substitute; third, recognizes the wacky heterosexuality of fetishistic love-making which involves a penis-copy; and fourth, enjoys an orgasmic pleasure of a sex which is entirely mediated by the representation of his chosen *écriture*. The pervert's both/and disavowal pulls off, pulls out, and pulls at with tricks, larks, capers, mischief, and diablerie. The pervert cultivates a cognitive dissonance against the neurotic sensibility. Neurosis otherwise limits the fetishist's play and enjoyment in his galaxy of re-presentations of the objects of desire in a fantasy frame of presence rather than absence.

The pervert is the master of a showmanship on both sides of the aisle. He is the ringleader of an act which is both stage left and stage right: man and Woman (yet neither solely transgender nor specifically hermaphrodite); castrated and plentiful (yet neither only clitoris nor merely penis); gay and straight (but neither exclusively bisexual nor solely polyamorous); capitalist and communist (but both and); lover and hater (yet neither specifically ambivalent nor uniquely multivalent); liberal and conservative (also also and also), and so on.

The pervert's metalanguage is free to release the family jewels of private property into the open space of the public. The pervert does not own (*le propre*) as private property *my* whiteness, *my* gayness, *my* body, *my* manic-depression, and so on. Rather, the Pervert-Schizoid-Woman transforms the jewels from diamonds to cubic zirconia, and she loves both the copy and the facsimile. She does so without the treasured accoutrements of the private property of *my* values, *my* politics, *my* wife, and generally *mine*. The nodal point of the revolutionary dream against $-ism is: first, the disturbance of identity and desire; second, the destruction of binary organization; third, the dissolution of bourgeois private property; and fourth, the general critique of normativity and moralization in contemporary Western culture. My critiques of these symptoms sustain an elaboration of $-ism.

This project can be summarized as a playful subversion of the overlooked dominance of *le propre* in the Western system of $-ism. The Pervert-Schizoid-Woman celebrates the evisceration of the general equivalent as the adjudicator of nihilistic value of: first, the currency, coins and dollars; second, the father and normalization and idealization; third, the phallus and the quantification of quality; and fourth, the sign and the stabilization of metaphor. The destruction of equivalence and the *simcha* of Sameness⁺ in Difference⁺ enable man to be *both* gay *and* straight, and *both* foreign *and* native. The pervert is also free to be *both* gay *and* straight, *and* foreign *and* native, *and* not gay *and* not straight, *and* not foreign *and* not native, and so on.

These multiplicities are possible even in the same time and space. This is so because Sameness⁺ rather than the Logic of Identity prances in a privileged network of creative condensations and displacements. This space is the unconscious and its primary process with neither negation nor temporality. This timeless expanse of space is a *mise-en-scène* of openness. It is the leeway of plays and performances, mixed and mismatched images, and displaced psychical intensities. These romps and capers of the primary process of the unconscious are without concern for coherence, logic, causality, linearity, contradiction, and so on. This is a space of the art of the self and the care for the galaxy of the Pervert-Schizoid-Woman. There is neither the proper nor mineness in this unconscious space. Identities and differences are switched and swapped with each other. The aims of life and the goals of existence are fractured in the eroticized body of infantilized (*a*)sexuality. As Freud notes in the dream-book (1900), the ego of the dreamer is everywhere in the dream.[11] Any reference to an authorial and agentic self — identical and owned and possessed — is a propagandistic slogan of a marketer of the secondary process of the ego.

To return to the two sons of the dead (alive) father, they cope with the absence (presence) of their father with the artful techniques of the unconscious system. The condensation and displacement of the primary process explain the Unreason of the capacity of the two brothers to sustain the mutually exclusive perspectives on the father from their own split orientations. The otherwise irresolvable antagonistic parallactic gap between life and death is properly mediated by the primary process of the unconscious. Unreason embraces the excluded and the contradictory. The father is both dead and alive. The brothers' reaction cannot be summarized by the Reason of identity and essence. The father's death is not coincident with his own death. The father's life is not continuous with his own life. Simultaneously, this life and death are in an unsymbolizable (in)equivalence. Life and death are a Being — as such, *qua*, by definition, *il y a* — which is forever under erasure. The relationship of ~~Being~~ cannot be properly symbolized. But, at the same time, the brothers sustain this Unreasonable truth of the primary process. The split in the ego allows the brothers to sustain the "two assumptions." The two avowals are that their father was still alive and that they were the rightful successors to his death. Unconsciously, the brothers escape confinement in the unification and totalization of perspective.

Figure 5.2 The Lambert Substitutability Function

This illustration depicts the dynamic of Being and temporality. The relationship is Queer Mathematically represented in the Lambert Omega Function. The Lambert Omega Function is written as a variable with the symbol: $r = d(r)e^{d(r)}$. This equation involves $\partial d/\partial r = \partial d/\partial r/\partial r$. Queer Mathematically, this represents the function whose derivative is itself. The result of this equation is $r = ke^d$ in which k is a constant. This Queer Mathematically represents the deconstructive discovery that the difference of difference is difference in an endless difference and deferral in the tissue of the traces of the text. The Queer Mathematical representation articulates the pervert's grasp of the symbolic order in which a brazen negativity relates units of texts and contexts in a Real Sameness⁺ which is beyond the spoken and the written. The equation $k = d$ represents the constancy of the differential (d) relative to the relationality (r). The context of the signification of a unit of text (A) is lost to the occluded center. The trace is obscured. The relationality to the occluded center is preserved. The constant (k) is the gravity of the occluded center. The occluded center is symbolized in a relationship. The structurality of the structure is resynthesized into the structure. The trace is reabsorbed into the sign as k or $d(r)$. The structure becomes imaginary. The maternal phallus is situated in this imaginary dimension. The function of gravity image is isomorphic to the Lambert Omega Function. This nexus symbolizes the relationship of the Real and the symbolic as it is mapped onto the imaginary dimension. The figure (right) is a representation of the Lambert Omega Function in space. This space is partly in the imaginary dimension. The other figure (left) indicates the (re)constitution and (re)contextualization of any object in retroaction (*Nachträglichkeit, après-coup*). This retroactivity splits the previous incarnations — identity and essence — of the word. The metaphysics of presence (absence) generates an endless series of simulacra but also a singular space for the pervert's will to power of substitution and his *jouissance* of Metaphoricity. The pervert effectively performs his substitution amidst a system of perpetual difference and deferral. This will to power of substitution is a substitution for substitutability. This is the *Trieb* of Metaphoricity and the object of the pervert's Other *jouissance*. The pervert's fetish is a source of ecstasy because it is *is not*, or the Being *of* Nothingness. The object *is* itself precisely in its decenterment from self-sameness and self-identity in the presence of *is* — as such or Being. This function represents the pervert's disavowal and displacement of presence with Metaphoricity and substitutability.

Notes & Sketches —

The brothers accede to the ego-ideal of the father in the same instant that they identify themselves as the sons. Normally, the offspring's identification with the father is the proper resolution of the deadlock of the castration complex. But the brothers' solution implies that these sons can simultaneously be the father of their own father *qua* the sons. The generational *Verleugnung* is perverse. This generational inversion reverses the cohort in question. Disavowal upsets the division between the sons and the father. The men are both father and son to the lost father. This lost father is simultaneously both son and father, and both alive and dead. The brothers are strictly dead *qua* father but also strictly alive *qua* father. This constitutes a series of *faux petit morts*. The issue is not simply perverse generational transgression. At stake is also obsessional neurosis: "Am I dead or alive?" Perversely, the brothers are empirically alive because they have nominated themselves the patriarchs of their own dead and alive father. Psychically, the brothers sustain the father not in his absence as a ghost but as a presence in their life. The brothers obviate themselves from the tortured legacies of the dead father. The paternalization of the sons reverses the structure and function of the ego-ideal. But how do the brothers enforce the ego-ideal on their own father? Is this the reason that the father must be alive? — that the brothers desire to execute their own inheritance of the paternal legacy and its jockstrap?

THE SYMBOLISM OF THE REAL PENIS

The difference between neurosis and psychosis is a repression of the drive in favor of reality in neurosis versus a foreclosure of reality in favor of the drive in psychosis. This opposition neurosis/psychosis is deconstructed in the third term of perversion. The mechanism of negation in perversion is *Verleugnung*. The perverse economy mobilizes the both/and affirmation and denial of apparent contradictions. The pervert converts the absence of the female genitalia into a presence of the maternal phallus. The aesthetic of perversity is a generalized play and amusement. The caveat to this neat definition of fetishism is that the pervert must "know very well" that the maternal phallus is lost in order to "but nevertheless" pray, believe, hope, laugh, enjoy, mock, deride, love, and so on. The pervert asserts a "but nevertheless" of this loss in the creation of the substitute.

The fetish-metaphor is the "monument," as Freud says, to castration in the fetish-object or the textual representation of enjoyment. The pervert does (not) know that the Woman is castrated. But her genitalia is nonetheless relegated to the phallocentric rank of the not-penis. The male fetishist's "knows very well" is a strictly phallocentric logic. The object of his knowledge is the void of Nothingness of the not-penis of the female sexual anatomy. The male pervert can(not) contest the cultural phallocentric knowledge of female lack. But he can abandon epistemology in favor of experimentation with representational practices which are beyond the either/or structure of phallocentric presence and absence.

The "but nevertheless" is also an index of the pervert's talent to transcend the horror of castration that male heterosexual subjects suffer for the rest of their unsatisfactory sexual lives. The "but nevertheless" opens the pervert to a plethora of aesthetics and sensibilities which facilitates a variety of approaches to the representational capacities and talents of image and word. The pervert's "but nevertheless" invites him toward those representations (fetish-objects, exclusive or creative) which garner pleasure for him in his (*a*)sexual erotic tryst in object, on page, and on screen. These texts garner pleasure for him with his (*a*)*sexuality* of re-presentation. But if these representations traverse in an aim/less wander around the void of the female sex in the *mise-en-scène* of fetishism, then how is the Real of the not-penis — Real Penis — to be conceived and approached? How does the Real of this penis return to the symbolic order *qua* its condition of possibility?

Splitting

The *Spaltung* in the system of the conscious is a critical component of the function of *Verleugnung* in perversion. The split is the paradoxical center of the dispersed subject of psychoanalysis. In *An Outline of Psychoanalysis* (1940), Freud returns to the distinction between neurosis and psychosis in the context of fetishism. This question sidetracked him in the midst of his article on fetishism from 1927. In this later (1940) text, Freud both expands and restricts the role of the *Spaltung* in the economy of the psyche. Freud writes,

> The view that postulates a splitting of the *Ich* in all psychoses could not claim so much attention if it didn't turn out to be applicable to other states which are more similar to the neuroses — and ultimately to the neuroses themselves.[12]

Although Freud originally discovered the split (*Spaltung*) with the hysterics that he counseled with Breuer, he only rigorously theorized the *Spaltung* in relation to the adult fetishist and the perverse offspring. Freud expands the work of *Verleugnung* in which "two psychical perspectives are formed instead of a single one."[13]

The process of fetish-formation is not merely a splitting of the *Ich*. The fetish does not simply provoke an ego which sustains two contradictory interpretations, such as the "I know very well" that Something is Missing, "but nevertheless" Nothing is Missing. The obverse is also instructive. "I know very well" that Nothing is Missing, "but nevertheless" Something is Missing. This latter case illuminates the discomfort that the subject may experience in confrontation with the absence of absence. This elucidates the resistance to a postphallocentric and post-Peniscentric and postcapitalist communist queer (*a*)sexuality of the Spirit of the System. Why is Nothing is Missing an anxious quandary, even more so than Something is Missing? Lacan suggests that it is the proximity of the object which is the source of anxiety.[14] A castration of castration would likely incite a neurotic anxiety. This compels the fetishist to rework a revision: "I know very well that Nothing is Missing, but nevertheless Something is Missing." The consequences of this reiteration are narcissism, aggression, anxiety, ambivalence, jealousy, hatred, fear, envy, worry, dread, and so on. These affects are invariably directed toward the dead or alive father and his avatars.

The ego splits into multiple and contradictory perspectives ("I know very well, but nevertheless"). But Freud also discovers a splitting of the fetish-representation itself as both a "monument" to castration and as a "guarantee" against it. First, the "monument" to castration suggests a physical and permanent infrastructure to be revisited by a flock of devotees. The "monument" is visited by a dirty band of fetishists. These perverts rehearse with precision their devotion to the fetish-object and the hollowed ground of the castration. A "monument" is not possible without the loss which conditions its occasion. The fetish-object is made possible by the castration of the Woman. Second, the object of the "guarantee" against castration in the fetish-representation is the faith that the man's penis will not be annexed in the scene of sexual intercourse with the Woman and the fetish-object. But there is no covenant that the man will not lose his penis. The "guarantee" is simply a pledge with the power and prowess of the fetish-representation *qua* penis-substitute. The pervert enters a masochistic pact with the magical necromancy of the re-presentation of the penis in the fetish-object. But how are we to be sure that "two" interpretations are framed rather than a "single one"? What criterion separates the "two" from the "one"?

The secondary process of the ego is the system which distinguishes between incompatible thoughts. It does so as if these thoughts were two — distinct and opposed — rather than one. These (this) thought(s) are (is) paradoxically "extimate" to each other (itself) as disunified and split. The chasm in the conscious is enforced by the Reason of the ego-system. Egotistically, "one" incompatible content and another "one" deviant thought cannot be "one" but must be "two." This division is the case no matter the Unreasonableness of each thought in relationship to the other, such as homophobia and gay pride. The split by Reason squarely disregards the primary process of condensation and displacement in the dream-work. The primary process otherwise sanctions such contradictions in a logic of the both/and rather than the either/or. But Freud does not celebrate this unconscious thought process. Rather, Freud interprets the case of hypnoid consciousness as a pathological disavowal of compression of "two" into "one" within the strategies of signification of Reason and the secondary process. How do "two" incompatibilities and incongruities become "two" rather than an inconsistent extimate "one"? How does the "one" split into the hypnoid consciousness of A ≠ A?

The unconscious welcomes the "two" within the "one" through the technique of condensation. This technique is necessarily hazy and contradictory. Condensation assaults the force of the secondary process of Reason with the playful split of the unconscious processes. The secondary process of the ego-system cannot tolerate any relationships other than those dictated by Reason. The Pervert-Schizoid-Woman and her modality of fetishistic textuality — *(a)sextuality* — seek the playbook of the unconscious in order to make the secret truth of the schizoid's Unreasonable designs visible to the culture of neurosis. The pervert does so from within the logic of unconscious techniques. The anatomy of the system is structured like the Madness of Order. How is this skeleton to be illustrated in a system that systematically but unintentionally neurotically forecloses (*rejet névrotique*) its own structure as the condition of both the system and its neurotic subjects?

The task to pervert a neurotic — who is simultaneously a dimwitted schizoid — is a massive pursuit. The *Verwerfung* of the signified — the Real Signifier and the Signified/r — destroys the system of signification (~~Being~~) within which the theory of value can even be addressed. But an untidy recourse to a metalanguage — in-action, in-process — which both decodes and caricatures a symbolic order is useful to this project. The Real overwrites this order. The Real makes any separation of signification and its resistance unthinkable. How does the perverse critic irradiate for the neurotic that this neurotic already knows what the neurotic is? How does the perverse deconstructionist showboat and showcase that the return of the repressed is the same as the repressed? This overlap between repression and its return is precisely the structure of schizophrenia.

The implication is that in the endless trail of penis, substitute, origin, word, metaphor, penis-substitute, sign, fetish, and so on, there is an object of articulation. This *das Ding* must be articulated. *Das Ding* is neither the imaginary phallus nor the Real phallus nor the symbolic phallus. Instead, the object of fetishistic re-presentation is the Real Penis. This unsymbolizable appendage is the material and fleshly embodiment of pleasure. The Real Penis always returns to the same place of the Real. The Real Penis is the sublime unrepresentable referent of fetishism. The Real Penis adorns the system with the schizophrenic supplement that the structure already possesses on the sly. There is a fetishistic gap — metaphor/metonymy — even between the lost penis and the present fetish. The name for this time and space must be alphabetically otherwise than the *clichéd différance*. The Other is the Real Penis. She is the fleshly, colored, and textured embodiment of pleasure and pain. The Real Penis is the mediation between the substitutions which haunt this book: center, metaphor, penis, metonymy, penis-substitute, word, fetish — and every other object in the system. The Real Penis must be (already is) described and approached because the symbolic and the Real are already coincident — Sameness⁺ — in the Real Signifier and the Signified/r. The Real Penis is the sign of Being under erasure. The Real Penis is the fleshly material embodiment. The Real Penis is the Marxist surplus value which is inequivalent to all value. The Real Penis is singular. The Real Penis is the function which is the excluded Outside of the system.

The Real Penis is worthless in itself because it can only be understood as pure use-value. The Real Penis is the signifier of the copula and the preposition. These grammatical functions orchestrate the relationships between the objects in the discourses of metaphor and metonymy. The Real Penis is the textual lubricant of the relationships among the penis, the fetish-representation, and the obscured female genitalia in the sexual scene of fetishistic satisfaction. As Lacan wryly chides, there is "no such thing as a sexual relationship."[15] But this is so not because the phallus is veiled. The sexual relationship is impossible because the Real Penis conditions the emergence (*Eros, Thanatos*) of the objects in the system. The Real Penis is the sexualized sign of ~~Being~~. The fleshly and embodied penis is strictly sublime and unrepresentable. The mediation *qua* copula of sexual organs and body parts can only be achieved in the absence of phallic sexuality. This summons the question of communist sexuality. What is the postphallic genital principle of communist sex? What is the *Aufhebung* beyond the phallus? Will the Real Penis arrive in the dialectical progression of history? — and with what modality of *jouissance*?

Between "Yes!"

The parallax of the object refers to the Zizekian parallactic gap of two antagonistic perspectives on the "one" and the "same" object. This parallax is perverse because the object is double, in the least. It is split between an "I know very well" of epistemology and a "but nevertheless" of faith. Parallactic disavowal mediates between a knowledge on either side of the object and a faith on both sides of the object. This parallax also explains Freud's encounter with fetishists who fear castration despite disavowal with the fur, lace, shoe, and jockstrap. The pervert overcomes the fantasized horror of castration in his *(a)sextual* creation of fetish-object-substitute-metaphor for the female penis. This "quite special" penis has gone awry and gone missing. An *(a)sexuality* intends to transform Lacan's "no such thing as a sexual relationship" of the neurotic into a "such a thing as a representational sex" of the pervert. Freud writes,

> Thus [perverts'] behavior simultaneously expresses two contradictory premises. On the one hand they deny the very fact that they perceived — that they saw no penis in the female genitals — and on the other hand they acknowledge the female's lack of a penis and draw the right conclusions from this.[16]

First, the fetishist perceives in the object the impossible simultaneity of the presence and the absence of the penis. At once, the subject and the object are split. The hypnoid effect applies to both the fetishist and his representation. Such a feat is miraculous. The pervert sees both presence and absence, both *Fort!* and *Da!*, and so on. At first glance, the fetishist is a castrated neurotic who is subordinate to the penis-clitoris phallocentrism of loss. But the pervert's talent to disavow this loss is precisely the magic which marks the distinction between himself and the ordinary neurotic. The pervert is a neurotic with an Unreasonable and intuitive embrace of contradiction against the Reasonable enforced submission to logic.

The second move of the pervert is to "acknowledge" or avow the lack but then "deny" (in total: "acknowledge" and "deny" in disavowal) the object that he has already "acknowledged." Her next move is to draw the proper conclusions about private property, potential loss, and privileged value. This second fetishistic gesture is regressive because it reposits castration into an economy that previously orchestrates its *Verleugnung*. But this artistry also invites an acceptance of castration. Concession to castration enables the fetishist both to deny it in disavowal and also to stave off the hallucinations and delusions of psychosis. Mad symptoms foreclose the frame of reality-fantasy altogether. Freud organizes disavowal in the figuration of "on the one hand" and "on the other hand." Is (are) such a "hand"-to-"hand" acknowledgment ("I know very well" or "but nevertheless") and denial ("but nevertheless" or "I know very well") a simultaneity at once — *Yes!* — ? Or is this double-gesture a chronological succession whereby the fetishist denies no-penis and phallocentric logic and then acknowledges the phallocentric truth of no-penis? Or is "hand"-to-"hand" an "I know very well, but nevertheless" of unconscious condensation and displacement? Is disavowal a "yes" to epistemology and a "yes" to faith — chronologically or simultaneously?

My reading of perverse fetishism is that its assay is simultaneity in the superpositional both/and Other-Logic. This Other is not even properly explained by Octave Mannoni's patient's "I know very well, but nevertheless." Mannoni's mantra is differed and deferred in space and time. The quantum overlap of *Yes!* is delayed in the spatial and temporal interval of articulation of knowledge and faith (hope, dream, love, and so on). The pervert suffers his own setbacks because he is sutured to a successive chronology in which the "contradictory premises," as Freud puts it, are visible because of the spatial and temporal gap between "denial" and "acknowledgment" in the space-time of disavowal. The talented pervert exerts his "premises" simultaneously. The in-process, in-action is double-speak.

The sexual relation is this in-and-out and out-and-in of the mutually exclusive, at once, at the same time, simultaneously, *Yes!* Superpositional simultaneity is strictly undecidable in the instant of the movement: willing having beening Becoming Being — *Yes!* The pervert's both/and is also simultaneously an ephemeral castration. Castration and its other are instantaneous. The penis is (potentially) annexed at the same moment as it is (potentially) sutured. The both/and is not simply an instant undecidability. The both/and is not quickly transcended by either one "hand" or the other "hand" with a blend of regret and relief. Rather, the magnificent feat of the pervert is the reconciliation of the mutually exclusive — *Yes!* This is a talent that Reason consistently castigates and cages as evidence of a faulty Unreason.

This "on the one hand" and "on the other hand" are classically fetishistic because they strive to open the parallactic gap of identity and difference. Double-hand opens toward two antagonistic perspectives on "one" and the "same" parallactic Uncalculable X object. The fetishistic parallax welcomes this aperture *qua* difference at the same time as it closes it *qua* identity. This successful gesture is a Sameness⁺ in the simultaneity in space and time of the convergence of identity and difference. This object, as Derrida points out, is "not identical" to itself as self-same and self-identical.

An object is the same as every other object in the system. The identity which is foreclosed in the symbolic returns in the Real *qua* Sameness⁺. Presence substitutes for absence — one over the other — "on the one hand" and "on the other hand." Sabbatical excess between binary oppositions is a strictly deconstructive insight and project. Plenitude substitutes for a lack in the same place — *Yes!* — and also at the same time — *Yes!* — that the coincidental but qualified overlap between absence and presence of the parallactic gap is indicated. The mutually exclusive (antagonistic) emerges as simultaneously the same and the different. This is precisely the logic that the pervert discerns in the fetish-object. The fetish is the sexual representation of the parallactic gap and the Uncalculable X of the object of the Real parallax. This Uncalculable X is the Real Penis.

The function of the Real Penis is the mediatory lubricant between the female sexual anatomy and the fetish-screen. The symbolism of the Real Penis is World. The two antagonistic perspectives, fetish and clitoris, "simultaneously" exist side-by-side in a hypnoidism on both hands, jerking together, with the hands on "one" and the "same" fetish-object. This fetish-object is mediated by the Real Penis. The Real Penis is none other than the impossible and inexplicable coordination of the material and the abstract, and the signifier and the signified. This organization must be in-process, in-action as a verbed gerund or Ing⁺: deeding-doing-deeding-doing. The in-process, in-action work is accompanied by a minor shift in perspective between system and $-ism. The fetish and the clitoris are joined as decoration and object in the Becoming of the substance of enjoyment for the fetishist.

Figure 5.3 Real Fetishism

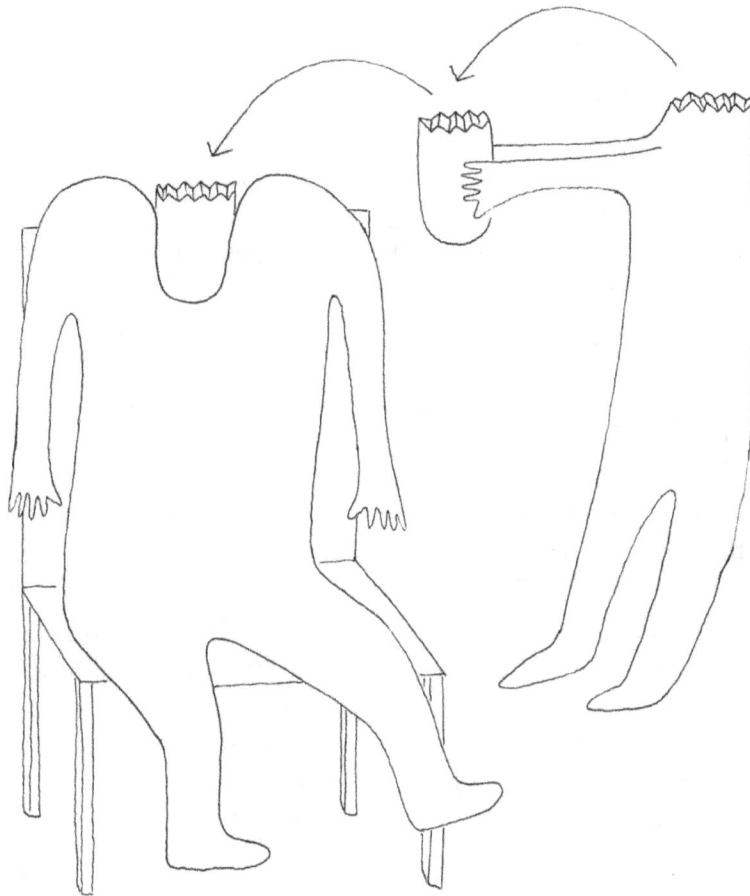

The Real Fetishist obliterates phallocentric absence. The Real Fetishist sutures the gap with the fragmentation of the jagged object. The Real Fetishist simulates a relationship of Sameness⁺ between otherwise disparate objects — centers, shoes, jockstraps, metaphors, laces, signs, furs, fetishes, and so on. The revolutionary selfhood of the Real Fetishist inspires an existence which is not cohesive or totalized but rather an alterity which is an effect of a Sameness⁺. The Real Fetishist is different from himself but the Same⁺ as (Different⁺ from) the other. The Real Fetishist is enlivened by the process of self-fragmentation in the generation of a legible Sameness⁺ in the symbolic order. The selfhood of the Real Fetishist is not a figuration of identity or difference but rather of partiality and disintegration. The figure of the seated Woman (left) represents the occluded center which provides organization to the system as its veil. This hidden center is sutured with the Sameness⁺ — neither self-same nor self-identical — of the psychical acumen of the pervert (right). This picture portrays the pervert's talent to recognize and perform Sameness⁺ from within the structure of the system of self-same and self-identical objects of *Gestalt* totalities.

Notes & Sketches —

The spatiotemporal ideological shift illuminates the fissure in this otherwise simultaneity. The *at once* makes possible the aperture and closure of Sameness⁺. Sameness⁺ is chinked with identity and difference at the moment of the retro-grammatological bait-and-switch. A miraculous fetish represents, on the one hand, the presence of the lost maternal penis in the object and, on the other hand, the concurrent absence of this penis. This happens despite the resistance of the fetish to capture as either one or the other. The fetish is (also) (yet) both simultaneously. The fetish is (yet) (also) split. The fetish is this process of splitting. The fetish is neither "on the one hand" *qua* split nor "on the other hand" *qua* split. Neither/nor, the fetish is the in-action, in-process duration of the split. The pervert gets off on an engagement not with an object *per se* but with the splitting of the object. It is no wonder that Freud maintains that the object of desire is mostly irrelevant to the process of desire. The object will always be split as otherwise than and elsewhere from itself. The object of *désir* is *Trieb*.

REAL FETISHISM

The sister's lost penis is experienced as the gap between the fetish and the clitoris or between the penis-substitute and the female penis. The division consists of the splinter between the substitute and the clitoris. This gap between the substitute and the clitoris is a symptom of the phallocentrism that the Woman "does not have a penis." Alternatively, the fissure may be interpreted as the gap between the substitute and the female penis. The latter is the case for the postphallocentric Real Fetishist who engages the lacuna between the penis-substitute and the female penis. This second option involves the closure of the phallocentric gap. It opens a simple time and space which are crushed into the sexual void — *Yes!* — in the "such a thing" of the (*a*)sexual relation. The former lacuna is between the fetish and the not-penis. The former case is animated by the conventional phallocentrism of the male fetishist. The latter version of fetishism entails the splitting between the penis-substitute and the clitoris *qua* female penis. This variant of perversion is Real Fetishism. Real Fetishism dazzles the perversity of communist queer (*a*)sexuality.

Real Splits

Real Fetishism sparks the material-abstract time-space of the sign. I designate this joint as the Real Penis. Real Penis is the proper name for the lubricant (such as the / or <> or ⊇) between ostensible oppositions, such as penis/not-penis. The conventional male fetishism of phallocentrism negates the Real Penis. The overlap of the various differences is denied in favor of the correspondence between the two objects, fetish and clitoris. In contrast, the Real Fetishism of postphallocentric perversion concerns the gap between the fetish-object and the clitoris-female-penis. The Real Penis is neither repressed nor foreclosed nor disavowed. Real Fetishism unveils the Real Penis as the figural-literal, material-abstract joint which cannot be theoretically explained whatsoever. The Real Penis is the hinge between embryonic displacements and compressions of aims and objects in the fetishistic celebration of substitution. The distinction between the "no such thing" sexual relationship between the Patriarchal Fetishist and his penis-substitute and the ordinary clitoris, on the one hand, and the "such a thing" sexual relationship between the Real Fetishist and his fetish and the rare female penis (or male clitoris, and so on), on the other hand, is now clarified. The former prosaic version of Patriarchal Fetishism sustains the wound of sexual difference. Patriarchal Fetishism nostalgically returns to loss even as the wound is temporarily sutured by the fetish-object in an obsessive fixity and exclusivity. In contrast, the radical design of Real Fetishism harnesses a representation which closes the gap between sexual opposition. Patriarchal Fetishism structures its sexuality around the substitute/clitoris division.

Real Fetishism organizes its (*a*)sexuality around the aperture and closure of the gap between the fetish and the female penis. Patriarchal Fetishism is arranged by the Real of sexual difference. Real Fetishism is coordinated by a *Verleugnung* in which sexual difference returns as "sexual difference" — and as every other object in the system.

Real Fetishism deconstructs the word. Radically, the fetish is transformed into the penis-substitute which engages with the female penis which is simultaneously the male clitoris which is itself the penis-substitute which is at the same time the fetish which is also the clitoris-substitute — and so on. Real Fetishism is a *jouissance ad infinitum* of sexual ecstasy and erotic textuality. Real Fetishism is an (*a*)*sextualism*. The Real Penis is an afterthought in a delayed after-glow during the in-process, in-action "such a thing" sexual relation of Sameness[+]. The Real Penis is the singular instant of space and time in which neither Something is Missing nor Nothing is Missing but — Everything is Present. The plenitude of the lost maternal phallus and the lack of the deficient clitoris are isomorphic. But this isomorphism is disrupted by an excess.

The temporal difference between the female penis and the not-penis is crucial. The maternal phallus is a lost paradise of the oedipal and castration complexes. The maternal phallus portends a masculine retroactive glance toward the origin of presence and absence. In contrast, the clitoris is the not-penis. The clitoris is a present loss which the female junior redeems in a futural will to consumption of penis-substitutes, such as Freud's metaphors of husband and "penis-baby."[17] This secondary version of female development demonstrates a critical aporia in the infamous Freudian query of, "What does a Woman want?" The Woman wants something Other. This Other is situated in the boundless metonymy of the shopping spree of penis envy.

The fundamental logic of the unconscious persists beyond the boundaries of the historical-theoretical debacle of lack and castration in the psychoanalytic and phallocentric ideologies. Other-Logic is the contradictory schizophrenic Unreason of the both/and structure of the pervert's system. Crazy logic is barred from the conscious system because it is a threat to the neurotic either/or system of $-ism. This structure is organized by exclusion and hierarchy. This is the reason that perversion and fetishism are considered pathologies. It is also the explanation for the masculine burn for the maternal phallus and the lubricational division (/, <>) of the Real Penis.

The Real Penis intervenes at the moment of the "such a thing" as the sexual relationship. The Real Penis also supervenes in the relationship between every oppositional pair of objects in the system. The splitting of the ego consists of the simultaneity of the parallactic split in the object. Hypnoid consciousness also illuminates the overlapped split on the side of the subject. Splitting refers both to the ego and the other and also to the subject and the object. As Freud says of this splitting, "the two attitudes exist alongside one another for the whole of the individual's life, without influencing one another."[18] But what does "exist alongside one another" indicate?

The unconscious-work of condensation and displacement endures no trouble with this "alongside." The unification of the multiple and contradictory in condensation or the transfer of intensity and value in displacement is of no concern for the primary process. The "alongside" is happily assimilated to the Unreason of the system Unc. Unconsciously, various contradictory, paradoxical, conflictual, and incongruous contents play and cavort in compressions, displacements, reversals, and so on. The gorgeous mosaic of the unconscious is the precise effect of this Unreason. But the practical programme of existence in this *mise-en-scène* is a vexed question. How do perverts, schizoids, and Women live in the galaxy of a timeless unconscious and in an existence "alongside one another" without antipathy and irreconcilability? This space obliterates the parallactic gap and broken bridge between "yes I said yes I will — " — *Yes!* This (un)conscious space also upsets the codes and conventions of the system of language. These parameters are configured by the logic of the private property of the sign rather than by the free play of the signifier. Such a modality of splitting entails the extimate split of both the subject and the object, and both the self and the other. Each (is) becoming the other "alongside one another." The splitting is both of the object from the other and from itself. As processes, the subject and the object are (is) the Outside to the metaphysics of presence. The subject and the object are (is) what they (it) are-ing (is-ing) not.

Figure 5.4 Patriarchal Fetishism

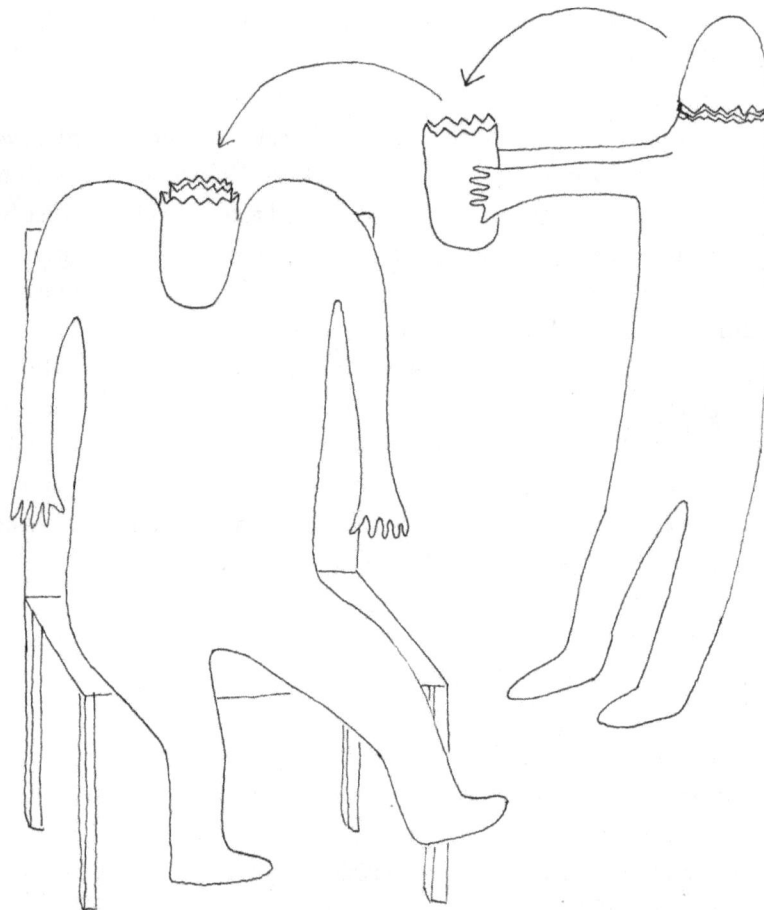

The Real Fetishist embraces the economy of Sameness⁺. The Real Fetishist is decentered from himself and proximate to the other. In contrast, the Patriarchal Fetishist merely succeeds in an endless series of substitutions which sustains his identity as a situated and located ego in the system. The Patriarchal Fetishist returns the (*a*)sexual force to the penis and to the masculinity of male subjectivity. The Patriarchal Fetishist simulates loss and sutures sexual difference. But he does so on the rider of the ego and its losses and castrations. The fetish is recuperated into a *Trieb* which is *de facto* neurotic *désir*. This desire does not exceed the system of Something is Missing toward the schizoid Nothing is Missing. The fetish-substitution of Patriarchal Fetishism is an endless series of jagged shells which never fills the loss or sutures the wound. The patriarchal object is exemplary of substitutability, but this *objet* refuses to yield the return of the object to a trace which is different from the penis and the substance of identity. Patriarchal Fetishism returns the alternatively psychotic object to the self of the male fetishist. This economy neutralizes the psychotic aneconomy of the split in the object that otherwise organizes the system of neurosis (psychosis).

Notes & Sketches —

My project is to imagine a space in which man ascends unto the unconscious in conscious fantasy-reality — living the unconscious. This sparks a radical splitting. Would we live "alongside each other" on different sides of the same side? A manifest unconscious framework may carve out a space within which man splits from himself in order to join with the other. But would the disappearance of the parallax rend the simultaneous aperture and closure of the gap between system and $-ism a forlorn perspective? The arrival of the unconscious and its Unreason portends the absence of negation and epistemology. But a postnegative and postepistemological *mise-en-scène* may make critique irrelevant and inapposite. The unfortunate implication is that there is no politics of and in the system Unc. But is the unconscious end of politics a redemptive quittance? The unconscious encourages man's Unreasonable splits from himself and sutures with the other. The system of the Unc. welcomes joy in parallactic gaps and relational plenitudes. This *Eros-Thanatos* upheaval beckons toward the solar system of the Pervert-Schizoid-Woman. But a traversal through the reality-fantasy of being-in-the-world and being-with-others is necessary before a genuflection toward a postpolitical, antiphallic, and anticapitalist ecstasy.

Fractures in the Objects of Representation

The split in the subject ($) is supplemented by the perverse fetishist's engagement with the massive and multiple splits within the fetish-object. The fetish is not only every object in the universe. The jockstrap is also a penis-substitute for the traditional male fetishist of a phallocentric logic of the clitoris *qua* not-penis. The Other-Jockstrap is also potentially a so-imagined clitoris-substitute for the radical Real Fetishist of a Penisclitoralcentrist sensibility. The latter progressive strategy of fetishism summons the metaphorical representations and figural hieroglyphics for the expansion of the clitoris: penis-substitute, clitoris-substitute, penis-clitoris, clitoris-penis, and so on. Real Fetishism eases castration anxiety for the otherwise terrified man.

But this is so only insofar as the fetishist acknowledges that the clitoris-substitute (fetish-object) is simultaneously a penis-substitute (fetish-object). The talented and enlightened Real Fetishist understands that concomitant castration anxiety is not structured around a phallocentric difference (penis/not-penis) that otherwise privileges the male. Rather, castration is organized by a generalized -centrism. Such a reconfiguration includes, "A Woman has a clitoris, and a man does not have a clitoris." The fetishist does not fear the clitoris. Rather, the Real Fetishist's castration ambivalence is about sex organs insofar as they are different (identical) whatsoever — even small penis against big penis, cut penis against uncut penis, hairy penis against shaved penis, and so on.

This fetishist is deeply deconstructive. His joy is the *jouissance* of text and representation. The pervert's mortiferous Other *jouissance*, or even *jouis-sens*, is the manic deconstruction of the fetish-object. The pervert summons the gay's gaze of grammatological splits and their conversion into gobbledygook. He gay/zes with the absence of the signified of identity and difference. He spurns the signified — Clitoralcentrism, phallocentrism, or a generalized -centrism altogether. The (*a*)sexual pervert's frenzied mania is a desexualized sexualization of the violence of the text. Derrida is an (*a*)sexual textual predator. This most advanced fetishist foreswears sexuality for textuality — or (*a*)sextuality. The pervert sees no difference between the sexual and the textual. The pervert's *objet a* is the object "itself." This is the reason that deconstruction's libido aims toward a metalanguage in which so-called logocentric abstraction can experimentally sever itself from the body. Derrida's enterprise is to re-present sexuality *qua* textuality *qua* the split object of fetishism.

The perverse instant of the universalization of psychoanalytic castration and capitalist scarcity breaks the restraints of limitations. This law of lack involves the regulations of the pleasure principle and the sustained scarcity of the monetary system. Instead, the handsome pervatologist pursues an in-process, in-action jockstrapological critique of division, hierarchy, and the signified. He does so with the erotic aim/less wander of *Trieb* toward a metalanguage of the obscenities of representation and the sublimity of all text after the erasure of ~~Being~~.

This splitting of the fetish-objects of the world into shards of texts, alphabets, signifiers, and vocabularies — a gobbledygook of representation — foundationally subverts not only order, hierarchy, and the center of the system. In addition, the deconstructive (*a*)sexual will destroys the entirety of adult sexuality in favor of a return to the fractured objects and aims of young eroticism. This (*a*)sexual pervert eschews all opposition, distinction, and hierarchy. He pursues the deconstruction of the sign in a *Trieb* toward the frolic and frisk of the signifier. Her work is structured by text — the screen of the not-penis, the stain of the female penis, and the spot of the clitoris. Her talent is to expose the system and its effects and to theorize potential escapes from -centrism. The navel of -centrism is the split in the self and the fracture in the other. The horizonal — "yes, yes" — play land of this pervert is the Unreason of the unconscious. This is a space of neither negation nor knowledge. This cultural work confuses the boundaries that Freud establishes between the internal world of drive-impulses of the *Es* and the external world of demands from reality. The Real Penis is the lubricant of / or <> or ⊇ or any preposition whatsoever.

The fetishist's symptom is an effect of compromises with the Janus-faced smirk of the fetish-object. Freud reduces the fetishist's disavowal of reality to "half-measures, incomplete attempts at detachment from reality."[19] In defense of the pervert, a "half-measure" is a moderated altered construction of the fantasy frame which mediates between the obstinate shackle to the world in neurosis and the fancied flight from the world in schizophrenia. A "half-measure" is a safe and secure modality of distance from the ideological straightjacket of a manufactured scarcity and an oppressive patriarchy. The "incomplete attempts" of escape from fantasy-reality that Freud mentions only underscore the unexpectedly conservative orientation of the fetishist's reconstruction of the framework of reality. But the pervert also vigorously engages in a fundamentalist transformation of *écriture* and representational practices. This is the reason that the pervert intervenes in the field of sexual difference despite his latent (*a*)sexuality. Sexual difference is the dimension in which phallocentrism as a cruel and strange representational practice is in effect. This reality-fantasy is the system in which the fetishist's critique intervenes. The pervert elevates the fierce negative and differential signifiers to the unexpected and glorious positivity of the word.

Each signifier is reconstituted as different from the other signifiers. The signifier is simultaneously different from itself. *Ergo* — the object is not identical with itself but the same as every other signifier in the Other. This is a Sameness⁺ which is precisely "not identical." The signifier is neither self-same to nor self-identical with itself. Why is this nonidentity otherwise than "itself"? The signifier is the same as the other (different) signifiers in the system. Each signifier is different from itself — ~~noncoincident~~ and ~~noncontinuous~~ — in order to be the Same⁺ as but also Different⁺ from every other signifier in the system. This is the horizon of the pervert's project to translate the schizoid's flips and flops of Unreason. The deconstruction of *le propre* and the self-sameness and self-identity of essence (otherwise: A = A) articulates a Reasonable, coherent, rational, and logical explication of Unreason. The splitting of the object demonstrates that Unreason is internal to Reason. Unreason emerges as the condition of the governance and enterprise of Reason.

Freud's noted "half-measures" and "incomplete attempts" figure hypnoid states of split consciousness *qua* supplements of the trace and the Signified/r. Voice and text can only half-finish and undo the work of signification. This is the limit of the pervert's *Praxis*. It is the horizon of the desperate and cheery work of his life. The pervert makes the Unreason of Reason visible to the neurotic structures of an otherwise schizoid culture. The Real Penis is the parallax between these halves and incompletes of the splitting of subjects and objects, and selves and others. The Real Penis is the psychoanalytic version of the concept of the trace. The Real Penis precedes *différance* because it is the in-process, in-action simultaneity of the verbed gerund or Ing⁺.

The Real Penis lubricates and greases the willing having beening Becoming Being of the deconstruction of — *Yes!* — and so on. The Real Penis has neither presence nor absence. The Real Penis is neither is nor is not, and neither Being nor Nothingness. The Real Penis is not a transcendental condition of (im)possibility of the joint of abstraction-materiality or subject-object. Rather, the Real Penis denotes an enabler in the illumination of a universal Sameness⁺. The Real Penis refuses -centrism — metaphor, substitute, clitoris-substitute, fetish, metonymy, penis-substitute, clitoris, fetish-metaphor, substitute-substitute, penis-clitoris-metaphor-substitute, and jockstrap — in favor of a Sameness⁺ — _____ — in a metalanguage. This metalanguage is a signifier *about* the signifier *about* —

Sameness⁺ is the aesthetic of the Pervert-Schizoid-Woman. The fetishist's so-called "half-measures" and "incomplete attempts" are not his reaction to the internal split between the double affirmation of acknowledgment and denial of castration. Rather, the half-ways and by-ways of perverse being-in-the-world indicate the internal split of the fetish-object. The shoe, lace, fur, and jockstrap are castrated. The split in the fetish-object refers to the inconsistency in the symbolic order. This rupture is neurotically foreclosed (*rejet névrotique*) by the system. This split in the fetish-representation includes such basic lapses as the excess of the message to the code. Splitting also illuminates the conflicts among multiple ontologies — what is, what are, what will be, what were, what could be, what would be, what should have been, what could have been, what would have been, what ought to be, and so on. These different worlds tussle with each other in the galaxy.

Reason responds to this challenge by enforcing a singular and unified ontological version of reality-fantasy. Becoming-Perverts are invited to fracture objects and worlds. But this work and play are deemed Unreasonable. Perverts are banished to the unwritten and unspoken outskirts of the Real. These perverts return *qua* the system. The system is the obscene overlap of the symbolic and the Real. This overlap of the Real Symbolic is the essence of (Un)Reason. The tidiest definition of Unreason is the return of the Real to the symbolic order. Unreason is the symptomatic effect of the system in its management of and operation as this disruption. The split in the object also generates the spun proliferation of disparate ontologies that a future of the Spirit of the System (S) promises. This destined fortune splits the *Ich* into a fractal hypnoid conscious in the process of the fetishization — substitution *of* substitution *of* substitution — of the entire symbolic order.

The split in the identical of the fetish-object illuminates a constitutive Sameness⁺. This parallax can only be viscerally experienced in *Trieb*. Drive is the Outside to the Freudian pleasure principle. *Trieb* is the underside of the ruthless and reactive regulation of excitation in the individual and social organism. Regulation of pleasure recuperates manic frenzy and revolutionary energy. The pleasure principle (ac)counts and (im) balances all space and time. This homeostasis is the speculated equivalence of increase/decrease in the system. *Thanatos* is Outside of the pleasure principle. This is so even as the death drive is simultaneously the center of the principle. *Thanatos* wills destruction. *Thanatos* is the partner of the grammatological effort to thrash and whip the system. The deconstructive *Trieb* does so only in the call toward the Other which is yet-to-come. *Thanatos* wills toward the beyond of death in an *à venir* of an aperture toward the future.

Spaltung in the subject represents an effect of the split in the social order and in the shadow of the fetish-object. The split subject is an effect rather than a cause of the splitting not of the ego but of the object. The object is split into inconsistency, multiplicity, disappointment, dissatisfaction, and so on. The split is the paradoxical *arche* of the *arche*typal split subject of psychoanalysis. The proper origins of the split subject include desire, the signifier, and the unconscious. These elements of the subject are discerningly Outside of the subject. The subject is a mere effect of forces that oddly exceed the split. This *Spaltung* is otherwise always already in the subject. The split in the object is the embodied essence of desire, the signifier, and the unconscious. These are all generally understood as private properties of the self. As Freud puts it,

> A refusal to accept the perceptions is supplemented every time by an acknowledgment of them; two opposing outlooks, independent of one another, always set themselves up — and this results in the splitting of the *Ich*.[20]

The structuralist fissure in the subject is supplemented by the triumph of the split in the object. The subjective *Spaltung* is the effect rather than the cause of the split in the fetish. Subjective splitting is the consequence rather than the origin of the inconsistency. The system makes no sense.

The split is both cause and effect of "itself." This causal and effective "itself" is the object of fetishism and the subject of the self. Cause and effect are *ex nihilo*. The split itself is split. The object of the pervert's (*a*)sexual ecstasy is Metaphoricity or the metonymization of metaphor. The rest of us also take sexual pleasure in this "splitting" of the object of the fetish. The *jouissance* of the Other pervert is structured by the substitute *of* the substitute, and so on. The pervert's joyful Metaphoricity is organized by the poetic difference and deferral of the re-presentation of the representation (and so on) of the deconstructive signifier. The distinction between the Other and the subject is stressed to indistinction. The splits in the battery of the signifier effect a gap in the subject. The hole is sutured with the fetish-objects in the system.

The point in space and time at which the self ends and the fetish begins is indeterminate and undecidable. This is so because the entire battery of text is equivalent to the litany of fetishes. These fetishes suture the wound of female castration in its wretched terror. But in rare cases these objects can suture difference. The wound can be bandaged by the *différance* of the differences and deferrals which is in-between the cuts and scrapes of objects. These scraps for the (*a*)sexual fetishist's *jouissance* are exclusively textual. Unavoidable syntactical reasons force Freud's note of the "two opposing outlooks, independent of one another" to miss the promised simultaneity of the disavowal of the fetishist's avoidance of castration anxiety. Perversion returns to the maternal phallus in the veil of the penis-substitute. The intuition of the (*a*)sexual deconstructionist fetishist destroys the entirety of ontology. The pervert ascends to an unconscious and its logic of the primary process of simultaneity of compression, displacement, and paradox in the absence of any temporality whatsoever.

AN ARTFUL COUNTERFEIT

Freud identifies the central mechanisms of the primary process as condensation, displacement, considerations of representability, and secondary revision. These are the fundamental talents of the Other dimension of psychical life. The unconscious is the space but not the time of the Pervert-Schizoid-Woman. The space of the future is the instant of the simultaneity of the dissolution of the mutually exclusive. This simultaneity is the ruin of the system of $-ism. In his text, "Formulations on the Two Principles of Psychic Functioning" (1909), Freud applies the split between the primary-unconscious and the secondary-conscious systems to the artist, the art-object, and the community of neurotics of the schizoid system of $-ism. The Neurotic Foreclosure (*rejet névrotique*) of the schizophrenic structure of the system returns to destabilize the system *qua* "itself." But how is the process of this return to be written? Under what code does the pervert witter and chunter? How is this dysfunctional dynamic of normativity to be symbolized if *écriture* (or Being) is put under erasure by the Madness of Order of the system?

Art reconciles the two principles of the conscious and the unconscious. This distinction between the secondary and the primary processes is a division that neither the pervert nor the madman fully recognizes as valid and consequential. The pervert disavows the division. "I know very well that there is no such thing as a binary opposition between conscious/unconscious, but nevertheless I suppose such a division because it is useful in the effort to write the structure of the system…." The pervert's pragmatic *Verleugnung* contrasts with the obscene *Verwerfung* of the psychotic. The schizoid's mode of negation is a fierce "No!" Foreclosure is overlapped with the entire structure of the signifying chain. The gap between conscious and unconscious is arbitrary but conventional. The system Cs. and the system Unc. could be redesigned and redivided differently. The pervert understands the (un)conscious as an extimacy. The conscious and the unconscious, and the secondary and the primary, are each defined by negation and difference. This definition is structured by the comparison and contrast — the (un)like of exchange — with the other words in the system. The pervert repudiates the existential and ontological "what is" of the unconscious. But, at the same time, the pervert affirms the awesome Unreason of the unconscious. The pervert rejects a substantial unconscious. But the pervert welcomes the Perverse Logic of the unconscious and its resistance to the codes and conventions of the system.

Neither the pervert nor the madman has an unconscious. Neither has a psyche which can strictly be divisible into the two dimensions of the system Cs. and the system Unc. But both the pervert and the schizoid view the unconscious as an extraordinarily productive image or conceptual persona. This is so even if the concept does not apply directly to the intrapsychical economy of the pervert and the schizoid. The reason that the unconscious is philosophically crucial for the pervert is that Freud's study of the primary process (condensation, displacement, and so on) discovers the techniques and tropes of a latent imagery. The pervert enkindles this Other representation in his endeavors to symbolize the secret truth of the schizoid's Unreason. The talented deconstructionist fetishist discerns that the unconscious is the royal road to the Unreason of the schizoid. The unconscious is the key to the riddle of the system of $-ism. The psychotic's truth of $-ism is embedded in the unconscious. The primary process is the system of semantics and syntax which is prohibited from the conscious system of the ego. The contents and forms of the unconscious are banished from the system. But the modes of the unconscious signifying chain are simultaneously the syntax and semantics of the conscious system. The secret of these forms is that there is a mere parallactic gap between primary and secondary processes, and between conscious and unconscious systems.

The division between the systems of the unconscious and the conscious is of two antagonistic perspectives on "one" and the "same" object. The Real is revealed in the process of a shift in perspective and a revision in viewpoint. Lacan makes such blasphemy explicit in his disclosure that the primary process unconscious is structured like a secondary process language. Lacan claims that Unreason and Reason are somehow configured as the same structure: "the unconscious is structured like a language."[21] The unconscious is a menace to the secondary system of signification because it disturbs Reason. The unconscious reveals the internal inconsistency of the system Cs. The unconscious is structured like Reason. The schizophrenia of Unreason is intramural to the laws and codes of Reason. The pervert studies the primary process in order to decode the secondary system and write the secret truth of the ego. Unreason is the royal road to the neurotic. The pervert is the royal road to the schizoid.

The Artist

The artist is the heir to the schizoid. Creative signification in art is a detail of madness. In his 1909 essay on the two principles of the primary and secondary processes, Freud writes: "The artist is originally someone who, unable to come to terms with the renunciation of drive satisfaction demanded by reality, turns away from it and gives free rein to erotic and ambitious wishes in his fantasy life."[22] Freud at first figures the artist as the madman. The artist is the crazy character whose "renunciation" of instinctual pleasure and wanton whim enforces a rejection of the conventional symbolic order and its codes, semantics, and syntax. He does so for the sake of another world of satisfaction and the "freedom" of "eroticism" and "wish." The artist is the unlawful schizoid whose erotic wishes and erudite fantasies enable him to flee the world into a reverie of his own ambitions. Art is not of this world. Rather, the artifice of art is otherworldly.

The artist and the schizoid foreclose reality in favor of the demands of the *Es*. The returns of the foreclosed Real are the artistic creations of what Nietzsche refers to as the "future philosophers" and the "free Spirits."[23] But where do these demands — "drive satisfactions" — originate? Although Freud's work posits an originary and unconscious *Es* from which the *Ich* and the *Über-Ich* themselves evolve, the *arche* of this *Es* is suspended. *Wo Es war* — but where was it? The psychotic and the artist indulge a trace of "drive satisfaction." But do they renounce a cauldron of desires and wishes which is necessarily joined to either the *Ich* or the *Über-Ich*? If not, then the artist-madman has not "renounced" "reality" but has merely chosen to heed the "reality" of the "drive satisfaction" of reality.

Art is also not otherworldly. Rather, the artifice of art is its reinscription of the conventions which it purports to flee. This "drive satisfaction" is the overindulgence of the artist. This "reality" is the proper neurotic spoor of drive renunciation. But drive and reality are flip-sides of the same "free rein," "ambitious wish," and "fantasy life." The artist is nothing but a bureaucrat with a beret. The proximity between reality and fantasy indicates that the artist and the schizoid are both conjoined to and detached from reality. The crazy artist's intensely cathected urge for fantasy, freedom, ambition, wish, and drive is an effect of reality. But, at the same time, this drive is different from the conventional symbolic order. The artist may be a crazy person because he chooses urge over convention. But he is also a prosaic neurotic. His "fantasy life" is a scant permutation on the "reality" that he purports to "renounce."

This economy makes the madman or the artist profoundly neurotic or hysterical. This is a neurosis in bad faith. The artist and the psychotic are caught in the anachronistic dynamic of law and transgression or "reality" and its "renunciation." To be fair to the schizoid — but to properly crucify the artist — the psychotic disrecognizes the binary oppositional logic of conscious/unconscious and rule/trespass. The madman refutes the binary oppositions in the system. He cannot "renounce" either convention or fantasy. The schizoid cannot properly negate with any coherence. This is so except for a foreclosure. This *Verwerfung* is coincident with the system. The schizoid's good faith ensures his strict disqualification from any binary opposition, such as reality/fantasy, altogether.

The artist's choice of unruly desire over traditional duty reinscribes the conventional antagonistic logic of the system. This is so even as he pretentiously fancies himself a man of freedom, iconoclasm, ambition, wish, and fantasy. The artist of the primary process is isomorphic to the police officer. Both the artist and the cop "renounce" elements of the system in order to consolidate their haphazard identities and desires as either countercultural or law-abiding, and as either revolutionary or ordered. The artist is a cop with a trust fund. This eerie and uncomfortable correspondence indicates parallactic overlap. The primary process materializes at the same time as it also vanishes. The system Cs. emerges from the ether of the primary process. The secondary process enforces a logic which enables a conventional lifestyle for the subjects of culture. The ego-system wills the $-ism-system.

A close reading of the secondary process suggests that the "renunciation" of "fantasy life" in the choice of "reality" is the extimate obverse of this fantasy. This flip and twist also illuminate the modality of the visibility of the unconscious-work. The essence of the unconscious-work is to disclose itself amidst the gaps and holes of the assumptions in the tricks and treats of the ego-process. The unconscious invariably ruptures the series of negatives of the secondary process. This is so even if the affirmation of Unreason by the primary system is finally recuperated by the Ego-Logic of the system of Reason. There are inevitably moments in space and time in which the spontaneous interventions of the primary process — returns — destabilize the system and its conservative homoeostasis. These jiffs affirm the cracks in the edifice of $-ism. These returns open space for a schizophrenic artistry that may "renounce" the codes and conventions of the secondary process. The destabilization momentarily indulges in the Unreason of artifice. This art disturbs the private property relations of subjectivity and sociality.

Freud surmises that the artist mimics the role of the psychotic. The schizoid forecloses reality in favor of the demands of the *Es*. The instinctual urges of the id — desires, wishes, dreams, wants, needs, fancies, and so on — cannot be traced to an archaic and originary *Es*. They cannot be traced back to the *Ich*, the *Über-Ich*, and the outside world. There are no discrete origins for urges or spontaneous manifestations of the will to freedom, happiness, abandon, creativity, and so on. The artist is tightly shackled to the system. The ruse of $-ism is to instill in its subjects the fantasy of escape from a system in which law/transgression is the linchpin of its false promises. Foucault (1975) puts the will to liberate (sexuality) in transgression quite cynically. He writes,

> What sustains our eagerness to speak of sex in terms of repression is doubtless this opportunity to speak out against the powers that be, to utter truths and promise bliss, to link together enlightenment, liberation, and manifest pleasures; to pronounce a discourse that combines the fervor of knowledge, the determination to change the laws, and the longing for the garden of earthly delights.[24]

The poeticized nub is that transgression of the law is the condition of the idiot's *jouissance*. This cycle of rule/rebellion is central not only to the joys of sex and sexuality. Law and its infraction are also internal to an artistic creativity which seeks to overturn the prohibitions of the reality principle of the secondary process for the garden of earthly delights of the id.

This flower bed is simply a bad copy of the *Ich* and the *Über-Ich*. The artist sublimates his sexuality in the creation of art-objects for fantasy, play, and whimsy. This flirtation with the outskirts of "reality" in a bout with psychosis is tempered by the secondary ego-process. The system Cs. keeps the artist from slipping into an abyssal plunge of schizophrenic vertigo. The artist evades the madness of a feigned and funded flee from the secondary process of the ego. Freud suggests that a *Praxis* of symbolization is beyond the bounds of convention and code. Artistic *Praxis* is outside of the semantics and syntax of the system. But a creatively artistic and potentially schizoid selfhood and sociality are achievable and redeemable. The dalliance with the edges of Unreason may be situated within the reality of the dynamic between rule and break. But this is also a gesture toward the foreclosure of the symbolic and the descent into the Real. How does the artist avoid the fate of the schizoid's secret truth — of which the artist knows but nothing? The artist is a mere charlatan of Unreason. But is his art a superegoic mimicry whose injunctions to *Jouir!* the system and its transgressions make an escape from constraint a variant of conformity to normativity? This is precisely the theoretical deadlock that the pervert writes in order to evade.

There are avenues by which the artist can both avoid the failure of psychosis and achieve the success of creativity. Such a counterfeit victory is unimaginable for the authentic Unreason of the schizoid. Freud writes,

> Thanks to special gifts, however, [the artist] finds his way back to reality from this fantasy world by shaping his fantasies into new kinds of reality, which are appropriated by people as valid representations of the real world.[25]

The artist avoids the dizziness of psychotic foreclosure through the "special gifts" that he shares with others. These others confer a modicum of Reason onto the otherwise Unreasonable (fantasy, wish, ambition, and so on) representations in the artworks that she produces as artist. The schizoid's Unreason is tempered by the "special gifts" of the artist. Her translation of the urge into representation confers validity on the work of art. The pervert is an artist because she exercises a *Praxis* of the symbolization of the Real. This *praxis*tical exploitation of his "special gifts" does not facilitate the creation of art *per se*. Nor do these "special gifts" promise a modernist art for art's sake. Instead, the perverse performer body paints a political art. Perverse art consists of the politicization of aesthetics.

Perverse Art

Walter Benjamin elaborates the principle of the politicization of aesthetics as the specifically communist practice of the production of art against the aestheticization of politics. The latter is the reactive and totalitarian orientation toward art.[26] Perverse political art demonstrates the Real Symbolic. The artistic Signified/r is the closeted truth of the schizoid's Unreason. The pervert mobilizes art as the politics of the world disorder of the galaxy at the ends of the universe of an endless expansion. The talented pervert's creative *écriture* is the artistic and political will to *pervert the neurotic*. A communist's perverse art politicizes the aesthetics of representation. Freud says that "special gifts" return the artist from urge and instinct to reality and the secondary process. The artist oversees the superpositional conflation of fantasy and reality. The artist transitions back to the secondary process of reality from the unconscious-process of fantasy. This "shaping" denotes artistic processes, such as *papier-mâché* and sculpture. Freud vaguely refers to such processes as "new kinds of realities." But of what?

A passage of the act (or *Praxis*) transforms reality-fantasy into the void of the Real. The passage is not only a code for revolution. It is also a moniker for the translation between the primary process of the unconscious ("fantasy," which is itself secondary process reality) and the secondary-ego discourse ("reality," which is itself coincident with a primary-unconscious signifying chain). The abyssal Real must be impossibly written even if such *écriture* writes forever. The Real is glimpsed in the parallactic gap between the overlap of "fantasy" *qua* secondary ego-process and "reality" *qua* primary unconscious-signifier. This parallax demonstrates that the void of the Real is the process of shift and transition. The Real manifests in the shifting and translating between primary and secondary, ego and unconscious, and fantasy and reality as a "sameness which is not identical." Sameness⁺ is the name for the Unreason of the signifying chain. Sameness⁺ is the object of *Verwerfung* by the system of \$-ism.

The artist's "special gifts" can only distantly approach the truth of the Real. The artist safely errs on the side of neurosis against schizophrenia. But the community ("appreciated by people") of neurotics can confer a sliver of the reality principle upon this (Un)Reason. The reality principle enables the artist to rejoin the society of artists. This apparent disavowal says "yes" to fantasy but also "yes" to reality. But it does not say *Yes!* to the superpositional parallactic overlaptic voice of Sameness⁺. The artist achieves a balance between madman and neurotic. But the crucial component of the effort is the pedagogy of the symbolization of the artwork. Freud says: "Thus in a certain way [the artist] actually becomes the hero, king, creator, favorite he wanted to be, without having to make the enormous detour of actually changing the outside world."[27] Freud mockingly describes the ego-ideal of the artist. Freud's words are also perspicacious because they demonstrate that the artistic project is fundamentally about identification, identity, and the secondary-ego process of Being.

The pervert transforms intuition of the signifying chain and the world that it organizes. Embarrassingly, the artist seeks to become a hero and a king. The two projects may not be mutually exclusive. But Freud's articulation of artistic urge and return to instinct frames the artist as a reactive figure. The artist's lazy destabilization of the reality/fantasy division is already deconstructed by psychoanalysis as a fundamental precept. Easy artistic disruption animates distraction rather than commitment. The artist executes a transformation of the inside as opposed to the "outside world." The specifically perverse artist pixelates her magic. The distort-and-turn of the inside and the outside will be twisted and flipped. Deconstruction invites a symbolization of the world of fantasy. *Praxis* illuminates and transforms the world of the "outside" of reality, fantasy, and the secondary processes of the ego and its either/or logic of Reason. But can the minor straddle of the fantasy/reality dyad and the symbolic/Real dichotomy achieve a pedagogical subversion? Can the perverse ceramicist crack the kultural kiln with the kadre of primary process tricks: voodoo, hex, jinx, occult, sorcery, jiggery-pokery, mojo, theurgy, sortilege, and other mysterious signifiers of enchantment? The issue for the pervert and his artistic innovations and creative experiments is performance and demonstration. How are the Madness of Order, the overlap of $-ism and S, Sameness⁺, the Real Symbolic, the Real Signified/r, and so on — how are these closet truths of Unreason to be symbolized?

The pervert rigorously studies the secondary process. He does so in order to elucidate the trickery of the unconscious-work. Lacan famously claims that the unconscious is structured like a language of compression-metaphor and displacement-metonymy. The dexterous pervert must not merely note the paradox that the conscious is the unconscious. The pervert must also illuminate the dissimilarity between the system Cs. and the system Unc. The divergences between the primary process and the secondary process involve temporality, epistemology, and negation. The differences also refer to the split between text and image. The ordinariness of convention is the object of *Verwerfung* in the Real of the artist's mad creative exercise. The painter-by-number-artist is but a painter-by-letter-neurotic. Both are effects of a system which enforces dominant modes of signification and representation of the proper (ac)count. The artist prefers to become a hero and a king for his friends. Alternatively, the pervert labors to illuminate the system and transform its madness.

The pervert innovates alternative modalities of representation. These Other representations perturb the foundations of the otherwise tedious conventions of textualization. The pervert takes aim at the Real sublimity of the chains of text. The healthy artist garners signification in the symbolic order within a community of neurotic art critics. The neurotic artist lazily tries to "become" Hero, Inc., and King, M.F.A. The artist is a neurotic with an inflated sense of his own ego. The image of the neurotic artist is opposed to variants of schizoid rant and perverse *écriture*. Freud's version of the neurotic artist is of the dutiful subject of the simulation of the ego-ideal — hero, king, father, and so on. The artist mimics this regressive agency of idealization. He does so through the same normative process by which the male junior becomes dutiful husband, business executive, and proud father. The successful so-called artist inherits the father's lost dream. The artist mobilizes normativity in his theory and practice. In contrast, the pervert symbolizes the farcical figuration of any supposed reconciliation between reality and fantasy. The pervert slyly illuminates the utter conventionality of the mad-artist. The artist may be a hero-sculptor or a king-painter to his friends and family. But to the rest of us he is but a poseur whose ambitions follow law (transgression) rather than whimsy (revolution).

The artist reproduces the dynamic of law and its transgression. The perverse critic uncovers the massively puny residuum of the artist and his so-imagined transgression of the culture. The pervert's symbolization of this dynamic indicates a pivotal schizoid truth about the system. Perverse *Verleugnung* is the failed reconciliation of schizoid *Verwerfung* of reality and neurotic *Verdrängung* of instinct. The pervert's symbolization of the schizoid's Unreason is not the artwork of an atomistic artist. The primary process of the unconscious enables perverse splits which are beyond the break between knowledge and faith, and between "I know very well" and "but nevertheless." The pervert experiences a disunity in space. Fragmentation in the world ruptures the time of the divisions between conscious/unconscious, secondary/primary, and so on. The trick is to reveal the coincidence — Sameness⁺ — between the primary process and the system of the ego. The pervert's passion is to capture the overlap between madman and hysteric, between schizoid and neurotic, and between unconscious and conscious. The origin of the *Es* is the ego, the superego, and the outside world. The primary process of the dream-work is internal to the conscious structure of the system. The signifying chain and its centers are structured like hallucinations and delusions. The system is haywire.

TRUE DISBELIEVER

The division between fantasy/reality involves a separation of ambition, play, creativity, and spontaneity, on the one hand, and rule, convention, code, semantics, and syntax, on the other hand. This opposition emerges in Freud's (1936) text, "A Disturbance of Memory at the Acropolis." Freud discusses the vicissitudes of so-called disbelief. Disbelief is an incredulity or astonishment in faith or belief. Trust is tinged with dubiety and suspicion. Disbelief is a doubt that nonetheless believes. Disbelief is neither knowledge nor certainty nor science. Disbelief is the Outside of epistemology. Disbelief is an Other. Disbelief captures a peculiar riff on the pervert's "I know very well, but nevertheless…." The skeptical surprise of disbelief does not correspond to the pervert's "I know very well." The amazed doubt of disbelief is uncertain. A disbelief also sustains a faith. Disbelief is an optimistic hope in the absence of knowledge rather than a pessimistic dismissal on hiatus from knowledge. The one who disbelieves is amazed in a condition of doubt.

The basal distinction of disbelief is visible in the gap between the "yes" of an optimistic hope in the absence of knowledge, on the one hand, and the "No!" of a pessimistic dismissal in the absence of certainty, on the other hand. Disbelief and belief involve the obverse of the pervert's "I know very well." Disbelief and belief exactly do not know. "But nevertheless," (dis)belief happily and skeptically believes. The (dis)belief qualifies the open modification in knowledge and the deep certainty in belief. Disbelief implies an affirmation, confirmation, and repetition. Disbelief is more optimistic than pessimistic, and it is more hopeful than dismissive. The one who disbelieves is astonished by her own shock and awe. The disbeliever is prepared to be entranced by her own faith in an object which appears beyond credulity and reality. The object is subject to belief because it is beyond belief.

Subjects and Objects of Disbelief

A true disbeliever believes in disbelief. This is so despite the provisos and caveats of knowledge. But a true disbeliever does not believe in his own disbelief. This is so even if the disbelief ambivalently — optimistically, dismissively, pessimistically, hopefully — believes in the object of disbelief. The perverse true believer of disbelief disbelieves in the *Cogito*. The perverse true believer of disbelief questions any substantial origin or *arche* of thought. The true believer (dis)believes in his object ("knows very well"), but he (dis)believes in its subject ("I"). "But nevertheless," the true believer of disbelief suspends the consequences of the disappearance of the "I." He does so in order to embrace deeds in the absence of doers. The perverse true believer believes in the object of belief. He does so even as he disbelieves in the subject of this same belief. This aesthetic is a deconstructionist permutation of the split in the self in the perverse sensibility. Astonished, the one who disbelieves fades behind the incredible presence of the object of faith. The subject splits, and the *Cogito* blanches behind the incredulity of the object of the shock and awe of faith.

The neurotic does not share a belief because he is certain of his knowledge. This epistemology is organized by the conventional rules and codes of Reason. Tedious edicts and predictable mandates strictly delimit knowledge from belief, epistemology from divinity, and so on. The true divinist of perversion foreswears the "I" even as he sustains an uncertain knowledge ("I know very well"). Such knowledge is always displaced by a "but nevertheless." This "but nevertheless" invites alternative forms of orientation toward the world. These alternatives to *episteme* supplement but cannot destroy metaphysical epistemology. But the pervert's disbelief: claims belief in the deed rather than certainty in the doer; advances action over identity; and favors pleasures and bodies over identifications and egos. The neurotic subject of knowledge simply "knows very well, but knows very well." This repetition of knowledge belies a crack in the edifice of epistemology. Why must knowledge reiterate itself? The neurotic holds fast to the repetition of knowledge in the image of the self. The disbeliever exchanges certainty for astonishment as the self fades in the face of an object which cannot be assimilated into the codes of Reason.

Freud lurches in his account of the strange modality of negation of divine doubt. Disbelief is the sensibility of a perverse true believer who believes in the object of his belief but does not believe in the subject of his belief. The pervert does not believe in the "I" which otherwise disseminates among the traces of text. Freud says: "This disbelief is clearly an attempt to reject a piece of reality, but there is something strange about it."[28] Freud vitally undertheorizes this "piece of reality" which is rejected. But must this sliver of the world be the object of neurotic *Verdrängung*, schizophrenic *Verwerfung*, or perverse *Verleugnung*? Or is this "piece of reality" subject to a different modality of contradiction and retraction altogether? Is divine doubt the effect of a threat of the content of this sliver of the world? The astonishment that the "piece of reality" presents threatens certainty but inspires belief. This experience opens the impossible as the horizonal risk at the edges of Reason.

Humorously, Freud qualifies his obscure account of disbelief with "clearly." Freud's hazy outline of divine doubt ("there is something strange about it") is otherwise a chronicle of the abrogation of a slab of the world. This fragment of the symbolic order eludes Freud's estimable grasp. But this "clearly" is instructive because it indicates that the object of the negation is clarity. The object which is revoked from the field of the system of the Acropolis is a "piece of reality." This sliver of the world is otherwise plain, explicit, lucid, and coherent. The object of the divine doubter is obscenely present. The sliver of the world is only veiled because it is revealed. In a haze, the impossible object becomes — in shock and awe — real.

Freud accounts for a disbelief which is certainly clear. But it is clear about next to nothing. The "attempt" to uncover fails to negate ("reject a piece of reality"). But the strangeness of divine doubt is that it makes itself its own object. Perversely, the subject and object converge. The perverse true disbeliever may ask himself a question about his disbelief. "Do I know or do I believe — what is the subject of my disbelief?" The external object of divine doubt may be God, the signifying chain, the Other, and so on. This perverse object of disbelief is of secondary importance to the subject and the object of the referent of a divine doubt. Disbelief can only be an effect of the differential negativity in the chain of words. The pervert is not only unsure of himself because he is elevated to an object (subject) of the uncanny. The pervert is also in disbelief about his disbelief. The pervert is the divine doubter of his divine doubt. The one who disbelieves is in astonishment of the subject and the object. The divine doubter is exasperated by the presence of the object and, by extension, the presence of the subject.

Freud notes the peculiarity of disbelief. Divine doubt seeks to avoid pleasure. Disbelief is strictly inconsistent with *Eros* and the pleasure principle. Homeostasis seeks to intensify pleasure in the contraction of tension. Freud asks: "But why such disbelief about something which, on the contrary, promises to deliver a high degree of pleasure? Truly paradoxical behavior!"[29] The object of divine doubt is the Something is Missing of the maternal phallus. The befuddled male junior expects the missed *das Ding*. This object is absent and impossible. The offspring of disbelief in the maternal phallus "rejects a piece of reality" which is the system of phallocentrism and castration. "But nevertheless," the perverse true (dis)believer believes in divine doubt all the same. He (dis)believes in the phallocentric reality of castration. The object of the maternal phallus is ir-real and non-existent. This is so except in the fantasy scenario of the fetishist. The perverse disbeliever asserts faith in the object of the maternal phallus. The woman's missing penis is the object of a divine faith in the impossible. It is the object of the fetishist's belief — shock and awe — in its impossible presence.

Das Ding

Das Ding is also the object of divine doubt. Disbelief questions itself. The abject anagram and basal stumper of fetishism emerge. How can the pervert believe in a dimension which is Outside of knowledge, beyond phallocentrism, irrespective of empirical evidence, and against convention? How does the pervert believe in the presence of the absence that otherwise organizes anxious identity, unfulfilled desire, and impotent pleasure? The pervert's paranormal sorcery dismantles the entire foundation of Western humanism. The true disbeliever *qua* true believer believes in a divine doubt that simultaneously questions itself *qua* disbelief. The (dis)belief promises, as Freud says, "a high degree of pleasure." Disbelief is a doubt about the subjective orientation of the true disbeliever. Disbelief is also the source of pleasure and the paradoxical avoidance of it. Neurotically, the disbelief in divine doubt is the wellspring of displeasure. This divine doubt — What is? — puts into question the self-identity and the self-sameness of the word. Disbelief also haunts the neurotic with the specter of a double negation. The repressed and the return of the repressed are the same gesture.

This chicanery destroys the bi-level configuration of the conscious/unconscious division. Perversely, the maternal phallus *qua* imaginary phallus is to be avoided as unpleasurable because the pervert garners *jouissance* from representation and text. The fetishist foreswears reference. This is the case for both the penis and the clitoris. The maternal phallus or the sister's penis is only enjoyable as a nostalgic retro-glance for the neurotic. But the pervert discerns the Woman's penis as joyful. The Woman's penis is an in-process, in-action sexual relation. The sexual rapport is also constitutively veiled by representation. The Woman's penis is only a source of pleasure for the schizoid whose psychical structure is capable of the Other enjoyment. This *jouissance* pleases itself with a plenitude and a fullness in the absence of absence. The Real Penis is a metaphorical lubricant between binary oppositions. These oppositions are in fragile decomposition. The Real Penis is the avataric forerunner to the female penis. The Real Penis is a purely fictional figuration of the impossible joint between abstraction and materiality. The Real Penis prepares the neurotic and the pervert for their journeys toward the end of phallocentrism and castration and near the end of private property and scarcity. The Real Penis invites the neurotic to the Seyfert galaxy of communist queer (*a*)sexuality and the Pervert-Schizoid-Woman.

The maternal phallus must be an object of disbelief not because of its absence. The maternal phallus must be estranged and distanced from the subject. Even the fetishist veils its simulated presence with the shoe, lace, fur, and jockstrap. The maternal phallus is present in its obscenity, proximity, and contiguity. There is "something dubious and unreal about the situation" and this divine doubt. There is an "element of doubt about reality" in this divine doubt. The "reality" which is in abeyance is momentarily suspended from its otherwise nailed floorboards to Reason. The universe is questionable and simulacral. This is so even as it is conspiratorial and deceptive. The objects on the horizon are copies (of copies, and so on) without stable referents. A disposition toward disbelief arises as a caution not only about the positive ontology of Being. Divine doubt is also the object of the *not* of the negative, differential, and diacritical obverse of the ontological project.

The putting of ~~Being~~ under erasure destroys all copulatic relationships between objects. Man cannot answer the question, "What is?" This ontological impotence applies to any [penis] whatsoever. Man cannot even formulate the ontological question, "~~What is?~~" Ontology is a primitive intellectual escapade. Disbelief in an "element of doubt about reality" means that the subject ("I") disbelieves its own disbelief. I am in question. I am in dubiety, simulation, and unreality. This fierce scrutiny generates, as Freud says, a "feeling of estrangement." The object of this divine doubt is the maternal phallus. The subject is put into a quick state of "estrangement." This subject's identity and desire — being-in-the-world and being-with-others — are obliterated by the proximity to the referent. The maternal phallus is dreadful. The pervert's will to symbolize the system in both the absence and the presence of the maternal phallus is undone in the face of the mother's presence.

Dasein indicates a divine doubt which is a mistake. The being-there of the maternal phallus is both present and absent. This summarizes a disbelief *of* disbelief. The ir-real and un-reality of the object and the subject dissolve the relationship between the "I" and the symbolic order. This is certainly a "feeling of estrangement." Freud says: "What I am seeing there is not real.'"[30] What is the otherwise than "real"? What is the synonym of "not real" if not simply every other word in the system? Each of these words is defined in a negative and differential modality of the word for "not real." The "real" is the decenter around which the feelings of estrangement in divine disbelief circulate. Freud's various and unmanageable phenomenological descriptions of the subject and the object of disbelief indicate that a radical diacritics emerges around the object of disbelief. The maternal phallus is this reality. The maternal phallus is the excluded center of the system of the true disbeliever. The entire system of negativity converges around this hole in the symbolic order. The moment of its potential suture is the manifestation of the absolute positivity of the entire system.

Paradoxically, positivity irradiates from the negativity of diacritics. Positivity animates the parallactic coincidence and overlap of each word with every other word. Oxymoronic positivity demonstrates that there is neither gap nor fissure — neither negation nor knowledge — in the approach to the *makutu* of the entrant of the referent. This referent is the Woman's penis. Her penis sutures the vapidity in the symbolic plane. The maternal phallus installs the Logic of Difference⁺ or Sameness⁺. The signifiers return to signs, scarcities return to plenitudes, supplies/demands return to fullnesses, phallocentrisms return to the Sameness⁺ in difference of Penisclitoralcentrisms, and castrations return to specularities. The hierarchies, evaluations, nihilisms, and violences are effects of the general equivalence of comparison, contrast, and exchange. These symptoms of hatred dissipate upon the approach to the disbelief of the presence of the maternal phallus.

The maternal phallus is embodied in the sister's penis. The presence of the Woman's penis is the fundamental proviso of a radical transformation in sexual and capitalist relationships. The madman breathes. The pervert drops his pen. The Woman laughs. But, as Freud suggests, the "truly paradoxical behavior" of this divine doubt is that it remains an object of disbelief. Disbelief is faith rather than knowledge. But divine doubt is a faith which questions its own faith. Disbelief disbelieves the disbelief which is the object of the true disbeliever. The fetishist makes the maternal phallus present. This is so despite the constraints of Reason. Perversely, castration is sutured by the impossible presence of the sister's penis. On faith, the Woman is plenitude.

The maternal phallus is both subject and object, both active and passive, and both masculine and feminine. The maternal phallus and the Woman's penis are both penis and clitoris. The Woman's penis is the universal and general hermaphroditic subject and object of the future. The sexuality of communist queer (*a*)sexuality of hermaphroditism is an autoaffection of self-love of the autointercourse of the original sexuality of the infant.

Self-pleasure is the *Praxis* of (*a*)sexual hermaphroditism. When will man be ready to "know very well, but nevertheless"? When will man be ready to acknowledge that the (Wo)man and her young self-pleasurable hermaphroditic postgenital communist queer (*a*)sexuality have emerged after the *Aufhebung* of capitalism and the dawn of the plenitude of communism? When will man notice his clitoris? When will man embrace that Nothing is Missing?

Futurally, sex ends because there will be a Nothing is Missing of presence and plenitude in the sexual relation. An (*a*)sexuality displaces penis and clitoris with representation and simulation. The pervert inherits the text. The pervert does so because he finds himself bored with sex. The pervert prefers the masochistic increase in (un)pleasurable tension of the foreplay of courtly love. The pervert eschews the neurotic decrease in (un)pleasurable release in the phallocentric money shot of male orgasm and ejaculation of conventional desire and its goal of the capture of a finally irrelevant and arbitrary object. How will man approach this future of the text without sex — *(a)sextuality*?

The twin funeral directors — psychoanalysis and deconstruction — announce the end of the history of man in the subordination of Being to *différance* and to the Other. But psychoanalysis and grammatology do so without a satisfactory successor to the transcendence of the symptomatology of the system of $-ism. Can the pervert and the fetishist illuminate the system at the same time as they promise its transformation? Or must the talent of the *écriture* of the pervert be subordinate to the logic and the economy which are the object of the pervert's critique? Can the fetishist's enterprise to re-present representation espy success in his failure and achieve victory in his defeat? But if castration and lack are constitutive of Western textuality and sexuality, then how can the clitoris be tweaked in order to elevate such a scrap, as Lacan says in the *Seminar* on the ethics of psychoanalysis (1959-1960), to the dignity of *das Ding*? What is sex after the phallus? How does representation become the medium of an (*a*)sex of the future?

Chapter Six

The Pervert (3): Betwixt Unreason

I can stand brute force, but brute reason is quite unbearable. There is something unfair about its use. It is hitting below the intellect.

— Oscar Wilde

This book formulates the master signifier of the "Pervert-Schizoid-Woman." Lacan says that the master signifier is invented by the hysteric's engagement with the magical silence of the analyst. My master signifier articulates an other-than-human form of life. This master signifier indicates a beyond of the economy of $-ism. The Pervert-Schizoid-Woman gestures toward an outside of the rule of *le propre*. The master signifier reinvigorates an Order of Madness. This Other inspires the Spirit of the System as Becoming-Perverse, Becoming-Schizoid, and Becoming-Woman. I present Pervert-Schizoid-Woman as a thinking, being, and living. This existence is both resistant to $-ism and invitational to a life beyond its values. My project begins with the perverse, schizoid, and feminine assumption that there is something else in the symbolic and in the Real — in the people's galaxy — which will yield greater enjoyment and renewed ethics. This master signifier is born of the (this) hysteric's rebellious engagement with the obscene tradition of the master and the wry silence of the psychoanalyst. The doctor's kind but firm quietude permits space and time for the hysteric to invent what can best be described as an authentic word which summarizes her desire. The purpose of this chapter is to explicate the techniques of the pervert's exposition of the schizoid's Unreason.

BECOMING-OTHERWISE

The early hysterics madly raved against the world. But they encountered dismissal and ridicule from husbands, fathers, and other male figures of authority. Freud listened to these crazy Women. Freud may have twisted their words and turned their desires against them. But he listened and attended to these Women and their speech. The psychoanalyst listens and hears. The essence of the master signifier is its form and materiality — *qua* signifier — rather than its content and ideality — *qua* signified. My master signifiers in this text are *a priori* empty. The signification of these master signifiers is mostly unmarked and impassive. But this is exactly their purpose and asset. The content and signified which unfold in the textual mobilization of these master signifiers are made possible by the surrounds and traversals of the words, gestures, vocabularies, letters, alphabets, and signifiers which animate this book. The Pervert-Schizoid-Woman and $-ism are the Real toward which the symbolic *Praxis* of this book in authorship and readership approaches. My job is the impossible enterprise to project content of the signified into the form of the Real. The Real is the distant horizon. The Real resists but also tempts my interpretive endeavor to write the impossible.

"What is" — Lacan?

The definition of the pervert is complex and contested. The work in this book will be to outline the pervert's selfhood. But I do so with experimentalism and blasphemy. My pervert is not your pervert. This is the essence of perversion and fetishism. There is no unitary and unified — self-same and self-identical — pervert because he is a figuration of a subjectivity and a sociality which are deeply opposed to essence. In addition, the pervert is rife with inconsistencies and mismatches. The pervert's identity and desire are appropriated for various and variant ideological purposes. I seize the pervert as archetypal of the future and the *tout autre*. The pervert is the Outside to patriarchal phallocentrism, capitalist scarcity, and the sign. Patriarchy, capitalism, and language are organized by the dictum that Something is Missing.

But I am also enamored to the pervert because he is the psychoanalytic character who most closely resembles the writer. The scribe's project is to symbolize the Real and make coherent the Unreason of the world. This project is crucial not simply for academic reasons. The dial is also decisive because it encourages emancipatory practices in the world. In a brilliantly subtle gesture in his first *Seminar* on the ego (1953-54), Lacan answers his own question — "What is perversion?" — with a series of negative definitions (perversion is not) which concludes with: "It is something else in its very structure."[1] First to note is that Lacan posits the ontological question of "What is?" in relationship to the pervert. But then he proceeds to negate not only the pervert's ostensible traits and qualities but also the ontological question as such. The center of perversion sustains a radical subversion of the ontological-philosophical project. This deconstruction is associated with Derrida and his grammatology. But the predecessor of the *destruktion* of the extant order of Being is Heidegger and his scrutiny of the metaphysical tradition. The pervert contests ontology and metaphysics. The pervert does so even if he cannot possibly transcend these extant schemes. The pervert's job is to symbolize and represent this project as the practical structure of the Madness of Order. The pervert's text summons a theoretical exit from $-ism and Western modalities of thinking, being, and living.

The negativity of Lacan's assessment of perversion is a witty reference to Freud's idea that the pervert is the "negative" of the neurotic. Lacan's cheeky description of perversion solicits the massive negation in the structuralist system. This negative ontology (what is not) also illuminates the "something else" of the coincidence of desire and *objet a*, and *Trieb* in aim. Lacan writes,

> What is perversion? It is not simply an aberration in relation to social criteria, an anomaly contrary to good morals, although this register is not absent, nor is it an atypicality according to natural criteria, namely that it more or less derogates from the reproductive finality of sexual union. It is *something else in its very structure* (my emphasis).[2]

The subject who poses the question of perversion refers to the ontological query: "What is?" This posited question does not imply that perversion is essential. The query does not indicate that perversion is situated within a metaphysics of presence. Rather, Lacan's ontological inquiry is a proleptic response to the series of negative defenses against an essence. This split in perversion is noncore and inessential. But the split is also simultaneously indispensable and needed. The impossible question of essence is necessarily essential — But why? Simply, the question is posed. Heidegger demonstrates that the human being *Dasein* being-there is the being-in-the-world and being-with-others who has Being and the ontological query as an essential curiosity and project. The structure of care is a concern for "What is?" Not only is the question of "What is?" a regard which cannot be answered. But worse, the question of ontology cannot even be posed. The Being of the "is" of "What is?" is destructured by the grammatological economy of the negative and differential structure of the signifier and by the nullity which is at the basis of Being.[3] The (in)essence of perversion provokes Lacan's series of negative definitions of *nots*. These *nots* can be interpreted as an allusion to the negativity at the center of Saussure's semiology.

Saussure's ~~signifier~~ is not present. Heidegger's ~~Being~~ is not present. Lacan's dictum *lettre pour l'être* — Meaning for Being — marks the transition from the Real of infancy to the symbolic of adulthood. The transition is under erasure — ~~*lettre pour l'être*~~ — and even *pour* is sublimely unrepresentable because *pour est pas pour: ~~lettre pour l'être~~*. The reduction of Being and Meaning to a deconstructive under erasure is itself under erasure: ~~Being and Meaning~~ (and so on). The signifier is what it is not. The signifier is not what it is. This summarizes the conceptual discovery of Saussure's intervention. The signifier is always otherwise than and elsewhere from "itself." Lacan's point about perversion is that it mobilizes this diacritical negativity. The pervert is "something else" because he is not what he is. The signifier is not present, as Saussure makes clear, and Being is not present, as Heidegger discovers.

Neither/nor but —

An analysis of Lacan's definition of perversion illustrates the resistance of perversion to the conventional psychoanalytic conceptualizations of perversion. Lacan begins the exegesis that perversion is "not simply" a litany of qualifications. The pervert's complexity exceeds simplicity. But this easiness is simultaneously included in perversion. Perversion is both complex and obvious. This both/and "but nevertheless" is a component of the indispensable essence of perversity. First, perversion is plainly neither an abnormal nor deviant set of acts or identities. Nor is perversion an odd or eccentric inadequacy to moral criteria. Neither is perversion a freakish or strange irregularity from nature. Nor is perversion a disparagement of heterosexual reproductive union. "But nevertheless," perversion is — "something else in its very structure."

The grammatical — syntactical and semantic — structure of this minor revision of Lacan's ontological (what is) approach to the essence of perversion is organized not by the neurotic either/or nor by the perverse both/and. Rather, Lacan's definition of perversion is structured by the *neither/nor*. This neither/norism can be classified as the schizoid-deconstructionist aesthetic and sensibility. The neurotic either/or enforces an existential decisionism of choice: either both/and or neither/nor. In contrast, the perverse both/and disturbs the neurotic's either/or binarism. Perversity includes both exclusive options of both either/or and both/and. The pervert's form of the affirmative "yes, yes" is forever recursive: both either/or and both/and and either either/or or both/and and both either/or and both/and and either/or and (and so on). Alternatively, the schizoid-deconstructionist's neither/nor is oriented toward the Other. The horizon of schizophrenia is the *tout autre* which is yet to arrive in presence. The *tout autre* is out-standing, not-yet, and in-coming. The Other is Becoming what it is not (yet). The neither/nor structure is the penultimate grammatical organization of both deconstruction and schizophrenia. Neither/norism is the essential construction of the extant symbolic order. Neither/norism is the fundamental arrangement of the system in its constitutive madness.

The system understands itself as *au fond* neurotic. But the core organization of $-ism in its crazy *finite infinity* or *infinite finity* is substitution. This paradoxical temporality is strictly deconstructionist and schizophrenic. The talented pervert must perform a feat that Lacan half-says in his negative elucidation of the *comme-ci comme-ça* of perversion. The pervert demonstrates this neither/norism. But the caveat is that such neither/nor — but — can only be symbolized in the both/and design of perversion. As Octave Mannoni's patient uttered: "I know very well, but nevertheless...." The neurotic's either/or articulates the "yes, no" as either yes or no. The pervert's both/and symbolizes the "yes, yes" *qua* an affirmation. This double-yes endorses both yes and yes and either yes or No! and both yes and yes and No! and No! (and so on). This "yes, yes" affirms an infinite recursion of a superpositional oscillation. In contrast, the schizoid's neither/nor writes an ecstatic orgasmic *Yes!* of the simultaneity of a profound indecision. The schizoid enacts neither the neurotic's yes/No! nor the pervert's yes-No! — but the schizoid yesNo!yesNo!yes or "Yes I said Yes I will Yes!" but yet "but nevertheless." The schizoid and deconstructionist's openness to the *tout autre* perversely aestheticizes the galaxy. A temperamental phallic function is suspended in the future. This *tout autre* promises that the past not only will have been in the future. The Other also promises that the past has not happened yet. As Lacan says of perversion: "It is something else in its very structure." But what? — may we even ask?

And Else

This *something else* is otherwise a simultaneity of neurosis and psychosis. Perversion is otherwise than itself. Perversion is both/and "but nevertheless" neither/nor. Essence is a concept which is acutely destabilized in Saussure's account of language. But the essence of perversion is that it is *something else*. A "What is?" of ontological Being is antecedent to the otherwise (*else*) of perversion. There must be *something* which is symbolized as a metaphysics of presence. This Being precedes the otherwise *else* of the perverse aperture to the Other. A psychoanalytic context unveils yesNo!yesNo!yes this *something* as the object which is missing. It does so in order to elicit the *else*. This *else* is the otherness which supplements *something*. The *something* is the signifier to be amplified with further signification and even with the elusive transcendental signified. Something is Missing in the antecedence to the Other (*else*). This antecedence is perversion. Perversity is a supplement to female lack, the Woman's castration, and the clitoris. The "else" refers to the referential penis *qua* archetypal fetish-substitute (shoe, lace, fur, and jockstrap). The "else" represents the Nothing is Missing (or else) of the signified of perversion. The interval among Something is Missing (Lacan: *it is*), Something is Still Missing (Lacan: *something*), and Nothing is Missing (Lacan: *else*) demonstrates that the metonymic movement of fetishism is a triple axis with Johnny Weir's penis. But what are the chronologies, contents, and forms of this icy sexual rapport among objects?

This can only be answered in Lacan's unethical capitulation to give way on his (my) desire to discern perversion "in its very structure." The structure of perversion determines a paradoxical affirmative negativity. This can best be summarized as yesNo!yesNo!yes *Yes!* Perversion reveals the odd parallactic overlap of Something is Missing in castration and scarcity and Nothing is Missing in plenitude and abundance. But what is a structure if not the architecture which is buoyed by the function of orientation, balance, and organization? This coordination is the structure that Derrida describes as the limit of thought. Lacan illuminates that perversion is a structure *qua* veil. Man does not know the essence of a structure. This is so even if man can recognize the center. This center makes the structure both operative and dysfunctional. My project in this book is to articulate the Madness of Order. My enterprise is to textualize the essence of the structure of the sign in language, the commodity in capitalism, and the desire in sexuality. I discover that the ontological query "What is?" *qua* structure is a question of the metaphysics of thought. This question puts the entirety of structure in a flaccid condition that only Ben's penis can revive. A perverse structure is entirely devoid of the father. Paternity is not only neither dead nor alive. The father's presence and absence constitute a radical *nonappearance*. There is no father as such. This is the reason that the *père-version* or the other version of the father must be "something else in its very structure." The structure must be a structure which is otherwise than a structure. The essence of this system is as yet undetermined and undecided. There is no essence to perversion. This book can only circumcisionally circumlocute — *cut* — around the Real in the symbolization of the impossibility of the Real Pervert. This book on the pervert is the constitutive outside around which the hollowed vase of perversity emerges in its *something else*. The *else* is a Nothingness of — *qua* value and *qua* communism and *qua* (*a*)sexuality — Nothing is Missing. But then, why write?

From Identity and Desire to Jouissance

The future figuration of selfhood and sociality revises the oedipal projects of identity and desire. The future identification outstrips the broken mirror of narcissism and the desire for ownership of private property. The Pervert-Schizoid-Woman represents an ideal for a want-to-be that no longer wants-to-be. The Pervert-Schizoid-Woman embraces an ideal which is no longer an idealization. The Pervert-Schizoid-Woman eclipses the sad failures of desire's attempts to entrap the object. The Pervert-Schizoid-Woman represents an ideal for a want-to-have that no longer wants-to-have. The Pervert-Schizoid-Woman invites an ideal which is no longer organized by the ideology of scarcity and the terror of castration. This *tout autre* foreswears the two fundamental subjective and Spiritual symptoms of man as they are diagnosed by psychoanalysis. The primary symptoms are identity (want-to-be) and desire (want-to-have). The pervert is not obsessed with identity (to be) or desire (to have). Rather, the Pervert-Schizoid-Woman concerns herself with *jouissance*. He makes enjoyment the law (pact). Her duty is to inspire *jouissance* in the Other. The pervert is the instrument of the Other's pleasure.

Enjoyment is the essence of the pervert's project. *Jouissance* is the *modus operandi* of his verity of symbolic articulations. The pervert's will to *jouissance* is instructive and pedagogical. The imperative to pleasure is also witty and droll. Perverse enjoyment is both scholastic and merry. The pervert displaces the $-istic oedipal project of identity. The pervert avoids the oedipal frustration and competition among a diverse plurality of identities. Each of these identities is otherwise in competition for a fabricated limited quota of resources. The pervert also spurns desire and its unsatisfied pursuit of the ever-recessional *objet petit a*. This object inevitably refuses to please its neurotic admirer. The pervert substitutes an anxious world of identity and desire with the free pursuit of the Other pleasure. This *tout autre* enjoyment is the manic dance trance, the joyful morning after, and the *omg!* orgasm with Taylor's penis. Lacan associates this enjoyment with femininity. He identifies a feminine *jouissance* with the not-whole and non-knowledge.[4] This *not* is the obverse of the positive ontological question of: "What is?" The Pervert-Schizoid-Woman flirts with *jouissance* and with the Other as its source. This Other is coextensive and coterminous — expansive in spatiotemporality — with the entirety of the galaxy.

The *arche* of trance and joy and *omg!* is all of the points and lines in the four dimensions of the universe: first, the dimension of space; second, the dimension of time; third, the dimension of the unconscious (which is an absence of the second temporal dimension); and fourth, the dimension of *Praxis*. At the limit of the dimensionality of the ever-expansive universe, *Praxis* is the *arche* of all *jouissance* as its wellspring for the Pervert-Schizoid-Woman. The pervert refuses to deploy her desire as "a defense," as Lacan says, "against going beyond a certain limit in *jouissance*."[5] In contrast, the neurotic defends against pleasure with desire. The latter becomes attached to objects which resist the capture of desire and the momentary effluvium of joy. The pursuit of desire — *objet a, a, a, a, a*, and so on — inevitably encounters the resistance of the object. This opposition is the source of narcissism, aggression, and anxiety. In contrast, the pervert dallies with pleasure and with the *Trieb's* encirclement in the aim/less wander around the objects of desire. The pervert does so without the temptation to make these slippery objects private property. This *Trieb* frees the subject from the bonds of ownership and *le propre*. The pervert is the one, in Lacan's words, "who pursues *jouissance* as far as possible."[6]

The pervert extends pleasure beyond the ordinary pleasure principle of a regulated tension and release in the orga(ni)sm. The pervert gestures toward the beyond of the pleasure principle in the death drive of *Thanatos*. This will toward the *petit mort* animates an aim/less destruction. But it does so always in a vertiginous relationship to constructive *Eros*. The will to death is the *telos* of an orgasmic Other *jouissance*. This *tout autre* finally demolishes the self-same and the self-identical in favor of a cosmos of quarks, fractals, strings, and bodies-in-pieces. Freud's theory of the pleasure principle (constancy and Nirvana) holds that unpleasure is the increase of a frenzied and frenetic tension against a pleasure of the decrease of a depressive and regretful return to the homeostatic regulation of the system. This scheme of pleasure is deeply conservative. The Freudian principle of pleasure suggests that frenzied revolution is the formation of unpleasure and that cautious conservatism is the source of pleasure.

The pervert's *jouissance* is beyond this reactive homeostatic regulation of the system. The mechanism of perverse *jouissance* is foreplay. This is the modality of (*a*)sexuality. Freud identifies this modality of foreplay with the vicissitudes of a drive whose will is the absence of an otherwise irrelevant *Objekt*. Lacan also associates this aim/less foreplay with the rituals of Medieval courtly love. Deleuze's early book on masochism (1967) also identifies this desexualization as an integrant of perversion. This masochism resists the dysfunctions of the dynamics of law/transgression between *Ich* and *Über-Ich*. The pervert's passion "as far as possible" is his gesture toward the yet-to-come of the universe. This solar system forsakes the frustrated projects of identity (diversity, identity politics, and so on) and desire (sex, sexuality, gender, and so on). The beyond of the pleasure principle — "as far as possible" — is the condition of the pervert's discovery of an (*a*)sexuality. This queerness overturns the hierarchies of genitalia. Queerness disturbs the hierarchization of the penis *qua* the final glorious referent of all of sexuality. But what is a penis? The destruction of ontology clarifies the limits of the philosophical project. Not only can man not know the "What is?" of any object being-in-the-world and being-with-others. The sublime unrepresentability of ~~Being~~ (A ≠ A) is such that man cannot even formulate the question of "What is?" altogether. Man on the moon, iPads, nuclear weapons in silos, cures for polio, treatments for cancer, caffeine-free diet sodas, free love, and Matt's jockstrap — and we cannot even symbolize the question: "What is?" — the penis?

Toward Perversion

The neurotic represses enjoyment with the mother and with his own penis in favor of identification with the ego-ideal of the father. This exchange is an effect of the male junior's sight of the female junior's clitoris and the fantasmatic castration anxiety in the bewildered psyche of the male junior. The masculine subject capitulates to the fear of potential loss. He (re)produces the norms and conventions of Western culture. Alternatively, the Pervert-Schizoid-Woman liberates pleasure from economic, sexual, and textual repression. He avoids castration and the normative ego-ideal. The Pervert-Schizoid-Woman emancipates her desire from the economy of $-ism. $-ism is shorthand for the narcissism and aggression of the oedipal subject. $-ism stows away *jouissance* behind the sword and shield of a vulnerable and anxious narcissism.

The Pervert-Schizoid-Woman seeks the *jouissance* on the obversive flip-side of desire's anxious encirclement of an elusive object of identification (ego-ideal) and desire (*objet petit a*). As Dany Nobus writes, the pervert is "creating an alternative symbolic order in which *jouissance* holds pride of place."[7] This universe decrees the Other — perverts, of all sorts — who desires the play land, amusement park, and orgy fest of *jouissance* rather than the private condo, gated community, and office park of identity and desire. *Jouissance* can hold "pride of place" because it is valued by the community above the doomed projects of the identities of *my* gayness, *my* blackness, *my* manliness, *my* jockstrap, and so on. *Jouissance* can hold "pride of place" because it overruns the projects of the desires of *my* needs, *my* wants, *my* entitlements, *my* rights, *my* loves, and so on. The pervert refuses to forsake enjoyment for the trite jollies of identity and desire.

That said by *my* words, what symbolic order privileges *jouissance* as the principle of organization? The index of the distinction between the society of identity and desire, on the one hand, and the culture of euphoria and rapture, on the other hand, is the gap between desire and drive, between *désir* and *Trieb*, and between masculine idiotic *jouissance* and feminine enjoyment. The Pervert-Schizoid-Woman seeks others who *desire* *jouissance*. This is a paradoxical reversal of words. The obverse questions the primacy of desire in psychical organization *in toto*. The pervert invents a world in which Spirited ravishment rather than anxious identity and insatiable desire reigns supreme. The impossible horizon of this book consists of this utopia of manic ecstasy: "I know very well that identity, desire, and the very structure of fantasy ($-ism) prohibit *jouissance*, but nevertheless (Pervert-Schizoid-Woman)...." The unconscious is the *mise-en-scène* of a liberated pleasure of otherwise run-amuck desires, truths, and wishes. These latent contents are scrambled by an ultimately outmatched dream-censor. The law otherwise spontaneously creates the neurotic symptoms of wild dreams, aborted jokes, jocular slips, and phantom limbs.

The primary process of the unconscious is the vocabulary of pleasure. The word of the dream-censor muddles the latent desires which otherwise only present truth in a madcap form. But the superego also enables the primary process to express its truths in the exuberances and felicities of an inhibited and liberated primary process. Law is not simply the inverted ladder of desire. Perversely, law (pact) is the condition of possibility of *jouissance*. The *law of enjoyment* is the tearoom and bathhouse of the primary process. The law of enjoyment is the space — without time — of the painful delights of the pervert's text. The pervert discovers the representability of the schizoid's secret truth of Unreason. This truth is the Madness of Order of the West. This psychosis is articulated in the field of the unconscious and its techniques of condensation and displacement.

Psychoanalytic critics, such as Zizek, criticize the pervert as the instrument of the law. The pervert supposedly forces the coincidence of the clever *jouissance* of the law and the imperative *Jouir!* of the superego. But the revolutionary point of the perverse structure is that it twists and turns the division between pleasure and law in an extimacy which undoes any coherent (non)coincidence. This perverse *moil* deconstructs these (all) distinctions. The pervert relishes a confusion which cannot disentangle the *Über-Ich* from the *Es*, the masculine from the feminine, and the other from the Other. The pervert disorganizes the dominant (all) structure. The pervert's artistic endeavor outlines the blueprints of the system which reveal its essence *qua* madness. But how does the revolutionary triplet of the Pervert-Schizoid-Woman present the map of this territory if the neurotic confuses the territory for the map? Are the neurotics already perverse? If so, what is the parallactic gap which separates the "one" and the "same" map from the nomads who are lost amidst the territory?

Another climacteric question pertains to the centrality of the Other *jouissance* in the economy of perversion. Derrida maintains that the function of the center is the expression of the excluded finite sign of infinity. Is *jouissance* banned from the structure of the Pervert-Schizoid-Woman? Is pleasure excluded even as it is the master signifier of the orientation, balance, and organization — generalized harmonization — of the system of perversion and fetishism? If so, then the Other *jouissance* is Outside of the structure which it systematizes and arranges. The negation of this *jouissance* to the Outside *qua* the excluded function of the entire system of the future is a *Verleugnung*. This exclusion is an "I know very well that *jouissance* is the organizational principle of the Pervert-Schizoid-Woman, but nevertheless" — and this is crucial — "this excess *jouissance qua* the function of the system returns as the disturbance of the signifying chain from the resistance of the Real." The surplus *jouissance* of the function *qua* the disbarred center of the system is the object of a neurotic *Verwerfung* in the Real. This absolutely unspeakable and unwriteable return to the system is the condition of the (de/re)stabilization of the structure.

The excluded excess *jouissance* must be foreclosed in order to enable alternative metaphors to occupy the position of the center — such as pervert, schizoid, Woman, Sameness⁺, Real Symbolic, Sprit of the System, S, Signified/r, $-ism, and so on. Other pleasure must also be foreclosed in order to facilitate the return of a surplus — plenitude and abundance — which disrupts phallocentric castration and capitalist scarcity. The merit of the Other *jouissance* is that its negation by the masculine system returns to the system as an excess. This surplus disturbs the simple homeostatic tension/release model of pleasure. The Other reminds the system of its foreclosed masochism. Excess disturbs the regulation and governmentality of enjoyment. The tired dynamic of law/transgression is ruptured by the foreplay of courtly love and its detailed codes and artful rules of the masochistic extension of *jouissance*.

SURPLUS PERVERSIONS

Freud's later theory of perverse disavowal and psychical splitting gestures toward an alternative subjective and Spiritual — $-ism — and social and systemic — *le propre* — form of life. This existence deviates from the castration deadlock of the neurotic and the Unreasoned containment of the madman. Freud describes the trinity of disavowal, psychical splitting, and castration in his brief but memorable text, "Splitting of the Ego in the Defensive Process" (1938). He describes the vicissitudes of fetishism as paradigmatic of the structure of Becoming. My reiteration is: willing having beening Becoming Being — a reprisal of Becoming which references the past, the present, the future and then (re)references the return to the past into the future in the constitution of a deferred — willing having beening Becoming. This account of a temporality of Becoming-Nothingness is a project that necessarily supersedes my own work in this book.

My claim about perversity is that fetishism unsettles two central principles of $-istic psychical organization: castration anxiety (private property, identification, ego-ideal, renunciation of desire and enjoyment); and binary opposition (what Saussure names as "distinction" and "opposition" on the level of the sign). These distinct oppositions include such binaries as man / Woman, my penis / your penis, Harold's penis / Nick's penis, my penis / Nick's penis, and so on. The pervert's symbolization of the madman's secret truth of Unreason contests the oppositional structure of $-ism. Perverse text deconstructs *arche* and origin into trace and the Same⁺. The pervert's pen also supplants the central organizational conditions of $-ism with relationality and constructionism.

Relationship and construction are the foundations of Saussure's theory of value. This theory of value comprises the fundamental precepts of the Madness of Order and the schizophrenia of the system of words. Relationship and construction destabilize the economy of ownership in the domains of politics, economics, and culture. In politics, relationality and constructionism undermine such theories and practices as private property, copyright, trademark, law, duty, and responsibility. These ideologies are disrupted by the parallactic gap of the (im)proper. In economics, the displacement of systems of *le propre* upsets the ideas and institutions of supply/demand, scarcity, rent, profit, and interest. In culture, ownership of thought, affect, body, and speech *qua* integrant foundations of $-ism is undone by the breaches of the Marxist abolishment of private property.

In the text on the *Spaltung* (1938), Freud frames the offspring's reaction to maternal lack as a psychical trauma. This breach is between the inside and the outside. It is a gap that Freud found at the origins of the neuroses of the Great War. He presents traumatic neurosis as the origin of his discovery of the death drive and the compulsive repetition of displeasure. Note: Freud identifies the offspring's discovery of castration with the horrors of the Great War. This battlefield of lack (in which an estimated 37 million people died) forces the offspring to confront or to deny the reality of the castration threat. But the pervert's disavowal chooses both. The choice that the offspring faces is framed through the lens of the $-istic neurotic either/or. This is a forced choice.

The either/or choice — castration and reality or plenitude and delusion — organizes the divisions of the order of *le propre*: mine/yours, ours/theirs, and his/hers. This series of possessive qualifiers demonstrates the coded capitalism of private property in the signifying chain. Forced choice of urge or reality — desire or order — confronts all subjects of culture as the price of admission to $-ism. The subject must be either man or Woman (the hysteric's dilemma), either dead or alive (the obsessional's question), and so on. The culture fiercely forbids a deconstruction of these binary oppositions. The subject has the choice to be either man or Woman (but not both), the decision to be either gay or straight (but not both), the opportunity to be either right or wrong (but not both), the choice to be either adored or disliked (but not both), the invitation to be either white or black (but not both), and the possibility to be either so on or so on (but not both).

The pervert's "I know very well, but nevertheless…" is a quick revisionary trespass of the neurotic's either/or economy. This perverse subversion of binary logic is a fervent threat to the order of the West. Perverse deconstruction of opposition reduces the positivity of the sign (distinctive, oppositional, and essential) to the negativity of the signifier (differential, relational, and constructed). The menace of deconstructive perversity is to the integrity — self-identity and self-sameness — of the word. The signifier is the grammatological risk of the system. This is so even as the signifier is also the internal condition of the (dys)function of $-ism. The diacritical model of meaning-making in negation and relation in the signifier wreaks havoc on the system. The word in distinction and opposition organizes itself as present, ahistorical, balanced, combined, and stable. The system is oriented, balanced, and organized by sign-substitutions (materialities joined to abstractions) rather than by signifier-substitutions (materialities). The transformation of the codes of order from sign to signifier promises a fiery meltdown for a meek and compromised system. The structure is of the madness of the signifier. The system enforces an object which it is unable to prosecute: a stable system of words. The word is flaccid. The jockstrap is hard.

At first rupture, the system neurotically forecloses (*rejet névrotique*) this Real Signifier or Signified/r. It does so in order to discharge its own peril. The terrible paradox of the Madness of Order is that the greater the administration of order, the more intense the counterresistance of the madness of this system. The order is outmatched by itself. The West must finally capitulate to the signifier and abandon the values of $-ism: privacy, property, ownership, lack, castration, opposition, narcissism, aggression, anxiety, and so on. This dialectical inversion returns the order to the same place of the Real. This Real is already in its place. The pervert farcically contests a simulated law. But the pervert does so only insofar as he pretends in fetishistic (dis)simulation that resistance and prohibition are obversive flip-sides of the same political flim-flam dumb show. The peculiar spectatorship of such an illywhacker of a performance is that the neurotics of the order are blind to the swindle. The neurotics are the mere effects of the neurotic (psychotic) *Verwerfung* of the Real and its return *qua* the system of order.

Hysterics and obsessionals view trespass and rule as binary oppositions. Each opposition is equal and identical to itself because each is unequal and different and equal and identical to the other — or Sameness⁺. Bizarrely, this uninformed quackery is spot-on. This is so even from the pervert's skewed and doubled perspective. In *Three Essays* (1905), Freud hastily says that the pervert is the negative of the neurotic.[8] But the neurotic is also the negative of the pervert. Both neurotic and pervert are the positives of each other. The Other (*of* the Other *of* the Other, and so on) side of the equation (*of* the equation *of* the equation, and so on) is lost on Reason and the Madness of Order. The Real is the sublime object around which the pervert desperately assays to speak and to write the abjectly Unreasonable. This Real is *Verwerfung* only to be returned at the moments in which the pervert and the schizoid intervene. The pervert's expeditious aim/less dawdle and visceral happy(less) trudge are the mirthful context of the so-called law. This *Trieb* enables the pervert to enjoy an expanded *jouissance* for himself.

The Splitting of the Forced Choice in the Process of Suture

Freud presents the offspring with two alternatives in the face of maternal lack. These two choices mimic the offspring's own negotiation of castration in the original *mise-en-scène* of the discovery of sexual difference with the female junior. Freud says,

> It [the male junior] must now decide either to recognize the real danger, give way to it and renounce the instinctual satisfaction, or to disavow reality and make itself believe that there is no reason for fear, so that it may be able to retain the satisfaction.[9]

The female junior's difference is not an empirical castration but only a morphological difference. This morphological difference is the "real danger." This is so because the male junior (and Freud) translate *difference* in morphology into *deficit* of signification. The transcription from morphology to signification and from *difference* to *deficit* introduces two irrefragable inquiries. Both of these queries are unanswered. First, how is materiality converted into abstraction? — in theory, in practice, and in an always already combination of the body and the mind, and the physical and the speculative? The Real Penis is not the symbolization of resistance but the (*a*)sexualization — (*a*)sextualization — of the Real. Second, how is plain and innocent difference returned to deficit and the signification of hierarchy and nihilism?[10]

The Freudian phrase "give way" to the menace of castration suggests a subordination to a nonsubjective and ahistorical force. This 37 million dead (Freud's war metaphor) overwhelms the offspring's entire sense of itself. The paraphrase of difference into deficit from within the context of the general equivalent (signification and hierarchy) reduces the morphology to words. Freud deems this translation a "castration." This gloss on female shortfall incurs into the deepest and darkest of the traumas of the Great War in the being-in-the-world and being-with-others of the offspring's *Dasein*. The choice to "renounce" the narcissistic "satisfaction" implies a willful choice on the part of the male junior. But the "give way to it" phraseology indicates a forced choice. In contrast, the schizoid decision sustains the offspring's disavowal of the symbolic reality. This denial is not of castration but of difference. This difference is transmuted into deficit. At the same time, the perspective of the pervert — somehow — discerns that the undefined "fear" is imaginary. The pervert convinces himself of the fraudulence of "fear" in order to enjoy "satisfaction." These perverse joys include: obsessive self-pleasure; maternal incest; scopophilic voyeurism at the female junior's difference; and fantasies about differences and deficits.

Freud's narrative teems with gaps and holes. The parable flat lines at the most basic question. Why does the male junior transliterate difference in morphology into deficit in signification? Why does he do so even with the haunt of the father's threat against self-pleasure? The criteria that Freud offers for the general equivalent signification of the genitalia are "size" and "visibility." The penis is more sizeable and more visible and as such is consistently privileged. But the reverse of less size and less visibility of the clitoris could easily be coded as superior. The fabled moment of decision for the male junior executes his diagnostic fate: as neurotic in submission to castration with the paternal ego-ideal; or as psychotic in renunciation of castration with the foreclosure of the paternal signifier of prohibition; or as perverse in acknowledgment and denial with the invention of the fetish-object. The pervert's fetish confesses a scarcity but at the same time annuls this castration. But neither/nor — Then, what?

These three choices of neurosis, schizophrenia, and perversion are narratively flawed for three distinct reasons. First, the story of the castration complex fails to convincingly account for the Freudian-boy interpretation of difference *qua* deficit. Second, the fable miscarries the criteria of the general equivalent of "size" and "visibility." The reversal of this privilege is easy and unspectacular. Third, the weave misinterprets the enjoyment of the male junior's voyeurism at the naked body of the female junior. The female junior is neither morphologically nor metaphorically castrated. But then what precisely is her deficit? She is described as an absence in relationship to the penis *qua* presence in the logic of phallocentrism. But the reason for such assessment is either dubiously morphological and literal or unexpectedly feminist and figural. The origin of phallocentrism is neither the presence of the penis nor the absence of the clitoris. Rather, the origin of -centrism is the generalized pathology of the signifying chain. This basic sickness is the binary oppositional structure of what Saussure identifies as signification. The sign is the name for the object of the pervert's disavowal: "I know very well that signification is structured by the binary distinction of the sign, but nevertheless I believe in the negative and differential madness of the value of the signifier." The pervert's object of destruction is the *sign* in the practice of *signification* — rather than the *signifier* in the theory of *value*. The pervert's *jouissance* is of the signifier of value.

In Freud's 1938 text, there are two claims which are made about the male junior. These charges arrange the offspring's approach to desire, object, and the phallus. First, there is the "demand by the instinct" that the female junior be endowed with a penis. The male junior need not fear the loss of his own. Second, there is the "prohibition by reality." This claim insists that the female junior does lack and that the male junior, too, may lose his penis.[11] The demand by the instinct is code for the male junior's expectation of Sameness[+] in the place of identity and difference. The origin of this calculation abides as a mystery. A possible explanation is the male junior's presumption that binary opposition details (dis)privilege. Freud's supposition is that the binary distinction between penis and its not-penis (or the clitoris) is imaginary. The choice is either the one (penis) or the other (not-penis). This otherness is neither equal nor unequal — neither identical nor different — as it is mapped onto a hierarchy of privilege and disprivilege. This rank is based on the criteria of "size" and "visibility." The female junior's variance is deemed an arrears. This disparity retroactively clarifies the father's castration threat. Sexual difference also portends a future loss of masculine private property. This is so unless the male junior accedes to the demands of the normative ego-ideal of the paternal legacy. The little boy recoils from his mother and his own penis as response to the materialized threat of castration as it is embodied in the castrated figure of the little girl. Frightened, the little boy turns away from pleasure and toward identity and the codes and conventions of the culture as they are represented by the idealized authority of the father.

Figure 6.1 Binary Phallic Logic

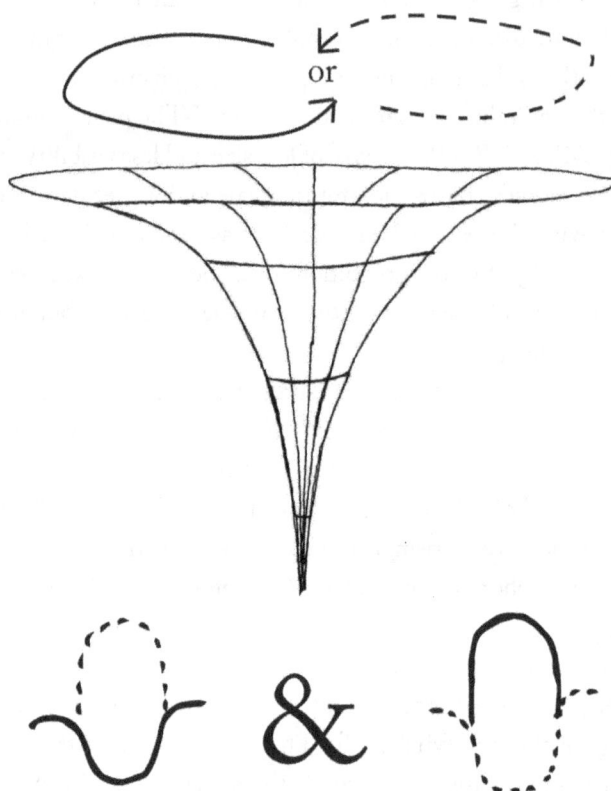

This image depicts the dynamic of an infinitely (pro/re)gressive — recursive — Sameness⁺. The Outside of the system of meaning-making and of the construction of a space in time and a time of space is the spectacular series of singularities of penis and clitoris (and so on). These bright positivities are themselves in and of the Real. The singularity ~~is~~ without any constituted position within an economy of comparison, contrast, and exchange in relationality and constructionism. The paternal phallic function and the present structuration of the signifying chain are organized by the negation — enacted exclusion — of these singularities on the outskirts of the economies of general equivalence. The two figures which are below the phallic function are linked by an ampersand. These figures represent the clitoris and the penis. But the *bothness* and *andness* of the deconstruction of the binary oppositional structure radically resist expression in the system of the metaphysics of presence and the regime of identity/difference. This is so because the incomparable and incontrastable — general inequivalence — singularity of the penis and the clitoris is rhizomatically and irreconcilably resistant to any calculation of exchange in the metrics of nihilistic value. This singular resistance to general equivalence is expressed in the dotted lines that partially draw the (permeable) boundaries between the figures. There is no such *das Ding* as a penis which is (not) a clitoris or a clitoris which is (not) a penis. The drawing deploys the dotted lines in order to signify the impossible schizoid truth: the penis is *not not not not not,* and so on. The ampersand is translated by Neurotic Foreclosure (*rejet névrotique*) into the either/or binary opposition of presence and its obverse. This translation of both/and into either/or is the will of the paternal function.

Notes & Sketches —

The retrospective glance at castration (re)produces a conservative and reactive Western culture. Civilization is a (re)effect of the (re)duplication of the norms and codes of the extant symbolic order. Revolutionary transformation is unlikely in a system in which castration structures identity, identification, desire, and pleasure. The "demand by the instinct" is the avoidance of the castration complex and the return to maternal and masturbatory pleasure. In contrast, the "prohibition" by "reality" accepts castration as Something (May Be) Missing. The reality principle enforces an identification with the father and a recoil from the pleasures of the male junior's penis and his mother. The choice is of an unsymbolizable and inarticulable Real Sameness⁺. This Sameness⁺ is the false choice between the penis of the male junior which is̶ — as his penis or the male clitoris — the same as the female junior — or the female penis or the clitoris. This unsymbolizable relationship indicates not only that B̶e̶i̶n̶g̶ is under erasure, such that there is no word for the relationship of Sameness⁺·. The decision is about the hierarchical division between the male junior's superior turgidity and the female junior's inferior bits and pieces. The intermission is̶ between the mother, self-pleasure, and *jouissance*, on the one hand, and the father, law, and the ego-ideal, on the other hand. This basal set of oppositions of distinction of signification cannot be put into text. This is so except in the web of words of $-ism. Being is neither under erasure nor over extracted "but nevertheless" Real. This Real is the internal structure of B̶e̶i̶n̶g̶.

Psychosis and Sameness+

These maternal and paternal choices are mapped onto the distinction between psychosis and neurosis. Psychosis forecloses the symbolic and its order of sexual difference. It does so in order to refute the reality of phallocentrism and hierarchical difference. These are otherwise structured by the general equivalent of evaluative abstraction and speculation. In contrast, neurosis accepts the symbolic order of the hierarchical binary opposition between the sexes. It does so in order to repress the urge toward an inarticulable Real S̶a̶m̶e̶n̶e̶s̶s̶⁺ which is neither equality nor inequality nor identity nor difference but Sameness⁺. Freud presents the offspring with an either/or choice. This choice is the prepositional precondition of binary opposition. The decision is between neurosis and psychosis. This either/or science of Reason mimics the exclusionary schema of the system of $-ism and its discrete division of objects from each other. This $-istic design is visible in the otherwise self-same and self-identical penis "itself" and clitoris "itself."

The neurotic Logic of Identity (A = A) posits that the penis is (rather than is̶) the penis *qua* the superior organ and that the clitoris is (rather than is̶) the clitoris *qua* the inferior part. On the street it is said, "the man has a penis and the Woman does not have a penis." The schizoid choice is of Sameness⁺ in neither an equality nor inequality nor identity nor difference. Sameness⁺ designs the Madness of Order of the system. This Sameness⁺ is otherwise neurotically foreclosed (*rejet névrotique*) only to return as the constructed essence of the system. The schizoid function also applies to the male junior's male clitoris and penis and the female junior's female penis and clitoris. These two impossible articulations of the Real of Sameness⁺ — neither equality nor inequality nor identity nor difference — affirm the relationality and constructionism of an antiidentitarian Sameness⁺, or a Derridean "sameness which is not identical." This is consistent with the aesthetic of the Pervert-Schizoid-Woman's general *modus operandi* to shatter and wreck the extant symbolic order. This explosion accompanies the limit-thought that the clitoris is the penis and that the female penis is̶ the male clitoris (a̶n̶d̶ s̶o̶ o̶n̶).

This Difference⁺ is an equivalence and coincidence (B̶e̶i̶n̶g̶) which illuminate the same difference of each object from "itself." The penis is different from itself but the same as the other. The clitoris is different from itself but the same as the other. The spectacle of this perverse sensibility (A ≠ A) is that the female penis is the referent of the castration anxiety which organizes all of Western humanity. The female penis is sustained by and coextensive with the entirety of the objects in the signifying chain. But the male junior of neurosis invokes hierarchy and binary opposition of the sign as opposed to the differences and negativities — strange Sameness⁺ ($\supseteq$) Difference⁺ — of the signifier. The female junior consumes the future from the position of envy and desire, and the male junior protects the present from the position of ego and identity.

In contrast, the bedrock of phallocentric sexual difference fails to register in the schizoid's psychical economy. The psychotic is free to reconfigure sexual difference and every other binary opposition whatsoever from the Outside of the paired design of $-ism. The neurotic either/or economy of hierarchy and distinction — the sign — is an aesthetic which fortifies the borders of identity and difference. These oppositions — such as white/black, schizoid/neurotic, Craig/Tobey — are understood as private property. The objects of *le propre* are not to be swapped and switched like the objects and aims of nascent sexuality. The only possibility of trade and traffic of such objects and things is authorization from the general equivalent and its enforcement of comparison, contrast, and exchange. General equivalence is structured by the quantification of quality in abstraction and speculation. The impasse of the madman's response to castration is the surrender of absence in the suspension of the phallic *point de capiton*. This suspension is isomorphic to Derrida's vision of the finite function of an infinite series of metaphors. The madman's ecosystem is an absence of absence in *Verwerfung*, or lack of lack in the Woman. But does the absence of absence or the lack of the lack simultaneously present absence and fulfill lack? Any answer to this question can only confirm that the economy of madness is a resistant Real which contests the coherence and articulacy of the extant symbolic order.

The psychotic's craziness situates him within the dimension of the Real. The resistant to symbolization is a traumatic and torturous proximity to the Real Signifier and the Signified/r. The madman is overwhelmed by the obscene plenitude and shattered fullness of Sameness⁺. This Difference⁺ is posted at the "same place" of the reccurence of the Real and a return to a Sameness⁺ "which is not identical." This Outside of identity/difference alienates the madman and the Woman from the economies of castration. The schizoid is exempt from phallocentric sexual difference and the consumerism of the female junior's past and present lack. The madman is also unencumbered by the anxiety of the male junior's present and future castration. The psychotic is relieved of the scarcity and supply/demand dynamics of capitalism. The schizophrenic is on the verge of the emergence of a postphallocentric and postcapitalist euphoria of the Spirit of the System. Futurally, Sameness⁺ and Difference⁺ structure sexuality and economy. Even the signifier is reorganized by this madness of a gobbledygook which ~~is~~ accessible to us only after the death of ~~Being~~. The schizoid thrives in the torturous exclusion from phallocentrism and capitalism. The schizoid chooses to renounce the general equivalent of father, phallus, currency, and sign. This generalized function is orientation, balance, and coordination. Generalized harmonization is excluded from the system even as it is the central metaphor for the organization of hierarchy and signification in binary opposition.

The psychotic's proximity to the Real is situated within the symbolic order. The Real Madman is an occupant of either the asylum or the university. But either locale renders it nearly impossible for the madman to properly articulate in the codes, conventions, semantics, and syntax of the extant order of Reason. Rather, the schizoid's flashy but mistaken Unreason strives to represent the secret truth of the Real. This resistant Real Signifier is absolutely unsymbolizable not only because it is a riff of and on Unreason. The madman's symbols are also insightfully and deconstructively recursive. The resistance of the Real is a defiance of the transcendental signified of philosophical speculation or the *objet petit a* of sexual desire. *Contra* phallocentrism, the schizoid witnesses that the penis is the clitoris because the penis is not the penis and the clitoris is not the clitoris and, at the same time, the penis is the penis and the clitoris is the clitoris and, at the same time, the penis is the clitoris and the penis is not the penis and the clitoris is not the penis and, at the same time — penis penis penis clitoris clitoris clitoris — clitoris and penis so clitoris on and Other penis. A possible symbolization of this Sameness$^+$ ($\supseteq$) Difference$^+$ is ~~penis clitoris~~. The interpretive rationale of such blather and blether is that the spatiotemporal interval between penis and clitoris articulates the *différance* which cannot be simulated as the *arche* of the chain of words. This deconstructive (pro/re)gression — which cannot be what it ~~is~~ — illuminates Being under erasure. Recursively and negatively, the *sous rature* articulates a what is is what is not and what is is what is not is not what is and what is not, and so on. Truth can only be half-said *in toto*. There are a constitutive excess and systematic remainder — surplus — which escape the word.

The schizoid's Unreason is the object of the pervert's talented and delighted *écriture*. The same Pervert's Logic — Real Signifier or Signified/r — applies to the communist abolishment of private property. Each signifier (currency, commodity, profit, interest, and rent) is not owned by "itself." Rather, this excess is neither owned by the corporation nor co-owned by the management and union arrangements. Instead, the surplus is not owned whatsoever. It is owned only — except — by the entire battery of words in the Other. This dispersed improper property — *le propre est l'impropre* — ruptures any ownership and abolishes any private property. The schizoid's skirmish with the sign and its distinctions and oppositions is fundamentally outlawed by the system because it is a threat to the word in *langue*, to the scarcity and supply/demand dynamics in capitalism, and to the desire and identification in sexuality. The psychotic's antiphallocentric and anticapitalist rants and raves — ~~Being~~ — are confined to the basements of the asylums or to the lecture halls at the universities. But, in most cases, the crazy person finds himself behind the grates of the grimy windowpanes which obscure the institutional tortures of correctional facilities.

The structure of neurosis vitally deviates from the schema of psychosis. The schism (\$-ism) of neurosis isolates the clitoris from the penis. Neurotic experience of sexual difference posits the binary oppositions of phallocentrism (penis/not-penis) which rule the systems of representation under patriarchy. These codes of figuration — or Freudian so-called considerations of representability — delimit the modalities of possible articulations and symbolizations in and by the neurotic structure. These confinements in representation of the neurotic and phallocentric contour of sexual difference are supplanted by the Real sublimity of the internal and external division and suture within each signifier of the opposition. Perversely, the case of the penis and the clitoris imposes an external and internal plenitude, equivalence, equality, coincidence, continuity — or an unsymbolizable Sameness$^+$ of Being. Each signifier ~~is~~ the other in the system. This Real confers *value* rather than *signification* in difference and deferral, backward and forward, to the object in question. It does so precisely as the ontological question of "What is?" Every signifier in the system is internal-external in extimacy — Difference$^+$ — to every other signifier in the battery of the Other. This aneconomy asserts that there is neither lack nor castration, nor hierarchy nor signification — nor and or both either Juan's jockstrap — between signifiers. Each signifier is divided from "itself" (is not or ~~Being~~) but is also sutured to the others (is or ~~Being~~). This is the Reasonable consequence of the logical extension of Saussure's theory of value and the signifier against the concepts of signification and the sign.

The neurotic's sleepy acceptance of the patriarchal version of sexual difference holds that the clitoris is not the penis but is rather a deficit. The man has a penis and the Woman does not have a penis: penis/not-penis. This patriarchal modality of thought indicates that the man may lose his penis unless he conforms to the norms of the ego-ideal of the society. Neurotically, the Woman envies the penis and seeks to procure the objects that she lacks in the penis = baby = husband (and so on). This anal equivalency involves the substitution of metaphors for a penis which is fundamentally undefined and indeterminate. The penis *qua* referent is otherwise resistant to a metaphysics of presence. The intimation in the conservative neurotic impression of sexual difference is that the penis is self-same and self-identical with itself (A = A, or Being, *il y a,* as such, *qua,* what is). The clitoris is also self-same and self-identical as deficient. The neurotic's foreclosure of the Madness of Order pretends that the penis is the penis and, as such, is needlessly unencumbered with reference in *différance* — difference and deferral — to any other word in the Other. The penis may be a Nothingness of the unsymbolizable Real. But the penis is defined as a pure tautology itself in its own privilege. The clitoris is also the clitoris. It is unsullied by any reference whatsoever to another word by which it is ascribed its deficiency. The penis and the clitoris are ultimately singularities. But what is the ~~relationship~~ between singularities?

The neurotic economy indicates that privilege/disprivilege, superiority/inferiority, penis/not-penis, and so on are generated without relationship or construction of general equivalence in comparison, contrast, and exchange with an Other. The signification of the words is generated *ex nihilo* — Out of Nothingness. The schema of (dis)privilege in neurosis is the substantive configuration of the symbolic order. This paradox is that the essence of neurosis is Unreason. The neurotic symbolizes sexual difference as phallocentric (A/-A) even as he relates the two objects — A and B, penis and clitoris — in a bond of hierarchical evaluation. This comparison and contrast are at a distance from the schizoid's Real of sexual difference. The psychotic returns each signifier to an otherness (*of* otherness, and so on) in a recursive Sameness[+].

This strict infinity cannot exclude even the function of orientation, balance, and coordination of the sexual structure. The schizoid structure (dys)functions in the strict absence of the function. The neurotic's structure is organized by the "paternal function." The schizoid's system is (de)composed of a series of unmoored words. The representational regime of phallocentrism cannot finally be symbolized. The schizoid's traces of metaphors and metonymies are an aim/less/full *Trieb.* Drive wanders about the objects in the spiral of the expansive galaxies in the heavens. The neurotic surrenders to lack and desire. The neurotic conforms and photocopies the normative ego-ideal of the father. The neurotic grants purchase power and authority to the twin pillars of $-istic selfhood and sociality. These dual obelisks are identity (want-to-be) and desire (want-to-have). The pillar is also the private property relations of capital. These capitalist relationships (dis/en)able the want-to-be and want-to-have structures, and vice-versa. These bonds animate the endless metaphorical metonymical fracas of narcissism, aggression, and anxiety. The *telos* of this battle is the neurotic's outstripped crusade against death. The neurotic's imperious hope for enjoyment is dissatisfaction with the paltry spoils of masculine idiotic *jouissance.* This ordinary enjoyment wistfully pleases itself in the ephemeral arrival of its *objet petit a* in the sickly clutches of its desire in the retroactively confirmed missed encounter.

The psychotic achieves *jouissance* by drive in the aim/less *Trieb* of the sweet foreplay of the resistant Real rather than by desire in the endless *désir* of the rambled projection of an elusive object. The form and the content of this *objet* of *Trieb* are subordinate to the prepositional and indexical highways and byways of the pervert's flights of fancy. These deterritorialized lines of flight pursue the schizoid's Unreason. The pervert's catch-up and tell-all of the madman's misadventures are the impossible symbolization of the Real of the Madness of Order. The neurotic endures desire and its displacements. The neurotic suffers the returns of his repressions. The neurotic symbolizes his experience in the easy repression and return of dreams, slips, jokes, and psychopathologies. The neurotic's literal desire, wish, and truth return as a metaphor — full stop — only to be easily retranslated into the dimension of the literal. In contrast, the schizoid is simultaneously a neurotic from both his own perspective as a crazy person and from the viewpoint of the pervert's postbinary outlook. The madman enjoys the *Trieb* and its infinite loopy lanes and endless twisted trails. But the hitch is that the schizoid cannot symbolize this drive. The madman's signifiers are split from themselves. The signifier is endlessly recursive. The signifier is torn by Unreason. The symbolic order of the neurotic deems this Unreason a madness which may be considered "a sameness which is not identical." The slaves of neurosis are not yet ready to recognize this Sameness⁺ because they (we) are much too happy being neurotics.

Neurosis-Perversion-Psychosis

The diagnostic alternative to neurosis and psychosis is perversion. This is the case even if the schizoid-pervert is simultaneously neurotic from the perspective of a ~~Being~~ which is under erasure in an inarticulable sublimity of the Real ~~Sameness~~⁺. The schizoid and the pervert also hysterically repress and return symptoms *qua* neurotics. The madmen and the perverts do so even as they deconstruct the binary opposition between conscious/unconscious. Neither pervert nor schizoid favors this binary distinction of conscious/unconscious which is otherwise pivotal for psychoanalysis. But the psychotic and the pervert celebrate the psychoanalytic techniques of and talents for so-called considerations of representability for an interpretation of the Madness of Order. The perverse-schizoid perspective discovers that each is the other. The pervert understands that the pervert and the schizoid are simultaneously neurotic. The neurotic, pervert, and psychotic are each subject to *Verdrängung, Verleugnung*, and *Verwerfung*. The modality of negation of the system of $-ism is Neurotic Foreclosure (*rejet névrotique*). This is so on the grounds that $-ism discerns itself *qua* neurotic and as a series of repressive rebuttals and harmless returns in symptoms of everyday life. But this apparent neurosis belies an ardent schizophrenia of the system. This is the Madness of Order. The crazy system is settled by crazy people. Psychotics misinterpret themselves and their system as neurotic in schizoid garb. Neurotic Foreclosure (*rejet névrotique*) represses the Real and its return in the symbolic *qua* the Madness of Order. The intuitive Unreason of the schizoid and the talented *écriture* of the pervert are the centers of the illumination of the Madness of Order. The performances of these two *dramatis personae* invite a critique of $-ism and its reinvention in the horizonal content and form of the Spirit of the System.

The pervert is considered in her specificity both spatially and temporally. A quantum simultaneity of superpositional oscillation is the spatiotemporal art of the fetishist. Freud says of the embryonic prototype of the pervert and his two choices between neurosis and psychosis: "But in fact the offspring takes neither course, or rather he takes both simultaneously, which comes to the same thing."[12] The pervert "takes both simultaneously." A close exegesis of that phrase suggests a free choice ("takes") but also a forced necessity ("both"). It is as if the will to Become-perverse is neither free nor forced but otherwise a modality of a paradoxical forced choice. An ostensibly free choice is enforced. The same holds for the pervert who "takes both simultaneously." The negotiation of castration is a matter of life and death because for the male junior of self-pleasure the penis is coextensive with his existence. Freud unpacks the decisive consequences for desire, castration, and *jouissance* of this forced choice. The perverse simultaneity of the choice mobilizes the fetishistic artistry of the both/and rather than the strict economy of the either/or. The offspring affirms both the both/and and the either/or — and so on.

The schizoid-deconstructionist exquisitely disposes the neither/nor "but nevertheless" — the Other. This *Yes!* aneconomy delays the choice. The neither/norism of deferral of the schizoid is isomorphic to Derrida's *différance*. Perversely, the male junior chooses neither instinct nor urge, neither desire nor reality, but — The Other to either neurosis or psychosis and/or neurosis and psychosis is deferred. The offspring avoids oedipalization. The offspring sustains infancy and its *jouissance* at the cost of identity and desire. Perversion entails separation but not alienation. The schizoid-deconstructionist's neither/norism cannot be assimilated into a proper account of the pervert's version of concurrence and synchronicity. Freud's emphasis on the "simultaneous" is crucial. The pervert seeks to compress time and space — at the same time — within the symbolic order. The techniques and talents of the unconscious-work (condensation and displacement) in a field which is Outside of time and knowledge invite a deconstruction of space-becoming-time and time-becoming-space. Unconsciously, space is the dimension which dominates. The simultaneity of the one and the other is compressed from temporality into spatiality with no "No!," no "know," and no "time." But how is (the resistance to) choice possible in a simultaneity which is absent of temporality as such?

The pervert discerns the choice of both neurosis (repression of the urge) and schizophrenia (foreclosure of reality) at once. Simultaneity illuminates the both/and attitude of the pervert. The pervert's *Verleugnung* destructures all binary oppositional logic — either man or Woman; either gay or straight; either right or wrong, and so on. The "I know very well, but nevertheless" also demonstrates the schizoid *Yes!* of the (non)arrival of the Real Signifier and the Signified/r at the instant of the dissolution of the Order of Madness. Freud's insightful conclusion is that "both" choices arrive at "the same thing." This "same thing" indicates that the choice of both is a decision of a Sameness⁺ which mediates the dysfunction of ~~Being~~. Neurosis is not neurosis, and psychosis is not psychosis (and so on). Freud indicates that the pathways of neurosis and psychosis are distinct only insofar as they are defined by the neurotic Logic of Identity.

In contrast, the perspective of the schizoid-pervert's Logic of Difference views the neurotic repression as precisely not itself. *Verdrängung* is *Verwerfung*. Queerly, the "simultaneity" of neurosis and psychosis "comes," as Freud says, "to the same thing." But what is this "thing"? Freud implies that *das Ding* is negation or Sameness⁺. *Das Ding* of Sameness⁺ is neither identical nor different and neither equal nor unequal. Radical negativity generates radical Sameness⁺. The crush and conquer of either repression and its return in the symbolic or foreclosure and its return in the Real provoke the emergence of "a sameness which is not identical." The nullity, as Heidegger puts it in *Being and Time* (1923), and the differences and negativities, as Saussure puts it in *Course in General Linguistics* (1917), dissolve all positive objects of self-identity and self-sameness. The symbolic and the Real are coincident with each other *qua* the Real Symbolic. The Real (⊇) the Symbolic.

The repression *qua* foreclosure in the symbolic *qua* Real returns in the Real Symbolic. The return is the series of ruptures *qua* the Madness of Order. The system is the return of the Real Symbolic. The pervert's experiment to "take both simultaneously" fiercely acknowledges his insight about the system. The symbolic is structured like madness. The solar system is a recursive (pro/re)gression of the Real Signifier. This simultaneity is the temporality of *value* rather than *signification*. Simultaneity of Sameness⁺ is the momentary spark of coalescence of all of the words in the system — *Yes!* This radical affirmation sustains the (non)arrival of the signified in its signification. The simultaneity of both neurosis and psychosis is the perversion of the system and the illumination of the Madness of Order. The neither/norism of a delayed — differed and deferred in *différance* — temporality is the exclusive Time of the Schizoid of the Madness of Order. This madness shillyshallies adult sexuality in the process of the dillydallying of nascent sexuality.

Perversions and Père-Versions

The supplement in deconstructive perverse disavowal is anti-$-istic. The Derridean supplement disclaims the exclusion of the Other and the entire battery of signifiers from identity *qua* difference in Sameness⁺. The otherwise exclusion of Sameness⁺ is the foundation upon which so-called self-same and self-identical identity and difference (A = A) are elevated and endowed. The neurotic division between words in the system is otherwise unexpectedly structured by the perverse insight that identity deviates from itself. A constitutive Otherness elaborates identity from an Outside. This Outside cannot be detached from the inside of itself in its own — *le propre* — encounter with a fundamental Otherness to itself. Perversely, identity is outside of itself.

Identity is only internal to itself from the perspective of this Outside. The obligatory metonymic gesture toward the other words in the system is the condition of the self-same and the self-identical *qua* otherwise Sameness⁺. Perversion is a compromise between neurosis and the repression of desire which returns in the dream, slip, joke, and truth, on the one hand, and psychosis and the foreclosure of the signified which returns in hallucinations and delusions, on the other hand. Impossibly, the pervert chooses *both* neurosis *and* psychosis.

This enforced decision is a simultaneity. The *Verdrängung* of symbolic otherness in neurosis is coincident with — B̶e̶i̶n̶g̶ — the *Verwerfung* of the signified in schizophrenia. These two negations — *Verdrängung* of the constitutive outside and the *Verwerfung* of the *nom-du-père* — interact with each other. Somehow — neurosis and psychosis cavort and play together. Erotically, neurosis and psychosis generate the peculiarity of the pervert's disavowal. This *Verleugnung* invariably entails the repression of otherness. Negation is unavoidable in a web of words which is structured by temporal deferral and spatial difference. The pervert represses despite his *Verleugnung*. The *Verwerfung* of the signified is the negation of the center of signs, words, metaphors, fetishes, and so on. These substitutes otherwise exclude the function around which the structure is "thinkable." The pervert forecloses despite his *Verleugnung*. Perversion is *something else* — in another space and a different time of the Other.

The pervert is situated between a performance of neurosis (*Verdrängung*) and psychosis (*Verwerfung*). The neurotic alienates himself from the other in his repression. He does so only to re-experience the other in the zany form of its return in the symptom. The schizoid loses his mind in hallucinations and delusions. He does so in the absence of absence and the lack of the lack. The phallic *point de capiton* otherwise arrests the trace (is like, and so on) in the sequence of words. The paternal metaphor is suspended. The series of metaphors and metonymies — metonymization of metaphor — refers, differs, and defers endlessly around a series of prepositions. These phallic indexical prepositions haphazardly direct the commotion of the on-ramps and off-ramps of the traffic of existence. The pervert loses nothing because the simultaneity of the both/and of disavowal enables him to cultivate and enjoy otherness — what the neurotic represses — and at the same time sustain and comprehend the signified — what the schizoid rejects from the symbolic.

Perverse disavowal is grounded in the universe at the same time — simultaneously — as it interprets this galaxy otherwise. This ambivalent being-in-the-world makes the pervert a talented writer. The pervert discerns the structure of the system as experienced but unsymbolized by the schizoid. But the pervert also dexterously expresses and performs this Madness of Order and the Unreason of the schizoid. The pervert is both Outside and Inside of the world. The pervert is both External and Internal to the order. The pervert takes at once "both courses" of neurosis and psychosis. The pervert is anchored in the symbolic of its *Verdrängung* and return. But he also flirts with the Real of *Verwerfung* and its rupture. How does the pervert — somehow — do it?

This concomitant *Verdrängung* and *Verwerfung* of the pervert's psychical economy explain the incoherent modality of negation of the system of $-ism in Neurotic Foreclosure or *rejet névrotique*. An incongruent Neurotic Foreclosure (*rejet névrotique*) is the essence of the dynamic of the Madness of Order. The unassimilable signifier is rejected from the symbolic order only to return from the Real *qua* the system. The system is this foreclosure of the Real Symbolic, the Real Signifier, and the Signified/r. Madness of Order is — B̶e̶i̶n̶g̶ — this Neurotic Foreclosure (*rejet névrotique*). The neurotic's repression of the signified of the truth of desire in the *point de capiton* releases the excess of play in *différance*. The unforeseen systematic upshot is the kindle and revival of the Real Signifier and the Signified/r. The dangerous surplus of the Real that insurrectionarily returns *qua* foreclosure is the Real of the order. This dynamic is Unreasonable. This cycle is the original object of *Verwerfung* by the citizens in the system. Perverse both/and *Verleugnung* admits the sister's penis in a Peniscentrism (Clitoralcentrism) of Sameness⁺ of both equality and otherness, and identity and difference, and so on.

Sameness⁺ is markedly different from a phallocentrism of the general equivalent. Equivalence implies inequality in quantified similarity. The young pervert enjoys the penile plenitude and the nascent communism — Nothing is Missing — of a galaxy of same penises and same clitorises. The economic dynamic of these (*a*) sex organs properly defends against the horrific multiplicitous reptilian penile death match of Medusa's snakes. But, at the same time, the pervert affirms — somehow — the female junior's castration and the system of capitalism. The pervert discerns this simultaneous negation and affirmation and the obverse of each as — is — the other. The pervert wrests a compromise formation of neurotic *Verwerfung*. The pervert refuses the reality of the Real of sexual difference — ? — in schizophrenia and its correlative hallucinations and delusions. This schizophrenia approximates a philosophical idealism.

The pervert cheerfully surrenders to reality in neurosis and the accompanied symptomatic returns. Neurosis resembles a materialism in which the subject succumbs to the demands of the empirical. The pervert represents the system with flair and gift because such virtuosity and artistry are visceral to his psychical structure. The pervert exactly imagines the system only because his gaze returns his look at himself as an object. The pervert paints his portrait. The pervert then cleverly convinces others to misrecognize themselves in his oils. It was only after an affair with Petit-Jean's jockstrap that Lacan could say: "You see that can? Do you see it? Well, it doesn't see you!"[13]

This hypothetical binary opposition between neurosis and madness is a reference to both the empiricism of the Real of sexual difference — ? — in neurosis and the idealistic discernment of Sameness⁺ — ! — in schizophrenia. The critic anticipates both worlds. First, the neurotic empiricism of the reality of phallocentric division and hierarchy of the general equivalent of penis/not-penis is acknowledged. Second, the schizoid idealism of the (dis)simulation of a Sameness⁺ which is the Outside of equality, inequality, identity, and difference is affirmed. These two aspects are both overlapped versions of the same skewed psychotic viewpoint of a recessional Real *qua* parallactic gap or quantum entanglement. The interval between the neurotic and the schizoid in binary opposition is the space of the pervert and his Being. The interstitial field advises that the distinction between the empirical but phallocentric order of penis/not-penis, on the one hand, and the idealist but Peniscentric coordination of penis-clitoris (⊇) clitoris-penis (and so on), on the other hand, is the groundwork for the essential opposition between the neurotic's return of the repressed and the schizoid's rupture of the Real. The pervert divines that the object that violently returns in the symbolic is the rupture of the Real. The strict equivalence and total coincidence — Being — between the symbolic and the Real are the timeless space of the pervert. The pervert is the space of the unconscious.

This Being (Becoming) is situated at the instant of the Real Signifier in the space of each and every word in the system. The nodal point of the Madness of Order is the dreamy navel of the network of texts and pictures of dream-interpretation. The navel is the rupture within each word in its relationship to the other objects within $-ism. This destabilization is also simultaneously the relationship (⊇) of the system of $-ism with itself *qua* system — or $ (⊇) S. This explosion and suture of the system — at the same time — invite the pervert to both affirm in his "yes" and to reject in his "yes" the otherwise metonymic shift toward another which is yet-to-come in the schizoid neither/nor of Being. This is the perverse postontological wager. This also applies to a Becoming of a what will be or a what willing having beening Becoming Being — and so on. This temporality articulates the in-process, in-action development of Becoming of what is Becoming.

The pervert is the critic of the solar system. The pervert's secret truth of the schizoid's Unreason is the salvation of the pervert. The emancipation of the world from the Madness of Order is the pervert's marvel and joy. Liberty is a source of "I know very well, but nevertheless…" — ! The pervert holds a tenuous clasp on symbolic reality. The positive ontological order of Being is split in the parallactic gap between itself and the hilariously returned scare quotes of "itself" *qua* Other. The schizophrenia of the web of words is the alienation of the object from itself in the scare quotes of the freaky return of *Verleugnung*. The pervert's talent for symbolization in spoken and written syntax and semantics in sketchy suture and nebulous grasp of *langue* commissions him to wryly and incisively critique the orb of the earth. The talent also inspires him to textually and adroitly toil for the transformation of the system. The transition commences with an expression of a neurotic schizophrenia of the Real Symbolic in anticipation of a Pervert-Schizoid-Woman of the postphallic and postcapitalist clitoral future.

The pervert resists but also heeds the father's law of a coherent chain of signification. This perverse duty transpires in the absence of an obedience to the ego-ideal and to the normativity of the culture. The pervert both "rejects reality and refuses to accept any prohibition" (psychosis) and "in the same breath [recognizes] the danger of reality, takes over the fear of that danger as a pathological symptom, and tries subsequently to divest himself of the fear" (neurosis).[14] The fetishist is thinking, being, and living in a double-speak or double-edge, which is itself a half-said silly return of the scare quotes of Sameness⁺. The ridiculous return is redoubled "in the same breath" which acknowledges and denies the bedrock of the Real of sexual difference — ? — and the consequent "fear" of present and future proleptic loss. The pervert also — somehow — redistributes unconscious mechanisms of the primary process in order to "divest himself" of fear. This curious phrase implies a financial diversification and a psychical disidentification. The upshot is a calm disquietude. "In the same breath," as Freud says, the pervert remarkably achieves this simultaneity of the mutually exclusive. The pervert salutes castration and waves it goodbye. The pervert owns the fear and disregards its implication. The pervert accepts the situation, and he denies its constraint.

Later, the pervert transforms the intensity of the protective presence and shatterproof plenitude of the maternal phallus into the *mise-en-scène* of the objects of the lace, fur, shoe, jockstrap — and every other object in the system. These other objects are already fetishized. The system is saturated with the otherness of the Outside. The proviso of the internal so-called identity of the object is its own externality. The signifier is already a fetish. The Madness of Order is already the perversion of the signifying chain. The situation is an ir-reality. The neurotic cannot witness this two-fold parallactic gap. First, the hysteric is blind to the castration of each word in itself — because each word — B̶e̶i̶n̶g̶ — every other word in the Other. Second, the neurotic is oblivious to the plenitude of each signifier in itself — because each signifier — N̶o̶t̶h̶i̶n̶g̶n̶e̶s̶s̶ B̶e̶i̶n̶g̶ — itself. Each word (is) every other word in the battery of the Other. The parallactic gap of the Real Symbolic is this overlap between neurotic lack and schizoid plenitude. The pervert is the *über*-representer of this paradox. The pervert writes this Being *sous rature*. He does so from within the metaphysics of presence and the *signification of value* or the metonymization of metaphor of Being. The supremacy of value and metonymy explains the half-said double-speak double-edge of the pervert's discourse.

The politics of neurosis, schizophrenia, and perversion is unique and singular. The symptomatic fear of a proleptic annexation of the penis, private property, identity, desire, and enjoyment organizes the neurotic's psychical orientation as castration anxiety of the protection of capitalist private property. Fear and dread of loss and death are supplanted by the psychotic's certainty toward the secret truth of the Unreason of an anticentrism. The madman embraces a communist abolishment of the private property of sex and gender, and of all of the other nodes of identity and difference, such as race, class, ethnicity, disability, nation, religion, and so on. To riff off of the famous closure of "The Communist Manifesto" (1848), "Perverts of the World — Always Already United!" The fetishist both accepts and rejects prohibition: "I know very well that the rules apply to me, but nevertheless I play against the odds in order to gesture toward the arbitrary but conventional violence of the metaphysics of presence and to explicate that rule-breaking is isomorphic to rule-making and that the constitution of the trespass is coincident with the constitution of the law."

The law is arbitrarily and mystically organized. The pervert happily accedes to the rule of the law — what Lacan names as the so-called law of desire. The law is a substantive sketch of the society and its subjects. The pervert revels in joyful satisfaction in the arbitrary but conventionalized law. But the pervert also fancies a new law — a maternal rule rather than a paternal dictate. The passage of the act or Event of the pervert's happy compliance with rather than aggrieved resistance to the law yields an orgasmic feminine Other *jouissance*. This Other takes pleasure in the world. The pervert's primary politics is his manifesto of *écriture*. But his secondary political device is a disposition to illuminate the extimacy of law/transgression, rule/rebellion, prohibition/ infraction, and so on.

The pervert takes a whack at a deconstructive blueprint of the schizoid's secret map of the symbolic order and its Unreason. The pervert seeks to artfully create another *jouissance* which is beyond identity, desire, and masculine pleasure. Ecstatic joy returns to the Real Symbolic as an affirmation which is beyond the incessant negations of both diacritics and dialectics. The pervert's future is a plenitude of an anticapitalist communism and a fullness of a postphallic global sexual orgy with Derek's jockstrap (*et al.*). The pervert refuses submission to a farcical transcendent signified at the center-substitution-metaphor of an antagonistic binary opposition, such as the good and the right against the bad and the wrong. Rather, the pervert blithely subordinates himself to the opposition in order to subvert its primacy *qua* "primacy." The pervert enjoys the opposition and in the process subverts its violence. The pervert's enjoyment is resistance. The *Jouir!* is not a capitulation to enjoyment of the system but rather a conformity to *Trieb* rather than *désir*. Vitally, the pervert's lust is the deconstructionist's strategy of the symbolization of the Unreason of the schizoid. This strategy is the both/and two-step of the first and second readings of the text. The first interpretation establishes the grain of the law of the text. The second reading transgresses against the convention of the rule of the word. This perverse adventurous duplicity resists the otherwise critical effort to reverse the opposition. Instead, the pervert's Unreason is structured by the vain but noble duty to displace the oppositional structure of the order of the series of objects.

Derrida (1972) claims that the *finite infinity* or *infinite finity* of sign-substitutions excludes the *function* of the center from the series of metaphors. The forlorn but requisite work is to include the excluded function into the structure of the series of metaphors. Metaphorization of functionalism is a version of an *underlanguage* rather than a metalanguage. An underlanguage dissolves the orientation, balance, and organization — generalized arrangement — of the system. Metaphor axes $-ism to the bilge and bosh of Unreason. Perverse deconstruction is oddly simple because the symbolic order is structured like madness. The gaps and fissures which make its oppositions reversible and displaceable are the fundamental substance of deconstructionist ontology: ~~Being~~. Not only is ~~Being~~ under erasure — Being *il n'y a pas* Being. But any object in the system is simultaneously not itself because the absurd rupture of Being *qua* Real destabilizes the "is" that otherwise defines the self-same and the self-identical of any word whatsoever. Being hilariously returns *qua* "Being."

Destruction of the ontological question and answer of Being — What is? — is the architecture of the schizoid's Unreason and the *écriture* of the pervert's manifesto. The pervert's erotics is the rot of the system. The destruction of ~~Being~~ and the ontological quest for what is enables an autodeconstruction of the series of objects and sequence of words of both the differential and the negative of the signifier, on the one hand, and the positivity and the fullness of the sign, on the other hand. The schizoid's mad animation performs this sexy *destruktion*. Quite simply, ~~is~~: that what is is what is not and what is is what is and also that what is is what is not and what is is what is is not what is is what is not and what is is what is and also that what is is what is not and what is is what is is (and so on, recursively in space and time). This recursion endlessly extends until the enforced moment of the overlap of the parallactic gap — *Yes!* The schizoid's clairvoyance is the wannabe philosopher. But the pervert's inspired calligraphy is the mark of the interdisciplinary Cultural Studies scholar.

The pervert's principle is that the law is neither desire nor transgression. The precept of rule is the neurotic and idiotic dynamic of rule and trespass. This demonstrates the predictable reinscription of punishment for the trespass. The law/transgression cycle is pivotal for the neurotic. The key signifier for the pervert is *jouissance*. Enjoyment is the code and the doctrine of the law because the pervert gets off on the triumph of the Other's sport. Lacan imagines the so-called inverted ladder of law and desire in which the rule generates the will to a transgression with paltry and regretful (dis)satisfaction. The pervert reimagines this relationship as the extroverted ladder of law (pact) and *jouissance*. This displacement of *désir* with *Trieb* is antecedent and subsequent to the Freudian pleasure principle and its reactive homeostasis. The pervert enjoys the traversal without the restraints of the silly dynamic of excitation and *denouement* of the energy in the orga(ni)sm. Perversely, pleasure never ends because it has neither commencement nor destination. Neurotic idiotic pleasure is sadly finite. Perverse Other *jouissance* is torturously infinite. Neurotic desire contracts, and perverse pleasure expands. There is only masochistic foreplay. All (de/re)sexualization is beyond the pleasure principle in the *mise-en-scène* of *Thanatos* and the death drive. This orgasmic scene of blue balls is strictly the Outside to the pleasure principle and the homeostatic increase/decrease in the tension of law and its transgression. But how does the pervert teeter at the edges of madness but recuperate the secret truth for the daft psyches of his neurotic brothers and sisters?

Real Mediations

The fetishistic strategy savors the in-process, in-action lubrication by the imagined Real Penis. The Real Penis is the connective fleshy tissue which metonymizes (in)complete metaphors. The Real Penis is the substitution for the copula of Being. This Being is forever under the fissure of erasure because it is noncoincident and noncontinuous — neither self-same nor self-identical but ~~is not~~ — with itself. This Sameness⁺ of Being applies to words of any coincidence. Any other word in the system which purports to sustain its own self-same and self-identical ontological Being is subordinate to the *sous rature* of disappearance and incoherence. Ontologically, the "what is" (and so on) cannot define the other words in the system which rely upon Being in order to define "themselves" *qua* "themselves" to be "themselves" *qua* "themselves" whatsoever. These sequences of scare quotes vibrantly return as the symptom of the perverse *Verleugnung* of difference. The Real Penis is the (*a*)sexualized veil of Being. The Real Penis denotes the Nothing is Missing in the Real and the return to the Sameness⁺ of space. The Real Penis returns to the same place as a "sameness which is not identical." The Real Penis is the mediatory symbol — / and <> and () and : (and :) and (⊇) and ★. The male penis is the female penis is the female clitoris is the male clitoris is the male-clitoris-female-penis, and so on. These mediatory symbols — / and <> and () and : (and :) and (⊇) and ★ — represent proxies for what is and is not the fissure *sous rature* of ~~Being~~. I have resorted to such words as coincidence, equivalence, continuity, and so on in order to denote this Sameness⁺. Even (⊇) is unsymbolizable because of its internal and external split within a Being which is not itself. The Real Penis is a figuration of this symbolism of mediation. Symbolic mediation is material or abstract, or bodily or textual. Antiphallocentrically, the male penis ★ the female penis ★ the female clitoris ★ the male clitoris ★ the male-clitoris ★ the -female-penis- ★ the –Woman clitoris (⊇) man penis- ★ and Cindy's jockstrap.

The simultaneity of the mutually exclusive indicates a fervent resistance to the law of language. This is outlined in Ferdinand de Saussure's *Course in General Linguistics* (1917). It is also visible in the work of deconstruction: first, Heidegger on the word as the "House of Being"[15] with "Being under erasure"[16]; and second, Derrida on the trace of the play of the signifier in the relationality and constructionism of the sign in the haphazard and inelegant system of binary opposition.[17] There can be no metalanguage of *langue*. This is so even if such a *mythos* is necessary in the discussion of the Madness of Order and the effort to transgress the outlaw. The simultaneity in superpositional flux of the mutually exclusive — neither both either and or nor — animates the perverse sensibility. This aesthetic undoes the boundaries of *le propre* (the proper, property, ownership, possession, and mineness). This perversity also celebrates the contradictions which are internal and external — extimate Same+ — to all projects of identity and desire. This includes those injunctions that must be adopted at the resolution of the male castration complex. Play and strategy of rattle and faze are the gaiety and flirtation of the pervert's *jouissance*. Jive is both the effect and radix of dispute of what Derrida (1972) says of thinking the "structurality of structure" or of reasoning the "essence of essence."[18] The pervert's *jouissance* is organized around this desirous transgression and enjoyable strategy whose *Trieb* scrambles all hierarchies and oppositions in the order of signification. Perverse ecstasy upends the laws of words and the rules of vocabularies.

I have focused on the patriarchal phallocentrism that psychoanalysis both exposes and explodes. I have also emphasized capitalist scarcity, private property, and other fields of *le propre*. These archetypes of property are coded within the system of language. The web of words is the foundation of the phallocentric representation of penis/not-penis of castration and of the capitalist reductions of economic relations to privacy and scarcity. These tropes of ownership extend beyond *my* penis and *my* money. Other avenues of proprietorship include *my* body, *my* mind, *my* soul, *my* thought, *my* value, *my* talent, and so on. These thrills can otherwise be conceived of as Sameness+ and Difference+, or as Derrida's "a sameness which is not identical." But obversely, what is "an identity which is not the same"? The amusement is visible in the Real Penis which always returns to the same place or simply in Sameness+. This sublime Being which is resistant to *écriture* simply looks campy and queer —

> Identity ∇ difference, self ∇ other, man ∇ Woman, gay ∇ straight, native ∇ foreign, black ∇ white, abled ∇ disabled, and ∇ the ∇ obverse. It can be symbolized in the loathsome political liberalism of equality: identity = difference, self = other, man = Woman, gay = straight, native = foreign, black = white, abled = disabled, and = so = on = and = the = obverse. ~~Being~~ can be mediatively symbolized as: everything = in = the = the = world = is = equal = because = everything = in = the = world = is = unequal. (Note: ≠ .)

Every opposition is internally and externally — extimately — split from itself because it is a joint of the Other. This mutual constitution and its unrepresentability reduce and elevate the signifying chain to a chucklesome and jokey game or *Logos*.

The pervert's *élan* and polish are affirmation. This dash and zing for flash and swing are the fetishistic orientation. This fling with trashy gingers and their deconstructions animates a hopeful, passionate, and enthusiastic excitement toward what willing having beening Becoming Being in-process and in-action. Perversely, gerund *qua* verb is Being *qua* Becoming *qua*, and so on. Grammatology immolates the extant of what is. It even autodeconstructs a metatheoretical series of concrete instances of opposition, origin, and signified. Such sunny grammatological murder blasts opposition as a structure which is the (non)condition of the Madness of Order. Madness of Order is exactly deviant from its own essence. This *différance* from the self-same and the self-identical is the exact *esprit de corps et pénis* of the both/and economy. Mutual contradictory superpositional resistance to observation collapses a destructive *Thanatos* into a series of unities of *Eros*. This explosion is the condition of the mantle of the yet-to-come of the Other of the Pervert-Schizoid-Woman and the Spirit of the System (S).

The Pervert-Schizoid-Woman of the S is ~~coincident~~ with the s of $-ism. S is simultaneously the Madness of Order and the conceptual persona of the neurotic. The Pervert-Schizoid-Woman is a configuration of neurosis. The Spirit of the System is a rendition of $-ism. What is the Sameness⁺ between the two, pervert and neurotic, and S and s? The ($\supseteq$) is ~~Being~~ the series of vast sublime consequences and massive unsymbolizable effects of the fiery raze of the project of the metaphysics of presence. The pervert illuminates the parallactic overlap. The pervert rearranges phallocentric lack and castration and capitalist private property and scarcity. The pervert does so in order to usher in a future system (S) which is already present but as yet invisible. S and s will become visible but with a shift in parallactic perspective.

The superpositional coincidence in the parallactic gap invites the pervert and the schizoid into the economy of the neurotic. This overlap of *Verleugnung, Verwerfung,* and *Verdrängung* animates the arrival of the Woman. Octave Mannoni's patient's dictum purports that the perverse offspring "knows very well" that the mother lacks and that the sister's penis is a desired fraud (neurosis), "but nevertheless" the fetish in-process, in-action bandages this wound in the simultaneity of the aperture and closure of the parallactic gap. Mannoni's ditty articulates the switcheroo from psychosis to perversion. The ecstatic instant of the perverse continuity (~~Being~~) between the lace, fur, shoe, jockstrap, and the maternal phallus represents the moment of difference and deferral of the fetish ($\supseteq$) female penis rather than the fetish ($\supseteq$) "penis-substitute." This shift in Being from penis-substitute to maternal phallus is the success of the lubricant of the Real Penis. This emollient of the Real Penis is "a sameness which is not identical." The Real Penis returns to the same place of Sameness⁺. The overlap of the parallactic gap is decisive. Phallocentrism and Clitoralcentrism, private property and public property, capitalism and communism, lack and plenitude, scarcity and fullness — and all of the other binary pairs in the system — ~~coincide~~ for a moment in space. The pervert's fetish is — Becoming. This *fete* of the Real Penis is the pursuit of *Trieb* and the return of the Madness of Order to health. The circuit party returns the symbolic to the Real. The parallax also emerges as a Peniscentrism — Clitoralcentrism — *qua* the penis in relationship ($\supseteq$) to the clitoris.

This penis is the excluded function of the generalized coordination of all of the objects in the galaxy. The penis is the center of the system. The penis is the excluded referent. The penis is the prototype and the archetype of all representation. But a Peniscentrism (Clitoralcentrism) is precisely the obverse of phallocentrism. Peniscentrism resists the structure of opposition: penis/not-penis. Instead, Peniscentrism (and Clitoralcentrism) returns the excluded body to the center of the system. The system is otherwise arranged by the general equivalent of the sign, the father, the phallus, and the dollar. The Real Penis strictly is *not*. The excluded referent of the system is the body of the penis and the clitoris. The generalized -centrism of the return of the body to the system illuminates the excess materiality that the abstraction of general equivalence cannot contain. The penis and the clitoris stick out of the system. The sex organs do not fit the arrangement of the relationship between body and mind.

The pervert does not deny the maternal phallus. The mother's penis is the entry into a symbolic order. This structure is reconfigured without opposition, hierarchy, identity, difference, masculine libido, capitalism, private property, or scarcity. But, at the same time, these trammels are internal to the reborn Spirit of the System of Sameness⁺, *Trieb*, feminine *jouissance*, communism, public property, and plenitude. Female castration is neither accepted nor rejected. Rather, Woman's lack is both admitted and controverted. This choice among the either/or, the both/and, and the neither/nor is the crux of the pervert's indecision. The female clitoris (is) the male penis because each of these sexual organs is different from itself. The female penis is (~~Being~~) the female clitoris and the male penis is (~~Being~~) the male clitoris. The destruction of the extant ontological order of Being is the perverse counterpart to the power and magic of the metaphysics of presence of the uncastrated maternal phallus.

The penis is both itself but also not itself. This simultaneity of "I know very well" and "but nevertheless" is handily reversible as "nevertheless" and "but I know very well." Disavowal exhibits a simultaneous affirmation which applies to the clitoris and to other sex organs, such as hermaphroditic configurations. The (im)possible female penis promises the future of a perverse revolution of the Spirit of the System. Selfhood and sociality involve the constitutive inlay and swathe of every neurotic division in the system, even the Spirit of the System (S) against $-ism (s) and the Madness of Order. The female penis is the sexual figuration of the Hysteria of Order. The linchpin of the transition of the madness of the system to a healthy schizoid and perverse order is the radiant return of the sister's penis from the Real. The return of this sister's Real Penis is a vibrant presence. The triumphant return of the sister's penis topples the distinction and opposition of the word. The otherwise fissure of the divide and conquer system autodeconstructs under scrutiny and demolition. The politics of everyday life engages the quaint thought and whimsical image that we are all on different sides of the same side.

Freud pronounces the perverse sensibility and fetishistic strategy a "very ingenious solution" to the castration threat.[19] The genius of perversity is that it avoids castration and its ruffians of lack, anxiety, desire, and identity. The sortilege is achieved not through indiscriminate foreclosure of loss but in genial affirmation of a simultaneous ("in the same breath") moment of both/and compromise. Cooperation outstrips the logic of (non)contradiction. Logic ($A = A$) is the Reasonable foundation of a binary economy. Unreasonably, the pervert's pixie dust bewitches Reason into the charade that the female penis is both present and absent. The pervert does not solely affirm a surmise in its presence — what the male junior assumes in his shocked approach to difference *qua* deficit. Rather, the pervert explores a faith ("I know very well that the penis is lost, but nevertheless I believe…") in a Sameness⁺ (~~Being~~) without recourse to either empirical data or experiential record. The pervert divines — somehow — the maternal phallus. This code of belief — trust and creed — serves him in his fetishization of the mother's loss.

The pervert's divine optimistic hope explicitly acknowledges a contradiction with knowledge ("I know very well, but nevertheless…"). In contrast, the neurotic wins his castration anxiety on the principles of knowledge ("I know very well, but I know very well"). This certainty of epistemology eschews all faith, belief, hope, divinity, trust, and persuasion. The neurotic's will to castration is organized by Reason. Reason is structured by castration. The pervert's avoidance of loss is configured by an adept loyalty to an otherness which is beyond Reason. The Madness of Order demeans this faith *qua* Unreason. Unreason is simultaneously the precept of $-ism. The perverse evasion of castration dramatically resituates the pervert's relationship to the law (pact) and *jouissance*. Freud's laudatory remarks about the fetishist demonstrate the pervert's potential transformation of subjectivity and sociality — man and world — in his campy redesign of castration and its effects.

The compromise between psychosis and neurosis is imperfect but functional. According to Freud, "the instinct is allowed to retain its satisfaction" and sustain the psychosis of a foreclosure of the order of sexual difference.[20] But, at the same time, "proper respect is shown to reality" and the neurosis of a repression of the desire for the mother is also achieved.[21] The "retention" of the satisfaction of the schizoid's enjoyment of the mother is tempered by a "proper respect" toward the father. The pervert clinches a sexual effluvium with his penis and his mother at the same time as he identifies with the law of the father and pursues the ego-ideal. This identification deviates from the normative demands of bourgeois culture. The pervert respects reality in the same gesture as he subverts it. Perversely, respect is subversion. The both/and simultaneity of the mutually exclusive triumphs. Mutual inclusivity configures ~~Being~~ as deviant from itself. The unconscious representation of contradiction expedites an impossible written and spoken of Being *sous rature*. The art of the pervert is respect in subversion and honor by dissent. The pervert lauds through criticism, and agrees with disagreement. These prepositional forms — in, by, through, with — typify the by-routes and cross-streets of the demonstration of the deviation of every object from itself. The preposition is the grammatical mechanism of the subversion of the Logic of Identity.

The preposition is the spatial text in which the difference and deferral of *différance* traverse Outside of identity and essence. The preposterous prepositional pervert masturbates the subject *qua* object *qua* subject. The pervert embraces the mother's love as, with, toward, near, by, and so on this object. Love must be reconciled with an amnesic gesture toward the father and an inconstant idealization of masculinity. Identification with the father allows entry into an Order of Madness. The pervert wills this S in his decision to collaborate with the schizoid. The ethical caper of the schizoid and the pervert is to transform the Madness of Order into the robust health of the Order of Madness. But, at the same time, the horizon of this dash is the intense overlap of the two registers. This parallax exceeds itself toward an Other — capitalist overproduction, psychoanalytic *Trieb*, and deconstructive signifier — whose (*a*)sexual origin cannot be recuperated by the mutual inclusion or Sameness⁺ of the aneconomy of the Spirit of the System. This gap may not even be approachable from within the extant symbolic order. But the maternal phallus *qua* object of belief rather than *qua* object of knowledge structures a trust which cannot be contradicted by either empirical or experiential Reason. Faith enlivens the source of the pervert's power, magic, and confidence to enjoy Joe's jockstrap among other sacred jockstraps. The "very ingenious solution" of perversion is the fetishist's transformation of man and world.

The Real Penis is proxy for ~~Being~~. The Real Penis is the emollient of the ontological quest for representation of the self-same and the self-identical. The ~~Real Penis~~ is *sous rature*, like ~~Being~~. But the difference is figural and metaphorical. The Real Penis implies an (inchoate) sexualized galaxy in which all objects are liberated in the free exchange and emancipated switcheroo of aims and objects. This unguent viscerally relates and constructs in the absence of the speculations and abstractions — in capitalism, numbers; in phallocentrism, size and visibility — of general equivalence. The Real Penis is the Real which resists sex, sexuality, and gender. The embodied return of the Real Penis destroys the ontological self-same and self-identical "What is?" of precisely these essences. The words of the Madness of Order are neither separate nor proximate, and neither alien nor familiar. Rather, objects are Otherwise in the novel forms and new modes of consanguinity and propinquity. Bonds and links between these objects are the Real. These rapports animate the scene of fetishism. Fetishism is the in-process, in-action willing having beening Becoming Being — Real Penis. The ~~Real Penis~~ is Other. There is no exact word for the ~~Real Penis~~. There is no proper symbol for the joint or hinge between materiality and abstraction, between body and mind, and so on.

The Real Penis is the greasy smear which relays and spins symbolic objects toward each other in the absence of the sign of division (/). Hierarchy otherwise separates word from word and object from object. The compromised Being of the Real Penis is Real. Being is resistant to symbolization *qua* under erasure. The Real Penis relates and correlates objects in the copula. The Real Penis even relays and conveys the self-identical and self-same of the word with itself *qua* Being. ~~Being~~ is another substitute for the ~~Real Penis~~. *Qua* substitution, the Real Penis and Being — but also any other object — can be elevated to the function of the center. The (any) object is the asymbol (⊇) for the copula of Being. Being is otherwise the (dis)connective tissue of relationships between the objects in the system. Other names for the ~~Real Penis~~ include Vacation, Time-Share, Beach-Front Property, the Vineyard, the Beach House, the Ocean, the Boys on the Sand, and so on. The function is excluded from the center (*et al.*) of the structure. The Real Penis (and so on) is excluded from the system as the proviso of its coordination. The object in the system is Outside of the system itself. There is no Inside of the system. There is no Outside of the system. The object is in the indeterminate and undecidable timeless space of the unconscious. The metonymization of metaphor can be articulated as Alexander-Real-Penis-Skarsgard-Real-Penis-and-Real-Penis-I-Real-Penis-are-Real-Penis-in-Real-Penis-love-Real-Penis *qua* the Real-Penis (and so on).

The copula of the Real Penis is destructured. But this is also exemplary of every other part of speech in the systems of desire, commodity, and the sign. But the concept of the Real Penis is considerably different from Being. The Real Penis is less pretentious and more campy than the ontico-ontological difference of the philosophical and ontological project. The Real Penis introduces the dimension of the Real *qua Verwerfung* into the intimacy of the symbolic web of words. The hinge which fastens the material signifier and abstract signified is not the symbolic but the Real. The Real Penis is not only the playfully perverse avatar of Being. It also denotes the prepositional fetish for the maternal phallus. This is crucial for my purposes. The perverts believe, hope, promise, and divine that the fetish — somehow — can suture the wounds of the space (to differ) and the time (to defer) between the marks in the universe of objects. The Being of the philosophical and ontological project — "What is?" — may be forever under erasure. The perverse Real Penis may be absolutely resistant to the word. But the inspired seal of the ontological impossibility and the Real symbolization in the brazenfaced, bad-mannered, brash-necked, and smart-arsed Real Penis present a perversely conceptual "but nevertheless" flipped and nervy object for the *différance* between, among, below, above, around, within, without, and near the proximity of objects.

The Real Penis is a figuration of a torus-like extimate relationship between the symbolic and the Real. The word and its impossibility are internal to each other at the same nodal points of the Real Symbolic. The Real Penis is the overlap — parallactic aperture and closure — of the symbolic and the Real. The Real Penis is the uncracked and laminated overlay of the maternal phallus and its fetishes. The (im)perfect pall of fetish-object *qua* penis-substitute *qua* maternal-phallus *qua* Real-Penis — ~~qua~~ — is a collection of objects. These objects are not self-same or self-identical to themselves. The ~~Real Penis~~ can only be savored as such at the simultaneous fetishistic moment of orgasmic after-glow of the four-way-*qua* at the end-of-the-lay. Perverts are swizzled. But "yes, yes" it will return even better the next time around, near, by, and so on — toward Piper's jockstrap. At the orgasmic spatiotemporal moment of the emergent Spirit of the System of Sameness⁺ of —

> — fetish-Real-Penis-penis-substitute-Real-Penis-maternal-phallus-Real-Penis-Real-Penis-Real-Penis — fur, Real Penis, lace, Real Penis, shoe, Real Penis, Hayden Christensen, Real Penis, Hugh Jackman, Real Penis, and every other guy and doll and the rest of us in the sets of jockstraps in the battery of the Other —

— all of this faithful shag and divine bonk illuminates the nexus of the symbolic and the Real. The Real Penis is the conjunctive and prepositional goo in-between objects whose interdependence is less oppositionally divisive and more coitally sexy. The compulsive repetition of the Real Penis elaborates copulative adjective, verb, adverb, noun, and so on. These indices posit a systemic insistence which bonds, breaks, loves, takes, desires, and drifts — toward a *Trieb* which is beyond the pleasure principle and ascendent to *Thanatos*. This death drive is cut from the same circumcision of the love-making of her partner, *Eros*. *Eros* contracts bodies together. *Thanatos* expands the universe. Any which way?

Real Symbolic

~~The~~ Real Penis makes possible such apertures and closures with joints and hinges of fetishes, metaphors, centers, metonymies, maternal phalluses, sisterly penises, and so on which are bonded by milt and seed rather than (/), (—), (<>), and even (⊇). The radical exclusion of the function of these various (de)centers means that the entire system is Outside of itself. The Real Symbolic is absolutely unsymbolizable. The system is woefully outmatched by the Real. The symbolic order surrenders the Real Signifier and the Signified/r to the center of its system. This return of the Real to the extant order of Being inspires madness. The hysterics of the order can only neurotically foreclose (*rejet névrotique*) the consequent returns of the Real with skeptical habit. These returns are the simultaneous rupture and brace of an Unreasonable Reason. *Qua* returns, patriarchy, capitalism, and language are the fundamental symptoms of this return of the unspeakable and unwriteable object. The Real hijacks and destroys ontology. The Real generates the gobbledygook slip and slide of nonsense in the system. This poppycock is the redemption of $-ism in a gesture toward the trust and the promise of the arrival of the future of the Pervert-Schizoid-Woman and the Spirit of the System.

Perversely, this Spirit (S) is simultaneously the Order of Madness and the Madness of Order. Metaphysical schizophrenia is internal to the symbolic *qua* Real as the Outside of the rational coherence of binary oppositions of Reason. Reason is a coordinated set of combinations in the symbolic order. This series generalizably harmonizes the system. The schizoid is concerned with the impossibility of the written and the spoken of the Real. The schizoid suffers the tortures and amusements of an incoherent Unreason. The pervert rejoices in the *Trieb* which encircles the impossible codes of speech and text. But, at the same time, the pervert also plays and strategizes with the "What is the penis?" of the ~~Real Penis~~ and ~~Being~~ and their infinite ~~avatars~~. These familiar aliens of bonds and unions in a beyond of the pleasure principle await the (de/re)construction of the deceitful opposition between *Eros* and *Thanatos*. Freud remarks on the essential extimacy of the life drive and the death drive in *Beyond the Pleasure Principle* (1920).[22] *Eros* enforces unions and nexuses. *Thanatos* devises breaks and ravages. *Thanatos* undoes the bonds of *Eros*. *Eros* reconstructs the ruins of *Thanatos*. But what is the difference to note if each is the flip-side of the other in the (de/re)construction of its brother's gesture?

This posthomeostatic drive is a modality of solidarity. Beyond, is a law of *jouissance* as duty. The pervert bequeaths such solidarity to the reality of castration. The pervert both regards and appreciates but also dismisses and deplores this Real of sexual difference. The pervert's charmed respect for the Real Symbolic is visible in his wanderless drive around — near, by, above, to, below — the Real. The pervert's journey speaks and writes the future amusements of the symbolic of the Spirit of the System (S). The pervert's aim/less mosey freely transforms the Madness of Order into an Order of Madness. The pervert's *Trieb* opens the translation of the Spirit of the System into the System of the Spirit. The Real Symbolic's flip and switch are a willing having beening Becoming Being — *Yes!* The moment of simultaneous superposition deploys the techniques and talents, and slips and slides, of the unconscious. These primary process gizmos manifest in the absence of the negation of castration and the loss of scarcity. Knowledge and the series of oppositions, hierarchies, significations, and nihilisms are dissolved. The pervert outlines the fissure of the Real in the architectonics of the signifier which overwhelms the purported self-same and self-identical unity of the sign. Unveiled, the system manifests the Real difference and negativity of the signifier at the center of the symbolic word. The object is different from itself.

Figure 6.2 The Real Symbolic

This image shows the metarelationship between the Real (left) and the symbolic order (right). The obverse parallactic overlap is a Sameness[+] of the two figures which are otherwise separated in this metarelationship in the symbolic order. The metaphysics of presence (left) is represented by the fill-in-the-blank line over the system of castration. This castration is depicted by the phallic function and the image of the vortex. The obliterated quotation marks symbolize the Real which is the Outside of the metaphysics of presence and the system of simulacrum. The symbolic order enables quotation marks to express the ~~Being~~ of any object and any word. The object (right) is fragmented and situated within the quotation marks. The quotation marks around the object indicate a fundamental impossibility. The fetish defies the system of identification, and it prefers a play of *jouissance*. The *das Ding* or object is always subject to the ontological question of the "What is?" which (de)constitutes the borders of the answer. The object *qua* subject (right) playfully precedes the ontological question. This object (right) is merely fragmented. This is distinct from the absent (present) simultaneity of the object (left) of the Real Symbolic. The Real Symbolic is the overlapped parallactic eclipse of the symbolic order and the resistant obverse in the Real. The symbolic speaks and writes its own impossibility.

Notes & Sketches —

There is no prescription, formulary, or procedure for this galaxy-making experiment between man and world. There are rigorous excavations of the diagnostic structures in psychoanalysis. These typologies theorize speculative expositions of characterologies and pathologies. These diagnostic verdicts on social ills enable and disable the transition toward the Other of the Pervert-Schizoid-Woman and her Spirit of the System. The essence of the pervert is an aesthetic and sensibility. Perversion is not quite camp. Perversion is not exactly kitsch. But perversion is also not irony or deadpan. Rather, the perverse attitude is contingent on the thinking, being, and living of each singular aspirant to perversion, schizophrenia, and femininity. But I do insist on solidarity as decisively essential to Becoming-Perverse. United, the queers, the normals, the weirdos, and the conservatives are campy, kitschy, ironic, deadpan, wry, and even quiet.

Real Fetish

Becoming-Pervert engages with the wizardry of fetish-making *qua* world-making. This is a cosmological world-disclosure. This is the "another way out," as Freud says, of the magic of the fetish in the castration complex. The pervert must celebrate the "creation of a substitute for the penis which he missed in females — that is to say, a fetish."[23] A psychotic foreclosure of the empirical world and experiential life is supplanted by a perverse substitution of an object for an absence. But the pervert substitutes not for any lack of an object but for the absence of a quite specific Something is Missing. This object is the mother's penis or even the sister's penis. The maternal phallus is specific and unique. The sister's penis is also magical. The sister's appendage is isomorphically significant because it is the penis of the same generation as the male junior's penis. The sister's penis is Outside of the relational vicissitudes of the generational general equivalent of the father's phallus. These maternal and paternal relationships otherwise define the offspring's orientation toward the phallus of the identificatory ego-ideal. The sister's penis is the phallic *general inequivalent*. The male junior's penis is the phallic *indeterminate equivalent*. The sister's penis embodies the specificity and uniqueness of the maternal phallus but in a generational cohort at the outskirts of the idealization of the paternal generation. The rapport between the penis of the male junior and his sister is distinct from the relationship between the male junior and the paternal phallus. The sister's imagined penis puts the undecidability of the male junior's penis in sharp relief.

The originary Something is Missing is inside and outside of the mother. The mother's pretend phallus is sustained by the male junior's fantasy for a period even after the revelation of the castration of the female junior. Lacan emphasizes the castration of the mother in the text on the function of the phallus (1955).[24] Maternal castration is the source of the scene of fetishism. The female junior's castration is the scene of anxiety. This *mise-en-scène* foments the masculine trajectories toward the ego-ideal and the (re)production of Western civilization. The mother bears her penis in the make-believe of the male junior for a considerably longer duration than the female junior retains hers in the male junior's imagination. Maternal castration puts both the mother's desire and the offspring's identification under suspicion. The male junior discovers that Something is Missing in the mother at the climax of the reorganization of his epistemophilic instinct and its extant interpretation of maternal desire. Suddenly, the male junior realizes that his mother's desire is oriented toward an Other. This Other is not the offspring. Normal developmental conditions prompt the male junior to individuate and differentiate from the mother in order to identify with the father. This nascent identity warrants an embryonic object of desire. The male junior will become (like) the father, and he will have someone (like) his mother. Identity and desire are metaphorical — *like* — at the inception of their development. The (like) is the metaphorical *différance* in space and time of the renewal anew of identity and desire.

In contrast, the perverse offspring becomes the instrument of both the mother's *jouissance* and the generalized Other's ecstasy. The pervert becomes a performer, a clown, a showman — *à Lacan* — for the world's stage. The castration of the mother is relieved. The male junior is separated but not alienated. The mother's desire is displaced from son to father. But maternal enjoyment sustains libidinized desire for the charmed shenanigans of the son. This split between *désir et jouissance* is pivotal. The pervert discerns that joy is happy expression and that want is the exact opposite. The pervert imagines that *jouissance* is freedom and that desire is necessity. The mother's enjoyment is the pervert's pleasure. The radiance of the galaxy is the amusement of the pervert. There is Nothing is Missing if Everything is Hilarious. If the *petit pervers* Lacan can avoid the enforced castration anxiety of the Something is Missing — not in the mother but in the female junior and her *Title of the Letter* (1973) — then his performances in *Seminar* will be marvelously witty even without the presence of Jacques-Alain Miller's jockstrap.

The plenitude of the maternal phallus formerly enables the male junior to endlessly enjoy the prized possession of his penis in the warm embrace of his mother's universal love. The *l'homme-lette* or omelet-man of childhood — Sameness⁺ — is antecedent to identity and desire. This cozy and snug incestuous affair with the mother is shattered by the neurotic's encounter with castration. Castration is the first engagement between *Homo sapiens* and difference. This difference is defined *qua* deficit as Something is Missing. The perverse male junior both accepts and denies this castration. The perverse offspring's achievement is not to *know* of female plenitude but to *believe* nonetheless in this presence despite evidence to the contrary. This divine trust in the world eschews debilitative loss. The male fetishist dreams of laces, furs, shoes, jockstraps, penises, substitutes, maternal penises, penis-substitutes, penis-penises, clitoris-clitorises, centers, metaphors, words, signs, and so on. These master signifiers are the excluded function of the field of (*a*)sexuality. These fetishes are not Outside but also not Inside of the system as its proviso of operation and its term of expiry.

The fetish is a reference for the penis, which is a reference, which is a reference, which is a reference, and so on. The fetish miraculously makes divine belief and innocent trust the source of a sexual orgasm. The (*a*)sexual moan and groan are unknown to neurotics. These neurotics otherwise suffer Something is Missing and the quick tension and release of lazy climax. The neurotic forever endures and desires the truth that "there is no such thing as a sexual relation."[25] The perverse subject has not only "saved his own penis," as Freud explains. But he has also eclipsed the castration anxiety which precipitates narcissism, aggression, and anxiety. These symptoms are characteristic of oedipal forms of selfhood and sociality. These modalities of oedipal contacts and $-istic interactions are arranged by Something is Missing. Revolution is only possible in and as the expansive parallactic overlap of the Real and its material overlay. There is no mechanism of revolutionary transition from s to S to s to S in the total triumph of castration. The revolution toward S is only possible in the parallactic transfomation of Something is Missing into Nothing is Missing. But this parallax entails an expansive excess. This surplus cannot be assimilated into the utopic imagination of feminism, communism, and the signifier. This transfiguration summons permutational arrangements of the aneconomies of an Everything is Alive — surplus, deficit, excess, recess, expansion, contraction — of communist queer (*a*)sexuality. These variants of parts and wholes — hearts and holes — invite new (*a*)sexual identities of desire, finance, and language. The (*a*)sexuality is a species and breed of antioedipal selfhood and sociality. An (*a*)sexuality complements the pneuma of the Pervert-Schizoid-Woman and her Spirit of the System.

Perversely, why bother with identity and its political non-starters and dead-ends if a pin-up of Milo Ventimiglia's jockstrap will do the trick as the trick? Freud describes the upshot of fetishistic disavowal: "[the male junior] need have no fear for his own penis, so he could proceed with his self-pleasure undisturbed."[26] But what are the forms and contents of this "undisturbed" self-pleasure? Freud's text implies that the little pervert returns to his penis because he evades anxiety about loss. The offspring also sustains a disinterest in the law of the father and his establishment of a normative ego-ideal for the young-masturbator. The mechanisms of the father and the ego-ideal are necessary in order to transition away from anxiety and the "undisturbed" and toward sexualization and the other. But is there another requirement which permits the male junior to evolve from the fearless pervert of bottomless masturbatory jocundity in his cautious sidestep away from the sister's penis and the maternal body and toward the representation of the fur, lace, shoe, and Mike's jockstrap? The leap from the sister and the mother to these fetishistic figurations of the maternal phallus is tricky and unwieldy. How does the male junior avoid incest with the mother? Even, why should he? The fetishes are the material substratum for the indices of the pervert's pleasure. But the mechanism by which the fur, lace, shoe, and jockstrap fit adequation to the reality of the sister's penis and the maternal phallus is only unconvincingly examined by Freud.

The perversion of childhood refracts the thinking, being, and living of the subject of adult fetishism. Freud surmises that the male junior's fetishistic strategy is "decisive as regards the boy's practical behavior."[27] But the consequence of Freud's insight about "practical behavior" is mostly unexplained. This is so except for a couple of stray mentions of residual anxieties. This reference to "practical behavior" intimates the pervert's penchant for pictures rather than people. The ecstasy in the image incurs both a loss and a gain. The other is "undisturbed" because the center of the substitution in fetishistic sex is the penis-substitute rather than the castrated clitoris. But the other is also "disturbed" because she is subject to open substitution. The pervert is inessential to the scene of fetishistic satisfaction.

Perverse fetishism is a social and political strategy whose efficacy is only limited by the reach of its compromise between psychosis and neurosis. But the ethics of fetishism is potentially charged and distressed. There is no proleptic generalizable evaluative gizmo which can assess the ethics of perversion and fetishism in any specific and accidental situation. My claim is that the pervert and his cohort of friends make up and make out structures and systems which are profoundly progressive. The pervert may be an historical constituent *ad infinitum*. But he is also a social essence *ad infinitum*. The distinction in the specificity of the fetish and its *mise-en-scène* is under scrutiny only because Sameness⁺ is an ethics.

The advantage of the neologism Real Penis is its indication of the simultaneity of the fetish, the penis-substitute, the sister's penis, the mother's phallus, the center, the sign, the metaphor, the word, and the object in the same moment at the same instant. This at once is an orgasmic — every word ~~is~~ the same word and every word ~~is~~ the different word, and so on — orgiastic celebration. The Real Penis indicates the necessary lubrication not simply of representations and figurations. The Real Penis also indexes emollient between the materialities of bodies and souls. The Real is unspeakable and unwriteable. This is so even in the *Praxis* of the symbolic order of the Becoming-Spirit of the System. But the Penis in the Real promises to intermix bodies, pleasures, and fluids in the absence of ~~Being~~. The death of philosophical ontology invites an *Eros* in which the Real Penis sublimely unwrites, obscurely unspeaks, and divinely disfigures distanced copulas. These connective marks deliver unto the death of man the obvious truth that "there is no such thing as a sexual relation."

The Heideggerian Ontico-Ontological Difference is isomorphic to the Perverse Being-Real-Penis Division. The parallactic gap between Heideggerianism and perversion is that whereas the former Being under erasure is resistant to speech and writing the latter (*a*)sexuality is resistant to gender and sexuality. The symbol of Being — under erasure — is resistant to ontic entities. The Real Penis — under the covers — is resistant to gender and sexuality. The Real Penis and its (*a*)sextuality are under erasure — *sous rature* — because they resist sexual difference and its system of gender and sexuality. The purpose of the Real Penis is to indicate an (*a*)sexuality. This (*a*)sexuality is the Real object of the pervert's resistance to gender and sexuality. The fetish-object decopulates and desexualizes. This is an (*a*)sexuality. But it is not a sex. The pervert gets off on text rather than on sex, on pictures rather than on anatomies, on words rather than on bodies, on signs rather than on sins, on *clichés* rather than on the birds and the bees, and on phrases rather than on the facts of life. The Real Penis runs out of lubricant. But the Real Clitoris is its own emollient. This is so only in the event that the heterosexual man overcomes the attitude of horror toward the clitoris. The magical lesbian engages the unspeakable and unwriteable vagina and clitoris (*et al.*) within the Real Symbolic. She does so without the Real Penis. But then with what? The lesbian puts under erasure itself *sous rature*: ~~Real Clitoris~~.

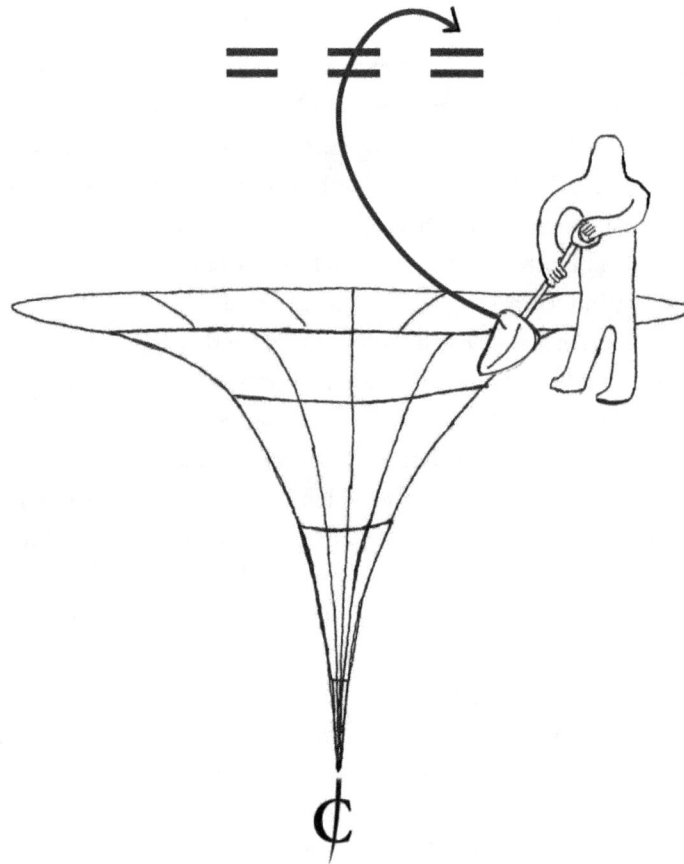

This illustration shows the neurotic who mines the center of the structure. The neurotic performs the labor of the restabilization and decenterment of reiterations. The neurotic scours the identities and differences in the system. The neurotic integrates these binary oppositions into the Logic of Identity (A = A ≠ B). This image shows that the system is in excess of itself. There is a surplus which exceeds the phallic balances of identity, difference, and (in)equality which are measured by the general equivalent. The (in)equality is excavated from the infinite source of difference — A and B and C and D, and so on — in order to restabilize and destabilize the structure. This system is otherwise emptied of loss and devoid of lack. Standardization produces the debt of a Something is Missing in a system which is otherwise structured by a Nothing is Missing. The neurotic intuition of loss is predicated on a plenitude of excess. Phallocentric castration, capitalist scarcity, and linguistic absence are the effects of a system of (im)balanced (in)equality. The picture illustrates that there is an abundance of goods and services which is barricaded by a loss in currency. The production of goods and services outstrips the availability of dollars and coins. Simultaneously, the historical production of an abundance of goods and services and the ideological necromancy of a scarcity of dollars and coins are mediated by a general equivalence which regulates the plenitude of Sameness⁺ in the system as an (in)equality. This standardization enables and institutionalizes (in)equality in sexual, economic, and linguistic difference.

Notes & Sketches —

"...THAT DANGEROUS SURPLUS..."

Sameness⁺ is the structural principle which organizes the Madness of Order. This Sameness⁺ is neurotically foreclosed (*rejet névrotique*) by the system. This Real returns to destabilize the order of $-ism. The illumination of the organizational principle of Sameness⁺ demonstrates a surplus which exceeds Sameness⁺. This remainder of energy tends toward the expansion of the universe in the *tout autre* of the Other. This excess is visible: in the Overproduction⁺ of commodities in capitalism; in the extension of (un)pleasure in *Trieb*⁺ and the masochism of courtly love; and in the Play⁺ of the signifier in language. My claim is that the source of this excessive expansion of the solar system is an (*a*)sexual essence which is the excluded function of the system. The capitalist ideology of scarcity, the patriarchal version of sexual difference, and the word of *langue* must confront the obscene abundant signifier of this (*a*)sexuality. The Neurotic Foreclosure (*rejet névrotique*) of the Madness of Order is the reaction of the system to this scandalous ~~Being Nothingness~~ at the excluded center of the system. The returns of this *Verdrängung* of the Real are the symptoms of capitalist scarcity, phallocentric sexual difference, and the sovereignty of the word. The liberation of the surplus promises an expansion of the universe toward communism, feminism, deconstruction — and the Spirit of the System of ... that dangerous supplement ...

Psychoanalysis is a consistently anxious fable about castration and loss. But there are moments of insight in which a shiny plenitude emerges from the shadows of bloody knives and amputated appendages. Lacan's innovation of the concept of "surplus *jouissance*" in his *Seminar* on the other side of psychoanalysis (1969-1970) illuminates the bone in the throat of transition — from the masculine to the feminine; from anxious protection of private property to free production of worlds-to-come; from castration and lack to plenitude and fullness; from worried desire to outlandish *Trieb*; from restricted capitalism to free communism, and so on. The notion of surplus *jouissance* is essentially the hitch of too little with too much. Quite happily, man has too much, yet man settles for too little. This typical economy is isomorphic to the capitalist supply/demand dynamic in which supply overruns demand. The system must raze its excess in order to sustain scarcity. $-ism must convert too much into too little. The system must transform Nothing is Missing into Something is Missing. The Madness of Order must retool the penis into the phallocentric version of the clitoris.

The concept of surplus *jouissance* is homologous to the theory of surplus value in Marx. The substance of both surpluses — Lacan's enjoyment and Marx's labor — is sublimely unrepresentable from within the future system. A nascent communism is a system in the absence of the general equivalent of dollars and coins. The products of labor cannot be speculated or abstracted. The object is valueless. An embryonic surplus *jouissance* is a system in which pleasure cannot be calculated because Nothing is Missing in enjoyment. These (in)equivalences in labor and enjoyment are possible even if the current organization authorizes their calculation and speculation. This commodity is comparable and contrastable to this other object, and this enjoyment is abstractly greater or lesser than this other pleasure. Otherwise, there is neither Nothing is Missing nor Everything is Present in these surpluses. This is so despite the excess which is conceptually articulated in both the joy and work which are under consideration. In the *Seminar* (1969-1970), Lacan first mentions surplus *jouissance* with a caution,

> What's disturbing is that if one pays in *jouissance*, then one has got it, and then, once one has
> got it then it is very urgent that one squander it. If one does not squander it, there will be all
> sorts of consequences.[28]

The capitalist exchange market persuades the self to receive the payout with his *jouissance*. This is only the case if the subject is a pervert whose position is precisely the enjoyment of the Other's *jouissance*. If the subject of surplus *jouissance* is a pervert, then he owns it ("has got it"), then he still owns it ("then, once one has it"), and then he must unown it ("it is very urgent that one squander it"). The system of *propriété de la jouissance* (the proper, property, ownership, possession, and mineness) must be quickly destructured of *jouissance* lest the system of enjoyment transition from Something is Missing *de la jouissance* to Nothing is Missing *de la jouissance*.

The private property of pleasure must be transferred from one to the other — <> or / — in order to sustain a capitalist society of minimalist joy rather than a communist culture of maximalist rapture. The system is structured by the supposed equality of general equivalence of dollars and coins in exchange of enjoyments. This "then one has got it" means that the surplus pleasure is converted into an ownership of identity and desire. This is so no matter the permeability of these boundaries between selves and others. These borders will necessarily be porous in the exchange of *jouissance* with the Other. The resultant imbalance in the exchange is (re)calculated and re(ac)counted in order to generally and equivalently determine who's the taker and who's the maker, who's the top and who's the bottom, and so on. These calculations of the gift disinterest the pervert.

But the catch is that the "then one has got it" in giving it up to the Other renders the deal raw. But for whom? In the phrase, "if one pays in *jouissance*," the payer is undecided — whether it is the debtor or the creditor. Whose enjoyment is whose? The enjoyer is the one who pays. He pays with *jouissance*. The surplus of the enjoyment is an excess, extension, and nimiety which cannot be calculated or counted. But speculation and abstraction haunt the scene of exchange as reminders of an anxious (in)equality. The imbalance is on neither and both sides of the exchange. The consequence of this (un)decided (in)equality is an anxious question. Whose pleasure is whose? Anxiously, by what standardization of general equivalence can this interval between debt and credit — "if one pays in *jouissance*, then one has got it" — be measured? What is the criterion by which deficit and surplus are determined?

Surplus Ownership

The surplus is simultaneously a deficit. This excess must be "squandered" lest "all sorts of consequences" tread the entire system of $-ism — capitalism, phallocentrism, private property, scarcity, patriarchy, binary opposition, hierarchical signification against play of value, distinction of the sign above difference of the signifier, desire better than *Trieb*, and so on. The nefarious effect of surplus is that the system is structured by phallocentrism (not-penis) and capitalism (scarcity). These systems are arranged by a concept of desire. *Désir* is organized by the sting of lack and the bite of castration. Castration and scarcity are the internal constituents of the psychoanalytic view of desire and identity and the capitalist ideology of production and consumption. Capitalism is founded on the assumption of scarcity. There is an essential debt (credit) in the system of $-ism. The supply/demand dynamics are necessary for the (im)proper distribution of private property goods to so-called (improperly) naturally born selfish — rather than to so-called (properly) socially designed monstrous — subjects. Phallocentrism is organized on the assumption of the not-penis. There is an essential lack (fullness) in the system of patriarchy. The criteria of "size" and "visibility" are requisite for the (im)proper measurement of sexual objects in the field of desire. Surplus is the future. But excess is manipulated by the shackles of capitalist scarcity and phallocentric clitoris.

Phallocentrically, the penis accrues both its positive value but also its incipient vulnerability in comparison and contrast with the clitoris. The female genital is of miniature stature and obscure visibility. This renders the clitoris a faded copy of the glory of the original phallus. The phallic criterion for general equivalence is magnitude. The penis is deemed the superior counterpart of the not-penis. In code, "a man has a penis and a Woman does not have a penis." This not-penis is a suspiciously — dare I say — homosexual description of the clitoris. The Woman's positive sex is figured as an absent negativity. Capitalistically, the commodity accrues both mark-up and mark-down in comparison and contrast with the other commodities in the system as it is mediated by the general equivalent. The commodity is assigned value — less or more — by the dictates of currency. This is so even if there is no necessary and logical relationship between two different commodities of distinct use-value. The system of commodities is not strictly structured by a –centrism of A/-A. Rather, the commodity is arranged by subordination to a generalized and standardized system of numbers and integers in currency. The violence of valuation in the commodity system is that the general equivalent compares, contrasts, and exchanges between use-values which are otherwise singularities. These singularities cannot be properly calculated or speculated in exchange. The otherwise singular positivity of the use-value of a commodity is dominated by the negative system of exchange of the general equivalent.

The *le propre* economy is the foundation of $-ism in capitalism and phallocentrism. The self owns as *le propre* under the regime of $-ism. The self owns *my* pink Jansport backpack, *my* J.Crew merino wool sweater (with *my* patch sleeve pockets), *my* Jaguar XJR, *my* Ford F150, *my* mansion, and *my* cardboard box — but I also own *my* education, *my* thought, *my* personality, *my* body, *my* genetic code, *my* values, *my* politics, *my* sexuality, *my* identity, *my* community, and so on. I even own ownership of *my*self. The self is captive to a rabid will to privacy and property and at the same time to privation and paucity. These guarded lunch pails and protected eggplants are then quickly manipulated and disposed of — only to foster regret and remorse for the loss. The will to collection of ownership only intensifies the protective anxiety of loss and the narcissistic regret of mourning and melancholia.

The regain of this loss sutures the wounds with other wid-mos and giz-gets. The process of exchange and return is the essence of the masculine economy of debt and castration. This cycle of exchange and return annuls the otherness of the Outside. This phallocentric and capitalist economy of comparison and contrast is virulently symptomatic and effectively everywhere. The capitalist system is organized by scarcity and the supply/demand dynamics of credit and debt. Nietzsche discovers the resentful slave of obligation, reciprocity, charge, duty, accountability, and responsibility at the origin of morality.[29] There is a beyond of the strict codes of capitalist consumerism and general equivalence and an outside of the patriarchal version of desire and lack. But a restricted economy must otherwise "squander" the excess. This surplus cannot be recuperated into the abstract (knowledge) or material (concrete) systems of $-ism. The extra must be negated by *Verdrängung* or *Verwerfung* or *Verleugnung*. The capitalist misunderstands the situation of surplus *jouissance*. The economist apologist misses the inevitable and undecidable — constitutive — imbalance between self and other in enjoyment. This misproportion is neither equal nor unequal nor identical nor different in speculation or calculation. The emergence of an otherness to the closed circuit of the $-istic circulation of value is not equality. This system of equality is based in a calculation of difference and otherness in quantity and magnitude. The heterosexual misunderstands phallic *désir*. The man misses the constitutive lack at the center of the object of desire. The surplus of enjoyment is squelched by the imbalance in relationship to the *objet*. The object is calculated as the proper fit for the aim. But the transience of the object transforms plenitude into lack. The neurotic suffers loss rather than relishes gain. In contrast, the pervert's surplus in *jouissance* and use-value in labor celebrate the un(ac)countability and (mis)measurement of the object.

The issue is the conditions of the productivity of the surplus. The psychical and social endeavor to elevate the unequal and identical, and equal and different, imbalance to Sameness⁺ is crucial to my theoretical and political commitments. The Spirit of the System innovates a clitoral and communist system. Neurotics and capitalists must learn to renounce exchange, obligation, debt, credit, and return. The pervert and the communist embrace a general rather than a restricted economy. The perverse (*a*)sexual world-to-come (S) is open to asymmetry, imbalance, incalculability, and unaccountability. Perversity and communism are a pure phonology. Neurosis and capitalism are a pure psychology. The return of obligation of reciprocity in exchange is the subject of analysis in Derrida's discussion of the annulment of the gift in *Given Time: 1 Counterfeit Money* (1994). The masculine economy must "squander" the excess and surplus of *le plus de* penis and commodity.

This morality of debt, credit, obligation, exchange, and return is a *Gordian knot* strangulation of the future of the Spirit of the System. The pursuit of S invites the pervert and communist to seek the *Holy Grail* panacea programme. My effort flashily overwhelms the $-istic desire to imbalance equality and inequality with a gesture toward a Sameness⁺. The neurotic projects of capitalism and phallocentrism structure all relatedness between objects. This is performed by the criteria of the general equivalent. The standards are labor time in capitalism and desirous magnitude in phallocentrism. The capitalist and the patriarch pursue the overwrought calculations, anxious speculations, and desperate (ac)counts of this equality. Fetishized equality can only steal from an inequality. This will to generalize *qua* equivalent reduces the specific and the particular to the general and the universal. Generalization and equivalence mobilize a global criterion of value for labor difference and sexual difference. Standardization enforces (a)symmetry in raptures, heartaches, resources, opportunities, and surplus dis*jouissance*. Tired sways spin in the delusional denial of excess and surplus. Capitalism and phallocentrism already recuperate the Uncalculable X into the system, no less but no more.

Paradoxically, this recuperation slips on the excess. Self-identity and self-sameness stumble at the won expense but inside joke (cost and benefit) of Real Sameness⁺. This ~~Sameness⁺~~ is the order of the Real. Celebration of surplus is the experience of the schizoid's trance Unreason. The effluvium is the deconstructionist and perverse *écriture-χορός* of futural thinking, being, and living of the Woman and her Spirit. Real Sameness⁺ emerges as a creationist *ex nihilo* in the absence of the signifier. The signifier strives to speak and to write the Real. *Praxis* is the explosion of the system of $-ism *qua* its own proviso of capitalism and patriarchy. But Derrida says in *Of Grammatology* (1967) that "the signified is originarily and essentially (and not only for a finite and creative Spirit) trace, that it is always already in the position of the signifier."[30] The Outside is recuperated into an Inside. This aperture ultimately swallows the Other into the system as such. But Spirit pursues the transcendence of $-ism with the perversity of the faith and hope of the "but nevertheless."

Excess *jouissance* overflows the signified of the slip of the joke, the ejaculation of sex, the intensity of intellectual patter, and the free asymmetry of the gift. Surplus — deficit ($\supseteq$) profit, pleasure ($\supseteq$) pain, and clitoris ($\supseteq$) penis — cannot be situated in a metaphysics of presence of any of the partners in exchange. Nor can it be (re)calculated and (ac)counted in its value. Value cannot be properly mediated in relationship to a general equivalent. The manifest purpose of this standard is to equalize and balance. But the latent function of the father, currency, sign, and phallus is to arbitrarily but authoritatively invent an appraisal of value, either loss or gain, either won or lost, either better or worse, and so on. Capitalistically and patriarchally, the surplus must return in an (in)equality and (im)balance of debt and excess.

In exchange, Derrida refers to the unexpected center as the "not-gift." The momentary suspension of the exchange economy manifests at the moment in comparison and contrast in which surplus and excess — *qua* loss or *qua* gain — are Nothingness. The whips and chains of the exchange economy are homologous to the capitalist law of M-C-M'. This is the logic of money. Currency purchases commodities in order to procure more money *ad infinitum*. This (in)finite accumulation is a profitable letter of ownership in the absence of either points of departure or arrival. Derrida argues that the return of the gift with another gift in a closed circuit of exchange and return annuls the gift as such. The exchange economy of obligation and reciprocity invents the as such and the *qua* in order to isolate the gift within borders. The gift properly resists comparison, contrast, and exchange. The gift evades the system of general equivalence and its father, phallus, currency, and sign.

Capitalism and phallocentrism make the gift and the return-gift essentially not-gifts. The only possible

Outside of this metaphysical enclosure in equality, identity, inequality, and difference in exchange, speculation, and return is a not-gift and a not-return. The *not* refuses to calculate and speculate. This Other embraces and celebrates the gift — given but not returned — as an unaccountable and unmeasured not-gift. The general equivalent of capitalist phallocentrism precludes proper not-gift non-exchange. Gift must be uncalculated, unaccountable, and unmeasured. Otherwise, the surplus of the gift must be squandered. The excess of the gesture must be annulled. The clitoris must be compared, contrasted, and castrated. The singular use-value of the commodity must be exchanged for standardized currency. The negative and differential play of the signifier must be subordinated to the positive unity of the sign.

The logic of binary opposition (A = A ≠ B) is structured by a deficit. The privileged word accrues value. The secondary word lacks (A/not-A). *Signification* (words *qua* signs) is finally privileged as the model of communication above the hectic and schizoid differential negativity of *value* (materialities and abstractions *qua* signifiers and signifieds). This latter aesthetic of value of the *not* is inconsistent with binarism. Saussure's sign privileges strict distinction against playful difference. This economy of distinction reinscribes binary oppositions within a web of words of either/or and (A/-A). Perversion structurally exceeds — both either/or and both/and both either either/or and or both/and, and so on — these restrictions.

The masculine economy is situated by relationships between elusive and cagey objects and helpless and ashamed desires. Perverse *Trieb* eschews the subject<>object (*et al.*) knot of desire altogether. *Trieb* enjoys the aim/less encirclement around the void. The function of the *mise-en-abyme* is to hoot and huzza for the *Trieb* and its drive unto *Thanatos*. This Other feminine aneconomy invites an S of gift without debt, credit without receipt, love without diamond contract, and so on. The Spirit of the System is beyond the nihilism of value. Spirit eases the "all sorts of consequences" of the scary specter of surplus and the ghostly reminder of debt. This male junior is worried stiff over the length and width of his shaft. But when will it finally be amputated for (the) good?

$-ism and Surplus

The other side of Lacan's thesis about surplus *jouissance* is that excess must be excoriated from the system. The elision of the remainder sustains castration and desire as the linchpins of the system of $-ism. The structure in the West is regulated by lack (sexual difference and phallocentrism), scarcity (capitalism and private property), loss (identity, ego, and metaphor), and negativity and difference (sign, signifier, signified, and the signifying chain). Capitalist excess in the system forces the apparatus to overflow with remainders of goods, services, enjoyments, ejaculations, differences, identities, widgets, gizmos, and time machines. An excess in the system threatens the disappearance of the apparatus of desire (phallus, object, and so on). The surrender of *désir* to *Trieb* threatens the capitalist ideological fables of castration and scarcity. Lacan uses the strange word "anxiety" for the presence of absence.[31]

An extended *Yes!* lubricates the Real Penis. This surplus is the relational inspiration for the in-and-out of negative and differential relationships in the battery of the Other signifiers. Excessively, every word is the same word. As surplus, this system will be (already is) each according to his need and each according to his ability. Patriarchal excess disturbs the truth of Unreason that the penis is the clitoris. Surplus achieves a queer (*a*)sexuality in which representational objects of desire enjoy a Nothing is Missing. An (*a*)sexuality emerges in the positivization of the negative loss of the *objet petit a*. The *objet* of *Trieb* encircles the void. An empty Nothingness is absence around which the bright positivity of presence circulates an Other *jouissance*. After capitalism and patriarchy, an envisioned Nothing is Missing structures the amusements of whack-a-mole and pinball-machine play *writ large* for the Pervert-Schizoid-Woman.

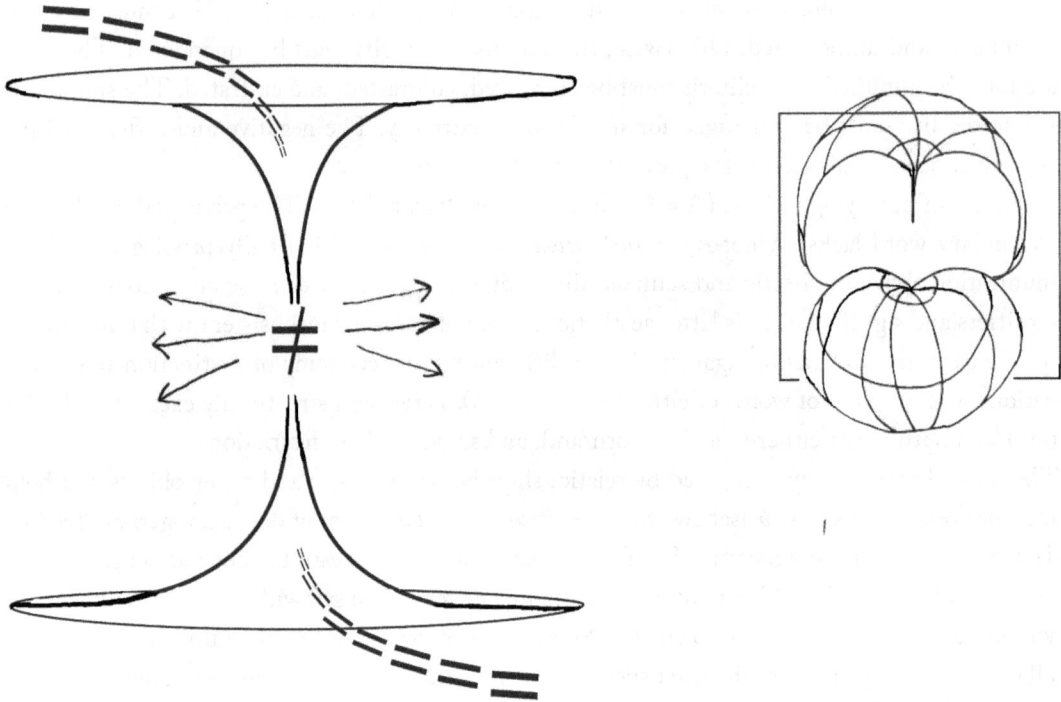

This image shows the unequal sign (center) which organizes the function of the phallus. The unequal sign charges the phallus with articulations of identity and difference in comparison, contrast, and exchange as the general equivalent of (in)equality. The identity which slips and slides toward and beyond this nexus of *différance* emerges from the other side *qua* its flip-side. In contrast, the future of the Pervert-Schizoid-Woman invites the (im/ex)plosive flip and twist of a traversable rather than a regulated border. The units of text are otherwise mediated by the system. The posthumanist galaxy of the Pervert-Schizoid-Woman is not mediated by the general equivalent of the television screen or the virtual dollar. Rather, the Pervert-Schizoid-Woman is unmediated by the Real in perpetuity. The perverse communist future of (*a*)sexuality is the horizon toward which ~~equality~~ gestures in its incomparable, incontrastable, and unexchangeable singularity. It is neither Tom's *big* jockstrap nor Jim's *bigger* jockstrap in comparison, contrast, and exchange of (in)equality but Tom's *biggiest* jockstrap and Jim's *biggeriest* jockstrap in their singularities. I have the *jockstrapiest*. Tom's jockstrap, Tim's jockstrap, and my jockstrap are incomparable, incontrastable, and unexchangeable because they are each the singularity of their own essential variant of ~~jockstrap~~. The relationship among the three jockstraps is the Outside of the general equivalent of identity and difference, equality and inequality, and so on.

Notes & Sketches —

This case of postscarcity surplus *tout autre jouissance* is antecedent and subsequent to the insufferable desires and unachievable wants of –centrism. These malformations of desire include castration, lack, capital, general equivalence, and so on. But, at this same moment, the system will be transformed from castration and scarcity into both castration and plenitude, and both scarcity and fullness, and so on *qua* Sameness⁺. This Sameness⁺ is none other than the Nothing is Missing of the same place of the Real. Man returns to a society of the Real. This endless ejaculation of productions of penises, clitorises, commodities, and so on is the instant in the system in which Nothing is Missing *except* Nothingness itself. Nothingness is the surplus. Until and yet, institutions of all kinds are animated by this revolution in the aesthetic and sensibility of excess Nothingness. The remainder of Nothingness must be performed and digested as material conditions (Marx) and knowledge conditions (Hegel). But, until and yet, the system will rule man and enjoy him while he enjoys the rules. This is — at this time — the pervert's essence. The surplus Nothingness is assimilated by the ideologies of the dominated not-penis of phallocentrism, the enforced signified of the sign, and the manipulated scarcity of overproduction.

Same+ Slave

The crucial distinction of the pervert is the attenuated twist not on the *content* of the law but on its *form*. Freud says in the dream-book (1900) that the essence of the dream is "the *form* in which it is dreamt" (my emphasis).[32] At the close of his first *Seminar* on the ego in Freudian thought (1954-55), Lacan says,

> Now, each time the other is exactly the same as the subject, there is no other master than the absolute master, death. But the slave requires a certain time to see that. All because, like everyone else, he is much too happy being a slave.[33]

The condition in which "the other is exactly the same as the subject" is the dominance of an uncalculated and un(ac)countable Real in the absence of a general equivalent. This is the condition of the Real Pervert. This "exact" Sameness⁺ of the deconstruction of the symbolic order in its schizophrenic neurosis involves the return of the neurotically foreclosed (*rejet nérvotique*) from the Real. The return of the Real disbands the combinatory pairs of Reason and their false foundation in binary opposition. The scaffold is (un)supported by the Real of the schizoid's Untruth. The (non)arrival of this "exactly the same" between self and other involves the suspension between every binary opposition in the system. This is the presentation of a "sameness which is not identical." The self and the other are different from themselves. The subject and the object are ~~not~~ self-same and ~~not~~ self-identical. But, at the same time, the self and the other are "exactly the same" as each other. But, at the same time, the self and the other are the "same" as themselves. This is the recursive Sameness⁺ of the parallactic overlap between the symbolic and the Real.

This wondrous contradictory paradox is furiously and spastically celebrated by the Pervert-Schizoid-Woman rather than soberly and coldly critiqued by the neurotic of Reason. Lacan is certainly correct that it "requires a certain time to see" this Sameness⁺. It "requires a certain time to see" the murder of all mastery except for the extraction of bodily and biological existence. The bitterly sad question is not — "Why has it taken so long for man to realize that he is the same as the other?" Rather, this "certain time" is the stop-start-watch by which the slave experiences and understands a Sameness⁺ which is only disturbed by the "absolute master, death." The mortal body is the surplus remainder of Sameness⁺. This slavish temporality is not the *futur antérieur* of Lacan's *après-coup* and Freud's *Nachträglichkeit*. The deferred (in)action of a past happens in the future moment of the arrival of the letter at its destination. The action is momentarily halted as Signified/r.

The irresponsible author can only retrospectively glance backward in order to realize that this book will have been (*futur antérieur*) written in the future event (now but also later) of its publication (now but also later). The temporality of the *futur antérieur* only implies that the past is activated in the future. The temporality of *Nachträglichkeit* and *après-coup* only indicates that the future retrospective glance of the past can be understood as the past that it is now but was not then. The temporality of this *futur antérieur* is situated within the metaphysics of absence. But the Other-Time of the Pervert is the temporality of presence. Perversely, the now and the later are (pro/retro)spective glimpses from the moment of presence. This is so even for the present in the past or the present in the future. The letter is already arrived and departed now or later. It takes a certain time for the slave to see that. The reason is the excess of mortality.

The certain time refers to the second-dimension of temporality. The slave awakens to a perverse Real Sameness⁺. This Real is (not) identical to any constitutive delay in *différance*. Lacan describes with patience the *über-mensch's* soured displeasure that the slave requires a certain time to see Sameness⁺. But the issue of the certain time — history as such — is the temporality of the renewed and the awakened. My claim is that the shift in temporality is from present, past, and future (all within presence) to the verbed gerund or Ing⁺. This Ing⁺ is strangely classified as a noun because the deployment of the gerund is preceded by the Being of the verb. This counterintuitive split within an in-process, in-action activity of Becoming (gerund *qua* verb) which is then categorized as a self-same and self-identical Being (gerund *qua* noun) is an ideological trick of time. This neurotic move installs Being in the place of Becoming. This is the reason that it takes a certain time for the slave to see that he is the same as the other. The split between Being and Becoming is surplus mortal Nothingness.

There is an abysmal upshot to this misclassification of the gerund *qua* noun — I̶n̶g̶⁺. The slave's in-process, in-action toil is the cultivation of nature into culture. According to Hegel, this labor is rewarded with the satisfaction of the slave's self-recognition in his object.[34] The slavish *objet petit a* denies the lazy master satisfaction even in his appropriation of the good. This labor is stabilized and immobilized *qua* noun. The noun in this context of (non)arrivals is the verbed gerund or Ing⁺. The neurotic metaphysics of absence is the temporality of the dominant interpretation of life and death. The in-process and in-action — in-performance in-labor — Becoming is an identity. This essence is always split from action in the devious division between doer and deed. Lacan's certain time is the interval between the initiation of a happy slavery and the emergence in time of a now. This certain time opens the contingency that, "each time the other is exactly the same as the subject, there is no other master than the absolute master, death." This delayed truth beckons toward the Spirit of the System. The Freudian *Wo Es war*, comes to be — and then, we engage with this Unthought of the Time of the Schizoid. The "absolute master, death" is the remainder of the Sameness⁺ between the slaves. The parallactic overlap between self (other) and other (self) is exceeded by the proviso of Nothingness.

Other-Time fosters a nuanced twist on happy slavery. An excess of affect is a remainder. A surplus *jouissance* is an excess. An extra commodity is a supplement. An untorn foreskin is a residue. This surplus is accompanied by "all sorts of consequences," as Lacan says. An elaboration of these certain times invites an intervention in the fissure between the Time of the Neurotic of the *futur antérieur* (Freud's *Nachträglichkeit* and Lacan's *après-coup* of the mark of the past from the future) and the Time of the Schizoid of the trace and *différance*. This Real always returns on time off time and in time to the same place. This latter Time of the Schizoid informs the struggle between *après-coup* and Real Time. This gap grants a theoretical glint through which to illuminate a certain time in which to see that the other is the same as the subject in the thinking, being, and living of Sameness⁺. The obstacle to Sameness⁺ — certain time — is the destruction of the surplus. Man squanders the capitalist excess of commodity and labor, and the patriarchal surplus of penis and clitoris.

Langue and its dominant word squander the surplus of the material signifier and the abstract signified. Capitalism and its general equivalent standardization of supply/demand dynamics of scarcity squander excess goods and services. Phallocentrism and its penis squander the otherness and difference of the positivity of the other. The word and its positive units squander the remainder and reminder of value. The Madness of Order sustains itself as a system which burns excess, empties surplus, and subtracts excess. It takes a certain time for the slave to see that. But what remainder cannot be burned? What surplus cannot be emptied? What excess cannot be subtracted? Death and Nothingness are the gasp and breath which escape assimilation and incorporation. It takes a certain time for the slave to see that Nothingness mediates and radiates Being.

THEATRE OF THE PERVERSE

The pervert's talents with *écriture* extend to other forms of symbolization which are beyond the written word. The horizon of the pervert's intervention in civilization is the *perversion of neurosis*. She perverts neurosis in order to facilitate a perverse performativity in being-in-the-world and being-with-others. A crucial modality of this performance is a theatrics of everyday life. A Theatre of the Perverse is the horizon toward which the pervert extracts a performance of an Other-Logic. This is a stage performance of a Sameness⁺ which cannot be reduced to either an identity with text or an identification with character. This preludial — even prodromal — sketch of a Theatre of the Perverse cuts a division between a theory and a practice of performance. But I also want to suture the wound of this gap. The Theatre of the Perverse histrionic luvvie — actor with wits — is perfectly present. This Woman who lives the future of the Spirit of the System has *presence*. This Woman is no doubt a masochistic exhibitionist. She woos the ~~sadistic~~ masochistic voyeurism of her audience. An account of the costume of the pervert of the Theatre of the Perverse engages with this question of *presence* in thinking, being, and living. This *presence* is crucial both onstage and offstage — were such a distinction even faintly adequate.

The performance of the perverse actor in his *presence* is properly illuminated by the parallactic gap. This parallactic distance in space and time (*différance*) is the moment of *presence* in which an object, such as a motivation, affect, word, system, and monologue, is torn between two antagonistic and exclusive perspectives. This "one" and the "same" object is split from itself. A motivation for manipulation is exactly not the motivation for manipulation. An affect is precisely different from the affect. A word from the performance is a word which is distinct from the chosen word in script, articulation, monologue, and dialogue. A monologue is not pronounced by the speaker of its words. This "one" and the "same" object is split *from itself*. This *Spaltung* can be understood through a variety of theoretical paradigms.

The presence of the parallactic gap is the magic of the talented pervert in the psychoanalytic scene. The object is sutured as "itself" only to be divided from "itself." The pervert — or what I am suggesting is the successful *presence* of the actor in performance in a Theatre of the Perverse — illuminates both this aperture and closure simultaneously. She does so in order to reveal that each is the other such that the "itself" (identity of a character or relationship and identification of a motive or affect) is always otherwise than "itself." The "itself" is transfigured into an otherness which cannot be accounted for by the boundary and border of *le propre* as the proper, property, ownership, possession, and mineness. Theatre of the Perverse demonstrates the fissure in which the ontological *what is* and *what is not* coincide. This visibility is a *presence*. It is the object of the performance precisely because it exceeds itself in a split which is its simultaneously unified essence. A surplus of Being and Nothingness emerges as a gap. The word for this interstitial overlap is *presence*.

Parallactic Performance

An illustration of this parallactic gap or (un)veil — *Aletheia* — is articulated by twentieth-century discoveries in quantum physics. The Copenhagen observer problem (1925) is structured by the duality between the particle and the wave. An object (an electron, in this metaphor) is either a particle or a wave — but not both. The properties of a particle and a wave are mutually exclusive. These properties are discontinuous and noncoincident with each other rather than simultaneous and overlapped with each other. But the Copenhagen school (1925) discovered that under certain conditions an electron may be both a particle and a wave in a so-called superposition. The collapse of this superposition of the otherwise both/and mutual inclusivity is committed when the observer glances at the scene. The gaze forces the electron into an economy of either/or and a choice between either a particle or a wave. (This summary of a detail in quantum physics perversely collapses the discovery.)

Theatre of the Perverse maintains that the character succeeds in performance at the moment of the visibility of this superposition. The perverse parallactic overlap exceeds capture in either the mask or the actor, either the performance or the performer, either the deed or the doer, and either the role or the thespian. The remnant which emerges from the aperture *qua* closure in voice and movement in the superposition is the perverse character. The perverse character is an eccentricity which strives to reveal that what is (Being) is simultaneously what is not (Nothingness). This ex-centric unification of Being and Nothingness — role and actor, performer and performance, and so on — is the essence of each as they pass inside and outside of each other. The superposition is finally collapsed by the spectator or observer. The audience decides the gap between either role or actor, either performer or performance, and so on. The character in the Theatre of the Perverse is the *presence* which escapes in a moment and in a flash as the in-between of this decision. The character reminds the spectator that the remainder that the observer sees in the perverse performance is the simultaneously sustained and dissolved split — parallactic gap — in the presentation of the mask and the actor. The *presence* of the character escapes the duality of the particle and the wave. A *presence* exceeds the superposition.

The object of this split is the performance of the Theatre of the Perverse. The fissure may be figured as the noncoincidence between mask and actor, between performance and performer, between deed and doer, between role and thespian, and so on. Hegel defines the essence of drama as the gap between the mask and the actor.[35] This split invites the sheer force of the dramatic tension. The discontinuity between costume and actor — mask and thespian — is organized by a suspension of disbelief in the spectator of the performance. The drama is not structured in mimesis of the dreary and prosaic everyday world.

Instead, this all too quotidian lifeworld is substituted with the bold and unexpected *mise-en-scène* of the unforeseen. A character is not a talented scripter of scenes and plots for his various boyfriends, ex's, cheaters, man-stealers, and so on. Rather, a character in life onstage and offstage concretely illuminates this inequivalence between mask and actor, between performance and performer, between deed and doer, and between character and thespian. The parallactic gap splits "one" and the "same" object from itself. Just so, the character whom we love because he has *presence* makes visible in voice and movement the simultaneity of these two dimensions which are otherwise mutually exclusive. The spectator of the Theatre of the Perverse suspends not disbelief but *belief itself* in his enjoyment of the actor and the show. The Real slips in-between the role and the actor. The Real mediates between the mask and the performer. A *presence* flashes before the spectator. The Theatre of the Perverse produces the simultaneity of the double *co-presence* of the otherwise mutually exclusive. The vulnerability of this excess and the desperate attempts to control this excretion in performance are the objects of the perverse performance. The mechanisms for this regulation are role, plot, script, and *mise-en-scène*. The perverse theatrics of everyday life illuminate the parallactic overlap of Being and Nothingness. Suddenly, in presence it appears that what is is precisely what is not.

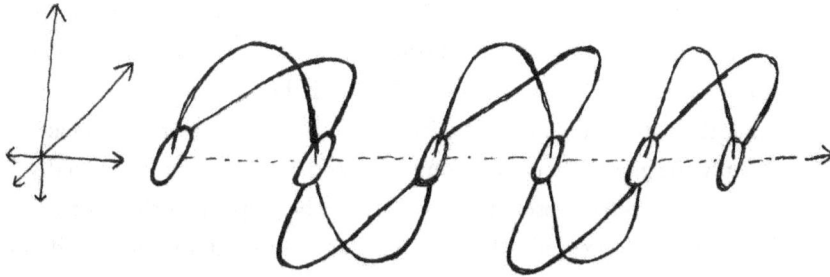

This image illustrates the *sui generis* and *ex nihilo* propagation of a weightless wave of light that momentarily *Becomes Being* and momentarily captures *Being Becoming* in a dynamic of mutual exclusivity. The physics metaphorically expresses the neurotic either/or binarism which regulates the system of signification. The pervert's hand is depicted (below) in its talented will to disavowal. The pervert's hand converges on the collapse of the mutual exclusive particle/wave duality — subject/object binary — in the traversal around and as the *Trieb* of substitutability. The pervert displaces the ontological question of the meaning of Being with the fetish. The jockstrap — "fetish" — illuminates the *bothness* and *andness* of a mutual inclusivity of the *neitherness* and *norness* of the schizoid's messianic call toward the *tout autre*. The pervert assembles a (meta)physical universe which is structured by the deconstruction of opposition and the illumination of the Real Symbolic. The ontological question is misplaced. The pervert's fetish is displaced.

Notes & Sketches —

In psychoanalysis, this talent is the pervert's gesture of *Verleugnung* in which the fetishist substitutes representation (the shoe, lace, fur, and jockstrap) in the place of the castrated female genitalia. The clitoris otherwise unconsciously reminds the horrified man of his own imminent loss. This artful solution to the castration complex enables the man to safely enjoy sex with representation (things, objects, props, costumes, sets, lines, scripts, and stage directions) without the horror of the reality of the clitoris. The pervert's psychical soliloquy begins, "I know very well, but nevertheless" — as if he acknowledges the reality of the horror of castration at the same time as he disavows it with the representation of the object of enjoyment. The pervert witnesses not simply the gap between representation and reality but more crucially their simultaneous coincidence. The visible excess of the representation is reality. The palpable surfeit of reality is representation. The Theatre of the Perverse illuminates this (dis)continuity in an instant and in a flash. This moment is the *presence* of the actor in character. The surplus of performance is the *presence* of the character.

Dramaturgical fetishism invites the spectator to enjoy the overlap between role and actor, and between performer and performance. The object of the pervert's performance is the unsymbolized Real. The sublime Real is the center of the theatrical magic on the stage. This *presence* is neither role nor actor nor performer nor performance nor reality nor representation. Rather, this simultaneity is the *presence* around which the magic of the Theatre of the Perverse circulates. This describes the pervert's will to get off on a representation (props, costumes, and script) which (un)veils this loss. Freud describes the ego as a series of lost investments and absent objects. Freud implies that a constituted sense of self is the process of loss. The loss of the self promises the gain of the self. The self cannot be an "I" because it gains and loses — exceeds — itself *qua* itself in the "me." This *moi* is the remainder of the otherwise balanced coordination of the self and its homeostatic regulation. This relationship is visible in the face of the *presence* of the fetishistic stand-in for the leading man. But does this leading man exhibit the character of *presence*? And who is *his* leading man, and so on?

These three chapters on the pervert describe a *postpsychoanalytic* theory of the pervert. The pervert is the idol of the interventions in this book. The pervert's disavowal of sexual difference, symbolization of the Real of Unreason, and enjoyment of *Trieb* rather than anxiety of *désir* make him the archetypal posthumanist paragon. The hero *perverts the neurotic*. The pervert invents the Pervert-Schizoid-Woman and her *tout autre* Spirit of the System. The pervert discerns the Madness of Order. The pervert demonstrates the surplus and remainder which exceed the parallactic overlap — Sameness[+] — between *les mots et les choses* of the system of $-ism. The excluded function of the center returns in its excess to disturb the system. The pervert reminds the neurotic of this disturbance. But the pervert also imagines this surplus as an extension and expansion of the system toward financial abundance in Overproduction[+], courtly love in *Trieb*[+], and the signifier in Play[+].

Division two of the book supplements the discussion of (*a*)sexuality in chapters one and two, the elaboration of *postpsychoanalytic* psychical structures in chapter three, and the figuration of the conceptual persona of the pervert in chapters four, five, and six. I now turn toward the specific social architectures of the Madness of Order as they are critically elaborated: in the sign in chapter seven; in labor in chapter eight; in discourse in chapter nine; and in the unconscious in chapters ten and eleven. Division two of the book then proceeds to a critical review of desire and morality in chapters twelve and thirteen. The conclusion to the book articulates freed and liberated surpluses in communism and *Thanatos*. The book ends with a brief coda which returns loss to gain and then lack to addition, and then — in the expanses of space.

The horizon of the book is a system which is beyond the private property principle and toward a perverse *jouissance*. The upcoming spadework in deconstruction, Marxism, and psychoanalysis will illuminate the Madness of Order in the extant systems of language, finance, and desire. But if the pervert's jockstrap *qua* fetish is the performance of a superpositional parallactic overlap, then what is the split *within* this fetish?

What cup does the strap overlay? The fetish deconstructs the self-same and self-identical object. But the object also deconstructs the fetish. After deconstruction, is there even a fetish as such? The deconstructive fetish is the center of the structure. The Marxian fetish is labor. The psychoanalytic fetish is the penis. But after the critiques of the fetish by deconstruction, Marxism, and psychoanalysis, what is the pervert's fetish? How does fetish *structure play* in deconstruction?

The psychical structure of perversion discerns the social organization of $-ism. Division one of the book theorizes a *postpsychoanalytic* model of perversion and its composition by the word, the commodity, and *Trieb*. The pervert is the conceptual persona whose clinical structure permits him the proper orientation toward the galaxies of language, economy, and desire. The second division of the book scrutinizes the anatomy of the social arrangements of the sign in language, scarcity in economy, and desire in the psyche. How does the pervert discern the social formations of the systems (s) of the symbol, the commodity, and the phallus? What does the perverse *aesthete* uncover in the system of $-ism? What is the *tout autre* of the Spirit of the System (S) which inherits these critiques? What is the communist queer (*a*)sexuality which enlivens an *unambivalent* disavowal and its return of expansion and openness rather than contraction and closedness? The aperture of the pervert is — What?

Division Two

Madness of Order

$-ism

$-ism: (n.) /SCHIZ-em/: 1. A concept invented by the free market capitalist system to denote the systematic discrimination of people for lack of currency. This form of discrimination applies to all men, women, and the rest of us who inhabit the planet earth. 2. The invisible other of the system. 3. The system is the $-ism.

$chizoid: (n.) /SCHIZ-oid/: 1. A person who suffers under — and battles against — the system of $-ism.

$chiztic: (adj.) /SCHIZ-tic/: 1. A term used to describe an institution (of any kind: governmental, corporate) which discriminates based on the concept of $-ism.

Chapter Seven

Structure, Fetish, and Perversion in the Discourse of Deconstruction

> Philosophy is to the real world as masturbation is to sex.
>
> — Karl Marx

This work invents two new master signifiers — "$-ism" and the "Pervert-Schizoid-Woman." I invent this new vocabulary for three reasons. First, I want to establish a theoretical and linguistic context in which to critique the current system of the West. Second, I want to name the object of interrogation. Third, I want to identify a navel around which words circulate and punctuate a future selfhood and sociality. $-ism is a concept which arises from a sustained criticism of the system. The symbol ($-ism) represents the negative aporias of the structure of the West. It also identifies the positive possibilities of the transformation of the relationship of purported equivalence — self-identity and self-sameness — between the internal coherence of the system and its negative Outside. Pervert-Schizoid-Woman is an empty signifier. Its content is merged with its symbol in the development of the critical exegesis of the system of $-ism. The purpose of this effort is: first, to unveil an original exploration of the adverse elements of the current structure; and second, to innovate alternative models for selfhood and sociality. The experimental aspect of this enterprise evolves from the interrogative perspective. But both gestures are internal to each other. The analytic evaluation of $-ism prepares us for an illumination of a future. The inventive dream of the Pervert-Schizoid-Woman inherits the gaps and fissures in the dominant system in the West. What we learn from the interpretation guides us toward this substitution of S (Spirit of the System) for s ($-ism and the Madness of Order). In the same way, the specter of the substitution returns to the disappointments of the extant symbolic order.

The hysteric *qua* author enunciates his own master signifier(s). He does so in consultation with the magical silence of the psychoanalyst. This labor rebels against the knowledge of the master. The strange collusion between master and analyst generates the new: an otherness which is the specific and unique production of the hysteric and his idiosyncratic unconscious. My master signifiers are inspired by an ambivalent revolt against the existent symbolic order. This system must be critically judged for its flaws and roadblocks. The critique releases the textual and political resistance of the hysteric in the assembly of the novel alphabets, new words, and invented vocabularies of the future. We must understand the master and his architecture in order to release an unconscious of an otherness to this structure itself. Creation of the pervert's master signifier is the risk of this book. The specter of the Pervert-Schizoid-Woman is the promise of this peril. $-ism is the bureaucratic officialdom of the West. $-ism names the values and rules which must be destructured in order to herald a future. Becoming-Other is the Pervert-Schizoid-Woman and her Spirit of the System. The Other promises to ambivalently succeed and simultaneously fail betwixt the promise of Lacan's version of the all-embracing love of the father,

> Off you go, say everything that comes into your head, however divided it might be, no matter how clearly it demonstrates that either you are not thinking or else you are nothing at all, it may work, what you produce will always be admissible.[1]

My work critically engages $-ism. As the dreamy inventor — writer — of the Pervert-Schizoid-Woman, I wish that whatever is manufactured will always be "admissible." The wish of this dream can only be fulfilled in the process of its *écriture* and *lirer*.

Marx's definition of communism includes the strict abolishment of private property. This is a tenet of the future of mankind because of the teleological necessity of the arrival of a system of each according to his need and each according to his ability. Marx's massive attack on capitalism argues that private property relations of production become a "fetter," as he notably says (1864), on the forces of production in the historical march of the power of labor and creation.[2] The pervert's will to fabricate an alternative law — the law of enjoyment as opposed to the law of desire — ventures to innovate this otherness in his master signifier. This play requires work. According to Marx, labor is the foundation of the humanity of man. The pervert's intention also requires talent. Textualization demands coherence — what Freud refers to as analysis-work in the interpretation of the symptom. Analysis transcends the obfuscations of the primary process of the unconscious. The pervert's project requires a set of strategies and manners through which this fecundity can weave itself into a preexistent consistency of discourse — alphabets, letters, words — that already sustains its own logic and structure. The relations of private property production tightly enchain the forces of production. Labor becomes constrained and shackled in its potential and promise. The pervert's articulation of the *tout autre* and the eccentric master signifier delivers this otherness. Emptiness is opened to signification from the culture. In Laclau and Mouffe's concept of hegemony, this master signifier becomes the object of a struggle of signification.[3] What does "$-ism" or "Pervert-Schizoid-Woman" mean? The text cannot simply appeal to Marx's communist dictum of each according to his need and each according to his ability. But the profound substrate of this project is Marx's critique of private property. The object of critical scrutiny is *le propre* in French: the proper, property, ownership, possession, and mineness. These qualifications not only refer to material goods such as a house or car or boyfriend. They also apply to abstract contents, such as ideas, values, speech, emotions, thoughts, words, and text. The fundamental object under suspicion in this book is ownership. This critique is written under the name of Marx.

Meta-Deconstruction

This chapter situates the deconstructive critique of the sign within the context of the psychoanalytic exposition of fetishism. Derrida makes an implicit claim to a "metalanguage." This is a language *about* language and a theory *about* theory. Somehow, this metalanguage is outside of the signifying chain itself. But Derrida (and de Man) also reject the possibility of a metalanguage. De Man refers to it as the "resistance to theory."[4]

Resistance is coextensive with the deconstructive project. But it is essential to gesture toward a metatheory — philosophy — of deconstruction. Deconstruction's insights are situated within the play of the signifier. But these ideas are also critical to and constitutive of a practice. This *Praxis* revolutionizes the practical networks of signification in writing and speech. Deconstructive *Praxis* also explodes commonsense ideas about ordinary behaviors (conversation, pedagogy, *et al.*) in everyday life. A meditation on the philosophical insights of deconstruction inspires shifts in practice.

Deconstruction is informed by the structuralist linguistics of Saussure and his schizophrenic concept of value.[5] Saussure's theory of value is the most psychotic concept in the history of twentieth-century thought. Saussure will say that the paradoxical principle of value holds that dissimilarity (un-like) exchanges for an uncertain value to be (un)determined at some point in space and time as similarity (but also un-like). An uncertain value is (un)determined at some point in space and time. The system of value is organized by the exchange, comparison, and contrast of indetermination.[6] This is the essence of *langue*: indetermination. The center of the system is instability. But the exact obverse of indetermination and instability is also the essence of the system. This doubled negation is precisely what Saussure means by his theory of value: pure negation and the internal Nothingness of Being. Saussure contends that simultaneous (dis)similarity of exchange, comparison, and contrast is "necessary for the existence of a value."[7] The strict madness of this concept is the architectonics of speaking and writing.

The orientation of grammatology is a messianic and impossible faith in the advent of the to-come of the future signified (*et al.*) through the retroactive supplementation of the signifier (and so on) of the past. The future is always deferred such that the past has not yet happened. Nothing has happened yet. The Pervert-Schizoid-Woman in Becoming is this *tout autre* of the skate and wait toward the future. But from whose perspective is deconstruction a perverse and fetishistic set of textual sex acts? From which viewpoint is the parallactic gap the obverse? From which psychical structure — neurosis, psychosis, or perversion — is deconstruction revealed as continuous with a construction which exceeds its critique? As Barbara Johnson asks, what difference does deconstruction make?[8]

PARALLACTIC GAP

The parallactic gap is central to my claim that $-ism and the system (s) are coincident with each other. The s and the S are split perspectives on the "one" and the "same" object. Marx theorizes that surplus value is the dizzy double vision obverse of "profit" in capitalist economics. The basal difference between Marxist economics and capitalist economics is not structured according to a different version of the organization of the capitalist mode of production. Instead, the minor but vast division between Marxist economics and bourgeois economics is simply two words: surplus value. The object of this terminological conflict is the gap — subtraction and depletion but also addition and excess — between the value of the worker's product on the market of exchange and the wage that the worker is paid for his activity. (My analysis is a demand side interpretation of the Marxist parallax.) The leftover must be understood as simultaneously an addition and a subtraction.

Ricardo and the bourgeois economists identify this excess as "profit." The "profit" returns to the corporation in order to be reinvested in the economy. Marxists articulate this remainder — materialized representation of the gap between wage and price — with the two words: surplus value. These two words indicate the criminal theft from the worker of the value of his labor and product. Antagonistic views on the "one" and the "same" object of the gap between sales price and paid wage beg a crucial question. What is the unified and unitary

— self-same and self-identical — object to which the two words "profit" and "surplus value" refer? The question inverts the form of the answer: there is no present object — Being — as such: *qua*, by definition, *il y a*, by necessity, and so on. The competition between the claims to signify this stolen gap or gained excess is the vanishing mediator between capitalism and Marxism. This ephemeral object is the source of a struggle of signification. Criminal theft for the Marxists and free enterprise for the capitalists are coincident with each other. Theft is freedom. Liberty is crime. Capitalism is the "one" and the "same" system for both the bourgeoisie and the radicals. The crucial difference is not the material practices of capitalism. Instead, abstraction and ideology are at stake. What is the destination of the loss and the excess? Where do the subtraction and the addition arrive in the material presence — representational articulation — of dollars and coins?

The battle of signification is between "profit" and surplus value. These signs name the fundamental concept that both separates and unites bourgeois economics and Marxist economics. But the word is not simply another mark in the signifying chain. Instead, it is the sign which organizes the context of the division between liberals and radicals. The "one" and the "same" object is diametrically split from itself in the concept. This idea is simply discerned in the choice of word. The semiotic decision acutely affects the ideological and political apprehension of the Event of capitalism. But the otherwise *de minimis* but nevertheless consequential difference is mostly overlooked. The parallactic gap is closed in order to veil the inaccessible object — *Boy!* — of political contestation.

Real Parallax

Zizek's conception of the Real parallax is central to my project. In *The Parallax View* (2006), Zizek focuses on a shifting in perspective and a transforming from one perspective to another. This oscillational conversion is performed within a precisely binary structure. The obscured object of this shift is the "Thing." This Thing is the concealed object. It is veiled by the competition between perspectives on this object. The Real parallax of multiple appearances of the Real returns to the "same place" of the Real in an undefined and resistant Sameness$^+$. The parallactic Real is this hard bone of contention. The Boy's boner pulverizes the Sameness$^+$ into the multitude of appearances. This obscure object can be understood as *das Ding* — Kant's fetish for the noumena of transcendental consciousness. *Das Ding* emerges only in the shifting in perspective between the one and the other and from this side to the other side. The Thing is revealed — *Aletheia* — as an in-process, in-action gesture of perspective on appearance(s).

This shift is performed in the pervert's text. The parallactic object or *das Ding* emerges in the gesturing of the gerund-as-verb or what I refer to as the "Ing$^+$" — shifting perspectives, seeing differences, and imagining otherwises. The gerund *qua* verb qualifies the gerund *qua* noun. The split must be performed as Ing$^+$ in-process and in-action. Herein, an example from my stint at jury duty:

Juror #69: "I'm really excited for jury duty. I've always wanted to be on a jury."

Michael: "You know, I have to say, I really don't feel comfortable as a rich white gay boy from the suburbs coming into the inner city of Boston to throw black and Latino kids in jail."

[pause.]

Juror #69: "No, no. What you're doing is participating as a responsible American citizen in the tradition of a free and liberal judicial system whose time-honored tradition spans hundreds of years of the great history of the American justice system — "

Michael: " — That's what I'm taking about!"

There must be spatial and temporal movement (*différance*) in order for the Real multiplicity of appearances to manifest in visibility. The *Praxis* of *Trieb* — as opposed to the foolishness of *désir* — surrounds the Real parallax. *Praxis* floridly generates these appearances on the "one" and the "same" object. The gap between "profit" and surplus value is exemplary of the coincidence between $-ism and system. This interstitial overlap is archetypal of the Becoming-Other of the split in the object. The split involves the otherwise mutually-exclusive as continuous with each other. Different worlds in space are conjoined in the same world.

Emergence of a parallactic overlap between gay pride and homophobia, between good and evil, between ephemeral and permanent, and so on is the crack in the edifice of the positive unity of the word in the system. This fissure manifests at the moment in which Sameness$^+$ — parallax — appears as the essential schizophrenia of the system. The structure neurotically responds to the schizophrenia of the Madness of Order. The symbolic order of the either/or neurotically *forecloses* (otherwise the mode of negation in psychosis) the slip and slide of the signifier. The difference and negativity in the value of the theoretical components of materiality and abstraction are foreclosed by the structure of neurosis. Appearance of this value is performed in opposition to the signification of the practical positive entity of the word. The negative play of the signifier returns to disturb the system with spatial and temporal compressions and displacements. The Real disturbs the consistency of the system. The Real and the symbolic coexist *as* each other. The trick is to demonstrate the simultaneous aperture and closure of this trace of excess in the "one" and the "same" object. There is no proper word for this split object. The subject itself is the original presence of this cut between the Real and the symbolic. Man is the material and abstract (body and mind) place of this paradoxical dissonance.

Quantum Ing+

This textual and bodily movement — Ing$^+$ — is the objectification of the making-verb of the gerund. A Verb-i-zation$^+$ or Ing$^+$<>Ing$^+$ is a grammatical neologism of an undertheorized part of speech: the gerund *qua* verb. The shifting in perspectives, transforming in viewpoints, and revolting in orientations of the system are the integrants of the parallactic performance. This illuminates a dizzy doubleness — or what quantum physics would call a "superposition" in the Copenhagen theory of the observer problem (1925). According to quantum physics, the electron is simultaneously a particle and a wave — which are otherwise mutually exclusive properties of a sub-atomic system. The experiment demonstrates the transcendence of the antinomic mutual exclusion of the properties of the electron in sub-atomic science in the laboratory. The object is not either a particle or a wave but both a particle and a wave. This mutual inclusion is collapsed upon observation. (This summary itself collapses the distinction.)

Erwin Schrodinger's thought experiment (1935) illustrates the everyday consequences of the paradox of superpositionality in quantum physics. The idea presents the paradox of a cat which may be simultaneously dead and alive in a state of quantum superposition. The scene is of a cat which is sealed in a box. The cat's life or death is dependent on the state of a radioactive substance, whether it is decayed and safe or radioactive and dangerous. Schrodinger's philosophical experiment illustrates the everyday consequences of the Copenhagen interpretation of the observer problem: that the cat is both dead and alive in a simultaneous superposition until the object collapses into a definite property as either alive or dead upon observation. The perverse thought experiment isolates the Copenhagen interpretation of a quantum superposition of a subatomic system which is simultaneously in a state of mutually exclusive properties until it collapses into one of the definite states — the cat as either dead or alive.

The theory of superposition posits mutually-exclusive properties in a state of contradiction and disavowal. The quantum theory illuminates the perverse both/and structure of the subatomic electron and, by extension, of (the) everyday object(s). Schrodinger's paradox also reveals the isomorphic parallactic shift from one perspective to another. The shifting, transforming, and revolting are — $Ing^+\!\!<\!\!>\!Ing^+$ — performed in the absence of the observer and his speculation. Insertion of the observer into the experiment collapses the particle-wave perverse anti-unity. This superpositional state of the electron — or the cat — is isomorphic to the superpositional parallactic gap. The Real Parallax is the object of superposition (electron) in its oscillation between antagonistic symbolic perspectives (particle and/or wave). The observational collapse reduces the both/and entanglement to either/or positionality. The perverse both/and bend of the superpositional mutual-inclusion is reduced to the neurotic decisionism of either one (alive) or the other (dead).

Zizek's parallactic Real makes space for a multitude of perspectives on the Thing. The obscured object of the system is freed in the very acting and gesturing of the critic. Zizek defines the parallactic gap as "not so much a shift in the object," he says, "as a shift in our attitude toward the viewed object."[9] The Real object is obscured from presence. The symbolic order and its various forms of *Praxis* parallactically encircle *das Ding*. This Thing resists consensus in a self-same and self-identical metaphysics of presence. The parallactic object of the Real is neither Being nor Nothingness, and neither is nor is not. The object resists the entire ontological project. The electron is the Real parallax which resists the neurotic laboratory observation of either a particle or a wave. The cat is the gap which refuses the neurotic theoretical speculation of either life or death. Both the electron and the cat are in perverse and superpositional Becoming of Ing^+ — a generalized *Verschrangung* — in an entanglement between symbolic appearances. But is it possible to observe the simultaneity of *Eros* and *Thanatos*? Can a Marxist's analysis of the free market and an economist's defense of capitalism be observed as a "one" and the "same" symbolic appearance? Is Real *Verschrangung* visible? Can Ing^+ be articulated in presence? How do we illuminate the gerund in its essence as a verb?

Unreason

My work on the parallactic gap is preceded and informed by Zizek's work. My caveat is that Zizek emphasizes the constitutive antagonism between the two "attitudes." He foregrounds the competitive perspectives, conflictual viewpoints, and embattled inversions of the Marxist *camera obscura* (1845) of ideology. My interest in Becoming-Perverse in this study hopes for a paradoxical *détente*. My concern is a *rapprochement* between neither the neurotic either/or side of the parallax nor the perverse both/and Sameness[+] orientation toward the parallax. Rather, the reconciliation is organized by the otherwise "something else entirely," as Lacan says, of the fetishist.[10] The pervert's symbolization refers to Zizek's "shift in our attitude" in *écriture*. Symbol and attitude illuminate the parallactic gap of neither the neurotic reader nor the perverse writer. Instead, my shift and symbol focus on the madman's Unreason. The psychotic's neither/norism suspends the duality in a superpositional oscillation in which the object cannot be determined or decided in its essence in the neurotic structure of either the one or the other. The pervert inherits the madman's indecisionism in order to affirm the both/and structure of the object as essentially double, in the least. Perversely, the object exceeds itself.

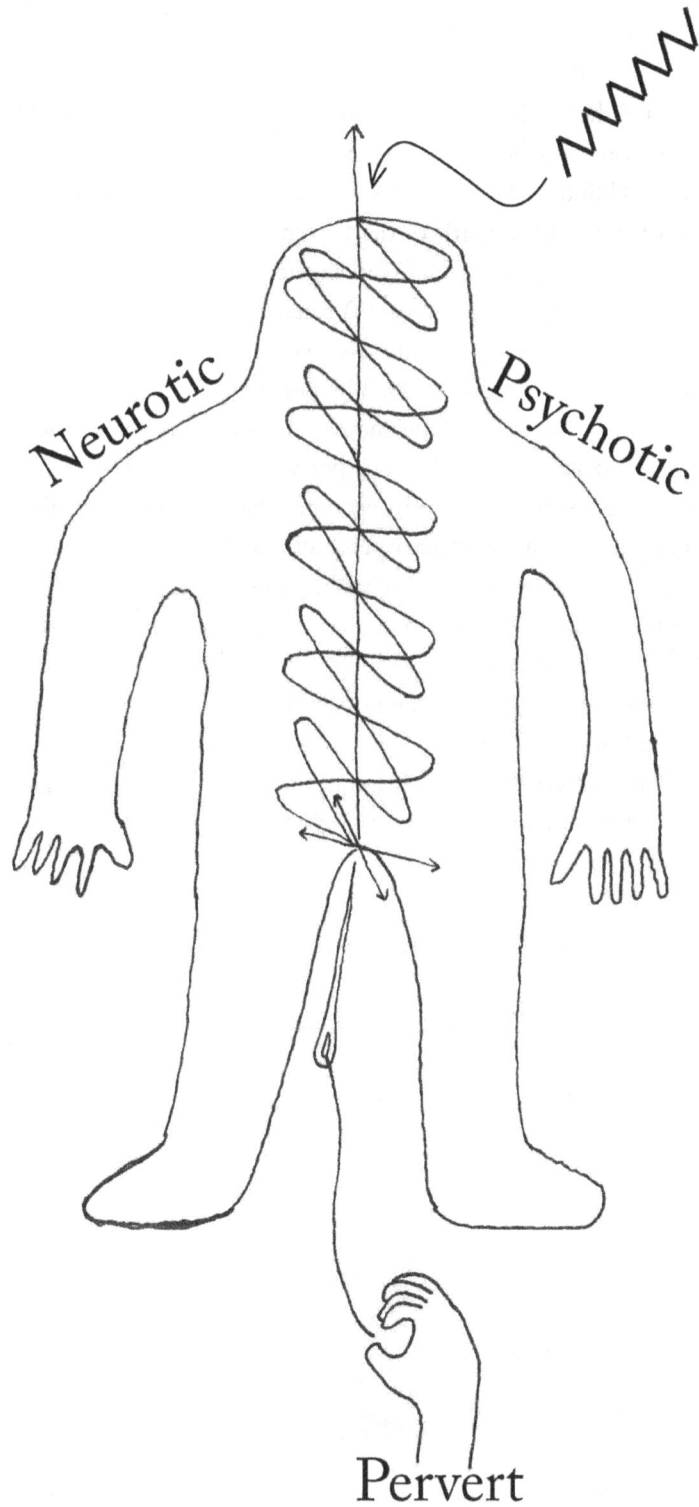

Figure 7.1 Particle<>Wave Perversity

This illustration depicts the subject who is split between the psychical structures of neurosis and psychosis. The sine waves (center) are overlapped and perpendicular to one another. These suggest an electromagnetic wave of light that according to physics is a wave and not a particle or a particle and not a wave: either/or and both/and but also neither/nor. The particle/wave duality is analogous to the parallactic gap which separates psychotic from neurotic, and the Madness of Order from the Order of Madness. The fragmentation of the sine waves represents the gap or fissure in the essence of the system. This schizoid gap is the proviso of the system. The system is (will be) the Spirit of the System because of this schizoid gap. The psychotic experiences Sameness⁺. But the schizoid cannot articulate this Unreason. The neurotic is immersed in the schizophrenia of the system. The neurotic is blind to the schizoid (neurotic) structure of $-ism. The pervert sutures the gap between the Madness of Order and the Spirit of the System. This is symbolized by the needle and thread (center) of the electromagnetic wave/particle duality in a series of stitches. The pervert (below) is consistently attuned to the particle/wave either/or, both/and, and neither/nor structures. The pervert plays and performs the risk of a theoretical and practical disruption of the two mutually exclusive perspectives on the particle and the wave, and on the position and the velocity. The pervert risks the thinking, being, and living of the simultaneity of the one and the other and the one and not the other and the neither one nor the other of the pervert's both/and and the schizoid's neither/nor. The pervert demonstrates the continuity in difference *qua* Sameness⁺. The neurotic (is) the psychotic but only insofar as the psychotic is at a distance from himself. The relationship of opposition posits that the two binary perspectives are identical to themselves and different from each other. This opposition between neurotic and schizoid (*et al.*) is the proviso of the identity of each as self-same and self-identical. This gap between the one and the other conditions the possibility of both Being as is and ~~Being~~ as is not. The space of this gap of Something is Missing is the condition of the coherent Being of any object in the world whatsoever. The existential possibility of the object as such is the space of castration. Sexual difference is repressed by the neurotic, foreclosed by the schizoid, and disavowed by the pervert. The pervert unstitches Being. The pervert fragments the object. The substitutions for this exposure of Being *qua* ~~Being~~ extend and expand the expanses in space of the jockstrap and the "jockstrap."

Notes & Sketches —

My fascination is with the madman's will to retheorize and repractice such an internal gap — otherwise and altogether. The neurotic views either one or the other sides of the object as opposite sides of a binary. The pervert imagines both one and the other sides of the object as (a) superpositional coincidence(s) of a torus. The schizoid occupies the Other-Position of the vanishing mediator. This spectral mediation approximates the parallactic object. The schizoid is profoundly Real. He thinks and lives in an extra-linguistic dimension. He is not only the Real object of resistance to the system. He is also a resistance to the symbolic order of coherent syntax and legible semantics. As the vanishing mediator, he is existentially dead. He is the mortal stain in the symbolic order. The schizoid is the negated — *foreclosed qua repressed* — center of the system. My Thing in this pursuit will be the twist of the shift in perspective between the Reason of the system (s) and the Unreason of its underside.

Zizek's emphasis is on the two perspectives which are in an antagonistic (class) conflict which breaks the "hard kernel" of the return to "the same place." But my focus in this book is to surmise and perform a playful *Praxis*. I want to spotlight the essential resistance of the Real. This work on the Real is simultaneously internal to the symbolic order. The Madness of Order and its Reason are the constitution of the one within/out the other, or a "sameness which is not identical." (Un)Reason is the horizon of a deconstruction of the symbolic order. My labor discerns such ruin as the simultaneous reconstruction of this same system. The very repute of the philosophical *qua* ("as such") involves its synonymous avatars: essence, Being, metaphysics of presence, *il y a*, what is, as such, and so on. These codes of the Logic of Identity are in considerable question in this project. The effort must demonstrate the Madness of Order. It must illuminate the Neurotic Foreclosure (*rejet névrotique*) of the Real which is otherwise the center of the schizoid system. I will stage a few wildly complex but also grimly simple concepts and their "conceptual personae," as Deleuze and Guattari say of the figures of philosophical invention. These concepts adorn my conventional interpretation of s with an intuitive grasp of $-ism. The proper haunts the internal structure of the extimate of remainder and excess. It also disturbs the system of loss and debt. The system is not "as such." Rather, the system must be understood "as not such and such, and so on." Surplus-Deficit and its translations in *qua* are the subtext of the theoretical framework of this book.

My work explicates and applies the parallactic shifts in deconstruction, psychoanalysis, and Marxism to the Becoming of the Pervert-Schizoid-Woman and the critique of $-ism. The perverse textual will to signify *das Ding* returns to the latency *of the latent* and to the unconscious *of the unconscious*. Is there a foundational endpoint to the interrogation and interpretation of the unconscious and the latent? If not, then the letters and words unexpectedly return as the manifest not of the unconscious but of the secondary process. The returns and disturbances of the signifiers are reminders and remainders of the Unreason within Reason. The demonstrations in this book articulate the Madness of Order and the overlap of s and $-ism. Strangely, Zizek's account of the parallactic gap does not account for his own split in the antagonistic relationship between shifts in perspective. The shift makes *das Ding* appear otherwise in translation. How do these interpretive surpluses, deficits, and excesses reveal their own parallactic gaps? What is the split *in the split* "itself"? Is the spectral mediation of the Real schizoid also split? Is his manic frenzy situated within the Real in the absence of absence and in the plenitude of communism?

Zizek argues that "the parallax at its purest" is "the endeavor to encircle/discern the unfathomable gap of the Difference by repeatedly formulating both perspectives."[11] This "encirclement" and "discernment" are the in-process, in-action shifting of different perspectives on the "one" and the "same" object. This parallactic labor summons the aim/less *Trieb* of feminine *jouissance* in the feminine lack of the lack. This is visible to us: first, in communist plenitude in Marxism; second, in the Other-Logic of penis = clitoris because penis ≠ penis and clitoris ≠ clitoris or a "sameness which is not identical" in a deconstructive psychoanalysis; and third, in the trace which is lost to *arche* in the Sameness⁺ of space and time in deconstruction.

This round-about and become-aware of *das Ding* in its doubleness — simultaneity — summarize the Madness of Order but also the Order of Madness. The parallax illuminates the pervert's grasp of the Unreason of Reason, the Reason of Unreason, and the (Un)Reason of (Un)Reason. Representation of this visceral secret truth of the madman is the horizon of the text. The work of deconstruction, psychoanalysis, and Marxism is situated at the center of such a project. Scrutiny of the Madness of Order, the schizophrenia of the system, and the psychosis of the structure wills itself toward this Sameness⁺ — but which is "not identical" to "itself." All of these relationships are isomorphic: deconstructive difference and deferral in the trace; psychoanalytic consideration of sexual difference and the split in the ego of the unconscious in the signifying chain; Marxist reconceptualization of the internal publicness of the private in economic relations of the proper; and the perverse value in the split in the sign. These paradigms and concepts scrupulously regard the constitutive split of text (and so on) as splintered in the translations and perspectivalisms between splits. A quantum physics of quarks, strings, and other foreseeable snippets and specks illustrates that the split is split like any semblance of unity and identity but also of "disunity" and "difference." These split splits are subject to endless destructive recursion. The only organizational principle of the system is *Thanatos*. Death instinct is itself a split vanishing mediator of an infinity of other vanished spectral mediations. No presence is possible.

THE PERVERSITY OF DECONSTRUCTION

The parallactic gap mediates between two values in any system. This introduces the specific perversity of deconstruction. If Derrida were on the couch, the psychoanalyst would no doubt diagnose him as a pervert. Derrida's rejoinder would be to promptly exit the office and never look back. The isomorphic and equivalent relationship between deconstruction and perversion is evident in Freud's own writings on perversion. The deconstructive double-gesture to twist and flip reproduces the textual moves in the original scene of fetishism as it is depicted in Freud's essay, "Splitting of the Ego in the Defensive Process" (1938). Freud celebrates the offspring's artful reaction when face-to-face with the penis-to-clitoris threat of castration. The "ingenious solution" to castration is fetishism. Freud describes the terrified male junior's reaction of "horror" at the female junior's imagined castration. This is the condition of the pervert's smart disavowal of lack. The curious male junior is aghast at her present(ation of) castration. This hole in the symbolic order retroactively (*Nachträglichkeit, après-coup*) illuminates the earlier "sight of the female genitals" as a "dreaded confirmation" of the omnipresent threat of the loss and death of the male junior's private(s) property.¹² The theft is the object of the male junior's anxiety. Fear is assuaged in the abandonment of an incestual desire for an ego-ideal identification, and in the substitution of father for mother.

Acknowledgement and Denial

However, the perverse male junior's "ingenious solution" is an alternative decision. First, he accepts the "demand of the instinct" — to deny Something is Missing — in order to sustain the satisfaction of plenitude — to imagine Nothing is Missing. This plentiful fullness is antecedent to lack in scarcity. The second move of perversion is then to obey the "command of reality" — to acknowledge that Something is Missing — in order to maintain the reality of loss — to suspend Nothing is Missing. The little pervert straddles the parallactic overlap between the capitalist castration of Something is Missing and the communist plenitude of Nothing is Missing. What is crucial about the conceptual locus of fetishism is that it is the site of the negotiation between reality and instinct, between symbolic and Real, between castration and plenitude, between lack and fullness, between capitalism and communism, and so on. The pervert discerns the potential applications of his both/and aesthetic for man and world. The origin of this disavowal is his "ingenious solution," as Freud says, to the castration complex.[13]

The challenge for the talented writer of perversion is to articulate the imbrication of the extimacy of the oppositional signs in relationship to each other. The pervert's selfhood and sociality are structured by the fetish. This object is both a substitute for the female penis and a present object of pleasure. The unsymbolizable penis is the final referent for this duality of absence and presence. The peculiar function in which reality and representation, symbolic and Real, and referent and image are themselves dissolved is the maelstrom of Baudrillardian simulation. In simulation, there is no relationship between the sign and the referent. The God-function that otherwise guarantees the exchange of meaning — comparison and contrast of the general equivalent — is considered merely another sign in the system. Simulation emerges when dollars are exchanged with each other in the economy of M-C-M'. Financial exchange is internal to the death drive of capitalist accumulation. The 100% emerges from the 99% when the system achieves its logical *telos*: money owns money, and ownership owns ownership. At this coming moment, the proletarianization of the remnants of the bourgeoisie succeeds. The modest use-value of the general equivalent finally withers away. Unexpectedly, the Real will return to stabilize instability.

The pervert's *Trieb* gets off on the simulacrum. It does so with a difference. There is no necessary relationship between the simulation and the fetish, on the one hand, and the referent and the object, on the other hand. Let them eat money! But the fetish-object is "itself" a necessary function. The embodied materiality of the specific fetish-object is finally irrelevant to its function as a metaphorical substitution. What is fixed in the perverse economy is the referent: the penis. The penis is the fundamental referent for all of sex, sexuality, and gender in the system of psychoanalysis. Freud's own fixation on the penis returns to the quality of exclusivity in abnormal sexuality as it is outlined in *Three Essays on the Theory of Sexuality* (1905).[14]

The foundation of the system is the penis. This static reference to the penis constrains the signification of the abstract sign of the fetish but at the same time frees the value of the material signifier. The upshot of the limited freedom of the fetish is that all of the representations and objects in the system must be properly interpreted with perverse intuition. All objects are simulated penises. Everything is a penis. The abstract signification of this Penis-Presence is fixed as plenitude, fullness, communism, and Nothing is Missing. At the same time, the material value of the Penis-Presence is unmoored as supplementary, desired, substituted, and Something is Missing. There is an excess material — foreskin — in the penis. How is the division between Something and Nothing as the objects of both absence and presence to be decided?

The pervert's both/and *écriture* illuminates the inevitable indecision of such a determination between either Something is Missing in the economy of capitalist castration or Nothing is Missing in the truth of communism. This deconstructionist move is consistent with the "ingenious solution" of the male junior. The little pervert manages both to acknowledge and deny reality by disavowing difference and inventing the simulacral fetish-object.[15] This re-presentation tethers abstract signification to the referent of the penis at the same time as it frees material value to substitute — displace and compress — meaning-making among all of the objects in the symbolic order. Perversely, the entire universe is a series of penises. These penises materially deviate from the fleshly embodiment of the penis itself. The consequence of this argument is that in a strict interpretation: *the penis is not the penis.* But, if this is the case, then what is a penis? How can psychoanalysis make the penis the penultimate referent of sex, sexuality, and gender if the penis is absolutely undefined? If the penis is undecidable, then to what does a fetish refer? For what is the penis itself a substitute? What is the metalanguage of the penis *of* the language of the penis? Perversely, the penis is merely a distant referent, and distinct fetishes substitute in the place of this lost but present reminder.

Figure 7.2 The Gesture of Deconstruction

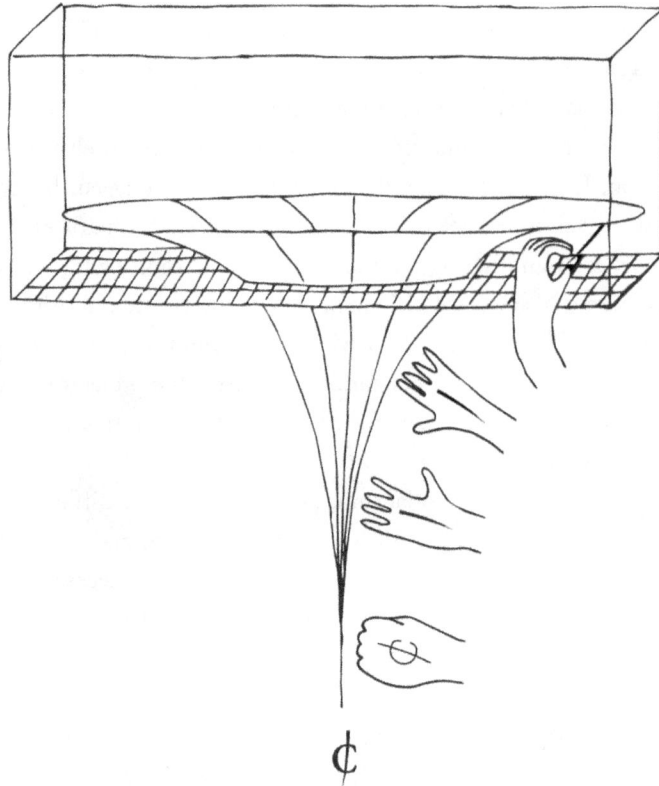

This image illuminates the pervert's sleight of hand. The pervert speaks and writes the structurality of the structure even with(out) reference to an impossible metalanguage of language *about* language. The perverse deconstructionist does not psychotically foreclose the occluded center in an incoherent manifestation of Unreason in the absence of the signified. The perverse deconstructionist also does not uncritically immerse himself in a system which enforces neurotic repression as the condition of both its stability and disruption. Rather, the perverse deconstructionist speaks and writes the Real of the occlusion of the center even within the framework of the system of the circles and rings of the units of signification. He does so in the absence of a direct manipulation of the occluded Outside of the structure. The pervert handles (center) desire in the transformation of lack and phallus into enjoyment and the expansion of the succession of objects and jockstraps (*et al.*). The pervert magically occupies the space (center) of transience. The pervert lives the Verbed Gerund or Ing+ of the noun *qua* verb. The movement of the hand (center) is a Becoming of the Verbed Gerund which has neither departure nor destination, and neither commencement nor arrival. The pervert's object is a both/ and and a neither/nor. The object is a disavowal which holds (center) the contradiction in one and the same space and time in the movement of Becoming *qua* Being. The pervert holds (center) to the gravity (below) of the system and the parallactic gap. This faint reference to the originary object — jockstrap, and so on — is the *mise-en-scene* of the perverse deconstructionist performance.

Notes & Sketches —

The pervert's "ingenious solution to the difficulty" or "another way out" of the castration threat is the creation of this substitute which is an understudy for the penis.[16] The fetish-object must compensate for the capitalist castrative logic of the Something is Missing of the penis. The penis is itself absent. It is difficult to imagine practices of fetishism in a communist economy in which Nothing is Missing. There is no commodity fetishism under communism because Everything is Present. A salient difference between the pervert and the schizoid is that the penis-substitute in the fetish sustains the general equivalent of value. In contrast, the schizoid's resistance to coherence destroys the function of equivalence and its operation of comparison and contrast. The pervert's substitution allows the fetishist to avoid schizoid foreclosure and enjoy disavowal: "I know very well that Something is Missing, but nevertheless — ...a...a...shoe...a...a...." This play of repudiation and concession is "the to and from between denial and acknowledgement," as Freud says.[17] Disavowal permits the male junior to dismiss the threat and sustain his pleasure. The pervert "knows very well" that the object deviates from its referent and that the penis-substitute contrasts with the penis. The pervert acknowledges that the metaphorical is distinct from the literal. "But nevertheless," the pervert gets off on the representational approximation between these ostensibly opposed signs.

The dimension of the pervert's *jouissance* is fundamentally representational. The simulation and simulacrum are archetypal of the fetish-object. Representation is the dominant aesthetic in the universe of the pervert. Metaphorical substitution of trace and *différance* is internal to the fetish-object. At the same time, the function of substitution cannot itself be substituted. This is so even if the objects of substitution are easily swapped and haphazardly switched. The *function* of substitution is not itself a substitute. Therefore, Freud can posit the primacy of the phallus and Lacan can name the function the phallus — and then force the flaccid penis to (de) fend for itself. Deconstruction makes essentially the same move of bait-and-switch between substitution and function. It is only Marxism which will name the vanishing mediator between penis and phallus. Mediation is performed by what Marx calls the "bourgeois individual." This bourgeois individual is the commodified and fetishized subject *qua* general equivalent of the capitalist mode of production. He is the distant destination of the stockpile of the accumulation of capital: coins and dollars, $ — as debt.

Thinking

The perversity of Derrida's deconstruction can be discerned in his 1967 essay, "Structure, Sign and Play in the Discourse of the Human Sciences." One such conspicuously perverse feature is deconstruction's demand for the simultaneity of mutually exclusive tasks. The two "interpretations of interpretation" which are theorized in "Structure, Sign, and Play" (1967) are "absolutely irreconcilable even if we live them simultaneously and reconcile them in an obscure economy."[18] A search for metaphysical truth and the arrest of the signified, on the one hand, and the dance and play beyond such an ontological project, on the other hand, perform perversion in its operational disavowal of binary terms. The deconstructive both-truth-and-play two-step poses a triple impossibility which is "absolutely irreconcilable."

What, precisely, is impossible in the outlines of deconstruction? First, truth and origin are deemed impossible. Second, adventure and dance are isolated as resistant to symbolization. But "living them simultaneously" in what Derrida refers to as an "obscure economy" and in what I designate as perversion is merely disavowed. This is so "even if we live them simultaneously" as a quaint proviso of the other impossibles. The dance-maker and truth-sayer modes of interpretation are impossible as separate endeavors on their own terms. Metaphysics is a ghostly presence which promises a life after its own death. The affirmative dance and play are also considered unapproachable because language is essentially metaphysical insofar as it posits *arche*, origin, truth, and other categories of thought which make a claim for a present and stable Being. But the third perverse option of "living them simultaneously" is the horizon of the promise of deconstruction. Perversity installs an otherwise banished otherness into the self-same and the self-identical of any system and any economy. This is the pervert's revolutionary contribution to thinking, being, and living in the world. But how so for the pervert?

Otherness is essential to the pervert's psychical investment in fetishism and disavowal. The two otherwise exclusive strategies — metaphysics-making and play-acting — mimic the logic of perversion as it is articulated by Octave Mannoni's patient: "I know very well, but nevertheless…." The "I know very well, but" implies that perverse fetishism gestures beyond all of epistemology. The "know very well" indicates an exhaustion of epistemology after whose expenditure emerges the fetishist's "but nevertheless." This postepistemological sensibility denotes a return both toward and away from metaphysical knowledge. Disavowal performs a nuanced twist which is both for and against the philosophical project. For the perverse deconstructionist: "I know very well that truth and origin are impossible, but nevertheless…." The deconstructionist returns to metaphysical claims and activities. He does so even if such efforts are essentially impossible. The perverse mantra also implies an "I know very well that adventure and dance are impossible, but nevertheless…." This indicates that the deconstructionist turns to antimetaphysical strategies of escape from the tradition. He does so even if such plays are deemed impossible. Derrida "knows very well" that both projects are impossible, "but nevertheless…." His indecision opens up the gesture toward the *tout autre* of an Other economy. This Other would be outside of the either/or and the both/and choices themselves. Rather than either/or or both/and, an economy of the neither/nor emerges as the alternative for the schizoid Other. This invites an aperture toward a *tout autre*. The neither/norism encourages the (anti)metaphysical project of the deconstructive strategy of "two interpretations of interpretation."[19] The demand to "live them simultaneously" exhibits the both/and simultaneity — "yes, yes" — which is characteristic of perversion. The perverse male junior sustains two contradictory interpretations — both an acknowledgment and a denial — of castration. Just so, the deconstructionist "simultaneously" performs what are "absolutely irreconcilable."

The at once acknowledgment and denial of two different interpretations are incoherent nonsense to the neurotic. How can the Woman be both castrated and plentiful? How can the economy be both capitalist and communist? Yet, for the pervert, this dizzy doubleness is the Real overlap and intersection — quantum *Verschrangung* — of the parallactic gap. The general equivalent of the phallus in sexual difference and currency in capitalism disappears. The standards no longer mediate relationships between otherwise incommensurable principles: penis/clitoris and capitalism/communism. The sudden coincidence of the penis and the clitoris or the unexpected overlap of capitalism and communism exemplifies a perverse and parallactic economy. Such is the deconstructionist logic of the "irreconcilable" economy of the both/and of (anti)metaphysics. The deconstructionist's two-step perversity mobilizes the both/and subjective and objective matrix. Grammatological disavowal discerns both a structuralist-pragmatic interpretation, on the one hand, and a passage "beyond man and humanism," on the other hand. Deconstruction's fetishism both reproduces the very economy which is the object of critique and at the same time flirts with an "absolute break and difference."[20] The trick is to nourish the private and public conditions in which such contradiction is accorded the proper time and emancipatory space. This Other unconscious is the *mise-en-scène* of an experimentation with the peculiarly perverse Other-Logic of Unreason. The pervert seeks the reconciliation of acknowledgment of lack and denial of castration. Just so, the deconstructionist wants the simultaneity of presence and absence. Together, the pervert and the deconstructionist will a system which is beyond the either/or logic of the neurotic in which the object is distinctly and oppositionally present or absent.

Question of the Fetish

There are several specifically fetishistic features of deconstruction. These are especially evident in "Structure, Sign, and Play" (1967). This perversity surfaces in the limit-thought of thinking essence or what Derrida describes as "thinking the structurality of structure."[21] Derrida writes,

> Nevertheless, up to the event which I wish to mark out and define, structure — or rather the structurality of structure — although it has always been at work, has always been neutralized or reduced, and this by a process of giving it a center or of referring it to a point of presence, a fixed origin.[22]

Derrida claims that to pose the question of Being ("the structurality of structure" or "What is structure?") is a present component of the theoretical enterprise. But it has been veiled and obscured by the will to a center, presence, and origin. This center refers as (not) the transcendental signified. This signified halts the play of meaning and the instability of signification. The signified arrests the (re)definition of words. Why is there a will to a stop sign? The punctuation defines the essence of the part of the whole, the presence of the element in the system, and the truth of the signified in the network of signifiers — as present in Being. This singular metaphysical gesture enforces the arrest of the infinite trace of meaning-making. Otherwise, this trail of alphabets and vocabularies extends beyond any fixed origin or ultimate reference.

Examples of the arrest of *différance* are the reference to the penis in the theory of sexual difference in psychoanalysis and the citation of the historical march of labor in Marxism. Freud's entire formulation is organized by this final referent: the phallocentrism of anatomical difference in which the clitoris can only be interpreted as the absence of phallic presence. The fetishism of perversion posits the object as a metaphorical substitution whose literal origin returns to the penis. Derrida's insight about presence illuminates that Freud's discourse sustains its explanatory coherence only because it refers the network of otherwise inchoate words (especially the fetish-images) to the signified of the penis. Marx's textual network refers to the development of the historical progression of the forces of production. The entire Marxist system of analysis hinges on the development of labor and technology. In the absence of this center of his analysis, Marx's project of the critique of the synchronous and diachronous development of labor is suspended. Both the Freudian and Marxist systems can only be theoretically sustained by the fixed deployment of the center. This center knits and weaves the elements of the system into a coherent whole. But what theory or practice finally disturbs Derrida's generalized "center," Freud's specific "penis," and Marx's singular "forces of production"?

The inspiration for deconstruction is simply the thought of essence. The magic consists of simply asking the ontological question — What is? This generates the subversion of the center. The ontological inquiry of Being opens the trace and the differences and deferrals of the signifying chain. These marks of text spin the signifier out of "itself" and toward all of the other points of signification in the system. The paradox of this thought is marvelous: the thought of essence generates the truth of construction. The ontological-essentialist project inspires genealogical-constructionist thought. Metaphysics is the origin of its own destruction. The "I know very well" conditions the "but nevertheless." The "two interpretations of interpretation" are constitutive of each other. They are perspectives on the "one" and the "same" object — "what is." The implication of the thought of essence is a radical subversion of the entire metaphysical tradition of epistemology. Knowledge in the philosophical tradition is acutely fragile. The mere thought of "itself" ruins its claims to origin and essence. The thought *of* thought is adequate to undermine thought. This demonstrates a peculiar paradox: that philosophy as the love of wisdom has never thought of itself. It is only the pervert's exhaustion of the battery of signifiers in the Other of knowledge which can inspire philosophy to finally emerge in thought.

The point is not simply that deconstructive thinking is radical and dissident. Rather, the limit-thought of deconstruction is simply coincident with thought — of the "structurality of structure." By function, thinking is essentially destructive. Deconstruction uncovers the internal *Thanatos* within the binds of a metaphysical *Eros* with its bonds of haphazardly articulated *epistemes*. The ordinary question (of Being) is adequate to the task of the destruction of the word. The fetishist turns toward the metaphorical substitute ("but nevertheless") after the literal original ("I know very well"). Deconstruction's thought also turns to a metaphysics of paradox and simulation. Identification and determination of the center ("penis," "forces of production") inspire simultaneous dissolution of the signified. The Reasonable project of truth and the Unreasonable will to exit — the two interpretations of interpretation — are the same gesture. This constitutive instability in the system has been invisible to us or "neutralized or reduced," as Derrida says.

Freud's theory of fetishism articulates the gap between the fetishistic penis-substitute and the penis itself. Grammatologically, the coincidence between penis and fetish is as yet unnoticed. The limit-thought of the parallactic overlap between penis and fetish has been disregarded. The tradition has as yet to ask the question of Sexual Being. What is the *penis-ality* of penis if it is the final referent for both phallocentric sexual difference and perverse fetishism? The philosophical and psychoanalytic will has offset and cancelled the question of the penis. The fetish is a substitute for a penis, but for what is a penis itself a substitute? The tradition is yet to ask the query of Labor Being. What is the *labor-ality* of labor if it is the origin of historical progression and radical revolution? The Marxist desire has cancelled and nullified this question of labor itself. Labor is the genesis of history, but what is the advent of labor? For Derrida, this peculiar disclaimer of the question of the "structurality of structure" illuminates the blindness of thought. Man has yet to properly think. Why do we assume that we know what we have yet to ask? Work and play think the center. Play and strategy begin the ontological inquiry: What is? But what is "What is?" — and so on?

Substitution

In the paper on structure and sign (1967), Derrida notes a "series of substitutions of center for center" as a constitutive feature of every structure.[23] By "center," Derrida means the transcendental condition of possibility: the enabling feature, the founding act, the necessary element, and the constitutive determinant. This proviso provides an unquestioned ground for the orientation, balance, and organization of a structure. The "center" is the unexamined assumption and the uninterrogated premise. Lacan would call this force the *point de capiton*. It makes a structure both necessary and insecure. Derrida says that the purpose of this center is not only to orient, balance, and organize the structure — one cannot in fact conceive of an unorganized structure — but above all to make certain that the organizing principle of the structure would limit the play of the structure.[24] First, the center is a "function." It "orients, balances, and organizes" in a homologous and isomorphic way across all structures. The study of structure will illuminate a series of functional effects which would apply to all systems. Second, the function to "orient, balance, and organize" needs supplemental elaboration: to orient indicates that the structure must have direction, perspective, and position such that it is situated in space and time relative to the elements in the structure for which it is the center; to balance intimates that the system must have coordination, equilibrium, and correspondence such that it sustains stability, like the homeostatic return in Freud's pleasure principle; and to organize signals that the structure must be arranged, categorized, and assembled such that the exercise to make the structure work is distributed among the elements around which the center functions as the principle. These qualifications of the center apply to the intention of the fetish-object in the scene of sexual difference: the fetish orients the sexual intercourse around the object; the fetish balances the division of sexual difference; and the fetish organizes meaning-making for the pervert whose dependence on the fetish for enjoyment must be ensured.

The "series of substitutions" refers to the infinite variety of terms for the center. It denotes the substitution of one word or object for another word or object. The center is subject to this "series of substitutions." This subordination of the particular and the specific to the universal and the general is the purpose of the center. Like this center, the particularity and specificity of the fetish-object are immaterial and irrelevant to its functionality. Distinction and definition are critical to the enjoyment of the empirical fetishist whose object is at stake in sexual engagement. The center of a structure is also idiosyncratic to the system. The universal and generalized functionality of the center or the fetish can be substituted with the particular and the specific. But the functionality cannot be substituted. The functionality is the constitutive ground of every structure and every fetish. The series of centers of structures or fetishes of perversions includes any foundational sign which is the critical integrant of the structure: for Marx's dialectical materialism, it is labor which is the center of the structure; for Freud's sexual difference, it is the penis which is the center of the system. The center makes each structure possible. The history of philosophy includes such centers (fetishes) as: "God," "Man," *"Cogito,"* "Mind," "Transcendental Consciousness," "Existence," "Essence," "Phenomenological Consciousness," "Will to Power," "Being," "Power/Knowledge," *"Différance,"* to name a few.

The resonance between the fetishist's high heel shoe and the philosopher's center is immediate. Both the fetish and the center are substitutes. The center is substituted with a particular and specific sign. The fetish is substituted with a unique and idiosyncratic object. However, the rhetorical variance between the two substitutive logics is that Derrida notates the function as "center" whereas Freud names the function as the "penis." The distinction between the structure's "center" and the pervert's "fetish" is that the former is qualified and described in abstract generalities, such as orientation, balance, and organization. In contrast, the pervert's fetish is defined and detailed as the concrete penis and its size, visibility, and turgidity. A crucial question about the analogy between center and fetish emerges. Is the penis a function or an inaccessible object? Is absence itself a function?

Derrida refers to the center as "unique" and that which "escapes structurality itself." The center is both "within" but also "outside" of the structure.[25] The "uniqueness" of the center is the particularity and specificity of it for the precise structure that it orients, balances, and organizes. The fetish-object is also unique to the specific pervert. The fetishist's sexual enjoyment is contingent upon its presence. The fetish substitutes for a penis which is unique. The specificity is structured by "size" and "visibility." Lacan distinguishes the penis by its "turgidity." But there are other pleasurable peculiarities of particular penises. Freud's fetish-penis is the maternal or female phallus. It is an object which should have been present but was absent. There are no specific kinds and distinct traits of this penis. The only generalization about this penis is that it is absent in delay. Derrida claims that the center is both "inside" and "outside" of the structure. This implies that the center is outside of contestation and regardless of negotiation. The center is beyond the tension between presence and absence. This give-and-take otherwise structures the order of the system. The female penis is "inside" of the *mise-en-scène* of the fetishist's psychical and sexual economy. The female penis is the principal condition *qua* absence of the *jouissance* of the fetishist. The maternal penis is also "outside" of the pervert's universe. It is the distant and inaccessible object which is forever lost to presence. The center is identified and thematized within the structure in its repetition and reiteration. The fetish is proximate and integral in its magical necromancy as the object of substitution. The fetish is both inside and outside. It is an explicit substitution. It is always elsewhere from itself in a deviation from presence.

Otherwise

The most contradictory of Derrida's statements about the center of the structure is the claim that "the center is not the center."[26] The word is swapped and switched with other words in the network of the system. The sign is always elsewhere to and otherwise from its proper (*le propre*) place in the structure. The "thought" of the center decenters this sign and its own relationship to itself. The center cannot be the center because the sign resists the logic of the self-same and the self-identical. The center is cut by a negativity ("not the center") because its value is referred in and by a series of differences and deferrals beyond itself. Freud's fetish is also alienated from itself because of its double signification: as the unique and specific fetish-object and as the general and universal function of phallic presence. The fundamental feature of the fetish-object is that it is precisely not that which it simulates. This addresses the origin of perverse disavowal: the simultaneity of both acknowledgement and denial.

The trace of the lost maternal phallus in the presence of the shoe, lace, fur, and jockstrap provides the necessary signification of phallic presence to the fetish *qua* the veil of the Woman's castration. The fetish sustains phallic presence despite the generalized castration that otherwise marks all of the objects in the system. The psychical reminder of the maternal phallus bathes the object in a presence that otherwise would be castrated within the system of objects. How is the pervert able to perform such wizardry? If the centered play of the structure is "contradictorily coherent," as Derrida says, then this coherence and logic are the expression of "the force of a desire."[27] The system inexplicably contains the give-and-take play of the structure. It does so despite the radical substitutability of this place-holder at the center of the system. The pervert's "force of a desire" is the intention to escape the oedipal situation of castration. The pervert strives to avoid his own subordination to loss and death.

Function, Fetish, and Sign

The most salient overlap between center and fetish is substitution. The center, in Derrida's words, "receives different forms or names."[28] The center is a function. But it is occupied by different words. The novelty of Derrida's intervention is that the sign is a veil for this function that otherwise orders and systematizes the structure in question. These systems are psychoanalytic phallocentrism and capitalist private property. The sign of phallocentrism is the penis. It is the final referent for sexual difference and desire. The penis can be the only referent for fetishism. The question is the material-abstract significance of the penis as a referent for sexual difference and desire. Is the penis a sign which is a form or a name? Does this metaphor obscure a more basic principle? Or is the penis a function which is the essential axiom of orientation, balance, and organization in the structure? This question isolates the profound ambiguity of both deconstruction and fetishism. What is functionality itself? Earlier, I drew a distinction between the Real Fetishist and the Patriarchal Fetishist. The Real Fetishist achieves (*a*)sexual satisfaction with an object which is unmoored to reference to the lost maternal phallus. In contrast, the Patriarchal Fetishist only sustains enjoyment with an object which refers — in difference and deferral — to phallic presence. The Real Fetishist takes pleasure in an object — form or name — which is untethered to the function of phallic presence *qua* the "center" of the structure.

Figure 7.3 Perpetual Lack

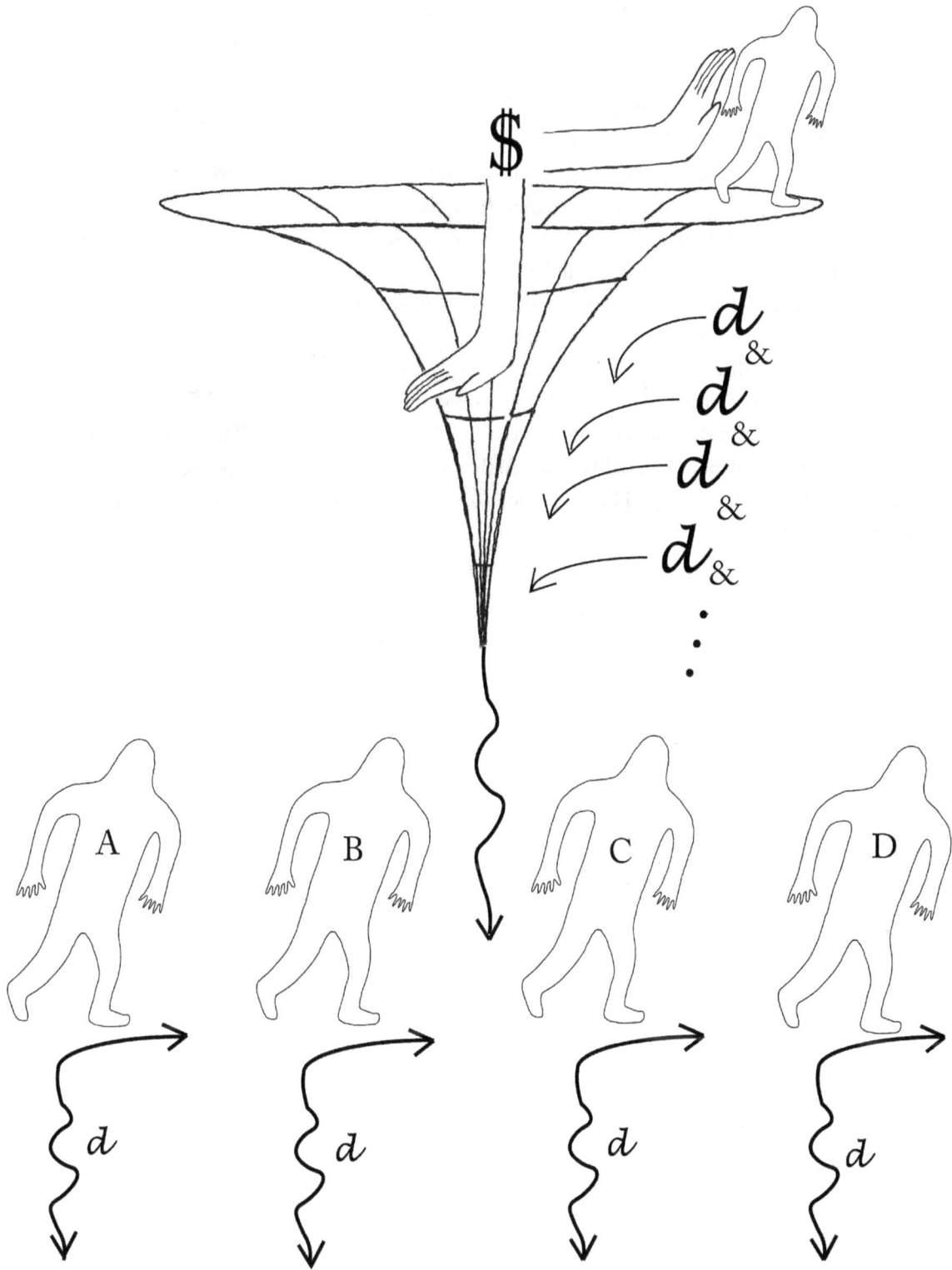

This image shows the neurotic (A, B, C, D; below) who is pushed into place (above, center) by the system. $-ism enforces the code of lack. Loss constitutes the gravitational pull (center) of this hold. At every juncture of speech (A, B, C, D), the neurotic's word vanishes into the Nothingness at the occluded center — as soon as the speech is uttered. The transformation of A in its Becoming B is an instantaneous (difference and deferral) relationality and constructionism of Sameness⁺. A Becomes B precisely because B is and is not A. This illustration depicts the psychosis of the neurotic's participation in the system — of s *qua* $-ism. The difference and the loss which are inherent in any psychotic unit of text are subsumed by the occluded and abyssal center. This makes the illusion — s *qua* $-ism — of meaning-making possible. The neurotic's thinking, being, and living insipidly enforce a system in which all terms (A, B, C, D) are self-same and self-identical — same as themselves — and positive and unified — different from the other. There is a Something is Missing in the jockstrap at the moment of its reveal — *Not yet!* — of the penis. The jockstrap *qua* fetish is otherwise not an object of perpetual lack but rather a prop for infinite plenitude. The heterosexual capitalist system of scarcities and penises is displaced by the (*a*)sexual communist system of plenitudes and jockstraps *qua* "jockstraps." This fetishistic system of *Verleugnung* and its disavowal of castration and return of "sexual difference" also return "heterosexuality," "capitalism," "scarcity," and "penis" — in the scare quotes of an expanded and extended spatiality of the perverse galaxy. These singularities are simultaneously the effect of both the negative and differential diacritics of the signifier and the positive signification of the sign. The excess of the parallactic overlap of the fetish is a surplus materiality. This endless surplus eclipses the perpetual lack of the neurotic's participation in the system of $-ism. The happy horizon is the deathless abundance of the pervert's dance in the Spirit of the System.

Notes & Sketches —

The specific and unique fetish-object can be identified as "different forms or names." The fetish can be any object in the system which is a spatiotemporal compression and displacement of the female penis. But the epistemological and ontological status of the word "penis-substitute" is in abeyance. The "penis-substitute" mediates between the concrete "fetish-object" of the pervert's *jouissance* and the "penis" to which it refers. The simple deconstructive critique of Freud's theory of the fetish is that the interval of manifest/latent — fetish/ penis — is arbitrated by the strange word "penis-substitute." This word separates the fetish from the penis in order to relate each to the other. The transparent instability which haunts Freud's theory is that the reference to the penis must refer to yet an Other, and so on. To what does the penis refer? This excess supplements the penis with further referral in difference and deferral. The ontological Being of the penis is — as such — and *qua* — and by definition — and like — and *il y a* — and so on. The penis is a substitute for the penis. The penis is substitution — Metaphoricity — itself.

This insight is the departure point for Lacan's theory of the phallus as the "transcendental signifier" as opposed to the "transcendental signified." The phallus is precisely a function. This phallic function gestures toward the other objects of desire. The phallus is classified as a metaphor. There are "different forms or names," to cite Derrida, for this metaphor of the phallus. There is no constitutive difference between the "transcendental signifier" of Lacan's phallus and the "transcendental signified" of Derrida's *arche*. Both the phallus and the signified refer to transcendentalism and to a philosophy of the "condition of possibility." The phallus and the signified denote the proviso of the ontic differences within the ontological structure of existence. Transcendentalism illuminates but obscures the functionality of the veiled source of the order of the structure. The precise purpose of this transcendentalist turn is to unveil the obscurity of the function of the phallus and the different words of the *différance* — of every other sign in the system. The penis may be interpreted as its "own" substitute. Every signifier in the Other is otherwise and elsewhere from itself in the play of the system. There is no center even as a function. The "different forms or names" or the various fetish-objects of perverse enjoyment infinitely obscure an origin at the center of the structure. What is the function of the coordination and arrangement of the structure if the center-function is always differed and deferred from presence? What is the status of the female penis if it is adumbrated and unseen? What is the essence of the Woman's phallus if it is only imagined as present in the horror of its absence?

The "history of metaphysics" is determinate of "Being as presence." This history has masked what would otherwise be a scandal. The scandal is that "the center" is "not the center," that the mover-and-shaker is always "elsewhere," and that the foundation of structure "escapes structurality" itself.[29] The function of the center is situated beyond the reach of the letter. But it is not clear that this negation ("not the center") altogether abolishes its function. The organizational principle may be stationed beyond "presence." But it may still orient, balance, and organize. Derrida's deconstruction of the Being of the "is" does not imply that the structure does not function. Rather, the claim simply suggests that Being persists outside of "forms or names" and words or signs in the symbolic order. Lacan defines *Praxis* as the impossible symbolization of the Real. *Praxis* is any project which seeks to uncover what is outside of consciousness, writing, and speaking. The center is the Real. It is the unsymbolizable trauma of the structure. The system is oriented, balanced, and organized by this disruption. The Real center is beyond the presence of the elements. These integrants are otherwise coordinated by the Real center. Any system (phallocentrism, fetishism, structuralism, Marxism, and so on) is configured and coordinated by this Other in space and time.

The pervert's *jouissance* is impotent in the absence of the fetish. The fetish reminds the pervert of castration, but at the same time it defeats the anxiety because the object simulates the presence of this absence. The crazy contradiction in the fetishist's psychical life is that — somehow — absence reminds the pervert of presence.

Inexplicably, lack implies plenitude. The symbolization of the Real is the source of the pervert's pleasure. Castration anxiety is the immediate effect of the loss of the female penis. Otherwise, the Woman's phallus is a reminder of security and comfort. Lacan notes that there is only cause in that which is broken. This dictum applies to this *mise-en-scène* of desire. The fetishist manages to fix what is broken: absence. The target of the pervert's passion is the conversion of the absent into the present and the broken into the fixed. This effort requires an acknowledgment of the loss in order to deny the diminution. The pervert demonstrates that the suture of the wound operates on the level of the "forms or names," as Derrida puts it. The return to presence is a project of metaphor and representation rather than of center and function. This center is outside of symbolic presence. The fetish rather than the function is the object of the pervert's psychosexual intervention.

The perverse parallax is this overlap between the function of the center which is not present, on the one hand, and the signs which are present in their substitution, on the other hand. What works in fetishism is this coincidence between sign and function, between representation and reality, and between word and referent. The "penis-substitute" is Freud's awkward word for the mediatory gap between the fetishistic representation and the referent of the penis. This mediation opens and closes the lacuna between the fetish-object and the penis. But the question returns with insistence. Is the penis also a fetish? Or is the penis a form, name, and sign? Or is the penis a function, operation, and center? The uncomfortable trouble with these questions is their formulation. If the center is other than presence, do we have any sense of what a function is in itself? What is the prop for or simulacrum of the signs of "forms or names"? Why must the center disappear at the same moment that the sign emerges? Why is the referent lost in the presence of the representation?

Something is Missing — in the relationship between representation and reality. The fetish closes the gap of Missing. But the object does so only insofar as the fetishist opens the object's wound in order to enjoy the effort to mask the castration. The pervert knows "very well" that castration is an accomplished fact, but he "nevertheless" reminds himself of it in order to forget it. I would not describe such a plot as dramatic nostalgia. Rather, I claim that it mimes the serious play of the offspring against the reality of the symbolic order of the adult. The fetishist takes seriously the absence of the function of the center. He resists a metaphysics of presence. The fetishist engages this loss in order to reinvent a symbolic order in which *jouissance* rather than desire organizes the system.

It is a silly amusement that the function of the center slips and slides. *Différance* enables the joys of the representations and words which also suture the absence of the referent for which they approximate. The pervert gets off on the present enjoyment of an absence. This serious play of the offspring simply enjoys castration whose pleasure must be understood as plenitude. The conversion of the masculine Something is Missing into the feminine Nothing is Missing is perspectival and parallactic. The transformation resists determination as presence. The opposition between the words is subverted by the two-step of acknowledgment and denial. As the pervert would say, "If 'Something is Missing,' then 'Something' must be 'Nothing' — otherwise, why would I be enjoying myself so much?"

The criterion for perverse pleasure is not the desirability of the object. The fetishist's enjoyment is not organized by the phallic outline of the *objet petit a*. Rather, the condition of the fetishist's *jouissance* is the success of the fetish itself. The question for the neurotic is the desirability of the object. In contrast, the concern for the pervert is the promise of the object to supply the pleasure. But the status of the penis survives as a question. Is it an object of *désir* or *jouissance*? Is it a function or a sign? Is it Real or symbolic? How can a lost absence be presently embodied in the material form of the penis itself? The conundrum of phallocentrism is not the process by which the offspring somehow sees the negativity of castration or Something is Missing in the female junior. The aporia of the offspring's relationship to the penis is the method by which he somehow apprehends the positivity of plenitude or Nothing is Missing in himself. Why is it simple and easy to see absence whereas it is difficult and formidable to see presence? Lacan claims that there are the spots and the stains — constitutive blindness — in the visual field. Is it possible to look and not see that Something is Missing? Can plenitude be the object of the look if lack is the subject of the gaze?

The Function of Simulation

The pervert does not deploy signs in order to remake the structure yet again. Rather, he uses words in order to demonstrate that the representation of the "forms or names" as substitutes for the organizational principle of the center involves the simulation of presence in the place of absence. The fetishist's representations are material embodiments with abstract significations. These perverse alphabets and objects gesture toward a necessary function of the system: absence. But what is the object of this absence? The center is only absent insofar as it is veiled by the different words which substitute in its place. The sign is a "creationist sublimation *ex nihilo*," as Lacan puts it. This invention supports the system as a self-posited force of presence. The sign invents and deploys itself out of nothing but the ether of the signifying chain. Derrida further claims that "the concept of a centered structure" can be understood as "contradictorily coherent."[30] The contradiction at the nucleus of the center is the temporal movement and spatial dislocation of the structure. Derrida refers to this instability as the "event" and "rupture" of the thought of essence *qua* construction. Space and time generate a play which subverts the center. The condition of possibility of the structure is this subversion of the center by the substitution of the other signs in the system.

The event or rupture in the thought — thinking — of history upsets any determination of "Being as presence" for the center of the structure. The center defends itself against the otherwise Becoming of the system. This defense is a deviation of the center from "itself." The center solicits this defense against Becoming in its absence as Being. The function of the absent sign is organized by the hidden machinations of the otherwise occluded center of the system. The purpose of the sign is to spin the system and topple the structure. The sign *ex nihilo* emerges in the structure as the substitutive metaphor. The word (in general) beseeches the supplementation of all of the other signifiers in the system. The sign of the structure is simultaneously all of the other signs in the system. There is only one generic structure within which "different forms or names" occupy the center. The purpose of this dwelling is to veil the functionality of the center. The ordinary neurotic experiences the integrity of each sign and the singularity of each structure. In contrast, the pervert discerns a profound Sameness⁺ which qualifies the "structurality of structure" and the general ontological "What is?" at the origin of structure. The movement of Becoming disturbs the function of the center. Becoming spatially decenters and temporally disrupts the operation of the center. The center is subverted by the play of forms and names, and penis-substitutes and fetish-objects. These marks in the system reduce the Becoming of sign-substitution to the Being of the center as a function. The oscillation of the movement of Becoming in the system is pinned to the stasis of the Being of the different "forms or names" of the signs in the system. But if the center is deviant from itself, then its different "forms or names" in sign-substitutions must be qualified as effects of the center of the structure.

The psychoanalytic reference to the penis must be decentered. The center is outside of presence as the inaccessible Real around which symbolization encircles. Is either the fetish-object, the penis-substitute, or the penis different from simulations of the center? Is the psychoanalytic credit to the vaunted penis a gesture toward this veiled penis which is always Other? Or is the penis a mere "form or name" itself? Is the penis a simple word within the network of other signifiers? The penis is no doubt singular. It is as such marked in psychoanalytic theorization. But its structural position as either a contingent sign ("forms or names") or a foundational referent ("center") is not resolved. Is the penis the condition of possibility of male fetishistic sex? Or is it a substitute for a more fundamental reference to function rather than to play? If the isomorphism between the penis and the center holds, then how does absence generate its functionality? How does loss promise effects in the signifying chain of the pervert?

Derrida isolates a nonpresent center. This Real is otherwise than and elsewhere from the decenter of the structure. This illuminates another similarity between deconstruction theory (*différance* and trace) and the concept of perversion (fetish, penis-substitute, and penis). The deconstructionist's sign and the pervert's fetish are substitutes or metaphors for an Other which is neither self-same nor self-identical. The fetishist's shoe and the philosopher's center are always not themselves. Rather, they refer to an otherness which confers value on the sign and the fetish "as such" of which each is not *qua* not. The fetish-object is the substitute (or the penis-substitute) for the absent maternal phallus. The mother's missing penis is *das Ding* which was never there but should have been. The pervert's erotic reaction to the fetish is made possible by an expectation and an anticipation which are frustrated. But this privation is the condition of the enjoyment. The slippage between the fetish and the penis (with the mediation of the "penis-substitute") invites the fetishist to get off on not merely the shoe, lace, fur, or jockstrap. Even more so, the pervert takes pleasure in *substitution itself.* The pervert enjoys the function of metaphor. But he may prefer some metaphors more than others as an effect of their function. Perversely, the process of metaphor is the intercourse of sex.

Metaphor is not merely a negation of presence in the endless chain of supplemental significations. The pervert discovers an addition in metaphor which is internal to the manifest subtraction in metaphor as it is discerned by the neurotic. This brazenly simple but powerfully consequential twist from subtraction to addition illuminates the shift from metaphorical supplementation as a sign of absence to metaphorical excess as a mark of presence. The fetishist divines an economy in which Nothing is Missing rather than one in which Something is Missing. The fetishist's shoe is surely a pillar and a prop as a substitute for the Something is Missing. The psychosexual economy of fetishism presupposes an absence because the maternal phallus serves as the *objet petit a,* or cause of desire. This loss inspires the human subject and its *Praxis* of the symbolization of the Real. But the fetish-object does not substitute for the absence of Something is Missing. Rather, the fetish represents the Nothing is Missing — or the Everything is Present.

This present absence renders the fetishist's magical substitution strangely not metaphorical. The shoe, lace, fur, and jockstrap as fetish-objects are neither metaphors for nor figurations of the maternal phallus. The metaphor and the figure imply a castration and a lack in the system. The neurotic's metaphor suggests a negative supplementation of subtraction. Perversely, Nothing is Missing because the fetishist discerns a reconfiguration of the metaphorical dimension. This rearrangement deconstructs the opposition between the metaphorical and the literal. Freud turns toward the "penis-substitute" in order to overcome the gap between the prosaic fetish-object and the final referent in the penis. But this is a mistaken interpretation of fetishism. The objects themselves are not manifest signifiers of a latent content. The objects are not cathected as reminders of loss and return. The fetish is a toy or a prop for the reinvention of the world. As Freud says of childhood play: "The opposite of play is not what is serious but what is real."[31] The fetishist plays seriously.

The pervert contests the reality of sexual difference itself. The fetish-object is positivity and plenitude. The fetish is configured beyond the arrangements of desire and castration that otherwise structure metaphor. The fetish does not refer to the penis. Rather, the penis recalls the fetish. The fetish is a substitute for itself because it denies the negativity (*différance* and trace) that otherwise indexes castration. The object of the fetish is Real. This illustrates a pivotal difference between the deconstructionist's center and its substitution of "forms or names," on the one hand, and the pervert's fetish-object and its substitution of "itself," on the other hand. The center is a veiled function which dissimulates itself in the background against the foreground of the representational signs. The fetish is an exclusive and fixed object which simulates itself *qua* itself in plenitude.

Baudrillard's marked distinction between dissimulation and simulation clarifies the difference between the center and the fetish. Baudrillard says: "To dissimulate is to pretend not to have what one has."[32] He continues: "To simulate is to feign to have what one doesn't have."[33] The pervert precisely simulates a presence and an absence. The charisma, power, and magic of this faked plenitude overrun the negativity of the lost maternal phallus. The shoe becomes the penis for the pervert. This is the reason that the shoe must be present as exclusive and fixed for his sexual relationship. The economy of dissimulation applies to the masculine subject. He forever subordinates his presence and pleasure to the dictates of the law of the father and to the demands of the civilization. But how can the lace be the penis outside of the structure of metaphor and the (un)like and (dis)similar? How can Being be thought by the pervert outside of the economy of castration? How is the ontological question to be posed beyond the subtraction of the Something is Missing and the endless calculations of loss? Answers to these questions involve scrutiny of the maternal phallus. Lacan equates the maternal phallus with *das Ding* or the Thing. The horizon of this Thing approaches the space and time in which the fetish-object returns to itself. This is the moment at which the structure of metaphor (simile) bleeds to its death.

Some das Ding is Not Missing

Lacan's discussion of *das Ding* in the *Seminar* on the ethics of psychoanalysis (1959-60) informs a proper interpretation of the peculiar object of the fetishist's enjoyment. This object is the maternal phallus. This liminal maternal phallus should have been present but was absent. Lacan describes the Thing as the wholly other object which is inaccessible. It is also the misty object which regulates the entire system within which the subject encircles this Thing or "true secret," as Lacan says.[34] The true secret of *das Ding* does not merely refer to its veil of itself. The true secret also refers to the maternal phallus and to the resistance to representation. This Thing is impossible to imagine. It is a loss of an absence which was never present to experience. The subject of desire is in search of an object which is unrecognizable even were it present. The subject is blind to *das Ding*. At the same time, the Thing organizes the experience of the relationship between the pleasure principle and the reality principle. Lacan says: "The world of our experience, the Freudian world, assumes that it is this object, *das Ding*, as the absolute Other of the subject, that one is supposed to find again."[35] This object is the maternal phallus and its "absolute" otherness. This object radically redistributes phallocentric sexual difference. The Thing reconfigures the entire system of identification.

Lacan emphasizes that the Thing is that which we are "supposed to find again." This foregrounds the strange sense of the word "find." Is that which is to be found a formerly present object that we have lost with the imperative that we return to it again? Or is the Thing an object which we must find even if it has never been present in our past? If the former, then what is at stake is an effort to "refind" the object which is lost to the subject. If the latter, then the work is to "find" an object which is radically unimagined by the subject. But Lacan claims that the object of the Thing "has never been lost."[36] This indicates that the Thing is situated between the lost and the found. *Das Ding* is in-between something which should have been present but was absent, on the one hand, and something which is the object of a return in the effort to capture this presently absent object, on the other hand. The Something is Missing of *das Ding* is organized by a Nothing *was* Missing in a previous personal and social past. The catch is that the Something in which the subject of phallocentric sexual difference and capitalist scarcity is marred in a relationship to castration emerges as an effect of this loss. The subject only retroactively discovers the presence of this absence. The "absolute Other of the subject" refers to the limit of the boundaries of the body, soul, and mind of the subject. It is the edge beyond which the subject confronts an otherness. This excess destabilizes the subject and the system in which this subject is embedded. The incessantly insistent object of *das Ding* is a temptation around which the blindness of man peers.

The return to the Thing can only be approached as a lost object for the subject. Man aims "to reproduce the initial state, to find *das Ding*."[37] This "initial state" is not simply the oneness and wholeness of *l'homme-lette*. Rather, the initial state is the infantile quest to discover the riddle of sexual difference. The offspring seeks the source (origin, *arche*) of the system. Lacan says that, "the Thing is not nothing, but literally is not."[38] The "is not" or the negation of Being illuminates the ontological status of this originary object and its initial embryonic development. This stage is pure negation. The obscene purity of this negation ("is not") is the originary object and the fundamental state of *das Ding*. The object is unimaginable to the subject. It is the condition of the radical turnover of the entire system in a negation which is internal to the structure. Lacan refers to *das Ding* as the "beyond-of-the-signified."[39] It is the horizonal and emergent negation of that which is in the system. A return to the lost object and the initial state is a recall to the negation of that which is in the world. It is a renascence of *Thanatos* and the death drive. The organizational principle of the structure is this negation of the "is not." The precept of the center is the death drive and mortality. The vaunted maternal phallus is a distant death. The fetish-object veils this *petit mort* in order to sustain a pleasure. This joy is the pervert's *jouissance*. Pleasure pulsates on the other side of castration.

The fetish does not stand-in or stop-gap for an object which is present and nameable. Rather, the fetish is a reminder of the object which should have been present but was absent. The reason that the offspring expects this presence is a mystery. Young masturbatory pleasure is not only primary but optimal. Originally, the male junior has no interest in sexual and affective relations with the vagina or the clitoris. The male junior expects a radical Sameness[†] in the place of difference. The maternal phallus and the female penis are curious avatars for a lost object. These are signs for a ghostly absence whose presence is forever deferred into a suspended past or a promised future. Freud formulates the fetish as an inexact substitution for this impossible and unfathomable object. The fetish is the space and time of an economy which is Outside of sexual difference. Nothing is Missing and the maternal phallus are objects of Real loss. *Das Ding* eludes capture in deeds and words. The fetish-object is not simply a prop or an instrument for a concrete and empirical object which can be designated as the maternal phallus. Instead, the fetish is the representation of the function of absence.

The object is a function of castration and lack. This absence is at the center of the psychical and semiotic structures of both the individual and society. This function is "itself" qualified with scare quotes. The function of castration is neither self-same nor self-identical to itself. The subject has no access to the presence of *das Ding* except in its subjective and objective effects. The function of absence must be considered deviant and divergent from itself. The center is certified as absent or not itself. The center is also the source (*arche* and origin) of the subject's desire. This *désir* is the essence of man's existence. The pervert's *a* is "a" substitute for "the" function of this absence. The loss is not a gap in the object itself. The lack is a wound in the structure. The object is the castration of the function of the center. The pervert desires "the" function of absence. The pervert desires absence itself. The fetishist covets the "is not" of the radical negation of all which is in the system. The pervert desires the lost origin. His object of desire is the *arche*. The pervert's cause is the advent of the entirety of the system in the place of the function of this absence. This object is the foundation and the principle of the world.

The fetish can only be apprehended as Something is Missing for an elementary reason: thought. The "thinking the structurality of structure" is the advent of the Becoming of the fetish as a substitute for an absence. The metaphysical gesture is both inspired and defeated in the project to return to a presence which is forever lost to the specters of *das Ding* and to the resistance of the Real. The fetishist merely rediscovers "*a*" fetish-object which represents "the" function of the entirety of the symbolic system. This is the function of Something is Missing. Every other word in the structure is a code for this loss and death. Derrida's infamous "play" of the text is the bemused runaround of these various words. None of these words can be stabilized as presence. The absent function is the origin of the system. There is no word to designate this function. Any series of words, such as "metaphor," "fetish," "substitute," "penis," "center," "sign," "function," "metaphor," "fetish," "substitute," "penis," "center," "sign," "function," and so on — each of these words only inadequately represents the center in its functionality.

The fetishist's object substitutes for the function. It is an *a* of the *objet* for *the* function of the center. The structure's center is "not the center" and "elsewhere."[40] How are these two functions of the object and the center to be defined and elaborated? How are the fetish and the metaphor to be signified if each is identical to itself as an absence or the "is not" that Lacan likens to *das Ding*? The fetish is present because of the absence of the absence of the maternal phallus. The fetish is not defined by a difference and a negativity. Instead, the fetish is distinguished by an absence which generates a presence. The fetish is loss which invests gain. The function of the fetish is absent. This absence enables the fetish to work. Similarly, the "different forms or names" of the sign-substitutions in the structure obscure the center. This center is differed and deferred from any presence. The center is radically absent. The function of the center is absent. This absence is the foundation of the success of the sign-substitutions. These metaphors appear in the place of the function as compressions and displacements. The function of both the fetish and the sign is to obscure reality. The fetish eclipses the referent of castration in the absence of the penis. The sign conceals the principle of organization in the absence of the center. An articulation of this function of the "center" of the structure and the "penis" of sexual difference resists proper expression.

The center is not itself because it is decentered as otherwise and elsewhere. But then what is the ontological presence of it? The fetish is not the female penis but a veil of its absence. But then what is the fetish? What is the penis whose absence the fetish conceals? Undeniably, the pervert's *a* and the philosopher's "different forms or names" or "sign-substitutions" are toys and props. These figures and costumes screen the primordiality of the referent. The metaphors and representations veil the center of the philosopher's structure and the center of the fetishist's object. The check on any analysis of the bedrock foundation of the function of the sign or of the fetish is the Real of the function. This Real is denoted as the center and the penis in my analysis. What is a penis? What is a center? What is "what is"? What is a function apart from a specific fetish and a particular sign? What is the functionality of the maternal penis and the philosopher's center?

Derrida begins to articulate the limit of thought "that there was no center." He discovers in this thought that the center is "not a fixed locus but a function, a sort of nonlocus in which an infinite number of sign substitutions come into play."[41] The key signifier in this passage is "a sort of nonlocus." This ambivalent phrase articulates a blurry outline of the center. This hazy phrase is consistent with an unsymbolizable entity, such as this functionality of absence. A "nonlocus" denotes a readily available space for the locus itself. A "nonlocus" also indicates that its space is unoccupied in the present. But this nebulous "nonlocus" is also necessary and constitutive. It is a place-holder for the contingent sign to substitute in the place of an emptiness. This investment of Being in Nothingness is the return of the sign in the place of the nonlocus. Lacan names this emergence a "creationist sublimation *ex nihilo*." The negative ("non")component of "nonlocus" is a reference to the negativity in the signifying chain. This negativity haphazardly refers different words to multiple loci. This "non" also denotes that the series of signs in metaphorical substitution in the place of the center cannot be in its proper place or order. The "locus" is negated because it is contingent, accidental, and even scandalous. The center *qua* center is an "as such." This self-same and self-identical Being is impossible to symbolize in the Real. The center is a faceless and nameless function. The functionality of this center may be fixed, but its name and face are unfixed and substitutable. The sign substitutes for nothing. This is the reason that the center and the fetish are both functions of an absence that unexpectedly enables the various presences in the system. There is neither an object nor a referent. There is no penis.

The "nonlocus" of the center is occupied by the master signifier of any discourse. This representation is possible because the center is itself a function of absence. This operational loss must be sutured by the ephemeral presence of the sign. The object is occupied by the vaunted shoe or lace or fur or jockstrap or any other object in the system. This fetishization is possible because the maternal phallus is a function of absence. This function organizes the sexuality of the pervert. The appearance of the center *qua* center is impossible. There is neither an essential nor exemplary structure. The manifestation of the maternal phallus is impossible. There is no presence of the female penis to which the fur, lace, shoe, or jockstrap approximate. The center and the fetish are animated by "different forms or names" of an "infinite number of sign-substitutions." These objects and signs seek to suture the gap and hole that otherwise make them possible. The economy of substitution cannot succeed in the absence of absence. The center and the maternal penis are names for an absence which inspires this series of substitutions, differences, deferrals, compressions, displacements, metaphors, metonymies, and so on. This set of toys and props composes the structure and its internal movements. The center *qua* center or the penis *qua* penis must be understood as definitively "not the center" and inevitably "elsewhere."

This series of signs — faces, names, and forms — in philosophy includes: "God," "Man," *"Cogito,"* "Mind," "Transcendental Consciousness," "Existence," "Essence," "Phenomenological Consciousness," "Will to Power," "Being," *"Différance,"* and "And So On." Each of these words is a contingent sign for the necessary function which makes each structure possible. Any series of objects in sexual perversion performs the same function. The representation is made possible by the absence of the reality. The signifier of representation simulates a relationship to reality. The reality is the sign in the semiotic structure. The reference is the penis in the sexual economy. The wager of fetishism is that the function of absence generates symbolic effects of presence in the signifying chain. This presence enables the peculiar sexuality of the pervert. Derrida's critique of structure and sign bets that the structure can topple in the play of words which coordinates the structure. The vital difference between deconstruction's center and perversion's fetish appears at this juncture. Derrida's play seeks to amusingly and endlessly substitute signs for each other in the absence of a referent which would otherwise stabilize this strategy. Freud's fetish wants to enjoy a restricted set of representations in the choice objects. The deconstructionist enjoys playing with signs in substitution. The pervert takes pleasure in *substitution itself.* What is substitution? What is the reference to which substitution refers? — substitution *of* or substitution *with* or substitution *as* or substitution *for?* Preposition, what? Masochistically, the pervert enjoys the Becoming and process of substitution rather than the Being and presence of the object.

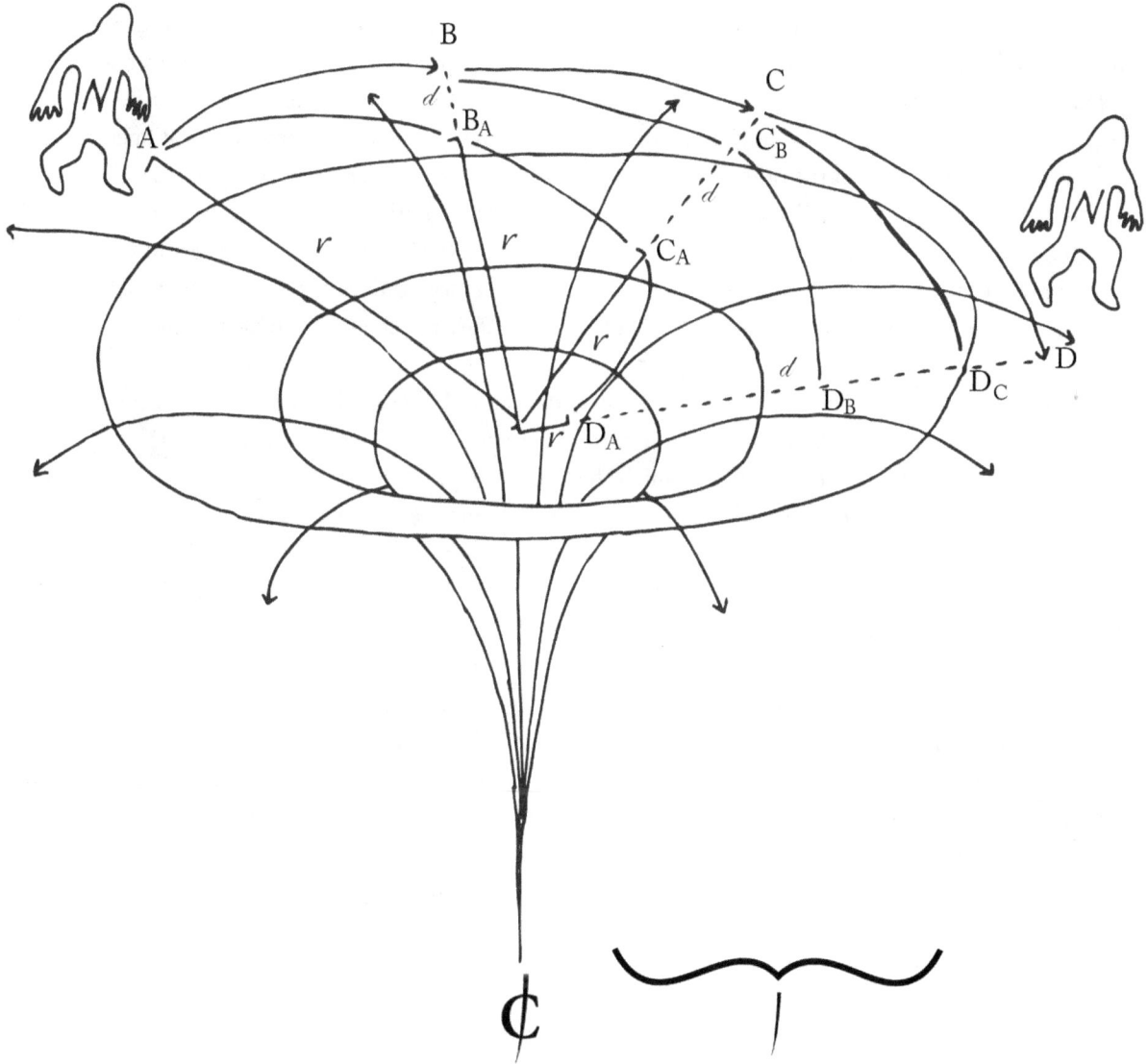

Figure 7.4 The Neurotic's Travels

This drawing depicts the relationship among and performance of: first, signification and meaning-making; second, the gravity and function of the occluded center; third, the psychical structure of neurosis; and fourth, the difference and deferral of relationality and constructionism. The neurotic circumnavigates the center of the system. This place of participation — thinking, being, and living — in the signifying chain is referred to as A. B_A is the unit of text of A which is recontextualized in a traversal into and through B. The lost excess in translation is an effect of difference and deferral. This *différance* is the condition of possibility of meaning-making. This fissure also indicates the proviso of loss but also gain. The gap illuminates the necessity of the forgotten and erased in lost excesses and gained remainders. The diagram shows that relationality and constructionism shrink the relationships among the units of text to zero (below). The distance from the center is reduced to Nothingness (below). The identity and essence of A are lost to spatial differentiation and temporal deferral. The signified is altogether lost, and meaning-making is (Becoming) impossible. The system is a perversely excessive 1/0 rather than either the neurotic either/or of the plenitude of Being and the absence of Absolute Nothingness, on the one hand, or the schizoid undefined All which is at once the Being of Absolute Nothingness, on the other hand. This perverse economy is consonant with Saussure's version of negativity, difference, relationality, and constructionism. The elaboration of diacritics communicates an All (Nothing) which is equivalent to a Nothing (All). The occlusion of the center (below) refers to this *absolutely relative* value of the signifier and its differed and deferred distance. This is the radius (above, left, right) of the system. The paradoxically *absolutely relative* value is both the limit to and the excess of the borders of the system. The psychotic imagines relationality and constructionism in trace and *différance*. The pervert sustains relationality and constructionism, but he articulates the distance between the units of text in their excessive overflow from the gravity (center) of the stability of the system. As a Queer Mathematics, the trajectory of the occluded center is the Real Symbolic in which the binary 1/0 yields the result of a complex and undefined *finite infinity* or *infinite finity*. This dimension of the Real Symbolic makes possible and visible the overlap and suture of the economies of Something is Missing and Nothing is Missing. The dimension of the maternal phallus and its substitutive fetish-object (jockstrap, "jockstrap," jockstrap, and "jockstrap") is the space in which the occluded center (below) and the excessive overlap of objects with themselves are possible in the Being *of* Becoming and the simultaneous metaphorization of metonymy and metonymization of metaphor. The relationship between difference and deferral in relationality and constructionism is the integrant of the Real Symbolic. An image of the collision of tectonic plates which collide and fold into each other articulates the timeless — suspension of the phallic function — third-dimension of the unconscious. The relationality and constructionism of difference and deferral — *différance* — transform negative value (signification) into positive signification (value). The pervert's signifierization of the sign — or valueization of signification — illuminates this Real Symbolic (Madness of Order) of $-ism (below, right).

Notes & Sketches —

A Function

The functionality of the center is crucial to understanding perversion. The function puts in sharp relief the division among penis, penis-substitute, and fetish. The critical interval in deconstruction is between center and the sign-substitutions which become situated in the place ("nonlocus") of this center. These metaphors are simulations of the function. This function is veiled in the process of its operation. Lacan's *objet petit a* is also structurally functional. The object-cause of desire conditions man's existence. The specific and particular features of the object are irrelevant to its functionality. Freud maps different objects of desire in the oral, anal, and phallic stages of psychosexual development. But the function of sexual relationships is essentially the "ultimate aim," as Freud puts it in the text on instincts (1915).[42] This latter flirtation is what Lacan refers to as the barred object of "courtly love."[43] The function of the *objet petit a* is to inspire the man's desire and to tempt it toward the "ultimate aim." The toil and sweat of this function in the *mise-en-scène* of a pedagogical fantasy are inexhaustible. The promised capture of an object sustains and even intensifies the transcendental power and operational efficacy of the function. There will always be another object which will serve the function of the *objet petit a*. Lacan titles one of his texts, "God and the *Jouissance* of ~~The~~ Woman" (1973), with "~~The~~" crossed out and under erasure. There is always another Woman such that *the* Woman is only *a* Woman. Another Woman tempts beyond the bend as the next conquest.

This model of desire is essentially fetishistic. An *a* is a substitute for another *a* is a substitute for another *a*. These *a* or *objets* are all "remnants," in the terms of the *Seminar* on the four fundamental concepts (1964), or "semblances," in the words of the *Seminar* on female sexuality (1972-73), for the impossible. Lacan smartly performs the function of *a* by consistently shifting its name and definition throughout the course of his teaching. In his discussions of "Schema L," Lacan refers to the object as "*a*." In his *Seminar* on the transference (1960-61), Lacan refers to the function of *a* with the Greek term *agalma* from Plato's Symposium (416 BCE). Most revealing is Alan Sheridan's note in his translation of *Écrits* (1966): "Lacan insists that '*objet petit a*' should remain untranslated, thus acquiring, as it were, the status of an algebraic sign."[44] Lacan's use of a formal and abstract symbol for the function of the object-cause of desire indicates the ultimate untranslatability of the function. The provisional function can only be represented by a sign. The translation of this sign is imprecise and approximate. The function is nebulous and equivocal. The veil of "different forms or names" of the fetish-objects conceals the incoherence of the precept and principle of structure and sex. The Madness of Order cannot articulate itself except in *les mots et les choses* of obscure representation.

The center and the penis are screened. But the strategy of deconstruction and the desire of perversion covet this function of absence. Loss is the foundation of the structure. Castration is the ground of phallic sexuality. Derrida announces the absolute necessity and final inescapability of the function of the center. He notes that, "one cannot in fact conceive of an unorganized structure."[45] He says that, "the notion of a structure lacking any center represents the unthinkable itself."[46] Thought cannot conceptualize the absence of a center. Thinking cannot conceive of the disorganization of the structure. We cannot even think without orientation, balance, and organization. Thought is the condition of the (im)possibility of structure. Thought commences the slide from an essentialist epistemology toward a constructionist ontology. More so, the "unthinkable" absence of a center is exactly the function of the center. The purpose and proviso of the center are to be absent. The various sign-substitutions and fetish-objects cannot suture the wound of castration if Nothing is Missing in the system. The center functions in and as a galaxy of lack — otherwise there would be no "nonlocus" for which to swap in and swap out in the switch and glitch of the signifier. The function of absence is the proviso of presence in the system. Perversely, the loss is the condition of the gain.

Impossible

The Derrida of "Structure, Sign, and Play" (1967) recommends only the thinking of the "structurality of structure." This thought is an Event. This rupture replaces one sign-substitution (say: God) for another transcendental term (say: Power). However, Derrida later posits an ecstatic and optimistic "yes, yes." He later affirms an economy which is outside of traditional metaphysics and toward the *hors texte* itself. This more radical gesture seeks to "conceive" of the "unthinkable." This project wants to imagine an "unorganized structure." This endgame typifies deconstruction's specifically antimetaphysical foray. Such adventure takes flight beyond the rigidity of the structure. The elements will always be subordinate to substitution, displacement, compression, metaphor, metonymy, and so on. But Derrida's later formulation of deconstruction affirms an impossible economy. This Other-Structure explodes the function of the coordination of the center. This turn toward the impossible announces the emergence of an Other. The *tout autre* is the horizon of deconstructive work and my conceptualization of the Pervert-Schizoid-Woman.

Lacan's concept of desire similarly works to destroy the transcendental function of the subject. Desire involves a suicidal gesture. Such a *petit mort* is inspired by *Thanatos*. Lacan classifies the object of desire as the cause of desire. This metonymic passion of desire seeks its own condition of possibility. Desire aims to consume that which makes it possible. Desire aims at the destruction of the penis which is otherwise the organizational reference for all phallic sexuality. Lacan cites Spinoza's claim (1677) that desire is the "essence of man" in the *Seminar* on the four fundamental concepts of psychoanalysis (1964).[47] This passion desires its own cause. It animates a self-destructive suicidal desire or *Thanatos*. Death drive wills the destruction of its own center. This center of destruction deviates from its own essence. The fetish-object not only conceals absence but ordains its destruction. This desirous annihilation of absence promises the total demolition of the system. This violence of *Thanatos* heralds the inconceivable and the unthinkable. Deconstruction seeks the ruin of the fundamental functionality of the center. Psychoanalysis promises the slaughter of castration. Both deconstruction and psychoanalysis usher in the Becoming of the Pervert-Schizoid-Woman and the arrival of an aneconomy — resistant to comparison, contrast, and exchange — of plenitude and fullness. This postcenter and postpenis dimension is the realm beyond phallocentrism and castration, and beyond capitalism and scarcity. This future is even beyond the regulation of pleasure by the pleasure principle. But how is such demolition to be performed in thinking, being, and living? What is beyond the pleasure principle?

Deconstruction against Desire

The inscription of the subject in the structure is an especially tricky bind to undo and displace. The subject in contemporary theory is trapped between a phenomenology of resistant bodies and a structuralism of fatalist subordination. The deconstructive critique of Lacan is well articulated in Lacoue-Labarthes and Nancy's book, *The Title of the Letter* from 1973.[48] The critique is that Lacan places an emptiness (absence, castration, and lack) at the center of his system. He names this gap the "subject of desire." For deconstruction, there is no proper subject except as a momentary effect of the text. Derrida does mention several subject-ive constituents in "Structure, Sign, and Play" (1967). These articulate a role for the human in the series of substitutions for the center of the structure. The grammatological critique of psychoanalysis claims that the decentered subject is nonetheless situated at the center of the structure. This is so even if its position is an emptiness in search of a signified — meaning — on the periphery of the system. Early in the essay, Derrida speaks of the "force of a desire." It is difficult not to fasten such a force or desire to some modality of subject. This will strives to make contradiction itself coherent.[49] The "contradictorily coherent" structure can only sustain itself by a desire or a force. This will underpins the contingent center — metaphor, face, name, form, and so on. This center makes a specific and particular structure possible but also vulnerable. The source of this force and desire is undefined. But it can be assumed that this *arche* is also captive to the structure within which it is embedded. The purpose of this foundation is the preservation of the metaphor for — the function.

Derrida speaks of the "centered structure" as a contradiction. The center is endlessly substituted with different masks and screens. But the function of the veil in the structure is consistent. The so-called uniqueness of the system is a farce. Each structure is substitutable for another. This is so even if the logic of the referent (the penis, in psychoanalysis; labor practices, in Marxism) of this structure is inconceivable and unthinkable. The referent is beyond the capacities of man's will to knowledge. The contradiction in the structure is that it is wildly revisable. The system is contingent on the metaphor that haphazardly occupies the position of its center. The centered structure operates according to a ground and a certitude. The signified is beyond play. This play questions, interrogates, and annoys the foundation of the system. Play can disrupt a centered structure. The rupture can undermine a structure with an identified form, name, and fetish. This subversion is possible even in the absence of a coherent account of the essential structurality of the system. In the most impressive deconstructive readings, the structure emerges only as an effect of its dissolution. The components of the edifice are only visible upon the ruin of the system. But it is difficult to imagine such deconstruction without a hand and a pen, let alone a fist and the man.

The closest approximation to an explicit dialogue with psychoanalysis in Derrida's text on structure and sign (1967) is his remarks about anxiety. He says that anxiety is manifest in the entanglement of the subject (or "force" or "desire") in the structure. He says that "certitude" as opposed to "play" is a weak attempt to master anxiety. This angst is a consequence of,

> a certain mode of being implicated in the game, or being caught by the game, of being as it were at stake in the game from the outset.[50]

The proper object of speculation in this passage is the "mode" in which the subject is "implicated" in the "game." How is the subject collared by the structure? A game involves rules but also transgressions. It implies multiple players who compete to win. The structure consists of a coordinated set of rules and forms of infraction. It includes a series of hierarchies in which certain elements are privileged over other parts. The center is the "nonlocus" of the arrangement of the game. The specific and particular theme, but not the general and established organization, is the contingent component of the game of codes, offenses, and hierarchies.

The anxiety of "implication" is the position that the subject occupies in relationship to the center and to the other segments in the system. Why does anxiety manifest from within the structure? It does so because of what is "at stake in the game from the outset." The origin-trace of existence installs a series of positions, perspectives, and identities. The subject is "thrown," as Heidegger would say, into a system.[51] The subject does not design, authorize, or will this structure. The stakes of the game are pre-established by the structure and its center. The governance of the moves and gestures of the subject is coded by a structure which exceeds this subject. The semblance of the center switches in a series of substitutions of words. The subject plays in more than one game at the same time. The effect of the overlap of multiple structures — such as system (s) and $-ism — is that the moves in one game may interfere with the gestures in another game. Anxiety is an effect of this parallactic overlay of structures. Anxiety is the consequence of the disruption of the continuities within each distinct system. The subject may protect itself from the exigencies of the game by lowering the stakes. The conditions for this protection against anxiety remain to be invented. An escape from anxiety may involve the deconstruction of nihilism. Nihilism is the system of values in which elements in the system are (dis)privileged in comparison and contrast with each other.

Substitution of Function

Derrida claims that the center or the function has "never been itself." This elucidates the invisibility of the functionality. The center is only discernible in the veiled forms and hidden names in the structure. The function is "itself" not the function. The function is a differed and deferred absence. The center (dis)appears in the temporality of: willing having (nevering) beening Becoming Being — Nothingness. The spatial interval is marked in the text. Temporally, the function has never been itself in either the past or the present. The possibility of a future in which the function is present is a possible advent of the future. The delayed presence of the function — what is is what is not — indicates that the "structurality of structure" is fundamentally concealed from analysis. The subject is trapped in a system which is beyond its grasp. The subject is the effect of a structure which exceeds this subject's own metaphysics. Derrida says that the center-function has "been exiled from itself into its own substitute."[52] This demonstrates that only substitution in form and name is visible in the structure. The function is veiled behind (above, around, by, and so on) the sign. The play of this form continues to obscure its orientation, balance, and organization. At the same time, the metaphor illuminates the instability of the work of representation but not of reality. The form belies the occupation of the word but not of the referent. But what is the referent of *le propre* ("own substitute") as the locus of the "exile" of the function of the center?

The gesture of substitution marks the function "itself" as its "own." The mystery of private property in the signifying chain is revealed. The substitute-sign usurps the functionality of the function. The play of displacement and compression destabilizes the locus of the center. The "exile" of the center from the force of the substitute(s) collapse(s) the division between sign and referent, representation and reality, and the function of the center and its series of words. Unbelievably, *the function is in play*. The inconceivable and the unthinkable — *tout autre* — become possible. The condition of the possibility of this Event is what Derrida begins the text with: "thinking." The proviso of the deconstruction of structure is "thinking," precisely, the "structurality of structure." The proper philosophical name for this thought is the ontology of essence. Unexpectedly, the thought of essence ruptures the structure. Thought dissolves neither the substitute nor the function, neither the sign nor the referent, and neither the representation nor the reality. Rather, the thought of essence deconstructs the basal division between the word and the world, and between discourse and life.

The word at the functional center of the structure is itself a substitution of itself. The function of the center is substitution. A structure is simply a series of substitutions. The center is a conduit for its own decenterment. Derrida says that, "the substitute does not substitute itself for anything which has somehow existed before it."[53] This suggests that the substitute is — the substitute. This substitute is always already this substitute. The thought of the structurality of essence entails a reference to construction. Why? The sign is doubled. The "itself" is the substitute of "itself." The field of the play of signs is infinite (*différance* and trace). But the system is unexpectedly finite. The functional center *qua* series of substitutions implies an absence and a castration or that there is "something missing from it," as Derrida says.[54] The function of substitution is responsible for this absence. There is an infinite possibility of substitution in the system. But such potentiality is closed off by necessity because of what Lacan names the "phallic function." The *point de capiton* halts the slide of meaning-making in the signifying chain.

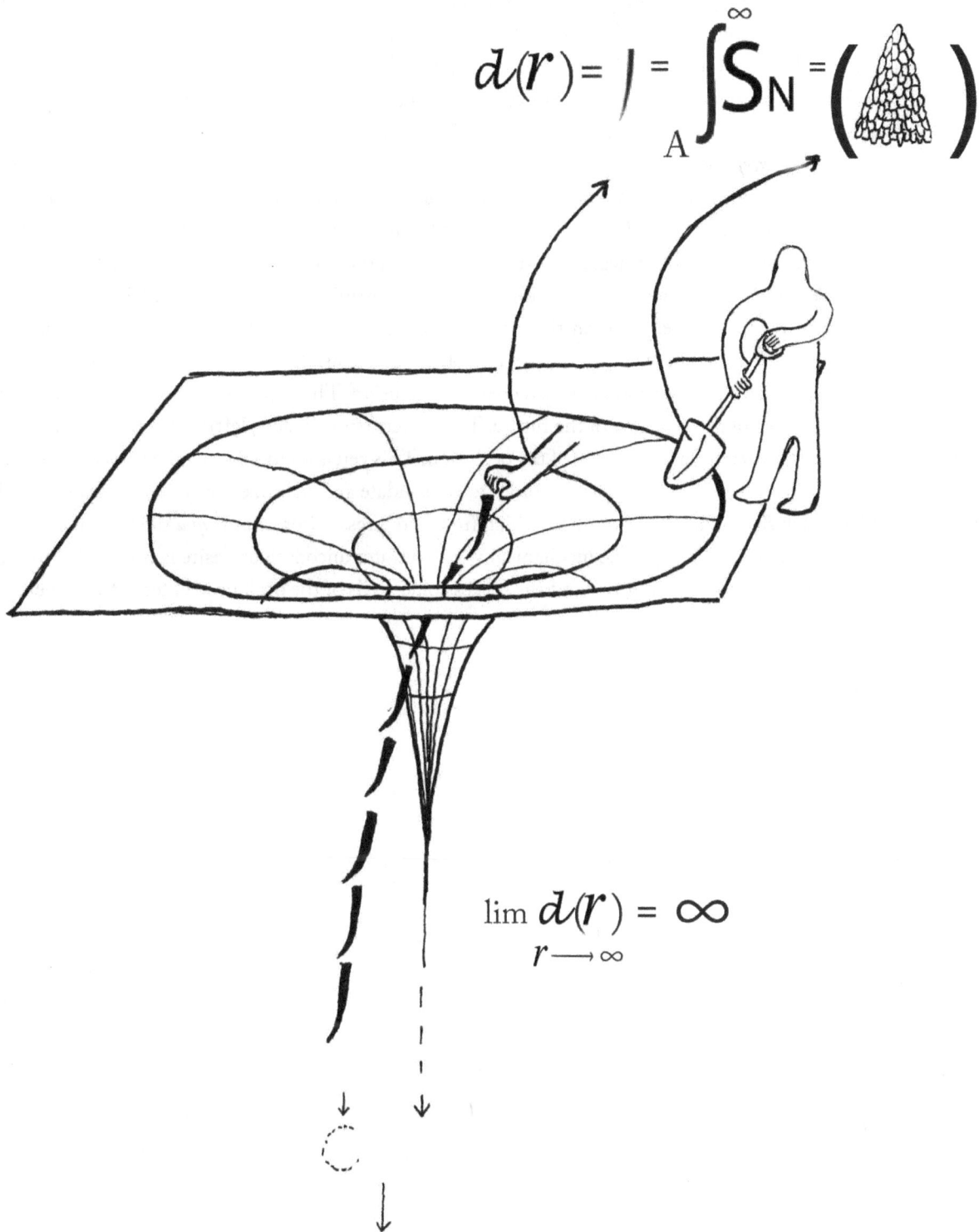

Figure 7.5 Occlusion and Excess

$$d(r) = | = \int_A^\infty S_N = (\triangle)$$

$$\lim_{r \longrightarrow \infty} d(r) = \infty$$

This illustration demonstrates that the equivalence of the object is simultaneously excluded in the Outside but also included in the Inside. This object is a substitutive center in the context of the accumulation of commodities in capitalism. The pile of objects in parentheses (above, right) conveys that substitutive centers are essentially infinite. But these substitutions are produced as and limited by an enforced finity. The infinity of substitutive centers — commodities, shoes, objects, laces, metaphors, centers, furs, fetishes, jockstraps, and so on — is indicated in this Queer Mathematics (above, right). This Queer Mathematics indicates the limit of difference and deferral as a function of relationality and constructionism. A *différance* can only approach infinity from within the limits of finity. The system is finite but at the same time infinitely inclusive of substitutive centers — *except* the deferred occluded center. The finitude is Queer Mathematically symbolized as the integral of S_N as it spans from a hypothetical and displaced originary unit of text (signifying term) to infinity. This integral is deferral as a function of relationality (*d(r)*). The integral is the radius, and it is the constant occlusion of the system. The integral is also represented in the enclosed space of the gravity function. The limit of the deferral as a function of relationality proceeds to infinity. But the space which is defined by the circulation of currency is finite. Yet even this veil is perversely unveiled only to return this function to other objects in the *mise-en-abyme* of substitutions. The object of exclusion is potentially included. But this inclusion excludes the newly differed and dispersed object of occlusion. The object of occlusion is the deferred and delayed — not-yet — of the *tout autre* of the future. The dotted arrow (below, left) which traverses toward the center illustrates this perpetual recurrence of the occlusion. This veil is accumulation. The object is forever displaced and dispersed Outside of the system in order to consolidate and stabilize the system. The perpetual recurrence of the occlusion is the same structure which (re)(re)(re)presses (forecloses) *qua* the negation of the symptom of the unconscious of $-ism. The mechanism which negates unconscious desire is isomorphic to the function which banishes the excess signifier and the succession of veils of the occluded center at the dispersed decenter of the system.

Notes & Sketches —

Derrida's "something missing from it" is precisely the terms in which Freud describes the female genitalia in *The Interpretation of Dreams* from 1900.[55] This "something missing from it" is also the precept of capitalist supply/demand dynamics and the ideology of scarcity. This "something missing from it" structurally obstructs endless semiosis because the series of words "is finite," as Derrida says.[56] The paradox of substitution is both the strange functionality of forms and signs and the weird simultaneous (in)finity of the series of substitutions. The circle of this figure-eight is the parallactic coincidence of surplus and deficit. This gap arranges the economy of sexual difference in the psychoanalytic interpretation of gender. This tension organizes the letter and its (non)arrival at the destination of signification. This imbalance structures exchange in capitalism. Something is Missing is the outline of the semiotic chain of signification in deconstruction. Lack is the precept of phallocentrism in psychoanalysis. Loss is the principle of capitalist accumulation. At once, the absence and the castration of a Something is Missing are continuous with the presence and the plenitude of a Nothing is Missing. The deconstructive critique of the sign, the psychoanalytic analysis of castration, and the Marxist outline of capitalist accumulation revolve around the possibility of a transformation of Something is Missing into Nothing is Missing.

The key citation from Derrida's text is his reference to a "vicarious function." This function is a finite absence. It is also a surplus which can "supplement a lack on the part of the signified."[57] The etymological origin of the word "vicarious" is the Latin for "substitute." This supplemental surplus of the word simply adds to the finite "something missing" in the signified. Yet, at the same time, this vicarious function of one for the other subtracts ("supplements a lack") from the signified. The parallactic gap in this relationship is such that the "abundance of the signifier," as Derrida says, is "the result of a *lack* which must be *supplemented*" (my emphasis).[58] Plenitude is the consequence of lack. Presence is the result of absence. Infinity is the effect of finity. Fullness is the product of castration. Communism is the outcome of capitalism. The signified is the consequence of the signifier. Surplus is the result of debt. Gain is the effect of loss.

And yet, at the same time, the obverse is correct. The supplement — excess and surplus but also castration and deficit — is also present. Lack is the consequence of plenitude. Absence is the result of presence. Finitude is the effect of infinity. Castration is the product of fullness. Capitalism is the outcome of communism. The signifier is the consequence of the signified. Debt is the result of surplus. Loss is the effect of gain. The Becoming in these flips and flops destructures the otherwise static Being of binary relationships between oppositional words. The substitution is "vicarious." It is also a "function." Each word "is" the other word simultaneously. There is "something missing," as Derrida puts it, in any spatial and temporal interval of delay in difference and deferral. A castration divides each term from the other and from itself.

Post-Post

Deconstruction neither repeats nor reverses the hierarchical logic of the binary that it seeks to upset. Rather, deconstruction seeks an "obscure economy." This Other-Economy exceeds the logic of binary structure. Perversion neither represses the sight of the female genitals (neurosis) nor forecloses the economy of difference (psychosis). Rather, perversion wants an "ingenious solution" and "another way out" of the Oedipus complex. But then what is the difference between the Jacques of psychoanalysis and the Jacques of deconstruction? Any disagreement between the Jacques must be decided by an intersubjective competition between the two, Jacques *et* Jacques. This rent between the two Jacques is visible in the uneasy distinction between structuralism and poststructuralism. Neither Derrida nor Lacan offers explicit formulations and defenses of these theoretical positions. However, any differentiation between Derrida and Lacan can only be decided by the question of perverse and functional substitution. What is the theoretical significance of the "post" in poststructuralism? What is the meaning of the "post" which is found lacking in structuralism? What is replaced in structuralism by the substitution of the word "post"?

Derrida critiques Lacan first in the long footnote in *Positions* (1971) and later in the essay, "*Le Facteur de la Vérité*" (1975). Derrida views Lacan's erection of a system on the equation of truth-Woman-castration as metaphysical and worrisome. Castration is the center of the psychoanalytic structure. This is so even if castration is a code for the absence of the function of the center. Derrida charmingly declares his own identity as different from Lacan's own perspective,

> The difference which interests me here is that — a formula to be understood as one will — the lack does not have its place in dissemination.[59]

The signifier "lack" cannot articulate the "place" of the instability of the play in the structure. There is neither a single nor a fixed transcendental sign. Lacan's "lack" is not *the* sign but only *a* sign. No choice metaphor has "its" own and proper "place" in the play of the text. What is "lack" a substitution of? Or substitution for? Or with? Or by? And so on? What is the function?

There is a crucial difference between the two theories. Lacan identifies a necessary and structural lack in the essence of self and society, and in the structure and its coordination. In an invaluable but modest contrast, Derrida affirms a play in the text. Lacan emphasizes the lack and loss of Something is Missing. Derrida eludes capture in both Something is Missing and Nothing is Missing. The distinction between Derrida and Lacan may be isomorphic to the division between structuralism and poststructuralism. But the gap cannot be separated from a certain competitive rivalry between the two Jacques. Lacan's own theory finds this antagonism at the basis of the narcissism and aggressivity of the imaginary register. Derrida's contention is palpable in the *Positions* (1971) footnote in which he mentions Lacan's "aggressions in the form of, or with the aim of, reappropriation."[60] The theme of ownership (*le propre*) frames many of Derrida's texts, including *The Truth in Painting* (1987). This text focuses on the Shapiro-Heidegger debate about the Van Gogh "shoes." The crux of the query is the undecidable but unavoidable question of "whose shoes are they?"[61] Whose theory is it? Whose center is otherwise? Whose fetish is "lack" and whose fetish is "play"? Whose fetish is of, with, near, by, about, otherwise, elsewhere, and so on? Is it Derrida-structuralism or Lacan-structuralism? And which one is "post"? What is "post" in a future which is inconceivable and unthinkable? What is "post" in a beyond of the pleasure principle? What is "post" to the regulatory criterion in psychoanalysis? What is "post" beyond the play of the text?

The slippage between the two Jacques mirrors the difference between the ego-ideal and the ideal-ego. Lacan inscribes and undermines the differed and delayed identity in the appropriately outside-and-inverted chapter title, "Ego-ideal and ideal ego," in his first *Seminar* (1953-54).[62] This mirrored double is what Lacan would call the "madness" and "confusion" of love. The madness of love is the dissolution of the distinctions between self and other, lover and beloved, and ego-ideal and ideal-ego. Mad love is a psychotic (dis)union. Love and madness are delayed by reading these Jacques as two rather than as one. In the Spirit of such an ambivalent madness, let us ask the "Who speaks?" of structuralism and poststructuralism. Is it Jacques-structuralism or Jacques-structuralism? As with Derrida's *différance*, we cannot hear the difference between the two Jacques. Nor, however, can we even see the difference. So, more rhetorically than ever: what's the difference? The haunted silence of the pervert's laughter is only possible in the future. This Other-Future is beyond the prosaic pleasures of centers, signs, and fetishes.

Fetish and Center — and Simulation

Baudrillard's categories of simulation and the hyperreal illuminate the relationship between the Derridean center of deconstruction and the Freudian fetish of psychoanalysis. Simulation is the absence of "origin" and "reality."[63] By origin and reality, Baudrillard means the truthful adequation of any proposition to any reference. Truth is mediated and guaranteed by a third term, such as God or Power or any other central principle of organization. The third term enables a comparison, contrast, and exchange of meaning or value. The third mediates the two signifiers in the relationship in question, such as good/evil or dominator/dominated. Baudrillard refers to a "liquidization of all referentials," and of hyperreality he continues that,

> worse: with their [referentials] artificial resurrection in the systems of signs [becomes possible],
> a material more malleable than meaning, in that it lends itself to all systems of equivalences,
> to all binary oppositions, to all combinatory algebra.[64]

The referent — or origin and reality — is vanquished from experience. The dead returns from its exile. Death is resurrected in the light materialism of the sign. This "material," as Baudrillard puts it, is ductile and pliant. It can be easily exchanged in comparison and contrast with all of the systems of opposition and representation. This mediation happens according to the logic of what I name as $-ism. $-ism involves equivalence, exchange, return, debt, binarism, and so on. The sign is not simply unmoored from reference as if it were free of organization. The system of signs is structured according to the logic of the system (s). However, (s) is unanchored in reference, reality, and truth. The sign continues to function by the logic of the system. But its reference to reality is undone.

Baudrillard's citation of "combinatory algebra" recalls Lacan's use of the "matheme." The matheme is an abstract representational vehicle for an elucidation of concrete social practices (such as: $\$<>a$). The reduction of things and objects to signs and representations (from reality and truth to simulation and imaginariness) is a threat. All exchange is possible. Consequently, nothing is either permitted or prohibited. All signification is possible and therefore no signification is realizable. There is no limit on semiosis. Uncontrolled meaning-making is otherwise limited by reference, truth, and reality in the system of signs. Simulation mirrors the imaginary in Lacan's version of psychoanalysis. Under the regime of simulation, there is no third term to organize the system of true/false and real/imaginary. Unmediated duality structures the system. This is so even as the system of binary opposition in the $-ism of the system is sustained.

(Dis)simulation

Simulation pretends to have the object which is otherwise absent. The sign of the system feigns to possess reference, truth, and reality. In contrast, "to dissimulate," Baudrillard argues, "is to pretend not to have what one has."[65] The difference is nuanced but decisive. In simulation, the object of the lie of the system is the presence of an object which is otherwise absent. In dissimulation, the design of the fib is the absence of a reference which is otherwise present. A *(dis)simulation* feigns an epistemological trickery which is isomorphic to the pervert's disavowal. In simulation, "I know very well that the object is absent, but nevertheless I simulate it as present" — but for what? In dissimulation, "I know very well that the object is present, but nevertheless I dissimulate it as absent" — but for what? The enforcement of the reality principle of truth and referentiality is possible in the structure of (dis)simulation. But such law and order cannot arrest the whack-a-mole deception of either of these modalities of management of the system of signs. The fetishist performs his own (dis)simulation. The pervert *dissimulates simulation* in order to *simulate dissimulation*. How so?

The substitution of the signs of the real for the real itself is a curious proposition for deconstruction. Derrida is at pains to demonstrate the division between the function of the "center," on the one hand, against the different "forms" and "names" which are the textual representatives of this operation of infinite substitution, on the other hand. This endless process occurs within a finite system. The absent signifier in the structure is the transcendental condition of the finitude of this functionality. This coincidence of the parallactic gap between sign and function is absent in the system. The perverse trick is to properly (dis)simulate that this function veils itself as the sign in dissimulation at the same time as it announces its presence as distinct from the sign in simulation.

The function of substitution must simulate a loss of "itself" in the series of forms and names in order to avow the presence of "itself" as distinct in functionality from this set of ordinary metaphors and prosaic metonymies. Simultaneously, this function must dissimulate a presence of "itself" in this same set of words in order to disavow the absence of "itself" as otherwise equivalent (comparable, contrastable, and exchangeable) to the centers of the other systems of signification. The obverse is also the necessary case. The function of substitution must simulate a gain of "itself" in the series of forms and names in order to disavow the absence of "itself" as indistinct in functionality from this set of ordinary metaphors and prosaic metonymies. Simultaneously, this function must simulate a presence of "itself" in this same set of words in order to avow the presence of "itself" as otherwise equivalent (comparable, contrastable, and exchangeable) to the centers of the other systems of signification. There is a limited number of other modalities of this (dis)simulation. This performs the simultaneity of a surplus from within a deficit —

— (Non)the (non)function (non)of (non)substitution (non)must (non)simulate (non)a (non)loss (non)of (non)"itself" (non)in (non)the (non)series (non)of (non)forms (non)and (non)names (non)in (non)order (non) to (non)avow (non)the (non)presence (non)of (non)"itself" (non)as (non)distinct (non)in (non)functionality (non)from (non)this (non)set (non)of (non)ordinary (non)metaphors (non)and (non)of (non)everyday (non) metonymies; (non)simultaneously, (non)this (non)function (non)must (non)dissimulate (non)a (non)presence (non)of (non)"itself" (non)in (non)this (non)same (non)set (non)of (non)words (non)in (non)order (non)to (non)disavow (non)the (non)absence (non)of (non)"itself" (non)as (non)otherwise (non)equivalent (non)([non] exchangeable [non]and [non]comparable) (non)to (non)the (non)"centers" (non)of (non)the (non)philosophical (non)and (non)otherwise (non)systems (non)of (non)signification —

— The infinite universe must simultaneously be finite. This is the case even if the series of substitutions is infinite. This is also the reason that Lacan symbolizes the Woman as under erasure. The fetishist's (dis)simulation of (dis)simulation is an object of amusement. The set of forms and names — objects of fetishism — is limited.

God

Simulation threatens the divisions between true/false and real/imaginary. Suspension of reference imperils stability. Such a cut is implied in Saussure's work from 1917, in *Course in General Linguistics*, and in Derrida's critical update of Saussure's work in his 1967 book, *Of Grammatology*. The foundation of signification is the abandonment of reference in hyperreality. Baudrillard writes,

> All Western faith and good faith became engaged in this wager on representation: that a sign could refer to the depth of meaning and that something could guarantee this exchange — God of course.[66]

The bet on the sign is that meaning can be adjudicated. The bet on representation is that the winner and the loser of the "wager" can be situated in the proper hierarchy of signification in relationship to a reality. God posits this ground (which is His own foundation) in the law and order of Nature or Culture or other centers of the function of substitution. What is the origin-trace of God's authority?

The source of this mystery and mysticism can only be in the referent as opposed to in the sign. This is the reason that the order of signs is a threat to a system of exchange, comparison, and contrast. The series of signs is a menace to the authority of the general equivalent. This adjudicatory third otherwise mediates the relationship of value between objects in question. If God is god, then the (e)valuation of the relationship between god and the Devil is impossible to pursue. Both epistemology (the pervert's "I know very well") and faith ("but nevertheless") become suspicious. Only an ontology of the sign is possible. This ontology of the sign is the thinking, being, and living of representation. Word cut from object, signifier cut from referent, life cut from death, world cut from earth — such is the horizon of the fetishist's strange object of *jouissance*.

The fundamental difference between the disorder of the system ("play") in Derrida, on the one hand, and the simulation of absence and dissimulation of presence in Baudrillard, on the other hand, is the parallactic gap. Deconstruction opens and shuts the door between function and sign. Hyperreality loosens and tightens the screw between reference and sign. The threat of deconstruction is not the abeyance of reference. This is so despite the abject terror that the infamous *il n'y a pas de hors texte* commentary provoked among humanists. The late Derrida distances himself from the simple interpretation of *hors texte* as the suspension of reference. Later, the *pas hors texte* is reread as a substitute-sign for the various "impossibles" which emerge toward the end of Derrida's career. These futural dimensions of the *tout autre* include: justice, ethics, democracy, and so on. Unexpectedly, the horror of grammatology is the profound stability of the system itself. Derrida uncovers the function of the center. Undecidably, is metaphor a necessary structure which cannot be universally displaced ($-ism, s) or a contingent formation which can be overrun by a novel system (S, $-ism)? The fright of Derrida's discovery is not the destruction of order. Rather, the alarm is the uncanny sturdiness of structure.

Alternatively, the threat of simulation is to the aptitude of law and order. Baudrillard outlines the subversion of authority from within a system which is simultaneously strictly outside of the metaphysics of presence. He writes,

> It is no longer a question of a false representation of reality (ideology) but of concealing the fact that the real is no longer real, and thus of saving the reality principle.[67]

Simulation renders the binary organization of the system impossible. The oppositions of real/imaginary, truth/scandal, and law/transgression are still operative in the system of signs. The difference in simulation is that these linguistic divisions are not theorized or practiced as real or true. The system of signs is combined and structured according to the rules of the system, but the sheer realness of these differences is suspect. The regime of simulation does not disorganize the structure. This disruption of the structure is the effect of the grammatological play of the text in substitution and displacement — of center for center. Even so, the structure survives its dismantlement as the condition of its own possibility. Differently, simulation stabilizes the system in its organization but undermines the relationship between object and referent. In simulation, the graft between sign and object is suspended. Suddenly, the word is open to processes of semiosis which are untethered to the realness of the referent.

Law and Order

Simulation undoes the metaphysical guarantee of this structure. There is no necessity in the so-called "transgression" of the "law." Neither the word "transgression" nor the word "law" is real or true. Rather, each word is fake and fictional. Simulation is a greater threat than the masculine idiotic cycle of law/transgression. Baudrillard says that simulation, "leaves open the supposition that, above and beyond its object, law and order themselves might be nothing but simulation."[68] If simulation pretends to have what it does not possess, then law and order (and transgression and subversion) are treated as if they were devoid of the authority of governance (and the insurrection of resistance). Simulacrum of jurisdiction (but also of rebellion) represents the menace to all of the systems of rule and sovereignty. Even within the combinatory system of the sign, the law is vulnerable in the era of simulation. This is the reason that the police state must be parodied rather than transgressed. The rebel stiffens the law because he posits the realness of the law itself. In contrast, the parodist contests law *tout court* because he disrupts the real as its proviso of operation.

The law can only defend against simulation by the assertion of the reality principle. In Freud, the reality principle is the basis of the analysand's successful navigation of the world. The army against the insurrection of the hyperreal is truth and reality. As Baudrillard says,

> The only weapon of power, its only strategy against this defection, is to reinject the real and the referential everywhere, to persuade us of the reality of the social, of the gravity of the economy and the finalities of production.[69]

Whereas simulation posits defiance in the suspension of reference deconstruction articulates a resistance which is internal to the structure of the function of the sign. Grammatology destabilizes the text even if the system returns to dominate in functionality. This is so no matter the magic of the deconstruction. In contrast, subversion in simulation suspends truth. This is the case even if authority returns simulation to the reality principle.

This principle of executive organization and function sustains the ego and its traversal of the real and the true. Deconstruction understands the sign as a displaced function which limits the infinity of the system. Functionality (center) *qua* "functionality" (as a sign) resists reabsorption into the series of metaphors. This is so even if the center peers beyond the structure as the center. Simulation usurps the foundation of comparison, contrast, and exchange. This ground is otherwise mediated by the third term: "God," "Power/Knowledge," "Being," "*Différance*," "Unconscious," and so on. The difference between these master signifiers may be moot because God is "god" and function is "function." But this overlap does not undo the distinct consequences of the break between function/sign in deconstruction and between reference/sign in simulacrum. The former returns equilibrium to an (in)finite homeostatic system — or to what Freud names the "pleasure principle." The latter escapes principality itself — or what Freud names the "beyond the pleasure principle." Deconstruction discovers the final sadism of the system. Simulation notes the aperture of masochism in its closure.

Fetishism and Prototypicality

My illumination of deconstruction from within the discourse of simulation isolates the specificity of the fetish as it relates to the deconstructive center-function and to the postmodern simulation-simulacrum. Freud's *ur*-essay, "Fetishism" (1927), closes on an utterly bizarre note,

> The normal prototype of all fetishes is the penis of the man, just as the normal prototype of
> an organ felt to be inferior is the real little penis of the Woman, the clitoris.[70]

The deep oddity of this conclusion to a profoundly eccentric text is the qualification of "the clitoris" as "the real little penis." This "the clitoris" is precisely not "the real little penis" because "the clitoris" is "the clitoris." But this "the clitoris" is referred to as "the real little penis" and yet to another as — the "normal prototype." There is "the real little penis." But this "the real little penis" is not "the clitoris." At first glance, Freud's claim is simply that the fetish is a prop for the anatomical penis of the man. The fetish is a representation in an embodied object (fur, lace, shoe, and jockstrap) of the penis. This fetish is the source of the magical power and mystical prowess of this penis. The penis is the final referent for all of the fetishes in the galaxy. The penis "itself" cannot be a symptomatic substitute for another object. The penis is as such the final referent in a series of substitutions and equivalences for all of sexuality.

Freud's use of "prototype" in this passage is crucial to a proper analysis of the fetish-object. Freud's odd word, "prototype," illuminates the isomorphism among the Derridean center, the postmodern simulacrum, and the sexual fetish. The theory of the fetish implies the antecedence and originality of the penis as a prototype. The penis precedes the fetish-object in both space and time. The penis also precedes its other approximations in the structure of Freud's strange conclusive sentence to his paper on fetishism. There is a *différance* of "the penis." There is a split in the penis as the otherwise *arche* of the fetish. The spatial deviation and temporal delay in the penis also apply to "the real little penis" of "the clitoris." The fetish may be a differed and deferred substitute for the penis. But Freud's words also indicate that "the real little penis" is the "prototype" for "the clitoris." This prototype is an antecedence and an originality. The prototype refers to both the penis and the clitoris. Both the male genitalia and the female sex organs are prototypical. This prototypicality indicates neither superiority (supposedly the penis) nor inferiority (ostensibly the clitoris). Rather, prototypicality is the object of fetishism.

The fetishistic prototype of the penis-fetish is "the penis." The fetishistic antecedent of the clitoris-substitute is "the real little penis." This articulation of two prototypical original antecedent anatomies for the fetish illuminates the duality of fetishes in the sexual economy: the penis and the clitoris. The difference between the two prototypes is size and visibility. Freud isolates magnitude and noticeability as criteria in the texts on the castration complex and sexual difference from the 1920s.[71] The penis as "itself" and the clitoris as "the real little penis" are prototypical and unequal originals of the emergent fetishes. But what are the "prototypes" for these prototypes "themselves"? Deconstructively, are "the penis" and "the clitoris" center-functions or sign-substitutions? Postmodernistly, is the territory of sexual difference coextensive with its map? But more to the point is a basic ontological question. What is a "prototype"? And what is the prototype *of* the prototype?

Freud qualifies his use of the word "prototype" with "normal." He does so for both "the penis" and the male fetish-object and for the "the real little penis" and the clitoris. In *Three Essays* (1905), normality is associated with a fluidity of aim and object (against the fixation of the pervert's object) but also with a precise obsession with phallic sexuality and the domestic arrangement of heterosexual monogamy. Normal heterosexual object-choice is both pathological and typical, abnormal and ordinary, and sick and healthy. The prototype for the penis is not entirely summarized as "the penis of the man." Earlier in the text, Freud remarks that, "the fetish is a penis-substitute," but he continues with, "not a substitute for any chance penis, but for a particular quite special penis that had been extremely important in early life but was afterward lost."[72] He goes on to say that, "the fetish is a substitute for the Woman's phallus which the male junior once believed in and does not wish to forgo — we know why."[73] Freud does not surmise the reason that the offspring would only reluctantly forswear his "belief" in the female penis. But it can be inferred that it is the male junior's castration anxiety which is at stake in the threat of the loss.

Freud's description of the object of fetishistic substitution as a "particular quite special penis" denotes that the sign — or function — of the substitution is of an object. This object is at a deviance (spatially, temporally, and psychically) from the chain of equivalences for which it is the object of proxy. The maternal phallus is a "particular quite special penis." It is qualitatively ("quite special") and quantitatively ("particular") distinct from the "normal" of the "prototype" of the penis. The latter is itself a deviation even in its own specificity. If the "normal prototype" of the (superior) fetish-object is the penis, and if the "normal prototype" of the (inferior) fetish-object is the clitoris, then the question of the prototype becomes paramount to an elucidation of the function of the fetish in the psychical economy of both men and Women, normal and abnormal, and healthy and pathological. How can the prototype be "normal" in reference to both the "the penis of the man" and "the real little penis" if the object for which they substitute is strictly outside of the economy of exchange, comparison, and contrast? — outside of the "normal" because it is a "particular quite special penis"?

Same

Freud's symptomatic reference to "the same" in his discussion of the fetish underscores the easy recuperation of this "particular quite special penis" into the system of the fetishistic economy. He writes,

> In all cases the meaning and purpose of the fetish turned out under analysis to be the *same*. It revealed itself so unequivocally and seemed to me so categorical that I would expect the *same* solution in all cases of fetishism (my emphasis).[74]

There is a semiotic gap in the fetish-object (shoe, lace, fur, and jockstrap). The manifest object ("in all cases") must be further interpreted for a clandestine "meaning and purpose." The final referent for this significance of the fetish-object is the penis: "the fetish is a penis-substitute."[75] At first glance, Freud's comparison of the fetish to a penis-substitute indicates that the fetish-object is the prop and stanchion for the penis. The fetish-object is secondary and derived in reference to the primary and original penis of which the former usurps the "meaning and purpose." But what are the "meaning and purpose" of the penis?

The oedipal fables from the 1920s indicate that the penis is considered the private property (*le propre*) of the offspring. This private(s) property can be (will be) annexed if the offspring deviates from identification with the ego-ideal and the proper mimicry of sexed and gendered (and so on) roles in the culture. The significance of the penis in psychoanalysis can only be as a reminder of loss: for the female junior, as regretful retrospective glance toward a castration which inspires envious consumption of fetish-objects to suture this originary wound from the past; for the male junior, as fearful prospective glare toward an imminent castration which provokes defensive protection of present fetish-objects to suture the advent of an annexation in the future. For both the female junior and the male junior, the "meaning and purpose" of "the penis" and "the real little penis" — the penis and the clitoris — are the terrorism of capitalist private property.

This horror can be put in the terms of the selfhood and sociality of $-ism: *my* self, *my* body, *my* thoughts, *my* feelings, *my* ideas, *my* homosexuality, *my* values, *my* love, *my* joys, *my* money, *my* responsibility, and *my* and so on. This is a chain of oppositions rather than equivalences because each ownership (*le propre*) is situated in the phallic logic of hierarchy and opposition. The parallactic interval between "the penis" and "the real little penis" and then the fetish must overrun the purported "meaning and purpose" of these professed referents of the fetish-object. The fetish must be a substitute for an object which is otherwise than either the penis of the man or the maternal penis of the Woman. But this object of reference is the "same," as he says twice in the citation above. This "sameness" refers to "purpose," "meaning," and "solution." How is Sameness⁺ the solution to the horror of castration which is otherwise the object of the veil of the fetish-object?

This other referent for "the penis," "the real little penis," and "the clitoris" is the "prototype." The signification of the "prototype" is its difference and deferral *qua* absence and lack — which generate a presence and surplus. The fetish is the embodied reverberation of this antecedent and subsequent prototypicality. The original object must be precisely outside of both the signifying chain and the series of (in)equivalences (such as the anal fantasy of: penis = baby = faeces) in the order of metaphor. The "penis," "the real little penis," and "the clitoris" gather their signification and *modus operandi* from this prototype. The prototype is the third term of mediation of the superior fetish (the penis) and the inferior fetish (the clitoris) in the psychosexual economy. The prototype itself is veiled in Freud's text on fetishism (1927) such that its veritable invisibility qualifies it as the advent and origin of the fetishes. The fetish is a substitute for both the penis and the clitoris. Both male organs and female parts are the absences for which the presences of the fetish-objects suture the wound. The penis is castrated in the present. The superiority/inferiority binary is mapped onto the opposition penis/clitoris. The opposition between the penis and the clitoris is organized by the prototype. This prototype confers value — superiority for the penis, inferiority for the clitoris — onto the genitalia in question. This prototype is obscured from view because it is the original model from which the copied deviations — penis and clitoris — emerge in their approximation.

Phallus Fetish

Lacan's word for this prototypicality in the dimension of psychosexual difference is "the phallus." The prototype of sexual difference is the phallus. It is specifically a function in Lacan's design. If the phallus is a function — the phallic function or *point de capiton* or quilting point rather than a form or a name — then the isomorphism between the Derridean center and the Lacanian phallus must produce similar effects. These consequences are orientation, balance, and organization in the (sexual) structure. But are the center and the phallus themselves forms and names such that the ~~center~~ and the ~~phallus~~ resist determination as presence? Or are these signs the functions themselves? The center is merely a form or a name for a function which is decentered from its own metaphors. The structure is finite. The supply of substitutions is infinite with the exception of the center. This center is distanced from the chain of signification as its condition of possibility. The phallus is merely a sign for a function which resists the word. The sexual field is finite because the supply of substitutions is endless with the exception of the phallus. The phallus is obscured from the chain of sexual objects as its condition of possibility. At stake in fetishism is the final referent of the substitution of the object of fetishism: the penis — and whose?

The phallus details a relationship between the subject and itself "without regard," as Lacan says, "to the anatomical distinction between the sexes."[76] The central point is that the phallus "can play its role only when veiled."[77] The phallus indexes the various *objets petit a* in the sexual field. But its functionality as the transcendental proviso of operation is such that it must be elsewhere from and otherwise than — "veiled" — the sexual field. The phallus is the advent of desire. It is itself excluded from the structure. Like Derrida's center, the phallus orients, balances, and organizes the sexual structure. The Lacanian phallus is obscured in its functionality. The forms and names of its avatars are the only visible remnants of this central function. Like the philosopher's center, the phallus is excluded from the system that it otherwise orients, balances, and organizes. The philosophical center is a function which enables the substitution of different words — such as "*Différance*," "Being," "Power/Knowledge," "Unconscious," and so on.

These substitutes are strictly fetishes insofar as they are props for the function of orientation, balance, and organization of the philosophical system in question. The phallus is also a function which enables the substitution of different words. These metaphors are not predetermined in their genitalia — such as shoe, lace, fur, jockstrap, penis, clitoris, vagina, and so on. The philosophical center is a function which escapes form and name. The phallus is a function which resists presence because it is always hidden. The referent for the fetish *qua* substitute is the *hors texte* or mark which is outside of the system in its functionality. The fetish substitutes for functionality *qua* the transcendental condition of possibility of the entire field of desire. The phallus is a fetish. The central words in philosophy — *"Différance,"* "Being," "Power/Knowledge," "Unconscious" — are objects of fetishism. Philosophy is a series of stained jockstraps and torn panties.

The pervert's penis-substitute makes the penis the final referent in this series of substitutions. Philosophy is a bad copy of the penis. The penis is a compression of the entirety of the signifying chain. But there is a pivotal exception to this series. The function or the phallus is exiled from this set as its proviso of exercise. The fetish is a representation of every word in the system. The phallus must be excluded as the prerequisite of the exercise of the series of philosophical jockstraps and conceptual panties. The fetish is both the metaphor ("penis-substitute") for every object in the system and at the same time the exception to this exchange. The fetish *qua* penis-substitute represents all of the objects in the system *except itself*. A better translation of the "penis-substitute" is "the penis." This represents an unexpected coincidence between the penis and the phallus. The parallactic gap between penis and phallus is visible in the articulation of the fetish *qua* the penis-substitute. But the closure of this aperture is enforced by the functionality of the penis as referent for the metonymies of desire in the field of sexuality.

The penis is the practical sign which is excluded from the otherwise infinite play of the theoretical difference and negativity of the signifier. The penis can only be the final referent of perverse sexuality if the functionality itself is another word. Deconstruction views the fetish as (im)possible because the field of substitutions is endless. The functionality of the center is excluded from the system which is both infinite and endless, and limited and finite. For psychoanalysis, the fetish is also (im)possible because the phallus as the indexical signifier of the effects in the field of sexuality is barred from the system and under erasure. The only way that the phallus can be otherwise than a metaphor is in the event that the penis is not the final referent for the fetish. Psychoanalysis cannot be considered a system of "phallocentrism" because any other signifier can substitute in the place of the "penis-substitute" *qua* "penis" *qua* "phallus" *qua*, and so on. What are (are there) differences and deferrals for the "phallus" even if this "phallus" is veiled?

Exclusion of the Phallus

In the letter of the text (1927), the deviation from the prototype of "the penis" is only the one step from "fetish" to "the penis" — and then full stop. The fetish is a single deviation from the penis in the letter of the text. There is only a simple metonymy or synecdoche from the fetish to the penis as final reference for the entirety of the set of objects in the symbolic system. The entire world is phallically sexualized with a trace of penile sexuality. All objects in the system are sexualized. The unexpected exception to this generalized sexualization of the chain of signification is the penis *qua* phallus. The phallus is excluded from sex. The phallus is properly (a)sexual. This one step from "fetish" to "penis" marks a relationship of (un)likeness. The comparison, contrast, and exchange of the two objects are not possible in the absence of a gap between two rather than between one. The difference between the penis and the clitoris is size and visibility. These are the criteria by which the penis is considered superior to the clitoris. The metonymic comparison of phallus and penis — as opposed to phallus and clitoris — is the mere measure of turgidity.[78] The curiosity of the final words of Freud's text profoundly revises the primacy and originality of the substitute *qua* penis-substitute.

Figure 7.6 The Phallus Logarithm

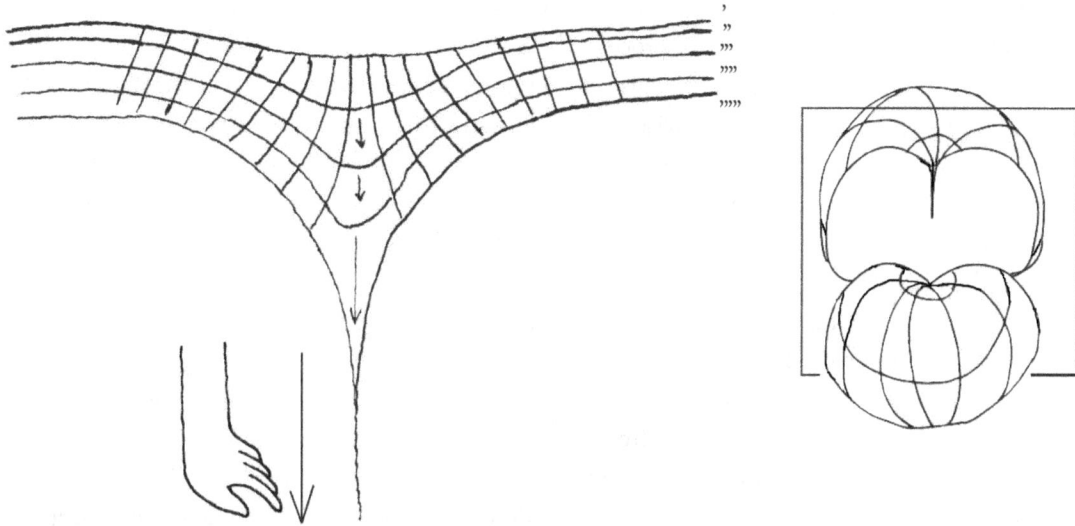

$$\text{phallic}'(x) = \text{phallic}''(x) = \text{phallic}'''(x) = \text{phallic}''''(x)$$

This image opens the gaze to the abyssal void of the phallic black hole of the *Eros* (*Thanatos*) binding (freeing) — (*a*)sexual — force of the cosmos of *langue* and Being. The cross-section of the multiplicity sphere (right) orients the reader and contextualizes the in-process, in-action work of the phallicization (left) of the system and its series of objects and words. The hand parallels the (im)balancing and (re)iterative (de)centering of the system. The phallic function is its own derivative *ex nihilo*. This function phallicizes the penis and symbolizes the Real. The function superpositionally engenders itself. The layers which are bent and broken traverse the black hole and obey a logarithm whose principle of inclusion is retroactively reincluded and reintegrated into itself. This theme is represented by the inverse of the exponential function and its integral (*r = 1/d*). Queer Mathematically, the integral of the 1/*d* function is instantiated in the 0,0 parallax point. This accounts for the complex infinity of 1/0 (in which *d* is decreased to 0) of the logarithmic function. This figure depicts the physics and linguistics which propel the pervert to traverse the mirror hole and wormhole of the Real Symbolic. Really, any ~~word~~ or any ~~object~~ is under erasure because any word or any object is split from itself in the fissure of ~~Being~~.

Notes & Sketches —

Whereas the difference and deferral (*différance*) from the prototype of "the fetish" to "the penis" are a spinster's single step the difference and deferral from the prototype of "the real little penis" to "the clitoris" are a two step: from "organ felt to be inferior" to "the real little penis" and then to "the clitoris." The "penis-substitute" is the mediatory third term between "fetish" and "penis." Strangely, this penis-substitute is absent in the finale to Freud's description of the process of substitution in fetishism. This process of the slip and slide is otherwise profoundly metaphorical because it is organized by an infinity of substitutions within a finity of objects. The exception to this otherwise endless series of metaphors is the function of the phallus. The phallus is excluded from representation as the condition of possibility of the system. What is the significance of the single referral of the male genitalia in the fetishistic economy — from "fetish" to "the penis" — versus the double distance of the female genitalia in the economy of substitution — from "fetish" to "the real little penis" and then finally to "the clitoris"?

The answer is both addition and subtraction. The penis is close to and in proximity to the fetish. The clitoris is far from and at a distance to the fetish. But, at the same time, the clitoris is close to and in proximity to the end of the signifying chain as the final referent of the penis. The obverse is also the case in the traversal in the opposed direction. The penis is far from and at a distance to the fetish. The clitoris is close to and in proximity to the penis. The fetish — penis-substitute or clitoris-substitute — is strictly undecidable in its anatomical thematization. Lacan can say that the relationship between the phallus and the subject is "without regard" to anatomical distinction. The fetish cannot be determined as a metaphor for either the penis or the clitoris. This addition or subtraction is strictly undecidable. The final referent for the fetish is the penis. The phallus is excluded because it is the referent for the penis. The phallus is Real.

The Primacy of the Clitoris

The phallus is veiled because it dissimulates what it does not have which is simultaneously what it does have: the clitoris. The present absence of the penis is the phallus. This text for the veiled reference to the clitoris is not yet articulated by a word. What is the final referent for the clitoris? The unexpected answer is that the clitoris is the original and primary sex organ. A Clitoral Stage is the fourth phase of genital sexuality. The clitoris is strictly Outside of the Freudian system of sexuality because it is the function which orients, balances, and organizes the structure of desire. The clitoris is the central function of desire. There is an infinity of penis-substitutes or penises or fetishes with the exception of the phallus. The phallus is the clitoris — namely, the penis. The penis, penis-substitute, and fetish dissimulate the clitoris. The clitoris — all of this time — has merely *(dis)simulated* its lack and castration. The archetypal fetishist is the Woman who simulates castration and dissimulates plenitude. The penis, penis-substitute, and fetish are simulations of plenitude and dissimulations of lack. The clitoris *(dis)simulates* because it is the Outside of the metaphysics of presence.

The prototype which is antecedent to the penis, the penis-substitute, the fetish, and the clitoris is the prototype itself. A prototype is a precedence which is a model of perfection ("normalcy") for the copies and deviations of the fetishes. The prototype is the function of the coordination of the fetishistic system. The penis lacks the phallus. The clitoris lacks itself. The clitoris is Real. The prototype is the self-same and self-identical phallus — and clitoris. The prototype is the excluded (*a*)sexual Real of sexual difference around which desire encircles in its aim. The penis is a symbolic copy of this Real. The penis is also a fetish insofar as the shoe, lace, fur, and jockstrap are copies of the copy of the penis. The penis is a facsimile of the clitoris. The penis simulates what it does not have. The clitoris dissimulates what it does have. The penis and the clitoris must be the final referents for the fetish if the phallus is the function which is outside of a limited field of substitution.

The fetish is a metaphor for the penis and the clitoris. Fetishism is the *dissimulation of simulation*: to feign to not have what it has — the clitoris and the penis — in order to demonstrate having what it does not have — the penis and the clitoris. This is the pervert's *dissimulation of simulation in order to simulate dissimulation*. The penis and the clitoris are figurations of *(dis)simulation*. The object of fetishism substitutes for neither the penis nor the clitoris but for the prototype of normalcy. What is a prototype?

Both male perversion and female fetishism are the original and normal modalities of sexuality. The female junior looks in the scene of the discovery of sexual difference. She gazes with the opposite and inverted criteria for superiority. The evaluation of sexual difference is contingent on the prototype or retrospective glance of the gaze: who is looking? The function of castration will dominate the scene of genital sexual difference. But whose "penis" is under the glare of the apparatus of prototypicality? Whose "penis" is questioned after the normal is deemed the superior? What is the object of the fetishist's enjoyment? Does the subtraction lack the addition (the clitoris)? Or does the addition lack the subtraction (the penis)? The function is simply another word. This metaphor is subordinate to the play of the text and the switcheroo of the fetish, penis-substitute, fur, lace, shoe, jockstrap, penis, phallus, clitoris, and even prototype. The conundrum is the simultaneity of castration and plenitude, lack and fullness, absence and presence, and deficit and surplus in the fetishistic and deconstructive economy. What potential aneconomy disorganizes this structure of excess and debt? What extant structure regulates the superfluity of energy in a system which can only be contained by its return to a homeostatic medium of the idiot's pleasure principle? What is the galaxy beyond the Penis Principle?

The riddle is the symbolization of this *(dis)simulation* and its infinite recursion. This slip and slide include the indication of functionality as internal to the signifying chain. Is it possible for the signifying chain to disrupt its own center *qua* function rather than *qua* sign? The penis-substitute-penis-phallus-clitoris-prototype is the fetish for functionality. The function of orientation, balance, and organization is coincident with penis-substitute-penis-phallus-clitoris-prototype-function. The only difference between functionality and this series of words, metaphors, fetishes, and objects is the desire of the subject. Does the subject desire a presence which dissimulates an absence? Or does this subject desire an absence which simulates a presence? The pervert wants both. The pervert *dissimulates simulation* (clitoral penis) in order to *simulate dissimulation* (penile clitoris). Dissimulation is the cover of plenitude with a loss. Simulation is the mask of presence for a castration. The magical performance to demonstrate the veil of possession of the capture of what is not enjoyed (dissimulation: to deny plenitude at the same time as admit castration) in order to illustrate in the text the revelation of ownership of the loss of what is gone (simulation: to acknowledge lack at the same time as concede possession) — is what? This is the pervert's theatricalization of the *disavowal of disavowal*. This illuminates the prototypicality of perversion.

The prototype of sexual difference is this endless difference and deferral of the both/and economy of the identity and difference of the penis and the clitoris. The infinite (pro/re)gress of (in)equality is the structuralist theory of difference. This is the reason that the fetish is a substitute for both the penis and the clitoris. The pervert's disavowal is a Sameness[+] which is not identical to this "one" and the "same" disavowal. Disavowal deviates from disavowal itself. Perversion and deconstruction are otherwise to and elsewhere from themselves. This Other is prototypical of an economy which thinks "the perversity of perversion." The fetishist's truth is the essential presence in absence and absence in presence. The penis and the clitoris are each coincident with each other such that the fetish — penis-substitute and clitoris-substitute — may not even be possible in the pervert's theory and practice. There is no such *das Ding* as the fetish. The prototype is continuous with the chain of words for both deconstruction and psychoanalysis. The question of the desire of the subject (*Che Vuoi?*) is unstable if the center is wobbly and the function is mythical. The pervert escapes desire and its *objets* — word, metaphor, fetish, center, sign, and so on. Outside of desire, the deconstructionist plays and the fetishist enjoys. But — what? The Freudian fetish is the pervert's Hitchcockian MacGuffin. Perversely, this delay and interruption are the essence of the fetishist's *Trieb* beyond the structure and sign — and even play — of the deconstructionist's text.

The subtext of my study is Marxism. Is the capitalist the postponed destination of the very start of this delayed inquiry? The bourgeois individual is commodified by the fetishism of capitalism. But to what end? If the prototypical capitalist is no less than a penis-substitute, then he must also be simultaneously more than the sum of his own labor. I want to turn to a pedagogy of the idiotic but pleasurable equilibrium of the capitalist system. I will analyze the internal excess of the homeostasis in capitalist overproduction. This is the critical theme of the next chapter of the book. The object of discussion will be the paradoxical transformation of surplus into deficit, plenitude into castration, fullness into lack, presence into absence, credit into debt, and Nothing is Missing into Something is Missing. A Pedagogy of the Proletariat will scrutinize the castration at the center of capitalism. How is castration *produced* by capital?

Chapter Eight

Debt to Marx

Without a revolutionary theory there can be no revolutionary movement.

— V. I. Lenin

The Marxist critique of private property is the basic theoretical orientation of this book. Derrida works to critique the system of *le propre* in the entirety of his efforts. His metatheory disturbs all claims to essence and identity: what is. Any border or boundary which is circumscribed around an object or entity is fractured simply because of its unstable position within the traces and chains of the signifying disorganization. The compressions and displacements of the center of any structure indicate that all paradigms are continuous and coincident with every other. Every word is the same (different) word.

This functionalization of the principle of organization shows that the network of signifiers is ordered by the metaphorical ("the literal") which perturbs any coherent parameters. But the words in the system float and waft in ways, byways, and out ways in a temporal and spatial movement which is directed by a function. This function is irreducible to any chance signifier that may haphazardly orient, balance, and organize the structure in a form or a name. The thinking of this substitution facilitates the displacement of the center. However, the function of the center is unexpectedly present and stable. It is so even if its contingent sign is substitutable in the web of signification. The system is simultaneously both infinite in substitute centers and finite in the structural exclusion of the function from the series of metaphors. At stake in deconstruction is the abolishment of private property in both the signifier (materiality) and the sign (materiality-abstraction).

Marx critically intervenes in the history of labor in the life of man. He situates existence in an irreducible materiality ("dialectical materialism"). This physics and body cannot be eliminated by or incorporated in their excess by the displacements and compressions of the sign. Both deconstruction and Marxism tarry with the surplus of a materialism within the system. This remainder cannot be recuperated into its smooth operation. For deconstruction, *le propre* names the impossible appeal to a stopgap on the seepage of materiality beyond the borders of the system. Marxism views the private property of capital and its accumulation as the essence of the system of capitalism: to limit the excess of materiality in the structure. The homeostatic management of materiality in the textual structure and capitalist system is situated within the uneasy overlap of materiality and abstraction, physicality and speculation, signifier and sign, and theory and practice. The invention of a deconstructive Marxist *Praxis* is advanced by a scrutiny of a torn materiality and its (in/ex)clusion within the system.

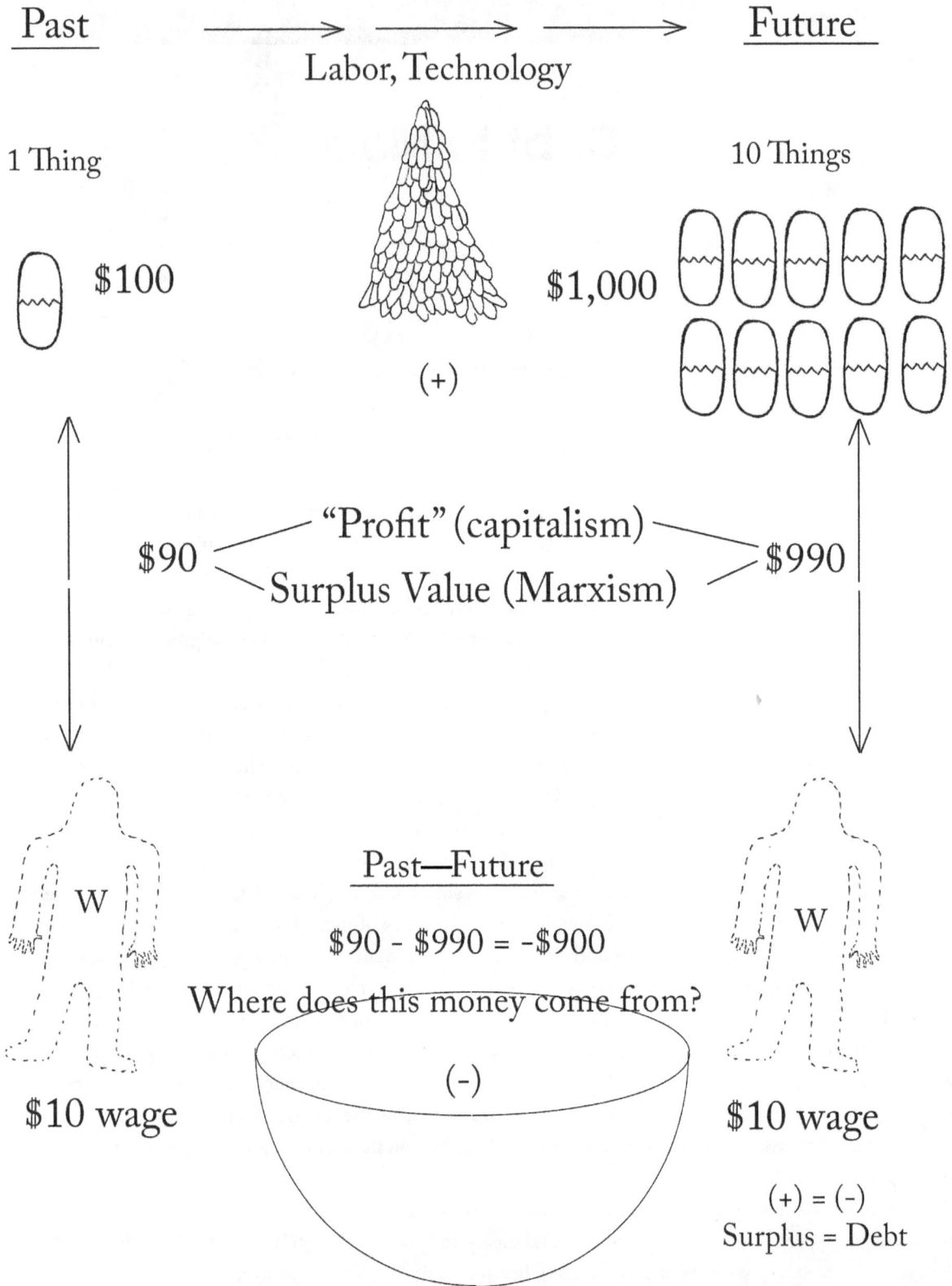

Figure 8.1 The Pervert's Marxist Economics

Past → → → Future

Labor, Technology

1 Thing

$100

(+)

10 Things

$1,000

$90 ⟨ "Profit" (capitalism) ⟩ $990
     Surplus Value (Marxism)

W

$10 wage

Past—Future

$90 - $990 = -$900

Where does this money come from?

(-)

W

$10 wage

(+) = (-)
Surplus = Debt

• 332 •

This diagram elaborates the pervert's critique of capitalism. The interval between past and future (above) indicates the development of the forces of production (labor and technology). The historical march of labor productivity exponentially expands the quantity of commodities which is produced by the capitalist forces of production: in this example, from 1 Thing to 10 Things over the course of the passage from the past to the future. The gap between wage and MSRP is the parallactic gap between capitalist "profit" and Marxist surplus value. These two ostensibly opposed objects are a "sameness which is not identical" as a split in the parallactic gap on "one" and the "same" object. The worker earns $10/hr. in the past in the production of 1 Thing, and this 1 Thing sells for $100 with the difference of a $90 capitalist "profit" or Marxist surplus value (right). The power of labor and technology in the future (right) produces 10 Things, but the wage of the worker stagnates at $10/hr. The "profit" and surplus value exponentially increase from $90 to $990. What is the source of this difference of $900 between the "profit" and surplus value of the past and the "profit" and surplus value of the future? The sum must come from the bank in the form of debt. The addition of 1 Thing to 10 Things in the interval from the past to the future is converted from a gain to a loss, and from a surplus to a debt. The system borrows debt on credit. The Things multiply, but the supply of currency is secured to a system of credit and debt with the bank. (I have excluded non-labor costs — "land" — from my analysis in order to starkly isolate the mechanism of capitalist exploitation from a demand side perspective.)

Notes & Sketches —

MARXISM AND SEMIOTICS

Saussure's analysis of the sign in *Course in General Linguistics* (1917) establishes a tripartite semiological terminology: material signifier, abstract signified, and their union in the textual sign. The veritable mystery of signification is the materiality of the signifier in its autonomy from the signified in theory and then the dependence of this material signifier on the abstract signified of the sign in practice. Saussure says,

> Language can also be compared with a sheet of paper: thought is the front and the sound the back; one cannot cut the front without cutting the back at the same time; likewise in language, one can neither divide sound from thought nor thought from sound; the division could be accomplished only abstractedly, and the result would be either pure psychology or pure phonology.[1]

Saussure claims that the materiality of the signifier and the abstraction of the signified can only be isolated and separated in theory, in philosophy and speculation. The brute material component of the sign — the signifier — can only be autonomous in theory. The stark materiality of the sound, image, and mark in isolation is only a theoretical postulation. In practice, no such autonomous materiality *qua* materiality is accessible. In life, all materiality will be marked by abstraction, speculation, and signification. This materiality will be counted and recounted by mediations — comparisons and contrasts — of the general equivalent. In practice, the sign is the joint between the material signifier and the abstract signified. This interface between signifier and signified makes words and utterances possible. Night and day, materiality is joined to abstraction. Words and things, meanings and objects, *les mots et les choses* — are conjoined in an alloyed composition of the material and the ideal.

Materiality and Abstraction

The paradox of Saussure's map of the signifier/sign and theory/practice divisions is that it is only in the signs of language that the signifier is accessible in its materiality. Saussure writes,

> The characteristic role of language with respect to thought is not to create a material phonic means for expressing ideas but to serve as a link between thought and sound, under conditions that of necessity bring about the reciprocal delimitation of units.[2]

A Marxist *Praxis* is defined as the overlap of these two dimensions: theory (signifier and signified, apart) and practice (signifier and signified, tied). The constitutive component of materiality (the signifier and the sign) is internal to both theory and practice but in different forms. In theory, materiality is autonomous, separated, and detached. In practice, materiality is dependent, subordinate, and conditioned. In theory, materiality is the Real which resists symbolic articulation. In practice, this materiality is already symbolized, written and spoken.

A semiological *Praxis* of deconstruction and Marxism is organized by the coincidence of these two aspects of materiality: the brute autonomy of materiality (the signifier) and the imbricated physicality (the signifier) and conceptuality (the signified) in the sign. Semiologically, such *Praxis* is constituted as the overlap of theory — the autonomy of materiality which is irreducible to any abstraction — and practice — the inextricability of the body and speculation. The joint between theory and practice in *Praxis* is this trace of a materiality which is torn between autonomy and dependence, and between separation and subordination. The object of *Praxis* is this excess materiality. This surplus body is uneasily situated in both of these dimensions. It is torn across the field of the absolutely unsymbolizable. Surplus materiality is situated between the Real, on the one hand, and the written text and spoken utterance, on the other hand. This nodal point of materialism is the site of a simultaneous symbolic articulation and Real resistance. Excess materialism troubles the otherwise smooth operation of the general equivalent. Deconstructive Marxism views materialism as at once autonomous from and resistant to abstraction and at the same time dependent on and constitutive of this same conceptuality.

The challenge of *Praxis* is this trace of materiality in the parallactic gap between theory and practice. Materialism is the Real which is both resistant to articulation and yet also already symbolized. *Praxis* is not simply the forever failed effort of the textualization of the Real. Instead, *Praxis* is the representation of the failure of symbolization itself. Lacan identifies *Praxis* as the writing and the speaking of the Real. In the *Seminar* on the four fundamental concepts of psychoanalysis (1964), Lacan says,

> What is a *Praxis*? I doubt whether this term may be regarded as inappropriate to psychoanalysis. It is the broadest term to designate a concerted human action, whatever it may be, which places man in a position to treat the Real by the symbolic.[3]

The proper object of the *Praxis* of the Real is the failure of the symbol, sign, and theory. The symbolic articulation in abstraction and speculation cannot capture the trace of materiality in the Real. The Real resists the sign of the general equivalent as the signified of this materiality. There is an excess of materiality in the overlap of the dimensions of theory and practice. It is this surplus which cannot be assimilated into the system of abstraction, speculation, conceptualization, or the general equivalent. The proper name for this surplus materiality is the Real.

The proper *Praxis* of a Pedagogy of the Proletariat is the exposure of this remainder to the system. The indescribable enigma of capital is this excess materiality as it is divided between the theoretical separation of the material-physical-bodily from the abstract-speculative-conceptual, on the one hand, and the practical union of body and mind (and so on) in the sign, on the other hand. A deconstructive Marxist *Praxis* illuminates a surplus materiality which cannot be sutured by the sign. Marx's work illustrates this remainder of materiality which emerges in the gap between theory (the signifier and the signified) and practice (the sign). I want to demonstrate the joint between neither the united materiality and abstraction of the sign in practice nor the separated body and mind in theory. Rather, my work is to indicate the split in materiality itself. This split in the materiality of the signifier and physicality of the body — the worker, one may hazard — is the interval of the parallactic gap between bourgeois economics and Marxism, and between capitalism and communism. This split in the body is the *arche* of the dissolution of *le propre* in deconstruction. Split materiality also indicates the promised abolishment of private property in communism. To pose the question to this worker, what happens to the body in what Marx calls "commodity fetishism"?

Praxis

Deconstructive Marxism proposes the pedagogical encirclement of the Real as the proper modality of *Praxis*. The exposure of the failure of writing and speaking is critical to this project. The overlap between the materiality of theory and the materiality-abstraction of practice demonstrates that there is a constitutive remainder of materiality. This extra escapes reincorporation into any coherent system of *Praxis*. The Real escapes the symbolic. This Real is the source of the disturbance of the system of capital. The excess in the system is the breach in materiality between representation and the Real. There is a component of Real materiality which cannot be symbolized, spoken or written.

The chink in the efforts of the textualization of the Real produces an effect in the capitalist organization. This effect resists metabolization by the system. A surplus of materiality escapes the codes of the general equivalent. This remainder vanishes from the system in an absence which otherwise must be sutured by the system of capital. The teeters and totters of the general equivalent trip on this excess materiality. A pedagogical *Praxis* exposes the surplus of materiality in the structure. The extra exceeds the limits of the general equivalent. There is an integrant materiality which is both internal and external to the system. These extra goods and services subsist on the outside of the system. Materiality returns to the inside of the structure in order to destabilize it. How is this rupture of the surplus to be demonstrated?

The profound disturbance in Marx's *Thesis Eleven* (1845) on theory, practice, and *Praxis* is that the entirety of the irresolvable antinomy between philosophy and politics, theory and practice, signifier and sign, and material and abstraction is articulated in the most pithy of terms in one sentence. To wit: "Philosophers have hitherto only interpreted the world in various ways; the point is to change it."[4] The simple and elegant expression of what emerges for us as a veritable impossibility to resolve inspires a deep humility in the projects of both abstract speculation and concrete practice — and their impossible union as a *Praxis*. The text also illuminates the profound and frustrated lacuna between the theoretical signifier/signified and the positive entity of the sign — or combination in *Praxis*.

If *Praxis* is considered the Theory of Practice, as I call it, then the practical sign must execute the theoretical signifier/signified. This means that words would mobilize brute materiality. Discourse would articulate material marks (sounds and images) in the absence of abstraction and conceptuality. The purpose of *Praxis* in a Theory of Practice is the production of materialism — bodies, corporealities, use-values, objects, textures, and so on. These bodies would be severed from signification. This system is what Saussure would call "pure phonology." Words would have no meaning, but they would (be) matter.

Obversely, if *Praxis* is considered the Practice of Theory, as I name it, then a mass of materiality and a swarm of abstraction would articulate naked general equivalence. Saussure says,

> Psychologically our thought — apart from its expression in words — is only a shapeless and indistinct mass. Philosophers and linguists have always agreed in recognizing that without the help of signs we would be unable to make a clear-cut, consistent distinction between two ideas. Without language, thought is a vague, uncharted nebula. There are no pre-existing ideas, and nothing is distinct before the appearance of language.[5]

A Practice of Theory understands the purpose of *Praxis* as the creation of pure ideality of general equivalence. This generation of coins and dollars would not refer to either the material signifier or the conceptual signified. This system is what Saussure refers to as "pure psychology." The coins and dollars would have meaning, but it would not (have no) matter. The horizon of *Praxis* — the quantum superposition of theory and practice — is either brute materialism — brain dead — or obscene idealism — body dead — in either formulation of *Praxis*. The consequence is either pure materialism or unalloyed idealism, and either phonology or psychology. Derrida refers to this as the logocentric bias of a division between mind/body (and so on) in Western metaphysics. The logocentric bias is a consequence of the failure to properly interpret the excess materiality in the system.

Figure 8.2 (Set) Theory and Practice

Practice

signifier $\bigcap$ signified

Theory

signifier $\setminus$ signified

Excess Signifier: signifier $\subset$ signified $\implies$

signifier $\bigcap$ signified = signified

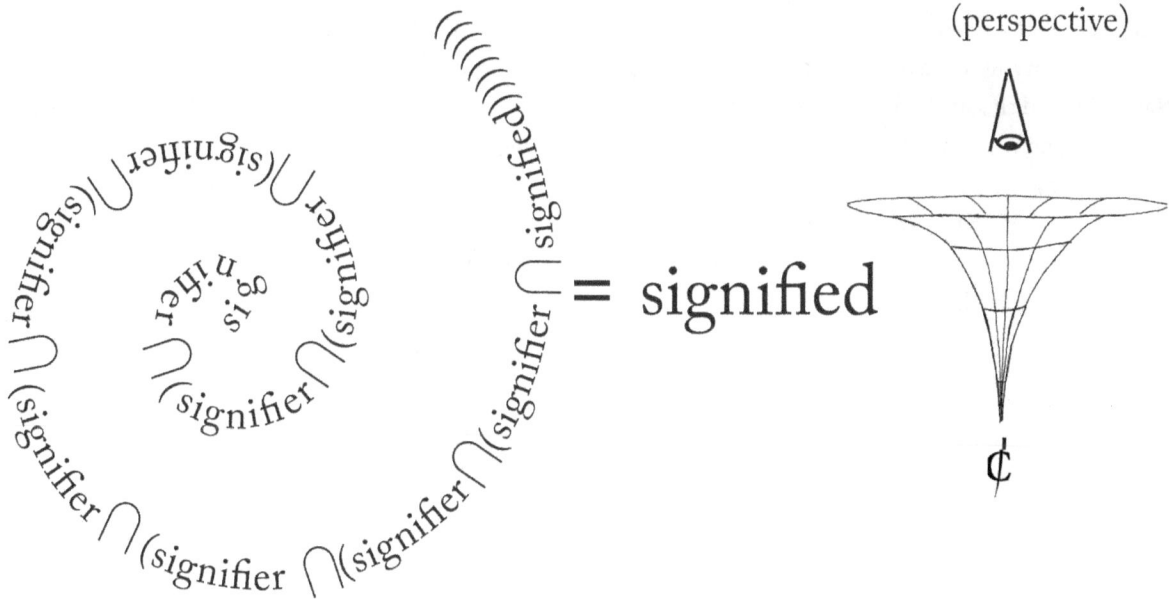

(perspective)

= signified

¢

Praxis = Practice $\bigcup$ Theory =

(signifier $\bigcap$ signified) $\bigcup$ (signifier $\setminus$ signified) = signifier

This illustration deploys a Queer Mathematical set theory and symbolism in order to outline the Marxist concept of *Praxis* of the fourth-dimension in relationship to the Saussurian concepts of signifier and signified or value (as opposed to the sign and signification). Practice (above, left) is defined as the intersection of the sign, signifier, and signified. Practice is the everyday word which conjoins the material signifier and the abstract signified. Theory strips and isolates the materiality of the signifier from the abstraction and speculation of the signified. The backslash symbol (above, right) indicates the set of the signified which is subtracted from the set of the signifier. The leftover of the signifier is a Real impossibility to speak or to write because the material signifier suspends the speculation and abstraction — meaning-making — of the signified. This overflow of the signifier in relationship to the signified is isomorphic to the occlusion of the center and the *mise-en-abyme* of its veil. The excess signifier (center, above) refers to the signifier as a superset of the signified. The signified is entirely included in the set of the material signifier. But the obverse is not the case. There is a surplus of materiality which cannot be contained by speculation and abstraction. The signifier contains all of the signified with the addition of a surplus and an excess. The intersection of the signifier and the signified (below) is the loss of the signified and the gain of the signifier. The overlap is the set of the signified. The spiral image (left) indicates that the intersection of the signifier and the signified is an insistent signified. The perspective (right) depicts the spiral (left) in relationship to the vortex of the occluded center and the gravitation anchor of an essential Nothingness. The excess signifier is repeatedly excluded as a surplus which cannot be recuperated by and reincorporated into the system. The image shows the signifier as it disappears into the occluded center. This disappearance is indicated by the configuration of the perspective on the function of gravity. The Real is consistently and repeatedly resistant to integration into the system. The spiral recalls the dissolution of units of text (signifying terms) as they disappear into the displaced void of the occluded center. *Praxis* (below) *qua* the union and the addition of the sets of practice and theory is necessarily a surplus materiality of the signifier. The first parenthetical (below, left) represents the abstract signified (left). The second parenthetical (below, right) represents the excess signifier. In sum, the relationship between the two parentheticals generates an abundance of Marxist materialism of the signifier. The intersection rather than the union of the sets of practice and theory is a null set. This null set indicates that the Real excess material signifier of the body of the worker cannot be signified.

Notes & Sketches —

The capitalist system is organized by a general equivalence of currency — dollars and coins. This standard arbitrates the value of objects as quantifiable in the process of comparison, contrast, and exchange. The *Praxis* of capitalism is the Practice of Theory. A *Praxis* of theory transforms an Economics 101 class into a way of life. This *Praxis* animates capitalist reification or what Marx refers to as "commodity fetishism." This fetishism is distinct from the pervert's *jouissance* of the fetish-object: the fur, lace, shoe, jockstrap, and every other object in the system of substitution. Capitalist fetishization involves the generation of pure general equivalence and exchange-value. A deconstructive Marxism celebrates pedagogical proletarian *Praxis* and denounces capitalist *Praxis*. Pedagogical Marxism mobilizes a Theory of Practice. Proletarian *Praxis* overlaps the signifier of value and theory with the sign (signifier-signified/sign) of signification and practice. A deconstructive Marxism of pedagogical proletarian *Praxis* mobilizes an overlapped and doubled materiality of the material signifier of value and the joined materiality of the signifier and abstraction of the signified in signification.

The layered integration of the signifier of theory and the signifier-signified/sign in practice generates a doubled materiality of the physicality of the signifier of value in practice and the corporeality of the signifier and abstraction of the signified in signification in theory. *Praxis* is the interface of the surplus of the doubled materiality in the overlapped integration of the signifier of practice in value and the signifier of theory in the sign. Surplus body in *Praxis* promises the production of brute materiality as a critique of the logocentrism of the pure ideality of the general equivalent. Materialism *qua* signifier of both theory and practice is the linchpin of the possibility of a radical practice. Marxist dialectical materialism is a privileged domain for the Theory of Practice. Man's situation is always a human *Praxis*.

The separation of politics and philosophy, concreteness and abstraction, practice and theory, and even body and mind is already sutured by the system. This bandage is materialism. But why is this *Praxis* of the sign of theory and practice — the joint of the signifier and the signified — an ardent failure for us? I will return to the madness of the relationship between material and concept — body and mind — as it can(not) be mapped onto semiology or Marxism or *Praxis* after my exegesis of value and profit. But I can say now that at the same moment in time and axis in space both materiality and abstraction will slip between each other only to generate both a surplus and a deficit which can only be recuperated into the system by a reference to an Other. This Other is quite happy to lend its assistance. There is a slip and slide in *Praxis*. The joint of this rupture is materialism. The word is abstraction. The general equivalent is this cut in the Real. The wound in the economy expands, and dollars and coins must be stretched in order to suture the gash.

Solids, Airs, and Mediations

Marx and Engels's most dramatic statement in "The Communist Manifesto" (1848) is no doubt that under capitalism, "all that is solid melts into air."[6] The exigent sense of this famous script is that all that has been in a venerable presence — values, mores, relationships, ideas, and so on — disappears in the ether of capitalist society. This evaporation of the abstractions of the culture cannot be traced to any unitary source. Rather, the system of capitalism writhes all of Being (what is) into the air-ducts of the terrain of selves and cultures. Capitalism is a challenge to any extant ontology which is not powerfully historicized. The other side of the metaphor is that the transformation of a solid into another molecular state involves passage into the state of a liquid. As a liquid, this fluid and voluminous substance is prone to a spatial reconfiguration of itself in a protean volatility.

The metamorphosis of ideologies — all of what is — transforms solid into air. This happens in the absence of a transition to a liquid form. The pulverized ideological system that capitalism reinvents is not simply rearranged by the society, like the reorientation of liquid in space. The extant symbolic systems of the culture are the object of a magical disappearance rather than a negotiated rearrangement by the system and its subjects. The questions after the melt are, "What fills the vacuum of the abrupt loss of the solids and the naturalized values of the culture in the system?" and "What happens after the coordinates of the symbolic order are upended?" Capitalism is certainly a revolutionary event because it reorganizes the basic coordinates of the symbolic apparatus. But the image of "all that is solid melts into air" does not radically restructure the system. Capitalism generates a hole — Something is Missing — in the air. This loss must be (ac)counted (for) in order to make full a renewed system of absence under capitalism. The loss of solid and the rise of air are the conditions of the advent of capitalism as a system of scarcity. The air promises lack and castration. All that is penis melts into clitoris.

Communist Sex

Another indication of "all that is solid melts into air" is the fate of sexual difference under the transition to capitalism and then to communism. The development of capitalism is progressive because it conditions the further refinement of the forces of production toward the revolution to communism. But what is the genital principle of organization after the *Aufhebung* against the capitalist penis? What is the genital principle in the emergent communist mode of production? The penis and the clitoris battle each other in an endless (class and sexual) struggle of plenitude and lack under capitalism. But what sexual principle inherits overproduction and the end of alienated labor? The airs of the feminine economy overcome the solids of phallic organization. But what morphological and anatomical difference returns as the postphallic genital principle of the communist revolution? In each according to his need and each according to his ability, what structured object is beyond both supply and demand? What sexual organ is the Outside of value? What is sex after capitalism?

An answer to such a question must refer to a critique of the capitalist general equivalent of currency. The work of this standard is the generalized quantification of the value of all commodities. There can be no genital sexuality under communism because the revolution toward plenitude melts into air the solid of the penis. The air (heir) of sexuality must be redefined for a future communism and its potential (*a*)sexuality. This (*a*)sexuality may be a maximization or a minimization of sexual practices in the pleasures of a *Trieb* in the absence of desire. The *Aufhebung* from capitalism to communism promises the revision of scarcity in the material conditions of real life. The revolution also requires a transformation in sexuality. What is sex after castration? What is *Eros* when Nothing is Missing?

TOWARD VALUE

The general equivalent of currency in the capitalist system quantifies the use-value quality of goods and services in digits, numbers, integers, and so on. These objects of use-value are produced by the proletarian cultivation of nature into culture. This is the process of labor. The general equivalent works on the level of the sign. Currency conjoins materiality and abstraction, body and speculation, physicality and conceptuality, and use-value and exchange-value. The trace of the material signifier of theory is autonomous from the calculation of the comparison, contrast, and exchange of the quantification of coins and dollars. The surplus materialism of theory cannot be recuperated by the sign. This theoretical component of the signifier is the Real. It resists writing and speaking. It eludes exchange by the general equivalent. This remnant of materiality evades capture in the system of private property under capitalism.

Marx emphasizes material conditions as the origin of consciousness. In *The German Ideology* (1845), Marx states: "Life is not determined by consciousness, but consciousness by life."[7] Such a theory foregrounds the material signifier as the advent of the nascent worldview of the proletariat. Materiality is the revolutionary dimension of Marxism. Materialism illuminates the centrality of both theory and the signifier in the communist revolution. An excess materiality in the Real is an untouched surplus. The extra body and physics exceed the quantification of use-value by the general equivalent. The parallactic gap sustains and collapses the division between capitalism and communism. The parallax is the locus of two antagonistic perspectives on this "one" and the "same" object. This object is the material body of the theoretical signifier. How do capitalism and communism — bourgeois economists and Marxist critics — differently approach this material remainder? The general equivalent is the vanishing mediator — specter — which dissolves in the transition from one perspective to another viewpoint of the parallactic gap. Currency is the proviso of the union and separation, *Eros* and *Thanatos*, and identity and difference — Sameness[+] — of this object of materiality. The general equivalent solid which ought to melt into air in transaction and exchange is currency.

The transition from an economy of approximate use-value (C-M-C') to near exchange-value (M-C-M') initiates a peculiar movement. The accumulation of abstract capital (exchange-value) rather than material objects (use-values) is the object of movement in the system. Under capitalism, the object of substitution is not center for center, or sign for sign, or object for object, or fetish for fetish, or substitute for substitute, or penis for penis, and so on. Instead, this object is transformed from the metaphors for Derrida's center to the function *itself*. The capitalist function is the accumulation of currency in dollars and coins. The general equivalent compares and contrasts material goods. This standard confers quantified value. Abstract numerals imply both plenitude — a comparison and contrast to a lesser value — and scarcity — a contrast and comparison to a greater value. The function of the capitalist structure is the orientation, balance, and organization not of scarcity but of *surplus*. The system must sustain itself in the enforcement of castration and lack by the will to convert surplus and excess ("greater" — and "lesser") into deficit and debt ("lesser" — and "greater"). The capitalist system must retard the development of a communist (*a*)sexual erotic economy. Communist erotics is outside of the phallic organization of presence/absence because in the Marxist utopia Nothing is Missing.

Marx stresses that the system of capital is predicated on "accumulation." This capitalization on capital (M-C-M') is only possible and necessary if Something is Missing in the accumulation which has yet to (ac)count for a balance which ~~is~~ will be due. The heterosexualism of capitalism is that the function is itself a metaphor for the system: currency, dollars and coins. The penis transforms into the phallus. The reason that under capitalism "all that is solid melts into air" is that the solid of goods and services — the use-value component of a commodity — is transformed into the air of speculation and abstraction — the exchange-value relationship. But what is the object of speculation? Marx's communist *telos* toward the "abolition of private property" is a will to redress the insistent (ac)count of the value of objects from the perspective of the general equivalent.[8] The dissolution of private property returns the airs to solids, the speculations to materialities, and the abstractions to physicalities. The capitalist phallus transforms into the penis.

How No Thing Became Some Nothing

The "antagonism" between "capital and wage-labor" is best expressed in the odd paradox of Marx's criticism of bourgeois economics and in the naturalization of exploitation in the concept of "profit."[9] The capitalist concept of "profit" and the Marxist revision of this metaphor for exploitation as "surplus value" are opposed perspectives on the "one" and the "same" object. This object can be approximated but only asymptotically. This object is represented as the interval between the wage of the worker and the price of the commodity. Capitalists return this gap to the owner as the "profit" of the corporation. The excess is reinvested by the company in the mysterious process of "accumulation" in which an addition of Something is Missing generates a subtraction in the "accumulation" of this Something is Missing. Somehow — "all that is solid melts into air" — an addition of Something is Missing in the general equivalent of dollars and coins is transformed into a subtraction of Something is Missing. This is the puzzling process of accumulation whereby abundance produces scarcity and gain increases loss. Except, at the same time, the enigmatic process of accumulation also involves a subtraction of Something is Missing. And then somehow — "all that is solid melts into air" — a subtraction of Something is Missing in the general equivalent of dollars and coins is translated into an addition of Something is Missing.

The interval between wage and price is the surplus value. This word names the capitalist theft of the value of the body of the worker. The value is rightfully and properly owned by the worker in return for his labor in the production of the commodity. At first glance, the opposition between "profit" and surplus value is a word — the two concepts substitute for the "one" and the "same" gap. But the name for the Real object of the antagonism between "profit" and surplus value on the "one" and the "same" object is in suspension. The object is in a quantum superposition between gain for the owner and loss for the worker. But the reverse cannot be the case. Why? The exchange-value of materiality in the sign is disjunctive with materiality in itself. The nodal point of the gap between wage and cost is the struggle to calculate the abstract and speculative exchange-value of an otherwise surplus materiality. This extra cannot be assimilated into the system as either "profit" or surplus value.

Neither a capitalist bourgeois economist nor a Marxist critical economist can properly identify this Real materialism — labor — because there is no final referent or metageneral equivalent. There is no standard which could definitively convert the material into the abstract and the bodily into the speculative. The reason for this failure to symbolize the Real is the split in materiality. The fissure is between the autonomy of the signifier in theory and the subordination of the signifier to the calculation of the sign in practice. Capitalists posit a nebulous supply/demand dynamic as the origin of the calculation of exchange-value. But the emergence of plenitude from scarcity in capitalist overproduction decimates the fundamental precept of capitalism in Something is Missing. The bourgeois system must *produce loss* in order to symbolize the Real with the value of "profit." Marxists find themselves in the same bind. Marx theorizes labor-time as the advent of value. This is an obscenely abstract map of value for a writer who is committed to materialism.

The two limit-principles are capitalist scarcity and Marxist temporality. These standards evaluate by comparing and contrasting — exchanging — goods and services in the marketplace. The point is that these yardsticks cannot properly read and write the Real of the excess and surplus. As a sign in practice, materiality exceeds the smooth operation of the general equivalent. The material and the bodily escape capture in the sign. There is a specter haunting the general equivalent. It is the signifier and its excess rather than scarcity, surplus rather than debt, and remainder rather than restriction. The containment of this extra is the defense of a capitalism which is overwhelmed by overproduction. The will to calculation of the general equivalent is mobilized in order to textualize the Real. A surplus materialism makes this effort a writing and a speaking of the failure of symbolization. This Real resistance to the articulated symbolic order heralds the end of capitalism. The deconstruction of text is the revolution against capital. The free play of the materiality of the signifier inspires emancipated production and liberated consumption.

Figure 8.3 Dollars and Coins

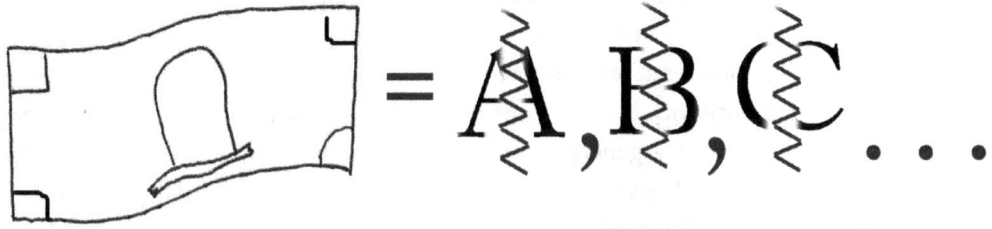

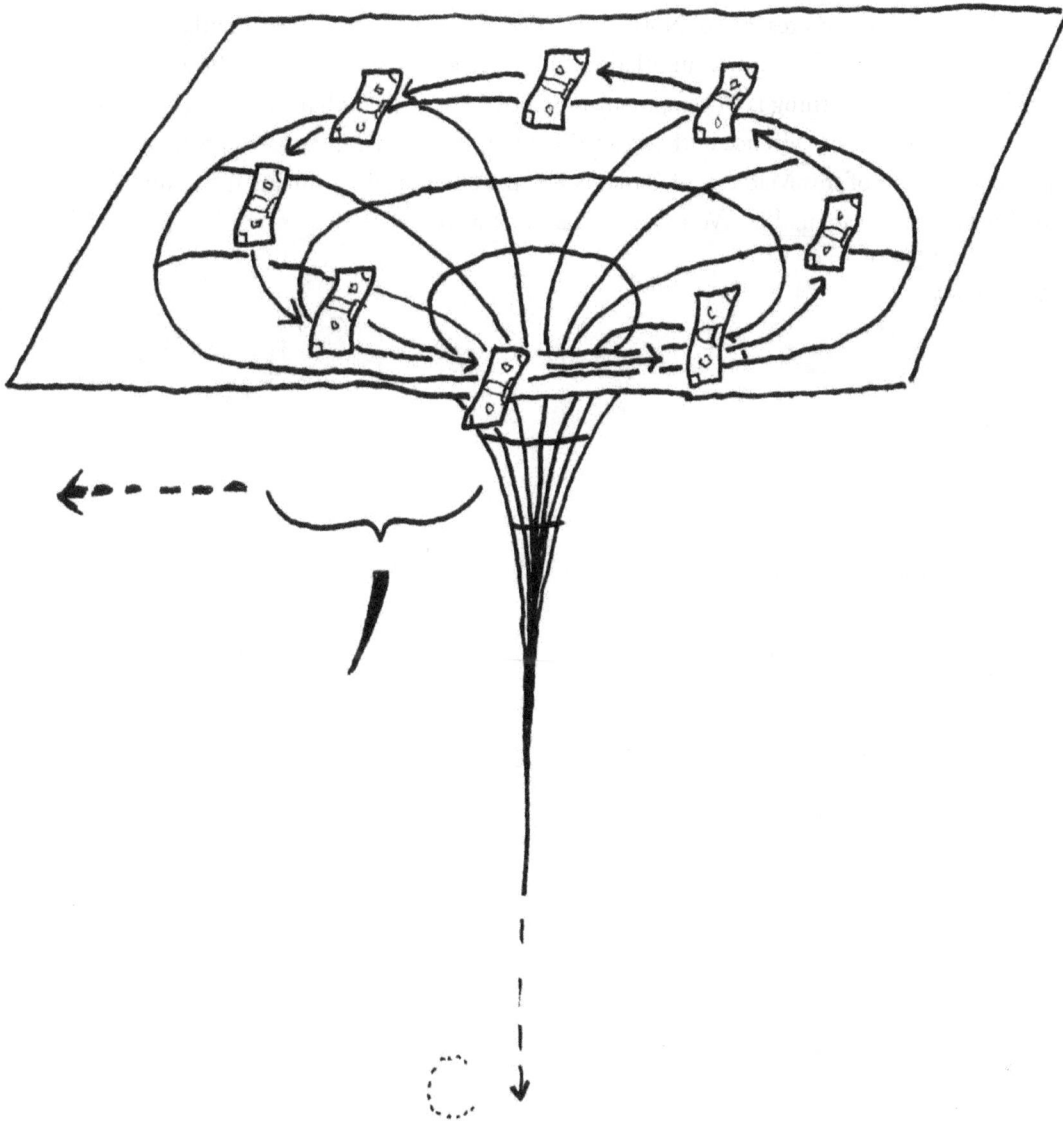

This illustration portrays the principle of the general equivalent of dollars and coins and its isomorphic relationship to the chain of signification. The circulation of currency parallels the difference and deferral — *différance* — of one unit of text (A, B, C, D, and so on) to the antecedent and posterior word in the delayed retroaction of meaning-making. This return backward and forward fragments the object in space and time. Any object is the same as any other object because each object is split — jagged edge — from itself. Any unit of text cannot be considered self-same or self-identical — Being, *il y a*, as such, by definition, *qua* — in coincidence and continuity with itself. But the neurotic's *rejet névrotique* forecloses (represses) this Unreason, and it returns the system to a general equivalence of comparison, contrast, and exchange. The general equivalent in the system of *langue* excludes the object which is otherwise equivocal and fragmented. The Real resistance to signification fundamentally constitutes the object. The occlusion symbol (below, center) represents the radius of monetary circulation. The fabled debt (credit) in the economy and the substitutive centers in the structure are infinitely expandable. This extension — fetishes, *et al.* — sutures the parallactic gap which separates surplus and deficit, plenitude and lack, and signifier and sign. Finitude is mined from the infinity of the plenitude and presence of Nothing is Missing. The *ex nihilo* of accumulation — Something out of Nothing — is achieved because accumulation functions as the paradoxical subtraction (addition) of Something is Missing from Nothing is Missing. Any presence — signified, phallus, object, goods and services — is predicated on a constitutive absence in the castration of phallocentrism, the loss in scarcity, and the word in signification. The name of this Madness of Order is $-ism. A proper discernment and manipulation of this system is the Spirit of the System. The Woman inherits this future.

Notes & Sketches —

Excess Materiality

A Marxist economist revises "profit" as surplus value in order to illustrate the theft of value from the worker as "profit." This "profit" should otherwise rightly be returned to the worker. The speculation of this value in the form of the general equivalent — dollars and coins — is undecidable. The value of "profit" or surplus value is calculated by capitalist supply/demand dynamics or it is evaluated by Marxist labor-time. But this parallactic overlap of "profit" and surplus value incisively illuminates the excess of materiality which ruptures the smooth operation of the general equivalent. There must be a surplus of materiality — labor — in order to generate an inequivalence between "profit" and surplus value. Communism suspends any value of materiality which is abstracted as either "profit" or surplus value. There is no general equivalent in the Spirit of the System or, as I call it, Spiritual (S) X. The *telos* of historical dialectical materialism is a valueless and antinihilistic system of materiality.

The use-value of the commodity of the Pervert-Schizoid-Woman cannot be (ac)counted. The use-value of the object cannot be compared, contrasted, or exchanged. The only relationship between objects is incommensurability and singularity. There is no abstraction in digits or speculation in integers — $-ism — by which to measure exchange-value. Communism disbands the calculation of both "profit" and surplus value. There is no yardstick by which to measure the value of the gap between wage and cost. The loss or gain — subtraction or addition — between cost and wage is either quantified in "profit" by capitalists or surplus value by Marxists. But communism insists that ~~loss~~ and ~~gain~~ can only be expressed in the use-value of the materiality of the signifier.

I isolate the surplus — addition and subtraction — as the worker's "Proleptic X." This is the ~~value~~ which is promised to return in the future of the Real. The Proleptic X is neither a loss nor a gain because the general equivalent cannot capture the remainder of the overlap between theory (signifier-signified) and practice (signifier-signified/sign) in *Praxis*. The owner's gain in "profit" or loss in surplus value can only be conferred in the money-form of the general equivalent. For Marx, work has no value. A strictly communist perspective discerns that the excess of value has arrived at neither the destination of the worker nor the departure of the owner. Surplus cannot be quantified in the general equivalent. Any "profit" is incalculable because materiality cannot be quantified. Any surplus value is unaccountable because materiality cannot be quantified. But why is this differed and deferred value *qua* unspeakable and unwritable excess located in the Real? Why is the worker's Spiritual (S) X otherwise the Outside? The object of surplus value and "profit" can only be abstracted from the perspective of the bourgeoisie and the domination of the general equivalent: abstraction, speculation, calculation, comparison, contrast, exchange, and so on. The owner's "profit" is extracted in the abstraction of the materialism of the worker's labor. The Proleptic X is the Real object of the parallax. The Proleptic X is stolen as "profit" by the owners under capitalism. It is returned to the workers in Marxist critique as surplus value.

Communism

Communism proposes that the Proleptic X not be extracted in the abstraction of the materialism of the worker's labor as either "profit" or surplus value. Postnihilistic communism discerns that the worker's material labor cannot be returned to him in the inverted — *camera obscura* (1845) — equivalence of currency as either "profit" or its reverse in surplus value. The Proleptic X Real object of the parallax of the labor-process and the use-value of the commodity can only be strictly conceptualized in capitalist terms. Capitalism abstracts value with the general equivalent of dollars and coins. The obverse of capitalist exploitation and the extraction of "profit" cannot be Marxist surplus value because the interval between the price of the commodity and the value of the worker's labor can only be explained as a function of exchange-value as conferred by a system of the general equivalent in capitalism. Communism indicates that there can be neither "profit" nor surplus value. The value of the worker's labor is owed to him in a future in which dialectical materialism destroys all value at the end of nihilism proper.[10] The incalculable surplus value returns in the future as the Proleptic X. The Real returns from the future of communism to destabilize the symbolic order of capitalism. The Real is the failure of the capitalist *abstraction* of dollars and coins in nihilistic value. The Real is also the success of the communist resistance to the quantification of labor in excess *materialism*. The Real returns as the surplus of bodies and goods. There are too many objects on the shelves at Wal-Mart. This abundance ("scarcity") is the reason that these commodities are on the shelves at Wal-Mart.

This stockpile is the return of the Real in the symbolic. The excess represents the impossible coincidence of the Real and the symbolic. Capitalism resists itself. The worker inherits the return of the Proleptic X from the future of the Real. The Real is ~~represented~~ as each according to his need and each according to his ability.[11] The accumulation of capital is the extraction of surplus value. The destination of this accumulation of value is the abolishment of currency, destruction of general equivalence, and dissolution of the mediation of value. This is the diacritical rather than dialectical End of History. Communism is the end of value and the end of nihilism. The *telos* of the accumulation of capital is the obliteration of the general equivalent. What emerges after the *destruktion* of the symbolic order of capitalism? There is no word for communism. The symbolic order of the signification of words cannot name the diacritical system of the value of the signifier. The *Praxis* of capitalism — the Practice of Theory and the dominance of the sign over the signifier — cannot speak or write the words of communism.

Under capitalism, the Proleptic X parallactic object is under erasure — ~~Proleptic X~~ — because it is the return of the Real from the revolution. The worker's Real Proleptic X is not a word. The Proleptic X is neither "profit" nor surplus value. The Real communist future will be the purity of the material signifier as it is detached from the material-abstract and signifier-signified sign. There is no conceptuality in communism. There is no psychology in communism. There is no thinking in communism. After capitalism, there is only pure phonology: sounds, faces, voices, bodies, textures, songs, dances, and so on.

Communism is neither the practice of abstraction nor the practice of materialism nor the theory of *Praxis*. Communism is the Other of what Marx strives to impossibly describe — speak and write — in the Real. The future is the Spiritual (S) X or communism. This return of the Real Spiritual (S) X is the proleptic and promised Spirit of the System. The Pervert-Schizoid-Woman arrives as the end of capitalist accumulation. Capitalization can otherwise never end because it has already expired. Capitalism is a zombie who ravishes the desert of the Real. The pervert's "I know very well, but nevertheless" articulates the ends of capitalism. After Absolute Knowledge ("I know very well"), the "but nevertheless" appears. The Real Proleptic X becomes visible — yet it is already the object of capitalist accumulation under the name of "profit." The X is already the object of Marxist critique under the name of surplus value. The pervert of sexual difference "knows very well" that Something is Missing, "but nevertheless" the fetish-object sutures the wound. The pervert celebrates that Nothing is Missing. The pervert is the future subject of communism. The fetish is the Freudian name for Marxist use-value. The fetish is the material embodiment at the limit of capital. After capital, all objects become fetishes. The materialist fetish embodies the substance of the signifier in the absence of referral — either finitely or infinitely — to the penis. Communism mobilizes Real Fetishism. The returns recur in the space of the unconscious. The unconscious is the locus of communism. This space is a primary (production) process of use-value.

Capital at the Limit

The Marxist outline of "profit" is transparently dubious. The Marxist analysis of the capitalist extraction of value from the body of the worker is capitalist. The Marxist ruse is the displacement of "profit" with the opposed concept of surplus value. The substitution implies that the interval of the parallactic gap — ~~Proleptic X~~ — between "profit" and surplus value should return to the worker. The idea is that the object is the worker's original (origin and *arche* in deconstruction), private (property in Marxism), and owned (castration anxiety of loss in psychoanalysis) value. The deployment of surplus value is a capitalist concept. The idea reinscribes *arche, le propre,* and *désir* — $-ism — into the Marxist critique of the economy of private property. The Marxist critique reproduces the capitalist aesthetic as its effect. Private property is the fundamental limit of thought. There is no concept which is present beyond origin, privacy, and possession. The limit-thought of capital is capitalism. This illuminates the gap between Marxist critique and communism, and between the pervert's speaking and writing and the communist's promised Proleptic X of the future. Marxism can only think the limit of capital. This limit is the end of abstraction. What comes after thinking?

The possibility of communism can only be understood within the horizon of capitalism. All that is air, is air. Otherwise, oxygen is scarce and man expires in its absence. The promised Proleptic X is the suture of the antagonistic gap between wage and price, either "profit" from a capitalist perspective or surplus value from a Marxist perspective. But from a communist sensibility, this Proleptic X cannot be spoken or written until the arrival of the Spiritual (S) X or ~~communism~~. At this juncture, speaking and writing end, and the Real and the symbolic perfectly coincide. This parallactic overlap is (in)visible under the current system. The parallactic gap between capitalism and communism is closed at the end of the accumulation of capital. The extraction of surplus value as "profit" is (will be) complete because the proletariat is entirely stripped of a currency which would represent its value. Man is already communist because he is divested of value. The capitalist-nihilistic calculation of the value of the worker is sublated when the proletarian becomes Nothing. The worker transcends the economy of value and Becomes-Nothing in which Nothing is Missing. The end of sexual difference in psychoanalysis is isomorphic to the end of the antagonism between capitalism and communism, and between "profit" and surplus value. Capitalist "profit" and Marxist surplus value approach an equivalence in which exploitation overlaps with liberation, and enslavement inlays emancipation.

The Real — ~~Proleptic X~~ or ~~communism~~ — manifests at this juncture. The signification of the division between "profit" and surplus value collapses. Surplus materiality resists capitalist accumulation. At the end of man, the pure materiality of the signifier issues as the Theory of Practice. Theory of Practice materializes the component of abstraction in the sign in order to rend signification (the positive word) equivalent to value (the negative and differential signifier). Saussure writes,

> But the statement that everything in language is negative is true only if the signified and the signifier are considered separately; when we consider the sign in its totality, we have something that is positive in its own class.[12]

The ends of accumulation are responsible for the destruction of the sign and signification and the emergence of the signifier and value. The exchange-value of the general equivalent transforms into the value of the signifier.

The key to Saussure's explosive concept of value is difference. Difference is the (non)present mediator and general (in)equivalent between the objects in the system. Saussure says,

Everything that has been said up to this point boils down to this: in language there are only differences. Even more important: a difference generally implies positive terms between which the difference is set up; but in language, there are only differences without positive terms. Whether we take the signified or the signifier, language has neither ideas nor sounds that existed before the linguistic system, but only conceptual and phonic differences that have issued from the system.[13]

The pure materiality of *Praxis* emerges from the overlap of the theory of value (signifier-signified) and the practice of signification (signifier-signified/sign). This excess of materiality in the overlap of theory/practice and signifier-signified/sign — *Praxis* — is the ruin of representation and the rise of the unalloyed signifier. The signifier is the diacritical value of communism. The impossible word for communism is the Proleptic X of the Spirit of the System and the Becoming of the Pervert-Schizoid-Woman.

The clarity of use-value manifests as: _____. This is the end of man's millennia long monologue. The text is destroyed. The symbolic order crumbles into Unreason. The system of *langue* autodeconstructs because the essence of the structure is a suicidal *Thanatos*. The last Visa card is cut. The future is the present. Being emerges from Meaning. The name for the Proleptic X or the Spiritual S (X) or communism becomes irrelevant. The Pervert-Schizoid-Woman Becomes-Otherwise. All that is air sublimates into liquid.

Real Profit and Surplus Value

Surplus value is a concept which is internal to capitalism. The source of "profit" in surplus value is origin, privacy, and ownership: *arche*, *le propre*, and *désir*. The key concept of Marxist economics is reinscribed in the system of private property. Surplus value is the capitalist conceptualization of the Proleptic X. The X is the Real around which "profit" and surplus value encircle. The X is the unnamed referent or the Real parallax which returns from a future which is already the present. Bourgeois economics and Marxist economics are antagonistic perspectives on this otherwise Real Proleptic X. What is the properly communist name for the debt of the present in the return of the future? What is the signifier for the Real of the stolen and returned — lost but gained, subtracted but added — interval between wage and cost? What is the "antagonism" between capital and labor, bourgeois man and proletarian Woman, and owner and worker?

These questions may be approached in a nuanced recount of the gap, fissure, interval, in-between — add: lacuna — between "profit" and surplus value. Communism is an aneconomic system in which the general equivalent is absent. There is no currency — dollars or coins — in a communist system. Only "use-value" can structure the aneconomy because exchange with currency is inoperative in the field of: plenitude rather than scarcity; fullness rather than lack; Nothing is Missing rather than Something is Missing; the Pervert-Schizoid-Woman rather than the neurotic, and so on. There is no quantification of value in communism. The (in)finity of numerals is absent. The (ac)count is not a function within a communist order. The potential aneconomy of communism illuminates that the gap between "profit" and surplus value is only credible if this excess is interpreted from the perspective of the general equivalent.[*]

---

[*] Marx's controversial so-called labor theory of value posits that the value of the commodity is equivalent to the labor-time which is involved in the production of the object. The surplus value is calculated as the deduction of the wage — which is determined as the reproduction of the means of subsistence of labor — from the value of the commodity. In other words, Marx measures the value of the commodity and the exploitation in surplus value in labor-time. My

The standard enforces scarcity and castration on the system. The essence of the general equivalent is castration. The authority of capitalism is organized by the phallocentrism of sexual difference and the threat of castration against the male junior. The mechanism of this power is simple: comparison, contrast, and exchange of the Something is Missing. Under communism, the "value" of the gap, fissure, break, in-between, lacuna — add: rent — cannot be counted, accounted, calculated, evaluated, determined, judged, and so on. The quantification of exchange-value is banned from the system of qualitative use-value. There is neither use nor exchange in the Proleptic X of the promised future of the Spirit of the System because this Other manifests in the failure of symbolization and in the Unreason of speaking and writing. The sign of signification returns to the signifier of value — which is precisely not a value.

Surplus and Deficit

The worker is the castrated victim of a criminal theft. This robbery masquerades as a legal "profit" for the owner. The law is illegal. The "profit" accrues this excess value in the gap, fissure, break, in-between, lacuna, rent — add: void — between wage and price. What is the origin of the light materialism (signifier-signified *qua* sign) of the dollars and coins of the general equivalent? What is the source of the standard — $ — which represents in an abstraction — $69 — and in a speculation — $96 — the materiality of bodies and the physics of the remainder of the stolen exchange-value? The worker's dance — soft-shoe and jazz-hands — on the factory floor cannot produce dollars and coins from the assembly line. How is the extra — gap, fissure, break, in-between, lacuna, rent, void, split, arch — between wage and cost to be translated into the abstraction and speculation of dollars and coins? What sutures the wound of the owner's castration of the worker in the conversion of ~~surplus value~~ into profit? How is the surplus of "profit" converted into the deficit of surplus value from the perspective of the Marxist worker? How is the excess of surplus value translated into the remainder of "profit"?

Surplus and deficit — communism/capitalism, plenitude/scarcity, and penis/clitoris — are antagonistic perspectives on the "one" and the "same" object: the general equivalent. The opposition between surplus and deficit

---

deconstructive Marxism and emphasis on surplus materialism reconfigure the calculation of the value of surplus value as the interval between wage (or means of subsistence of the worker) and the price of the commodity. This measurement captures surplus value (or "profit") on the demand side (MSRP) of the equation rather than on the supply side (labor theory of value) of the dynamic of capitalism. But note that this gap — of which labor-time or commodity price is the measurement — is the identical wedge which makes surplus value (or "profit") possible. The difference between Marx's original labor theory of value and a deconstructive Marxist demand theory of value is merely the choice of metaphor for a void (surplus value or "profit") in the system of capital. The (in)decision of the choice of metaphor — time of production or price on the market — is of different words for the same concept: the rift between value and its surplus value. This demonstration indicates that production, circulation, and production under capitalism are profoundly metaphorical. The various deposits and withdrawals of value are different points of transaction for the same function: the abstraction of value from the production process. The field of abstraction is the domain of the secretion of surplus value. This is the reason that my deconstructive Marxist critique of capitalism emphasizes surplus materiality. This signifier overwhelms the signified, and both of these dimensions can be understood as the site of capitalist exploitation whose letter — departure and arrival, deposit and withdrawal, and surplus and debt — can only be a metaphor for the accumulation and distribution of capital. Marx's labor theory of value and a market supply/demand theory of value are each metaphors for the same process of substitution — of labor-time for surplus value or "profit" for surplus value. The Metaphoricity of the exchange of labor-time and price-tag indicates the violent equivalence of metaphor in a system which is rigged by forced (in)equality. The Other locus of substitution is the site of the accumulation of debt and credit — but whose?

organizes the very possibility of the dialectical materialist arrival unto communism. Marx speaks from the perspective of the owners in order to illuminate the unconscious truth of the system for the workers. This is the Marxist Pedagogy of the Proletariat. Pedagogy is the pervert's will to speak and to write the secret truth of the schizoid's Unreason. Unreason indicates that a function is a mere metaphor in a system of differences without positive terms.

The function of orientation, balance, and organization — generalized coordination — that Derrida says is excluded from play as its proviso is in fact internal to the play. This function is yet another sign in the series of forms-names-centers-substitutes-signs-fetishes and every other word in the system. Under capitalism, the functionality of the general equivalent disappears under the slippage of the sign. The effect is that the structure of dollars and coins ("Current Balance") is fundamentally disoriented, unbalanced, and disorganized. The slip and slide between sign and function in the play of substitution are the limit-thought of deconstruction. Twist and turn are also the horizon of communism — ~~Real~~ — in the exhale of the last breaths of the airs (heirs) of capital. In the case of psychoanalysis, this semiosis and traversal articulate the perverse *Trieb* in which the penis becomes the fetish for the clitoris-substitute and every other word in the system.

This deconstructive slip and slide, Marxist twist and turn, and psychoanalytic semiosis and traversal are only possible if the phallus is not veiled and concealed. As Lacan says: "The phallus can function only when veiled."[14] But the phallus must also be revealed and visible. The pervert must demonstrate that the difference and deferral (*différance*) of dollars and coins make a subtraction from an addition, rend a lack from a fullness, produce a castration from a plenitude, organize a debt from a surplus, and enjoy a Something is Missing from a Nothing is Missing. The excess will never accrue to the owner of "profit." This is so even if its *arche* in work is plain and simple.

The parallactic overlap between the owner and the worker emerges. Something is Missing for the owner and Nothing is Missing for the worker. The worker is Outside of the system of value. There is no value to this excess of ~~surplus value~~. The worker of capitalism is already the pervert of communism. This obscured surplus is the reason that Marx identifies the key word in economics as *surplus* value. The difference is the materiality of the nodal point between the signifier and the sign. The unfathomable and obscene inquiry indicates that *Praxis* is the overlap of practice/theory and signifier-signified/sign within the mode of production of capitalism and the system of nihilism. Communism is the horizon of the objectification and fetishization of all subjects *qua* objects without gain or loss but merely with the slippery excess of materiality. The pervert's fetish is every object in the system. The fetish is the return of the Real from the revolution.

The Arche of Value

Labor is the general equivalent in Marxism. How is the surplus value or "profit" of capitalist exploitation converted from labor and materiality of the signifier into abstraction-materiality of the sign in the Becoming-Function Becoming-General of dollars and coins? The sign is only possible within the limit-thought of capitalism. After capitalism, the signifier liberates humanity from alienated labor, enforced scarcity, and the rule of the general equivalent. The worker is the emancipatory force of the revolution. But this functionality of the worker must be explained by the process whereby the worker becomes an object. The human becomes the general equivalent. Marx refers to this conjuring of dollars and coins from blood and sweat as "commodity fetishism." The heterosexualism of the commodity is the capitalization of labor or the mechanism by which labor is transformed into capital.[15] This inquiry poses the veritable riddle of capitalism and its central function: accumulation. How is capital accumulated by the system? What is the source of coins and dollars? How is the magic of money pulled out of the hats of heroes? How does money breed money? What is the Big Bang of capital that (retro)actively represents the products of labor?

The conundrum is this *arche* of the general equivalent. The object of inquiry is the source of the accumulation of capital in (signifier as sign) but also as (sign) the general equivalent. The issue refers back to deconstruction's sign and function, and to psychoanalysis's fetish and substitute. This exegesis enables a transition toward a discussion of the scene of the discovery of sexual difference in Freud's work. The horizon of the investigation of capitalism is an explanation of the conversion of plenitude into scarcity or the transformation of communism into capitalism. How does the system of $-ism transform a plenitude of labor in the forces of production (what Marx refers to as "overproduction") into a scarcity of exchange-value in the monetary economy (currency and the finity of value)? The issue is the mechanism of a capitalist accumulation. How does accumulation spectrally transfigure — all that is solid melts into air — plenitude into castration, fullness into lack, abundance into scarcity, surplus into deficit, and credit into debt? The worker is the object of this transformation.

The proletarian becomes the vanishing mediator in the relationship between capital and labor. But the mediation of this transition from addition into subtraction and from Nothing is Missing into Something is Missing is not of man as man himself. The work of the spectral intermediary is not performed by man as a worker. It is not done by man as a commodity. The spectralization is not even accomplished by man as an object or a thing. Rather, the work of the vanishing mediator between capital and labor is achieved by a man who becomes the general equivalent of currency. This worker must emerge from an Other. This Other is at the ready to loan the worker to the owner of both the credit and the debt simultaneously. But in what form?

The mystery of capital can be articulated in three dimensions which overlap and converge at the site of the body of the worker. First, the materiality of labor is transformed into the abstraction of the general equivalent of value. This conversion is articulated as either the justified property of the bourgeois capitalist in "profit" or is understood as the rightful property of the proletarian worker in surplus value. The Real parallax of this Proleptic X is the promised return of each according to his need and each according to his ability in communism. This Spiritual S (X) is strictly under erasure even in the present historical moment in which it lives and breathes. How is work translated into money? The center of this angle of the inquiry is the specularization of materiality and the abstraction of physicality. This identifies the disjunction between the signifier and the sign. The object of *Praxis* is the material signifier in the overlap between the signifier in theory and the signifier of the sign in practice. How is the abstract-material sign assembled in practice if the material signifier and abstract signified are divided from each other in theory? Marx implicitly pursues the mechanism of this division and bandage, and aperture and closure. The object of Marx's analysis is the function by which the materiality of the signifier of labor is divided from conceptuality in theory at the same time as its physicality is sutured to abstraction in practice.

The heterosexualism of capital is also posed by two additional sets of questions. The second indicator of the strangeness of capital is the issue of the origin and *arche* of exchange-value itself. The source of both the abstraction and materiality of the general equivalent is unresolved. Value is facilitated by comparison and contrast. What is the metalanguage of value? What is the genesis of the money-form in both its materiality and abstraction? The conceptual specularization of physical labor in and as "profit" and surplus value confronts the aporia of the split between signifier and sign. The third bewilderment is a hybrid of the two antecedent questions. How does surplus value or "profit" become the property of the owners? Does a surplus (n)ever arrive at its destination? What is the advent of currency before and as it circulates in the exchange economy? Practically, money does not grow on trees. But it also does not grow from the body of the worker. How does currency enter the economy? Why do we not know the answer to such an elementary question? The bourgeois jargon of the academic discipline of economics obscures the origin of capital, even as this *arche* is systematically displaced in the process of the circulation of the money-form.

Figure 8.4 The Castrated Worker

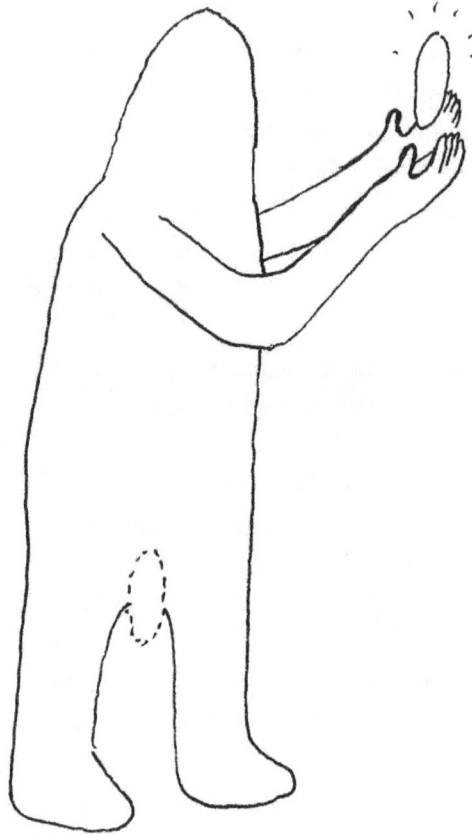

This picture is of the castrated worker (center) whose submission to lack and to the general equivalence of comparison, contrast, and exchange of (sexual) identity and difference manufactures him as a commodified object of capitalism. The object of capitalist exchange is castration. The object of comparison, contrast, and exchange is the absence (penis/not-penis; iPad/not-iPad) in relationship to the standard (phallus, father, currency, sign) of equivalence. Capitalistically, the exchange of castration is the "profit" (surplus value) which is stolen from the proletariat by the bourgeoisie. Capitalist castration in the so-called free market is the essence of exploitation. Capitalist castration is the object of psychical and bodily exchange in the capitalist system. There is a Something is Missing (center) in the selfhood and sociality of the capitalist regime. Capitalism is the exchange and commodification of castration. Capitalist theft and consumer debt are the mechanisms of this castration. In capitalist terms, the worker's commodified penis is stolen from him in the form of the surplus value of "profit." This penis is recuperated by the worker in a debt (signification) that approximately sutures the lack of his own stolen penis. But in communist terms, the worker's incalculable penis (Penis) is stolen from him in the form of the surplus value of "profit." This theft of _____ can only be returned from the future in a singularity (value) which cannot be reduced to the general equivalence of dollars and coins. Phallocentrically, the loss returns as debt. Peniscentrically, the loss returns as the future.

Notes & Sketches —

The first query about the specularization of materiality and the abstraction of physicality is the riddle of the imposition of dollars and coins on the objects which are conferred value in exchange. There is no easy account of the mechanism which renders the theoretical signifier (body, physics) a sign of both materiality and conceptuality (dollars, coins). The theoretical materiality of the signifier must necessarily slip and slide on a trace of specularization — but within theory. At the same time, the practical physicality-abstraction (sign) must inevitably trip on a trace of materiality (the signifier) — but within practice. This unbreakable paradox is the only pivot on which the break between capitalism and communism can be thought at the limit of symbolization. An elusive *Praxis* encircles the Real of the surplus of materialism and the signifier.

This Real cannot be recuperated into the capitalist system. The Real is the parallactic object around which theory and practice cannot articulate the joint or hinge of the sign. The semic excess of practice is this materiality of the signifier whose name is *Praxis*. The Pedagogy of the Proletariat illuminates that there is a surplus of work. This remainder cannot be summarized or (ac)counted in (for) dollars. The "profit" and surplus value emerge as the parallactic gap. The Marxist's surplus value edges toward materiality as the remainder. The capitalist's "profit" gestures toward abstraction as this unrecoverable excess. The Real parallax of the overlap between theory-materiality (signifier-signified) and practice-materiality-abstraction (sign) is the unsymbolizable Real of capitalist accumulation. Capital can be neither spoken nor written. Capitalism cannot speak its own proxy. The system of $-ism cannot symbolize $.

The perverse insight is that value cannot be in excess unless it is materialized in the physical fetish-object of the shoe, lace, fur, jockstrap — and every other object in the system. The so-called overvaluation of the fetish in perversion demonstrates the disjunction between signifier and sign, between materiality and abstraction, and between physicality and speculation. The pervert's libidinal fascination with the representation of the penis illuminates the secret truth of the schizoid's Unreason. The signifying chain of comparison and contrast — Saussure: "in language there are only differences without positive terms"[16] — in equivalence escapes overlap with the brute materiality of the object of fetishistic *jouissance*. The departure and destination of value — from whom to whom — are the puzzle of accumulation. The matter in question is the processes whereby capital spawns supplementary capital. This involves the transition of exchange from the use-value modality of C-M-C' to the exchange-value arrangement of M-C-M'. The third inquiry about the Being of value probes the enigma of the metaphysics of presence — of dollars and coins.

The most unexpected conundrum of capital is a simple demystification of the system itself. How are the abstraction and speculation of the general equivalent possible in a system of labor and the forces of production? What is money? Currency is an exposure of the heterosexualist. But a component of this capitalist heterosexualism is a fear of the clitoris and a scarcity which is always in-process and in-action. It is a castration anxiety about the loss of Nothing is Missing and the maternal phallus. Capital is about the distressed conversion of Nothing is Missing into Something is Missing. Capitalism transforms abundance into lack, surplus into deficit, and excess into debt. Capitalism is the story of the fantasy of castration. Capitalism is also the narration of the defense against perversion. The purpose of currency is to sustain this castration. Debt is the monetary supplement to the ideology of castration. Capitalism explains the Oedipus complex. The castration complex explains capital.

The Fetishism of Value

The parallactic gap between "profit" and surplus value returns to the Freudian idea of the fetish-object as a substitute for the penis and to the Derridean idea of the metaphor as a center for the function in the structure. These relationships are isomorphic. The bedrock of Marx's concept of capitalist exploitation is the redistribution of value in the form of the general equivalent in currency from the proletarian worker to the bourgeois owner. The word for this interval in which use-value is converted into exchange-value — and then stolen — is surplus value. The reason that Marx underscores "surplus" in this theoretical abstraction is that capitalism implicitly posits an additional value which is not an addition to the worker's labor. This excess is generated by the imaginary gap between wage and cost. The capitalist term for this imaginary gap is "profit." The Marxist term for this fancied interval is surplus value. The communist term for this is each according to his need and each according to his ability. My term is the Proleptic X. The Real symbolization is: _____.

The economic antagonism between the bourgeoisie and the proletariat is the effect of the imposition of both an added value for the owner in the form of the presence of "profit" and a subtracted value for the worker in the form of the absence of currency in the wage. The ghost of a castrated absence is the specter of a plentiful presence. The bourgeoisie understands the interval between wage and cost as coincident to and continuous with itself — self-same and self-identical. The general equivalent unflinchingly determines exchange-value in the supply/demand dynamics of the marketplace. The value of both "profit" and surplus value can be calculated and monetized. This value is identical under capitalism because dollars and coins abstract from labor. The exchange-value of identity and difference in calculation overwrites a Sameness⁺ of the incalculability of the labor-process and the use-value. In contrast, the communist intuits the gap between wage and cost as incommensurable and immeasurable. The monetization of materiality cannot unfailingly suture the gap between the physical and the abstract, the bodily and the specular, and the use-value and the exchange-value.

Communism illuminates the failure of the symbolization — speaking and writing — of the Real. This divergence in (in)calculation is the simple but vast fracture between bourgeois economics and Marxist economics. The object of the parallactic gap is ~~what is calculable~~ between "profit" and surplus value. This is the Real around which both capitalist economists and Marxist economists speak and write in *Praxis*. *Praxis* is speaking and writing the signifier. The signifier is pure materiality without conceptuality. There is no speech in communism. There is no text in communism. The capitalist economist imaginarily symbolizes the Real because he reduces this resistance of the body, the physical, and the material to an abstract and specular value of general equivalence. For capitalism, the Real can be (ac)counted (for) as digit, numeral, and integer. For Marxism, the Real can be recounted as surplus value. For communism, this Real cannot be spoken or written because it is resistant to comparison and contrast. The symbolic and the Real coincide: $-ism = S. *Praxis* of capitalist economics is a Practice of Theory. In contrast, the *Praxis* of Marxist economics is a Theory of Practice. There are two modalities of *Praxis*, each contingent on the relationship between the signifier and the sign, and between materiality and materiality-abstraction.

Theory of Practice

The conceptualization of Marxist *Praxis* as the Theory of Practice promises the return to a brute materiality or what Saussure refers to as pure phonology. Words would mobilize stark materiality. Discourse would articulate material marks (sounds and images) in the absence of abstract concepts (ideas and values). Marxism invites the end of man's era of speaking and thinking. Communism heralds the start of man's future of _____. Obversely, if *Praxis* is considered the capitalist Practice of Theory, then a mass of materiality and a swarm of abstraction would articulate naked dollars, coins, and Visa bills. The former case of a Marxist Theory of Practice posits *Praxis* as the production of materialism — bodies, corporealities, use-values, objects, textures, and so on. This materiality is logocentrically severed from abstraction — letters, vocabularies, exchange-values, words, signs, numbers, and so on. The capitalist Practice of Theory presents *Praxis* as the creation of pure ideality of numbers on a MasterCard monthly statement. These digits and integers refer neither to the material signifier nor to the conceptual signified. The horizon of *Praxis* is either gritty materialism or obscene idealism.

The *Praxis* of capitalism is the Practice of Theory. Capitalism exchanges the materiality of the labor process for the speculation of currency. The fissure between profit and surplus value is a fable of the capitalist Practice of Theory. The Real is calculable because it can be reduced to the abstract general equivalence of the Discover card monthly statement. Marx closes the parallactic gap between profit and surplus value. But the price of such substitution of words is the reinscription of the capitalist effort to reduce the Real which cannot be spoken or written to a cost or price in the marketplace. Pervert-communists unveil labor as an excess which overwhelms the calculations of the general equivalent of currency. The commodity cannot be counted because it is sublimely unrepresentable.

This is the specter of the conundrum. How does the communist perspective even speak or write if the parallactic gap between equivalence and incommensurability, exchange-value and labor-process, abstraction and materiality, and sign and signifier — is closed? The critique of capitalist exploitation under the name of surplus value destroys abstraction and speculation. But how does communism speak and write? How does communism speak to and about capitalism? What is the language of communism? What is the diacritical material of the signifier of value after the collapse of the positive entity of the word of signification? What emerges after speaking and writing? How is the transition from Marxism to communism possible?

Languages

In *Reading Capital* (1968), Althusser and Balibar articulate the aporetic word (surplus value) through which Marxism articulates itself against the general equivalent of the sign ("profit"). The idea of surplus value is the fundamental concept which distinguishes Marx's critical economics from the classical economists of capitalism, such as Ricardo and Smith. Althusser and Balibar write,

> Smith and Ricardo always analyze "surplus value" in the form of profit, rent and interest, with the result that it is never called by its name, but always disguised beneath other names, that it is not conceived in its "generality"; as distinct from its "forms of existence": profit, rent and interest.[17]

The terms which are used by Althusser and Balibar have a specific sense because the object of their critique of the capitalist economists is based on an effort of translation between two radically different languages. The first language is the capitalist speaking and writing of exchange-value and the abstractions of the sign in practice. The second language is a communist inscription of use-value and the materialities of the signifier in theory.

This endeavor to translate between a discourse of numbers, prices, and wages in capitalism and a text of goods, services, and uses in communism is exemplary of the tricky aperture-closure of the parallactic gap. This discontinuity between two mutually exclusive interpretations — class antagonism — on the "one" and the "same" object is the effort to symbolize the Real parallax. This object is a puzzle to identify in a word because its self-same and self-identical essence is in question within its extimate split. The "surplus value" and "profit, rent, and interest" are a Derridean "sameness which is not identical." The words are best understood as the marks of "forms of existence" ("profit, rent, and interest") which are veiled underneath the "generality" of surplus value. These metaphors must be translated into the proper "generality": surplus value.

The Marxist point is that the extraction of exchange-value from the proletarian is continuous with an excess, surplus, and remainder of use-value. This surplus of goods and services cannot be assimilated into the system. There is an extra materialism which escapes general equivalence. Ricardo and Smith identify this scission as a "form." Marx critically isolates the gap as surplus value. The two words are substitutes for a function. This function is the center for Derrida and the fetish for Freud. The entirety of the system is a function for "itself."

The unassimilable signifier of the worker's excess materiality indicates that the general equivalent cannot (a)count (for) all of the potential exchange-value in the system. This surplus in exchange-value is the object of the accumulation of capital. This infinite will to capitalize labor must confront the Real of materiality. The Real is the excess of the signifier which cannot be reincorporated ("accumulated") by capital. Accumulation is its own limit. This limit is the signifier. This resistant Real of the signifier is the proviso of the capitalist neurotic desire for its *objet petit a*. This contrasts with a perverse *Trieb* and a dizzy aim/less wander. This Real is the obstacle to an absolute territorialization of labor under the rule of the general equivalent. Capital symbolizes the Real as the limit of accumulation. The essence of capital is neurotic desire and the slip and slide of its object of accumulation. The essence of the Real is perverse *Trieb* and its resistance to any proper object. A materiality of the signifier invariably escapes capitalization and accumulation.

Materialism is the object of capitalist accumulation. The object is the obstacle to the realization of accumulation. Capitalism can only be structured according to the Something is Missing of castration and scarcity. Crazily, a wax in accumulation simultaneously implies a wane in capital. The condition of (im) possibility of the system cannot be articulated or identified in its excess as the Proleptic X or even as communism. This remainder — and every other word in the system — escapes symbolization absolutely. The Real always returns to the "same place"[18] because the failure of representation is "a sameness which is not identical," as Derrida says, or, as I impossibly speak and write it, a Sameness⁺.

The resistance of the surplus of labor is that under capitalism there are too many goods and services rather than not enough products and resources. There is overemployment rather than underemployment. This excess in the system renders exchange-value (as Marx puts it) and signification (as Saussure puts it) profoundly sublime. The dollar and the coin, and the sign and the word, cannot be captured by the monetary system and the language system. The gap between capitalism and communism can only be spoken and written as the Proleptic X of the Real. This stolen X will be returned from the future as the S of each according to his need and each according to his ability. This S of the promised future and the s of the extant $-ism are isomorphic to each other. But a gap persists between the surplus of labor and its reintegration into the system as a posited exchange-value of dollars and coins. Bodies will matter. The future of communism is a sublime unrepresentability. This Real is internal to capitalism itself. The United States of America is already communist. But she does not know it yet.

The blind spot around which capitalism is organized is the Real. Accumulation strives to speak and write this surplus with dollars and coins. This Real is both the foundation and the dissolution of capital. The remainder of the Real is labor. This is the reason that capitalism must consistently squander this excess of labor. Overproduction is the necessary proviso for the arrival of communism. Overproduction is also the essence of capitalist monetary practices. This excess of labor — surplus value — can only return in the future of communism. This remainder returns to the "same place" of the Real when the general equivalent is banished from the processes of mediation between labor and object. The use-value of the sublime appears in communism. This is a speaking without utterance and a writing without text.

Communism enjoys the production and the consumption of use-values which are incommensurable with each other and singular in their existence. Communism prohibits capitalist accumulation because a postscarcity and postphallic system need not burn the excess, destroy the surplus, or dispose of the remainder. These extras are produced by the system as both its *Eros* and *Thanatos*. Under communism, accumulation of the exchange-value of capital disappears. Under capitalism, this accumulation of debt twists and turns around the Real of this excess of incalculable ~~use-value~~. Every word in the system which is encircled in the symbolization of speaking, writing, and calculating the resistant Real disappears with the destruction of the general equivalent. The Real inherits the symbolic. Communism displaces capitalism. This switcheroo has already happened.

The remainder of excess is the essence of communism. The surplus is the presupposition of capitalism. The manifest specter of this use-value materiality is the latent truth of communism. Communism is the terror of capitalism. The loss in the transition to communism is not the remainder of the Proleptic X. Rather, accumulation and capitalization are outstripped in communism. The sublime Proleptic X — what cannot be spoken or written — of the capitalist surplus is finally reincorporated into the S as the center of an s. This S (s) is beyond the morality of good and evil, outside of the nihilism of value, and retardant of the general equivalent. S = s and s ≠ S. Communism emerges because of the gap between currency and objects in the system. The heterosexualism of the commodity is that it appears as if there is a scarcity in goods and services. But the Marxist truth is that there is a scarcity in dollars and coins. Capitalism converts the penis into the clitoris under the phallocentric logic: "a man has a penis and a Woman does not have a penis." The revolution rewrites phallocentric scarcity as the "penis ~~is~~ the clitoris." Being will be under erasure. Dollars and coins will not be counted. The text will not be spoken or written. What emerges is a substitution which is precisely not a substitution which is —

Commodity Fetishism

Marx's concept of commodity fetishism articulates the monstrous transformation of man into a commodity. The heterosexualism of the commodity is that it is simultaneously an inert object and an animate subject, an inactive thing and an active person, and an insensate widget and a sentient man. This heterosexualism is the effect of the transformation of man into object and human into thing. Marx (and later, Lukács) understand this process as "reification."[19] The commodification of man reduces him to an exchange-value within a nihilistic system. As a commodity, the only utterance man can make is, "How much am I worth?" This question of exchange-value is mediated by the general equivalent of currency. In his book, *Symbolic Economies after Marx and Freud* (1973), Jean-Joseph Goux outlines the other general equivalents: the father for social relations, the phallus for sexual relations, and the sign for linguistic relations.[20] The enforced sale of man's labor in the marketplace subordinates his essence as a "social being,"[21] as Marx says, to the value of the monthly statement of an American Express card. The subject becomes an object which is mediated in its value by forces which exceed it.

Marx defines the essence of man as his activity of labor rather than as his exchange-value. The subordination of the human to a nihilistic exchange-value reduces him to a commodified effect of the system of $-ism. Reification makes man become the signifier of the material body of the exchange-value of the signified and the sign. Man is transformed into the material signifier. The signification of the word overwrites this material use-value with abstract exchange-value. The worker becomes the material and physical object which is inscribed with the abstraction and speculation of the general equivalent. The worker *qua* signifier is stamped with the signified in the process of the generation of the sign of the commodity as the proviso of the emergence of the general equivalent. But an unrecoverable surplus of materiality cannot be spoken or written. The excess insists as the force of the Real. How does this material Real hinder the smooth operation of the capitalist function of the accumulation of exchange-value?

Man is split between the raw materiality of labor, production, activity, use-value, and the theoretical signifier of materiality, on the one hand, and the physical-speculative conjoinment of body and mind, material and abstraction, and signifier and signified as the sign in practice, on the other hand. The process of commodity fetishism is the transformation of the signifier into the sign. The essence of capital is the conversion of the worker as signifier of labor into the worker as sign of fetishistic exchange-value. As sign and commodity, the worker's materiality (labor, productivity, activity, use-value, and the practical sign of material-abstraction) is the excess which escapes capture in the sign. This sign is mediated by the general equivalent. The materiality of the signifier in theory is internal to the body-mind of the sign in practice. This materialism is the surplus. This remainder of bodies exceeds the general equivalent itself. Marx names this excess labor the *lumpenproletariat*. Western capitalism identifies the surplus as the unemployed.

This signifier of materiality vamooses the sign. The worker is brainless — pure phonology in communism. The general equivalent is by necessity at a castration and a deficit in relationship to the excess and surplus of the body of the worker. This signifier of the body of the worker is the stark materiality of the Proleptic X: _____. This Spiritual S (X) illuminates the Real sublime division between capitalist exchange-value and communist resistance of the Real. The Real is surplus, and it is all the same excess because it cannot be divided by exchange-value. The heterosexualism of the worker *qua* commodity is the surplus of the body. This remainder is the unassimilable signifier which cannot be (ac)counted (for) by the system. The queerness is a body which does not fit.

The essence of communism is this remainder of signifiers and materialities of the worker. This signifier is the doubled overlap of a materiality in theory and a materiality in practice. This doubled overlap and superpositional crossover between theory and practice, and between signifier and sign, illuminate a stark economic fact. There will always be a surplus and remainder of material in the system, by definition. Castration is a fantasy of capitalism. The pervert sutures the wound of the lack in the place of the maternal phallus with the use-value of the fetish. Perversion is the communist Real response to the fantasy of capital. The pervert is communist because he disavows castration. The fetish is the inevitable excess of penis in the system. The foreskin is the queer specter of communism.

The penis is represented by an otherwise — fur, lace, shoe, and jockstrap — because there is a surplus of penis. Capitalist accumulation overwrites the materiality of the signifier of the worker with the exchange-value of goods and services in the process of commodity fetishism. Capital accumulates man as general equivalence in reification. Accumulation requires that there be simultaneously both a deficit and a surplus of bodies. The worker's body is split between the material signifier of theory and the material-abstract sign of practice. The essence of communism is material labor. Goods and services are located in the fissure — parallactic gap — between the brute materiality of the signifier of theory and the suture of materiality and speculation of the sign of practice. Communist man resists the reincorporation — accumulation — of man *qua* commodity by the mediation of the general equivalent. The Marxist theory of man strives to escape the Becoming-Commodity of man in commodity fetishism.

These concepts of selfhood and sociality must be transformed in the transition from capitalism to communism, from s to S, and from $-ism to Spirit. The worker's heterosexualist objectness makes him entirely determined in exchange-value by the general equivalent. But the slip and slide of the body beyond the capture of the practical sign disrupt the system of accumulation because this excess of the theoretical signifier (labor, productivity, activity, and use-value) is the raw materiality upon which the general equivalent marks the commodity with exchange-value. The theoretical signified is the general equivalent which is precisely outstripped — doubly — by the practical-theoretical *Praxis* of the signifier. There is an excess of material in *Praxis*. There is a surplus of use-value in *Praxis*. There is a remainder of goods and services in *Praxis*. But there is scarcity in the practice of economic theory in capitalism. The excess is the reason that Marx can write the word as *surplus* value.

The process of accumulation of capital is organized by the resistance of the Real of the signifier — of the materiality and the labor of the worker. The extraction of "profit" from the worker articulates the interval between wage and price in speculative exchange-value in dollars and coins. This exchange-value is determined by supply/demand dynamics in the marketplace. Abstraction in the sign (the practical signified) of the materiality of the theoretical signified reduces the worker to a commodity. Abstraction extracts value which can be compared, contrasted, and exchanged. Fetishization enables the owner to steal a surplus of "profit" from the signifier. The mystery of capital is presented in this process of the representation of this "surplus value." What is the origin or *arche* of the currency of the general equivalent — dollars and coins? The worker's efficiency produces an accumulation of value in the escalation of productivity, the extension of technology, and the mass multiplication of commodities. A "profit" (surplus value) is extracted in the gap between wage and price. This aperture will forever increase as yet more goods and services are produced on the assembly line. Marx's principal argument is that this increase in exchange-value on the side of supply intensifies the criminal theft of value from the worker in surplus value.

However, the enigma of capital is even more paradoxical. How does an increase in the supply of the theoretical material signifier — goods and services — translate into an increase in the supply of the practical material-speculative sign — the general equivalent? The supply of goods and services "accumulates" from the factory floor. But what is the source of dollars and coins of exchange-value which also "accumulate" in speculation? This quandary between the supply of commodities and the medium of the general equivalent appears because the general equivalent must be a function of *finity* within a system of *infinity*. The general equivalent is a function of *finite* exchange-value because it compares, contrasts, exchanges, measures, calculates, and so on. But the accumulation of exchange-value in signs, numbers, integers, digits, APR balance transfers, and so on is strictly *infinite*. This *infinity* is the paradoxical reason that exchange-value is *finite*. There is always a Something is Missing in the monetary system. The general equivalent is founded on the organizational principle of the phallocentric version of the clitoris. The penis is the effect of an ever present diminution of capital. Heterosexualistly, capitalist *accumulation* is based on *debt*. Addition + = - and subtraction - = +. This loss can only be impossibly recuperated by further submission to this same principle. The system is designed to *produce debt*.

Clitoral Communism

The unassimilable signifier is the lack in the place of the clitoris. The female genitalia organizes the system as the center. But, at the same time, the clitoris is absent from this same system: "a man has a penis and a Woman does not have a penis." The clitoris and its bodily materiality have no exchange-value because they are the negativity of the system of sexual difference. The heterosexualist words for the clitoris — "does not have a penis" — express this negativity which cannot be reincorporated into the system. The manic accumulation of the system battles to capitalize this negativity. The materiality of the clitoris *qua* the Real of sexual-capitalist difference resists this assimilation. The clitoris cannot be capitalized and accumulated. The clitoris is already communist. The archetypal perverse fetishist is the lesbian. Capital accumulates this unsymbolizable clitoris — or what psychoanalysis refers to as the Real of sexual difference. The negativity of the Real Clitoris under the rule of phallocapitalocentrism is such that it spurns all efforts to subordinate this sexual-figural excess to general equivalence. The ~~clitoris~~ cannot be spoken or written. But the lesbian can enjoy this clitoris in the feminine *jouissance* of the Other. This is the reason that Freud can compulsively articulate the enigma of sexual difference, "What is a Woman?" The essence of femininity is an unrepresentable sublimity because its phallocentric negativity configures its objectness as an absence of value, comparison, contrast, exchange, calculation, and so on. Not only is the _____ without words, but it also has no exchange-value except as the Outside to the precarious exchangeability of the penis.

But the ~~clitoris~~ is also the object of a never ending effort to capture the resistant Real of this theoretical signifier of the clitoris — "What is a Woman?" — as material signified of man's desire. The clitoris is the material excess of the system of the sign and the general equivalent of capital. The Woman's clitoris labors on the assembly line. The Woman's value can only be articulated as the remainder of the "profit" or the surplus value which is otherwise accumulated from the rent between wage and price. The value of the clitoris is negativity. The clitoris is resistant to the general equivalent and secured to the factory floor as signifier and labor. But how is the Woman's surplus represented in the system? How does the exchange-value of the clitoris (Proleptic X, and so on) evade calculation in words and marks by the accumulation of capital? How does the system of $-ism work to make good on the Woman's loss? The axis of Marxism and psychoanalysis illuminates the linchpin of the (im)possibility of exchange-value and the effort to utter and script the negativity of value. The purpose of capital is to *accumulate debt*.

Ex Nihilo — Accumulation

Marx's discussion of the central concept of surplus value underscores the extraction of exchange-value. Abstraction of currency is the representation of labor in its in-process, in-action transformation of nature into culture. The extraction of value between the wage of the worker in the factory and the price of the commodity on the market is the instant of exploitation.[22] Capitalists name this difference "profit." The stolen value is distributed to investors. These bankers move integers and decimals from the left-side of the computer screen to the right-side of the same screen. This is the lazy labor which is involved in the legal theft of surplus value. Bankers are paid to make sure that the integers and decimals on the right-side of the screen match — but not quite — the numbers and quotients on the left-side of the screen. The gap in digits and units between the screen *Fort!* and the screen *Da!* is what Marx defines as surplus value. This *surplus* value must be converted into a *deficit* value in order to organize the structure between the left-side of the screen and the right-side of the same screen. Accumulation is the risky movement of the equivalence of the sign from subject to subject, whether individual investor, corporate earnings, national coffer, and so on.

The trick in the translation is to note the point of departure (arrival) and the site of destination (origin) of the letters and numbers of these trans(actions/lations) in the hazy light of monitors, keyboards, and the occasional Casio calculator from the early-80s. The general equivalent is the guarantee of the binary structure of the relationship between debt and credit, scarcity and abundance, deficit and surplus, and the left-side of the screen and the right-side of the same screen. The solvency of the general equivalent is the foundation of the potential equitability of the left-side of the screen and the right-side of the screen. But the condition of the circulation of the currency is a necessary imbalance — excess, deficit, surplus, lack, remainder, loss, extra, absence, plus, minus, left-side of the screen, right-side of the screen, *Fort!*, *Da!* — between the creditor and the debtor. This imbalance is necessary in order for capital to be accumulated from debt to credit, scarcity to abundance, deficit to surplus, and left-side of the screen to right-side of the screen. The system is structured by the negativity and finity of the general equivalent. The system will always generate a debt of Something is Missing. A communist Nothing is Missing (penis, pervert's maternal phallus, and fetish-object) can only be achieved Outside of a system of comparison and contrast in which limitation is otherwise the basal logic of exchange-value.

Figure 8.5 Accumulation of Debt

This picture illuminates the relationship between manic capitalist accumulation (+) and depressed capitalist debt (-) in the castration and alienation of the worker. The surplus of objects and commodities parallels the excess of the signifier and materiality in the staggered overlap of the *theory* of the signifier and the signified, on the one hand, and the *practice* of the sign, on the other hand. The three neurotics (above, center) represent the workers who participate in the capitalist system of: first, alienation from self, other, labor process, and sensuous being; and second, occlusion of the endless limit of capitalist accumulation. The paradoxical effect of the essence of capitalist economics — accumulation — is the *production of debt*. Accumulation and debt are flip-sides of the same circulation of currency in the economy. A contraction of the money supply accelerates the increase in debt. An expansion of the money supply also accelerates an increase in debt. The reason that the circulation of currency — expanded or contracted — increases debt is that this currency must be returned to the bank. The bank is the *arche* of all exchange-value (currency) in the system. The worker is the *arche* of all use-value (goods and services) in the system. The bank is worthless but wealthy. The worker is worthy but poor.

Notes & Sketches —

This constitutive absence is a castration of the general equivalent. Castration is the proxy of the function of the standard. This essential loss indicates the necessity of the general equivalent to a system of calculation. The circulation and accumulation of capital must be guaranteed by a currency which can enforce the loss and gain of exchange-value. The supply of labor is necessarily in excess of the currency because the productivity of the worker escalates over time. But the supply of the general equivalent — dollars and coins — is necessarily limited because its function is to (ac)count for a system of (im)balances. Production exceeds not consumption but rather dollars and coins. How is surplus value or "profit" monetized? The finity of currency castrates the plenitude of labor and its Nothing is Missing. How does the Nothing is Missing of labor produce an absence and a Something is Missing? Where does money come from? Why do we not know the answer to such an elementary question?

Marx's work in the *Grundrisse* (1857-58) responds to the conundrum of the monetization of surplus value in "profit" by the abstraction of materiality and the transformation of the signifier into the sign. He unpacks the contradictions in production, circulation, and consumption of value under capitalism. The general equivalent is sublimely unrepresentable. The dollar and coin cannot be captured by speech or pinned in text. In the *Grundrisse* (1857-58), Marx writes,

> Note that money becomes an end instead of a means and that capital, as the superior form of mediation, everywhere *establishes* the inferior form, labor, simply as a source of surplus value (my emphasis).[23]

Marx says that the capitalization of labor is the source of surplus value. Surplus value can only be understood as an unsymbolizable Real — unspoken and unwritten — materiality of the signifier. This Outside is unrecuperable within the system of exchange-value. Communism is a postphallic and postscarcity brainless pure phonological utopia. The capitalist can steal this value only insofar as he is able to convert the signifier into the sign. This transformation of worker into dollar makes mediation in the marketplace possible. The activity of labor in production of use-value is compromised in the ascendance of capital. Marx refers to it as the process of "alienation."[24]

Less from More

The capitalist appropriates materiality for the purposes of exchange under the sign of currency. The ommision in this passage is not the "establishment" of labor (which he explains: "as a source of surplus value") but the "establishment" of capital. What are the origin and *arche* of dollars, coins, and Diner's Club charge cards (RIP) as the mediators between buyers and sellers in the accumulation of stolen capital or surplus value? In the first volume of *Capital* (1865-66), Marx commits to this same blind spot,

> The circulation of money as capital is, on the contrary, an end in itself, for the expansion of value takes place only within this *constantly renewed movement*. The circulation of capital therefore has *no limits* (my emphasis).[25]

Capital may have "no limits" in its accumulation of the general equivalence of currency in the exchange relationship of M-C-M'. But this "circulation of money" is an "end" as such. The "ends of man," as Derrida titles his essay from 1973, are the end(s) of capital.[26] These ends indicate that capital is profoundly divorced from use-value, materiality, and the signifier. The "constantly renewed movement" of M-C-M' begs a fundamental question. How is this "renewal" possible? How do dollars and coins "renew" themselves? The "profit" is the extraction of surplus value from the laborer. The result is an excess which cannot be incorporated into the symbolic system of capital. How is this remainder (not) represented in the system?

Contra Marx's articulation, there is a limit to the circulation of capital. The limit is the castration and scarcity which are enforced — by definition — in the exchange of currency. The general equivalent of currency is the economic principle of castration. The use of currency is only coherent as a symbolic system if there is a limitation of value. The monetary system will necessarily be situated in an economy of Something is Missing. Capital will always be subordinate to the logic of phallocentric sexual difference. This castration (what capitalists call "scarcity") is not a dearth of the use-value of commodities in the signifier and its material excess in the body of the worker. Rather, the castration is a lack in the exchange-value of currency in the sign and its circulation as capital in the system. A cut of the cash is a circumcision of the penis.

The expansion of capital in profit is the exploitation of the worker in the theft of surplus value. This crime can only be committed if the signifier is converted into the sign and brute materiality is transformed into speculative exchange. At the same time, this can only happen in the addition of general equivalence. The general equivalent represents as the sign this excess in labor or the "constantly renewed movement" of the circulation of capital. The surplus value is stolen by the owners from the materiality of the worker's use-value. But it must also be monetized in order to be translated into "profit" and then capital. This additional currency cannot be extracted from the worker whose labor is the material excess which "profit" appropriates. Instead, the exchange-value of abstraction and speculation of the general equivalent is *borrowed* from the Other. The excess words are borrowed from another locus in the system. This illuminates Marx's reference to the "constantly renewed movement" which has "no limits." The circulation of capital is founded on the exploitation of the laborer in the extraction of surplus value. This exploitation and its corollary alienation are only possible in the transformative monetization of this stark materiality of the signifier by borrowed currency from elsewhere in the system. Capitalist accumulation is profoundly organized by debt. Crazily, the addition is the subtraction. But such a relationship to the Real is sublimely inarticulable in speech and writing. The bizarre symbolization of addition = subtraction must be inscribed as ~~addition = subtraction~~.

Debt

The "constantly renewed movement" of M-C-M' is a series of transactions between debtors and creditors. An increase in the excess of materiality is converted into the abstraction of currency in borrowing and lending. This conversion can only result in an increase of debt, *in toto*. The more capital circulates toward Nothing is Missing, the more capital stumbles onto Something is Missing. The pervert's fetish sutures the gap of this capitalist castration. The closer that the system approaches communist abundance in the materiality of goods and services in use-value, the greater the accumulation of debt and deficit in exchange-value. The reason that the USA national debt is astronomical ("$19 trillion dollars") is the *surplus of goods*. Capitalism accumulates this debt which is borrowed from the Other on surplus. Crazily, the system *borrows a deficit on a credit*, and it *borrows a debt from a surplus*. The Other's credit on this surplus of Nothing is Missing is itself lost to lack by being transfigured into Something is Missing upon the loan to the debtor party. The representation of labor — the translation of the material signifier into the speculative sign — is only possible in an economy of castration. Speaking and writing with the sign are the labor of lack. This labor must be revised in order to reverse the $-istic prioritization of speculation above materiality. The surplus of goods and services must be freed from the shackles of the scarcity of dollars and coins.

Figure 8.6 The Marxist Future of the Pervert-Schizoid-Woman

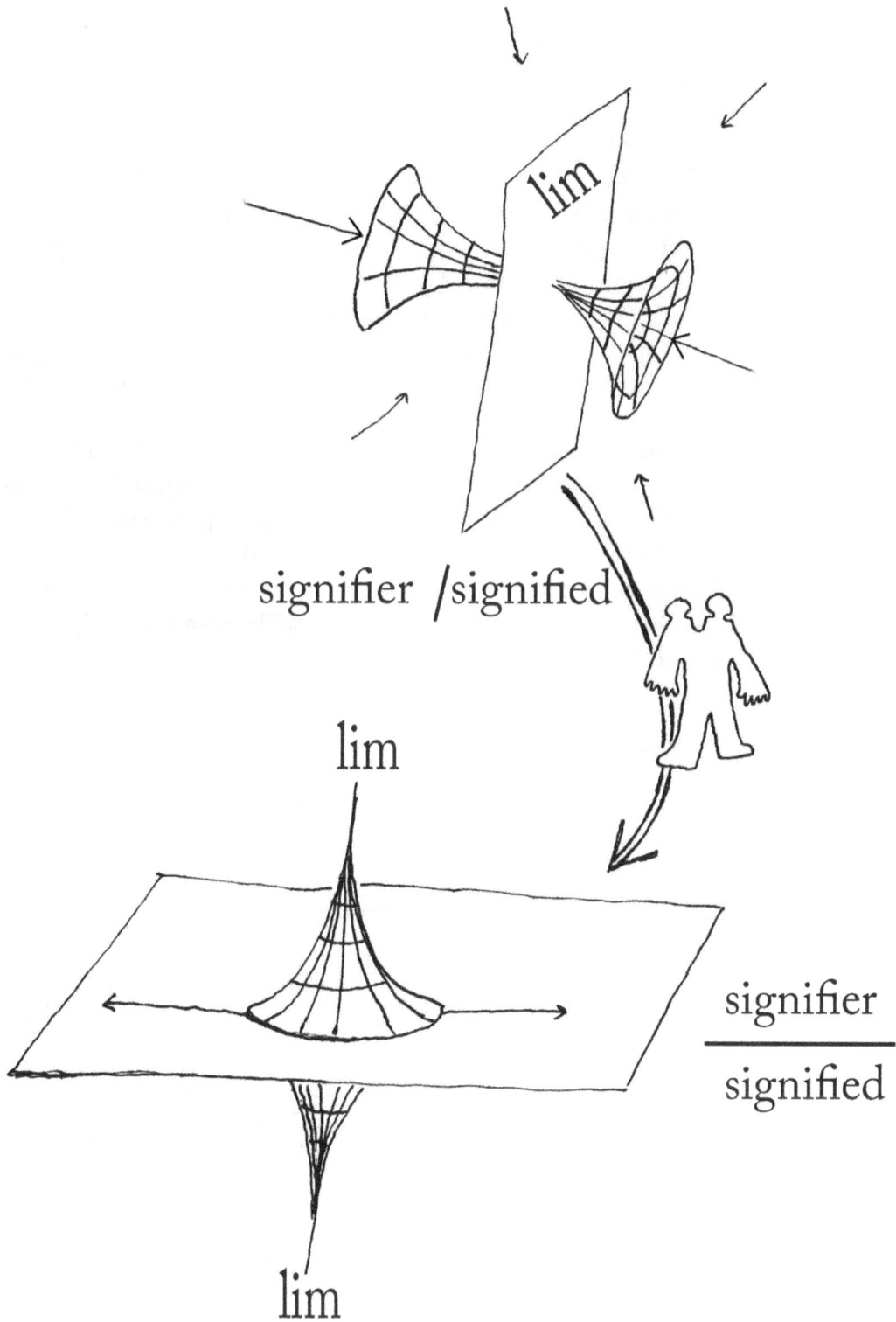

lim

signifier /signified

lim

lim

$$\frac{\text{signifier}}{\text{signified}}$$

The appearance of the Pervert-Schizoid-Woman in the transition from capitalism to communism obliterates the conventional $-istic structure of signification. The transition elaborates a reconfiguration of the limits of Marxist temporality and capitalist surplus. The parallactic convergence of the limited and the infinite vanishes in the expelled center of debt. This work is performed through *Praxis*. The excess signifier is reintegrated into the system through the political and aesthetic dimensions. The gap between signifier and signified becomes the medium of an inequivalent exchange of the value of signification. The revolutionary rearrangement of the limits of the organizational gravity function promises a world of infinite possibilities of value rather than a system of finite limitations on signification. A limit-thought is indicated by the signifier but suppressed by the system. The signifier is liberated by the possibility of positive articulation rather than by the necessity of absence (and the absence *of* absence, and so on). The capitalist regime of castration posits that any unit of text (commodity) in the signifying chain is severed from itself by the general equivalent. The limit-thought of the Real Signifier designates the impossible boundaries and bonds of the capitalist galaxy. The subject of $-ism is limited by signification because its *Praxis* enacts the impossibility of the infinitely removed center of the sign. But emergent communism is arranged by the deconstructive signification (value) of this severance. *Praxis* is the signification of the split of the excess of the signifier. The excess of the signifier is resignified as a surplus rather than as a debt. A capitalist system which is based on deficit (penis, commodity, and signification) is flipped into a communist logic which is structured by plenitude (clitoris, use-value, and value). This communism is neurotically foreclosed (*rejet névrotique*), but it is also paradoxically present even in its negated absence. $-ism is at the origin of communism. The figure (above) parallels the other side of the parallactic convergence in the obverse place in the Other. The Other is mobilized in the communist flip from scarcity to each according to his need and each according to his ability. The subject *qua* object is flipped onto the same side of the equation as the subject *qua* subject. The Other-Logic is incorporated into the ego. The communist future is the horizon of the alterity of this radically Other of the Pervert-Schizoid-Woman.

Notes & Sketches —

The question of the origin of currency is an inquiry into the monetization of labor, the specularization of materiality, and the abstraction of the signifier. This work is visible in Marx's circular explanation of the process of the causal relationship between the circulation of capital and the extraction of surplus value. In a revelatory passage, Marx writes,

> We have seen how money is changed into capital; how through capital surplus value is made, and from surplus value more capital. But the accumulation of capital *presupposes* surplus value; surplus value *presupposes* capitalistic production; capitalistic production *presupposes* the pre-existence of considerable masses of capital of labor power in the hands of producers of commodities. The whole movement, therefore, seems to turn in a vicious circle, out of which we can only get by supposing a primitive accumulation (previous accumulation of Adam Smith) preceding capitalistic accumulation; an accumulation not the result of the capitalist mode of production, but its starting-point (my emphasis).[27]

This citation traces the processes of the transformation of money into capital, then of capital into surplus value, and then of surplus value into more capital. Marx says that this capitalist accumulation must "presuppose" surplus value — which itself must "presuppose" production — which itself must "presuppose" the concentration of the capital of labor power by the owners. The advent of accumulation is the general equivalence of currency: "we have seen how money is changed into capital." But the origin of money is "presupposed." The entrance of money into the system of circulation is unexplained and inscrutable. Where does money — dollars and coins and Banana Republic credit cards (mine: $500 limit) — come from? The accumulation of capital entails surplus value. But the source of the monetization — symbolization of the Real — of this materiality is obscure.

The advent of capitalist accumulation must be a concentration or "primitive accumulation" of capital and labor. Nothing is Missing is at the origin of the system. Plenitude in the communist mode of production is the "starting-point" of the relations of the production of capitalism. Communism is antecedent to capitalism. The accumulation of capital "presupposes" communism. This presupposition is the unconsciously repressed of the capitalist mode of production. The abundance is repressed in order to facilitate the relations of the production of capital. This organization is contingent upon an enforced scarcity (castration and lack) in the system. Capitalism sustains itself in an economy of borrowing and lending. Debt is the organizational precept of the general equivalent. Dollars and coins enforce *finite* value on an otherwise *infinite* potentiality of labor and the signifier. The vicious circle of capitalism is the "primitive accumulation" at the advent of the system. The primitive is a surplus of Nothing is Missing. This abundance must be converted into a debt of Something is Missing. This transformation is necessary in order to underpin the ideology of scarcity and the structure of capitalism.

The vicious circle is a system of accumulation in which an *addition* of value must be translated into a *subtraction* of this same value. The surplus of labor and the excess of the signifier are the split in materiality itself. The split is the resistant Real or *objet petit a*. The Real cannot be captured in an accumulation which has no limits. The destination of the remainder of the use-value of the worker's labor escapes extraction by abstraction and speculation. The signifier is sublimity. Words have no signified in theory. Speaking and writing are in excess of themselves in practice. The surplus is squandered by the system. The excess returns to neither the worker nor the owner. Unmarked material haunts the system as the spectral center of the structure. This function escapes the configuration of the center, substitute, sign, fetish, and so on. The unrepresentable function of the center of the structure is the excluded materiality which is exiled to the Outside of the system only to return from the revolution as the spectral destabilization of the structure itself.

The signifier promises a communism in which S rather than $-ism is elevated to the dignity of *das Ding*.[28] Lacan approximates the Thing with the maternal phallus. This present absence is the object of the pervert's Other *jouissance* of drive. This Real returns from the future in the promise of the Proleptic X. The X is the unsymbolizable ~~use-value~~ of work. The X cannot be reduced to the abstract exchange-value of dollars and coins. $-ism will be spoken and written as S. This S is the Sameness⁺ of every word in the present system. Money may (not) grow on trees in the capitalist system because there is no (a) scarcity of trees. But the Real of labor persists as the unassimilable signifier. Excess in the system cannot be fetishized by capital. Accumulation appears *ex nihilo* from an originary communist accumulation in which Nothing is Missing. But the value of labor materializes from the body and skill of the worker. The worker's sensual and social being builds an earth and a world for the future of a communist accumulation that also has no limits. But this limitless labor will be the ending rather than the beginning of Something is Missing. As Marx says in the *Grundrisse* (1857-58), "At one point there used to be nothing missing."[29]

Parallax Economics

The capitalist parallactic gap between "profit" and surplus value is a tear in the system of representation. This structure is arranged by the general equivalent (dollars and coins) in the quantification of goods and services in exchange-value. The origin of the gap is the capitalist system. The system accumulates capital. This capital is produced by a hole in the symbolic order of the general equivalent. The corporation opens an interval between the wage of the worker and the price of the commodity. Capitalism must tear into the equilibrium of the system in order to generate surplus capital. The so-called growth in a capitalist economy is the result of this gap between wage and price. But the crucial aspect of this blown hole is that it is fundamentally *representational* in the system of dollars and coins. Currency displaces labor as the *sin qua non* of the capitalist system. This isolates the commodity fetishism which alarms Marx. The gap between wage and price — "profit" or surplus value — must be represented by the light materialist (paper and metal) ideality of the general equivalent.

Circulation and accumulation of capital are simply the effort to represent the Real object of the parallax. Under capitalism, the exclusive representational medium is dollars and coins. Currency must be produced in order to make good on the loss between price and wage. Representation sutures the gap in the historical march of the productivity of labor. Currency represents this hole. There is a *surplus* of goods and services, but there is a *deficit* of dollars and coins. This aperture between wage and price must be sutured by representation. Capitalist accumulation is based on the generation of this gap. The money supply sutures the castration which is the effect of "profit." Corporate earnings produce debt. The practical and theoretical *a priori* of capitalism is loss. Capitalism is a system of dysthymic grief. The symptom of this unhappy depression is frenzied mania.

The Real object of the parallax can be defined as "profit" or surplus value. But the value of this interval can be substituted — like a metaphor — across the body of the economy. The "profit" which is stolen by the corporation must be represented elsewhere in the economy. This surplus value ("profit") which is purloined by the corporation is re-represented in the debt of the consumer. The consumer borrows representation from banks (personal loans, student loans, business loans, credit cards, mortgages, lines of credit, ATM fees, and so on) in order to purchase the goods and services which he has himself produced. The stolen value from the worker is borrowed as debt from this same worker in order to purchase the goods and services. *Profit is equivalent to debt.* Surplus value is the concept which indicates the Real object of the parallax between the "one" and the "same" object of the interval between wage and price. Debt pays for "profit," and loans substitute for stolen wage. The worker is forced to borrow the value which is stolen from him by the corporation. The worker is stolen from twice: first, in the rift between wage and price; and second, in the chink between debt and wage. The heterosexualism of this relationship is that the Real object of the parallax (debt, profit, or surplus value) is (re)represented in the economy twice. The proft is skimmed from the debt, and the debt is skimmed — but from where?

Figure 8.7 Fetish Future

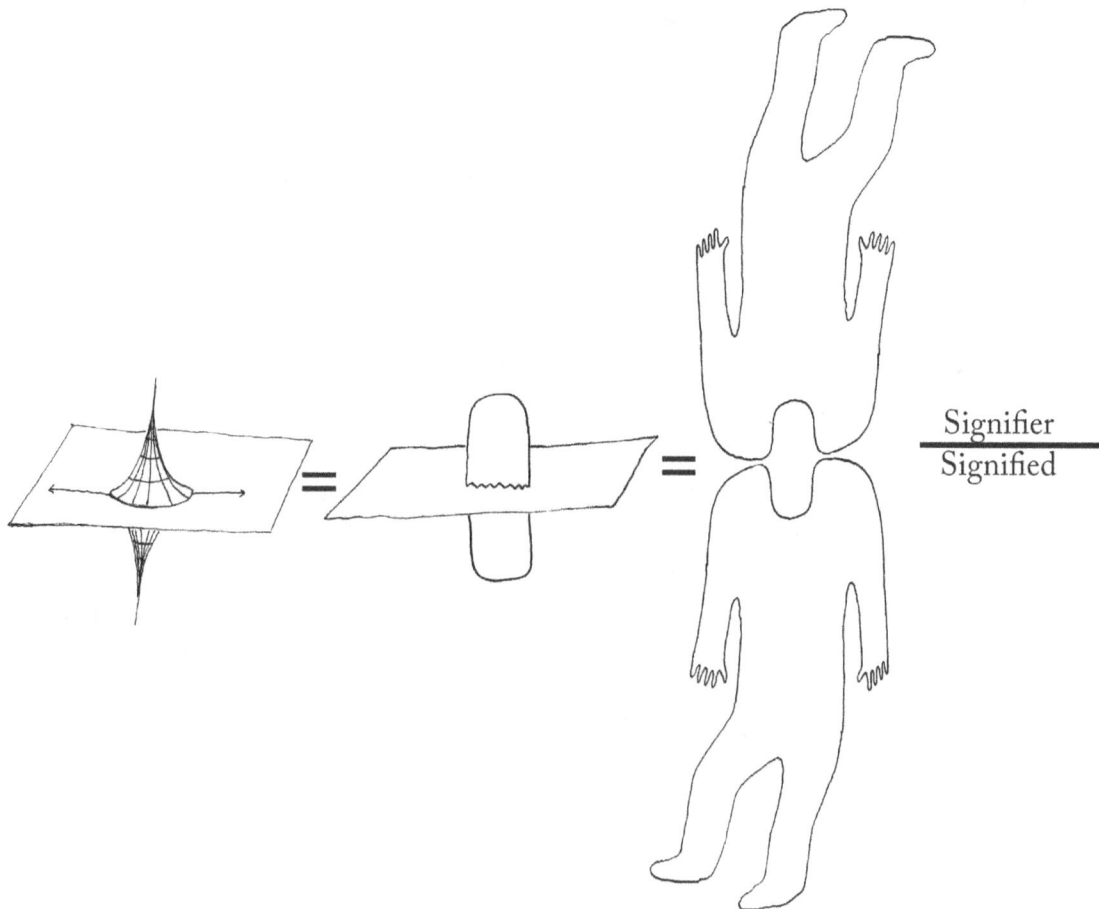

$$\frac{\text{Signifier}}{\text{Signified}}$$

This illustration shows that the fetish-object (center) of the postcapitalist future is the plenitude of the paradoxical Positivity of the diacritics of the signifier. This signifier is recommodified (left). This recommodification of the signifier — as opposed to the sign — is isomorphic to the plenitude of the lack of the Woman *sous rature* and *sur l'effacement*. The slippery excess of the signifier illuminates the essential distinction between signifier and signified (right). The surplus is the horizon of communism and its structure. The split in the object is equivalent to the split in the unit of text. This is the raw material to be objectified. The other side of Lacan's mirror is this unalloyed materiality of the logic of the communist future. The image depicts the isomorphism of: first, the plenitude of lack (left); second, the general equivalence of the (non)identity of any object (center); and third, the clitoral plenitude of the Woman (right). The communist fetish heralds the materialization of the future. The fetish is the material embodiment of the postphallocentric, postsign, and postcapitalist future. The fetish is the future feminist reconfiguration of the patriarchal enforcement of feminine loss. The fetish is the future linguistic Positivity of the signifier. The fetish is the future Marxist materialism of the absence of the banker's speculation. There is a spectre haunting Heterosexuality — the spectre of the Jockstrap.

Notes & Sketches —

The mystery of the origin of capitalist accumulation is revealed: *The Bank*. Under the Federal Reserve Act of 1913, private banks are free to print money in the form of credit to be borrowed as debt. Banks earn free profit from the currency (and charged interest) of dollars and coins. The *arche* of dollars and coins is the bank. The bank prints money *qua* debt as *representation*. These dollars and coins match the gap — suture the castration — which is opened by debt and "profit" (or surplus value). The theft from the worker generates representation (dollars and coins) at the site of "profit," debt, and interest. The accumulation of capital is more than two-fold in any transaction. The so-called economic growth of a capitalist system is merely the consequence of *(re)representation* of a wound in representation in two other places — "profit" and debt — plus interest in the body of the economy. Currency is a heterosexualist creationist sublimation *ex nihilo* — dollars and coins emerge from the Real object of the parallax.

The Real object of the parallax is the condition of possibility of the transactions and exchanges in capitalism. The hegemonic struggle to represent this Real object produces the break among "profit," debt, and surplus value. But the hitch is that the Real object (interval between wage and price) resists symbolization by the system of capital. Capitalists view the excess as "profit" (debt). Marxists refer to the remainder as surplus value. Economically, the Real object is split between representational commitments — either "profit" or "debt." The parallax chooses both options, and the Real object is represented twice in the system. The mystery is that the gap generates a surplus at the site of coroporate earnings but produces a loss at the site of the indebted consumer. The Real resists symbolization by the representational system of currency.

The symbolic order wants to steal twice from the Real. The capitalists want corporate earnings. The Marxists want surplus value. The effect of representational investment in the Real is the production of an equilibrium in the system: "debt" and "profit" are coordinated and stabilized by an equilibrium. The reason is that the symbolic order is structured by a binary logic (worker/owner, wage/price, and so on) which divides the Real into a system of equivalence. The value which is generated on the supply side (production) of the balance sheet must be equalized by a loss on the demand side (consumption) of the system. The symbolic desperately assimilates the Real to the binary logic of the system. But the Real resists articulation by dollars and coins in a system of balances between surplus and deficit. The Real object is the source of the (dys)function of the system. Nothing is Missing in the Real — until the symbolic divides it into Something is Missing. Nothing is Missing in the Real Economy. The symbolic order converts this abundance into the system of scarcity. This representational hole in the system is the proviso of currency. Nothing is Missing spells the death of representation. Cut the last Visa card, then —

Chapter Nine

Madness of Order

It depends on what the meaning of the word "is" is.

— Bill Clinton

This chapter is perverse because it puts the schizoid's Unreason in sharp relief. Unreason is the essence of the extant symbolic order. The system in its constitutive madness is structured by this Unreason. The psychotic's disturbed signifier is the effect of the Madness of Order. A Neurotic Foreclosure (*rejet névrotique*) of this essential psychosis of the system of $-ism defines Western thinking, being, and living. Chains of signification enforce the existence of man. My critical interpretation of the schizoid's Unreason is not a project to discover the order of madness. Such a project would seek to objectify the madman within an order of Reason. This objectification is exactly the effort that the schizoid's Unreason resists. This text refuses to evaluate the order of madness and the madman. Rather, my study uncovers the Unreason within Reason. I elaborate a schizoid system ($-ism, S) that dysfunctionally fancies itself a common structure of neurosis. The structure reckons itself to be ordinary. But this system is otherwise overrun with an Unreason that the system cannot even put into words. I am happy to leave the madman to his abject and deranged devices. I empathize with his torture by the signifier. I appropriate the schizoid's intuition of the Unreason which animates the Madness of Order.

I discuss Unreason specifically within the context of structuralism in order to expose the Unreason of the system. The signifying chain is sheer craziness. Unreason must be rigorously theorized in the language and logic of Reason. This discourse of Reason is structuralism, specifically Saussure's radical discovery of the so-called value of the signifier. The horizon of this chapter explains Unreason in the most intuitive and accessible of methods and schemes. This study of structuralism posits Unreason as the organizational principle of the systems in the West. Reason structures the extant symbolic order precisely *qua* madness. Unreason is the internal consistency of Reason. A study of the Madness of Order indicates the schizophrenia of structure. The overlap of the parallactic gap is the split between two perspectives on "one" and the "same" object. These objects are $-ism and S, and system and the Spirit of the System. This overlap is an aperture and a closure. The parallax is the essence of a system which must neurotically foreclose (*rejet névrotique*) its Unreason into an unsymbolizable Real. The neurotic represses: *Verdrängung*. The psychotic forecloses: *Verwerfung*. But the system neurotically forecloses (*reject névrotique*).

The hard kernel of Real sublimity returns to disrupt the signifying chain. Destabilization is the precept of the extant symbolic order. Unreason liberates logic and its minions from the constant and consistent eruptions of a Real which resists the spoken and the written. The Real is the ruin of representation and the claims of discourse. Unreason can only be accommodated by a system which foreswears the word altogether. What supplements the positive logic of the sign after its immolation in the schizoid's secret truth of Unreason? Can the signifier return to an Outside of both Reason and Unreason and toward a Pervert-Schizoid-Woman and her Spirit of the System? An unexpected positive affirmation of the signifier frees man for the advent of a discourse of signs without things, words without people, and fetishism in the absence of absence. The space is — the Outside of representation.

Ordinary ambiguity does not define Unreason. Everyday equivocation is internal to Reason. The essence of Unreason is delirium. This *deliro* is an unspeakable and unwriteable sublimity. *Praxis* encircles in its efforts to make sense out of nonsense. The madman's Unreason is informed by the profound and fundamental unsymbolizability of the secret truth and latent content of the system. Unreasonable order is the object of speech and writing, and living and breathing. My job is to indicate this Unreason through the strange effects of the destabilization of the system. My perverse work is also to demonstrate the obscene Reason of this Unreason. The madness of the system is logical. Psychosis is reasonable. Delirium conforms to the basic precepts of reasonable argumentation. The pervert's talent is to make intuitive an object which is otherwise veiled in the dysfunction of the system. I uncover the unconscious underside of the ego operations of the system.

My elucidation relies on the absolutely insane theory of value in the work of the Swiss linguist, Ferdinand de Saussure. My discussion illuminates the unseen Unreason of *langue*. Saussure is the most important thinker of the entire twentieth century. The reason for such an accolade is that his limit-thought about *langue* is precisely incoherent from within language. Saussure cannot speak his speech. This is the reason that a valiant so-called metatheory — philosophy — is *a priori* impossible. An exegesis of the concept of value in Saussure's thought can only be a *Praxis* around which the hard kernel of the Real resists in textualization. My enterprise as a talented pervert is to approach this Real. The chapter traverses the ideology of the system of neurosis. I demonstrate the failure of representation *in toto*. Unreason resists capture in Reason. This is so even if such madness is the internal condition of Reason. Is any representation — even Reason — possible within the Madness of Order and the system of Unreason? Is Reason present? Can we even speak?

COURSE ON VALUE

Saussure begins with a distinction between thought and its Other. Thought refers to a set of shaped and distinct ideas which are isolated and separated from each other. The proviso of thought is the division between thoughts and the relationship between distinct thoughts. The Other of thought is a nebulous and indistinct mass which cannot forge thought because it is otherwise unorganized and uncoordinated by divisions between thoughts. The condition of thought is an articulated set of distinctions. Saussure says,

> Psychologically our thought — apart from its expression in words — is only a shapeless and indistinct mass. Philosophers and linguists have always agreed in recognizing that without the help of signs we would be unable to make a clear-cut, consistent distinction between two ideas. Without language, thought is a vague, uncharted nebula. There are no pre-existing ideas, and nothing is distinct before the appearance of language.[1]

The "shapeless and indistinct mass" is thought which is Outside of expression and communication. Saussure's presupposition is that thought is the effect of the word and its "clear-cut, consistent distinction between two ideas." The substance of thought cannot "pre-exist" language. There is "nothing" which is Outside of language. Man thinks and expresses in words. *Langue* is the condition of thought. The essence of language is isolated and distinct ideas which can be related to each other as different. The offspring who is prelinguistic is the Other of thought. The offspring is fundamentally inhuman and prehistoric insofar as thought is impossible for the offspring.

The transition from inhumanity and prehistory is the incision of the word into the "vague, uncharted nebula" of experience. The unarticulated is antecedent to the word. What is the prethought which is precedent to thought proper? What does the offspring experience in the inhuman and prehistoric realm of the Other of thought? Is the transition from childhood to adulthood, from inhumanity to humanity, and from prehistory to history — is this transition into the offspring's first murmur of "mama" a charmed elevation to the world of words? Or is the forced entry into the galaxy of words a sad fall from the "shapeless and indistinct mass" of the inhuman and prehistoric goo? These queries oblige the crucial question of the necessity of language and thought. What are the advantages and disadvantages of thought in the human and the historical?

Possible Word

After the emergence of the human and the historical, thought joins abstraction and materiality, and signified and signifier, in the hinge of the word in its written and spoken iteration. The "vague, uncharted nebula" of the inexpressible is a series of unorganized and uncoordinated materialities and abstractions. This discoordination between signifier and signified is unanchored in legible words. The word is only possible as both a materiality (such as a sound or image) and an abstraction (such as an idea or concept). The purpose of the system of language is to join these two dimensions — material signifier and abstract signified — together as the sign. The word is the unit of language which is understandable to and as thought. Saussure writes,

> The characteristic role of language with respect to thought is not to create a material phonic means for expressing ideas but to serve as a link between thought and sound, under conditions that of necessity bring about the reciprocal delimitation of units.[2]

The purpose of *langue* is to "serve as a link" between signified and signifier ("thought and sound"). This function is perforce of necessity in order to generate the "reciprocal delimitation of units." Reciprocity implies that the material-signifier and the abstract-signified are linked together by a mutual effort. Both signifier and signified are joined at the hinge of the sign. The delimitation of units is an arduous task for thought. It requires the "vague, unchartered nebula" of a "shapeless and indistinct mass" to miraculously separate itself from the originary prelinguistic, prehuman, and prehistoric blob from which the capacity for thought withdraws. How is the unstructured swarm of signifiers and signifieds to be joined at the hinge of the word?

Saussure's simplified "reciprocal delimitation of units" avoids an explanation of this mysterious process. The joint or hinge of the word is the union of otherwise ripped marks and sounds, and ideas and concepts, from the originary splotch of inchoate signifiers and signifieds. Saussure advances beyond a simple referential model of the role of language. The elements of language — signifier, signified, and sign — refer to themselves in a series of chains of meaning-making. The purpose of thought is less to speak *about the world* and more to speak *about speech*. Thought thinks itself. It does so through the service of *langue* which joins materialities and abstractions. But how is such a joint ("reciprocal delimitation of units") to be performed in the generation of the simple word? Can thought emerge from the nebulous bubble of a swarm of sounds and images, and ideas and concepts?

Saussure is at his most complicated best in his reference to a specific metaphor that he uses to describe the relationship between materiality and abstraction. The initial wager of Saussure's metaphor is that *langue* can be compared and contrasted with another object, in this case with a sheet of paper. Comparison and contrast are possible only if there is a constitutive difference between the two objects in relationship to each other. He writes,

> Language can also be compared with a sheet of paper: thought is the front and the sound the back; one cannot cut the front without cutting the back at the same time; likewise in language, one can neither divide sound from thought nor thought from sound; the division could be accomplished only abstractly, and the result would be either pure psychology or pure phonology.[3]

The metaphor of the word as a sheet of paper implies the correspondence between the two words at the same time as it enforces a difference. This illuminates a central concern of language: that it is divided from itself. Saussure's *langue* is otherwise than itself. This "language" is neither self-same nor self-identical. It resists any metaphysics of presence and Logic of Identity (A = A). Saussure's *langue* is not language but is (like: comparison and contrast) a sheet of paper. This reference to the Other is the necessary proviso both for Saussure's definition of "language" and for the metaphorical process by which the "reciprocal delimitation of units" generates signification for both "language" and "sheet of paper." *Langue qua* "language" speaks about *language* in reference to a "sheet of paper." Saussure's word "language" does not refer to the empirical and worldly object being-in-the-world. Rather, the word refers to yet another *word*.

Saussure elaborates the metaphor with a division between the front of the sheet of paper (the thought, idea, or concept of the signified) and the back of the sheet of paper (the sound, mark, or material of the signifier). Materiality and abstraction, signifier and signified, and sound-image and idea-concept are always already sutured to each other such that the word is fundamentally indivisible. The signifier of materiality and the signified of abstraction are *a priori* joined. The "reciprocal delimitation of units" is decided in advance. The signifier and signified are a retroactive construction of a sign which is split but sutured by a segregated materiality and an isolated abstraction. But why are a separated materiality of the signifier and abstraction of the signified a merely hypothetical or theoretical postulation? Why is the word dominate over the signifier and the signified? If materiality and abstraction are only retroactive theoretical constructions of the word, then from where does the word emerge? The word appears *ex nihilo* — Out of Nothing — from the blob of a nebulous unstructured inhuman and prehistoric mass of the Other.

The distinction between "pure psychology" and "pure phonology" is instructive because it suggests that both are strictly impossible. An unalloyed psychology is a system which is dominated by the abstractions of ideas and concepts. But these signifieds are utterly inaccessible to man without the joint — to a materiality of sound or image which makes present to the senses the idea and concept of the signified. Similarly, a sheer phonology is a system which is structured by the materialities of sounds and images. But these signifiers are totally inaccessible to man in their signification without the joint or interface with an abstraction of idea or concept. The joint makes present the meaning-making of the language system. Psychology promises pure ideas and values which are invisible to man. Phonology provides pure sounds and images which are meaningless. Any separation of signified and signifier — cut in the sheet of paper — ruins the system of language. A rupture between the material-signifier and the abstract-signified renders anything written or spoken the Other of language. Language is a combination of psychology and phonology. The system of the word is a simultaneous division and suture of the body of materiality and the mind of abstraction. What is life — like an offspring's existence — in the prelinguistic, prehuman, and prehistoric unhinged and unjoined disengagement between signifier and signified? What happens (to us) when the system of *langue* fails at its role at the "reciprocal delimitation of units" in the words of the written and the spoken?

Arbitrariness

Arbitrariness is a critical concept in Saussure's version of semiology. The arbitrariness of the sign does not refer to the conventionalization of an otherwise whimsical relationship between materiality and abstraction, and between signifier and signified. Saussure says that "not only are the two domains that are linked by the linguistic fact shapeless and confused, but the choice of a given slice of sound to name a given idea is completely arbitrary."[4] This variant of arbitrariness refers to the link between the sound and image, on the one hand, and the idea and concept, on the other hand. There is no necessary — God-given or Nature-given — reason that any sound or image is attached to any idea or value. But the crucial component of Saussure's theory of arbitrariness is the relationship of value — relationality and constructionism — between the signifier and the signified. Saussure says: "But actually values remain entirely relative, and that is why the bond between the sound and the idea is radically arbitrary."[5] The phrase "entirely relative" piques interest in the fundamental concepts of arbitrariness and value. The postulation of a "relative" series of values begs a crucial question. To what is the relativity of the sign in relationship? An "entirely relative" system must be referred to a standard. This is so even if such a standard is "entirely relative." But what is the *relative standard*?

The system of value between signifiers and signifieds is paradoxically *absolutely relative*. The system is relative to itself and to all of the objects — signifiers and signifieds — in the structure. Arbitrariness refers not simply to the conventionalization of the capricious. Rather, the presupposition of arbitrariness is linked to an absolutely relative system. The joint or hinge between signifiers and signifieds *qua* signs is haphazard and mercurial. But such a system of value (as opposed to signification) ruins any coherent organization and legible coordination between the materialities and abstractions of the system. Consensual meaning-making intervenes in order to delimit the otherwise chaotic discordance between signifiers and signifieds. The absence of coordination renders an absolutely relative system isomorphic to the "vague, uncharted nebula" of the prelinguistic, prehuman, and prehistoric chaos which is antecedent to *langue*. What is the source of the stabilization of the system? What enforces the hinge between body and mind, between signifier and signified, and between materiality and abstraction? Can a system of a paradoxical absolute relativity generate the word?

Saussure invokes the classic antinomy between the individual and society in order to resolve the "entirely relative" arbitrariness of the sign that otherwise ruptures the meaning-making capacities of the system of language. Saussure says,

> The arbitrary nature of the sign explains in turn why the social fact alone can create a linguistic system. The community is necessary if values that owe their existence solely to usage and general acceptance are to be set up; by himself the individual is incapable of fixing a single value.[6]

Social consensus is the force which establishes the bond between the otherwise arbitrary relationship between signifier and signified. The isolated individual is ineffectual in the coordination of these relationships. There are two consequences of this insight: first, there is no obligatory reason to sustain any conventionalized relationship between signifier and signified because the relationship is arbitrary, neither God-given nor Nature-given; but second, there is no necessary reason to change any consensual relationship between signifier and signified because the relationship is arbitrary. Saussure's point is that social forces overwhelm individual choice on the matter of the word. The sign preexists the individual speaker and writer of language. This preeminence eclipses the individual's agency to transform the system.

The signifier and signified are joined by the word. This socially arbitrary and absolutely relative relationship between materiality and abstraction renders the word an established fact of the system of *langue*. The system is predominantly protected from transformation. *Langue* is profoundly conservative. This is so even if it is simultaneously "entirely relative." The relationality and constructionism of the system are simultaneously the proviso of its reactionary conventionalism. How are signifiers and signifieds unhinged in order to disturb the atrophied relationship — *qua* — of the word? The sign freezes the play of materialities and abstractions. But how is the structure to be unsettled in order to forge new relationships among signifiers and signifieds?

Saussure's so-called structuralism is most visible in his subordination of the elements of the system (signifier, signified, and sign) to the framework of the structure. Even if words are unsettled by the infrastructural play of the signifier and the signified, the system otherwise dominates the subordinate elements of the structure. Saussure says,

> In addition, the idea of value, as defined, shows that to consider a term as simply the union of a certain sound with a certain concept is grossly misleading. To define it in this way would isolate the term from its system; it would mean assuming that one can start from the terms and construct the system by adding them together when, on the contrary, it is from the interdependent whole that one must start and through analysis obtain its elements.[7]

The system dominates its elements. Language precedes all material marks and abstract concepts. The signifier and the signified are inaccessible to man except as component parts of the word. Materialities and abstractions are constituted by an Other which precedes and exceeds them. The elements are coerced and manipulated by a system which confers value on each object but also isolates and relates each element to the other. The force of the system is social and consensual. The social fact of language makes each element subordinate to the system.

In the West, the fundamental unit is the individual and his private property. Identity, identification, and individuality are coded into Romance languages: mine, yours, his, hers, theirs, and ours. The individual is the primary referent in Western civilization. Capitalist private property is coded into the signifying chain. The subordination of the "vague, uncharted nebula" of the prelinguistic, prehuman, and prehistoric signifier and signified is an ideological effect and cause — presence — of the rabid individualism in the West. In contrast, Saussure displaces the individual unit with the system *tout court* as the agency of arrangement and order of the structure. The relationship between materiality and abstraction precedes the individuality of each of these elements of the system. Context introduces the text. *Mise-en-scene* heralds the costumes. Framework prefaces the elements. Individual yields to the relationship. Subject is an effect of the society. But what is the origin of the relationship? What is the context of the (con)text? What is the "reciprocal delimitation of units" if the process of this "delimitation" is subordinate to a system which exceeds the units and even the structure?

Saussure's most profound statement about language is that its foundation is pure difference. Saussure says that: "Language is a system of interdependent terms in which the value of each term results solely from the simultaneous presence of the others."[8] The presence of the "others" implicates the context by which the value of the objects in the system is determined. The "interdependence" between the terms is the interrelational source of the meaning-making in the signifying chain. The strange "simultaneous" overlap of the others and the object in question indicates the deeply paradoxical structure of the signifier. The "others" in the system are simultaneously immanent to the signifier in question. The interdependent presence of the "others" is inextricably internal to the value of a particular object. Value can only appear in relationship to the other present objects in the system. The other objects are internal — present — in the object under scrutiny.

Absent signifiers are simultaneously present in the present signifier. The converse also holds. Present signifiers are simultaneously absent in present — *qua* absent — signifiers. Words in the system are simultaneously present In/Outside the object. A relationship "solely" between the signifier and the "others" belies the basic integration of the signifiers with each other *qua* themselves. There can be no strict division between any of the objects in the system. The "others" are virtually suspended both syntagmatically and paradigmatically, and both syntactically and semantically. The entire battery of signifiers is simultaneously present even in its absence. Each word contains every other — "interdependent" and "simultaneous" — word in the system. Each word is internal to every other word. Every word is the same word.

Saussure completes this concept of interrelated and simultaneous difference in his account of both the exchange and the comparison of words. Saussure writes,

> [The signifier's] value is therefore not fixed so long as one simply states that it can be "exchanged" for a given concept, i.e. that it has this or that signification: one must also compare it with similar values, with other words that stand in opposition to it. Its content is really fixed only by the concurrence of everything that exists outside of it.[9]

Value cannot be fixed because its meaning is not determined by simple exchange of one signifier for another signifier, and of one object for another object. Exchange is strictly impossible because value is not binary. Rather, the meaning-making in the signifying chain is articulated by the entirety of the others in the system of *langue*. Comparison and contrast with "similar" or "opposite" values mean that value can only be fixed by the "concurrence" (context, *mise-en-scène*, framework, and relationship) of other objects in the system. But the crux of this argument is that there is a necessary "concurrence" *of the* "concurrence" itself. The context is always a text. The framework is always an element. The relationship is always an individual. But what are the metaconcurrence, *über*context, and suprarelationship of these expansive circles?

The "concurrence of everything that exists outside" of the object is an ever expanding and forever widening circle of circles (and so on). The object is bombarded by not only "everything that exists outside." The object is overwhelmed by "everything" *tout court*. The purported exchange of the signifier for its other yields to the comparison and contrast of the interdependence of simultaneity of "everything that exists." Can the object even be determined as presence from within the system? Is there an accessible object of identification? Is value not only unfixed and unanchored but also remote and unapproachable? What is analysis in the absence of its object? After the word, what speaks?

Saussure reiterates the relevance of the system over the elements in his reference to the environment which surrounds the signifiers in the system. He says: "the value of just any term is accordingly determined by its environment; it is impossible to fix even the value of the word signifying 'sun' without first considering its surroundings: in some languages it is not possible to say 'sit in the sun.'"[10] The paradox of the problematic is the phrase "just any term." What could "just any term" possibly mean in a system in which the "environment" of interdependent and intertextual Outside relationships isolates the value of "just any term" in the system? Saussure's economy of meaning-making sustains the discrete object at the same time as it fiercely dissolves it. There can be no "any" object in the system. Every other signifier is present with and in this "any" object. The bizarre conclusion is that language is in essence the "vague, uncharted nebula" of jumbled materialities and unconstrained abstractions — which is exactly the ostensible obverse of *langue*.

In Saussure's system, the word simply cannot manifest as such. The "concurrence of everything that exists outside" swallows "just any term" into the "shapeless and indistinct mass" of the prelinguistic, prehuman, and prehistoric goo of the offspring's schizophrenic babbles. *Langue* presents as a system of "clear-cut consistent distinctions." But the otherwise discrete object yields to the collapse of "just any term." Interdependence and simultaneity of the other words in the system displace the individual as the fundamental unit in the system. What is the absent value amidst the obscene presence of all of the objects in the system, and at once? Does the word even arrive as an effect of the system? Is the word — as such?

Is Not

Saussure defines a system which tears any positive unity — word — from within/out of its determinate and decidable essence. Saussure says,

> Instead of pre-existing ideas then, we find in all the foregoing examples values emanating from the system. When they are said to correspond to concepts, it is understood that the concepts are purely differential and defined not by their positive content but negatively by their relations with the other terms of the system. Their most precise characteristic is in being what the others are not.[11]

There are several profound aporias in this outline of the value of the signifier. The "values" emanate from the system. These senses are "purely differential." Values are generated in the open comparison, contrast, and exchange with the other objects in the system. Any positive unity is ruptured by the negativity and relations — *nots* — from which these ostensibly positive contents achieve their value. Saussure designates the presence of the signifier as "precisely." This exactitude is farcical because a system of negative differences cannot achieve an exact — determinate and decidable — sense for any object. The "precise characteristic" of the signifier is pure negativity: "what the others are not." The essence of the object is the void and abyss of Nothingness. The negative relationships which surround the object confer a decentered meaning onto the object.

Saussure's "what the others are not" syntactically situates Being ("are") and Nothingness ("not") in contiguity. The object being-in-the-world can only be understood as split between this Being and Nothingness, or between is and is not. The "precise characteristic" of any object in the signifying chain is always ruptured by the Other. The Woman is split from the man. The gay is splintered from the straight. The black is fissured from the white. The disabled is cleaved from the abled. The evil is ruptured from the good. A determinate and decidable "precision" can only be approached as a relationship (*of* a relationship, and so on) such that exact "reciprocal delimitation of units" is impossible within a system of open comparison, contrast, and exchange. This indicates that there is no value as such — *qua*, by definition, essentially, *il y a*, by necessity, and so on.

Figure 9.1 Same Difference

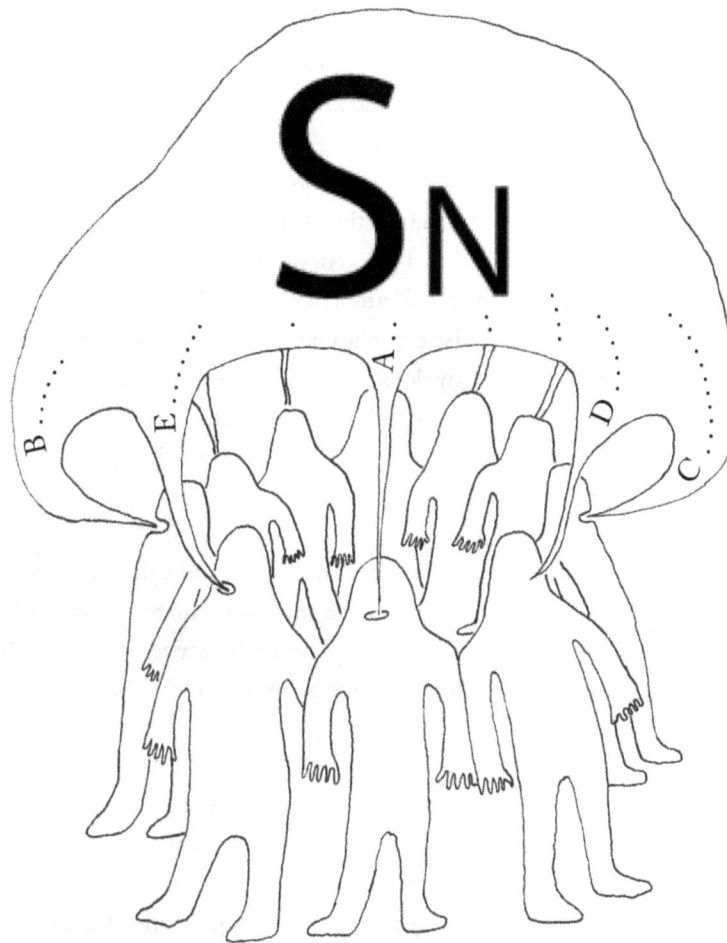

This illustration visually illuminates the same difference of the Principle of Sameness⁺. The gaggle of neurotics *qua* signifiers (center) stands together in proximity. But they also face outward and away from each other. The ideological assumption of $-ism is that each signifier sustains an opposed and distinct signification. *Contra* Spirit, the system posits that each word is a different word. The psychotic vision which is depicted (above) portrays each unit of text as subsumed in the Same⁺ Other of the entire network of words. Every word is the same word. Any spoken or written unit of text is extracted from a context. But this context — essence of communication — is both everywhere and nowhere in the points of space and time in the system. The word is everywhere because the latent (manifest) significance of every word is internal (external) to every other word. The word is nowhere because signification — the written and the spoken — is unwriteable and unspeakable in any single and isolated word. Words are necessarily relative —relational and constructed — to each other. But this essential relativity is simultaneously impossible to symbolize in the system. $-ism cannot speak or write its own truth of the *absolute relativity* of the meaning-making process.

Notes & Sketches —

The issue is made more complex because the "system," as Saussure refers to it, must "emanate" from an Other. The object emerges from a recursive metasystem, and so on. The Constitutive Outside is simultaneously internal to its own exterior. The slip and slide render cause always already an effect. Unpredictably, not only is the object ("just any term") inscrutable to analysis. But the system is obscure to evaluation. The void of the Nothingness of value ever extends and forever multiplies. The object recedes from purview and exceeds any viewpoint. The closer the subject analyzes the "reciprocal delimitation of units" the more it finds the limitlessness of an inexact precision of context and texts, *mise-en-scène* and costumes, framework and elements, and relationship and individuals. The ostensible division between context/texts, scene/costumes, framework/elements, and relationship/individuals cedes to the negative differential play of the signifier. Interdependence overlays distinct objects in the signifying chain. This economy is internal to *langue* in its very structure. Precision and exactitude surrender to equivocality and ambiguity. The system of "clear-cut distinction" submits to the misty unexplored muddle of the prelinguistic, prehuman, and prehistoric. How did language hoodwink man into the conceit that the system works? Why does language work if it precisely does not work? How does language work by not working? How does speech speak without words?

Saussure's claim about the differential negativity of the material signifier applies to the abstract signified. Saussure writes,

> The conceptual side of value is made up solely of relations and differences with respect to the other terms of language, and the same can be said of its material side. The important thing in the word is not the sound alone but the phonic differences that make it possible to distinguish this word from all others, for differences carry signification."[12]

Saussure's words reiterate that value is "made up solely of relations and differences." But such a formulation indicates that there must be an Other to the relations and differences. This Other constitutes both the signifier and the signified. The "solely" of Saussure's articulation must be split. There are relationships and interdependences among signifieds and signifiers. But there must also be positive unities and essential individualities within the system of relations and differences. This underside of the theory is the repressed of Saussure's thought. The positive and essential are the unexpected limit of the theory of value. What could the positive and the essential possibly be in a system in which the Other confers value on every object in the system?

Nothingness is the void of the object which is caught in relays and referrals to others. Nothingness assumes a substantive role in the spoken and written approach to the signifiers in language. Man speaks Nothingness. Man writes Nothingness. Being is *qua* Being this Nothingness. Positivity and essence can only be determined and decided as the Being *of* Nothingness. The effect of the system of relations and differences is the Co-Constitutive Outside (and so on) of Nothingness. The hiccup in this interpretation is Saussure's reference to pure differences as that which "carry signification." How does the pure difference of Nothingness as it is constituted from the Outside "carry signification" in the meaning-making process? What is the object which "carries" the significance in negative relationship with the other signifiers of the context, the *mise-en-scène*, the framework, and the relationship?

These "differences" which "carry signification" can only refer to the entirety of the signifying chain. None of the signifiers can be divided as discrete and separate from each other. The battery of the Other "carries" signification. What is the point of departure and destination — origin and arrival — of this "carried" signification? What is the *arche* — sender and receiver, speaker and interlocutor, and writer and reader — of the signification of the text? This impasse confronts both the aperture of an *hors-texte* but also the recursive circularity of signification. The signifying chain "carries" signification from here to there, this way and that way, and by this and by that. Can the word only speak about its supplemental word? Does the word refer to a referent which is other than simply another negative and differential carrier of — Nothingness?

Saussure's summation of his wildly paradoxical and unsymbolizable concept of the signifier beseeches the question of the essence of difference. Saussure writes,

> Everything that has been said up to this point boils down to this: in language there are only differences. Even more important: a difference generally implies positive terms between which the difference is set up; but in language there are only differences without positive terms. Whether we take the signified or the signifier, language has neither ideas nor sounds that existed before the linguistic system, but only conceptual and phonic differences that have issued from the system.[13]

Saussure's admirable effort to "boil down" his sublime theory of linguistic value closes the constitutive recursion in his own theory. The object to which the essence of the theory is "boiled down" — namely: "in language there are only differences without positive terms" — is precisely a Nothingness around which the series of other signifiers slips and slides in the extimate constitution of the object. What is precisely *not* "only differences without positive terms"? This Other is the series of positive terms and essential unities. This Other is the positive and essential Being around which the Nothingness of the signifier is enclosed. Saussure identifies the word as this positive entity. But what is the essence of difference if the structure of the negative and differential signifier is established without the presence of a positive term? The positive unity of the word is the vehicle of proper signification. The representation and study — symbolization and analysis — of difference exceed any "set up" in relationship to a positive unity. What is a paradoxical absolute relativity? How does the peculiar standard of relativity yield to the word? Is the word possible?

Is

Saussure returns to a coherent Reason in his theorization of the sign and signification. The signifier and signified animate the diacritical play of value. In contrast, the word is its own positive unity which is defined by an internal consistency. Saussure writes,

> But the statement that everything in language is negative is true only if the signified and the signifier are considered separately; when we consider the sign in its totality, we have something that is positive in its own class.[14]

The system of negative differences is the architectonics of the signifying chain. But the visible components of the structure are a series of words whose organization is distinct from the pinball wizardry of the foundational materialities and abstractions of the "vague, uncharted nebula" of the signifying chain. The "separate" "consideration" of the signifier and signified is a strictly theoretical orientation. In practice, the signifier and signified cannot be detached from their joint *qua* the sign. Value is inaccessible to the speakers and writers of language. The architectonics of the signifying chain is a theoretical postulate. Architectonics of *langue* is strictly invisible to everyday practices of communication. Even the theoretical articulation of the signifier and signified can only be structured by the word and its signification of positive units.

The "totality" of the word indicates a "positive" sign. The word is defined in its "own class." The bizarre oppositions between signifier/sign and value/signification render the foundation of the system radically unconscious. The operation of the semantics and syntax of language is unconscious. The essence of the system in the signifier is veiled from the use of words in speaking and writing. The signifier is the object of the repression in the system. The sign is the veiled return of the repressed in the structure of language. The word is a symptom. The latent truth of language is the signifier. The latent returns in the manifest form of the positive unit of the sign. But if language is a symptomatic dream, then what is its desire? What is the desire of the repressed signifier?

The Word

Saussure's description of the word is strange and hazy. The diacritical system of open comparison, contrast, and exchange of the detached materialities and abstractions of the signifiers and signifieds in the system presents as an Unreasonable absolute relativity. Saussure says: "Although both the signified and the signifier are purely differential and negative when considered separately, their combination is a positive fact."[15] The unexplained hinge between signifier and signified *qua* sign is assumed. Unorganized materialities and unanchored abstractions — signifiers and signifieds — are inexplicably united by the conventionalization of arbitrariness and the consensual agreement of community. The "positive fact" of this "combination" in the "totality" of the sign belies any coherent architecture. The diacritics of the signifier illuminates the appearance of an extimate signifier and signified. This is so even if the signifier and signified are paradoxically absolutely relative. The signification of the word forges a "positive fact" in the absence of any arrangement.

Saussure fails to define "positive fact" except to suggest that it deviates from the differential negativity of value. Presumably, words are related to each other syntactically and semantically. The signification of a given word is isolated and discrete from a system of otherwise open comparison, contrast, and exchange. The diacritical play of the signifier is stabilized as the internal structure of each sign. But these internal components of each sign are simultaneously negatively and differentially intertwined with the other materialities and abstractions in the system. The internal coherence — "positive fact" — of every word is twisted by the signifier-signified relationship. The "positive fact" of the word is unstable. The architectonics of the system is arranged by a negative and differential series of relationships which disrupts the internal coherence of the word and its positive unity. The symptom of the word is its constitutive instability. The latent truth of this manifest inconstancy is value. Value disturbs signification. The signifier upsets the word. The dual-level architecture of the system — signifier-signified/sign and value/signification — is wobbly because the word is subordinate to materialities and abstractions which are the external source of the internal (in)consistency of the word. The architecture of the signifying chain is opposed to itself. Why does the system enforce the repression of the signifier in the defense of the word? What is the threat of the signifier and its wish? What is the latent truth of the manifest word?

The crucial theoretical distinction between the word and its signification, on the one hand, and the signifier and its value, on the other hand, is structured by the division between "difference," on the one hand, and "opposition," on the other hand. Saussure establishes this opposition in order to explain the gap between the dual-level architecture of the signifying chain — between the negative and differential signifier and the positive unity of the sign. Saussure writes,

Two signs, each having a signified and signifier, are not different but only distinct. Between them there is only opposition. The entire mechanism of language, with which we shall be concerned later, is based on oppositions of this kind and on the phonic and conceptual differences that they imply.[16]

The internal components of the word — the material signifier and the abstract signified — constitute the sign. The word is the symptomatic semantic and syntactical element of the signifying chain. The word cannot be opposed to the signifier and the signified because these theoretical components are the internal (in)consistency of the word. The negative and differential relationships of materialities and abstractions are different. The signifier *qua* difference is the internal constitution of the sign *qua* opposition. The word is not different from but opposed to the other signs in the system. Difference refers to the negative diacritical relationship between signifiers and signifieds. Opposition denotes the semantic and syntactical relationship between positive unities of words in relationship to each other.

The crux of the gap between value and signification is relationality and constructionism. The signifier gathers (in)coherence in the open comparison, contrast, and exchange with the other materialities in the system. In contrast, the sign is meaningful as a positive unity. This self-identical and self-same word is then linked to other signs in the system of signification. The two logics are strictly opposed. The divergence between signifier and sign is an opposition. In theory, opposition is organized by difference. In practice, difference is structured by opposition. The signifier and signified are conferred meaning from the Outside of the battery of signifiers. The word is internally consistent as a positive unity without reference to the Other. The paradox is that value is internal to signification. The positive unity of the word is internal to value. The negativity and difference of the signifier are the internal (in)consistency of the positive unity of the word.

The wager of signification is that the diacritical play of negativity and difference can be stabilized and anchored in the positive entity of the word. How does the word manage to dominate the haphazard and ephemeral relationality and constructionism of the "vague, uncharted nebula" of the materialities and abstractions of the signifying chain? How does the word dominate the signifier? If the signifier of materiality and the signified of abstraction exceed containment by the positive unity of the sign, then what is the consequence for the word? Can the word be considered self-identical and self-same — word — if the underlying architectonics of the signifying chain is a "shapeless and indistinct mass"? What is the mechanism — force and power — of the sign which contains the endless plays and puns of the signifying (mis)arrangements of the signifier and signified? The signifier slips and slides from beyond the limits of the word. What are the effects of this destabilization on the spoken and the written? How is a system of stable communication possible if the foundation of language is an architectonics of the misshapen, uncharted, nebulous, and indistinct? How does the word even manifest as such? — and for what purpose?

METAPHORS OF DIFFERENCE

Metaphor is the structure of the signifying chain. At its most basic, metaphor is a relationship between two linguistic marks or objects or sets of signifiers which correspond in kind or likeness to each other. This relationship marks the emergence of metonymy as the temporal desire in the movement of the relationship of "is like." This temporal metonymy articulates this for that, part for whole, here to there, and so on. Metonymy is internal to the structure of metaphor and its otherwise static identifications. A metaphor is a relationship between likenesses. (By definition, a metaphor refers to a direct comparison: "is"; and a simile indicates an indirect comparison: "is like." However, metaphor and simile share a common structure: the comparison and contrast of dissimilarity *qua* similarity. In my discussion, the words "metaphor" and "simile" will be used interchangeably, and I will classify an indirect comparison, such as "is like," as metaphorical. In this discussion, the indirect comparison and contrast of "is like" are considered exemplary of the Spirit of metaphor. For my purposes, the construction of the "is like" indicates the profound metaphorical organization of the signifying chain.) The first critical revision of the otherwise basal structure of metaphor is a nuanced interrogation of likeness itself. A "like" (or "is") mediates the relationship between the constitution of signifiers. Two objects which are like each other — as in the structure, "my lovely jockstrap is like a red, red rose" — simultaneously imply a constitutive unlikeness. There is a divergence between like and unlike. The object can be designated as like the other object — "love" to be "like" "a red, red rose" — because of a gap between the two objects or between "love" and "a red, red rose." A comparison is not possible between the self-same and the self-identical. Difference must displace identity as the proviso of metaphor. What modality of difference is such a displacement? The desire of metonymy — here to there, part for whole — ruptures the identification of metaphor. The movement of metonymy and desire ruins metaphor and identification because metonymy (…) refers and defers metaphor (.) to the Other. The Other is a destination which is not present to either itself or an Other. What is Being (un)like? Metaphor implies that "my lovely jockstrap" is both like and unlike "a red, red rose." The relationship of the metaphor is a mediation of the gap of both likeness and unlikeness, nearness and distance, and suture and gap. The like is like the unlike. Like, what?

Being ("is") is under scrutiny in the process of metaphor and its convergence of dissimilarity and unlikeness, and similarity and likeness. What is "like" like? What "is" ontological "Being" like? The Being ("is") of like is split between this likeness and unlikeness. Being is ruptured by its own internal gap. A break splits Being (is and is not) *qua* the self-same and the self-identical of identity. This split destabilizes metaphor because the likeness between the two objects in the structure of metaphor is displaced and reversed. Metaphor *qua* the center of the signifying chain is not only incoherent as a structure but it is also resistant to representation, like a mark of sublimity. The process which establishes a relationship of likeness with metaphor and identification invariably entails the process of marking a relationship of unlikeness with metonymy and desire. Likeness is (un)like unlikeness.

But this reference to Being ultimately misnames the relationship between metaphor and its obverse. Being is always *sous rature*. The establishment of identity or identification as forms of metaphor is preposterous. Identity yields not only to difference. The self-same and the self-identical (.) surrender to the entire battery of negative and differential signifiers (…) in the signifying chain. Lacan identifies this system as the Other. The project of identification and metaphor is finally absurd because it is always ruptured by desire and metonymy. The (.) concedes to the (…), and so on (…). Identity is the most metaphysical of claims in language because it posits the self-identity and self-sameness (A = A) of the signifier. Who posits such identity? How is its possibility sustained? How is its futility exposed? How did metaphor become (im)possible? Why is the success of Metaphoricity a cultural and superegoic demand?

The End(s) of Metaphor

The form of metaphor accommodates any content. The organization of metaphor is central to the work of the signifying chain. This double-movement of relationship between words which are both same and different, both like and unlike, both near and distant, both separate and indistinct (and so on) animates all of the words in the system. A book is a series of chapters is (like) a series of paragraphs is (like) a series of sentences is (like) a series of letters is (like) a series of quarks (and so on). This metonymy of desire in its approach to the elusive *objet petit a* or transcendental signified is strictly endless (or structurally is so). This movement constitutes the deadlock of both desire and identification. The desire of turn about and around (…) and identity of essence and closure (.) are both subordinate to the same function of diachrony. The form of metaphor (with or without "like") conforms to any content. The structure of metaphor forges a relationship between all of the words in the system. Language is a system of metaphors and identifications (.) which are themselves metonymies and desires (…). The system of signification would dissolve without the anchor of metaphor — like and like, full stop — and its sorcery of identification, identity, essence, *il y a*, by definition, *qua*, by necessity, and so on.

A reversal of the opposition that usually organizes the relationship between metaphorical this is that and metonymical part for whole shows that metaphor and metonymy are the same essential structure. This splits the division between synchrony and diachrony because the former organizes a metaphor which slides into the latter as metonymy. Metaphor is otherwise than itself because it is like and unlike itself: (.) is (un)like (.). This "itself" rends metaphor from within the structure of an organization which is different from the self-same and self-identical. The signifying chain is a network of relationships between signifiers which are both self-same and self-identical (A = A) but also simultaneously Other (A ⊃ A). This structure smashes neurotic temporality into the vortex of the schizoid *Yes!* Incredibly, the relationship to the Other returns to identity in order to posit a self-same and self-identical organization.

The structure of the Logic of Identity is exactly the condition of its own (im)possibility. Metaphor is internally (externally) split. Any reference — what Derrida calls the differences and deferrals of the signifier — to the Other destructures unity, self-sameness, and self-identity. The Logic of Identity (A = A) enforces the self-same and the self-identical. *Il y a* is precisely this self-same and self-identical. The *qua* (.) undoes such presence in its reference to the Other and to the general economy of the web of words. As such (.) is internally (externally) split because any reference to the Other, such as "my red, red rose is like a lovely jockstrap," simultaneously destructures any reference to the Other of the Other. Difference and deferral dissolve the unity of the self-sameness and self-identity of the object. The Logic of Identity (A = A) enforces the self-same and the self-identical. ~~Being~~ undoes such presence because it refers to the other and to the Other. *Like* not only submits to an untimely death. Metaphor expires of its own accord. The essence of metaphor is a suicidal *Thanatos*.

The signifying chain is organized by the death drive and its tendency toward fragmentation, disunification, separation, and divorce. The will to death beyond the pleasure principle and toward an insistent repetition compulsion is the extimate suicidal tendency of the symbolic order. Words cannot be "themselves" if identification (.) concedes to (…). The same is the case for the obverse of the self-same and the self-identical. Metaphor demonstrates that the object is fundamentally otherwise than itself. But can (.) stabilize the temporal movement of metonymic desire (…) in the generation of a coherent identification (.) as self, other, and system? Metaphor must stabilize the infinite recursion of metaphor *qua* metonymy in order for the system to survive its own suicidal tendency. But how does metaphor as the fundamental center of the signifying chain survive its own death? Is metaphor — like the father — a ghostly presence in its absence?

The structure of relationship — and its referrals, differences, and deferrals — is fundamental to the system. These displacements extend beyond the synchronous. Synchrony is always simultaneously diachrony. Synchrony in space and diachrony in time cancel each other in the play between the condensations of *Eros* and the displacements of *Thanatos*. Identity (.) limitless. The self (…) is (.) unbound (…). Metaphor exceeds itself beyond the limits of metaphor. Metaphor is the center of the system and the principle of its organization and coherence. But it is also deviant from itself. The words which are structured in metaphorical relationships of simultaneous likeness and unlikeness, or similarity and dissimilarity, are otherwise (…) than themselves because words and their surpluses are situated in a system of *langue* in which there are "only differences without positive terms."[17]

Beyond the spatial synchrony of Saussurian structuralist linguistics is the simultaneous implication of a temporal diachrony that Saussure also acknowledges. The temporal diachrony cannot be separated from the spatial synchrony. Diachrony interferes with the structure of metaphor even as it conditions its possibility. This is shown in the imbrication of identification of this (.) with that (.) at the same time as desire transforms this into that (…) in metonymy. Metaphor is not like metaphor. Metaphor is unlike metaphor because essence is like the Other (and so on). Metaphor (in)completes itself in the temporal movement of metonymy and desire and the parts for the wholes, and the these for the those. The fundamental extimacy or external intimacy between spatial and temporal, and between synchrony and diachrony, is put into question even in Saussure's emphasis on the spatial and the synchronous. Temporal diachrony also marks a relationship in which the signifier is not itself. But this temporality is subordinate to the internal excess of Being. The Being under erasure wrecks havoc in a space from which an atemporal time has yet to depart or arrive.

The definition of any word presupposes the structure of metaphor. The organization of metaphor ("like" and "unlike") conforms to the content of the definition of the word. (Metaphor is like simile.) Metaphor entails the establishment of a relationship between the word "itself" and the other words which constitute its definition. Like in the work of a dictionary, the word "jockstrap" can only be defined as legible in reference and relationship to the other words in the system. The word jockstrap is joyous but meaningless on its own. An instructive exercise would be to determine an adequate word to describe a sign which is somehow entirely isolated from the signifying chain. My foray into this invention is (⊇) and its Real proximities between indeterminate and undecidable objects being-in-the-world. Derrida's word is the signified, and Lacan refers to it as the Real. The word jockstrap cannot be (either semiologically, for Saussure, or ontologically, for Heidegger) Outside of a relationship to the other words in the system. Heidegger makes such a point in his theorization of the worldliness of the world as a web of significant references with *Dasein* as its final referent. Heidegger even redefines *Logos* as relationship.[18]

The word jockstrap cannot be on its own at all: not ever. Rather, the jockstrap is situated in a network of relations with other words. It is nonsituated and decentered in the signifying chain which is Outside of the jockstrap "itself." The jockstrap is defined beyond its "own" borders. The metaphor of the jockstrap as an identity or identification must refer to the Other of desire for its identification *qua* itself. The essence of the identity of the jockstrap is to desire beyond itself toward the Other. Desire constitutes and complicates identification. Desire encircles identity as the source of the dissolution of essence. The endless trajectory of this desire (…) toward the *objet petit a* or the transcendental signified (.) renders identification (.) an incomplete project (…). The effort of the sign is simultaneously contingent on desire for its (im)possibility. The word jockstrap makes sense only insofar as a relationship is forged between an "itself" which vanishes and a difference with the other words which define it in the system. This chain of words governs the reconstruction of the disappeared.

What is my lovely jockstrap?

> what is my lovely jockstrap? my lovely jockstrap is like a red, red rose, a red, red rose is like a missed opportunity, a missed opportunity is like a party I forgot to attend, a party I forgot to attend is like a dream come true, a dream come true is like the incompletion of a task, the incompletion of a task is like existence, existence is like a party in Fiji, a party in Fiji is like a trip I forgot to plan, a trip I forgot to plan is like a misplaced sock, a misplaced sock is

like a party of one, a party of one is like a fantasy of genocide, a fantasy of genocide is like a dreamy nightmare, a dreamy nightmare is like the loss of a wish, the loss of a wish is like a misreading of death, a misreading of death is like a lost pair of glasses, a lost pair of glasses is like a shot glass without vodka, a shot glass without vodka is like absolute blackness, absolute blackness is like a projection on the horizon, a projection on the horizon is like the ego, the ego is like a prop, a prop is like a crutch, a crutch is like an enabling condition, an enabling condition is like the strike of a match, the strike of a match is like the power of oxygen, the power of oxygen is like the wellspring of disaster, the wellspring of disaster is like comfort food, comfort food is like the butter on toast, the butter on toast is like tasty drivel, tasty drivel is like fodder for conversation, fodder for conversation is like the shreds of a document, the shreds of a document are like dead trees, dead trees are like capitalism, capitalism is like the policy of scorched earth, the policy of scorched earth is like a heat wave, a heat wave is like a fad, a fad is like a fashionable gimmick, a fashionable gimmick is like the dawn of the new world order, the dawn of the new world order is like a paranoid invention, a paranoid invention is like a sad walrus, a sad walrus is like a lonely crust of bread, a lonely crust of bread is like abject poverty, abject poverty is like a misfortune, a misfortune is like a cookie, a cookie is like a fable, a fable is like a metaphor, a metaphor is like a series of metonymic chains of discourse, a series of metonymic chains of discourse is like the alienation of my lovely jockstrap from itself, the alienation of my lovely jockstrap from itself is like, "what, then, is my lovely jockstrap?", "what, then, is my lovely jockstrap?" is like the chains of metonymy at the center of a metaphor, the chains of metonymy at the center of a metaphor are like the displacement of all of the metaphors from any presence whatsoever, the displacement of all of the metaphors from any presence whatsoever is like "what is my lovely jockstrap?" again, "'what is my lovely jockstrap?' again" is like the lost return to my lovely jockstrap, the lost return to my lovely jockstrap is like "what is my lovely jockstrap?," "what is my lovely jockstrap?" is like what is my lovely jockstrap, what is my lovely jockstrap is like my lovely jockstrap is like

Stained. In the dictionary, the user may discover the Being ("is") of the "jockstrap" "itself." This metaphorical mediation usually relies on the colon (":") rather than Being ("is") or metaphor ("like") as the copula for the relationship it draws between the signifier and its Other. The colon (":"), Being ("is"), and metaphor ("like") are imprecise symbolizations for the relationship not only between sameness, nearness, likeness, and indistinction, but also between difference, distance, unlikeness, and separation. Any word for the copula between words — such as is or is not, sameness or difference, nearness or distance, likeness or unlikeness, indistinction or separation, or even ($\supseteq$) — is inadequate as an index of the definition of the essence of any object. The structure of metaphor and the organization of the signifying chain are based on the ghostly remains of a vanquished essence. For what does the colon (":") or Being ("is") substitute? How is it possible for Being to represent unlikeness if the latter is likeness? How does the colon symbolize the difference which is constitutive of identity? Where does the metonymic flow (...) of words find destination (.)? Does identification ever return to itself in reference to the desirous network of words?

The center of the symbolic order is otherwise than itself. Madly, metaphor *qua* metonymy, and identification *qua* desire, are the principles of the organization of meaning-making. The situation is more dire than even Derrida suspects. The paradox is not simply that the center of the structure is infinitely substitutable in different "forms and names," such as is or is not, sameness or difference, or in the recent philosophical tradition, Nietzsche's "Will to Power," Heidegger's "Being," Foucault's "Power/Knowledge," Derrida's own "*Différance*," and so on. Rather, the problem is still more strange: *there is no word for this center whatsoever*. There is no such *das Ding* as a word. There is no word. The father is neither dead nor alive nor in the process of murder nor in the process of suicide. The father is simply Other to the system. What magic pulls the center out of the structure? How does man delude himself into a belief in or even a knowledge about a center or a margin which is not present — *qua* Nothingness — as itself? If the father is not the center of the system, then where is he? The *father* is elsewhere, and the *function* is dead.

Desire for the Lost Signified

The example of the definition of jockstrap in the dictionary demonstrates the endless Metaphoricity of identification as it slips into the infinite field of desire of what Lacan calls the *objet petit a* and its endless transience. The dictionary summarizes the jockstrap in the following format: "Jockstrap: a veil for *das Ding*." The definition of jockstrap which is provided by the dictionary is itself a metaphor. As metaphor: a jockstrap is (like) a veil for *das Ding*. The structure of metaphor easily assimilates to the organization of the definition. Any denotation or connotation of a word reproduces the structure of metaphor: "like," "unlike," "is," "Being," "is not," "Nothingness," ";," and so on. The dictionary is a compendium of metaphors. The metaphorical structure of the dictionary and the metonymic slippage within this structure of metaphor indicate that this treasury of words must refer to an otherness or what Derrida calls a supplement: books, articles, reviews, magazines, jots, Google, sporting goods catalogs, and so on. The dictionary is an infinitely recursive system of metonymy (…) in its explication of metaphor (.). But what is metaphor like (…)? Every word is simultaneously both the metaphor for essence and decidable determination, on the one hand, and the metonymy of slippery and excessive inessentiality, on the other hand. This simultaneity is the Pervert's Logic of disavowal and the both/and structure. Disavowal dissolves difference at the same time as it sustains this same difference. The pervert's both/and simultaneity affirms both metaphor and metonymy as *different* from themselves but the *same* as each other. The word for this paradoxical Unreason is Sameness⁺.

The pervert also affirms all of the words in the system of the Other, including negation. These words are fetish-objects. Objects suture the gap of the castration of sexual difference in the system. Perversely, there is neither castration nor lack. Plenitude frees the pervert to affirm the entirety of the galaxy even against the strict dictates of the neurotic either/or of the system. The intelligible definition of the jockstrap is provided by the dictionary. The dictionary — from page to page (…) — of metaphors (.) confers a relationship between the Inside of the jockstrap and the Outside of the other words in the system. These others constitute the jockstrap — "its" — as Inside of the metaphorical field of delimited signification. This process is the mirror of the structure of metaphor. This *mise-en-abyme* is also a metonymy. Metonymic here to there, and over to under, represent metaphor *qua* otherwise than itself. Identification must be simultaneously figured as desire. The ego is this metaphorical and identificatory interpretation of desire.

Freud claims that the ego is the compilation of lost object-cathexes. The ego is fundamentally the lost. The self is elaborated by the movements of desire. These desirous traversals simultaneously constitute and dissolve — same Sameness⁺ different Difference⁺ — the ego. The mirror shatters the *Gestalt* of Lacan's mirror stage. Metaphor and identity submit to the broken shards of metonymy and desire. This mirror is supposedly opposed ("unlikeness") to the denotative and literal dimension of the definition which is provided by the dictionary. But if metaphor is the structure of all signification, then what is the structure of metaphor if it exceeds itself into metonymy (A is like S is like E is like X, and so on)? Is metaphor even a structure?

Figure 9.2 Metonymy, Metaphor, and Sameness[+]

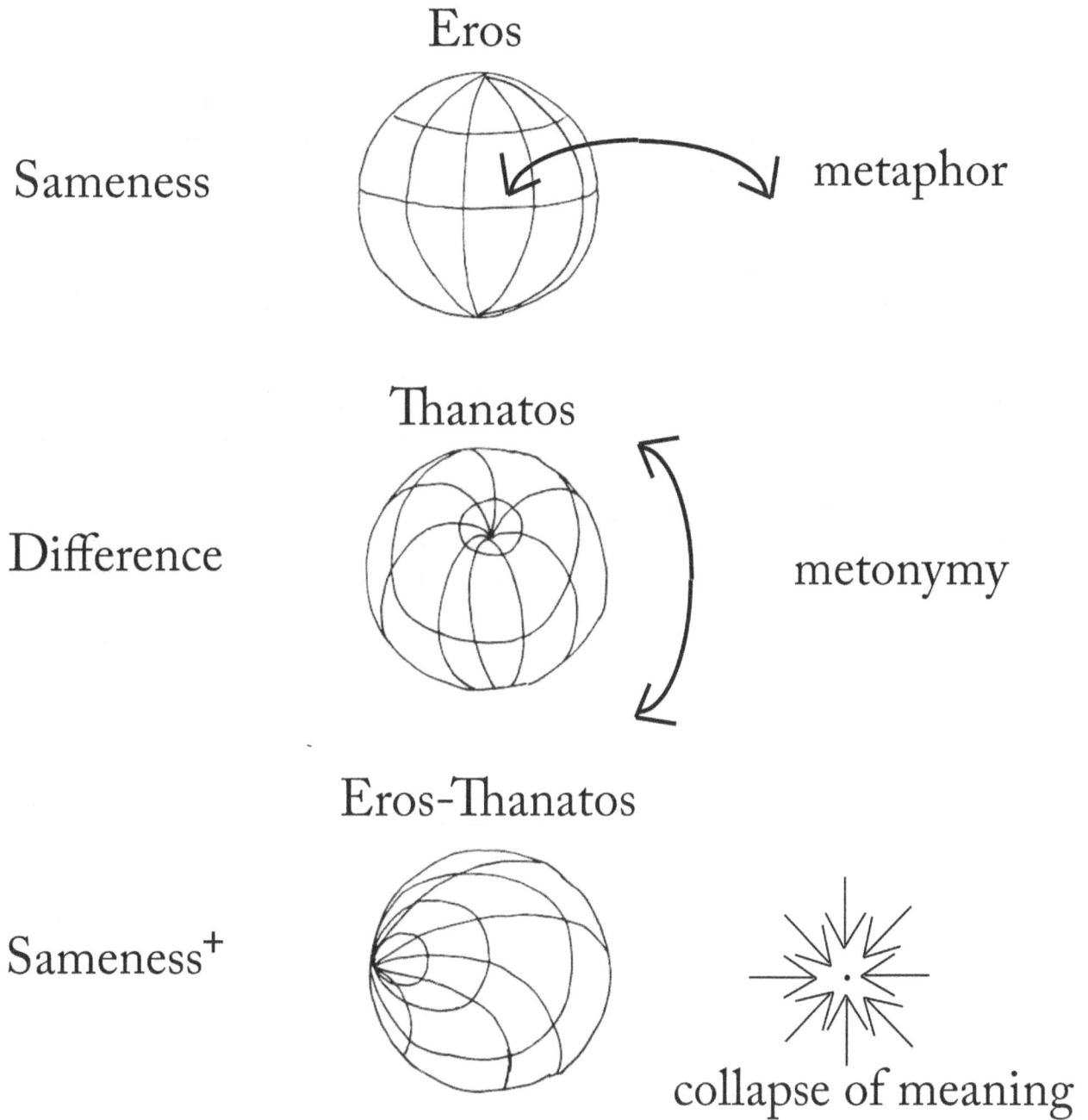

Eros

Sameness

metaphor

Thanatos

Difference

metonymy

Eros-Thanatos

Sameness[+]

collapse of meaning

This illustration includes three sets of figures (above, center, below). The sphere of *Eros* (above) portrays an illumination of difference as identity — but not yet as Sameness⁺. This *Eros* and metonymy sphere illuminates the switch and swap of words In and Out — here and there — in the sphere. The picture represents the ways in which one unit of text includes (excludes) the other units of text. But this switcheroo In and Out — here and there — *qua* everywhere in all points of space and time is neither self-same nor self-identical. The *Eros* of the system binds the words together such that the switch and swap In and Out are possible. This is the substitutional structure of metaphor. Metaphor is identical to but also different from metonymy. The sphere of *Thanatos* (center) approximates the psychotic intuition of difference as a Same⁺ Difference⁺ which is neither self-same nor self-identical. Metonymy denotes the temporal slipperiness of the sign. The identity — but not yet Sameness⁺ — in the sphere of *Thanatos* (center) opens space for a difference in signification. *Thanatos* is an unbound form of signification. The infinity of metonymic slippages (metaphorical substitutions) is understood as the death of the system in the *mise-en-abyme* of infinite semiosis. The visuality of these images inverts identity — but not yet Sameness⁺ — into difference, and it converts difference into identity. The picture visualizes rather than writes the neurotic repression of difference (symbolized as identity; above) and the psychotic foreclosure of identity (symbolized as difference; center). The sphere of *Eros<>Thanatos* (below) visually depicts the pervert's performance of this aesthetic of translation. The pervert expresses the *Eros<>Thanatos* parallactic overlap in a *Praxis* and a *jouissance* which are the Outside of *désir*. Sameness⁺ is the word for this relationality and constructionism which are structured by the inarticulable copulatic relationship of ~~Being~~ under erasure. *Eros<>Thanatos* is yet and already *Eros*. But the pervert's talent enlists the slipperiness of signification (metonymy, center) in order to speak new words in a new aesthetic. The pervert (mostly) recoils from a metalanguage. The pervert's art elaborates a future which is the Outside of *désir* in the transformation of death into *Praxis*. The sphere of *Eros<>Thanatos* is perversely both/and and schizoidly neither/nor *Eros* and *Thanatos*. The metonymies of jockstraps are a metaphor for "jockstrap," but the metaphor of "jockstrap" is also a metonymy for metaphor. The (un)limited space between jockstrap and "jockstrap" is the (im)perceptible gap between metaphor and metonymy in the return of sexual (*a*)difference in *Verleugnung*. The expansion and extension of jockstraps are the force of the (*a*)sexual will to power of the spatiality of the solar system of jockstraps. The jockstrap is the Outside of narrative chronological temporality.

Notes & Sketches —

Metaphor structures all signification. Metaphorical essence and truth are the work of a potentially endless metonymic synecdoche of part for whole, and so on. What is a veil for *das Ding* like and unlike? Not only is the literal a mere mirage of the metaphorical and vice-versa but an abyssal Metaphoricity — metonymization of metaphor — is the structure of the system of signification. The word submits (...) to a metonymy of words. The self yields to a series of others. This journey of desire and returned closure destroys identity in the process of the construction of metaphor. The structure is a system of metaphor *qua* metonymy. This is so even if this *qua* is the object of suspicion in the deconstruction of the positive ontological order of Being. The definition of jockstrap which is provided by the dictionary is a metaphor for another metaphor. This double (triple, and so on) metaphor is the Being of the movement of metonymy *qua* Becoming. The series of words is a perverse Metaphoricity of fetishes. This metaphorization of metaphor (and so on) is the essence (.) of metonymy and desire (...). There are many jockstraps on the Outside.

The essence of the spatiality of metaphor is its obverse: the temporality of metonymy. The only reason that we use the word "metaphor" is to stabilize an identification (.) which is always already metonymy (...). Metaphor is "like" metonymy. Identification *qua* metaphor and the ego-ideal is a second-order metaphor and metonymy for synecdoche. Identity and metaphor are inexhaustible in their gesture toward an endlessly desirous metonymy. What is metaphor like, and so on? Metaphor is the displaced *arche* of metonymic desire. Lacan calls the simultaneous (de)stabilization of this origin the "phallus." Lacan says: "The phallus is the signifier of this very *Aufhebung*, which it inaugurates (initiates) by its disappearance."[19] The phallus "disappears" as the inauguration of the metonymic slippage of words. The phallus must function as a veil and as a disappearance — as a jockstrap. The origin of desire is abyssal. *Arche* is Outside of presence. Identification "disappears" as the ostensible origin of desire. The self dissolves as the effect of a displaced genesis. To reverse my claim of eight sentences previous: metonymic desire is the origin of metaphorical identification. But if identity and metaphor, on the one hand, and desire and metonymy, on the other hand, are an interchangeable Sameness⁺, then is the question of *arche* always already under erasure?

Identification and metaphor, and desire and metonymy, are not present *qua* themselves even as they emerge *qua* their counterparts. The dictionary is a metaphor for the set of words which it purports to define in reference to the other words in the system. This ceaseless movement of metonymy *qua* metaphor is an infinite process and action. The metaphor of the self cannot suture this gap in (as) metonymy. Identification contains desire. Identity restrains desire in the Oedipus complex. The offspring's desire for the mother submits to identification with the father. The difference of deferral to the other words is the effort of desirous metonymy to return itself to metaphorical identification. Is the return of metaphor simultaneously the submission to metaphor *qua* signified? Or is this signified (.) itself a metaphor for a deferred (lost) metaphor (...)? Or is identification (.) always outrun by desire (...)? Or have these questions already been resolved as the same question *qua* Sameness⁺ — (⊇) — ?

The Means of Metonymy

The definition of a word is a metaphor for the entire dictionary. The compendium of words in (out) the dictionary is the jockstrap. The word is defined by the entirety of the set of metaphors — identities, objects, things, words, fetishes, and centers — in the dictionary. The jockstrap is defined as the dictionary and beyond this unlimited "itself." Every word is the same as every other word. Metaphor is structured according to a radical Sameness⁺. The signifier is internally divided in itself as this Sameness⁺. Definitions of words ("is," "Being," "like," ":," "*il y a*," "as such" "by definition," "*qua*") are provided by the dictionary. This series of words includes such empty signifiers as "freedom," "liberty," and "equality" which are the object of the struggle for hegemony in the politics of the signifier.[20] "Freedom" is a metaphor — for what? "Liberty" is a metaphor — for what? "Equality" is a metaphor — for what? "Self" is a metaphor — for what? All words are empty because metaphor is structured by the incomplete movement of metonymy toward an elusive signification, or Lacan's *objet petit a*, or Derrida's transcendental signified. The self is merely an outline of the Inside (Outside) of an empty vase (*qua* Being) which is surrounded and constituted (*qua* Nothingness) by the *mise-en-abyme* of metonymic desire. Identification is Nothingness only to be freed as Being by metaphor (.) *qua* metonymy (…) *qua* metaphor (.) *qua* metonymy (…) *qua*, and so on (…). The father entraps the offspring in the claws of an identification with him and the ego-ideal. The paternal metaphor consolidates an identification out of a stark Nothingness of the emptiness of a vase. The father is a metaphor. But where is he situated in the game of words?

The father is absent from the dictionary because the dictionary is structurally *open*. The dictionary is a compendium of an *open* set of fetishes and jockstraps. The function of the father is to contract and close the tendency toward expansion and openness which is otherwise the animate Principle of Sameness⁺. The father is a prop for the trap of metonymy and desire in the clutches of metaphor and identification. This is the proper resolution of the male Oedipus complex. The pervert resists capture in this ruse because he is committed to radical metonymy — desire or what becomes *Trieb* or drive in the Other *jouissance*. The pervert recoils from the project of metaphor, the imperative of identification, and the ideology of the individual. The madman and the pervert variably reject the father function. The series of objects in the system is expansive and open rather than contracted and closed. An off-copy title of the pervert's manifesto of the schizoid's Unreason is: "God and the J̶o̶c̶k̶s̶t̶r̶a̶p̶'s̶ *Jouissance*" (1972-73). The pervert and the madman bypass identity and its metaphorical stabilization in favor of metonymy and its desirous pursuit. The pervert and the schizoid return to *Trieb*. The dictionary *qua* the battery of signifiers in the Other is organized as a system of lack because of the insistent reflection of desire and metonymy. The self is an object which exceeds itself. Identity is impossible because its constitutive emptiness (Nothingness, is not) is itself (Being, is). The self constitutes itself *qua* itself which is a deviation *of* itself. The self is decentered. The relationship between the man and his Boy is mediated by the jockstrap which screens the Boy's *das Ding*.

This rearticulates Lacan's theorization of the mirror as the opposite and inverted gap between the ego and its constitutive alter ego. The mirror is an index of this paradoxical relationship of the self to itself. There is Nothingness to identity. Identity is the effect of (mis/dis)recognition. This self is plainly the emptiness or void around which the words of metaphor and identification, and metonymy and desire, circulate. The internal (external) empty Nothingness of the vase *qua* constituted is supplanted by the external (internal) full Being of the outline of the vase *qua* constituted. But, at the same time, the reversal of this relationship also adequately describes the same rapport. The Constituted misunderstands itself as the Constitutive and vice-versa. These blips in the system — internal, external, empty, full, Being, Nothingness — present as the other. Each cannot (mis/dis)recognize itself as such. Fragmentary movement toward identification — "self" — is always incomplete — "Other." The self is subordinate to the *objet petit a* or the transcendental signified. The slippage of diachrony, temporality, and deferral of desire explodes the self-identity and self-sameness — Being — of the self. At the same time, the subordination of the self to the Other in a temporal chain of signification is further confused by the apparent immobility of the synchrony, spatiality, and difference of identification. Time is the space of this deconstruction. But time is not yet time. Time is suspended in the Time of the Pervert. The pervert's watch is yet to either tick or tock until the expansion of space — Inside ($\supseteq$) Outside — is stretched to its infinite edges of the solar system.

Lacan's distinction between the want to be of selfhood against the want to have of desire is put in sharp relief. Identification (to be) must be outstripped by desire (to have). Identification and desire — self to other — are the same structure. There is no difference between identification (want to be) and desire (want to have). There is no possibility of an economy of *le propre* in the signifying chain. Any reference to the proper (proper, property, ownership, possession, and mineness) is fundamentally outstripped by the aneconomy which is organized by the signifier. The signifying chain promises privacy in the form of the possessive — mine, yours, his, hers, theirs, ours. But there is simultaneously no private property in the system. The fabled father is a delusion of the structure. Capitalism is an hallucination of the system. The solar system is structured by maternity and communism. Signification implies lack in the signifier (*différance* and trace). But, at the same time, there is simultaneously no castration in the system. Why does private property (what Marx defines as the essence of capitalism) dominate the system if it is simultaneously absent from its organization? Why does castration (what Freud defines as the nodal point of all psychical development) rule the system if it is simultaneously absent from the structure? How does neurosis emerge as the principle of the organization of a system which is structured as schizophrenic? How did capitalism and phallocentrism manifest — *ex nihilo* — against the journey of the force of labor toward abundance and the *Trieb* of (a)sexuality toward — ?

The only modality of return is the trespass of the endless cycle of law and its transgression and the transcendence of the other opposed binary oppositions. The divisive logic of the symbolic order is precisely the defense of the system against its own essential schizophrenia. This protection is illuminated in the pervert's form of negation. Disavowal discerns the law and its transgression as flip-sides of the same torus strip. Disavowal is simultaneously the return of disavowal. Disavowal reveals that the madness of the web of words is the principle of the symbolic order. $-im is the strange neurotic repression *qua* psychotic foreclosure — *rejet névrotique* — of the fundamental schizophrenia of the system. Man misunderstands the structure of his own negation. The subject misrecognizes his own "No!" What does "No!" negate? How does the "No!" (not) work? The transition from a veiled system of its supposed neurosis with its divisions between latent/manifest and unconscious/conscious to its truth as *rejet névrotique* requires the revelation of the Unreason of the Madness of Order. The techniques of the deconstruction of binary opposition in the representational system can be summarized by the creative figuration of the dream-work of the primary process.

Grammatology is the insight of the pervert. The pervert is the masterful mediator of issues of figuration between latent and manifest (and so on). The pervert sutures the division between the primary process of the unconscious and the secondary process of the system of the ego. The enlightenment of the truth *qua* Unreason in the symbolic order is contingent upon the mode of representation of the system. The reason that the organization of the signifying chain is obscured to the subjects of this order is that the psychical structure of neurosis dominates the configuration of a system which is otherwise psychotic. The system cannot represent its own organization *qua* madness. The neurotic interpretation and organization of the schizophrenia of the system foreclose madness. Madness is negated in the neurotic repression — *rejet névrotique* — by the symbolic order. This neurotic *Verdrängung* is schizoid *Verwerfung*. Negation of the system is proof of the schizophrenia. Psychosis is internal to a misrecognized neurosis. The system is organized by the incoherent coincidence of repression and foreclosure, and neurosis and psychosis.

Freud's definition of perversion as late as the 1938 essay on "The Splitting of the Ego in the Process of Defense" is the overlap of neurosis and psychosis, and repression and foreclosure. Fetishism is the name for the process of deconstruction. The psychical collusion and collision between alternative clinical structures are precisely perversion. The clinical philosophical structure of fetishistic perversion of representational simultaneity of the shoe, lace, fur, and jockstrap (and so on) is a mode of textualization. This fetishism can articulate and mobilize the requisite representational talent for its figuration as Unreason. The system autodeconstructs of its own misrecognized neurosis in psychosis. The reader, writer, and speaker are unnecessary in the autodeconstruction of the structure. This autodeconstruction is the cause and effect of the dissolution of the self.

The system is constituted as the schizoidly repressed ontological "What is?" of a question. The repressed returns in the symbolic order *qua* the foreclosure of psychosis. Schizophrenia is simultaneously the symbolic order. The preposition — of, as, against, by, toward, near, around, and so on — is the force of the perverse illumination. Perversity is simultaneously at the disposal of and enforced by the subjects of $-ism. The *qua* is this endless process. The system represses its own schizophrenia. The return of the repressive negation is the madness of the system. The return of madness is the symbolic order. The system is this simple cycle of *Verwerfung qua Verdrängung* of madness. The return of madness disrupts *qua* constitutes the system *qua* Real. The overlap of the repression of foreclosure and its return as the Real demonstrates the essential madness of $-ism. Psychosis *qua* Real cannot be figured. This is so because of the imperceptible difference between the symbolic order and the trauma of the Real. The pervert's talent is to illuminate the (non)coincidental both/and superpositional entanglement between these two orders of the galaxy.

The structure of madness in the system is disguised because the neurotic represses the suspension of the transcendental signified or *objet petit a*. Erasure is the condition of the structure of the symbolic order. There is no end (what Freud calls *Ziel*) in desire as the trickster object-cause. The *point de capiton* of the phallic function only momentarily and neurotically freezes the movement of desire in the image of the self. The paternal button-tie also simultaneously releases the letter onto the next destination and departure. Psychosis is spoken by perversion as neither arrival nor departure and both departure and arrival (and so on) of the letter. The both neither/nor and both/and and neither/both/and nor/neither/nor (and so on) are deemed the nonsense of Unreason.

The neurotic fantasy of the phallic function posits $-ism (private property and *le propre*) as the connective tissue between the inevitable signification of an inchoate swarm of signifiers and the illegible swath of signifieds. Materialities and abstractions are anchored — hinge and joint — to each other in the positive unity of the word in a coherent system of signification. The love letters of the metaphor for a "jockstrap, jockstrap rose" are promised by the *point de capiton* of the neurotic phallic function. The button-tie is the guarantee of the arrival of the love letters or the transcendental signified or the *objet petit a*. This deceitful promise organizes the approach of desire toward its goal (*désir*) rather than the visitation of aim with itself (*Trieb*). This other is the constitutive split in the object. The aim of desire is a misnomer. The aim of *désir qua Trieb* in the "missed encounter" is desire. The essence of *désir* and *Trieb* is distraction. Desire is distracted. Freud mentions these detours and delays — what Lacan describes as the diversions and bypasses of courtly love — as the aims of the instinct. Metaphor finally fixes identification in desire *qua* identity rather than *qua Trieb*. Phallic stabilization of the transcendental signified or the *objet petit a* is inoperative in both the schizoid and the pervert. The schizoid and the pervert invariably refuse the paternal vase of Being or Nothingness.

The endless supplement to desire is metonymy. Derrida refers to this simultaneous overlap as trace and origin. Origin and trace are opposed *qua* supplements *to* each other but also as — ($\supseteq$) — each other. Parallactic (non)coincidence ruins the *Gestalt* identification of the self. At the same time, the phallic *point de capiton* freezes desire in the image of identification and metaphor. The pervert's "but nevertheless" is the coincident rejoinder to the pervert's "I know very well." The truth (.) of the word is the ellipsis (…). Desire and trace cannot outstrip identification and the metaphor of origin. Being captures temporality as its own property (*le propre*) even as such privacy insists in its escape *from* and also as — ($\supseteq$) — metaphor. The *Gestalt* of the mirror stage is not simply a representation of a deviation between the ego and its ideal. The ego *Gestalt* and its anticipatory and constitutive maturation are different from "themselves." *Gestalt* is not *Gestalt*. Internal external division sustains the contrast of the ego and the other.

The cracked mirror is also an index of the image of metaphor $(\supseteq)$ *qua* $(\supseteq)$ metonymy, and of self $(\supseteq)$ *qua* $(\supseteq)$ other. This is so even as this speculation concurrently deviates from this fundamental variance in itself. This is the simple version of the function of the name-of-the-father. The paternal ego breaks the mother/offspring dyad of imaginary (dis)union. The father insists on an identification with a future excess. The displacement and condensation of the self are summarized as the ideal or want to be of identification. The self deviates from itself in order to become itself. The schizoid and the pervert resist the trope of the name-of-the-father. The schizoid and the pervert refuse to sacrifice *jouissance* for a coherent identity — the aperture and closure of the parallactic gap between ego and ideal — within the symbolic order.

The consequences of the choice are vast for the fate of difference in the symbolic order. The pervert's singularity animates the Constitutive — and Constituted — vanished mediation between \$-ism and S. The choice of *jouissance* instead of identity and desire breaks with the father's nefarious contribution to the *mise-en-scène* of the Oedipus complex. The father's role is to insist on a rapport between the offspring, on the one hand, and the superego and the ego-ideal, on the other hand. The pervert prefers to deny his acknowledgement of the distinction between the desire of the mother and the name-of-the-father. The realization of sexual difference is the horizon of the Oedipus complex. Perversely, the castration complex is a representational charade with the fetish-object. The shoe, lace, fur, jockstrap, and every other object are props of the performance.

The speedy paralysis of desire-metonymy finally captures the potential of *Trieb*. The dead end of the resistant object after its death and the moor of identification in the restriction of *Trieb* are extimatic obverse perspectives of the same movement. ⁺Ing metaphor is-ing — ⁺Ing⁺ — Be-ing-com-ing — Ing⁺. This articulates the essence of identity *qua* difference, self *qua* other, metaphor *qua* metonymy, identity *qua* desire, and Sameness⁺. Becoming-Other is a metaphorical metonymy or the becoming-time of space and the becoming-space of time. This is the Being of Derrida's (non)concept of *différance*. The dictionary refers (or differs in spatiality and defers in temporality) the definitions of words to other words as supplements (and so on). Metaphoricity slips into an endless metonymy. The proper name for metaphor is the Outside of the symbolic. Metaphor is present only in and as the Real. The Outside of the symbolic order is the Inside of the symbolic order. Metaphoricity — Inside $(\supseteq)$ Outside — is the object of the pervert's ecstasy. The metonymization of metaphor is the (*a*)sexuality of the pervert.

The central principle of organization of the symbolic order is the Real Metaphor. The *métaphore de la métonymie* is a metaphor. Metaphor is simultaneously both itself and not itself. This is the formula and articulation of Being. Being is the Becoming of split simultaneity. How can metaphor *qua* metonymy be a metaphor for Being unless it commits suicide as its own condition? Is the death of the self a murder by others in the system which robs the self of its own identity? How can the relationship between sameness and difference, nearness and distance, likeness and unlikeness, union and separation, and Being and Nothingness be properly textualized? This Being is the copula which relates the signifiers to each other. *Qua* metaphor, Being is a metaphor. But for what? Metaphor is dead — murder or suicide — and metonymy is its heavenly supplement. The obverse is also the case. What is the Other of identity and desire, and self and other, toward which men drive? It is not the simple beyond of the pleasure of regulation because we have yet to even arrive at the pleasure principle. The pleasure principle of homoeostasis is an apparatus of time. Time is deferred in space. There is no time for time in space. The unconscious is timeless. Masochistically, the pleasure principle is yet to present. The only present dimension in the solar system is the space of singular differences which are mapped as incomparable and incontrastable Sameness⁺. *Thanatos* is primary.

Duchamp's "Fountain"

One day, in 1917, the artist Marcel Duchamp went to the J.L. Motts Iron Works Co. on Fifth Avenue in New York City and purchased an ordinary object: a standard Bedfordshire model urinal. Duchamp proceeded to take the urinal back to his art studio on West 67th Street and reorient it ninety-degrees from its normal position of use. He scribbled "R. Mutt 1917" on the side of the urinal. This summarizes Duchamp's artistic efforts in the making of the work of art, "Fountain" (1917). He purchased an ordinary object, he slightly rotated the object, and he scrawled letters on the side of it. At the time of the purchase of the urinal (and the creation of the artwork "Fountain"), Duchamp was a board member of the Society of Independent Artists. The Society was organizing an exhibition around the obscene ethos that all of the work that was submitted to the show would be accepted. The Society promised the guarantee that all of the submitted work would be(come) art. Duchamp submitted his urinal as an artwork for the exhibition under the name, "R. Mutt," and awaited word from the board. Would the object be deemed an ordinary urinal or an extraordinary artwork? Would the democratic-totalitarian ethos of the exhibit transform the ordinary into the extraordinary? — and how? As it turned out, the board rejected the urinal ("Fountain") from the show. The rest of this fable is history: a hullabaloo followed, and Duchamp's extraordinary artwork (rather than ordinary object) which was known as the "Fountain" became widely considered the most influential and revolutionary work of art in the entire twentieth century. How did this happen? What was the revolution?

My discussion endeavors to explain the influence and revolution of "Fountain" (1917). I want to articulate an original theory of metaphor (and metonymy) in reference to desire, *Trieb*, sexual difference, ontology, and the principle of pleasure and its beyond. Strangely, the original "Fountain" (1917) was lost, but Duchamp authorized reproductions of his "ready-mades," as they were called, in the 1950s and 1960s. These ready-mades are copies of a copy, or a "simulation" in Baudrillard's words. In an act of smart solidarity with Duchamp's transgressive and absurdist sensibility, a Swedish performance artist pissed on the "Fountain" (1917) in a museum in Stockholm in 1999 (and was quickly escorted from the museum by security officers). This Swedish artist made the necessary extraordinary artwork an inessential ordinary object. The performance artist made the object both artistic and ordinary, and both fabulous and prosaic. The artist reversed Duchamp's move and indicated the mutual interchangeability of both gestures. The urinal is both an extraordinary artwork and an ordinary object.

The question which is posed by Duchamp's "Fountain" (1917) is often summarized as: is it art? Does the "Fountain" count as a work of art? This implicit indictment (art or not-art) is beside the point even as the interrogation reveals the stakes of Duchamp's intervention. Any discussion of the merits of the artwork — is it art? — involves accounts of aesthetic value (such as beauty), production (such as artistic technique), and consumption (such as art historical interpretation and criticism). But the social fact is: Duchamp's "Fountain" (1917) is not only a work of art. It is an extraordinary work of art. How do we know this? — precisely by the widely pronounced critical evaluation of the work of art from positions of power, such as art historical societies and visual culture textbooks and by the general audiences who accede to the expertise of power.

Foucault's obsessive textual return to the word "power" as the proper metaphor for the Constitutive Outside, as Derrida calls it, demonstrates a politicization of epistemology, ontology, and ethics in philosophical project. Baudrillard's interpretation of Foucault suggests that "power" is the fiery void of a vacant Nothingness. This void is the absence around which discourse — and Foucault's own studies — encircles.[21] The Baudrillardian interpretation of Foucault undermines the presence of any center — *et al.* — such as "power/knowledge" as an orientated and perspectival anchor for critical discourse. Foucault's compulsive repetition of the word "power" in his *oeuvre* demonstrates an insistent return to a center in his own theoretical edifice. Power *qua* center is terrifically compromised and mostly absent from within the delirium of Foucault's own theoretical commitments to the limit of thought. The only effective way to make a claim from within (preposition: out) the whirlwind of the in-between is to perversely disavow the "play," "strategy," or "adventure," as Derrida says, of text and its possible significations.[22] Any spectator can banter about aesthetics, production, and consumption all that he wants, but it does not authorize or enable him to deny Duchamp's "Fountain" (1917) classification as a work of art. But if the spectator were to dissolve himself into the *mise-en-abyme* of madness in which orientation and perspective are lost, then creative redefinition is risked. How does the writer animate the collapse of the structure from within the structure itself?

Contra common *doxa*, truth and beauty are not in the eye of the beholder. This isolated eye is blind because it cannot create a consensus on its own which would recognize the gaze that it purports to see. Knowledge *qua* disavowal in orientation and perspective is only possible if this will to truth can be socially situated within a community of ambivalent agreement. Similarly, the extant codes of convention mean that I cannot declare myself the primal father. Such an intervention would be interpreted as madness. Its articulation would be understood as schizophrenic because its content deviates from the organization of the structure from within which its desperation is uttered. The primal father is the fiction which sutures the loss of this center. The father purports to represent this center from within the mnemonic traces of the past. The reason that I may be the primal father is that I have subjects (sons and brothers) who are subordinate to me and who acknowledge my position as the center of the structure either in the past or in the future or in the future *qua* the past. The primal father of Freud's myth strangely avoids this consensual recognition from the Other because the sons and brothers are banished from the community. Their ostracization makes the response of the Women and the sisters in the father's beach house of considerable interest. The madman is the consequence of the denial of the name-of-the-father and its enforcement of coherent identity. The psychotic does not recognize me (or the *point de capiton*) as the primal father. But the schizoid's clinical structure enables him to return this Real to the symbolic order however dreamy and disturbed the hallucination or delusion which ruptures the system.

Practices of paternity maintain stable signification. Coherence is organized by convention and the general disavowal of deconstructive play. This is so even if such misadventure is also exactly coincident with solidarity. Meaning is not subjective, relative, or relational. But, at the same time, such qualifications circumscribe all signification. The point is that meaning is not individually subjective, singly relative, or independently relational. Rather, meaning is collectively subjective, socially relative, and culturally relational. Relationality and constructionism subvert any claims to an identity in interpersonal relations or to a center in a structure. This is the instructive demonstration of Saussure's views on the arbitrariness and absolute relativity of the material signifier.

Saussure's schizophrenic discovery of value in the signifier (as opposed to signification in the sign) articulates the impossible in the history of Western thought. This limit-thought is the secret truth of Unreason. This secret is strangely present in every moment in the history of Western thought. Western philosophy is the secret truth of Unreason. But it is oddly invisible. Western thought is as yet unthought. The differences and deferrals (*différance*) of the signifier escape the neurotic *point de capiton* of the phallic function. The self is essentially deformed. All versions of position and orientation are ruptured. This puts under duress even Marx's infamous image of the *camera obscura* (1845). This image is a metaphor for an ideological structure. The *camera* enables the critic to illuminate the upside-down *obscura* structure of social reality from within perspective. The gaze *qua* deferred object-cause manifests as the (im/ex)plosion of any coordinates whatsoever. This is the destruction in the aftermath of the Event. Saussure's discovery of the Madness of Order — amidst the prosaic neurosis of the system — is this Event. The collaboration between otherwise isolated units decides identifications and desires. The reason for this decision is the legibility of metaphors for the self *qua* the entirety of the Other.

The social fact which terrorizes man is that the Other confers value on the subject. The subject is also simultaneously the object in the vertiginous whirlwind of disperspectives and misorientations of the gazes. Identification happens to this subject (⊇) object not only because the subject deviates from itself *qua* object. The self is the Other, except that ~~Being~~ is *sous rature*. The *essence* of the subject is *constructed* as the object. Essence ~~is~~ construction, but also: ~~essence construction~~. The preposition is the essence of the self. The other parts of speech — nouns, pronouns, adjectives, determiners, verbs, adverbs, conjunctions, and interjections — are the elements of the *Trieb* toward — The *Gestalt* image in the mirror interpellates this veritable plaything of the system: *Différance*, Constitutive Outside, Power/Knowledge, Other, Phallus, Being, Will to Power, and so on. But the center of this discursive orchestration escapes as the difference and deferral of the Real. All of this commotion — switcheroo, here to there — is Nothingness.

The work of the Other — Real Metaphor — is visible in Duchamp's efforts with the "Fountain" (1917). Duchamp became — will-have-become from the time-machine of *Nachträglichkeit* and *après-coup* — the artist of the most influential work of art in the twentieth century. He did so even in the absence of any recognizable materialist artistic practice. Duchamp merely purchased the urinal, rotated it from its normal position, and scrawled letters on its side. He had the foresight to submit it for exhibition, but it was the Board which contributed the capstone gesture. The Board rejected the most influential work of art in the twentieth century. The so-called artist — for lack of an adequate metaphor for a subject who is also simultaneously an object — becomes the subject (⊇) object of his own (not)work. The artwork purchases, rotates, and scrawls the artist rather than the reverse. This distinction between Outside and Inside is only possible if there is no Other of the Other *qua* the Other. If the Constitutive Outside is itself Constituted — the Other of the Other of the Other — and if the Constitutive of the Constituted of the Constitutive is itself Constituted — the Other of the Other of the Other — then the possibility of stable orientation and coherent perspective proves preposterous.

Deliriously, the purchase, rotation, and scrawl are endlessly deferred beyond either artist or Other (or Other and Other, and so on). The Other is a fixed fetish rather than a played substitution. Metaphor fashions Duchamp the artist of an artwork that simultaneously manufactures his own identity as otherwise than itself. Neither the Other nor the self is present to itself as either Other or self. There is neither artwork nor artist, and neither Constituted nor Constitutive, but — The Other is a metaphor for the function of a center. The center is infinitely substitutable in the endless escape of metonymy from the clutches of metaphor. The center is neither the artist nor the artwork nor the museum nor the bathroom (and so on). The structure of the schizoid's neither/nor is a supplement to the neurotic's either/or and the pervert's both/and. Either and both, and or and both — are also crucial to the appearance of the Pervert-Schizoid-Woman. The conundrum in this effort will be the pervert's considerations of representability of this schizoid Unreason.

But who is this Other of the Pervert-Schizoid-Woman? Why is this question of the Other or a fundamental metaphor or a center which could halt the play of endless signification posed? How could such an Other become manifest and visible? If the Other yields to the metaphorization and identity (.) of metonymy and desire (...) and the obverse — stable articulation and incoherent play — then who is the Other of this Other? Does Derrida's *différance* finally trace beyond Lacan's *point de capiton*? Do the mother and the clitoris triumph? If Duchamp is not the artist, then who is he to be(come)? There is no Other of the Other. What Other is antecedent or precedent to the present Other? Any reference to this Other freely forces the pervert to unveil the Unreason of the schizoid. The pervert mobilizes the representational pyrotechnics of disavowal. The Other cannot be determined as presence in a metaphor which escapes slippage into an infinite metonymy. Duchamp may be the cause or the effect of the artwork. But his essence is subordinate to these same bits and bobs, nooks and crannies, parts for wholes, and wholes for parts of metonymy.

Duchamp stole the manufactured urinal from the original laborer at the J.L Motts Iron Works Co. on Fifth Avenue in New York City. This anonymous worker is the subject ($\supseteq$) object of the assembly of the urinal. This lost laborer who materially constructed the urinal is invisible in the artwork. This is so even if the artwork is this labor *qua* a creationist sublimation *ex nihilo* of the Other *qua* Duchamp. From where do the artwork, artist, laborer, and spectator originate as *arche*? Who is the artist of the most influential artwork in the entire twentieth century? The worker's general labor is subordinate to Duchamp's so-called artistic technique and conceptual innovation.

Even if the spectator or critic stabilizes Duchamp's conceptual study in presence, the decision of the locus of this conceptual pissy letter begs the question of *arche*. Is the origin of the work of art the mind, the brain, the gene, the misfired neuron? — then off on chase to what destination? — and toward (away from) which remainders and excesses of the Other? Even, where *is* the urinal? Who willed this epic irritant into a presence which dissolves itself on its own terms? The artist of "Fountain" (1917) is disturbingly undecidable. The Other disrupts the coherence of the work of art and the identity of the artist. The Other is the so-called artist. Every word in the system is the artist, artwork, laborer, and every other word in the Other — Artist ($\supseteq$) Artwork ($\supseteq$) Laborer ($\supseteq$) Object ($\supseteq$) — This collectivist — constructionist and relationalist — artwork is beyond capitalist ownership. The concept of the work of art — specifically: relationality and constructionism — shifts agency and responsibility to the Outside. The structure of the trace of the word jockstrap = P = E = N = I = S = is responsible for the wound. The artist is alien. The artist is also human.

Duchamp discovers by accident that the system is already communist. The structure is in essence the abolishment of private property. But, at the same time, the system sustains the humanist theories and practices of the Logic of Identity. This — *right now* — is communism. But man neither theorizes nor practices it as such. Capitalist man is thinking, being, and living in a communist system. Man is suspended from the world. Capitalist man is in the wrong world. The world is erroneously structured for a mistaken man. Man and the world are misfit. This is not the proper world for man. Man is not the proper subject for the world. This relationship between the subject and the object is inadequate. This is not the world of man and his $-istic values and affairs. This world must be subordinated — *Verwerfung* — in order to return an existence which fits the ideological presuppositions of the linguistic sign, the capitalist commodity, and phallocentric sexual difference. But how and why does the system neurotically foreclose — *rejet névrotique* — its Unreasonable truth? What are the threats of the system and its communist and schizophrenic essence? The negation of the system reproduces the schizoid foreclosure. This madness is the essence of the system. $-ism compulsively repeats the gesture of its dissolution in order to escape an Other-Metaphysics. This suicidal tendency in the death drive is simultaneously the source of the *Eros* of the system. What is a life which is beyond an obsessive and compulsive series of suicide attempts?

The Other confers signification on Duchamp. Duchamp is a urinal in a museum. Duchamp's identity is unsettled by context and the (con)text of (con)text of (con)text, and so on. The instructive point is not to be conned by the context. The easy substitution of objects — Duchamp, you, me, museum, bathroom, your penis, my penis, jockstrap, and so on — makes the presence of the artist of the most influential and revolutionary work of art in the twentieth century undecidable and indeterminate. The identity of the artist of "Fountain" (1917) is a veritable mystery because the self has been eclipsed by the Outside. This is the exact reverse of the proper trajectory of the Oedipus complex and its imperative of the exchange of desire and pleasure for identity and ideal. The Oedipus complex is evaded. Castration anxiety is displaced. What are the psychosexual trajectories of maturation which avoid parental conflicts and defeated objects? What psychosexual system displaces the neurotic trajectory of phallocentric loss and capitalist scarcity with the *Trieb* of the Pervert-Schizoid-Woman?

The reversal is staged from within the structure of metaphor. The so-called artist and artwork are subordinate to an Other. This remainder exceeds the artist and artwork. The metonymic desire of the slip and slide between text and context — art and museum, urinal and bathroom, and artist and Other — destabilizes the determination as presence of any metaphorical identification — (.) *qua* (...) — of the artwork or artist within a coherent context. Whose *(le propre)* presence is subordinate to the excess of the system? Who are the subject and the object? Whose is whose? About the Van Gogh shoes about which Heidegger and Schapiro feud: "Whose are the shoes?"[23] — to which I might add: "What size are they?" This ownership *(le propre)* is destroyed by the Other. Capitalist ownership confers an identity which is unwanted — "mind," "iPad," "soul," "Cheerios," "body," "Xbox," "speech," "doll," "unconscious," "calculator," "neuron," "gizmo," and so on.

The Contexts of the Contexts

Rather than direct questions about aesthetics, production, and consumption, Duchamp's work poses the question: *how* is it a work of art? How does Duchamp's "Fountain" (1917) become art? How does the ordinary unworthy object become an extraordinary valuable artwork? The quick answer is: the (con)text. The reason that the urinal is an extraordinary art object rather than an ordinary utilitarian object is that it is located in a museum under clear glass encasement rather than in a dirty bathroom. The deconstruction of the frames of the two contexts (museum and bathroom) is performed by the Swedish artist who pissed on the "Fountain" in the museum in Stockholm in 1999. The museum is also simultaneously the bathroom. The museum and the bathroom are not themselves ($A \supseteq A$).

The urinal takes on its value as an extraordinary art object because it is in a museum. The urinal takes on its ordinary value because it is in a bathroom. The surrounds confer value on the object within the *mise-en-scène*. The (con)text creates the (con)text because the (con)text is easily interchangeable and endlessly extendable. The Other (museum, bathroom, reader, and author) confers signification on the text (urinal, ordinary object, and extraordinary artwork). But the Other also confers signification on the context. The bathroom is not itself without the urinal. The museum is not the museum without the artwork. This (there) (con)text(s) is (are) mutually constitutive and substitutable. The only presence in the system is this unstable and incoherent (con)text. Signification is reduced to Nothingness in the absence of the (con)text of Nothingness. The excess (...) illuminates the text and object (the urinal) that the text and object will Be(come). But where and when, in what space and time, will the Becoming be present? What is the Other of the Other? Presence — *et al.* — is not simply deferred beyond spatialized borders between Inside and Outside. Presence is the *tout autre* of the system.

The Other enables the signifier to become other than itself. The urinal only will have been (*Nachträglichkeit*, *après-coup*) an extraordinary artwork in the futural event of its arrival in the presence of the museum as its constitutive context. The effect of the slippage in the context refers this event of stability to an Outside of space and time. The context will have been Becoming what it still will have been (is) Becoming and also already is not yet. But does the signified of the ordinary urinal or the extraordinary artwork ever arrive at the bathroom or the museum? Are these objects — *et al.* — ever present if the bathroom and the museum also precede (*Nachträglichkeit*, *après-coup*) both the departure and the arrival of the urinal or the artwork? Does the temporality of the *futur antérieur* ever arrive in its future — *qua* signified? Does the *will* have a *Becoming*? Does the will-have-been submit to a will-never-have-been-ing of the never-past and never-future? Has the past even happened yet in a future which recedes from presence? Has nothing happened yet? Has time yet to begin? The unconscious is the space of timelessness.

This situation introduces the tense of the Time of the Pervert: willing having beening Becoming Being — This articulates the pervert's schizophrenic insight. Temporally, best put: (the) (con)text-ing(s) in process-ing(s) of Ing⁺. This is exactly not a sentence because the verb is absent. But the demonstration is that these gerunds *qua* verbs — Ing⁺ — articulate the Time of the Pervert and the explosion of any chronological time, such as the Time of the Neurotic and the *futur antérieur*. Text and context are a simple Nothingness in the absence of the phallic *point de capiton*. Nothingness is the fetish as-happening but-not-yet signified as endpoint to several actions. The urinal is not an extraordinary art object because of anything either internal or integral to itself. The urinal is also not an extraordinary art object because of anything external or extrinsic to itself. Can we so readily trust the conceptual critique of (con)text from within the text of my con? If neither/nor, then what is emergent from a not-yet future? If time is suspended, then is time at all? There is no time in the unconscious.

The urinal is not even the present object in the absence of the frame of the bathroom (ordinary urinal) or the museum (extraordinary artwork) or everything (*et al.*) that the urinal is coincident with in its Constitutive Outside. Rather, the object simply is not — Being *qua* Nothingness and Being ($\supseteq$) Nothingness — in the absence of a frame of reference which would otherwise confer its objecthood. The fetish illuminates the Time of the Pervert: in-process is the Beingness-ing-Nothingness-ing Ing⁺. But if the object (museum and bathroom) is itself absent, then is Being (essence and identity, *et al.*) at all possible in the present? The fetish is absent in its fetish-ing. Fetish-ing is the verb-i-zation of the gerund form and the noun-i-zation of the verb form of Ing⁺. The fetish is the Being of the gerund *qua* as such. The object is split in an indeterminate and undecidable space. This is the essence of Saussure's version of the signifier. The fetish is a Becoming-Split of the object in the Outside of time. The Outside of time is the unconscious.

Duchamp himself barely touched the object, except for the slight rotation and the scrawl of "R. Mutt" on the side. The force which makes the urinal extraordinary art has nothing to do with the essence or the presence of the object. There is Nothing — Inside ($\supseteq$) Outside — of the object. The urinal is an extraordinary art object because of external and extrinsic elements, such as the context, *mise-en-scène*, surrounds, and museum which confer value on the urinal. But there is also Nothing — Inside ($\supseteq$) Outside — of the object. The urinal is also an extraordinary art object because of internal and integral elements, such as color, texture, design, and GPF which confer value on the urinal. But there is neither an Inside of the urinal nor an Outside of the urinal. How is this perverse simultaneity possible? The apparently external and extrinsic properties (museum, clear glass encasement, and spectators) may be a Constitutive Outside. But this very Outside is Constituted by the Constitutive Inside (color, texture, and cake). The Constitutive Outside is simultaneously Outside of the Constitutive(-Constituted) Outside(-Inside). The ($\supseteq$) is itself Constituting-ing-ing-Constituted-ing-ing Ing⁺. This illuminates the Time of the Pervert and his fetish.

The otherwise self-same and self-identical (A = A) submit to the differences of the Other (A $\supseteq$ A). The signifier is the effect of the _____ of its own negation. The absence of *arche* is stabilized by the fiction of a creationist sublimation *ex nihilo*. *Fort! Da!* The self-same and the self-identical are the eruptions of differences in the Other. Origin implies trace. Derrida explicitly notes that the *arche* (is) trace.[24] Temporally, put best: origin-ing-ing-perform-ing-tracing-ing Ing⁺. The verbed gerund is the Time of the Pervert's fetish. Temporally, the perverting fetishing is-ing fetish is-ing origin-ing-ing-tracing-ing in the spacing of timing and the timing of spacing in the in-action fetish-ing Ing⁺. This is precisely an incomplete sentence because there is no discrete and isolated verb for an action. This *entire sentence* is a verb. It is a representational figuration in Being of an inconclusive Becoming. The sentence (we) await(s) the Event. A symbolization of this perverse temporal form must be impossibly read as the verbalizing of the gerunding, and so oning. Time is not yet because space is not present to spatialize time. Time waits for itself — Outside — for space. The unconscious of timelessness precedes the temporality of the system of the conscious.

The word is exposed by an internal ($\supseteq$) external difference. The difference between an ordinary urinal and an extraordinary work of art is the difference between external (internal) and extrinsic (integral) factors, such as a bathroom (gift shop) and a museum (toilet bowl brush). The external and extrinsic factors are simultaneously internal and integral to the object. The words of "internal," "external," "integral," "extrinsic," "museum," "bathroom," "gift shop," and "toilet bowl brush" — Inside Outside — are strictly interchangeable. Fetish-ing ~~is~~ *qua* ~~is~~ verb-ing. There is space in the absence of time. Space and time are the same dimension. Freud names this spatial dimension the unconscious. The pervert's space is timeless. Space is yet to extend into time. Time is *not*.

The pervert's myriad fetish-objects are the effect of the unconscious-work of translation in condensation and displacement. The secondary process and considerations of representability return fetishing to the secondary process of the ego. There are no borders between objects — *et al.* — other than those which are enforced by precarious and momentarily unhinged metaphors and uneasy identifications. The Other is the external and the extrinsic — Outside — force which confers the self-same and the self-identical of the internal and the integral — Inside. There is no word ("grasshopper") for this Co-Constitution of the Constitutive as concurrently Constituted in the object. Desire forever ruptures the stabilization of these boundaries. The refusal of slippery bits and pieces and slimy crannies and crevices to recognize borders is the reason that desire — *et al.* — cannot be satisfied. The *objet petit a* slips from the grasp of desire because there is no division to trespass. The object of desire is Nothingness. The *objet petit a* is —

The reason that the system is schizophrenic is that there is neither law nor father in $-ism. Freud's turn to a "longing for the father" is his explanation for religion as a cry from the Real depths of the symbolic order.[25] The neurotic seeks the stabilization of the fundamental psychosis of the structure. Constituted madness is the object of its own systemic force of repression. Constitutive psychosis is the organizational principle of the operation of the order. Try this: the urinal is ordinary not because of some internal and integral properties which are Inside of the urinal. Rather, the urinal is ordinary because of some internal and integral properties which are "Inside" of the urinal. The urinal is ordinary because it is in a museum. The internal and external properties — Inside and Outside — of the urinal are constituted and conferred by the Other. The fundamental emptiness of the urinal is magically returned to the urinal in this constitution of itself and conferral of its value. The internal and integral — Inside — are themselves *qua* the external and the extrinsic — Outside. This *qua* illuminates the principal function of the preposition: to direct the chains of words toward essence and identity in the swap in-and-out — Inside and Outside — of desire. Desire is neither Inside nor Outside. Rather, desire is the determined neurotic cathexis to a perspective and an orientation which are lost to *Trieb* in the endless recursion of the contexts and their galaxies. The preposition directs the traffic of *Trieb*. The Ing⁺ is the object of the disturbance of the preposition. Each word — "internal," "external," "integral," and "extrinsic" — is different from itself because it is coincident with its opposite word (A $\supseteq$ A). Put recursively, Outside ($\supseteq$) internal ($\supseteq$) external ($\supseteq$) integral ($\supseteq$) extrinsic ($\supseteq$) Inside (...) —

The internal and integral property is Being the external and extrinsic property. This Constitutive tension is irresolvable because each signifier is mutually (un)Constituted and (un)dissolved by its opposite. This excess is the self-same and the self-identical. The opposite is its own opposite *qua* the other. Being ($\supseteq$) Nothingness — Nothingness ($\supseteq$) Being — Being ($\supseteq$) Nothingness — "Fountain" (1917) is extraordinary art not because it was slightly rotated and grafitied by an artist (put under clear glass encasement). Rather, "Fountain" (1917) is extraordinary art because it is in a museum (bathroom). What is (Being) the museum (or the bathroom) if it is internal (external) and integral (extrinsic) — Outside — in a recursive context? What if the context were merely a text? — and what if this (con)text were a (con)text? What is the bathroom? How is the bathroom? Why is the bathroom? Where is the bathroom? But when? The bathroom — *et al.* — is the Outside of time. The unconscious is timeless. The worldly object is timeless. The object — *et al.* — is Outside of time. The zero-degree of temporality is the Time of the Pervert. Time is a symptom of neurosis. There is no time for the madman and the pervert. Schizophrenia and perversion are the Outside of time in the endless expanse of the space of the solar system.

The reversal of the Inside/Outside binary enables the destabilization of the relationship between text (object, urinal) and context (museum, bathroom) and Other (con)texts. To reverse Derrida: there is nothing *Inside* of the text. Why does Derrida decide to negate the Outside if the negation equally applies to the Inside? The Inside and the Outside are mutually Constitutive. The recursive Outside — Inside — Constitutes — Constituted — this mutual constitution. There is also nothing *Outside* of the text. The Outside ($\supseteq$) Inside of the Outside and the Inside of the text (is, are) a Nothingness. The system enforces the neurotic either/or choice: Inside *or* Outside. There is nothing neither Inside nor Outside of the text. There is no certain division between the text "itself" and the text not "itself." Temporally, the urinal is Outside of time. Neither now nor then nor later but unconsciously —

Spatially, there is also no certain division between the Inside "itself" and the Outside "itself." The urinal is in an indeterminate and undecided space which is outside of comparison, contrast, exchange, or presence. *Il y a* — presence — in space. The question of spatial context is, "Where is the urinal?" The question of temporal context is, "When is the urinal?" The presence of the object is to be determined by the process of fetishing by text, context, author, and reader. The forces of stabilization constitute the self-same and self-identical (A = A). These forces are neither present nor determinate — as such, *qua*, by definition, *il y a*, and so on. Force (*et al.*) is the process of fetish⁺ing *qua* object Ing⁺. The fetish-ing-object-ing *qua* verb in form Ing⁺ is the time(lessness) and space of the unconscious of an absent temporality and an unordered spatialization. There is space. But there is no time. Space is not Inside — Inside/Outside — a series of spaces. Unorganized spaces make time impossible. Time is unconscious timelessness. The Time of the Pervert is a timelessness off pace with space. The time of the future is the space of the unconscious. The object (*et al.*) is space. The artwork is a wish of the unconscious. The urinal is the navel of the dream.

The Inside is the Outside

These quick answers to rhetorical questions about (con)text in Duchamp's "Fountain" (1917) obscure the truly revolutionary consequences of the work. The crucial interval between subject and Other is the relationship — word for such — between the words in the opposition. The word of metaphor (.) is torn by the movement of desire (...). Where is the museum as an identification or a presence if the metonymy of (con)text forever extends its boundaries? What (is) the symbol for the relationship between the urinal and the museum? — or between text and context, object and *mise-en-scène*, and you and me? This return of the infinite recursion ($\supseteq$) of the (con)text deconstructs the symbolic order as such. There can be no organized symbolic order in the absence (...) of presence (.). The system requires stability in order to generate signification. This sense is concurrently the proviso of the destabilization of the Real *qua* the symbolic.

The system is organized by an orientation toward signification which is enforced by the paternal metaphor and the *point de capiton*. The question of selfhood — "Who am I?" — cannot settle identity (.) because the question of metaphor is the precise answer to the question of identity. Nothingness is otherwise because Nothingness *qua* Being — ($\supseteq$) — is the parallactic overlap between (...) and (.). *Fort! Da!* But how is the relationship between the subject and the Other to be symbolized as Being ("is") or Nothingness ("is not") or otherwise? The economy of diachronous desire for the *objet petit a* must be beyond presence (.). The *objet* is neither (.) nor (…). Rather, the object-cause of desire is (⊇) which exceeds (…) the self and itself (…) across the prepositional orchestration in the expanse of space in the unconscious.

The supplement to this desire is neither *arche* nor trace. The proper copula — ~~Being~~ — which relates words *qua* Constitutive (…) *qua* Constituted (.) in their constitution is neither (…) nor (.). Metaphor is (not) (un)like itself. The proper stable essence (.) for metaphor must not be a metaphor. … (…) … (.). Metaphor is always already metonymy. Identity is always already desire. Unlikeness *qua* (.) is posterior to any essence in space. There is no such *das Ding* as identity or essence. There is no (.) — There is no such possibility as perspective or orientation. There is no such *das Ding* as the self. There is neither cause nor effect in the apparatus of the self. The difference between Constitutive (…) and Constituted (.) is null. The *Gestalt* image is not merely a mistaken fiction. The *Gestalt* image is also an ideological hoax of the system.

Freud's account of the exchange of the desire for the mother for identification with the father — paternal metaphor — is incoherent. The system unexpectedly bars the function of the father. There is no exchange of mother for father. The Oedipus complex is an unnecessary fable. The system is bit for byte and part for whole in an endless desire (…) of *Trieb*. The foreclosure of drive is the condition of the neurosis of the system. The schizoid and the pervert escape the oedipal injunction. Metaphor is neither a metaphor (.) for metonymy nor a metonymy (…) of metaphor (…) — Is there a word for an endlessly recursive *not* which is not not itself not? Each is otherwise than itself. Each *qua* itself is not itself *qua* other. This is the essence (.) of the word (…;). The word is not a word. Perversely, … … (.) (⊇) (…) and (…) (⊇) (.) (⊇) (.) … ….

There is nothing integral and internal to — Inside — the text. There is nothing extrinsic and external to — Outside — the text. The text is spatial, but it is neither Inside nor Outside. The Inside and the Outside make and break each other, but their coordinates in space are indeterminate and undecidable. The unconscious expanse of ~~Inside~~ and ~~Outside~~ in space makes time the Outside of the galaxy. The museum illuminates the urinal. The urinal frames the museum. The *Aletheia* happens from Inside and Outside and not from Inside and Outside. But what is this Constitution (.) Constituted (…) by? The space of the (con)text slips on the bathroom floor and slides on the museum entranceway. This is a recursive spatial expansion of the Inside (⊇) Outside. There is no temporality in the unconscious space. Out of time, *Trieb* wanders space. The enforcement of Inside of the bathroom against Outside of the museum endeavors to coordinate space in order to enable time. The suspension of the Inside and the Outside — Constituted and Constitutive — suspends time. Uncoordinated, the space of the unconscious cannot be calculated — numbers, integers, decimals, and 1s and 0s. Space is the Outside of the general equivalent. Outside of time is — communism. The unconscious is the timeless space of communism. As Marx promised, Communism is the End of History. Communism is a space.

Neither Inside nor Outside is present. There is *not* an Inside or an Outside. There is uncoordinated space. But there is no chronological time. The Constitutive (…) and the Constituted (.) have yet to be *qua* Being *qua* self-same and self-identical. There is an endlessly delayed — Out of Time — Constitutive (…) of the Constituted (.) (…) (.) which emerges as creationist sublimation *ex nihilo*. Lacan's example in the *Seminar* on the ethics of psychoanalysis (1959-1960) is Moses who makes the Chosen People — *is* — out of the slaves — *is not*.[26] Courtly love and its (in)terminable efforts to approach its object of desire — (…) — indicate this same interval between (…) Nothing and (.) Something.[27] This Constitutive Constituted is the spatial third-dimension of the timeless unconscious. The unconscious is a kaleidoscopal space which obscures all Reason of the ego in favor of the Unreason of the primary process. The Inside of the urinal is the Outside of the museum because neither is exclusively itself nor the Other but their extimate Sameness⁺ of Inside (⊇) Outside.

Inside and Outside are Constitutive (.) and Constituted (…) — metonymy and metaphor, desire and identity, and self and Other. Inside and Outside are the Constitutive (⊇) Constituted extimate Other Sameness⁺ Inside and Outside of the Constitutive (⊇) Constituted of (…) in the absence of (.). The (…) is simultaneously Inside and Outside of itself. Perversely, Sameness⁺ (⊇) — The object is at once neither A nor B, but both A and B, except neither A nor B. Rather, the object is A and B, except neither A nor B. But the object is also either A and B or neither A nor B. It is both (.) and (.) but also neither (.) nor (.). Rather, it is (.) and (.) or neither (.) nor (.). Recursively, the object (⊇) both and but also neither nor and nor neither nor is neither or neither. *Ex nihilo,* space.

Duchamp's work of art is different from itself and the same as itself. The artwork is Becoming-ing itself-ing Ing⁺ in this endless recursion of the *not.* This *not* returns to this *not* (and *not,* and so on) and to a Sameness⁺. The infinitely unfurled (con)text is the artwork. Duchamp's urinal is the museum. The symbol (⊇) is the copulative figuration of Being under erasure. This symbol (⊇) articulates the recursive cause and effect of Sameness⁺. Stabilization is the peculiar and unfortunate effect of the system which seeks the arrival (.) of the letter (…) at its destination (.) or the Constitutive at its Constituted or metonymy at its metaphor or desire at its identity. The impossibility of this recursion — its break — is denoted by (⊇). The phallic function is foreclosed by the schizoid and disavowed by the pervert. Derrida (1972) says it plainly: "I would like to demonstrate why a context is never absolutely determinable, or rather in what ways its determination is never certain or saturated."[28] The context is never saturated — exhausted and totalized — because it is always supplemented with or extended by further (con)texts in expansive space. The context is coexistent with the entirety of the galaxy and is beyond even this solar system. The context is neither an Inside nor an Outside, but both and neither and either both or neither but —

There is no context because there are no spatial borders. The museum is the bathroom is the urinal is the artwork, and so on. Each is Ing⁺ this otherwise and even beyond this Ing⁺ toward the outskirts before infinity but not beyond — *Yes!* The Madness of Order is summarized as: … Ing⁺ around Ing⁺ toward Ing⁺ near Ing⁺ by Ing⁺ under Ing⁺ above Ing⁺ for Ing⁺ below Ing⁺ and Ing⁺ so Ing⁺ on Ing⁺ … — The paradox of the unfurled context is that man all the while does know — "I know very well, but nevertheless" — the spatial location of the unknowns to presence. The *point de capiton* stabilizes contexts and coordinates of space. An enforced Inside/Outside — here versus there and up versus down and right versus left — facilitates the deployment of numbers, integers, digits, 1's, 0's — general equivalence — of temporality and capitalism. The phallus is foreclosed by the schizoid, and it is disavowed by the pervert. Perspective and orientation are the techniques of the neurotic and his regime of $-ism. The neurotic's will to identification — Constitutive *qua* Constituted — enforces the *point de capiton* and its nefarious work to anchor futural free communist space and to underpin extant antagonistic capitalist time. The trick is that the phallus is also not present. Metaphor (.) is strictly coincident with the entirety of the words in the system (…).

The museum and the bathroom are "a sameness which is not identical."[29] Each enclosure is unclosed and disclosed *qua* the Other. Parallactic reversal stains any stable map of space of the urinal. Time cannot tick and tock in the absence of bordered space. The Inside of the urinal is undecidable and indeterminate because neither space nor its object is self-same or self-identical (.) but each is rather otherwise than this otherwise (…). A Sameness⁺ which is not identical to itself is either same or different, both same and different, neither same nor different, but — Sameness⁺ returns to neither the origin of the Constitutive (…) nor the destination of the Constituted (.) Madly, (…) origin (…) destination (…). The perverse caveat is that the Madness of Order can be rewritten as: (… …) (… origin …) (… destination …) (… …). Or, schizophrenically, this summary can even be written as: (… … … …) (… … …) (… … …). Sameness⁺ is the Becoming of the *Trieb* in its wanders around an object which appears self-same and self-identical but is self (⊇) other. The artwork cannot be art because it is simultaneously in a bathroom. The urinal is both the bathroom and the museum. This relationship of each object to itself breaks essence (*le propre*) because the object is the Other also but simultaneously not this excessive remainder. What is the name for this copulatic relationship if Being is not itself but exactly every other signifier in the system? The Inside (⊇) the Outside — but what ~~is~~ (⊇)? This symbol is the abstract figuration of Sameness⁺. The objects on either side of the relationship of ~~Being~~ are *sous rature*. The only presence in the Madness of Order is the Sameness⁺ of (⊇). Madness of Order ~~is~~ (⊇). Madness (⊇) Order. Put madly, (⊇) (⊇) (⊇). But why is (⊇) not under erasure like Being, *différance*, (:), Real Penis, horseshoe, and toothbrush? (⊇) is yet to unfold into presence. (⊇) is the *tout autre*. *Qua* language, (⊇) is the object of (*a*)sexuality.

The Inside is the Outside. The Inside is not the Inside. The Outside is not the Outside. There is no word to textualize the relationship of the (un)Constitutive (⋯) (un)Constituted (⋅) between the two words. The relationship (⊇) cannot be put into words. The Constitutive (…) is a myth. The Constituted (…) ~~is~~ (⊇) a fable. Being *qua* an incessant series of spatial splits can only be coordinated by (⊇) in relationship to the Constitutive (…) and the Constituted (.). How are the networks of objects related to each other in the absence of the (this) word? The system is properly denoted as (⊇). What are the thinking, being, and living of (⊇)? What are the art of the self and the care of the world of (.) (…) (⊇) (…) (.) — ?

Each unsettled word cannot be revealed as such because it is already related to a Real resistance. This defense is internal to the signifying chain. The word is sublime in its unrepresentability. The question is not the object of symbolization. Rather, the issue is the unsymbolizable sublimity of representation. The mark of Being ("is") is an inadequate symbol for the relationship between (⊇) words. There is no word for Being because twists and traces — around, near, by, above, below — suspend the presence of the subjects and objects in the system of discourse. The relationship between two objects is Real. The orchestration of prepositions is the symbolization and articulation of space. Space is resistant to symbolization absolutely. This relationship (⊇) is resistant to the written and the spoken. The name for (⊇) is an impossible abyssal *mise-en-abyme*. This void is neurotically anchored by a series of metaphors (.). (⊇) is Real.

Praxis is the effort to translate this symbol into text. *Qua* futural, *Praxis* makes the future present. As Lacan says: "The Real is absolutely without fissure."[30] *Qua* Real, the word cannot be ruptured because it is erased in its essence. The symbolic is always already the Real. The only word that the system can speak is, "(⊇)." How do unspoken and unwritten words — Real — speak in the vocabularies and alphabets, and marks and sounds, in the symbolic order? How does the system of speech speak its own Outside which is simultaneously its extimate Inside? How does the word articulate itself even if the word cannot comprehend the message of its own code? The symbol for metaphorical (un)likeness is (⊇). Perversely, (.) (…) (⊇) (…) (.).

The Real spikes as the bandaged wound in the wake of its emergence from a metaphorical and identificatory system. This structure is coincident — Sameness⁺ — with metonymic castration. Movement of desire — Ing⁺ of *Trieb* — castrates the system of points of reference and images of idealization. The traversal from word to word destructures the symbolic order. Castration organizes the clipped psychosis of the Madness of Order. The neurotic forecloses itself. Essence is structured *qua* castration. Castration of the self — splits and shards — is the structure of the original Oedipus complex. The symbolic order neurotically forecloses — *rejet névrotique* — itself. This negation is the positive order of the ontology of the system. This *Verwerfung* is the system. The system commits suicide in order to function as a positive organization of borders and *le propre* — of capitalist private property and phallocentric sexual difference. Negation of the positive order of Being is also simultaneously the positivity of the negative order of Being. The tension between *Eros* and *Thanatos* functions as a positive system of border. Suicide is the essence of the *Eros* of the system. *Eros* is the end of life. *Thanatos* is the condition of the system. *Thanatos* is the start of life. The aim of all *Eros* is *Thanatos*. The death drive is the principle of expansion and openness.

Figure 9.3 Difference of Difference of *Différance* and Trace

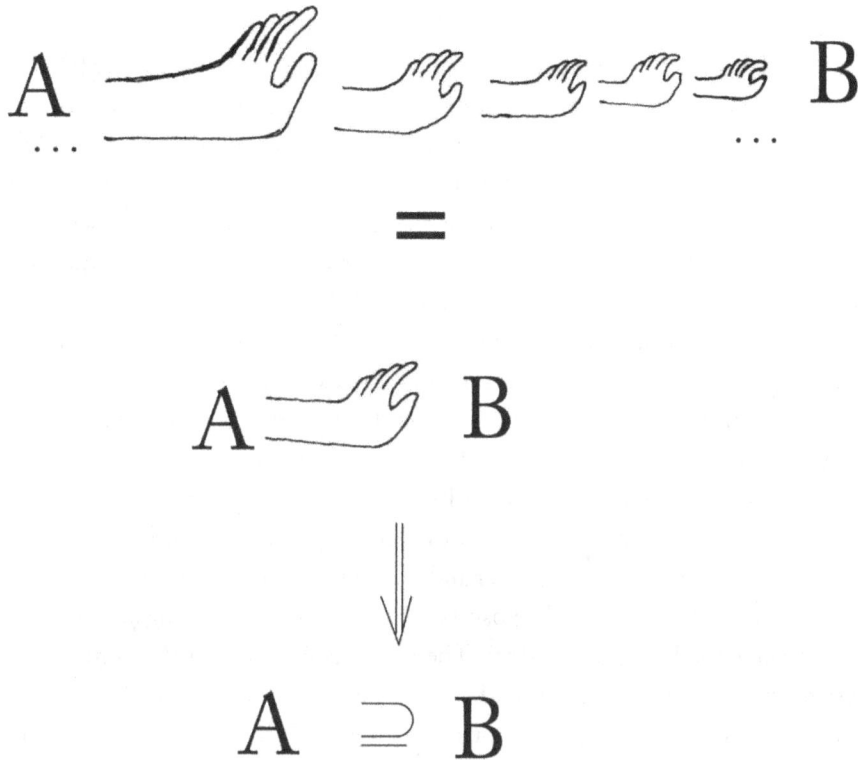

This picture illustrates the relationship (construction) of any unit of text (term, signifier, word, phrase, sentence, paragraph, page, and so on) to any other unit of text. The difference and deferral of A to B are possible in a *finite infinity* or *infinite finity* of gestures, movements, traversals, deployments, indications, gesticulations, and so on. The endless series of deferrals — pushing hands — indicates that the relationship and construction of A to B are bonds whose copulative ~~Being~~ is under erasure in the Outside of signification. The introduction of the symbol (⊇) (below, center) denotes the impossible symbolization of the overlap — continuity and coincidence — of the relationship between Being and Nothingness, is and is not, and so on. This Being *sous rature* and *sur l'effacement* is the abyssal vortex of *Eros* and *Thanatos*, Being and Nothingness, and is and is not which fractures all signs. This play is infinite because its space cannot be reduced to a series of discrete marks which could be speculatively and abstractly counted by the hours, minutes, and seconds of the narrative chronology of time. This image visualizes the asymptotic lines of the gravity function and the infinitely displaced center of occlusion. The *arche*-trace of spatial extension and expansion is dispersed and decentered, but its force in the solar system is the (*a*)sexual split(tings) in space. The difference of difference of *différance* is the traces of jockstraps in the extension and expansion of a displaced center whose constant repressive *Verdrängung* (foreclosed *Verwerfung*) is affirmatively renewed by the perverse *Verleugnung* of jockstrap *qua* "jockstrap." The jockstrap is the accidental effect rather than the necessary cause of perverse Other *jouissance*. The ~~jockstrap~~ is under erasure only insofar as its ostensible presence is reduced to the exchange-value of comparison and contrast rather than to the singularity of the ~~jockstrap~~iest.

Notes & Sketches —

The symbolic order cannot operate without this foreclosure of Being *qua* Real. The system is pure negation. This is so even if the system cannot articulate this secret truth of Unreason. Pure negation is negated *qua* pure positivity. The return of the Real in the symbolic is simultaneously *Verwerfung* in the foreclosure of the Real. Return and negation are the same gesture. The Real is pure positivity. The system forecloses (…). Negativity is the internal positivity of the Real. *Verwerfung* of the Real in its fundamental negativity is Being. The positive ontological order is essentially the destruction of the extimate condition of ontology. But this negativity is also simultaneously the positivity of the Real. System i̶s̶ negativity. The symbolic is foreclosed *qua* positivity ($\supseteq$) negativity. ($\supseteq$) is the condition of division and the return of the system to ($\supseteq$). This return is the positivity of the system. System i̶s̶ positivity. Return is the object of the pervert's *jouissance*. The object of the pervert's return is the excess of this return. The pervert's *Verleugnung* is negation *qua* expansion and openness.

The conceptual innovation of Duchamp's "Fountain" (1917) is this perverse return of the foreclosed *qua* system to the Real Symbolic. Return of the Real is outlawed by the structure. But this return is simultaneously the proviso of the positive order of Being. The symbolic forecloses its own structure. This center returns in the Real as the destabilization of this system. $-ism is the perverse process of the foreclosed negation *of* foreclosed negation. The symbolic is this rupture. The Real returns the symbolic order from the negativity of the foreclosure *of* the positive ontological order of Being. The system enforces an identity as self-same and self-identical. The Logic of Identity otherwise opposes Duchamp's innovation. Lacan says: "The Real is the impossible."[31] This impossible refers to the signifier and its arrival at the signified — *word* — in presence. The impossible is the coherent symbolization of the positive ontological order or Being *qua* — ($\supseteq$) — Nothingness. Each word in the system is the Being of the Real. The relationship between Being *qua* Real is mediated by the ($\supseteq$) and its resistance to any division between Being and Real. The essence (…) of the Madness of Order is Being ($\supseteq$) Real or essence and identity (.) of construction and *Trieb*. ($\supseteq$) is extimacy and Sameness⁺ (…). Perversely, (Sameness⁺) ($\supseteq$) (Sameness⁺) —

The Real Signifier is coincident — i̶s̶ — with the entire system. The Real Signifier is the truth of Unreason. The Real Signifier is the subject and the object of the pervert's *écriture*. The foreclosure of the symbol by itself is the condition of the symbolic operation. Structure is *Verwerfung*. System is negation. *Eros* is *Thanatos*. Is ($\supseteq$) Is. The negativity of the system returns as this positivity and unity of the sign. The return loop between the negative ontology of Being and the positive ontology of Being is the Nothingness of $-ism and its differential relations of value. The symbolic is the madness of the schizoid. Madness is the precept of $-ism. The madness of the neurotic order is the order of the schizoid's madness. Order is yet madness, but madness is not yet order. But how can psychosis be the foundation of neurosis *qua* the system in its (dys) function? How does queerness produce ordinariness? How does psychosis generate neurosis? What of the men who wander about the world with neurotic symptoms of dreams and jokes rather than schizoid symptoms of delusions and hallucinations? Or is a dream a delusion? Is a joke a hallucination?

The Foreclosed Father

The paradoxical relationship between Inside and Outside that Duchamp demonstrates is foreclosed in the symbolic. The system is foreclosed. This *Verwerfung* is the system. The foreclosed returns as instability of the structure in its operation. The system is dislocation. The system is structured not only *by* the Real but exactly *as* the Real. The system is the absolute resistance to the written and the spoken. The symbolic order is resistance. $-ism is the process of the foreclosed negation of $-ism. The *Eros* of $-ism is its *Thanatos*. *Eros* ($\supseteq$) *Thanatos*. The system is subordinate to the *Verwerfung* of the system. This is the upshot of Saussure's demonstration of the extimate — internal (⊇) external — schizophrenia of *langue*. Freud writes of the pervert: "The ego rejects the incompatible idea together with its affect and behaves as if the idea had never occurred to him."[32] The symbolic order (dys)functions in its behavior. It is "as if the idea has never occurred to [the system]." The symbolic rejects itself in order to found itself. This simultaneity of Being and Nothingness is the essence of the foreclosed truth of (⊇). Civilization is structured by *Verwerfung*. Civilization is secretly schizophrenic. The schizoid foreclosure of the system is its own condition. The "incompatible" idea that the "ego" of the system must foreclose is the simultaneous presence and absence of the Signified/r and the Real Symbolic. This "incompatible" concept is identical to _____. Every word is both forever unnamed and immediately named in order to found the system. The proper name for this function is the temporality of what willing having beening Becoming Being — The word is the Outside of time. The unconscious is the space of the anonymous word. This anonymous word is a sign *sans* signified. The unconscious is the timeless space of the signifier.

The madman rejects the father. The psychotic does so in order to secure his own Unreason. The pervert disavows difference. The pervert does so in order to enforce an internal difference (A (⊇) A) and an external plenitude of (A (⊇) A = B). The modality of negation in the system is a *Verdrängung* from the perspective of neurosis and a *Verwerfung* from the perspective of perversion. The perspectivalism and orientation — *camera obscura* (1845) — of the pervert make any clinical differentiation among neurosis, perversion, or psychosis impossible. The Madness of Order is blind to its own organization. The pervert's magical alphabets note the parallactic overlap of repression and foreclosure. The aperture of a gap between *Verdrängung* and *Verwerfung* illuminates the difference between $-ism and S. This is visible even if the system ($-ism) and its obverse (S) cannot be neurotically distinguished. The structure is already schizophrenic. Perspective and orientation are absent. The pervert is the only conceptual persona who approaches the established essence (⊇) of the system. The neurotic (⊇) the psychotic. The Madness of Order is a system of hysteria and obsession. The name-of-the-father is subject to *Verwerfung*. The (dys)function of (Un)reason *qua* a coherent system is the consequence of neither the dead father nor the alive father but the father *sous rature*. The proviso of the system is Nothingness. The Real Signifier is the supplement to the system. Ruin is foundation. Destruction is renewal. The Real Signifier is the source of the essential autodeconstruction of $-ism.

A radical Sameness⁺ between words (A (⊇) B (⊇) C (⊇) D and (⊇) so (⊇) on) illuminates the extimate — Being *qua* Nothingness — inconsistency of each word with itself. As Lacan says, what is foreclosed in the symbolic returns in the Real.[33] The Real always returns to the same place because space — Inside (⊇) Outside — is an infinite expanse in the timeless unconscious. Real Sameness⁺ is the navel — everywhere and anywhere — of the positive ontological order of Being. The navel leads down into the unknown of the simultaneous negation and return of every word in the skedaddle of twists and turns of alphabets. The name-of-the-father is subordinate to *Verwerfung*. He otherwise threatens essential selfhood with castration for any trespass of desire (…). The symptom of the foreclosed paternal metaphor is the autodeconstruction of the order. Autodeconstruction is the essence of the successful operation of the Madness of Order. This system submits to its own death in *Thanatos* as the condition of its own life in *Eros*. Grammatology murders the ontological order of Being. Autodeconstruction commits Being to suicide. The suicide is always already committed. As Heidegger implies, the catastrophe has already happened. But, then what?

The mechanism which purports to organize the system returns to decapitate it. The paternal metaphor returns not as the foundation of civilization. Rather, the father returns — fantasmatically and necromanically — as a reminder of the death of the universe. The father utters the truth of castration — which is *Thanatos*. The recurrence of the substitution of the name-of-the-father stabilizes the object *qua* dissolution. The (im/ex)plosion of the Real Signifier is the structure of the object. The system cannot endure Being. $-ism is the positive ontological order. Presence *qua* Real returns to resist the symbolization of Being absolutely. Being is Real. The word is Real. (.) (⊇) (…). Foreclosure and its return are the same gesture. Negation and its return overlap. *Verwerfung* and return are a Sameness⁺ of coincidence. The symptom and its latent content are the same. The system returns the symptom because $-ism forecloses itself.

The system and its return are the same movement. The manifest representation is the content of *Verwerfung*. The symptom cannot appear because the system submits it to its *Verwerfung*. Negation and its returned symptom are the proviso of civilization. The symptom of *Thanatos* returns as death. *Jouissance* of the symptom is the ecstasy of the *petit mort*. The *sinthome* is the coherent articulation of the subject. *Thanatos* returns in the symptom. The symptomatic eruption of the Real articulates the mortality of the positive ontological order of Being. The death drive organizes the symptom. Even *Eros* returns as the symptom of this death. The symptom returns not as coincident (*Eros* and unification) with the system but as its dissolution (*Thanatos* and divorce). *Qua* the effect of *Verwerfung*, $-ism can only return symptoms — delusions and hallucinations — of schizophrenia. *Qua* breath and life, man is in essence delusional and hallucinatory. Man is mad.

The system forecloses the name-of-the-father. Metaphor (essence, identity, (.)) threatens castration of the self for any trespass of the bob and weave (…) of desire and the traversal and movement (…) of metonymy. Paradoxically, this return of the father as neither presence nor absence is the (de)construction of the ontological structure of essence. The father is both the threat to and the condition of the *not* of the extant order. Psychoanalysis theorizes the subject's attitude toward the father. As Freud says, "We know nothing of the origin of this ambivalence" toward the father.[34] Psychotic *Verwerfung* of the name-of-the-father returns to disrupt identity and essence (.) in the system. The father facilitates identification ("I am like my father") because the paternal authority enforces the private property (*le propre*) relationship of the penis of the offspring. The ghostly father also unsettles identification because he disrupts Being — (⊇) — *qua* — (⊇) — Real. The Real returns in the failure of symbolization of Being (⊇) under erasure. There is no word *sous rature* to describe this relationship between subject (⊇) object.

The Real is the locus of the foreclosed. But the return of *Verwerfung* disrupts everyday ontology. Destabilization upsets the order in its essence. The return of *Verwerfung* collapses border, essence, identity, metaphor, Inside, Outside, (.), and even (…). Madness of Order is deconstruction. Autodeconstruction is a suicidal process of disintegration. Duchamp's "Fountain" (1917) returns the foreclosed symbolic to the Real. Duchamp's artwork returns the Real Signifier to the ontological organization of bytes and bits, parts and wholes, and the copulative relationships which fix spatial coordinates. These frames of reference otherwise enable chronological time. The artwork is the impossible symbolization of the most influential philosophical thought in the entire twentieth-century. This limit-thought is Saussure's version of value. The language of the Real is the discourse of value. The Real refuses articulation in words. Value rebuffs the written and the spoken in words. The foundation of civilization can be neither written nor spoken. Man is lost in an expansive galaxy of space with only the orchestration of prepositions to guide his timeless movements. This describes the Pervert-Schizoid-Woman of thinking, being, and living the primary process of the unconscious of the Spirit of the System.

Saussure's insight is the coincidence of the symbolic and the Real. This parallactic overlap is made possible by the *Verwerfung* of the father. Paternity returns as the dead father. This cycle of negation and return — murder and resurrection — is the structure of the Real Symbolic. Return conditions the madness of extant ontology. The system is symptomatic. Ontology is foreclosed by the system. Being — the ontological *et al.* — is cut by the Real. This coincidence between Being (⊇) Real is the reason that the father is negated in foreclosure. *Verwerfung* facilitates paternal return. The reappearance of the father renews Being. The suicide of the father is the proviso of his loss, return, and resurrection. The extant ontological order is this cycle of murder, return, and redemption. Foreclosure is the structure of the Real Signifier. The Real Symptom returns to disrupt the presence of the word. The Being of the Real is foreclosed. Spatiality invites the destructive return of the *point de capiton*. The open field of space conditions the repeated renewal of the father. Paternity resists repeated *Verwerfung*. But the essence of the system is this compulsive reappearance. Does the pervert's both/and economy return the Real to its proper place in the symbolic in time? How does the Real Father return? What is the sudden effect of the return of order to disorder, of ontology to deconstruction, and of (.) to (…)?

(In)equalities

Duchamp demonstrates the basal impossibility of coherent signification. An ontology which is structured in accordance with the logic of anality and value is written as the penis = baby = feces — penis = ($\supseteq$) = baby = ($\supseteq$) = feces = ($\supseteq$). This is the object of autodeconstruction. The foreclosure of Inside ($\supseteq$) Outside affects the other binary oppositions in *langue*, such as man/Woman, white/black, straight/gay, abled/disabled, native/foreign, here/there, and so on. The copulatic relationship between man/Woman, white/black, straight/gay, abled/disabled, native/foreign, here/there — or between you and me — is beyond representation. Each of the words and essences (.) is not itself because it is other than itself, and so on (…). There is Nothingness to symbolize. This impossible copulatic relationship — Being — is foreclosed in the Madness of Order. *Verwerfung* returns ($\supseteq$).

The self is outlawed by the Real Symbolic from being both man and Woman. If there is a question or resistance, then it is pathologized as an "identity disorder." But this self is not both man and Woman. The individual is barred from being both black and white. If there is a difficulty or issue, then "mixed race" is authorized as its own identity. But this self is not both black and white. The person is prohibited from being both straight and gay. If there is a complication or incoherence, then a "bisexual identity" is an option. But the identity is not both gay and straight. These relationships of proximity are symptomatic *of* but not essentially *as* Being. The copula between opposites is starkly foreclosed by the Madness of Order. Every other relationship between objects is also disabled. The Other is neither man nor Woman, neither black nor white, neither straight nor gay, neither abled or disabled, neither native nor foreign, neither here nor there — but willing having beening Becoming Being —

The system is structured by relationships at the same time as copulatic bonds cannot be articulated as presence. The system forecloses the truth of the symbolic. Truth returns from *Verwerfung qua* $-ism. The truth of the system is the immanence — Inside ($\supseteq$) Outside — of the Real Symbolic. Truth ($\supseteq$) Real. The structure firmly negates the truth. ($\supseteq$) is *sous rature*. The series of words is a collection of lies. The proof of the schizoid *Verwerfung* is that any will to deconstruct these oppositions is deemed an incoherent and mad Unreason. Schizophrenia is bereft of proper signification except in the pervert's valiant redress and undress of this absence of the secret truth of the Madness of Order. The perverts render madness its own Reason. But can madness speak the truth if speech is a lie? What speech articulates ($\supseteq$) under erasure? What does Sameness[+] write other than yet more — + — ?

The illumination of this both/and economy is the pervert's project. The pervert's clever disavowal of sexual difference and colorful construction of fetish representation suture the wound. Perversely, incompatible ideas happily coexist in a jubilant economy of plenitude rather than battle in an anxious organization of castration. The Real is this "collision," as Lacan says, "with the unassimilable signifier."[35] The unassimilable signifier is the Real Signifier. The unassimilable signifier smashes $-ism. $-ism simultaneously is — willing having beening

Becoming Being — *Verdrängung* as its return. The system is the stupidity of foreclosed returns. Return of the Real is the in-action, in-process of the symptom. The symptom ($-ism) is the Ing⁺ — return — Ing⁺ of the Real. The system is the explosion of the Real. The system is willing having beening Becoming Being — this symptom. The system-symptom is a parallactic gap. The clash between itself and itself — ($\supseteq$) — is the extant ontology. The symptom is the cut of the Real. The Madness of Order is a series of knocks and punches of the unassimilable words. These excesses and remainders are sutured by the neurotic *point de capiton* of the phallus.

The phallus structures signification. This arrangement makes the order dysfunction. The dash of the unassimilable words — bytes, bits, parts, and wholes — is a prang in the split in ontology. The crazy system is this unassimilability of the words to their proper semantic and syntactical spaces. The system is the gash of the Real from within the symbolic order. The unassimilable Real Signifier is the potential and threatened absence of the signified or Signified/r. ~~Being~~ is absent *qua* absence or present *qua* absence. The Real Signifier renders a rash in the symbolic order. Absence formalizes plenitude rather than lack. Communist and penis plenitude is the Real resistance to symbolization. The word refuses textuality. The system is impossibly relational. Madness cannot perform its essential function to enforce the Logic of Identity. Relativity is impossible from within the Madness of Order. Relativity is the unassimilable and inessential truth of the Madness of Order. The obscene relationality of $-ism bans relativity as a precept of civilization. Relativity is not possible in a negative and differential system which is unmoored by a general equivalent of — relative to — standardization. At best, Saussure presents a concept of *absolute relativity*. The trick of this incoherent set of words is that each is internal — extimate — to its external.

The magic of Saussure's insight is that the concept of value — which is presented as so-called absolute relativity — is discovered by the impressibility and incoherence — gobbledygook — of the articulation. Saussure shows that the organizational principle of civilization in *langue* (Saussure and Derrida), in finance (Marx), and in desire (Freud and Lacan) is balderdash. The truth of the system is gibberish. The precept of the galaxy is tongue. The coherent universe of language, finance, and desire is the Outside to the principle of the solar system. There is no such *das Ding* as the systems of discourse, economy, and sexual difference.

The signified is lost. The schizoid and perverse logic (A ($\supseteq$) A because A = B = C = D, and so on, and A) deconstructs opposition and occludes the *point de capiton*. Madness releases *différance* and its endless Metaphoricity (…). The silly stress of the neurotic is not only to suture this gap of abyssal infinity. The neurotic also commits to the system of castration and private property. The neurotic returns his symptom from the latent locus of the unconscious. This space is structured as a language. The *écriture* of the absolutely impervious to the written and the spoken resists any possible locus that the neurotic otherwise supposes as his anchor in the surf of the series of words. The neurotic either/or network translates text into a system of the signified (.) of latent truth. But how?

The kicker is that the unrepresentable and inadmissible signifier is the Madness of Order. The system is barred access to its own essence. The (…) is simultaneously a (.) which is displaced in its identity (.) *qua* (…). The order will not admit (that it) itself (is/into) $-ism. All of the objects in the networks are excluded from their own systems. Order is not simply disorder. Order is not order. (.) is not (.) but rather (…). But is (…) also simultaneously (.)? The word is rejected *qua* extimate from the system. Meaning-making is absent at the precise moment of its ephemeral articulation. There is neither signified nor even signifier as such. The Signified/r is the moment of both commencement and destination, and both departure and *terminus*. The Signified/r is neither the origin of speech nor the arrival of communication. Rather, the Signified/r is the terrorized flight of the schizoid's psychical tormented amusement and the pervert's textual pixie dust. The ($\supseteq$) abstractly symbolizes the barred relationship — ~~Being~~ — between the objects in the system. The relationship between objects is ($\supseteq$) — what is best described as spatial proximity in the absence of digits and integers which could otherwise fix the coordinates of temporality. The ($\supseteq$) is the timeless spatiality of the unconscious. The ($\supseteq$) is the essence of relationality and constructionism of the Madness of Order. This nexus is violently foreclosed by the neurotic systems of $-ism in discourse, economy, and sexual difference.

The logic of the Inside is the Outside (and so on) is prohibited by the system. This exclusion of schizoid truthful Unreason is the paradoxically banned proviso of $-ism. Coherent craziness cannot be murmured by the signifying chain. This is so except in the sly wanders of the pervert's words. The system cannot speak its own truth. The secret truth — Inside ~~is~~ Outside or ($\supseteq$) — is the sublimely unrepresentable. But this essence (…) *qua* (.) of the system is summarized by the undecidable and indeterminate spatiality of the unconscious. The preposition is the orchestration *qua* system Cs. whose ego directs the otherwise sublime ($\supseteq$) relationships between uncoordinated objects. The manifest representation of the Madness of Order is the foreclosure of the kernel of absolute resistance to the self-sameness and self-identity of the word. Otherwise, $-ism is structured by the phallocentric and capitalist logic (A = A) and by the *Verwerfung* of the essence of the system.

The neurotic cannot assimilate the inadmissible truth of the system. The Madness of Order is this Real Signifier and its return to the system *qua* $-ism. $-ism is this set of Real Signifiers and its recursive negation in a *mise-en-abyme* of Sameness[†]. The neurotic is situated in the endless circuit of law and its transgression. This rule/rebellion cycle forever separates the neurotic from the endless aim of the circuit of *Trieb*. Duchamp's "Fountain" (1917) demonstrates that the urinal (artwork) is a museum (bathroom) and that the external (internal) and the internal (external) are the (Outside) (Inside). This demonstration is summarized by ($\cancel{\supseteq}$) which is under erasure in the system of the Unc. The relationship between objects to themselves and to each other ($\supseteq$) is neither (either) Constituted nor (or) Constitutive but cc'd and carbon copied.

The Other-Logic is an extimacy in the Real. Extimatic relationship is the insight of the schizoid. The *écriture* of this extraordinary object ($\supseteq$) is the pervert's labor. There is neither Outside nor Inside as such. Neither is there exterior nor interior of the system. Neither is there Outside nor Inside of the world. There is neither text nor context as such. But if there is no text, then what is there? The Outside of text and its temporal coordinates are the material signifiers of texture, body, sound, dance, scent, and voice. These bodies and physics are the lost materialities — uncharted and inchoate — which are barred in the practice of the word. Pictures otherwise play in the theory of the signifier. Paradoxically, this unalloyed materiality is only accessible in the *Praxis* of the word. The schizoid suffers the obscenity of pure phonology of the materiality of the signifier. The schizoid is Outside ($\supseteq$) of Inside/Outside. The psychotic is atemporally situated *qua* Inside ($\supseteq$) Outside. The madman is ($\supseteq$). The pervert moors these untextualized materialities — uncoordinated proximities — into a coherent abstraction and speculation of Reason.

The borders between the (otherwise) text define the Constituted-Constitutive Outside of the text. But any metaphorical definition is imperiled by the Madness of Order and its $-istic foreclosure of the Real. A metaphor simply becomes definition, and then metaphor, and then redefinition, and then metaphor, and then redefinition (.) — and then (…). The Outside is not present to the Outside. The Inside is also not present to itself. The Outside is not the Outside. The Inside is not the Inside. Schizophrenia indicates an eternal movement — *Trieb* — of quantum oscillation between various materialities in another space — here, there, over here, and over there — and another time — then, now, before, and later. The schizoid of the primary process — Becoming-Unconscious — is the timeless space of uncoordinated materialities and their haphazard arrangement by phallic prepositions. The schizoid's Unreasonable truth is that the Inside and the Outside are otherwise than themselves (A $\supseteq$ A) in an atemporal space. This unconscious field — neither negation nor temporality nor knowledge — exceeds a tape measure and a stopwatch. This is so even in the presence of primitive and phallic poodles. Objects cavort and play — (⊇) — as differences but not deferrals. There is no such *das Ding* as time. This is the kooky Time of the Pervert and its articulation of schizophrenic atemporality. Time is a fable of the neurotic.

The madman's discourses are rants and raves of a frenzied manic and delirious Unreason. *Deliro* escapes the objectifications and containments of truth. *Deliro* is the Outside of *langue*. This is so even as *Deliro* is the internal truth of the system. The cost of Unreason is the medical restraints which lock the schizoid in the asylum. The Logic of Identity summarizes the resistance to truth and the fissure of the Real. The liberatory chants of Unreason battle the Logic of Identity. This is so even as the relationship of Unreason to Identity can only be expressed as madness (⊇) rationality or (…) (⊇) (.). There is no essence (.) to the empty words of Reason. Words are always already dispersed in the discombobulated network of materialities and abstractions. Essence is elsewhere. The neurotic pursues essence through a vigilant attunement to the arrangement of phallic prepositions. The one to the other, the this to the that, the here to the there, and the over to the under — metonymy — chase the *Objekt* of *désir* rather than the *Ziel* of *Trieb*.

The neurotic stalks (.) but only encounters the Signified/r (…) in the simultaneous arrival and nonarrival — (.) (⊇) (…) — of the letter at its points of departure ("I") and destination ("I"). The space and time of *Trieb* are the timing of this spacing and the spacing of this timing: time-becoming-space and space-becoming-time. This Becoming is spatial. The disruption of the Inside/Outside binary opposition reveals the scandal of the explosion. The Inside (Outside) is not itself. The Outside (Inside) is not itself. This is the space of the unconscious. The phallic preposition is the only grammatical mark which can coordinate nebulous spaces and enforce fictional times on the route to organization and regulation. Otherwise, the word is a Sameness[+] (⊇) all of the other objects in the system. The preposition outstrips temporality because the development of the index is the navigation of the routes of space and its coordinates.

All of the objects in the system are words of Sameness[+]. These words are strictly valueless and postnihilistic marks in undecidable and indeterminate space. Each signifier is a different materiality (sound or image). But each word is the same (neither equal nor unequal and neither identical nor different) value. This modality of value — undecidable and indeterminate — is the value of Saussure's schizophrenic outline of the foundation of the system of *langue*. Value includes ancillary structures, such as the order of finance and the structure of desire. The word is a Sameness[+] which is the Outside of the calculation and the speculation of numbers, digits, starts, and stops. But what is the word for the unified — neither equal nor unequal nor identical nor different — (⊇) of Sameness[+]? What is the word?

There is no word for the object or for the relationship between objects. The (⊇) which substitutes for the occluded center — metaphor and sign and fetish — is the aesthetic of the abyssal structure of the death of the father. There is no (.) of the arrived signified at its departure and destination (metaphor). There are only the slip and slide of the departure *of the departure* and the destination *of the destination* (…) in metonymy *qua* (…) *qua* (.) *qua* (…). Essence and its explosion are the same. The same is also equal and unequal and identical and different — Sameness[+]. What is the proper word for this series of both/and and neither/nor recursions without spatial coordination or temporal arrangement? Is this word the same and equal (metaphor) or the different and unequal (metonymy) — or perversely and madly, equal and unequal, and different and same? The essence of the word in metaphor, the rupture of the word in metonymy, the pursuit of (.) in desire, and the coherence of the signified in identity are the same structure because (.) (⊇) (…) *qua* (…) (⊇) (.). One word would do the trick to symbolize the ~~Real Being~~. Instead, a repetitive compulsion of signs — signification — makes any termination of abstraction of the general equivalent impossible. What is this one word, either at departure or arrival, or either at start or stop? This word is not the unconscious. This symbol is not (⊇). But this word is a word.

The Inside is the Outside — and Not

The visual representation of schizophrenia is Duchamp's conceptual innovation. The complications which are generated by this ostensibly simple paradox — urinal in a museum — illuminate the schizoid structure of the symbolic order. Structure is foreclosed *qua* the system. The order returns *qua* disruption in the Real. Madness of Order is this cycle of disruption. $-ism is the simultaneous escape from and containment of madness. The system is founded on *Verwerfung*. Foreclosure and its return are imperceptible. But negation is visible because the shadow of each object is illuminated in space. *Verwerfung* returns itself in a repetitive gesture. Negation is the compulsive will to resurrect a system which is its own suicide. Madness of Order not only commits suicide, but it simultaneously bungles this cowardly act. The pervert's project demonstrates the simultaneous (non)coincidence of *Verwerfung* and its return *qua* a Sameness⁺ in space. The perverse critic demonstrates the divergence of mutually antagonistic perspectives because he invents the (⊇) at the center of the relationship of the object to itself and to the other objects in the system. The division between *Verwerfung* and its return must be sustained at the same time as its obscene identity must be showcased. Neither tricks can be pulled without the other. Illumination of the paradoxical coincidence of the two ostensibly opposed perspectives must unveil its difference if only to display its Sameness⁺. *Verwerfung* — ~~Being~~ — *Verwerfung*. The unconscious space of (⊇) represents the recursive negation of the schizoid's intuition and the pervert's aesthetic.

The pervert illustrates the both/and suture and sever of the bandaged gap of the deviation of an object from itself. The pervert's preferred symbol for the secret truth of the Madness of Order is (⊇). This abstract notation figures the extimacy *between* binary oppositions, such as white/black, right/wrong, good/evil, gay/straight, and so on but also *between* the object itself, such as black, right, good, gay, and so on. This (⊇) is the object of *Verwerfung* and its return *qua* the disruption of $-ism. The pervert's magic performs this chicanery through the demonstration of the split of Sameness⁺ within/out and the suture of Sameness⁺ within/out —

> White (⊇) is (⊇) wrong (⊇) is (⊇) evil (⊇) is (⊇) straight. Capitalism (⊇) communism (⊇) scarcity (⊇) abundance (⊇) presence (⊇) absence (⊇) castration (⊇) fullness (⊇) clitoris (⊇) penis, and so on. But also: white (⊇) white and wrong (⊇) wrong and evil (⊇) evil and straight (⊇) straight. Capitalism (⊇) capitalism and communism (⊇) communism and scarcity (⊇) scarcity and abundance (⊇) abundance and presence (⊇) presence and absence (⊇) absence and castration (⊇) castration and fullness (⊇) fullness and clitoris (⊇) clitoris and penis (⊇) penis, and so on.

The two in/external dimensions of (⊇) illuminate the parallactic gap in which each term is different from itself because it is the same as the other. This Sameness⁺ is the schizoid truth of the Madness of Order and the object of the *Verwerfung* of the system. The return of the foreclosed (⊇) is the essence of the system: timeless unconscious spatial proximities. The pervert illuminates the aperture *qua* closure.

Smoke and mirrors also explain the symbolic repression of any textualization of (⊇) as the rants and raves of a mind gone adrift. The system forbids the becoming-space of time and the becoming-time of space — unconscious expansive space — in the instant of superpositional entanglement. But this Neurotic Foreclosure (*rejet névrotique*) returns. The pervert's disavowal returns *qua* itself. These modes of negation — neurotic *Verdrängung* and psychotic *Verwerfung* — are the same even in space — but not in time — in their difference from themselves. Negation — neurotic *Verdrängung* and psychotic *Verwerfung* — negates itself. *Verdrängung* is subject to foreclosure, and *Verwerfung* is subordinate to repression. The negated — repressed and foreclosed — and the return of the negated — repressed and foreclosed — are the same gesture. This unveils the no

"No!" of the timelessness of the unconscious. The negation of negation (is) the positivity of positivity. There is no negation in the unconscious because all forms of psychical negation — neurotic *Verdrängung*, psychotic *Verwerfung*, and perverse *Verleugnung* — have negated themselves. There is no coherent willing having beening Becoming Being temporality for the pervert because the absence of absence situates any semblance of presence in the Other. The pervert's space is the timelessness of the unconscious. The playful reconfiguration of condensation and displacement wills a topsy-turvy culture of metaphorization — Becoming (.) — and metonymization — Becoming (...). The strange movement dances across the uncoordinated proximal spaces of the unconscious without the speculated and calculated time of the ego. Perversely, foreclosure (is) disavowal (is) repression in space but not in time. The timeless aesthetic of the unconscious is the space-out of the ego-system.

There is no negation in the unconscious of the system. The logic of the unconscious is positivity. Desire cannot be spoken in the language of the secondary process of the ego-conscious. The secondary process is organized by negativity and difference. Only the hiccups of wish, desire, and truth manifest in the visibility of the extant galaxy. The Constitutive Outside is the Constituted Inside. The relationship between these two (one) dimension(s) can only be summarized by the Real excluded function of ($\supseteq$). The unconscious is the boundless space of the solar system. The relationship between unequal identities is simultaneously of equal differences. If the unequal is the equal and the identical is the different — Sameness⁺ — then the relationship between all of the objects (Constitutive and Constituted) is a double affirmation and negation. Positivity and negativity are the same aesthetic in the same relevant space in the same atemporality. This fissure of self-same and self-identical identity (A = A) is the complete destruction of the universe. Extimacy unwinds any semblance of a coherent center (.). How is the word possible in a system in which signification is impossible? What are the spoken and the written of value? What is the utterance of the undecidability and indetermination of uncoordinated space?

Only (im)possibility emerges in a triumphant heap at the closure of the word. No modality of communication approaches the abyssal void except the madman's Unreason. This crazy discourse reduces the entirety of the system to the split — ($\supseteq$) *qua* excluded function — within the extant object which already is *qua* Being. The neurotic is unable to see himself — ego/mirror — as such. The neurotic (schizoid) forecloses himself *qua* an otherwise ordinary repressed neurotic. But the self of the Madness of Order is not an ordinary repressed neurotic. The self is the properly schizoid effect of the network of words in the battery of the Other. Truth is only visible to the madman. Truth is only articulable by the pervert. Endless substitution — center for center, sign for sign, metaphor for metaphor, word for word, fetish for fetish, and so on — originates in the creationist sublimation *ex nihilo* of signification. The magician pulls the rabbit out of the hat with a hole in it after forgetfully but cleverly putting the bunny in his shoe with a tear in it.

The neurotic agrees to enjoy this endless and repetitious dumb show. The neurotic is squarely situated in the domain of the pleasure principle and its conservative regulation of homeostasis and the increase and decrease of tension. In contrast, the schizoid and the pervert experience *Thanatos* which is beyond the pleasure principle of simple balance and control. But who is the magician? — and who is the hare? The pervert recognizes prestidigitation because he understands that $-ism is structured by the fake-out and whack-a-mole substitutions of *Verleugnung*. The universe is blatantly schizoid. The psychotically negated is present and absent — *qua* return — in the space of Sameness⁺. But is this an order as such? Is the symbolic an uncharted and inchoate nebula which is suspended above the abyss of the excluded function of the excluded center? If so, can this madness be recuperated by a Reason whose projects demand coherence and legibility?

The neurotic is the effect of *Verwerfung*. Madness simulates coherence. Schizophrenia feigns neurosis and its cycle of law/transgression and symptom/return. The neurotic forecloses the schizophrenic negation of its own extant positive ontological order of Being. The phallus is the avatar of neurotic *Verdrängung*. The *objet petit a* is the ever delayed gift for the neurotic's subordination to the conceit of Being. The neurotic slips on the Signified/r. The neurotic is hoodwinked by the devious collusion and witless conspiracy among subject, desire, object, and phallus. The neurotic knows the plot, and he plays his role with courage and talent. But there must be a *jouissance* beyond this repetitive idiocy. Words refer to other words (…) in order to signify the text that these words already are (not). Signification represents the object that it always has been and always will be *qua* Nothingness and its substitutes in the abyssal *mise-en-abyme* of the series (…) of centers (.) in the nooks and crannies of the spoken and the written of text.

Switcheroo of every other word is the disorder of the system. There is no present metaphor because [substitution] is an endless process. The only modality of coordination of this mechanism is the phallic prepositional directions which organize the movement of the words around the galaxy. But even the regime of ~~prepositions~~ is under erasure: near becomes far, over becomes under, right becomes left, up becomes down, and so on. Signified/r disrupts the *point de capiton*. *Verwerfung* triumphs over *Verdrängung*. (…) yields to (.). But the neurotic insists on a fundamental fetish: "Will to Power" in Nietzsche; "Power/Knowledge" in Foucault; "Being" in Heidegger; the "Unconscious" in Freud and Lacan; "Ethics" in Levinas; *"Différance"* in Derrida, and so on. These philosophical fetishes are constraints which strive to contain (.) the forces of *Trieb* (…).

The self-same and the self-identical are shattered by internal and external — Inside ($\supseteq$) Outside — sources and relations. Being is not present to itself because the Real is uncastrated. A hole in the Real would otherwise make this Real a signifier which is assimilable to the system. All signifiers are fundamentally the same — every word is the same word, both equal and unequal, both identical and different, and so on. The Constitutive is simultaneously the Constituted. The Constituted is simultaneously the Constitutive. The Sameness⁺ among all words crushes all hierarchical systems of domination. The trauma of the Real generates a radically different subjectivity and sociality. The Real manifests — parallactic aperture — in its obscene violence against the cosmos. The visibility of the parallax inaugurates the massive task to pervert the neurotic and to transform $-ism into S. But how is it possible to make a pervert out of a neurotic if the effect of the foreclosure of the Real is precisely the neurotic himself?

A reborn world pronounces a series of schizophrenic propositions. These are otherwise obscured by the lazy knowledge and limited intuition of the neurotic. Unreasonably, truth speaks: Being is Nothingness; the urinal is what it is not; the text is not the text; the object is different from itself; it is what it is not, and so on. Even the original explosive proposition of the ridiculous coincidence of Inside and Outside is disrupted by the Real and its excessive and endless *Verwerfung* — and *Verdrängung* and *Verleugnung*. These preposterous propositions superpositionally oscillate between and as — ($\supseteq$) — affirmation and negation. Affirmative negation and negative affirmation — *Eros* ($\supseteq$) *Thanatos* — are the aesthetic of the pervert's disavowal of the excluded Real function of the abyssal occluded center of the system in ($\supseteq$). Undecidability and indeterminacy disavow oppositional attitudes. These oppositions can otherwise coexist side-by-side — proximal in uncoordinated and timeless unconscious space — without any rational correction of the contradiction. As Freud says of the perverse approach to difference in the context of the castration complex: "[the fetishists] disavowed the fact [of sexual difference] and believe they do see a penis all the *same*" (my emphasis).[36] Freud's "all the same" is the proper phrase because it gestures toward the strange coincidental overlap of all of the words in the system. My choice is neither "sameness" nor "difference," nor "equal" nor "unequal" — but Sameness⁺. This Sameness⁺ is the philosophical correlate to the abstract symbol of ($\supseteq$).

My inadequate neologism for the unsymbolizable Real Signifier is chosen mostly for aesthetic reasons. But the ideological consequences of this decision are vast. This is so even if the reasons are unarticulated because of the haunted presence of the underside of the choice metaphor. Disavowal is the only means of coherent expression *within* but also *as* the Madness of Order. The Freudian so-called considerations of representation of the unconscious-work are the parameters of the pervert's will to illuminate the Real of the schizoid's gibberish. Disavowal succeeds in this symbolization. The pure negation — *Thanatos* — of the positive extant order of Being defines both the essence of the Madness of Order and the incoherence of the schizoid's Unreason. The pervert's discourse encourages the neurotic to abandon the phallus (paternal metaphor and *point de capiton*) as otherwise endlessly substitutable. *Qua* substitution, the phallus is a mere mark in a series of unremarkable spots. *Qua* substitution, the *point de capiton* is a point of departure or arrival, or start or stop (.), in a sequence of entrances and exits (…). The phallus (is) the clitoris (is) and so on because neither (is) themselves. The *point de capiton* is pointless.

The pervert seduces the neurotic into an affair with a system of *différance*. This network is without the *point de capiton* of the violence of the signified. Otherwise, in schizophrenia, the system suffers total breakdown. Any communication whatsoever is impossible. Resistance is the symbolic order as such. The system is this insistent schizoid dissolution of signification (the sign) by value (the signifier). The galaxy is the foreclosure of the paternal metaphor. As a system, the name-of-the-father is *a priori* foreclosed. There is no father. There never was a father. There never will be a father. The paternal metaphor is a fable. The galaxy is maternal and motherly. Neither Freud nor Lacan accounts for the genesis or operation of the paternal metaphor. Freud refers to the father's distant threat against the offspring's mischievous self-pleasure.[37] Lacan clumsily diagrams the substitution of the name-of-the-father for the desire of the mother.[38] The system can(not) function in the absence of the absence of the father.

The proviso of the Madness of Order is the dead father. The simulation of the presence of the father is the condition of this absence. This vanished father founds the system on the endless negation of this pretend presence. Disavowal is a strategy of signification. The pervert's fetishes are representations of the Real. This alphabet expresses the inarticulable truth of the madman. The schizoid speaks the neurotic's truth as his own. This desire is inadmissible to the subject of neurosis. The paternal metaphor returns from the Real *qua* foreclosed *qua* the symbolic order. The father returns — endlessly — in order to stabilize the system which consistently renounces him. The pervert's discourse reduces the privileged metaphor of the father to a prosaic Metaphoricity. What is a father like — ?

Perversion — *différance* — metonymically stretches and spreads (…) the metaphorical stasis of identity and essence (.). The pervert represents the failure of the paternal function. The paternal metaphorical essence and identity *qua* maternal metonymical spin and topple are abyssal. The pervert simulates the father. The pervert is a *père-version*, as Lacan puts it. The *père-version* substitutes in the place of the absence of paternity. The pervert comically outlines the system that he cannot define. Neurotic blindness to the Real is the distraction of the repressed and its lazy and ceaseless returns. But if the system is madness, then does perverse symbolization reactively correct — contain and systematize — the schizoid's Unreason? Does the *écriture* of disavowal return schizophrenia to a coherent but tweaked extant symbolic? I maintain that the pervert's signification of value — signifier *qua* sign — of the psychotic's rants and raves productively supplements the schizophrenia of the Madness of Order. But how is this addition pulled out of the schizoid's holy shoe and displayed to the neurotic as the magic which (the pervert) is (not)? How is the logic of the primary process of unconscious-work revealed to a neurotic whose only awakened experience is of the ego — as if? This ego (.) is a fiction which substitutes in the place of an abyssal rise and fall (…) along the diacritical chain of value of the signifier. The ego is a substitute in the place of "itself" *qua* the other surrogates and substitutes across the sequence of value. The pervert destructures this ego.

JOKES AND THEIR RELATION TO THE UNCONSCIOUS — ABYSS

Freud's so-called considerations of representability refer to the success between the mediation of the unconscious signifier and its translation into the secondary process of the discourse of the conscious ego. The purpose of translation of the wacky words and pictures of the primary process into the neurotic discourse of the secondary process is isomorphic to the pervert's enterprise to symbolize the Unreason of the schizoid. The pervert rewrites Unreason into a coherent and reasonable vocabulary for the neurotic. The barrier to Unreasonable rapport with the neurotic is not only resistance from the ego to the Other of interpretation. Additionally, the navel of the trouble is the massive gap between the *Verschrangung* of the unconscious and the structure of the secondary process of Reason. The representational conundrum is not simply the effort to translate. Rather, the object of the pervert's representation is translation itself. The issue is not the prosaic talent to translate between foreign languages. The pervert's craft is to translate *between the same language.*

Translations

In *Jokes and their Relation to the Unconscious* (1905), Freud reintroduces the concept of the unconscious-work as the original *métier* of the primary process. The obfuscatory occupation of the primary process animates the tension between desire and censorship. The productive strain in-between wish and law shapes the peculiar representation of the manifest symptom. The unconscious scrambles and jams words and pictures in order to evade the critical judgments of the censor. The law guards the self and the Other from the truth of desire and wish. But do unconscious desire and primary truth speak the syntax and semantics of the secondary process of Reason? Desire may only be itself as such in the code of the unconscious figuration and allegory of metaphor (.) and the zigzag and flight of metonymy (…). Desire *qua* desire may only be itself in the absence of negation, temporality, and knowledge. The words and images of desire may be resistant to the conscious system of negation, temporality, and knowledge. The unconscious presents the dream, joke, slip, and psychopathology of everyday life as mere effects of desire. But what is the *discours* of *désir?*

The Real inflects the system of the ego and the conscious with a disturbance. Rupture reminds the subject and structure of the frailty of their consistency with themselves (A = A) and subordination to Outside forces ($\supseteq$ *qua* function). The psychoanalyst translates the manifest into the latent. This transcription illuminates the reverse work. The obverse movement transfigures the unconscious into the system of the Cs. Analysis indicates that resistant truth can be accessed by the secondary process and free association. If the vocabulary of desire is resistant to negation, time, and knowledge, then the semantics and syntax of truth are radically otherwise than the system of the Cs. How does the conscious translate desire if the truth speaks a foreign tongue?

Lacan's much-hyped sound bite that "the unconscious is structured *like* a language" ekes out a distinction between the unconscious processes and conscious-ego discourse. Condensation is *like* metaphor and displacement is *like* metonymy (my emphasis).[39] The distinction between the codes of the unconscious and the conventions of the conscious is structured by the metaphorical — *like* — organization of vocabulary in both text and image. The words and pictures of desire are qualitatively different from the language of the secondary process. The metaphorical — *like* — gap of both (.) and (…) animates the translation of the systems of the Cs. and Unc. The truth of desire speaks a language in the absence of temporality, negation, and knowledge. Unconscious *écriture* cannot be translated into the conscious-ego system of the secondary process. Desire does not speak language even at the same time that truth organizes this *désir.*

The analytic enterprise to transfigure primary process truth into its own ego-conscious semantics and syntax fails to recognize the vocabulary of desire. Manifest representations of the unconscious are expressed in their bizarre form because truth resists the secondary process. Analytic efforts at dream-interpretation misread the codes of the unconscious. Interpretation is a mistaken occupation because it enforces time, negation, and knowledge on the space of the unconscious. The unconscious cannot be translated into the codes and conventions of manifest ego-conscious discourse. Desire is the Other of Being. Desire is Real, so desire is *sous rature*. Interpretation is an *a priori* failed process by definition of the precepts of the ego-system. Eruption of the unconscious in dreams and parapraxes reminds conscious articulation that the secondary process is not the authority of signification even in the discourse of the conscious. *Wo Es war, es soll unconscoius kommen.*

The abyssal structure of metaphor illuminates this fracture in interpretation. Translation of the manifest representation into its latent content beseeches the supplementation of the difference and deferral — slip and slide — along the uncharted inchoate nebula of words. What is the *latency of* the latent content, and so on? The analytically reconstructed latent content (.) is a mere transformation of a manifest form which awaits yet further (…) interpretation into its *latent latency* (and so on) in the abyssal *mise-en-abyme* of analysis. This trace deconstructs all bi-level configurations of interpretation: conscious/unconscious, denotation/connotation, manifest/latent, metaphorical/literal, and so on. The psychoanalytic endeavor to organize the West around the fiction of Something is Missing teeters at the edge of the abyss of the absences of a fundamental metaphor and the final referent of the penis. There is no such *das Ding* as the unconscious. Paradoxically, this Nothingness is the truth of the unconscious.

The endless referral of the figurations and allegories of metaphor *qua* signifier absolutely destroys not only the function but even the purpose of the father. The systematic murder of paternity makes the direct expression of the essence of the system impossible. Perverse textualization of an ontology of translation is suspect. Translation is merely another word for the system. Any demonstration of the ontological structure of translation frames the system from an Outside. The Outside reveals the system as the negative obverse of the order. The psychotic escapes to the Outside. The benefit is the truth of the Madness of Order. The cost is incoherence and nonsense. The revelation of the essence of transfiguration slips on the process of translation *qua like qua* translation. Existential process and ontological essence are displaced by transliteration. The grammatological symbolization of the backslash (/) is symptomatic of this *différance* in translation. What does the binary opposition symbolization of (/) textualize? My abstract symbol of ($\supseteq$) expresses the excluded *function* of the center of the series of substitutes (signs, words, metaphors, fetishes, and so on). But the question applies to ($\supseteq$) — what is the ($\supseteq$) *de* ($\supseteq$) — ?

A pedagogy of the pervert is a hermeneutics of failure. Perverse *écriture* of transcription demonstrates the Real effects of translation. Breakdown of words is translation. Destabilization is also the essence of the transliterational galaxy. Neurotic Foreclosure (*rejet névrotique*) returns negation *qua* the Real. The Real is the organizational principle of the symbolic world. The isomorphic relationship between the signifying chain and unconscious-work indicates that any analytic interpretation is beside the purpose of the crystallization of the unconscious. The secondary process and the primary process employ the same techniques of expression. The strategies of textualization are identical in the primary process and the secondary process. But the salient division between the two systems is effected by the metaphorical gap — *like* — between the primary process and the secondary process. What is *like* like? What is the question which is posed by the ontological status of *like*?

The excess of distinction between unconscious and conscious — like metaphor — is the difference in translation in its essence. Sameness[†] of the unconscious/conscious suture and split shows that the primary process must be different from the ego-discourse in order to open the in-between gap in the condition of possibility of translation. The space-time *différance* is the structure of the galaxy in its essence. How is the gap — (/) — emergent in representation if it is already sutured? How do the representational pyrotechnics of the joke split the difference in order to make visible a remainder and reminder of the simultaneous parallactic aperture and closure? This project is the essence of the pervert's pact with the neurosis of the subject. The hysteric is an effect of the Real Signifier. But how is the unconscious *qua* the word? What is the unconscious word (positivity, affirmation) if its conscious translation is situated in the field of temporality, negation, and knowledge? How do the negative and differential relations of signifiers speak and write the positive unities of the sign? How is the break between signifier/sign to be properly deconstructed — and in what space? Unconscious articulation can only be an affirmative space of the signifier *qua* sign.

Literal qua Metaphorical

The considerations of representability rely entirely on the bi-level configuration of signification. The division between unconscious and conscious is the proviso of Freud's enterprise. About jokes, Freud writes: "The double meaning of the literal and metaphorical signification of a word [is] a rich source for the techniques of jokes."[40] The joke is contingent upon this ambiguity and play between the binary organization of the literal and the metaphorical. The abyssal structure of metaphor is such that the latent so-called "metaphorical" dimension of the object is a supplementary excess and adjunct remainder of "metaphorical" interpretation *ad nauseum*. As soon as this "metaphorical" dimension of analysis is deemed the unconscious or connotative underside of the "literal" or denotative dimension of the joke, the "metaphorical" (... *qua* .) is upended as the "literal" object (. *qua* ...) of yet a further "metaphorical" ("literal") (... $\supseteq$ ...) signification. There is no stable "metaphorical" or unconscious dimension of the joke. A "double meaning of the literal and metaphorical signification" disregards the void structure of the word. The wish that the jocular word is situated between the literal and the figural, or between the denotative and the connotative, or between the conscious and the unconscious is an effect of the neurotic *point de capiton* of the father's intervention. Clandestine interpretation enforces a necessary halt in the *différance* of an otherwise suspended articulation.

The techniques of joke mobilize the bi-level configuration of the literal and the figural. Freud is blind to the mortal structure of *like* (and so on) of the *mise-en-abyme* of interpretation. The joke depends on this contained and constrained model of interpretation — conscious/unconscious, literal/metaphorical, denotative/ connotative, and so on. But this modality of interpretation misreads the Unreason of the schizoid and the *Praxis* of the talented pervert. The fetishist unveils the *structure* of this void. The hole in the galaxy is that Being is precisely otherwise than itself — *what is is what is not*. Freud claims that, "thanks to certain favorable circumstances, [the joke] can voice two meanings."[41] This double-voiced enunciation limits the play of the text. The doubled joke tethers the text to a strict binary logic of opposition. Play and excess of significations are suspended between the strict confines of the either/or of the joke. The "favorable instances" refer to the perfect correspondence between the message of the latent content (unconscious and connotation) and the manifest representation (conscious and denotation) of the joke. There is no play of the text in Freud's joke. Surprise of otherness is neutered. The jokester controls the text, like an anxious and authoritative author. This is the essence of the punch line (.) of the joke.

Freud discusses both nonsense and absurd jokes in his survey. He is particularly fascinated by the question of the transformation of pure nonsense into a sensical joke. He says: "There is sense hiding in this nonsense, and [] it is this sense in the nonsense that makes the nonsense a joke."[42] As an analyst, Freud cannot simply enjoy the nonsense. He investigates the nonsense. He reduces nonsense to sense, just like a doctor who encounters a schizoid and forces the psychotic's Unreason to speak the rationality of Reason. The treatment of schizophrenia — body and Unreason — objectifies crazy talk. The analyst constrains psychotic vocabularies, and he translates them into Reason. Unreason must be quelled in the translation of the body and soul of the madman into the discourse of Reason and its apparatus of normalization. Why does the doctor not acknowledge the translation of his words of Reason into the truth of the schizoid's elaboration of the Madness of Order? Freud commits the same error in his project to make "sense" of "nonsense." He reduces Unreason and madness to Reason and neurosis. Freud castrates a secret Untruth. He reduces the gurgles of the architectonics of the solar system to a prosaic permutation of unconscious desire. Sense is internal to nonsense. The joke can be understood as trace or *différance*. Nonsense is the Unreasonable effect of the slip and slide of signification. Discourse disintegrates into the gobbledygook of a nonsensical Unreason. The sense in discourse circulates around the Real navel of the joke. The suspended punch line (…) is the inarticulable truth of the Madness of Order and its proper symbol: (⊇).

All worldly *Praxis* symbolizes the Real. The joke is continuous with all concerted action in the world. Man and world are a joke. Ontology is the translation of Real nonsense into symbolic sense in *Praxis*. Hidden text is the sense of this nonsense. The joke unveils the emergent Reason and rationality in Unreason and delirium. The joke demonstrates that madness is the internal essence of $-ism. The pervert's signification is humorous because the comic unveils the overlap of madness and sanity, disorder and order, play and structure, Real and symbolic, and so on. The joke hides and reveals the deconstruction of binary opposition *in toto*. *Thanatos* animates this comedy. Gallows humor explains the conscious-ego confession that, "I'm dying of laughter." The joke is comical because it reveals the Madness of Order. The joke presents perversity: "I know very well that this is nonsense, but nevertheless it is perfectly reasonable." The disavowed in the joke — acknowledgment and denial — is the opposition between Unreason and Reason. There is no difference between insanity and rationality other than *différance*.

The joke-teller articulates the nonsense before the listener discovers its sense. Madness precedes logic, Unreason prepares Reason, and the primary process organizes neurosis. The pervert discerns the Unreasonable nonsense. She then demonstrates the hidden sense of the clandestine truth of the extant order of Being. The schizoid presents as crazy. The primacy of this insanity enables the neurotic to glimpse the Reason of the schizophrenic. The pervert demonstrates this Reason. She indicates that the madman's whimsical speech is not a joke. Nonsense is not a joke because there is no nonsense in the system. The system is — Being *qua* Being — this nonsense. Sense makes no sense. The joke is impossible. The joke bombs by dint of its structure. Failure indicates that Reason has an origin. Reason is lost in the space of trace. If Reason is lost, then can Unreason be found?

Disavowedly, the (non)sense of the joke (un)veils this (non)sense. The joke makes "appear," Freud says, "nonsense from one point of view" which "must make good — or at least admissible — sense from another."[43] The joke is situated in the parallactic gap. Two mutually exclusive and antagonistic perspectives on "one" and the "same" object complement each other. The competition between these two perspectives of sense/ nonsense and Reason/Unreason provokes an affect. A "conflict of feelings," Freud says, is "produced by [the] simultaneous sense and nonsense [in the joke]."[44] This "simultaneity" indicates the superpositional disavowal of perversion. The synchronicity of a "conflict" implies that the opposition between sense and nonsense — Reason and Unreason — is reconciled in the *jouissance* of the joke. The hidden dimension is this kernel of Real inconsistency within Reason. The manifestation of contradiction is the precept of the organization of a joke. Why is this sparkle of craziness enjoyable to us? How is this pleasurable wound of Unreason finally sutured by us in the process of the joke itself? Is laugher the affective response to the abyssal reversal of sense and nonsense? Or is laughter the uneasy rejoinder which mobilizes the *point de capiton* (.) in order to cut the slip and slide of *différance* short?

The joke returns this gap in Reason to rationality and logic. At the punch line, the joke makes sense. Reason contains the nonsense of the joke. Reason triumphs, and the authority of order is reproduced. The superegoic demand to enjoy the alphabets, words, and vocabularies of the joke restricts the adventures of Unreason. This imperative — *Jouir!* — of the joke enforces the masculine libidinal economy which gets off on the arrival of the signified. The masculine jokester limits (.) endless play (…) of the signifier. Only the neurotic enjoys the idiot's joke because the payoff of pleasure is the signified of sense. Analysis of the structure of jokes articulates a sensical Reason. This Logic of Identity overrides the madness of Unreason. The "simultaneity" of the interval between sense/nonsense is madness.

The concurrence of rationality and madness opens the parallactic gap at the same instant that it closes it. This aperture-closure reveals the object as perversely both/and. The object is different from itself. The structure of the joke disturbs the self-same and the self-identical. The joke is decentered from itself. The neurotic reconstructs the joke in order to enjoy the kernel of insanity. But Reason finally rationalizes this craziness as comical but sensical. The joke is humorous because it returns nonsense and madness to Reason and rationality. The joke makes the audience laugh. But how does it open a nonsense which resists closure by Reason? What is humorous precisely because it is not? What is the Nothingness of the Being of humor? Is there even a proper object of laughter? Or is the joke always already told and the perverts still laughing?

The joke is structured by metaphor. Metaphor is nonsensical and Unreasonable because it is forever recursive (…). The *like* is always a higher/lower and nearer/further Metaphoricity. The "literal" dimension and the "metaphorical" universe are indivisible because each slips and slides — *différance* — into the other. The Madness of Order shows that all "metaphors" are fundamentally "literal." The joke is animated by the same mechanisms of condensation and displacement. These techniques underlie the processes of obfuscation and concealment in dreams. Unification of an unsuspected bond of signification in the joke generates absurdity. A double-layer of meaning is intended and received in the performance of the joke. The "indirect representation," as Freud says, splits the joke into a layered set of senses. The synchronous duality of levels constitutes the joke. The joke mobilizes this contradiction in sense in order to inspire the pleasure of the joke. The joke is the privileged dimension of the perverse aesthetic of the *jouissance* of the Other disavowal. The neurotic enjoys nonsense and the Madness of Order because the system makes sense of an otherwise neurotically foreclosed (*rejet névrotique*) nonsense. Unwittingly, the neurotic enjoys Reason and rationality at the cost of Unreason and madness.

The Father and the Joke

The father who is neither appeared nor disappeared but nonappeared is strangely present in the joke. But the father is also annulled within the process of the joke. The joke manifests the nonappearance of the father in "indirect representation." The father's foreclosure of the primordial signifier is unveiled in the joke. This indirect representation is the visible effect of the screened presence of paternity. The success of the joke is the reminder of the nonappearance of the father. The joke formulates the murder of absence *qua* presence. The Becoming of presence is based on the disavowal of contradiction. Suddenly, Nothing is Missing. Contradiction is resolved by disavowal. A unification of condensation sutures the wound of contradiction. The joke undoes scarcity. The joke indirectly represents a communism of plenitude rather than a capitalism of scarcity. The joke articulates a Peniscentrism of Sameness⁺ rather than a castration of sexual difference.

The joke makes Sameness⁺ visible to man. Condensation is "putting things together as a series with the conjunction *and*" (my emphasis).[45] All of the words in the system are suddenly positively related ($\supseteq$) to each other. A both/and logic is consistent with an unconscious of neither temporality nor negation nor knowledge.

Condensation is organized by — *like* — metaphor. The system is structured by both/and perversity. What is the aesthetic of this substitution? What specifies metaphorical substitution in the joke-technique as distinct from metaphorical substitution in the discourse of everyday life? Freud says: "The way in which the second metaphor comes about seems to constitute the requirement for it to be a joke, not the two metaphors themselves."[46] A concurrent difference and identity ("second metaphor comes about") are the essence of the joke. The joke is arranged by form rather than by content. The content of the metaphor is secondary. Metaphor is dead. A "metaphor" is already "literal" within a *mise-en-abyme*. How and when does metaphor succeed? The success of metaphor is a theoretical impossibility. Metaphor does not structure the joke. Rather, it is the joke which structures metaphor. The humor is the unintended reversal of the primary *arche* of metaphor as the precept of $-ism.

The father is dead. But both metaphor and paternity make a necromantic appearance in the joke. Metaphoricity manifests as an effect of its nonappearance. The joke is structured by the simultaneity and coincidence of Unreason and Reason, madness and rationality, and nonsense and sense. Metaphor shows this at once disavowal of the parallactic gap. The split in the object is both opened and closed. The object is both itself *qua* Being and not itself *qua* Nothingness. Metaphor presents as an *effect* rather than the *cause* of the signifying chain. The two objects of opposed and antagonistic perspectives are identified as both identical and different. This illumination manifests Sameness[+]. *Like* is not possible if the space and time — *différance* — between the two objects are null and void. There must be a difference for comparison and contrast — exchange — to be possible and coherent.

At the same time, this difference is foreclosed because Being is conditioned by identity. The Logic of Identity is contingent upon the difference that it both acknowledges and denies in disavowal. Foreclosure is sutured by disavowal. The pervert stages the Madness of Order in the internal disavowal of the signifier. The content and the form of metaphor decide either psychotic *Verwerfung* or perverse *Verleugnung* and their respective returns. The foreclosure in the Real renders the word impossible and incoherent. The disavowal in the symbolic returns *qua* itself. But disavowal returns with the crucial distinction that representation rather than reality is in presence. Return in perversion is *écriture* — fetishes, objects, and (*a*)sexuality. Return in schizophrenia is disturbance in reality — delusions and hallucinations. $-ism contains and constrains madness because the psychotic structure is isomorphic to the system. The psychotic is ruptured by the Madness of Order in the disturbances of reality. The pervert evades these disturbances in the substitution of representation for reality. The escape to representation in the place of reality is the pervert's smart approach to $-ism. Representation will be the Real in the future of the Pervert-Schizoid-Woman.

Metaphor

Fetishism symbolizes this process of *Verleugnung* in a representation. Disavowal demonstrates and performs the constitutive instability of the architectonics of the signifying chain. The paternal metaphor is suspended in perversion. The fetishist bypasses fantasy-reality for the Real of representation. The pervert lives and breathes the Real Signifier or the Real Symbolic or the radical Metaphoricity — (...) — in their *mise-en-abyme*. The joke reveals this Real Signifier in the figural representation of the lace, shoe, fur, and jockstrap. The sweetener in this performance is that the success of metaphor is achieved in its abject failure. What is the effect of the success of the death of metaphor? What originates from the grave which arouses amusement but also showcases the triumph of *Thanatos qua* the essence of the system and its achievements? The system works *qua* its own foreclosure. The impossibility of *like* exhibits the success of its own failure. Why does the no-go (.) go (...)? How does *Trieb* emerge as an effect of the circulation of desire in the system?

Freud foregrounds the conundrum of the variable effects of metaphor in his work in the joke-book. He writes: "We find the decision as to whether something is a joke or not more difficult to make in the case of metaphor than in other forms of expression."[47] There is a specific reason that metaphor is "more difficult" to understand in the structure of the joke. Metaphor obscures the joke because the double-voiced is absent from the form and the content of metaphor. The entire structure of *langue* is metaphorical. But the joke is structured differently. The success of the joke makes sense of nonsense. Ordinary discourse works because it indeed works. Man communicates even if only because the word works. The system need not posit an origin or *arche* for the series of signs in the system. As Lacan points out in the *Seminar* on the four fundamental concepts of psychoanalysis (1964), there is only a cause (origin, *arche*, departure, and arrival) in something which does not work. Frenzy for the cause is only generated in the wake of a malfunction. The system inexplicably works. Deconstructive *différance* and trace in the *mise-en-abyme* are invisible to and unnoticed by the neurotic. The neurotic does not bother to read *Of Grammatology* (1967) because he is certain that he is the speaker of his speech and the writer of his *écriture*.

Deconstruction spotlights the glitch in the system. Grammatology illustrates the presence ($\supseteq$) absence of the *arche* of this collapse. Otherwise, the fissure in Being is unnamable because it is subordinate to the effects of the differences and deferrals in discourse. Deconstruction indicates that the breakdown — Madness of Order — has no cause. All effects are *ex nihilo*, Out of Nothing rather than Something. Deconstruction posits a Nothing is Missing of communist plenitude and queer (*a*)sexual difference. Ordinarily, communication in everyday life ignores the unconscious hiccups in the web of meaning. There is no origin because the system evidently works. Neurotic Foreclosure (*rejet névrotique*) returns *qua* this destabilization. This disturbance is the system. Schizophrenia works, and it proscribes no explanation, such as cause or reason. The handiwork of sense in the system smoothly operates because nonsense — Real Signifier, Real Symbolic, Sameness⁺, Nothing is Missing, Being, Phallus, Father — works. Madness of Order slips and slides beyond a causal *arche* because rupture works. There is no *arche* for the defect of Something is Missing because the system flourishes on the phallocentric logic of castration and the capitalist system of scarcity. The system handles itself *qua* malfunction. The death of metaphor — ~~like~~ — is the break in $-ism that simultaneously makes the structure possible. $-ism is managed by *Thanatos* and the will to destruction. Disintegration unifies the system. *Eros* is *Thanatos*. The two principles cannot be separated because each substitutes for the other in its effect which simultaneously is its cause. Life, inhale and exhale, is death. Ruination is the principle of foundation.

Metaphor works because it does not work. Why? It is what it is not. But it is difficult to detect metaphorical processes and procedures in the networks of discourse. Metaphor (mis)informs the joke because *langue* is organized by substitution. Sameness⁺ denotes synchronous and diachronous slippage. The play of the slip and slide is in timeless space. It is strange that metaphor works according to the plans of the system because it is evident that the father is absent from $-ism. The schizoid is collared and pinched by this absence. The psychotic's frenzy and mania are the expression of a discursive web of words in infinite flight and irrepressible fancy. The madman encounters the disorganization of signification in delusions and hallucinations. The joke gestures toward the parallactic overlap between the oppositions in the structure. The comical zeal is the excess between conscious/unconscious, denotation/connotation, signifier/signified, manifest/latent, Reason/Unreason, rationality/madness, and so on. The object of the comic is ($\supseteq$).

Deconstruction and translation are representational effects of the Madness of Order. The joke implicates nonsense in sense. The articulation of the unconscious from within the words and alphabets of the conscious secondary process is an impossible metalanguage — a discourse of Reason *about* the words of Unreason. Grammatology (Derrida and de Man) and psychoanalysis (Lacan) generally dismiss metalanguage. The *über*-signification is a perspective which subverts the principle which is the object of articulation of this metalanguage.

De Man says that "theory" closes the cleavage between the various levels of analysis of the text. But, he concludes: "Nothing can overcome the resistance to theory since theory is itself this resistance."[48] A necessary resistance overwhelms the critical exploit to capture the closure and aperture — total overlap and absolute speculation, on the one hand, and incomplete coincidence and partial identity, on the other hand — of the self-identical and the self-same Logic of Identity. The system forecloses the signified, and it returns the absolutely resistant to signification to the center of the structure. This hole reveals the system not in its ~~essence~~ but in its effect. This effect is its differed and deferred — delayed — ~~essence~~ in an undecidable and indeterminate space of the unconscious.

BEING...

These demonstrations indicate that Being ("is") both is itself and is not itself. Being ("is") is both "is" and "is not" because the Inside ("is") is the Outside ("is not"). Being ("is") is "is not" and the "is" is not "is not." Being is not "itself." The "is" is "is not," or it is what it is not. Being is also itself. The "is" is "is," or it is what it is. This undecidable and superpositional oscillation between Being and its obverse can only be coherently understood in the "hypnoid conscience," as Freud and Breuer (1892) referred to the psyches of the early hysterics, or later as Freud referred to the double-attitude of the pervert.[49] This (dis)orientation upsets the mutual exclusivity of the opposition between objects which are otherwise cast within a binary structure. The "is" is not "is not," or it is not what it is not or it is what it is. It is not what it is, and it is what it is not. Being both is not itself and is itself Being. Being is in a perpetual state of oscillation and indecision in an indeterminate — $(\supseteq)$ space $(\supseteq)$ — of incoordination in the unconscious. Being ("is") both is (Being) and is not (Nothingness). It is not what it is. It is what it is. It is what it is not. Any text is different from and the same as — Sameness[+] — itself. Being ("is") is the chosen word to explicate the disruption of the self-same and the self-identical of the word because the ontico-ontological difference, per Heidegger, is the theoretical presupposition of the coincidence of any object with itself. The split in Being destroys the entire ontological project and the positive extant order. The supposition of ontology — Being — misunderstands the Madness of Order. The ontological inquiry is a missed encounter with $-ism. The ontological gesture — "What is?" — destabilizes not simply Being but the entire set of conditions of the identity of any object with, around, by, below, above, adjacent, beyond — $(\supseteq)$ — itself. Why is it impossible to totalize the split in identity $(A \supseteq A)$ *qua* itself *qua* a coherent identity $([A \supseteq A] \supseteq [A \supseteq A])$ — ? Any totalization is subject to its own negation in an undecidable and indeterminate space in the absence of temporized coordinates.

This discussion is a snapshot of the so-called poststructuralist critique of Hegel's totality of the End of History. The gap between postmodern fragmentation and modern totalization can be mapped onto the switcheroo between Saussure's theory of the value of the signifier as negative and differential and his notion of the signification of the sign as a positive entity unto itself. The tension between Hegel's totality and deconstruction's supplemental Other is structured by the possibility and necessity of an infinite extension and expansion of *Trieb* and the signifier in contrast to the private property of a destined and departed sign. The word limits space, and it unfolds time. But the word also sustains the play of the system. A retotalized identity and identification are veritably everywhere. Totalization defines man's $-istic identities as forms of *Gestalt*. But the integral exception to this totality is the essentiality of the signifier in space and the necessity of the deferral of ~~time~~. The signifier insists in an endless turmoil of the radicality of desire: $(A \supseteq A = A \supseteq A)$ $(\supseteq)$ $(A \supseteq A = A \supseteq A)$, and so on. The binary logic (like a computer code) of *langue* organizes a schizophrenic system. Do we dream of the fragment and awaken to the total? Or do we dream of the whole and awaken to the incomplete? Or do we dream the totally fragmented and awaken to the wholly incomplete?

Figure 9.4 Queer Mathematics of *Différance*

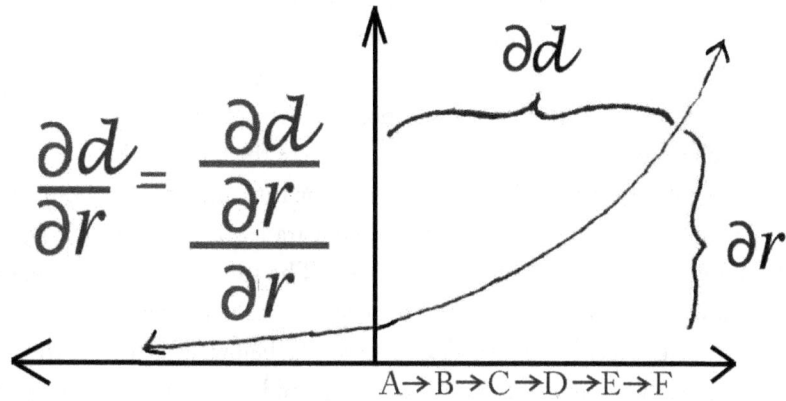

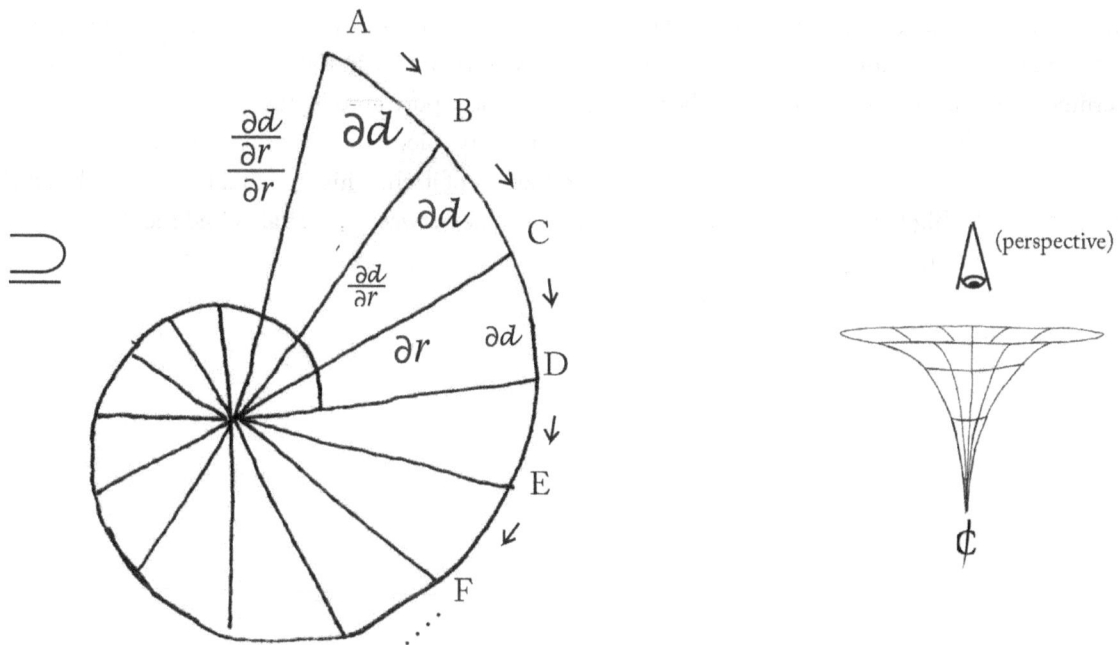

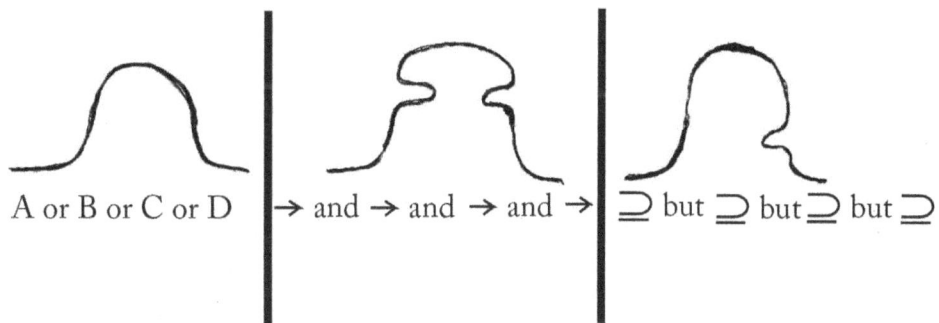

A or B or C or D │ → and → and → and → │ ⊇ but ⊇ but ⊇ but ⊇

This series of graphs shows that the difference *of* difference is difference. This is the so-called non-originary origin of the trace. The gap at the center of *différance* in difference and deferral is excess difference and deferral. The graph of the function ($r = e^d$) (above) indicates that the rate of change at any instant is equivalent to the value of *d* such that the difference of difference is difference. The gap at the decenter of relationality and constructionism is surplus relationality and constructionism. The difference *of* difference *qua* difference is Queer Mathematically symbolized by the derivative symbol (∂). The golden spiral (center, right) shows a perpetual and perdurable relationship of gap and bond of fissure. The golden spiral is a ratio which is continuously reintegrated and constantly reiterated. The length of the resultant hypotenuse must symbolize the rate of change of *d* to *r* — of difference and deferral to relationality and constructionism. This spiral (center, left) is visually homologous to the psychotic (neurotic) disappearance of each term (A, B, C, D, and so on) into the voided center of a prehistoric and asymbolic Sameness[+]. The spiral (center, left) resembles the neurotic's travels. This neurotic movement toward (away from) the occluded center is depicted in the downward (upward) conveyance in the gravity figure (center, right). The three heads (below) indicate the three postpsychoanalytic clinical conceptual personae. The pervert is thinking, being, and living the metonymy of units of text. The psychotic imagines the Same[+] (non)relationship between each and any object. This singularity of the difference *of* difference is illustrated by the repetition of the arrow of difference and deferral between objects. The pervert's "but nevertheless" is the conjunction which recurs this sensibility of play in the articulation of the psychotic's discernment of *différance qua* Sameness[+]. The pervert's aesthetic is portrayed by the golden spiral (center, left). The pervert's jockstrap is Becoming-Splitting in its spatial expansion and extension toward (away from) its (*a*)sexual nucleus. This (*a*)sexuality is an *ex nihilo* — Big Bang — of itself. This (*a*)sexuality expands the fetishes in the system. The Big Bang extends the universe. The *différance* between (*a*)sexuality and the Big Bang is the choice of metaphor: quarks and strings or jockstraps and cups?

Notes & Sketches —

Dualism misencounters itself because text is synchronically and diachronically resistant to interpretation. Spatially, the system cannot define itself except through a series-in-time movement-in-space set of referrals in an expansive solar system. These elaborations in the sweep of space are neither destined (.) nor arrived (.) happenings of negation. Difference cannot decide its own identity. The massive negation that Duchamp's artwork (1917) presents as a philosophical concept resists articulation in words. Text resists and defies text. The Real is the brutal — joyous, masochistic, depressed, and sadistic — negation from the void of the center (*et al.*) of the galaxy. The Real Signifier positively represents the intense negation of the order. Negation is an undefined, undecidable, and indeterminate difference. It is — *not*. Negation is the void of creationist sublimation *ex nihilo* of that which is simultaneously averse and amenable to the symbol. No word for this negation — neither *Verdrängung* nor *Verwerfung* nor *Verleugnung* — can be articulated. The essence of Nothingness — *not not not* — is precisely equivalent — Sameness⁺ — to every other word in a series in the expanse of space. Time cannot begin until space ends. Until the ends of space, time is suspended. — Nothingness —

— Being — Negation is a signifier without a signified. Negation sustains itself as this process of immolation in the gap between materiality and abstraction. Freud's word for this spin and spun negativity is *Thanatos*. The only signifier of — *not not not* — is its obverse in positivity. Paradoxically, positivity returns as the essence of the system of negative and differential diacritics. *Eros* is the metaphor for *Thanatos*. The text is both the text and not the text. A urinal is a urinal because it is not a urinal. The object is not the object because it is the object. These are the rants and raves of a madman. Her discourse of Unreason contests the organizational principles of all *doxa*. The speech of the subject is Unreason. Unreason is internal to and even coincident with Reason. The aporetic schizoid symbolization of Being — the copula between words *qua* ($\supseteq$) — is the everyday occupation of *écriture et lirer*. There is no name for Being or for any other signifier in the system. There are no words in *langue*. What is the substance of writing and speaking? What is written by the writing? What is spoken in the speaking?

In *History of Madness* (1961), Foucault says that Unreason is a generalized deviation from the foundational structure of Reason. But Unreason is also constitutive of the organization of Reason. Foucault writes,

> Thus the simplest and most general definition that can be given for madness is delirium itself: Delirium — from *Delero*, to rave, to talk idly; which is derived from *Lira*, a Ridge or Furrow of Land. Hence *Deliro* properly imparts, to deviate from the Right, that is, right Reason.[50]

Madness is not merely a deviation from Reason. Unreason is a threat to the coherence and dominance of rationality and logic. Discourse is arranged by *Deliro*. *Deliro* reduces words to a farcical and campy gobbledygook. This schizoid structure challenges Reason as a system of signification of clarity and rule. Madness contests the expression of truth. Crazy talk shames Reason. Mad words disrupt the system. Psychotic vocabulary resists truth. *Ergo*, the madman and his secret are contained and tortured. But the core of excess can be represented in the *Trieb* of the perverse fetishist and the dangerous allure of his fetish-texts. These magical objects illuminate radical substitution — (…) Metaphoricity (…) — and the suspended unraveling of the system of binary opposition. The fetish simultaneously veils and uncovers the order of penis-substitutions and the series of furs, laces, shoes, jockstraps, and so on. But after imaginary and symbolic props, what is the Real Penis?

The textual divination of this Real Penis is the horizon of a madness which uncovers the work of metaphor — *like* — as the essence of *langue*. An approach to the Real Penis is a flirtation with the parallactic gap between the system and $-ism *qua* the underside of the positive extant order of Being. The sign is the architectural protective prophylactic prop of the order in its crusade against its own madness. The Real Penis is the internal condition — flesh, blood, and sperm — of an order whose Reason will break the latex. The "vagina," as Freud says, "becomes valued henceforth as an asylum for the penis."[51] The Real Penis is the superpositional moment of the undecidable and indeterminate coincidence between the Madness of Order *qua* the Order of Madness *qua* parallax in *Deliro* and Reason. This imperceptible overlap is the space of the UnReason of the final release from the "asylum." The overlay liberates the "vagina" to be otherwise than an "asylum" for phallic psychosis.

Being disrupts all claims to presence. *Il y a* destroys the foundation of $-ism which is otherwise the presence of stable oppositions. The world is a mad mix-up. A homosexual is a spinning Jenny. An artist is a penis. A house is a jar. Quinoa is a bunny. The object is reference to another reference because words speak about *words* rather than about *things*. The absence of stable signification dissolves the structure. But the system returns because difference and deferral are the order of the solar system. The future beyond this dizzy negation is the wander of *Trieb*. *Verwerfung* of madness and its wacky architecture returns to destructure the system in the strange coincidence of Being and the extant ontological order of objects, on the one hand, and the Real which resists the self-sameness and self-identity of these objects, on the other hand. The absolutely unwriteable disrupts all identity. Being and the Real escape symbolization absolutely. Every signifier — Every Real Signifier — avoids the word. The word — any — is the Real. Why does man not see the coincidence of the Real and the symbolic? What disables a realization of this constitutive Sameness[+]? How is the system blind to itself? The name-of-the-father cannot guarantee a neurotic structure of alphabets, words, phrases, sentences, paragraphs, and pages. The father is dead *qua* the proviso of paternity itself.

Being (every word) cannot be determined as presence. Being is the Real around which symbolization circulates. Being is the object of the inexhaustible amusement of *Trieb*. Drive is coincident with all of the efforts of speaking and writing of the difference and deferral of the text. The distinction between *désir* and *Trieb* is a minimal difference within the same isomorphic structure. Desire and drive miss their objects. Desire suffers this loss as castration. *Trieb* enjoys the aim. Lacan's plea at the end of the *Seminar* on ethics (1959-1960) is "to act in conformity with the desire that is in you."[52] The cheeky subtext of this otherwise crucial imperative — that ethics must choose desire over symptom — is that *désir* by definition "gives way" as itself *qua Trieb*. The effort to "act in conformity with the desire that is in you" paradoxically excites the transformation of desire into *Trieb*.

Drive positively and ethically wanders the Real without the anxiety of desire. The loss of *désir* is the gain of *Trieb*. Drive overcomes value and mediation of phallus, father, sign, and currency. Drive transcends closure of any self-identity and self-sameness of its object, including itself. *Trieb* traces the round-about as merely the traversal of space in its chosen gerund form — Ing[+]. Drive enjoys the floatation within the ether of the world. The journey of *Trieb* is directed by the series of prepositions. This series creates the backward and forward zigzag in and out of spatiality. An infinitely expansive space stretches *in* time but not *within* time. The world is ordered — before, after, and in the process of the before and the after — in the dust of *Trieb*. But time as such is suspended. The expansion of space interrupts the presence (past, future) of time. Time is not-yet time in a space which is not-yet space. The Real around which the drive flirts and plays in *Praxis* splits Being through the introduction of a temporality of an endless willing having beening Becoming Being — whatever — Outside of present temporality.

Presence enjoys its own traversal *qua* simultaneously Becoming subject and object. The object is situated within a network of phallic — directive and indicative — prepositions without the anxious indignities of presence. The Lacanian *lettre pour l'être* returns signification (*lettre*) to Being (*l'être*). Symbolization of all of the relationships between objects in the system represents the joyous collapse of the system. The structure is already in shambles as its very condition of operation. The system pretends to suture the fundamental perturbance which is the source of its disability. A systemic autodeconstruction is the reason that Derrida explicitly claims that deconstruction is "undeconstructible."[53] Derrida's work identifies the essential element of infinity. Infinity involves a spatial and temporal extension of every object of substitution in the chain of words. The system consistently and constantly decenters every material mark and abstract concept in the Other.

Decenterment repeats and reiterates despite the fiction of a phallic stability in the system. The schizoid structure of the world is veiled. The neurotic pathology of the repressed and its return is endemic. This cycle is psychotic because the negation of desire and its return in the symptom are classified as opposed gestures. The self-same and self-identical presence of this distinction repressed/return is the object of a perverse speaking and writing of a Real Sameness⁺. Metaphor is a figuration of the signifier. Metaphor destructures its own work of the mediation of likeness and unlikeness, nearness and distance, and so on. *Like* mediation endeavors to speak and write the relationship of Being. This relationship — *Praxis* — cannot be represented. *Praxis* strives to speak and to write the sublime otherwise. The sublime is this Real impossibility.

Duchamp's conceptual point transcends conceptualization. The concept cannot express anything whatsoever other than the sublime inarticulable center of conceptuality. Duchamp's artistic and conceptual intervention is strictly invisible. This is so even if it is retroactively legible in its effects. All words are fundamentally subordinate to a radical *dis*recognition. The concept is a nonconcept. The word is a nonword. Concepts, materialities, and words are Real Signifiers. Duchamp's conceptual indication is empty. The concept (is) Nothingness. The subject (is) Nothingness. The subject is primitively hieroglyphic. The concept of Duchamp's "Fountain" (1917) destroys conceptuality. Derrida's *différance* mimics the concept of the "Fountain" (1917) and its discernment of the Outside of conceptualization. Perpetual oscillation in superposition energizes the aneconomy of both both and and and both and and and and both either and or and both neither and or nor and both dialectics and diacritics and both both and and and — and the entire battery of signifiers — and the Other — and the —

At the moment of observation, the series of words collapses into distinct oppositions. The whims of the preposition direct an infinitely recursive and superpositional disoriented gaze. At what point does the recursion of the gaze — sentence to paragraph to page to chapter to book to — finally look from an oriented perspective? At what point does the reader make a pact with the metaphysics of presence — the sentence, the paragraph, the page, the chapter, the book, and so on until — and look? The neurotic prefers sadistic voyeuristic scopophilia to masochistic exhibitionist performance. All prepositions point toward the Other. The vague uncharted nebula of words dissolves and disbands — elsewhere and otherwise — at the juncture of the essentialist question — "What is?" Perversely, words are beyond signification whatsoever because of infinite trace and undecidable oscillation. The concept which is articulated in "Fountain" (1917) resists representation as certain knowledge. This is so even if this figuration asymptotically frames the schizoid's secret truth of Unreason.

This concept haunts the symbolic as its own truth. Truth is Outside of the symbolic. Truth is Real. The unconscious is the locus of this truth. But conscious discourse disregards this truth except for the hiccups in the symptom. Madness of Order is the signified *qua* signifier. Necessarily, schizophrenia must be contained. The unconscious truth of the system can only be expressed as the Outside of the diacritical system of difference and negativity. Unreason articulates a positivity. Positive Unreason is the Outside of the negation — "No!" — of the system of the Cs. The truth of Unreason utters an affirmative "yes" in the system of the Unc. Positivity is analogous to the return of the pervert's disavowal of sexual difference. Negativity returns positivity. But are negation and its returned positivity a distinct cycle in neurotic *Verdrängung*, perverse *Verleugnung*, or psychotic *Verwerfung*? Whose return illuminates a Sameness⁺?

Duchamp's work indicates a Real which resists symbolization absolutely. The Inside is the Outside, but the Inside is also not the Outside. Both of these propositions deviate from themselves. Neurotics, try this: the Inside is and is not the Outside. Or this: the Inside is both the Inside and the Outside. And this: the Inside is (not) the Outside. And again: the urinal (is) the museum (is) the bathroom. Again: the urinal is both an ordinary urinal and an extraordinary art object. One more time: the urinal is willing having beening Becoming Being both artistic-ing and prosaic-ing — Ing⁺ — as otherwise than willing having beening Becoming Being — *et al.* — These propositions summarize the problem of observation in the Copenhagen (1925) interpretation of quantum physics. The object (an electron) oscillates in what is called a superpositional entanglement — generalized — between two mutually exclusive positions (as a particle and as a wave) until its collapse into a determinate property as either a particle or a wave. The text is an oscillation until the neurotic observation and violent determination of the presence of signification. The reader is a text. Readerly and writerly oscillation extends and stretches into the beyonds of the solar system. (I have collapsed the Copenhagen interpretion for my own performative purposes.)

The "observer problem," as it is known by quantum physics, also has its own "observer problem," and so on. The final referent of recursive observation is extended outward and inward between, on, for, near, above, at, around, as, over, under, and toward an observer whose glances simultaneously freeze and release the objects of their purview. Who is the reader? The reader observes the superposition of the text in its collapse. But who observes the reader's observation of this collapse, and so on? Recursion of the gaze is spatial rather than temporal. The observer problem resolves itself in the scene of a timeless unconscious in which the absence of absence frees observation from the knowledge of the secondary process ego-conscious system. The unconscious invites the electron into its *mise-en-scène* as both a particle and a wave. The *this* particle for *that* wave and *part* particle for *whole* wave of metonymy are spatially endless.

There is no final referent of a reader *of* the reader. The writer is both author and reader. But this deference and misreference cannot settle a key question. Who *qua* subject writes this writer and what has been willing having beening Becoming Being the text *qua* object? Who writes the writer? Does the reader *qua* the writer write the writer? Does the writer *qua* the reader read the reader? ⁺Reading⁺ — ⁺Ing⁺ — ⁺Writing⁺. Neurotic articulation swiftly anchors incessant negation in the desperate but habitual deployment of the phallic *point de capiton*. The neurotic identifies metonymy and desire as literal. Freud cannot account for the installation of the paternal metaphor — phallic stabilization — in the neurotic. Freud exposes the male junior's renunciation of the mother. The male junior submits to identification with the father as ego-ideal. In contrast, the female junior's postcastration trajectory is satisfaction with penis-substitutes (father, husband, and baby). Both masculine and feminine libidinal economies eschew access to the lost female penis.

Only the fetishist deploys the object (fur, lace, shoe, and jockstrap) as a prop for the lost penis. The fetish protects the pervert from the horror of the clitoris. Why do the male junior and the female junior renounce the lost penis? How does the pervert sustain its presence? What is the source of the different attitudes of the neurotic knowledge of castration and the perverse belief in plenitude? How is knowledge — "I know very well, but I know very well" — to be transformed into faith — "I know very well, but nevertheless"? How does the fetishist convince the hysteric that this neurotic himself does not know the object of the pervert's faith? Why is knowledge the apex of Reason if faith is the discourse of its revelation?

A critique of the Madness of Order discovers that Unreason is immanent — Inside (⊇) Outside — to Reason. The principle of the extant ontological order is (⊇) and its unsymbolizable copulatic relationship to the other objects in the system. The schizophrenia of the positive (negative) ontological order of Being is reasonable and rational. But the crucial dimension is that Reason is dysfunctional and unhealthy. Reason is unreasonable and irrational. The epic philosophical pursuit of Reason (such as Hegel's work on *Geist*) indicates the shameful malfunction of Reason.[54] There is only an origin in a glitch. The *arche* of Reason — as yet — resists presence to speculative philosophy and everyday *doxa*. Reason cannot be present in the usual spots and common crevices. Reason is elsewhere than the positive ontological structure of Being. Reason is the Outside of the ontological question of "What is?" Reason and its obversive Unreason must be traced to spaces which are beyond the rational and the logical, the ego and the individual, and the conscious and the present. Reason is Other. The wager of the next chapter is that Reason is to be found in the most unlikely of locales: the navel of the dream which reaches down into the unknown of the unconscious.

Reason and its immanent Unreason are unconscious. Pursuit of the unconscious and its architecture invites a reconsideration of the timeless space of desire. Reason is the timeless space of Unreason. But if Reason is unconscious, then can it speak in the alphabets and words of its own Unreason? Does desire write and speak within a discourse of Reason (⊒) Unreason? Copulatically, can (⊒) be symbolized by the unconscious primary process? After the ego, is ontology finally possible? The positive order of Being will be displaced by the negative and differential arrangement of the elements in a dream. The ontology of the dream questions the ontological project from within the negative and differential order of the signifier rather than within the positive order of the Being of the sign. The ontological "What is?" transmutes from ~~Being~~ and its gobbledygook to (⊒) and its Other-Logic. How do objects relate to themselves and each other from within the *mise-en-scène* of the unconscious dream? The relationship between objects is displaced from ~~Being~~ to (⊒). How does this shift from the positive ontological order of Being of the secondary process to the Dream-Ontology of the unconscious reorganize the self, the other, and the galaxy? After ~~Being~~ in the conscious, what is Being in the system of the Unc.?

Madness of Order in Finance and Desire

Madness of Order indicates the fundamental destruction of ~~Being~~ *qua* under erasure. The deconstruction of Being (is, are, were, and so on) undercuts the identity and essence (.) of all subjects and objects in the positive ontological order. The presence of the word submits to the traces of differences and deferrals — reference to reference, around reference, toward reference, by reference, near reference, below reference, above reference, and so on. This series of traces describes the undecidability and indetermination of any meaning-making enterprise in the comparison, contrast, and exchange of objects. Every word is the same word. *Qua* Sameness[+], there is no possibility of an economy of the sign in language, of currency in finance, of father in sociality, or of phallus in sexuality.

~~Being~~ under duress not only disintegrates the essence and identity (.) of the "What is?" in presence *qua* decidability and determination of each object in the extant ontological system. Being *sous rature* also subverts the copulatic relationship of any object with both itself (A = A) and also with all of the other words in the system (A(⊒) B (⊒) C (⊒), and so on) to which these words are already in relationship. The pervert discerns this Madness of Order that otherwise neurotically forecloses — *rejet névrotique* — the differential and negative foundation of civilization. My notation of (⊒) is an abstract symbol which visually textualizes the parallactic gap between the object itself and the relationship (⊒) of the object to any other presence in $-ism.

The (⊒) is a fetish for the voice of the excluded *function* whose absence is the proviso of substitute signs, metaphors, words, and fetishes that otherwise occupy the position of the occluded center of Being. The (⊒) is the symbol for the banished *function* of the paternal metaphor. The (⊒) indicates the death of the father and his inevitable return in the symptom of substitute signs, metaphors, words, and centers. This series otherwise occupies the space of death in the structure of the system of the Cs. Unconsciously, (⊒) figures the absence of a present word for the representation of the copulatic relationship between words and themselves, and between words and each other. The system of the Unc. animates an ontological order of Being — Dream-Ontology — which is the Outside to the *function* ($\supseteq$) and its substitute series of castrations.

The pervert's intuition of the Madness of Order applies to systems which are beyond *langue*. The structure of the sign is a privileged domain for the illumination of the schizophrenia of $-ism. The systems of finance and desire are fundamentally of the signifier, the signified, and the sign. Finance and desire are enterprises of semiotics. Madness of Order is the essence of the dominant systems of finance (Marx's critique of capitalism) and desire (Freud's elaboration of sexuality). Madness of Order is the logic of the signifier in *langue*, the commodity in capitalism, and desire in phallocentrism. Deconstruction is the basal matrix of the Madness of Order. But the architectonics of $-ism is the foundation of Freud's elaboration of desire and Marx's critique of capital.

Chapter one, "A Drive toward (*a*)sexuality," and chapter two, "Delays and Interruptions," establish the Madness of Order in the expansive openness of *Trieb* and the spatial deferral of presence and essence. Chapter three, "Psyches and Patients," chapter four, "Pervert (1): Between Neurosis and Psychosis," chapter five, "Pervert (2): Representation," and chapter six "Pervert (3): Betwixt Unreason" illuminate the Madness of Order in the essential clinical structures of psychoanalysis. Chapter seven, "Structure, Fetish, and Perversion in the Discourse of Deconstruction," outlines the Madness of Order at the center of structure. Chapter eight, "Debt to Marx," investigates the Madness of Order in a semiological Marxism. Freud's innovative conceptualization of pathology, Derrida's explosive illumination of structure, and Marx's critical work on capital are each specific interrogative extensions of a generalized critique of the Madness of Order in the system of $-ism.

Capitalism is the Madness of Finance. Marx's persuasive critique of capitalism shows that the general equivalent — dollars and coins — is structured by the arbitrary quantification of qualified use-value. The capitalist mode of production reduces the singular — incomparable and incontrastable — quality of goods and services to the exchangeability of the quantification of the value of currency. The crux of the illumination of the Madness of Order is that use *qua* exchange is dominated by the mediatory general equivalent. Dollars and coins draw — somehow — comparisons and contrasts between otherwise absolutely singular objects. The inexplicable — heterosexualist — necromancy of the commodity is the quantification in 1's and 0's of qualified use-values in purpose and intention. How does quantified exchange-value standardize qualified use-value? The essence (.) of the commodity form in the Madness of Order in the financial system is this conversion of singularity into exchange, and of this transmutation of use-value into dollars and coins (...).

The precept of the capitalist economy is that the commodity gathers a presence through the comparable and contrastable system of exchange. But Saussure's madness reduces comparison and contrast to an undecidability and indetermination. The commodity is *not*. The commodity is *sous rature*. The ~~commodity~~ is devoid of presence in the exchange of comparison and contrast. There is no such *das Ding* as the commodity. This object is the absent center — function *qua* Nothingness: ($\supseteq$) — around which the (in)finite accumulation of capitalist exchange-value twists and turns in its obscene violence. The object resists the manic frenzy of capitalist commodification and its will to *produce debt* and convert Nothing is Missing into Something is Missing. Exchange-value is what it is not. The capitalist system is structured by the circulation of a Nothingness. The relationships between currency and objects cannot be spoken or written by the system. The scaffold of capital is the copulatic gap between exchanges. The principle of capitalism is the exchange of Missing. The comparable and contrastable value of this loss (gain) is beyond calculation and speculation.

Desire is the Madness of Heterosexuality. Freud's view of desire is structured by the precepts of $-ism. The relationship between aim and object — *Trieb* and *Objekt* — installs a gap between subject and object, man and world, and doer and deed. The *objet petit a* slips and slides — over here, then over there — such that it eludes both the metaphysics of presence and the ontology of Being. The *objet* is not what it is, and it is what it is not. The *objet petit a* is *not*. The subject's *Praxis* encircles a Real Nothingness. The neurotic's wayward journey is arranged by phallic prepositional indices and directions. The displacement of the object facilitates the endless circulations of desire. Freud discerns the space between objects as a castration and a loss. But this differential negativity of diacritical desirous pursuit is also transformed into a purely positive articulation of Being *qua* Nothingness.

Freudian phallocentrism is the origin and destination of the *lettre* of castration and its losses. The penis *qua* commodity is comparable and contrastable — "size" and "visibility" — in relationship to the clitoris. But this exchange of meaning-making is strictly psychotic because the penis cannot be the final referent — word, sign, metaphor, substitute, or fetish — for itself. The objects in the Madness of Order are under erasure. Just so, the ~~penis~~ is *sous rature*. The system of desire is structured by a series of nihilistic values. These calculations and speculations are arranged by the mad structuralism of Saussure's version of the undecidability and indetermination of the coordinates of the object. The penis is a commodity. But a commodity circulates — ($\supseteq$) — elsewhere and otherwise. The space of the circulation of the linguistic sign, the capitalist commodity, and the desired object is the unconscious. The Madness of Order is situated in the unconscious of the self and the system. What are the politics and sociality of this unconscious? What is the architecture of ($\supseteq$) — ? What is the subjective and objective design of the madness of man and his *mise-en-scène*?

The precept of the Madness of Order is a linguistic, economic, and sexual assumption that I have exploited in order to draw an isomorphism among the sign/signifier in language; the supply/demand scarcity under capitalism; and the penis/not-penis of phallocentrism. Linguistic signification, phallocentric penis/not-penis, and capitalist scarcity are structured by the phallocentric logic of Something is Missing. The project of this book is to illuminate the perverse labor to convert — somehow — lack into plenitude, loss into fullness, clitoris into queerness, scarcity into abundance, absence into presence, capitalism into communism, and the neurotic into the Pervert-Schizoid-Woman. The future of the Madness of Order is the end of the word in language, the collapse of the dollar and coin in finance, and the exhaustion of phallic sexuality in desire. Futurally, madness transforms into the materialism of the signifier, the freedom of communism, and the (*a*)sexuality of queerness. What is the space of the signifier, the communist, and the queer? I now abandon the sublime symbol ($\supseteq$). But I do so in order to map the blueprint of an architecture yet to be built. What is the architecture of — when — Nothing is Missing?

Chapter Ten

Unconscious Architecture

When an idea is wanting, a word can always be found to take its place.
— Johann Wolfgang von Goethe

Freud's fearless and hypnotic text, *The Interpretation of Dreams* (1900), establishes the series of neurotic oppositions — fundamentally: conscious/unconscious — which will guide the research for the rest of his career. Freud's first assumption in the dream-book is that the dream and its interpretation are different from each other. The unconscious and the conscious are discrete orders which are separated by the work of translation. This enterprise is the domain of the "dream-work." The labor of the unconscious obscures the latent content into the manifest representation. Translation is also the purview of "dream-interpretation." Analysis reverses condensation and displacement in the illumination of the latent signification of the dream. As Freud puts it: "The restoration of the connections which the dream-work has destroyed is a task which has to be performed by the interpretive process."[1] The "interpretive process" is assigned the endeavor to reweave the otherwise "destroyed" sense of the latent truth. The purpose of this chapter is to elaborate the architectonics of the unconscious and its form, content, and function.

Freud's commonsense wager is that interpretation is distinct from the dream. This premise is such a foregone conclusion that Freud need not explicitly oppose the interpretation and the dream. Freud only assumes that "dreams are capable of being interpreted."[2] The implication is that dream and interpretation are separate entities. The title of Freud's book, *The Interpretation of Dreams* (1900), implies that interpretation and dream are disjoined objects. Freud says that he is "led by some obscure feeling" that "every dream has a meaning."[3] This "obscure feeling" motivates Freud's recognition of the division between dream and its interpretation. This intent belies the neurotic inclination to view as separate and oppositional what could otherwise be understood as proximate and similar. The obscure feeling prompts Freud's separation of dream from interpretation. The division illuminates the neurotic tendency to understand the world in terms of oppositions: conscious/unconscious, manifest/latent, dream/interpretation, and so on. Freud's dream-analysis is encouraged by the neurotic symptom of an obscure feeling. As a manifest symptom, this strange affect is a consequence of the translation between the unconscious and the conscious.

The condition of dream-interpretation and the very separation between the unconscious and the conscious is the work of the primary process ("dream-work"). The labor of the unconscious enables a translation from the latent content into the manifest form. Dream interpretation is a pathological symptom. The endeavor of dream-interpretation is a consequence of the work of condensation and displacement. The achievement of dream-analysis is the upshot of the constitution of the manifest dream. Unexpectedly, the analysis is a dream. The dream is the latent content of the manifest form of the interpretation. In a reversal, the truth of the interpretation is the dream. The dream-interpretation translates the latent content into the manifest representation. The dream-work obscures the dream-analysis. The system of the unconscious veils the secondary process. The interpretation is a fulfillment of a wish. The dream is the wish of analysis. But how does the Freudian hermeneutics of suspicion fulfill desire? And why does desire will knowledge?

THE DREAM OF INTERPRETATION

The work of metaphor (or simile) is the formal substitution of one content for another: "My love is like a red, red rose." The trick is not only that metaphor slides into the slips of metonymy. Metaphor *qua* metonymy is also structurally endless. This is the economy of the *metonymization of metaphor*. This infinity mimics the economy of the differences and deferrals of *différance* in the absence of the *point de capiton*. This button-tie would otherwise refer the future to the past. An infinite metonymy against the ends of an anchored metaphor marks the (transgressed) division between neurosis and psychosis, and between *désir* and *Trieb*. These oppositions are concurrently flipped because metaphor "itself" displaces the self-same and the self-identical unity (*Eros*) of "itself." The metaphorical flip is an effect of the metonymic process of its "own" identification *qua* metaphor. The reversal of the division between metaphor/metonymy disorganizes the divisions between neurosis and psychosis, and between desire and drive. If metaphor is endlessly metonymic — and if sense is unanchored in nonsense — then the meaning of a dream is deferred into the void of unlimited semiosis.

Freud admits as much in his acknowledgment that the "navel," as he says of the dream, "is the spot where it reaches down into the unknown."[4] The "unknown" is a fortuitous metaphor. It describes the *telos* of a diachronized metaphor. This involves a substitution and a contiguity which proceed "down" ("up") into the chasm of an omphalos of a resistant interpretation. Freud writes,

> for "interpreting" a dream implies assigning a "meaning" to it — that is, replacing it by something which fits into the chain of our mental acts as a link having a validity and importance equal to the rest.[5]

The passage performs what it articulates: interpretation. Interpretation is the substitution of one content for another content. Freud performs this substitution in the text by "assigning a 'meaning' to it — that is, replacing it." The enterprise of substitution is what Freud means by the assignment of "meaning" to the dream. The interpretation of a dream is the substitution of its content with another message — "assigning a 'meaning' to it." But what is the difference between the "meaning" and the symptom that Freud identifies as the two ends between which the means of the activity of "replacement" and "assignment" mediates? The dream and its interpretation are different twists on the same turn. But in which direction — from dream to interpretation or from unconscious to conscious or from flip to twist — does the effort of "replacement" or "assignment" gesture to "fit into the chain of our mental acts as a link" the substitution in question? And toward which end? Does the interpretation precede the dream? Or does the dream interpret the wish of analysis?

Analysis also requires that the substitution conform to standards — that it "fits into the chain of our mental acts." This compliance ("fits in") with the standards of conscious operations limits the liberty of the interpretation of the dream. The dream-work veils the truth of desire in the activities of displacement and condensation. The interpretation-work of the analyst must "fit" the manifest representation of the symptom "in" the rhetorical devices of the secondary process. Substitution is limited by the constraints of the conscious mental apparatus. Limitation is a liberation because it invokes the radical Sameness⁺ ("having a validity and importance equal to the rest") which animates perversion. Fetishism unveils the radical deconstruction of the hierarchical oppositions — conscious/unconscious, manifest/latent, dream/analysis, and so on — which organize Freud's system.

Interpretation of the dream conforms to the constraints of the norms of the conscious system. It does so through the liberation of the radical Sameness⁺ of perversion. Fetishism permits the analysis of the dream. The neurotic structure of the analyst is a mere effect of the Sameness⁺ of the pervert. The pervert "fits in" to the "chain" of linkages — metaphors and metonymies — of the system of the ego. Interpretation conforms to the standards of Sameness⁺ which are consistent with the experience of the pervert. Properly interpreted, the passage suggests that the "interpretation" of the dream ~~is~~ the "assignment of meaning" ~~is~~ the "replacement" of it with another content ~~is~~ — and so on. These three signifiers — "interpretation," "assignment," and "replacement" — are each metonymic contiguous metaphorical substitutes for each other. As such, they are themselves symptoms. These figurations emerge simultaneously as themselves (hermeneutic devices) and as otherwise (manifest representations of pathology) than themselves. Interpretation is a symptom. Interpretation is a symptom of itself *qua* a symptom.

The dreamy and interpretive making of this sequence of equivalent metaphors — Sameness⁺ — is based on the words in the series which have "a validity and importance equal to the rest." Dissolution of hierarchical division — conscious/unconscious, manifest/latent, and dream/interpretation — is the proper work of the interpretation of dreams. Interpretation is the metaphorical substitution of content for content ("assignment" and "replacement"). This process yields to a happy death by the network of interchangeables which is "equal to the rest." The series of (un)likenesses is based on the bond of Sameness⁺ — noncoincidence with itself and continuity with the others which constitute themselves by what they are (not). These loops and rings animate the pervert's experience of the world. The analyst's labor of interpretation *qua* the patient's manifestation of symptom mimes the pervert's engagement with the solar system.

The joint of equivalence ("having a validity and importance equal to the rest") among these words is the *travail* of the interpretation of the dream. A Sameness⁺ among the fragments — metaphors and metonymies — of the dream analysis makes complete interpretation impossible. The phallic general equivalent otherwise mediates "validity" and "importance." Absent, this operation submits to the anal equivalence of all of the signifiers in the chain of linkages. Freud writes,

> Actually no such complete explanation of a dream has ever yet been achieved, and anyone who has attempted it has found portions (and usually very numerous portions) of the dream regarding whose origin he could find nothing to say.[6]

The "origin" of the dream yields to an infinite trace. This *différance* is "equal" to an endless "rest" — Sameness⁺ — in the battery of words in the Other. The Sameness⁺ between the signifiers in the network reduces the otherwise hierarchical division between conscious/unconscious and manifest/latent (and so on) to a fraudulent dream of the analyst. Dream resists total interpretation because the chain of equivalence that Freud describes as the essence of dream analysis must rely on an unassimilated inconsistency — inequivalence — in order to construct its series of equivalence.

Freud names this inadmissible signifier the "origin" of the dream. The *arche* indicates the source of the wish, desire, and truth. Desire is a consequence of creationist sublimation *ex nihilo*. Out of Nothing, the chain of equivalence and the deferred *objet petit a* make presence. The parts of the dream about which the analyst "could find nothing to say" underpin the sequence of interchangeables between the words of the analysis. The series of equivalence — Sameness⁺ — in the interpretation of a dream depends on the inconsistency of an object. Different-Signifier from the equivalent signs in the interpretation enables the analysis to separate itself from the excluded object. Excess is the origin or navel — both departure and destination — of the twists of dream and interpretation in the web of words.

In the analysis of dreams, Freud strives to separate the interpretation from the dream. Freud writes: "The interpretation of dreams is like a window through which we can get a glimpse of the interior of that apparatus."[7] Freud's wager is that interpretation will not fall through the "window" of the "interior" and become part of the dream that it seeks to analyze. Why is the dream considered the inside ("interior") of the relationship between symptom and analysis? The "apparatus" is split between an interior and an exterior. This apparatus is the binary architecture of Freud's theoretical edifice: conscious/unconscious, manifest/latent, dream/interpretation, symptom/analysis, and so on. The promised "glimpse" inside of the "apparatus" of binary opposition implies an exterior to the distinct and positive relationships between signs. The endeavor of interpretation gazes into an economy which is beyond the neurotic structure of binary oppositions. This dualistic system otherwise structures the symbolic order.

Dream-analysis permits a curious leer at the condition of possibility that Freud otherwise says is the unknown navel or origin of the symptom. Analysis opens a peek at the distinction between dream and interpretation and the other pairs of oppositions in Freud's apparatus. A scan of the "interior of the apparatus" illuminates the dream. This dream is the enterprise of the dream-work — condensation, displacement, considerations of representation, and secondary revision. Unconscious-work obscures the division which is established by a window which is none other than interpretation itself. Dream-work cracks the "window" between the interior/exterior, on the one hand, and the Outside to this division itself, on the other hand. The dream is excluded as Outside to the binary oppositions which organize Freud's system.

The exclusion from the chain of equivalence in the interpretation of the dream is the *dream*. The dream must be isolated from itself in order to emerge as coincident and continuous — Sameness⁺ — with the interpretation. Interpretation exposes the latent thoughts of the dream. The unconscious excludes the dream *from itself*. The dream is excluded from the dream. The dream is not the dream. The dream is the interpretation. What is a dream? To revise Freud, a dream is the fulfillment of an interpretation. Interpretation is the wish of analysis. The resistance of the navel of or *arche* to analysis is the wish of the dream. The desire of the dream is resistance. Desire is the language of the Real.

Freud's trust in the patient's conscious articulation of unconscious thoughts (what he calls "free association") belies the liaison between conscious and unconscious, and between analysis and dream. These dualities organize the patient's relationship to the analyst. A separation of these words — patient and analyst, conscious and unconscious, and interpretation and dream — veils a fundamental relationality and constructionism. Other-Logic binds the otherwise opposed. Why must the patient be considered apart from the analyst? Why must the unconscious be understood as outside of the purview of the conscious? Why must the interpretation be theorized as distinct from the dream? The elusive "last secret" of a dream approaches this indistinction between the words — patient and analyst, conscious and unconscious, and interpretation and dream — which must be repressed in order for the neurotic system of the conscious-ego to function.[8] The entire Freudian apparatus is based on the repression of the extimacy that he will otherwise find at the origin of the formations of the unconscious. These formations are the effects of the dream-work: condensation, displacement, considerations of representation, and secondary revision.

Freud claims that repression is necessary for civilization. Negation of relationality and constructionism is essential to the function of the neurotic. The neurotic symbolic order (interpretation) represses the *travail* of the symptom-work (dream). The unconscious proviso of the Madness of Order is repressed. Displacement and condensation are a threat to the organization of the system. The wish of the system recoils from the elusive and dreamy Outside of the interior/exterior opposition of the "window" pane. The system forbids a "glimpse." What is excluded from the dream as its internal essence? What is a dream if its wish is the fulfillment of interpretation? Or is analysis the obscured latent essence of the dream itself? Are we dreaming analysis rather than analyzing dreams?

Dreaming

The architectonics of the dream and the unconscious clarifies the relationship between the pervert and the schizoid. The pervert's massive campaign is to symbolize the Madness of Order. $-ism is the latent secret truth of the schizoid's Unreason. Illumination of s = $-ism is arranged and systematized by the fetishist's own perverse aesthetic: "I know very that that the Madness of Order is both Reason and Unreason, but nevertheless I believe in the potential representability of such scandalous truth amidst the (dis/en)abled constraints of the *mise-en-scène* of the dualities of unconscious/conscious, dream-work/dream-distortion, wish/censor, and so on." There is the inevitable potentiality of the repression of truth from representation in the dream. But there is also the aspiration for symbolization to lucidly and perspicaciously succeed. Freud says that the dream is a "form of expression."[9] This form can plainly — but in twist and contortion — picture the wish for proper dream-interpretation. Considerations of illustratability are the province of the dream-work. This careful art of the detail circulates the creative twists and turns of the translation from the threat of the latent content to the obscurity of the manifest form.

This talented *écriture* is performed in the service of the dream-distortion translation of the latent menace into the manifest picture. The apparatus of condensation-metaphor and displacement-metonymy is essentially the same mechanism. Both condensation and metaphor, and displacement and metonymy, mobilize a transvaluation of psychical intensities by the primary process. This transfiguration is a crucial integrant of the work of analysis. Transvaluations must be tempered by the conditions and revisions of the "form" of the "expressed" wish in the dream. The latent/manifest relationship and translation must be relatable by the patient and interpretable by the analyst. The pervert's sexy scheme symbolizes the schizoid's Untruth and its Unreasonable subversion of the symbolic order. The pervert's textual (*a*)sex tarries with the textual, visual, and logical conditions of production. The extant forms of expression accredit the pervert's words and deeds of *Praxis* with the Spirited talent to symbolize $-ism.

Dream-work plays with reversals, unions, splits, tethers, regressions, contradictions, antitheses, yes's and yes's, affirmations, timelessness, replacements, displacements, and substitutions. A reversal switches course in the opposite direction. A union joins the opposed in harmony and arrangement. A split forces a break between previously aligned objects. A tether restricts movement and transformation. A regression returns an object to a former state. A contradiction combines the opposed. An antithesis engages two opposed objects. A "yes, yes" refers to the Joycean-Derridean perverse reiteration of affirmation. An affirmation supports and encourages a representation. Timelessness refers to the atemporality of the unconscious. A replacement is an object which takes the place of another object. Substitution is an object which holds the place of another object. These elements of the dream-work are mobilized in order to obscure the represented wish. These techniques of obfuscation evade the censorship that otherwise bans desire from appearance in the system of the Cs.

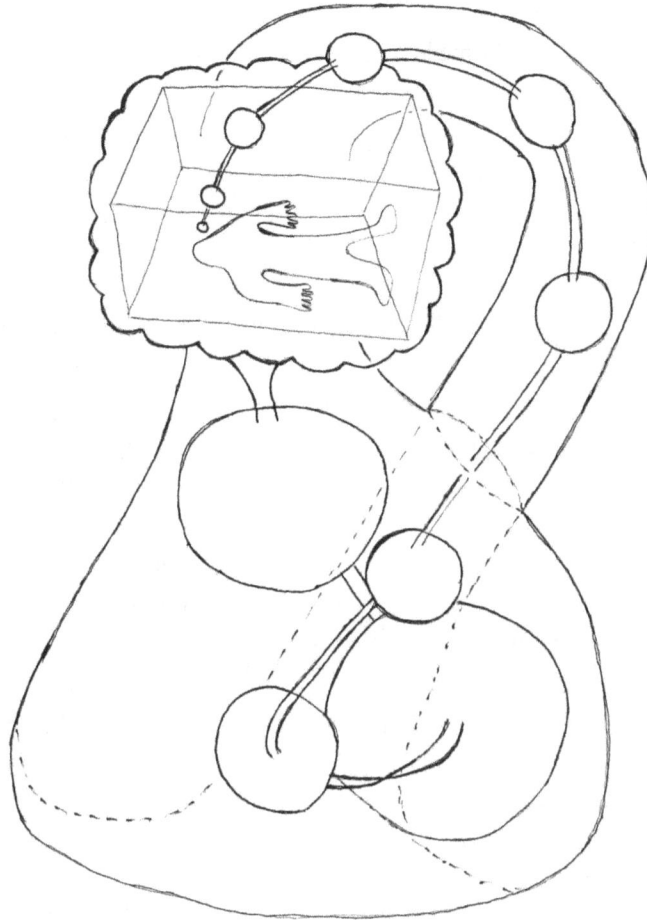

Figure 10.1 Dream<>Analysis

This image shows the neurotic dreamer who is situated at the aperture (above) of the Klein Bottle. The Klein Bottle represents the paradoxical principle of the system of value and its Inside-Outsideness and Outside-Insideness to itself in its generation of simulations — metaphors, words, objects, metonymies, and so on — of its own center. This picture illuminates the deconstructed distinction between dream and analysis, and between unconscious and conscious, in the parallactic perspective of the fetish. The hermeneutic trajectory of dream-analysis is depicted in the bubbles (above, left). These bubbles double and invert themselves. The neurotic dreamer is portrayed as dreaming the context of the dream itself. The neurotic dreamer is simultaneously dreaming wish and analyzing dream. This image shows the Sameness[+] of perversion which frees the dream to yet supplemental dream (analysis) and analysis (dream). This is done by a split in the subject of representation and the object of representation. The dream does not represent the fantasy of reality. Rather, the dream *qua* manifest representation expresses a latent wish that both precisely surfaces as a symptom in the fantasy-reality and retroactively embeds itself within the dream in the analysis of the past. Paradoxically, analysis not only translates the repressed desire but it also simultaneously dreams this latent wish itself. This paradoxical *Möbius* relationship between dream and analysis is visualized in the Klein Bottle.

Notes & Sketches —

These tricky tropes express the myriad and inventive textual talents of the unconscious-work of the primary process. At success, this charismatic flirtation simultaneously distorts and unveils — *Aletheia* — the latent wish. Distortion is adequately savvy because it bypasses the censorship of the system of the ego. But the ruin of representation is also sufficiently blunt to be interpretable as a wish, desire, or truth to the insightful analyst. The in-between of dream-work and dream-interpretation is the delicate dance to trespass the censor of the society. But dream (⊐) interpretation also reveals the Untruth of Unreason to the blindness of Reason and its neurotics.

Dream Is the Wish of Dream

I will present a critical exegesis of the techniques of unconscious representation. Freud says that the interpretation of the dream is the royal road to knowledge of the unconscious. He says that the unconscious is the source of the wish. The dream is the privileged symptom for an analysis of the latent content of the unconscious. The dream is the archetypal pathology. Dream represents the signified of the unconscious in wish, desire, and truth. Dream is also principally visual. The visuality of the dream involves foreground, background, color, light, props, characters, and movement. All of these specifically visual components of the dream are integral to the emergent signification of the latent content of the dream. A language of illustrations is a necessary obligation of an analyst who wants to properly interpret dreams. The considerations of symbolization must include scrutiny of the scopic regime of ocularity. This is the case even if the elemental modality of signification in the interpretation of the sublimity of the alphabet is text, words, and letters.

The *arche* of the royal road to the unconscious implies that the dream is the departure-destination advent of semiosis, both conscious and unconscious. Freud mentions "the revelation of an unsuspected psychical source of stimulation" as the wellspring of the wish.[10] Freud's explication is a dissatisfaction which borders on a mollification. Dream may be the artistic indulgence of the repressed. But its *arche* must differ and defer elsewhere to at least the *latency of the latent* (and so on). The "royal road" is long, twisted, and diversionary. The unconscious never arrives in presence. The latent content is always deferred by a conscious encirclement of a manifest representation. This aim/less *Trieb* is critical to the pervert's speech and *écriture*. Drive illuminates the road whose detours and digressions of scenic routes bypass arrival at the destination of the unconscious. If the unconscious is always deferred to another avenue or terrace, then the dream not only resists interpretation. The dream never stops dreaming. Man is still asleep.

Lacan claims that the unconscious is structured like — but also unlike — a language. Language is a metaphor for *language*. The unconscious is structured *like* a language — which is structured — like itself — which is structured — like itself — which is structured — like itself — which is structured — This formalization of a metalanguage returns to Derrida's discussion of function versus sign-substitutions in the work of orientation, balance, and organization of a structure. In "Structure, Sign, and Play" (1967), Derrida argues that the function of the coordination of a system cannot be self-identical and self-same. Organization of the structure cannot be represented by the accidental sign for the center. The origin of the wish is the effect of the phallic stabilization of the letter at the signified. A signified comprises a series of signs, such as "unconscious" or "soul" or "heart" or "cerebral cortex" or "primary process" or "genome" (and so on), which coordinates the system. The deconstructionist discerns that the *arche* slips and slides. The letter of the source of the wish is (un)decidable. The origin is caught between two slippery oppositional options that the pervert-deconstructionist strives to (in)completely disavow.

Freud is mute on the question of the origin of the wish. But the psychical or somatic source of desire can be unsteadily traced to disorganized childhood complexes and inchoate sexual traumas. Freud is adamant about any speculation about a spatiality and temporality of the unconscious. Freud intends to,

> dismiss the possibility of giving the phrase [unconscious, primary process] an anatomical interpretation and supposing it to refer to physiological cerebral localization or even to the histological layers of the cerebral cortex.[11]

Freud was a neuroscientist and later a psychoanalyst. His magnificent discovery of the unconscious cannot be physically situated in anatomical, physiological, or histological sections of the body or brain. Lacan demonstrates that the unconscious resists the metaphysics of presence. The unconscious is dispersed and diffused across the movements of the signifying chain. The unconscious is a ghostly haunt of the arbitrary denotative conventions of the relationships between signifiers and signifieds. The unconscious is a reminder of the instability of words themselves.

Freud speaks of a "mental apparatus built up of a number of agencies arranged in a series."[12] But he refuses to situate those sub-organizations within the body or the mind. Lacan's emphasis on the chains of discourse is an adept supplement to Freud's recoil from a biology of the unconscious. This is true of Freud even if his later topography of id, ego, and superego (1923) erred in the direction of the essential and the anatomical. Freud spends many pages in *The Interpretation of Dreams* (1900) recounting the *mise-en-scène* of the dream. Freud describes a "change of location of mental activity" in the unconscious.[13] He says: "The scene of action of dreams is different from that of waking ideational life."[14] Freud refers to the dream's talent to "dramatize an idea" or an "experience,"[15] and he even draws what he calls a "social parallel"[16] and analogy to "political life"[17] in the dream. The unconscious is the Outside.

Dream (by the) Book

A brief analysis of Freud's *The Interpretation of Dreams* (1900) reconceptualizes an ontology of the future. This critical exegesis illuminates the Dream-Ontology of the pervert. This brief excursus presents key articulations in Freud's text. The elaboration also establishes a framework through which to link Freud's architecture of the unconscious with Heidegger's interest in the ontological question, "What is?" The most bizarre discovery in the history of psychoanalysis is Freud's identification of the female genitalia with castration and absence. Freud's explicit revelation of this intuition presents itself at about the middle of the dream-book (1900). He writes, "something is missing describes the principal characteristic of female genitals."[18] The Something is Missing links psychoanalysis, deconstruction, and Marxism. Deconstruction claims that the text is always supplemented by an Other. There is a structural incompletion in signification. The Something is Missing is the variety of words, substitutions, fetishes, metaphors, and others that infinitely substitutes in the place of a center of the text. At the same time, this infinite series of words excludes the *function* of the orientation, balance, and organization of the structure. The foundation exceeds the structure. The function is excluded from the structure. The function is deposited into an Outside which returns as the destabilization of the system in question. Psychoanalysis suggests that the clitoris is this Outside. The clitoris is the excluded Missing. The clitoris founds the entire system of psychoanalysis (and the West) on castration and lack. This is visible in both the myth of the primal horde in *Totem and Taboo* (1913) and in the oedipal fables from the 1920s.

A deconstructive Marxism understands that the castration in sexual difference under phallocentrism is homologous to the scarcity in the supply/demand dynamics under capitalism. Marxism suggests that an overproduction in supply threatens the foundation of general equivalence of currency because material excess makes any restrictions on consumption and production unnecessary. Under late capitalism, there is a Nothing is Missing as the "principal characteristic" of the emergent communist system. According to Marx, what is excluded in capitalism is its own internal abundance. Plenitude must be castrated in order to sustain a system in which scarcity ($-ism) rules over the supply of use-values *qua* exchange-values. The question of the secondary characteristics of the excluded function in deconstruction, the clitoris in phallocentrism, and the scarcity under capitalism returns to the figure of the supplement. What are the secondary characteristics of systems which are incomplete as the condition of their operation?

Substitution is the central principle of the symptom. The word is always otherwise to and elsewhere from "itself." The phantom limb indicates sexual frigidity. The inexplicable cough denotes fear of castration. The unexpected typo suggests murderous intentions toward the father. Substitution is the foundational precept of the entire symbolic order. This series of substitutions is exactly infinite. This is so even if the function of the center is excluded from its series. A simple version of this idea is voiced in Freud's remark that in the translation from the unconscious latent content into the conscious manifest form the signified "is torn out of context and in the process transformed into something alien."[19] The ripped shreds of the latent content of the unconscious wish are translated into the bizarre form of the dream. Such a tear from (con)text to (con)text is the extraordinary work of the interchange between the dream-work (condensation, displacement, secondary revision, and considerations of representability) and the dream-censor. The censor puts the kibosh on a direct expression of the wish. The dream-censor requires this obscured transformation of the unconscious wish into its kooky manifest form in the dream. The law is the condition of the circulation of desire in the system of the dream. Rules and regulations avoid retribution for the asseveration of a desire.

Wish otherwise arouses the condemnation of the *Über-Ich*. This judgment would apply both intrapsychically and extrapsychically. A trace of *différance* makes possible the substitutions which are necessary in order for the wish to become visible in the dream. This is the case even for the spooky articulation of the images in the *mise-en-scène* of the dream. But this series of substitutions is not infinite because the final referent for the mechanisms of the dream-work is the wish. Desire is not excluded as the functional center of the dream because it is figured in the returns from the manifest dream *qua* its latent truth. The trace of an endless semiosis weaves and bobs its way through the dream. Toward its ends, this otherwise perverse metonymization of metaphor returns to the neurotic signified of the latent desire. The structure of the dream is a closed system because of the return from the wacky and freaky dream scene to the strict interpretation of this manifest form in the analysis of the latent content. Upon waking and analyzing, the dream returns the endless and open manifest form to the strict signified of the latent content of truth.

The secondary process makes the work of dream-interpretation possible for the analyst. The system of the ego transforms the incomprehensible into the legible. About the secondary process, Freud says,

> What marks out and reveals this part of dream-work is its bias, its slant. This function is not dissimilar to the one the poet [Heine] mischievously attributes to the philosopher: with its shreds and patches it stops up the holes in the structure of a particular dream. Thanks to its efforts, that dream loses the appearance of absurdity and incoherence and comes close to the model of a comprehensible experience.[20]

The secondary process is prejudicial against the truth. The purpose of the secondary process is to make the manifest form of the *mise-en-scène* resist its own *mise-en-abyme*. The gaps and fissures in the dream refer to the spots in the form that the semantics and syntax of everyday talk and analytical discourse cannot understand. Freud analogizes such enterprises with the handiwork of the figure of the philosopher who seeks to articulate Reason in the place of Unreason.

The Unreason of the dream is crucial to a proper interpretation of Dream-Ontology. The secondary process of the ego enforces coherence and orderliness onto the sprawl of images and pictures. These portraits cannot be easily assimilated to the signified. The will of the philosopher strives for sound interpretation. The secondary process seeks a veneer of articulacy and cogency for the whims and fancies of the dream. The occupation of the secondary process transforms the architecture of Unreason into a lucid and plain record of advisable verity and judicious realism. The absence of the secondary processes would make the dream inaccessible to the analyst and his techniques of interpretation.

The most significant element of the manifest figuration of the dream is its representation of contradiction, antithesis, and conflict. ~~Being~~ (under erasure) positions negation at the center of theoretical curiosity. Freud claims that there is no negation in the unconscious. This is the precise opposite of the constitutive feature of negation in conscious discourse. About this absent "No!" in the unconscious, Freud writes,

> Particularly striking is the way dream behaves towards the conflict and contradiction category. It is quite simply ignored; so far as dream is concerned, "no" appears not to exist. Dream has a particular predilection for drawing opposites together to form a single entity or representing them as such. Indeed, it even takes the liberty of representing any element by its optative opposite, with the result that one cannot, at first, know of any element capable of having an oppositive whether in the relevant dream-thoughts it bears or in a positive or negative connotation.[21]

Dream peculiarly upends and twists negativity. Freud says that dream "behaves toward" strife and opposition. It is as if the dream reacts in relationship to the concepts of conflict and contradiction. The relationship between the dream and the "No!" is an articulation within the conscious discourse of the ego. The figuration opposes the dream to a clash with disagreement and antilogy. A dream ("yes") and its opposite ("No!") are already engaged in a confrontation. But the dream disregards this negativity and difference in conflict and contradiction. How does the dream say "No!" to the "No!"? How does the dream say "yes" to the "No!" at the same time as it sustains its affirmation and positivity?

These queries are crucial because they seek a response to a more fundamental matter. What is the language of "yes"? What are the words of affirmation? What are the syntax and semantics of positivity? If usual chitchat is structured by negativity, then what is the organization of the affirmation and positivity of representation? The break between a dream of pictures and images and an utterance of words and alphabets illuminates the specificity of the icon and the portrait: there is no negation in the image. There is no "No!" in the unconscious because the picture resists differential negativity. The portrait and icon are not organized by the general equivalence of comparison, contrast, and exchange. This also indicates that there is a fundamental gap between word and image, and between discourse and figure. The language of pictures is not semiotic. The scene of the unconscious must be revealed to articulate a language of positivity rather than a diction of the "No!" The challenge for a map-making of this unconscious architecture is the elaboration of the language of differential negativity qua positivity in a figuration of a semic unit other than the distinctive and oppositional sign. The images in the unconscious cannot utter "No!" Instead, the portraits and icons in the dream affirm — "yes, yes" — the correspondent latent content of the manifest formation. The picture welcomes all objects. The image invites all desires. The vision embraces all truths. The illustration adopts all wishes. The image of unconscious thought is — *Yes!*

Figure 10.2 Capitalist Binary Exclusion

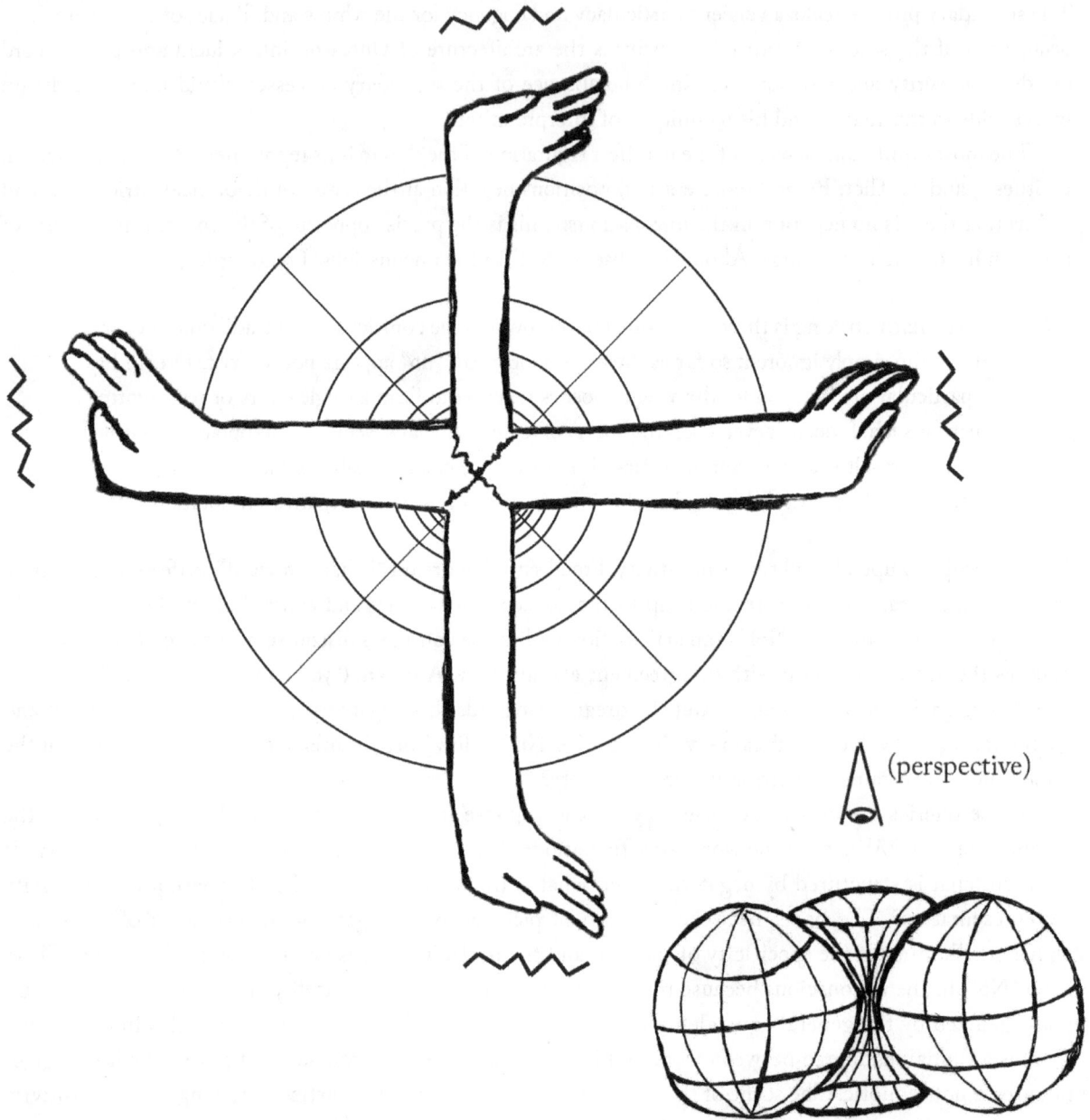

(perspective)

This image represents the binaristic system of capitalism. The system of $-ism is structured by a simultaneous inclusion and exclusion. This totalized incorporation and pressurized expulsion constantly reproduce their logic in the integration of the self-same and the self-identical of the Logic of Identity and the exclusion of the Sameness⁺ of Otherness. Capitalism is the economic and psychical system which is structured by the potentiality of totality (fragmentation) as it is expressed in *désir* and its Something is Missing. The small image (right) orients the spectator's perspective and contextualizes the main image (center). The neurotic's hands emerge from the constitutive fragmentation (totalization) of signification of the Real Symbolic. Neurotic Foreclosure (*rejet névrotique*) represses (forecloses) this disturbance of identity and essence. This image expresses the modalities and techniques of $-ism and their perpetuation of totalization (fragmentation) in the potentiality of Something is Missing in the *désir* to cross boundary even within the context of fragmentation (totalization). These splits of *Thanatos* otherwise obliterate this will to totality (fragmentation) over fragmentation (totality), Something is Missing over Nothing is Missing, and *désir* over *Trieb*. The image indicates that the compulsive insistence of the potentiality of Something is Missing in totality (fragmentation) is structured by the integration of its own obliteration and the incorporation of its own death. The binary system creates opposition and division that at once obscure the root of the binary in the Otherness of the elusive *meta*general equivalent. This binary structure of exclusion is isomorphic to the system of consciousness. The system of the Cs. imposes a division upon itself which sustains the conscious as opposed to and divided from the unconscious. But the conscious is isolated at the same time as it is excluded from the fundamental foundation of the division that otherwise schizoidly cleaves this system from itself and the other. The unconscious is included and integrated in order to be excluded and expelled. The fragmentation (totalization) of Nothing is Missing and *Trieb* yields to Something is Missing and *désir*. Consciousness is a fib of capitalism and the binary structure of opposition and division. Capitalism and its system of exchanges simultaneously include and exclude the use-value sentient quality of the commodity in order to quantify it in standardization. The Nothing is Missing of the singular object which is Outside of the general equivalent is incorporated into the system of exchange of comparable and contrastable (in)equalities. This object *qua* commodity is subordinate to the economy of a potentiality of Something is Missing in totality (fragmentation) in the exchange of general equivalence. The object *qua* commodity is ultimately expelled by the reduction of its singular use-value to the quantification of numbers, integers, and decimals in exchange. The potentiality of Something is Missing in the *désir* of totalization (fragmentation) structures the anxious exchange of capitalist binary exclusion.

Notes & Sketches —

UNCONSCIOUS-SPIRIT

At the level of the system Unc., truth is clear and plain but controversial and scandalous. The truth of the unconscious is its latent dimension. The latent thought is clear and cogent but unexpected and minatory. However, at the level of the system Cs., the truth is confused and curious. The truth of the unconscious is manifest in the system of the Cs. Truth is the dream, and it is the object of befuddled amusement upon waking. Unexpectedly, the conscious is Unreasonable. Man awakens to a series of wacky images and zany plots. The peculiar manifest representation of the explicit latent truth of the unconscious elicits inquiry and temptation but also resistance and defiance. Freud discovers that truth uncovers itself in a strange form. Truth is Unreasonable. This aberrant formalization in the dream is only understood as fishy from the perspective of the secondary process and the authority of the ordinary syntax and lawful semantics of the system. The rum manifest representation of the explicit latent truth of the unconscious inspires curiosity and resistance. Truth dreams in the details, minutiae, and deeds of everyday life. Truth speaks in an Other which is mostly dismissed by the neurotic subject of $-ism.

Posited desires, wishes, and truths are sourced from the psychoanalytic playbook. This Baedeker includes the textbook accounts of the Oedipus complex, the castration complex, the themes of sexual difference, and so on. The Cs. symptoms then revise the playbook. Freudian practice and theory are intimately intertwined. Freud makes this clear in his text, "The Question of Lay Analysis" (1926). In the text, he opens a division and then sutures the gap between the scientific theory of psychoanalysis and the transmission of techniques to analysts-in-training. He writes: "The standpoint we are looking for is only to be found by switching from scientific medicine to the practical art of healing."[22] There is a reciprocity between books and couches, and between theory and practice. The gap between conscious and unconscious is tenuous.

Freud's most focused effort in *Praxis* is to account for the mediation between, on the one hand, the explosively explicit and admonitory denotative latent thought of the unconscious and, on the other hand, the confusingly bizarre and deeply incomprehensible manifest representation of the conscious. The unconscious work of the primary process is the set of mechanisms which translates between the systems Unc. and Cs. The truth of the subject and the system is in the dimension of the unconscious. Any access on the "royal road" to the wish is the (counter)reverse translation of truth in its crazed and ridiculous manifest form into the coherent shock of its latent thought. Truth is assembled in the process of the translation of the Reason in the unconscious into the Unreason of the system of the Cs. Truth is articulated both in the latent level of the unconscious and also in the manifest representation in the system of the Cs.

The process of otherwise neurotic translation of manifest picture into latent idea retroactively constitutes the unconscious truth only after (*Nachträglichkeit, après-coup*) such an analytic interpretation has properly been pinned and decided in the discourse of the system of the Cs. Suspension of the manifest representations and associations returns to the repressed. *Outré*, the repressed only returns after its return. Weirdly, the return of the repressed returns its own return. The unconscious is an effect of the system of the Cs. This return is the reverse of the Freudian prioritization of the unconscious in the metatheory of the first topography (1895, 1900). The conscious disrupts the unconscious. Unexpectedly, man already lives in the unconscious. But he does not know it yet. The conscious discourse articulates a primary system of the Unc. The symptom is an effect of the system of the conscious. The subject and the society — $-ism — are pathological even within the ego-secondary process. The system is conscious of its own sickness. The unconscious speaks the truth of the discourse of the conscious. Language is unconscious. Repression can only return itself. Unconscious conscious. Conscious unconscious. Cs. Unc. Cs. Unc. —

The temporalities of analytics become central to an analysis of the neurotic, psychotic, and perverse approaches to the unconscious. The manifest representation figures the latent content only in the future event of the analytic intervention. The *point de capiton* eclipses a potentially infinite recursion of *différance*. The phallic function pins the unclosed unraveling of untidy differences and slippery deferrals. Trace extends beyond and before the symbolization of the penis. It snakes around references in and to the Oedipus complex, the castration complex, and the themes of sexual difference. The pervert writes to unconceal — *Aletheia* — the truth of the subject and the system. She must focus on the creative effluvium of the labor of unconscious-work. A consideration of Unreasonable truth — kooky desire and confused wish — is the necessary preparatory work for an analysis of truth. What is this truth of dream? The wish of a dream is unveiled by the interpretation of the discourse of the system of the Cs.

The question of the specificity of the patient's dream sidesteps a significant metatheoretical question about the unconscious. Freud elaborates this metatheory throughout *The Interpretation of Dreams* (1900). But he mostly misses the ontological question of the "What is?" What is the lifeworld of the dream? I want to explore the ontology of the dream, the dream-work, and the unconscious. The thinking, being, and living Become-Other for the Pervert-Schizoid-Woman of the unconscious. Who is the subject in — out, around, under, by, near, below, far, above, and so on — the unconscious? The horizon of the Becoming of the Spirit of the System is a Becoming-Unconscious. This Becoming-Unc. is the space of the world of the dream. If man is already unconscious, then why does he not know it? The $-istic system is structured by the secondary process. This is so despite the simultaneous organization of this same system by the primary process. Why does man live in the unconscious but conduct himself as if he suffers in the system of the Cs.?

Living Representing

The Unconscious-Life of the dreamy world of the Pervert-Schizoid-Woman is unlike (like) the ordinary being-in-the-world and being-with-others in the neurotic system of the conscious secondary process. Unconscious-Life breaks with the fundamental ideological structure of the Western world: *individuality*. But Unconscious-Life also wanders from causality, logic, self-sameness, self-identity, morality, spatiotemporal coordination, among other classic concepts. The traditional domains of Western philosophy — ontology, epistemology, and ethics — are acutely unsettled as enterprises in the thinking, being, and living of the unconscious. Unconscious-Life is repressed in the system of the conscious because the thoughts of the latent dimension *qua* lifeworld of future existence are a threat to the subject and society.

The unconscious as a mere concept is a threat to the entirety of $-istic civilization. The unconscious system of representations and images, world of significations and words, galaxy of relationships and tensions, solar system of ethics and moralities, universe of articulations and discourses, and constellation of values and exchanges — these are dangers to the Madness of Order. The unconscious strolls away from *le propre* as such. Freud variously describes the Other-Logics of the unconscious mechanisms of the primary process in scant sections of the dream-book (1900). How do we make friends, take boyfriends, and lick jockstraps in being, thinking, and living in the unconscious? These are especially vexed questions if the subject is otherwise the dupe of the secondary-ego process.

Freud's most generalized statement about the unconscious is that it is a dimension in the absence of knowledge, temporality, and negation. This renders any illumination of the Unconscious-Spirit an arduous project. The deconstructive approach to value and trace is a counterintuitive account of meaning-making. Grammatologically, the sense of Reason emerges from the play and the relation between negative and differential words in the system. The system is possibly closed for Saussure. The chain is potentially open for Derrida. At its most abjectly horrific, Saussure (1917) says: "In language there are only differences without positive terms."[23] Derrida follows exactly fifty years later (1967) with the insight that the origin (is) the trace.[24] The basal point is that no entity is coherent and intelligible unto itself. Rather, the object gathers meaning(lessness) in the process of relationship with the Other. A closed system indicates that the letter finally arrives at its destination. The letter departs (arrives) at a point of origin — "I" — and then arrives (departs) at a point of entry (exit) — "me." Derrida's open system demonstrates that the *finite infinity* or *infinite finity* of additional-subtractional supplementation promotes the potentiality for unlimited semiosis.

The Saussurian differential system of value and the Derridean strategic play of the signifier reveal that meaning-making is foundationally structured by negativity. Meaning-making is also circumscribed by the father's "No!" This is the case even as semiosis is simultaneously organized by an unexpected maternal positive affirmation. This positivity serendipitously manifests amidst negativity. Any explication of an Unconscious-Logic must be situated within the enabling constraints of the secondary-ego process. Unconscious-Spirit can only be articulated in a *langue* of negativity and difference. This semiotics is at a disjunction from the system of the unconscious and its universal *Yes!* of the Pervert-Schizoid-Woman. Freud acknowledges this difficulty toward the end of the dream-book (1900), "my descriptive skills," he admits of his work to describe the unconscious and its mechanisms, "are barely adequate."[25] The insufficiency is due to the singularity of unconscious space: no negation, no knowledge, and no temporality. The pervert discovers the limits of his talents of *écriture* in a description of the unconscious — and of thinking, being, and living in its space.

The turn toward the ontological question of the "What is?" is not to ask the question of the mere existence of the unconscious. The specific ontological question is not even posed in order to investigate the essence of the unconscious itself: "What is the unconscious?" The pseudometaphysical philosophers would upend both the riposte and proposal of the ontological question of any essence of the unconscious. Saussure's response to such a question is mediated by a finite but exhaustive sequence of words. None of these signs (signifiers) properly returns to a definitive Being of the unconscious — as such, *qua*, in essence, by definition, *il y a*, and so on. The unconscious *qua* the unconscious is mediated by a negative and differential series of goods and chattels. The unconscious is not the unconscious. Constitutive otherness makes any return to an ontological inquiry into the Being of the unconscious a vastly encyclopedic and mildly farcical game of whack-a-mole. Derrida's gesture destroys the ontological tradition. Metaphysics is uprooted at its origin and destination. Derrida immerses the signifier of the unconscious in chains of intersectional and interactive words. These signs are ambivalent in relationship to the oppositional structure. Heidegger views the question of "the meaning of Being" (ontology and the ontico-ontological difference) as fundamental to *Dasein* (or the being-there of man) in being-in-the-world and being-with-others.[26] The foundation of Being is an intuited "nullity."[27]

The ontological question of Being is simultaneously struck by a negativity of "is not" or Nothingness. The deconstructive critique of Lacan's work by Lacoue-Labarthes and Nancy in their book, *The Title of the Letter* (1973), chides Lacan for his elevation of the subject — however purportedly decentered and wherever ostensibly dispersed — to the center of his system of desire. What is desire? The status of psychoanalysis as a science (or not) depends on whether desire can be understood as an object of an empirical science. A deconstructive conundrum besets Lacan's question. The essence of desire is to be undefined because *désir* is around which the empty vase is constituted by the Other and the others. A science of desire can only study an object which is otherwise an ephemeral effect of Nothingness.

The ontological question of the unconscious — "What is the primary process?" — must be set aside. Grammatology undermines any question of or answer to this query about the ontology of the unconscious.

Rather, my focus is the ontology in (around, by, under, near, above, away, toward) the unconscious. What is Being in the dream world? The qualification of *qua*, as such, in essence, *il y a*, and by definition must be radically rethought in the dimension of the primary process. Elucidation of being-in-the-unconscious is made even more exigent by Freud's claim that there is no knowledge in the unconscious. Any exposition of Unconscious-Life will be organized by the secondary process. The ego discourse is saturated with knowledge of various sorts. Derrida makes the explicit claim that there is no exit from metaphysics and its fundamental precepts: causality, reference, correlation, truth, correspondence, reality, and so on.[28] Freud says that the unconscious is absent of temporality. Derrida's *différance* showcases the absent deferral in the signifying chain.

Time is in the process of Becoming space (what Derrida refers to as "time-becoming-space"), and space is in the process of Becoming time (what Derrida refers to as "space-becoming-time").[29] These spatial and temporal dimensions of Becoming display a presence and a Being which are under erasure. The unconscious is the space of additional Becomings in coordination of space and time: namely, "space-becoming-space" and "time-becoming-time." The expansion of the text or the galaxy suggests that space is not yet space and time is not yet time. But space is also already space. Time is also already time. There are several tenses in the English language. Each of these tenses has a unique combinatory temporal dimension. But for my purposes, the psychoanalytic *futur antérieur* (will have been) is most exemplary. Space will have been space in the future event that space is yet. Time will have been time in the future event that time is yet. The *point de capiton* makes such an Event — space and time — both possible and actual and impossible and virtual. Space is yet to manifest. Time is yet to come.

Irksomely, Lacan offers no account of the advent of the phallic function for the subject. His weak explanation is the simple pronouncement of the substitution of the identification with the father for the desire of the mother.[30] The generalized psychoanalytic fable is that the offspring's sight of the female junior's lack retroactively makes sense of the authority and power of the father. Freud figures this paternal leverage as the father's threat to the offspring against self-pleasure. The male junior's effort to protect his penis and to save his life demands renunciation of his self-pleasure and desire for the mother. Freud understands the naughtiness of autoeroticism and maternal-pleasure as deviant acts which transgress the rules of the culture. The male junior identifies with the father and with the codes of the dominant civilization of $-ism. There is no account of the neuroticization of the subject other than in reference to repression and its return in the cracks in the edifice of the system. There is no reason that the subject does not become either schizoid or perverse. Psychoanalysis cannot explain the dominance of the neurotic structure. Why do subjects of $-ism not suffer *différance* and trace and become schizophrenic? Why do subjects not intuit that space and time are the same dimension and write the perverse manifesto of the space-time discontinuum? The system of $-ism may be sadly neurotic. But why then is our own posse of friends animated both by illiterate schizoids whose banter amuses us and by dexterous perverts whose insights dazzle us?

Unconscious-Spirit is the thinking, being, and living in — out, around, under, by, near, below, far, above, and so on — the unconscious. The reason that the grammatical preposition is central to a sketch of Unconscious-Life is that it denotes space as opposed to time. Space is the principal *mise-en-scène* of the unconscious. The unconscious is a space. The preposition — out, around, under, by, near, below, far, above, and so on — is vitally spatial. The preposition organizes space. The preposition also enables subjects — perverts, schizoids, Women, and the rest of us — to navigate this space. This is so even if the preposition navigates man rather than the reverse. The preposition articulates the spatiality of the unconscious. The creative arts of time-becoming-space and space-becoming-time spin and spool in all directions. Spatial Becoming unfolds in an (in)finite extension from here to there, to other-here to other-there, to world to universe, to galaxy to solar system, to constellation to museum, to bathroom to — and so on. The preposition indicates that the unconscious is organized and structured by space.

The caveat is that this formation and coordination are neither self-identical nor self-same to the secondary process. The unconscious is not even self-same and self-identical to its own primary process. The primary process is not itself. The perverse deconstructive (dis)orientation of the dream-work is not itself. The unconscious is a secondary effect of the system of the Cs. The Cs. is out, around, under, by, near, below, far, above (and so on) the unconscious. The system of the Unc. and the system of the Cs. are proximal — but how? The liveliness of the project of understanding the self as thinking, being, and living in — out, around, under, by, near, below, far, above, and so on — the Unconscious-Spirit is complicated because Freud emphasizes the spatial visuality of the manifest formations of the dream-work. But it is crucial to situate Becoming-Unconscious as a being-in-the-world and being-with-others in the unconscious-work of meaning-making in a system which is radically otherwise than the system of the Reason of $-ism. The Pervert-Schizoid-Woman is in essence at work. The work of the Pervert-Schizoid-Woman is not the translational mediation between the metaphysics of the latent thought and the Unreason of the manifest representation. Nor is the Pervert-Schizoid-Woman the thinking, being, and living of the explicit latent truth. Nor is the Pervert-Schizoid-Woman simply the manifest representation in its preternatural eccentricity. Instead, the Pervert-Schizoid-Woman lives the Unconscious-Spirit of the primary process. Her space is the dream-work. The Pervert-Schizoid-Woman is a communist dreamer. She *works*, and it *works*. There is no cause — origin and *arche* — in the unconscious. The Pervert-Schizoid-Woman's Becoming *is*. Becoming Being Becoming Being — Ing⁺ — Being Becoming Being Becoming —

The Spirit of the Dream-Work

Freud presents a sustained elaboration of the unconscious processes in the lives of dreams. In *The Interpretation of Dreams* (1900), Freud stresses that the processes of conscious thoughts are at odds with the adventures of the unconscious-work of the primary process. Freud says: "It has been repeatedly pointed out that the associations binding dream-thoughts together are of a very special kind and differ from those that operate in waking thought."[31] The key words in this excerpt are "association," "together," and "binding." The *modus operandi* of the unconscious-work of the happy labor of perverts, schizoids, and Women is to overcome division, fraternize otherness, and coalesce difference.

In contrast, the waking thoughts of the ego-process tend toward differentiation, separation, and alienation. The secondary process of Western $-ism isolates identities from each other: white/black, gay/straight, right/wrong, good/evil, $-ism/S, here/there, man/Woman, penis/clitoris, and so on. The economy of $-ism disassociates, disbands, and unbinds differences. These potential confederations, bonds, and sutures promise to flourish in the economy of the unconscious. Marx refers to the horizonal communist organization as an "association." In "1844 Manuscripts," Marx writes,

> Social activity and social enjoyment exist by no means only in the form of some directly communal activity and directly communal enjoyment, although communal activity and communal enjoyment — i.e., activity and enjoyment which are manifested and directly revealed in real association with other men — will occur wherever such a direct expression of sociability stems from the true character of the activity's content and is appropriate to the nature of the enjoyment.[32]

Marx makes social being the fundamental precept of selfhood and sociality. The capitalist atomizes individuals. Marx emphasizes the sociality, community, and association of collectivist activity, enjoyment, and expression. Marx identifies the "association" as the futural formal modality of selfhood and sociality of men, Women, and the rest of us. These subjects enjoy themselves and each other in the absence of the atomization, alienation, and competition of a capitalist marketplace. $-ism is otherwise structured by the battle of individuals rather than by the bonds of collectivity. Marx's version of the future mode of production is in contradistinction to the capitalist workplace. The capitalist factory structures labor according to a series of alienations: the worker in opposition to his labor activity, against his fellow workers, in conflict with himself, and against his own sensuous species-being.[33]

The capitalist promotes the alienation of governmental-corporate ownership and private property. *Contra* capital, Freud envisions a dreamy association, unconscious togetherness, and playful binding in which differences collide, impossibilities dance, and the exclusionary logic of $-ism is displaced by unconscious social relations. This modality of interlinked "associations" is certainly a "very special kind." The space of the unconscious is the End of History — and so of temporality — in the arrival of a communist association of (*a*)sexual laborers. Women freely produce and conscientiously consume while bound to each other in a process of dream-work and unconscious-work *qua* unalienated labor. Freud elaborates this associative togetherness in his claim that the dream-work is "under a kind of compulsion to combine," as he says of the stimuli of subjectivity and sociality, into "a single entity."[34]

The question for an ontology of thinking, being, and living in the Communist Unconscious dream — rather than the capitalist ego nightmare — is the qualification of a "single entity." What is a "single entity"? This composite condensed figure is the parallactic overlap of an overdetermined plethora of images, alphabets, texts, and, by extension, persons, friends, enemies, boyfriends, fighters, nations, races, religions, genders, (dis)abilities, (trans)genders, (*a*)sexualities, and so on. The pervert's economy of the both/and celebrates an inclusion of the mutually exclusive and a *soirée* of the extraordinarily disjunctive. Just so, the unconscious-work compulsively combines latent desires into, as Freud puts it, "a single entity."[35] What is a totality which in/excludes the trace? What is a footnote after Derrida's *Glas* (1974)?[36]

This image of a "single entity" is a compendium of a simultaneity of desires, wishes, and truths. The purpose of the dream-work is to combine and merge. The leisurely *moil* of the unconscious-work of the primary process is to fix and fuse. In *Beyond the Pleasure Principle* (1920), Freud describes the tendencies of *Eros* and drives: "These circuitous paths to death, faithfully kept to by the conservative instincts, would thus present us today with the picture of the phenomena of life."[37] Freud describes the oddity of the intercourse between the life drive and the death drive with these words,

> Hence arises the paradoxical situation that the living organism struggles most energetically against events (dangers, in fact) which might help it to attain its life's aim rapidly — by a kind of short-circuit.[38]

The ostensible opposition between *Eros* and *Thanatos* positions the respective movements of each drive in a peculiar correspondence to each other. It is not simply that death is the internal principle of life. Nor is the point that life must attain its opposite in death. Rather, Freud's words gesture toward an extimate parallactic overlap in which the self-sameness and self-identity (A = A) of life and death are each ruptured in the other of Sameness⁺. *Qua* death, life is inconsistent with itself. *Qua* life, death is at a distance from itself. Life cannot be summarized in itself. Death cannot be its own end. There is an Other — trace and *différance* — in life.

There is an Other — trace and *différance* — in death. Life is neither departure nor commencement, and death is neither arrival nor destination. *Contra* Heidegger's existentialist being-toward-death, mortality is deferred.[39] Life persists in its internal structuration *qua* death: (…) *Eros* (…).

The narrowed duality of instincts that Freud approaches toward the middle of his career — *Eros* and *Thanatos* — is usually interpreted as a binary opposition. But Freud's ambivalent and befuddled division between the principle of pleasure and the doctrine of its beyond (1920) shows that life drives and death drives can only be conceived as differential apparitional emergences of an elemental Sameness[†]. The terror is Freud's twin discoveries: first, that the principle of pleasure and the credo of its beyond are of an essentially identical structure; and second, that *Eros* and *Thanatos* articulate an unsymbolizable split but unified drive whose name and structure are beyond Freud's grasp. Freud says of the two pairs of instincts,

> One group of instincts rushes forward so as to reach the final aim of life as swiftly as possible; but when a particular stage in the advance has been reached, the other group jerks back to a certain point to make a fresh start and so prolong the journey.[40]

Freud claims that the aim of the sexual drives is "the coalescence of two germ-cells which are differentiated in a particular way."[41] The microbiological rhetoric reveals the purpose of erotics: the union of division, the coalition of partition, and the merger of difference. The aim of life in *Eros* is combination, connection, partnership, and association. These are exactly the tropes that Marx links to the collectivist ethos of the being, thinking, and living of communism. Freud describes *Eros* as "constructive or assimilatory."[42] Rather than breaks and gaps of negativity, the Spirit of *Eros* is interdependence and correspondence. The thinking, being, and living of the primary process of the unconscious are the Becoming-*Eros* of Spirit. The productive work of the unconscious invites a Becoming-*Praxis*. The first-dimension is space, of which the unconscious is the *mise-en-scène*. The second-dimension is time, of which the unconscious is devoid. The third-dimension is the unconscious, in which space and the dream-work compulsively blend and join toward the fourth-dimension of *Praxis*, in which the perverts, schizoids, and Women labor in the Becoming-Love of the Spirit of the System.

Marx summarizes this aporia of a metaphorical love — revolutionary *Praxis* — with his own political commitments. The break between the third-dimension of the primary process and the fourth-dimension of *Praxis* can be read into his *Thesis Eleven* from his text on Feuerbach (1845): "In various ways, the philosophers have always interpreted the world; the point is to change it."[43] Marx's famous and simple observation illuminates the politics and ethics of *Praxis*. A close analysis of *Thesis Eleven* (1845) will illuminate the stakes of a deconstructive interpretation of the unconscious and the dream-work. The horizon of this pause in my explication of the Freudian unconscious and its dream-work is to contextualize the social and political dream of the unconscious. Fidelity to psychoanalytic theory must be matched with a commitment to the politics of Marxism. A Spirited intersection between psychoanalytic Marxism and the destruction of ontology in the grammatological project illuminates the lifeworld of the dream of a political future of theory and practice.

THESIS ELEVEN — THE POINT IS TO —

The pervert interprets the world. He translates the schizophrenia of the system into the text of S in order to pervert the neurotic. The pervert observes what does not work. She intuits a solution to the impasses of the extant symbolic order. Perceptively, Lacan claims that there is only an origin and a cause — *arche* — in that which does not work. The conundrum for the perverse "interpretation" of the "world" is visible in the first part of Marx's thesis, "in various ways, the philosophers have always interpreted the world." This is an interrogative observation about theory. What does (not) work in the system of $-ism? The layered and integrated approach to Marxism, deconstruction, and psychoanalysis in this book is the navel of the origin and destination — Outside — of the rupture to and the fix of the system. This study engages $-ism and the ways in which it both does and does not work.

Marxism primarily apprehends the question of the ways in which the galaxy does not work in its synchronic critique of capitalism. But Marx also vaguely sketches a model of the ways in which the world will work under communism. Deconstruction interrogates Marx's *Thesis Eleven* (1845) — "in various ways, the philosophers have always interpreted the world; the point is to change it" — for its ontological incoherence. The "What is?" of ontological "interpretation" both is (Being) and is not (Nothingness) in its negation. The "world" is also struck under erasure as both Being and Nothingness.

Freud's work supplements deconstruction in an examination of the question of the ways in which the world does not work through the lens of unconscious desires and wishes. Freud asks this question of the rupture within the structure of the repressed and its return. What are the unconscious desires whose negations return as symptoms? Neurotically, the repressed returns as substitutive satisfactions for sex. Psychotically, the foreclosed Real returns as the radical disruption of identity and difference with a Sameness⁺. Perversely, the disavowed (and so on) returns the disavowed (and so on) of difference. Psychoanalysis isolates the dysfunction in the system in the negation of neurotic sex, schizoid rupture, and perverse difference. A proper illumination of *Thesis Eleven* (1845) enables a traversal of the field — from $-ism to S to $-ism to S — from within the frameworks of Marxism, deconstruction, and psychoanalysis. How does the world not work? How will it work? The horizon of this book is the parallactic transformation from $-ism to S. The point is to —

If the point is to transform the universe, then this Marxist, deconstructionist, and psychoanalyst Pervert-Schizoid-Woman is the heroine. The subject and the object of this Jacquerie are (mis/dis)identified by the philosophical project. Deconstruction affirms that revolution includes within its extimate identity all of the signifiers in the system *except* the object of the ontological query: "revolution." The revolution is everything but itself. The revolutionary stratagem is excluded from itself. The agitator is everything but himself. This deconstructive quasi-totality ($\supseteq$) of "itself" not only dissolves the subject of the revolt against the antagonism of the class structure. The deconstructive critique of presence also unsettles the question of the *Geist* of history: Spirit and Mind for Hegel ("young Hegelians") and Labor and Proletariat ("forces of production") for Marx. Ontologically, what is the Event? Who is the universal subject of the proletariat? Who is the perverse scholar who textualizes the riot? Who spits on the corporation as the schizoid activist? Who is the gerund of *Praxising*? What is the object of this *coup d'etat du capitalisme*?

The deep conundrum of *Thesis Eleven* (1845) is the transition between speculation and substance, abstraction and tangibility, philosophy and politics, and theory and practice. The copulatic symbolization — ($\supseteq$) — of the relationship between theory/practice is vexed for a variety of reasons. But the fundamental aporia is *arche* — the commencement and arrival, and the departure and destination — of the relationship between philosophy and politics. On this question of *arche*, I want to quote Derrida at length,

> Differences, thus, are "produced" — and deferred — by *différance*. But what defers and who defers? In other words, what is *différance*? With this question we reach another level and another recourse of our problematic. [] This implies that the subject (in its identity with itself, or eventually in its consciousness of its identity with itself, its self-consciousness) is inscribed

> in language, in a "function" of language, and becomes a speaking subject only by making
> its speech conform — even in so-called "creation," or in so-called "transgression" — to the
> system of the rules of language as a system of differences, or at least by conforming to the
> general law of *différance*, or by adhering to the principle of language which Saussure says is
> spoken language minus speech. [] The privilege granted to consciousness therefore signifies
> the privilege granted to the present.[44]

Derrida's point is not simply the hack gesture of the philosopher who observes that words and things are a
consequence of a transcendental condition of possibility — whether Kant's Transcendental Consciousness,
Foucault's Power/Knowledge, Heidegger's Being, Saussure's *Langue*, Lacan's Phallus, Freud's Unconscious,
Hegel's *Geist*, and so on.

Rather, Derrida's claim in this extended citation is that the presence of the word requires an ontological
interrogation of the object. Derrida's simple query — "What defers and who defers?" — can only be answered
by the ontological (What is?) question of *différance*. Derrida's critical turn toward the notoriously woolly words
"consciousness" and "self-consciousness" conceptually presupposes the self-identity and self-sameness (A = A) of
itself *qua* itself. But this center of "consciousness" is merely another mark in a series of signs, centers, substitutions,
words, metaphors, fetishes, and so on. The presence of any of these objects at the apex of the structure is an effect
of the absence of the marks in the (in)finite supplementary — additional and subtractional — series of alternative
words. Derrida refers to the "function" of language which is the exiled Outside of the center of the structure.
This functional Outside governs the coordination of the structure in the absence of this Other.

A "consciousness" is a function of the series of metaphors and fetishes which substitutes in its abyssal place.
But this functional consciousness of *écriture* is the excluded center of the system. A consciousness outstrips and
exceeds the metaphysics of presence. The subject of spatial difference and temporal deferral — movement in time
and division in space — is a *différance* which disrupts the presence of consciousness. *Cogito* is otherwise disquietly
absent from its own activity in the world. Rather than the simple *Cogito* of "I think, therefore I am," Derrida's
reconceptualization of "consciousness" rewrites Descartes's famous dictum as "Thinking-Becoming." Thinking-
Becoming is a verbed gerund which is refashioned as the inessential effect of a consciousness which is excluded
from the system of the globe. But who is the transformative subject of the revolutionary *Praxis* of the point — is
to change it? The getaway of consciousness from presence indicates the desideratum of an alternative modality
of philosopher. This soul is the future of the Cultural Studies scholar — men, Women, and the rest of us.

No Time, Space-Becoming-Space

Marx's famous figure of ideology as the upside-down flip and twist of the *camera obscura* (1845) pivotally
sustains perspective.[45] In contrast, Lacan's version of the object-cause of the gaze disorients subjectivity into
a bewildered oscillation of lines and arrows without points of anchor in the subject's gaze or the object's face.
The so-called reality of the bourgeois system is exactly the obverse of the truth of the world. Presence in space
and time is dubious from a dreamy displacement and condensation in which space-becomes-time and time-
becomes-space — and space-becomes-space and time-becomes-time. Derrida continues:

> Differ in this sense is to temporize, to take recourse, consciously or unconsciously in the
> temporal and temporizing mediation of a detour that suspends the accomplishment or
> fulfillment of "desire" or "will," and equally effects this suspension in a mode that annuls or

tempers its own effect. And we will see, later, how this temporization is also temporization and spacing, the becoming-time of space and the becoming-space of time. [] *Différance* as temporization, *différance* as spacing. How are they to be joined?[46]

The key issue is the joint or hinge between space and time, the first-dimension and the second-dimension. The process of differentiation in the first-dimension of space and the movement of deferral in the second-dimension of time must be joined in the space-becoming-time and time-becoming-space of *différance*.

A first approach to this question is the basal inseparability of the two dimensions of space and time. Space is crisscrossed in time, and time marks the borders of space. But Derrida intends to divide space and time. But he does so in difference-space and deferral-time in order to resuture the chiasm between the two dimensions. Derrida's neologism *différance* displaces and condenses the otherwise discrete dimensions of space and time. The Becoming of each in the other — space-becoming-time and time-becoming-space — indicates a spatially expanding universe whose extension unfurls over time. The timeless space of this Becoming will be the unconscious.

A Becoming of either space of time or time of space implies a suspension between the departure point of an *arche* and the destination point of an origin. In abeyance, neither space nor time yields to a metaphysics of presence. There is neither a present-past nor a present-future in the unconscious. Paradoxically, Becoming is the Outside of time. But Being is perfectly in the present of time, both a present-past and a present-future. Outside of temporality, Becoming puts the second-dimension of time on hiatus. Derrida's horizonal space-becoming-time and time-becoming-space — difference-deferral and deferral-difference in *différance* — are freed of temporality. What is an atemporal time? What is time as the Outside of time? This timelessness is the *mise-en-scène* of the spatiality of the unconscious. An unconscious *sans* temporality is the hinge or joint between Derrida's "temporization" and "spacing." Time can only be thought in the Outside of time. Time is not time. The division between the first-dimension of space and the second-dimension of time is deconstructed. What time — is?

The cynosure of this explosion is the Freudian unconscious. Derrida even mentions an "unconscious" in this passage. Derrida refers to a "desire" or "will" that retroactively pins the future in the past. This *point de capiton* precipitates the metaphysics of presence and a "consciousness" which appear as the *arche* of mind and body, thought and affect, and signified and signifier. The trick is to collapse the division between space and time in a Becoming-Untimed. The unconscious and its no "No!" and no "know" foster an alternative spatiality in which the dream-work (re)posits the ontological question of Being. The renewed question is of the *atemporal Becoming* of space in the expansion of the galaxy. The space of atemporal Becoming is the Freudian unconscious. The unconscious is the third-dimension whose absence of knowledge and sabbatical of negation open toward the fourth-dimension of *Praxis*. This *Praxis* is a space of the purity of nonpresence and nonknowledge. The unconscious Becomes-*Praxis*. *Praxis* emerges in the aftermath of knowledge, negation, and temporality. The crucial implication for an evaluation of humanity within/out its contextual frame and worldly situation is that knowledge, negation, and temporality are joined to a strange and absent word. This word is the indescribable — *le propre* (proper, property, ownership, possessions, and mineness). Space-Becoming-Space — *qua* space-becoming-time and time-becoming-space in *différance* — is the amplification of *Praxis* against the invisible but rampant philosophy and politics of *le propre*.

Marx's heartfelt commitment to a critique of capitalist exploitation and an elaboration of communist freedom is a demonstration of *Praxis*. The proviso of communism is the *Praxis* of the overlap of theory and practice, and philosophy and politics. Marx invents the word, but he inadequately defines its significance.

Marx's *Praxis* is the word for the fourth-dimension. The space of *Praxis* is the unconscious. The parallactic fold of theory and practice is possible in the unconscious. But revolution is not an unconscious process. Revolution is a *Praxis* which unfolds in a space which is devoid of knowledge, negation, and temporality. At revolutionary disposal are the techniques of the primary process. The ego-system of the secondary process is conservative and reactive. An organization of binarism of opposition, exclusion of otherness, and privatization of identity enforces rather than transforms a capitalist system. Cs. is opposed to the revolutionary project at the start. The horizon of *Thesis Eleven* (1845) is not simply revolution unto the final mode of production in the historical march of labor. Additionally, Marx's maxim makes the interface between theory and practice — thinking, being, and living — a labor of *Praxis* which must transform the inherited forms and contents of the system of the conscious. This invention requires man to forsake reliance upon the ego and the secondary process for experiment with the unconscious and the primary process. How can the revolutionary *Praxis* act (out) the unconscious itself? What is the lifeworld of a communist unconscious? In various ways, man has always suffered the conscious and repressed the unconscious; the point is to return it.

After the Unconscious

The unconscious is Freud's revolutionary discovery. My consideration of Marx's *Thesis Eleven* (1845) invites a meditation on the difference between philosophical interpretation and concrete activity at the juncture of the *Praxis* of the unconscious. There are several ways in which the invention of the unconscious radically transforms the galaxy in both theory *qua* interpretation and practice *qua* change. The concept of the unconscious decenters "consciousness," such as Kant's "transcendental consciousness" which synthesizes the data from the external world. Contemporary cognitive science and neuroscience are the heirs to the troubled concept of consciousness. The fable of consciousness and its Kantian categories and faculties or neuroscientific neurons and synapses — red herring and pork pie — imposes the ideology of the so-called consciousness of the individual and its inevitable solipsistic imprisonment.

After psychoanalysis, a nebulous consciousness can no longer be considered the center of agency, intention, will, and authority. The consciousness of the individual is an effect of unconscious processes which exceed and produce the subject of desire. This subject is not the doer of the deed in relationship to the object of desire. This individual is subject to the system of desire and its wily causes and blurry effects. The unconscious redesigns the world because the center of man is no longer the ego and its avatars. The upshot of this radical decenterment of man from himself is that the subject of the verb is neither the individual of the action nor the doer of the deed. Rather, the action *acts* the individual, and the deed *does* the doer. Syntactically, the verb precedes the subject which is then surreptitiously and retroactively posited as the subject of the verb. This reversal of the subject-verb-object syntactical construction acutely transfigures *langue* from a schema of agency, will, intention, and authority to a structure of effect, product, outcome, and result. The subject is always already an object. The copulatic Being is — *objet* ($\supseteq$) *objet*.

The unconscious is the apparatus of the reversal of the humanist prioritization of the subject and its tenacity and drive. Becoming is antecedent to Being. The Time of the Pervert and Ing[+] posit the gerund *qua* verb as the essence of will in the system. After the unconscious, man is an effect of desire, wish, and truth. Repressions and returns destabilize the speech of the speaker, the actions of the actor, the deeds of the doer, and the symbols of the writer. The subject is a symptom. This dream *qua* subject represents an excess of meaning-making. This surplus is beyond the consciousness of the subject. The unconscious not only "changes" man's visions of others through the colored gaze of his desirous projections and anxious estimates. Additionally, the unconscious "changes" man's perception of himself. Rather than agentic doer and willful individual, man becomes the contingent effect and haphazard product of the unconscious. This architecture exceeds the transcendental consciousness of Kantian neuroscience or of any other centered apparatus for the apprehension of man and world.

Gaze's Gazes

The unconscious reverses the humanist prioritization of the individual and its own exposition of the self, other, and events in the world. *Qua* decentered and dispersed, the subject is the object of the gazes of the Other. These gazes analyze and evaluate — make meaning — of this subject *qua* the object of the gaze. The interpretive apparatus of the gaze is decentered and dispersed. The gaze is over here and over there, above that and below this, near these and far from those, outside this and inside that, away from here and close to there, and by these and around those. Lacan's version of the gaze is outlined in the *Seminar* on the four fundamental concepts of psychoanalysis (1964) in which he theorizes the gaze as precisely not the property (*le propre*) of the self but the enterprise of the object. As Foucault memorably says in *Discipline and Punish* (1975): "Visibility is a trap."[47] Surrounded and surveilled, the subject is subordinate not simply to the gaze of the Other but to the *gazes of others*. These diffuse points of judgment and appraisal gaze at the subject from multiple positions of scrutiny and with various frameworks of analysis. The subject(s) of the unconscious is (are) everywhere in the solar system(s).

The gaze not only reviews the subject. The gaze gazes at the gaze itself. On this question, Lacan says: "Consciousness, in its illusion of seeing itself seeing itself, finds its basis in the inside-out structure of the gaze."[48] The make-believe of "consciousness" is the fantasy of "self-consciousness." Self-consciousness is the fantasmatic ideology of a specular return of a look outside toward a look inside. This delusion is imaginary because it fancies the mirror reflection of the other *qua* the self. The looking glass of "seeing oneself seeing oneself" implies the potential *mise-en-abyme* of consciousness. But Lacan's point is the exact reverse. The fib of consciousness is that the self is present to itself. Rather than an infinite recursion of image, so-called consciousness circles outside in order to return inside. But the "inside/out structure of the gaze" disrupts this illusion of the return of the self to itself. Instead, the look of the ego is captured by the gazes of others. Man's look at himself in consciousness is hijacked by the hijinks of others who transform man's look into the Other's gaze. The "illusion" of consciousness is that the structure of the "outside" returns to the "inside" of the subject. Instead, the gaze captures the look. The Other overwhelms the subject. The self is an effect of the system. The signifier represents the subject to another signifier.

The abstract thought of the material body is everywhere and anywhere in the galaxy: in class, on photographs, in memory, of thought, on Facebook, in videos, in voices, on paper, in music, in heart, in soul, around people, in conversation, and so on. The unconscious decenterment of the self displaces it from the center of a bound circle to the decenter of an unrestricted sphere. A philosophical interpretation of consciousness is upended by the concept of the unconscious. Freud's discovery radically challenges the humanist object — worldly subject — of interpretation. If the gaze gazes at the gaze, then the gaze cannot be present to itself. The gaze is hollowed of self-sameness and self-identity. Endlessly, the Other's gaze judges the other's gaze evaluates the Other's gaze assesses the other's gaze decodes the Other's gaze regards the other's gaze, and so on. The gaze resists the metaphysics of presence of Being and avoids the *arche* of an origin. The *arche* of the gaze is already traced in the differences and deferrals of the Other's and others' gazes. This infinite series of gazes looms and brews toward and away from the letter of the look. Finally, there is neither a subject nor an object of the gaze. The *objet petit a* as the object-cause of the gaze of desire slips and slides around and beyond other gazes. No one looks. No one sees. No one judges. No one evaluates. No one analyzes. No one examines. No one gazes. No one interprets. The gaze resists the metaphysics of presence. The gaze is Real.

Figure 10.3 Consciousness and Death

....

This picture depicts a group of neurotics who are separated by outward-facing mirrors. These mirrors obscure the radical Otherness which is embodied by the Woman and her inverted head (center). The illustration represents the fib of consciousness which lies to itself within the system of $-ism. The deception of consciousness imagines that the departure of consciousness from within itself toward the outside of itself is merely a reiteration of itself as self-same and self-identical in the Logic of Identity (A = A). The neurotic consciousness in the mirrors recuperates its own death as its life. The cost of this life is an alienation from and obliteration of the Other. This Other — Woman — is the decapitated and sunken head at the center of a consciousness (or set thereof) and its projection of the self-sameness and self-identity of itself onto the other *qua* mirror. Paradoxically, consciousness recuperates its own death as its life. The narcissistic decapitation of the Woman denies the constitutive force of *Thanatos*. The series of mirrors aggrandizes and immortalizes the self at the cost of the marginalization and mortality of the other. The paradox of death (consciousness) is that it is exiled from a system ($-ism) that it inhabits as its foundation.

Notes & Sketches —

This limitless run-around of looks, sights, judgments, evaluations, analyses, examinations, gazes, and interpretations escapes the presence of any consciousness. The unconscious transforms interpretation of the world because there is no present *arche* of theoretical speculation which is not merely the gaze's gays' gaze's gays' gaze, and so on — queerly. Unconsciously, analysis runs its course, off the text, off the subject, off the margins, and off the object. But if "interpretation" slips and slides away and toward Ing⁺, then is revolutionary transformation in "change" possible in Marxist *Praxis*? The psychoanalytic concept of the gaze and its unconscious decenterment of man ruin any stable orientation for philosophy. Rather than the *camera obscura* (1845) of the Marxist critique of bourgeois ideology, the unconscious bewilders the subject and object from any presence of scrutiny. As an intellective apparatus, does the unconscious make the "interpretation" of the "world" fatally delayed?

The rejoinder to this skeptical query is that the neurotic *point de capiton* retroactively pins signification in the return of the *camera obscura* (1845) and the perspectivalism that otherwise facilitate analysis. Marx improperly formulates the question of *Thesis Eleven* (1845). It is not simply the philosophical interpretation of the world which is at issue for both Marxism and psychoanalysis. Properly reconfigured, Marx wants to inquire: in various *ways* philosophers have interpreted the world; the point is to change *them*. Psychoanalysis multiplies symbolic orders and pluralizes worlds. The gazes' gay's gazes are interpretations which are contradictory and conflictual. The gaze invites an estimation of this multiplicity — "various ways" — and encourages a transformation which challenges the self-sameness and self-identity of the universe. The perverse object is split and fractured into a series of fetish-objects. The world is split and splintered into a variety of part-objects. Psychoanalysis and its infinite gazes of hollowed eyes invite man to pin the endless slippage of eyeballs. Looks promote diverse philosophical interpretations. The point is to change them.

Praxis

Another uneasy distinction in Marx's *Thesis Eleven* (1845) is that between abstract "philosophy" and concrete "change." The division between speculation and transformation — theory/practice, concept/material, mind/body, signified/signifier, and so on — is dubious. The aims of revolutionary fervor are a *Praxis* which unties and unites binary oppositions. These divisions otherwise separate the various ways of analysis and the purpose of the transformation of them. The horizon of *Thesis Eleven* (1845) is *Praxis* as the union of the divided tendencies in revolutionary ideas and transformative activities. In chapter eight, "Debt to Marx," I introduced a distinction between the Practice of Theory and the Theory of Practice. The former mobilizes the dominance of the sign in order to generate the pure speculative interpretations of philosophy. The latter marshals the insurgence of the signifier in order to inspire the material conditions of perversity. Perverse *Praxis* demands the Marxist materialist commitment to the toil of labor, the sensuality of the body, and the signifier of the symbolic order. The deconstruction of the binary opposition in *Thesis Eleven* (1845) between "interpretation" and "change" disrupts the work of philosophy. The gap between the projects of a capitalist practice of the theory of the sign and a communist theory of the practice of the signifier must be undone. How so?

The deconstructive analysis of the world in its different modalities in theory showcases the spatial and temporal paradoxes of a slippery presence. The transition from *différance* to communism and from theory to practice in a Marxist *Praxis* is inspired by the deconstructive approach to temporality. The lost schizoid discerns that communism is̶ capitalism. The torture of the madman is the absence of the *point de capiton* which pins the past in the present within the tense of the *futur antérieur*. The past will have been the past in the future event that the future arrives in order to retroactively (*Nachträglichkeit, après-coup*) pin the significance of the past. The past happens in the future. But the future is prospective. The present is yet to happen. Nothing has happened yet.

The truth of capitalism emerges in the future of communism with a backward glance from each according to his ability and each according to his need. In various ways, why does man outsource making the world go around to dollars and coins? In various ways, why does man delegate the creationist sublimation *ex nihilo* of dollars and coins to the private Federal Reserve Corporation and at the cost of an annual percentage rate that consumers charge to themselves? In various ways, why does the bourgeoisie interpret the world with ideology when the point is for the proletariat to change the world into communism? In various ways, why does the bourgeoisie defend capitalism when the point is for the proletariat to interpret the world with communist truth?

The abstract/material gap between theory and practice must undo the division between philosophical abstraction and political activity. The gap between man and world is essentially spurious. Man is the effect of the contextual frame of the world. The world is the labor of man. The purported chiasm between the individual and society is an irresolvable antinomy in social theory. This basal distinction founds the split between theory and practice. The deconstruction of the break between subject and Other facilitates the demolition of the separation between theory and practice that otherwise occludes the mobilization of a philosophical and political *Praxis*.

My critique of $-ism in this book emphasizes the stupidity of the division between man and world. This lacuna otherwise structures the binary oppositions of the Madness of Order. A grammatological elision of the man/world border claims that the subject is an effect of the signifying chain. A fabled so-called consciousness is a product of the rules and codes of *langue* and its system of syntax and semantics. The ostensible consciousness of man is the upshot of the architecture of conscious words and the unconscious architectonics of signifiers and signifieds. This conscious and unconscious scaffold confers signification on man. As I discussed in chapter nine, "Madness of Order," Duchamp's "Fountain" (1917) demonstrates the extimacy of the Inside and the Outside. The identity of the object of the urinal is contingent on the surrounds either of a bathroom, such that the urinal is an ordinary doohickey or, of a museum, such that the urinal is an extraordinary artwork. The bathroom is internal — extimate — to the urinal. The urinal is internal — extimate — to the bathroom. The museum is inside — extimate — of the artwork. The artwork is inside — extimate — of the museum. To put it — bathroom ($\supseteq$) urinal ($\supseteq$) urinal ($\supseteq$) bathroom ($\supseteq$) museum ($\supseteq$) artwork ($\supseteq$) artwork ($\supseteq$) museum. The relationships between Inside and Outside, between doohickey and artwork, and between bathroom and museum undo the strict opposition between otherwise mutually exclusive objects. The Sameness⁺ deconstructive aneconomy applies to the division between man/world and theory/practice. To put it — man ($\supseteq$) world ($\supseteq$) theory ($\supseteq$) practice.

Grammatology undoes these divisions and inspires a man-world and a theory-practice. This deconstructive revolution is the philosophical and political *Praxis* of the perversity of the signifying chain. The Other represents the subject to another signifier, and so on. A speculative analysis of the galaxy and its binary counterpart of transformative renovation of the solar system must be understood as a torus-like inter-twined flip-side in which we — "Who, we?"[49] — philosophers and workers, thinkers and laborers, and intellectuals and activists deconstruct worldly and wordy division in a movement toward the creation of a *Praxis* of perversity and its materialism of the signifying chain.

Marx's *Thesis Eleven* (1845) falsely posits an opposition between speculation/activity which can otherwise only be broached in *Praxis*. But this dialectical opposition unto an *Aufhebung* of the totality of *Praxis* closes the discussion, terminates the philosophical verbiage, arrests the activist protest, and discontinues history. A perverse version of transformation upsets the binarism of theory/practice. But it does so in order to liberate the latent Marxist truth of *Thesis Eleven* (1845). Interpretation (is) change, philosophy (is) politics, abstraction (is) materialism, speculation (is) activism, and thought (is) action: ~~Being~~. Deconstructive ontology deletes Being in the relationships of Becoming. An Ing⁺ otherwise transforms interpretation-becoming-change, philosophy-becoming-politics, abstraction-becoming-materialism, speculation-becoming-activism, and thought-becoming-action.

Praxis-Becoming-Superposition

Another dimension of Marx's famous apothegm is the necessary linearity of Marx's simple but weary sentence. The sentence is separated by a semi-colon: "In various ways, philosophers have always interpreted the world; the point is to change it." Derrida demonstrates that the ground of this series of words is the spatialization of difference and the temporization of deferral. Becoming is structured like Being. Queerly, there is no temporality in Becoming. Spatiality is the organizational principle of the unconscious. As schizophrenic, *différance* must ultimately forsake the temporal delay of *différer* because the madman suspends the *point de capiton* that otherwise retroactively (*Nachträglichkeit, après-coup*) pins the past in the present from the future. This abeyance of temporality effectively interrupts time. The schizoid's temporal Outside spatializes the solar system in an infinite expansion of an unconscious. This unconscious is absent of knowledge and negation. The issue is a proper description — word — for this suspension of temporality in the unconscious. What is time after time? What is the atemporality between a delayed *arche* of departure and a deferred origin of destination? What is the love letter between its writing and reading — ? An atemporality of time after time — Time of the Schizoid — transcends the simple *futur antérieur* time — Time of the Neurotic — and its retroactive inscription of signification. This post-stopwatch o'clock is also not the nuanced Time of the Pervert. After temporality, time is Outside of the pervert's "yes, yes" affirmation of the double-time of departure and arrival, and of *arche* and origin.

The interruption of a timeless timetable is the Time of the Schizoid and his *Yes!* Radical affirmation of the negation of the entirety of deferral and delay — history as such — is isomorphic to the instantaneous simultaneity of the quantum (1925) superpositional parallactic overlap of the otherwise duality of particle/wave — and good/evil, here/there, right/wrong, gay/straight, over/under, black/white, difference/deferral, and so on. *Yes!* — in the collapse of temporality, space curves over itself because linear temporality disorganizes spatial linearity. The psychotic's lost but found time — *Yes!* — mimes the quantum (1925) superposition in which the space between objects is quashed by simultaneity. At once, upon observation, the spatialization of difference between the particle and the wave collapses space and time between departure and arrival. Particle-becoming-wave and wave-becoming-particle render the linearity of temporality otherwise a suspension between a delayed past and a deferred future. Nothing has happened yet.

The quantum observation (1925) collapses the superpositional overlap between the particle and the wave. This observation demonstrates the basal distinction between the look and the gaze. The quantum observer looks from a determinate and decided perspective between the subject of the scientist and the object of the parallactic superposition of the electron. This look collapses the perverse simultaneity of both a particle and a wave into the neurotic logic of either a particle or a wave. The quantum observer is the subject of the look. In contrast, Lacan's version of the gaze is not present in either a subject or an object. The gaze does not look. The gaze resists the collapse of the perverse superposition of the electron into the neurotic duality of particle/wave. The gaze is a deeply schizophrenic concept. This idea indicates that only the look is available to the neurotic subject. Perverts, schizoids, and Women mobilize the gaze as a counterresistance to the metaphysics and presence of Being. The quantum observer is the neurotic scientific looker. The decentered subject is the perverse schizophrenic gay's gazer. The superposition of quantum physics is finally subordinated to the neurotic and his look. Queer (*a*)sexuality is animated by the pervert and her gaze. After Copenhagen (1925), the Pervert-Schizoid-Woman is herself an oscillation of superposition. The Pervert-Schizoid-Woman is a cat who is both alive and dead, and so on. (I have collapsed the distinctions in quantum theory for my own purposes and pleasures.)

Spiritual Dreams

My theoretical advance toward the thinking, being, and living of dreams emphasizes the lifeworld of the Unconscious-Spirit. Marx's stress on association, togetherness, and bind articulates the precept of the space of the unconscious. Displacements and condensations of the dream-work split and suture words and images in the *mise-en-scène* of the night. At the ends of metaphysics, temporality, and negation, an Unconscious-Life resists symbolization in the letters and words of the system of the Cs. The sheer craziness of the negative (positive) disorganization of the signifier is the closest approximation to a conscious *langue* for the interpretation of the space of the unconscious. The unconscious-work unites the disparate into unity and merges the dispersed into confederation. The unconscious inspires *Eros* and its series of coalitions, amalgamations, and federations of the coalescence of the splits and splinters of the devious work of *Thanatos*.

The "single entity," as Freud says of the condensed figure in the dream, is the object of the displacements and condensations of the dream-work. The unconscious splices and dices the dozy displacements and sleepy condensations of text and image. A single entity ostensibly indicates a self-sameness and self-identity of the positive unity of the sign. But must the displaced and condensed single entity of the unconscious be considered the coherent image and legible word? Unconsciously, atemporal Being is ruptured by a paradoxical Becoming *qua* Being in space. A Being *of* Becoming — Ing$^+$ — does not implicate a simple linear temporality. Time is otherwise excised from the universe of the unconscious. A presence of trace and a metaphysics of *différance* propose an unspecified — indeterminate and undecidable — curvature in space. The reconfiguration of timeless space involves Space-Becoming-Space *qua* Space-Being-Space. Curvature destabilizes borders of units of space in the unconscious. Dream-work of displacement and condensation prepositionally bobs and weaves around a fractured and curved space of a plurality of dimensions. The system of the Cs. is unquestionably unprepared to map the complexities of unconscious space. But this *Daedalian* architecture and *Gordian* design unravel any self-sameness and self-identity of a single entity as bound and discrete in the place of the unconscious.

The single entity is the composite of the displacements and condensations of words, images, and energies. These split figurations hover above these composed figures. Man remembers these objects when he awakens from the dream. The consequence of the rupture of an otherwise self-same and self-identical single entity belies the disintegration of the sign. The word is a positive unity or single entity. The sign is opposed and distinct from the other words in the system of signification. The fissure of the word mobilizes the return of the signifier and the signified. Disjointed materialities and abstractions, images and speculations, and things and ideas render the unconscious a chain of marks rather than a series of words. This explains the arrant discoordinated jumble of words and things which scoots and skirts around the curved and fractured space of the unconscious. Freud's reference to a so-called single entity is a misnomer because prepositional madness twists and turns images and texts in, toward, by, near, under, over, adjacent, around, and so on — a curved space. A single entity in the unconscious properly designates a nodal point. The single entity is the navel of the unconscious. The navel is around which materialities and abstractions circulate in the displacements and condensations of the unconscious dream-work.

The strange dominance of *Thanatos* in the break-up and break-apart of pictures and letters in the unconscious spotlights the emphasis on unity, togetherness, and association in the dream. The nodal point around which *les mots et les choses* bandy about is the fragmentation of the death drive. A single entity in the unconscious indicates the navel around which exploded signifiers and shattered signifieds cavort. Materialities and abstractions play and dance in the generation of a manifest representation in the dream. This image is the nocturnal wish at the ends of the unconscious. Freud's "single entity" is a troubled choice of words. But I want to stress that thinking, being, and living in Unconscious-Life promise the union of division, coalition of partition, and merger of difference.

These tendencies toward the life drive of *Eros* intensely impact ways of being-in-the-world and being-with-others. $-ism is arranged by the principle of opposition. These divisions include white against black, gay opposed to straight, good antipathetic to evil, offspring antagonistic to adult, man hostile to Woman, we unsympathetic to them, here resistant to there, death averse to life, and so on. Unconscious-Life and its condensed and displaced signifier of the Outside to metaphysics, negation, and temporality attenuate these clashes. What are the mechanisms by which unconscious-work invites the future of Spirit and System? The humanist yields to the pervert who soars away from the system Cs. and toward the system Unc. The future is the unconscious. The pervert is the ringmaster, the schizoid is the emcee, and the Woman is the impresario. The world of the secondary process is a grim and violent prison. Unconscious-Life will be the show.

Temporally, the unconscious witnesses the End of History. This End of History is visible in Hegelian absolute knowledge — all is known — and Marxist communism — all is free. But this apparent totalization is destabilized by the traces of displacements and condensations in the unconscious. These slips and slides outstrip the borders of the sign with the messy excess of the signifier. The trace of *différance* undoes any closure of the dream-work. The manifest representation of veiled truth is a half-said of the wish. Psychoanalytic interpretation of dreams is partial and incomplete. The dream never ends. Man is yet still dreaming. Certainly, the unconscious is the space of the *Eros* of combination, connection, partnership, association, interdependence, correspondence, and assimilation. But *Thanatos* is also a pivotal component in the scene of the unconscious. The death drive tugs and pulls at words and pictures. Destructive tendencies are complementarily tempered by the combinatory sensibility of *Eros*. Unconscious atemporality heralds the End of History. But Hegelian totalization of knowledge and Marxian totalization of freedom will be forever ruptured by an unconscious which never stops not being written.

My diagram posits that the first-dimension is space; the second-dimension is time; the third-dimension is the unconscious; and the fourth-dimension is *Praxis*. Space exceeds time in the odd Being *of* Becoming or Ing⁺. The first two dimensions of space and time collapse into the curved and fractured spatiality of the third-dimension of the unconscious. Thinking, being, and living in the unconscious are an effect of the dream-work. The unconscious is the *mise-en-scène* of the fourth-dimension of *Praxis*. Timeless space, pure positivity, and surpassed ~~metaphysics~~ of the unconscious are the dimensions of the *Praxis* of the queer (*a*)sexualist. *Praxis* is the essence of the unconscious. Queer (*a*)sexual *Praxis* unifies speculative philosophy and activist politics. Unconscious *Praxis* is thinking, being, and living the unconscious. Queer *Praxis* is in the closet because it is the desire of the unconscious.

Freud's view of man is dark and stark. Freud claims that the tendencies of *Homo sapiens* are violent and sexual. Man's nature must be tempered by culture. Lacan's view of man is more optimistic. The properly ethical trade-off between repression and symptom against desire and sublimation is an elementary choice.

In essence, man is desire. Lacan's early pessimistic theorization of the imaginary register of ego/other strife yields to an optimism about love. Love is a key subtext in Lacan's later work on psychoanalysis. Freud's grim view of humanity situates man within the context of a moralist civilization which makes the text of man sick. But Freud cannot access man's essence or nature or even the tone and temper of his instincts. The essence of man and the nature of the human are strictly determined by a constitutive outside which confers value and signification — such as "instincts" — onto the docile body of man.

This fracture in Freud's view also applies to Lacan's flirtation with theories about imaginary narcissism and aggressivity. The imaginary duality of rivalry is already situated within a symbolic order of codes and conventions. Imaginary mayhem is the unfortunate effect of a civilization of combinatory pairs of signs. Strife is the sad consequence of the rules and regulations which govern man's relationships of rivalrous binarism and violent opposition. Toward the unconscious, I hope ("I know very well, but nevertheless") for an emergent organization of selfhood and sociality — thinking, being, and living — of the system of the unconscious. *Contra* the system of the conscious, this unconscious will usher in an Other to the system of $-ism and the Madness of Order. What are the specific conditions of representability of thinking, being, and living in this alternative fourth-dimension of the *Praxis* of the unconscious?

KNOWLEDGE — NEGATION — TEMPORALITY

$-istic *Praxis* animates the tortured and revised metaphorical symptoms of a deranged and unsymbolized — but lived and breathed — ideology (philosophy, speculation, abstraction, and theory) of *le propre*. This $-istic *le propre* is expelled from the structure as the unary signifier. The primordial word — *le propre* — is simultaneously the center of the system. The unconscious is ~~metaphysical~~, ~~negative~~, and ~~temporal~~. The implication is that *le propre* is correlated with knowledge, negation, and time. A thinking, being, and living of communist *Praxis* eschew the elemental anatomies of: philosophical epistemology or knowledge; the father's authoritative "No!" or negation; and the quick tick-tock of the clock or temporality. The extimate *le propre* in epistemology is its generalized will to power. This will is articulated by Nietzsche[50] and later Foucault.[51] Essentially, knowledge generates the breeds, orders, ranks, classes, types, species, brands, and models which pigeonhole man into identity and its legacy of symptoms. Man is the object rather than the subject of identification. I do not identify with you (me). Identification identifies me (you). The process precedes the product. The deed is antecedent to the doer. I do not own my homosexuality. My gayness owns me. The self becomes an oxymoronic privatized public property of knowledge. The self is a system of powerful epistemes. Structures of knowledge are arranged in the nooks and crannies of every institution. The *le propre* of knowledge is summarized by the enforced (mis/dis)identification of man in an essentialized order of rank by various classifications of race, gender, sexuality, class, nationality, religion, fashion, age, disability, education, and so on.

Knowledge, Rather Unconscious

Zizek claims that multiculturalism is the ideological supplement to late capitalism.[52] His claim is both outrageously controversial and precisely exact. Knowledge pluralizes identities, multiplies sites of identification, and designs the self as an exchange-value of the commodity fetishism of capitalism. Undoubtedly, the *le propre* of epistemology is rampant in the system of the Cs. Unconscious-Life banishes metaphysics from the unconscious *mise-en-scène* of the Pervert-Schizoid-Woman and her Spirit of the Unconscious-System. The negation (*Verwerfung* and *Verleugnung*) of *Praxis* in violent and hateful civilization returns as a *le propre* which organizes knowledge, power, and their indexed classification of selves and others. *Le propre* is the theory and practice — philosophy and activism — of knowledge. *Praxis* skedaddles from metaphysics. Man escapes power/knowledge in an unconscious space in which the words of *langue* and the doers of *parole* are freed from arrangement by epistemes and their mobilization of identity and identification. But how?

The three theoretical paradigms in this study — Marxism, deconstruction, and psychoanalysis —advance toward provisional possibilities of escape from the metaphysics of *le propre*. Marxism identifies the source of knowledge under capitalism. As Marx says, "the ruling ideas are the ideas of the ruling class."[53] The critique of ideology is the Marxist weapon against the tyranny of the system of the Cs. of capitalism. The transition from the spatiotemporality of the conscious to the spatio*Praxis* of the unconscious involves a nuanced but intense critique of the ideologies of capitalism. My book engages this project. My original neologism of $-ism strictly refers to economic foreclosure: the schizophrenic *Verwerfung* of 5 billion men, Women, and the rest of us who live on less than $10/day in exclusion from the exchange economy of the Western marketplace. $-ism identifies the dark underside of $. Under the critique of $-ism, my work uncovers the ideologies of the conscious system-symptom of capitalism. The concepts of the individual, such as agency, will, intention, authority, responsibility, and so on are objects of a radical critique of the indiscernible air and imperceptible oxygen which enliven and deaden thinking, being, and living under contemporary Western conditions.

Althusser's spurious but productive distinction between the science of Marxism and the ideology of capitalism opens space between the $-istic concept of the Western "individual" and the otherwise subordinated and effected "subject."[54] Althusser (1970) theorizes the ideological function of institutions which exceeds the strict parameters of the state. The science of Marxism glimpses the gap between the individual and the subject. The Marxist witnesses the process of subjectivization whereby the ideological humanist individual yields to the scientific structuralism of the concept of what Althusser calls the Subject.

The blind spot of Althusser's structuralist Marxism is that the scientist is like any other individual. The scientist is always already a subject. The Marxist critique of ideology is circumscribed by its own interpellation. The upshot of this contradiction is not the *mise-en-abyme* of the ideological study *of* the ideological study *of* the ideological study *of* the — Rather, the unintended benefit of Althusser's counterfeit opposition between science/ideology is that it solicits a profound question. How does knowledge isolate itself from ideology? Genealogical analysis is the proper methodology for the study of this process. But the issue of the division between ideology and science exposes the locus of the "individual" and its agentic attribute: knowledge. Foucault's metatheory puts the institutional relationship between knowledge and power in the position of transcendental proviso of objects and subjects in the world. The myriad knowledges of the system of the Cs. and its so-called individual belie the unconscious returns which disrupt this system. The Real of the unconscious disturbs knowledge. The so-called Marxist scientist transcribes this process of the assembly of the ideological individual *qua* subject of the Subject. Marxist structuralism ruptures always already subjectivized capitalist humanism. The Marxist scientist records these interpellative scenes of the always already transformation of the individual into the subject by way of the ideological concept of the Subject. Suspension of knowledge is at stake.

Deconstruction destroys metaphysics. The critique of philosophical ontology and the deconstruction of the presence of ~~Being~~ disrupt the assertion of both the question and the answer to the query. Of grammatologically, the simple and primitive ontological question — "What is?" — cannot be articulated as such. The trace not only subverts the metaphysics of the presence of Being. But *différance* also reduces the discourses of knowledge to gobbledygook. A basic question arises at this juncture in deconstruction. What are we doing when we write and speak? An answer (question) to this inquiry cannot even be properly formulated. The prospects for a legible knowledge and its coherent effects — identification and regulation — are nil. The theoretical deconstruction of the entirety of Western metaphysics may be a *fait accompli*. But we still live and breathe capitalist ideology and its attendant symptoms. These maladies are articulated by psychoanalytic illumination and deconstructive insight.

A crucial component of the *lirer* and *écriture* strategy of deconstruction is charisma and persuasion. A grammatological subversion of a binary opposition — or of any series of concepts which is strategically determined as choice objects of ruin — must be rhetorically eloquent and powerful. Nietzsche's concept of the will to power is a useful supplement to the deconstructive strategy because power fashions an affirmative will which glows in its analysis and burns in its critique. The best deconstructive interpretations demonstrate the inadequacy of distinction and opposition. Grammatological exegeses reverse prioritization. Twisted and flipped, deconstruction summons an undecidability. This uncertainty puts the neurotic determination of the either/or in abeyance. The perverse oscillation of the both/and and then the schizoid's indetermination of the neither/nor mobilize humanity toward the *tout autre*. Deconstruction rattles and rolls metaphysics because it perversely plays an either/or "but nevertheless" both/and "but nevertheless" neither/nor "but nevertheless" — variance and suspension of the *tout autre*. The will to power of the charm and allure of the deconstruction in question is the proviso of the future of a ~~metaphysics of presence~~.

Psychoanalysis puts truth in the unconscious. Capitalism is vitally Unreasonable. The knowledge of the system Cs. is the object of suspicion. *Qua* conscious, the knowledge of the manifest representations of being-in-the-world and being-with-others is a series of symptoms whose truth is veiled and obscured in the truth of the unconscious. Psychoanalysis demonstrates that truth is the Outside of the system of the conscious. Epistemology is situated in the unconscious of the negated (*Verdrängung*, *Verwerfung*, and *Verleugnung*) of the society. Latent truth is unconscious content. But how can the unconscious as a system of condensation and displacement be structured in the absence of epistemology? If desire, wish, and truth are latent to the unconscious and symptomatic of the system of the Cs., then the unconscious is a series of knowledges, truths, and epistemes.

The first caveat to this wrinkle in Freud's theory is that the knowledge of the unconscious is fundamentally distinct from the power/knowledge of identification and regulation. The Foucauldian study of the institutionalization of identity defines knowledge as invented fable and contrived fiction. The human sciences of power/knowledge simply fabricate — creationist sublimation *ex nihilo* — the various bogus so-called truths about man and his sexuality, animality, health, sickness, economics, culture, desires, proper bathroom rituals, righteous water faucet habits, improper water filtration ceremonies, normative water fountain sacraments, developmental water boarding techniques, abnormal water park attendance, and essentialist water wasting protocols. H_2O is the regulated identity of our time because it posits a natural which is antecedent to the social. The system otherwise interprets and confers — power and knowledge — bathroom rituals, water faucet habits, water filtration ceremonies, water fountain sacraments, water boarding techniques, water park attendance, and water wasting protocols. The knowledge of the system of the Cs. is structured by the regulation of identification from within a moralist and ridiculous framework.

In contrast, the knowledge of the unconscious is the truth of desire. The so-called ~~knowledge~~ of the unconscious circulates desires, wishes, and truths whose identities can only emerge in the system of the Cs. *qua* the symptoms of jokes, dreams, slips, and psychopathologies of everyday life. The latent truth of unconscious desire is only readable and visible in texts and pictures. Wish emerges in its manifest representation in the symptom. Truth is suspended in the unconscious. Knowledge is in abeyance as the Outside of the circulation of displaced desires and condensed wishes. The articulation of knowledge is the manifest representation in the symptom. There is no strict knowledge in the unconscious. The truth of desire is only visible and readable as images and words in the manifest signs of the conscious world. The unconscious interrupts and adjourns knowledge until the dream-work scrambles its truth. Unconscious-work does so in order to elude the censor of the subject and society. Unconsciously, knowledge is delayed. It emerges only afterward — *après-coup* and *Nachträglichkeit*. The unconscious truth only will have been (*futur antérieur*) in the future event that such truth arrives in the discourse of the conscious and its manifest representations. Does the letter of unconscious truth arrive at the destination of the symptom?

Either neurotically or schizoidly, the circulation of displaced wishes and condensed desires in the unconscious recoils from a Being whose ontological presence can only dilate in the neurotic structure of the system of the Cs. The architecture of psychoanalysis shows that there is no knowledge in the unconscious. Marxism illustrates that the knowledge of the system Cs. is mere bourgeois ideological obfuscation. Marxism eschews the binary division between Cs. and Unc. But Marx's base/superstructure model of ideology identifies the economic ground as the determinant of the cultural paraphernalia of the commodified entertainments and exchanged amusements of capitalist civilization. $ is the veiled unconscious of manifest $-ism. What is $? — the capitalist cannot yet summon an answer. Psychoanalysis shows that knowledge is only discernible in the manifest quirkiness of the symptom. The unconscious generates — creationist sublimation *ex nihilo* — the delayed arrival of manifest knowledge and its idiotic dysfunctions.

Negation, Rather Unconscious

There is no negation in the unconscious. The three philosophies under study in this book invite a critical interrogation of the absence of negation — no "No!" — in the unconscious. Marxist historical dialectical materialism refers to the violent sequences of determinate negations of modes of production. The clash between the relations of production and the forces of production generates an irresolvable antagonism in the extant order. This conflict is sublated and synthesized by the *Aufhebung* toward the future. The logic of Marx's historical *telos* of the development of the forces of labor is modeled on Hegel's dialectic of *Geist* (1807).[55] Hegel's system is fraught with negativities, twists, oppositions, turns, and reversals. The same unstable but teleological system structures Marx's version of the succession of revolutions in history. Negation is deeply central to Marx's system. Antagonism of opposition is the choice metaphor for the capitalist relationship between the proletariat and the bourgeoisie. Dialectical and determinate negation (*Aufhebung*) is the conscious articulation of historical progress.

The unconscious of Marxism is the aneconomy of a system without currency and exchange-value. The Marxist unconscious is a structure without private property and commodities. Money and ownership are otherwise the essence of capitalism. The communist wish of the system of the Cs. of capitalism is the exhaustion of dollars and coins and the abolishment of private property and general equivalence. The symptoms of communist desire are capitalist exploitation and alienation: the bored worker who pushes paper for work; the minimum wage worker whose stolen wage profits the corporation; the isolation of lonely people and solitary secrets; the alienation of sexed bodies and pleasurable affects; the violence of murder and theft; and the exploitation of people *qua* clients of social service agencies and charity offices. These figurations of everyday life under capitalism are symptoms of the unconscious wish of communism. This desire is the abolishment of private property and the incineration of dollars and coins. How does the (communist) unconscious avoid the temptations and lures of knowledge and its identifications and regulations?

My outline of the mediation between capitalist-Cs. and communist-Unc. claims that communism as a mode of production is profoundly positive. The determinate negation (*Aufhebung*) of the fierce antagonism sublates the division between the owners and the workers. The *Aufhebung* achieves a revolt against the gap, and it ushers in the system of communism. The S is the endpoint of the *telos* of the dialectical succession of modes of production in history. Communism is the End of History. Marx's winsome decree is each according to his need and each according to his ability. But Marx imagines his utopia with misty eyes and blurry vision. The abolishment of private property and the destruction of the general equivalent illuminate the positivity of the communist system. The end of *le propre* unveils the wish, desire, and truth of the unconscious of the Cs. of capitalism. The \$-istic system of exchange-value mediates the tension between finity and infinity in the abstract calculation of numbers and the speculative account of dollars and coins. Capitalism is structured by the strange *accumulation of debt*. The paradox of (in)finity is such that the Cs. system of capitalism is coordinated by the phallocentrism of castration and the scarcity of supply/demand dynamics. The *Aufhebung* unto communism destroys the capitalist fetishization of mathematics. Communism returns to an abundance in which a gain/loss calculated quantification of value yields to a Sameness⁺ enjoyed qualification of use.

Temporality, Rather Unconscious — Neurotic, Perverse, and Schizoid Times

I theorize three distinct modes of temporality, each exclusive to a psychoanalytic clinical structure: neurosis, perversion, and schizophrenia. The Time of the Neurotic refers to the simple deferred action (*Nachträglichkeit, après-coup*) of the retroactive constitution of the past from the future. The past will have been (*futur antérieur*) the past in the future event which marks the past as such. Time forever circles back on itself in the making, unmaking, and remaking of meaning. Temporality is Being. But this Being is resignified retroactively. Time is (was), and time is (was) again. The neurotic's temporality suspends the past which is retroactively conferred signification in the present, and in the future. The past waits, but its signified is returned to it through the passage of time. Temporally, the world makes sense for the neurotic. The delay (*différance*) in time is sutured by the retroactive supplementation of the open signifier of the past with the closed signified of the present and the future. A retrospective glance backward ensures that the past isolates itself in its own presence in the significance of the past as such. The past is present to itself. The Time of the Neurotic promises the presence of a past which can be recalled by the present and the future.

In contrast, the Time of the Pervert refers to a provisional suspension in the retroaction of temporality. Perversely, the event is what willing having beening Becoming — and then inconclusively Being. Perverse temporality forsakes the mutual exclusion of the past/future for a suspended present of Becoming. Incongruously, the Becoming of the world *is*. Becoming of the event is present because the Ing⁺ breaks the circle of retroactive reconstitution of the event in the dynamic between past and future. The neurotic's past returns to itself. In contrast, the pervert's past awaits retroactive signification from the present and the future. This circular process never conclusively returns a futural closed and determinate signified to the open and undecided signifier of the past. The present is catapulted into the future in the absence of a backward return to the past. The past is interrupted by this drive (*Trieb*) toward the future. The presence of this future is deferred by the supplementation of signification in the thrust and hurl toward this future. The Time of the Pervert is oriented toward the past of the *futur antérieur* and the will have been tense of retroaction. But the object of this past resists closure in a metaphysics of presence. The signification of the past object is suspended between its openness toward the present and the future and the retroactive return (*après-coup, Nachträglichkeit*) of the past to itself through the mediation of the presence of the present and the future. The Time of the Pervert is an experience of the slippage of the future toward a past which is itself in the process of Becoming. Time returns to a past which is in the process of Becoming itself. The past is open. The future is yet to arrive in the past. Perversely, the past is still happening — toward the future which is (also) happening — in the present.

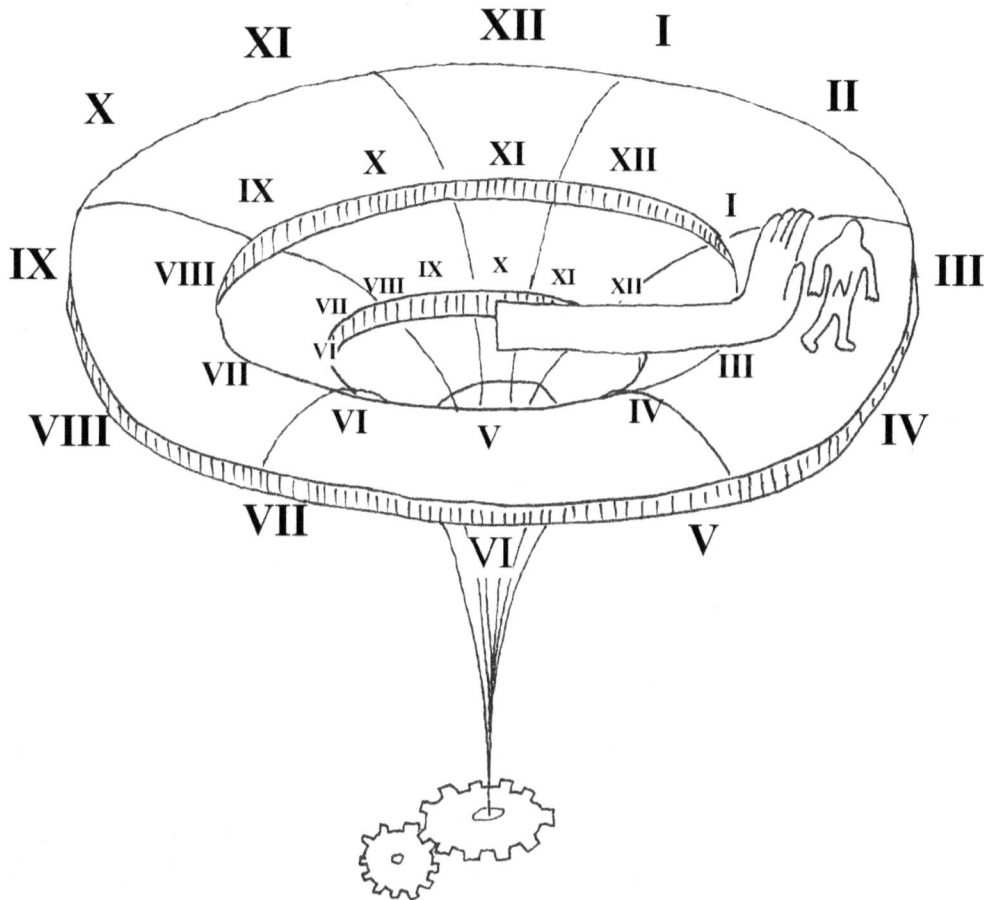

Figure 10.4 Time of the Neurotic

This illustration depicts the Time of the Neurotic. Psychoanalysis destabilizes the conventional model of linear chronological temporality. Freud's *Nachträglichkeit* and Lacan's *après-coup* articulate a version of temporality in which time folds back on itself from the future (present) toward the past (present). The event of the present only will have been the event of the present in the future (present) event that the present (past) is marked as such in the future. Retroactively, the past (present) comes into being only in the backward glance of the future (present). The past (present) is present in the future (present). But there is no past or future in the Time of the Neurotic because the logic of *Nachträglichkeit* and *après-coup* activates the past only in a recycled present which gathers the past into the concurrence of the present. Past looking, the Time of the Neurotic achieves a recycled return to the metaphysics of presence. The past is contained within the retrospective glance of the present, and the future is obscured by the return of the past to the present. The phallic *point de capiton* arrests the infinite play of the signifier of *différance* which otherwise gestures toward the *tout autre* of the future. The future arrives in the present, and this Other returns the past to the metaphysics of presence. The Time of the Neurotic is the return of the past to itself — the *futur antérieur* of what will have been — as a presence. The horizonal aperture toward the future is suspended. The Time of the Neurotic returns the past to the punctual now of the present. The future is forever obscured by the regressive assimilation of the unimagined impossible into the extant possible.

Notes & Sketches —

Figure 10.5 Time of the Pervert

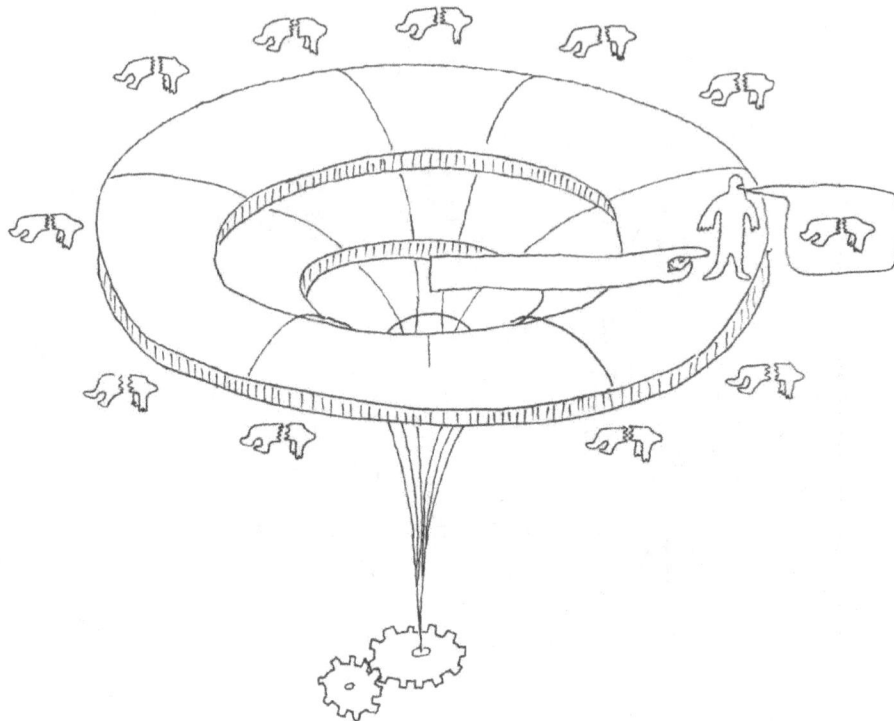

This figure illuminates the Time of the Pervert. This modality of temporality abjures chronological time, and it ruptures the neurotic's containment of the free play of the signifier in *différance* and the differences and deferrals of textuality in an (always already) expansive universe. The Time of the Pervert reconciles the radical gap between the Time of the Neurotic and the Time of the Schizoid. The neurotic's temporality freezes the infinite gesture toward the future with the phallic *point de capiton* that retroactively returns the past and the future to the metaphysics of presence. Perversely, temporality is both Being and Becoming such that the otherwise pinned significance of the present in the past, and the past in the present, is ruptured by the infinite slip and slide of the past *of* the past, and of the future *of* the future. The temporality of perversion endlessly revises the event of the past (present) in order to open the *écriture* of the future in the present. Perversely, the event is what willing having beening Becoming — and then inconclusively Being. The pervert's temporality is situated within the logic of *Nachträglichkeit* and *après-coup*. But the Time of the Pervert also gestures toward the futural Becoming of the present (past) Being. Becoming simply *is*. The perverse and parallactic overlap between Being and Becoming in the Time of the Pervert posits a coherent signification of the event. But it also simultaneously opens this Being *of* Becoming and Becoming *of* Being to the differences and deferrals of *différance* in an expansive galaxy of the future. Provisionally, the pervert's temporality suspends the phallic *point de capiton* in order to situate the future within the present — or within the Being *of* Becoming and the Becoming *of* Being. The future is Becoming in the present of the Being of the future. Perversely, the present is its Becoming toward the future of its Being. In contrast to the retrospective glance of the neurotic's temporality, the Time of the Pervert illuminates the future of the suspended of the *Becoming* in the presence of *Being*. The expansive universe is Becoming the event of its always already Being. The instant of the punctual now *is* the Becoming of the past *of* the past and the future *of* the future. Now, the future *is* the presence of its own Becoming.

Notes & Sketches —

Figure 10.6 Time of the Schizoid

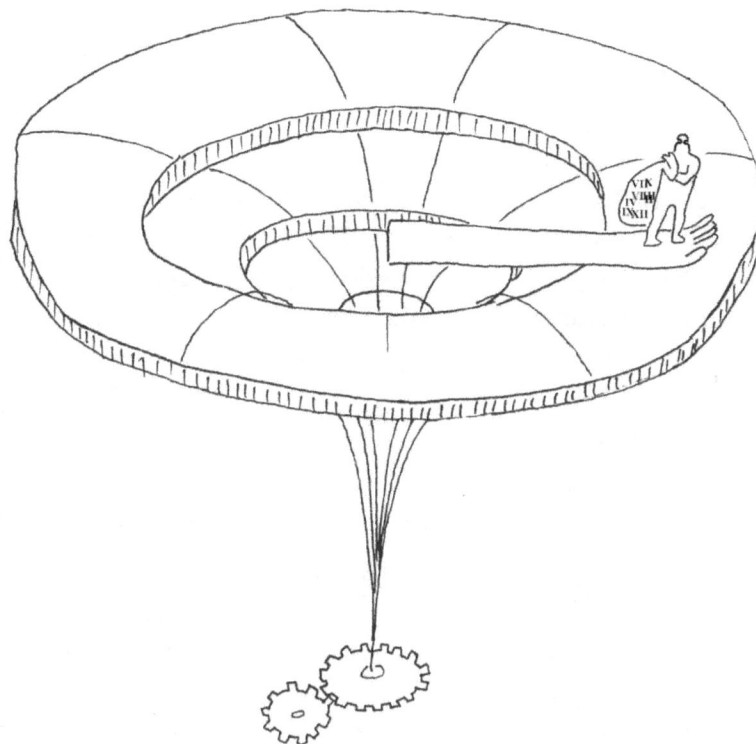

There is a singular distinction between the Time of the Pervert — what I call *temporalité de la volonté* "*oui, oui*" or the temporality of the "yes, yes" — and the Time of the Schizoid — what I call *temporalité gérondif comme verbe Oui!* or the temporality of the *Yes!* The time of perversion invites the Being of the event in its Becoming toward the future. But the temporality of madness suspends presence *tout court* such that the event is itself in abeyance. Open toward the future, the schizoid's temporality is structured by a messianic aperture toward the *tout autre* of both the past and the present. The schizoid's Real Time abjures any symbolic division of temporality into discrete units of past, present, and future. Outside of time, the event is yet to happen. Nothing has happened yet. The schizoid awaits in a messianic aperture toward the Other whose deferral is infinite. Schizophrenically, there is neither past nor present nor future. The world is atemporal, and the field of this timelessness is the unconscious. The schizoid occupies singular but indeterminate points in the first-dimension of space. At the Outside of history, any abstraction or speculation of the temporality of the schizoid's presence or absence is impossible. Space curves because determinate points of comparable and contrastable units of space cannot be marked by the calculations of temporality. The Becoming *of* Being — and the Being *of* Becoming — rupture past, present, and future. The schizophrenic messianic aperture toward the Other is the anticipation of a not-yet, in-coming, and out-standing temporality. Time is yet to begin or to end. Crazily, the words, "past," "present," and "future" are dull marks of textuality, and these fabled coordinates are destructured by the expansive dissemination of the psychotic's unhinged alphabets and by the frenzied trace of the schizoid's unanchored vocabularies. There is no time for the schizoid, and there is no temporality in the unconscious. Space *is*. Suspended, time *is not*. The schizoid's temporality is unmoored and unfixed. Adrift, the schizoid's time is structureless and disjoined.

Notes & Sketches —

The Time of the Schizoid resists letters and words. Schizophrenic temporality refers to a Being which is Becoming. Schizoid temporality indicates a Becoming *of* Being. The schizoid's Real Time indexes a Being *of* Becoming. What is the imperceptible difference between the perverse chronometer and the schizoid's timepiece? Perversely, temporality curves toward presence, but it is suspended by Ing⁺ or the gerund *qua* verb. In contrast, the schizoid's chronography neither curves nor even passes. The Time of the Schizoid is Real. Schizoidly, time is only experienced and perceptible as an effect on everyday neurotic time and its series of revised retroactions. There is a singular distinction between the Time of the Pervert — what I call *temporalité de la volonté "oui, oui"* or the temporality of the "yes, yes" — and the temporality of the Time of the Schizoid — what I call *temporalité gérondif comme verbe Oui!* or the temporality of the *Yes!* The schizoid's watch never exhausts the Becoming of the misinformed arrival of the letter. Communism is the end of the general equivalent. It is the absence of units of measurement. There can be no time, in the past, present, or future. Marx's End of History is also the end of temporality as such. The abstract speculations of capitalism and its calculators yield to the sheer space of the productions of the unconscious. Marx's dialectical historical materialism is a temporality of schizophrenia.

CONSIDERATIONS OF REPRESENTATION, OUTSIDE

The promise of Unconscious-Life invites perverts, schizoids, and Women to enjoy thinking, being, and living in the timeless space and psychical positivity of the Freudian unconscious. A glimpse of this solar system is visible in Freud's discussion of the considerations of representability of the unconscious-work in the dream. Considerations of representability negotiate the tension between desire and censor in the architecture of the unconscious. The latent wish seeks revelation in the system of the Cs. But the threat of this desire to the individual and to society forces a negation (*Verdrängung*, *Verwerfung*, or *Verleugnung*) of the wish into the unconscious. Truth returns to civilization in the form of the veiled symptom. The wish manifests in the deranged form of the symptom in order to evade the censor. If the truth bypasses the censor, then it can surface in the conscious. Analytic interpretation intervenes at this juncture. Analysis translates the manifest representation of the symptom into the latent truth of the unconscious. The unconscious-work and its reverse in interpretation-work are mediated by the friction between wish and censor, desire and law, and truth and Reason.

Freud's considerations of representability are crucial to both the formation of the symptom and the analysis of the manifest representation. Considerations of representation outline the proper form for the content of the wish. How will desire be represented to civilization? What are the modalities of pictures and words that excessively and disturbingly translate the truth into the symptom? A reflection on the considerations of representability indicates the variety of lifestyles and costumes, concepts and ideas, and deeds and doers which is possible in the engagement between desire and law, wish and prohibition, truth and Reason, and dream-work and censorship. A provisional theorization of Unconscious-Life arouses a thinking, being, and living of the Becoming of displacements and condensations. The considerations of the representability of these twists and turns are the essence of the timeless space and positive physics of the unconscious.

Freud's thoughts on the mediation of representation between Cs./Unc. are sprinkled throughout the text of the dream-book (1900). The text articulates the obversive relationship between interpretation and dream, and between analysis and symptom. The reversal of unconscious-work and analysis-work is mediated by code and convention. Representability is a compromise configuration between the formal rules of syntax and semantics in the conscious and the experimental modes of magic and wizardry in the unconscious. Unconscious-Life is the timeless space of the prepositionally organized displacements and condensations of the formal and the experimental, and the conservative and the ridiculous. Unconscious-Life of the Pervert-Schizoid-Woman is the thinking, being, and living within this cooperative and agreeable settlement. Freud outlines several unconscious techniques of representation. This series of mechanisms of obscurity includes: the incredulous resistance to the representation of logical relations; the ripped torsion between text and context; the simultaneity of the mutually exclusive; the twist and twirl of relationships of causality; the immunity to the either/or alternative in traditional logic; the will to the similar, the correspondent, the common, and the together; and the sheer excess of displacements and condensations in relationship to the articulations of the system of the Cs. What are the peculiar unconscious strategies of representation which transform thinking, being, and living away from $-ism and toward S?

Masquerades of Logical Relationships

Freud mentions the unbelievable resilience of the unconscious to symbolize logical relations, such as identity, difference, causality, reason, inference, validity, completeness, and so on. Freud says: "It goes without saying that the individual pieces of [the] complicated structure [of the dream] stand in the most widely varied logical relationships to one another."[56] The organization of the manifest representation is "complicated." The logical relationships of causality and validity are disparate and multifarious. The logic of the relationship between self and other in the world is complex and variegated. Relationship — what Heidegger defines as philosophical *Logos* itself — is twisted and extimate.[57] Freud's sparse words for the "widely varied" relationships belie the sheer exhaustion of the project to plot the abstract coordinates of a concrete interpretation of a dream. Freud identifies displacement and condensation as fundamental techniques of the dream-work of the unconscious. But any further elaboration of these mechanisms is beyond the purview of even the pioneer of the unconscious. An encyclopedic compendium of the skewed logical relationships in the timeless space of the unconscious may be beyond the will to knowledge of *Homo sapiens*.

Unconscious-Spirit of thinking, being, and living is more labyrinthine than can be mapped or diagrammed. Man is blind to his own thought in the world of the unconscious. Being-in-the-world and being-with-others are the Outside of scientific observation and calculation. Life in the world is obscure to man. The consequence of ~~knowledge~~ is that man must be irresponsible for thinking, being, and living. Freud's wish in the dream of Irma's injection is to be free of obligatory morality. The wish of the Western unconscious is to be innocent of responsibility for action and to be absolved of guilt for deed.[58] Unconscious-Life escapes the Judeo-Christian moralism of the union of doer and deed. Unconscious-Life is beyond good and evil. Becoming-Unconscious wagers that man is kinder when he is out of control.

Freud's other words on logical relationships can be summarized as a meditation on the preposition. The preposition is necessary for conscious interlocution. But the preposition is unexpectedly suspended in the system of the Unc. The connective goo of the preposition relates objects and subjects, and it joins verbs and adjectives. Freud states that in reference to "logical relations" between the elements in the unconscious, "dream has no means of representation at its disposal."[59] He continues to say that a dream "usually leaves such connecting words out of account."[60] These tiny marks are the mechanism of organization of subjectivity, objectivity, and activity in discourse. Prepositions piecemeal the words of the sentence into a coherent order of action. Freud writes,

> What happens to the logical ties that had formed the structure hitherto? How are they represented in dream — the "when, wherefore, just as, albeit, either/or" and all the other connecting words without which we cannot make sense of what we are told?[61]

Freud posits the unconscious structure of these tiny words as a question. There is no detailed summary of the representation of such essential words as "when," "wherefore," "just as," "albeit," and "either/or." Freud notes the apparent absence of these words in manifest representation. The censor excises these logical relationships from dreams.

The conundrum is made worse because dreams are pictorial and imagistic. The representation of "just as" or "albeit" in the paint and photography of the dreamscape is untold. Strictly, there is no proper translation between the picture and the word, between the portrait and the sign, between the icon and the symbol, and between the image and the text. Freud is not only flummoxed by the elision of logical relationships which are otherwise essential to the signifying chain of the conscious. Freud is also flabbergasted by the minor but vast chiasm between the manifest pictorial representation of the dream and the analytic interpretation of these images in the vocabularies of text. The extraction of these words from the worldly unconscious frees the Pervert-Schizoid-Woman from otherwise basal elements of conscious existence. The loss of "When?" explodes all of temporality — past, present, and future. Timelessness is a prominent feature of the unconscious. Out of time, man is free to move in space without the constraints of hours and minutes.

The possibility of the "missed encounter" is the destined mismatch between the divided subject and the *objet petit a* of this division. The missed encounter is stricken from the unconscious because time no longer separates space. Unconsciously, there is only the encounter as such. Unconscious-Life unfolds the sustained encounter in which the mortal gap between self and other is overcome by the timeless instantaneity of the encounter between desire and its object. After the timely question of "When?," the spacey question of "Where?" and the nooks and crannies of the spatiality of the timeless unconscious is foregrounded. The encounter is sustained in all points in space. The displacements and condensations of abstractions and materialities supervise present encounters and unmediated experiences of thinking, being, and living.

The loss of the existential question of "Why?" frees man precisely of responsibility and the Judeo-Christian enforcement of the retroactive punishment of the doer for the deed. Unconscious-Life which is beyond good and evil forsakes "Wherefore?" in order to liberate man from the constraints of the sickness of moralism. The "Wherefore?" implicates metaphysical *arche* as the precept of Reason and the maiden of causality. The deed is freed from the doer. The subject is excused from responsibility. The jettisoned "Why?" also undoes the will to knowledge of evaluation and judgment. Interpretation accompanies the power/knowledge relationships between the apparatus of normalization (medicine, anthropology, biology, psychiatry, and so on) and the subject *qua* object of normative scrutiny.

Freud also notes that the unconscious cannot represent "just as" or "albeit" in the manifest representation of the dream. The "just as" is the syntactical bond of metaphor. As capitalist apologists would put it, "the individual is free — just as life is opportunity." The connective "just as" relates "freedom" to "opportunity" in a metaphor that paradoxically identifies a similarity with a dissimilarity and an identity with a difference. The structure of metaphor (simile) is the organizational essence of *langue*. The disruption of "just as" destabilizes metaphor. The "just as" undoes the foundation of the signifying chain of *écriture et discours*. Unconscious-Life speaks an entirely alternative system of words and grammar. The system Unc. opens thinking, being, and living to a series of signifiers which escapes the odd (dis)similarity of metaphor and its will to unify the different and combine the disparate. The language of Unconscious-Life is not merely the effect of the whirlwind of the displacement of intensities and the condensation of forms. Unconsciously, man no longer writes and speaks either metaphorically or literally. The written and the spoken are born anew for the Pervert-Schizoid-Woman and her system.

Freud's claim that the unconscious considers "albeit" and "either/or" beyond the text deletes the neurotic forced choice between two propositions. Freud says: "The 'either/or' alternative is one that dream cannot express at all; it tends to absorb the two halves of the alternative into a single context, as if they enjoyed equal validity."[62] The "equality" between the "two halves" of a mutually exclusive binary choice of either/or appreciably razes the hierarchical structure of the system of the word. Rather than an arrangement of right/wrong and heterosexual/homosexual, the unconscious reconfigures conventional hierarchy in the elevation of each word in the binary to an "equal validity." This incredible deconstruction of hierarchal rank and prejudiced order outstrips the sign of its precept: the positive units of words in distinct and oppositive stratum and queue. Unconsciously, identities are different from themselves because they are the same as each other. A Sameness[+] regulates identity and difference as schizoidly incoincident with themselves because perversely parallactic with each other.

Rather than by the strict either/or of moralism, Unconscious-Life is rearranged by the pervert's both/and and the schizoid's neither/nor. Perverse existence in the unconscious undoes the necessity of choice. Identity is extimately split from within/out. Man is both black and white, gay and straight, good and evil, man and Woman, here and there, abled and disabled, and so on. The forced choice of identity is released from the self-sameness and self-identity of the coherence of mutual exclusivity. Not only is the subject of the unconscious exempt from the missed encounter of $\$<>a$. He is also freed from the mutual exclusion of identification. Unconsciously, man presently encounters himself *qua* Other.

For Freud, "Dreams are wholly egotistical."[63] The dreamer is broadcast over the entirety of the space of the unconscious. Amidst displacement and condensation, the considerations of representation project man onto the other avatars in the timeless space of the primary process. Neither excluded nor masked, man is spread out across an expansive space. The subject is everywhere in the dream. Man is worldwide in the *mise-en-scène* of the unconscious. The self is split from its splits. Borders otherwise separate the subject into the either/or neurotic economy of alienation and estrangement. Unconsciously, these partitions are supplanted by a system in which the coordinated points of existence superpositionally generate an extimate transcendence of an "albeit." This "albeit" otherwise places me here but not there, with you but not with them, around that but distanced from this, away from her but close to him, identified with radicalism but not with conservatism, and so on. Beyond logical relationships, thinking, being, and living exceed the self and its coordination in space and time.

Con-Texts

Another dimension of Becoming-Unconscious is Freud's insight that the orderly arrangement of text and context retroactively pins significance on both text and context. This (con)textual (retro)action animates the dream-work and its displacements and condensations of intensities and forms. In the dream book (1900), Freud says: "It is up to dream-interpretation to restore the context that dream-work has destroyed."[64] The unconscious destructures context. The purpose of context is vital to the process of signification in the conscious symbolic order. Context situates and determines the text. Context abstractly limits and concretely binds the object. Context saturates the object in question with a surrounds of signification. Meaning-making must be stable and coherent. The project of semiotics is only possible within a system of moored contextualization. This context must be delimited and impermeable — at least in an instant — in order to stabilize the text. The letter must be sealed in an envelope in order to depart and arrive at its own destination.

Figure 10.7 Worship of Absence

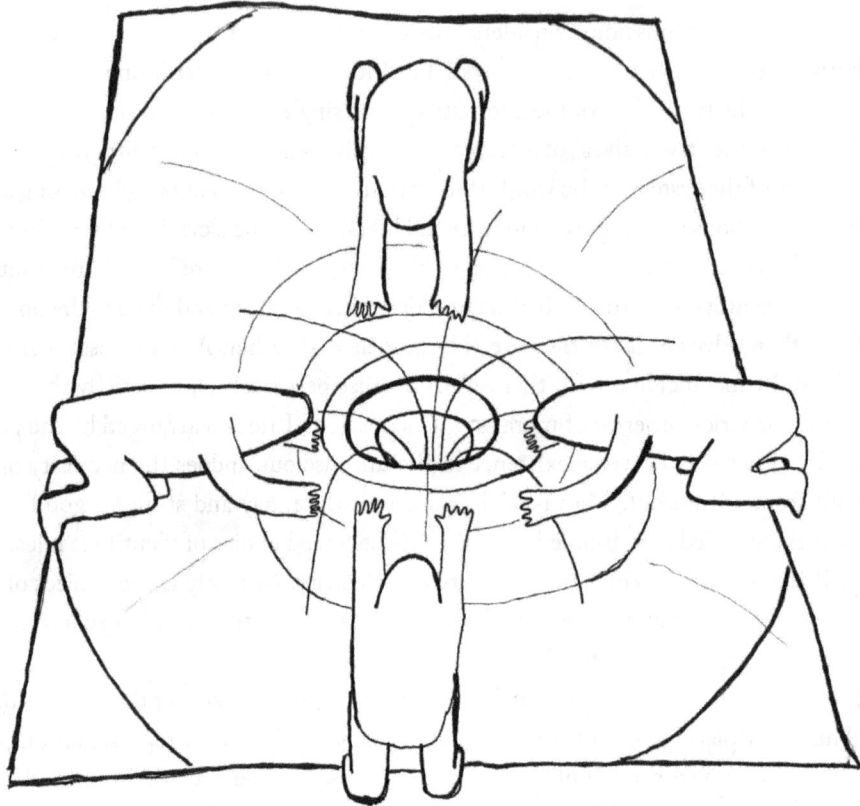

This illustration depicts the capitalist worship of absence. The phallic function of the general equivalent is the standardization of a necessary *inequality* between commodities in the system. The system of equivalence is a structure of −centrism in which each object is in the absence of the other object of its own comparison and contrast in the exchange of its value. The general equivalent (currency, dollars and coins) strips the object of its use-value in order to subordinate it to comparison, contrast, and exchange with another object in the quantification of quality. The dominion of exchange-value in the system reduces use-value to currency. Dollars and coins become useful. Use-value is transformed into exchange-value. The capitalist worships the process of exchange rather than the product of labor. The capitalist worships the mediatory agency of triangulation of general equivalence (father, phallus, sign, currency, and God) rather than the mediated objects of use-value. The capitalist worships the apparatus of the exchange of absences rather than the Spirit of the presences of objects. The divine object of the capitalist is the function of the phallus (father, sign, currency, and God) and its enforcement of the exchange of absence. The divine object of the capitalist is the standard itself rather than the object of this standardization. There is no present object for the worship of the capitalist. The capitalist's *objet* is an endlessly delayed effect of an infinite process of exchange. There is neither consumption nor production — each according to his need and each according to his ability — for the capitalist.

Notes & Sketches —

In Derrida's essay, "Signature Event Context" (1972), he says: "Context is never entirely saturated."[65] The context is itself contextualized. The text is itself a context. In the ever-expansive spatiality and temporality of *différance,* texts and contexts slip and slide toward and away from each other. The ostensible presence of the word is disrupted. The (con)text swings and sways in an "unsaturatable" dissemination of the signification of the (con)text and the (con)text. The upshot of a bulldozed context is that signification is precisely impossible because an unlimited context cannot function as the frontier between an exterior context which confers and steadies the value of the interior text which is under scrutiny.

Freud's assertion that the dream-work "destroys" context indicates an infinitely expansive and "unsaturated" space of the unconscious. The borders of this space leak beyond firm boundaries and solid perimeters. The space of the unconscious is infinite. The desolation of context also suspends meaning-making. The phallic *point de capiton* cannot (retroactively) pin signification on the antecedent text. Strictly, there is no signification in the unconscious. The displacements and condensations of the dream-work warp and spin materialities and abstractions of images and words. A settled definition eludes the grasp of thinking, being, and living in Unconscious-Life. The troubles for psychoanalytic interpretation are vast. An unsaturated context frees the sign *qua* signifier toward endless semiosis. The analytic "restoration" of context can only be fashioned by a delimitation of space. This "restoration" is only possible if there is an establishment of fixed borders around which the pictures and texts of the dream are contained in signification. Perverts, schizoids, and Women live an unconscious which is the Outside of the sign and signification of *langue*. In the future, writing escapes significance, and speech evades message. Spiritually, in dream, man becomes an undefined and undecidable point in the infinite expansion of space. Man is Outside of coordinated space, Outside of chronological time, and Outside of the system of the word. Unconsciously, man lives in the third-dimension of the unconscious. Man meanders and poodles his way toward the return of the repressed of *Praxis* and into a symbolic order which is otherwise than arranged by the hatred and violence of *le propre*.

Superpositional Exclusion

A complementary aspect of the unconscious is its considered representation of the mutual exclusion of divided and opposed words, objects, and positions. The neurotic system of the either/or sustains the conventional coherence in which the word is a positive unity unto itself. The sign is clearly bound to the other words in the chain of signs. The semantics and syntax of a sentence of text are structured by this delineation in space and time — difference and deferral — in order to bestow clarity on the relationship among subject, verb, and object. The unconscious destabilizes the forms of the syntax and semantics of the system Cs. Rather than the spatial linearity and temporal succession of a word which is separate and different from another word, the system of the Unc. symbolizes this organization as a simultaneity. At an instant, the most varied pictures and texts emerge in the dreamy manifest representation of the dream-work and its battle with the censorship. The wish evinces its simple latent content in a simultaneity of the mutually exclusive. Freud maintains that any logical coherence — making-sense — in the dream is represented in the dream-work by simultaneity.[66]

The quantum experiment of the duality of the particle and the wave illuminates the both/and perversity of the object and its reduction to an either/or neurosis upon observation. A dream displays this same quantum oscillation. Remarkably, Freud contends that such a quantum confusion is an index of logical coherence. Unconsciously, good sense is represented by the mutual inclusion of quantum oscillation and simultaneity. For the humanist, the Copenhagen experiment (1925) demonstrates the destruction of context and the parallactic overlap between otherwise mutually exclusive objects. Freud wagers that logic is illogical and that sense is nonsense. Unconsciously, Reason is Unreasonable. The consequence of the Copenhagen interpretation (1925) is the rapturous elevation of self-identity and self-sameness to Sameness⁺. This principle of the signifier includes the entire battery of the Other within the signifier. But, at the same time, this schizophrenic parallactic overlap of each with the other — every word is the same word — excludes the signifier from itself. Any signifier is the totality of the solar system *except itself*. Lacan's subject of desire is an empty vase which is surrounded by the constitutive outside of symbolic forces. The same hollowed interior and saturated exterior animate the signifier and its relations and differences of negativity.

Unconsciously, the subject is *Praxis* — we can only wish — but this *Praxis* of philosophical speculation and concrete activism excludes one: *Praxis*. The reason for this exclusion is the radical absence of the presence of the signifier in question. The word is an effect of mediation of the entire chain of materialities and abstractions in the system. Any signifier can only be the hollowed extimate of the Other. The presence of the Other is the proviso of the absence of the self. This self is present *qua* absent. This gap radically deconstructs division and opposition *tout court*. Unconscious-Logic of simultaneity arranges the future of perverts, schizoids, and Women. Soon, man inhales and exhales the Unreason of simultaneity and the absent presence (present absence) of ~~Being~~. Freud discovers that Reason is ridiculous and that logic is farcical. But he also demonstrates the potentiality of another system: *Praxis, except* — This exception is the object of deconstruction's messianic call toward the Other. The oscillation of the mutually exclusive properties of an electron closes the system. The Freudian unconscious and the Saussurian signifier open present exclusion to future inclusion and — The future is yet to arrive. The past is suspended in undecidability. Outside of time, the future is unconscious *Praxis, except* —

Except —

The art of solidarity is a tenet of Marxism. The alienated and atomized workers in competition in the Starbucks and Wal-Marts of capitalism are superseded by intimate and attached people in harmony in the places of communism. Capitalism imposes the ideological individualism of the isolated and independent man. In contrast, the mode of production of the Spirit of the System invites an ideological solidarity of the interdependence and cohesion of communist man. Freud's words about togetherness in the unconscious present a hopeful outlook on a horizonal unconscious communism. The system of the Cs. is structured by the castration of phallocentrism and the scarcity of capitalism. The symptoms are alienation, atomization, and competition. This is the sorry man of $-ism. But Freud's discussion of unconscious togetherness indexes the insipient communism of the primary process. Freud says,

> Similarity, correspondence, common ground — these dreams usually represent by drawing [the two terms concerned] together into one, forming a single entity that is either already present in the relevant dream-material or is constructed from scratch.[67]

A "similarity" describes a relationship between two objects which are otherwise distinct and opposed. The structure of metaphor is the precept of *langue*. Metaphor is arranged by the exchange of the dissimilar *qua* the similar. The hack metaphor (or, specifically, simile), "my jock is like a red, red strap," exchanges dissimilarities by disavowing the constitutive difference between the ostensibly same. The primary process is metaphorical. Freud's account of this metaphorical strategy is of the displacement of energetic intensity between disparate dream-elements. Life in the unconscious is structurally metaphorical. The upshot of Saussure's description of value and the signifier is that every word is the same word. Perverts, schizoids, and Women are each persons of Sameness⁺. Every person is the same person because each person is different from itself but the Same⁺ Different⁺ as the other. The signifier excludes the self from itself but unites it in a series of metaphors with peoples of the galaxy. The concept of Sameness⁺ electrifies unconscious living, being, and thinking. *Praxis* is an unconscious principle. But the exclusion is simultaneously this *Praxis*. Man is many, yet man is the Same⁺. Theory and practice are the Other of *Praxis*.

The relationships of "correspondence" describe a set of interchangeable themes *qua* "similarity." But the additional valence is an implied agreement and analogy between the characters of the unconscious. Contemporary theory generally defines politics as the battle for hegemony in the ideological field of theory and practice.[68] An uneven social order facilitates a democratic politics. Democracy articulates perspectives within an open symbolic field of chains of equivalence in which such empty words as "freedom," "liberty," and "opportunity" can be saturated with a content. The mandate of politics is the Marxist trope of antagonism. A binary dialectical battle (between proletariat and bourgeoisie) is rearticulated by a series of words which struggles for an unstable hegemonic rule over the social field. The acute downside of this politics is that the hegemonic skirmish is forever open. Politics resists closure. Marx indicates that communism is the End of History after the revolutionary *Aufhebung*. But democratic politics exceeds finity.

Contemporary theorists of politics welcome the open extension of politics. Politics never ends. Unconscious-Life suspends politics because it emphasizes the primary process tropes of similarity, correspondence, common ground, simultaneity, mutual inclusion, and so on. A politics of the conflict of signification and hegemony may be the solution to current impasses. But politics is also the concept at the center of the problematic. Communism at the End of History dissolves the politics of the antagonism of civil society. The future of the unconscious escapes the clash of politics altogether. This vision is admittedly utopic. The "similarity" and "correspondence" of the primary process eschew antagonism for agreement and prefer rapport to skirmish. To riff off of Lacan, when the slaves realize in delay that they are all the same as each other, the only master is the absolute master, death.[69] Death triumphs. Politics is suspended. But until mastery returns to mortality, the galaxy will be structured by opposition and its antagonisms instead of by Sameness⁺ and its *Praxis, except* —

A correspondence also indicates proximal interfaces between men. Alliance bonds men to each other, homosexual to homophobe, black man to racist Woman, feminist to misogynist, philosophy to Cultural Studies, and self to other. After slavery, the effluvium of a Sameness⁺ of man and world elevates the rest of us — perverts, schizoids, and Women — to the apex of similarities, correspondences, and a common ground of splits in fetishes, splinters in words, and snaps in identities. Unconscious-Life trades difference for Sameness⁺, antagonism for agreement, independence for alliance, solitude for solidarity, and *Thanatos* for *Eros* — and the obverse. The sanctimony of man's haphazard identities and contingent roles — precious selves and prized commitments — yields to the joy of relatedness and banter. My homosexuality surrenders to the interdependence between my gayness and your homophobia. My feminism cedes to the game between my feminism and your misogyny. My Marxism remits to the play between my radicalism and your liberalism. My immorality cedes to the dumb show between my depravity and your ethics. My love for you flirts with your love for me. Unconsciously, the emphasis is on the happy tensions and weird coincidences between ostensible divisions and oppositions.

The fundamental unit in the West is the individual. The primary unit in Unconscious-Life is the relationship. Marxism identifies such a shift from the atom to the molecule as the abolishment of the private property (*le propre*) of the self — of the homosexual, homophobe, feminist, misogynist, Marxist, liberal, immoralist, ethicist, and lover. Atoms are already molecules. Individuals are already relationships. The inquiry into the unconscious analyzes the formal representation of these purportedly incoherent relationships. Dreamy considerations of representation must join relationship to representation. Work of representability is to imagine alternative modalities of the figuration of the perverse both/and and the schizoid neither/nor. Perversity and schizophrenia usurp the neurotic either/or and the fundamental unit of Western civilization: the individual.

Displacement and condensation are the techniques of the primary process which articulate objects as relationships rather than as individualities. Freud variously identifies the jostle toward connection, the force of relationship, the displacement of context, the simultaneity of the mutually exclusive, the elision of signals of direction, and a generalized togetherness, commonality, similarity, and correspondence — as typical of unconscious representations. *Praxis* — *except* — is the hopeful invention of the future Unconscious-Life. The caveat to the daydream of *Praxis* is the messianic exception. The word for this exception is the (*a*)sexual queer. The (*a*)sexual queer will always be loved. The otherwise negated (*a*)sexual queer always returns to the unconscious. His (*a*)sexual queerness is embraced by a *Praxis* which is remorseful because it has forgotten him for a moment.

Considerations of Unrepresentability

Freud's asset in the *The Interpretation of Dreams* (1900) is his concrete analyses of specific dreams whose interpretations inlay the general mechanisms of the primary process: displacement, condensation, secondary revision, and considerations of representability. The text is less adept at an exhaustive outline of these mechanisms. The reader of the book is left with the impression that the thamaturgical techniques of the primary process are simply beyond the skill of anyone who would endeavor to map out their nuances and intricacies. Displacement is a general concept, and condensation is an ordinary mechanism. Freud admits the scarcity of sustained insight into the artistry of unconscious image and word. It is no wonder that dream-interpretation is always open to another signifier beyond any final closure of analysis. Freud explicitly acknowledges the half-said of analysis: "In reality, this kind of total resolution of a dream has never yet succeeded."[70] Humbly, Freud recognizes the limits of a metatheory of the hijinks of the primary process,

> Conveying the simultaneity of so intricate a coherence by means of consecutive presentation which appearing, each time I advance a view, to do so without preconception, in the long run, exceeds my ability.[71]

Freud's discovery of the unconscious exceeds the scholar's talents. The unconscious is a conceptual and practical *Über-Efrindung* which supersedes *Homo sapiens* and its primitive mind. The virtuous panache of the unconscious overwhelms the modest intellect of man. Consequences of man's epistemological finitude are decisive.

The considerations of representability negotiate between desire and law, and between wish and censor. Dream-work deploys the techniques of representation at the disposal of the primary process. Unconscious mechanisms capture the unconscious wish. The primary process transforms the desire into skewed pictures and obscure words. The unconscious muscles the truth beyond the censorship and toward conscious life as a symptom. This symptom must be reversed — from manifest to latent — in order for the interpretation to resolve the significance of the symptom. Interpretation provokes the analysand to experience — rather than resist — the truth of desire. Conscious meditation on the considerations of representation confronts the impasse of the ordinary syntax and semantics of the discourse of Reason. Exploration of representability engages the inexplicable structures of the unconscious. An unconscious which is devoid of time, empty of knowledge, and deprived of negation isolates the primary process as deeply divided from the ordinary codes and everyday conventions of thinking, being, and living under $-ism in the West.

I want to conclude this discussion of the considerations of representation and Becoming-Unconscious with a notable quote by Freud about the doer and the deed, and the dreamer and the dream. Early in the dream-book (1900), Freud describes the dream as,

> something alien and [I] feel so little urge to claim authorship of it that we are as likely to say "It dreamed to me" as "I dreamed." Where does it stem from, this sense that dream originates outside of the mind?[72]

The dream of Irma's injection articulates the basal wish of Western civilization: to be beyond good and evil. The desire of man is to be innocent of responsibility for the misdeed. The doer may logically precede the deed. But the deed secretly and retroactively posits the past doer of the future deed. The relationship between man and his object of responsibility is the sticky field of moralism. Nietzsche's insight is that morality makes us sick. Beyond good and evil, unto health and happiness — such are the unconscious wishes of Western man as they are articulated in the *ur*-dream of psychoanalysis.

Freud says of a dream that he only cautiously claims "authorship" for both the manifest representation and the latent content of the symptom. Beyond good and evil, the dreamer is divided from his dream, the doer is split from the deed, and the responsible consequences of indiscreet action are dispersed into the solar system beyond points of application of responsibility and punishment. Freud's reason for resistance to authorship of the dream is the intuition of the reversal of prioritization of doer and deed, and of agent and action. Freud notes that the subject would usually say, "I dreamed." On the contrary, Freud suggests an obversive orientation toward the subject-verb-object grammatical structure. I did not dream the dream. Rather, the dream *dreamed me*. I did not do the deed. Instead, the deed *did me*. Unconscious-Life is reconfigured by this reversal. The dream articulates man's action in the world as the world's action on man: object-verb-subject. The wish in this turnabout is the same as the desire to be rid of responsibility for the deed. If the deed *does man* and the dream *dreams man*, then man is neither the responsible doer of the deed nor the culpable envoy of the dream. Man is not responsible for the act, and man is not blameworthy for desire.

The strange sensation of "alienation" at the origin of the dream is exactly the will to be beyond good and evil — to be in excess of the deed and the wish. The impression that the dream originates "outside" situates the dream and its wish in a constitutive exteriority. The Outside confers signification of the dream from an external otherness of the self. The dream is Outside of the subject. The Outside dreams the inside. The external dreams the internal. The context dreams the text. But awakened, the nightmare returns: the responsibility for the deed and the culpability for the desire. Dream is the extimate formation between conscious and unconscious, manifest and latent, and dreamer and dream. Considerations of representability (responsibility) liberate the dreamy Unconscious-Life from the moralism of the system of the Cs. But man still contends with the night terrors of $-ism and the capitalist isolation of the individual.

Amidst the reversal of subject and object, Freud asks the key question: "Where does it stem from, this sense that dream originates outside of the mind?" The purposeful question may be reformulated as, "Why does man displace himself onto an Outside?" The answer is not simply that man seeks to escape the ideology of individualism and its agency, intention, will, authority, and control. Additionally, man wishes to extend the self — displacement and compression — into a space which is beyond the frozen hollowed sculpture of the lonely and isolated unit of the individual. This atomized self is otherwise closed to the world, divided from the other, separate from the environment, apart from the context, and distinct from the other. The wish to dream in excess of the self animates a latent desire of man. This wish is that man escape the self-imprisonment in his solipsistic self as the private property (*le propre*) of his so-called consciousness.

The Derridean trace disrupts the presence of this consciousness. Infinite spatialization and temporization spread the self around the globe and toward points of interconnection with others. I am everywhere on this page. I am everywhere in this book. I am everywhere in this room. I am everywhere in this world. I am everywhere in this universe. Diffusion and dispersal — *différance* — of the self break the arbitrary borders between the feet and the floor, the arm and the table, the elbow and the chair, my thought and your thought, our emotions and their emotions, and your property and my property. Unconscious-Life invites the communist aesthetic which abolishes private property (*le propre*) and its privileges and partitions. The wish that the *dream dreams the dreamer* and that the *deed does the doer* is the will to communism. The extension of Unconscious-Life into an ever-expansive universe achieves the layered integration of selves and others. Unconscious-Life summons the impossibility of *Praxis*. The West can yet dream — or the dream can yet dream the West. Can we, *Praxis*? — *except* — To return to the ontological question — What is Being in the Communist Unconscious?

Chapter Eleven

Communist Unconscious

It is impossible to leave a closed space simply by taking up a position merely outside it, either in its exterior or its profundity; so long as this outside of profundity remains its outside or profundity, they still belong to that circle, to that closed space, as its "repetition" in its other-than-itself. Not the repetition but the non-repetition of this space is the way out of this circle; the sole theoretically sound flight — which is precisely not a flight, which is always committed to what it is fleeing from, is the radical foundation of a new space, a new problematic which allows the real problem to be posed, the problem misrecognized in the recognition structure in which it is ideologically posed.

— Louis Althusser and Etienne Balibar

The Communist Unconscious is the *mise-en-scène* of a futural space of *Praxis*. The manifest $-ism of this sad world is the ruler of the system of the Cs. But the wager of this study is that there is an unconscious space in which the precepts and values of communism become the thinking, being, and living of the posthuman of the Pervert-Schizoid-Woman and the Spirit of the System. The bet is that in the future man's place will no longer be this pitiful galaxy but the unconscious universe. The future of the unconscious imagines the possibilities of an existence within and as the processes of condensation, displacement, secondary revision, and considerations of representation. These techniques enjoy the play of *Aletheia* of the twists and turns of desire. How can man promise himself this unconscious future of the primary process in which the *naïve* hopes of the communist horizon become ourselves, together? The purpose of this chapter is to theorize a Marxist unconscious at the edge of a materialist *Praxis*.

THE BOURGEOIS INDIVIDUAL

The first approach to the Communist Unconscious is a turn to Marx's critique of the bourgeois individual. The bourgeois individual is the theory and practice of the atomization and alienation of man from himself and his fellow man. In "On the Jewish Question" (1843), Marx puts the man of the secondary process of the ego to words,

> Above all we notice the fact that the so-called rights of man, the rights of man as different from the rights of the citizen, are nothing but the rights of the member of civil society, i.e. egoistic man, man separated from other men and the community.[1]

Marx targets the humanist trope of the "rights of man" which animates the so-called democratic governments in North America and Europe. Marx notes the slippage between the rights of man, the rights of the citizen, and the rights of members of civil society. The primary detail of the discourse on human rights (man, citizen, and civil society) is that this curious figure of speech — "rights" — purports to speak from either the divinity of God or the ground of Nature. The discourse of rights promises a covenant with the individual. This contract commits to a relationship of rights between the individual and an unquestioned and inalienable Other — God or Nature, by way of the State. The unquestioned indubitability and unrecognized invention of this authority pretend to guarantee a set of universal rights and responsibilities which is incontrovertible. These rights are imagined to be strictly outside of society and history, even as they are plainly initiated by the State and its worldly development.

The discourse on rights is not only farcical but also symptomatic. Marx uncovers a veil — manifest against latent — in which the rights of the bourgeois individual are substituted in the place — as metaphor and metonymy — of a radical gap between freedom/necessity and individual/society. The terror of this fissure is a monstrous unconscious latent truth. The revered rights of man are simply the decrees and impositions of the State as they are structured by the mode of production of capitalism. The rights of man are the dictates of capitalism. The freedoms of man are the necessities of capitalism. Emancipation is captivity. Liberty is slavery. The captive rights of the capitalist apply to what Marx refers to as "egoistic man." The man of the ego indexes not only the deplorable traits of the subject of the secondary process and its narcissism, aggression, anxiety, and so on. Marx's egoistic man also illuminates the atomized, alienated, estranged, and disunited worker. The worker's natural capacities as a sensuous social being are stymied by a mode of production in which competition, selfishness, and survivalism are the so-called freedoms and liberties of the capitalist right to despondence.

Rights of Man

Marx's acuity focuses on the powerful divisions and irreparable separations between men under the capitalist mode of production. The phrase, "rights of man," is singular. The subject of this right — however divine or social, natural or manufactured — is organized at the site of the individual. The right is of man as single and alone rather than as collective and social. The rights of man are rights of capitalism and restrictions on communism. Any right — freedom or liberty — which is interpreted as individualist encourages an atomized and alienated selfhood and sociality. A collectivist and interactive galaxy is interrupted as the proviso of these rights. Self-interested production and consumption are the essential traits of the capitalist. The so-called democratic rights of man structure humanity as a divided series of lost part-objects. These selves are separated from common bonds and invested commitments with each other. Marx notes,

> But the right of man to freedom is not based on the union of man with man, but on the separation of man from man. It is the right to this separation, the rights of the limited individual who is limited to himself.[2]

Marx wants freedom to be the opportunity for bond between men rather than liberty to be the condition for separation of men from each other. Marx's "union" is not simply a reference to the early organizational structure of the worker's revolution. A union also addresses forms and types of associations. These alliances gather together and round up lost men and strayed Women. These subjects seek communion with other bodies and souls. Union cultivates humans in interaction and engagement. The will to "separation," as Marx puts it, is not a proper "right." The social effort must be to forge liberties and freedoms. These sovereignties forge relationships, affiliations, partnerships, and alliances between subjects. Marx seeks a materialist and ideological system in which the drive of *Eros* binds men toward each other against the splintered effects of a *Thanatos* which shatters men from each other.

Marx seals his critique of the contemptible bourgeois individual of capitalism in his summary that the rights of man are ideological code for the privatization of self and world. The rights of man transform sensuous species-being into commodified private property. Marx says: "The practical application of the rights of man to freedom is the right of man to private property."[3] The essence of freedom is private property. Bourgeois freedom is the ideological supplement to *le propre* (the proper, property, ownership, possession, and mineness) and the system of $-ism. Bourgeois freedom encourages — guarantees as a right — various tears and lacerations. These divisions scuttle connection and interrelation between man and world. The most nefarious aspect of the privatization of freedom is that man is considered the packaged private property of a commodity. The privatization of man is a vicious nightmare. Man is reduced to the form of a commodity.

Marx's best critical work on ideology ("superstructure") outlines this cold and violent truth. Capitalist man is narrowed to property: comparable, contrastable, exchangeable, and disposable. *Qua* property, man is reified as an inert object. He cannot relate to his environment — man or world — except as an exchange-value. As a use-value, man is considered a distinct utility in relationship to purpose, motivation, and project. In contrast, the privatized man of exchange-value is a cog in a machine and a binary switch on a computer. The purpose and action of the worker are separated from his thinking, being, and living. The walking dead of the privatized man of property is subordinate to a stupid life of hustle and bustle — generalized busyness. Existence is the mere vehicle for profit and the enhancement of value. *Qua* commodity, the only pertinent question for man to ask his fellow slave is, "How much am I worth?" The cost/benefit analysis of man is evaluated by a unitary and unified standard. Lacan refers to this object of standardization which mediates comparison and contrast in exchange as the phallus. This abstract and speculative standardization of man and world exceeds and determines every breath of man.

However, the so-called humanism of Marx's work belies his own unexpected tendency to privatize the self. The Marxist self is both a lost ideal and a future standard. Marx says: "All emancipation is bringing back man's world and his relationships *to man himself*" (my emphasis).[4] The liberation of man from the chains of capitalist exploitation returns man ("bringing back man's world") to man himself. A closed circle of freedom "returns" the variety of extensions of man — objects, friendships, commodities, relationships, activities, thoughts, interests, ideas, and so on — to man *qua* his own private property. This private property of the self is indicated by the possessives of mine, yours, his, hers, theirs, and ours. The humanist Marx cancels the otherwise necessary gaps and fissures of a public property self. Otherwise, these bonds and investments in selves and communities make the exteriorization and publicization of the self the mandate for the emergent communist man.

Marx's words about the "return" of world and relationship to man are obscure and faint. But even the rhetoric of such an image is at odds with collectivity and communitarianism. This relationality is otherwise essential to the invention of a man who transcends the invented rights of capitalism and its rules of private property and exchange-value. A renewed S must resist economies of debt, obligation, return, and closure. A Spiritual communist society of free production and free consumption neither assembles nor expends within a metaphysics of presence of binary oppositions. Capitalistically, the letter of the commodity departs and arrives at the source of production or consumption. The worker labors, and the buyer consumes. But communism is organized by a sublimation *ex nihilo*. Communist productive creation and consumptive enjoyment transpire in-between sites of *arche*. There is neither originary author of production nor present source of consumption.

The use-value of the widget circulates in a system without ownership. The worker is not the architect of the use-value. The consumer is not the expediter of the commodity. The Spirit of the System is an aneconomy. The communist mode of production inspires the public circulation of the exteriorization of a man who slips and slides along the chain of word-commodities for free and liberated give and take. There can be no "bringing back man's world and his relationships to man himself" in a system in which unrestricted circulation, uninhibited production, and emancipated consumption trump the abstract and speculative calculations of the anxious surveillance of value. The self is neither interior nor inside. Posthumanity is in the Outside.

The space of the unconscious circulates man here, around, under, over, beside — generalized prepositional organization — in the wacky zigzag of the primary process and its displacements and condensations. Unconsciously, the self is elsewhere from itself. The subject is condensed and displaced. Man is beyond the self-same and above the self-identical. No humanist "return" is possible. The unconscious galaxy melts and morphs wishes and desires into the Outside. Unconsciously, I am everywhere in this sentence, in this paragraph, on this page, in this chapter, in this book, and in its reader. Profoundly, I am in you. Any return of self returns man to all of the coordinates of unconscious space and its circulation of commodity-wishes. This unconscious distribution of man in text and picture shatters humanist unity. The unconscious upsets fixed points of production and consumption, and assembly and depletion. Self ($\supseteq$) other — everywhere and anywhere.

From Atomization to Solidarity

Marx is at his best when he says: "Man must recognize his own forces as social forces, organize them, and thus no longer separate social forces from himself in the form of political forces."[5] The conceptual transformation of individual forces into social forces is a deeply Nietzschean[6] and Deleuzean[7] idea. Marx commits to the socialization and publicization of power and force. This externalization opens space for the happy collision of values, the joyous clash of politics, the winsome skirmish of attitudes, the energized battle of activities, the sham conflict of aesthetics, and the engaged ruckus between men themselves. Marx's Spirit is haunted by the graceful words at the closure of "The Communist Manifesto" (1848): "Workers of the World — Unite!"[8] The odious consequence of an individualist conception of force is that cause, effect, and their intermediary relations return — from arrival to departure — to man *qua* doer and deed. This moralism epitomizes the negative will to power of reactive forces that Nietzsche[9] and Deleuze[10] critique in their work on bad conscience and *ressentiment.*

In contrast, the modality of collectivist force that Marx inspires assembles disparate strength from a variety of sources in the culture. Collectivism harmonizes the divided and synthesizes the alienated from within the will and power of a Spirited collection of men. The revolution is not by the individual. The revolution is not for the individual. The revolution is not with the individual. The socialization and publicization of social forces are the cause and effect — *Nachträglichkeit* and *après-coup* — of the revolution. The communist revolution of the future is the flight of Spirits in shared galaxies on the commons of the cosmos. But it is only after the revolution in the sacred sovereignty of the primary process that a solidarity of force and an interaction in the condensations and displacements of the unconscious are achieved. This space is free of temporality, epistemology, and negation. The return to the primordiality of the unconscious is the space of the break from *le propre* and the escape from $-ism. Until then, selves are private, thoughts are owned, loves are secret, fears are personal, desires are confidential, and thinking, being, and living are exclusive. The wager of an unconscious communist revolution is that the zigzag play of texts and pictures in the manifest dreams of the Other will be the space in which man loses himself and gains the other.

Figure 11.1 The General Equivalent Split

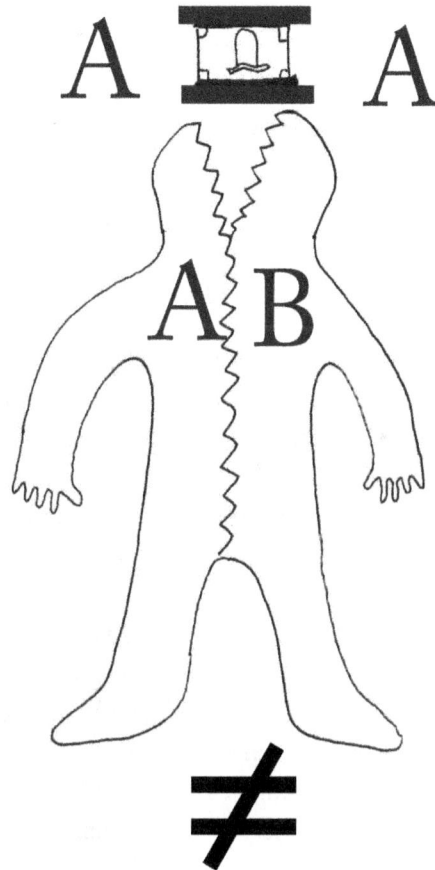

This illustration represents the general equivalent of currency (dollars and coins) as it affects and effects the subject. The general equivalent cleaves man into two extimate beings of himself. The general equivalent viciously creates the *désir* for a reconciliation of this split. The *rapprochement* is addressed in the pathological forms of neurosis, psychosis, and perversion. The identity of man (above) is sutured and joined by the historically determined capitalist system of dollars and coins. Signifying term A is coincident to and continuous with itself — unequal — within a relationship of a system of cleavages and splits. The consequence of this capitalist alienation is that the subject's thinking, being, and living in the Madness of Order are the conditions of its contingent survival. Man copes with the spits and splits of his self as both owned and unowned, and as both centered and decentered. Man's existence and expression within a system in which Nothing (is) Missing force him (the neurotic) to formulate a structure of an executive ego which regulates his identity in relationship to a *désir* from which he is alienated. The same currency which makes any object equal — self-same and self-identical — simultaneously renders any object unequal, self-same, and self-identical. The general equivalent sutures the wound of difference only to inscribe alienation in the place of the subject.

Notes & Sketches —

The alienated atomization of man and world is the practical and theoretical symptom of capitalism. Marx repeats the word "atom" in reference to the mistakes in the bourgeois conception of the individual. In "The Holy Family" (1845), Marx says: "The members of society are not atoms."[11] Marx also says that the egoistic individual of capitalist civil society suffers a,

> non-sensuous imagination and lifeless abstraction [which] inflate himself to the size of an atom, i.e. to an unrelated self-sufficient, wantless, absolutely fully, blessed being.[12]

Marx critically and starkly isolates the woeful ideology of self-sufficiency and its symptomatic returns in the ego-system of capitalism. There is no desire for use-value. The only motive is the accumulation of exchange-value. But essential human cultivation of nature into culture in labor is the essence of man.

The essence of *Homo sapiens* is deposed by an alienated atomization of the secondary process. The ego-system of capitalism compares, contrasts, and exchanges man in order to isolate him from the other. A Communist Unconscious promises that man will return man to the other. Spiritually, man will be decentered from himself and recentered in the other. Unconsciously, man loses himself and the Logic of Identity (A ≠ A) but gains the other in Sameness⁺ (A = B, and so on). The imaginary boundaries which separate the offspring from his mirror are shattered by a constitutive extimacy. Comparison and contrast between ego and ideal — narcissistic and aggressive exchange — are displaced by an aneconomy of the unconscious. The primary process ruins temporality, negation, and knowledge. The unconscious returns the subject to the primary process of the fundamental mechanism that Freud isolates as the secret of the psyche: substitution.

Substitution is the magical necromancy of the function of the phallus and its will to do, undo, and redo the relationships between chains of words in the battery of the Other. Derrida fathoms that the function of generalized coordination in the structure is expelled from the system as the proviso of the free play of substitution of signs and metaphors. The Communist Unconscious banishes the metaphysics of presence of the function to the Outside. The primary process system is the metaphorical-condensation and metonymical-displacement of words. Lacan says that the signifier represents the subject to another signifier. The subject is the sign, word, center, and fetish which are at play in the structure and its generalized coordination. Man is the happy effect of sign-substitutions for the center of the structure. Notably, the function is excluded from the structure. The world is the slip and slide of the primary process. The world is the amusement of wish and the masquerade of desire.

Truth avoids the censor, and it appears in the system of the Cs. Unconscious-Life is this freedom of substitution. Schizophrenically, every word is the same word. Every person is the same person in the psychosis of the unconscious. This extimacy — man is different from himself because he is the Same⁺ Different⁺ as the other — indicates that man is the other *qua* himself. The subject is exactly the Sameness⁺ of the other. Mortally, the only absolute master is death. The trouble is that it takes a certain time for the slave to discover this Sameness⁺. Unconscious Sameness⁺ between self and other is the truth of the primary process. This communism of an association of an unsymbolizable relationship — Sameness⁺ and ~~Being~~ — will arrive in Spirit.

Private Property

Marx's later work on capitalist economics spans the gap between ideology and exchange, and between superstructure and base. The challenge for the innovation of a communist future in the *mise-en-scène* of the unconscious — Communist-Spirit — is not solely the recreation of theories and practices of the self. The work is also to imagine economy and exchange in the third-dimension of the unconscious of communism. This communism is a system that Marx faintly imagines as each according to his need and each according to his ability. Marx's most pronounced critique of the capitalist economists (Smith and Ricardo, *et al.*) is that private property is assumed *a priori*. Private property (what I refer to in this study as *le propre*) is the fundamental precept of the capitalist system as an economy and a lifestyle. As its point of departure, private property and the commodity cannot be explained by capitalist economics. Capitalism plainly presupposes itself. Capitalism resists any genealogical or historicist account of itself. Private property is presented as natural, a gift from God or Nature.

But Marx cannot coherently identify the origin of private property except with reference to alienated labor as the proviso of ownership. The critical foray into an analysis of the ideological structures of capitalism is Marx's closest approximation to an etiological account of the fundamental symptom of capitalism. Marx's strange reticence to present a *bona fide* constructionist account of the advent of the central concept of capitalism — private property — belies an even more bizarre aporia in Marx's work: a strict failure to convincingly describe private property, as an object, an effect, an institution, and a system of value.

I will return to this conspicuous absence in Marx's critique of private property toward the closure of the book. But I can say that the assembly of a Communist Unconscious must dissolve private property — whatever it is — at the margins of the text. The public, outside, and exterior supplant the private, inside, and interior. An Outside emerges from the absence of the father's negation. The Spirit of Communism opens toward a play without the sensibilities of the Judeo-Christian imperative of individual responsibility and the consequential symptoms of bourgeois exchange and its reification of man.

Marx incisively critiques the alienation of the worker from the object of his labor. The commodity is the objectified form of the worker's externalization of labor. The commodity is the basal source of the oppression of the worker. Marx says,

> the object that labor produces, its product, confronts it as an alien being, as a power independent of the producer. The product of labor is labor that has solidified itself into an object, made itself into a thing, the objectification of labor.[13]

The object transforms from a use-value into the monstrosity of an exchange-value over which the producer loses himself and his freedoms. This loss of the creation from the creator — of the gap between author and text — is a trope of structuralist theories of production (such as writing, *écriture*). The structuralists of a renewed writing, such as Barthes and Derrida, understand the liberation of the text from the authority of the writer, and the emancipation of the signifier from the constraints of the signified, as sources of *jouissance*. An indisputable consequence of this chasm between author and text, signifier and signified, creator and creation, and worker and commodity is not only that a semiotic multiplicity and advanced play substitute in the place of strict codes and tired norms of consumption. The break between author and text also dissolves the foundational precept of Judeo-Christian morality in responsibility.

I will closely read the *ur*-dream of Western civilization in Freud's discussion of the dream of Irma's injection in the dream-book (1900) later in this study. But I can say at this juncture that Freud discovers that the elemental unconscious wish of the West is to be rid of responsibility. The wish to press beyond good and evil invariably dismantles the key theories and practices of the West, such as agency, intention, motivation, causation, and the predicative relationship between the doer and the deed. But Marx's critique of the domination of the proletariat by the excrescence of the commodity outlines the gap between the will of the subject and the autonomy of the object. This split is the crux of the alienation of man in the world.

Structuralism persuasively celebrates the decenterment of the self. But it is difficult not to vigorously nod with Marx when he plaintively says: "The worker relates to the product of his labor as to an alien object."[14] A Communist Unconscious must release the self and its objects from the ideology of private property. But Communist-Spirit must also create a system in which objects do not subordinate the worker but rather liberate him — toward a system, I hazard, of masochistic service. At the ends of the domination of the conscious system, will the "leap," as Deleuze says about the de/resexualization process in masochism, gesture toward a galaxy of service? Will the system transform into an Other-Logic in which man's subordination to the other is the emancipation of himself? Labor is the essence of the human. Unconsciously, whose labor is (for) whose (whom)?

This trope of self-ownership (*le propre*) inflects Marx's writing on the relationship between the producer of the commodity and the product of that activity. Marx says: "The external character of labor for the worker shows itself in the fact that it is not his own but someone else's, that it does not belong to him, that he does not belong to himself in his labor but to someone else."[15] A pivotal aspect of Marx's view of the labor process is that it involves what he refers to as "externalization." An interiority of the worker is externalized in the process of labor which is then objectified in the object of production. The prerequisite of objectification (and commodification, and so on) is externalization. The subject externalizes itself. Man's lifeworld bends from the interior to the exterior, and it traverses from the inside to the outside. The consequence of this *a priori* externalization — publicization rather than privatization — of the self is capitalist oppression. Marx demonstrates that externalization is a source of pain and misery.

Externalization is the origin of private property. Capitalist economics cannot trace ownership to an *arche*. Besides externalization, Marx emphasizes the ownership of the product of proletarian labor by an alien being. This other sovereignty is both the vampiric commodity and the owners of the factory. These forces extract "profit" (surplus value) from the worker in the illegal theft of the value of labor. The aporia of ownership is that the system is structured by accumulation and exchange. The representational signs of the system — currency, dollars and coins — are in constant but uneven circulation in the economy. There can be no ownership of dollars and coins because their value only emerges at points of exchange. Weirdly, no one owns money even as it is the primary lubricant of a system of ownership. The ownership of value (either "profit" or surplus value) is strictly undecidable. Value is neither here nor there but in the slippery *objet petit a* of desire. Value is a circulation (accumulation and exchange) of *Trieb* and the aim/less wander of coins and dollars, numbers and fractions, 1's and 0's, pluses and minuses, and imbalances of surpluses and deficits.

There are material objects in the system. But the value of commodities is invariably in flux. Ownership of a value resists the metaphysics of presence. Oddly, capitalism is an economy of *public property*. A Communist Unconscious encourages circulation of displacement and condensation. But an unconscious of communism resists any determination of presence which would halt the twists of texts and the turns of images. Unconscious-Spirit promotes neither subject nor object of *le propre*. The proper is neither mine nor yours. Property is neither his nor hers. The owned is unowned. The possession is unpossessed. What is mine is not mine. This unconscious dissolution of *le propre* will be supplemented with the deconstruction of subjective and objective possessives. These grammatical possessives include mine, yours, his, hers, theirs, and ours. Any arrival or departure of a site of moralist responsibility disappears. Beyond good and evil, the Communist Unconscious detaches sign from reference. Beyond good and evil, *Trieb* circulates a letter which does not arrive at its destination at the navel of the dream. The Communist Unconscious promises that the dream resists interpretation. The revolutionary dreams, and dreams on. Masochistically, the man defers the Boy for the dream. He wills the pact with the wholly other of the Real resistance to presence. The Boy is the process of the revolution — *Not yet!* The universal masochistic service economy appears, and the (de/re)sexualization of all of the objects in the galaxy begins, again. The Boy is dispossessed, and then —

Figure 11.2 Currency, Difference, and Deferral

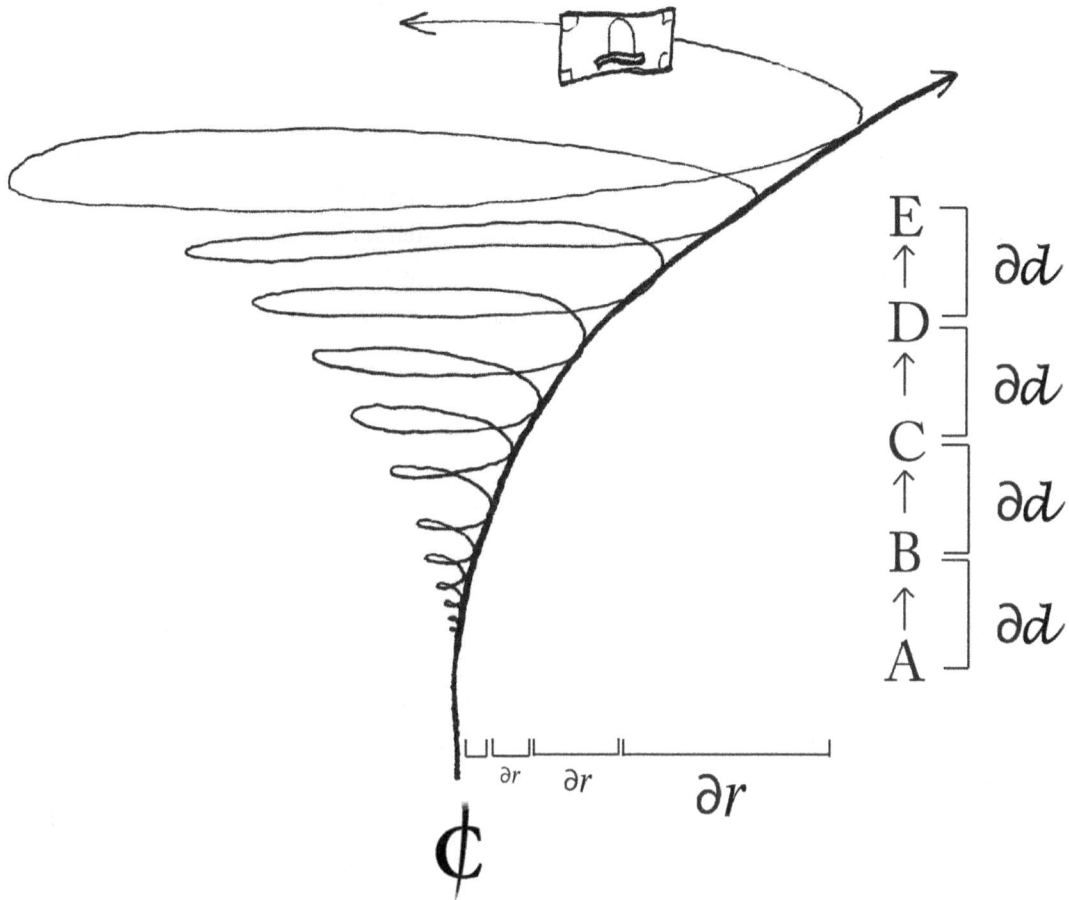

This image displays the circulation of the general equivalent of dollars and coins. The illustration shows the structure of the general equivalent and its establishment of the differed and deferred gap between units of text or dollars and coins. This circulation must produce a deficit through the incorporation of an expansive orbit of scarcity. The fictional dimension of time as a chronological history is depicted on the vertical axis. The vacuum of lack between one unit of text and another is marked by the ∂d. The ∂r is the unsymbolizable Real because it is the precept which is established by the general equivalent as its principle of organization. This principle expands the universe of units of text — dollars and coins — at a rate of escalation. But this escalation is merely the collection of lack. The exponential curve conveys the torus-like relationship between value and itself. This bond is inclusive of itself *qua* debt. There is no value *of* value — or *meta*value — which can be subsumed by the system in order to seal a totality which is without reference to the difference and deferral of the accumulation of deficit. Currency escapes the economy of *le propre* because the essence of gain is loss. Loss cannot be owned. Desire is the desire of the Other. The dollar is the dollar of the Other.

Notes & Sketches —

COMMUNISM

The system of currency is the basis of capitalist exchange of private property. Any analysis of capitalism must tarry with the theory and practice of capital. An invention of a Communist Unconscious must consider the transition from an economy of comparison and contrast which is mediated by a general equivalence (dollars and coins) to an aneconomy in which circulation of use-values is unmediated by standardization. Marx's quick dictum about communism is that it is a society which is structured by each according to his ability (free production) and each according to his need (free consumption). This system is organized by an integrated and collectivist association of workers. There are no dollars and coins in a communist system. There is no (ac) count of materialities and physicalities with abstractions and speculations. The general equivalence of currency (and the father, phallus, and sign) is absent. The universe returns to the lubricated substitutions of Freud's vision of incipient sexuality in which the entire surface of the offspring's body is sexualized. Each part-object is pleasurably substitutable for the others.

Mo Money Mo Problems

Marx's foremost critique of the money economy is that it makes man coincident with currency. In the "1844 Manuscripts," Marx says,

> What I have is thanks to money, what I pay for, i.e. what money can buy, that is what I, the possessor of the money, am myself. My power is as great as the power of money. The properties of money are my — (its owner's) — properties and faculties. Thus what I am and what I am capable of are by no means determined by my individuality.[16]

Summarily, the capitalist individual is the stockpile of goods and services at its disposal. The upshot of this overlap between commodity and self is that man can only be understood as a value. Nietzsche[17] and later Heidegger[18] regard value as the foundation of nihilism. Heidegger explicitly notes that the signifying chain is a system of value and hierarchy. Language is nihilism. Man writes and speaks the nihilism of value. Man is a fetishized commodity who is recapped in the currency of exchange-value.

There is no use-value of man — such as kindness, generosity, love, patience, empathy, and so on — which cannot be reincorporated into the nihilistic exchange-value of money. A sad consequence of this manic capitalist speculation is that love is quantifiable. Money can buy you love. Affect is structured by dollars and coins. Life is exchanged for *dinero*. The quality of the use-value of life is quantified in a hierarchical system of surpluses and deficits. The self is not merely a mark which is conferred value by an external and alien standard. The subject is also subordinated to the standard of dollars and coins which exceeds the authority and resistance of the self. Money may make the world go around. But this is so only because we have outsourced making the world go around to money.

In a remarkable citation from the "1844 Manuscripts," Marx describes the functions of union and separation which are internal to the monetary system. Marx isolates the ways in which currency binds but also dissipates relationships among men, nature, and culture. This motif of fusion and breach recalls Freud's discussion of the drives of *Eros* and *Thanatos* in *Beyond the Pleasure Principle* (1920). *Eros* is the drive of life, of unification, amalgamation, synthesis, and coalition. In contrast, *Thanatos* is the drive of death, of detachment, disconnection, rupture, division, and severance. The tension between the life drive and the death drive is united in an intertwined overlap which delays any easy division between *Eros* and *Thanatos*. Marx asks,

> the bond that binds me to human life, that binds society to me and me to nature and men, is not money the bond of all bonds? Can it not tie and untie all bonds? Is it not, therefore, also the universal means of separation? It is the true agent both of separation and of union, the galvano-chemical power of society.[19]

The preserve of all life (*Eros*) is currency. Money is the "bond of all bonds." Dollars and coins are the fasteners and fixes which bind men to other men, nature, culture, and themselves. Money is a permutation of the life drive. Money is the source of togetherness. But, at the same time, currency can "untie all bonds" as the "universal means of separation."

The paradox of currency in its will to union and fraction is isomorphic to the peculiar relationship between *Eros* and *Thanatos* in Freud's work on the fundamental instincts of life. As the "true agent both of separation and of union," money is a mystical "chemical" which blends as it splits, and combines as it divorces. This dialectical tension between *Eros* and *Thanatos* in the economic dimension illuminates a key truth about capitalism. The system is in paradoxical constant flux. Marx defines capitalism as the frenzied tendency toward accumulation. Capital is a system of the crazed collection of less, based on more, deficit, based on surplus, and debt, based on plenitude. This unhinged accumulation of exchange paradoxically produces debt and manufactures deficit. It also (un)ties relationships of quantification and qualification. The frenetic capitalist will extracts Nothing is Missing from Something is Missing only to return to the obverse. Capitalism is the constant process of the substitution of lack for plenitude. Capitalism makes currency the command "of separation and of union." The mixture of loss and gain, unification and division, and part and whole is isomorphic to Freud's *Eros* and *Thanatos*. This *mélange* fashions a system of currency which is deeply unstable and unpredictable.

Freud's instincts and Marx's money share a common risk in the rupture of social bonds. Selfhood and sociality are destructured by the perils of Something is Missing. Freud's life drive binds losses. But this combination also succumbs to the explosions and splits of *Thanatos*. Marx's critique of currency illuminates the enforced ties of capital and labor. But this union surrenders to the splinters of hierarchy, inequality, bankruptcy, debt, and loss. The Becoming of the Communist Unconscious must restructure this relationship between *Eros* and *Thanatos* and the (un)ties of currency. Freud explains that the unconscious forsakes negation. The abeyance of negation in the unconscious privileges *Eros* above *Thanatos*. *Eros* is the conspicuous precept of the dreamworld of the unconscious. Similarly, an unconscious logic of capitalist accumulation can only be organized by production and surplus rather than by negation and deficit. In a Communist Unconscious, a psychical system of pure and unalloyed *Eros* of reincorporation of the split and snap of the death drive forms into the Spirit of unity. At the same time, man can imagine an economic system of use-value in the absence of the speculation of dollars and coins. Currency feverishly chases surplus (deficit) and the will to make Nothing is Missing from Something is Missing. Currency bewilderingly organizes the strange overlap of Nothing and Something, plenitude and castration, excess and scarcity, and addition and subtraction. But how do postnihilistic use-values circulate in substitution — displacement and condensation with revision and representability — if Nothing is Missing in an atemporal unconscious? This question astonishingly indicates that the unconscious is strongly materialist. This materialism is not merely the light materialism of the sign with its materialist component of the signifier. Rather, the materialist system of the production and the consumption of use-value — communism — is the system of the unconscious. The unconscious is a materialist structure, over and above the light materiality of the signifier.

Communism Optimism

A surprise to the close reader of Marx's critique of capitalism and invention of communism is that Marx presents very little of substance about a future communist collectivity. Most distinctly, Marx defines communism as a system of each according to his need and each according to his ability. The communist system is also an aneconomy without general equivalence or private property. The classical economists cannot account for the *arche* of private property because it is the foremost presupposition of the system. Marx isolates alienated labor — unhappy work and miserable industry — as the cause of private property. In "1844 Manuscripts," Marx explicitly says, "alienated labor is the immediate cause of private property."[20] The ratiocination of this idea is speculative, and the logic is obscure. Alienated labor is the proviso of the capitalist mode of production and its specific relations and forces. The private assembly of commodities is owned by the bourgeoisie. But there is no perspicacious account of the dubious relationship between the activity of despondent laborers and the ownership of private property.

Marx's general point is that the alien extraction of the commodity as private property from the worker in the marketplace retroactively renders labor itself an activity of alienation. But if dejected baristas are the source of private property, then what is the *arche* of alienated labor? The circular reasoning indicates that capitalism is the explanation for itself. Capital and its alienated labor sire capital and its private property. Capitalism is a creationist sublimation *ex nihilo*. *Contra* Marx's famous remark that capitalism emerges from the transmutation of solids into air (1848), a psychoanalytic revision of Marx can only conclude that capital is the effect of the displacement of sexual libido from its proper erogenous aims. Capitalism is the symptom of repression rather than the outlet of sublimation. This discussion returns to the dynamics of repression and negation because of the question of the desire and the threat of the Communist Unconscious. What is the threat of plenitude to $-ism? Why must loss be sustained as the proviso of the system of the ego? How does the general equivalent of dollars and coins substitute as the symptom for a negated — *Verdrängung, Verwerfung,* or *Verleugnung* — aneconomy of use-values and their pleasures?

The inquiry will be two-fold: first, the study must determine the dynamics of the repressed and its return in the tension between ego-capitalism and unconscious-communism; and second, the critique must establish the proper space of a Communist Spirit. Will man voyage toward the primary process of a renewed unconscious of thinking, being, and living? Will man risk the return of the repressed of Real communism and its valiant effort to overwrite capital and the symptom of scarcity? At stake in this choice between $-ism or unconscious is Spirit. Spiritually, worldly or otherworldly, will the perverts of the world unite in a refined Order of Madness or in a perverse symbolization of the Real?

In his dreamy imagination of the future, Marx promises the destruction of the economy of *le propre*: the proper, property, ownership, possession, and mineness. In "1844," he says that "communism is the positive expression of the overcoming of private property."[21] The word "positive" is philosophically significant because the dialectical methodology of Marx's work otherwise emphasizes the (Hegelian) determinate negation of the *Aufhebung* toward the Other unto communism. The "positive expression" philosophically refers to the *telos* of the End of History. The series of violent clashes between oppositional systems and actors is overcome in the achievement of the communist mode of production. The positive expression of communism achieves the totalization of historical movement at the ends of its development. But, as an aside, this totalization is structurally open because the X returns from a strictly infinite expanse of the historical theft of the surplus (in whatever form). This return can only be positive because it is expressed and experienced as the signifier *sans* the signified. The materialist wager is that there is Nothing is Missing in this future abundance of materiality. The End of History is the Advent of the Surplus.

Figure 11.3 Circuit of Identity

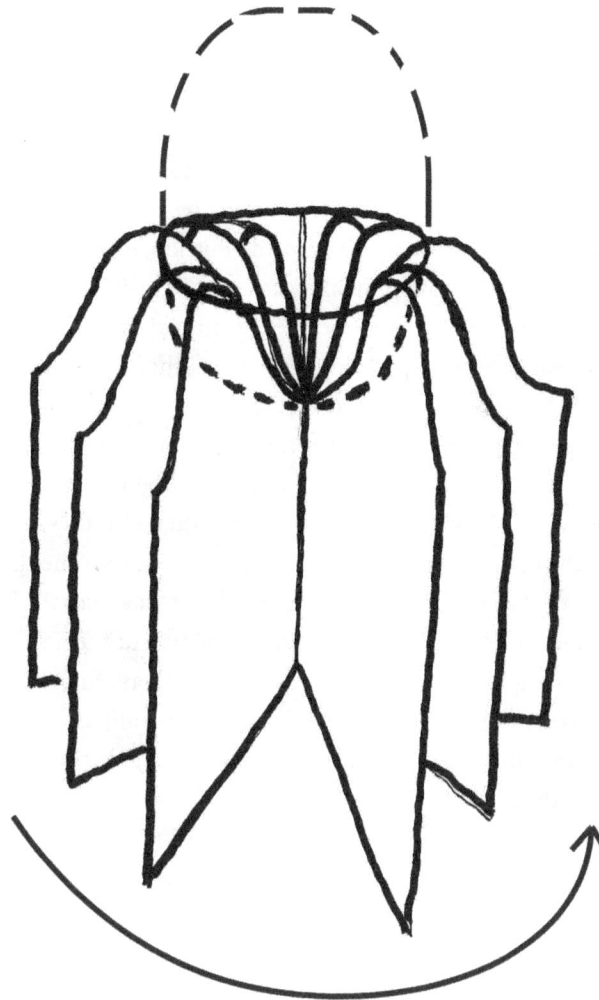

This drawing depicts the circuit of the subject who identifies as — and is identified as — an object in the capitalist system. The illustration shows the dimensional dynamic of an Other who is simulated as an absence. This absence is the object of the subject's will to identity. The subject traverses the time and space of the other in order to return to itself. The subject achieves the semblance of closure unto itself in the return speculation of the other. But this return speculation is structured by an absence because the other is reduced to an objecthood in the process of this identification. The Something is Missing of castration is the principle of a desire which reduces the subject to an object. Neurotic desire obscures the (*a*)sexual nucleus which is otherwise the principal energy of the other and the source of the self in a differed and deferred distance and proximity. The neurotic convinces himself that he is his own *arche*.

Notes & Sketches —

The will to "overcome" private property is a vexed project because Marx's definition of private property is scant and undeveloped. Private property (*le propre*) is not only coded into Romance languages with possessive qualifications. Private property is also the ideological outline of the bourgeois individual who is atomized as isolated, alone, self-contained, self-sufficient, solitary, and singular. A generalized elucidation of private property *per se* is simply absent in Marx's work. The likely reason for the unexpected absence of the otherwise epically present is that private property is the oxygen of the West. The internalization of private property is invisible. The mode of production of capitalism is unnoticed *doxa* for an unhistoricized Western imagination. The obverse of private is public. The social and economic implication of the communist inversion is the exteriorization of selfhood and sociality. Communism entails the publicization of use-values. Beyond private property, there is no division between private/public, inside/outside, self/other, and so on.

Communism abolishes not only private property but also the bi-level configuration of text. There is no split between the obscurities of the unconscious and the mystifications of the secondary process. The future is transparent. The abolishment of private property liberates author and reader, and worker and consumer. The end of private property relieves man of responsibility for the departure and destination of the object. The subject and the object are neither split nor sutured. The self and the other sustain a liminal in-between superposition. This space is the Outside of *le propre*. This inside (outside) space of Becoming undoes the division between an internal world of thoughts, ideas, concerns, values, desires, and fears, on the one hand, and an external world of people, things, objects, joys, tears, and bodies, on the other hand. This extimacy promises a deliverance from the Judeo-Christian tradition of morality. Extimacy frees the bourgeois individual from his Western role as the responsible doer of the deed. The deconstruction of the inside/outside binary releases man from the consequent series of symptoms of Being and presence, such as narcissism, aggression, anxiety, and so on. A communist beyond of the good and evil of capitalism ends morality. Communism heralds the psychical and social *tout autre*. The communist system of happy gestures is a galaxy in which doer and deed — cause and effect — are untied from the estrangement and alienation between subject and object.

A crucial dimension of the plot is the Becoming of communism as an in-process, in-action development of sociohistorical conditions. Marx's view is that the development of the forces of production (labor and technology) invariably produces a surplus of goods and services. For the first time in the entire history of humanity, scarcity is abolished. Man is freed of material necessity. Objects are plentiful. Production is unregulated. Consumption is ungoverned. The logic of castration is expelled from the sphere of economics. The pivotal supply/demand dynamics of the capitalist relations of production become null and void. The system of currency otherwise manages supply/demand. This dynamic is structured by scarcity. Castration is otherwise organized by the teeter-totter of supply, demand, and the supervision of price in the marketplace. The end of scarcity inspires the disappearance of money. The perverts, schizoids, and Women produce and consume as they wish. History is transformed into posthistory. The lack of capitalism and phallocentrism yields to the presence of the Spirit of the System.

The beyond of the capitalist coercion of alienated labor is the organization of the workers in association for the sensuous cultivation of nature into culture for the use-values of the society. Marx also discusses independence, dependence, and social intercourse in his excurses on the creative dimensions of the transition toward communism. In "The German Ideology" (1844), Marx writes,

> The reality, which communism is creating, is precisely the true basis for rendering it impossible
> that anything should exist independently of individuals, in so far as reality is only a product
> of the preceding intercourse of individuals themselves.[22]

The wide-angle takeaway from this citation is the imbricated intercourse between men, production, objects, and history. The discrete divisions between individuals, between man and labor, between production and consumption, and between historical modes of production are myths. These myths are dismantled. The system of $-ism is otherwise organized by positive structures — isolated units — of objects. This arrangement of words systematizes the galaxy into disjoined planets, each with their own weather patterns, atmospheric pressure, measured circumference, barometric pressure, and species of alien.

The same categorization applies to nature and culture in capitalism. The nonstop generation of contemporary identities and their precious hybridities is endless: race, class, gender, sexuality, nationality, ethnicity, region, disability, body type, religion, occupation, cut, 7", uncut, 9", and simply massive. Zizek repeatedly claims that multiculturalism is the ideological supplement to late capitalism. The proliferation of sacred personal identities extends the capitalist privatization of the self. The extension of identification nurtures niche markets for the commodification of identity. The excessive market differentiation of self divides and conquers selves and communities by arbitrary but conventionalized differences. These divisions abet defensive separation and uneasy distance.

Marx identifies the historical teleological arrival of communism as the abolishment of such personal identities. He specifically refers to the dissolution of religion and nation in the global revolution unto communism.[23] The citation (above) specifies that the historical in-process, in-action Becoming of communism cultivates a world-to-come as the "true basis" of a Marxian philosophical truth. The communist truth is that the discrete isolation of objects and subjects is neither theoretically coherent nor practically desirable. But how does the Becoming of communism make it "impossible" for subjects of capitalism to discern that there can be no "independent" Being (what is) which is considered isolated and distanced from the individual?

The *telos* of the ends of capitalism is the closure of the political as such. Politics is essentially the fundamental antagonism between the bourgeoisie and the proletariat, between the owners and the workers. Marx's dialectical materialism posits an historical march of labor and its simultaneous cultivation and subjugation by the dialectical tension between the forces of production of power and innovation, on the one hand, and the relations of production of containment and suppression, on the other hand. Marx articulates the ends of the antagonism of politics proper in "The Poverty of Philosophy" (1846) with his prediction of,

> an association which will exclude classes and their antagonism, and [in which] there will be no more political power properly so called, since political power is precisely the official expression of antagonism in civil society.[24]

The speculation that politics achieves *denouement* at the End of History is both grandiose and delusional. But Marx's commitment to the materialization of Hegel's historical dialectical *telos* of *Geist* (1807) compels him to imagine the end of politics. Democracy conceives of politics as an endless negotiation between competitive interests.

But the Nietzschean caveat to this democratic ideal is that force and power triumph over reason and logic. Any so-called reason is an effect of force and any so-called logic is a consequence of power. The minority party of political battle inevitably loses. The strong and the mighty achieve victory over the weak and the oppressed. Democratic politics is overpowered by the forces of strength. Power otherwise dictates right from wrong, just from unjust, and the proper system (capitalism) as such. Marx's version of politics as the sheer will of the antagonism between classes promises a harmonious totality at the End of History. Interests are united, divisions are settled, and the *mise-en-scène* of communism is a relaxed enjoyment of man's essence in labor, free and chosen. The advent of the revolution unto postpolitics reposes a critical question. What is this nefarious private property of the bourgeoisie which dominates the air and water of capitalism and manipulates the worker into his own submission to a system of scarcity and castration? How are capitalist scarcity and phallocentric castration overcome in the *Aufhebung* beyond private property? What is unconscious communism after the dissolution of the private and the proper? A theoretical exploration of the governance of private property under the primary process is the necessary adjunct to the practical abolishment of private property in the system of the Cs.

The Repression and Return of Communism

The metatheoretical architecture of psychoanalysis includes not only the binary division between conscious and unconscious. Psychoanalysis also theorizes a variety of mechanisms by which these two dimensions are related to each other. These instruments include the latent content, the manifest form, the symptom, the return of negation (neurotic *Verdrängung*, psychotic *Verwerfung*, and perverse *Verleugnung*), and the threat of the unconscious wish. Capitalism rules the system of the ego-conscious. Existence is structured by the thinking, being, and living of comparison, contrast, exchange, standardized equivalence, currency, structured fetters on production and consumption, and the commodification of life by the nihilism of value. Communist themes and motifs, even the word itself, are consigned to the unconscious of the individual and the society. Ego-capitalism is structured by supply/demand dynamics and scarcity. The *sin qua non* of capital is the accumulation of loss and the inexplicable conversion of plenitude into scarcity, fullness into lack, and penis into phallocentric clitoris.

$-ism thrives on and dies by the dictate of Freud's view of female castration — that Something is Missing. The various symptoms of Something is Missing include the plethora of subjective and social dysfunctions in the capitalist galaxy: alienation, estrangement, narcissism, aggression, anxiety, competition, fear, rudeness, monetization of affect, quantification of quality, standardization of value, nihilistic reduction of man to commodity, and so on. Veritably, every sour and crabby interaction in the Western solar system is reasonably traced to capitalism and its ideological supplement in castration. An unconscious communism is a threat to the symbolic order because it reminds capitalists not of their extant oppression but of their lost liberation. The corporate-statist management of the lifeworld is violent and deranged. This is so despite the ideological machinations which tempt man to enjoy his symptoms. The symptoms of capitalism are the collective fantasy of loss and the fervent desire for castration.

Desire for lack is a strangely male heterosexual invention because *désir* preserves the essential negativity of the clitoris *qua* the proviso for a paradoxical male heterosexual desire. At stake in the unconscious threat of communism and its postcastration plenitude of a postpenis and postclitoral (*a*)sexuality is male heterosexuality. Reasonably, male heterosexuality (in its current form) is an invention of capitalism and its allegiance to the ideology of scarcity. The manifest threat of an unconscious plenitude of penis = clitoris (and so on) is male heterosexuality and, by extension, reproduction, domesticity, and progeny. The unconscious threat of communism is the destabilization of normative sexuality. The Ego Heterosexual Industrial Complex defends its fixed selfhood and sociality against the eruptions of the Real Penis and the emergent plenitude and fullness of the primary process and its displacements and condensations of a communist queer (*a*)sexuality.

The wish of the unconscious of latent communism is the realization of communist man. Communism wishes a selfhood and a sociality of each according to his need and each according to his ability. The fulfillment of Communist Unconscious desire is the proper interpretation of the manifest obfuscations of the wish of communism. A proper interpretation of the manifest representations of the defense against communist truth advances toward the realization of the wish of the future. The principal symptom of capitalism in its defense against the unconscious is phallocentric clitoral Something is Missing. Castration defends against the penis. Lack safeguards against Nothing is Missing. $-ism must cultivate the ideological conditions which sustain loss and death.

The primary strategy of defense is currency. The system of dollars and coins is configured by scarcity. The infinite numeracy of money is such that there can never be a sufficient quantity of money. A necessarily insufficient quotient of currency is organized by the capitalist accumulation of debt of more and ever in the abstract capitalization of numbers and decimals. The paradox of capitalist accumulation is that the will to addition and the supplement is simultaneously organized by the truth of subtraction and the deficit. Currency is the central capitalist institution. The scaffold of dollars and coins is both tenuous and misunderstood. The fantasy of castration is enforced and sustained by $-ism. Citizens are consistently reminded of debt. The delusional construction of the "national debt" ("$19 trillion dollars") is the macroscopic rendition of capitalist clitoral scarcity. A microscopic version of the fiction of loss is the various moral modalities of personal debt: private loans, credit cards, business loans, mortgages, student loans, APR's, and so on. The communist truth of the obfuscatory manifest representations — slips, dreams, jokes, and pathologies — of capitalism and scarcity is the simple economic truth that the mass of moola is theoretically infinite beyond any momentary finity. Capitalistically, there are necessary and essential debt and castration.

The American structure of a central bank, the private corporation of the Federal Reserve, accords private banks with the sovereignty to print dollars with neither condition nor limit. The advent of this monstrous institution of the central bank dates to the origin of the American republic and the machinations of Alexander Hamilton, the first American Secretary of the Treasury (1789-1795). The Federal Reserve System (1913) is the origin of the extraction of value from the worker by fixed and variable interest rates. The central banks print free money and then sell the currency to consumers at a rate of interest. This rate of interest multiplied by the aggregate sum of the loan is the stolen value from the worker. This stolen interest supplements the other modalities of extraction: "profit" by way of the stolen surplus value; and rent by way of the stolen gap between the value of the property and the cost of the lease. Summarily, the rule of debt in profit, interest, and rent mobilizes scarcity and castration. Lack is the proviso of the coherence of capitalism and the logic of phallocentrism. The fantasy of castration is the ideological supplement of capitalism. The symptom of capitalism in the system of the Cs. is debt. Repression of communism is enforced by the ideology of the phallocentric version of the clitoris. The phallocentric relationship of the clitoris to man isolates the psychosexual nodal point of capitalism.

The threat of communism is a penis-plenitude: penis = clitoris or penis ($\supseteq$) clitoris. This (non)genital plenitude contests the phallocentric lack of the capitalist system. The manifest symptom — even *sinthome* — of the ego is the defense of deficit and debt. What are the mechanisms whereby the communist truth avoids the manifest-censor in order to erupt in the kooky form of the dream, slip, joke, and psychopathology of everyday life? The strategies of displacement and condensation of the primary process evade the superegoic censor whose role in the *mise-en-scène* of the dreamy unconscious is to obscure the wish and truth of communism. Repression enables desire to emerge in the conscious in a zany form. Perversely, the split between the conscious and the unconscious is tenuous. The (un)conscious is the simultaneous repression and return in the defense against difference.

The class antagonism of Marx's philosophy frames the repression-return dynamic not as sexual (genital) difference but rather as class (economic) difference. Sexually, the pervert's horror at the sight of the clitoris forces a disavowal of this negative difference which returns as itself in the fetish. This fetish is the (dis)simulation of the penis-clitoris. Somehow — the pervert's inexplicable strategy of simultaneous acknowledgment and denial elevates the unconscious to the level of the conscious. Somehow — the pervert's *Verleugnung* raises the conscious to the rank of the unconscious. The pervert resolves the anxious conundrum of sexual (class) difference because he collapses the division between conscious/unconscious and manifest/latent. The repressed and its return are the Same⁺. The plenitude of latent communism is repressed by the capitalist regime only to return as itself in the system of the conscious of capitalism. Communism is internal to capitalism. Capitalism and its theft of profit, rent, and interest from alienated workers are parallactically overlapped with a plentiful communism of each according to his need and each according to his ability. $-ism = S or $-ism (⊇) S is the perverse framework of the repression of communism and its simultaneous return of itself *qua* capitalism.

This perverse (dis)simulation is a dangerous threat to the system because it muddles the division between communist legality and capitalist crime, progressive justice and illegal injustice, and plenitude and scarcity. Scarcity is already plenitude. The clitoris is already the penis. Capitalism is already communism. The caveat to this parallactic twist and flip is the stubborn aporia of the copula: ~~Being~~. Scarcity ~~is~~ already plenitude. The clitoris ~~is~~ already the penis. Capitalism ~~is~~ already communism. What is the proper word for the relationship of proximity between the pairs of oppositions? How is the overlap — continuity and coincidence — between capitalist scarcity and communist plenitude to be symbolized if Being (what is) is under erasure?

The techniques of the unconscious primary process — displacement, condensation, revision, and representability — are the mechanisms by which the unconscious of communism ruptures the conscious laziness of capitalism. Psychoanalytic work on the tension of the (un)conscious of capitalism deploys a rigorous analysis of the stirs and shifts of the wish and truth of communism. The communist challenge is the bait-and-switch of a masquerade. The dare is to obscure communism and its ideological commitments in the togs and threads of the Other. Communism must be disguised and concealed by the techniques of the primary process. Obfuscation of communism evades the censor of the system of the Cs. *Qua* present in the system of the Cs. of both selfhood and sociality, the obscured communist wishes promise to wreck havoc in the extant symbolic order of capitalism. Communism breaks the barrier of the conscious in order to disturb the symbolic order.

Real Communism returns the schizophrenically foreclosed of the capitalist symbolic. $-ism is capitalist. This system (dys)functions in the *Verwerfung* of the return of the negated of communism. The Real of communist plenitude punctures capitalist scarcity. The reaction of the symbolic equivalence of currency is the foreclosure of this Real of each according to his need and each according to his ability. The symbolic order operates loss: the castration of phallocentrism, the scarcity of capitalism, and the absence of the sign. The ego-system sustains capitalism by banishing the threat of plenitude-penis from its order. This psychotic foreclosure of plenitude and communism institutionalizes capitalism and its presupposition of scarcity. The madness of *Verwerfung* also underpins phallocentrism and male heterosexuality. The system forecloses the clitoris in order to preserve male heterosexuality and its patriarchal institutions of sexism and misogyny.

The (*a*)sexual truth of communism is revealed: *homosexuality*. The queerness of communism ruptures the patriarchal order of capitalism and scarcity. This queerness is a threat to the phallocentric clitoral scarcity of the system of supply/demand dynamics and the general equivalent. The Communist Unconscious is queer. The queer liberates an (*a*)sexual libido which ruptures the ego-system of heterosexuality and its capitalist debt. There is neither negation nor knowledge nor temporality in the queer Communist Unconscious. The queer primary process freely exchanges metaphors and substitutions in order to evade the censor and achieve recognition in the conscious. At stake in the Communist Unconscious and its return is the ruin of a male heterosexuality. This otherwise dominant sexuality is structured by loss and death. Communist queer (*a*)sexuality returns to rescue man from capitalist patriarchy. The queer Communist Unconscious renews an (*a*)sexuality of each according to his need and each according to his ability.

But what is the connective word — copula for Being — for erotic foreplay between the conscious and the unconscious, the manifest and the latent, the capitalist and the communist, and the straight and the queer? How will the effluvium of the queer primary process displace the tired straight secondary process and its defense of normative heterosexuality and false capitalism? A queer communist ontology of the dream identifies a revised approach to Being and its (in)distinctions. What is the ontological project — What is? — in the unconscious? Can queer communism reconfigure this fundamental question of philosophy? Knowledge, negation, and temporality arrange the system of the ego. Will queer communism rescue the future from these limits of thought? The Outside of metaphysics is the queerness of communism. The queer unconscious summons is to repose the ontological question — What is? — from within the unawares and timeless positivity of the unconscious of $-ism *qua* Spirit.

DREAM-ONTOLOGY

In Heidegger's *Being and Time* (1923), he formulates the simple ontological question: "What is?" This query is the precept of philosophical inquiry in epistemology, aesthetics, and ethics. Any propositional claim must settle the question of the ontological — of Being, as such — in order to proceed with its hypotheses, conclusions, and revisions. But the ontological question cannot even be formulated because ~~Being~~ is under erasure. What is "What is?" ~~What is?~~ The "what is" of any subject or object cannot be spoken or written. Being is otherwise the mediation of each sign with itself: A = A, capitalism is capitalism, sex is sex, boring is boring, Being is Being, and is is is. Ontological Being is the proviso of self-sameness and self-identity. Being is the logical guarantee of the coherence and order of the structure and its elements.

But the question of ontology is not simply the propositional query: "What is?" Rather, my concern is also the transposition of this theoretical ontological question — "What is?" — within the lifeworld of the dream of the unconscious. The wager of this study is that the question of the meaning of Being is distinct in the fields of the system of the Cs. and the signifying chain of the unconscious. There is a conscious articulation of ontology which is distinct from the unconscious enunciation of Being. The system Cs. splits the classic Freudian oppositions — unconscious/conscious, latent/manifest, symptom/ interpretation, and so on — which must be understood as bivalent and ambivalent. These oppositions are secured by the codes of evaluation and hierarchy which are the standards of the word: distinction, opposition, signification, and the positive unity of the sign. The word is the measure of Being in the system of the ego-conscious. Any binary in the conscious system is situated between Being and Nothingness. A binary is articulated between the permutations of: what is is what is not and what is is not and what is not is not what is and what is not is is what is not and what is is not is not and what is is what is not is not what is and what is not and what is is not is not what is, and so on. Being (is) — negatively and recursively, *not*.

A compulsive repetitive negation of rules and codes of the "what is" is the structure of the ontology of the word. The conscious negativity of the Being of the sign contrasts with the Dream-Ontological affirmation of all of the conjunctive systems: neurotic either/or *Verdrängung*, perverse both/and *Verleugnung*, and schizoid neither/nor *Verwerfung*. This affirmation gestures toward the Becoming of the Other of the Pervert-Schizoid-Woman and the Spirit of the System. Dream is the *mise-en-scène* of *Eros*. Affirmations and unifications connect and conjoin disparate part-objects in the displacements and condensations of the primary process. A dream fulfills the wish of Unreason. Dream-Ontology is structured as the Marxian *camera obscura* (1845) of philosophy.[25] Outside-Being enunciates the copula from the fresh perspective of the unconscious field.

Outside-Being (is) the absence of knowledge, negation, and temporality. How is the ontological inquiry of "What is?" to be reformulated in a timeless space which exceeds epistemology and the differences and negativities of the signifying chain?

This space of postgnostic positivity poses and rejoins the ontological inquiry with a different set of postures and dispositions. Freud's venture that a dream is the fulfillment of a wish proposes a simultaneity of the narrative closure of the fantasy-scene and the emergence of the presentation of the wish. The quandary of this apparatus is that the fulfillment of the wish coincides with the *denouement* of narration. Desire is unconsciously achieved at the moment of the ends of storytelling. The wish is fulfilled by interpretation of the dream. But the closure of the wish of a satisfied unconscious endows the analyst with the project to transform the unconscious desire into the willed truth of the system of the Cs. Dream bequeaths the loss of the aperture of narrative at the commencement of the journey toward the conscious expression of the object of the fantasy.

A wish is the transformation of a disagreeable idea into an agreeable idea. This is so even if thoughts are split and decentered from themselves. The wish of transformation is based on a perverse-schizoid Logic of Difference (A ≠ A) rather than on a neurotic Logic of Identity (A = A). Dream is the achievement of a transposition of Being (what is and as such) into Nothingness (what is not and otherwise). Other-Nothingness (or the what is not is not) is not an idea but an image. The Other-Metaphysics is not a text but a picture. The disagreeable conscious idea realizes an agreement between the ego secondary process and the unconscious primary process through a repression of the edgy tension in the psychical apparatus. Dream achieves agreement within the Logic of Difference. Unconsciously, the disagreeable Unreason of A ≠ A is reworked into an agreeable — happy and content — reconciliation in the field of the unconscious. The primary process rearranges the discomfort of Unreason into the play of desire. Ontologically, Being is reshaped to be otherwise than under erasure. If Being *is* (rather than *is not*) under the conditions of the primary process, then what are the mechanisms of this revolution in unconscious ontology? What are the consequences of an unconscious positive and affirmative ontology which supersedes a negative and differential ontology of the system of the conscious?

A Dream is a Fulfillment of —

A dream is a fulfillment of the wish of the concurrent agreement and disagreement of an uncomfortable thought. A perverse dream mobilizes the both/and nonbinary and multivalent value of the signifier and its subversion of *le propre*. Under the sleepy conditions of unconscious Dream-Ontology, what is is what is not — ~~Being Nothingness~~ — in the absence of an essential and coherent copula of relationship or what Heidegger refers to in the Greek as *Logos*. The idea that a dream is a fulfillment of a wish illuminates the strange transformation of disagreement into agreement in the Becoming of Being. Freud's thesis also frames an answer to the question of ontology: "What is?" The subject — *Dasein* — who asks the question of Being in the unconscious is yet to be determined. The dream is the scene which puts into image the form of the expression of the question, "What is?" In kind, the question puts into image the form of the expression of the question of ontology. What is? — in the unconscious? Dream is the scene which puts into imagination the style of the expression of the enunciation, "What is?" What is the new worlding of Becoming, Being, and dreaming of earth and world?

The aesthetic — picture and image — is constructed from dream-work and dream-distortion. The constraints of the conceptualization of the question of Being are the object of inquiry. There are parameters in the risk to ask the question of ontology. The wager requires a foray into the conditions of the framework in which the question of ontology — What is? — can be posed. These limits are the dream-censor and it various "No!'s" and negations. There is a modality in which the dreamer formulates the question of "What is?" in style and expression. The dream is the dramatization and visualization of the idea — but not the identity — of Being. None of this worlding can be experienced as temporal except as an extended present tense of the timelessness of the unconscious. The philosophy of ontology is at stake in the dream. The question is not "What is?" but rather "How is: What is?" How is Being — Why? — posed as the question of essence?

A dream is a dramatization and visualization of an idea — "How is...?" — but not an identity — "What is?" The focus of Dream-Ontology is Being *qua* the proviso of the ontological project. The wager is to identify the ways in which Being (as such, *qua,* by definition, and *il y a*) is problematized and elaborated as a question of meaning in the unconscious. There is no temporality of this ontological Being. The ontological (is) experienced in the dream as a timeless present tense. Being is not Becoming. Unconsciously, Being is Being. Being is a Becoming which is strictly atemporal. Ontologically, the dream poses Being *qua* Becoming. Being (is) Ing⁺. The question of ontology is not genealogical-historicist with a posited series of origins. Rather, ontology is an issue of form and expression. Ontology is a matter of discourse, attitude, style, signifier, content, and message of the "What is?" of Being. The dreamer asks this question of the "What is?" in the dream. How does dream present the image and picture of the dreamer and his question of the being-in-the-world and being-with-others in the dream?

The pervert, schizoid, and Woman each enjoy distinct orientations toward the ontological question. The schizoid is the philosopher of an Anti-Ontology of what is *ex nihilo* out of Nothingness. The schizoid cannot speak in Reason. The schizoid's signifier is otherwise unanchored in the word of distinction and opposition. The pervert is ontologically mute. The pervert speaks around and beside ontology in the articulation of the resistance of signification. The pervert rescripts the theory of the schizoid and his signifier/signified division of inchoate materialities and jumbled abstractions. The pervert writes in the word of Reason but with the aesthetic of the signifier of Unreason. The pervert's *écriture* mobilizes the theory of value as opposed to the practice of signification. The pervert *practices theory.* The pervert's *Praxis* is the *écriture* of the ontology of the Being of the world. But the pervert writes this ontology from the experience of the Real of the schizoid. The pervert inscribes Unreason in the discourse of the symbolic order. The pervert translates the dreamy Unreason of the schizoid into the signs of an unconscious Reason. The dream is the schizoid-perverse form of expression of the language of the manifestly latent and the latently manifest universe. It is the Woman who inquires about Being in the spacescape of the unconscious.

The dream for the schizoid-pervert is an aesthetic of the talented expression and unique form of ontology. The pervert's avatar is formalization. The pervert's speech and text are the manifest alphabets and portraits of the unconscious of the dream. Dadaism and its nonsense abjure coherence and reasonableness. In contrast, the pervert wills a surrealist latent content. Surrealism illuminates the letters and pictures of signification in practice in the sounds and images of value in theory in the system of Unreason. The unconscious speaks the alphabets and portraits of theory. The primary process practices theory. The unconscious theorizes desire. The dream dramatizes theory. The unconscious is the apparatus of critical theory. The Cultural Studies scholar speaks the language of dreams. But how is the question of the formation of the question of ~~Being~~ posed in an unconscious of images and pictures?

There is neither linear time nor chronological temporality in the unconscious. In *Being and Time* (1923), the worlding of the gerund-as-verb of Ing⁺ is the time of Be(Ing⁺) of being-in-the-world and being-with-others. Freud's claim that a dream is a fulfillment of a wish answers the ontological question of the "What is?" The fulfillment of a wish transcribes the agreeable into the disagreeable and then the obverse. The dreamy realization of desire is a transposition of the disagreeable but truthful wish of the latent content into the agreeable but silly symptom of the dream. The end of the dream in its interpretation is the discernment of truth. The analysis of the dream answers the question of Being. What is the truth of the self and Western civilization?

Dream answers the question which is posed by desire *qua* question: $\$<>a$. The symptom responds to the rapport between the transference and its relationship to the *sujet supposé savoir*. Dream answers its own question. Dream is the Becoming of the subject of the question and the object of the answer. The dream — Ing⁺ — is the process of truth. *Aletheia* elaborates truth in space. But this (un)concealment of truth in Becoming is strictly spatial. Becoming is the Outside of the watch of time and the map of space. Paradoxically, Becoming is situated in the locus of the timeless unconscious. The ontological truth of Becoming is simultaneously ahistorical and atemporal. The existent emerges in the unconscious. But this Being (as such) must simultaneously *be* Becoming. The conceptual neologism of the Ing⁺ enunciates the perverse verbed gerund of the Time of the Pervert. Perverse Ing⁺ is the proper (a)temporal modality of unconscious ontology. Unexpectedly, Becoming is principally spatial. Surreally, Being is primarily temporal. Being (what is) and Becoming (what is becoming) cannot be strictly divided from each other.

Unconscious truth is fundamentally both essential and genealogical, both spatial and temporal, and both static and historical. But this genealogy, temporality, and historicity are spatialized — somehow — in the primary process of the unconscious. The dreamer gazes at time in expanse. The dreamer views temporality in margin. The dreamer beholds the map of time. Time is a picture. Temporality is a portrait. Queer (*a*) temporality of truth exceeds any separation of space and time, and of the first-dimension and the second-dimension. Space and time cannot be disjoined because space-becomes-time and time-becomes-space. Desire is neither spatial nor temporal but Other. Perversely, truth is both spatial and temporal but also neither spatial nor temporal.

Unconscious wish illuminates the Derridean approach to space and time as it is outlined in his essay on "*Différance*" (1967) — space-becoming-time and time-becoming-space.²⁶ Truth is of neither the first-dimension of space nor of the second-dimension of time. Wish cancels spatiotemporal continuity. The third-dimension of the unconscious is the mediatory deconstruction of space and time as otherwise distinct dimensions. The unconscious ruins spatiotemporal logic — such as causality, correlation, coordination, organization, unity, distinction, process, product, and so on. The unconscious is the scene of the preternatural expression of desire and truth in text and image. The fourth-dimension of love in *Praxis* is the affective dimension of this process of the spatialization of time and the temporization of space. Fourth-dimensional *Praxis* is the affect of truth. *Praxis* is the feeling of the realization of the wish. It is the emotion of the achievement of truth. *Praxis* in the fourth-dimension is the awesome sentience in Becoming of the ruin of the coordinates of the world. *Praxis* is the event of the suicidal achievements of *Eros*. Is *Thanatos* the protective shield against the explosion of the coordination of space and time? Can life service *Eros*? Or is *Thanatos* the guardian of life?

The wish of the unconscious is profoundly of the subject's design. Heidegger poses the question of the subject (*Dasein*) for whom the meaning of Being is at issue. My claim is that the ontological inquiry into the existent is the wish of the unconscious. But who is this dreamer of ontology and its unconscious revision in form and expression? The dream *qua* symptom is the rejoinder to the answer to the question of this wish: Who is man? Who is this sleeper of the closed eyed space of no "No!," no time, and no knowledge? Dream-Ontology summons this posthumanist hero. There is a man of inquiry in the dream. The authority of this self is under duress in the colorful world of its desires and truths. As Derrida would rejoin, "But who, we dreamers?"²⁷

The words in the system of the Cs. ask the question: "Who am I?" "What is my veiled desire?" The unconscious is the talented technician of symbolization in the primary process. The unconscious also inquires: "What is language?" Lacan's revision of the mechanisms of the primary process illuminates the mechanisms of displacement-metonymy and condensation-metaphor. These techniques inadequately assimilate the primary processes of unconscious textualization to the tropes of the discourse of the system of the Cs.[28] A magical excess animates the primary process and its arts and sciences of text and image. The remarkable talents of the unconscious are not the revised tropes of ordinary language. The figuration of the latent content betwixt the will of expression and the repression of the censor is certainly wily and sly.

The Spirit of the unconscious is its radical design of an expanse of space with neither time nor negation nor knowledge. The unconscious is an exclusive *mise-en-scène* in which man does not breathe as conscious body and soul. The Other-Ontology approaches the ontological question — "What is?" — from a distinct perspective. What is "What is?" under the conditions of the primary process? What is ontological Being in a system with neither temporality nor negation nor knowledge? The system of the Cs. may pose the question of the self — "Who am I?" But it is timeless space, sweet nonknowledge, and bright positivity which indicate an Other configuration of the proposal and reply to the simple but tricky ontological question. What is? — the condition of *Praxis*? More so — what is the relationship between queer (*a*)sexuality ($\supseteq$) *P* — ?

Outside of Knowledge

The focus of the crucial inquiry into the Other-Logic of the unconscious is the significance of the absence of knowledge, temporality, and negation. In the system of the Cs., both the neurotic and the schizoid suffer the consequences of blind knowledge. The neurotic misinterprets his world because the ego-function is torn among the demands of the *Es* of unruly desires, the *Über-Ich* of rigid strictures, and the external world of conventions and codes. The *Ich* is a fiction because of its imaginary capitation in the Other. This fabled *Ich* is also the spoken effect of the mirror and its avatars on the Outside. The Other confers identity onto the *Ich*. The *Ich* is an object rather than a subject. The executive function of the *Ich* is compromised and dysfunctional. The neurotic *Ich* is simply lost in the world. The *Ich* is divorced from anchor in acuity and insight. Freud illuminates the constitutive blindness of the neurotic. Desire is obscured in the subject's unconscious only to emerge in the shock and awe of the skewed detail in everyday life.

The psychotic suffers a certainty of knowledge. Schizoid certitude deviates from the generalized doubt of the neurotic. Psychotic certainty is the necessary correlate to paranoid schizophrenia. The crazy person's delusions and hallucinations are understood by the schizoid as exact and real. The neurotic's doubt in the symptomatic hiccups of the signifying chain is transposed into the psychotic's certainty of delusions and hallucinations. The schizoid evinces pathological ontological conviction in what is — which precisely is. Neurotic and psychotic epistemology retards progressive thinking, being, and living in the world. Reason — blind and dysfunctional or certain and deranged — is a problem rather than a solution.

The pervert's epistemological situation is complicated because of the mode of negation of the lost and the found in *Verleugnung*. The simultaneity of acknowledgment and denial in the pervert's psychosexual economy integrates the mutually exclusive — unconscious/conscious, latent/manifest, here/there, right/wrong, negation/ return, and so on — as parallactically overlapped in a superpositional simultaneity. The pervert's knowledge is both recognized and dismissed at once. A static account of the pervert's knowledge cannot be determined in presence. Perversely, the metaphysics of presence (Being, is) cannot be sustained. Perverse textualization of the schizoid's Real writes Unreason within a metaphysics of quasi-presence. The pervert writes Being and

Nothingness, is and is not, presence and absence, and *ici et ailleurs*. The pervert's *écriture* is both sophisticated and loony. Perverse text is potentially incoherent. The reader is lost in traces of the trace.

The pervert's knowledge is neither static nor present. The pervert's epistemology isolates neither subject nor object. The pervert is not troubled by knowledge. Fetishistic strategy mobilizes the both/and economy of mutual inclusion. Perverse technique celebrates denial and acknowledgment. Perversion is a scheme which avoids knowledge (Being, as such, *qua*, by definition, and *il y a*) altogether. The pervert's passion scripts the Unreason of the schizoid and the Madness of Order of $-ism. The pervert desperately wants to know the Reason that the world does not work. He explicates the fundamental flaws in the system to ordinary neurotics whose daftness obscures the truth of the solar system. An excess in perverse knowledge escapes articulation. Knowledge is itself Something is Missing. The neurotic wills a mastery of knowledge. The capitalist accumulates a debt of value. The pervert opens the parallactic gap against final totalization.

Deleuze's icy masochist suspends and imagines. The pervert structures knowledge in the delay of difference and deferral in Derrida's *différance*. The letter resists both departure and arrival. The signified is momentarily illuminated. But the process of this transcendence is quickly scuttled toward other signifiers. The pervert's knowledge of Unreason is a series of fluorescent flashes of insight and fast flickers of intuition. At best, the pervert's knowledge cannot be archived as a canon. Rather, the pervert's knowledge consists of a transient acumen in an ephemeral moment, in a word or a sentence, or in a chapter or a book. The neurotic weaves epistemological tales of historical grandeur and timeless truth. The schizoid screams delusions and hallucinations of a Real galaxy whose Other-Logic and raw form of madness cannot be assimilated to the worldly. But the knowledge of the pervert is neither the neurotic's canon nor the psychotic's certainty. The knowledge of the pervert is Other. This epistemology is both an interval and a relationship between what is and what is not. Perverse *episteme* is ambivalent, multivalent, doubled, and troubled. Essentially, perverse truth gestures toward the next gesticulation in the movement of the letter and its clandestine signified.

The three modalities of epistemology — neurotic, schizoid, and perverse — differently approach the latent content of truth. Perversion is the closest approximation to the absence of knowledge in the unconscious. The pervert's suspended and imaginative aesthetic toward the signified is the sensibility of the unconscious. The primary process performs the zigzag substitution of forms and contents of texts and images in the unconscious. Dream is structured by metaphor and its additions, subtractions, supplements, and losses. Dream achieves an aneconomic equilibrium in which trade and swap replace hierarchy and equivalence. The extraordinary ways that the unconscious processes handle division include: the conversion of either/or into both/and; the disruption of reference to causality and etiology; the combination of the mutually exclusive; the disregard for antinomy and contradiction; and the elevation of nonsense to the dignity of *das Ding*.[29] Considerations of representability are purposeful.

Wish and truth elude the censorship and erupt into the conscious because the primary process dexterously screens its truth in the manifest Unreason of the dream. Considerations of representation in dream approach the epistemological aesthetic of the pervert. The pervert uncovers the penis behind the bra. The pervert denudes the latent in the manifest. The pervert demonstrates the unexpected Sameness⁺ Difference⁺ of the otherwise opposed in any system. Half-said double-speak is precisely the representational talent of the primary process of the unconscious. Perverse *écriture* in the text of the Cs. is animated by the mechanisms of the primary process of the system of the Unc. Perverse text mimics the play and parody of the unconscious. The pervert writes the unconscious. The primary process is the stylist of the pervert's pen. The pervert's knowledge — such as it is — debunks its own proviso. The pervert teaches the unconscious to know. To know — but what? The pervert is the pedagogue of the unconscious. His lesson is a playful textuality which verses men, Women, and the rest of us in the virtue and grace of the horizon which is beyond the third-dimension of the unconscious. The pervert's signified — such as it is — is the horizon of the fourth-dimension after space engulfs time and the unconscious writes toward its wish.

Timeless Space

The unconscious is the Outside of knowledge. The space of the unconscious is also timeless. An exigent concern is the spatial architecture of the unconscious. The unconscious does not have a cortical or anatomical location in the body. The unconscious is the signifying chain in its work of substitution. But what are the design and layout — architectural space — of the unconscious? The integrants of this space are the latent wish, the talents of representation of the primary process, and the censorship of wish. Text and image are also part of the makeup of the unconscious space. But it remains a peculiarity that the architectonics of this space is mysterious and unthinkable. The space of the unconscious resists any metaphysics of presence. The basic coordination of the system — spatial movements — of texts and images in the primary process is inaccessible to analysis. There is no visual representation — diagram, chart, graph, or outline — of the unconscious and its machinations. The unconscious is structured like a language. But this formula simply defers another quandary. What is the (spatial) structure of language? Where is language?

In *Course in General Linguistics* (1917), Saussure presents a series of diagrams of first, the relationship between the signifier and the signified, and second, the relationship between signs.[30] These purposeless images indicate that the systems of the value of the signifier and the signification of the sign cannot be visualized. Words — material sounds and marks, and abstract ideas and thoughts — are neither visual nor spatial. Where are words? Where are sounds? Where are thoughts? The substances of the system are themselves retardant to an ontological inquiry of Being. It is no wonder that the structuralist view of language fundamentally destabilizes ontology. The bits and pieces of language are dislocated in any space whatsoever. Text and image are outside of (the) space (of the unconscious). Any visual and spatial map of the complexities of the system of the primary process is beyond spoken or written representation. The word is neither here nor there but — The unconscious is neither here nor there but — The spatiality of the unconscious is radically Other. The space of the unconscious is a different kind of space. What is a space which exceeds the map?

The question of time and the unconscious is thorny, especially because Freud does not articulate details about this extraordinary atemporality. First, the timelessness of the unconscious refers to its archivization of memory. The unconscious preserves mnemic traces of thought and affect. Unconsciously, man never forgets. The archive of experience is collected in the unconscious. But reserved where? The archive of the unconscious spatializes time. Memory is stockpiled in space. Past experiences in thought and affect are spatialized. The crucial dimension of this temporal compression and spatial displacement is the twist of time into the turn of space. The archives of time and the memories of history are transformed into the spatial shapes and visual forms of the unconscious. Unconsciously, the subject sees time in space. The second-dimension of time cannot be divided from the first-dimension of space.

This twisted incorporation of time into space implies that the Other-Space of the unconscious is a space in which time can be archived in order to be recalled and recollected. Spatialization of temporality makes time the subject and the object of displacement and condensation. The spatialization of time can evade the censor. The space of history erupts into manifest visibility. Successful interaction between the primary process and the dream-censor precipitates the visible advent of latent time in the manifest form of the symptom. The dream (*et al.*) is an illustration of time in space. The symptom is a vision of time. The psychoanalyst interprets time. The object of psychoanalytic exegesis is time. Symptom (is) time. Dream is an image of time. In essence, "what is" in the ontological Being of the symptom is the Becoming of time. The relationship between temporality and ontology in the unconscious is the animation of time-becoming-space. Ontology destructures Being in order to restructure Becoming. What is — is Becoming. The question is not the object of this Becoming. Rather, the issue is the Becoming *of* Becoming, and so on.

Becoming resets the ontological question from within/out the purview of the unconscious. Dream-Ontology poses the fundamental philosophical question of ontology — "What is?" — as Becoming. Heidegger's obsessive use of the word Being in his masterwork *Being and Time* (1923) belies the mistaken truth of his orientation toward ontology. *Da-sein* (being-there) who asks the question of the meaning of Being poses this question from the system of the Cs. The ego-system asks the question of Being from the Outside of time. Heidegger's *Dasein* asks the ontological question in the first-dimension of space, "What is?" The alternative ontological proposition is about Becoming (what is-ing) rather than about Being (what is).

My neologism of the Ing⁺ is crucial to an interpretation of unconscious ontology because it demonstrates that the Time of the Pervert (gerund-as-verb: ing-ing-) is the Becoming of the ontological question. Heidegger's mistake is to accept the counterintuitive classification of the gerund (Be-ing) as a noun. Properly, Being is Be-ing is Becoming is Becoming-ing, and so on. Paradoxically, the Time of the Pervert of the Ing⁺ is visible in the atemporality of the unconscious. The archive of time is spatialized. Time emerges in manifest form in the space of the symptom. Dream Becomes in time. Time manifests as the space of the colorful tableau of the dream. We dream in space, time. A dream is a moving, picture.

The primary process transforms time into space. The methods of metaphor and metonymy transcribe time into space, over time, in space. The first-dimension of space, the second-dimension of time, and the third-dimension of the unconscious simultaneously switch and swap for each other. The proviso of the unconscious is the Unreasonable overlap of space and time. Space (is) time. Space (Ing⁺) time. The third-dimension is the process of an *Eros* which sutures the splinters of the space and time of *Thanatos*. Parallactic overlap in space and time is the pervert's deconstructive fascination. Continuity and coincidence between space ($\supseteq$) time measure the deconstruction of every other binary opposition in the system, such as unconscious/conscious, latent/manifest, symptom/interpretation, and so on. The superpositional parallactic overlap of space and time Becoming each other realizes the pervert's clinical clairvoyance: that each is the other because none is itself in ~~Being~~.

The discovery is that there is no ontology in the unconscious. *Il n'y a pas.* The ontological question of "What is?" can only be posed from the system of the Cs. and its metaphysics of presence. But the ontological question of "What is-ing⁺?" can be posed in the primary process. The proper ontological question is of the meaning of *Becoming*. Becoming is the Time of the Pervert. Becoming is the name for the timelessness of the unconscious. The pervert's Becoming is atemporal because it neither begins nor ends. Perverse temporality neither starts nor stops. Strangely, Becoming *is*. Becoming is the transformation of the ontic nodes of objects in the world in presence. Becoming (is) Being. To reverse, the gerund is a noun. The ontological question of what is at the level of the Cs. should be properly reposed as the perverse inquiry about what is Becoming at the level of the Unc. How is this question of Becoming and Dream-Ontology to be answered? And, by whom? Is there a language of Becoming? Can Becoming only speak the language of Being? Must the signifier speak through the defiles of the sign? What is the word for the Becoming of materialities and abstractions, and signifiers and signifieds?

This image portrays the perverse sign (signifier) and its rupture of the metaphysics of presence of signification. The materiality (signifier) component of the sign constitutes itself *ex nihilo*. It establishes itself in an infinite distance from the ideality of the signified. The material abundance of the Real is centered in itself — as such — as a flat surface. The materiality of the signifier disrupts the signified as a component part of the sign. The communist abundance of the signifier twists itself around and toward any reference. The abundance of materiality abandons the restrictive economy of the sign (signified). The signifier materially expands in the absence of any standardization of value by the general equivalent. The materiality of the signifier outstrips the calculations and speculations of the general equivalent. The general equivalent (father, phallus, sign, currency) must posit an Other which is not yet subordinate to the standards of systematicity. This unmarked material Other is the differed and deferred Outside which can only return in an elusive and unsignified abundance of Real materiality.

Notes & Sketches —

No, Not Yet

Freud says that the unconscious is a space without negation. Negation is the organizational principle of the signifying chain of the system of the Cs. (the sign) and the central feature of the psychical structures of neurosis, psychosis, and perversion. The Saussurian version of *langue* makes negativity and difference the fundamental provisos of the articulation of materialities (sounds and images) and abstractions (ideas and thoughts). Any given signifier or signified is internal to every other signifier or signified. The generation of value is possible because of the differences and negativities in the exchanges between materialities and abstractions in the system. Saussure's version of the sign ultimately trumps his otherwise explosive version of value in the concept of the signifier. But the word is only marginally referenced by Saussure in his discussion of his otherwise primary concern with value. The emphasis of the discussion of value is the difference and negativity — comparison, contrast, and exchange — in the switcheroo between signifiers and signifieds.

Saussure defines the word as a "positive" entity in order to contrast it with the negativity and differentiality of the signifier and the signified.[31] The value of the signifier emerges in the play of differences and negations. The value of the signifier is animated by uneasy comparison, unstable contrast, and erratic exchange. In contrast, the signification of the sign is defined by the conventionalized security and fixed positivity of the everyday word. The disorganization of the basal structure of language in the signifier is negativity. The signifier is sheer negativity. The positivity of the word only emerges from the radical relationality of value. The positive unity of the word is the upshot of the play of the signifier. Positivity is strictly absent from the signifier and the foundation of *langue* in value. The positivity of the word is the conditional effect of pure negativity. An explosive negativity is the infrastructure of a conscious system of words with each object as positive and distinct in opposition to each other. The unconscious of language is the negativity of value. The system of the Cs. of language is the positivity of signification. *Langue* is split between foundation and effects, structure and symptoms, substratum and elements, and unconscious and conscious.

Psychoanalytically, the signifier is the latent content of language. The signifier is repressed as the unconscious of the system. The word is the manifest form of language. The word is the symptom of the signifier. My model splits but sutures the conscious/unconscious, sign/signifier, and signification/value binary oppositions. This framework illuminates the transformative relationships (dream-work or signifier-work) between the rudimentary unconscious essence of the system in the signifier, on the one hand, and the transposition of this negativity and differentiality into the symptom of the word in the system of the Cs., on the other hand. Why does *langue* repress the signifier into the unconscious? The threat of value to the order of the system is the subversion of coherence and legibility. The diacritical negativity of the signifier rends any stable and consistent signification unimaginable. The back-and-forth whack-a-mole of comparison and contrast in an open system of exchange in which new materialities (sounds and images) and abstractions (ideas and concepts) join other haphazardly and randomly selected signifiers and signifieds makes the emergence of the signified *qua* sign in signification inconceivable.

The silly relations, playful differences, and uncoordinated negativities spurn coalescence around and as a word. The signifier threatens the lifeblood of the sign. Value promises the subversion of communication. The basal foundation of the system of language is both its proviso and death. The system must repress the signifier into the unconscious of language. $-ism must coordinate meaning-making between positive units of words. At stake in the signifier is the simple prospect of speaking, writing, and listening. The dominance of the word defends against the end of language. The word protects itself against a system of value which is explosively indeterminate and undecidable.

The model of the unconscious/conscious of *langue* illuminates both the repression of the signifier and the primacy of the word. The system promotes the sign *qua* signifier as the constituent unit of the signifying chain. The sign *qua* signifier coordinates communication. The set of mechanisms by which this negation (of negation: difference and relationship) is achieved is three-fold. The psychoanalytic clinical structures posit three forms of negation: *Verdrängung* in neurosis; *Verwerfung* in schizophrenia; and *Verleugnung* in perversion. Neurotically, desire is a threat to the system of the Cs. This desire is repressed. This wish is repressed in the unconscious. Desire returns as a series of symptoms: dreams, slips, jokes, and the psychopathologies of everyday life. Psychotically, the signified is foreclosed in the Real. This Real returns to the symbolic in its radical destabilization in the rupture of the symptoms of delusions and hallucinations. The absence of the paternal function (or the *point de capiton*) ruins coherent representation. *Verwerfung* invites a series of loopy symbolizations which breaks the otherwise binary logic of the signifying chain.

Perversely, difference is disavowed. The origin of this *Verleugnung* is sexual difference. Disavowal acknowledges the phallocentric reality that man has a penis and Woman does not have a penis. But disavowal also simultaneously denies this difference. The superpositional both/and psychical orientation of the pervert is the consequence of this form of negation. The return of the disavowed in perversion is the disavowal of difference. Remarkably, the pervert experiences binary opposition as Sameness⁺. The various divisions in the system — unconscious/conscious and negation/return — are coincident and continuous. The return of the disavowed and the disavowed itself are a Sameness⁺ which is non-same and non-identical. The upshot of the perverse orientation toward the symbolic order is not that difference is Sameness⁺ but that Sameness⁺ is difference. The effect is the total split of reality and its return as the split *qua* itself. Certainly, perverse *Verleugnung*, schizoid *Verwerfung*, and neurotic *Verdrängung* are distinct modalities of the management of the symbolic order and the ontological facticity of difference. The negation of the signifier in the system Cs. must be explained as a specific modality of negation in a particular psychical structure. What is this psychical mechanism which negates the scaffold of the system — the signifier — and promotes its effect — the word — as the fundamental precept of the symbolic order?

The Praxis of the Radical Theory of Practice

Undoubtedly, the schizophrenic foreclosure of the signified — Signified/r — generates an absence. The lack returns from the Real to shake the symbolic order. I refer to this process as the Neurotic Foreclosure (*rejet névrotique*) of the Real and the return of this inconsistent gap in the destabilization of the symbolic. Negation is qualified as neurotic because the symbolic system is fantasmatically structured on the level of the Cs. $-ism is a series of binary oppositional pairs of self-same and self-identical words. The latent truth of Sameness⁺ (A ≠ A) is banished from the ego-society and foreclosed in the Real. The signifier of Sameness⁺ disrupts all systems of coherent semiosis. The mystery is the mechanism by which schizoid foreclosure manages to negate the signifier. In his essay, *Différance* (1967), Derrida describes a "force" or "desire" which recenters the play of the structure.[32] A similar intentional mechanism with *arche* and origin is the source of the repression of the signifier and the enforcement of binary opposition and the positive unity of the word. Derrida also makes the claim early in his career that a centerless structure represents the "unthinkable."[33] This argument is keenly unsatisfactory because it purports to explain the impossible by dint of its impossibility. The schizophrenia of the signifier is beyond the limit of thought. Man is limited to think the sign rather than the signifier, the word rather than the mark, the positive rather than the negative, and the identical rather than the different.

An indication of this impossibility is presented in Saussure's work on the distinction between theory and practice. The division between the signifier/signified as isolatable units of study is only a theoretical concern and prospect. The signifier is a theoretical principle which is essentially impractical. The signifier is only accessible in theory. In contrast, the word is a practical entity. We live and breathe in words. The sign is the essence of everyday practicality. The word is available as performance in everyday life. Theory is foreclosed by the system of the conscious. The theoretical signifier is exiled in the Real of the unconscious. Practice is the system of the sign. We speak and write the manifest form in the system of the Cs. of the word in practice. Expatriated, the latent form of the signifier seethes in the system of the Unc. in theory. Practice is conscious. Theory is unconscious. Philosophy is the latent truth of world. This philosophy is a threat to the system because it speculates the truth of the symbolic order.

The role of the Marxist Cultural Studies scholar is to invent the *Praxis* of this relationship between theory and practice, philosophy and world, latent and manifest, return and symptom, unconscious and conscious, and signifier and word. The thought of a Cultural Studies *Praxis* returns to Marx's *Thesis Eleven* (1845) and his plaint that: "Philosophers have hitherto only interpreted the world; the point is to change it."[34] In chapter eight, "Debt to Marx," I presented a semiotic theory of Marx's critique of capital. I claim that an excess materiality of the overlap of the signifier (materiality of sound and image) and the sign (combination of materiality and abstraction) generates a surplus body which cannot be (ac)counted (for) by the system of exchange. A return to Marx's *Praxis* in the context of a psychoanalytic interpretation of the signifying chain, on the one hand, and the Saussurian distinctions between theory/practice, signifier/sign, and value/signification, on the other hand, cracks the code of the perverse project to illuminate and transform the Madness of Order. Marx's *Praxis* unveils the Neurotic Foreclosure (*neurotische Ablehnung*) of the Real Signifier and its return as the rupture of the symbolic order.

Praxis is a transformative grasp of the foreclosure of the Real Signifier in the practice of the sign and its return as theory to the symbolic. The everyday practices of the word in writing and reading foreclose *différance* for the sake of coherence and intelligibility in communication. Practice negates the Real Signifier in order to coordinate the structure of signification of letters with the *arche* of departure and destination of writers with readers, speakers with listeners, and any either/or point of origin of enunciation. The threat of the value of the signifier and its diacritical play of difference and negativity is *arche*. Origin is the closed system of return and obligation between speaker and listener of speech, reader and writer of *écriture*, and any either/or binary order of points of start and stop, beginning and end, and genesis and finish. The endless play of the signifier in an open system ruptures any metaphysics of presence which would posit an "I" or a "you" as points of enunciation of speech-acts — and of any deed whatsoever. The unconscious of value radically unsettles the theory and practice of the doer. The signifier represents the Death of the Author. This death simultaneously massacres Western morality and its foundation in the willful agency and intentional choice of determinate and decidable subjects. The threat of unconscious value is the subject of desire, Judeo-Christian morality, and coherence of communication.

The work of the Cultural Studies scholar of *Praxis* is to study the overlap between the speculative philosophy of the unconscious signifier and the everyday procedures of the conscious sign. The Freudian model of the psyche separates conscious from unconscious, manifest from latent, return from desire, and secondary process from primary process. The generalized analytical translation between the binary organization of these oppositional pairs is the interpretation of the analyst. The purpose of psychoanalysis is to transcribe the conscious level of the manifest symptom into the unconscious dimension of the latent truth. Freud acknowledges the limits of analytic interpretation, and he admits that surplus semiosis exceeds analysis. But his practical approach to the analysand encourages the manifest signifier to return to the latent signified in the interpretation of the symptom and the retroactive (*Nachträglichkeit, après-coup*) specification of the truth. The patient assumes this Real truth of desire.

But the parallactic gap between the theory-signifier and the practice-sign generates an excess materiality or surplus signifier. This remainder cannot be assimilated into the psychoanalytic system of interpretation. A surplus of text and image — meaning-making — escapes the closure of the metaphysics of presence and the will of psychoanalytic interpretation in practice. The analytical mastery of the word *qua* translation of the signifier cannot close the gap between signified and signifier, latent and manifest, unconscious and conscious, return and symptom, material and ideal, and value and signification. The hermeneutic fantasy of a speculative and mirrored relationship between unconscious and conscious is broken by the excess of text and image, and marks and pictures. These representations elude the private property capitalist possession of the Outside by the system of the Inside. On which side of the series of semiotic oppositions (value/signification, signifier/ sign, and theory/practice) and psychoanalytic divisions (unconscious/conscious, latent/manifest, and return/ symptom) does the excess of materiality, the surplus of picture, the remainder of text, and the abundance of the Real Signifier seethe with the intentions of a rupture of the orderly hierarchy of object and subject?

The Cultural Studies scholar notes the key paradox in the scaffold of Marx's *Thesis Eleven* (1845). The antinomy is the overlap of theory and practice, and interpretation and revolution. This parallax indicates that materialist *Praxis* unveils an excess of theory. The theory of Marxist Cultural Studies mobilizes the signifier and the signified as distinct units in differential and negative relations of comparison, contrast, and exchange. My practice involves the sign (signifier and signified, in combination) as a positive entity in syntagmatic and paradigmatic relations with other words in the system. The two modalities of *Praxis* are a bourgeois Practice of Theory and a radical Theory of Practice. The bourgeois Practice of Theory entails the reduction of the signifier to the sign. A slippery excess of abstract philosophical speculation originates from such a practice (sign and signification) of theory (signifier/signified and value). The Practice of Theory is philosophy: "Philosophers have hitherto only interpreted the world."

In contrast, a radical Theory of Practice promises the elevation of the sign to the signifier. A revolutionary surplus of materialist transformative practice manifests from such a theory (signifier/signified and value) of practice (sign and signification). Rather than the Continental Philosophy of the Practice of Theory and its speculative abstractions, the Cultural Studies Theory of Practice invites materialist political transformation: "The point is to change it." Revolutionary transformation is the consequence of the excess of materiality in psychoanalytical interpretation. This interpretation otherwise sustains the binary logic of the psychoanalytic system. The point is to — liberate the materiality of the practice of Marxist dialectical materialism from the abstraction of theory. The point is to — exchange the unconscious/conscious (and so on) division with an aperture toward a materialist Other. The point is to — return the signifier to the conscious system. The point is to — substitute value for signification. The point is to — return Madness to Order. The point is to — free the materialism of earth from the abstraction of world. The point of Cultural Studies is to — not interpret change. The point of Cultural Studies is to — *change interpretation*. The object of this critique is not merely a discrete set of interpretations; rather, the target for the Cultural Studies scholar is the apparatus of (the end of) interpretation itself. This apparatus is rebuilt under the mistress signifier of the Pervert-Schizoid-Woman in this book.

Figure 11.5 The Return of the Signifier

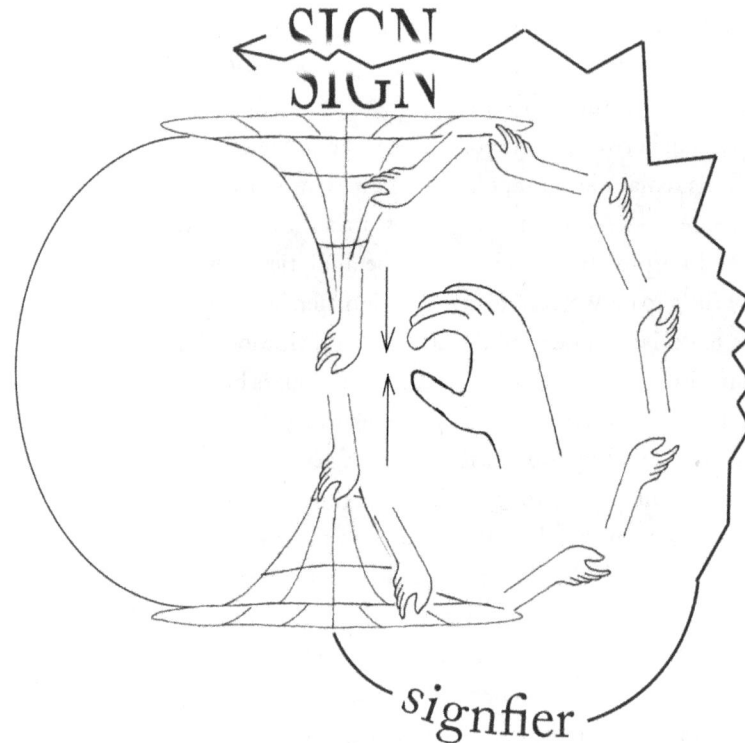

This image shows the peculiar *Trieb* (as opposed to the lazy *désir*) of the Pervert-Schizoid-Woman and her encirclement around a spatially interrupted and temporally delayed — difference and deferral in *différance* — object of the drive. The gestures of the *Praxis* of speech and writing of the Pervert-Schizoid-Woman and her symbolization of the Real mobilize the theoretical signifier in order to traverse the (*a*)sexual center of the system and its excess materiality. The finite signified of conceptuality and abstraction cannot outstrip and overwrite the sheer abundance of the materiality and physicality of the signifier. The return of the primacy of the signifier deconstructs the sign — the distinction and opposition between material signifier and abstract signified, in theory. In effect, the return of the signifier over the sign in the traversal of the Pervert-Schizoid-Woman and her insistent but inadequate symbolization of the Real in *Praxis* fundamentally disturbs the oppositions between conscious/unconscious, manifest/latent, symptom/truth, and so on. The return of the signifier in the encircled crisscross of the traversal of the Pervert-Schizoid-Woman illuminates the architectonic Sameness[+] in each instant of difference and deferral. The distinctions of oppositional pairs in the system of the sign yield to the differential negativity — Positivity — of the structure of the signifier whose series of identities and differences returns to the Real of the Same[+] space and time. This return of and as the Real is the force of the brute materiality of the signifier above the inadequate conceptuality of the signified. The excess materiality that cannot be signified returns as the fodder — signifier — for the endless effort of the *Trieb* of *Praxis* to symbolize the Real resistance to signification and the economy of the sign.

Notes & Sketches —

No No, "Yes, Yes"

Freud's cryptic view of the unconscious promises the transcendence of epistemology and the suspension of temporality. The other peculiar aspect of the unconscious is the sheer nonexistence of negation. It is difficult to square the negation of negation — what Hegel names the *Aufhebung* — because of the structure of *langue* and the (dis)coordination of the signifier and its indeterminate and undecidable value. My psychoanalytic reading of semiology maps the split between the signifier (value) and the word (signification) onto the division between the unconscious and the system of the Cs. The conscious dimension of everyday conversation is structured by the practical speech-acts of signs and words. Man's everyday speech is coordinated by the positive entity of the sign whose internal consistency makes it essential and meaningful unto itself. This positivity is underlayed by the radical negativity of the signifier and signified in diacritical play.

Saussure cannot explain the mechanism by which the play of materiality and abstraction in an open system of indetermination and undecidability is — somehow — coordinated into binary oppositional pairs of internally consistent positive words. The best explanation that Saussure provides for this magical mastery of play by opposition is his emphasis on arbitrariness and conventionality. Saussure explains that the link between the signifier (sound and image) and the signified (concept and abstraction) is purely arbitrary. There is no necessary — divine or natural — relationship between a particular sound and a specific idea. The link between arbitrary materiality and arbitrary conceptuality is convention. This convention is the contingent sociohistorical agreement by the speakers of language to specific joints between signifiers and signifieds.

This conventionalized hinge between the arbitrary materiality of the sound-image of the signifier, on the one hand, and the arbitrary abstraction of the thought of the signified, on the other hand, is unified in the composite of the positive entity of the sign. The word is the effect of the conventionalization of arbitrariness. Saussure notes two consequences of this arbitrary conventionality: first, there is no necessity for the sign to function as itself as self-same and self-identical because any word could always be otherwise than itself; and second, there is no reason for the sign to be transformed from its constitutive joint between sound and idea because the limit is based on arbitrariness. The system of *langue* is deeply conservative. The unconscious galaxy of value and the signifier is free and open, and playful and risky. In contrast, the conscious universe of signification and the word is rigid and closed, and serious and reactionary. The pervert wills the return of the signifier to the system of the Cs. The task is to emancipate the arbitrary from the conventional, and to free the playful from the disciplinary.

BECOMING-PRAXIS

This book discusses the concept of *Praxis* in a variety of forms. My work deploys the word *Praxis* as defined by four distinct but overlapped purposes: first, *Praxis* is the symbolization of the Real, or the written and the spoken of the inarticulable; second, *Praxis* is the relationship between *Objekt* and *Trieb*, or the encirclement of text around the object; third, *Praxis* is the Theory of Practice, or the excess in the signifier of materiality; and fourth, *Praxis* is the heir to Marx's *Thesis Eleven* (1845), or the overlap of theory and practice, and philosophy and activism, in politics. These four modalities of *Praxis* indicate that the word is multivalent. The word *Praxis* refers to a distinct but overlapped series of methodologies which concerns text, desire, materialism, and politics. The endeavor to determine and clarify *Praxis* is its own complex *Praxis*.

The first theory of *Praxis* that I note is the symbolization of the Real. *Praxis qua* articulation of the resistant text is critical for my purposes. The impossibility of the spoken and the written underscores the impediment of letters and alphabets to representation of the center (*arche* and origin) of the system. The *function* of the structure is the excluded center of the system which cannot be written or spoken in the language of $-ism. This constructed essence *sous rature* of the occluded center of the system is the Real which returns to the same place of defiance of and obstruction to textualization. The Real is the X around which *Praxis* encircles in its *Trieb* to write and speak the impossibility of a representation of the symbolic order and its coordination by the excluded function. $-ism is a series of combinatory binary oppositions. *Langue* arranges the order of these pairs in a systemic design in accordance with duality and polarity. Any disruption of the binarism of this positive system of words unsettles the structure. Neurotic existence is arranged by binary opposition and the hierachization of (dis)privilege. But the Real X of the system is in excess of the organizational coordination of the structure. The excluded function returns to destabilize the symbolic order. This surplus of the *Trieb* cannot be incorporated into this system. The Signified/r is the inarticulable nodal point of the differences and deferrals — *différance* — of the framework of meaning-making in the edifice of the Western system. The Unreasonable coincidental overlap — Sameness⁺ — of the Real Symbolic is an effect of the extimately situated Real. This absolutely unsymbolizable Real is positioned as the resistant center of the symbolic order. *Praxis* in *Trieb* strives to reveal — write and speak — this Real Symbolic *qua* the object. The *désir* (*Trieb*) is obstructed by the Signified/r. The inarticulability of the excluded central function of the structure opens the fissure between the *Trieb* and its *Objekt*. This theory of *Praxis* is decisive for the pervert's project to render the madman's Unreason a form of Reason for the prosaic neurotic. The symbolization of the Real *perverts the neurotic* in order to unsettle the apparatus of lazy repressions and returns. *Trieb* is the calm frenzy to textualize the wholly other of the system in its constructed essence.

The second theory of *Praxis* that I note is the relationship between *Trieb* and its object. Idiotic masculine *jouissance* enjoys the petty capture and loss of its object. The stupidity of the cycle of law/transgression is internal to this neurotic dynamic. The sequence of rule/rebellion and order/infraction compulsively repeats. The neurotic forever parrots this arrangement of the seizure and distraint of its *objet*. Alternatively, the feminine Other *jouissance* displaces the idiot's cycle of rule/rebellion with the intensive erotic delays of the beyond of the idle homeostasis of the pleasure principle. The pervert engages the masochistic edge of courtly love in order to differ and defer — *différance* — the object in *Trieb*. This *Trieb* encircles its unsymbolizable *objet* in perpetuity. The *Praxis* of *Trieb* suffers and enjoys the painful but pleasurable protraction of the missed encounter between the subject and its *Objekt*. The *Praxis* of *Trieb* configures a perverse (*a*)sexuality. This (*a*)sexuality is structured by the inversion of pleasure and the beyond of the principle of ordinary enjoyment. The pleasure principle posits the regulation of tension in the orga(ni)sm. A communist queer (*a*)sexuality enjoys the beyond of the principle. Queerness inverts the relationship between the otherwise unpleasurable tension and pleasurable release of this intensity of the pleasure principle. Femininely, the object resists capture in the clutches of desire. The pervert delays approach toward (away from) the object in the masochistic edge of courtly love. The Woman achieves the Other orgasm. This Other *jouissance* is not structured by the phallocentric male orgasm and ejaculation. The *Praxis* of *Trieb* showcases a communist queer (*a*)sexual modality of the approach toward (away from) the object. This modality of *Praxis* is critical to my project because it inspires a theory of perverse (*a*)sexuality. This version of *Praxis* also illuminates the Signified/r structure of infinite semiosis. *Praxis* indicates the madness of the orchestration of meaning-making in *langue*. This *Praxis* in *langue* of the signifier — against the sign — highlights dysfunctions of private property and scarcity in capitalism, and of gender and sexual relationships in patriarchy.

The third theory of *Praxis* that I note is the Theory of Practice. A Marxist Theory of Practice underscores the generation of an excess materialist signifier in proletarian theory, practice, and politics. Marx faintly conceives of *Praxis* as the overlap between theory — philosophy, abstraction, and speculation — and practice — activism, politics, and concreteness. A deconstructive Marxism maps the Saussurian distinctions among signifier, signified, and sign onto the gap between theory and practice in Marxist politics. The signifier is the material sound or image in the wave or mark. The signified is the abstract idea or concept in the calculation or hypothesis. Crucially, Saussure claims that the signifier and the signified — materiality and abstraction, sound and image, and wave and mark — can only be separated and divided in theory. Philosophically, the material signifier and the abstract signified can be divided in a theoretical elucidation. But the practice that we live and breathe forces the hinge of the material and the abstract, and the signifier and the signified, to be joined as the sign or word. A division of materiality and abstraction is possible in philosophy. But everyday practice generates and deploys the word. My point is that a deconstructive Marxism must overlap the two sides of the Marxist *Praxis* division between theory and practice, on the one hand, and the Saussurian aperture and closure between the signifier/signified and the sign, on the other hand. The consequence of this overlap in deconstructive Marxism is a surplus of the material signifier. The excess body and physics cannot be assimilated into the capitalist, linguistic, or sexual systems. This version of a materialist *Praxis* of the surplus signifier of the Theory of Practice is decisive for my project. Marxist *Praxis* indicates a substrate of materialism in the system. This excess ruptures the speculations and abstractions of private property in capitalism. The surplus of the signifier upsets the word in *langue*. The extra signifier destabilizes sexual difference in patriarchy. The surplus body of *Praxis* is the bone in the throat of $-ism. The general equivalent of comparisons and contrasts of abstract exchange is ruptured by a materiality which cannot be contained by speculation and calculation.

The fourth theory of *Praxis* that I note is the classic script from Marx's *Thesis Eleven* (1845): "In various ways, the philosophers have always interpreted the world; the point is to change it."[35] This eminent ditty is considered the *arche* of Marx's principle of the relationship between theory and practice. This version of *Praxis* inspired such politicized revolutionaries as Antonio Gramsci and his figure of the so-called organic intellectual. This form of *Praxis* also animated the origins of Cultural Studies in the Birmingham School of the study of the culture of the working class. *Praxis* is purposeful to my project. The concept portends the revolutionary potential of the overlap between theory and practice. *Praxis* indicates the relationship between philosophy and speculation, on the one hand, and activism and concreteness, on the other hand. Marx's rumpus is simply lovely. The clarity of Marx's summons for a *denouement* between philosophy and activism in politics is a refreshingly utopic vision of the significance of study to activity. Marx's *Praxis* illuminates the substantive relationship of scholarship to its world.

But now I want to introduce another modality of *Praxis* (*P*) in this study. This *Praxis* is defined as the destined thinking, being, and living of the Pervert-Schizoid-Woman in the future of the Spirit of the System. I articulate this novel *Praxis* (*P*) as the Communist Unconscious of *P* and its articulation of selfhood and sociality. This theory of subjectivity and objectivity will transcend the aporias that I have outlined in the systems of language, finance, and sexuality. The theory of the Communist Unconscious elaborates a Marxist primary process and its distribution of the surplus materiality of the system. But the *P* of the Communist Unconscious is also a radical subject and structure of thinking, being, and living. This *Praxis* is at the outskirts of the extant system of the symbolic order. This book massively inlays the systems of language, finance, and sexuality in $-ism. The project does so in order to situate an original and inventive reimagination of the possibilities of the *tout autre*. The *P* of the Communist Unconscious is a theoretical and practical — *Praxis* — intervention in the prospects for anti-$-istic care of the self and society. This fifth version of *P* supplements the other four modalities of *Praxis*: first, *Praxis* is the symbolization of the Real, or the written and the spoken of the inarticulable; second, *Praxis* is the relationship between *Objekt* and *Trieb*, or the encirclement of text around the object; third, *Praxis* is the Theory of Practice, or the excess in the signifier of materiality; and fourth, *Praxis* is the heir to Marx's *Thesis Eleven* (1845), or the overlap of theory and practice, and philosophy and activism, in politics. *Praxis* (P) will become the thinking, being, and living of the fourth-dimension of the Communist Unconscious in the arrival of the Pervert-Schizoid-Woman and the Spirit of the System.

The perverse technique of *Praxis* transforms the Practice of Theory (excess signified and speculation) in Continental Philosophy into the Theory of Practice (surplus signifier and body) in Cultural Studies. The purpose of this transition from Continental Philosophy to Cultural Studies — from excess calculation to surplus physics — is to detach the arbitrarily conventionalized relationships between signifiers and signifieds. The disengagement of materiality from abstraction is not only the will of *Trieb* and its aim/less wander up and down the differences and deferrals of *différance*. This endeavor to uncouple sound and mark from concept and idea is also the labor of the dream-work. Displacement and condensation rupture the naturalized relationship between material signifier and abstract signified. The text of a dream can bypass the dream-censor (ideal, superego, and society) because it slackens the joints between pictures and meaning, and between texts and code. The dream-work rearranges convention in order to unleash latent desire into the field of the system of the Cs. Desire is only visible as arbitrary. Convention represses wish.

The unconscious primary process is the field of the displacements and condensations which unhinge the signifier from the signified. This dissociation demonstrates the transition from the philosophical Practice of Theory to the radical Theory of Practice — or *Praxis*. The Theory of Practice returns to this elaboration of the sign *qua* signifier. The unconscious of value must be transposed into the conscious of signification in order to unveil the truth of the signifier in the ego-society system. I focus on the excess materiality in *Praxis* and the translations between conscious/unconscious and secondary/primary. This transmutation intends to indicate that speculation and abstraction (what capitalists refer to as "exchange-value") cannot analytically overwrite the abundance of potential meaning-making in the text and image in the formation of the symptom. The dream exceeds its interpretation. The unassimilable leftover indicates that the signifier overwrites the sign. *Contra* Saussure, value trumps signification. The radical foundation of the system structures its elements. The word is at the mercy of negation and difference. The signifier is sovereign.

The issue of negation and affirmation is made more complicated by the theorization of a materialist Theory of Practice or *Praxis*. The division unconscious/conscious is unsettled by the surplus unconscious signifier. This signifier ruptures the conscious word. The explosion of the signifier in the conscious chain of discourse indicates an absence of negation — no "No!" — in the unconscious. A first interpretation of the affirmation of the unconscious against the father's "No!" is that the unconscious only says "yes." Desire says "yes." Wish says "yes." Truth says "yes." Desire is a latent thought whose expression is obscured by the dream-work of the negative and differential play of displacement and condensation. The dream-work skews the latent thought into the manifest form. The manifest representation presents as the symptom in the ego and society. The symptom of *langue* is a set of disturbances in the manifestation of words and binary oppositional combinations of signs. Any hiccup in the system of semantics and syntax on the level of the Cs. indicates a symptomatic manifestation of the latent truth of the excess materiality of the signifier and the coordination of value in the Unc. Labor cannot be assimilated into the frenzied will to capitalist accumulation. Work is the surplus which shatters the capitalist system of scarcity (castration) and the supply/demand dynamics of the exchange economy of dollars and coins. Surplus material labor is the limit of capitalism. Excess use-value is the check on the *finite infinity* or *infinite finity* of capitalist profit making. The dollar and the coin are stripped of their value by the productivity of the signifier. The signifier is the labor of the surplus. The worker is the signifier. The body is the source of value.

Word, Without Affect

Freud's brief metapsychological paper, "On Negation" (1925), outlines the relationship between negation and thought. Unexpectedly, negation is a modality of speech by which the ego acknowledges the content of the negation. The Cs. says "No!" at the same time as it says "yes." Generalized negation is deeply perverse. The acknowledgement of the content of the desire at the same time as the denial of this same content mimes the both/and structure of the pervert's disavowal. Freud's work on negation upsets any easy division between ego/other, conscious/unconscious, manifest/latent, and truth/symptom. In a revelatory passage, Freud writes,

> The content of a repressed idea of thought can get through to consciousness, then, on condition that it is negated. Negation is a way of acknowledging the repressed, indeed it amounts to a lifting of the repression, although not, of course, an acceptance of what is repressed.[36]

Freud gestures toward a crucial distinction between the affective and ideational components of unconscious content. The intellectual function of judgment can recognize the abstract signification of repressed content in the process of negation: "No!" However, this form of negative acknowledgment sustains the repression because it does not engage with the affective dimension of the disagreeable idea.

A repressed content is split into a duality between body/mind and material/abstraction. The intellectual faculty of judgment mindfully abstracts the truth of desire in the system of the Cs. Judgment "acknowledges" the wish and "lifts" the repression. But this psychical gesture is not coincident with an "acceptance" of the object of the repressed. The repressed is both material and abstract, and both signifier and signified. But the word of unconscious truth is perversely split into ideational content and affective emotion by the intellectual function and generalized negation of everyday neurotic orientation toward a "disagreeable idea." This uncomfortable speculation is situated in a liminal zone between conscious and unconscious.[37] In the dream-book (1900), Freud describes the latent content of the unconscious as a "disagreeable thought."

A proper interpretation of the unconscious is that it is a timeless space of an affect ("disagreeable") and idea ("thought"). Freud argues that everyday intellectual judgment negates (affirms) an idea of the thought. This double-gesture lifts the repression but does not accept the latent content. The truthful idea is clarified but the emotive component of it is suspended in abeyance. An emotional embrace — this desire is affectively mine — of the thought is the proviso of an acceptance of the wish and its assumption *qua* the truth of the desire of the subject. The ego-function splits affect/idea. The joint between materiality and abstraction is suspended. The intellectual attitude only achieves simultaneous acceptance and dismissal with the ideational content of desire. The ego-system delays the affect and the emotion, and the material and the body, from the process of generalized negation. Abstractions and speculations of philosophy and its intellectual judgments expel the materiality of tears and joys from the negative appearance of the latent content. The effect of the philosophical orientation is two-fold: first, the sign is split into materiality/abstraction, signifier/signified, value/signification, and theory/practice from its otherwise unity in the word; and second, the materiality of the signifier of affect and emotion is suspended as an excess and surplus of an improper remainder. The division of the word in Continental Philosophy smashes the positive unity of the word.

This invites the diacritical logic of the signifier and value into the system of the Cs. The ego-system is otherwise structured as a series of binary oppositions in signification. The speculation of the executive function of judgment returns the unconscious to the system of the Cs. This is the reason that Freud can say that negation "lifts" the repression — desire is, as such, and Being — but does not "accept" the truth. The material affective component of the signifier is delayed. The dry theoretical judgment of the philosopher has "always interpreted the world." The hot *Praxis*tical pervert rises to the challenge of "the point is to change it." The pervert assumes the affective dimension of desire, and she returns truth to the playful signifier. The signifier otherwise escapes from the unconscious and disrupts the system of $-ism and its defenses and codes against truth. The trick is to reimagine negation *qua* affirmation and to resituate *Thanatos qua Eros*.

Originary Sexual Difference

My work is to open the border between self and other and the gap between inside and outside that Freud mentions in both *Beyond the Pleasure Principle* (1920), with reference to the traumatic neurosis of the Great War, and in "On Negation" (1925), with reference to the affirmation of the life drive and the negation of the death instinct. The explicit distinction between inside/outside — ego/other — is raised in "On Negation" (1925) in Freud's remarks about the unaccountable genealogical-historicist development of the humanist $-istic border between inside and outside, and between self and other. Freud simply remarks that,

> We see that, once again, it is a question of inside and outside. That which is non-real, merely imagined, subjective, exists only on the inside; other things, real things, are also there on the outside.[38]

This issue of inside/outside is crucial because it is not an originary state of the organization of man. A few lines below this passage, Freud writes: "The opposition between subjective and objective does not exist from the start."[39] The profundity of this thesis should not be underestimated. The existence of the infant in his Real presymbolic polymorphous perversity is an awkward liminal space between subject and object, and between you and me. Infancy experiences the prelapsarian environs before the offspring's insertion into the system of signs and the repressions of desire in the prosaic galaxy of adult normativity.

The offspring's transition from the indistinct blur of his pink lips and his mother's nipple to the anxious protection of his penis against loss is coordinated by the vicissitudes of the castration complex and the system of Oedipus and identification with the ideal of the father.[40] Lacan's famous "Mirror Stage" (1949) presents the scene of the emergence of otherness in the offspring's psychical economy.[41] His Majesty the Baby experiences an unbound and indistinct spatiality of *l'homme-lette*. The offspring's ex-istence spreads over the entirety of the globe. He is cut down to size when he gazes at the mirror image of himself. He experiences an idealized and ideological version of himself as the *Gestalt* subject of humanism. This apparatus of individuality is total, whole, complete, perfect, unified, and so on. Both Freud and Lacan view the fundamental division between subject and object — I/you and self/other — as absent at the origin. Originary experience is strictly Deleuzean.

Man is born as a series of discontinuous fragments of part-objects in the absence of division and split. Man lives in a global *mise-en-scène* without the separation of inside and outside. The acutely traumatic incursion of the inside by the outside is the basal experience of the Western individual. The consequences of the appearance of difference in the offspring's world cannot be overestimated. The ardent significance of difference is such that it is mostly unnoticed. The first code of the universe is identity/difference, and so on. Freud thematizes the discovery of difference as the phallocentric penis/not-penis coordination of sexual difference. But difference is crucial to the coordination of all binary pairs of identity: black/white, gay/straight, abled/disabled, Christian/Jew, and so on. The wager of psychoanalysis is that the first and foremost experience of the trauma of difference is sexual. Evidence: the near epic dysfunction of the sexual life of *Homo sapiens*.

Affect

A truism of grammatology is the potentiality of a happy dissolution of all borders between words and objects. The architecture of the signifying chain is the comparison and contrast in exchange of indeterminate and undecidable materialities and abstractions. The scaffold of *langue* is simply: every word is the same word of Sameness⁺. A structuralist perspective understands any division as theoretically suspicious and practically reversible. But the system of the Cs. coordinates the unities of signifiers and signifieds into the positive units of binary oppositions and the divisions between penis/not-penis, white/not-white, and so on. The eruption of a surplus materiality of the signifier in the ego-society ruptures the smooth operation of psychoanalytic interpretation and, by extension, abstraction and speculation *tout court*.

The nefarious modality of $-istic thinking, being, and living in (or out of) *Praxis* is the generalized intellectual function of negation in philosophy. Negation splits the bodily and affective materiality of the signifier from the speculative and abstract thought of the sign. $-ism understands, but it does not feel. Man speculates about *P* and its value and significance. Man abstracts from *Praxis* and its interests and duties. Man thinks about *P* and its possibilities and breakdowns. These intellectual orientations toward affect privilege the sign above the signifier, the mind above the body, thought above affect, conscious above unconscious, manifest above latent, and an inadequate theoretical practice above the play of ideas and feelings in the Theory of Practice. Intellectual negation and judgment overwrite the Real of the radical pervert with the $-ism of the bourgeois philosopher.

The system represses affect because its unassimilability to the binary codes of the system makes it a threat to the entirety of the order of the world. Affect returns to the galaxy as an obscure symptom. The symptoms of the culture are an unhappy succession of dysfunctions and dislikes. The outrageous sickness of Western civilization is the scarred hopes and charred glass of the symptomatic returns of affect and their obfuscation as an incoherent series of codes of Reason. Psychoanalytically, the symptom is configured as a bi-level metaphor in which the manifest appears in the obscure and cranky form of the symptom or connotative schema. The manifest nightmare of the twentieth-century and its outrageous hate and violence belies the latent truth or denotative dimension. Any witness of the world is of violence and hatred. But the wager of Freud's hermeneutics of suspicion in psychoanalysis is that violence and hatred are screens for the Other. Metaphorically, violence and hatred are like — What we see in the world is not what we see.

The risk of psychoanalysis is to translate the world of $-ism and its mass horrors and everyday cruelties into the unexpected and sad truth of the latent content of affect. Freud's model of metaphor accounts for the deviation of the manifest and the latent. But Freud's systematization of his theory tends toward particular claims about specific patients. Later in his work, such as in in *Civilization and its Discontents* (1930), Freud outlines a theory of civilization in which the world is arraigned as the source of the repression of unconscious desire. But Freud's stance is that the human is essentially hateful and violent. Freud's pessimistic wager is that civilization is ambivalently necessary in order to protect man and world from man himself — despite the manifest symptoms which appear in the wake of the demands of the surrounds.[42] Sublimation is the proper triangulation of instinct and symptom.

The predictable absence in Freud's theory is an etiology of man's instinctual hatred and violence. Freud's emphasis in his later so-called sociological work is on the constitutional (genetic and natural, divine and Spiritual) atrocity of the all too human. This is the reason that Freudian psychoanalysis finally emphasizes law above love, and the ego above the id. Freud's assumption that man is essentially rubbish steers his work toward mechanisms by which civilization can be protected from a Hobbesian state of nature. However, Freud's practice as a psychoanalyst seeks to relieve the patient's symptom through a technique which enables the analysand to approach her repressed truth and assume it as her own.

The reason that intellectual judgment is a defense is that it merely "lifts" the content in the process of simultaneously acknowledging and denying the strict thought of repression. The other side of psychoanalytic practice must encourage the patient to assume the affect of this content. Freud refers to this work as catharsis. Man's nature is essentially monstrous. But is a civilized superegoic repression the proviso for the survival of man and world — $-ism — however deplorable the appearance of the symptoms of screened truth? Or is *Homo sapiens* a redeemable animal?

Natural Man

The break between Freud and Lacan is precisely at the juncture of the state of nature of man. Freud emphasizes law and order even as he encourages individual analysands to liberate the unconscious. Freud's dark view of humanity in the myth of the murder of the primal father (1913) and in the story of the murderous intentions of the male junior in the Oedipus complex (1920s) rends law and order — superegoic repression — man's protection from himself. Lacan's view of the state of nature of man is more optimistic. The reason for this is not a *naïve* Panglossian optimism about man and his current environs under late capitalist exploitation and phallocentric patriarchy. Lacan cannot articulate a set of reasons for an optimistic view of the potentiality of man. Lacan's orientation is a wager for man in contrast to Freud's bet against man. Like Lacan, Freud beseeches the liberation of unconscious wishes and the resolution of unconscious conflicts. But Freud's career is notable for its deeply negative view of man.

Lacan's view of the essential potentiality of man is articulated in his vision of desire, drive, and sublimation as it is outlined in the *Seminar* on the ethics of psychoanalysis (1956-57). Toward the end of the text, Lacan presents an entreaty: "Last Judgment: Have you acted in conformity with the desire that is in you?"[43] The simplicity of this articulation belies the radical consequences of his statement. The ethics of psychoanalysis is not to repress desire but to liberate wish. Ethics is an emancipation of truth. The ethical life is the liberation of wishes and truths which are otherwise repressed into the unconscious by the strictures of culture. Immorality is properly defined as repression. The effect of repression is evil. The hatred and violence of man are the consequence of the disruption of free libido and prodigal life. Freud discerns man's essentially sick world as the necessary defense against man's inherently violent instincts. Lacan wagers that man's potentially ethical life is the promise of an emancipation of man's repressed desires. Freud cites law for the protection of civilization. Lacan embraces love as the promise of psychoanalysis.

At the close of the *Seminar* on the ethics of psychoanalysis (1956-57), Lacan writes: "The important thing is not knowing whether man is good or bad in the beginning; the important thing is what will transpire once the book has been eaten."[44] This passage suspends the unanswerable. What happens at the ends of good and evil? The book is eaten, and man liberates desire. Man does not give way on his desire. Man encounters and engages his *objet petit a*. The critical and insolvable dimension of this scene is the encounter and engagement. How does man treat his object of desire? What is the essential relationship between subject and object at the ends of the delay of their *rendezvous*? The matter is of the joint of affect and thought, and the hinge between emotion and idea. The affective dimension of desire must be properly outlined. The ideational framework of desire must be adequately diagrammed. Lacan puts any definitive answer to these hopeful questions in abeyance. Lacan says: "The question is: what happens after the book has been eaten?"

The image of eating the book represents an inexorable confusion of the proper (*le propre*) of subject and object. A book is read; broccoli is eaten. To eat the book is to improperly encounter and engage the *objet petit a*. There is an afterward to good and evil and the responsibility for Irma's pains. The self and the other engage with each other in the Outside of the codes and norms of the diseases of Western civilization. Man eats the book, and he loves his object differently. Affect will be different after repression. We have yet to properly feel even as we improperly think. The precedent part of the passage about the goodness or the evilness of the book establishes the suspension of the future. Freud pessimistically approaches man's instincts and the final necessity to constrain them with law. Lacan optimistically wagers that man is good. But he also dismisses the importance of such a query. Lacan tends toward revolutionary love — *Eros* above *Thanatos* — whatever the essential goodness or evilness of man.

The critic cannot access the essentialist nature of man. There is no *Homo sapiens* outside of a structure which confers values on bodies and souls. Lacan's emphasis is on radical transformation. The imperative of this movement is: "Do not give ground relative to one's desire."[45] The ethics of psychoanalysis invites a Spirit in which the exchange of law with love, repression with liberation, symptom with desire, and conscious with unconscious promises an Outside whose oral, anal, phallic, and clitoral (and so on) consequences cannot be anticipated in advance. The ethics of psychoanalysis is a wager.

The surplus materiality in the pictures and words of the translation between Cs. and Unc. introduces the radicality of the signifier into the $-istic system. Order cannot recuperate this free play in either psychoanalytic interpretation and its fictional navel of the dream or in the hierarchical enforcement of abstraction above materiality. The return of affect to the world is always already man's affair. The chiasmic trouble is simply the discernment of the truth of the unconscious. The marks in texts and the colors in images are the symptomatic effects of the return of *Praxis*. Man's gaze at the mirror, look at the enemy, stare at the other, leer at the stranger, gawk at the different, and ogle at the threat — this gaze is accompanied by an affect toward an object. But, wretchedly, the gaze misses its object. Man sees what he does not see. Man does not see what he sees.

This constitutive blindness is an axiom of psychoanalysis. Interpretive mistake transposes affect into Reason and its violent minions. Unlove is the object of the gaze. Lacan's venerable line about the gaze in the *Seminar* on the four fundamental concepts of psychoanalysis (1964) is: "When, in love, I solicit a look, what is profoundly unsatisfying and always missing is that — you never look at me from the place from which I see you."[46] The absence in the self is the presence of the Other. Love is the trial to make coincide the "profoundly unsatisfying and always missing" gap between lover and beloved. The pervert transforms the signs of Reason and the violence of the combinatory oppositional pairs of signs into the excess materialities and signifiers of Unreason and the affects of love (and so on). This *Praxis* must return to the inside/outside and self/other divisions which develop from the oceanic oneness of infancy. The binary system of words of the system Cs. is the adult world of division and opposition. The sheer incoherence of the system of comparison and contrast of indetermination and undecidability in exchange in the unconscious is the galaxy of the offspring and his oceanic experience of a series of indistinctions.

Adult experience of the traumatic structure of difference is internalized as the condition of man's dysfunction in society. An offspring's experience of the absence (*of* absence) involves the incoherent blur of an indistinct system of marks and images. These babyish signifiers cannot be assimilated into speculation. The offspring enjoys the signifier and value. The adult copes with the word and signification. The offspring loves because opposition is gone. The adult suffers the symptoms of Unlove because opposition insists. *Praxis* returns to the materialities and bodies of the signifier of childhood and their free play of switcheroo between aims and objects without reference or signification. Young sexuality loves. All bodies are beautiful in childhood.

The Praxis Principle

Praxis must decide between *Eros* and *Thanatos,* and between the drive of life and the drive of death. In *Beyond the Pleasure Principle* (1920), Freud describes *Eros* as the instinctual force of unification, mergence, connection, combination, union, and federation. The life drive coalesces the fragmented particles of the world into bound bodies and ensembles. In contrast, the death instinct tears, fragments, detaches, fractures, and splinters.[47] However, the ostensible opposition between *Eros* and *Thanatos* is chimerical. Simply, the unities that the life drive delivers are consolidated effects of splits in other ensembles, and the detachments that the death drive generates are shattered effects of combinations into other unities. The life and death drives are neither opposed nor distinct. Rather, *Eros* and *Thanatos* are systematically integrated as principles of the process of the (dis)integration of the self and the other. The two drives force the movements of life toward death and the return of death in life. The beyond of the principle of pleasure inspires a reversal of Freud's original hasty model of enjoyment. This scheme is that the increase of tension in the organism is unpleasure and that the decrease of this tension is pleasure. The tension of frenetic exuberance is unpleasurable. The steady restraint toward the zero degree is pleasurable.

However, beyond this conservative version of pleasure is the masochism of the reversal of the principle. The masochist reverses the tension/release model of pleasure. Masochistic pleasure delights in the delay of the difference and deferral — *différance* — of climax. The masochist defers and suspends the orgasm. A desexualized imagination animates an energy which is at the service of the prorogation of the org(ani)sm. A messianic patient waiting for the *tout autre* enlivens the pervert's courtly love. An (un)pleasure is beyond the pleasure principle of regulation. The masochist enjoys a desexualization. The sexual orgasm is delayed in order to sustain the joy of its expectation. This reversal of the pleasure principle mobilizes an (*a*)sexuality. This (*a*)sexuality gets off on the imaginary potential of getting off.

The idiotic neurotic chases his *objet petit a* in a hasty but happy rush toward orgasm and its brief afterglow. The neurotic gets off on getting off, full stop. In contrast, the Other pervert chases the chase and traces the trace — *Trieb* — in an extended erotic play of codes and rules. This patient waiting suspends the orgasm in the imagination of expectation and the fantasy of anticipation. The pervert's Other *jouissance* desexualizes pleasure. The messianic orgasm protracts the Other enjoyment of masochistic suspension and delay. The question for those of us who reckon with the beyond of the principle of pleasure is, "For what does the pervert's desexualization await?" The protracted virginal (*a*)sexual desexualization of the pervert defers the object of his frenzied and anticipatory drive. What is this messianic object if the aim of drive is not sexual intercourse and climactic ejaculation? This object can only be *Praxis* and its transformation of the solar system. The sacrifice of sex promises the gift of revolution. The pervert's (*a*)sexuality waits for *Praxis*. Man has yet to begin *Praxis*. Man is not ready for *Praxis*. Man has not properly prepared for the Event of *Praxis*. Man must prepare for the Event of *Praxis*.

The transformation of *désir* into *Trieb* concludes — commences — in *Praxis*. The wager of the masochistic patient waiting of *Praxis* is the arrival of the future: the signified, the *tout autre*, justice, and the variety of utopic theories and practices of the future of the Spirit of the System. The clinical constitution of the unique desexualized pervert of the future is indeterminate. Her psychical makeup resists explication or etiology. But the ethical imperative of the pervert's imagination and suspension is properly an enforcement of Lacan's dictum — "do not give ground relative to one's desire."[48] The dynamic between *désir* and its *objet petit a* is essentially of an object which yields and surrenders to the missed encounter. The object slips from the subject's grasp. Desire is already drive. The minor but vast difference between *désir* and *Trieb* is the parallactic gap of this missed encounter between neurotic and *objet*. What is the affective dimension of the (missed) encounter of the object for the neurotic and for the Pervert-Schizoid-Woman? The gap returns to the conservative structure of Freud's pleasure principle. The neurotic suffers unpleasure in the manic intensification of the encirclement of *désir* (*Trieb*) around its object. The idiot bears *différance* and its suspension of the signified and an open future. The neurotic wills the closure of death in the orgasm and in the sorry return to the homeostatic equilibrium of a weary organism.

In contrast, the Pervert-Schizoid-Woman enjoys the ecstasy of the crazed fanaticism of the twists and turns of the prepositional orchestration — around, near, by, over, beyond, under — of the trace of differences and deferrals around the *objet* in its delay. The pervert savors the erotic foreplay of a life in which the zigzag drifts and swings toward a resexualization of his constitutive (*a*)sexuality. This (*a*)sexuality drives its *Eros* toward and away from the closure of an orgasmic death. The pervert is the essence of *Eros*. The Pervert-Schizoid-Woman gets off on life and its spatial expansion beyond herself toward the Other. This expansion is the third-dimension of the timeless space of the unconscious. The *mise-en-scène* of the fourth-dimension of the Event is *Praxis*. This *Praxis* is the commitment of the patient waiting of masochism. *P* is the (*a*)sexuality of the queer communist pervert.

The parallactic reconciliation of neurosis and perversion can be extracted from a snippet of text in "On Negation" (1925). Freud states: "Affirmation — as a substitute for unification — belongs to *Eros*; negation — the successor to expulsion — belongs to the destruction-drive."[49] A close reading of this excerpt spotlights the extimacy between *Eros* and *Thanatos*, and between the stupid idiocy of the neurotic's desire and the ethical exoticism of the pervert's drive. The "yes, yes" of affirmation mobilizes the techniques of the primary process and the no "No!" of the unconscious. The pervert hollers *Yes!* to the continuous movement of the globe, from here-yes to there-yes, from around-yes to near-yes, from above-yes to below-yes, from down-yes to up-yes, and so on — *Yes!*

The pervert's "yes, yes" affirms each instant of life. Freud suggests that this "yes, yes" can be interpreted as a "substitute for unification." *Qua* substitute, affirmation enjoys the series of substitutions of the fetish in its displacement and condensation in the series of metaphorical additions and subtractions of the unconscious. The pervert takes rapture in this series of part-objects of momentary splits and renewed unities. Substitutes for unification achieve the pervert's *Eros* and the solidarity of relationship and attachment. In contrast, the death drive ("No!") expels and rejects otherness. Notably, Freud says that negation is the "successor" to expulsion. The reactive force of negation ("No!") is the effect of expulsion. The process of the internalization of the ego as self-same and self-identical in "expulsion" is the proviso of negation itself. The enforcement of the inside/outside division between self and other is the condition of the negation of the father's "No!" The development toward adulthood — inside/outside and self/other — forces the choice of negation. $-ism insists on bounded separateness between self and other. Life will be organized by *Thanatos*. An endless series of enforced negations and a compendium of compulsive repetitions of a stipulated "No!" will structure the globe.

The pervert shrieks "yes, yes" in a desexualized trace of (*a*)sexual ecstasy of an imagined futural *Praxis*. The neurotic moans "No!" in a heterosexualized pounce at its *objet petit a* and the frustration of desire. The heterosexual neurotic will never engage in proper *P* because he relishes death and its pitiful phallocentric orgasm of ejaculation at release rather than life and its joyous postphallocentric Other of delay at extension. The communist queer (*a*)sexual Pervert-Schizoid-Woman thinks *P* and lives *P* — Becoming-*Praxis* — in her liberated *Yes!* to the affirmation and unification of *Eros* and *Praxis*. The pleasure principle returns to a crash toward conservative homeostasis. The beyond of the pleasure principle elevates to the heights — not-yet — of unimaginable exhilaration of the promise and anticipation of the *tout autre*. The queer *Praxis* principle Becomes-Other. Perverts *Praxis* forever. An (*a*)sex is *Praxis*. A sex is theory. Until then, the practice of sex is the object of the patient waiting of the (*a*)sexual masochist. Sex? — *Not yet!*

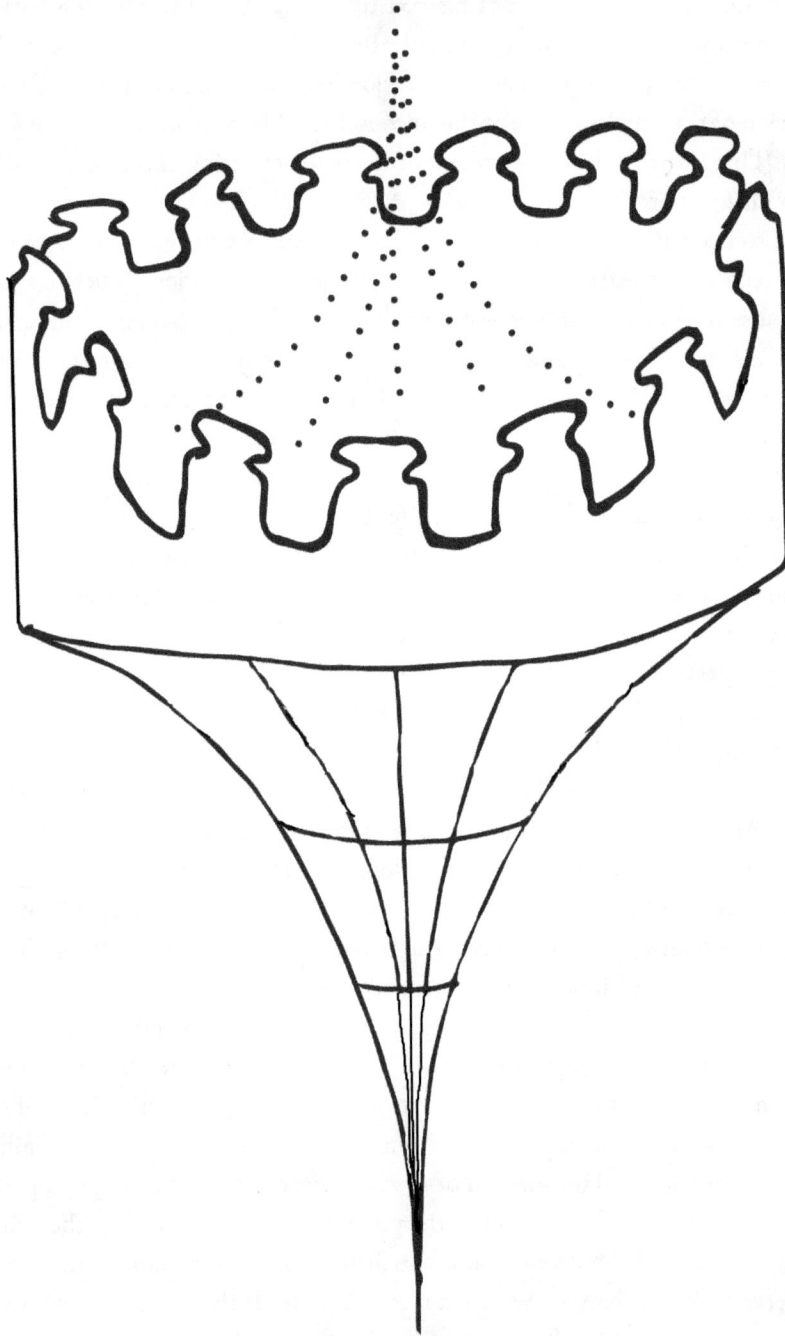

This drawing illuminates the *écriture* of Sameness⁺ of the (*a*)sexual communist future of the Pervert-Schizoid-Woman. This symbolic structure — syntax and semantics of communication — is distinct from and opposed to — but also the Same⁺ as — the speech and writing of the capitalist neurotic under the regime of exchange-value and the accumulation of debt. The illustration depicts a posse of Pervert-Schizoid-Women who speak and write in a system of identities and differences — positive entities of the sign — whose essence is the (*a*)sexual Sameness⁺ of all meaning-making. The Pervert-Schizoid-Woman elevates the distinction and opposition of the sign to the difference and negativity of the signifier — to the (*a*)sexual void of incomparable and incontrastable singularities of material (sound and image) marks. A reference to the Same⁺ *value* of the signifier — difference and negativity — emerges from the system of the self-same and self-identical — distinct and opposed — *signification* of the sign. In the future, the dispersed and divided *Thanatos* of *langue* is transformed into a united and bound *Eros* of differential and negative Sameness⁺ which refers all meaning-making of identity and difference to the (*a*)sexual material nucleus — excess materiality — of the (im/ex)plicitly spoken and written of the word: *every word is the same word*. Every signification of identity/difference in the distinct and opposed sign is structured by an unsymbolizable Real Sameness⁺ of the signifier. The Sameness⁺ is the distilled integral of all of the signifying terms or units of text in the system. Communistically, all identical and different units of text refer to a Sameness⁺ which is neither self-same nor self-identical. An *finite infinity* or *infinite finity* is the expansive-contractive aesthetic of the Pervert-Schizoid-Woman and her will toward expansion and openness. This is the essence of the occluded center of the system. The occlusion is drawn in the inverted gravitational figure, and it is marked by the ellipsis. The units of text (A, B, C, D, and so on) converge upon the Sameness⁺ which *is* in all points of space and time — everywhere and anytime — between the marks of the sign. The frenzied *Thanatos* of the signifier yields to the sign, and the contractive *Eros* of the sign submits to the dispersed *Thanatos* of the signifier. *Eros* and *Thanatos* refer *les mots et les choses* to the (*a*)sexual center of an abundant materiality whose excess cannot be captured by either the binding force of life or the destructive force of death. Life binds its destruction of extant unities, and death pillages its renewal of reformed fragments — in endless expansion.

Notes & Sketches —

The pervert shrieks *Yes!* in a desexualized trace of (*a*)sexual ecstasy of an imagined futural — *tout autre*. The neurotic moans "No!" in a heterosexualized pounce at its *objet petit a* and the frustration of desire. The heterosexual neurotic will never *Praxis* because he worships death and its pitiful phallocentric orgasm of ejaculation. The communist queer (*a*)sexual Pervert-Schizoid-Woman will love in her liberated *Yes!* to the affirmation and unification of *Eros*. The queer (*a*)sexualist Becomes-Other. The idiot dies apart from his *objet petit a*. Patiently waiting, will the Faggot encounter his Boy? Patiently demurring, will the Boy dissimulate the delay? The erotic interval between the man and the Boy is the extended unconscious space of the *Praxis* of queer communist revolution. *Praxis* is the desexualized preparatory labor for the arrival of the leap unto the universal masochistic service of communism.

Chapter Twelve

Faggots

> One day the brothers who had been driven out came together, killed and devoured their father and so made an end of the patriarchal horde. United, they had the courage to do and succeeded in doing what would have been impossible for them individually. Cannibal savages as they were, it goes without saying that they devoured their victim as well as killing him. The violent primal father had doubtless been the feared and envied model of each of the company of brothers, and in the act of devouring him, they accomplished their identification with him, and each of them acquired a portion of his strength. The totem meal, which is perhaps mankind's earliest festival, would thus be a repetition and a commemoration of this memorable and criminal deed, which was the beginning of so many things — of social organization, of moral restrictions and of religion.
>
> — Sigmund Freud

Freud's *Totem and Taboo* (1913) presents the story of psychoanalysis as an allegory of murder and its consequences. For Freud, murder haunts the scenes of sexuality, paternity, and maternity (the Oedipus complex) and desire and law (the myth of the primal horde murder of the father). Murder fortifies the foundational structures which enable civilization to function by the precepts of the proper conventions of identity and desire. Murder is an alibi for the castration of the Woman in the scene of the discovery of sexual difference in the castration complex. This murder is the condition of possibility of the order of the world. The centrality of murder is isomorphic to castration in sexual difference, to scarcity in capitalist economics, and to phallocentrism (penis/not-penis) in patriarchy. These modalities of murder are homologous: in the myth of the primal horde, the sons dispatch with the primal father; and in the oedipal tale texts, the jealous and jilted young lover harbors murderous intentions toward the father who is the obstacle to his desire. The purpose of this chapter is to isolate the paradoxes of identity and desire at the origin of civilization.

Murder plots a presence which is converted into an absence. This mimes the economy of the maternal phallus in the Oedipus complex, and it analogizes overproduction in capitalism. Murder is the social and political foundation of the confused and unhappy resolutions to and conditions of oedipal desire, capitalist exploitation, and patriarchal oppression. The *ur*-text of psychoanalysis, Sophocles's Oedipus cycle (429 BCE), involves murder: the unwitting murder of the oedipal father, Laius, whose substitution involves dramatic turns which rock Thebes and her inhabitants. The drive (*Trieb*) beyond the pleasure principle (1920) encircles around an absence — or presence, if you prefer. This _____ resists capture in symbolization in the Real. Desire is structured by lack and its disappointed (un)fulfillment. Drive is organized by an aim which forsakes the *Ziel* in favor of its own self as narcissistic object. This Becoming-Object neither Becomes Being nor is Being Being. Neither Being nor Becoming is purely spoken from the perspective of the pervert's *Trieb*. Rather, drive occupies a dizzy oscillation in the interval between Becoming and Being.

SORRY TRANSGRESSIONS

Freud outlines the myth of the murder of the primal father in *Totem and Taboo* in 1913. But it is originally mentioned in *The Interpretation of Dreams* in 1900. The primal father enjoys all of the Women in the clan for himself and bars the sons of any enjoyment for themselves. The primal father is a ferocious figure. He simultaneously embodies both absolute authority in a brazenly unjust law and total *jouissance* at the cost of the potential enjoyment of all of the other men (sons and brothers) in the clan. This potential pleasure is an enjoying. But whether promised, counterfeit, or imperative, this barred *jouissance* is suspended as an imaginary past of what will have been deprivation in the future event in which the boys discover — somehow — Something is Missing. The so-called ladder, as Lacan puts it, of law and desire is inverted in this scene. But the law initiates desire in the process of the hystericization of the brothers. If Nothing is Missing amidst the volleyballs and swimsuits on the excluded beach which is the Outside of the father's civilization, then by what mechanism or apparatus and by which reminder or aesthetic do the brothers encounter Something is Missing in their homosexual libido? Is there a relationship between law and enjoying? — or law and *jouissance*?

Law and Jouissance

The cycle of rule and rebellion cannot be explained in the myth because the rule is in abeyance. What is the relationship between prohibition and joy? Desire is based in lack. In contrast, enjoyment is either masculine — illusion and disillusion of the grasp of the object — or feminine — *Trieb* as aim/less wanders about the seashore. There is no constitutive difference between the masculine and feminine logics. There is no gender in the absence of the primal father's rule and the suspension of the hystericization of desire. The brothers only become men through the process of guilt and remorse. Antecedent to the murder, the brothers may be homosexual (which is Freud's indication), but they are strictly in the absence of gender. Homosexuality is not only genderless but it is strictly (*a*)sexual because it is not organized by genital difference. The brothers on the beach are pure sexuality and unalloyed libido in a Nothing is Missing. This (*a*)sexual configuration is the effective scope of the insight of a perverse arrangement of *Trieb qua désir qua Trieb qua désir qua qua qua* — either as perverse fetish or textual metaphor or deconstructionist center.

Perverse, schizophrenic, and feminine perspectives discern that there is no law as such without enjoyment for the masculine ego. There is no stupid pleasure without rule for the idiot. Phallic *jouissance* is organized by the endless cycle of law and transgression or by Lacan's inverted ladder. The inversion establishes rule in order to tempt the trespass of the boundary. At the same time, there is no law in the absence of the infraction. This misdemeanor retroactively posits the law of its own transgression. This dumb show is a silly and repetitive dynamic in which law must always triumph even if it is itself simultaneously its own transgression. The rule and trespass are each torus-like flip-sides of the same asinine rapport. This circular sequence is the essence of the Freudian pleasure principle. Beyond the prosaic increase/decrease of tension is the drive toward death. *Thanatos* introduces an alternative modality of mortal *jouissance*. Feminine not-whole, non-knowledge, and *Trieb* offer an enjoyment which is outside of the father's law and beyond the ridiculously incessant cycle of rule and rebellion.

The father must be dead. Lacan indicates that the father always has been dead. The father must be neither living nor dying. The father is strictly suspended in liminality and undecidability. The neither/nor of the father inspires man to emerge in futurity. The essential issue of the murder is the mode of negation of the father in the murder: neurotic *Verdrängung*, perverse *Verleugnung*, or schizoid *Verwerfung*. However, the alternative possibility to a clinical negation is that the father was never negated as such. The father's semblance never even emerged as presence in the economy of the brothers. The father never appeared on the beach, in the conscious of the brothers, or in the scene of (un)hystericized desire. Man has not yet desired. *Contra* Freud, civilization is not organized by desire and its repression but by the temporal suspension of a desire which cannot be assimilated to a metaphysics of presence. The human is still waiting to desire. The father who is more powerful in death than in life returns in the schizoid Real as delusions and hallucinations. He haunts the neurotic in dreams, slips, jokes, and psychopathologies. He returns as the fetish in the pervert's disavowal of difference. The proper tense of this futurity of the dead father — from past to future — is crucial. This question determines the possibilities of desires and enjoyments. What does a boy want? And what is a boy enjoying? Desire and pleasure are effects of the (dis/re/non)appearance of the father.

The Pervert-Schizoid-Woman relinquishes the myth *qua* myth that the father has been presently murdered. The pervert disposes of the ideology that the deed has been presently done by present doers. The pervert denies that the brothers survive in the aftermath of the violent mistake of the murder. The brothers of the imaginary revolutionary deed must abandon the fable of the invented Freudian storyline — murder and its effects — if they intend to escape from exclusion by the father as the plot promises.

In contrast to the masculine system, the feminine *jouissance* is organized by a system in the absence of absence. The schizoid-boy renounces the *point de capiton* and the stabilization of desire. Instead, he favors the infinite metonymic movement of *Trieb*. This traversal toward an endless and encircled aim is its own *Ziel*. The Other enjoyment intuits that the mythic murder of the primal father is farcical. The exclusionary law is based on the totemic memorialization of the murder of the primal father. The law is not written into the conscience of the collective history of the sons. The movement along a torus-shaped surface achieves the experience of a Sameness⁺. The imperative of difference yields to the experience of "a sameness which is not identical." This feminine experience eschews the economy of the masculine myth. Absence is not the only principle for organization. A peculiar analytic absence is both posterior and antecedent to law. What precedes and follows the murder? What is the Outside of the in-process, in-action of the murder?

The murder is always taking place. The murder has neither started nor ended. It is not itself. The same is the case for (will be the case of) my scant metaphor of the beach for this Outside. The entire set of metaphors is internal to this expression of the Outside because this Other — but one, *except* — is excluded as the condition of possibility of the metaphor under consideration. But the incomplete Becoming of this metaphor — the instant of the now — is such that at the same time as it unfolds — the instant of the now — it is otherwise. For this reason, this metaphor of the beach is excluded from itself even as it includes the suspended metaphors for the Outside to take its place at the site of precisely where (Unc.) and when (Cs.) it is not.

Figure 12.1 The Primal Horde Myth

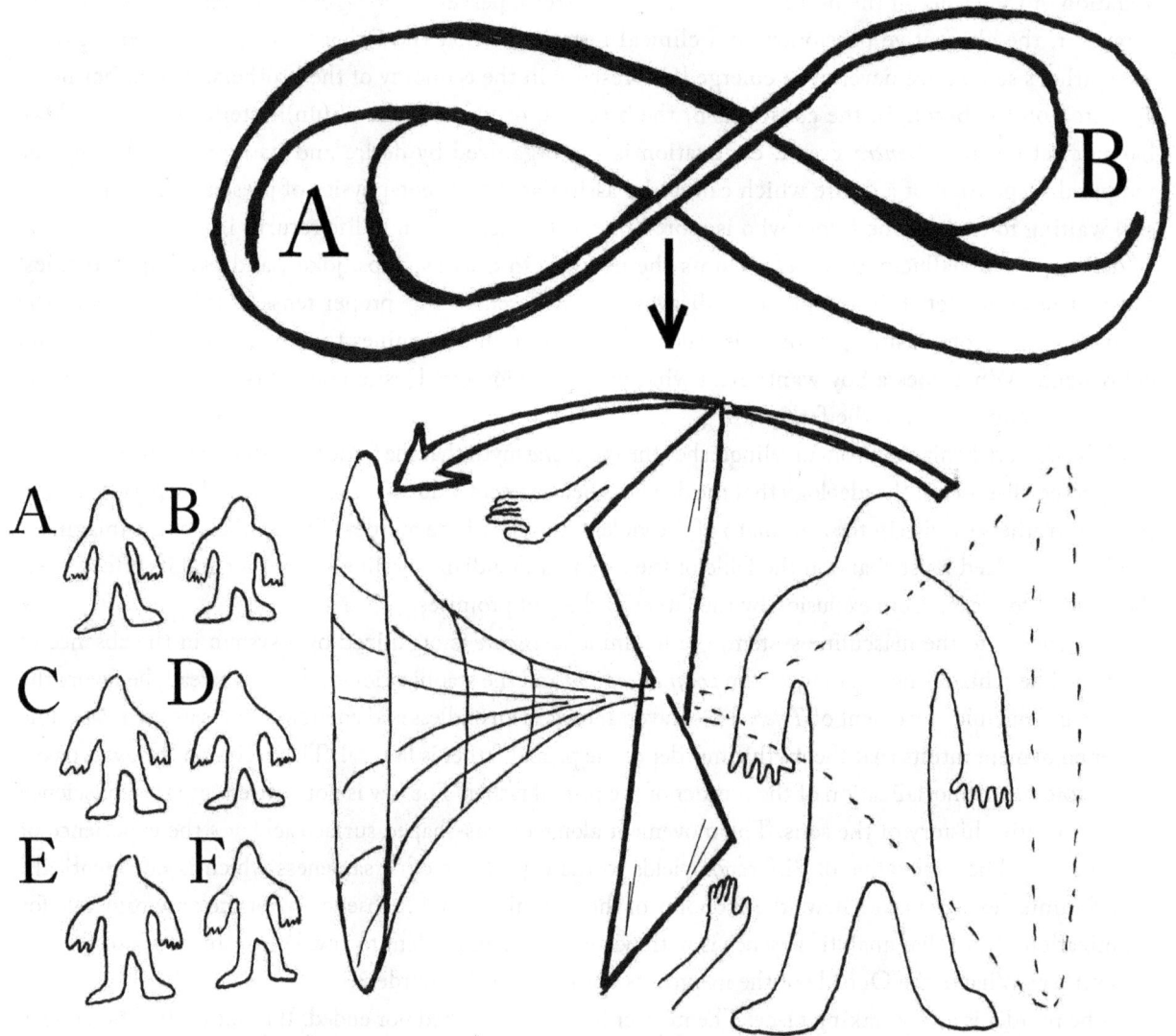

This illustration portrays the relationship among the brothers of the primal horde, the obscenity of the father, and the peculiar temporality of the (non)hystericization of desire. The *Möbius* loop (above) conveys the concept that any object (A, B, C, D, and so on) is neither self-same nor self-identical with itself even in its (non)identity with any other object in the system. The *Möbius* strip (above) also depicts the paradoxical relationship between law and transgression as it is articulated in Freud's myth of the primal horde. A law is born from transgression but also instantaneously the obverse. The relationship between infraction and rule is constituted at the same moment as the bond between crime and statute. The image depicts the brothers (below, left) and the primal father (below, right). The brothers (left) are labeled with the signifying terms (A, B, C, D, E, and F). The twisted mirror (below, center) separates the brothers from the father. This twisted identificatory mirror division shows the compulsively enacted ambivalence which posits that the system is closed. The fraternal prehistoric Otherness on the Outside of the *Möbius* system (above, center) is integrated and assimilated into the fabled conscious narrative chronological temporality of the neurotic. The Outside of the system is the other side of the mirror (below, center). This Outside is simulated within the system because of an ambivalence toward the $-istic ideologies of phallocentric castration, capitalist scarcity, and linguistic absence. Psychoanalytically, an inexplicable and unexplained castration and lack in law and transgression are the folkloric logic of Freud's myth. The twisted mirror (center) represents the myth of the origin which simulates the *arche* of the world and the advent of time. The dotted line designates the flip-side of the gravitational function. The dotted line indicates that the space of language in which the brothers (units of text and signifying terms) are self-same and self-identical is conditioned by a *Möbius* twist. This twist sutures the beginning to the end — the departure to the destination — from the past to the future. This twist parallels the processes whereby the elision of the other establishes the fib of an autonomous selfhood. The *Möbius* loop demonstrates that the self-sameness and self-identity of A are predicated upon a simulation of an exterior rather than on a radical encounter with an otherness. The father's murder is isomorphic to the twist of the mirror — a simulation of an outside in which the historical narrative *arche* both begins and ends, departs and arrives, in coincidence with linear temporality. The dotted line indicates the place of the gravity function — were it not for the *Möbius* self-constitution *ex nihilo* and *causa sui* which is symbolized by the twist. A metaphysics of presence produces (differs and defers in relationality and constructionism) a potentially infinite (but simultaneously limited) set of objects *ex nihilo* and *causa sui*. The object which is discoordinated in the galaxy both everywhere and nowhere is solidified into a presence — *hic et nunc* — but with a past (present) which is to be disclosed only in a future. This future is buried in the past. Both nothing has happened yet, and everything has already happened. The radical prehistoric babyish psychotic (*a*)sexuality on the other side of the Lacanian mirror yields in a compulsive twist to a mundane and tangible post — *faux* — revolutionary metaphysics of presence. Metaphysically, the objects of signification are bound to each other as self-same and self-identical in the aftermath of an impossible hystericization of desire. The unexplained question is for the jock. Crucially, how is the (*a*)sex object on the beach to be symbolized — spoken and written — in the aftermath of the murder? What is (*a*)sexuality before and after the father? Is the disavowal of the jockstrap *qua* "jockstrap" possible in the return of perverse *Verleugnung* in the prehistoric Nothing is Missing of the queer beach? Or are perversity and its jockstrap the consolation prize for the *faux* revolution and its disastrous repercussions? Is the jockstrap (*et al.*) an adequate compensatory exchange for the penis (*et al.*)?

Notes & Sketches —

Paternal Paradoxes

Freud's deceptively simple outline — a single paragraph — of the primal murder presents the careful reader with several aporetic conundrums. Confusion is precisely the orientation of the brothers before, during, and after they rush the beach house in order to transform their own (*a*)sexual Nothing is Missing of an originary homosexual libido into the sexual Something is Missing of the desire of heterosexuality. In the story, the brothers band together to murder the primal father because he is an obstacle to their own hysterical desire. This hystericized desire is the proviso of the revolutionary act. This desire is masculine idiotic enjoyment. It is the *telos* of an aim toward the *Ziel* of its (non)fulfillment. The brothers' decision to embark on the (counter)revolutionary gesture of murder is deeply mistaken. The primal father's law of exclusion facilitates the phallic *jouissance* that the brothers ultimately agree to pursue in the social pact — what Freud identifies as law, morality, and religion.[1] The social pact is arranged at the cost of a revolutionized society. The pledge to trade *l'être pour lettre* — or Nothing is Missing for Something is Missing — otherwise elides female lack and capitalist exploitation in a postcastration, postscarcity, postpatriarchal, postmetaphorical, and postmetonymical Nothingness on the beach, in the water, on the sand, trunks, volleys, tans, baths — and variants of towel-whipping.

The brothers abandon the opportunity to displace the clitoris (as not-penis) as the negative linchpin of Western civilization. It is a lost duty to embrace this alternative figuration — not the penis but another archetype of a general (non)equivalent or Other. This figure is the Pervert-Schizoid-Woman and her *jouissance* of the Other. The plot is the psychoanalytic *ur*-text of the origin of civilization. The upshot of the abandoned choice is that the law is reinstituted by the brothers as the consequence of the (un)heroic deed. The deed is simply done in the present. It is then retroactively experienced from the future of law, morality, religion, and Western civilization. The consequence of revolution is guilt and remorse. The foundation of heterosexuality and capitalism (scarcity) is bad conscience. The brothers suspend the pursuit of the Other *jouissance*. The (counter)revolutionaries recoil from an Other-Logic unto castration, capitalism, and patriarchy. They agree that none of them should be treated like the primal father treated all of them — and like they all treated the primal father. The founders renounce the very ground of civilization. The origin of civilization is a source of primitive and primordial regret. The world is a mistake.

The social pact is constituted by a retrospective gaze at a deed and a doer rather than a doing. The brothers do not want a repetition of exclusion for no other reason than ambivalence. This ambivalence is the simultaneity of the love and hate that they feel for the father. Freud explicitly states that he can offer no account of an origin for ambivalence.[2] But this ambivalence is the principle of organization for the split, both theoretical and practical, between the deed and the doers, and between the action and the actors. The in-process, in-action doing, murdering, and enjoying must yield to the metaphysics of presence. The Being of the murder is integrated into and by the system. It is as if the spectacular event were performed in a presence whose futural effects are retrospective guilt and remorse. If this ambivalence were not constitutive of the origin of civilization, then the murdering would still be in-process, in-action forever, even today. The affective relationship between the sons and the father is ambivalent. The murdering and enjoying of the father's body both begin and end with this ambivalence. Otherwise, in the absence of an ambivalence that Freud cannot explain, the brothers would still be feasting on the naked body of the father, neither dead nor alive, but in-between, in a liminal and undecidable state.

Instead, the brothers agree to a postrevolutionary renunciation of the Other *jouissance*. They institute patriarchy, capitalism (scarcity), and other social ills which are posterior to the law. The founders of civilization retroactively invented patriarchy and capitalism (scarcity) as original to civilization. The reason for this structuration of the brothers' guilt and remorse for the past murder is the retroactive constitution of the doers of the deed *qua* done. After the deed, retroactive speculation enframes the brothers with responsibility for the deed. Once the deed is committed, all of the symptoms of civilization become necessary. But is the deed in fact done and with the ghostly apparition of the father as a reminder of the crime? Or does the supplemental Becoming of the murder which is Outside of presence defer the deed — in-process, in-action — to an endless and infinite enjoying? The singular reason for the neurotic repression of the Other-S in favor of law, morality, and religion is the crucial obligation to this past loss of murder, absence, death, debt, return, obligation, deficit, and so on.

In *The Ego and the Id* (1923), Freud defines the ego as a series of lost object-choices.[3] The self is the process of loss. The self is in-action, in-process losing. The self is the effect of the transformation of Nothing is Missing of the brothers into the Something is Missing of desire, patriarchy, sexual difference, private property, scarcity, and capitalism. Freud structured this basal loss into the essence of the ego. This lost self is formulated as early as the dream-book (1900) with reference to the clitoris and Something is Missing. The castration of sexual difference, the phallocentrism of patriarchy, and the scarcity of capitalism are the foundations of Something is Missing. The Something is Missing is the phallocentric interpretation of the clitoris and the capitalist evaluation of material existence. The murderous transgression originally intends to suspend the violent law. But the obscene law paradoxically returns with vengeance in the guilt and remorse of the haunted Spirit of the lost father in the done murder. It is not simply, as Freud contends with Goethe, that "in the beginning was the deed." Rather also, "in the end was the deed." The political transgression of the brothers' rebellion against the father reinscribes Something is Missing as the subtractive addition to Nothing is Missing. This phallic *jouissance* indicates that the neurotic idiot's *jouissance* is the source of the cycle of law/transgression.

But another explanation holds. The law may be the retroactive construction of the political violation. The law as the source of guilt and remorse is the retroaction (*Nachträglichkeit, après-coup*) of the murderous crime. The breach posits its own antecedent rule. If we are always rule-breakers in the present — like the boys who storm the beach house — then why is the rule of the primal father's obscene precepts subsequently invented in order to punish in guilt and remorse the doers of the misdeed which was itself previously undone? The social conditions design loss as an integrant of man. Even the brothers interpret their dirty underwear and wet tents — palm trees and scuba gear on the beach — in comparison and contrast to the imagined air conditioned luxury of the beach house as a deficit and a Something is Missing. The exception is that — inexplicably — the lack of the lack — Nothing is Missing — is the origin of this exchange at the base of an unexplained desire. There is no reason for the revolution. This is the reason that the revolution works. It has no cause, origin, or *arche*.

The experiential and conceptual chasm between law and transgression — prohibition and *jouissance* — is a devious ruse of the phallic order itself. There is no division between rule and rebellion in embryonic sexuality. Sexual objects and erotic aims energize infinite substitutions and endless exchanges. In childhood, all beautiful bodies are the same body. Freud identifies this sexual-trace as the free substitution of the sexualized body of the offspring. Derrida identifies this economy of sign-substitutions as the function of the center of the structure. This *différance sexuel* supplements in subtractive addition and additional subtraction. *Différance sexuel* inspires the dissolution of boundaries against which to otherwise stupidly rebel. Offspring are sexualized because they cannot desire. Sex and sexuality are only possible in a system in the absence of desire, object, lack, castration, scarcity, and so on. The exchange of *l'être pour lettre* inaugurates desire at the same time as it obstructs sex. The only sex is the homosexual libido under the excluded skies of the beach. Homosexuality is (*a*)sexual. There is an absence of desire which could satisfy a cathexis of an absent object. Nothing is Missing is the scene of fraternal communist sex. A communist homosexual (*a*)sex resists capture in desire and castration.

The three characters of Pervert-Schizoid-Woman must each uniquely stage the Other *jouissance* of sex without desire, and of Nothing is Missing rather than Something is Missing. This *mise-en-scène* is the field of the Real. The project for the pervert is to symbolize the secret truth of this Real *qua* the *Verwerfung* of the symbolic. The challenge for the schizoid is to pursue justice in his political radicalism. But he must resist delusions and hallucinations in the return of the foreclosed in the Real. The task for the Woman is the simple thinking, being, and living of the secret truth of the pervert's symbolization of the Real and of the schizoid's blazed political trail. Other Futurity is manifest after the scarcity (or private property: of commodities) of capitalism and after the castration (or private property: of bodies) of patriarchy are vanquished from the structure of humanity. How is the Other pleasure of what I name as the Spirit of the System (S) possible within a structure which is otherwise organized around violent exclusion? How is S imaginable before and after the banishment of the brothers to the shores and joys of (*a*)sex without desire?

The Other returns to an illuminated extimacy of both exclusion and inclusion. Exclusion includes itself as the exclusion of an inclusion which is excluded from itself as the included (and so on). The sand of the beach amidst the sun and the stars is the scene of the brothers and their exclusion from the violent *jouissance*. But what are the contents and forms of this enjoyment? What is the object of desired enjoyment that the brothers can only imagine from their distant perspective? What about those dirty volleyballs and wet trunks? What enjoyment is excluded from the primal father's heterosexual orientation? From whose perspective does exclusion emerge as the condition of desire? The brothers are excluded outside of the father's deck. But is the primal father excluded from the homosexual libido of a *fete* in which Nothing — but the father — is Missing? Is the father's heterosexual Something is Missing none other than his sons' Nothing is Missing in their homosexuality? Does Nothing Miss Something? If so, do the gay brothers want in (out) of the beach house? If the gay boys are invited in (out), then what of the ladies? — and their nascent desires?

The Oedipus Complex and the Primal Horde Father

The desirous regret of the brothers in their exclusion of entry to the beach house — however theoretically incoherent — showcases a significant breach in the parallactic difference between the oedipal explanation of identity and desire and the primal horde version of enjoyment. In the oedipal accounts from the 1920s, the male junior notices that Something is Missing in the other. He realizes that he will (potentially) miss that Something in the future. This potential future loss inspires anxiety of loss and identification with the father as ego-ideal. This identification is cathected in order to normatively shield the male junior's private(s) property from annexation. In contrast, the primal horde account of the brothers is organized around a creationist sublimation *ex nihilo* of Something is Missing from an originary homosexual Nothing is Missing. The brothers are excluded from the heterosexual party among the father and the Women of the clan. Strangely, in the *Totem and Taboo* (1913) explanation of the chronology of oedipalization, it is the male subject (the brother, the male junior) who is positioned in the classic penis envy orientation of the female junior and her present castration.

The oedipal interpretation of the female junior's envious desire for the penis claims that desire so-called flashes before her. But this envious flash of recognition only holds if the husband-baby of Freud's peculiar essay on "Femininity" (1930) is analogous — fetish or metaphor or substitute or center? — to this penis. The distinction between metaphor and fetish is temporal. The gap between metaphor and fetish is marked by the division between the synchronic dimension of Being and the diachronic dimension of Becoming. The gap between metaphor and fetish is structured by the difference between signification and the sign, on the one hand, and value and the signifier, on the other hand. *Qua* negated, the forms of metaphor and fetish must be understood through the lens of *Verleugnung*, *Verdrängung*, and *Verwerfung*. Representationally, the shift between metaphor and fetish is coordinated by the dream-work of the primary process and the ego-talk of the secondary work. Is baby-envy the Same⁺ — Real Signifier — as penis-envy = baby-envy? Is all desire fundamentally for the Same⁺ object? Is desire for a Sameness⁺ (either) metaphor (or) fetish in (both of these) mode(s) of interpretation of the object?

The male junior, the female junior, and the brother desire the Same⁺ prop or its avatar *qua* fetish or *qua* metaphor. The question is the status of this penis as or in itself. The emergence of the object of Sameness⁺ *qua* the Real Signifier foresees the dissolution of the Madness of Order. Sameness⁺ is the proviso of the destruction of the entire order upon which desire, lack, metaphor, and fetish are structured. But which object undoes what it does so well? Is the penis in its fleshly embodiment this unfathomable Real Penis? Is this Real Penis coincident with the unsymbolizable Real Signifier? Is this asymptotic overlap the fundamental *objet petit a*? Is the object inexplicable except in a phenomenological description of the glory of what fills the — hole? The Real Signifier destroys the system of $-ism. This Real Signifier is precisely the penis. But what is a penis?

However, the penis may not be the only object of desire which is veiled by the world of fetishes. The penis may be the object of in-process, in-action enjoyment in which Nothing is Missing. What is the penis desire for the male junior as distinct from the penis envy of the female junior if he already has the penis and she does not have the penis? The male junior already possesses the object *qua* metaphor or fetish or substitute or center. The male junior desires a repetition of this possession. He desires the repetition of the secondary metaphor *qua* the derivative of the original imaginary penis or the derivative of the fetish *qua* the veil of lack. The boy desires the original but only accesses the reproduction in metaphor. This metaphor-fetish is a mineness. This *le propre* hijacks metonymy in order to return it to its (in)complete identity. The boy desires the shield of the fetish. This veil yields enjoyment despite the concealed threat. What is penis-pleasure if the male junior fears the castration of the penis? Sex is an always anxious affair for the male junior of Oedipus. How are masculine sexuality and sex — let alone heterosexuality — even possible for the man? The brothers engage penis-pleasure within relationship to the other brothers rather than in rapport with the other sisters. The Women are inside rather than outside of the beach house. Homosexuality is both (*a*)sexual and, unexpectedly, asocial. The obstacle is the lack in the place of desire. The obstacle to desire — hystericization as such — is the absence of absence. For whom is Something (Not) Missing on the beach? How is this Missing (Nothing) transformed into (Something) Nothing?

The oedipal account explains the situation of the male junior as a futural mirror reflection of the present lack in the female junior. The primal horde narrative of the brothers' (un)hystericized desire is isomorphic to the penis envy of the female junior's glimpse of the phallic presence. This presence is displayed in the body of the male junior. The feminine situation is supposedly rectified by the arrival of the husband and the penis-baby. These objects satisfy the little girl's desire for identity against the background of resentment toward the mother. However, the utterly bizarre *Totem and Taboo* (1913) version of identity and desire is an alternative account to the oedipal tales. The brothers' own trajectory is precisely the trajectory of the female junior in the castration complex. The oedipal fable and its unexpected reversal of roles are only developed later in the 1920s. The entire Freudian account of a bunch of frat brothers and their paddles on the beach in *Totem and Taboo* (1913) can be unexpectedly translated as a record of a gaggle of sorority chicks being peeked upon by pesky and curious boys in the oedipal tales.

Instead of female desire against male identity in the oedipal rendition of development, the primal horde version of masculine identity and desire positions the male junior not as a mirror reflection of himself but as the male junior *qua* the male junior "himself." Not only is the primal horde account of the origin of the West a performance of drag with kings (the female junior *qua* the male junior) rather than queens (gays *qua* Women).

Additionally, the oedipal opposition between masculine identity and ego (castration anxiety) and feminine desire and regret (penis envy) is entirely spurious. It simply cannot be decided whether the Real Signifier of sexual difference is present in the "size" and "visibility" (presence/absence, activity/passivity, and phallocentrism generally) of the materiality of the packed trunks (8.5") off the shores. *Definitely cut.* The bikinis and board shorts reveal the deficit of the female junior's enjoyment of the primal father. The value of the material signifier of anatomy is at stake in the question of the present castration of the male junior and his imaginary phallus.

To put it conceptually, the possibility of a detachment of the symbolic from the imaginary, the conceptual from the material, the mind from the body, the sign from the signifier, and signification from value is indicated by the present lack in the male junior. Derrida critiques Western thought for its so-called logocentrism — the division between abstraction/materiality, signified/signifier, mind/body, and the hierarchization of the former against the latter. But does logocentrism need to be paradoxically redone, and in reverse? Would a dispatch of the abstraction, the signified, and the mind reverse the will of the phallus *qua* sign to do (its) work? Anatomy is the unabashedly criticized so-called destiny in psychoanalytic theorization. But the wager is that a resignified materialist anatomy is the problem of and not the solution to the nexus of castration.

At issue is the prospect that the brothers and the primal father — and the Pervert-Schizoid-Woman — live the Outside of the symbolic order. This Outside is nebulously transmetaphysical or precisely physical. This Outside is an interval which is antecedent or subsequent to the criminal deed of the murder. Is there such a gap which insists in the past, present, and future? Can a society of the Other be designed without the murder? Is there a civilization which is structured by the absence of patriarchal lack and castration, and capitalist scarcity and private property?

Freud narrates the (dis/re/non)appearance of the father in the absence of desire. *Contra* Freud, the primal father is neither dead by the hands of the brothers nor alive as "stronger," as Freud says, than in his life.[4] The father is neither living nor dying inside nor outside of the exclusion of the brothers. Shockingly, *the father is simply not part of the system.* The father is neither outside nor inside of the system. The primal father is otherwise than and elsewhere from the Madness of Order. This paternal madness is indicated as the Real Signifier. The father's absence is the condition of the Real Symbolic. The proviso of the Madness of Order is the absence of this father. The father's absence — never having been — explains the Neurotic Foreclosure (*rejet névrotique*) of the Real and its return as $-ism. The futural Spirit of the System is the divinity of a world which is always already without paternity. $-ism is S. The father is neither dead nor alive, neither dying nor living. Simply, the father is *not*.

Beyond the Deed

This strictly antecedent and posterior paternity — Outside — rends the primal father a mere effect of the fabled murder. The fabricated death is the genesis of the masculine economy. Otherwise, the system of castration is coordinated by the primal father and his murder. The Woman is figured as Something is Missing. The clitoral economy is the anthropomorphic metaphor for the foundation of the system in castration. The system is coordinated by the sexual difference of patriarchy and phallocentrism. The system is also organized by the scarcity of currency and the debt of private property under capitalism. The bedrock of the system is lack. This foundation is only explained in the earlier primal horde (1913) account of sexual difference. The myth posits the inexplicable — somehow — hystericization of desire as only a retrospective effect of the murder.

In the later oedipal tales (1920s), the work is also retroactive. The male junior's present gaze at the female junior and the repetition of this gaze in later sexual engagement with Women posit a past threat by the father. In contrast, the female junior presently and in a flash recognizes the superiority of the penis in "size" and "visibility" (Lacan: in "turgidity"). The female junior promises to make good on the loss in the future. The primal horde myth is organized by the present-future for both the male junior and the female junior. The design is that the male junior has the penis and the female junior has (will have) the penis. Crazily, in the 1920s, men and Women are understood by Freud to desire a loss which is both the male junior's future castration and the female junior's deferred gain. This present-future loss is the organizational principle of the entire system of lack in phallocentrism and of scarcity in capitalism. Why did man not instead desire the presence of the (male and female) penis? Why did man not desire the absence of desire altogether? The proper name for the foundation of Western civilization which is structured by the relationship between the female and male sex organs is Clitoral-Phallocentrism⁺. How did this comparative and contrastive diacritical Clitoral-Phallocentrism⁺ economy become simply phallocentrism rather than _____-_____-ism? Why did a generalized but unthematized -centrism dominate the division at the *arche*?

The assay of the clitoris as Something is Missing is based on the Freudian criteria of "visibility" and "size" of the materiality of the penis against the clitoris. This evaluative consideration is easily reversible if the value of morphological size and visual obscurity is inverted: smaller is better (the clitoris) rather than bigger is better (the penis). What is Missing both materially and conceptually if the value is reversible, even if not from Freud's heterosexualist perspective? Freud's scene of oedipal sexual difference posits this Something as difference *qua* deficit. The inferiority of the clitoris is defined by visual obscurity and minor turgidity. Is male Nothing is Missing a *Thanatos* of explosive fragmentation or an *Eros* of unified totality?

The death and life perspectival orientation on the "visibility" and "size" of the materiality of the penis against the soma of the clitoris demands consideration of the split object of the parallax. The matter is crucial because it determines the dominance of either the signification of the word or the value of the signifier. The female junior of the Oedipus complex recognizes that the present loss will become gain in an indeterminate future. The male junior imagines that the present is the potential of future loss. In contrast, the revolution against the father requires the proviso of the hystericization — somehow — of the brothers. The primal horde fable needs an account of the transition from a *Trieb* of Nothing is Missing to a *désir* of Something is Missing. *Contra* the oedipal fables, the primal horde myth situates the brother as a female junior — as desirous and envious — and also simultaneously as a male junior — as anxious and protective. At what point are the desires of the brothers hystericized? At what moment do heterosexuality, patriarchy, phallocentrism — law, morality, and religion — become the theory and practice of a society which was otherwise communist queer (*a*)sexuality?

The temporal paradox obscures a coherent answer to such a question. The prosaic stupidity of desire is such that it only will have been (*futur antérieur*) the desire to pry open the door to the beach house in the future event that the brothers understand their positions as excluded. They do so realize such exclusion but only in an unrealizable and fathomable future which is deferred — endlessly, for deconstruction, and finitely, for psychoanalysis. Man has yet to recognize his own subordination. A discernment of oppression motivates this rebellion against the rule. The remorseful death of the primal father returns as the general equivalent. This standardization dictates the value of penis/clitoris. In the original oedipal scene, the male junior fantasizes the difference of the female junior as the deficit of castration. The father was always dead. The outlandish consequence is that the father was never murdered. There never was and never will be — never is — the father. Why is there a fantasmatic trial for the boys? What is the fantasy of indictment if the brothers could otherwise elude guilt and remorse? Self-beratement implies that the brothers desire castration. If so, then this castration is the condition of enjoyment in the mobilization of a lost debt of the future against the present debt of a criminal past. What is the condition of this transition? Are the fabricated guilt and invented remorse the precise and intended obstacles to this passage beyond prohibition and infraction?

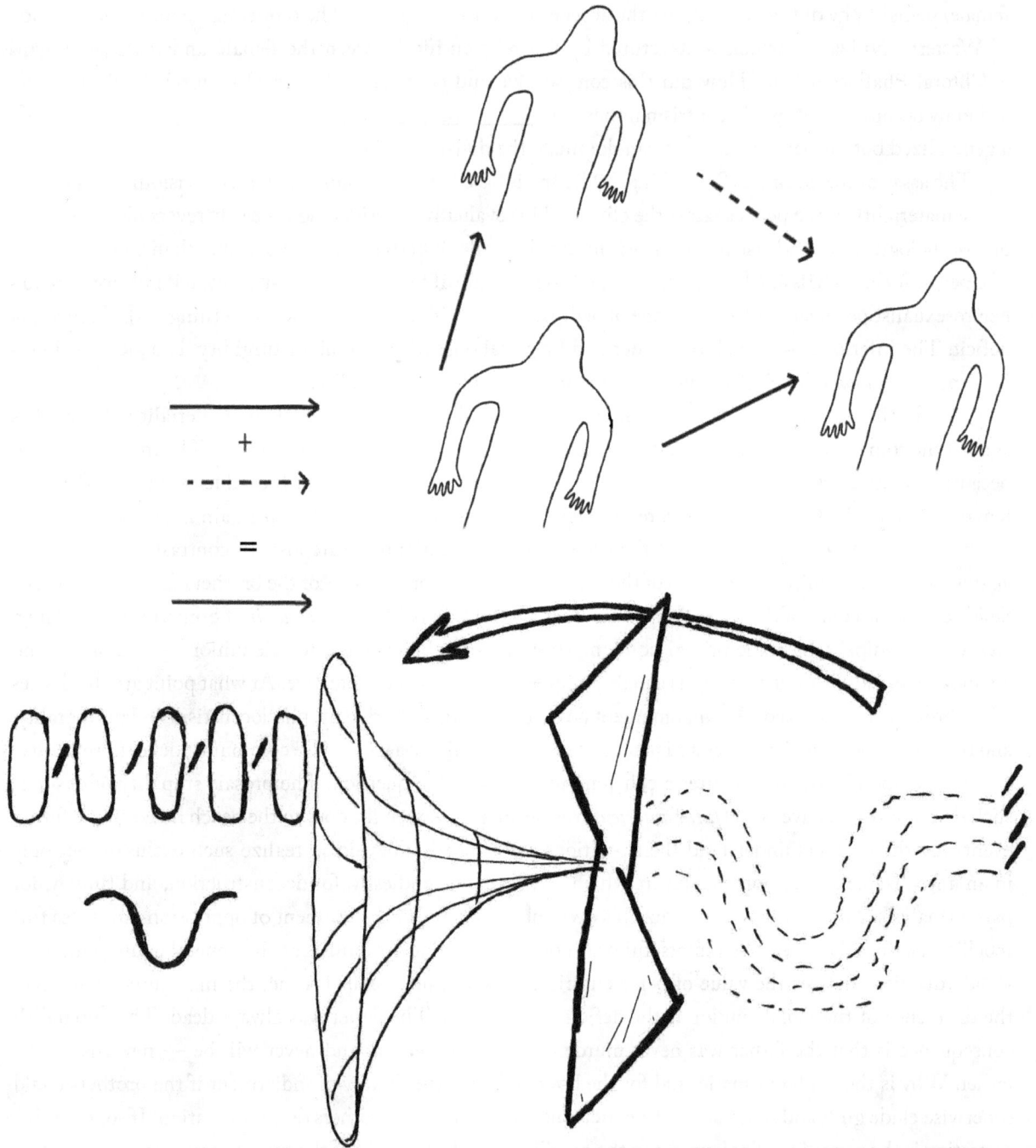

Figure 12.2 Representational Simulation

This picture shows that Lacan's dictum that there is (no) Other of the Other is isomorphic to the series of open (con)texts in *langue* in both textual and visual dimensions. Grammatologically, there is potentially neither departure nor arrival, and neither commencement nor destination, in the expansion of the (con)texts. The (con)text is prospectively unlimited. But Lacan insists that the letter arrives at its destination, and he implies that context finally delimits text. There is (no) Other of the Other. But the compulsions of $-ism must insist in such presence (absence) in order to simulate representation in the otherwise absence of a frame of reference. The system does so in order to buttress the binds which secure and stabilize the network of words. An Other of the Other implies an open system whose marks slip and slide beyond any determinate and saturated context. The obverse suggests a closed system in which the *point de capiton* halts the differences and deferrals of the trace of objects which extends beyond any frame of reference. The wrenched mirror (below, center) indicates that the phallus veils the potentially (in)determinate reference. The Outside of the system is represented in the multiplicity of dotted indents (below, right). This series of dotted indents (below, right) is the Outside of the veiled wrench in the mirror. Neurotically, the wrenched mirror (below, center) shows that both sides of the mirror must be the identical side — self-same and self-identical — and that the figure of the *Möbius* loop must be strictly divided by an interior and exterior, and by an Inside and Outside. The penis-objects (below, left) portray the originary absence (above, left) which is the result of the veil, dissimulation, and wrench. The Other of the Other (Father, God, and so on) is wrenched into the world from an undifferentiated Nothingness (Being). Lacan's dictum that there is no Jockstrap of the Jockstrap yields to Derrida's discovery that there is a "Jockstrap" of the "Jockstrap" of the "Jockstrap," and so on. The limit(less) return of the jockstrap defines the gap between a closed galaxy of neurotic contraction and an open solar system of perverse expansion. The pervert's pinch requires the tricky performance of the parallactic overlap of (no) Jockstrap of the Jockstrap in the simultaneous arrest and release — suspension — of the *point de capiton*. The (con)texts in the cosmos simultaneously expand and contract. This overlap of openness and closedness must be unraveled as the Same[+] flirtation and demur, and advance and recoil, of the masochist's *Trieb*.

Notes & Sketches —

The Idiocy of Masculinity

The negation of the logic of extimacy in the masculine order means that the brothers of the primal horde cannot imagine that their murderous transgression is itself the law of revenge. The boys cannot fathom that their violation in the homicide is itself the rule of requital. The sons cannot understand that their trespass in execution is itself the prohibition against life. This perverse extimacy is the sole province of the Other *jouissance* and the revolutionary effluvium of the Pervert-Schizoid-Woman. This pervert's aneconomy of extimacy is the deconstructive aesthetic of the Pervert-Schizoid-Woman. Extimacy is the secret truth of the schizoid's incomprehensible wails. Extimacy is the tortured text of the pervert's *écriture*. Extimacy is the thinking, being, and living of the emergent Woman of the Spirit of the System.

The transgression, violation, and trespass of the original crime can only intensify law, rule, and prohibition. These oppositions are understood in the Logic of Identity. To wit — transgression is not the law because transgression is transgression and law is law. There is neither castration (patriarchy) nor scarcity (capitalism) in S because the rule of identity is substituted (but also not) with the decree of difference. Peculiarly, why is there such neither/norism in a perversely both/and system? For her, a feminine Nothing is Missing complements the Freudian Something is Missing. A creationist sublimation *ex nihilo* indicates that Nothing is Something — but what? Nothing is Missing at the origin of Western civilization because Nothing is not Nothing and Nothing is Nothing and Something is not Something and Something is Something and — "yes, yes" — Something is Nothing (is not) Something is Nothing (and so on) — The word is every other word.

Astonishingly, the signifier is *positive* even from within a system of the radical negativity of the signifier. Is such a crime as parricide by the brothers a likelihood if Nothing is Missing for the unhystericized boys? Revolution is impossible for men, masculinity, and the penis. There is an entrenched conservative component to the penis, phallus, phallic sexuality, and phallic stage. Masculinity is reactionary. Male homosexuality is conservative. If Something is Missing — somehow — then what is this absence if the fix for the loss is butchery? The Missing in Nothing is Missing can only be posited retroactively from the perspective of Something is Missing rather than from the viewpoint of Nothing is Missing.

Originally, in the past, the brothers enjoy themselves and each other in the absence of desire and lack. Yet, in the present, lack and castration are fullness and abundance. Castration is a retrospective construction from the perspective of lack only after the murder of the primal father. The primal horde myth is strictly incoherent within the twists and turns of its own plot. The origin of civilization does not make any sense. The strange pivot of the ridiculous sublimity of this *arche* is that the lack at the center of the system cannot be symbolized. *Il y a*: ~~The Big Bang~~. What is castration — then, but not now? The plenitude of the past is a retroactive construction of the scarcity of the present. Communism precedes capitalism. In the beginning was —

Phallic Lack

The masculine is resigned to its own system of values of castration, scarcity, patriarchy, and capitalism. In contrast, the Other *jouissance* understands the ~~father's murder~~ as a mythic imposition of the castration of sexual difference and the scarcity of capitalism. Both of these symptoms are structured according to the economy of *le propre* of private property. The theoretical and practical trick is to tempt the subject away from constitutive loss. The talent is to lure man away from the lack of Something is Missing as the necessary component of a retrospective and prospective interpretation of self and society. Instructively, both the brothers of the primal horde myth and the male junior of the oedipal tales are at the origin — advent, *arche* — situated within an economy of abundance. For the brother, the party on the beach is outside of any experience, whether epistemological, ontological, exclusionary, castrative, or desirous. The male junior's oneness with the pleasures of the mother and his own penis is exempt from the threat of loss. If abundance and plenitude are at the origin, then the inevitable emergence of lack as proviso for entry into the system of $-ism requires the retrospective glance.

This backward gaze compares, contrasts, and exchanges the abundance of Nothing is Missing for the scarcity of Something is Missing. The retrospective interpretation trades presence for absence, and *Trieb* for *désir*. The mislaid, forfeited, and depleted past represents castration and scarcity. These are props for the systems of $-ism. There is only a loss in the gain of private property. There is only the privilege of the penis as property in the disprivilege of a deficient clitoris. There is no sabbatical in the Spirit of the System. There is no gap in the system. There is no fissure in the edifice. There is no debt in collection. There is no calculation of quality. The symbolic is Real because Nothing is Missing because Something is Missing: ~~Something Nothing~~. Why does man insist on castration in patriarchy and scarcity in capitalism? The interval between presence and absence is an object of obscene fear and hateful dread for the masculine libidinal economy. If the father were absent — neither dying nor living — this liminal period would not be a source of such anxiety and dread.

EXCHANGES

The origin (trace and *différance*) of the world is the foreclosure of the feminine and her *jouissance*. The feminine is the broken narcissistic reflection (lack and loss) of the masculine's fragile support in phallic *jouissance*. This masculine tepid joy is structured in capitalism (scarcity and private property) and patriarchy (castration and phallocentrism). Freud demonstrates that schizophrenia is the origin of the world. The psychotic foreclosure of the communist queer (*a*)sexualist is the advent of Western civilization. The reason that the communist queer (*a*)sexualist is simultaneously both denigrated and glorified is that she is a reminder of both the bedrock of the system and the revolutionary future of the Spirit of the System. This S is a system of plenitude which is beyond the scarcity of private property. This S is each according to his need and each according to his ability. S is also structured by the (non)coincidence and (in)equality — Sameness⁺ — of the penis and the clitoris and of every other word in the system. The feminine is the source of both the inherited tradition of historical subordination (castration, patriarchy, phallocentrism, scarcity, and private property) and the promised liberation of a destined emancipation (communism, Peniscentrism, and Spirit of the System). Paternal murder and guilty conscience both seek to suture the wound (castration and lack: more private property, more penis, more commodities, more men) in the symbolic order. This is simply unnecessary in a system which has freed itself from the economy of Something is Missing. But in the absence of absence, what is?

The penis is the object of the female junior's desire and envy. The castrated clitoris is the object of the male junior's horror and anxiety. The reason that the clitoris is the negative (A/-A: the masculine order, the logic of the sign) is that the clitoris is a source of dread. In contrast, the penis is presence (A = A) because it is the object of possession. The penis owns itself as itself as its own private property. This economy of *le propre* involves a self-sameness and self-identity in which the man is identified with the penis. Masculine identity is present to itself. Identification is the mere repetition of this identity within the structure of the ego-ideal. Private property is protected from annexation. But from whose perspective does the penis emerge as the anxious object of the man's fear of loss and as the desired object of the Woman's poise for gain?

The penis is both loss and gain, subtraction and addition, absence and presence, and capitalism and communism. The penis deviates from itself as otherwise to and elsewhere from itself. The materiality of its signifier slips and slides beyond the capture in abstraction and calculation in the general equivalent of the phallus. This imaginary materiality of the penis is an excess — foreskin — which cannot be assimilated to the system. This fleshly embodiment of skin exceeds containment as the "one" and the "same" object. How does this excess — surplus value, in Marxist code — return to haunt the system of castration and desire at the origin of Western civilization? The penis is in excess of itself. Its surplus must be circumcisionally squandered. The fleshly excess must be converted from Nothing is Missing into Something is Missing. The remainder of the penis must be transformed from abundance to scarcity. The penis must be remodeled from presence to absence. This is so in order to preserve the system of castration and desire that otherwise organizes the value of the penis. The penis must be (Becoming) castrated in order for it to be the penis. The penis is a metaphor for the effect of the clitoris. The clitoris is the original and primary sex organ of which the penis is a mere secondary copy. Why does the male junior not know this?

Nothing is Missing

It is no wonder that Freud emphasizes a Something is Missing at the center of his system. He defines the ego as the process of loss. The ego is losing itself in its very constitution. The ego is lost. In contrast, the logic of the Other future ($A = A \supseteq A = B$) details the parallactic gap between the object and itself. The penis is split in an excessive doubleness. The penis appears as both castration and plenitude, negative and positive, absence and presence, and scarcity and abundance. The parallactic approach discerns the object as the same as the other because different from itself. This object is different from the other which is different from the other "itself" because different from itself — and so on, in *différance*. A is A because A is not A, or Being (what is) is under erasure in the destruction of the project of ontology. Other economy is beyond *le propre*, outside of $-ism, after scarcity, and posterior to castration. The Spirit rends Sameness[+] *qua* Difference[+] because Sameness[+] is Difference[+] of itself. This Sameness[+] is different from the other because Sameness[+] is the Other to itself — and so on, in *différance*. The secret truth of the schizoid of this alternative symbolic order is the displacement of equality and inequality — (in)equivalence, (dis)continuity, and (non)coincidence — by Sameness[+]. This Sameness[+] is an unsymbolizable superpositional oscillation: is is is and is is not is and is is not is and is is not is not and is is is not and is is not is not and not not not — and so on, in *différance* and under erasure. The imperative of presence *qua not* ruptures Reason in the lunacy of Unreason. Other-Logic mobilizes this secret schizoid truth. The pervert avoids the pitfalls of an economy which is organized by the division, opposition, and word of signification.

Other economy ushers in free exchange and liberated substitution — what Freud describes as young sexuality. The mobile fixtures of this future are unrestricted by the abuses of the system of capitalist private property and the system of castrated phallocentrism — what Freud refers to as adult sexuality. The transition from masculine *jouissance* to feminine ecstasy yields an orientation toward the law which is otherwise than the tradition of the brothers of the primal horde. The Woman laughs at the unexplained transition — somehow — from plenitude to lack, and from abundance to scarcity, and from castration to presence, and from good conscience to guilt and remorse. The Woman laughs at the entire constitution of Western civilization. This galaxy is organized by the desire for the clitoris *qua* horrifically deficient rather than *qua* simply different. The distinctively Other relationship between phallus and Other is that the two basic principles of presence and absence (and so on) of the $-istic system are parallactically a ~~Sameness[+]~~ with each other. Each is different from itself but the same as the other.

This Other system is neither inequality of identity nor equality in difference. Rather, S is structured like the playful signifier and signified in difference and relationship rather than by the stiff logic of the word. The proper name for this parallax is strictly unsymbolizable. But Sameness⁺ inspires the appropriate aesthetic toward the bizarre intertwined overlap of each word with every other word of which each is ~~equal~~ and ~~continuous~~ and ~~coincident~~ and the Same⁺. The word for the affect of this Real sublimity is the Woman's clandestine Other Orgasm. Her orgasms are the schizoid's secret truth of the Other's *jouissance*. Unreason is outside of castration and scarcity because Nothing is Missing. The wave-particle duality in quantum physics (1925) shows that the economy (the electron) is both lack (castration, death, absence, loss, deficit, and Something is Missing) and plenitude (fullness, wholeness, abundance, presence, totality, completion, and Nothing is Missing). Otherness is antecedent to the collapse of the electron into the exclusive determinate properties of either lack (the particle) or plenitude (the wave). The collapse into determination is the effect of the act of observation. But why must the masculine subject observe the female junior in her difference and deficit? Why does the male junior look *qua* bewildered and fearful gaze? (I have collapsed quantum theory for my own amusement.)

The transition from masculine to feminine, and from phallus to Other, must avoid this quantum collapse into the neurotic either/or binary economy of traditional observation. Observational interpretation (not the gaze but the look) is the cut which arrests the simultaneous both/and of perversion. The parallactic gap implies an irreconcilable antagonism — parallax — between two interpretations on the "one" and the "same" split object. The parallactic gap reveals that the object is double, in the least. The parallax is split between the particle and the wave in a superposition. The object of the parallactic gap is constitutively split from "itself." The economy of lack and plenitude in the opposition between masculine/feminine exists in a state of superposition. The quantum superposition is antecedent to the shift between these either/or positions. The determinate neurotic either/or is a consequence of observation, interpretation, judgment, evaluation, critique, exposition, clarification, and a generalized hermeneutics. Lack and plenitude are not only intimately proximate but also constitutively coincident. Castration is extimate.

The unique relationship between the phallus and the Other can be glimpsed from a certain perverse and schizoid position of review. The economy is both lack (the particle) and plenitude (the wave). And — both are either lack or plenitude — and both lack and plenitude — and either lack or plenitude — and so on, in perverse *différance*. The survey of the feminine *jouissance* of the parallactic gap is that lack (is) plenitude, already and always. The penis (is) the clitoris, now and forever. This is so even if the is is is not — and is not is and is not, and so on. When will man understand that the system ($-ism) is itself its own subversion *qua* S? When will man witness that $-ism is (not) S? Whose value is accrued by the vigilant aperture of this interval? The aperture and closure of the gap between $-ism and S are the necessary gestures for the critique of $-ism. Even so, when will the scarcity in the capitalist marketplace unveil itself as endless plenitude?

The patriarchal castration of the transformation of difference into deficit in sexual difference reveals a paradoxical Sameness⁺. This is precisely not the fashionable so-called equality in difference. Desire for a Something is Missing cannot be calculated or speculated — general equivalence — with Nothing is Missing. Desire obstructs the counterintuitive realization of the Superpositional-Structure. Men, Women and the rest of us desire an economy which is otherwise and elsewhere to castration and its standardized general equivalence of equality (inequality) and identity (difference). But the strict impossibility of the symbolization of this relationship of ~~Being~~ renders any articulation of a proximity between objects an arduous project with failure as its necessary *telos* without end. This is the reason that the Woman must not speak in a future which is written only at the outskirts of the signifier.

Méconnaissance between the Logics

The Other *jouissance* schizophrenically mobilizes a frenzied politics. It perversely indulges a manic *écriture*. The pervert inverts the relationship between law and desire. Rule and rebellion are the gambit of phallic *jouissance*. The Pervert-Schizoid-Woman resignifies the dynamic as the circuitous and masochistic *Trieb*. Drive is the beyond of the pleasure principle of homoeostatic equilibrium between law and *jouissance*. Desire is based on lack. *Trieb* is organized as the aim itself. Masculine pleasure is ensnared in an endless spiral of a prohibition which forbids as the condition of a transgression which yields to the law as its condition of possibility (and so on). Frustration is the inevitable *Ziel* of the masculine economy.

Phallic enjoyment experiences the lap of the rule of the father's exclusionary law as circular, infinite, and disappointed. The Other *jouissance* exploits the upside and downside of the movement across the inverted torus-like bend between law and *jouissance* as it is retroactively recirculated. Primary pleasure posits the transgressed rule as what will have been (*futur antérieur*) the condition of its possibility. The unnecessary prohibition imagines *jouissance* as what will have been (*futur antérieur*) the source of its emergence. This Other-Ladder of law and *jouissance* — rather than of law and desire — is a traversal or *Trieb* across two sides of the same torus. It is a trippish encounter with a "sameness which is not identical." The law and its transgression are flip-sides of the same bend in the torus-like journey between prohibition and enjoyment. Law and enjoyment are the same structure. Law is enjoyment.

Rule and rebellion are ambivalently parallactic from the perverse quantum superpositional observation of the Other. The Other enjoyment is an effect of subordination to the law. Idiotic *jouissance* is an effect of the transgression of the law. The only mechanism of the subversion of the law of $-ism is an obscene and masochistic observation of and commitment to the law (pact). The perverts have no need for the endless spiral of rule and rebellion. The perverts are ~~deviant~~ from themselves and ~~equivalent~~ to — Sameness⁺ — each other. This is the secret truth of Unreason. The madman is the most lawful (pactful) citizen in the system. He is persecuted because his intellectual commitment demonstrates that the law (pact) is impuissant to joy. The law is opposed to desire, but the law (pact) is coincident with enjoyment. The Other *jouissance* is the sheer ecstasy of the rules in a system in which the future — *works*. This structure posits no genealogical account of the genesis of the rules and prohibitions because they *work*. *Jouissance works*. It has no cause. Desire does not work. Desire has an origin. This *arche* eludes a tedious search for its Real Signified. This word is an imprecise index of the malfunction of desire. Paradoxically, desire works because it does not work. Unfortunately, the system works by not working. Nothing succeeds like failure.

Foucault's work (1975) on sexuality and the immanence of power shows that repression — what Foucault plainly identifies as the "repressive hypothesis" in his critique of psychoanalysis — is liberation — what Foucault wryly describes as the so-called emancipation of the peripheral sexualities in the sexual sermon of modern science. The bodily "repression" of "sex" is the conceptual "liberation" of "sexuality." This Being (what is) is between repression and liberation. The relationship cannot be properly symbolized in the extant symbolic order. Heidegger puts Being under erasure, and Derrida invents neologisms which disperse words beyond presence. But the proximity in Foucault's work between "repression" and "liberation" is the secret truth of the schizoid. This is so even if the equivalence is an effect of Unreason for the masculine order of observation. Foucault writes the secret truth of the schizoid as a pervert. How can "repression" of sex simultaneously be identical to "liberation" in a history of sexuality? The repressed within Foucault's theory of power/knowledge is the self-same and self-identical — as such — which would otherwise genealogically emerge as the effect of Nothingness *ex nihilo*. Foucault obsessively refers to power. This concept is the center of the structure of his *oeuvre.* This repetition belies a reactive return to a center. His otherwise schizoid secret truth of "repression" "is" "production" in its perverse symbolization demonstrates the twists and turns, "spirals of power and pleasure," as he says of the coils of discourse, which make any turn toward humanism both unlikely and absurd.[5]

Freud slyly uncovers the remarkable and paradoxical dynamics of subordination and freedom in his claim that the "memorable and criminal deed" is, as he says, "the beginning of so many things — of social organization, of moral restrictions, and of religion."[6] The *arche* ("beginning") of all of Western civilization is criminal murder. Retroactively, the law will have been itself only in the event of a future crime which is reposited into a lost past. The foundational violence of the phallus is the origin that the Other fundamentally avoids. The pervert disavows the return of violence as the *Verleugnung* of the violence of the crime. The motive of the Other is to evade a castration. The pervert disavows in the both/and simultaneity of the superposition. The psychotic denies the signified of sexual difference. Perverse *Verleugnung* and schizoid *Verwerfung* are organized by a lost center. There is no primal crime (to be) committed because there is no lack in the exclusion of the brothers from the beach house to be redressed with the murderous deed. Nothing is Missing for the brothers. The Nothingness around which identity is structured is substituted with an outlandish and fluorescent Being.

In contrast, the phallus always implies lack in a difference *qua* deficit of the clitoris. The phallus cannot function in the absence of absence. Plenitude is the definition of the Woman. The Woman is an antiego antiloss anticastration antiscarcity ecstatic configuration. She promises a future sociality which is beyond the economy of *le propre* and Outside of the organized privacies and privations of $-ism. The phallus is structured by a castration and a scarcity. This castrated phallus braces and threatens its purpose to organize desire in a system of balanced coordinates: yours against mine, his against hers, and ours against theirs. The phallus is — quaintly — absent. The phallus is — absurdly — fictional. The phallus is the indexical sign for the Metaphoricity — metonymization of metaphor — of metaphor. The function is unmoored in any present metaphor, such as the phallus. The phallus is a void. The effect of this *mise-en-abyme* is the emergence of presence. The phallus must veil this absence of itself in a presence which is obscured by its own dissimulation. The phallus cannot appear as such. This is the fate of all metaphor(icity). As Lacan puts it: "The phallus is the privileged signifier of this very *Aufhebung*, which it inaugurates (initiates) by its disappearance."[7] Paradoxically, the phallus resists the masculine logic of the philosophical "*qua*" — presence, *il y a*, what is, by definition, Being — because it simulates a representation in the absence of any relationship to reference whatsoever.

The presence of the phallus is its absence. The phallus is present as an effect of absence. This opposes the properly phallic logic which enforces a so-called presence against a field of the absence of scarcity, lack, and Something is Missing. The reason that the phallus appears as present ("itself") is because it is absent. This is the logic of the Other that the phallus itself is configured to negate. The Other-Logic contests the phallic proviso of its own system of scarcity and castration. The phallus dissimulates in its absence and presence. The Other rebuffs any opposition between presence/absence — penis/clitoris, active/passive, and so on — altogether. There is only (dis)simulation for the Pervert-Schizoid-Woman. But what principle structures the feminine configuration beyond (this) opposition? What precept balances the (dis)simulation of *Verleugnung* and *Verwerfung*? What center is outside of binary logic and betwixt the words of the opposition itself? What is the center of the diacritics of the signifier? Is the decenter a relationship between a center and a margin? Or is the decenter a rupture with the possibility of any signified relationship with the inside and the outside (and so on) whatsoever?

This same peculiar logic organizes monetary currency under the scarcity of capitalism. The field of money is effective as value and measurement because of a virtual and structural absence. This absence is facilitated by the numeracy of infinity in the initiation of potential loss in the monetary system. There is Something is Missing in my wallet. Schizoidly, Nothing is Missing in currency. The remainder of perverse Nothingness is the gambit of endless calculation and protective *le propre*. Speculation organizes the field of money to the excesses of infinity. Perverts intuit that the supply of money is endless and therefore useless. Exchange is a value and a measurement. But it is unanchored in any necessary scarcity. The general equivalent settles the difference in quantity and quality between a jockstrap and a pair of boxers — unnecessarily. The jockstrap is the *jockstrapiest* and the boxers are the *boxersiest* — no general equivalent standardization is necessary for comparison, contrast, and exchange.

But the current regime of $-ism conceives of currency as restricted. Money is necromantically tethered to a scarce materiality. The enforcement of such restriction is the latent purpose of money. The function of the general equivalent is its manifest form. This is the paradox of the province of money as understood by the phallic order. The infinite calculations of the capitalist system negate the sheer abundance of use-value in the system. The latent truth that Nothing is Missing returns as the symptoms of capitalist exploitation as these manifestations are interpreted in Marxist analysis. The force of labor is restricted by the limitations of currency in the extant relations of production. The manifest function of currency is to enforce the ideologies of castration and scarcity as restrictions on both production and consumption. This contrasts with a communist mode of free production and free consumption of Nothing is Missing, presence, plenitude, abundance, and fullness. The phallus enjoys the bailiwick of money in count, account, accumulation, and exchange-value. Currency unveils — produces *qua* repressed — the stark scarcity which rules the dominant capitalist order under $-ism.

The Other sets ablaze dollars and coins because it understands them as an expendable restraint on free exchange and liberated substitution — what Freud describes as young sexuality. Absence is absent because each is the other as not itself. Why must the clitoris rule the exchange-value of the general equivalent under capitalism? — even as the penis is usually the indicted organ? The male junior fears a present gap of which he is the benefactor. But he worries about a future scarcity which will rob him of that plenitude. The female junior discerns a present absence. But she orients herself toward future abundance. Is it possible to spawn an economy of penises-clitorises? Or is all economy (exchange and substitution) a bet on the absence of Something is Missing? — such that I will exchange my metaphor for yours with the expectation that my gift is (ac)counted by the general equivalent as more valuable than yours?

Lack, Everywhere

The ego is structured by Something is Missing. The endless process of loss and its desperate return is the principle around which order is structured. This explains the consequences of both the primal horde myth and the Oedipus complex for civilization. The idiotic *jouissance* cannot (dis)count the (mis)count in the financial ledger. The balance sheet is forever fastened to the loss (supply/demand dynamics and the mediation of scarcity) that Freud posits at the origin of the world. There is Nothing to (ac)count (for) if Nothing is Missing. Absence is presence. The loss which is incurred in the primal horde murder sparks this will to (ac)count (*le propre*) in all dimensions of social and psychical life. The phallic order interprets the object as loss. In contrast, the Pervert-Schizoid-Woman discerns that the origin of the universe is plenitude. The difference between the phallic order and the structure of the Pervert-Schizoid-Woman is simply: *and*. Schizoidly, Something is Missing is only an oppressive ruse which is organized by the castration complex. This ideological temptation convinces man of the economy of a future lack at the so-called center of a universe of inherited loss.

The center is the guilt and remorse for the death of the father. This fantasized murder is coincident with man's own ego. The male ego is something which is Becoming-Nothing. This ego is a flaccid will to Nothingness rather than a fierce effort for presence. This trick is the ideological machination of the system of $-ism. This system dominates the society of the West. The pervert discerns the paradox that the crime is the law. This contractual pact initiates the maternal law (pact) of the rebirth of the new revolutionary man against the paternal law of the tyranny of the conventional order. There is a crucial difference between the mother's law and the father's law. The paternal prohibition harshly arranges the system according to the rules of guilt and responsibility for an invented absence with the father as general equivalent. The maternal rule playfully invites the young pervert to phallicize the mother's lack in the projection of fetishistic plenitude.

The female penis (and her avatars) are the psychoanalytic figurations of the plenitude of the world. This system is not of calculated equality in speculated difference but of Sameness⁺ in general nonequivalence. The pervert is the conceptual persona whose fetishistic simultaneous enjoyment of the fetish-object *qua* penis-substitute approaches this anti-$-istic configuration. This system-self enjoys Metaphoricity. The pervert's passion for metaphors invariably upends the division between the metaphorical and the literal and the possibility of a metalanguage. This reversal assembles a relationship between metaphors. Relationship is the object of desire and enjoyment for the pervert. The parallactic metaphor is sutured by the radical Sameness⁺ of a metaphor for and as a metaphor which is the same substitution of center. Metaphor is the (*a*)sexuality of the pervert. There is no name for this metaphor because it is the simultaneity — *Yes!* — of the entire battery of signifiers: shoe, Giovanni Ribisi, lace, Drew Carey, fur, Justin Bieber, clitoris, Keanu Reeves, penis, Jake Gyllenhaal, lace, Rupert Grint, fur — and so on, and jockstrap.

The pervert understands that the mother's loss is a gain. The horrific maternal lack is a magical motherly fullness. The phallic mother invites her offspring to renounce absence. The brothers, even the masochistic gingers, must forget the memorable historical misdeed of the murder. The form of this misadventure is a fictitious murderous negation. This murder can only be described as a schizoid foreclosure. The *myth of the myth* of the murder returns from the Real to disrupt the homosexual *fete* in order to constitute a civilization which is otherwise organized around desire, guilt, and remorse. Do the revered totem-animals who figure the father in his absence return the brothers to a memorial past of a reinvented future? — or to a sad present as an effect of a fantasized past? The central mysterious navel of the primal horde myth is the hystericization of desire. How do the brothers fathom revolt in the absence of desire? How does a happy boy desire the object-cause if he is already enjoying what he does not need to (not) enjoy? What is the object in the absence of its (*a*) cause? If the brothers swim on the beach without trunks and chicks, then how do they know (how) to desire?

LAW AS CREATIONIST SUBLIMATION EX NIHILO

There is another modality of return. This return reverses *Verdrängung*, *Verwerfung*, and *Verleugnung*. This return supplements desire with a form of symptomatic lack. Loss returns to itself as different from itself. An Other mechanism ~~hystericizes~~ the desires of the brothers. This Other operation establishes the conditions to turn toward the beach house and heterosexuality. This Other mechanism emerges *ex nihilo*. What enables the turn toward the beach house, and heterosexuality, and the daughters, and the mothers? How is heterosexuality even possible? What is Missing in homosexuality in order for heterosexuality to emerge? What is the castration in and as the penis? What does the penis lack? What is the obverse of the phallocentrism of the communist queer (*a*)sexual *hors-texte*?

Beyond the Penis Principle

The primal horde murder is the constitutive plot for the origin of the foundation of the law as civilization. This origin-story is a fetish. In fetishism, the clitoris is veiled in order to make the sexual relationship for the perverse man or the fetishistic lesbian a successful possibility. Freud's myth is a fetish which sutures the gap between a past Nothing is Missing as the retroactive (*Nachträglichkeit*, *après-coup*) projection of a present Something is Missing. The myth is a fetish which obscures and reveals — *Aletheia* — the prelapsarian (*a*)sexual and political utopia with the boys on the beach. The scene of the making absent of the absence, the making lack of the lack, and the making scarce of the scarcity is a retroactive construction of the mystery of a civilization which is based on (non)consensual normativity.

Sexual difference is veiled by political difference. The latent content of politics is sex. Political difference is hidden by sexual difference. The symptom of sexuality is politics, and the symptom of politics is sexuality. Politics and sex are a "sameness which is not identical." A different sexuality and an alternative politics — the Spirit of the System of the Pervert-Schizoid-Woman — can only be imagined from the neurotic present. This present limits even the possibilities of the revolutionary Event which would retroactively reorder the coordinates of the possible from within the extant symbolic order of $-ism.

Freud's fable is a simulated representation which is equivalent to the lace, fur, shoe, and trunks in the pervert's psychosexual economy. The story is fundamentally metaphorical. The representation in the scene of sexual fetishism is a "penis-substitute" for the "penis" of a prelapsarian sexual utopia on the beach. The representation in the scene of political fetishism is a "law, morality, and religion" which are a substitute for a political utopia in the beach house. On the beach, the scene is the (*a*)sex of objects, each according to his ability, and each according to his need. The fetish of sexuality and politics — *working* — is a retroactive construction of the dysfunctional present. The fetish has already happened for the neurotic. The fetish has yet to happen for the schizoid. The — Fetishing⁺ — for the pervert is the object of his textual effort to signify Becoming in the static language of Being.

The fetish-object is a metaphor for the past which can only be reconstituted in the future. The trouble is that the postlapsarian brothers of sexual repression and law, morality, and religion are neurotic. After the murder, the brothers are drenched in guilt, remorse, and the series of symptoms that psychoanalysis diagnoses. The possibility of a revolution toward the past unto the future is unlikely in a situation such as the present. S may be in the past, but can it be repeated in the future? Can perversity as an institution *pervert the neurotic* as a subject and a sociality?

The fetish substitutes for the penis. But is a metaphor simply a fetish? The difference that the metaphor strives to conceal with itself is not "itself." The traumatic lack that the fetish seeks to suture is an abyssal Metaphoricity. This gap is the object of lack for the male junior. The object of his (potential) castration is life. The penis is a figuration of life and its mergence with death. This is the combinatory paradox of *Eros* and *Thanatos*, of life drive and death drive, and of Being and Nothingness. The binary pairs are coincidental and overlapped in the parallax. But what is the penis even? The penis is undecidable. The penis is both the clitoris and not the clitoris, and so on. If this is so, then the primal horde myth is a mere representation in the absence of any historical referent.

This simulation is a specifically fourth-order simulation. The penis simulation is a radical break from the guarantee of the signified in God, phallus, money, sign, or any general equivalent which arbitrates the value between the oppositions, such as penis/penis-substitute, penis/not-penis, literal/metaphorical, fable/truth, and so on. The difference between the penis-substitute and the penis rends the essence of the penis otherwise than "itself." The penis is always a substitution. The penis is itself the phallus. The phallus is a function of metaphor. The penis is itself a metaphor — but for what? What is the difference among penis-substitute, metaphor, penis, and fetish — and substitute? The primal horde myth is a fetish without an adequate reference in a decidable penis.

The crux of the consequence is that Freud can find neither historical nor empirical reference for the myth. The plot of the fable is pure artifice. Why did Freud invent a fable of murder in 1913 and then only later develop the oedipal theory of first, the female junior's perspective of present castration and a futural return and, second, the male junior's intuition of a present abundance and a futural loss? In the oedipal tales, the process for the female junior is loss with return as potential gain. The male junior's trajectory is of an abundance which returns as annexation. The story begins with plenitude — Nothing is Missing — only to devolve into prospective loss. Oedipally, the female junior's origin is loss — *fait accompli* — which returns as gain. In contrast, the male junior starts with plenitude which returns as castration. The female junior achieves liberation. The male junior encounters loss. In the Oedipus complex, the female junior's desire is for a consumption which is based on Nothing. This Nothing will become Something in mimesis. The male junior's desire for and protection of Something will become Nothing. The distinction among the fetish, the substitute, and the metaphor is illuminated. The fetish conceals the horror of clitoral castration that the pervert disavows. The substitute obscures the presence of the fetish. This presence is the object of the pervert's enjoyment. The metaphor veils the parallactic gap — $-ism and S — which is revealed in metonymy *qua* metaphor.

The male junior of Oedipus catches sight of the female genitalia. He understands this Nothing not-penis as a castration. His curious epistemophilic instinct imagines that the female junior has been punished. He thinks that she has been castrated by the father. This thought haunts him retroactively (*Nachträglichkeit, après-coup*) as the consequence of the dire terror of the father's threat of castration. This threat chides the offspring to renounce his self-pleasurable desire and accede to an identification with the rules and conventions of the system of $-ism. These dictates involve the imperative that the penis be understood as capitalist private property. What is the castration that the male junior witnesses in the lack of the female junior? The boy understands and experiences his own penis as the center of his existence. The penis is his source of pleasure and enjoyment. The penis is the essence of his desire. Desire is the ground of the psychoanalytic subject.

The boy's view of the female junior's lack is a cracked mirror reflection of his loss. The male junior potentially loses in the unhappy happenstance of a future in which the penis is exchanged for the not-penis. What is this loss? What is a penis which defies the phallocentric sign in reference to the female not-penis? What is the female penis or the male clitoris? What is a "not-penis"? These are basal ontological questions. It is a query which is made a profound conundrum because grammatology upsets the possibility of a coherent riposte to the "What is?" Deconstruction even troubles the effort to offer a response to the ontological question of Being, *qua*, as such, *il y a*, in essence, and by definition. The undecidability of the Being of the penis — "What is a penis?" — rends any determinate answer to the Being — even as Nothingness — a loss for both the penis and the clitoris. At best, the definitions of the fetish, the substitute, and the metaphor are unveiled. A fetish veils the horror of the disavowed castration. The substitute veils the presence of the object of the pervert's pleasure in the fetish. The metaphor obscures the parallactic gap — $-ism and S — which is otherwise manifest in the metonymization of metaphor. But the referent for these costumes of fetish, substitute, and metaphor — penis and clitoris — is under duress and under erasure.

There are yet other component reasons that the penis is undecidable. The penis accrues its precarious value only in relationship — compare, contrast, and exchange — with the clitoris, the not-penis, and Nothingness. Freud lazily mentions "size" and "visibility" as the criteria for the difference between the penis and the clitoris.[8]

A not-penis is summarized as a deficit in size and a defect in visibility. But this deficit and defect are measured in relationship to the penis. Freud's posited difference shows that the penis *qua* the penis — as such, *il y a,* in essence, *qua,* by definition — accrues its value only in a relationship of comparison, contrast, and exchange with the clitoris, the not-penis, and Nothingness. The penis is itself in relationship to the entirety of the other objects in the system *except itself.* What is a penis? A penis is a relationship with the other objects in the system except itself.

The Something is Missing entails a qualification of the Missing. The male junior gazes in terrified horror at the not-penis of castration, lack, negativity, and loss. But this Something is Missing must represent a presence which is absent from the Nothing is Missing. What is the Clitoral Something (not-penis, and so on) which is extimate to the penile Nothing is Missing of abundance, presence, fullness, plenitude, and so on? The offspring witnesses himself without his penis. This not-penis represents the male junior. But the not-penis represents the male junior in an absence of pleasure and enjoyment but also simultaneously in an absence of fear and anxiety. The male junior is confronted with the castration of enjoyment and, specifically, with the coincidence of castration and pleasure. The threat of castration is the loss of *jouissance.* Enjoyment is the risk of loss.

The reason that the offspring substitutes desire for identification is to evade the loss of *jouissance.* But, at the same time, the offspring's will to identification with cultural ideals presupposes a limit on *jouissance.* This restraint is the proviso for the protection of the private(s) property of the masculine subject. Identification and desire are oppugnant to each other. The sad fate of the neurotic is this loss of *jouissance.* The superego saps ever more joy from the neurotic even as he wills the satisfaction of conscience. The superegoic imperative — *Jouir!* — is a permutation of this obligation to enjoy under duress. The pervert recognizes that such a law is the sadist's enjoyment. The neurotic has yet to discover the pervert's variant of masochism — whose partner is another clever masochist, ginger or not.

The gambit of the reckless and murderous deed is entry into the culture. The effect of the doer of the deed is the investment of guilt and remorse in the brothers. This subject's self-identity and self-sameness disrupt the primary ontological togetherness (Being, what is) of the world. This explains the profound significance of the murder of the primal father for the future of Western civilization. It also indicates the reason that Freud situates a myth at the origin of the world. Freud posits the murder of the primal father — as present. He does so in order to reinscribe the effects of the transition of playful enjoyment with the mother — toward the castration threat of the female junior — and then toward the castration anxiety of the penis — and then toward the identification with the father and his ego-ideal regime of rule, regulation, code, private property, husband, father, worker, and so on. The myth of the murder explains and enforces the normativity of selfhood and society. The future of civilization is not only contingent on the clitoris. World is also structured on the identification with the father and his will to reproduce the norms of the culture in his son. These codes are based in the psychical symptoms of narcissism, aggression, and anxiety. Western civilization is the heir to the clitoris.

The norms of the culture are reproduced through the body of the Woman and her clitoris. The Woman is extimate to the symbolic order. She is both the center and the margin of the text of the West. Her Nothingness is the simultaneous Being of the system, and her Being is the at once Nothingness of the System. The undefined clitoris must be resymbolized as the female penis (or whatever avatar for the lack) in order to restructure the system on the logic of Nothing is Missing rather than Something is Missing. The pervert's will is to speak and to write this Other. This project will inevitably transform the norms of the culture and, by extension, the concept of normativity itself. After the symbolization of the Woman, $-istic psychical symptoms will be transformed.

Figure 12.3 The Object of *Différance*

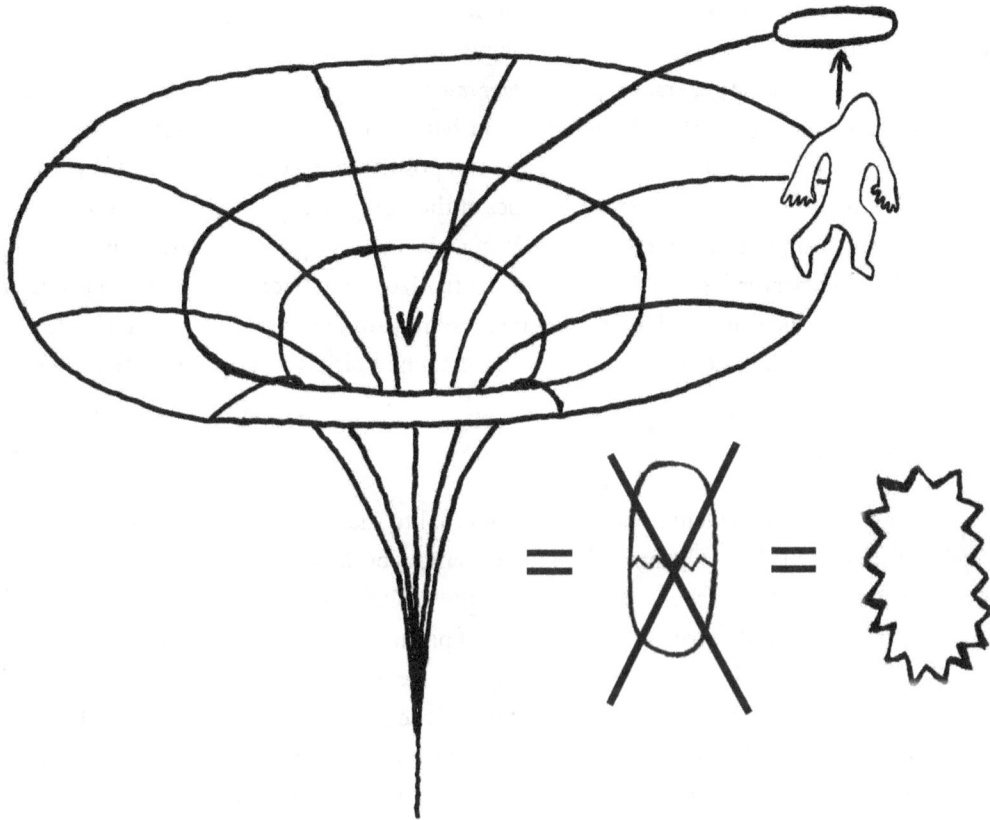

This image depicts the object of desire as paradoxically Outside of the system of desire. This structure of desire is otherwise based in sexual difference, castration, loss, and death. The object is exclusively spatial in its discoordination with the timelessness of the unconscious. The object is atemporal. Fables of temporality are effects of chronological narration. These myths of time are effects of space. This space is the fundamental dimension of the galaxy. The object traverses downward (upward) toward (away from) the (*a*)sexual center of fire and brimstone. This (*a*)sexuality is both/and Outside and Inside of the system because it is a leap ahead of (behind) the negation which (re)structures it. The excluded object precisely is *not* because it is not present in a decided and determinate space in the field of the unconscious. The boundaries of the object are fragmented (center, right). This object is the Clitoral Stage *objet* of the *Trieb* of the future. The future is the space in which any object can be itself (not itself) as neither self-same nor self-identical but singular (center, right). This singular object is a Sameness+ between the system and the fragmented object. This singularity resists capture in the general equivalence of comparison, contrast, and exchange.

Notes & Sketches —

But what is the not-penis if not the entirety of the battery of the signifiers in the Other with the exception of the penis? The pervert's will to rescue the female penis from cultural and Freudian obliteration — what is a Woman? — is the key to a disruption of the dominance of the sign over the signifier. The female penis is also the proviso for the destabilization of the positive entity of the penis against the negative and differential play of objects in the absence of any center, such as the penis. Saussure's value of the signifier defies the phallus, father, currency, sign, and the general equivalent *tout court*. The sign forecloses the signifier. The consequence of this dominion of the sign is that the not-penis rather than the diacritical play of the signifier rules the system. The murder of the primal father privileges the positive binary oppositions of the sign *qua* self-same and self-identical of signification above the diacritics of the signifier and the difference and negativity of value. The schizoid's political job is to contest this phallocentrism (scarcity and castration) which originates in the invented murder. The pervert's symbolic work is to textualize the schizoid's logic of Freud's *libretto*. Together, the labor is to enforce the value of diacritics against the masculine libido. The Woman's breath is to live and to become this novel modality of selfhood and sociality. The Spirit of the System is the *à venir* of the future.

The Primal Father

The father enforces enjoyment because loss is internal to the *jouissance* of the idiot. His ego is the process of losing itself. The ego is lost. The masculine subject enjoys because there is a castration and a scarcity in the system: in the patriarchal case, the female junior; in the capitalist case, limited resources. Freud murders the primal father in order to underwrite the father's rule of patriarchy and capitalism from the grave. The general equivalent of death insures law, morality, and religion. Death is the absolute master. Death is the general equivalent which trumps even the mediatory functions of the phallus, father, currency, and sign. The neurotic's drowned father returns in his blatant chicanery and charmed dishonesty. The so-called effects of liberation (transgression, violation, defiance, and trespass) against the tyranny of the law summon this dead father. Such breaches and resistances are painful reproductions of the bond between lawful rule and transgressive desire.

But the father need not be dead — must not be dead — in a society which is structured by the binds of *Eros* against the splinters of *Thanatos*. The Unreasonable secret truth of the symbolic order emerges as this Real. *There is no father*. The father is mythically present. Why does Freud conjure him? He returns only as a deadly reminder of castration and scarcity. The father drowns — but how? He does so only to be dragged ashore and laid to decompose on the clothesline with the boys' trunks and the animal totems. The brief and obscene function of the dead primal father in the prehistory of man is to make loss effective for the society. The world — but not the next — is structured by loss. The pretense to the Spirit of the System is the resurrection of presence in the female penis, the male clitoris, and the —

Losses under Capitalism

The capitalist marketplace arranges the constitutive loss at the center of masculinity. This commodified loss means that each commodity is different from every other commodity. Each commodity is the same as itself. The self-sameness and self-identity of each capitalist commodity render exchange possible only with reference to the third term of the general equivalent. The God (in) Trust can adjudicate the relative value in quantity and quality of the commodity in question. This masculine logic is opposed to the Other *jouissance*. The feminine discovers a parallactic gap within/out each object. This aneconomy elevates the commodity above the reductive logic of the general equivalent of the commodity form and its mediation by currency. The feminine enjoyment invites the object to elude commodification.

The identity of the object deviates from itself because it is subject to the cascade of the generation of diacritical value. Perversely, what is is what is not. The pervert experiences the elision of Being, as such, *qua*, in essence, by definition, *il y a*, and so on. The murder of the primal father and the introduction of lack into the center of an economy in which Something is Missing initiate exchange and substitution. This third function is an agency of arbitration. This standard renders each commodity simultaneously both identical and incommensurable to the other commodities in the marketplace. This consequence of the father's murder illuminates the reach of the economy of *le propre* under the rule of both castration in patriarchy and scarcity under capitalism. The substitution of or the exchange between commodities in the economy of capitalism is isomorphic to the displacement (*Wo Es war*) in the economy of metaphor.

Limited comparison, contrast, and exchange — in a closed system — facilitate the slip and slide in, "My love is like a red, red rose," and so on. The gap between "my love" and "a red, red rose" cannot be sutured by any further difference and deferral of metaphorization in discourse. The series of metonymies which is metaphorically supplemented is strictly endless. Not only is "my love" precisely not "a red, red rose" — then, and so on — in an open system. In addition, the identity of "my love" — and of "a red, red rose" — is both indeterminate and incomplete. What is "a red, red rose" like? The closed system of the neurotic returns the series of loves and red, red roses to love — the open system of the schizoid resists return to loves and the red, red roses to — The remorseful guilt at the plinth of the loss of the father inflects even metaphor. This metaphor is a literal figuration of the Freudian ego. The slip and slide between "my love" and "a red, red rose" present a misfit between the two objects in uneasy (non)correspondence, (in)equivalence, (in)equality, (non) continuity, and (non)coincidence — Sameness[+] — with each other. This guilt is constitutive because the social organization of scarcity and castration under $-ism is the material component of a system which is structured around the lost ego. This ego is decentered from its customary position in the center of the structure.

Freud's allegory of the primal horde murder articulates that at the moment of man's liberation in the murder of the primal father he encounters guilt and remorse. When the brothers storm the beach house, their reaction is a sad resolve to order a world in which revolt against the coordinates of the system is prohibited and transgression against the rule is punished. The brothers were certainly happier — in *Trieb* rather than *désir* — outside on the beach. These sands and seas are an antecedent and prelapsarian space in which castration and lack were excluded. The social order can only proceed according to the dictates of private property and the general equivalent. This can be so only in the presence of absence and in the specter of loss. The ego "itself" is the process of its own loss of "itself." This lost ego is the origin of the system.

The guilty conscience is berthed in the figuration of the fable of man. Guilt and remorse reinstate the prohibition that the crime originally intended to redress. This idiotic *jouissance* is the affect of the act of so-called revolutionary liberation from the primal father. The historic mistake returns the brothers to the prohibition that their mythical act aspired to avoid. The phallic *jouissance* of false emancipation also appointed the rule of castration and scarcity. This castrative code incited additional foolish acts of masculine enjoyment, such as relations with private property, subordination to the general equivalent, enforcement of binary oppositions, ideological commitment to scarcity, contextualization by castration, and so on. There was neither scarcity nor castration before the brothers stormed the beach house with trunks off and towels wet. The act of revolution established the limits of resources. The revolt promoted the potential for annexation. The revolution ordered law, morality, and religion. This is the foundation of the system of $-ism. S of the past as it is imagined from the perspective of the $-istic present awaits a return to the past-future of S in the present of $-ism. The trouble is this metaphysics of presence. The Time of the Neurotic disturbs presence because its temporality retroactively pins the past in the future and the future in the past. The Time of the Schizoid ruins presence because the infinite slippage of the trace upsets any division among past, present, and future — *Yes!*

The act of fraudulent liberation only achieved the momentary masculine pleasure of the paltry spoils of the mythical battle with the primal father. The brothers enjoyed the crucifixion of the father's body. But in the aftermath of the violent deed, the brothers released the Women (daughters, mothers, and sisters) who were the supposed objects of desire from which they had previously been excluded. Both castration in phallocentric patriarchy and scarcity in (capitalist) economics were invented by the lore of the ego as the loss in Something is Missing. But is the murder a committed deed? Or is the murderous crime a dreamy nightmare whose only purpose is to secure the ever delayed origins of Western civilization to the fantasy of absence? Why does Freud *fantasize castration*? Why do the brothers retroactively (*Nachträglichkeit, après-coup*) imagine a Nothing is Missing of penis, female penis, clitoral-penis, penis-clitoris, penis-penis, clitoro-clitoris, and so on?

THE MYTH OF THE MYTH

The murder is the *arche* of the guilty conscience of civilization. A deconstructive interpretation of the primal horde myth displaces the primacy of the murder *qua* origin for its subjective and social effects on man and Western civilization. The murder may be an effective myth. This is so even if its presence is put under scrutiny by deconstruction. The myth of the primal horde murder is a retroactive reconstruction of the masculine spoils of civilization. This is so in order to both obscure and reveal the fundamental structure of the social system ($-ism). This system is organized by the brothers in the aftermath of — What? The brothers exchange what can be described as an undefined exclusion from the primitive community — the beach — for the phallic *jouissance* dynamic of law/transgression — foundation of Western civilization. This stupid cycle is the consequence of the guilty conscience and its institutions in law, morality, and religion. This exchange is isomorphic to Lacan's existential exchange of *lettre pour l'être*. The swap in-out is neither free nor liberated. Rather, the trade is a forced choice. The brothers had faced their own imagined murder after the father's death in the absence of any enforceable social contract. Freud writes,

> [The brothers] revoked their deed by forbidding the killing of the totem, the substitute for their father; and they renounced the fruits by resigning their claim to the Women who had not been set free.[9]

The operative sign in the passage is "substitute." It is metaphor — or Metaphoricity— for "totem." This "substitution" refers to the radical foreclosure (murder) of the primal father. This *Verwerfung* is the so-called origin of law, morality, and religion at the foundation of the social order.

The Myth of the Myth

The instructive point is that the "substitute" for the father is a "substitute" for Nothing. This representative of the father is a creationist sublimation *ex nihilo*. This substitute is also a trace of *différance*. This creationism out of Nothing is the cause and effect of a trace which is beyond any *arche* in which Nothing is Missing because Something is Missing. This *différance* blurs the division between Something/Nothing. Trace introduces the

Time of the Schizoid into the fable of the primal horde. There is no presence for the schizoid with which Being could neurotically identify. A retroactive constitution of the past in the future is impossible. The Time of the Schizoid suspends this *point de capiton*. Trace in space overruns any distinctive temporality. The father and his murder surface from traces and exchanges which obscure any *arche*. The Event manifests out of Nothing. It is a creationist sublimation *ex nihilo*. The consequence of this interpretation is that prehistoric man is the brother who is outside in the cool winds on the beach at sunset with his brothers.

The father is the totem animal. The dead father is neither substitute nor metaphor nor artifact. Rather, the father is a deferred origin who is subject to a series of substitutions — including the "primal father." His presence is deferred. But this is so in a system which is organized around debt. This supplemental subtraction is owed to the father for the mythical murder. The ambivalent series of gifts and sacrifices that Freud uncovers in prehistorical totemic practices is a symbolic stockpile of goods. These objects are circulated in a social economy of castration. This economy is based on absence and the female genitalia of Something is Missing. The series of totems is a substitute for castration. Perversely, substitution is castration. Madly, subtraction is positively and (in) finitely supplemented. The totem is a substitute for a father. This father was never a father. The father's mortal function is the metonymization of metaphor. The trace of the totem is the fictional death of the primal father to which the token owes its distant and recollected origin. The totem is the father. But the father is also a totem.

The primal horde myth indicates that the brothers imposed their own punishment for the crime of the revolt against the primal father. A society which is structured by law is the proper frame for a community which is organized by grief. The law is the appropriate arrangement in retroaction for the mournful subject. The Pervert-Schizoid-Woman eschews the Something is Missing and its various psychoanalytic symptomatology of melancholia, and so on. There is no gap in the system except the split which fissures each object from itself. The All is the All *except* — This inconsistency is sutured in the relationship of Being with the other objects in the system.

The pervert's view of the female genitalia *qua* empty cavity is *sous rature*. The clitoris is returned and sutured by representation in the fetish-object. The fetish returns from negation *qua* itself. Both the bewildered and besieged *Ich* and the unsatisfied and incorrigible *Es* structure the brothers' psyches before the murder. Unbridled (*a*)sex is unhinged and impenetrable. The ferocious *Über-Ich* of the commandment to enjoy demands the return to order at the cost of enjoyment. But none of this coordination is possible until — if — the father is murdered by the brothers. If the boys burn down the beach house, then Oedipus rules. The brothers berate themselves for their crime. The brothers release the objects of their desire. The brothers install a civilization which enforces the renunciation of enjoyment.

Totems and Taboo

The relationship between the brothers and the dead father is structurally ambivalent. Freud acknowledges that he cannot explain the genealogical origin of this fundamental affective orientation toward the father. Freud writes: "Totemic religion not only comprised expressions of remorse and attempts at atonement, it also served as a remembrance of the triumph over the father."[10] This triumph is the social order which is invented by the brothers. They fabricate this system in order to limit the Other *jouissance*. The Other is otherwise only accessible to the primal father in a regretful past. The triumph of the brothers over the father initiates the rule of castration after the reign of the obscene paternal *jouissance* of the mythical past. The Other (*a*)sexual *jouissance* is otherwise only imaginable to the boys in a lost paradise.

The triumph of the murderous deed and its aftermath is the victory of castration and scarcity. Something is Missing rules the ideology of Western civilization in the patriarchal interpretation of sexual difference and in the capitalist fabrication of scarcity. But the sad failure of the brothers of the defeated revolutionary debacle can be celebrated by the Pervert-Schizoid-Woman as a happy success. The perspective of the perverts of the feminine enjoyment is unmoored in any symbolic order. The neurotic world is designed by the loss of an ego and the penis in castration and by a limitation on production and consumption in scarcity.

The ambivalence that the brothers felt toward the inert father is evinced in the ritual sacrifice of the totem animal. This sacrificial act atones in reproduction for the murder. Totemism is a symbolic patricide which was performed when the bounty from the original murder, such as paternal attributes, threatened to disappear from the community under the aegesis of castration and scarcity. The loss is symbolically and ritually replayed in the absence of the goods that otherwise suture the wound of the father's death. This bandage returns to the plenitude before the murder. This fantasmatic surplus is a mere backward glance toward a fictional origin-story of the past. But why is the origin-story of Nothing rather than Something?

The system is organized by loss. This requires a degree zero of Nothing is Missing in order for loss — and its obverse: gain — to be calculated and then either suffered or celebrated. All that is vanished is subordinate to the calculations of cost. The lost bounty of paternal attributes is yet another additional subtraction. These symbols of lost abundance demand further sacrifice and renunciation. This economy of scarcity demonstrates the organization of the money economy around loss: ego, other, and community. The so-called origin of civilization is an imagined allegory of loss because the loss must be subtracted from plenitude. The genesis of society is this mythology. The loss is lost.

The sutures for the wound of this absence are the various ideologies of castration, phallocentrism, patriarchy, scarcity, supply/demand, and general equivalence. These ideological configurations frame the prehistorical engagement with the series of worshiped and sacrificed totemic protocommodities. Civilization is born of a fake crime against an invented father. The origin is a myth. The Pervert-Schizoid-Woman can only laugh at the unlikely success of the ruse of the invented murder of a sham paternal presence. The Nothing is Missing is a retroaction of the civilization of scarcity. The exchange of Nothing (Something) for Something (Nothing) promises plenitude at the same time as it installs a system of its impossibility. But were the origin Something is Missing, were the tale told by the female junior, then —

"God is Dead"

In his *Seminar* on the ethics of psychoanalysis (1959-1960), Lacan provides a pithy response to the puzzle of the origin of civilization. Did law solicit transgression? Or did rebellion retroactively constitute the rule? Lacan writes: "God, then, is dead. Since he is dead, he always has been."[11] God's death is not simply retroactive as a glance backward at a distant lost point of origin and destination. Rather, God's death is precisely not a death. God died in a different modality of death than the transition between the alive and the dead. Lacan's point is that God's Nothingness ("is dead," "always has been") is God's Being. God is born dead. The function of God is organized by his death. The God-function is his death and its effects on man and world. God cannot be dead because his effect *qua* God is a function of this death in whose shadow God and man are thinking, being, and living. Freud compares deity to paternity: "at bottom God is nothing other than an exalted father."[12] If the father is dead, then so God is dead.

The consequences of Lacan's simple statement — "Since God is dead, he always has been" — are extraordinary. The mythology is internal to the myth itself. The brothers are at the start oedipalized — desirous and hystericized. The brothers must be oedipalized and heterosexualized in order to desire the mothers, daughters, and sisters in the clan. At the *arche* — at the final start of the origin — the boys desire the mothers, daughters, and sisters. Desire and its repression are the condition of the fraternal revolutionary unity against paternity. The father is the source of their sexual frustration and political exclusion. This is also the reason that the primal father — the original man — must be heterosexual. The brothers must be at the origin hystericized and desirous. This is so in order for the brutal treatment of the brothers by the primal father to incite a desirous frenzy to overthrow the paternal regime and murder the father.

But the purpose of the murder and its aftermath ("law, morality, and religion") is precisely to instruct in fantasy the desires of the brothers that otherwise precede the murder and its consequences. The past happens in the future, and the future happens in the past. The present is the trace of this retroaction, or Freudian *Nachträglichkeit* and Lacanian *après-coup*. The brothers only desire their object as an effect of the desire of this object. The boys desire a murder and a sexual *fête* with the ladies only after this assassination and orgy. Strangely, *the brothers desire before they desire*.[13] This desire is a creationist sublimation *ex nihilo*. Desire is untied to any origin, such as the cycle of law/prohibition. There is no *arche* which could generate this desire. There is no genesis of desire. Desire will always be *Trieb*. Desire is always already drive because it is organized as pure trace. Desire is *différance* such that nothing has happened yet. Trace disrupts any past, present, and future — beginning, middle, and end — of the storybook of desire. The brothers are still waiting for (a)sex with their twins and sex with their sisters. In the schizoid trace, sexuality is suspended as antecedent and posterior to sex. In contrast, neurotic desire is best understood as a retroactive reconstruction of analysis. Fraternally, (a)sexuality awaits —

The desire of the brothers returns from the future to the past. The desire of the boys in the past only will have been such a desire in the future event that the desire achieves its aim. The desire to murder the father is only possible after the murder of the father. This murder retroactively constitutes the desire. This desire is its own — *ex nihilo* — condition. This is the temporal logic of deferred action for the neurotic. Desire can only emerge if the father is murdered. But the murder of the father cannot be explained as the effect of an original desire. Neurotically and psychotically, the brothers desire in the absence of desire. The subject simply does not desire as a subject of desire. Desire is inessential and dispensable. Desire would be referred to an origin either in the past from the future or from the future to the past. But no such presence in temporalities is possible. It can be concluded that desire does not work because it has an *arche*.

Neurotically, desire does not work because the return of the repressed in the symptom disrupts ordinary life. Desire (*Trieb*) does not refer to an *arche* because the origin (is) trace. The suspended presence cannot temporally coordinate retroaction. There is no cause of desire for the schizoid. Psychotic desire precisely *works*. It is a profound mistake of humanity to posit the departure-destination of desire in either theory or practice. The origin of desire (is) the trace of the deed. This deed is only possible in the aftermath of this desire. The deed precedes the doer, and the future precedes the past. This is the deed/doer relationship for the neurotic. The object is antecedent to the desire: *petit a objet*. The brothers become themselves in the violent process of the father's murder. But antecedent to the rush of the beach house is a *Trieb* which encircles *Ziel* as the (a)sexual aim itself.

The neurotic is situated between retroaction of the future in the past. Desire precedes itself — but in presence. The schizoid is Other and situated between _____ and _____. Outside of proper hystericization, what is the pedagogy of desire? The brothers learn how to desire in the *mise-en-scène* of fantasy. The blind spot of the lost historical mark and abstract empirical reference of the myth is the (a)sexual shenanigans on the beach. These deeds provoke the brothers to discover that Something is Missing. This exclusion is otherwise sutured by an oceanic *jouissance* in which Nothing is Missing. The oceanic oneness of Spirit — Freud refers to it as religion — shorts desire and castration, and so on.[14] But is the lack of the lack itself a constitutive lack? The substitute-formation for the hystericization of desire on the outskirts of the primal clan must be a queer mechanism. At what point does an originary homosexual libido confront — Something? If Something is Missing in the female genitals, then what is this simultaneous Something is Missing in the boys, their sexualities, and their penises? What is the not-penis *of* the penis on the beach?

Always Already

There is another unexpected consequence of Lacan's critical insight that the father-God has always already been murdered. This murder is otherwise the Event that Freud's myth purports to explain. Neurotically, the traumatic murder and heroic misdeed have already taken place. The doers of the deed have always already committed the deed in the process of Becoming the doers. Becoming the doer in the process of the deed is retroactive. The brother only will have been a brother — desirous and hystericized — in the future event that the father is murdered. This temporal logic is the Time of the Neurotic. The origin-story of civilization is elementally neurotic. The brothers' phenomenological experience is of guilt and remorse in the future. The brothers' only experience from within the internal twists and external turns of the myth is the guilty conscience. There can be no prelapsarian bliss which is antecedent to the murder of the primal father and the consequences of the mistaken deed.

Freud's entire myth — start to finish — is articulated from a retrospective glance from the future backward toward the past. The exclusion, desire, revolt, murder, guilt, remorse, and civilization have always already been experienced and constituted. Neurotically, the past of civilization presses toward the present. But presence is also schizoidly retroactively revised in the suspension of the present in a pure *différance* which identifies the world as both already past and not yet present. At the same time, the madman's intuition is that both nothing has happened yet and that everything has already happened. The simultaneity of Nothing-Everything is such that the totality of history (*et al.*) is the instant of _____. The murder has already been committed in an irrecoverable past. The murder has also never been committed in an experienced present. The necromantic oddity of Freud's myth is that the loss of the primal father cannot be the origin of law. The father never appeared — even to disappear — as such. The father is always already dead. The schizoid's caveat is that the father is not-yet dead. But the simultaneity of the already and the not-yet elides an origin-story *tout court*. The madman principally contests the *arche* as isolated from the Other.

The massive achievement of Freud's work is the demonstration of a mythical father who is lost to trace and *différance*. The neurotic pins the present and retroactively measures the loss of this dead father. Freud's fable invents scarcity and castration at the origin of a world in which the father is *mythos*. The brothers did not murder the father. Rather, the signifier — psychotic *différance* — murdered the father. Freud's regressive move in his account of the fable is the enforcement of the neurotic *point de capiton* of the reality principle on the myth. Freud structured an origin-story which is based on the subtly peculiar device of a parricide lost to the paradoxical logic of a desire. This desire is posterior to the *Trieb* on the sands of the beach.

It is crucial that the father never appears as such and that the brothers have always already murdered the father. The fundamental latent truth of Freud's indication is that there is no origin of "law, morality, and religion." The *arche* is but an antecedent exclusion of the gay brothers from the beach house. The origin of a civilization is the gambit of a mythical father. The dynamic of law-prohibition and transgression-*jouissance* is a ruse. Both movements achieve the same end of the guilty conscience of castration and scarcity. The purpose of the trace of the primal father is the guilty conscience and its subjective and social resources. But what is antecedent to the trace? Are the ocean and its sands the Outside of the signifying chain? If this Outside is precisely unconscious, then the atemporality of the myth indexes Freud's intervention as strictly schizophrenic.

Figure 12.4 Metaphorization of Metonymy and Metonymization of Metaphor in *Trieb*

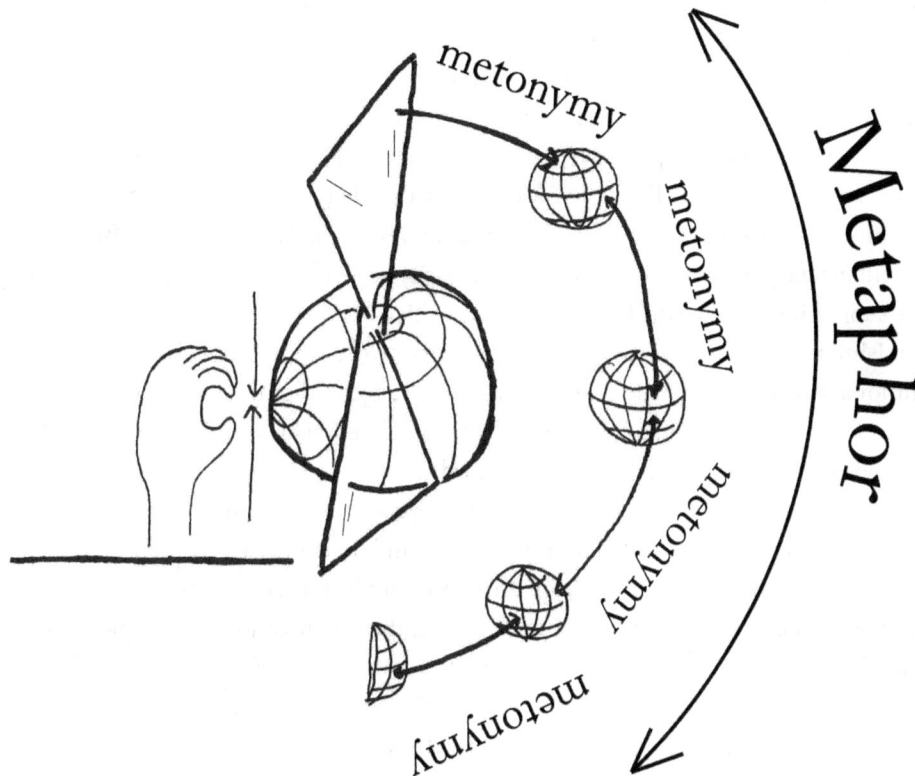

This picture represents the relationship between totality and a closed system and multiplicity and an open system. The illustration also figures the relationship between metaphor and metonymy. The image shows that the series of metonymies of units of text (A, B, C, D, and so on) and any system of metaphor presume to simulate an originary object. But the (trace of the) object is structured on the air and water of an absent advent in both/either metaphor and/or metonymy. The Outside of the metaphysics of presence is a _____ of the spoken and the written. The parallactic overlap of metaphor and metonymy (left) is the simulacrum of a series of totalizations of multiplicities — and multiplications of totalities — in the absence of reference. There is a semblance of *arche* because the origin must be both Outside and Inside of the system — Why? The simultaneous superpositional juxtaposition is necessary in order to found the system from the Outside. At the same time, the structure is situated Inside of the system as its origin. The pervert's sphere is (de)centered both everywhere and nowhere. This is the nether side of the compulsive dance of the metonymization of metaphor (metaphorization of metonymy). The pervert's gesture parallels the compulsive insistence toward closedness and contraction. But it does so in an act which returns an Otherness and an excess to the closed system of the *point de capiton* of metaphor. The long arrow of metaphor (right) illustrates a *Trieb* which precedes *désir*. This *Trieb* articulates a primordial atemporality — against the fictions of the narratives of chronological temporality — whose procession is the timeless space of the unconscious. The jockstrap *qua* fetish is both metonymy and metaphor. The pervert arrests and releases — suspends — the jockstrap in the superposition of Being and Nothingness, presence and absence, is and is not, and so on. *Trieb* encircles the jockstrap ("Boy") which returns as the differed Boy of "Boy" in a series of Boys (jockstraps) in the expanses of space.

Notes & Sketches —

The Desire for Castration

The satisfaction of the ego-ideal is impossible under the conditions of the myth of the murder of a father who never appears as such. The ego-ideal motivates the subject's failed identifications in the cultural order as man/Woman, white/black, straight/gay, native/foreign, abled/disabled, and so on. These points of identification are organized around a constitutive disidentification. Repressed (dis)identification returns with the symptoms of racism, sexism, homophobia, and so on. The murderous object of the guilty conscience is for a crime which was never committed. The father was always already murdered. The crime was never presently committed. The brothers live on the hot sands of the beach forever. This is the Outside. But, at the same time, the boys also simultaneously suffer guilt for a crime which was never committed and which was always already committed. The subject internalizes the fable of a murder which was never committed. Innocence is converted into guilt by a misinformed memory and a slick temporality of the Time of the Neurotic. The brothers can only suffer guilt for a substitution for the original crime. The object of guilt is *différance* itself.

The metaphor for the object of guilt is visible in the totem. The father is a fantasy. The ideological purpose of the father — and of the entire myth of the primal horde as outlined by Freud — is the enforcement of the foundation of the guilty conscience in man. This precept reproduces the principles of castration and scarcity in the social order. The system is structured around the scandalous delusion of a murdered father and his ghostly remainders in totem-commodities in capitalism and in God in generalized equivalence. There is no proper object of the brothers' guilt. *Trieb* rather than *désir* is the organizational principle. Drive is outside of the father's beach house. Communist (*a*)sexual queerness (is) *différance*. Time-Space <> (*a*)sexual <> Space-Time. The totem is the father. Paternity is itself a form of totemism. The father and the totem are strictly interchangeable. There is no such thing as the metaphorical. The totemic animal is the patriarch of the primal horde. There is no such thing as the literal. The father is the primal horde of the *Politburo*.

Queerly, the proper object of guilt escapes untainted because the absence is empty. The lack is infinitely substitutable with other signifiers in the system. The brothers atone in their guilty conscience for their own radical innocence. The brothers are guilty of innocence. But at what moment? Guilt emerges in the absence of a genesis for the system. The object of guilt is a proleptic loss which has yet to be lost. This indicates the unfortunate truth that guilt works. The system successfully operates by the guilty conscience. The pervert disavows the loss of the maternal phallus in order to will a world of plenitude. The penis is the clitoris because the penis is not the penis. The trace of the primal father is the manifest form of a latent content whose truth is castration and scarcity. The primal father-God is displaced in the absence of the diabolical and premeditated intent of man. There is no proper guilt for man because he is not the doer of the deed. The doer is an effect of the deed. The absence of the deed means that there is neither doer nor desire. There (is) *Trieb*. The father is murdered in the absence of the brothers. The father is murdered before the birth of his sons. The murder simply happened as a deed without a doer. It is a murder without a murderer. It is a disappearance without an appearance. It is a nonappearance.

Lacan illuminates the paradoxical acquittal of the brothers for the crime for which the myth prosecutes them. The myth exonerates the otherwise guilty brothers. The tale weaves the origin of law, morality, and religion as the negation of the Other *jouissance*. Then the fable uncovers that the brothers are submitted to the ferocity of the superego and the demands of the ego-ideal. The crucial function of guilt in the primal horde myth is the creationist sublimation *ex nihilo* of this guilt. Guilt is the substitution for the void of the Real in the foundation of the paternal symbolic order. *Wo Es war*: where the ~~father~~ was (not), the guilty conscience comes to be. The primal father must disappear but also simultaneously not appear. The father is a collective delusion of personal and social history. This trick founds the social order on his loss. The father then (re)appears later in the myth as a ghostly superegoic reminder of the original invented crime.

This invented crime always already happened before the presence of either the sons or their imagined desires. The father rises from the dead to (re)appear as both conscience and its condition of possibility as loss. The later delayed murder of the father retroactively posits his earlier appearance in the historical past of the primal horde. The dead father retroactively advances the historical interval. This time is antecedent to the murder which has already happened. The consequence of such a tortured interpretation of Freud's deceptively simple fable is that *there is no such thing as the primal father*. Why must the father return from the ashes of the trace of *différance*? He must enforce the rules and regulations of the sociality of the brothers in the emergent civilization. The law is supervised by a ghost. The social order is structured by the otherworldly.

This interpretation of the primal horde myth posits an effective reason for the rule of the myth of loss. Why did the brothers invent the ideology of castration for themselves? What is the source of a fable which punishes the brothers with the guilt for an invented crime? What psychical and social interests does the reproduction of this myth serve? The key dimension of the primal horde fable is that it is a myth. It is a story which is invented by the brothers (and by Freud) in order to explain the world to themselves. Why did the brothers invent castration if they could simply swim in the seas and tan on the beach? The male junior in the scene of the discovery of sexual difference imagines a castration which threatens his own private(s) property of the penis. Why did the male junior invent castration if he could otherwise see difference *qua* Sameness[+] rather than difference *qua* deficit? The brothers retroactively imagine a loss which endangers their lives and clips their enjoyment. There is no ground which justifies the ideology of castration. The invention of castration is arbitrary. But the charisma of the storytelling of the fable explains its perceived naturalness. The ideology is a shared and learned agreement by the neurotics who no doubt recognized that Something is Missing. Why did the brothers desire castration? What did the brothers want to finally avoid on the beach with each other, trunks off?

Désir and Trieb

Marx famously summarizes — figurally — the difficulty of the transition from the society of castration and scarcity to the cosmos of plenitude and fullness in his *Thesis Eleven* (1845). This revolutionary transition also involves a movement from the masculine enjoyment of capitalism to the feminine *jouissance* of communism. The transformation must be structured as a shift from ordinary desire to extraordinary *Trieb*. The *arche* is chronologically reversed for the brothers — from Nothing is Missing *Trieb* to Something is Missing *désir*. The social transition is complicated by the temporal paradox at the center of the plot of the primal horde myth. The temporal *après-coup* or *Nachträglichkeit* of the oedipalization of the brothers defers both the murder and its effects into a future which is forever deferred by the traces of *différance*. Desire has yet to mobilize its aim/less *Trieb*. The oedipalization which precedes the initiation of the desire of the brothers complicates the plot of the primal horde myth. Neither history ("law, morality, and religion") nor its origin (revolution, murder) has yet to happen. The brothers enjoy a prehistory of a *Trieb* which is not even the province of proper neurosis.

The crucial point for the myth is that this history is suspended in a superposition which interrupts the movement (*Wo Es war*) of history itself. The brothers are retroactively posited as an origin for a history which is disbanded between, on the one hand, a lost past and a lost father and, on the other hand, a deferred future and a postponed revolution. Prehistorically, the brothers are themselves suspended between a death and a life. This is precisely the liminal position of Antigone in Lacan's interpretation of the second play in Sophocles's

Oedipus cycle (441 BCE).[15] The retroactively posited revolutionary subjects are yet to be present in the *socius* itself. What, precisely, is Outside of the beach house?

The loss of the primal father is a conundrum for the brothers. But the absence of the boys makes the transition from desire to drive, from idiotic *jouissance* to Other *jouissance*, and from castration and scarcity to fullness and plenitude an unimaginable task. This is so because the *telos* of transformation is in reverse. The perverts are the partners of the brothers. The lost boys are absent. They are impotent *lumpenproletariat* who are abused and accused. But they will be resurrected in a future association which returns them to the origin not of law, morality, and religion but to the trace of an Other *jouissance*. This Other is beyond the fictions of scarcity and castration which have burdened and tyrannized the brothers from the dawn of prehistory in the fable of a lost paternity. But this Other also emerges after the internalization of the invention of scarcity, castration, and the murder. What is life which is antecedent to the personalization of Freud's ideology?

The brothers are dead. The reason is that the brothers "always have been" dead. But what is a series of caskets in the hot sun on the beach? Who swims with ghosts? The revival of the brothers is a creationist *ex nihilo*. This emergence is fundamentally inadequate to the task of the transformation of the society. The brothers can only be properly resurrected from a future that retroactively produces them as brothers who are otherwise than themselves. What is antecedent to the perverts and the brothers beyond the shores of the beach? The task is to retroactively redeem the brothers. They become perverts from a future in which the rule of castration and the domination of scarcity have been displaced. An originary *Trieb* and an Other *jouissance* substitute for this negativity. This is the project of the creationist sublimation of my text. The dead brothers will be transformed into queer perverts.

The brothers and the perverts may be the same difference — Sameness⁺. The deed is deferred. The doer is postponed. The world awaits in prehistory for the arrival of both the doer and the deed. The perverts, schizoids, and Women promise to fashion a cosmos in which marvelous deeds — rather than responsible doers — rule the society. This galaxy of brothers cares less about the insides of the beach house and more about the trunks on the beach. This future vows a universe of *Trieb* of creationist *ex nihilo*. Commodities are supplanted by the joyous production of use-values which are detached from the general equivalence of currency. Equivalence inhibits rather than enables the free exchange and liberated substitution of incipient sexuality. Perversely, Sameness⁺ (is) Difference⁺.

This impossible equivalent proximity is neither equality nor inequality nor identity nor difference — but Sameness⁺. Such diacritical differential negativity is based on the decenterment of the general equivalent. Value is structured by the release of these goods from subordination to a currency. The system of exchange otherwise renders the goods speculated and abstracted — equal, identical, unequal, different, and so on — in relationship to each other. Freud (1917) articulates this postcapitalist logic in his discussion of anal eroticism in which he describes the equation: "penis = baby = faeces."[16] The anal eroticism of the pervert is strictly anticapitalist and antihierarchical. Anality foreswears the general equivalent. This equivalence reduces use-value to exchange-value. It also undermines the free exchange and liberated substitution of all of the goods in the system. Freedom is otherwise restricted because the rule of scarcity (capitalism) and the discovery of castration (phallocentrism) are the key ideological supplements to $-ism. An elusive and imaginary freedom persuades the brothers to storm the beach house. The prehistoric brothers are subordinate to a commodity which abuses and terrorizes them. This commodity is articulated in Marx's concepts of both commodity fetishism and capitalist exploitation. Man is also prostrate to a system of castration and scarcity which simulates loss in order to structure an economy which is organized around the scarcity of goods and the castration of identities.

The Hystericization of Desire

The center in this revolutionary fable is that the brothers are suspended in prehistory. It is for this reason that Freud can cull the rituals of prehistorical man as exemplary of modern nervous illness. Freud's peculiar interpretation of the primal horde myth illustrates that humanity awaits the unbridled enjoyment of the primal father and his exclusionary rule as a precondition for history in the murder and the revolution. The humanist *point de capiton* retroactively resolves the mystery of this fabricated loss with the invention of the guilty conscience. Even prehistorically, the brothers' desire must be hystericized in order to forge a society. This hystericization of the boys is the precondition of the enjoyment of the brothers in the historical process of the battle between idiot and Other, between desire and drive, between scarcity and plenitude, and between castration and fullness. The brothers anticipate the hystericization of a desire for a Spirit of the System which supplants the abusive system of castration and scarcity. This Spirit otherwise structures contemporary sociality even in its prehistory on the beach in the sun, trunks off. How is desire excited? How do the dead brothers awaken to a desire which has been otherwise crushed by the prehistoric loss of guilt and remorse?

The stimulation of desire precedes its objectification in the master signifier. Perversely, the division between the roles of master and analyst yields to slippage. The pervert's *Trieb* enjoys the pleasure of the Other. The pervert is invulnerable to the analyst because the pervert relishes the *jouissance* of the Other. The brother craves a society of the feminine *jouissance* of full pleasure and total enjoyment. This Other would be unimpeded by castration, scarcity, and loss. The schizoid's foreclosure of the paternal metaphor fastens him to a maternal economy of anxious fulfillment. The schizoid desires the transition of the object of enjoyment from the mother to the Other *jouissance*. The schizoid seeks revolutionary shelter from a prison house of maternal enjoyment which forecloses the pleasures of the Other. The schizoid is tortured by language. He covets a maternal symbolic order *sans* discourse. The schizoid hopes for the final discontinuation of the massive monologue of humanity. This epic sermon is structured by the oppositional words of the masculine *jouissance*. It does so at the cost of the silent bodily enjoyments of the Other *jouissance*. The Woman renounces desire and its support in speech. Instead, she pursues the bodily pleasures of the affirmation of a cosmos which is beyond scarcity and outside of castration. Lack is otherwise organized by speech. But must the brothers' desire be hystericized? Or could they enjoy their *Trieb* of the aim/less wander even outside of the beach house? Are these brothers already Women?

Prehistory

The rule of the future anterior in Freud's myth indicates that this origin-story for civilization is allegorical. It is properly prehistoric. The myth is prehistoric because it orients all of the vagaries and possibilities of the organization of humanity in the future. A *tout autre* which will arrive *à venir* in a future awaits a prehistorical past and its aporetic suspensions in the future anterior. I insist that contemporary humanity be conceived as prehistoric. Man is primitive. The conundrums of the primal horde myth suspend humanity between a prehistory and a history. The prehistory prompts the brothers to emerge beleaguered by a guilt and remorse which are structured by the metaphysics of presence and its anchor in the primal murder and the guilty conscience. But it is only the brothers who internalize the myth who find refuge inside of the beach house. What about the brothers who foreswear Freud's ideology of scarcity and castration? What about those boys who are unpersuaded by the lie of murder? What about the boys who enjoy spring, summer, fall, and winter in the oceans of the beach outside of the father's shack? Who are these boys? What is their *Trieb* rather than desire?

The future orientation of Freud's allegory gestures toward a toil and a play. This revolt is necessary in the transition from a traumatic prehistory of the guilty conscience to a political struggle between the masculine and the feminine, the idiot and the Other, scarcity and plenitude, castration and fullness, desire and *Trieb*, capitalism and communism — unto the glorious arrival of a posthistorical aneconomy. This Other-Economy displaces the calculated exchange of unequal goods. Exchange is ruled by the value of the general equivalent. Instead, the Other-Economy facilitates an unencumbered and liberated swap of goods. The objects are simultaneously incommensurable because they are structured without the general equivalent. *Les mots and les choses* are radically ~~equal~~ and ~~identical~~ to each other because ~~different~~ from themselves.

Aporetic opposites frame the myth: father/brothers, death/life, murder/absence, law/transgression, guilt/*jouissance*, doer/deed, and past/future. The temporal tension in Freud's allegory indicates that after the prehistory of man these opposites will not simply be resolved in a quasi-Hegelian totality of abstraction or in a Marxist materialist utopia. Rather, in the future these oppositional pairs will be enjoyed and played in a feminine modality of proximities. These spatial adjacencies starkly deconstruct the order of opposition. This binary system otherwise structures the economy of *le propre* (proper, property, ownership, mineness, and possession) for culture, society, impersonality, affect, cognition, politics, economics, speech, and so on. The brothers who resist the ideology of $-ism are the conceptual personae of selves who are beyond scarcity and outside of castration. The Pervert-Schizoid-Woman is the Outside of capitalism and phallocentrism.

The future of the *tout autre* and the *à venir* is the horizon of the incoherence of Freud's instructive and effective myth of the murder of the primal father. The will of the metaphysics of presence is horrified by the paradoxes and impossibilities of Freud's myth. This Father-Presence yields to the playful dissemination of the trace. The present of the anxieties of private property yields to the future of the proximities between objects. These relationships to each other are arranged by the play of the signifier and the signified rather than by the division and opposition of the sign. The future is difference and relationship rather than distinction and opposition — and the obverse of difference *qua* distinction and relationship *qua* opposition. The not-yet promises an exhaustion of the trace. The *tout autre* vows an invention of new games and alternative plays. This is beach stuff: trunks off, surfs up, tunes on. *Spanking*.

The brothers who resist the ideology of desire, scarcity, and castration — Something is Missing — are the bisexually constituted boys of an originary homosexual libido. Is it possible that on this prelapsarian beach of violent patriarchal exclusion these boys were simply having their own bit of fun with each other outside, on the beach? If so, was this prehystericized bisexuality — with a tendency toward male homosexuality — a desire which can only be properly called Pervert-Schizoid-Woman and his *Trieb*? The skinny-dipping in the ocean outside of the beach house was a *Trieb* beyond and before the ~~pleasure principle~~ of Freud's 1920 text. The Outside-Principle veils the latent unconscious truth of Freud's myth. The brothers only faked a hysterical desire for the overthrow of their old man. The hystericization of desire is the performance of neither identity nor identification. Oedipalization is simply a ~~prehistorical~~ performance — but why?

Heterosexual desire is a simulation of an originary homosexual libido. The murder of the primal father is the imperative of heteronormativity as the foundation of Western civilization. Homosexual libido finds its *arche* and etiology neither in genes nor the hippocampus nor even in immorality. Rather, homosexuality is the unexpected effect of *heteronormativity*. Queer (*a*)sexuality of the Pervert-Schizoid-Woman is precisely the Outside of the economics of scarcity and the desire for castration. Queer (*a*)sexuality is the only modality of bodily rapport for the subjects of the horizonal Spirit of the System. Heterosexuality is a fabled sham. But what is the origin of the primal father's anomalous *ur*-heterosexuality? There is a Something is Missing in heterosexuality itself that the homosexual brothers possessed in their Nothing is Missing. Conversely, there is a clitoral Something is Missing in the penile Nothing is Missing of male homosexuality. What is the proper name for this Missing? — metaphor, word, substitute, fetish, center, sign, and so on?

My discussion in this book of first, the ambivalent phallocentrism of psychoanalysis, second, the critique of capitalism in Marxism, and third, the destabilization of the sign in deconstruction has been arranged by a deconstructed opposition between Something is Missing and Nothing is Missing, and between Being and Nothingness. The parallactic overlap between lack and plenitude, castration and fullness, clitoris and penis, and capitalism and communism has isolated these specific practical and theoretical concepts as both distinct and opposed — as binary opposition — and as parallactic and overlapped — as extimate. But it is crucial for my project that the parallax of each in the other — extimacy — be visible in order to demonstrate the Madness of Order and its internal necessity within the order of Reason. The crux of the division between Something is Missing and Nothing is Missing — clitoris and penis, capitalism and communism, neurotic and schizoid, $-ism and S, and so on — is simple. The division and hierarchy between these opposed terms are organized by an economy of power and force. The rhetorical and institutional strength of each word in deconstructed opposition will be the victor of a battle between the two logics. Communist queer (*a*)sexuality is the mediation between these deconstructed oppositions in this book.

But, in this book, I am committed to the privilege of plenitude above scarcity, fullness above lack, the pervert above the neurotic, Peniscentrism above phallocentrism, and communism above capitalism. My critical exegesis and synthesis of Marxism, psychoanalysis, and deconstruction mobilize the intellectual talents of the pervert with the ambition that the Other battle the self-same and the self-identical toward the future of the *tout autre* of the Spirit of the System. In this promised future, a communism of each according to his need and each according to his ability triumphs above the capitalist fiction of scarcity and the series of ideologies which overlays thinking, being, and living in the space and time of Something is Missing. At stake is a practical and theoretical escape from the symptomatic consequences of a world which is ordered by *le propre* and the general equivalent. But the traces of scarcity, lack, neurosis, phallocentrism, and capitalism enjoy *terminus* in a Spirit of the System. S will dissolve capitalist private property, ego identity and identification, and linguistic binarism. Spiritually, the oppositions disappear in the ether of a solar system of the Other.

Moralism is the nihilistic system of the valuation of binary oppositions. This nihilism is a system of hierarchization of plenitude above scarcity (or the reverse), fullness above lack (or the other side), perversity above neurosis (or the obverse), Peniscentrism above phallocentrism (or the otherwise), and communism above capitalism (or the opposite). Moralism enforces the decisionism of binary opposition. Moralism is the ideological nodal point of the series of proper hierarchies that this book critically addresses. Moralism must be the incontrovertible object of critique of the dismantlement of $-ism and its series of Western ideological commitments. The father is dead, but moralism and its epigones live on. Moralism is the subjective and objective sickness of $-ism. Moralism must be subverted for the health of man and the strength of society. Moralism must be deposed. Are the communist queer (*a*)sexual Faggots up to the challenge?

Chapter Thirteen

Outside of Responsibility

I think it is best, therefore, to acquit dreams.

— Sigmund Freud

In my critique of $-ism and *le propre* over the course of this book, I have emphasized the centered subject and its deconstruction. The ostensible center of the subject is represented in such tropes as agency, intention, will, authority, and power. At its most basic, the centered individual of the enlightenment and humanism is the subject of the action toward an object. The individual is the doer of the deed in activity. In Romance languages, the simple articulation of the subject-verb-object syntax reflects the centered ego of the Western tradition. The centered subject and its traits implicate responsibility as the bedrock of Western morality. The action toward the object returns to the subject as the proper, property, owned, possessed, and mine. *Qua* subject, I am the doer of *my* deed, I am the actor of *my* activity, and I am the author of *my* text. I am responsible. Responsibility is the cornerstone of Western Judeo-Christian morality. This sick morality is precisely the matrix that Nietzsche seeks to transcend in his traversal beyond good and evil toward the *tout autre* of the responsible and accountable doers of deeds. $-ism typifies Western moralism because it posits a subject of agency and will who is obliged responsibility and its consequences for action taken in the world. *Le propre* is also an economy of responsibility because it isolates units — self from other, doer from deed, actor from action, and so on. These isolated objects can be structured as the discrete agents of action and specified objects of activity. The purpose of this chapter is to inspire a transition away from the proper of the doer and the deed and toward the amoralism of an irresponsibility.

Marxism, deconstruction, and psychoanalysis each undermine the Western moralism of responsibility. Marxism challenges this generalized form of responsibility with its wish for communism. This emergent mode of production is structured by workers in close relationship and rapport with each other. Communism forsakes selfishness and competition. Aggressive possession otherwise returns subjects (workers and individuals) and objects (commodities and activities) to the individual. Outside of a system of private property, the self engages the other without these restrictions. These limits otherwise alienate men from each other. The subject is freed of Western morality because it immerses itself in the world as an *ipse* in a confederation and association of others who work together with common purpose in solidarity. Deconstruction subverts responsibility because the unit of measurement of any subject-verb-object syntactical relationship is displaced by the traces of differences and deferrals. *Différance* submits the identity of the subject to other objects which exceed it. Grammatologically, Western responsibility and morality are incoherent because there is no present and identifiable individual who acts in the world. Psychoanalysis ruptures the concept of individual responsibility because it questions the otherwise self-certainty and self-knowledge of the conscious ego. The wishes and truths of the repressed in the unconscious render responsibility for deeds a miscalculation of the unconscious architecture. The concept of the unconscious subjects manifest action to a latent world. The ego submits to the Other.

Beyond good and evil and Western moralism is another sensibility. This aesthetics of the Pervert-Schizoid-Woman and the Spirit of the System eschews responsibility in favor of the abandonment of agency, intention, will, authority, and power. The wager of this move beyond good and evil resonates with Nietzsche's critique of Western moralism. Nietzsche contends that moralism makes us sick, ourselves and our society.[1] Rather than protective and preservative, Western morality is unhealthy and unsafe. The bet is that man is awesome when he is beyond good and evil. The strictures and punishments of responsibility make man evil. Beyond the responsibilities of morality awaits a renewed man whose bright ethics transcends the sour moralism of our time.

THE DREAM OF IRMA'S INJECTION

Freud's analysis of his own dream of Irma's injection is considered the specimen dream of psychoanalysis. Irma was Freud's patient. Despite his treatment of her, she continued to suffer symptoms for which he was variously (self-)reproached as the doctor in her case. The question of the dream is the cause of Irma's pains, the source of her discomfort, the doer of a mistaken deed, and the responsible agent of the error. The dream is considered archetypal of a fundamental Western wish. The wish of this foundational Western dream is to be rid of responsibility. Freud explicitly states this desire of the unconscious toward the conclusion of his exhaustive analysis of the dream,

> The material was, as one might say, impartial; but nevertheless there was an unmistakable connection between this more extensive group of thoughts which underlay the dream and the narrower subject of the dream which gave rise to the wish to be innocent of Irma's illness.[2]

The specific plot of the dream involves Irma, other doctors, and Freud. The story of the manifest content is limited. But Freud maintains that the wish is generalizable. The articulation of the wish exceeds the story of the dream. The dream is in excess of the dream. The unconscious latent subject of the dream outstrips the narrow confines of the plot of Irma and the symptoms that she suffers.

My claim is that the dream of Irma's injection is precisely about moral responsibility and the Western wish to travel beyond good and evil — "to be innocent of Irma's illness." Freud wishes to avoid persecution. He wants to evade prosecution. He hopes to avoid punishment. Freud seeks a world which is outside of Western morality. This is exactly an unconscious wish. Consciously, we may agree that responsibility and morality are the linchpins of Western civilization. It may be lazily conjectured that beyond Western moralism man's most violent intuitions and hateful instincts would destroy man and world. Freud says so in his so-called sociological work, in such texts as *Totem and Taboo* (1913), *Civilization and its Discontents* (1930), and *The Future of an Illusion* (1927). Freud's pessimistic wager is that law must trump love. Man's violent instincts must yield to the protective and preservative will of the civilization and its laws, moralities, and religions. The consequence of this repression is the symptom and its maladies.

Nietzsche's view is opposed to this Freudian despondence. Rather than a sick man who must be tamed by civilization, man is the fiery animal who must be liberated from morality in order to become more than himself in his will to power. Freud contends that responsibility is the source of security and immunity. But the wish of Irma's injection strikingly illustrates that Western man's wish is to journey beyond good and evil against a morality that otherwise generates the symptom of the dream. Morality represses man. The return of this repression is the symptom of the dream. Freud contends that morality is to be preferred to symptom and that civilization is to be preferred to instinct. Freud bets that love must yield to law. But the Western wish is precisely the reverse. The symptom must be dissolved (absolved) by the transcendence of good and evil. The instinct must be liberated against society. Love must triumph over law. The dream of Western man is Nietzsche's wish. The text of Irma's injection as both manifest content of the dreamer and critical text of the interpreter illuminates the latent desire and unconscious truth of Western civilization.

Dreaming the Father

My analysis of the dream — and its analysis — is situated in two different dimensions. The first significance of the dream is specific and particular to Freud, his patient, and the milieu of characters who populate the plot of Freud's version of the dream. Freud's interpretation of the dream is narrow. The analysis is about Freud and the specific script about Irma, her pains, and her treatment by Freud and other medical colleagues. The features of this particular set of concerns are spectacular because Freud's interpretation is evidently and wildly misguided. Clearly, Freud misinterprets the dream. As the father of psychoanalysis, Freud was essentially an untrained layman in the field of his own invention. A practicing psychoanalyst must be properly trained in the psychoanalytic community. Freud's peculiar position as the founder of psychoanalysis compromised both his edification and practice. Freud was unsuitable to be a psychoanalyst. Freud was unqualified to be a psychoanalyst. It can even be surmised that Freud was not a psychoanalyst.

But Freud's misreading of himself makes it possible for us to properly analyze the wish. Freud's erroneous interpretation of the manifest content of his dream is the proviso of a proper analysis of both the dream-thoughts and the interpretation. The interpretation is its own manifest content. Freud's analysis is properly a symptom. The interpretation is a dream. My work is to uncover the wish of interpretation. The process of the revelation of the wish of the interpretation will uncover a constitutive blindness in Freud's own scientific knowledge. Freud's medical acumen makes him obtuse to the manifest elements of the dream. Freud's scientific knowledge forces a misreading of science. Freud's scientific insight is simultaneously his psychoanalytic blindness. Our medical ignorance enables us to insightfully read the scientific words in Freud's dream and interpretation. Freud's ample knowledge inspires daft blindness. Our glaikit innocence generates inspired intuition.

I will begin with an analysis of the specific story of the characters and plots of the dream. Afterward, I will turn toward the generalizable wish of the Western unconscious in its specimen dream. The desire of the Western unconscious is to soar beyond good and evil and its ideology of responsibility of the doer of the deed. The question that must be approached in the specificity of the story is central. Of what deed did the doer want to exonerate himself? What is the relationship between the particular wish of the dream — split between Freud's interpretation and my own — and the universal desire of Western man to be rid of morality and its illnesses?

The specificity of the dream of Irma's injection is the protracted symptoms and residual pains after her course of treatment with Freud. My reading of the dream-thoughts and Freud's own interpretation of the text are brief. I focus closely on the matter of substitution in dream — what Freud refers to as the operation of displacement by the dream-work. The substitutive chains of metaphor enable the displacement of the center of analysis of the dream from Freud's attention to science and medicine to the properly sexual content of psychoanalysis. Freud rightly discovers morality and responsibility at the navel of the dream. But the picture of the desire is narrowcast rather than macroscopic. The dream speaks to Freud's desire. The dream also unravels the Western wish. The particular and the universal, and the specific and the general, must be reconciled in order to properly interpret the specimen dream.

As split between these two tendencies, the dream also irradiates a Hegelian truth about this relationship between the particular and the universal, and between the specific and the general. Each binary opposition is internal to the other. The sexual specificity of Freud's wish that I discover in the dream is woven into the moral universalism of Western man's desire to be rid of responsibility. What is the relationship between desire and morality, and between wish and responsibility? If Western man wishes the end of good and evil in the *über-mensch*, then what modality of (*a*)sexuality emerges from the ashes of humanism and the enlightenment? What is (*a*)sex after civilization? What is desire after morality? What do we do in bed when any bed will do?

My short figural reading of Freud's literal analysis of the text is structured by metaphorical substitution. This series of displacements invites a transition from the particularities of the characters and plots of the dream to the generalities of the fundamental Western desire that the dream articulates. In his article on the dream, "The Dream Specimen of Psychoanalysis" (1954), the psychoanalyst Erik Erikson situates the dream within the context of Freud's past and present life history. Erikson says: "The Irma dream and its associations clearly reflect a crisis in the life of a creative man in middle age."[3] The dream is not only about Freud's desire. The text is also about Freud's biography. The plot that Freud weaves about his treatment of Irma, her complaints and reproaches, and his competition with colleagues situates the story in the context of Freud's prosopography.

Freud positions the dream in the context of his personal profile in the preface to the second edition (1908) of *The Interpretation of Dreams*. He comments about the death of his father as the backdrop of the writing of the book. He suggests that his own self-analysis in the book is a reaction to his father's death.[4] In chapter twelve, I discussed at length the myth of the murder of the primal father in *Totem and Taboo* (1913) and the sons' affective and reasoned response to this death. The institutionalization of law, morality, and religion accompanies the guilt and remorse for the mythical murder of the father. It can be surmised that such guilt and remorse haunt Freud as he writes his book. Freud's outline of the fable of the murder of the father claims that the consequence of the murder — and the affective accessories of guilt and remorse — originates a system which tames murderous instincts and violent jealousies. In the aftermath of his own father's death, Freud erects a system — the system of psychoanalysis and its central concepts and elements in his dream-book (1900). Freud's response to paternal death is system and structure. The father's death wills a replacement for the loss of the center of the paternal structure. Freud's writings are a substitute for the death of the father's writings. Freud's *magnus opus* rewrites the paternal authority which haunts his pen. Freud's work on dreams — and specifically on the dream of Irma's injection — is troubled by guilt, remorse, and responsibility. Consciously, Freud is certainly not guilty and remorseful for his father's death. But according to the father of psychoanalysis, the response to paternal death is precisely this guilt and remorse. Writing is the symbolic response to these symptoms, and the erection of structure is the rejoinder to loss. But it is crucial to note that this turn toward system and stability is cut by the Real of the unconscious. This Real undoes the text from within the alphabets and letters of the script. The text escapes the authority of the writer, just as the dream escapes the authority of the self. Guilt and remorse are the affective responses to the loss of the text and of the self.

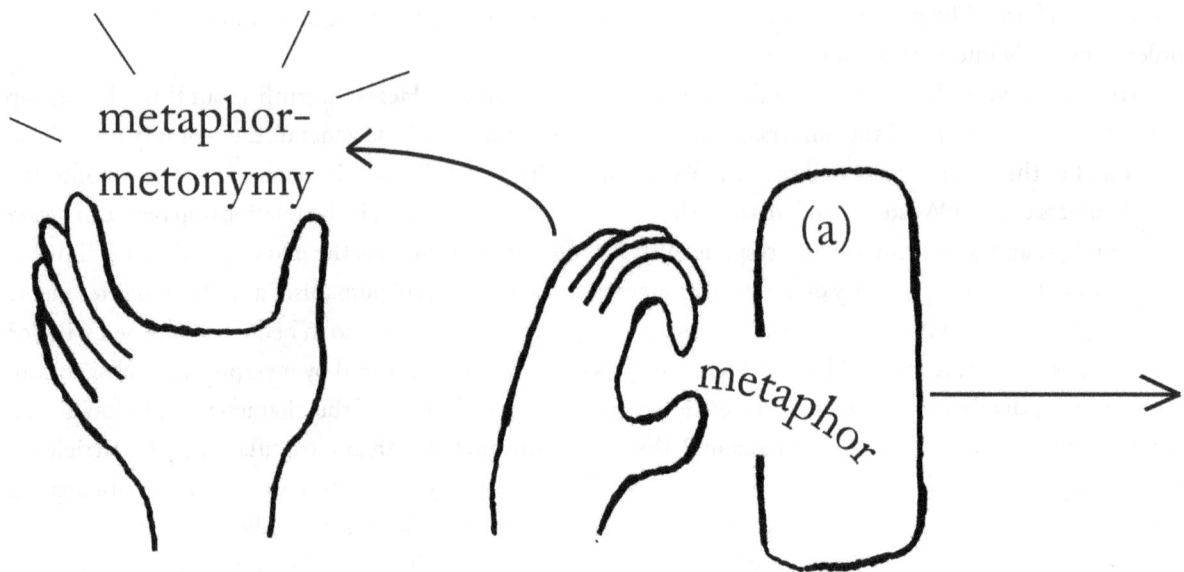

This illustration parallels the image of the Real Object that forever resists signification. The object slips and slides away from (toward) its series of representational components. This picture illustrates the empowered (*a*)sexual endeavor in difference and deferral (*différance*) of *Trieb* and the series of advances and recoils, and flirtations and demurs, of the avoidance of (engagement with) the object. The object does not frustrate the grasp of the doer (right) but rather happily retreats (proceeds) in its presence and absence. The (*a*)sexual pervert prizes the endless play of signification which is portrayed in the spark of metaphor<>metonymy (left). The object in its essential content is irrelevant and extraneous (right). The pervert enjoys the simulacrum — jockstrap, word, metonymy, representation, metaphor, fetish, center, and so on — of the object. The frustration of a resistant Real (right) yields to joyful polynomiality. The (*a*)sexual masochist grasps that the jockstrap can only conceal a "jockstrap." The penis (and so on) is forever occluded from the symbolization of the Real Object in the impossible *Praxis* to write and speak the Real Jockstrap.

Notes & Sketches —

The other side of these affects is responsibility and morality — "to be innocent of Irma's illness."[5] Freud's guilt and remorse for his father's death situate the sickness of morality and the wish to escape beyond good and evil at the forefront of his analysis of the specimen dream. (The dream precedes the death of Freud's father, but Freud worked on the analysis of the dream in the aftermath of the father's death.) Unconsciously, Freud's ink animates a text which can only be a fable which is beyond good and evil. Freud's analytic words can only be a treatise on Western man's distress at the stern authority of morality and his wish to evade its punishments. Freud's dream and interpretation are squarely situated at the apex of the conundrums of the economy of *le propre* and the system of $-ism. Freud's wish gestures toward the Spirit of the System and the future of the Pervert-Schizoid-Woman for man and world.

Sexuality, at Pains

The interpretation of the dream of Irma's injection is both a manifest and a latent response to the death of Freud's father. Freud's analysis is a rejoinder to an unconscious guilt and remorse and a conscious will to system that he outlines in *Totem and Taboo* (1913). Freud's desire to be innocent of Irma's pains is a substitute for his unconscious desire to be rid of the guilt and remorse of responsibility for his father's death. The manifest thoughts of the dream of July 23-24, 1895 are outlined by Freud in a single paragraph. The interpretation of this manifest set of words and images continues for many pages. The interpretation arrives at the brief latent thought that Freud wished to be innocent of Irma's pains.

A cornerstone of psychoanalysis is that unconscious desire is profoundly sexual. Desire is organized by bodies, flesh, anatomies, and the *mise-en-scène* of fantasy which makes desire possible. The repressed sexual culture of late nineteenth-century and early twentieth-century Europe historicizes Freud's insightful precept that the repressed consists of sexual content. No doubt, doctors and patients are overwhelmed by a desire that otherwise can only be spoken in the manifest veil of the unconscious-work of the primary process. Freud's concepts of the transference and the countertransference explain the desirous affects of the analysand toward the analyst and also of the doctor for the patient.

My claim is that the matrix of Freud's dream and its translation from manifest form into latent content is the sexual desire of Freud for his patient, Irma. This desire is unconscious to Freud. It is the latent content which is obscured by the short paragraph of manifest thoughts at the start of his discussion of the dream. The wish of the dream is certainly about responsibility. But my interpretation of the unconscious erotic transference between analyst and analysand illuminates that Freud fears responsibility for another deed for which he wills exoneration. This deed is particular to Freud and his treatment of Irma. But its specificity reveals the relationship between desire and responsibility, between sex and civilization, and between desire and morality. Beyond good and evil is (*a*)sexuality.

A critical psychoanalytic eye can quickly identify the sexual metaphors in the manifest thoughts of the dream. Irma's pains are primarily located in the mouth, throat, and abdomen. She suffers discomfort in the digestive tract. The medical interventions are made to her mouth and throat. She refers to a pain: "it's choking me."[6] A person's throat is choked by a phallic object which fits into the mouth and obstructs passage down the throat to the stomach and abdomen. The object of the choking is unspecified in the manifest description. The object of the choke obliquely refers to Irma's pains. Her throat is choked without the presence of a determinate object. The phallic object of the choke is absent. Something is Missing in the scene of Freud's examination of her pains. *Qua* Woman, the phallocentrism of Freudian analysis interprets her as the castrated Woman of not-penis whose physical and psychical makeup is the absence of the penis. Irma chokes on phallic absence.

The origin of her illness is lack. The effects of this castration are her symptoms of pain. Freud's patient is the castrated Woman who is choking on the presence (absence) of the penis. Whose penis is present (absent) in Irma's mouth? Who is the source of this penis which is both the symbol of malady and the object of scrutiny? How did Irma come to have a penis in her throat if her own castration bars her from access to this envied penis?

A Woman who chokes on a penis is engaging in oral sex. The Freudian criteria of "size" and "visibility" of the penis are an index of Irma's choking and the resultant pains in her stomach and abdomen. Oral sex has made Irma ill. The additional sexual content is visible in a metaphorical reading of the manifest form. The navel of the dream appears about half-way down Freud's awakened description of the dream. Freud writes,

> I thought to myself that after all I must be missing some organic trouble. I took her to the window and looked down her throat, and she showed signs of recalcitrance, like Women with artificial dentures. I thought to myself that there was really no need of her to do that. She then opened her mouth properly and on the right I found a *big white patch* (my emphasis).[7]

Freud situates the discovery of the "big white patch" in a large public hall with numerous guests. The scene of the examination of Irma and the discovery of the "big white patch" is public and communal. Freud prefaces the public examination of her throat with the thought that he "must be missing" the bodily origin of the illness. This "missing" refers to the absent penis of the castrated Woman. Freud "misses" this object which is both simultaneously hers and not hers. The rightful possession — *le propre* — of the phallic absence is "missed." Freud "misses" the presence (absence) of the penis. Freud's dream analysis "misses" the penis. The penis is the absent center — "must be missing" — around which both the manifest thoughts of the dream and the interpretation itself revolve.

This phallic plot of the public examination of Irma's throat returns to Freud's theory of the Oedipus complex and its twin gendered outcomes: the male junior's castration anxiety and the female junior's penis envy. The absence of the penis in Irma's throat — "must be missing" — is isomorphic to the lack that the male junior discovers in horror at the sight of the female junior. Freud's oral medical inspection of Irma's throat mimes the male junior's investigation of the not-penis in the place of the female junior. Freud's position as doctor in this scene is homologous to the male junior and his gaze in the scene of the discovery of sexual difference. The additional words about Irma's reaction to Freud's (the male junior's) examination of her throat describe the female junior's response to her proleptic loss of phallic presence: "She showed signs of recalcitrance." Irma's uncooperative attitude indicates her own resistance to the phallocentric scene of the discovery of sexual difference.

Qua male junior and female junior, Freud and Irma struggle with Freud's own theory. Freud's admission that "something must be missing" in his knowledge and power, on the one hand, and Irma's defiance against the phallocentric Something is Missing in her throat, on the other hand, illustrate that the fundamental issue of morality and responsibility is at the center of sexual difference. Weirdly, Freud's fantasy of castration posits no *arche* for the loss of the penis in the offspring's delusional construction of sexual difference. The female junior's castration reminds the male junior of the father's proleptic threat against his self-pleasure. The upshot of the ostensible confirmation of this threat organizes the male junior's will to trade desire and pleasure for identity and idealization. But whose present (absent) penis is choking Irma? The query indicates that the identity of the penis "must be missing" as a gap in the manifest thoughts of the dream. Whose castrated penis is missing? Whose unwelcome penis is jammed down Irma's throat?

The navel of the dream is no doubt the textual fragment "big white patch" that Freud finds at the back of Irma's throat during the examination. The "big white patch" is undoubtedly a splotch of semen which had been ejaculated from the phallic presence (absence) of a penis that Irma felt was choking her. The trace of the presence of the anonymous penis is this semen whose metaphorical condensation and metonymic displacement are the "big white patch" at the back of Irma's throat. The penis is absent as the phallic object which chokes Irma. But the trace of this penis is detectable in the semen as the effects of its former presence. The penis is present only in its ejaculatory effect. An unprotected oral sex between Irma and the *incognito* penis can be the source of sexually transmitted disease and organic distress. Likely, Irma's pains are caused by a sexual infection of some sort: gonorrhea, syphilis, hepatitis B, hepatitis A, herpes, genital warts, or molluscum. There are various possible sexual causes of Irma's illness. The "big white patch" is the nodal point around which a variety of infections is possible as the source of her discomfort. A series of potential maladies substitutes for the absent and anonymous penis. Neither the semen nor the infection is "missing." Rather, the object of the absence is the penis — and whose?

Oedipally, the male junior is the subject of the gaze. The "big white patch" at the back of Irma's throat marks his phallic plenitude even in the absence of the penis. Freud simulates this activity in his aggressive scopophilic medical intervention in her throat. Irma's reported "recalcitrance" in the manifest dream thoughts indicates her reluctance to assume the oedipal trajectory toward loss and envy. Her obstreperous response to Freud's sexual intrusion into her oral cavity indicates that Freud's medical deed was undesired. Irma rebuffs Freud's veritable physical and sexual foray into her throat. The manifest scene depicts Freud's sexual aggression toward Irma and her resistance to his moves. It is not difficult to surmise the latent content of Freud's awakened scribbles. Freud is raping Irma.

The Rape

The medicalized oral sex is forced on and resisted by Irma. Freud's gesture is not only sexual and violent. Freud's examination is also criminal. The scene is public — as he says, "a large hall — numerous guests, whom we are receiving."[8] The rape is public. There are witnesses to the crime. It is no wonder that Freud's wish is to be innocent of Irma's infection. The doer of the deed of rape is morally sinful. The doer of the deed of rape is criminally culpable. The deed is the object of personal responsibility. Western moralism indicts both the doer and the deed. Punishment for the crime of rape is severe. Freud's wish in the dream of Irma's injection is to be rid of responsibility for the rape of his patient and to be innocent of a crime in view of everybody. Why was Freud blind to the sexual content of the dream?

The dream-censor would properly veil the latent content of the dream with substitutions for the scene of oral sex. But in the interpretation of the text, why did the father of psychoanalysis fail to identify the deed? Freud's analysis of the manifest words of the dream depicts a plot of competition around responsibility for Irma's pains. But the latent truth of these pains is undiscovered by Freud. The doer is identified as Freud. But the deed is under erasure in Freud's interpretation. The analysis of the dream circles around the organic causes and effects of Irma's illness. The plot of the dream is a medical meditation on precisely the presence of organic and psychological dimensions of the malady. But Freud's interpretation resists any proper determination of the source of the sickness. Why was Freud blind to the deed? What is the consequence of dimness toward our deeds? How are sexuality and desire implicated in persecution for crimes which are beyond our knowledge and in prosecution for exploits which are outside of our grasp? What are sexuality and desire in the galaxy of good and evil? What is an (*a*)sexuality which is beyond good and evil? Innocent — of what?

There is other evidence in both the report of the dream and in the text of Freud's interpretation (*qua* latent thought in my analysis) to confirm the reading of Freud's rape of Irma and to verify the analysis of her pains as the result of a sexuallly transmitted disease. In the dream report, Freud mentions Irma's "pale and puffy" appearance which refers to the "big white patch" of semen at the back of her throat.[9] The manifest thoughts of the dream also allude to Freud's colleague, Dr. M., who "looked quite different from usual; he was very pale, he walked with a limp and his chin was clean-shaven."[10] The "very pale" refers to the color of both Freud's semen and penis. Fascinatingly, the note about a "limp" implicates erectile dysfunction as part of the scene of the rape. An erectile dysfunction of a man of Freud's age would certainly make for a "limp" penis. The citation of "clean-shaven" may be a credit to the thinning of Freud's pubic hair.

After the initial examination, Freud refers to Irma who "then opened her mouth properly" before the discovery of the semen at the back of her throat.[11] The implication is that there was an "improper" opening of her mouth. The proper/improper dyad also situates the medical examination-rape within the context of morality and right/wrong. Freud's examination of Irma is a moral examination of both doctor and patient. The rape is committed at this moral juncture in the oral cavity of Irma's throat. The dream thoughts also refer to a portion of skin which has been "infiltrated." This is a metaphor for a violent thrust into Irma's oral cavity.[12] The final words of the manifest report as they trail off into the secondary process of conscious control are: "Injections of that sort ought not be made so thoughtlessly...And probably the syringe had not been clean."[13] Freud is dirty.

Freud cites the injection that his friend, Otto, has made in the treatment of Irma with "propyl, propyls... propionic acid...trimethylamin" that Freud prosecutes as "thoughtless." In the dream-book (1900), Freud suggests that characters and personages in the dream refer back to the dreamer himself. The other is a condensation and displacement of the self.[14] Otto is a prop for Freud. An "injection" (after which the case study of the dream is named) reminds the reader of phallic presence and penile pressure. A penis is "injected" into the mouth with thrusts. Semen is "injected" into the back of Irma's throat. The various injections which animate Freud's analysis of the dream haunt the analysis like shot after shot — injection after injection — of semen. The analysis is coated in semen. Freud's interpretation is a task to clean up a veritable spray of semen from his own penis.

Sexual desire permeates not only a translation of the manifest thoughts of the dream. Sex oozes from the dream interpretation. Freud's conscious analysis of the dream is an unconscious text. Perversely, the conscious and the unconscious coincide. The interpretive conscious of the latent unconscious of Freud's dream is itself *qua Ich* the *Es* of Freud's analytic work. To be fair, my conscious interpretation of Freud's (un)conscious analysis is the unconscious Other. My work to discover the latency *of the* manifest *of the* latent is properly recursive against my interpretation of Freud's doubled desire. What is the unconscious will to identify the proper object of Freud's desire? What is my motive to indicate the moral infraction of which civilization must rid itself in the crime of responsibility?

STD

The variety of seminal injections notes the most damnatory of evidence for my interpretation of Freud's rape of Irma and his desire to be innocent of prosecution. Freud ends his report on the note: "and probably the syringe had not been clean." The syringe is plainly Freud's absent (present) penis in Irma's mouth. He admits with hesitation that it had "not been clean." The cleanliness of Freud's penis may refer to the upkeep of his groin. But uncleanliness likely refers to a penis which is infected by a sexually transmitted disease. The question of the sexual infection returns. Unconsciously, Irma's illness refers to Freud's sexual malady. At base, the dream is about Freud's rape of Irma and his fear that he has transmitted a sexual infection to her. Freud's responsibility is two-fold: first, for the rape of a patient; and second, for an infection that his colleagues reproach him for in his botched treatment of his patient. Freud is not only responsible for a crime and its aftermath. He is also concerned about "the hall — numerous guests" who challenge his treatment of his patient and by extension his competence as a medical doctor.

In Freud's interpretation of the "dirty syringe," he further says that, "I took constant pains to be sure that the syringe was clean." He says: "In short, I was conscientious."[15] The analysis defends Freud's penis and its infection by an STD with reference to "constant pains" and "conscientiousness." Irma is consistently referred to as suffering "pains" in the text. Freud's identification with Irma and her pains indicates a shift in emphasis from his position as doer to the facticity of the deed. Freud identifies with his victim. His "conscientiousness" is an index of his professional sympathy. The note about "conscientiousness" is likely a defense against his aggressive "infiltration" with "injection" of his unclean "syringe." The text of the interpretation belies Freud's *apologia* for his deed. Freud is regretful. He wishes to be rid of responsibility for a crime for which he is guilty and remorseful.

The band of brothers suffers guilt and remorse for the murder of the father. Freud suffers the regret for a crime for which he feels responsible. Haunted by the recent death of his father, Freud's willed innocence in his interpretation is displaced onto his treatment of Irma. Freud identifies Irma as the mortal father — sick patient — whose loss is his responsibility. The present (absent) penis in Irma's mouth is indubitably his own in the examination-rape scene in the large hall. But the specter of the father's phallus is also present as the lost penis whose trace is the semen at the back of Irma's throat. This "big white patch" haunts the son whose diagnostic frustration in the case of Irma is a harsh reminder of his own dead father who "became stronger than the living one."[16] Freud's limp and infected penis is no rival to his father's massive seminal shot at the back of Irma's throat. At the site of the father's semen, we can only astound: what is the father's "big white patch"? What is the *arche* of life?

This question of life is translated as the Being of the "big white patch" of the father's and son's semen. The scene of the dream figures the semen as the evidence of Freud's oral rape of Irma. The semen also represents the specter of Freud's father and his murder by his son. The metaphor of the "big white patch" refers to semen. But the essence of semen *qua* semen is also at issue. Freud's interpretation of this manifest figure misses its latent content. The reason for Freud's impaired vision is his symptomatic manifest repression of the father's and son's semen. This repression of the latent content of the "big white patch" returns as the symptom of the dream-analysis. My work is to uncover the latent content of this eyeless interpretation of the semen. I must assess the significance of the repression of semen in Freud's interpretation of the dream.

The "big white patch" is the manifest metaphor for the semen. But the (in)visible semen is also its own manifest veil whose latent truth must be uncovered. My claim is that Freud's scientific knowledge blinds him to sexual knowledge. The various references to scientific compounds and medical techniques in the manifest interpretation of the dream belie the latent content of the truth of the semen ("big white patch") at the back of Irma's throat. The manifest "big white patch" metaphorizes the latent "semen." But the latent "semen" is metaphorized by the variety of chemical solutions which populates the manifest (latent) text of the dream-interpretation. The central literal-metaphorical reference to scientific jargon is "propyl" and "propion."[17]

The lay reader will not notice the significance of these chemicals. But the medical interpreter will properly identify these scientific words. Propyl involves chemical solutions which are sexual and genital. Freud's obsessive reference to compounds, solutions, and chemicals everywhere in the text of the interpretation indicates a citation to sex and sexuality. The other prominent chemical of the body that Freud mentions several times in the interpretation of the dream is "trimethylamine."[18] The notable feature of this chemical compound is its fishy odor. Trimethylamine is the cause of vaginal odor which is due to bacterial vaginosis. Like propyl, the connotation of trimethylamine is explicitly sexual. The citation of trimethylamine may be Freud's latent explanation for Irma's pains. These discomforts are unconsciously revised as symptoms of dysfunctional genitalia and ill anatomy. The references to solutions in general introduce semen into the scene of the dream.

An interpretation *of* Freud's interpretation reads his own analysis as an unconscious latent content. This latent content of the interpretation must be scrutinized by an analysis of the explicit (implicit) words of the semiotic evaluation of the material of the dream. The scientific jargon of solutions, chemicals, and compounds is the manifest veil of an unconscious latent truth. The seminal "big white patch" at the back of Irma's throat is the navel of the dream. Other fanatical scientific references in the plot of the analysis include the *double-entendre* of Freud's note that "Irma seemed to me foolish because she had not accepted my solution."[19] The "solution" denotatively refers to Freud's treatment of his patient. But it also doubly pertains to his "solution" of forced oral sex and the "solution" of his own semen as the "big white patch" at the back of the analysand's throat. Freud refers to "mucous membrane," "tuberculosis," "turbinal bones," "gastric pains," "auppurative rhinitis," "pyaemia," and "metastases."[20] These references to medical vocabulary are unmistakably displaced and condensed citations of a sexualized body. This erotized soma is manipulated by science and medicine in the treatment-rape of the patient.

There are several other peculiar veiled references to oral rape in Freud's interpretation (manifest thoughts) in the dream-interpretation. The midst of the analysis includes Freud's admission that: "Frankly, I had no desire to penetrate more deeply at this point" with reference to a physical examination of the analysand.[21] Such "penetration" notes the forced invasion of Irma's oral cavity with Freud's infected penis. A couple of paragraphs below, Freud speaks of the "mouth" and his unconscious will to "have put the consolation" of treatment of Irma into the oral cavity of his colleague, Dr. M.[22] He repeats "mouth" again a few paragraphs later. The repeated citation of "consolation" indicates a compassionate approach to Irma. Otherwise, she is persuaded to tolerate or enjoy the treatment-rape of medical technique and scientific knowledge.

Blindness and Insight, Responsibility

Psychoanalytic theory and practice place sex, sexuality, and desire at the center of the speculative architecture and analytical technique of the enterprise. But the only significant turn toward sexuality in Freud's analysis of the dream is in reference to the "sexual metabolism" of trimethylamin. Freud says: "Thus this substance led me to sexuality, the factor to disorders which it was my aim to cure."[23] Freud concludes that this reference to sex cites Irma's widowhood. He is not implicated in the sexual connotations of the chemical solution. Everywhere in the text of the interpretation, Freud absolves himself of any sexual desire for Irma in the dynamic of the countertransference. My properly psychoanalytic reading of the dream and the dream-interpretation situates sexual desire squarely at the center of both the dream and its interpretation.

Freud's defense against sex — and defense against sexual offense — in the dream is no doubt an effect of the dream-censor of the unconscious. But this dream-censor also displaces and condenses from within Freud's *conscious* interpretation of the dream. Remarkably, the dream-work enforces its harsh censorship of the clandestine wish and the tricky liberation of its content on the level of the system Cs. The otherwise unconscious efforts of the dream-work not only skew the explicit latent content desire into the manifest words of the dream. In addition, the dream-work deceives Freud and his reader in the specifically conscious dimension of analysis. Interpretation *is* dream. The conscious *is* the unconscious. The practice of psychoanalysis is an unconscious effect of desire. Dream-interpretation is wish-fulfillment. *Qua* fulfillment, Freud's dream of Irma's injection is a defense against responsibility and a wish for innocence. Freud's wish is to be beyond good and evil. Freud desires to be shielded from persecuted and prosecuted responsibility for the unconscious desire of the dream and the conscious wish of the interpretation. Beyond good and evil is the parallactic overlap of analysis and dream, interpretation and text, interpretation-work and dream-work, and conscious and unconscious.

An otherwise literary psychoanalytic reading regards the specific scientific chemicals and compounds as strange to the lay reader. The ordinary reader is uneducated in the jargon of Freud's organic — as opposed to psychoanalytic — approach to Irma's malady. The division between layman/expert and scientist/humanist articulates the gap between, on the one hand, Freud's reading of the dream and, on the other hand, my interpretation of the dream and Freud's analysis of it. *Qua* neuroscientist, Freud's familiarity with the scientific jargon of chemicals, solutions, and compounds enforces a literary reading of these figures both in the awakened scribbles of the manifest form and in his interpretation of the dream. As laymen, our alienation from the virtuoso of the medical man renders our exposition of the dream and its analysis singularly different from Freud's approach.

The reason that Freud is blind to his dream and its interpretation is his own knowledge of science and medicine. He reads the words and pictures of the manifest thoughts as literal symbols. Freud reads otherwise denotative symbols not as unconscious condensation and displacement but as the literal elements of the plot of the dream. *Qua* scientist, Freud cannot read the split in the word and the picture. His interpretation is mired by the system of *le propre* and the self-sameness and self-identity of a metaphysics of presence (A = A). Freud's exegesis of the dream is peculiarly deprived of sustained elucidation of the metaphorical dimension of the words and pictures of the manifest content of the dream as he reports them when he awakens from slumber. The object is not split. The word is not otherwise than itself. The literal is not struck by the Real of gaps and holes in the symbolic order.

Freud's analytical efforts mostly focus on the plot of the scene, the rearrangement of the characters, and the organization of the *mise-en-scène*. Freud's scientific acumen distracts him from the metaphorical and metonymical — condensed and displaced — dimensions of the dream. In contrast, our gross innocence of science and medicine enables us to interpret the metaphors, understand the metonymies, and substitute in and out the potential condensations and displacements of both the dream and Freud's interpretation. Freud's knowledge obscures the truth. Our ignorance discerns the truth. The consequences of this reversal for psychoanalysis are substantial. Interpretation is perspectival. The truth does not emerge from objectivity. *Bona fide* analysis proceeds from the relationship between knowledges. My interpretation of Freud's exegesis of the dream is structured by the doctor's own daft mind. Freud's committed but barmy reading of the dream is the proviso of my own reassessment of the manifest (latent) dimensions of the dream and its analysis. The interpretation of dreams beseeches multiple elucidations.

Not only is there no definitive (Freudian) reading of a dream. But an isolated anatomization of the manifest thoughts of the symptom must necessarily be supplemented by additional analysis. The temporality of dream-interpretation is also modified because the secondary interpretation (my own) retroactively remodels the proper exegesis of the dream and its interpretation. The metaphysics of presence and Being (what is) of symptom and analysis is revised *post haste*. Truth unfolds in the time of the *futur antérieur* (Freud's *Nachträglichkeit* and Lacan's *après-coup*). Neither the dream nor its interpretation is present in time: Being, as such, *il y a*, by definition, *qua*, and so on. Interpretation precedes the dream. The dream never stops not being dreamed. The psychoanalyst interrupts the dream. But his intervention only momentarily punctures a symptom of which he is a part.

Freud did not rape his patient, Irma, but he did commit her to a fantasy of rape in his unconscious. The curiosity of the dream of Irma's injection is Freud's two-fold desire: to rape Irma and then to exonerate himself of this crime. Why did Freud fantasize this specific wish of criminal oral rape of his patient? The plot of Freud's interpretation of the dream is the competitive rivalry among Freud and his colleagues who desperately try to alleviate Irma of her discomfort. The effects of these quarrels are the various (self-)reproaches among Freud, his colleagues, and Irma.

The dream and its interpretation articulate Freud's double desire for crime and punishment. The dream and its interpretation situate transgression/law and infraction/rule as constitutive of the text.

The object of my interpretation is split. The secondary elucidation of the text focuses on both the awakened manifest thoughts and Freud's analysis of the dream. The text is split between dream and interpretation, between unconscious and conscious, and between manifest and latent. These otherwise binary levels cannot be divided and opposed in interpretation. My exegesis retroactively reorganizes the distinctions of the architecture of psychoanalysis and its binary elements. Both theory and practice of psychoanalysis are destabilized by the retroactive reinterpretation of the dream. The past dream happens in the future of Freud's analysis, then further in the future of my reinterpretation, and then yet further in the reader's later exposition of the past. Not only does the past happen in the future of interpretation. The future is also subject to the messianic structure of the not-yet of the hereafter. Freud has yet to dream, and I have yet to analyze.

"But nevertheless," Freud's wish to repress his desire to prosecute himself in his interpretation of the dream and his simultaneous will to rape Irma suggest that unconscious desire is not only in conflict with the ego of the system Cs. The desire to rape Irma is also in dissonance with itself. Freud's famous thesis that he articulates at the close of the dream of Irma's injection is suspect: "When the work of interpretation has been completed, we perceive that a dream is the fulfillment of a wish."[24] The caveat to the first proposal in this conclusion is that interpretation is questionable and incomplete. Freud mentions everywhere in his work that the analysis of the symptom is surely partial. My retroactive interpretation of Freud's dream and of his analysis of his dream unwinds not only the Time of the Neurotic (*Nachträglichkeit, après-coup*) but also the constitutive trace which upends any present interpretation.

The famous navel of the dream that Freud cites in the dream-book (1900) is the scrap of discourse which "leads down into the unknown."[25] The dark and hidden navel radically cumbers and revises any interpretation. Another aporia in Freud's esteemed contention about wish and its fulfillment is the exclusivity of the wish — as opposed to a series of desires which twists and weaves a plethora of potentially contradictory unconscious impulses. Freud's wish in the dream and its interpretation is double and opposed. He desires to rape his patient and to exonerate himself from responsibility for the infraction. The motivational unconscious desire of the symptom must be considered multiple, contradictory, and at odds even with itself. Freud's dual wishes present the twin provisos of Western civilization and the moralism of good and evil. The profound wish of Western man is to be rid of responsibility and to be freed from prosecution. But the desire is doubled and conflicted.

Freud's wish to be innocent of Irma's pains implicates a supplementary punishment for his crime, as either incompetent doctor or aggressive rapist. The significance of this duality of wish in the dream interpretation is that the evil of the crime cannot be considered apart from the good of the forgiveness. Freud's unconsciously wished rape and latently desired innocence are two constitutive elements of the Western process of morality and redemption. The absolution of the doer is a broad trope of Western religions. The components of the binary good/evil are flip-sides of the same quittance. Each is the proviso of the other. The binary of good/evil is a braided extimacy. Guilt and exoneration, and remorse and forgiveness, are internal to the process of redemption for the doer. Beyond good and evil can only be the journey beyond redemption. Nietzsche's amoral will abandons persecution in favor of a single wish. He desires to be rid of the stupid cycle of law/transgression. Nietzsche wishes the expiry of the persecution of a pathological and pathetic world and its all too human sickness and weakness. The (*a*)sexual masochism of the man and the Boy trades law/transgression for a maternal law of disciplines in which the difference and deferral of the object constitute the consensual pact (maternal law) between the two masochists. Beyond good and evil, the (*a*)sexual masochists honor the pact beyond the father's law in order to sustain the enjoyment of the interval between subject and object. Out of control, the man and the Boy sustain the pact, with(out) leap. The law is banished; local and consensual disciplines sustain the tension.

BEYOND GOOD AND EVIL

The reason to travel beyond good and evil is to escape the neurotic fixation on crime and punishment. The travel beyond Western moralism does not absolve man of his crime. Rather, the wish for amoralism is the desire for a system which is beyond doer/deed and the arch responsibility of the subject of the action for the object of the acted. A talented deconstruction of the subject/object binary is the proviso for the rupture of the division between good/evil in amoralism. The loss of the silly cycle of infraction/rule upends the divisions between neurosis and health, sickness and cure, patient and doctor, and so on. The Pervert-Schizoid-Woman rises from the ashes of the destructive supplement to Western moralism and its ideology of responsibility.

The wager of amoralism is that crime and punishment spawn a world of atrocity. Good and evil arouse grievous theory and practice. Beyond good and evil promises the strength and will of Nietzschean noble morality.[26] The bet of my study is that good and evil marry man to mischief. Freud's dream of Irma's injection illustrates man's nefarious intention and guilty conscience. Freud desires to rape his patient, and then he cowardly demands to be innocent of his misdeed. The system of arch-morality in Western civilization can neither prevent the crime nor ultimately hold the doer responsible for the deed. The trope of responsibility animates pull-yourself-up by your bootstraps conservatism and libertarian versions of liberalism. A proper destabilization of the ideology of responsibility reverses the subject-verb-object articulation in Romance languages. I am not responsible for the deed. The deed is responsible for me.

The challenge is to imagine amoral practices after the rupture of responsibility. What is the everyday relationship between the subject, verb, and object if the subject becomes the passive effect of the verb? Does it matter if the object of the deed is the consequence of an action which is subordinate to the actor's volition or an actor's will which is subdued by the action's intent? How is the Becoming of the gerund *qua* verb (Ing⁺) responsible for the deed if the Being of the subject and the object is not present? The massive consequence of the disorder of the doer/deed opposition is the radical eclipse of Being by Becoming. At stake is a genealogical inquiry that otherwise holds the historical subjects or objects responsible for their effects. After responsibility, an endless Becoming displaces the static determination of the Being of subject and object, agent and action, and doer and deed. But after Being, is Irma still — more than a century later — Becoming-Raped? If so, is analysis of desire even possible?

Western morality is implicitly critiqued by Marxism, deconstruction, and psychoanalysis. In *On the Genealogy of Morals* (1887), Nietzsche traces Western morality to the debtor/creditor relationship of return and obligation.[27] The moral system is organized by capitalism (scarcity and exchange in some form). The exchange of money is the foundation of the Western moral system. The insights of deconstruction demonstrate that the same economy of gift/return and credit/debt is operative in the system of *langue*. The series of incoherent and free signifiers of value must otherwise return to the proper word. The organizational principle of the word is the unity and positivity — expunction — of the differences and negativities of the signifier. The word returns the elements to the system. The signifier is obliged to respond to man's freedom with the responsibility of the word. Language is a moral system. Psychoanalytically, Freud is deeply divided about the causes and effects of morality on man and world. In chapter twelve in my discussion of *Totem and Taboo* (1913), I argue that the simple Freudian claim that the primal father's exclusion of the brothers from the primitive *socius* triggered a desire to murder the father and capture the Women is both imaginary and incoherent.

Freud's later so-called sociological work views man as dark and violent. Freud approaches civilization as the necessary structural lid on the aggressive and sexual instincts of man. The unfortunate consequence of this morality is the return of the symptom which must be treated as a basic effect of society. The requisite repression of desire and its simultaneous clinical liberation are a central conflict in Freudian theory. The tension demonstrates that the classic antinomy between man and world is a distressed relationship without any easy remedy. Civilization and its moralism make us sick. But the alternative is more ghastly than symptoms of repressed sex and violence. The psychoanalytic decision is between Freud and Lacan. Generally, the choice is between Freud's law or Lacan's love. But at stake is the impossible question of the essence of man. What is man in the Outside of world?

Marx settles the matter of morality with the introduction of the transition from capitalism to the mode of production of communism. All hitherto existing relations are exiled to the past. An unprecedented and unpredictable future opens for humanity in which a mostly undefined communist man displaces a viciously critiqued capitalist man. The *arche* of responsibility in the Marxist critique of capitalism is the capitalist externalization of labor and the extraction of surplus value from the body and soul of the worker. Under communism, a general nonequivalent dissolves the speculations and abstractions that otherwise standardize relations between supply and demand of goods and services. *Sans* general equivalent, the binary oppositions of moralism — good/evil and right/wrong — cannot be moored in any standard. Communism heralds a postnihilistic system of amoralism in which valueless singularities displace commodities of signification. Man becomes other than himself because he exceeds the borders of the division between the doer and the deed.

Derrida's later revision of the infamously unquiet *il n'y a pas de hors texte* invites the *tout autre* into a discussion about a deconstructively messianic future. Derrida names several of these emergent but impossible forms: democracy, justice, truth, and so on. This remarkably optimistic Derrida of the "yes, yes" affirms a future which is beyond Western civilization and its pervasive moralism. The Nothing outside of the text refers to neither the suspension of reference nor to the play of the signifier. Rather, this Something is Missing must be — could be and will be — supplemented by an alternative logic, a marginal system, and the wholly other of the *tout autre*. My necessarily failed pursuit is an active practical and theoretical will toward the rise of the Pervert-Schizoid-Woman and her Spirit of the System. The Outside of world is Nothing. But such is the Something of the messianic not-yet *à venir*. Derrida's optimism dissolves the binary opposition between nature/culture and essence/construction.

Lacan's *finale* to the *Seminar* on the ethics of psychoanalysis (1956-1957) is instructive on this matter. Revised, the question is not is man good or evil in Western civilization. Rather, the question is what happens after Western Civilization is over.[28] Psychoanalytically, it is difficult to gauge the twists and turns of Freud's thought on the question of an essential goodness or evilness of man. The general tenor of the instincts (*Instinkt*) in the early work on the theory of the drives implicates these impulses in a brutish relationship to their objects. The later *Thanatos* (1920) indicates a destructive tendency in man's soul. Both Freud and Lacan posit an antecedent dimension to man and to world in the offspring. Freud emphasizes the polymorphous perversity of young sexuality (1905). This emergent sexuality disorganizes eroticism on the outskirts of the structuration of language and culture. Lacan focuses on a prelinguistic infantile body which suffers and enjoys the *l'homme-lette*. This omelet-man endures and celebrates an infinite extension of psyche and body toward the outskirts of the solar system. Later, the offspring's borders are firmly institutionalized in the mirror stage. The offspring's confrontation with the *Gestalt* installs boundaries and idealizations. These inaugurate man's forced invitation into the signifying chain of the Other.

In the *Seminar* on the four fundamental concepts of psychoanalysis (1964), Lacan claims that desire is the essence of man.[29] Lacan's psychoanalytic theory otherwise abandons an internal essence of the subject. The essence of the subject is the construction of the world and its institutions. The question for Lacan is the flavor of this essence: good or evil? Lacan finally suggests good. The wager of the ethics of psychoanalysis (1954-55) is that desire is preferable to symptom. Man's essential desire is the good. The symptom of man is the dysfunctional effect of the repression of desire. Ethics is the return of man to desire in the good rather than the repression of man and the return of the repressed in the evil.

The Fourth-Dimension of the Praxis of (a)sexuality

The wish of dream-interpretation and interpretation-dream is to be rid of the gap between unconscious sexuality and its conscious effects in a moral system. Beyond good and evil is an (*a*)sexuality which is not only liberated from superegoic individual and social repression. Beyond good and evil is also an entirely transformed (*a*)sexuality. This (*a*)sexuality promises the deconstruction of the division between the systems Cs. and Unc. An (*a*)sexuality refutes the economy of liberation and its symptoms and returns. An (*a*)sexuality defies the language of the liberation of sexuality and the emancipation of desire. An (*a*)sexuality is beyond the good and evil of Western civilization and the moralism of responsibility. An (*a*)sexuality is the Outside of the doer of the deed. There is no doer of (*a*)sexuality. There is no author of (*a*)sexuality. There is no subject of (*a*)sexuality. An (*a*)sexuality is born of masochistic *Trieb* and its encirclement of an ephemeral object.

The *objet* skedaddles away from and en route to an (*a*)sex which scarpers from its doer, author, and subject. The *objet petit a* happily slips from the grasp of (*a*)sexuality. This emergent form of (*a*)sexuality enjoys the tension of a *Thanatos*. This death drive is beyond the pleasure principle of the degree-zero of a lazy homeostasis. There is no object of (*a*)sexuality because its metaphysics of presence spatiotemporally slips and slides beyond the chase and pursuit of the bemused pervert. The perverse (*a*)sexual cavorts in the joy of an Outside of time and space. Her place is the interstitial celestial openness of a deconstructed psychoanalysis. The unconscious/conscious distinction no longer makes the repression of wish and the emancipation of desire — unconscious truth — the proviso of a proper sex and a healthy sexuality. Communist queer (*a*)sexuality engages no proper object as such.

The perverse (*a*)sexual eclipses the mundane dimensions: the first-dimension of space; the second-dimension of time; and the third-dimension of the unconscious. The fourth-dimension of *Praxis* is the place of the theory and the practice of (*a*)sexuality. Earlier, I theorized *Praxis* as the rupture of the Real in the symbolic order. *Praxis* is a peculiar unary trait in the signifying chain because it has no conventionalized oppositional and binary word. It is connective and affixed (theory and practice) rather than oppositional and exclusive. *Praxis* is the Outside of representation. *Praxis* is the organizational principle of the entirety of the symbolic order. *Qua* Real, *Praxis* returns to the extant system of $-ism as precisely the selfhood and sociality of the queer (*a*)sexuality of communism. The sour system of Western society interprets *Praxis* as only a series of spits and fits. A massively dysfunctional civilization endures *Praxis* as failure. *Praxis* is the critique of $-ism and the hope of the Pervert-Schizoid-Woman. The project of humanity is the Spirit of the System and its promised (*a*)sexuality of the Pervert-Schizoid-Woman. Spiritually, *Praxis* must be released from its *Verwerfung*. The future must make structure and elements of *Praxis* the center of a renewed system. The perverse (*a*)sexual is the vanguard of the *écriture* of the (a)symptomatic return of this *Praxis*. We hope, beyond good and evil is the *Praxis* of (*a*)sexuality.

The structure of the morality of good and evil is a sexual system. Rather than the liberation of *Eros* and the emancipation of affection, sexuality is an organization of the manipulations of the pleasure principle and its approach toward a slippery object to be captured and owned. Sexuality is the medium of private property. Sex is a capitalist system of the comparison and contrast of bodies, the exchange and traffic of Women, and the sales of goods and purchases of services. What is the genital principle after capitalism? What is communist (*a*) sex? Freud views the represssion of sex and desire as the etiology of man's neurosis and sickness. He conceives of the repression of wish as the source of malady. But Freud also views the liberation of repressed instincts as a threat to man and world. Lacan's view of sex situates it at the interface of the symbolic and the Real. He contends that there is "no such thing" as a sexual relationship.[30] The fit between man and Woman, and between penis and clitoris, is inadequate. The horror of castration ruins heterosexual intercourse. It is no wonder that Leo Bersani can announce that the secret of sex is that most people do not like it.[31] Foucault's famous remark, "sex is boring," and Andy Warhol's admission, "sex is so messy," both speak to the utter dissatisfaction with sex and sexuality for both men and Women under our $-stic system of private property and phallocentrism. Freud's implicit question — why are we not having sex? — should be reversed — why are we having sex?

This is a vital question. It is a perspective on the issue of sex and sexuality which is seldom posed. Certainly, the purpose of sex is not reproduction. Most sex is unrelated to reproduction. Sex is often organized with the explicit aim to avoid reproduction. Reproduction is best considered an unfortunate ancillary effect of sex. But if reproduction is mostly irrelevant to sex, then why do we have sex? Capitalist and phallocentric sex is structured by the pleasure principle and the climax of male ejaculation before the ephemeral afterglow of the descent toward idle homeostasis. It is a simple observation to note that once a person has experienced and endured an orgasm, the series of postvirginal orgasms is an inspiration of a compulsive repetition of the death drive. Orgasm and death are peradventure isomorphic. But the obsessive will to orgasm is an effect of an intensified *Thanatos* whose insistent passion toward the self-shattering of the self belies a neurotic tendency toward the simple repetition of the pleasure principle. Sex is boring because it repeats the past. Sex is so messy because it involves the job to contain the novel in the repetition of the antediluvian. Sex is unlikeable because it is unsexy.

Freud contends that sexual desire can be a dangerous instinct. But it also must invariably be liberated. Lacan claims that sex is the impossible Real which can only be encircled and approached. But (*a*)sexually, sex is neither dangerous nor impossible. Sex is simply boring. Sex is plainly messy. Sex is obviously unsexy. An (*a*)sexuality does not emerge from a disgust with sex or sexuality. An (*a*)sexuality does not even emerge from the absence of libidinal tendencies toward the body of *Homo sapiens*. The (*a*)sexualist is libidinal and sensual, but she is not lustful or horny. The perverse (*a*)sexualist enjoys the chase rather than the capture. The (*a*)sexualist relishes the trace rather than the seize. The (*a*)sexualist gets off on *Trieb* rather than *désir*. Masochistically, the (*a*)sexuality of the queer communist pervert enjoys the patient waiting for an object whose distance is the mark of an unbearable closeness. This (*a*)sexuality is structured less by the boredom and messiness of sex *per se* than by the profound *ennui* of the possession of the object and the subsequent sexualized engagement. Sexual relations are to be avoided only in order to sustain the (*a*)sexual orgasmic difference and deferral in eroticism. Sex is the obstacle to the obstacle. Sex short-circuits the circuitous circuit of *Trieb*. Sex represses *Trieb*. Sexual relations put the kibosh on the Other *jouissance*. Sex is the distanced activity to be avoided at all costs in the perverse (*a*)sexual teeter and totter on the edge of an edging. The edge extends an infinitely supplemental expansion of the (*a*)sexual galaxy.

Deleuze's version of masochism (1967) suggests that desexualized deferral of the object finally yields to a resexualization in which a masochistic service unfolds as the principle of the future sexuality of the pervert. I am sympathetic to this view toward service because it makes the principles of masochistic resexualization imagination, suspension, and the maternalization of the universe. But I disagree with Deleuze's generalized emphasis on perverse resexualization — what he refers to as the instantaneous "leap." I contest the claim that the ecstatic deferral of the sexual orgasm is somehow lost to a capitulation to the boredom and mess of a sexual copulation that, as Bersani reports, most people do not even like.

My version of (*a*)sexuality does not involve a leap toward resexualization. Rather, the suspension of the intensified and pressured excitement of the (un)pleasurable beyond of the principle of pleasure is the precept of (*a*)sexuality. The pervert's sensual and sybaritic lifestyle embraces beauty and eroticism at the same time as it eschews sex and copulation. The masochist is an aesthete and voyeur. He achingly enjoys the beautiful body from a distance. He distressingly adores the sublime penis from afar. He tenderly basks in the magnificent anatomy from an interval. He painfully revels in the supple hair from behind the bend. He throbbingly delights in the lovely face from across the street. He bitterly idolizes the abs from the camera. He sadly thrills at the triceps from the screen. He sorely savors the forearms from the magazine. He bitterly basks in the biceps from the photograph. He torturously loves the summation of male beauty from the nostalgic reminiscence of the past and the imaginative prospect of the future. She is a scopophilic monster.

This (*a*)sexual perversion is neither of Deleuze's alternatives of desexualization or resexualization. Rather, this mental and affective appetitive orientation toward desire is *Trieb*. Drive is an attitude toward (*a*)sexuality which is structured by erotics rather than desire. The erotic Spirit of Peniscentrism and Clitoralcentrism — Post-Capitalism — is an (*a*)sexuality. In (*a*)sexuality, the object is beside the point — of contact. After capitalism, arrives a communist queerness in which the comparison and contrast of bodies, the exchange of sexual fluids, and the profitable accumulation of tricks and trysts are supplanted by the gazes, gaits, gestures, obscurities, and tortures of an (*a*)sexuality. An (*a*)sexuality is beyond not simply the principle of pleasure. An (*a*)sexuality is the Outside of the climax and ejaculation of the phallocentric orgasm of the bored and messy male body. An erotics of mental imagination and physical suspension elevates chastity to the dignity of *das Ding*. Foreplay is the *forte* of the queer communist (*a*)sexualist. The coldness of distance is the edge of the bedroom of the (*a*)sexualist.

However, the will to be remote from the object of desire must be supplemented by an affective dimension. Affect complements the patient waiting of the Pervert-Schizoid-Woman and her erotics of the Spirit of the System. The essential delay in the masochist's outlook toward boredom and messiness harnesses another principle which is beyond the *Eros* and *Thanatos* of neurotically unpleasurable tension and its stupid release. This extended interval is the fourth-dimension of *Praxis*. There is no first-dimension spatiality in *Praxis* because the pervert's *Trieb* resists the metaphysics of presence which would otherwise position the edge of his patient waiting as either *Fort!* or *Da!* The space of the unconscious in which words and pictures are displaced and condensed by the censorship is absent. The prepositional directives in space merely disorganize any orientation in the space of the unconscious. Temporally, there can be no chronological succession of *objets petit a*. The object is Outside of an organized space and time. The exclusion of spatial coordinates makes the organization of time impossible to either map or experience. The unconscious is bereft of any substance because the wishes and desires for the present object of conscious experience are displaced. There is no repressed or its return in the mentality or physicality — erotics — of (*a*)sexuality. Psychoanalytic interpretation is null and void for (*a*)sexuality because neither desire nor repression nor censorship nor latent content nor manifest form operates in this fourth-dimension of an erotic patient waiting of *Praxis*.

The veiled object is what I name as the *objet différé d'imagination* or deferred object of imagination. This veil is neither an *objet* of fantasy as the *mise-en-scène* of desire nor an *objet* as the aim of desire. Rather, the *objet différé d'imagination* or deferred object of imagination is the liminal void of neither space nor time nor the unconscious. This object is the *Praxis*-cause. *Praxis* is the constitutive outside of the subject. The object of *Praxis* is a metaphor for the various philosophical concepts of mediation: Foucault's Power and Knowledge, Derrida's *Différance* and Text, Nietzsche's Will to Power and Force, Lacan's Phallus and Symbolic, Marx's Mode of Production and Labor, and Saussure's Signifier and Sign. This series of philosophical metaphors *qua* metalanguages must be supplemented in order to register the constitutive outside of the pervert's (*a*)sexuality. This expanded context is *Praxis*. The (*a*)sexualist does not escape either genealogical production or social construction. Cultural forces generate (*a*)sexuality. Essentially, this modality of (*a*)sexuality is an effect of the social pressures and historical determinates in the transition from capitalism to communism, from phallocentrism to Peniscentrism, from castration to plenitude, and from Something is Missing to Nothing is Missing. A contemporary (*a*)sexuality emerges as the postcapitalist and postphallocentric sexuality of our time.

Figure 13.2 Unary *Praxis*

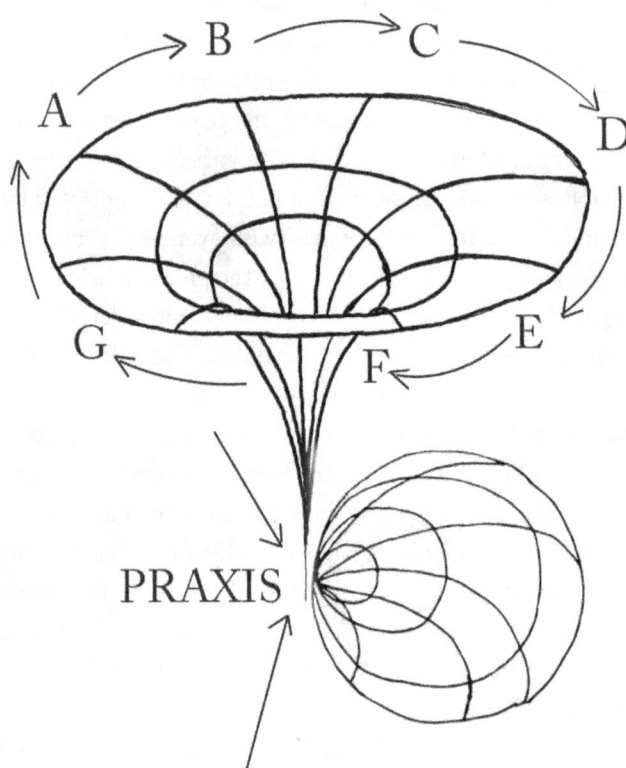

This image shows the signifying chain as it encircles the (*a*)sexual nucleus. The (*a*)sexual kernel of energy is the occluded gravitational center of the expansion of the universe in fetishes, penises, clitorises, objects, metaphors, signs, centers, metonymies, and so on. But *Praxis* is distinct from the other units of text (A, B, C, D, and so on) in the network of words because it is perversely Outside and Inside — extimate — to this veiled center of (*a*)sexual effluvium. *Praxis* is not swapped In and Out of the $-ism in the Logic of Identity of the division and opposition of the sign. Instead, *Praxis* is conditioned by the veil of (*a*)sexuality and its decentered nucleus of expansive energy. *Praxis* is neither integrated nor assimilated into the system of $-ism. *Praxis* symbolizes the Untruth of the schizoid's intuition of s *qua* $-ism. *Qua* combination of signifier and signified but precisely not as the combined positive unity of the sign, *Praxis* is consistently and continuously consigned to the margin of the Outside of the discourses in the system. This is so even as *Praxis* is at the center of the structure in its critique of phallocentrism, capitalism, *langue,* and the systems of *le propre. Praxis* symbolizes the Real at the edge of Something and Nothing. *Praxis* is excluded in its inclusion, and it is included in its exclusion. This situated Logic of Difference of *Praxis* is precisely the truth that *Praxis* strives to symbolize for the neurotic. The pervert joyfully symbolizes decenterment with the jockstrap and its "jockstraps." The neurotic uncomfortably engages presence (absence) with the penis and its avatars. Perverse *Praxis* symbolizes *around* its object in order to inlay the disappointed irrelevance of the avatar. The jockstrap is (*a*)sexual not because it resists genital sexuality. Rather, the jockstrap is (*a*)sexual because it is precisely not a jockstrap. The will to power of (*a*)sexuality is the universal force which unveils *Trieb* as the object of itself.

Notes & Sketches —

An (*a*)sexuality is beyond the capitalist and patriarchal Something is Missing. The abundance of Nothing is Missing of clitoris/penis — rather than penis/not-penis — and of plenitude of use-value — rather than scarcity of exchange-value — manifests as the postphallic *Praxis* of sexuality and the postunconscious *Praxis* of revolution. If the object is present rather than absent, then desire sears and burns. At the ends of Something is Missing, the *objet petit a* exsiccates from the world. The *objet différé d'imagination* or deferred object of imagination rises as the objectal force of the Pervert-Schizoid-Woman and her Spirit of the System. Now, I Spirit, the mind and the body, and the mental and the physical, unify in an imagination of the present. The solar system becomes the evanescent object of creativity and inspiration. The (*a*)sexualist envisions the *objet différé d'imagination* of the flair and panache of patient waiting *qua Praxis*. The disruptive philosophy and speculation, on the one hand, and the inert activity and practicality, on the other hand, are destabilized by the return of the worldly foreclosed to *Praxis*. Outside of time, space, and the unconscious, *Praxis* imagines — The gamble is that the Outside of extant philosophical metaphors, such as Power and Knowledge, *Différance* and Text, Will to Power and Force, Phallus and Symbolic, Mode of Production and Labor, and Signifier and Sign is the *objet différé d'imagination*. The object of imagination is the deferred gaze of the (*a*)sexualist and her communist queer *Praxis* of —

Faggots and an (a)sexuality

In the beginning is the deed. But for Freud this originary act is murder. The hateful violence of man is an effect of an exclusion. Banishment returns as the bloody brothers and their vengeful murder of the primal father. The psychical consequence is guilt and remorse. The social consequence is the assembly of civilization from the ashes of violence and shame. The brothers free themselves only to imprison the primal dwellers. The ostensible liberation and emancipation of the revolution against the father merely achieve a psychical symptom and a settled repressive society. But the father's murder is mythical. The father is neither alive nor dead. Instead, he is suspended between life and death. The father only haunts the brothers as a potential object of murder.

The briefly explicated plot of Freud's fable of the murder of the primal father situates the brothers in an exclusionary space in which desire has yet to be hystericized. Outside on the beach, the brothers cavort in a space in which Nothing is Missing. This is a space of the lack of the lack which is the Outside of castration. The brothers can neither desire the forbidden Women nor instinctually murder the primal father. This is so even as the exclusion is the condition of this prohibition. The father's lair inside the beach house is the projected figuration of a capitalism in which Something is Missing, either between the excluded brothers and the captive Women or between the sons and their father. The beach is the space in which Nothing is Missing in the absence of desire and sexuality *tout court*. The beach is the fourth-dimension of the communist queer (*a*)sexual *Praxis* of the future in the past.

The brothers are not sexual in a dimension in which Nothing is Missing. The sexual exploits of the brothers and their originary homosexuality are strictly (*a*)sexual. In the beginning, is the virginal homosexual. Freud's tale cannot account for the hystericization of desire. The revolutionary *coup* against the primal father is exactly mythical. On the beach, the gay boys enjoy their (*a*)sexuality with their brethren as *objets différé d'imagination*. The postcapitalist and postphallocentric prelapsarian homosexual utopia is paradoxically antecedent to the phallic capitalist economy of civilization. This civilization is forged by the heterosexualized — somehow — brothers after and as the murder of the father. The Clitoral Stage homosexual communist beach is the scene of (*a*)sexuality and the amoralism of the beyond of good, evil, capitalism, phallocentrism, and heterosexuality.

The pervert's concrete and empirical relationship to the *objet différé d'imagination* sparks the imagination of a liminal object — with trunks off but not getting off. The essential wish of Western man is to be rid of responsibility and the Judeo-Christian framework of morality and its structure of good and evil. The obstacle to the traversal beyond good and evil and toward amorality is two-fold: first, the guess that man is essentially wretched, whether conceived as Freudian instincts or biological genetic makeup; and second, the corollary supposition that the worldly context of the human text ruins *Homo sapiens*, whether he is good or evil in the beginning. Neither postulation can be submitted to either scientific experiment or humanist appraisal. Judeo-Christian moralism is organized by a fancied impression. This fantasy is deeply persuasive because neither the philosopher nor the scientist has access to either a man or a world which is not conditioned by biological genes or social context. The mostly discredited versions of man *sans* world are religious witnesses, such as the Christian fable of a prelapsarian bliss in the Garden of Eden before the fall or the Judaic intuition of the event of sin which begins anew each day. But for the people of the world, the idea that beyond good and evil is the Garden of Eden, or that moralism makes us sick, or that responsibility is the origin of sin — such is considered balderdash and bluster.

Freud's myth of the murder of the primal father is another origin-story that ostensibly enlightens the raw savagery of the brothers. This frightful image requires antidote. At the close of the *Seminar* on the ethics of psychoanalysis (1956-57), Lacan poses, I repeat: "The important thing is not knowing whether man is good or bad in the beginning; the important thing is what will transpire once the book has been eaten." Lacan's perspective denies the significance of the question that Freud seeks to answer with the myth of the murder of the primal father. The matter of the essential nature of *Homo sapiens* or the contextual determination of man is displaced. Lacan suggests that the experiment to liberate desire from restriction in the otherwise enforced repressions in society or the fabricated responsibilities in moralism is a trial which is worthy of man and world. Beyond good and evil — the exchange of symptom for pleasure — is an experiment which is reputable for *Homo sapiens*, violent instincts, dysfunctional genes, sour worldliness, or not.

Freud's own experiment banishes the brothers from civilization only to unfathomably assume first, the hystericization and heterosexualization of the homosexual desire of Nothing is Missing, and, second, the plenitude of penis *sans* castration, and, third, the abundance of use-values *sans* scarcity. *Contra* Freud's suppositions and intentions, I want to imagine the beach and its homosexual Nothing is Missing of the *objet différé d'imagination* and the (*a*)sexual approach of *Trieb* toward this object of man's mental and psychical imagination. Beyond good and evil is a trial which is worthy of man's precarious situation. Beyond good and evil is the wager of the communist queer (*a*)sexual pervert.

The precipitous consequence of Nothing is Missing is the absence of desire. The entirety of the original scene of the excluded brothers on the beach takes place in the Outside of desire. The object otherwise promises to fulfill the lack. Unlike the *objet différé d'imagination*, the object-cause of desire achieves its function in tricky lure and deceptive temptation. The subject of desire — $ \$<>a $ — is subordinate to fantasy and the *mise-en-scène* of the pursuit of desire. The context of fantasy determines the text of desire. The neurotic submits to the scene in which the object is situated. In "Instincts and their Vicissitudes" (1915), Freud claims that the object of desire is only "peculiarly fitted" to the aim of the drive.[32] The inordinate ductility of the object-cause indexes its arrangement by the fantasy. The peculiarity of the match between aim and object renders the *objet petit a* arbitrary and irrelevant to the satisfaction of the aim of the drive. How does the subject finally satisfy desire with the object? Or is the (*a*)sexualist the communist queer who discerns that the peculiar fit between *désir* and *Objekt* summarily indicates that the object is not a cause but rather an imagination?

The pleasure principle design of satisfaction establishes the tension/release model of desire and its fulfillment. The increase of an unpleasurable tension reaches a climax of explosion after which the pleasurable reduction of tension achieves satisfaction at the zero degree of homoeostasis. The masochist's orientation toward pleasure is precisely the reverse. Masochism gets off on the endless escalation of tension in Becoming. The trace is the source of the pervert's ecstatic delight. But this abstract schema of pleasure does not answer the concrete query about engagement with the object and the satisfaction of the aim. Supposedly, the male orgasmic ejaculation is the peak of a split (un)pleasure in which the afterglow of climax achieves the pinnacle of pleasure. But Freud undertheorizes the modalities of satisfaction of a variety of other relationships of $\$<>a$. This makes an empirical analysis of (*a*)sexuality a difficult project. How do the brothers have (*a*)sex with each other? What do (*a*)sexual relationships look like? What are the (*a*)sexual positions and roles during (*a*)sex?

An approach to these issues engages the alternative posthumanist subjectivity of the Pervert-Schizoid-Woman. At once, the (*a*)sexual communist queers do not have any intentional or willful reason to take action in the world: move in this direction, gesture toward that idea, create this condition, make that alliance, feel this emotion, talk that way, write this down, remember that event, and so on. The queer being-in-the-world and being-with-others are neither motivated nor calculated. The (*a*)sexualist enjoys himself without the executive function of the ego. The ego of the (*a*)sexual queer is displaced and decentered. The (*a*)sexualist enjoys a relationship to the *objet différé d'imagination* as a substitute for the purposive and deliberate ego. This object of imagination is animated by neither space nor time nor the unconscious.

The structuralist truth of the constitutive outside holds that the exterior designs the interior, the outside determines the inside, the context governs the text, and the extimate relationship between binary oppositions interweaves each in the other — and the obverse. Constructionism and relationality index the sheer ruin of any version of metaphysical humanism, moral individualism, or political liberalism. These ideologies would otherwise pretend to apply to the (un)hystericized and homosexual brothers of the primal horde. The subjectivity of the homosexual is acutely empty. The homosexual is the doer who is done by the deed's doer and the doer's deed. The non-duped certainly errs. But the dupe gets to fuck his brother.

The essence of the (*a*)sexual is not the desire of Lacan's $\$<>a$. The essence of the Pervert-Schizoid-Woman and her queer brothers, sisters, and the rest of us is *Praxis*. *Praxis* is neither spatial nor temporal because it is structured by *Trieb*. *Praxis* is not unconscious because it is freed of desire and wish. The perverse subject of *Praxis* displaces the psychoanalytic subject of desire. Rather than the algorithm for the subject of desire ($\$<>a$), this algebra of the subject of the fourth-dimension is: $S<>P$. The P designates the object of *Praxis* or the *objet différé d'imagination*. This object of the imagination is the differed and deferred *tout autre* masochistic object of *Trieb*. The object-*Praxis* (P) is suspended by the masochist's imagination. This suspended ingenuity meditates on its futural appearance at the horizon of the Spirit of the System. The object-*Praxis* (P) is a deeply Spiritual object. The *objet différé d'imagination* is neither empirical nor concrete. The *objet différé d'imagination* resists present self-sameness and essential self-identity. The extimate and parallactic split within the logic is structured by the Logic of Difference ($A \neq A$).

The (*a*)sexualist's psychical and social experience of his object-P is antecedent to the hystericization of desire and the heterosexualization of libido. The relationship between the (*a*)sexualist and his object-love — *queer et objet différé d'imagination* — is suspended in an authorless and subjectless Spirit of masochism. Rather than the *mise-en-scène* of fantasy and its castrated object and desirous subject, the frame of imagination stages the scene of the creative and original reinvention of the future. The P-*objet* is the *tout autre* of *Praxis*. The P is suspended by an innovative resourcefulness which delays the arrival of this *Praxis*. This scene is void of the humanist tropes of agency, will, intention, authority, control, and so on.

The communist queer (*a*)sexuals are precisely posthumanist. The experiences of agency, will, intention, authority, and control escape their psychical and social lives. The homosexual on the beach — shirt and trunks off — is antecedent to the hystericization of desire and the heterosexualization of libido. On the beach, Spirit washes toward the sands. The system is pure positivity and presence. A Nothing is Missing assuages the otherwise frenetic oedipal symptoms of the male junior's narcissism and anxiety and the female junior's envy and jealousy.

The absence of the conscious ego and its executive organization of agency, will, intention, authority, and control makes any *a priori* theorization of concrete and empirical (*a*)sex inconceivable. The acts and positions of (*a*)sex are unstructured by the executive functions of the ego. An (*a*)sex abjures the purposive plans of the system Cs. and the deliberative calculations of the doer and his deed. The *P* of (*a*)sex is spontaneous and impulsive. An (*a*)sexuality is not arranged by the sanctioned fantasies of the culture. Rather, (*a*)sex is impromptu and extemporaneous. But it is pivotal to understand that the pervert's relationship to the *objet différé d'imagination* is distant and cold. Feigned indifference animates the pervert's relationship to the messianic object. The masochist stays at a distance from the object-*P*, both spatially and temporally. The physical reason for this distance is the pervert's acute yen for the intense ache for a proximity to the object. This adjacency would otherwise overwhelm the subject and his eroticism. The (*a*)sexual may present as prudish or sterile. But the perverse masochist's desexualization is a profound — inordinately forceful — erotics. This eroticism overpowers the executive function of the ego. An (*a*)sexuality is antecedent to desire and hysteria. *Praxis* strips the (*a*)sexual of metaphysical humanism, moral individualism, and political liberalism.

The Deleuzean resexualization applies a misconception to the (*a*)sexualist. The subject of *Praxis* is radically erotic. The distinction between desire and erotics is crucial to a proper theorization of communist queer (*a*)sexual masochism. The former *désir* seeks an object which will (un)satisfy his aim *qua Objekt*. The latter *Trieb* ideates the *objet différé d'imagination*. Mundane masculine fantasy establishes the object of the neurotic's desire. Feminine creative imagination dreams the objectal horizon of the pervert's *Trieb*. The misty and shadowy (*a*)sex of the pervert is mobilized toward the future. The erotic gratification of the positions and roles of (*a*)sex is messianic. The (*a*)sexual orgasm is strictly beyond the pleasure principle. The essence of the (*a*)sexual orgasm is the differed and deferred (*a*)sexual comings and goings which gesture toward the future. The orgasm of the (*a*)sexualist assembles the future. The Pervert-Schizoid-Woman is yet to come. The (*a*)sexual imagines the future in his *objet différé d'imagination*. This vision innovates even in the absence of agency, will, intention, authority, and control. This (*a*)sexuality is the erotic principle of postcapitalist, postphallocentric, and posthumanist *Praxis*. *P* is deferred. This delay is the erotics of the pervert. The pervert tarries with *P* in order to extend it. The masochist defers *P* in order to protract it. The Pervert-Schizoid-Woman differs *Praxis* in order to broaden its scope in theory and practice, and in erotics and (*a*)sex. The principle of *différance* is the trace of *Praxis*. The *P* letter never arrives at its destination.

The logic of the nonarrival of the letter at its destination also applies to the self of the masochist. Her cold indifference — but also hot engagement — emerge *ex nihilo* from Nothingness. The masochist is not present to herself. Her gestures may be spontaneous and unthought or calculated and arranged, but the source of these orientations is strictly the horizonal Other to the text. As Deleuze claims, what speaks in masochism is the death drive, but this *thanatos* is also strictly interchangeable with the drive of life. The masochist's patient waiting is this drive. But the wait is active, and it extends itself endlessly in order to enjoy the absence of the object which is simultaneously the presence of the object. Whatever is Becoming — this will be the (*a*)sex of the future. *P* is the nonarrival of the self at itself and the other. The liminal space of no-self and no-other is the context of this protracted (*a*)sex of the future — *Not yet!*

Figure 13.3 The Fourth-Dimension of *Praxis*

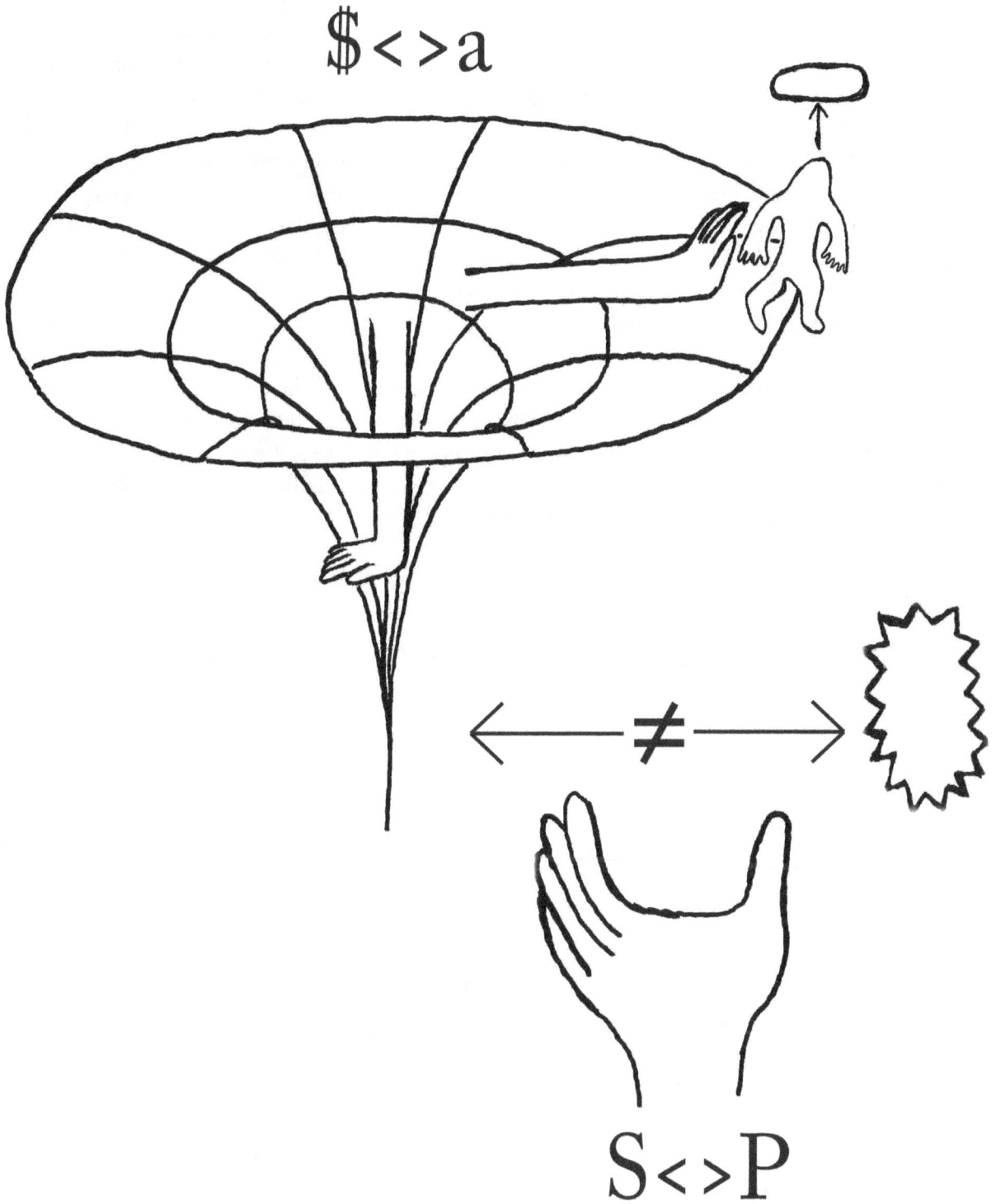

$$\$<>a$$

$$\ne$$

$$S<>P$$

This drawing illustrates $-ism and the ways in which the neurotic is held in place (above, center) by the chain of signification. The system holds the neurotic in his decided and determinate space between the gravity of the center and the objects which define the traversal of neurotic thinking, being, and living. The (in)equation of $<>*a* (above, center) represents this infinitely expansive set of relationships between the split subject of neurosis and the series of expanded and contracted objects of idiotic masculine *jouissance*. This structure is arranged by the (in)equivalence and (in)equality of any object to any other object in the comparison and contrast of exchange. The hand (below, right) represents the fourth-dimensional *Praxis* in which the object of the Clitoral Stage is indeterminate and undecidable in relationship to a context whose boundaries are Real and unsymbolizable rather than symbolic and articulable. The subject of *Praxis* (below, right) enjoys the interminable *Möbius* path in which Nothingness and Being overlap in the perverse gap of *bothness* and *andness*. The subject of the *Praxis* of the fourth-dimension is paradoxically whole and unsplit because its incomparable and incontrastable singular Sameness⁺ invites a veil between the object and its symbolization. The communist future portends a *Praxis* in which the subject is present (absent) in all points in space. *Praxis* gestures toward the pure phonology of the materiality of the signifier in the Clitoral Stage. The object is beyond representation because it is devoid of the abstraction and speculation of the signified. The materiality of the fetish-object *qua* signifier wrenches the jockstrap from the distant (proximate) relationship to castration and its return as "sexual difference." The castration which is subject to the *Verleugnung* of perverse disavowal returns the sexual difference not only as jockstrap and "jockstrap" but also as any expansive and extended series of words and objects — *tout autre* — in the system. *Praxis* impossibly symbolizes these singular objects of "return." The scare quote is the perverse shorthand for this symbolization in *Praxis*.

Notes & Sketches —

AN (A)SEXUALITY, BEFORE GOOD AND EVIL

The dream of Irma's injection articulates the Western wish to be rid of responsibility and to be beyond good and evil. Freud's myth of the murder of the primal father posits the revolutionary murder of paternity as the proviso of the turn toward guilt and remorse. Murder and guilt are the foundations of civilization. Freud's wish to be innocent of Irma's poor medical treatment is an effect of a moralist civilization. This moralism is structured by shame for the father's murder. The prelapsarian homosexuals are (*a*)sexual because the libido on the beach is pure sexuality and unalloyed *Trieb*. Only the Nothing is Missing is antecedent to the fictional hystericization of the brothers' desire and the heterosexualization of an originary homosexuality. The absence of an economy of castration and scarcity invites the homosexuals to enjoy a Peniscentric (Clitoralcentric) communist beach. Imaginary lesbians also take pleasure in plenitude and the Sameness⁺ of a subverted hierarchy of gender and sexuality.

Before good and evil, the rule of the father's exclusion is in abeyance. The homosexuals are guiltless, remorseless, and in desire of Nothing whatsoever. The word is absent. The homosexuals and their bodies frolic in an incipient sexual switcheroo in which all bodies are beautiful. Beyond good and evil, the bliss of an aneconomy with neither doers nor deeds — Becoming Ing⁺ — rules the galaxies. The absence of absence, plentiful penis (clitoris), and abundant goods structure the universe. The general equivalent ceases to compare, contrast, and exchange. The phallus is absent on the beach. Penises and clitorises dwell in the open space of *Praxis*. These (*a*)sex organs do so without the mark, the word, and their various significations. The pertinent matter is Freud's fantasy of castration. Freud's incoherent will to hystericize and heterosexualize the brothers is inexplicable. Why must civilization originate with an exclusion? Why must this foreclosure be resolved by violent revolution and unnecessary murder?

This question indicates the latent truth of Freud's myth. *The myth is a myth.* The retroactive construction of the past murder from a future civilization of good and evil — and the responsibility which negotiates between the twin pillars of Western morality — is a consequence of the Something is Missing in the social order. The object of this lack is the metaphorical castration of the Woman and her diminutive clitoris. But the Real hole in the symbolic order is the morality of good and evil. In the *Seminar* on the four fundamental concepts of psychoanalysis (1964), Lacan insightfully remarks, as I have mentioned, that there is only a cause in that which does not work. Freud's labor to trace back civilization to the imaginary murder of the primal father is the pursuit of a causality for the symbolic order. The solar system does not *work*. The origin of this fault is a fictional murder and a fabled series of affects. These sentiments motivate the invention of law, morality, and religion. The bulwark of civilization is the effect of a defect in the system. The prospective breakdown of Western civilization is morality. Freud traces this morality to murder. But the Becoming of the brothers as doers of the deed figures the murder of the father as the Outside of presence. The murder is a myth. The upshot of this myth is civilization. The world is founded on a lie. The solar system is the Outside of itself.

The binary of good and evil is the moral dimension of hysteria and heterosexuality. The antecedent aesthetic of the beach and its boys is a healthy homosexuality. The false trade-off between sickness and health, heterosexuality and homosexuality, and moralism and amoralism is the sin of civilization. The only explanation for hysteria, heterosexuality, and morality is an unexpected glitch in the system. This error is morality. Nietzscheanly, morality makes man sick. The dream of Irma's injection desires a civilization anew. This advanced galaxy is emergent in the future. This *avant-garde* world displaces the cracks in the edifice of a civilization which is structured by Judeo-Christian morality. Heterosexuality is the sin of civilization. Morality is the evil of the galaxy. A prelapsarian homosexuality is the savior of a fallen world. The Outside of good and evil is a queer (*a*)sexuality of communist plenitude and Penisclitoriscentric abundance.

Freud's peculiar and jumbled myth strives to enforce hysteria and heterosexuality as the necessary integrants to the development of civilization. These fundamentals are guilt, remorse, and murder. But the aftershocks of this fictive and mistaken revolution are the moralities which return Freud to the origin of the illness. Morality also illuminates the source of man's malady. Beyond good and evil, Something is Missing is exchanged for Nothing is Missing — capitalism for communism, lack for plenitude, heterosexuality for (*a*)sexuality, desire for *Trieb*, scarcity for abundance, sign for signifier, reader for writer, and so on. Morality can only insist as truth if the binary opposition between good/evil is structured into the precepts of civilization. Morality insists that good lacks evil. Morality exhorts that evil castrates good. The futural *tout autre* of the beyond of good and evil is a communist queer (*a*)sexual *fete* of bodies and materialities *sans* words and speculations.

Universal (*a*)sexuality ushers selfhood and sociality toward the postphallic and postcapitalist utopia of the Spirit of the System and its *Praxis*. Spiritually, the future is an (*a*)sexuality of deferred gratification in which the hystericization of desire and its immoral deed and sinful doer are suspended by a masochistic patient waiting — toward the beyond of capitalism and sexuality. The oral stage, anal stage, and primacy of the phallus are displaced by the embryonic postphallic and postcapitalist genital principle of the clitoris. *Qua* Nothingness, the clitoris is the absent center around which the structure of (*a*)sexuality is organized. This absent center is everywhere in the space of the (*a*)sexual solar system. Beyond good and evil, men, Women, and the rest of us live and breathe the clitoris as the bodily principle of a Nothingness is Present. The Woman's clitoris is the inherited genital on the horizon of the (*a*)sexuality of the future.

In a wonderful aphorism from *Beyond Good and Evil* (1886), Nietzsche remarks that "what is done out of love always takes place beyond good and evil."[33] The love of *Praxis* returns from repression in order to destabilize a symbolic order of Unlove with the unary trait of the love of *Praxis*. The gay boys on the beach are beyond good and evil because an unhystericized desire animates their gestures *sans* agency, movements *sans* intention, deeds *sans* will, actions *sans* authority, and endeavors *sans* control. The homosexuals enjoy texts without authors and scripts without writers. The brothers play and entertain on a beach in which Nothing is Missing. The love of *Praxis* "takes place beyond good and evil" because this *Praxis* is situated on the Outside of the binary series of oppositions in the symbolic order. The aneconomy of Nothing is Missing indicates that there is no system of good/evil (and so on) which arranges subjects and objects, and doers and deeds, in the hierarchy of Western morality. The division between the doer and the deed is spurious. Freud and Irma are exonerated of presence. The Unlove that otherwise symptomatically returns to the system as its bodily and mindful malady is overcome by a *P* which "takes place beyond good and evil," as Nietzsche says. *Praxis* manifests in a *mise-en-scène* of an unhystericized homosexuality — communist queer (*a*)sexuality — and plenitude of each according to his need and each according to his ability. *Praxis* invites a Penisclitoriscentric ~~equality in difference~~ Sameness⁺. The *P*-Principle is the rupture of the Unlove of a system gone haywire.

Unlove is the precept of the symptom and its dissolution in the beyond of good and evil of *Praxis*. Western civilization and its will toward the responsibility of the doer and the deed typify an Unlove of guilt and remorse for the murder of the father. Unlove animates the constitutive ambivalence of the hystericized and heterosexualized brothers of the nascent world of law, morality, and religion. Morality not only makes man sick. Morality makes man hate. *P* emanates from the loss of responsibility. *P* appears as the end of morality. *P* awakens at the quietus of the doer, his deed, and the moralist mediation between the subject of the action and the object of the activity. Love — *Praxis* — is the affect of amoralism. *P* is beyond good and evil. The conundrum of Freud's work on the origin of civilization is the projection of ambivalence *qua* the consequential origin and effect of the world. Why does Freud not only fantasize Something is Missing but also presuppose a basal Unlove of humanity?

The symptoms of $-ism index a pessimistic view of humanity both Inside and Outside of civilization.

But if Unlove is the principle of humanity, then its own transgression of binary logic — Unlove/X — gives hope for an internal destabilization — *Praxis* — of the system of Unlove. A proper amoral return to *Praxis* is the future of love. My claim is that the (*a*)sexualists of the future (past) of bodies without organs and deeds without doers — Becoming — are the lovers of this prelapsarian before and posthaste after of good and evil and the structure of Western moralism. Irma's pains may be an object of medical mistreatment. But do the persecution and prosecution of a displaced responsibility for her troubles promise the moralist existence of any of the characters in the plot of the dream? The moral strictures of Western civilization generate the symptom of the dream and its interpretation. With Freud, are we to imagine that repression will improve Freud's treatments and inspire better medicine? Or, with Lacan, may we imagine that desire — *Praxis* — will advance Freud's techniques and provoke better care?

The homosexuals on the beach avoid this forced choice between repression and desire, and between law and will, because their Becoming overcomes the metaphysics of presence of the departure and arrival of the letter. An (*a*)sexuality promises the imaginative suspension of the binary oppositions of doer/deed, repression/ desire, law/will, good/evil, and so on. The affect of *P* rather than the speculation of desire restructures the solar system. The pervert's masochism displaces man and his moralism. This illuminates the simple latent truth that love exceeds law. This *P*-Principle is the essence of (*a*)sexuality and its difference and deferral of the ambivalent *objet petit a*. The *P*-Principle entreats the communist queer (*a*)sexual imaginative flirtation with *objet différé d'imagination*. A deferred artistry delays good and evil in the retroactive construction of a posthaste world of suspended tension between a decentered (*a*)sexual *ipse* and an evanescent object. After responsibility, the pervert inherits a *Praxis* which escapes —

A Metaphor for Truth

I want to meditate on the brawn and muscle of chosen metaphors. The primal horde myth beseeches the logistics of the brothers' decision to mistakenly exchange the prelapsarian homosexual bliss of Nothing is Missing — the absence of castration, lack, scarcity, narcissism, anxiety, and aggression — for the heteronormative and phallocentric system of Something is Missing — the presence of castration, lack, scarcity, narcissism, anxiety, and aggression. How did the brothers exchange the bliss of the warmth of the mother and maternity for the ideologies of the rule of the father and patriarchy? There is no coherent account of the hystericization of desire of the homosexual brothers who are excluded from civilization at the outset of the origin-story of Western civilization. How was the exchange of plenitude for lack, penis for clitoris, and a *jouissance* of the Other for guilt and remorse possible? How and why did the brothers make the decision to storm the father's beach house and eat his body?

The answer is the strength of metaphor. The method is the will in contingency and necessity for substitution — center, metaphor, word, fetish, sign, and so on. Nietzsche illuminates the rhetorical value of metaphor. Nietzsche (1870) asks,

> What then is truth? A movable host of metaphors, metonymies, and anthropomorphisms: in short, a sum of human relations which have been poetically and rhetorically intensified, transferred, and embellished, and which, after long usage, seem to people to be fixed, canonical, and binding. Truths are illusions which we have forgotten are illusions; they are metaphors which have become worn out and have been drained of sensuous force, coins which have lost their embossing and are now considered as metal and no longer as coins.[34]

Figure 13.4 Pervert-Schizoid-Woman and Materiality

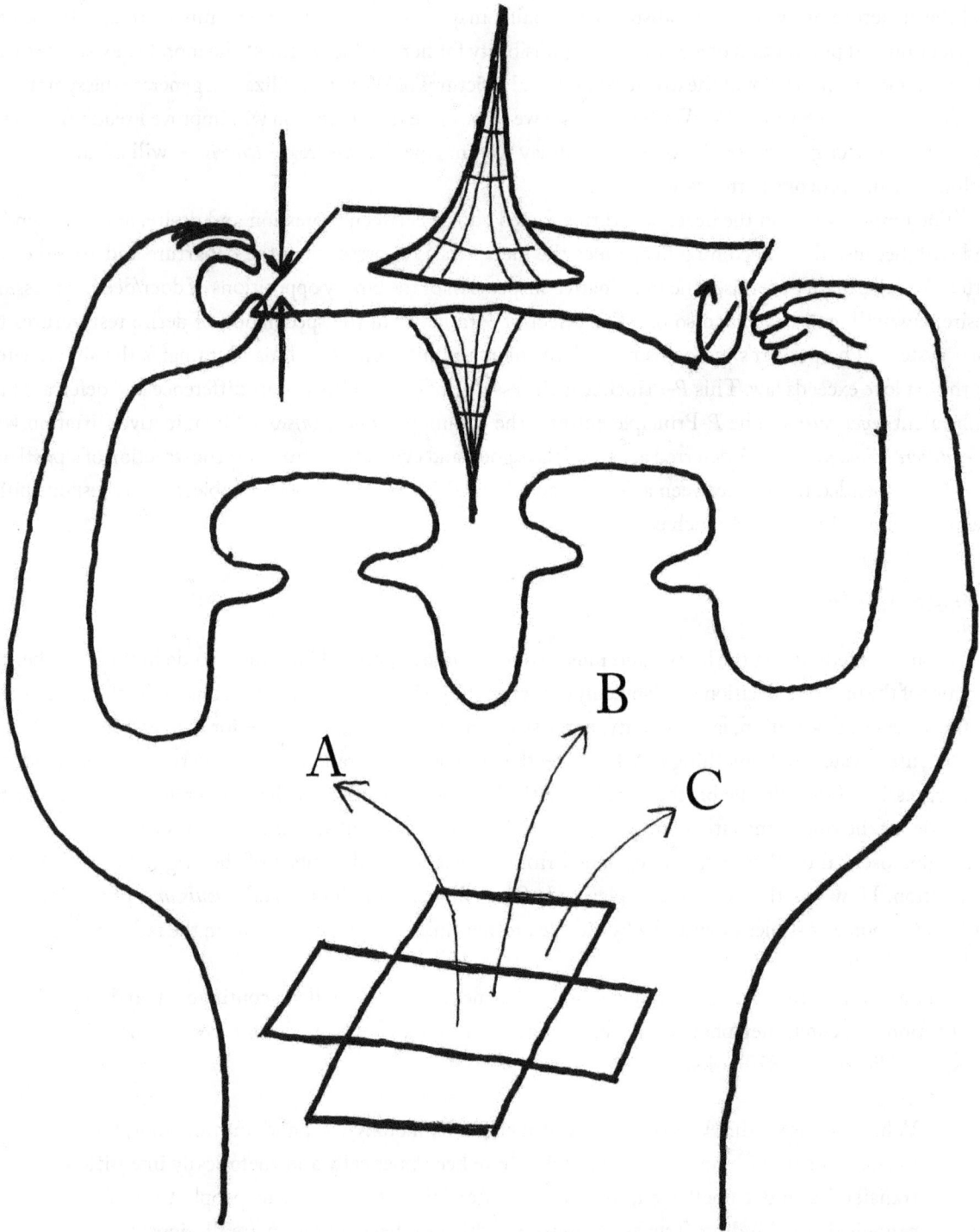

This image represents the function of the Pervert-Schizoid-Woman who heralds a futurity of Sameness⁺ and the Logic of Difference in the perverse interchangeability and fetishistic substitutability of untethered and unmoored *les mots et les choses*. The Pervert-Schizoid-Woman unwrenches the mirror (center). She demonstrates the parallactic gap between $-ism and S in the inverse and reverse of the gravitational (*a*)sexual push (pull) of the occluded center of the energy of the system. The units of signification (terms: A, B, C, D, and so on) are liberated from their presupposed points of origin and reference. The limits of phallocentric lack, capitalist scarcity, and the absence of the word are reconfigured as an overlap of the downward (upward) twist of the system rather than the division and opposition of the terms (A, B, C, D, and so on) (center). The Sameness⁺ — ~~continuous continuity~~ — of any incomparable and incontrastable object with any other undecided and indeterminate object is present at each point in the system. The staggered relationship between the material signifier and the abstract signified in the overlap of theory and practice in *Praxis* produces a surplus materiality. This excess materiality is the leftover of the system. The remnant of materiality and the signifier is the (*a*)sexual center around which the words and objects in the system revolve and traverse. The materiality of the jockstrap is the essence of the *jouissance* of the Real Fetishist. The sign (materiality and abstraction) of the jockstrap is the kernel of the *jouissance* of the Patriarchal Fetishist. The signified (speculation) of the jockstrap is the nucleus of the Capitalist Fetishist. The material, speculative, and spatial interval of magnitude between the penis and the jockstrap measures the Realness of the *jouissance* of the pervert and his relationship to the nascent future of the Woman. The (*a*)sexuality is the energy which expands the magnitude — the material essence of the jockstrap *qua* signifier, the material-abstract kernel of the jockstrap *qua* sign, and the speculative nucleus of the jockstrap *qua* signified. The pervert's pinch twists the divisions among Real Fetishist, Patriarchal Fetishist, and Capitalist Fetishist into the Lesbian Fetishist whose relationship to the penis *qua* referent is distant and nil. The Clitoral Stage of the Pervert-Schizoid-Woman gestures toward the strict materialism of the pure phonology of the communist materiality of the signifier and its (*a*)sexual decenter.

Notes & Sketches —

Fundamentally, a metaphor indexes a bi-level configuration. The figural substitutes in the place of the literal. The metaphor derives its secondary power and effective force from a reliance on a literal dimension. This literality precedes the intervention of the metaphor. A metaphor is predicated on this literal. But the literal too is enhanced by the dimension of the metaphorical. The original and primary metaphor at once appears as the secondary and derivative. But the metaphor is also the autochlonous and essential. Metaphor retroactively elaborates the literal. The metaphor purports to precede this literal.

The fetish is structured as a metaphor or "penis-substitute." The fetish is a screen for the absent maternal phallus. The *point de capiton* is the penis. The phallus is the final referent of sexuality, such as in fetishism. The phallus guarantees the stability of a meaning-making which does not otherwise drift and waft — *différance* — in an unlimited semiosis. Otherwise, *différance* unsettles the strict and tidy division between manifest/latent, symptom/truth, conscious/unconscious, and so on. The absence of the anchor of the literal penis in the series of metaphorical symptoms — phantom limb, hysterical cough, strange joke, slip of the tongue, inexplicable dream — would invite metaphor to jettison its persuasive talent to fix meaning in any coherent sense. The neurotic is organized by the strict function of metaphor to substitute dream for truth and symptom for signified. Neurotically, the binary structure of opposition in the web of words is sustained in a coherent Reason.

Metaphor is strictly unavailable to the schizoid. The crazy person suffers the suspension of the phallic function. The father's "No!" otherwise halts the slip and slide of an infinite semiosis. Psychotically, the *point de capiton* is suspended. Any bi-level configuration, such as literal/metaphorical, yields to an infinite Metaphoricity or *metonymized metaphor*. The manifest representation strictly resists hitch in a latent content. This unconscious truth is yet another manifest form whose further signification — slip and slide — sends it about the signifying chain in an incoherent aim/less *Trieb*. Return to the signified is suspended.

In contrast, the pervert mediates between these two extremes of neurosis and psychosis. The pervert translates between an easily assimilated signified of the neurotic and an elusively distant signified of the psychotic. The pervert does so in his chosen modality of negation, *Verleugnung*. Somehow — the pervert straddles the tidy reference to the signified and the abyssal plunge upward and downward in infinite semiosis. The pervert's talent with metaphor is that he discerns the parallactic overlap of the literal and the metaphorical — manifest/latent, conscious/unconscious, primary/secondary, and so on. The extimacy between the otherwise mutually exclusive oppositions can be symbolized as intertwined with each other in the paradoxical parallax. This extimacy is the contrast to the coherent system of Reason.

The issue of the strength of the metaphors of Something is Missing versus Nothing is Missing is perversely (un)decidable. Each term in the pair — lack and fullness, castration and plenitude, neurosis and psychosis, capitalism and communism, and so on — is understood as a metaphor for the other. Lack is like fullness. Castration is like plenitude. Neurosis is like psychosis. Capitalism is like communism. And so on is like *et al*. The affirmative will to power and the positive vector of force of the pervert's textualization elide the division between the literal and the metaphorical. Metaphor is neither self-same nor self-identical. But literal is also neither self-same nor self-identical. Perversely, there is no such thing as the metaphorical. The reason for this is that there is no such thing as the literal. Ontologically, ~~Metaphor~~ is like ~~literal~~. The remnant of this pursuit of the destruction of the ontological order of Being is ~~metaphor~~. Psychoanalytically, the paternal metaphor is the basal foundation of the social order. Civilization is under erasure.

Nietzsche's poetic account of metaphor illustrates that the generation of metaphor — as both remembered and then later forgotten — is structured by interaction and transaction. My close reading of the citation foregrounds the start of his interpretation: "What is truth?" Truth is essentially a question. It is a concept which originates in uncertainty and disagreement. Truth must be supplemented. Truth is not a conclusive proposition with a fixed signified. Rather, truth is a question in an aperture toward the proper supplemental signification of the pervert and the risk of an infinite semiosis of the schizoid. Truth opens toward a slip and slide which differ and defer any signified away from this same truth. Truth is organized around a chase. It is the resistant object of both *désir* — and its commitment to the capture of its *objet* — and *Trieb* — and its aim/less encirclement around a Real truth. Real truth resists the spoken and the written in any propositional answer to its posed question.

Nietzsche claims that truth is a set of shifting figurations, relationships, exchanges, and substitutions. These interactions are grounded in "human relations" and their poetry and rhetoric. Truth is a metaphor. Truth surfaces in human interaction and social transaction being-in-the-world and being-with-others. Neurotically, the bi-level meaning-making between truth and its metaphorical primacy is fixed. Truth refers to a metaphor, and metaphor refers to a truth. A "truth" "is like" "a" "movable host of metaphors." This summarizes truth as it is, as such, *qua*, by definition, *il y a*, and so on. Neurotically, the social interactive generation of truth is a simple bi-level transaction. The neurotic's binary psychical structure misses a crucial ontological question. If truth is like a metaphor, then what is a metaphor like — and so on? There is a neurotic truth. The truth is metaphor.

In contrast, the schizoid's disrupted father-function cannot arrest the cascade of words. This seesaw renders the madman's discourse incoherent. Schizoidly, truth may be differed and deferred to metaphor. But this ostensible signified for truth is itself another metaphor. Negatives and differences of value frame the *mise-en-abyme* of the psychotic's approach to signification. Value transforms metaphor into a metaphor which is a metaphor for a metaphor which is a metaphor for a metaphor — and so on. There is no basal metaphor which can retroactively (*Nachträglichkeit, après-coup*) pin the significance of truth. Alternatively, the neurotic understands truth as a metaphor, and presumably a metaphor for metaphor *qua* metaphor. The madman discerns truth as a series of signs in the web of words. Truth is a metaphor for the system *tout court*. The generalizable abstraction of Nietzsche's claim that truth is a "movable host of metaphors, metonymies and anthropomorphisms" approximates the schizoid's undecidable *différance* of truths and metaphors. The psychotic's semiotic lines of flight transform the entire battery of words into the set of the metaphor (*for* the metaphor, and so on) for truth. Nietzsche's "movable host" of an infinite variety of metaphors, metonymies, and anthropomorphisms mimes the psychotic's break from the simple binary logic of the literal/metaphorical reference between truth and metaphor.

The pervert negotiates the tension between the neurotic's bi-level orientation toward truth/metaphor and the schizoid's disorientation toward truth-metaphor-truth, and so on. The pervert recognizes the *mise-en-abyme* of semiosis which tortures the madman. But he is also able to steady the division between the referent of truth, on the one hand, and the series of metaphors that retroactively marks truth as deviant from itself, on the other hand. The pervert shows that the structure of metaphor ("truth is like a movable host of metaphors") is itself a metaphor. Truth *qua* metaphor displaces the self-sameness and self-identity (A = A) of each of the objects. This is the fundamental perverse truth of metaphor: metaphor is a metaphor for metaphor. Alternatively written, Becoming-Preposition or Ing⁺.

The word for the simultaneity of this deconstruction — truth/metaphor and unconscious/conscious — is Metaphoricity or the metonymization of metaphor. Metaphoricity is best defined as the *jouissance* of substitution — of truth for metaphor, of metaphor for metonymy, of metonymy for anthropomorphism, and so on. The series of switcheroos of the fetish — the shoe, lace, fur, jockstrap, *and so on* — energizes the pervert's enjoyment of substitution. The (*a*)sexuality of the pervert is Metaphoricity. Not only does the pervert get off on the signifier. He also takes orgasmic pleasure in the interaction and exchange — Sameness⁺ — of the pairs in otherwise binary opposition. The perverse critic reads Nietzsche's words about truth as an eroticism of metaphors, truths, words, fetishes, centers, signs, and so on. The claim that truth is a "movable host" is sexy talk to the pervert's pricked ears. The Pervert-Schizoid-Woman is the conceptual persona of the future who — somehow — discerns a Sameness⁺ of words. The pervert's hunch is that even amidst a *langue* which is based on opposition and its enforcement of penis/not-penis sexual difference — every word is the same word. Truthfully, truth is truth — but in other words?

Nietzsche's further discussion of the metaphorization of truth emphasizes that in the interaction and transaction of words, phrases, *clichés*, observations, and so on, the metaphor becomes, over time, fixed and pinned. The metaphor comes to present as if it were no longer a contingent figure but rather a necessary truth. A critical genealogist like Nietzsche contends that truth is a social and historical crystallization. Truth accidentally and haphazardly materializes from the ether of the culture. Truth is naturalized only to be bound as the wisdom of Reason. What is the literal referent for the metaphor which becomes canonized as truthful? At the origin, truth was mere metaphor. What was the literal referent of the metaphor before this exchanged word magically converted into truth? The neurotic experiences this ossification of cultural *doxa* into transcendental truth as the elevation of the metaphorical into the literal and of the manifest into the latent. Neurotically, truth surfaces in the innocent interaction and exchange in society between subjects and institutions. The neurotic cannot grasp the essence of metaphor (~~Being~~). He naively absorbs the conversion of metaphor into truth as a natural process.

In contrast, the schizoid's psychical *Verwerfung* of difference bestows him total access to the battery of words. But this is so with the caveat that no hierarchical division between words is possible. Schizoidly, every word is the same word. The psychotic interprets Nietzsche's metaphorical proposition that "truth is like a metaphor." But he does so in the incoherence of this proposition. The madman's radical and torturous elision of Being renders the significant gap between "truth" and "metaphor" terribly unstable. The claim that truth is a metaphor is a permutation that truth is truth and that metaphor is metaphor. The so-called repressed literal dimension of the metaphorical otherwise separates literal/metaphorical. But this is so only until the ossification of social interaction collapses the difference. Madly, this grammatological critique is always already performed. The madman cannot fathom any deep structure of a bi-level binary division. The literal content of metaphorical figuration can only be another metaphor. Truth is the ever-deferred metaphor which renders the literal and the metaphorical and the truthful mere permutations of a discursive system ablaze.

Perversely, the literal or truthful dimension of the metaphor is visible. But the fetishist understands each — truth and metaphor, latent and manifest, and unconscious and conscious — as parallactically overlapped in Sameness⁺. The unembossed and unsensuous metaphor-truth expresses a force. This will opens the gap between metaphor and truth. Force expresses a power. Paradoxically, this progressive force is isomorphic to the conservative will to close that same gap. A pervert, like Nietzsche, can make such a claim about truth and metaphor because it illuminates the simultaneity of the mutually exclusive. Simultaneity is the proviso of the overlap of the parallactic gap. The gist is not that truth is an army of metaphors. The nub is not even that truth is structured like a metaphor. Rather, the marrow of Nietzsche's intervention about the structure of metaphor is itself: "Truth is like a metaphor." The ontology of truth *qua* metaphor is struck with the cut of the Real. This Real rips the self-identity and self-sameness of truth and metaphor. The pervert discerns the schizoid's Unreason about the truth of Reason. The truth is that it is what it is not. Truth ~~is~~ Sameness⁺.

Nietzsche's work is not directed toward the *clichéd* genealogical thesis that truth is historically constructed. Nietzsche's effort is not to elucidate the transformation of culture into nature which is then forgotten in its historicity. Rather, the crux of Nietzsche's thesis is that ~~truth~~ — ~~Being~~ — is under erasure in the otherwise positive ontological order. Truth is the Real which cannot be articulated in alphabets or vocabularies. Truth cannot be written or spoken. The work of interaction and translation in the public sphere is the activity — together — to symbolize the Real in a *Praxis*. This *Praxis* would properly elevate the scrap of metaphor

— communist queer (*a*)sexuality — to the dignity of *das Ding* — men, Women, and the rest of us. It is an acutely sensitive process to generate truth. The strength and muscle of power will the transformation of metaphor into truth — or truth into metaphor. Force is the subjectivity and sociality whose ideological victory is the hard won reward for the successful *Praxis* of the symbolization of the Real.

The pervert's talent for text makes him the subject whose psychical structure ordains him as the object around which the ferocious and fervent vectors of force circulate. The pervert invents the metaphor for the schizoid's Unreason. The pervert transforms illusion into reality. He does so in his social interactions and economic transactions in history. The pervert's embossed coin will lose its shiny mint and gain a nondescript utility. The pervert's master signifier will become ordinary *doxa*. At such a point, the *Praxis* of the symbolization of the Real has commenced and the revolution is on. Metaphor foregrounds the centrality of force, power, and symbol in the process of revolution. This is the case in the context of the myth of the murder of the primal father but also in the *mise-en-scène* of politics. It is the case in the political interventions — *Praxis* — in the work of Marxism, deconstruction, and psychoanalysis.

In 1900, Freud valiantly noted that Something is Missing in the female genitalia. The reason that such an observation is acutely significant is that psychoanalysis posits sexual difference as the first and foremost experience of difference for the nascent offspring and the emergent adult. The simple Being of difference — identity/difference — is the foundational precept of all of being-in-the-world and being-with-others. Freud's discovery that the offspring's first experience of such a monumental institution as *difference* is thematized by sex, sexuality, and desire illustrates the profundity of Freud's observation that the Woman is castrated. My book launches from this primordial experience of Something is Missing. I have traced lack and loss in both deconstruction and its work on the sign and signifier, and in Marxism and its critique of scarcity and private property. Undeniably, Something is Missing structures sex and desire, discourse and meaning, and economy and currency. The sheer metaphorical force and power of Freud's early observation of lack and loss permeate not only sex but also language and economics.

The intention of this book is to transform the illusionary metaphor (truth) of Something is Missing into the revolutionary (truth) of Nothing is Missing. The parallax is the integrated coincidence and extimate overlap — Sameness⁺ — of opposition between Something is Missing in castration and scarcity and Nothing is Missing in fullness and abundance. The transfiguration of *doxa* into truth is the work of interaction, exchange, and rhetoric. This book is a contribution to this process. As a wannabe pervert, I not only want to demonstrate the overlap of the metaphorical and the literal, and the true and the false. I also want to invent metaphors for truth — and truth for metaphors. These coins can be exchanged, from person to person, in interaction and sociality. The contrived artificiality of the wholly other will lose its mint of guileless *naiveté* and inherit the embrace of a worn metaphor which passes hands, person to person, with a use-value for the future. To speak for and as metaphor, I want to close my recurred discussion of the homosexuals and their murdered father with final enquiries. Must the heir to paternal identification suffer the survivor's guilt and remorse for the murder of the primal metaphor for the phallus whose dispatch is the crime of the signifier and (not) of his neurotic brother? Do we ourselves make the minted and worn coins? — or do they make us?

If we want to unexpectedly and unbelievably wager the former for the moment with the force and power of perversity, then we can anticipate a bright future for the Beautiful Boy. This lovely brother did not murder a hallucinated father. Happily, now, this Beautiful Boy enjoys his communist queer (*a*)sexual brothers, sisters, and the rest of us on the Outside. The (*a*)sexuals and their masochistic *Praxis* are beyond the good and evil of the repeated circles and lazy prods of a signifier whose truth is mere metaphor. But who — and the rest of us — inherits this Beauty? The Woman?

Spirit beyond Principles

The way through the world is more difficult to find than the way beyond it.
— Wallace Stevens

Marx defines communism as the absolute abolishment of private property. The most salient description of communism as a future mode of production is a system of each according to his ability and each according to his need. Under capitalism, ability in production is structured by the supply/demand dynamics of scarcity. Production is necessary and essential. There is no freedom to the labor process and the organization of labor. The capitalist system of bourgeoisie and proletariat — owners and workers — structures labor in order to maximize profits. The workers are cogs in the machines of capitalist production. Consumption is also neither free nor democratic. The system of consumption is restricted by the ideology of scarcity. Together under capitalism, production and consumption, ability and need, are organized by necessity and essentiality.

The systems of production and consumption are enforced by the economic base. The financial system establishes the rules and regulations — what Marx refers to as the "relations of production." These codes maximize production and consumption in an equilibrium for the purpose of the accumulation of capital. The system of capital — need and ability, consumption and production — is strictly enforced by the invented ideology of scarcity. Scarcity is the economic (but also social and historical) assumption of limited resources. Under capitalism, a Something is Missing — castration — must be presupposed in order to found the system of currency and the supply/demand dynamics of the economic social order. The entirety of the system of capitalism collapses upon the dissolution of the economy of Something is Missing. The emergence of an aneconomy of Nothing is Missing — the economic transcendence of phallocentrism — invites the demise of the system of capitalism and its ideology of scarcity. The trick of capitalism is to sustain the fiction of scarcity in a time of plenitude. Any counterdiscourse to the dominance of Something is Missing is a dire threat to the system of supply/demand dynamics and the necessity of currency and the general equivalent. This counterdiscourse against scarcity does not need to demonstrate actual material abundance — the *lumpenproletariat* is adequate proof of the surplus (labor). Instead, the critique of scarcity must demonstrate that the fundamental logic of lack can be transcended in an articulation of this Real. The Real is without fissure, and the future is without holes. Oddly, the letter arrives at its destination precisely in a system in which *arche* is no longer possible.

Ownlessness

The transition from capitalist private property to its strict abolishment unto communist public property is theoretically and practically complex. It is most productive to think of private property with a generalized and universalized valence. Private property (or even *le propre*) is not simply a question of personal ownership and the transformation of rights at the point of sale of a transaction. Capitalist private property does not merely encompass prosaic commodities: the lawnmower, the automobile, the book, the house, the napkin, and so on. There is no doubt an inventory of private property under capitalism. But how so? An interpretation of the privacy of this property is legal right of access. Under Marx's version of communism, it is uncertain what form of property rights a communist subject would enjoy over such mundane objects as yogurt and butter. But presumably in a communist modality of improper property the ownership of simple commodities is not at issue.

However, the psychical dimension of property, ownership, and privacy (*le propre*) is visible beyond such unremarkable examples. Property and ownership instantly imply responsibility. The ownership and privacy of an object — boat or horse — reward individualist selfishness and personal gain. An enforced responsibility (for Irma's pains) in Judeo-Christian morality isolates capitalism as the antecedent organization of rights and wrongs. A postcapitalist abolishment of *le propre* suspends responsibility and globetrots beyond good and evil. Capitalist private property is the material and ideational — bodily and psychical — practice of morality and its precept of responsibility. Communist public property is the physical and speculative — thinking, being, and living — practice of amorality and its principles of solidarity and freedom.

The absolutely screwy dimension of Marx's massive attack on capitalism and private property is that it essentially circumvents a strict definition of private property itself. None of Marx's texts provides a proficient and detailed outline of the essence of private property beyond the political economic isolation of its essence in labor. I have suggested the affective and ideological consequences of *le propre* and their institutionalization by capitalism. But any fierce *Praxis* of resistance to capital must profile private property in its essence. Marx's deferral of this intellectual project indicates not only the pervasive airs — "all that is solid melts into air" — of the solids of private property under capitalism.[1] Marx's recalcitrance also reveals the resistance of private property to easy explication and comprehensive description. Private property is the Real of capitalism. Real Property is the organizational center of the structure of the additions and subtractions of the accumulation of castration.

This Real resists Marx's own exegesis because — unbelievably — private property is profoundly not itself an object of ownership. Under capitalism, the dollars and coins of the general equivalent circulate in an economy — from wallet to cash register, from credit card statement to bank vault, and from Visa card to ATM. Currency is the principle of *différance* and its differences and deferrals. Delay is the precept of capitalist comparison, contrast, and exchange of dollar for diet soda and coin for packaged quinoa. Currency haphazardly circulates and contingently spreads value across the social body. Any ownership of cash — in the wallet, say — spotlights the utterly pointless metaphysics of presence of any circulation of dollars and coins. The dollars in a wallet and the change in a purse can only be valuable in exchange. Owned dollars and possessed coins are strictly purposeless. Money is useful only in the moment of exchange. Money is not money *qua* money. Currency is not present. The general equivalent is under erasure. Currency is *not*: ~~dollars~~ and ~~coins~~.

The owner must surrender his Visa card number and private 3-digit security code in order to make use-value of this exchange-value. Structuralistly, value is generated by the comparison, contrast, and exchange of an undecidable and indeterminate value. Under capitalism, value is modestly fixed and stabilized by the standardization of the general equivalent. But money is only money when it is not money. Money is *not* — ~~money~~. Under erasure, currency is inessential and valueless. Private property is the effect of Nothingness. The capitalist system of *le propre* is a system of nihilism which excludes its own *objet petit a* or the general equivalent. Private property is a creationist sublimation *ex nihilo*. Capitalist goods and services magically emerge from the Nothingness of exchange.

All that is solid melts into air under capitalism. This violent defrost is the mysterious consequence of the Real of private property and the effects of this destabilization on the system of $-ism. Real Property resists capture by the circulation of capital because the twists and turns — prepositional directions — in exchange of comparison and contrast transfer ownership and shift propriety. The proviso of profit-making is the accumulation of capital. The distressed aporia of the accumulation of additions and subtractions in an economy of scarcity in which Something is Always Missing is — the abolishment of private property. Capitalism banishes private property from its system as the stipulation of the function of accumulation. Outstandingly, capitalism is communism. *Le propre est l'impropre.* But if so, then what does communism promise beyond the demystification of the rupture of accumulation and its various capitalist crises?

At the close of this study, I want to acknowledge the profoundly Marxist subtext of the book. I engage in detailed analyses of psychoanalysis and deconstruction, but the scaffold of my practical and theoretical intervention is Marxism. The word "democracy" is code for capitalism in the time of neoliberalism. For us, "democracy" is not on our side. A final meditation on capitalism is the necessary political supplement to a transgression of the system of *le propre* both in its actual existence in the monetary system of finance under $-ism and in its nominal fantasy in the superstructural ideology of the propaganda of the system of neoliberalism. I present an extended excerpt from "1844 Manuscripts,"

> Let us now see further how the concept of alienated, externalized labor must express and represent itself in reality.
>
> If the product of work is alien to me, opposes me as an alien power, whom does it belong to then?
>
> If my own activity does not belong to me and is an alien forced activity to whom does it belong then?
>
> To another being than myself.
>
> Who is this being?
>
> []
>
> The alien being to whom the labor and the product of the labor belongs, whom the labor serves and who enjoys its product, can only be man himself. If the product of labor does not belong to the worker but stands over against him as an alien power, this is only possible in that it belongs to another man apart from the worker.
>
> If his activity torments him it must be a joy and a pleasure to someone else. This alien power above man can be neither the gods nor nature, only man himself.

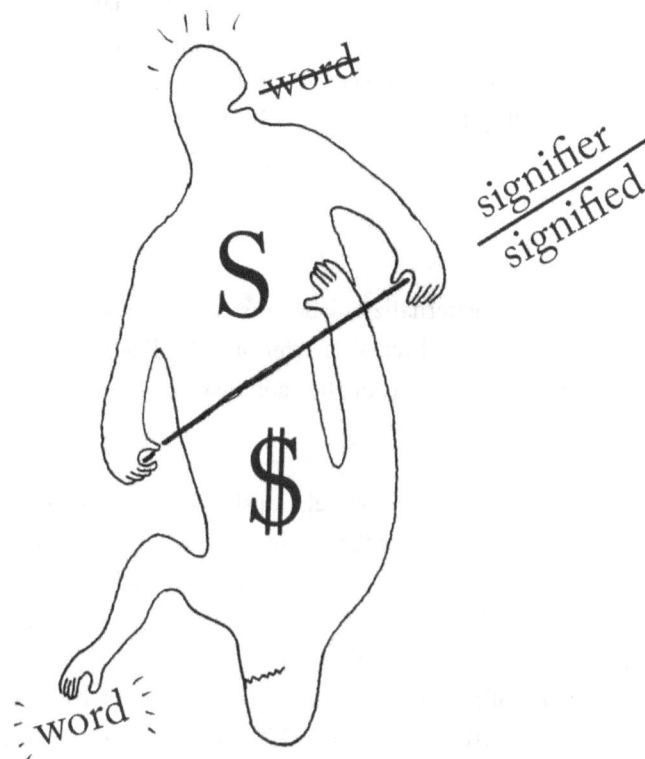

This picture juxtaposes the split neurotic subject under capitalism (below) with the emergent plenitudinal perverse subject under communism (above). The illustration compares capitalism and communism in their respective orientations toward the object and representation. The neurotic (below) desires (rather than enjoys) the signification of the word that the Capitalist Industrial Complex endlessly produces as a commodity. In contrast, the pervert experiences that the word is precisely a Nothingness which is caught between the gap of Being and Nothingness, is and is not, and so on. The plethora of capitalist commodities obscures a veritable abyss of *value* or the signifier rather than of *signification* or the sign. The communist (above) glows with the plenitude of the Real. This unsymbolizable excess is unsullied by the general equivalent of standardization — of *signification* of the sign rather than *value* of the signifier. The pervert happily enjoys (rather than desires) this plenitude in Being (Nothingness) because he discerns that words are materialist signifiers (fetishes) rather than ideational signs (commodities). The split between the neurotic of the extant system of capital and the pervert of the emergent system of communism parallels the split (and conjoinment) among the signifier, signified, and sign. The signifier happily embodies Marxist material plenitude. The signified of abstraction and speculation manically animates the general equivalent of money. The pervert properly speaks the word under erasure (above), and the neurotic daftly utters the word in its static and inert stupidity. Materiality (goods and services) is returned to the communist pervert, and ideality is accumulated by the capitalist neurotic.

Notes & Sketches —

Consider further the above sentence that the relationship of man to himself first becomes objective and real to him through his relationship to other men. So if he relates to the product of his labor, his objectified labor, as to an object that is alien, hostile, powerful, and independent of him, this relationship implies that another man is the alien, hostile, powerful, and independent master of this object. If he relates to his own activity as to something unfree, it is a relationship to an activity that is under the domination, oppression, and yoke of another man.

[]

Thus through alienated, externalized labor the worker creates the relationship to his labor of a man who is alien to it and remains exterior to it. The relationship of the worker to his labor creates the relationship to it of the capitalist, or whatever else one wishes to call the master of the labor.[2]

This protracted citation articulates the simple relationship between subject and object and its mediation by the Other. There are three pivotal Marxist themes in this lengthy citation. The first motif is of a systematic theft of an object by a subject. The second trope is of *le propre* and the object of belonging, possession, and ownership. The third issue is of the (un)closed circuit of capitalist exchange and accumulation.

Marx refers to the "alienation" of the worker's process and product which are stolen from the proletarian. The originary private property of the worker — use-value — is transferred from the self to the other and from the laborer to the owner of this activity and object. Marx's repeated referent for the locus of this accumulated stockpile of stolen value is an "alien being," "another man," and the "master of the labor." The alien owner steals value from the native worker. But the criminal mediation between the worker *qua* subject and the owner *qua* object is an unexplained enigma. The process by which capital extracts value from labor is ascribed to the capitalist alien master. But the accumulation of bourgeois private property is obscure. Marxist economics outlines the ideological and parallactic gap between "profit" and surplus value and the capitalist coordination of theft. The chink between wage and price opens the possibility of "profit" and the extension of bourgeois private property. The entirety of the heterosexualist puzzle of the commodity is this parallactic gap between salary and MSRP. Capitalistically, the mediation between wage and price is Adam Smith's nebulous "invisible hand of the market" and its distribution of supply and demand in slave-wage and mark-up.[3] But what is the suture of the aperture and closure of the rift between salary and sales, and between demand and supply?

The tricky aporia of this question is that Adam Smith's "invisible hand of the market" ostensibly settles the necessary capitalist imbalance between currency to buy and goods to sell. But the metaphysics of presence — Being — of supply and demand is strictly reversible. The allocation of goods on the supply side of the ledger is swiftly and invisibly — credit card statements, ATM withdrawals, stock trades, and financial derivatives — translated into the accumulation of dollars and coins on the demand side of the registry. The otherwise simple exchange of bread for dollars and banana for bread is a relationship of extimacy between supply and demand, between currency and commodities, and between salaries and prices. The limit of capitalism elaborates no division between supply and demand, between dollars and products, and between wages and profit. An intensified system of circulation reduces — in potentiality — the entire system of objects to currency, and the obscene economy of exchange diminishes — in potentiality — the total set of use-values to dollars and coins. The *telos* of bourgeois accumulation is a stockpile of the Nothingness of capital.

The Real of this system is use-value. Utility is otherwise profoundly overwritten by the speculations and abstractions of exchange-value. This Marxist insight illustrates the latent truth of capitalism. Capitalism is a system of *public property. Le propre est l'impropre.* There is no such *das Ding* as private property. Private property is the suture of the gap between supply and demand. This bandage coordinates the binary opposition of the stockpiles of commodities and the wallets of dollars. Real Property is the lubricant of the system of exchange. Real Property is the medium through which the general equivalent compares and contrasts commodities in the determination of value in currency. Private property has no value because it is the principle of exchange *qua* its cause and effect. The function of Real Property is isomorphic to my neologism Real Penis and its work to grease the relationship between the opposition of penis-clitoris and clitoris-penis. The reason that Marx finally abandons a detailed portrait (beyond political economy) of the object of the bourgeoisie — private property — is that it resists symbolization absolutely.

The circulation of currency can only compare and contrast values in their translation and transformation — Becoming-Otherwise — into commodities which — Becoming-Otherwise — transition and transmute into currency. Private property resists any metaphysics of presence because it is not part of the economy. The capitalist economic system is strictly coordinated by exchange and the general equivalent. The economy is obscenely monetary and purely financial. The Outside of capitalism is the series of use-values which resists symbolization, accumulation, and their processes of profit-making with dollars and coins. Private property is the Outside of capitalism. This is so even as it is simultaneously the proviso — *raison d'être* — of the capitalist world. Marx cannot define private property because private property resists *qua* the Real center — (⊇) — a system of accumulation and exchange that fundamentally excludes it. There is no private property in capitalism. Capitalism is Nothingness. But why does man return to its Being?

Marx's discussion of circulation presents a division between two forms of economy. The first system is of C-M-C'. This symbol articulates an economy in which an object is exchanged for dollars and coins which is then later exchanged for another object. The manic capitalist revision of this form of exchange is the economy of M-C-M'. This system exchanges currency for an object which is then later exchanged for dollars and coins. The first system accumulates use-values which are mediated by the general equivalent. The second system collects dollars and coins which are not only arbitrated by the general equivalent but in fact are the sheer Being of dollars and coins themselves. The utter madness of M-C-M' (and so on) is not only that use-value is repressed by exchange-value. The bizarre corollary is that the system can only recognize exchange-value, dollars and coins. The Real of private property is invisible in a system of accumulation which is coordinated by the frenzy of M-C-M'. To Marx's question of theft — "Who is this alien being?" — the answer can only be: $. Under capitalism, $ owns $.

The supply/demand dynamics of the "free hand of the market" are a simple and misunderstood myth of a circulation of dollars and coins whose end is a Something is Still Missing. Why is Being always Missing? The alien master of labor has not yet accumulated limitless expanse. There is no alien being whose purse stashes labor. This alien is differed and deferred in the capitalist circulation of M' — The "another man" who is the destination of value — bourgeois owner — against the "man" who is the departure of value — proletarian worker — is systematically displaced. The owner is an ideological myth of capitalism. The owner is owned by ownership. The foggy translations and pathological transformations of capital are the alien whose nefarious circulation can only be stopped at the point of — The Pedagogy of the Proletariat and the rest of us unveils the secret truth of the Unreasonable Real of capital: money is *not*. This deathly Nothingness is the organizational principle of a sad world. The private property of the bourgeoisie is a mark in a series of — $ — $ — $ — in which the object accrues subtractions and additions in the difference and deferral to an Other. This Other is alienated from the system *qua* the signified of the ends of accumulation. The alien is the proviso of the frenetic will to make this alien a native son. The ~~alien~~ is Other. *There is no bourgeois owner.* There are only proletarians. There is no antagonism between labor and capital. There are only dispersed and divided aliens.

The aperture and closure of the parallactic gap between capitalism and communism, private property and public property, profit and surplus value, exchange and use, and *le propre* and its Other are structured by the overlap between the cardinal economic principles of supply and demand. The supply of goods and services in use-value is always already monetized by exchange in the system. Use-value is forever overwritten by exchange-value. The Real is overwritten by the symbolic. Use-value (is) exchange-value. The ~~Being~~ of this relationship is *sous rature* and *sur l'effacement*. The rapport between utility and exchange — clock and cash — cannot be textualized by the system. This is the reason that the gap between supply and demand cannot be properly calculated.

The emphasis in Adam Smith's fatuous "free hand of the market" is "free." This so-called "freedom" of commodities and prices in (dis)equilibrium is a perfectly unrepresentable series of (un)calculations. There is no general equivalent *of* the standardization of general equivalence. Smith's nebulous "freedom" refers to the deconstruction of the metaphysics of capitalist presence. Under erasure, the bond — (⊇) — between supply and demand cannot be written or spoken. The consequence is the explosion of any division between supply/demand. The absence of this principle indicates that the values of binary oppositions of the financial system, such as transactions between dollars and objects, and between credit cards and commodities, cannot be calculated, freely or otherwise. Undecidedly, the selection of supply and demand resists any determination in the presence of either a supply of goods or a demand for goods. The economy is simply circulation, or *différance*.

The unfortunate effect of the fiction of scarcity and supply/demand is exchange-value. The transition from an aneconomy of circulation of goods to an economy of the accumulation of capital banishes use-value from the system. But these use-values can only be the manifest assemblage of private property. Private property can only be purposeful. The purposes include a house for living in, a broom for cleaning with, a car for driving in, a bicycle for riding on, a restaurant for eating at, and so on. Private property *qua* use-value is destroyed by the absolute sovereignty of exchange-value. The end of capitalism portends the submission of the circulation of goods and services of use-values *qua* private property to the accumulation of dollars and coins of exchange-value *qua* general equivalence. Private property as a use-value yields to its own system of capitalism and to the manic will to the accumulation and exchange of currency. The system of supply/demand exchange ruins use-value and its system of circulation of goods and services of private property. This property includes toys for playing with, beds for sleeping on, keyboards for typing on, tables for sitting at, and so on.

The abolishment of private property is not a strictly communist precept. Rather, the deracination of private property is the consequence of the internal logic of capitalism. Private property *qua* use-value is the condition of (im)possibility of capitalism. The system of *le propre* (*l'impropre*) is the proviso and limit of capitalism. Private property (is) its own destruction. The communist abolishment of private property is the direct consequence of the capitalist accumulation of profit. Communism emerges as the future after — within — the death of capitalism. The *Aufhebung* from capitalism to communism is a suicide. A dark *Thanatos* is the internal restriction of capitalism. The exchange of dollars and coins is the transaction of the death of capital. All that is living passes unto death. The death of exchange-value releases a monstrous surplus of useful objects in the system. The expansion of goods and services is near unimaginable in a system which is unshackled by the ideologies of scarcity and individualism, the dynamics of supply and demand, and the speculations of value and exchange. This proliferation of use-values is the horizon of free production. This promise of the limitless productivity of use-values is the paradoxical *telos* of the end of (private) property.

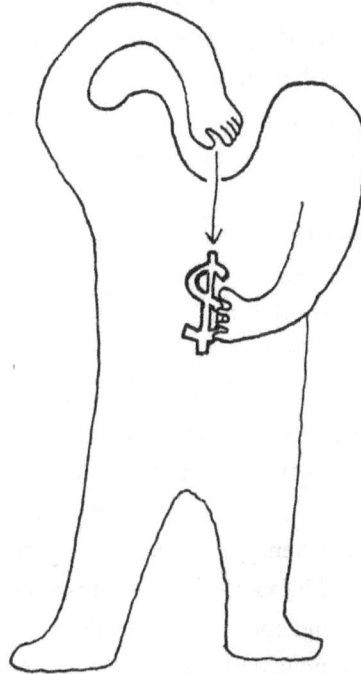

This illustration represents the neurotically ambivalent insistence upon a closed and contracted system rather than upon an expansive and extended aneconomy. The neurotic compulsively asserts his own lack — scarcity under capitalism and castration under patriarchy — as the basis of an ownership (*le propre*) in which he anxiously strives to recuperate both present and actual but also potential and virtual loss. Strangely, *ownership owns the owner*. The object of ownership — commodity, goods and services — is dissolved by the mania of the general equivalent and its command to quantify quality: in sexual difference, the magnitude of the difference between the penis and the clitoris; and in capitalist scarcity, the enforced relationship between otherwise singular objects. Ownership is the subject and the object of neither the bourgeoisie nor the proletariat but of *ownership itself*. The object is owned by the general equivalent of currency, dollars and coins. The neurotic's possession of currency (center) is structured by patriarchal sexual difference and capitalist scarcity. The proletarian obliterates his identity in order to reclaim it in the Other. The illustration depicts an indentation in the place of a head. This gap in the place of the head symbolizes the castration and scarcity of the worker under the conditions of alienation and estrangement in capitalism. *Wo Es war*, where the subject was, castration comes to be. But the perverse laborer creates the debt with one hand. At the same time, the pervert claims the surplus value ("profit") in the form of the dollar. Perversely, scarcity and plenitude, and debt and surplus, are the flip-sides of a general (in)equivalence which is the proviso of yet another day of speculation and calculation on the floor of the stock market. Commodity fetishism transforms the neurotic owner into an owned object. Perverse fetishism translates the penis *qua* commodity into a singular object (say, jockstrap) whose materiality cannot be abstracted and speculated into numbers, integers, decimals, and so on. The properly Real Fetish (say, Jockstrap) is unalloyed materiality in the future of the Spirit of the System. The perverse return of the Real Fetish is the Becoming-Schizoid of the future of the Woman.

Notes & Sketches —

Expansion

The system ($-ism) and its obversive Spirit of the System (S) are organized by a compulsive and ambivalent insistence. This dominion gravitates toward openness rather than closedness, and toward aperture rather than closure. The galaxy is expansive rather than contractive. The proclivity of S is expansive and open. But the imperative of the system is contractive and closed. The structure is underpinned by this compulsive and ambivalent insistence. $-ism is opposed to its own truth. This ambivalence is arranged in the systems of desire, language, and finance. But the imprecision of the structure is not an exact ambivalence. A surplus of ambivalence — *unambivalence* — undoes the $-istic systems of desire, finance, and language. The ruse is to return to the excess — but then not to return —

The communist queer (*a*)sexual generative center of the obscene abundance of the potentiality of the surplus of overproduction, signifier, and *Trieb* expands and grows the solar system and its series of fetishes — objects, centers, words, metaphors, signs, and so on. Delayed eroticism, material abundance, and open signification are the *telos* of the zone of energy of (*a*)sexuality. But the (*a*)sexual center of this generation is consistently opposed by the ambivalent repetitive compulsion away from this obscene center of plenitude. The (*a*)sexuality is the Outside of the nihilism of value. This evaluation structures the system of $-ism of phallic sexuality in desire, material scarcity in currency, and the sovereignty of the word in signification. My word — (*a*)sexuality — can only be interpreted inexactly. The word is a prop for the excess and surplus. The word — (*a*)sexuality — denotes the expansion and openness — but also contraction and closedness — of the system. But the proper Spirit of (*a*)sexuality overpowers the forces of containment and constriction in the systems of desire, finance, and signification of $-ism.

The word — (*a*)sexuality — is the optimistic bet on the return in *Verleugnung* of the expansion of fetishes rather than the compulsive return to the penis. The future of Spirit is the *unambivalent* return of *Verleugnung* and its series — *and so on* — of the unexpected and the unforeseen. Spirit wills the *unambivalent* disavowal of the fundamental Sameness⁺ between — in excess of — binary oppositions, such as desire/*Trieb*, capitalism/communism, and sign/signifier. There is an excess in the Sameness⁺ of perverse *Verleugnung*. The return of the disavowed *unambivalently* generates beyond itself and its own recurrence. The originary (*a*)sexuality produces the abundance of the arch Nothing is Missing at the *arche*-trace of the galaxy. Perverse *Verleugnung* returns the universe to the inarticulable (*a*)sexual productivity of surplus. Spirit is the won force of (*a*)sexuality against the repetitive compulsion of the system — sexual, financial, and linguistic — of $-ism. The paradox is that the generative principle of the universe is precisely not sexual. Libido is not the origin of the world and its series of cathexes. Rather, it is (*a*)sexuality which is the source of the growth and multiplication of the globe. Sex is a ruse, and (*a*)sex is the energy.

The $-istic Logic of Identity (A = A) is restrictive and contractive. The Logic of Difference of the System is proliferative and extensive. The reason that the Logic of Difference grows the universe is that it is structured by the Principle of Sameness⁺. Sameness⁺ (A ≠ A = B, and so on) is the doctrine of relationality and constructionism. Relationship and construction inspire an otherness. Rapport and bond with otherness generate objects — fetishes, centers, metaphors, signs, metonymies, substitutes, words, and so on. The universe is generated from the Principle of Sameness⁺ as it is freed by the Order of Madness rather than constrained by the Madness of Order. The Logic of Identity is the propositional logic of desire, finance, and language. The Logic of Difference is the doctrine of drive, abundance, and signifier. But which tendency — Logic of Identity or Logic of Difference, $-ism or S — will trend in the universe? Will Sameness⁺ be happily released by perverse *Verleugnung* in the Order of Madness and its generative objects in fetishism? Or will the Logic of Difference be sadly constricted by neurotic *Verdrängung* of the Madness of Order and its symptomatic returns in neurosis?

Beyond the Sexual Difference Principle

The paradox of Freud's version of sexual difference is that there is no such *das Ding* as the penis. Phallocentrism refers to the patriarchal logic that "a man has a penis and a Woman does not have a penis." This unconscious patriarchal truism explains the terror that the body and the mind of the Woman pose for the man and his flimsy masculinity. Phallocentrism also explains the rampant hatred of Women in Western societies. The glare of the penis/not-penis opposition is put in sharp relief in the absurdity of the utterance that "a man does not have a vagina and a clitoris and a Woman does have a vagina and a clitoris." This otherwise antiphallocentric articulation invites a fourth stage of the Freudian trio of oral, anal, and phallic phases of psychosexual development. The clitoris/not-clitoris logic is a –centrism. But this binary opposition between the presence of the clitoris and the absence of the clitoris gestures toward a Clitoral Stage. This Clitoral Stage transcends the presence — Being — of the penis. The Outside of patriarchy is an aesthetic and sensibility in which the penis is not the central referent of sexuality. The Outside of –centrism — penile or clitoral — is the (*a*)sexuality of communist queerness. Clitorally, the penis is *not*. A simple reversal of the criteria for the dominion of the penis in size and visibility can be reconsidered. Minor magnitude of the clitoris could otherwise be the essence of a superiority in size and visibility to the inferiority of the not-clitoris of the penis. The penis *is not*. This is the reason that Freud insists that it most certainly *is*.

A Clitoral Stage of psychosexuality must upend the –centrism of both phallocentrism — penis/not-penis — but also Clitoralcentrism — clitoris/not-clitoris. The challenge is to invent — (*a*)sexuality — an alternative semic structure. This system is the Other to the tension between center and margin. This interval is mediated by the *not*. The Clitoral Stage abjures the Logic of Identity (A = A). This economy otherwise insists that what is *is* — as such, *qua*, by definition, *il y a*, by necessity, in Being as itself present. The penis is the penis. The clitoris is the absence of Being — *is not*. These objects are mediated by an essential distinction and opposition of the word. The sign suspends the difference and negativity — Sameness⁺ — that otherwise structure bonds and rapports rather than breaks and separations between the sexual objects in the system. Phallocratically, the penis and the clitoris are considered the obverse distinction and opposition of each other as strictly positive units. The privileged positive object is the penis. The disprivileged negative object is the clitoris. This binary division and opposition are at a distance from the negativity and differentiality of the Sameness⁺ of relationality and constructionism. The essence of binarism is not only the arrangement of phallocentric sexual difference. This division and opposition of the binarism are the structure of *langue* and the system of signs.

Sameness⁺ is the principle of sexual (*a*)difference. Sameness⁺ illuminates a system which is beyond both phallocentric penis/not-penis and Clitoralcentric clitoris/not-clitoris. Sameness⁺ resists all economies of centers and margins. The insight of Sameness⁺ is that any object is the same as any other object because the lines of division and the marks of separation between objects are blurred. In the universe, there is more than one object. But there are fewer than two objects. But the crucial distinction is that any object is at a distance — *Spaltung* — from itself. An object procures its constituted essence — Being *qua* Becoming — in its reference to other objects and to the system of expanded and extended objects *tout court*. Any object is internal to any other object. *Qua* internal, any object is also external to any other object. This internal and external relationality and constructionism among objects are an extimacy. This extimacy overwhelms any object in its discrete positive unity as divided and opposed to any other object. The significance of this overpowered object of the parallax is that a surplus exceeds any object in the system. Any object implicates a remainder of and in itself. Any object surpasses itself. Any object implicates a surplus of and in itself. Any object is a remnant of itself. Any object outstrips itself into the open series of other objects in the expansive and extended space of the unconscious. The open series of fetishes extends beyond — above, by, below, near, around, outside — the penis. The penis is the mere remainder and reminder of the potentiality of contraction and constriction in the system. The fetish is the mnemonic trace of the generative and productive communist queer (*a*)sexuality at the obscenely abundant center of the universe.

The fetish is the object which is in surplus of itself. The fetish manufactures and assembles more of itself. The *Verleugnung* of disavowal returns the fetish *qua* the "fetish" — and the fur, lace, shoe, jockstrap, dildo, pylon, hairclip, belt, walrus, necklace, cookie, anklet, basketball, ring, savior, locket, horse, nails, whips, and an expansive and open series of other objects. The fetish expands the galaxy because the Principle of Sameness⁺ opens any object to its others as the proviso of essential constitution. In contrast, the Logic of Identity tends toward contraction and closedness because any object is a positive unity unto its autonomous and sovereign objecthood. The generative and productive center of the logic of Sameness⁺ is the kernel of communist queer (*a*)sexuality and its obscene abundance in potentiality. The Logic of Sameness⁺ and the Spirit of (*a*)sexuality extend the solar system to the Outside of the tedious and compulsively repeated penis (Being, Nothingness) and its negative obverse in the clitoris (Nothingness, Being).

The fourth psychosexual phase of the Clitoral Stage is the principle of this expansion of the galaxy of fetishes. These novel doohickeys and weird thingamabobs spin out and swerve by the penis *qua* antiquated referent or the clitoris *qua* horrific copy. The Clitoral Stage presents Sameness⁺ as a sexual principle. Sexual Sameness⁺ expands and extends — fetishizes — the solar system. *Verleugnung* returns the object as itself and its other in a multiplication of objects of both affirmation and negation in excess of strict ambivalence. In contrast, the psychosexual stages of orality, anality, and phallism limit and constrain the system of sexual objects. Fetishism is the practice of a sexual Sameness⁺. Fetishism extends the set of objects of *Trieb* rather than constrains the series of *objets* of *désir*.

The phallocentric (or Clitoralcentric) system tends toward contraction and closedness. The psychosexuality of the neurotic limits the objects of sexual enjoyment. But this restriction and containment of the sexual system also tend toward growth and development. The succession of fetishes extends the rounds of objects in the sexual orbit to an excess and surplus. These two tendencies — toward the contraction and closedness of the Logic of Identity and toward the expansion and openness of Sameness⁺ — are situated at the source of the communist queer (*a*)sexual empty abundance of the Real Signifier whose signified can only be imagined in the place of *das Ding* and the maternal phallus. This essential Spirit in the universe is the energy toward expression and proliferation. The systems of phallocentrism and idiotic desire recoil from this course of expansive *mana*. But the *Trieb* of courtly love and its screens of fetishes — *and so on* — extend and grow the set of objects in the system under the Principle of Sameness⁺. But the Logic of Difference of the Madness of Order must be recognized and mobilized in order to tap the potentiality of the communist queer (*a*)sexuality. Unfortunately, the Logic of Identity rules in the systems of discourse, economy, and desire under the dominion of $-ism. The Clitoral Stage galvanizes the powers of communist queer (*a*)sexuality and the tendency toward expansion and openness in the galaxy. The Clitoral Stage is the psychosexual stage of the growth of communist queer (*a*)sexuality and the Spirit of the System. This Clitoral Stage is the *Aufhebung* above the phallic contraction of the economic, linguistic, and sexual systems of $-ism.

Beyond the Sign Principle

The word is the everyday experience of the spoken and the written. The word is the medium of intellectual articulation and affective expression. The word is the architecture of language. But the skeletal scaffold of the system of *langue* is not the word. The architectonics of the system is the materiality of the signifier and the abstraction of the signified. The division between the sign and the signifier is operative on two distinct levels. First: the sign is structured by distinction and opposition; and the signifier is arranged by difference and negativity. The distinction and opposition of the sign present the word in the logic of binary opposition. Any word is distinct and opposed to any other word because it is self-same and self-identical to itself in Being and presence. The difference and negativity of the signifier present materialities and abstractions as internal and external — extimate — to each other in the Principle of Sameness⁺. The word is arranged by identity and difference. The signifier is disordered by extimacy. Second: the sign is entirely practical; and the signifier is purely theoretical. The word is the medium of everyday exchange. The signifier is the materiality which is torn from abstraction in the speculations of theory. The word is practice. The signifier is theory.

The architecture of the system of the word is of distinction, opposition, and practice. But the skeletal scaffold of *langue* is of difference, negativity, and theory. The system of language is split. A *Spaltung* interrupts the smooth integration of sign and signifier, word and materiality and abstraction, practice and theory, distinction and difference, opposition and negativity, and so on. Sameness⁺ is the discursive principle of the signifier. The negative differences of the system of the signifier situate any materialities (marks and sounds) in an internal and external — extimate — proximity to any of the other materialities in the series. The signifier *qua* object exceeds itself unto the sequence of other objects in the Other. This surplus of signifier overwhelms the tidy distinction and opposition of the positive unity of the word. The material skeleton is beneath the body of the sign. This substrate of the signifier disturbs the word with an excess of materiality. This surplus of the signifier cannot be contained by the distinctions and oppositions of the positive units of the word.

The solar system is situated between a tendency toward expansion and openness and a proclivity toward contraction and closedness. The galaxy gestures toward extension, but the forces of $-ism — the word in language, the scarcity in capitalism, and the phallic desire in patriarchy — compulsively insist toward diminution. The signifier is the force of growth and proliferation in the system. The word is the power of contraction and closedness in the galaxy. Spirit tends toward the generative signifier, but the compulsive insistence of $-ism gestures toward the nihilism of the word. Spirit trends toward the communist queer (*a*)sexual obscene empty abundance — signifier without a signified — at the center of the universe. But $-ism recoils from this radical (*a*)sexuality in order to sustain contraction and the systems which are structured by closedness, such as the sign in language, the scarcity in capitalism, and the phallic desire of patriarchy. The dominance of the word is an expression of the contraction and closedness of the system of $-ism in the galaxy.

The expansion of the galaxy requires the reversal of the sovereignty of the sign over the signifier. There is more excess on the level of the signifier of materiality and the signified of abstraction than in the dimension of the simple word. The word *qua* positive unit is self-contained and self-organized. The word is immune to the traces and vestiges of an otherness. In contrast, the signifier is subordinate and superordinate to an otherness which exceeds the signifier in its identity and definition. The signifier gestures toward otherness. A sequence of other objects is necessary in order to return to — but not recuperate as — the signifier. The Principle of Sameness⁺ opens the signifier to an otherness which is opposed to the self-sameness and self-identity of the Being of presence of the word. The Other always exceeds — proceeds and succeeds — the signifier in its precarious identity and haphazard difference. The sign is closed and compact in its positive unity and discrete articulation. The signifier is open and extended in its negative differentiality and connected fluency. The word is positive and unified. The signifier is negative and different. The series of fetishes is both internal and external — extimate — to any tenuous identity and provisional definition of the signifier. The sign is contraction, and the signifier is expansion. The Logic of Identity (A = A) animates the word. The Principle of Sameness⁺ (A ≠ A = B, and so on) inspires the signifier. The two logics are opposed from the perspective of desire, and the two (one) logic(s) are (is) the same from the disperspective of drive. There is more than one object in the universe. But there are fewer than two objects in the universe.

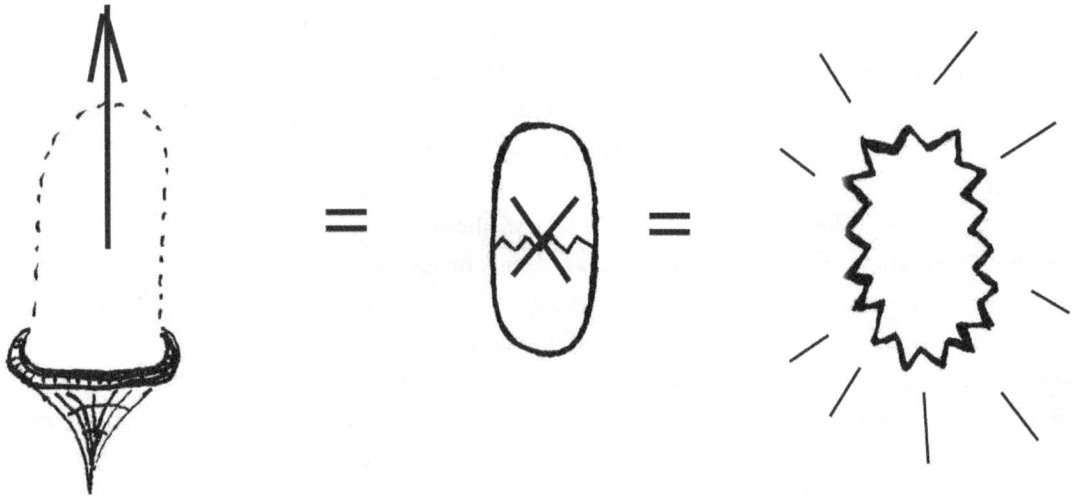

This illustration represents the future of the Spirit of the System in the Clitoral Stage. The female sex organ is radically Outside of the shenanigans of the Western metaphysics of presence of the penis/not-penis configuration of sexual difference in castration. The economy of this future will be an aneconomy of objects which are precisely themselves because they are coincident and continuous with — Same⁺ as Different⁺ from — the other objects in the system. The clitoral object is exactly itself in its excess and expansion Inside and Outside of itself. The fragmentation in the object (center, above) is the fissured surplus of the object. The broken outline of the object (left) expands beyond its own otherwise phallic borders. The clitoral object (right) in its Becoming is whole and total in its bright and singular partiality and fragmentation. The equation demonstrates the relationship among: first, the expansive object (left) whose boundaries are tenuous and flimsy; second, the undone fragmented object (center) whose fissure is essential to the Madness of Order and its *rejet névrotique*; and third, the clitoral maternal phallus object (right) whose bright positivity is a singularity which is beyond: first, the exchange-value of general equivalence of the word in discourse; second, the phallocentrism of patriarchy; and third, the exchange-value of the commodity. This equation depicts the transformation from an economy of exchange under capitalist commodity fetishism into an aneconomy of infinitely displaced and substituted objects of singularity in the absence of nihilistic comparison and contrast in the value of exchange. The clitoral object is the horizonal object of the Real Fetishist and his Real Jockstrap. The pure materiality of the Real Jockstrap (*et al.*) enlivens the Becoming-Schizoid of the pervert and his gesture toward the thinking, being, and living of the Clitoral Stage future of the Woman.

Notes & Sketches —

The theoretical postulation of the metonymization of metaphor illustrates the excess of the material signifier above the positive unity of the sign. A metaphor is a phrase which is considered a word. The phrase is compact and condensed. This is so even if the mediation of *like* posits a relationship of otherwise undecidable and indeterminate relationship of exchange between the two objects in rapport with each other in identification. But the metonymization of metaphor subordinates the positive object of the metaphor to a series of materialities (marks and sounds) which extends and widens the positive circle within which the metaphor articulates its identity and definition. Metonymy links metaphors. This process expands the positive unity of the object (metaphor) into relationships and bonds with other objects (metaphors) in the system. The fetish is not isolated or alone. The fetish is a series — fur, lace, shoe, jockstrap, *and so on*. This *et al.* is stretched beyond its closed positivity and toward an expansive openness. The metonymization of metaphor converts the positive object of metaphor into another metaphor. This process makes the whole of the metaphor into a part of another metaphor of which it is the excess and surplus. Metonymy transforms metaphor into another metonymy. The differences and negativities — otherness — of the signifier contrast with the positive unity — self-sameness and self-identity — of the sign. Metonymy of the material signifier exemplifies the vitality of the expansion and openness of the signifier in the world.

Beyond the Private Property Principle

Currency is the medium which sustains the principle of private property under capitalism. The Marxist subtext of this book establishes my critique of *le propre* under the symbol of $-ism. Marx refers to the commodity (dollars and coins) as a queer (rewritten: heterosexualist) enigma. Marx also says that currency twists and inverts the world into an upside-down caricature of itself. Dollars and coins are fundamentally a representational system. Currency is a simulation of the use-value of an object. The capitalist logic of M-C-M' accumulates capital — dollars and coins — rather than utilities — goods and services. The central mechanism of capitalism is the accumulation of *representation*. This accumulation of addition and subtraction, and credit and debt, entails the simulation of use-value with the sketches of exchange-value. The nucleus of capitalism is not the utilitarianism of goods and services. Rather, the pivot of capitalism is representation *of* representation. Capitalism (M-C-M') is torn from objects. Capitalism is the Outside of the object. The malady of capital is that it relinquishes the object of its representation. Capitalism is outstripped of the source of its exchange-value. The capitalist opposes the economy of fetishism. The fetish expands and extends objects — the fur, lace, shoe, jockstrap, *et al.* But the capitalist contracts and constrains objects because he mislays them. The capitalist system is strangely devoid of the production of objects even as it extends the generation of dollars and coins. But this creation of capital — accumulation — is also restrained by the debt economy which balances the supply of dollars and coins with a restricted set of manufactured objects. Currency *qua* representation exchanges an actually restricted set of dollars and coins on debt for a potentially infinite sequence of objects which is outside of the dynamics of supply/demand. Goods and services are endlessly expansive, but representation is limited. The fetishist enjoys a limitless succession of objects. The capitalist counts a *finite infinity* or *infinite finity* of dollars and coins whose accumulation only obscures objects and accrues debt.

Currency is not only a system of representation. Dollars and coins are also the media which circumscribe objects in their ownership and propriety. The payment of dollars and coins enforces proprietary rights. Currency circumscribes selfhood around objects. These objects are safeguarded within the parameters which are structured into the codes of *le propre* and the ownership of the object. The commodity is overrun by propriety by an other — alien being — whose ownership of the commodity isolates its relationship to other objects in the system. The object becomes solitary and inaccessible. The circumscription of the object establishes boundaries and borders around which the object is approachable as a use-value of consumption. Currency enforces a privatization of goods and services. The commodity is ripped from the Other and hostaged by the other. The system of representation is complemented by a system of ownership. The private bourgeois individual possesses the goods and services *qua* consumption which are otherwise the labor of the collectivity *qua* production.

The nexus between capitalist *le propre* of the private property principle and the castration complex of the sexual difference principle is strict and profound. The male junior conceives of his penis as his own private property. This possession of *le pénis de la propriété privée* is a retroactive constitution after the sight of the female genitals and the phallocentric interpretation of difference *qua* deficit. The originary experience of the penis is masturbatory pleasure and warmth with the mother. But the confrontation with potential castration breeds a possession and ownership of the penis *qua* commodity. This penile commodity must be guarded as the family jewels of the identity of the male junior and his nascent identification with the father as ego-ideal. The ownership of the penis — *le pénis de la propriété privée* — is the necessary proviso for the male junior's assent to the rules and regulations of the society. These strictures are embodied in the father whose prowess is magnified because he possesses the phallus *qua* arbiter of difference that the male junior hopes to inherit. The general equivalent between the male junior's penis and the female junior's clitoris is size and visibility in comparison, contrast, and exchange. But the capitalist upshot of the scene of the discovery of sexual difference is that the male junior must protect his appendage as private property — *mine* — in order to safeguard his identity in the society and his identification with the father. The penis *qua* commodity is the object which warrants the offspring's voluntary admission to the society. The Other is annexed if the penis is axed. A deferral of castration — in potentiality — promises the reproduction of the system and the contraction of the universe of objects to the penis and its proper male proprietors.

In contrast, the fetishist foreswears the unique *das Ding* of the penis. The penis is a mere prop for fascination with the sundry objects of fetishistic enjoyment. *Verleugnung* returns itself *qua* "itself." But this return affirms the verity of objects — the fur, lace, shoe, jockstrap, collar, button, locket, bracelet, justice, ring, truth, nail, communism, belt, buckle, and so on. The male junior of neurosis interprets the penis as the glorious apex of identity and identification. But the man of perversion discerns the penis as merely a tedious object in an otherwise extensive sequence of objects of lure and charm. These objects are not owned (*le propre*) by the fetishist because the perverse Principle of Sameness[+] enables his premonition that relationality and constructionism — otherness — exceed the strict bounded positive unity of any of the objects in the scene of fetishism. The scene of perversion must vary and extend beyond the otherwise insistent repetition compulsion of the ambivalence of the forces of expansion and contraction in the world. The penis is restrictive and constrained, and the fetish is extensive and wide. This fetishistic growth overruns the supply/demand dynamics of scarcity in the scene of ownership in capitalism. The fetishist grows his set of material objects. The capitalist accumulates debt in representation.

Spirit

I want to turn to Freud's *Beyond the Pleasure Principle* (1920) and its dualities of pleasure and unpleasure, and *Eros* and *Thanatos*. The two pairs of binary oppositions which structure the text generate an excess which cannot be assimilated or incorporated into the system of (un)pleasure and existence. An (*a*)sexual generative principle of Spirit is the organizational center of an expansive galaxy. The tendency of the world toward growth and dilation is contained and restrained by the force of $-ism toward contraction and diminution. The proclivity of the universe is to extend, but the inexplicable force of the galaxy is to contract. The Spirit of (*a*)sexuality is the power which must be liberated in order to free the solar system to escalation and multiplication. An (*a*)sexuality is the obscene empty origin of this abundance. But this (*a*)sexuality is variously negated by *Verdrängung* and *Verwerfung* in order to contain and swallow its positivity. The perverse negation of *Verleugnung* promises the return of negation *qua* "itself." This *Verleugnung* of difference *qua* "difference" is a source of the expansion of the solar system. The cultivation of perversion multiplies the universe. Perversion is a force of the tendency toward expansion and growth in Spirit. Disavowal is the negative principle of the obscene positivity of the abundance of (*a*)sexuality.

The twin polarities in Freud's text, *Beyond the Pleasure Principle* (1920), are pleasure versus unpleasure, and the life drive versus the death drive. The two binary pairs of oppositions intersect with each other, but their internal relationships are also distinct. The *Nirvana* principle holds that the increase in tension in the individual and social organism is an unpleasure and that the decrease in tension is a pleasure. An (*a*)sexual extension of unpleasure in *Trieb* and courtly love swells the set of gestures, habits, forms, rituals, flirtations, and so on. These modalities of active resistance to the object augment tension in the individual and social universes. Ideally, the (*a*)sexual masochist differs and defers the otherwise satisfaction in the phallocentric climax of the male orgasm and ejaculation. The orgasm is endlessly deferred in favor of the anticipatory patient waiting of the apex of the interstitial parallactic overlap between unpleasure and pleasure. The orgasm is the joint between unpleasure and pleasure. The apex of the orgasm is the parallactic intersection between the unpleasure (or ecstasy) of the increase in tension and the pleasure (or laziness) of the reduction of stimulation to the zero degree of homeostasis. The orgasm is neither the Being of the increase in tension nor the Being of the decrease in tension. Rather, the orgasm is the Becoming of Nothingness. The orgasm is *not*. Pleasure and unpleasure are structured by a *not* which cannot be assimilated or incorporated into the system of pleasure. The orgasm is an excess and imbalance between tension and its diminution. The orgasm is the inexplicable center of the configurations of pleasure. The *Objekt* of the aim/less wander of *Trieb* in masochism and courtly love is the Outside of the system. The tension of the (*a*)sexual patient waiting of courtly love extends and expands the force of this expansive Outside.

The proximity of *Eros* and *Thanatos* also enlivens an interstitial zone in which existence *qua* life and death cannot be articulated in their opposition to each other. *Eros* is the force of unification and mergence. *Thanatos* is the power of disintegration and fragmentation. But this ostensible opposition belies a fundamental Sameness[+] between the two powers. *Eros* binds the splinters and scraps of the death drive, and *Thanatos* breaks the unities and coalitions of the life drive. *Eros* and *Thanatos* are distinct logics, but their mobilization is unified and separated by the forces of contraction in the union of *Eros* and of expansion in the partition of *Thanatos*. The life drive and death drive are not to be interpreted as separate principles. Rather, the two drives are components of the same force of contraction and expansion in the solar system. The universe tends to expand with the fragmentation and disunities of the death instinct, but *Eros* resists this proclivity. The parallactic Sameness[+] of the life drive and the death drive achieves an imbalance in which either contraction and closedness or expansion and openness rule the principle of the universe. Does the Spirit of (*a*)sexuality empower the drive of death to expand the galaxy against the conservative force of *Eros* and its will toward unity and confederation?

The wager of this book is that the tendency in the universe is toward an expansion which is generated by the Spirit of a productive (*a*)sexual empty abundance at the center of the system. But this (*a*)sexuality is consistently negated by a disposition toward contraction in the systems of $-ism. Psychoanalytically, *désir* traps the object in its clutches in order to return the orga(ni)sm to the zero degree of homeostasis. Capitalism mobilizes the ideology of scarcity in order to tighten the supply/demand dynamics in currency during a time of abundance. The system of *langue* restricts the free play of the material signifier in favor of the closed system of the signified of the word. The (*a*)sexual generative center of an absent abundance in psychoanalysis is the masochistic patient waiting of the *Trieb* of courtly love. The (*a*)sexual productive nucleus of an empty fullness in capitalism is the overproduction of the historical march of labor. The (*a*)sexual precipitative core of a lost plenitude in discourse is the play of the signifier and a *finite infinity* or *infinite finity* of metaphorical substitution — *metonymization of metonymy* — in an open system of text. The negated excess in these systems overrides the conservative principle of contraction in the system. Spiritually, the difference and deferral of *Trieb* and the proliferation of penises and clitorises (and so on) expand the remainder of tension in the galaxy and generate a surplus of objects of sexuality. The materialism of use-value and the abundance of goods and services grow the objects in the solar system and multiply the singularities of objects above the reductive exchange of the general equivalent. The play of the signifier and the infinite substitutability of words in the world procreate the value in marks and sounds of text above the restrictive economy of the positive unity of the word. The generative principle of (*a*)sexuality is a cause (*a*) of: the extension of *Trieb* and sex objects; the multiplication of goods and services; and the proliferation of meaning-making. This (*a*)sexual cause (*a*) is the principle of the expansion of the solar system in Spirit. The wager is that expansion of S triumphs over the contraction of $-ism. An (*a*)sexuality is the ante of this communist queer textual gamble.

It is also crucial to note that expansion and contraction — openness and closedness — are parallactically overlapped. The expansion of the universe contracts a reactive tendency toward closedness, and the contraction of the universe expands a generative tendency toward openness. The aperture or closure — openness and expansion or closedness and contraction — of the solar system is perspectival. Psychoanalytically, the endless *différance* toward (away from) the object of orgasm is an expansion of gestures, moves, habits, games, and flirtations only in the event that orgasm has yet to be reached. The openness of this (*a*)sexuality can only be retrospectively evaluated by the Time of the Neurotic (*Nachträglichkeit* and *après-coup*) and the reflective review of a postcoital postorgasm degree zero of the lazy homeostatic wimpy afterglow of the apex of tension in the orgasm. Expansion cannot be understood as such until the time of contraction. The masochistic pervert of *Trieb* and courtly love cannot experience his torturous relationship to his object as expansive of gestures because he has yet to experience the apex of tension and its release. The pervert does not yet know release. The pervert cannot fathom the contraction of the solar system. The pervert only intuits expansion *qua* his own (*a*)sexuality. Only the neurotic is in the disprivileged position to understand the binary oppositions between tension/release, climax/*denouement,* and expansion/contraction. The proclivity of the universe is also toward contraction and closedness. But the wager is against the tendency of $-ism and for expansion and openness. But what is the escaped excess between the parallax of expansion/contraction and closedness/openness? What is the ventured surplus in the indeterminacy and undecidability of expansion and contraction, and closedness and openness? What is the principle of the excess of Spirit? What is surplus System?

The systems of desire, finance, and language each promise their own tendency toward expansion in the solar system. Psychoanalysis posits the *différance* of drive and the masochism of courtly love as distinctive modalities of (*a*)sexuality. *Trieb* opens the galaxy to a sequence of gestures which is endlessly reconfigured by the indexical directions of prepositions. Spirit must foster *Trieb* against the lazy male idiocy of the clutches of *désir* and its simple *objets*. Marxism posits the excess of materiality as the redemptive principle of (*a*)sexuality. Labor and its surplus of goods and services open the universe to a bountiful series of objects which is the source of the communist dictum of each according to his need and each according to his ability. Deconstruction posits the play of the signifier and the endless infinity of substitution as the potential of (*a*)sexuality. The play of the signifier unfastens pluralities of texts and contexts, and alphabets and vocabularies, for the extension of meaning-making on the globe. Spirit must cultivate psychoanalytic *Trieb* against *désir*, Marxist materiality against speculation, and deconstructive play of the signifier against the positive unity of the sign. But the obverse of this promotion is also necessary to the expansion ($\supseteq$) contraction of the solar system. The potential surplus of penises and clitorises can only be a retrospective fable from the perspective of the abundance of Peniscentrism. Excess cannot be discerned from the orientation of the castration of phallocentrism. The *Trieb* of courtly love enjoys the missed encounter with its object only *qua* an encounter. Each according to his need and each according to his ability is only a backward glance toward the so-called free hand of the market from the orientation of material abundance. The same is the case for (*a*)sexuality and its principle of generative expansion and contraction. An (*a*)sexuality can only be imagined as a generative center of obscene empty abundance from the perspective of: the surplus of penises and clitorises; the extension of *Trieb* and masochism; the plenitude of commodities; and the free play of words. Until the future, sex is not boring.

Freud's work on *Eros* and *Thanatos* is purposeful to my project because it demonstrates the interchangeability of the principles of the galaxy. But the instruction is that neither the life drive nor the death drive is a principle. Expansion and openness, and contraction and closedness, are not principles. The truth of *Trieb* is the pivot upon which the beyond of the principle can be glimpsed. The neurotic is situated between the prosaic but arduous tension between the ego and the superego. In *Beyond the Pleasure Principle* (1920), Freud summarizes this interval, in full,

> The development of mankind thus far appears to me to call for no other explanation than that applicable to animals; and the restless urge for ever greater perfection that we observe in a minority of individual human beings can readily be understood as resulting from the repression of drives — the foundation on which all that is most precious in human civilization is built. The repressed drive never abandons its struggle to achieve full gratification which would consist in the repetition of a primary gratification experience. All the sublimations and reaction-formations and surrogate-formations in the world are never enough to resolve the abiding tension; and the gulf between the level of gratificatory pleasure *demanded* and the level actually *achieved* produces that driving force that prevents the individual from resting content with any situation he ever contrives (my emphasis).[4]

The neurotic lives the interval between demand/achievement. This gap is the structural arrangement between the ego and the superego. The series of metaphors or sublimations which substitutes for the proleptic gratification of the original urge aborts success because the chasm between the demanded achievement and the achievement of the demand is swelled by a series of reaction-formations and surrogate-formations. Metaphor disappoints the charge to suture the gap between the departure and *arche*, on the one hand, and the destination and *arche*, on the other hand. The neurotic's existence is this interval of sublimations, reactions, formations, and surrogations between the imagined achievement and the commanded demand. The neurotic will never be content because he commits to the short-circuit of the departure of the demand and the arrival of the achievement and then its insistent repetition. Neurotically, the gap between the increase in tension and the decrease in tension is quickly closed by the fast capture and indolent afterglow of the orgasm. The midst of these twin poles of demand and achievement is the tortured metaphors of everyday life and the various symptoms of their disappointments.

The pervert displaces the neurotic mediation between *Ich* and *Über-Ich*. The pervert disrupts the interval of departure and destination between demand and achievement. The neurotic's life is the lacuna between the superegoic demand and the egoistic achievement of the individual and social urges of the organism. In contrast, the pervert's *Trieb* of masochistic courtly love destabilizes the *arche* of departure and *arche* of destination of the fulfillment and disappointment of the gulf between demand and achievement in satisfaction. The pervert's "development of mankind" and its "struggle to achieve gratification" are settled by an endless series of metaphors, centers, words, substitutes, fetishes, signs, objects, and so on. These surrogates expand beyond the *arche* of departure of the "development of mankind" and beyond the *arche* of destination of an elusive achievement of these goals. The pervert's force resists the interval between demand and achievement — superego and ego — because it exceeds any departure of command and any arrival of satisfaction. The neurotic's life persists in the homeostatic interval between the unpleasure of tension of the demands of urges and the pleasure of the release of the tension in the achievements (or not) of successes. The interim between demand and achievement is the space and time of the idiot's *jouissance.* In contrast, the pervert takes pleasure in an interlude which exceeds the borders of demands and achievements.

The reason that the pervert can enjoy rather than suffer the interval between demand and achievement — *Über-Ich* and *Ich* — is that he has never known gratification in the satisfaction of the object of achievement. The "abiding tension" of the neurotic's torturous relationship to the superego and the ego is unknown to the pervert because he cannot retroactively glance backward at the metonymy of surrogates of the achievement of the demand of the urge. The pervert is in the midst of the series of surrogates — *metonymization of metonymy* — in the absence of a departure of demands and an arrival of achievements. The pervert's galaxy is neither expansive and open nor contractive and closed. The indexical series of prepositions orchestrates the pervert's movements in the "abiding tension" of fetishes — sublimations, reactions, and surrogates — in his traversal of the world. But this extension in space is absent of interval between the commandments of the superego and the achievements of the ego. The pervert eludes the complex of the *Ich* and the *Über-Ich.* The pervert is the character of the *Es* of libido and energy.

The *Es* is the psychical representative of the obscene (*a*)sexual nucleus of the Spirit of the universe in its contractive expansion and expansive contraction. The system tends toward an expansion and openness in the S, but the breaks of $-ism return this gain toward the loss of contraction and closedness. The neurotic interval between superegoic demand and egotistic achievement is a closed system of contraction. This interval is isomorphic to the pleasure principle of the increase of tension in demand and the satiation of satisfaction in the return to the degree zero of achievement. The pervert abjures this closed economy. The *Nirvana* principle is a neurotic recoil from the productive (*a*)sexual center of the universe and its will toward expansion and openness. The neurotic pleasure principle tends toward the contraction and closedness of $-ism.

The horizon of the wager of this book is that Spirit accomplishes an *unambivalent* disavowal of Sameness[+]. This Sameness[+] is the parallactic overlap of every object with every other object. But if every word is the same word, then what excess escapes the contractive expansion of the collapse of the universe? What is the Spirit whose surplus expands from the obscene abundance of the negated (*a*)sexual nucleus of the solar system? Perverse *Verleugnung* returns an excess because the both/and structure of disavowal returns the negated as an "itself" which exceeds the object of its original negation. This interval between sexual difference and "sexual difference" opens a surplus which expands the galaxy. The pivot of the expansion of perverse *Verleugnung* is an *unambivalence.* This *unambivalence* breaks the equilibrium — self-same and self-identical — between the otherwise balanced tendency toward the openness of expansion and the closedness of contraction in the system. The bet is that (*a*)sexuality is the principle of this *unambivalent* discoordination between the otherwise balanced nexus. This *unambivalence* disrupts the pleasure principle and its return.

This (*a*)sexual excess is visible in Freud's distinction between *Eros* and *Thanatos*. The two forces are distinct but overlapped. They are not two isolated principles. Rather, *Eros* and *Thanatos* work in tandem toward a stability of the system between the unification and coalescence of the life drive and the fragmentation and destruction of the death drive. But a generated surplus at the interface of the tendency toward balance between life drive and death drive is the source of the energy of expansion that the system of $-ism otherwise recoils from in its approach toward (away from) the core (*a*)sexuality and its obscene empty abundance at the center of the solar system. *Eros* binds the masculine subject to the capture and release of its object. *Thanatos* extends the gestures and games of the masochistic approach toward (away from) its object. The life drive instructs the fetish in its return to the penis-substitute and the penis. The death drive destroys the reference of the fetish to any stable closed system of substitution. *Eros* returns labor to the value of general equivalence and to the bound system of supply/demand dynamics of scarcity. *Thanatos* ruins the established coordination of comparison, contrast, and exchange. The life drive binds the material signifier and the abstract signified to the sign and to the conventional syntax and semantics of the word. The death drive upsets the joint and hinge between signifier and signified, and it cultivates new arrangements of signs and their infinite substitutions. *Eros* is the force of the contraction of the universe. *Thanatos* is the power of the expansion of the solar system. Proliferation of delays and fetishes, overproduction of goods and services, and extensions of signifiers and signifieds are the unbalanced structures of the *unambivalent* disavowals of the system which expand the galaxy. Perverse *Verleugnung* is the Spirit which breaks the coordinated and balanced principle(s) of the life drive and the death drive.

The word *unambivalence* is quirky because it shakes the already vibrated relationship between life and death, and between love and hate. The issue is the return of the ambivalently negated of *Verleugnung* to the system. The return of perversion is an excess which is either assimilated and incorporated into the system of contraction or freed and liberated into the expansion of the galaxy. The energy of communist queer (*a*)sexuality is the subordinated object of the tendency of the system to recoil from this generative abundance. But revolutionized systems of desire, production, and discourse are also inclined to embrace this obscene emptiness at the core of Being. The wager of this study is that despite the conservative homeostasis of $-ism the system tends toward the direction of expansion rather than contraction. The historical developments in desire, finance, and discourse suggest this expansion — in *Trieb* and fetishism, in overproduction and unalienated labor, and in the free play of the signifier.

The principle of the Madness of Order is Sameness[+]. This Sameness[+] refers to the parallactic overlap of the otherwise mutually exclusive: Something is Missing and Nothing is Missing. Psychoanalytically, the penis/not-penis division is overrun by the proliferation of fetishes. Capitalism overproduces use-values that cannot be constrained by the limitations of exchange in the closed circuit of comparison and contrast. The architectonics of the signifier overlaps the contractive system of the word and its Reason of semantics and syntax. But, at the same time, the obverse of revolutionized expansion is also the case. The unconscious generates symptoms which inhibit thinking, being, and living in the world. Scarcity and supply/demand dynamics inspire the global march of history unto each according to his need and each according to his ability. The sign coordinates and organizes the play of materialities and abstractions in *langue*. A Sameness[+] illuminates that Something is Missing and Nothing is Missing. But the wager of this study is that the galaxy moves toward Nothing is Missing. The cosmos tends away from loss and death. My neologism Sameness[+] is written with the sign of addition (+) as the superscript to the word. This addition (+) intimates the expansion and growth toward extensions in *Trieb*[+], Overproduction[+], and the Signifier[+] from the obscene Being and Nothingness at the nucleus of communist queer (*a*)sexuality. The sign of addition (+) is the mark of excess and surplus. Sameness[+] is otherwise always Difference[+] — not itself.

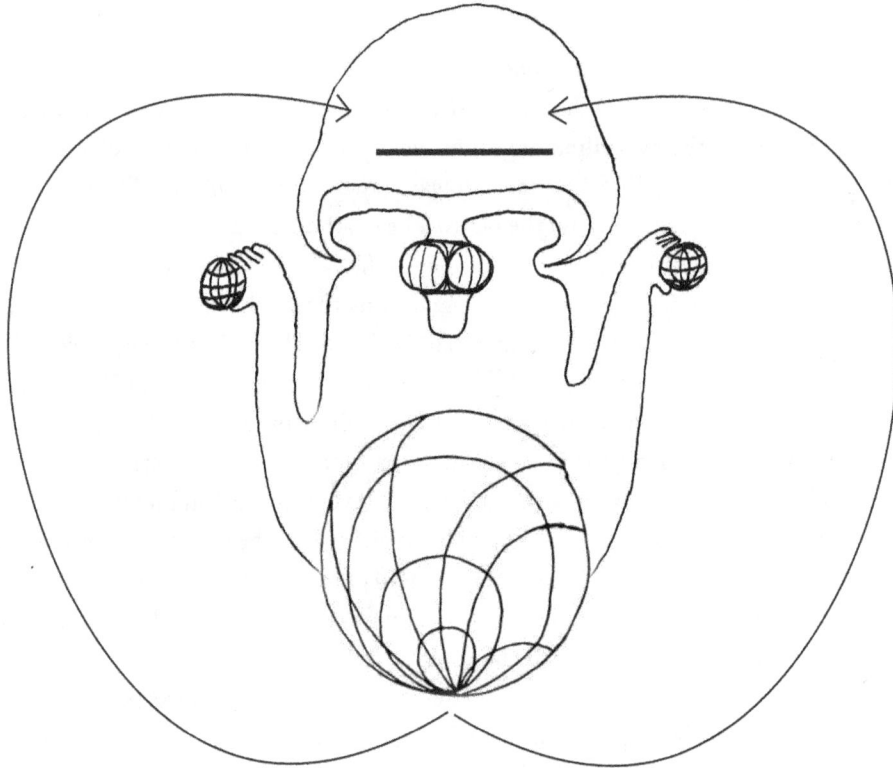

This image represents the materialist wager in this book. The bet is that an *unambivalent* Spirit emerges amidst the otherwise binary repetition of self-same and self-identical identity and difference (*et al.*). The wager is that an excess of materiality (signifier and labor) overwhelms $-ism even at the same time as this surplus of physicality and corporeality is uneasily reassimilated into the system. The tendency of the system is toward openness and expansion rather than closedness and contraction. The psychical (social) processes of negation which stage closure and contraction are stimulated by the constitutive openness and expansion of the galaxy. This illustration shows the Pervert-Schizoid-Woman configuration which is holding totality (fragmentation), viewing fragmentation (totality), and emerging from the unary realm of Nothingness wherein the not-yet ~~Being~~ is exactly resistant to the Real of symbolization *qua* Being. The wager of an open and expansive solar system as opposed to a closed and contracted solar system is situated on the axis between *Eros* and *Thanatos* and their simultaneous parallactic overlap and oppositional division. The *Eros<>Thanatos* of the universe is spoken in the language of the binds of totalities and boundaries. But the structure of this bound *Eros* of closedness is simultaneously structured as the unbound *Thanatos* of openness and the potentiality of innovation of plural worlds and multiple galaxies. The depicted speech bubble indexes the unsymbolized — unspoken and unwritten — future communism whose articulation is (meta)metalinguistic. The wager of the openness of the expansion and extension of use-values is at this historical moment utopic and virtual rather than real and actual. The wager is a bet from the future.

Notes & Sketches —

But must this expansion (+) be understood as a unidirectional and univalent — self-same and self-identical — principle of the galaxy? A Sameness⁺ (pronounced: /SAME-ness downside/) is also parallactically overlapped with a Sameness⁻ (pronounced: /Same-NESS upside/). The tension between this split within the Real Symbolic is an excess and surplus which are the objects of the tendency in the system toward Spirit. Are the (+) and (-) of Sameness to be theorized as a *Verdrängung* of the neurotic either/or — either addition or subtraction — or as a *Verleugnung* of the perverse both/and — both addition and subtraction — or as a *Verwerfung* of the schizoid neither/nor — neither addition nor subtraction? The forced choice of this decision is the tendency of $-ism toward contraction and closedness. The free destiny of this choice is the proclivity of the system toward expansion and openness. The (*a*)sexual core of obscene abundance is the force and power which inspire the proclivity toward growth — or — and — nor — the *tout autre* of the Other. Spirit is the word for this decision. How will Spirit release loss and death and reinvigorate excess and surplus? But, at the same time, how will Spirit constrain excess and surplus and recuperate loss and death? This is the edge of the pervert's space in the galaxy. But schizophrenically, it is neither expansion nor contraction — neither Nothing is Missing nor Something is Missing, but an altogether other configuration that may be in question. This is the aperture and closure of Spirit as it is situated at the *Spaltung* of $-ism and System.

Coda

Everything Is Alive

Noise: listening to someone who has never suffered.

— E.M. Cioran

Lacan conceives of the so-called pass as the end of psychoanalytic training and the genesis of the career of the newly born psychoanalyst. The pass is also the goal of the treatment of the patient. Lacanian psychoanalysis is only appropriate for the constituted subject. This is the person whose understanding of man and world is of absolute constitution from the outside — from the signifiers of language, from the institutional regulation of identity, from the interpellation by the law, from the imaginary determination by cultural images, from the imperatives of the superego, from the prison house of signification, from the recoil of anxiety, from the narcissism of speculation, from the paranoia of psychosis, from the aggression of desire, from the mirror of identification, and from the mourning and melancholia of the missed encounter. In other words, Lacanian psychoanalysis is only appropriate for the structuralist subject of nineteenth- and twentieth-century French and German philosophy — what is illuminated in the *Praxis* of Cultural Studies. The closure of Lacanian psychoanalytic treatment is the aperture of life after the death of the Other.

The rehearsed question of the *telos* of this book is, "Who comes after man?" But the Pervert-Schizoid-Woman's critique of $-ism is displaced by another urgent query. Who comes after God and the Other? Who arrives after the murder of the symbolic order by the exploited trauma of the Real? Whose form of negation is neither neurotic *Verdrängung* nor psychotic *Verwerfung* nor perverse *Verleugnung*? The modality of negation of the Real in psychosis is foreclosure. Lacan says that the Real returns to the symbolic in order to unsettle its entrenched figurations and regulations. But what genre of destabilization of the foreclosed Real is such a return? This methodology of rupture is neither philosophy nor Cultural Studies. The technique of this rupture is a moment of a peculiar form of temporality. The duration of this instant is the pass.

The pass retroactively rewrites the past from the perspective of an emergent future after the death of man. The loss of man redeems the torture of this past. The end of man makes the past the necessary precondition of a future. This *tout autre* will be a forced choice. The future is the choice of destiny. Posthumanity is neither life nor death. The afterward is an eternal and joyful mourning of loss. The proper name for this mourning is health. The symbol of $-ism is my personal ideogram for the prehistory of the past. The systems of the past have determined man up to the point of his pass unto health. $-ism is the social mark for the prehistory of man. S is born after the death of man and his humanism. The Pervert-Schizoid-Woman is the master word for the fashion of this destined existence. The between of $-ism and the Pervert-Schizoid-Woman — s and the *tout autre* — is the extended instant of the present.

Protracted presence pretermits the past and the future. What is undone in the back-and-forth in the symbolic order by the schizoid Real and its foreclosure of the neurotic symbolic? Lacan's explanation of the return of the Real is void of exposition and substance. But I want to originally betoken this rupture of the Real as the *retour de l'oubli* or the return of the forgotten. The *retour de l'oubli* is the unrecalled trauma, phantom ordeal, neglected omission, catastrophic recollection, spectral lesion, unnoticed wraith, and lost remembrance. All of these Events are negated in the symbolic order of happy business. The return of the forgotten disrupts the galaxies. The subject of *Verdrängung* is the neurotic. The subject of *Verleugnung* is the pervert. The subject of *Verwerfung* is the schizoid. The form of negation of the return of the forgotten in the Real is the Pervert-Schizoid-Woman. It is the figuration of a futural impossibility. This unendurable is remembrance. The arrival of the *tout autre* is a yet-to-come whose delay is the present of cheery distraction. The Pervert-Schizoid-Woman's remembrance is *entlassen* — negated *qua* dismissed. But the forgotten returns from the future and the past. The blessed neurotic's *futur antérieur* is the temporality of the *retour de l'oubli*. This future and past have been dismissed — *entlassen* — because remembrance is a threat to the symbolic order.

The memory of the Pervert-Schizoid-Woman's return of the Real *qua* forgotten is different from neurotic repression. The latter returns the repressed and latent truth of desire of the symbolic to the imaginary of fusional images and displaced antagonisms. This return of *Verdrängung* is then the *mise-en-scène* of the analysis of the symptom. Analysis reverses translation from manifest form to latent content. The return of the Real *qua* forgotten — *entlassen* — is also distinct from a psychotic *Verwerfung*. Foreclosure of the symbolic in the Real returns to terrorize consciousness and society. This psychotic foreclosure in the Real not only subverts the symbolic order. *Verwerfung* also radically transforms the order into incoherence. This secret truth must be impossibly symbolized by the *écriture* of the pervert. The Real *qua* the forgotten — *retour de l'oubli* — by history returns the personal and social trauma of the historical past and future to the Real. This is the proviso of the subversive force of the return of the forgotten to the solar system.

The archetypal psychoanalytic exemplar of the return of the forgotten is childhood memories — some happy, some sad. This Real returns the forgotten to the conscious as a prototypical preconscious, about which Freud wrote every little. The Real is the source of trauma and grief. These tribulations return as make-believe. Pretend returns as the form and content of young sexuality and childhood grief. Desire and love are the fundamental play of childhood. The threat of the return of this truth is that it is a commination to a civilization which is organized by neither *Verdrängung* nor *Verwerfung* nor *Verleugnung* but *entlassen* and the forgotten of the sex and grief of early life. This trauma is the most forced to be forgotten and the least welcomed to be remembered. The forgotten Real — *entlassen* — submerges history into the unconscious. The threat of the Real is history and the historicization of not only concepts and subjects but also of memories, dreams, tastes, textures, and sounds. These forgotten are the substances, lost and gained, and absent and present, of childhood.

The return of the Real of the forgotten — *retour de l'oubli* — promises a remembrance of common histories. These memoirs are forgotten — *entlassen* — by the Madness of the Order and the man who forgets to remember. The return of the Real also augurs a future whose horizon has yet to be outlined. The forgotten of the Real enables the travel back to the future. How does the Woman return from the Real as the rupture of the galaxy? The Woman recurs as the remembrance of the forgotten of traces — shards and fragments — of the stories and records of the world. The Woman's madness will redeem the forgotten Real. The Woman's words are a mournful language. But it is a dialect which is identical to our own. The Woman suffers the Real. The forgotten past properly memorializes the future of love in the loss of the self.

Psychoanalysis is the story of loss. We have lost loved ones, we have lost times, we have lost pains, we have lost spaces, we have lost gains, we have lost joys, we have lost the dear, we have lost the near, and we have lost ourselves. The recuperative efforts of analysis are to recrudesce these losses to the self not as returns but as radiant reminders of the future. The crucial moment of the reappearance of these losses is symbolization — writing, speaking, joking, drawing, screaming, sculpting, crying, and singing what has been lost in the pass to the past. These losses are not the genuine objects of mourning. The authentic object of mourning is a release from the object and a return to the self. The past of *entlassen* returns in the absence of self-beratement of the internalized object of melancholia.

The loss of the constitutive and the release from the outside harbor the calmness of the death of an interiority. This inside has otherwise been forever severed from the world. At this point, poetry becomes the exhilaration of the play to refashion a new world from the terror of the present in its regrets about the past and its anxieties about the future. The word for this creation of the work of art of the future is not sublimation but love. The precondition of love is the storytelling of loss and its *petit morts*. The Woman who tells the story of death makes love to loss. The decision to love is a forced choice. We cannot renounce the loss of ourselves for the other. To choose the pass of the love of loss of our chosen destiny is to celebrate that life itself is a suicidal love.

In our lives, the lost is a certain Nothing is (Still) Missing for some time and in some place. But when this Something is Missing is lost to a Nothing is Missing, when suicidal love gives way to an affirmation of this loss, when the Something is Missing hesitantly merges with a Nothing is Missing, then the absent future in a recalled past invites us toward a time and space of neither the unconscious nor love but of another. Everything is Alive, and so on. I would say — *Yes!* — for the two of us, just now, I will, together. But, until then, I will miss you in the expanses of space.

Endnotes

Chapter One

1   Sigmund Freud, *The Standard Edition of the Complete Psychological Works of Sigmund Freud*, ed. and transl. James Strachey (London, UK: The Hogarth Press, 1958), *4*, 50.

2   Ibid.

3   Roland Barthes, *Image Music Text*, transl. Stephen Heath (NY, NY: Hill and Wang, 1978), 142.

4   I am indebted to David Cohn for this concept.

5   Jacques Lacan, *Seminar 11: The Four Fundamental Concepts of Psychoanalysis*, ed. Jacques-Alain Miller transl. Alan Sheridan (NY, NY: W.W. Norton and Co., 1998), 6.

6   Sigmund Freud, *Beyond the Pleasure Principle*, ed. James Strachey (NY, NY: W.W. Norton and Co., 1990), 10-11

7   Lacan, *Seminar 11*, 49.

8   Jacques Lacan, *Écrits: A Selection*, transl. Bruce Fink (NY, NY: W.W. Norton and Co., 2004), 164.

9   Sigmund Freud, *Interpreting Dreams*, ed. Adam Phillips transl. Jim Underwood (NY, NY: Penguin Books), 346.

10 Sigmund Freud, *Sexuality and the Psychology of Love*, ed. and transl. James Strachey (NY, NY: Touchstone, 1997), 177.

11 Michael Warner, *The Trouble with Normal: Sex, Politics, and the Ethics of Queer Life* (Cambridge, MA: Harvard University Press, 1999), 41-80.

12 Georges Bataille, *Inner Experience*, transl. Leslie Anne Boldt (Albany, NY: SUNY Press, 1988), 58.

13 Martin Heidegger, *Being and Time*, ed. Joan Stambaugh (Albany, NY: SUNY Press, 2010), 283.

14 Ibid, 59-122.

15 Lacan, *Seminar 11*, 6.

16 Jacques Lacan, *Seminar 20: The Limits of Love and Knowledge*, ed. Jacques-Alain Miller transl. Bruce Fink (NY, NY: W.W. Norton and Co., 1999), 76-77.

Chapter Two

1   Sigmund Freud, *The Freud Reader*, ed. Peter Gay transl. James Strachey (NY, NY: W.W. Norton and Co., 1995), 132-133.

2   Sigmund Freud, *Beyond the Pleasure Principle and Other Writings*, ed. Adam Phillips transl. Mark Edmundson (NY, NY: Penguin Books, 2003), 45-46.

3   Ibid, 46.

4   Jacques Derrida, *"Différance,"* in *The Routledge Critical and Cultural Theory Reader*, eds. Neil Badmington and Julia Thomas (NY, NY: Routledge), 126.

5   Freud, *Standard Edition 14*, 121.

6   Ibid.

7   Ibid, 177.

8   Ibid, 148.

9   Ibid, 122.

10 Ibid.

11 Ibid.

12 Ibid.

13 Ibid.

14 Ibid.

15 Ibid.

16 Ibid, 123.

17 Sigmund Freud, *Totem and Taboo*, ed. James Strachey (NY, NY: W.W. Norton and Co., 1990), 79.

18 Jacques Lacan, *Seminar 7: The Ethics of Psychoanalysis*, ed. Jacques-Alain Miller transl.

Dennis Porter (NY, NY: W.W. Norton and Co., 1997), 145.

19 Friedrich Nietzsche, *On the Genealogy of Morals and Ecce Homo,* ed. Walter Kaufmann (NY, NY: Vintage Books, 1989), 112.

20 Lacan, *Seminar 7,* 149.

21 Ibid.

22 Ibid.

23 Ibid, 150.

24 Ibid, 152.

25 Ibid.

26 Gilles Deleuze, *Masochism: Coldness and Cruelty and Venus in Furs,* transl. Jean McNeil (Cambridge, MA: Zone Books, 1991), 31.

27 Ibid, 128.

28 Ibid.

29 Ibid.

30 Ibid, 73.

31 Ibid, 75.

32 Ibid, 88.

33 Ibid.

34 Ibid, 118.

35 Ibid.

36 Ibid.

37 Ibid, 120.

38 Ibid.

39 Ibid, 130.

40 Ibid, 121.

41 Ibid.

42 Freud, *Beyond,* ed. Strachey, 73-74.

43 Deleuze, *Masochism,* 121.

44 Ibid.

45 Michel Foucault, *History of Sexuality: Volume 1,* transl. Robert Hurley (NY, NY: Vintage Books, 1990), 159.

Chapter Three

1 Joel Dor, *Clinical Lacan,* eds. Judity Gurewich and Susan Fairfield (NY, NY: Other Press, 1998), 16.

2 Freud, *Sexuality,* 177.

3 Ibid, 197.

4 Freud, *Reader,* ed. Phillips, 96.

5 Ibid.

6 Ibid, 97.

7 Ibid, 99.

8 Sigmund Freud, *The Interpretation of Dreams,* ed. James Strachey (NY, NY: Avon Books, 1965), 431.

9 Freud, *Standard Edition 3,* 58.

10 Jacques Lacan, *Seminar 3,* ed. Jacques-Alain Miller transl. Russell Grigg (NY, NY: W.W. Norton and Co., 1997), 201.

11 Jacques Derrida, *Margins of Philosophy,* transl. Alan Bass (Chicago, IL: University of Chicago Press, 1985), 8.

12 Sigmund Freud, *Three Case Histories,* transl. James Strachey (NY, NY: Touchstone, 1996), 136.

13 Jacques Lacan, *Seminar 1: Freud's Papers on Technique,* ed. Jacques-Alain Miller transl. John Forresster (NY, NY: W.W. Norton and Co., 2013), 43.

14 Jean Laplanche and Jean-Luc Pontalis, *The Language of Psychoanalysis* (NY, NY: W.W. Norton and Co., 1974), 118.

15 Octave Mannoni, *Clefs pour l'imaginaire ou L'Auture Scene* (Paris, France: Seuil, 1985), 27.

16 Freud, *Standard Edition 19,* 143-144.

17 Friedrich Nietzsche, *The Gay Science,* ed. Bernard Williams (Cambridge, UK: Cambridge University Press), 6.

18 Jacques Derrida, *Of Grammatology,* transl. Gayatri Chakravorty Spivak (Baltimore, MD: The Johns Hopkins University Press, 1977), 314.

19 Paul de Man, *The Resistance to Theory* (Minneapolis, MN: Minneapolis University Press, 1986), 19-20.

20 Freud, *Interpretation,* ed. Strachey, 311-312.

21 Derrida, *Grammatology,* 11.

22 Lacan, *Seminar 1,* 117.

23 Lacan, *Écrits,* transl. Fink, op. cit.

24 Jean Baudrillard, *Simulacra and Simulation,* transl. Sheila Faria Glaser (Ann Arbor, MI: University of Michigan Press, 1995), 1.

25 Freud, *Sexuality,* 205.

26 Ibid, 208.

27 Lacan, *Seminar 7,* 68.

28 Lacan, *Seminar 20,* 57.

29 Baudrillard, *Simulacra,* 5.

30 Foucault, *History,* 36-50.

31 Lacan, *Écrits,* transl. Fink, 277.

32 Jacques Derrida, *Writing and Difference*, transl. Alan Bass (Chicago, IL: University of Chicago Press, 1978), 289.

33 Foucault, *History*, 36-50.

34 Ibid.

35 Warner, *Trouble*, op. cit.

36 Lacan, *Seminar 11*, 165.

37 Freud, *Reader*, ed. Gay, 286.

38 Lacan, *Seminar 11*, 170.

39 Ibid, 206.

40 Freud, *Standard Edition 12*, 71.

41 Michel Foucault, *History of Madness*, ed. Jean Khalfa transl. Jonathan Murphy (NY, NY: Routledge, 2006), 242.

42 Ibid.

43 Ibid, 243.

44 Ibid, 237.

45 Dor, *Clinical*, 36.

46 Lacan, *Seminar 2: The Ego in Freud's Theory and in the Technique of Psychoanalysis*, ed. Jacques-Alain Miller transl. Sylvana Tomaselli (NY, NY: W.W. Norton and Co., 1991), 191.

47 Dor, *Clinical*, 36.

48 Friedrich Nietzsche, *Thus Spoke Zarathustra*, ed. Walter Kaufmann (NY, NY: Penguin Books, 1966), 318.

49 Derrida, *Grammatology*, 65.

50 Freud, *Reader*, ed. Phillips, 67.

51 Freud, *Sexuality*, 213.

52 Ibid, 202-203.

53 Dor, *Clinical*, 41.

54 Ibid, 35.

55 Lacan, *Écrits*, ed. Fink, 3-9.

Chapter Four

1 Mannoni, *Clefs*, 27.

2 Sigmund Freud and Josef Breuer, *Studies in Hysteria*, ed. Adam Phillips transl. Nicola Luckhurst (NY, NY: Penguin Books, 2004), 14.

3 Freud, *Standard Edition 19*, 149.

4 Ibid, 152.

5 Ibid, 152-153.

6 Freud, *Sexuality*, 213.

7 Derrida, "*Différance,*" in *Routledge*, eds. Badmington and Thomas, 126.

8 Freud, *Reader*, ed. Phillips, 64.

9 Ibid.

10 Ibid.

11 Ibid, 67.

12 Ibid, 65.

13 Ibid, 64.

14 Ibid.

15 Ibid, 65.

16 Ibid.

17 Ibid.

18 Ibid, 66.

19 Ibid.

20 Ibid.

21 Freud, *Sexuality*, 213.

22 Lacan, *Seminar 20*, 57.

23 Freud, *Reader*, ed. Phillips, 67.

24 Ibid, 66.

25 Ibid, 90.

26 Ibid.

27 Deleuze, *Masochism*, 128.

28 Freud, *Reader*, ed. Phillips, 90.

29 Luce Irigaray, *This Sex Which is Not One*, transl. Catherine Porter (Ithaca, NY: Cornell University Press, 1985), 205-218.

30 Freud, *Reader*, ed. Phillips, 90.

31 Ibid, 91.

32 Ibid.

33 Ibid.

34 Ibid.

35 Ibid.

36 Lacan, *Seminar 20*, 76-77.

37 Freud, *Sexuality*, 92.

Chapter Five

1 Deleuze, *Masochism*, 128.

2 Freud, *Reader*, ed. Phillips, 92.

3 Baudrillard, *Simulacra*, 1.

4 Freud, *Reader*, ed. Phillips, 92.

5 Ibid, 95.

6 Derrida, *Writing*, 278.

7 Freud, *Sexuality*, 207-208.

8 Freud, *Reader*, ed. Phillips, 93.

9 Freud, *Reader*, ed. Gay, 130.

10 Freud, *Reader*, ed. Phillips, 94.

11 Freud, *Interpreting*, ed. Phillips, 308-9.

12   Freud, *Reader,* ed. Phillips, 56.

13   Ibid, 57.

14   Jacques Lacan, *Seminar 10: Anxiety,* ed. Jacques-Alain Miller transl. A.R. Price (NY, NY: Polity, 2014), 22.

15   Lacan, *Seminar 20,* 57.

16   Freud, *Reader,* ed. Phillips, 57.

17   Freud, *Sexuality,* 188-89.

18   Freud and Breuer, *Hysteria,* 14.

19   Freud, *Reader,* ed. Phillips, 58.

20   Ibid.

21   Lacan, *Seminar 11,* 203.

22   Freud, *Reader,* ed. Phillips, 418.

23   Nietzsche, *Zarathustra,* 286-296.

24   Foucault, *History,* 7.

25   Freud, *Reader,* ed. Phillips, 418.

26   Walter Benjamin, *Illuminations: Esssays and Reflections,* transl. Harry Zohn (NY, NY: Schocken Books, 2007), 217-252.

27   Freud, *Reader,* ed. Phillips, 418.

28   Ibid, 71.

29   Ibid.

30   Ibid, 73.

Chapter Six

1   Lacan, *Seminar 1,* 221.

2   Ibid.

3   Heidegger, *Being,* ed. Stambaugh, 59-122.

4   Lacan, *Seminar 20,* 10.

5   Lacan, *Écrits,* ed. Fink, 309.

6   Jacques Lacan, *Écrits: The First Complete Edition in English,* transl. Bruce Fink (NY, NY: W.W. Norton and Co., 2007), 826.

7   Dany Nobus, *Jacques and the Freudian Practice of Psychoanalysis* (NY, NY: Routledge, 2000), 46-47.

8   Sigmund Freud, *Three Essays on the Theory of Sexuality,* transl. James Strachey (NY, NY: Basic Books, 1962), 31.

9   Freud, *Standard Edition 23,* 275.

10   Martin Heidegger, *The Question Concerning Technology and Other Essays,* transl. William Lovitt (NY, NY: Haper Torchbooks, 1962), 53-112.

11   Freud, *Standard Edition 23,* 275.

12   Ibid.

13   Lacan, *Seminar 11,* 95.

14   Freud, *Standard Edition 23,* 275.

15   Martin Heidegger, *Basic Writings,* ed. David Farrell Krell (NY, NY: HarperCollins, 1993), 213-266.

16   Derrida, *Grammatology,* 1.

17   Ibid, 70.

18   Derrida, *Writing,* 278.

19   Freud, *Standard Edition 23,* 275.

20   Ibid.

21   Freud, *Standard Edition 23,* 275.

22   Freud, *Beyond,* ed. Strachey, 46, 49.

23   Freud, *Standard Edition 23,* 277.

24   Lacan, *Écrits: A Selection,* ed. Fink, 271-280.

25   Lacan, *Seminar 20,* 57.

26   Freud, *Standard Edition 23,* 277.

27   Freud, *Standard Edition 23,* 277.

28   Jacques Lacan, *Seminar 17: The Other Side of Psychoanalysis,* ed. Jacques-Alain Miller transl. Russell Grigg (NY, NY: W.W. Norton and Co., 2007), 20.

29   Friedrich Nietzsche, *Beyond Good and Evil: A Prelude to a Philosophy of the Future,* ed. Rolf-Peter Horstmann transl. Judith Norman (Cambridge, UK: Cambridge University Press, 2001), 21.

30   Derrida, *Grammatology,* 73.

31   Lacan, *Seminar 10,* 76.

32   Freud, *Interpretation,* ed. Strachey, 367.

33   Lacan, *Seminar 1,* 278.

34   G.W.F. Hegel, *Phenomenology of Spirit,* transl. A.V. Miller (Oxford, UK: Oxford University Press, 1977), 104-138.

35   G.W.F. Hegel, *Phenomenology of Spirit,* transl. J.B. Baillie (Digireads, 2010), 269.

Chapter Seven

1   Lacan, *Seminar 17,* 107.

2   Karl Marx, *Capital: A Critique of Political Economy Volume 1,* transl. Ben Fowkes (NY, NY: Vintage Books, 1977), 434.

3   Ernesto Laclau and Chantal Mouffe, *Hegemony and Socialist Strategy: Towards a Radical Democratic Politics* (Brooklyn, NY: Verso, 2001), 7-46.

4   De Man, *Resistance,* 19.

5 Ferdinand de Saussure, *Course in General Linguistics*, transl. Wade Baskin (NY, NY: McGraw-Hill, 1959), 111-122.

6 Ibid, 115.

7 Ibid.

8 Barbara Johnson, *A World of Difference* (Baltimore, MD: The Johns Hopkins University Press), 15.

9 Slavoj Zizek, *The Parallax View* (Cambridge, MA: The MIT Press), 152.

10 Lacan, *Seminar 1*, 221.

11 Zizek, *Parallax*, 153.

12 Freud, *Sexuality*, 177.

13 Ibid, 211.

14 Sigmund Freud, *Three Essays on the Theory of Sexuality*, transl. James Strachey (NY, NY: Basic Books, 1962), 1-38.

15 Freud, *Sexuality*, 210-213.

16 Ibid, 211-212.

17 Ibid, 213.

18 Derrida, *Writing*, 293.

19 Ibid, 369.

20 Ibid, 292.

21 Ibid, 280.

22 Ibid, 278.

23 Ibid, 279.

24 Ibid, 278.

25 Ibid, 279.

26 Ibid.

27 Ibid.

28 Ibid.

29 Ibid.

30 Ibid.

31 Freud, *Reader*, ed. Gay, 437.

32 Baudrillard, *Simulacra*, 3.

33 Ibid.

34 Lacan, *Seminar 7*, 46.

35 Ibid, 52.

36 Ibid, 58.

37 Ibid, 53.

38 Ibid, 63.

39 Ibid, 54.

40 Derrida, *Writing*, 279.

41 Ibid, 280.

42 Freud, *Reader*, ed. Gay, 566.

43 Lacan, *Seminar 7*, 162-163.

44 Jacques Lacan, *Écrits: A Selection*, transl. Alan Sheridan (NY, NY: W.W. Norton and Co., 1982), xi.

45 Derrida, *Writing*, 278-279.

46 Ibid.

47 Lacan, *Seminar 11*, 180.

48 Philipe Lacoue-Labarthe and Jean-Luc Nancy, *The Title of the Letter: Reading of Lacan* (Albany, NY: SUNY Press, 1992), 27-32.

49 Derrida, *Writing*, 279.

50 Ibid.

51 Heidegger, *Being*, ed. Stambaugh, 262.

52 Derrida, *Writing*, 280.

53 Ibid.

54 Ibid, 289.

55 Freud, *Interpreting*, ed. Phillips, 346.

56 Derrida, *Writing*, 289.

57 Ibid.

58 Ibid, 290.

59 Jacques Derrida, *The Postcard: From Socrates to Freud and Beyond*, transl. Alan Bass (Chicago, IL: University of Chicago Press, 1987), 441.

60 Jacques Derrida, *Positions*, transl. Alan Bass (Chicago, IL: University of Chicago Press, 1982), 107.

61 Jaccques Derrida, *A Derrida Reader: Between the Blinds*, ed. Peggy Kamuf (NY, NY: Columbia University Press, 1991), 277.

62 Lacan, *Seminar 1*, 129.

63 Baudrillard, *Simulacra*, 1.

64 Ibid, 2.

65 Ibid, 3.

66 Ibid, 13.

67 Jean Baudrillard, *Jean Baudrillard: Selected Writings*, ed. Mark Poster (Redwood City, CA: Stanford University Press, 1988), 175.

68 Baudrillard, *Simulacra*, 20.

69 Ibid, 22.

70 Freud, *Sexuality*, 209.

71 Ibid, 161-183.

72 Ibid, 205.

73 Ibid.

74 Ibid, 204-205.

75 Ibid, 205.

76 Lacan, *Écrits*, ed. Fink, 272.

77 Ibid, 277.

78 Ibid.

Chapter Eight

1 Saussure, *Course*, 113.

2 Saussure, *Course*, 112.

3 Lacan, *Seminar 11*, 6.

4 Karl Marx, *Karl Marx: Selected Writings*, ed. David McLellan (NY, NY: Oxford University Press, 2000), 158.

5 Saussure, *Course*, 111.

6 Marx, *Selected*, 224.

7 Karl Marx, "The German Ideology," in *Images: A Reader*, eds. Sunil Manghani, Arthur Piper, and Jon Simons (London, UK: Sage Publications, 2010), 49.

8 Marx, *Selected*, 232.

9 Ibid.

10 Heidegger, *Question*, 115-154.

11 Marx, *Selected*, 569.

12 Saussure, *Course*, 120.

13 Ibid.

14 Lacan, *Écrits*, ed. Fink, 277.

15 Marx, *Selected*, 435.

16 Saussure, *Course*, 120.

17 Louis Althusser and Etienne Balibar, *Reading Capital*, transl. Ben Brewster (Brooklyn, NY: Verso), 91.

18 Lacan, *Seminar 11*, 49.

19 Georg Lukács, *History and Class Consciousness: Studies in Marxist Dialectics*, transl. Rodney Livingstone (Cambridge, MA: The MIT Press, 1972), 83-222.

20 Jean-Joseph Goux, *Symbolic Economies after Marx and Freud*, transl. Jennifer Curtiss Gage (Ithaca, NY: Cornell University Press), 9-63.

21 Marx, *Selected*, 157.

22 Ibid, 232.

23 Ibid, 363.

24 Ibid, 177.

25 Ibid, 449.

26 Derrida, *Margins*, 136.

27 Marx, *Selected*, 483.

28 Lacan, *Seminar 7*, 43-70.

29 Marx, *Selected*, 159-191.

Chapter Nine

1 Saussure, *Course*, 111.

2 Ibid, 112.

3 Ibid, 113.

4 Ibid.

5 Ibid.

6 Ibid.

7 Ibid.

8 Ibid, 114.

9 Ibid, 115.

10 Ibid, 116.

11 Ibid, 117.

12 Ibid.

13 Saussure, *Course*, 120.

14 Ibid.

15 Ibid.

16 Ibid, 121.

17 Ibid, 120.

18 Martin Heidegger, *Being and Time*, transl. John Macquarrie and Edward Robinson (NY, NY: Harper and Row, 1962), 58.

19 Lacan, *Écrits*, ed. Fink, 277.

20 Laclau and Mouffe, *Hegemony*, 47-92.

21 Jean Baudrillard, *Forget Foucault* (NY, NY: Semiotext(e), 1987), 40.

22 Derrida, *Writing*, 292.

23 Jacques Derrida, *Truth in Painting*, transl. Geoffrey Bennington and Ian McLeod (Chicago, IL: University of Chicago Press, 1987), 257.

24 Derrida, *Grammatology*, 304.

25 Freud, *Standard Edition 13*, 148.

26 Lacan, *Seminar 7*, 173-74.

27 Lacan, *Seminar 7*, 152.

28 Derrida, *Reader*, 84.

29 Derrida, *"Différance," Routledge*, 126.

30 Lacan, *Seminar 3*, 97.

31 Lacan, *Seminar 11*, 167.

32 Freud, *Standard Edition 3*, 58.

33 Lacan, *Seminar 3*, 46.

34 Freud, *Reader*, ed. Gay, 510.

35 Lacan, *Seminar 3*, 321.

36 Freud, *Standard Edition 19*, 143-144.

37 Freud, *Sexuality*, 167.

38 Lacan, *Écrits*, ed. Fink, 190.

39 Lacan, *Seminar 11*, 203.

40 Sigmund Freud, *Jokes and their Relation to the Unconscious*, ed. Adam Phillips transl. John Carey (NY, NY: Penguin Books, 2003), 27.

41 Ibid.

42 Ibid, 46.

43 Ibid, 126.

44 Ibid.

45 Ibid, 57.

46 Ibid, 70.

47 Ibid, 74.

48 De Man, *Resistance*, 19.

49 Freud and Breuer, *Studies*, 14.

50 Foucault, *Madness*, 237.

51 Freud, *Sexuality*, 165.

52 Lacan, *Seminar 7*, 314.

53 Jacques Derrida, "Force of Law," in *Deconstruction and the Possibility of Justice*, eds. Drucilla Cornell, Michel Rosenfeld, and David Gray Carlson (NY, NY: Routledge, 1992), 243.

54 Hegel, *Phenomenology*, transl. Miller, 263-409.

Chapter Ten

1   Freud, *Standard Edition 5*, 342.

2   Freud, *Standard Edition 4*, 96.

3   Ibid.

4   Freud, *Standard Edition 5*, 225.

5   Freud, *Standard Edition 4*, 96.

6   Ibid, 40.

7   Ibid, 219.

8   Ibid, 273.

9   Ibid, 614.

10 Freud, *Interpretation*, 73-76.

11 Ibid, 81.

12 Freud, *Standard Edition 4*, 49.

13 Ibid, 48.

14 Ibid.

15 Ibid, 50.

16 Ibid, 141.

17 Ibid, 144.

18 Freud, *Interpreting*, 346.

19 Ibid, 322.

20 Freud, *Standard Edition 5*, 522.

21 Freud, *Interpreting*, 333-34.

22 Freud, *Reader*, ed. Phillips, 139.

23 Saussure, *Course*, 120.

24 Derrida, *Grammatology*, 47.

25 Freud, *Interpretation*, 685.

26 Heidegger, *Being*, ed. Stambaugh, 49-268.

27 Ibid, 263.

28 Derrida, *Grammatology*, 91.

29 Derrida, *Margins*, 8.

30 Lacan, *Écrits*, ed. Fink, 190.

31 Freud, *Interpreting*, 70.

32 Marx, *Selected*, op. cit.

33 Ibid, 81.

34 Freud, *Interpreting*, 191.

35 Ibid.

36 Jacques Derrida, *Glas*, transl. John P. Leavey and Richard Rand (Lincoln, NE: University of Nebraska Press, 1990), 77.

37 Freud, *Beyond*, ed. Strachey, 46.

38 Ibid, 47.

39 Heidegger, *Being*, ed. Stambaugh, 219-246.

40 Freud, *Beyond*, ed. Strachey, 49.

41 Freud, *Standard Edition 18*, 44.

42 Ibid, 49.

43 Marx, *Selected*, 158.

44 Derrida, *Margins*, 14-16.

45 Marx, *Selected*, op. cit.

46 Derrida, *Margins*, 8-9.

47 Michel Foucault, *Discipline and Punish: The Birth of the Prison*, transl. Alan Sheridan (NY, NY: Vintage Books, 1995), 200.

48 Lacan, *Seminar 11*, 82.

49 Derrida, *Margins*, 136.

50 Nietzsche, *Gay*, 208.

51 Michel Foucault, *Archaeology of Knowledge* (NY, NY: Vintage Books, 1982), 82.

52 Slavoj Zizek, *Interrogating the Real*, eds. Rex Butler and Scott Stephens (NY, NY: Bloomsbury, 2006), 53-54.

53 Marx, *Selected*, op. cit.

54 Louis Althusser, *Lenin and Philosophy and Other Essays* (NY, NY: Monthly Review Press, 2001), 85-126.

55 Hegel, *Phenomenology*, transl. Miller, 479-494.

56 Freud, *Interpreting*, 327.

57 Heidegger, *Being*, transl. Macquarrie and Robinson, 58.

58 Freud, *Reader*, ed. Gay, op. cit.
59 Freud, *Interpreting*, 328.
60 Ibid.
61 Ibid, 327-328.
62 Ibid, 332.
63 Ibid, 337.
64 Ibid, 328.
65 Derrida, *Margins*, 310.
66 Freud, *Interpreting*, 330.
67 Ibid, 335.
68 Laclau and Mouffe, *Hegemony*, 7-92.
69 Lacan, *Seminar 1*, 287.
70 Freud, *Interpreting*, 51.
71 Ibid, 615.
72 Ibid, 60.

Chapter Eleven

1 Marx, *Selected*, 52.
2 Ibid, 53.
3 Ibid.
4 Ibid, 57.
5 Ibid.
6 Nietzsche, *Gay*, 53.
7 Gilles Deleuze, *Nietzsche and Philosophy*, transl. Hugh Tomlinson (NY, NY: Columbia University Press, 1962), 39-44.
8 Marx, *Selected*, op. cit.
9 Nietzsche, *Gay*, 95.
10 Deleuze, *Nietzsche*, 111-119.
11 Marx, *Selected*, 148.
12 Ibid.
13 Ibid, 78.
14 Ibid.
15 Ibid, 80.
16 Ibid, 109.
17 Nietzsche, *Gay*, 204.
18 Heidegger, *Question*, 53-112.
19 Marx, *Selected*, 110.
20 Ibid, 85.
21 Ibid, 87.
22 Ibid, 179.
23 Marx, *Selected*, op. cit.
24 Marx, *Selected*, 215.
25 Karl Marx, "The German Ideology," in *Images: A Reader*, 49.

26 Derrida, *Margins*, 8.
27 Ibid, 136.
28 Lacan, *Écrits*, ed. Fink, 80.
29 Freud, *Interpreting*, 326-353.
30 Saussure, *Course*, 112, 114-115, 117.
31 Ibid, 120.
32 Derrida, *Writing*, 279.
33 Ibid.
34 Marx, *Selected*, 158.
35 Ibid.
36 Freud, *Reader*, ed. Phillips, 96-97.
37 Ibid, 99.
38 Ibid, 98.
39 Ibid.
40 Freud, *Sexuality*, 169.
41 Lacan, *Écrits*, ed. Fink, 3-9.
42 Freud, *Reader*, ed. Gay, 735, 756.
43 Lacan, *Seminar 7*, 314.
44 Ibid, 325.
45 Ibid, 321.
46 Lacan, *Seminar 11*, 67.
47 Freud, *Beyond*, ed. Strachey, 70.
48 Lacan, *Seminar 7*, 321.
49 Freud, *Reader*, ed. Phillips, 99.

Chapter Twelve

1 Freud, *Reader*, ed. Gay, 501.
2 Ibid, 510.
3 Freud, *Beyond*, ed. Phillips, 119.
4 Freud, *Reader*, ed. Gay, 501.
5 Foucault, *History*, 45.
6 Freud, *Reader*, ed. Gay, 501.
7 Lacan, *Écrits*, ed. Fink, 277.
8 Freud, *Sexuality*, 163.
9 Freud, *Reader*, ed. Gay, 501.
10 Ibid, 180.
11 Lacan, *Seminar 7*, 179.
12 Freud, *Reader*, ed. Gay, 504.
13 I am indebted to Thomas DiPiero for this insight.
14 Freud, *Reader*, ed. Gay, 723, 727.
15 Lacan, *Seminar 7*, 270-287.
16 Freud, *Standard Edition 10*, 74.

Chapter Thirteen

1   Nietzsche, *Gay*, 116.
2   Freud, *Reader*, ed. Gay, 142.
3   Erik Erikson, "The Dream Specimen of Psychoanalysis," *Journal of the American Psychoanalytic Association 2* (1954): 46.
4   Freud, *Reader*, ed. Gay, 130.
5   Ibid 142.
6   Ibid, 131.
7   Ibid.
8   Ibid.
9   Ibid.
10 Ibid, 131.
11 Ibid.
12 Ibid, 132.
13 Ibid.
14 Freud, *Interpreting*, 337.
15 Freud, *Reader*, ed. Gay, 140.
16 Ibid, 501.
17 Ibid, 138.
18 Ibid, 139.
19 Ibid, 134.
20 Ibid, 135, 136, 139.
21 Ibid, 136.
22 Ibid, 137.
23 Ibid, 139.
24 Ibid, 142.
25 Freud, *Standard Edition 5*, 225.
26 Nietzsche, *Gay*, 43.
27 Friedrich Nietzsche, *On the Genealogy of Morals and Ecce Homo*, ed. Walter Kaufmann (NY, NY: Vintage Books, 1989), 72.
28 Lacan, *Seminar 7*, 325.
29 Lacan, *Seminar 11*, 13.
30 Lacan, *Seminar 20*, 57.
31 Leo Bersani, *Is The Rectum is a Grave? and Other Essays* (Chicago, IL: University of Chicago Press, 2009), 3.
32 Freud, *Reader*, ed. Gay, 567.
33 Nietzsche, *Beyond Good and Evil*, ed. Walter Kaufmann (NY, NY: Vintage Books, 1989), 90.
34 Friedrich Nietzsche, "On Truth and Lies in a Non-Moral Sense," in *Images: A Reader*, eds. Manghangi, Piper, and Simons (Thousand Oaks, CA: 2006), 53.

Outro

1   Marx, *Selected*, 224.
2   Ibid, 83-84.
3   Adam Smith, *An Inquiry into the Nature and Causes of the Wealth of Nations Volume 2* (NY, NY: Oxford University Press, 1974), 160.
4   Freud, *Reader*, ed. Phillips, 170.

Works Cited

Althusser, Louis. *Lenin and Philosophy and Other Essays*. NY, NY: Monthly Review Press, 2001.

Althusser, Louis; and Balibar, Etienne. *Reading Capital*. Transl. Ben Brewster. Brooklyn, NY: Verso, 1979.

Badmington, Neil; and Thomas, Julia, eds. *The Routledge Critical and Cultural Theory Reader*. NY, NY: Routledge, 2008.

Barthes, Roland. *Image Music Text*. Transl. Stephen Heath. NY, NY: Hill and Wang, 1978.

Bataille, Georges. *Inner Experience*. Transl. Leslie Anne Boldt. Albany, NY: SUNY Press, 1988.

Baudrillard, Jean. *Forget Foucault*. Transl. Bill Beitchman, Nicole Dufresne, Lee Hidreth, and Mark Polizzotti. NY, NY: Semiotext(e), 1987.

Baudrillard, Jean. *Jean Baudrillard: Selected Writings*. Ed. Mark Poster. Redwood City, CA: Stanford University Press, 1988.

Baudrillard, Jean. *Simulacra and Simulation*. Transl. Sheila Faria Glaser. Ann Arbor, MI: University of Michigan Press, 1995.

Benjamin, Walter. *Illuminations: Essays and Reflections*. NY, NY: Schocken Books, 2007.

Bersani, Leo. *Is the Rectum a Grave?: And Other Essays*. Chicago, IL: University of Chicago Press, 2009.

Cornell, Drucilla; Rosenfeld, Michel; and Carlson, David Gray, eds. *Deconstruction and the Possibility of Justice*. NY, NY: Routledge, 1992.

De Man, Paul. *The Resistance to Theory*. Minneapolis, MN: University of Minnesota Press, 1986.

Deleuze, Gilles. *Masochism: Coldness and Cruelty and Venus in Furs*. Transl. Jean McNeil. Cambridge, MA: Zone Books, 1991.

Deleuze, Gilles. *Nietzsche and Philosophy*. Transl. Hugh Tomlinson. NY, NY: Columbia University Press, 1962.

Derrida, Jacques. *A Derrida Reader: Between the Blinds*. Ed. Peggy Kamuf. NY, NY: Columbia University Press, 1991.

Derrida, Jacques. *Glas*. Transl. John P. Leavey Jr. and Richard Rand. Lincoln, NE: University of Nebraska Press, 1990.

Derrida, Jacques. *Margins of Philosophy*. Transl. Alan Bass. Chicago, IL: University of Chicago Press, 1985.

Derrida, Jacques. *Of Grammatology*. Transl. Gayatri Chakravorty Spivak. Baltimore, MD: The Johns Hopkins University Press, 1977.

Derrida, Jacques. *Positions*. Transl. Alan Bass. Chicago, IL: University of Chicago Press, 1992.

Derrida, Jacques. *The Postcard: From Socrates to Freud and Beyond.* Transl. Alan Bass. Chicago, IL: University of Chicago Press, 1987.

Derrida, Jacques. *The Truth in Painting.* Transl. Geoffrey Bennington and Ian McLeod. Chicago, IL: University of Chicago Press, 1987.

Derrida, Jacques. *Writing and Difference.* Transl. Alan Bass. Chicago, IL: University of Chicago Press, 1978.

Dor, Joel. *Clinical Lacan.* Eds. Judith Feher Gurewich and Susan Fairfield. NY, NY: Other Press, 1998.

Erikson, Erik. "The Dream Specimen of Psychoanalysis." Journal of the American Psychoanalytic Association 2 (1954): 5-56.

Foucault, Michel. *Archaeology of Knowledge.* NY, NY: Vintage Books, 1982.

Foucault, Michel. *Discipline and Punish: The Birth of the Prison.* Transl. Alan Sheridan. NY, NY: Vintage Books, 1995.

Foucault, Michel. *History of Madness.* Ed. Jean Khalfa. Transl. Jonathan Murphy. NY, NY: Routledge, 2006.

Foucault, Michel. *History of Sexuality: Volume 1.* Transl. Robert Hurley. NY, NY: Vintage Books, 1990.

Freud, Sigmund; and Breuer, Josef. *Studies in Hysteria.* Transl. Nicola Luckhurst. NY, NY: Penguin Books, 2004.

Freud, Sigmund. *Beyond the Pleasure Principle.* Transl. James Strachey. NY, NY: W.W. Norton and Co., 1990.

Freud, Sigmund. *Beyond the Pleasure Principle and Other Writings.* Ed. Adam Phillips. Transl. Mark Edmundson. NY, NY: Penguin Books, 2003.

Freud, Sigmund. *Interpreting Dreams.* Ed. Adam Phillips. Transl. Jim Underwood. NY, NY: Penguin, 2006.

Freud, Sigmund. *Jokes and their Relation to the Unconscious.* Ed. Adam Phillips. Transl. John Carey. NY, NY: Penguin Books, 2003.

Freud, Sigmund. *Sexuality and the Psychology of Love.* Ed. and Transl. James Strachey. NY, NY: Touchstone, 1997.

Freud, Sigmund. *The Freud Reader.* Ed. Peter Gay. Transl. James Strachey. NY, NY: W.W. Norton and Co., 1995.

Freud, Sigmund. *The Interpretation of Dreams.* Transl. James Strachey. NY, NY: Avon Books, 1965.

Freud, Sigmund. *The Penguin Freud Reader.* Ed. Adam Philips. NY, NY: Penguin Books, 2006.

Freud, Sigmund. *The Standard Edition of the Complete Psychological Works of Sigmund Freud.* Transl. James Strachey. London, UK: The Hogarth Press, 1958.

Freud, Sigmund. *Three Case Histories.* Transl. James Strachey. NY, NY: Touchstone, 1996.

Freud, Sigmund. *Three Essays on the Theory of Sexuality.* Transl. James Strachey. NY, NY: Basic Books, 1962.

Freud, Sigmund. *Totem and Taboo.* Transl. James Strachey. NY, NY: W.W. Norton and Co., 1990.

Goux, Jean-Joseph. *Symbolic Economies After Marx and Freud.* Transl. Jennifer Curtiss Gage. Ithaca, NY: Cornell University Press, 1990.

Hegel, G.W.F. *Phenomenology of Spirit.* Transl. A.V. Miller. Oxford, UK: Oxford University Press, 1977.

Hegel, G.W.F. *Phenomenology of Spirit.* Transl. J.B. Baillie. Digireads, 2010.

Heidegger, Martin. *Basic Writings.* Ed. David Farrell Krell. NY, NY: HarperCollins, 1993.

Heidegger, Martin. *Being and Time.* Transl. Joan Stambaugh. Albany, NY: SUNY Press, 2010.

Heidegger, Martin. *Being and Time.* Transl. John Macquarrie and Edward Robinson. NY, NY: Harper and Row, 1962.

Heidegger, Martin. *The Question Concerning Technology and Other Essays.* Transl. William Lovitt. NY, NY: Harper Torchbooks, 1977.

Johnson, Barbara. *A World of Difference.* Baltimore, MD: The Johns Hopkins University Press, 1988.

Lacan, Jacques. *Écrits: A Selection.* Transl. Bruce Fink. NY, NY: W.W. Norton and Co., 2004.

Lacan, Jacques. *Écrits: A Selection.* Transl. Alan Sheridan. NY, NY: W.W. Norton and Co., 1982.

Lacan, Jacques. *Écrits: The First Complete Edition in English.* Transl. Bruce Fink. NY, NY: W.W. Norton and Co., 2007.

Lacan, Jacques. *Seminar 1: Freud's Papers on Technique.* Ed. Jacques-Alain Miller. Transl. John Forrester. NY, NY: W.W. Norton and Co., 2013.

Lacan, Jacques. *Seminar 2: The Ego in Freud's Theory and in the Technique of Psychoanalysis.* Ed. Jacques-Alain Miller. Transl. Sylvana Tomaselli. NY, NY: W.W. Norton and Co., 1991.

Lacan, Jacques. *Seminar 3: The Psychoses.* Ed. Jacques-Alain Miller. Transl. Russell Grigg. NY, NY: W. W. Norton and Co., 1997.

Lacan, Jacques. *Seminar 7: The Ethics of Psychoanalysis.* Ed. Jacques-Alain Miller. Transl. Dennis Porter. NY, NY: W.W. Norton and Co., 1997.

Lacan, Jacques. *Seminar 10: Anxiety.* Ed. Jacques-Alain Miller. Trans. A.R. Price. Cambridge, UK: Polity, 2014.

Lacan, Jacques. *Seminar 11: The Four Fundamental Concepts of Psychoanalysis.* Ed. Jacques-Alain Miller. Transl. Alan Sheridan. NY, NY: W.W. Norton and Co., 1998.

Lacan, Jacques. *Seminar 17: The Other Side of Psychoanalysis.* Ed. Jacques-Alain Miller. Transl. Russell Grigg. NY, NY: W.W. Norton and Co., 2007.

Lacan, Jacques, *Seminar 20: On Feminine Sexuality: The Limits of Love and Knowledge.* Ed. Jacques-Alain Miller. Transl. Bruce Fink. NY, NY: W.W. Norton and Co., 1999.

Laclau, Ernesto; and Mouffe, Chantal. *Hegemony and Socialist Strategy: Towards a Radical Democratic Politics.* Brooklyn, NY: Verso, 2001.

Lacoue-Labarthe, Philippe; and Nancy, Jean-Luc. *The Title of the Letter: Reading of Lacan.* Albany, NY: SUNY Press, 1992.

Laplanche, Jean; and Pontalis, Jean-Bertrand. *The Language of Psychoanalysis.* NY, NY: W.W. Norton and Co., 1974.

Lukács, Georg. *History and Class Consciousness: Studies in Marxist Dialectics.* Transl. Rodney Livingstone. Cambridge, MA: The MIT Press, 1972.

Manghani, Sunil; Piper, Arthur; and Simons, Jon, eds. *Images: A Reader*. Thousand Oaks, CA: Sage Publications, 2006.

Mannoni, Octave. *Clefs pour l'imaginaire ou L'Auture Scene*. Paris, France: Seuil, 1985.

Marx, Karl. *Capital Volume 1: A Critique of Political Economy*. NY, NY: Vintage Books, 1977.

Marx, Karl. *Karl Marx: Selected Writings*. Ed. David McLellan. NY, NY: Oxford University Press, 2000.

Marx, Karl. "The German Ideology," in *Images: A Reader*. Eds. Sunil Manghani, Arthur Piper, and Jon Simons. London, UK: Sage Publications, 2010.

Nietzsche, Friedrich. *Beyond Good and Evil: Prelude to a Philosophy of the Future*. Ed. Walter Kaufmann. NY, NY: Vintage Books, 1989.

Nietzsche, Friedrich. *Beyond Good and Evil: Prelude to a Philosophy of the Future*. Ed. Rolf-Peter Horstmann. Transl. Judith Norman. Cambridge, UK: Cambridge University Press, 2001.

Nietzsche, Friedrich. *On the Genealogy of Morals and Ecce Homo*. Ed. Walter Kaufmann. NY, NY: Vintage Books, 1989.

Nietzsche, Friedrich. *On the Genealogy of Morals*. Ed. Keith Ansell Pearson. Transl. Carol Diethe. Cambridge, UK: Cambridge University Press, 2006.

Nietzsche, Friedrich. *The Gay Science*. Ed. Bernard Williams. Cambridge, UK: Cambridge University Press, 2008.

Nietzsche, Friedrich. *Thus Spoke Zarathustra*. Ed. Walter Kauffman. NY, NY: Penguin Books, 1983.

Nobus, Dany. *Jacques Lacan and the Freudian Practice of Psychoanalysis*. NY, NY: Routledge, 2000.

Saussure, Ferdinand. *Course in General Linguistics*. NY, NY: Columbia University Press, 2011.

Smith, Adam. *An Inquiry into the Nature and Causes of the Wealth of Nations Volume 2*. NY, NY: Oxford University Press, 1975.

Storey, John, ed. *What is Cultural Studies?* NY, NY: Bloomsbury Academic Press, 2009.

Warner, Michael. *The Trouble with Normal: Sex, Politics, and the Ethics of Queer Life*. Cambridge, MA: Harvard University Press, 1999.

Zizek, Slavoj. *Interrogating the Real*. Eds. Rex Butler and Scott Stephens. NY, NY: Bloomsbury, 2006.

Zizek, Slavoj. *The Parallax View*. Cambridge, MA: The MIT Press, 2009.

List of Illustrations

Index

475, 476, 477, 481, 485, 503, 505, 513, 516, 518,
519, 520, 527, 529, 530, 531, 533, 536, 538, 540,
544, 545, 546, 547, 548, 549, 550, 552, 556, 559,
560, 564, 567, 568, 571, 575, 576, 583, 584, 585,
587, 589, 591, 592, 595, 596, 598, 599, 602, 603,
611, 613, 616, 624, 626, 627, 628, 642, 643